CANADA

Lake Superior

MINNESOTA

MICHIGAN

Lake Huron

Minneapolis St. Paul

WISCONSIN

Lake Michigan

Lake Ontario
Rochester

NEW YORK

VERMONT
Burlington
Montpelier   NEW   Portland
                 HAMPSHIRE
                 Concord   Manchester

Milwaukee
Madison

Grand
Rapids   Flint

Albany   Worcester   Boston
          Springfield   MASSACHUSETTS
Syracuse   Providence
          Hartford   RHODE ISLAND
                      CONNECTICUT

IOWA
Cedar
Rapids
Rockford

Warren Sterling Heights
Lansing   Detroit
        Livonia
Ann Arbor

Lake
Erie
Cleveland

Buffalo

PENNSYLVANIA
Youngstown

Erie

New Haven
Bridgeport
Stamford
Newark   New York
Trenton   Jersey City

Des Moines
Iowa
City
Omaha

Chicago
Gary South
      Bend
Fort Wayne

Davenport

Toledo

Akron

Harrisburg

Pittsburgh

Philadelphia
NEW JERSEY
Dover
DELAWARE

Peoria

Columbus

Baltimore

Kansas
City
MISSOURI
opeka
wrence
Kansas City
Jefferson City

Independence

Springfield

Columbia

St. Louis

ILLINOIS

Urbana

Springfield

OHIO

Dayton
Cincinnati

INDIANA
Indianapolis
Bloomington

Louisville
Evansville

Frankfort

Lexington

WEST
VIRGINIA
Charleston

WASHINGTON   Annapolis
D.C.
Alexandria   MARYLAND

VIRGINIA
Richmond

Hampton
Newport News   Norfolk
Portsmouth   Virginia Beach
              Chesapeake

KENTUCKY

Roanoke

Tulsa
Fayetteville

Springfield

Knoxville

Greensboro Durham
Winston-   Raleigh
Salem
Asheville   NORTH CAROLINA
         Charlotte

ARKANSAS

Little Rock

Nashville   TENNESSEE
Chattanooga

Memphis

Huntsville

Greenville

Columbia

SOUTH CAROLINA

ATLANTIC   OCEAN

Oxford

Birmingham
University

Atlanta
Athens

Charleston

MISSISSIPPI   ALABAMA
Montgomery

GEORGIA
Macon

Shreveport

Jackson

Columbus

Savannah

Mobile
Pensacola

Tallahassee Jacksonville

Gainesville

LOUISIANA

Baton
Rouge   Biloxi

Beaumont
Houston

New Orleans

Orlando

Galveston

Tampa
St. Petersburg   FLORIDA

Gulf of Mexico

Hialeah   Fort Lauderdale
          Hollywood
          Miami

URBAN POPULATION CENTERS

⊡ Over 5,000,000

■ 1,000,000–5,000,000

▣ 500,000–1,000,000

○ 100,000–500,000

☆ State capitals

△ Major university
    centers

0   300 Miles

0   300 Kilometers

American History

A SURVEY

"The American Environment"
essays by William Cronon, *Yale University*

EIGHTH EDITION

American History

A SURVEY

Alan Brinkley
Columbia University

Richard N. Current
Emeritus, University of North Carolina at Greensboro

Frank Freidel
Emeritus, Harvard University

T. Harry Williams
late of Louisiana State University

McGraw-Hill, Inc.
New York St. Louis San Francisco Auckland Bogotá
Caracas Lisbon London Madrid Mexico Milan
Montreal New Delhi Paris San Juan Singapore
Sydney Tokyo Toronto

American History

A SURVEY

4 5 6 7 8 9 0 DOW DOW 9 5 4 3

ISBN 0-07-015026-5

This book was set in Bembo by Americomp.
The editors were Christopher J. Rogers, David Follmer, and Cecilia Gardner;
the production supervisor was Kathryn Porzio.
The cover was designed by Jo Jones.
The photo editors were Elyse Rieder and Kathy Bendo.
R. R. Donnelley & Sons Company was printer and binder.

Cover illustration: Thomas Hart Benton, *July Hay,* 1943. Oil and egg tempera on composition board, 38 x 26¾ inches. The Metropolitan Museum of Art, George A. Hearn Fund, 1943 (43.159.1).

Library of Congress Cataloging-in-Publication Data

American history: a survey / Alan Brinkley . . . [et al.].—
    8th ed.
        p.   cm.
    Includes bibliographical references and index.
    ISBN 0-07-015026-5
    1. United States—History.   I. Brinkley, Alan.
E178.1.A492   1991
973—dc20   90-42172

About the Authors

Alan Brinkley is professor of American history at Columbia University. He has also taught at the City University of New York Graduate School, Harvard University, and the Massachusetts Institute of Technology. He is a graduate of Princeton University, received his Ph.D. from Harvard, and has been awarded fellowships by the John Simon Guggenheim Foundation, the Woodrow Wilson Center for International Scholars, the American Council of Learned Societies, and the National Endowment for the Humanities. He is the author of *Voices of Protest: Huey Long, Father Coughlin, and the Great Depression*, for which he won the American Book Award in 1983. He is coauthor of *America in the Twentieth Century* and has published many articles, essays, and reviews.

Richard N. Current is University Distinguished Professor of History Emeritus at the University of North Carolina at Greensboro. He is coauthor of the Bancroft Prize-winning *Lincoln the President*. His books include: *Those Terrible Carpetbaggers; The Lincoln Nobody Knows; Daniel Webster and the Rise of National Conservatism*; and *Phi Beta Kappa in American Life*. Professor Current has lectured on United States history in Europe, Asia, South America, Australia, and Antarctica. He has been a Fulbright Lecturer at the University of Munich and the University of Chile at Santiago and has served as Harmsworth Professor of American History at Oxford. He is past president of the Southern Historical Association.

Frank Freidel is Charles Warren Professor of American History Emeritus at Harvard University and Bullitt Professor of American History Emeritus at the University of Washington. Among his books are *Franklin D. Roosevelt: A Rendezvous with Destiny; F.D.R. and the South*; four volumes on Roosevelt covering his life to July, 1933; and *Our Country's Presidents*. He has been Harmsworth Professor of American History at Oxford, has lectured on American history on five continents, including Antarctica, and has held Guggenheim and National Endowment for the Humanities fellowships. He is a past president of the Organization of American Historians and the New England Historical Association.

T. Harry Williams was Boyd Professor of History at Louisiana State University. He was awarded both the 1969 Pulitzer Prize and National Book Award for his biography of *Huey Long*. His books include: *Lincoln and His Generals; Lincoln and the Radicals; P. G. T. Beauregard; Americans at War; Romance and Realism in Southern Politics; Hayes of the Twenty-Third; McClellan, Sherman, and Grant; The Union Sundered*; and *The Union Restored*. Professor Williams was a Harmsworth Professor of American History at Oxford and President of both the Southern Historical Association and the Organization of American Historians.

Contents

APPENDICES   *i*

Maps:

Documents and Tables:

Preface

The history of the United States is the story of many peoples living together in a single land. This book attempts to depict the extraordinary diversity of the American people over the nearly four centuries since the arrival of the first European settlers in what is now the United States. It also tries to explain their long struggle to forge a just society and a unified nation out of many distinct cultures. No single work can hope to tell the full story of any nation. In the case of the United States—a country of almost unparalleled diversity, in which change has occurred at such constant and dizzying speed that historical time seems almost to have accelerated— that task is particularly difficult. Nevertheless, this book attempts to present as full a picture as possible of the remarkable history of the American nation and its people.

Four broad themes shape the contents of this work. First, we have told the story of the nation's political institutions and the way they have evolved in response to changing circumstances, changing popular expectations, and the achievements and failures of leaders. Second, we have examined the development of America's role in the world, from its position as a weak dependency of the British and Spanish empires to its rise to international preeminence. Third, we have recounted the story of the development of the American economy, from its simple agrarian beginnings through its rise to industrial greatness to its troubled transition into a still uncertain postindustrial future. And fourth, we have described how the American people have lived: how they found their way to the New World, how they developed socially and culturally, how they responded to political and economic changes, and how groups that were divided by class, race, ethnicity, religion, region, and gender struggled to find ways of living together in a single society.

In preparing this new edition, we have continued and expanded our efforts to present a history of the United States that not only tells the traditional stories of great public events but also reveals those areas of the nation's past that historians have only relatively recently begun to explore. We have tried, above all, to show the way the nation's public history and its social history have interacted with and shaped each other. Readers familiar with earlier editions of this book will notice several obvious changes: a substantial selection of new photographs, maps, and charts; material on the very recent past; expanded and updated bibliographies; a new essay on the origins of segregation in the series entitled "Where Historians Disagree"; and a series of seven important new essays by the historian William Cronon designed to introduce readers to the emerging field of environmental history.

As always, however, the most important changes are those in the narrative itself. In this edition, we have expanded our efforts to incorporate into the story of the past the results of important new scholarship in many fields. We have increased our coverage of women's history throughout the book. We have substantially revised the first three chapters in response to new scholarship in pre-Columbian and early American history. We have greatly expanded and revised our treatment of the history of Native Americans throughout the volume in an effort to explore both their own, distinctive history and some of the ways in which that history has helped shape the larger story of the whole American nation (Chapters 1-8, 12, 13, 16, 21, 26, 27, 31). We have added new material on the history of Hispanic Americans (Chapters 25, 27, 31, 32).

This is the first edition of this book to be published under the auspices of McGraw-Hill, which acquired the college division of Random House/Alfred A. Knopf, the original publishers of *American History: A Survey*, in 1988. We are grateful to Alfred A. Knopf, Inc., for its long support of this book and its long commitment to editorial and scholarly quality.

We are also grateful to McGraw-Hill for continuing that support and commitment. We owe a special debt of gratitude to the many members of the editorial and production staff of Random House/Knopf who have moved with the books to McGraw-Hill and who have skillfully shepherded this new edition through the transition. We are particularly grateful to David Follmer, Cecilia Gardner, Kathy Bendo, and Elyse Rieder.

As always, we have benefited immensely from the efforts of scholars who, at our request, read and commented on the seventh edition of this book and whose suggestions were of incalculable value to us in preparing the eighth. We are also grateful to those students and teachers who have used this book over the past four years and who have offered us their unsolicited comments, suggestions, criticisms, and corrections. We hope they will continue to provide us with their reactions by sending them to us in care of the College Division, McGraw-Hill, Inc., 1221 Avenue of the Americas, New York, NY 10020. We will do our best to respond constructively to their suggestions.

Alan Brinkley

Richard N. Current

Frank Freidel

T. Harry Williams

American History

A SURVEY

Text within image: Their rype corne. / Their greene corne. / Corne newly sprong. / Their sitting at meate. / the place of solemne prayer / The house wherin the Tombe of their Herounds standeth. / SECOTON / A Ceremony in their prayers w strange gestures and songs dansing abowt posts carued on the topps lyke mens faces.

***The Indian Village of Secoton* (c. 1585), by John White**
The English explorer John White created this illustration of life among the Eastern Woodland
Indians in coastal North Carolina. It shows the diversified agriculture practiced by the natives:
squash, tobacco, and three varieties of corn. The hunters shown in nearby woods suggest another
element of the native economy. At bottom right, Indians perform a religious ritual, which White
describes as "strange gestures and songs." (*British Museum*)

CHAPTER 1

The Age of Discovery

The discovery of America did not begin with Christopher Columbus. It began many thousands of years earlier when human beings first crossed an ancient land bridge over the Bering Strait into what is now Alaska and—almost certainly without realizing it—began to people a new continent. No one is certain when these migrations began; recent estimates suggest that they started between 14,000 and 16,000 years ago, but some scholars believe the first crossings were much earlier. They were probably a result of the development of new stone tools—spears and other hunting implements—that made possible the pursuit of the large animals that regularly crossed between Asia and North America.

Year after year, a few at a time, these nomadic peoples—all of them apparently drawn from a Mongolian stock similar to that of modern-day eastern Siberia—entered the new continent and moved ever deeper into its heart. Ultimately, perhaps as early as 8,000 B.C., the migrations reached the southern tip of South America. By the end of the fifteenth century A.D., when the first important contact with Europeans occurred, America was the home of many millions of men and women. Scholars estimate that well over 10 million people lived in South America by 1500 and that perhaps 4 million lived in the territory that now constitutes the United States.

America Before Columbus

The warming of the earth that ended the Ice Age about 10,000 years ago created the distinctive geographic regions that characterize the American continents today. As settlement spread, the peoples of different regions began to adapt themselves to their surroundings and to create distinctive civilizations appropriate to their particular climates and resources. All American societies shared a common racial background, and many had significant contact with one another. But there was as much variety among the civilizations of the Americas as among the civilizations of Europe, Asia, and Africa.

The Civilizations of the South

The most elaborate of these societies emerged in South and Central America and in Mexico. In Peru, the Incas created a powerful empire of perhaps 6 million people. They developed a complex political system and a large network of paved roads that welded together the populations of many tribes under a single rule. In Central America and on the Yucatán peninsula of Mexico, the Mayas built a sophisticated culture with a written language, a numerical system similar to the Arabic (and superior to the Roman), an

1

Tenochtitlán—The Aztec Capital
This is a modern re-creation of the central square of Tenochtitlán, which was dominated by great pyramids comparable in size to those of ancient Egypt. The Aztec pyramids, however, served not as burial monuments but as the sites for human sacrifices on an epic scale. When the Spanish *conquistadore* Hernando Cortés entered Tenochtitlán in 1521, he found a rack in the central square that contained the skulls of about 100,000 sacrificial victims. Mexico City stands today on the site of the Aztec capital. (American Museum of Natural History)

accurate calendar, and an advanced agricultural system. They were succeeded by the Aztecs, a once-nomadic warrior tribe from the north. In the late thirteenth century, the Aztecs established a precarious rule over much of central and southern Mexico and built elaborate administrative, educational, and medical systems comparable to the most advanced in Europe at the time. The Aztecs also developed a harsh religion that required human sacrifice. Their Spanish conquerors discovered the skulls of 100,000 victims in one location when they arrived in 1519—which is one reason that many Europeans came to consider the Aztecs "savages" despite their impressive accomplishments (and despite the holy wars and witch burnings in the Christian world, which suggest that the Aztecs were not alone in finding religious justification for homicide).

The economies of these societies were based primarily on agriculture, but there were also substantial cities in which lived, among others, many of the warriors and priests who ruled the empires and formed their hereditary elites. Some of these cities were as large as the greatest capitals of Europe. Tenochtitlán, the Aztec capital built on the site of present-day Mexico City, had a population of over 100,000 in 1500 and an impressive complex of majestic public buildings—including temples equal in size to the great pyramids of Egypt. The Mayas (at Mayapan and elsewhere) and the Incas (in such cities as Cuzco and Machu Picchu) produced similarly elaborate settlements with striking religious and ceremonial structures of their own. These achievements are all the more remarkable for having been achieved without some of the important technologies that Asian and European civilizations possessed. The Incas, for example, never had any system of writing or any equivalent for paper. And as late as the sixteenth century, no American society had yet developed wheeled vehicles.

The Civilizations of the North

The peoples north of Mexico—in the lands that became the United States and Canada—did not develop empires as large or political systems as elaborate as those of the Incas, Mayas, and Aztecs. They did, however, build complex civilizations of great variety. In the northern regions of the continent emerged societies that subsisted on hunting, gathering, fishing, or some combination of the three: the Eskimos of the Arctic Circle, who fished and hunted seals and whose civilization spanned thousands of miles of largely frozen land, which residents traversed by dog sled; the big-game hunters of the northern forests, who led highly nomadic lives based on pursuit of moose and caribou; the tribes of the Pacific Northwest, whose principal occupation was salmon fishing, who created substantial permanent settlements along the coast, and who engaged in constant and often violent competition with one another for access to natural resources; and a group of tribes spread through relatively arid regions of the Far West who developed successful communities, many of them quite wealthy and densely populated, based on fishing, hunting small game, and gathering edible seeds, roots, and other plant materials.

Other societies in North America were primarily agricultural. Among the most developed were those in the Southwest. The people of that region built large irrigation systems to allow farming on their relatively dry land, and they constructed substantial towns that became centers of trade, crafts, and religious and civic ritual. Their densely populated settlements at Chaco Canyon and elsewhere consisted of stone and adobe terraced structures, known today as *pueblos,* many of which resembled large apartment buildings in size and design. In the Great Plains region, too, most tribes were engaged in sedentary farming (corn and other grains) and lived in substantial permanent settlements, although there were some small nomadic tribes that subsisted by hunting buffalo. (Only in the eighteenth century, after Europeans had introduced the horse to North America, did buffalo hunting begin to support a large population in the region; at that point, many once-

sedentary farmers left the land to pursue the great migratory buffalo herds.)

The eastern third of what is now the United States—much of it covered with forests and inhabited by people who have thus become known as the Woodland Indians—had the greatest food resources of any region of the continent. It supported a large array of tribes, most of whom engaged in farming, hunting, gathering, and fishing simultaneously. In the South there were for a time substantial permanent settlements and large trading networks based on the corn and other grains grown in the rich lands of the Mississippi River valley. As in the Southwest, cities emerged as trading and political centers. Among them was Cahokia (near present-day St. Louis), which at its peak in A.D. 1200 had a population of 40,000 and contained a great complex of large earthen mounds comparable to those found in the Aztec empire in Mexico.

The agricultural societies of the Northeast were more mobile than were those in other regions. Farming techniques there were designed to exploit the land quickly rather than to develop permanent settlements. Natives often cleared the land by setting forest fires or cutting into trees to kill them. They then planted crops—corn, beans, squash, pumpkins, and others—among the dead or blackened trunks. After a few years, when the land became exhausted or the filth from a settlement began to accumulate, they moved on and established themselves elsewhere. In some parts of eastern North America, villages dispersed every winter and families foraged for themselves in the wilderness until warm weather returned; those who had survived the perilous season then reassembled to begin farming again.

Many of the tribes living east of the Mississippi River were linked together loosely by common linguistic roots. The largest of these language groups consisted of the Algonquin tribes, which lived along the Atlantic seaboard from Canada to Virginia. More elaborately organized was the Iroquois Confederation, which took shape in the mid-fifteenth century and was centered in what is now upstate New York. The Iroquois included at least five distinct northern "nations"—the Seneca, Cayuga, Onondaga, Oneida, and Mohawk—and had links as well with the Cherokees and the Tuscaroras farther south, in the Carolinas and Georgia. The third largest language group—Muskogean—consisted of the tribes in the southernmost region of the Eastern seaboard: the Chickasaws, Choctaws, Creeks, and Seminoles. Yet alliances among the various Indian societies (even among those with common languages) were fragile,

Principal Subsistence Patterns of Early Native Peoples of North America

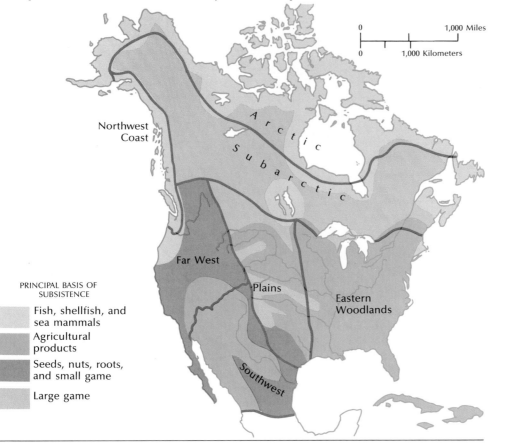

since the peoples of the Americas did not think of themselves as members of a single civilization. When Europeans arrived and began to threaten their way of life, Indians generally viewed the threat in terms of how it affected their own community and tribe, not how it affected any larger "Indian nation." Only rarely did tribes unite in opposition to white encroachments.

Given the enormous diversity of economic, social, and political structures among the North American Indians, large generalizations about their cultures are difficult. But in the last centuries before the arrival of Europeans, native Americans—like peoples in other areas of the world—were experiencing an agricultural revolution. In all regions of the United States (if in varying degrees from place to place), tribes were becoming more sedentary and were developing new sources of food, clothing, and shelter. Most regions were experiencing significant population growth. And virtually all were developing the sorts of elaborate social customs and rituals that only

relatively stationary societies can produce. Religion was as important to Indian society as it was to most other cultures and was usually closely bound up with the natural world on which the tribes depended. Native Americans worshiped many gods, whom they associated variously with crops, game, forests, rivers, and other elements of nature. Some tribes created elaborate, brightly colored totems as part of their religious ritual; most staged large festivals on such important occasions as harvests or major hunts.

Also as in other parts of the world, the societies of North America tended to divide tasks according to sex. All tribes assigned women the jobs of caring for children, preparing meals, and gathering certain foods. But the allocation of other tasks varied from one society to another. Some tribal groups (notably the Pueblos of the Southwest) reserved farming tasks almost entirely for men. Among others (including the Algonquins, the Iroquois, and the Muskogean), women tended the fields, while men engaged in hunting, warfare, or clearing land. Iroquois women and

Indians of New France
The drawing is by the cartographer Charles Bécard de Granville, who was employed by the French government to make maps of their territories in North America. Granville also produced drawings of the flora and fauna of the region and of the natives he encountered. This depiction of Indian hunters traveling by river dates from approximately 1701. (Gilcrease Institute)

children were often left alone for extended periods while men were away hunting or fighting battles. As a result, women tended to control the social and economic organization of the settlements and played powerful roles within families (which in many tribes were traced back "matrilineally," or through the mother's line).

Europe Looks Westward

Europeans were almost entirely unaware of the existence of the Americas before the fifteenth century. A few early wanderers—Leif Ericson, an eleventh-century Norse seaman, and perhaps others—had glimpsed parts of the New World and had demonstrated that Europeans were capable of crossing the ocean to reach it. But even if their discoveries had become common knowledge (and they did not), there would have been little incentive for others to follow, for Europe in the Middle Ages (roughly A.D. 500–1500) was not an adventurous civilization. Divided into innumerable small duchies and kingdoms, its outlook was overwhelmingly provincial. Subsistence agriculture predominated, and commerce was limited; few merchants looked beyond the boundaries of their own regions. Although the Roman Catholic church exercised a measure of spiritual authority over most of the continent, and although the

Holy Roman Empire provided at least a nominal political center, power was for the most part so widely dispersed that no single leader was capable of launching great ventures. Gradually, however, conditions in Europe changed, so that by the late fifteenth century interest in overseas exploration had grown.

Commerce and Nationalism

Two important and related changes provided the first incentive for Europeans to look toward new lands. One was a result of the significant growth in Europe's population in the fifteenth century. The Black Death, a catastrophic epidemic of the bubonic plague that began in Constantinople in 1347, had decimated Europe, killing (according to some estimates) more than half the people of the continent and debilitating its already limited economy. But a century and a half later, the population had rebounded. With that growth came a rise in land values, a reawakening of commerce, and a general increase in prosperity. Affluent landlords were becoming eager to purchase goods from distant regions, and a new merchant class was emerging to meet their demand. As trade increased, and as advances in navigation and shipbuilding made long-distance sea travel more feasible, interest in developing new markets, finding new products, and opening new trade routes rapidly increased.

Paralleling the rise of commerce in Europe, and in part responsible for it, was the rise of new gov-

The Cognoscenti
This detail from a fifteenth-century Flemish painting depicts English navigators and scholars gathered to discuss the possibilities for transoceanic trade routes. On the table are maps, drawings, and some of the new navigational devices that made possible the great explorations of the era. (National Gallery, London)

ernments that were far more united and powerful than the feeble political entities of the feudal past. In the western areas of Europe in particular, where the authority of the distant pope and the even more distant Holy Roman emperor were necessarily weak, strong new monarchs were emerging and creating centralized nation-states, with national courts, national armies, and—perhaps most important— national tax systems. As these ambitious kings and queens consolidated their power and increased their wealth, they became eager to enhance the commercial growth of their nations.

Ever since the early fourteenth century, when Marco Polo and other adventurers had returned from the Orient bearing exotic goods (spices, cloths, dyes) and even more exotic tales, Europeans who dreamed of commercial glory had dreamed above all of trade

with the East. For two centuries, that trade had been limited by the difficulties of the long, arduous overland journey to the Asian courts. But in the fourteenth century, as the maritime talents of several western European societies increased, there began to be serious talk of finding a faster, safer sea route to the Orient. Such dreams gradually found a receptive audience in the courts of the new monarchs. By the late fifteenth century, some of them were ready to finance daring voyages of exploration.

The first to do so were the Portuguese. Their maritime preeminence in the fifteenth century was in large part the work of one man, Prince Henry the Navigator, who devoted much of his life to nautical studies and the promotion of exploration. Henry's own principal interest was not in finding a sea route to Asia, but in exploring the western coast of Africa—

where he dreamed of establishing a Christian empire to aid in his country's wars against the Moors of northern Africa and where he hoped to find new stores of gold. But the explorations he began, while they did not fulfill his own hopes, ultimately led farther than he had dreamed. Some of Henry's mariners went as far south as Cape Verde, on Africa's west coast. After his death in 1460, Portuguese explorers carried on his work and advanced farther still. In 1486, Bartholomeu Díaz rounded the southern tip of Africa (the Cape of Good Hope); and in 1497–1498 Vasco da Gama proceeded all the way around the cape to India. In 1500, the next fleet bound for India, under the command of Pedro Cabral, was blown westward off its southerly course and happened upon the coast of Brazil. But by then, another man, in the service of another country, had already encountered the New World.

Christopher Columbus

Christopher Columbus, who was born and reared in Genoa, Italy, obtained most of his early seafaring knowledge and experience in the service of the Portuguese. As a young man, he became intrigued with the possibility, already under discussion in many seafaring circles, of reaching the Orient by going not east but west. Columbus was an industrious student of geography, and his wide readings convinced him that the Atlantic could provide easier passage to the Orient than either the existing land routes or the arduous sea route around southern Africa. Columbus's optimism rested on several basic misconceptions. He concluded that the world was far smaller than it actually is. He also believed that the Asian continent extended farther eastward than it actually does. He assumed, therefore, that the western ocean was narrow enough to be crossed on a relatively brief voyage. It did not occur to him that anything lay to the west between Europe and the lands of Asia.

Columbus failed to convince the leaders of Portugal of the feasibility of his plan; the Portuguese were more interested in establishing their route to the East around Africa. So Columbus turned from Portugal to Spain. Although the Spaniards were not yet as advanced a maritime people as the Portuguese, they were at least as energetic and ambitious. And in the fifteenth century they, like other European nations, were busy establishing a strong nation-state. The marriage of Spain's two most powerful regional rulers, Ferdinand of Aragon and Isabella of Castile, had produced the strongest monarchy in Europe.

Like other young monarchies, it would soon grow eager to demonstrate its strength by sponsoring new commercial ventures.

Columbus appealed to Queen Isabella for support—men, money, and ships—for his proposed westward voyage. The project would, he promised, extend the sway of Christianity to new lands and, perhaps more important to Isabella, help Spain in its emerging competition with Portugal. For a time, the queen was more interested in consolidating both Christianity and her own power at home; but in 1492 she finally felt secure enough to turn her gaze to foreign ventures. In that year, the Moorish stronghold of Granada fell to the Spanish armies, and the last Muslims were driven from the country; at the same time, the Jews of Spain—the only other significant non-Christian element in the population—were forced to choose between conversion to Christianity and emigrating. Confident now of her position within her own nation, Isabella finally agreed to Columbus's request.

Commanding ninety men and three ships—the *Niña,* the *Pinta,* and the *Santa Maria*—Columbus left Spain in August 1492 and sailed west into the Atlantic on what he thought was a straight course for Japan. Ten weeks later, he sighted land and assumed he had reached his target. In fact, he had landed on an island in the Bahamas. When he pushed on and encountered Cuba, he assumed he had reached China. He returned to Spain in triumph, bringing with him several captured natives as evidence of his achievement. (He called the natives "Indians" because he believed they were from the East Indies in the Pacific.)

Columbus did not, however, bring back to Spain what he had promised. He had no news of the great khan's court in China; nor did he have any samples of the fabled wealth of the Indies. And so a year later, he tried again, this time with a much larger expedition. As before, he headed into the Caribbean, discovering several other islands and leaving a small and shortlived colony on Hispaniola. On a third voyage, in 1498, he finally reached the mainland and cruised along the northern coast of South America. When he passed the mouth of the Orinoco River (in present-day Venezuela), he concluded for the first time that what he had discovered was not in fact an island off the coast of China, as he had assumed, but a separate continent; such a large freshwater stream, he realized, could emerge only from a large body of land. Still, he remained convinced that Asia was only a short distance away. And although he failed in his efforts to sail around the northeastern coast of South America to the Indies (he was blocked by the Isthmus

European Journeys of Exploration and Conquest

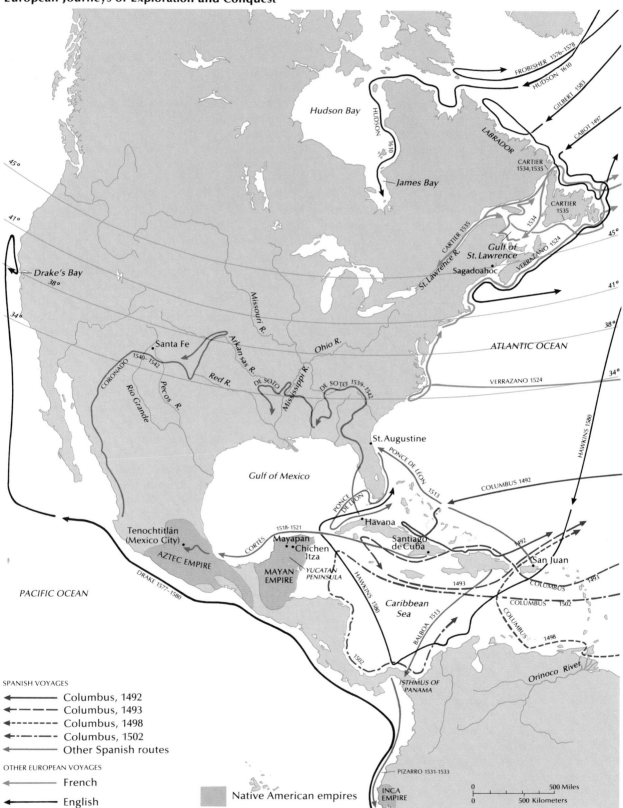

SPANISH VOYAGES

———⟶ Columbus, 1492
– – –⟶ Columbus, 1493
- - - -⟶ Columbus, 1498
–·–·–⟶ Columbus, 1502
———⟵ Other Spanish routes

OTHER EUROPEAN VOYAGES

———⟶ French
———⟶ English

Native American empires

45°
41°
34°
38°

Drake's Bay
38°

Missouri R.

Santa Fe

CORONADO 1540–1542

Rio Grande

Pecos R.

Arkansas R.

Red R.

Ohio R.

DE SOTO

Mississippi R.

DE SOTO 1539–1542

St. Augustine

PONCE DE LEON 1513
PONCE DE LEON

Gulf of Mexico

Havana

Tenochtitlán
(Mexico City)

AZTEC EMPIRE

1518–1521
CORTÉS

Mayapan
•Chichen
Itza

MAYAN
EMPIRE

YUCATAN
PENINSULA

DRAKE 1577–1580

PACIFIC OCEAN

Santiago
de Cuba

HAWKINS 1560

*Caribbean
Sea*

1493

1502

BALBOA 1513

1502

San Juan

1492

COLUMBUS 1493

COLUMBUS 1502

COLUMBUS 1498

COLUMBUS 1492

Orinoco River

ISTHMUS OF
PANAMA

PIZARRO 1531–1533

INCA
EMPIRE

Hudson Bay

HUDSON
1610

James Bay

FROBISHER 1576–1578

HUDSON 1610

GILBERT 1583

CABOT 1497

LABRADOR

CARTIER
1534, 1535

CARTIER
1535

1534

CARTIER 1535

St. Lawrence R.

*Gulf of
St. Lawrence*

VERRAZANO 1524

Sagadoahoc

VERRAZANO 1524

ATLANTIC OCEAN

HAWKINS 1560

45°

41°

38°

34°

0   500 Miles
0   500 Kilometers

Columbus's Third Voyage to America, 1498
This engraving is a sixteenth-century re-creation by the Flemish engraver Theodore de Bry of an earlier drawing. It shows Columbus's third expedition to the New World as it encountered natives near the island of Margarita, off the coast of Venezuela. Columbus's men received three pounds of pearls from the natives (the Indian canoes are shown here filled with pearl oysters) in exchange for some pieces of pottery, and then sailed on.   (New York Public Library)

of Panama), he returned to Spain believing that he had explored at least the fringes of the Far East. He continued to believe that until the day he died.

Columbus's celebrated accomplishments made him a popular hero for a time, but he ended his life in obscurity. Ultimately he was even denied the honor of giving his name to the land he had discovered. That distinction went instead to a Florentine merchant, Amerigo Vespucci, a passenger on a later Portuguese expedition to the New World who wrote a

series of vivid (if largely fictitious) descriptions of the lands he visited.

Columbus has been celebrated for centuries as the "Admiral of the Ocean Sea" (a title he struggled to have officially bestowed on him during his lifetime) and as a representative of the new, secular, scientific impulses of Renaissance Europe. But Columbus was also a deeply religious man, even something of a mystic, and his voyages were inspired as much by his conviction that he was fulfilling a divine mission as by his interest in geography and trade. A strong believer in biblical prophecies, he came to see himself as a man destined to advance the coming of the millennium. "God made me the messenger of the new heaven and the new earth," he wrote near the end of his life, "and he showed me the spot where to find it." A similar combination of secular and religious passions lay behind many subsequent efforts at exploration and settlement of the New World.

Partly as a result of Columbus's initiative, Spain began to devote greater resources and energy to maritime exploration and gradually replaced Portugal as the foremost seafaring nation. The Spaniard Vasco de Balboa fought his way across the Isthmus of Panama (1513) and became the first European to gaze westward upon the great ocean that separated America from China and the Indies. Seeking access to that ocean, Ferdinand Magellan, a Portuguese in Spanish employ, found the strait that now bears his name at the southern end of South America, struggled through the stormy narrows and into the ocean (so calm by contrast that he christened it the Pacific), then proceeded to the Philippines. There Magellan died in a conflict with the natives, but his expedition went on to complete the first known circumnavigation of the globe (1519–1522). By 1550, Spaniards had explored the coasts of North America as far north as Oregon in the west and Labrador in the east.

The Conquistadores

In time, Spanish explorers in the New World stopped thinking of America simply as an obstacle to their search for a route to the East. They began instead to consider it a possible source of wealth rivaling and even surpassing the original Indies. On the basis of Columbus's discoveries, the Spanish claimed for themselves the whole of the New World, except for a piece of it (today's Brazil) that was reserved by a papal decree for the Portuguese. By the mid-sixteenth century, the Spanish were well on their way to establishing a substantial American empire.

The early Spanish colonists, beginning with those Columbus brought on his second voyage, settled on the islands of the Caribbean, where they tried to enslave the Indians and find gold. They had little luck at either endeavor. But then, in 1518, Hernando Cortés, who had been a Spanish government official in Cuba for fourteen years and who had to that point achieved little success, decided to lead a small military expedition (about 600 men) into Mexico after hearing stories of great treasures there. He met strong and resourceful resistance from the Aztecs and their powerful emperor Montezuma; his first assault on Tenochtitlán, the Aztec capital, failed. But Cortés and his army had, unknowingly, unleashed an assault on the Aztecs far more devastating than military at-

Cortés in the New World
An Aztec artist created this image of Hernando Cortés in Mexico. Cortés is visible at upper left, on horseback, wielding a sword. Other images suggest the destruction his arrival produced among the Aztecs. One of the most brutal and successful of the Spanish *conquistadores,* Cortés burned his ships upon landing at Vera Cruz (where he founded a city) in 1519 to prevent his men from turning back. In 1521, he captured the Aztec capital, Tenochtitlán, after a long siege.
(Apostolic Library, Vatican City)

tack: they had exposed the natives to smallpox. An epidemic of that disease decimated the population and made it possible for the Spanish to triumph in their second attempt at conquest. Through his ruthless suppression of the surviving natives, Cortés established a lasting reputation as the most brutal of the Spanish *conquistadores* (conquerors).

The news that silver was to be found in Mexico turned the attention of other Spaniards to the mainland. From the island colonies and from the mother country, a wave of *conquistadores* descended on Mexico in search of fortune—a movement comparable in some ways to the nineteenth-century gold rushes elsewhere in the world, but much more vicious. Francisco Pizarro, who conquered Peru (1532–1538) and revealed to the world the wealth of the Incas, opened the way for other advances into South America.

The story of the Spanish warriors is one of great military daring and achievement. It is also a story of remarkable brutality and greed. The *conquistadores* subjugated and, in some areas, virtually exterminated the native populations. In this horrible way, they made possible the creation of a vast Spanish empire in the New World.

The Spanish Empire

Spanish exploration, conquest, and colonization in America was primarily a work of private enterprise, carried on by individual leaders, with little direct support from the government at home. Those who wished to launch expeditions to the New World had first to get licenses from the crown. By the terms of the licenses, the monarch received a fifth of any wealth found or produced in the new colonies. The organizers of the colonies retained a tenth of that wealth. They also received generous estates, other lands to divide among their followers, and the right to make use of native labor. But a license did no more than confer rights; colonizers had to equip and finance their expeditions on their own and assume the full risk of loss or ruin. They might succeed and make a fortune; they might fail—through shipwreck, natural disaster, incompetence, or bad luck—and lose everything, including their lives, as many adventurers did. The New World did not always attract good or intelligent settlers, but in the beginning it seldom attracted the fainthearted.

The first Spaniards to arrive in the New World, the *conquistadores,* were interested in only one thing: getting rich. More specifically, they were eager to exploit the American stores of gold and silver. And in that, they were fabulously successful. For three hundred years, beginning in the sixteenth century, the mines in Spanish America yielded more than ten times as much gold and silver as the rest of the world's mines together. These riches made Spain for a time the wealthiest and most powerful nation on earth.

After the first wave of conquest, however, most Spanish settlers in America traveled to the New World for other reasons, which were of more lasting importance to the future of America. Many went in hopes of creating a profitable agricultural economy in America. And unlike the *conquistadores,* who left little but destruction behind them, they helped establish elements of European civilization in America that permanently altered both the landscape and the social structure. Other Spaniards went to America to spread the Christian religion. Indeed, after the era of the *conquistadores* came to a close in the 1540s, the missionary impulse became one of the principal motives for European emigration to America, and priests or friars accompanied all colonizing ventures. Through the work of zealous missionaries, the gospel of the Catholic church ultimately extended throughout South and Central America and Mexico.

By the end of the sixteenth century, the Spanish empire had become one of the largest in the history of the world. It included the islands of the Caribbean and the coastal areas of South America that had been the targets of the first Spanish expeditions. It extended to Mexico and southern North America, where a second wave of European colonizers had established outposts. The Spanish fort established in 1565 at St. Augustine, Florida, became the first permanent European settlement in the present-day United States. Spanish missionaries ventured even farther north in the following years—at times reaching as far as the Chesapeake Bay—although they established no lasting presence in those areas. The Spanish empire spread southward and westward as well: into the land mass of South America—Chile, Argentina, and Peru—which was the target of a third Spanish military thrust. In 1580, when the Spanish and Portuguese monarchies temporarily united, Brazil came under Spanish jurisdiction as well. The Spanish empire now spread from Florida and Mexico to

Spanish America

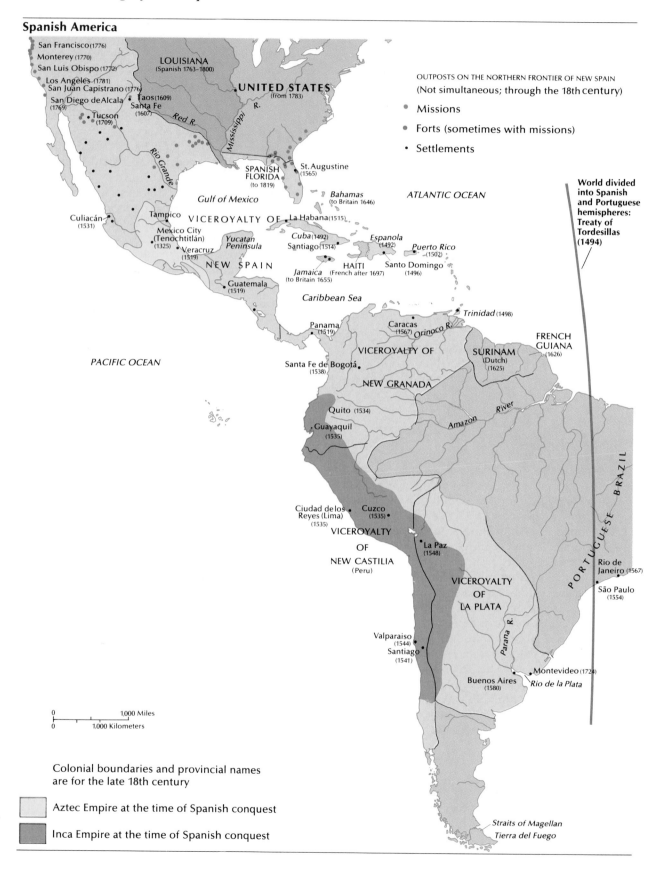

San Francisco (1776)
Monterey (1770)
San Luis Obispo (1772)
Los Angeles (1781)
San Juan Capistrano (1776)
San Diego de Alcala (1769)
Tucson (1709)
Taos (1609)
Santa Fe (1607)

LOUISIANA
(Spanish 1763–1800)

UNITED STATES
(from 1783)

Red R.
Rio Grande
Mississippi R.

OUTPOSTS ON THE NORTHERN FRONTIER OF NEW SPAIN
(Not simultaneous; through the 18th century)

● Missions

● Forts (sometimes with missions)

• Settlements

SPANISH
FLORIDA
(to 1819)

St. Augustine
(1565)

Gulf of Mexico

Bahamas
(to Britain 1646)

ATLANTIC OCEAN

Culiacán
(1531)

Tampico

VICEROYALTY OF

La Habana (1515)

Mexico City
(Tenochtitlán)
(1325)
Veracruz
(1519)

*Yucatan
Peninsula*

Cuba (1492)
Santiago (1514)

Espanola
(1492)

Puerto Rico
(1502)

World divided
into Spanish
and Portuguese
hemispheres:
Treaty of
Tordesillas
(1494)

NEW SPAIN

Guatemala
(1519)

Jamaica
(to Britain 1655)

HAITI
(French after 1697)

Santo Domingo
(1496)

Caribbean Sea

Panama
(1519)

Caracas
(1567)

Orinoco R.

Trinidad (1498)

VICEROYALTY OF

SURINAM
(Dutch)
(1625)

FRENCH
GUIANA
(1626)

PACIFIC OCEAN

Santa Fe de Bogotá
(1538)

NEW GRANADA

Quito (1534)

Guayaquil
(1535)

Amazon   River

P
O
R
T
U
G
U
E
S
E
  B R A Z I L

Ciudad de los
Reyes (Lima)
(1535)

Cuzco
(1535)

VICEROYALTY

OF

NEW CASTILIA

(Peru)

La Paz
(1548)

Rio de
Janeiro (1567)

São Paulo
(1554)

VICEROYALTY
OF
LA PLATA

Valparaiso
(1544)
Santiago
(1541)

Parana R.

Montevideo (1724)
Rio de la Plata

Buenos Aires
(1580)

0   1,000 Miles
0   1,000 Kilometers

Colonial boundaries and provincial names
are for the late 18th century

Aztec Empire at the time of Spanish conquest

Inca Empire at the time of Spanish conquest

Straits of Magellan
Tierra del Fuego

Cape Horn at the tip of South America, Spain's power stood unchallenged.

It was, however, a colonial empire very different politically from the one the English would establish in North America beginning in the early seventeenth century. Although the earliest Spanish ventures in the New World had operated largely independent of the throne, by the end of the sixteenth century the monarchy had established an elaborate hierarchical system by which its authority extended directly into the governance of local communities. Colonists had few opportunities to establish political institutions independent of the crown. The British administration of North America, by contrast, would be far looser and more casual; and European settlers there would quickly develop a political system in which the monarch often played an indirect, even a nominal, role.

There was also a significant economic difference. The Spanish were far more successful than the British would be in extracting great surface wealth—gold and silver—from their American colonies. But for that very reason, they concentrated relatively less energy on making agriculture and commerce profitable in their colonies. The problem was compounded by the unusually strict and inflexible commercial policies of the Spanish government. To enforce the collection of duties and to provide protection against pirates, the government required all trade with the colonies to be carried on through a single Spanish port and only a few colonial ports, in fleets making but two voyages a year. The system stifled the economic development of the New World. The British colonies, in contrast, faced far fewer restrictions and ultimately produced a large, flexible, and flourishing commercial economy that would sustain prosperity in North America long after the depletion of the gold and silver supplies had begun to debilitate the economies to the south. The Spanish emphasis on surface riches had an ultimately stifling impact on Spain itself as well. The supply of easy wealth from America weakened the incentive to promote domestic economic growth. That was one reason why Spain remained far less developed than its northern European rivals and why its relative power declined so quickly and dramatically in the seventeenth century.

Above all, perhaps, there was a demographic difference between the Spanish empire in America and the colonies to the north. Almost from the beginning, the English, Dutch, and French colonies in North America were centered on farming and permanent settlement and emphasized family life.

A Mohawk Settlement
This 1590 engraving by the Flemish artist Theodore de-Bry shows a Mohawk settlement in which native women and men engage in a variety of domestic tasks. DeBry never visited America. He published a series of books on the New World illustrated with copies of paintings and drawings of American Indians by the English explorer John White and the French traveler Jacques Le Moyne de Morgues. For many Europeans, deBry provided the only information available about native societies in America. (The American Museum of Natural History)

Hence, the Europeans in North America reproduced rapidly after their first difficult years and in time came to outnumber the natives. The Spanish, by contrast, ruled their empire but did not people it. In the first century of settlement, fewer than 250,000 settlers in the Spanish colonies were from Spain itself or from any other European country. Only about 200,000 more arrived in the first half of the seventeenth century. Most of the settlers came from various outposts of Spanish civilization in the Atlantic—the Azores, the Cape Verde Islands, and elsewhere; but even with these additional sources, the number of European settlers in Spanish America remained relatively small. Despite the ravages of disease and war, the vast majority of the population continued to consist of natives. The Spanish, in other words, imposed a small ruling class upon a much larger existing population; they did not create a self-contained European society in the New World as the English would attempt to do in the north. The story of the Spanish empire, therefore, is the story of a collision between and then a commingling of two cultures that had been developing for centuries along completely different lines.

The Meeting of Cultures

Even in the Spanish empire, where the lines separating the races grew far less distinct than they were in the English colonies to the north, European and native cultures never entirely merged. Indeed, significant differences remain today between European and Indian cultures throughout South and Central America. Nevertheless, the arrival of whites launched a process of interaction between different peoples that left no one unchanged.

That Europeans were exploring the Americas at all was in large part a result of their early contacts with the natives, from whom they gained their first knowledge of the rich deposits of gold and silver that drew so many Spaniards and Portuguese to the New World. From that moment on, the history of the Americas became one of increasing levels of exchanges—some beneficial, some catastrophic—among different peoples and cultures. (See "The American Environment," pp. 121–124.)

The first and perhaps most profound result of this exchange was the importation of European diseases to the New World. It would be difficult to exaggerate the consequences of the exposure of native Americans to such illnesses as influenza, measles, typhus, and above all smallpox—diseases to which Europeans had over time developed at least a partial immunity but to which native Americans were tragically vulnerable. Millions died. Native groups inhabiting some of the large Caribbean islands and some areas of Mexico were virtually extinct within fifty years of their first contact with whites; on Hispaniola—where the Dominican Republic and Haiti are today and where Columbus landed and established a small, short-lived colony in the 1490s—the native population quickly declined from approximately 1 million to about 500. In the Mayan

areas of Mexico, as much as 95 percent of the population perished within a few years of their first contact with the Spanish. Some groups fared better than others; many (although not all) of the tribes north of Mexico, whose contact with European settlers came later and was often less intimate, were spared the worst of the epidemics. But for most areas of the New World, this was a demographic catastrophe at least as grave as, and in many places far worse than, the Black Death that had killed about one-third of the population of Europe two centuries before.

The decimation of native populations in the southern regions of the Americas was not, however, purely a result of this inadvertent exposure to infection. It was also a result of the *conquistadores*' quite deliberate policy of subjugation and extermination. Their brutality was in part a reflection of the ruthlessness with which Europeans waged war in all parts of the world. It was also a result of their conviction that the natives were "savages"—uncivilized peoples who could be treated as somehow not fully human. Paradoxically, it was a consquence, too, of the high level of development of some native societies. Had the natives truly been as primitive and disorganized as Europeans wanted to believe, there would have been little need to destroy them. But organized into substantial empires, they posed a serious threat to the *conquistadores*' ambitions. That, more than anything else, accounts for the thoroughness with which the Spanish set about obliterating native cultures. They razed cities and dismantled temples and monuments. They destroyed records and documents (one reason why modern scholars have been able to learn so little about the histories of these native societies). They systematically killed Indian warriors, leaders, priests, and organized elites. They tried, in short, to eliminate the underpinnings of existing civilizations so as to bring the native population fully under Spanish control and to remove all obstacles to the spread of Christianity. By the 1540s, the combined effects of European diseases and European military brutality had all but destroyed the empires of Mexico and South America and allowed the Spanish to exert their authority with few organized challenges from the Indians.

Not all aspects of the exchange were so disastrous to the natives. The Europeans introduced to America important new crops (among them sugar and bananas), domestic livestock (cattle, pigs, and sheep), and perhaps most significantly the horse, which had disappeared from the Western Hemisphere in the Ice Age and now returned aboard Spanish ships in the sixteenth century. These imports were generally intended for the use of the Europeans themselves. But Indian tribes soon learned to cultivate the new crops, and European livestock proliferated rapidly and spread widely among tribes that in the past had possessed virtually no domesticated animals other than dogs. The horse, in particular, became central to the lives of many natives and transformed their societies.

The exchange was at least as important (and far more beneficial) to the Europeans. In both North and South America, the arriving white peoples learned new agricultural techniques from the natives, techniques often far better adapted to the demands of the new land than those they had brought with them from Europe. They discovered new crops, above all maize (corn), which Columbus took back to Europe from his first trip to America and which soon became an important staple in Europe itself as well as among European settlers in the New World. Such foods as squash, pumpkins, beans, sweet potatoes, tomatoes, peppers, and potatoes all found their way into European diets by way of native Americans. These and other American crops revolutionized European agriculture, enabling farmers to feed more people with more nutritious foods. That, in turn, facilitated the growth of the European population and the transformation of the European economy. Agricultural discoveries, in other words, ultimately proved far more important to the future of Europe than the gold and silver the *conquistadores* valued so highly.

In South America, Central America, and Mexico, a society emerged in which Europeans and natives lived in intimate, if unequal, contact with one another. As a result, Indians adopted many features of European civilization, although seldom did those features survive the transfer to America unchanged. Many natives gradually came to speak Spanish or Portuguese, but in the process they created a range of dialects, fusing European words with their own linguistic traditions. Gradually, European missionaries—through a combination of persuasion and coercion—spread Catholicism through most areas of the Spanish empire. But native Christians tended to combine the new religion with features of their old ones, creating a hybrid of faiths that was, while essentially Christian, nevertheless distinctively American.

Colonial officials were expected to take their wives with them to America, but among the ordinary settlers—the majority—European men outnumbered European women by at least ten to one. Not surprisingly, therefore, the Spanish immigrants had substantial sexual contact with native women. Intermarriage became frequent, and before long the population of the colonies came to be dominated (numerically, at least) by people of mixed race, or *mestizos*.

The frequency of intermarriage suggests a number of important aspects of the emerging society of the Spanish empire. It reveals, of course, that men living alone in a strange land craved female companionship and the satisfactions of family life and that they sought those things in the only places they could—among the native population. It reflects the desperate need for labor among the white settlers, including the domestic labor that native wives could provide; in some cases, therefore, intermarriage was a form of labor recruitment. And it suggests why the lines separating the races in the areas of Spanish settlement did not remain as distinct as they did in the later English and French colonies, which were peopled largely by families and in which intermarriage was consequently rare.

Intermarriage was not just a result of the needs and desires of white men. It required, too, at least some measure of acquiescence among native women. Some Indian women opposed marriages to white men and entered them only under coercion. But the extent of intermarriage suggests that not all women resisted. The condition of the sixteenth-century native population and the traditions of the South American tribes may suggest why. By the time white settlement began in earnest in Mexico and South and Central America, many Indian societies were already depleted, and the population decline continued rapidly thereafter. Much of this decrease was a result of disease, which affected men and women equally; but much of it was a result of warfare and enslavement, the burden of which fell disproportionately on men. The sex ratio within the native population, therefore, was seriously out of balance, and Indian women who married white colonists may have been responding to the shortage of native men. There were also long-established customs of intermarriage among some Indian tribes as a way of forming or cementing alliances. Since many Indians considered the white settlers little more foreign than some rival native groups, that custom probably contributed to the frequency of intermarriage as well.

Natives were the principal labor source for the Europeans. Virtually all the commercial, agricultural, and mining enterprises of the Spanish and Portuguese colonists depended on an Indian work force. Different forms of labor recruitment emerged in different areas of the empire. In some places, Indians were sold into slavery. More often, colonists used a coercive wage system closely related, but not identical, to slavery, by which Indians worked in the mines and on the plantations under duress for fixed periods, unable to leave without the consent of their employers. These indentured work forces survived in some areas of the South American mainland for many centuries. So central was the need for native labor that European settlers requesting land grants, or *encomienda*, from imperial authorities generally asked for title not to vacant tracts of territory but to particular Indian villages, which could become a source of labor and tribute to the usually absentee landlords.

Yet even that was not, in the end, enough to meet the labor needs of the colonists—particularly since the native population had declined (and in some places virtually vanished) because of disease and war. As early as 1502, therefore, European settlers began importing slaves from Africa.

Africa and America

Most of the black men and women who were sent forcibly to America came from a large region in west Africa below the Sahara Desert, known as Guinea. Like other continents, Africa was the home of a wide variety of peoples and cultures. And since over half of all the immigrants to the New World between 1500 and 1800 were Africans, those cultures greatly affected the character of American civilization. Europeans and white Americans came to portray African

society as primitive and uncivilized (in part to justify the enslavement of Africa's people). But most Africans were, in fact, civilized peoples with well-developed economies and political systems.

Human beings began settling in west Africa at least 10,000 years ago. By the fifteenth century, they had developed extensive civilizations and complex political systems. The residents of upper Guinea had substantial commercial contact with the Mediterranean world—trading ivory, gold, and slaves for finished goods—and, largely as a result, became early converts to Islam. After the collapse of the ancient kingdom of Ghana around A.D. 1100, they created the even larger empire of Mali, which survived well into the fifteenth century and whose great trading center at Timbuktu became fabled as a meeting place of the peoples of many lands and a center of education.

Farther south, Africans were more isolated from Europe and the Mediterranean and were more politically fragmented. The central social unit was the village, which usually consisted of members of an extended family group. Some groups of villages united in small kingdoms—among them Benin, Congo, and Songhay. But no large empires emerged in the south comparable to the Ghana and Mali kingdoms farther north. Nevertheless, these southern societies developed extensive trade—in woven fabrics, ceramics, wooden and iron goods, as well as crops and livestock—both among themselves and, to a lesser degree, with the outside world.

The African civilizations naturally developed economies that reflected the climates and resources of their lands. In upper Guinea, fishing and rice culti-

The Great Mosque of Djenné, Mali

Djenné emerged in the Middle Ages as one of the two principal urban centers of Mali. (The other was Timbuktu.) It was a center of scholarship and commerce, "large, flourishing and prosperous," one African writer of the time wrote, "rich, and blessed and favoured by heaven. God has granted this spot all his favours, as a natural and innate thing." After Islam spread into northern and central Africa, Djenné also became a religious center and the site of this striking mosque, which still stands today. (Eugene Gordon)

vation, supplemented by the extensive trade with Mediterranean lands, were the foundation of the economy. Farther south, Africans grew wheat and other food crops, raised livestock, and fished. There were some more nomadic tribes in the interior, which subsisted largely on hunting and gathering and developed less elaborate social systems. But most Africans were sedentary people, linked together in an elaborate network of political and economic relationships.

As in many Indian societies in America, but in contrast to Europe, African families tended to be matrilineal. People traced their heredity through and inherited property from their mothers. When couples married, the husband left his own family to join the family of his wife. Like virtually all other peoples, Africans divided work by sex, but the nature of that division varied greatly from place to place. Women played a major role, often the dominant role, in trade; in many areas, they were the principal farmers (while the men hunted, fished, and raised livestock); and everywhere, they managed child care and food preparation. Most tribes also divided political power by sex, with men choosing leaders and systems for managing male affairs and women choosing parallel leaders to handle female matters. Tribal chiefs were generally men (although in some places there was a female counterpart), but the position customarily passed down not to the chief's son, but to the son of the chief's eldest sister. African societies, in short, were characterized by a greater degree of equality between the sexes than those of most other parts of the world.

In those areas of west Africa where indigenous religions had survived the spread of Islam (which included most of the lands south of the empire of Mali), people worshiped many gods, whom they associated with various aspects of the natural world and whose spirits they believed lived in trees, rocks, forests, and streams. Most Africans also developed forms of ancestor worship and took great care in tracing family lineage; the most revered priests (who were often also important social and political leaders as well) were generally the oldest people.

African societies were elaborately hierarchical. Small elites of priests and nobles stood at the top. Most people belonged to the large middle group of farmers, traders, crafts workers, and others. At the bottom of society were slaves—men and women who were put into bondage after being captured in wars or because of criminal behavior or as a result of unpaid debts. Slavery was not usually permanent; peo-

ple were often in bondage for a fixed term, and in the meantime retained certain legal protections (including the right to marry). Their children, moreover, did not inherit their parents' condition of bondage. The slavery that Africans would experience at the hands of the Europeans was to be very different; but the existence of slavery among Africans themselves facilitated their enslavement by Europeans.

The African slave trade long preceded European settlement in the New World. As early as the eighth century, west Africans began selling slaves to traders from the Mediterranean, who were responding to a demand from elite families who wanted black men and women as domestic servants as well as to more general labor shortages in some areas of Europe and north Africa. When Portuguese sailors began exploring the coast of Africa in the fifteenth century, they too bought slaves—usually criminals and people captured in war—and took them back to Portugal, where there was a small but steady demand.

In the sixteenth century, however, the market for slaves grew dramatically as a result of the growing European demand for sugar cane. The small areas of sugar cultivation in the Mediterranean were proving inadequate, and production soon moved to new areas: to the island of Madeira off the African coast, which became a Portuguese colony, and not long thereafter to the Caribbean islands and Brazil. Sugar was a labor-intensive crop, and the demand for black workers in these new areas of cultivation was high. European slave traders found a ready supply along the coast of west Africa (and some areas of east Africa as well), where kingdoms warred with one another in an effort to capture potential slaves to exchange for European goods. At first the slave traders were overwhelmingly Portuguese and, to a lesser extent, Spanish. By the seventeenth century, the Dutch had won control of most of the market. In the eighteenth century, the English dominated it; by then, slavery had spread well beyond its original locations in the Caribbean and South America and into the English colonies to the north.

The Arrival of the English

England's first documented contact with the New World came only five years after Spain's. In 1497, John Cabot (like Columbus a native of Genoa) sailed to the northeastern coast of North America on an expedition sponsored by King Henry VII. Other English navigators, continuing Cabot's unsuccessful search for a northwest passage through the New World to the Orient, explored other areas of North America during the sixteenth century. But while England claimed dominion over the lands its explorers surveyed, nearly a century passed before the English made any serious efforts to establish colonies there. Like other European nations, England had to experience an internal transformation before it could begin settling new lands. That transformation, spurred by a combination of economic and cultural changes, occurred in the sixteenth century.

The Commercial Incentive

Part of the attraction of the New World to the English was its newness, its contrast to their own troubled land. America seemed a place where human settlement could start anew, where a perfect society could be created that was unencumbered by the flaws and inequities of the Old World. Such dreams began to emerge in England only a few years after Columbus's discovery. They found classic expression in Sir Thomas More's *Utopia* (published in Latin in 1516, translated into English thirty-five years later), which described a mythical and nearly perfect society on an imaginary island supposedly discovered by a companion of Amerigo Vespucci in the waters of the New World.

More's picture of an ideal community was, among other things, a comment on the social and economic evils of the England of his own time. Tudor England, despite its literary glory (it produced, among much else, the works of Shakespeare) and its adventurous spirit, was in many ways a troubled nation. The English people suffered from the frequent and costly European wars in which their government became engaged. They suffered from almost constant religious strife within their own land. And they suffered above all from a harsh economic transformation of the countryside. Because the worldwide demand for wool was growing rapidly (neither cotton nor silk having yet become a major source of cloth), many landowners were finding it profitable to convert their land from fields for crops to pastures for sheep. The result was a significant growth in the wool trade—but that meant that land tilled at one time by serfs and later by rent-paying tenants was steadily enclosed for sheep runs and taken away from the farmers.

Thousands of evicted tenants roamed the countryside in gangs, begging (and at times robbing) and alarming the more fortunate householders through whose communities they passed. The government passed various laws designed to halt enclosures, relieve the worthy poor, and compel the able-bodied or "sturdy beggars" to work. Such laws had little effect. The enclosure movement continued unabated, and relatively few of the dislocated farmers could find reemployment in raising sheep or manufacturing wool.

The enclosure movement had a more general impact as well. The population of England was growing steadily in the sixteenth century—from 3 million in 1485 to 4 million in 1603—but the food supply was not increasing proportionately. In some respects, it was actually declining, as land was moved from cultivation. Both because of the dislocation of farmers and the restriction of the food supply, therefore, the nation had a serious problem of surplus population.

Amid this growing distress, a rising class of merchant capitalists was prospering from the expansion of foreign trade. At first, England had exported little except raw wool; but new merchant-capitalists helped create a domestic cloth industry that allowed them to begin marketing finished goods. They gathered up raw material, put it out for spinning and weaving in individual households, and sold the cloth both in England and abroad. At first, most exporters did business almost entirely as individuals—except for their membership in the Company of Merchant Adventurers, which regulated some of the activities of its members and secured trading privileges for them. In time, however, merchants developed more formally collective enterprises and formed chartered companies. Each such enterprise operated on the basis of a charter acquired from the monarch, which gave the company a monopoly for trading in a particular region. Among the first of these were the Muscovy Company (1555), the Levant Company (1581), the Barbary Company (1585), the Guinea Company (1588), and the East India Company (1600). Some were simply regulated associations of individual traders, similar to the Merchant Adventurers, each member doing business separately. Others were joint-stock companies, similar in some respects to modern corporations, with stockholders sharing risk and profit on either single ventures or, as became more common, on a permanent basis. These investors often made fantastic profits from the exchange of English manufactures, especially woolens, for exotic goods; and they felt a powerful urge to continue the expansion of their profitable trade.

Central to this drive was the emergence of a new concept of economic life known as mercantilism, which was gaining favor throughout Europe. Mercantilism rested on the assumption that the nation as a whole, not the individuals within it, was the principal actor in the economy, and that the goal of economic activity should be to increase the nation's total wealth. Mercantilists believed that the world's wealth was finite; that one person or nation could grow rich only at the expense of another; and that a nation's economic health depended, therefore, on extracting as much wealth as possible from foreign lands and exporting as little as possible from home. Thomas Mun produced one of the classic statements of this economic philosophy in 1664, when he published *England's Treasure by Foreign Trade*. By then, however, mercantilism had already been shaping English economic life for many years.

The principles of mercantilism guided the economic policies of virtually all the great nation-states that were emerging in Europe in the sixteenth and seventeenth centuries. It greatly enhanced the position of the new merchant-capitalists, whose overseas ventures were thought to benefit the entire nation and to be worthy of government assistance. It also increased the competition among nations. Every European state was trying to find markets for its exports while trying to limit its imports. One result was the increased attractiveness of acquiring colonies, which could become the source of needed goods that a country might otherwise have to buy from other nations.

In England, the mercantilistic program thrived at first on the basis of the flourishing wool trade with the European continent, and particularly with the great cloth market in Antwerp. Beginning in the 1550s, however, that glutted market collapsed, and English merchants found themselves obliged to look elsewhere for overseas trade. The establishment of colonies seemed to be a ready answer to that problem, as well as to others, as the Oxford clergyman Richard Hakluyt argued in a series of explorers' narratives and in a 1584 essay on "western planting," which established him as the outstanding English propagandist for colonization. Colonies would, Hakluyt argued, serve many useful purposes. They would, of course, create new markets for English goods. But they would also help alleviate poverty and unemployment. The colonies themselves would siphon off the surplus population. For the poor who remained in England "idly to the annoy of the whole state," there would be

new work as a result of the prosperity the colonies would create. Perhaps most important, colonial commerce would allow England to acquire products for which the nation had previously been dependent on foreigners—products such as lumber, naval stores, and, above all, silver and gold.

The Religious Incentive

In addition to these economic motives for colonization, there were religious ones, rooted in the events of the European and English Reformations. The Protestant Reformation began in Germany in 1517, when Martin Luther openly challenged some of the basic practices and beliefs of the Roman Catholic church—until then, the supreme religious authority and also one of the strongest political authorities throughout western Europe. Luther, an Augustinian monk and ordained priest, challenged the Catholic belief that salvation could be achieved through good works or through the church itself. He denied the church's claim that God communicated to the world through the pope and the clergy. The Bible, not the church, was the authentic voice of God, Luther claimed; and salvation was to be found not through "works" or through the formal practice of religion, but through faith alone. Luther's challenge quickly won him a wide following among ordinary men and women in northern Europe. He himself insisted that he was not revolting against the church, that his purpose was to reform it from within. But when the pope excommunicated him in 1520, Luther expressed open defiance and began the process that would ultimately lead his followers out of the Catholic church entirely. A schism within European Christianity had begun that was never to be healed.

As the spirit of the Reformation spread rapidly throughout Europe, creating intellectual ferment and (in some places) war, other dissidents began offering other alternatives to orthodox Catholicism. The Swiss theologian John Calvin was, after Luther, the most influential reformer and went even further than Luther had in rejecting the Catholic belief that human institutions could affect an individual's prospects for salvation. Calvin introduced the doctrine of predestination. God "elected" some people to be saved and condemned others to damnation; each person's destiny was determined before birth, and no one could change that predetermined fate. While individuals could not alter their destinies, however, they could strive to know them. This tenet became the most powerful element of Calvin's religion. Those who accepted his teachings came to believe that the way they led their lives might reveal to them their chances of salvation. A wicked or useless existence would be a sign of damnation; saintliness, diligence, and success could be signs of grace. Calvinism created anxieties among its followers, to be sure; but it also produced a strong incentive to lead virtuous, productive lives. The new creed spread rapidly throughout nothern Europe and produced (among other groups) the Huguenots in France and the Puritans in England.

The English Reformation began, however, less as a result of these doctrinal revolts than because of a political dispute between the king and the pope. In 1529 King Henry VIII, angered by the refusal of the pope to grant him a divorce from his Spanish wife (who had failed to bear him the son he desperately wanted), broke England's ties with the Catholic church and established himself as the head of the Christian faith in his country. He made relatively few other changes in English Christianity, however. After his death the survival of Protestantism remained for a time in doubt, especially when Henry's Catholic daughter Mary ascended the throne. Mary quickly restored England's allegiance to Rome and harshly persecuted those who refused to return to the Catholic fold. Many Protestants were executed (the reason for the queen's enduring nickname, "Bloody Mary"); others fled to the continent, where they came into contact with the most radical ideas of the Reformation. Mary died in 1558, and her half-sister, Elizabeth, became England's sovereign. Elizabeth once again severed the nation's connection with the Catholic church (and, along with it, an alliance with Spain that Mary had forged).

The Church of England, as the official religion was now known, satisfied the political objectives of the queen, but it failed to satisfy the religious desires of many English Christians. To large groups of Catholics, it was an affront to their traditional faith; they continued to claim allegiance to the pope. To others, affected by the teachings of the European Reformation, it was a church that had abandoned Rome without abandoning Rome's offensive beliefs and practices. Under Elizabeth, the church began to change theologically and to incorporate some of the tenets of the Calvinist faith, but never enough to satisfy its critics—particularly the many exiles who had fled the country under Mary and who now returned, bringing their new, more radical religious

Elizabeth I
The Flemish artist Marcus Gheeraerts the younger moved to England in 1568 (along with his father, also a painter) as a Protestant refugee from his homeland. In approximately 1593 he painted this portrait of the English queen, portraying her as she was seen by many of her contemporaries: a strong, confident ruler presiding over an ambitious, expansionist nation. She stands here on a map of England. (National Portrait Gallery, London)

ideas with them. They continued to clamor for reforms that would "purify" the church; accordingly, they became known as "Puritans."

A few Puritans took what were, by the standards of the time, genuinely radical positions. They were known as Separatists, and they were determined to worship as they pleased in their own independent congregations, a determination that flew in the face of English law—which outlawed unauthorized religious meetings, required all subjects to attend regular

Anglican services, and levied taxes to support the established church. Their radicalism was visible in other ways as well, including their rejection of prevailing assumptions about the proper religious roles of women. Many Separatist sects, perhaps most prominently the Quakers, permitted women to serve as preachers and to assume a prominence in other religious matters that would have been impossible in the established church.

Most Puritans did not wish to leave the Church of England. Still, their demands were by no means modest. They wanted to simplify Anglican forms of worship. They wanted to reduce the power of the bishops, who were appointed by the crown and who were, in many cases, openly corrupt and highly extravagant. Perhaps above all they wanted to reform the local clergy, a group composed in large part of greedy, uneducated men with little interest in (or knowledge of) theology. The Puritans wished, in short, to see the church give more attention to its spiritual role and less to its temporal ambitions. No less than the Separatists, they grew increasingly frustrated by the refusal of either the political or ecclesiastical hierarchies to respond to their demands.

Puritan discontent, already festering, grew rapidly after the death of Elizabeth, the last of the Tudors, and the accession of James I, the first of the Stuarts, in 1603. A Scotsman, the new king was widely considered a foreigner. A learned man, he was nevertheless a poor politician—"the wisest fool in Christendom," some called him. Convinced that kings ruled by divine right, James made it clear from the start that he intended to govern as he pleased. He quickly antagonized the Puritans, a group that included most of the rising businessmen, by resorting to illegal and arbitrary taxation, by favoring English Catholics in the granting of charters and other favors, and by supporting "high church" forms of ceremony. By the early seventeenth century, therefore, a growing number of religious nonconformists were beginning to look for places of refuge outside the kingdom. When combined with the other economic and social incentives for colonization, these religious discontents helped turn England's gaze to distant lands.

The English in Ireland

England's first experience with colonization came not in the New World, but in a land separated from Britain only by a narrow stretch of sea: Ireland. The English had long laid claim to the island and had for many years maintained small settlements in the area around Dublin. But it was only in the second half of the sixteenth century that serious efforts at large-scale colonization began. Through the 1560s and 1570s, would-be colonists moved through the country, capturing territory and attempting to subdue the native population. In the process they developed many of the assumptions that would guide later English colonists in America.

The most important of these assumptions was that the native population of Ireland—approximately 1 million people, loyal to the Catholic church, with their own language and their own culture—was a collection of wild, vicious, and ignorant savages. The Irish lived in ways that the English believed crude and wasteful, and they fought back against the intruders with a ferocity that the English considered barbaric. Such people could not be tamed, the English concluded. They certainly could not be assimilated into English society. They must, therefore, be suppressed, isolated, and if necessary destroyed.

Whatever barbarities the Irish may have inflicted on the colonizers were more than matched by the English in return. Sir Humphrey Gilbert, who was later to establish the first British colony in the New World (an unsuccessful venture in Newfoundland), served for a time as governor of one Irish district and suppressed rebellions by the natives with extraordinary viciousness. Gilbert was an educated and ostensibly civilized man; yet by looking on the natives as people somehow less than human, and therefore not entitled to whatever decencies civilized people reserved for their treatment of one another, he managed to justify, both to himself and to others, such atrocities as beheading Irish soldiers after they were killed in battle. In dealing with "savages," the English believed, any tactics could be excused. Gilbert himself, Sir Walter Raleigh, Sir Richard Grenville, and others active in Ireland in the mid-sixteenth century derived from their experiences there an outlook they would take with them to America, where similarly vicious efforts to subdue and subjugate the natives ultimately succeeded—as they never did in Ireland.

The Irish experience led the English to another important (and related) assumption about colonization: that English settlements in distant lands must retain a rigid separation from the native populations.

In Ireland, English colonizers established what they called "plantations," transplantings of English society to a foreign land. Unlike the Spanish in America, the English in Ireland did not try simply to rule a subdued native population; they tried to build a complete society of their own, peopled with emigrants from England itself. The new society would exist within a "pale of settlement," an area physically separated from the natives. That concept, too, they would take with them to the New World, even though in Ireland, as later in America, the separation of peoples and the preservation of "pure" English culture proved impossible.

The French and the Dutch in America

English settlers in America, unlike those in Ireland, were to encounter not only natives but also rival Europeans who were, like them, driven by mercantilist ideas to establish economic outposts abroad. To the south and southwest were the scattered North American outposts of the Spanish empire, which, despite a peace it had negotiated with England in 1604, continued to look on the English as intruders. For many years, the English in their settlements along the coast could not feel entirely safe from attack by Spanish ships.

Other and more formidable rivals were appearing in the northern parts of the continent in the early sixteenth century: the French. France founded its first permanent settlement in America at Quebec in 1608, less than a year after the English had started their first at Jamestown, but the French colony's population grew very slowly. Few French Catholics felt any inclination to leave their homeland, and those French Protestants who might have wished to emigrate were excluded from the colony. The French, however, exercised an influence in the New World disproportionate to their numbers, largely because of their relationships with native Americans.

Unlike the English, who for many years hugged the coastline and traded with the Indians of the interior through intermediaries, the French forged close, direct ties with natives deep inside the continent. French Jesuit missionaries were among the first to penetrate Indian societies and established some of the first contacts between the two peoples. More important still were the *coureurs de bois*—adventurous fur traders and trappers—who also penetrated far into the wilderness and developed an extensive trade that

became one of the underpinnings of the French colonial economy.

The fur trade was, in fact, more an Indian than a French enterprise. The *coureurs de bois* were, in many ways, little more than middlemen between the Algonquin, Montagnais, and Huron Indians who hunted the fur-bearing animals, processed their pelts, and transported the furs in their own canoes and toboggans. The French traders were able to function only to the degree that they could form partnerships with the Indians, and that they succeeded was often a result of their ability to become virtually a part of native society, living among the Indians and at times marrying Indian women. The fur trade helped open the way for the other elements of the French presence in North America: the agricultural estates (or *seigneuries*) along the St. Lawrence River, the development of trade and military centers at Quebec and Montreal, and the creation of an alliance with the Algonquins and others that enabled the French to compete with the more numerous British in the contest for control of North America. That alliance also brought the French into conflict with the Iroquois, the Algonquins' ancient enemies, who were assuming the central role in the English fur trade. An early result of these tensions was a 1609 attack led by Samuel de Champlain, the founder of Quebec, on a band of Mohawks, apparently at the instigation of his Algonquin trading partners.

Besides the Spanish and the French, the English were soon to find in the New World another European rival, the Dutch. Holland in the early seventeenth century, having won its independence from Spain, was one of the leading trading nations of the world. Its merchant fleet was larger than England's, and its traders were active not only in Europe but also in Africa, Asia, and—increasingly—America. In 1609 an English explorer in the employ of the Dutch, Henry Hudson, sailed up the river that was to be named for him in what is now New York State, convinced for a time that he had found the long-sought water route through the continent to the Pacific. He had not found it, of course; but his explorations led to a Dutch claim on territory in America and to the establishment of a permanent Dutch presence in the New World.

For more than a decade after Hudson's voyage, the Dutch maintained an active trade in furs in and around New York. Not long after the first two permanent English colonies took root in Jamestown and Plymouth, the Dutch created a wedge between them when the Dutch West India Company estab-

Cartier in Canada
This early engraving of the French explorer Jacques Cartier shows him leading a group of settlers into what is now Canada. Cartier made three voyages of exploration to the New World between 1534 and 1542. On the last he attempted unsuccessfully to establish a permanent European colony along the St. Lawrence River, which he had discovered. Unlike some of the early English colonizing efforts, Cartier's included women as well as men—as this illustration reveals.   (Huntington Library)

lished in 1624 a series of permanent trading posts on the Hudson, Delaware, and Connecticut rivers. The company actively encouraged settlement of the region—not just from Holland itself, but from such other parts of northern Europe as Germany, Sweden, and Finland. It transported whole families to the New World and granted vast feudal estates to *patroons* who would bring still more immigrants to America. The result was the colony of New Netherland and its principal town, New Amsterdam, on Manhattan Island. Its population, diverse as it was, remained relatively small; the colony was only loosely united, with chronically weak leadership. It would ultimately prove a much less serious rival than the French to English domination of the region.

The First English Settlements

The first permanent English settlement in the New World was established at Jamestown, in Virginia, in 1607. But for nearly thirty years before that, English merchants and adventurers had been engaged in a series of failed efforts to create colonies in America.

Through much of the sixteenth century, the English had harbored mixed feelings about the New World. They were aware of its existence and intrigued by its possibilities. And like other European peoples, they were—under the leadership of their brilliant and popular ruler, Elizabeth I—developing a strong sense of nationalism that encouraged dreams of expansion into America. At the same time, however, England was leery of Spain, which remained

Roanoke

A drawing by one of the English colonists in the ill-fated Roanoke expedition of 1585 became the basis for this engraving by Theodore DeBry, published in England in 1590. A small European ship carrying settlers approaches the island of Roanoke, at left. The wreckage of several larger vessels farther out to sea and the presence of Indian settlements on the mainland and on Roanoke itself suggest some of the perils the settlers encountered.   (New York Public Library)

the dominant force in America and, it seemed, the dominant naval power in Europe. Even after Elizabeth dissolved the Anglo-Spanish alliance that her predecessor, Mary, had created, England remained for a time cowed by the Spanish threat.

All of that changed in the course of the 1570s and 1580s. English "sea dogs" such as Sir Francis Drake won nationwide fame for their successful raids on Spanish merchant ships and raised confidence about England's ability to challenge Spanish sea power. Far more important was a single event: the attempted invasion of England by the Spanish Armada in 1588. Philip II, the powerful Spanish king who had recently united his nation with Portugal, was determined to subjugate his annoying English rival—to end its challenges to Spanish commercial supremacy and to bring the nation back into the Catholic church.

He assembled one of the largest military fleets in the history of warfare to carry his troops across the English Channel and into England itself. Philip's bold venture turned into a fiasco when the smaller English fleet, taking advantage of its greater maneuverability and of the English seafarers' superior knowledge of the waters, dispersed the Armada and, in a single stroke, ended Spain's domination of the Atlantic. The most important inhibition the English had retained about establishing themselves in the New World was now removed.

The pioneers of English colonization were Sir Humphrey Gilbert and his half-brother Sir Walter Raleigh—both friends of Queen Elizabeth, and both veterans of earlier colonial efforts in Ireland. Even before the defeat of the Armada, Gilbert was insisting at court that English bases in America would give

SIGNIFICANT EVENTS

14,000–12,000 B.C.   Asians begin migrating to North America across the Bering Straits (p. 1)

1000 A.D.   Scandinavian explorers establish temporary settlement in Newfoundland (p. 5)

1347   Black Death begins in Europe (p. 5)

1420s   Portuguese explorers travel down west coast of Africa in search of sea route to Asia (p. 7)

1492   Columbus sails west from Spain in search of Asia, reaches Bahama Islands in the Caribbean (p. 7)

1494   Treaty of Tordesillas divides New World between Spain and Portugal (p. 10)

1497   John Cabot establishes first English claim in North America (p. 17)

1517   Martin Luther challenges Catholic church, sparking Protestant Reformation in Europe (p. 14)

1518–1530   Smallpox epidemic ravages Indian societies of Central and South America (p. 14)

1519–1522   Magellan expedition circumnavigates globe (p. 10)

1521   Cortés captures Tenochtitlán and conquers Aztec Empire in Mexico (p. 10)

1533   Pizarro captures Cuzco and conquers Incas in Peru (p. 11)

1558   Elizabeth I ascends English throne (p. 20)

1565   St. Augustine founded in Florida (p. 11)

1566   English conquest of Ireland begins (p. 21)

1585   "Lost Colony" established on Roanoke Island (p. 25)

1603   James I succeeds Elizabeth I in England (p. 26)

1606   James I establishes Virginia Company, divided between groups at London and Plymouth (p. 26)

still greater opportunities for sapping the power of Spain. In 1578 he obtained from Elizabeth a patent granting him, for six years, the exclusive right "to inhabit and possess at his choice all remote and heathen lands not in the actual possession of any Christian prince."

That same year, Gilbert and Raleigh, with seven ships and nearly 400 men, set out to establish a base in the New World. Storms turned them back before they had crossed the ocean. It took Gilbert five years to raise enough money to try again. Then, in 1583, he sailed with a second and smaller expedition, reached Newfoundland, and took possession of it in the queen's name. He proceeded southward along the coast, looking for a good place to build a military outpost that might eventually grow into a profitable colony, of which he would be proprietor. Once more a storm defeated him. This time his ship sank, and he was lost at sea.

Raleigh was undeterred. The next year, he secured from Elizabeth a six-year grant similar to Gilbert's and sent a small group of men on an expedition to explore the North American coast. They returned with two captive Indians and glowing reports of what they had seen. They were particularly enthusiastic about an island the natives called Roanoke and

about the area of the mainland just beyond it (in what is now North Carolina). Raleigh, an astute politician, received permission from Elizabeth to name the entire region "Virginia" in honor of Elizabeth, "the Virgin Queen." He hoped for financial aid in return, but Elizabeth offered none. So Raleigh turned to private investors to finance another expedition.

In 1585 Raleigh recruited his cousin, Sir Richard Grenville, to lead a group of men (most of them from the English plantations in Ireland) to Roanoke to establish a colony. Grenville deposited the settlers on the island, remained long enough to antagonize the natives by razing an Indian village as retaliation for a minor theft, and returned to England. The following spring, with expected supplies and reinforcements from England long overdue, Sir Francis Drake unexpectedly arrived in Roanoke. The colonists boarded his ships and left.

Raleigh tried again in 1587, sending an expedition carrying ninety-one men, seventeen women (two of them pregnant), and nine children—the nucleus, he hoped, of a viable "plantation." The settlers landed on Roanoke and attempted to take up where the first group of colonists had left off. (Shortly after arriving, one of the women—the daughter of the commander of the expedition, John White—gave

Wildlife in the New World

Sometime in the 1590s, after he had retired from the seas, John White published these sketches of the wildlife he had encountered during one of his voyages to the New World. They portray a diamondback terrapin and a swallowtail butterfly. White was one of the original explorers and colonists at Roanoke, but he was away in England when his daughter and granddaughter (Virginia Dare, the first English child born in America) vanished along with the rest of the settlers.   (British Museum)

birth to a daughter, Virginia Dare, the first American-born child of English parents.) White returned to England after several weeks (leaving his daughter and granddaughter behind) in search of supplies and additional settlers; he hoped to return in a few months. But the hostilities with Spain intervened, and White did not return to the island for three years. When he did, in 1590, he found the island utterly deserted, with no clue to the fate of the settlers other than the cryptic inscription "Croatoan" carved on a post. Some have argued that the colonists

were slaughtered by the Indians in retaliation for Grenville's (and perhaps their own) hostilities. Others have contended that they left their settlement and joined native society, ultimately becoming entirely assimilated. But no conclusive solution to the mystery of the "Lost Colony" has ever been found.

The Roanoke disaster marked the end of Sir Walter Raleigh's involvement in English colonization of the New World. In 1603, when James I succeeded Elizabeth to the throne, Raleigh was accused of plotting against the king, stripped of his monopoly, and imprisoned for more than a decade. Finally (after being released for one last ill-fated maritime expedition) he was executed by the king in 1618. No later colonizer would receive grants of land in the New World as vast or undefined as those Raleigh and Gilbert had acquired. Despite the discouraging example of their experiences, the colonizing impulse remained very much alive.

In the first years of the seventeenth century, a group of London merchants to whom Raleigh had assigned his charter rights decided to renew the attempt at colonization in Virginia. A rival group of merchants, from Plymouth and other West Country towns, were also interested in American ventures and were sponsoring voyages of exploration farther north, up to Newfoundland, where West Country fishermen had been going for many years. In 1606 James I issued a new charter, which divided America between the two groups. The London group got the exclusive right to colonize in the south, and the Plymouth merchants received the same right in the north. The settlers were to retain all the "liberties, franchises, and immunities" that belonged to English citizens at home. Through the efforts of these and other companies, the first enduring English colonies would be planted in America.

SUGGESTED READINGS

American Indians.   Wilcomb E. Washburn, *The Indian in America* (1975); James H. Merrell, *The Indians' New World* (1989); Bruce G. Trigger, *Natives and Newcomers* (1985); Carl Sauer, *Sixteenth-Century North America* (1985); Francis Jennings, *The Invasion of America: Indians, Colonialism, and the Cant of Conquest* (1975); Neal Salisbury, *Manitou and Providence: Indians, Europeans, and the Making of New England* (1982); Nathan Wachtel, *The Vision of the Vanquished* (1977); Kenneth MacGowan and J. A. Hester, Jr., *Early Man in the New World* (1950); Harold E. Driver, *Indians of North America*, 2nd ed. (1970); Francisco Guerra, *The Pre-Columbian Mind* (1971); Gary B. Nash, *Red, White, and Black,* rev. ed. (1982); Alfred W. Crosby, Jr., *The Colum-* *bian Exchange: Biological and Cultural Consequences of 1492* (1972); Henry Warner Bowden, *American Indians and Christian Missions* (1982); James Axtell, *The European and the Indian: Essays in the Ethnohistory of Colonial North America* (1981), and *The Invasion Within: The Contest of Cultures in Colonial North America* (1985); J. D. Jennings, ed., *Ancient North America* (1983); R. F. Spencer, J. D. Jennings, et al., *The Native Americans* (1978); Christopher L. Miller, *Prophetic Worlds: Indians and Whites on the Columbia Plateau* (1985).

European Explorations and Spanish America.   Samuel Eliot Morison, *Admiral of the Ocean Sea*, 2 vols. (1942), *The*

European Discovery of America: The Northern Voyages (1971), and *The European Discovery of America: The Southern Voyages* (1974); J. H. Parry, *The Age of Reconnaissance* (1963); David B. Quinn, *North America from Earliest Discovery to First Settlements* (1977); Charles Gibson, *Spain in America* (1966); James Lockhart, *Spanish Peru, 1532–1560: A Colonial Society* (1968); James Lang, *Conquest and Commerce: Spain and England in the Americas* (1975); J. H. Elliott, *The Old World and the New, 1492–1650* (1970); William H. Prescott, *History of the Conquest of Mexico*, 3 vols. (1843).

England Looks West. W. H. McNeill, *The Rise of the West* (1963); J. H. Parry, *Europe and the New World, 1415–1715* (1949) and *The Age of Reconnaissance* (1963); Wallace Notestein, *The English People on the Eve of Colonization, 1603–1630* (1954); Peter Laslett, *The World We Have Lost* (1965); Carl Bridenbaugh, *Vexed and Troubled Englishmen, 1590–1642* (1968); Patrick Collinson, *The Elizabethan Puritan Movement* (1967); C. H. George and Katherine George, *The Protestant Mind of the English Reformation* (1961); Michael Walzer, *The Revolution of the Saints* (1965); Keith Thomas, *Religion and the Decline of Magic* (1971); David Quinn, *The Elizabethans and the Irish* (1966); Nicholas Canny, *The Elizabethan Conquest of Ireland* (1976) and *Kingdom and Colony: Ireland in the Atlantic World* (1988); Lawrence Stone, *The Crisis of the Aristocracy* (1965); Margaret Spufford, *Contrasting Communities* (1974); David Underdown, *Pride's Purge* (1985); Christopher Hill, *The Century of Revolution, 1603–1714* (1961).

First English Colonies. Keith Wrightson, *English Society, 1580–1680* (1982); David B. Quinn, *The Roanoke Voyages, 1584–1590*, 2 vols. (1955), *Raleigh and the British Empire* (1947), and *Set Fair for Roanoke* (1985); Karen Ordahl Kupperman, *Roanoke: The Abandoned Colony* (1984).

Detail from *Penn's Treaty* (c. 1830), by Edward Hicks
Hicks was a minister in Bucks County, Pennsylvania, who won wide renown in the early nineteenth century for his primitive paintings of the American past. This idealized depiction of William Penn's treaty with the Indians is one example. (*Abby Aldrich Rockefeller Folk Art Museum, Colonial Williamsburg Foundation*)

CHAPTER 2

⬎ ⬆ ⬏

The English "Transplantations"

⬎ ⬆ ⬏

The Roanoke fiasco dampened the colonizing enthusiasm in England—for a time. But the lures of the New World—the presumably vast riches, the abundant land, the religious freedom, the change to begin anew—were too strong to be suppressed for very long. Such propagandizers as Richard Hakluyt kept the image of America alive in English society; and by the early seventeenth century, the effort to establish permanent colonies in the New World resumed.

The first few of these new efforts were much like the earlier, failed ones. They were largely private ventures, with little planning or direction from the English government. They were small, fragile, and generally unprepared for the hardships they were to face. And although they survived, unlike the Roanoke experiment, they at first met with similar disasters.

Three conditions in particular shaped the character of the first English settlements. First, the colonies were business enterprises. The colonists remained directly responsible to the private companies that had financed them, and one of their principal concerns from the beginning was to produce a profit for their corporate sponsors. Second, the English colonies, unlike the Spanish, were designed to be "transplantations" of societies from the Old World to the New. (Hence the term "plantation," which was used to describe most of the first settlements.) As in Ireland, there were few efforts to blend English society with the society of the natives. The Europeans attempted, as far as they could, to isolate themselves from the Indians and create enclosed societies that would be entirely their own. They seldom succeeded completely, but the effort shaped their communities nevertheless. And third, because the colonies were tied only indirectly to the crown (which chartered the private companies but took little interest in them thereafter), they began from the start to develop their own political and social institutions. However much the settlers may have wished simply to transplant English society to the New World, they were, in fact, developing a distinctive American society.

The Early Chesapeake

Once James I had issued his 1606 charters to the London and Plymouth Companies, the principal obstacle to founding new American colonies was, as usual, money. The Plymouth group made an early, unsuccessful attempt to establish a colony at Sagadoahoc, on the coast of Maine; but in the aftermath of that failure, it largely abandoned its colonizing efforts. The London Company, by contrast, moved quickly and decisively under the direction of the wealthy merchant Sir Thomas Smith. Only a few months after receiving its charter, the company launched a colonizing expedition headed for Virginia—a party of 144 men aboard three ships, the *Godspeed*, the *Discovery*, and the *Susan Constant*.

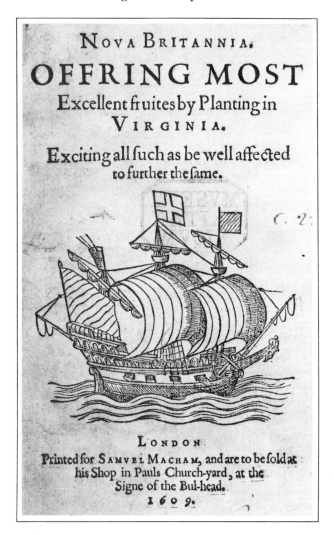

Recruiting for the Colonies, 1609
This is the title page for a pamphlet that describes the attractions of settlement in the New World. Most accounts of the "excellent fruites" of life in Virginia were, like this one, written by people who had never seen America but who shared the excitement that the colonies inspired among the early seventeenth-century English. (New York Public Library)

The Founding of Jamestown

Only 104 men survived the journey. They reached the American coast in the spring of 1607, sailed into the Chesapeake Bay and up a river they named the James, and established their colony on a peninsula extending from the river's northern bank. They named it Jamestown.

The settlers had chosen their site poorly. In an effort to avoid the mistakes of Roanoke (whose res-

idents were assumed to have been murdered by Indians) and select an easily defended location, they chose an inland setting that they believed would offer them security. But the site was low and swampy, intolerably hot and humid in the summer, and prey to outbreaks of malaria. It was surrounded by thick woods, which were difficult to clear for cultivation. And it encroached on the territories of powerful local Indians, a confederation led by the imperial chief Powhatan.

The result could hardly have been more disastrous. For seventeen years, one wave of settlers after another attempted to make Jamestown a habitable and profitable colony. Every effort failed. The town became instead a place of misery and death; and the London Company, which had sponsored it in the hope of vast profits, saw itself drained of funds and saddled with endless losses. All that could be said of Jamestown at the end of this first period of its existence was that it had survived.

The initial colonists, too many of whom were adventurous gentlemen and too few of whom were willing laborers, ran into serious difficulties from the moment they landed. Much like the Indians to the south, who had succumbed quickly to European diseases when first exposed to them, these English settlers had had no prior exposure to the infections of the new land and were highly vulnerable to local diseases. Malaria, in particular, debilitated the colony. Even when it did not kill, it so weakened its victims that they could do virtually no work. The promoters in London added to the problems by demanding a quick return on their investment, which diverted the colonists' energies into futile searches for gold and only slightly more successful efforts to pile up lumber, tar, pitch, and iron for export. These energies would have been better spent on growing food and establishing a new society.

The London Company's emphasis on immediate profits weakened the colony in another way. The promoters had little interest in creating a family-centered community, and they sent few women to Jamestown. The absence of women made it difficult for the settlers to establish any semblance of a "society." The English were seldom able (and perhaps also unwilling) to intermarry with native women, and hence Jamestown was at first an entirely male settlement. Without women, settlers could not establish real households, could not order their domestic lives, and had difficulty feeling any sense of a permanent stake in the community.

Greed and rootlessness contributed to the failure

to grow sufficient food; inadequate diets contributed to the colonists' vulnerability to disease; the ravages of disease made it difficult for the settlers to recover from their early mistakes. The result was a community without the means to sustain itself. By January 1608, when ships appeared with additional men and supplies, all but 38 of the first 104 colonists were dead.

Jamestown, now facing extinction, survived the crisis largely as a result of the efforts of twenty-seven-year-old Captain John Smith, a famous world traveler, hero of his own, implausible narratives of hairsbreadth escapes from both Turks and Indians, but a sensible and capable man. Leadership in the colony

Captain John Smith

John Smith was famous in England long before he became the leader and (many believe) the savior of the English settlement at Jamestown. According to his own immodest accounts, he had spent much of his youth in eastern Europe fighting in wars against the Turks and was even a slave in Turkey for a time. He returned to England from Virginia in 1609 but made one additional journey to North America five years later. In the years prior to his death in 1631, he wrote numerous books recounting and embellishing on his experiences. (Library of Congress)

had been divided among the several members of a council who quarreled continually until the fall of 1608, when Smith, as council president, asserted his will. He imposed work and order on the community. He also organized raids on neighboring Indian villages to steal food and kidnap natives. During the colony's second winter, fewer than a dozen (in a population of about 200) died. By the summer of 1609, when Smith was deposed from the council and returned to England for the treatment of a serious powder burn, the colony was showing promise of survival.

Reorganization

The London Company (now calling itself the Virginia Company) was, in the meantime, dreaming of bigger things. In 1609, it obtained a new charter from the king, which increased its power over the colony and enlarged its area. It raised additional capital by selling stock to "adventurers," who would remain in England but share in future profits. It attracted new settlers by offering additional stock to "planters" who were willing to migrate at their own expense. And it provided free passage to Virginia for poorer people who would agree to serve the company for seven years.

The company envisioned Jamestown as a communal venture. Under its new charter, the company itself would hold title to all land in Jamestown and would control all trade with the colony for seven years. The settlers would contribute their labor to the common enterprise and draw upon a company storehouse for subsistence. At the end of the seven years, the profits would be divided among the stockholders. In the spring of 1609, confident that it was now poised to transform Jamestown into a vibrant, successful venture, the company launched a "great fleet" of nine vessels with about 600 people (including some women and children) aboard—headed for Virginia.

Disaster followed. One of the Virginia-bound ships was lost at sea in a hurricane. Another ran aground on one of the Bermuda islands and was unable to free itself for months. Many of those who reached Jamestown, still weak from their long and stormy voyage, succumbed to fevers before winter came. That winter of 1609–1610 became known as the "starving time," a period worse than anything before. The local Indians, antagonized by John Smith's raids and other hostile actions by the early English settlers, killed off the livestock in the woods and kept the colonists barricaded within their palisade. The Europeans lived on what they could find: "dogs, cats, rats, snakes, toadstools, horsehides," and even the "corpses of dead men," as one survivor recalled. When the migrants who had run aground and been stranded on Bermuda finally arrived in Jamestown the following May, they found only about 60 people (out of 500 residents the previous summer) still alive—and even those were so weakened by the ordeal that they seemed scarcely human. There seemed no point in staying on. The new arrivals took the survivors onto their ship, abandoned the settlement, and sailed downriver for home.

That might have been the end of Jamestown had it not been for a strange twist of fate. As the refugees proceeded down the James toward the Chesapeake, they met an English ship coming up the river—part of a fleet bringing supplies and the colony's first governor, Lord De La Warr. The departing settlers agreed to return to Jamestown. New relief expeditions with hundreds of colonists soon began to arrive, and the effort to turn a profit in Jamestown resumed.

De La Warr and his successors (Sir Thomas Dale and Sir Thomas Gates) imposed a harsh and rigid discipline on the colony. They organized settlers into work gangs; they sentenced offenders to be flogged, hanged, or broken on the wheel. But this communal system of labor did not function effectively for long. Settlers often evaded work, "presuming that howsoever the harvest prospered, the general store must maintain them." Well before the end of the seven-year "communal" period designated by the Virginia Company, Governor Dale concluded that the colony would fare better if the colonists had personal incentives to work. He began to permit the private ownership and cultivation of land. Landowners would repay the company with part-time work and contributions of grain to its storehouses.

Under the leadership of these first governors, Virginia was not always a happy place. But it survived and even expanded. New settlements began lining the river above and below Jamestown. That was partly because of the order and discipline the governors at times managed to impose and because of the increased military assaults on the local Indian tribes to protect the new settlements. But it was also because the colonists had at last discovered a marketable crop—tobacco.

Europeans had become aware of tobacco soon after Columbus's first return from the West Indies, where he had seen the Cuban natives smoking small cigars (*tabacos*), which they inserted in the nostril. By the early seventeenth century, tobacco from the Spanish colonies was already in wide use in Europe. Sir Walter Raleigh had popularized the smoking habit, and the demand for tobacco soared despite objections on both hygienic and economic grounds. Some critics denounced it as a poisonous weed, the cause of many diseases. King James I himself led the attack with *A Counterblaste to Tobacco* (1604), in which he urged his people not to imitate "the barbarous and beastly manners of the wild, godless, and slavish Indians, especially in so vile and stinking a custom." Other critics were concerned because England's tobacco purchases meant a drain of English gold to the Spanish importers.

Then in 1612, the Jamestown planter John Rolfe began to experiment in Virginia with a harsh strain of tobacco that local Indians had been growing for years. The soil and climate were well suited to the crop; and Rolfe obtained seeds from the Spanish colonies and began growing tobacco of high quality in Virginia. It found ready buyers in England. Tobacco cultivation quickly spread up and down the James. The character of this tobacco economy—its profitability, its uncertainty, its land and labor demands—transformed Chesapeake society in fundamental ways.

Of most immediate importance, perhaps, was the pressure tobacco cultivation created for territorial expansion. Tobacco growers needed large areas of farmland to grow their crops; and because tobacco exhausted the soil after only a few years, the demand for land increased even more. English farmers began establishing plantations deeper and deeper in the interior, isolating themselves from the center of European settlement at Jamestown and encroaching on territory the natives considered their own.

Expansion

Even the discovery of tobacco cultivation was not enough to help the Virginia Company. At the end of the seven-year communal period in 1616, there were still no profits to divide, only land and debts. Nevertheless, the promoters continued to hope that the tobacco trade would allow them finally to turn the corner. In 1618, they launched a last great campaign to attract settlers and make the colony profitable.

The tobacco economy created a heavy demand not only for land but for labor. To entice new laborers to the colony, the company established what they

Growth of the Chesapeake, 1607–1750

Boundary claimed by Lord Baltimore, 1632

PENNSYLVANIA

Boundary settlement, 1750

Frederick
(1648)

Baltimore
(1729)

MARYLAND

Potomac R.

Providence
(Annapolis)
(c.1648)

Wilmington
(Fort Christina)
(1638)
WEST JERSEY

Dover
(1717)

LOWER
COUNTIES
OF DELAWARE

Fredericksburg
(1671)

Rappahannock R.

Chesapeake Bay

St. Marys (1634)

VIRGINIA

Fort Royal

Richmond
(1645)

Fort Charles

James R.

Williamsburg (Middle Plantation)
(1633)

Fort Henry

Jamestown
(1607)

Yorktown
(1631)

Newport News
(1621)

Norfolk
(1682)

Fort Christianna

NORTH CAROLINA

Elizabeth City
(1634)

Albemarle
Sound

0   50 Miles
0   50 Kilometers

Virginia Colony	Granville Proprietary
Fairfax Proprietary	(1649) Date settlement founded
To Lord Baltimore, 1632	

called the "headright" system. Headrights were fifty-acre grants of land, which settlers could acquire in a variety of ways. Those who already lived in the colony received 100 acres apiece. Each new settler received a single headright for himself or herself. This system encouraged family groups to migrate together, since the more family members traveled to America, the larger the landholding the family would receive. In addition, anyone (new settler or old) who paid for the passage of other immigrants to Virginia would receive an additional headright for each new arrival—thus, it was hoped, inducing the prosperous to import new laborers to America. Hence wealthy settlers often received headrights for themselves, for members of their families, and for the servants they imported to work for them. Some colonists were able as a result to assemble sizable plantations. In

return, they contributed a small quitrent (one shilling a year for each headright) to the company.

The company added other incentives as well. To diversify the colonial economy, it transported ironworkers and other skilled craftsmen to Virginia. In 1619, it sent 100 English women to the colony (which was still overwhelmingly male) to become the wives of male colonists. (The women could be purchased for 120 pounds of tobacco and enjoyed a status somewhere between indentured servants and free people, depending on the good will—or lack of it—of their husbands.) It promised the colonists the full rights of Englishmen (as provided in the original charter of 1606), an end to the strict and arbitrary rule of the communal years, and even a share in self-government. On July 30, 1619, in the Jamestown church, delegates from the various communities met as the House of Burgesses to consider, along with the governor and his council, the enactment of laws for the colony. It was the first meeting of an elected legislature, a representative assembly, within what was to become the United States.

A month later, there occurred in Virginia another event that established a very different but no less momentous precedent. As John Rolfe recorded, "about the latter end of August" a Dutch ship brought in "20 and odd Negroes." The status and fate of these first Africans in the English colonies remains obscure. There is some reason to believe that the colonists did not consider them slaves, that they thought of them as servants to be held for a term of years and then freed, like the white servants with whom the planters were already familiar. For a time, moreover, the use of black labor remained limited. Although Africans continued to trickle steadily into the colony, planters continued to prefer European indentured servants until at least the 1670s, when such servants began to become scarce and expensive. But whether or not anyone realized it at the time, the small group of blacks who arrived in 1619 marked a first step toward the enslavement of Africans within what was to be the American republic.

The expansion of the colony was able to proceed only because of effective suppression of the local Indians, who tried persistently to drive the English setters away. For two years, Sir Thomas Dale led unrelenting assaults against the Powhatan Indians and in the process kidnapped the great chief Powhatan's daughter Pocahontas. When Powhatan refused to ransom her, she converted to Christianity and in 1614 married John Rolfe. (Pocahontas accompanied her husband back to England, where, as a Christian con-

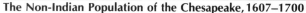

The Non-Indian Population of the Chesapeake, 1607–1700

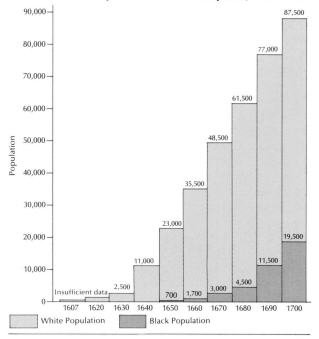

White Population   Black Population

bankruptcy. In 1624, James I revoked the company's charter, and the colony at last came under the control of the crown. So it would remain until 1776.

With the stabilization of Virginia's English sponsorship and the suppression of the Indian threat, the colony finally seemed secure. It had weathered a series of disasters and had established itself as a permanent settlement. It had developed a cash crop that promised at least modest profits. It had established a rudimentary representative government. And it could now realistically hope for future growth and prosperity. But these successes had come at a terrible cost. In 1624, the white population of Virginia stood at 1,300. Over the preceding seventeen years, more than 8,500 white settlers had arrived in the colony. More than 80 percent of them—7,200 people—had died.

Maryland and the Calverts

Maryland was founded under circumstances very different from those of Virginia, but it developed in ways markedly like its neighbor to the south. The similarities in climate and topography in the end proved more important than the contrasts in politics and religion.

Like Massachusetts, Maryland emerged in part from the desire of a religious minority in England to establish a refuge from discrimination. In this case, the minority was not dissenting Protestants but Roman Catholics. The new colony was the dream of George Calvert, the first Lord Baltimore, a recent convert to Catholicism and a shrewd businessman. Calvert envisioned establishing a colony both as a great speculative venture in real estate and as a retreat for English Catholics oppressed by the Anglican establishment at home. He experimented first with a settlement in Newfoundland; but after spending one frigid winter there, he traveled south to the Chesapeake and decided to relocate his colony there.

First, however, he had to return to England and win a charter from King Charles I (who succeeded to the throne on the death of his father, James I, in 1625). Winning a charter was a long process, and Calvert died while negotiations were still under way. But in 1632, his son Cecilius, the second Lord Baltimore, finally received a charter and made plans to continue the work his father had begun.

The Maryland charter was remarkable not only for the extent of the territory it granted to Calvert— an area that encompassed parts of Pennsylvania, Del-

vert and a gracious woman, she stirred interest in projects to "civilize" the Indians. She died while abroad.) At that point, Powhatan ceased his attacks on the English in the face of overwhelming odds. But his death several years later marked the beginning of the end of the short-lived tranquility. Powhatan's brother, Opechancanough, became head of the native confederacy and resumed the effort to defend tribal lands from European encroachments. He particularly resented the continuing intrusions of English merchants and missionaries into his villages. And so the Indians under Opechancanough secretly began to plan the elimination of the intruders. On a March morning in 1622, tribesmen called on the white settlements as if to offer goods for sale, then suddenly attacked. Not until 347 whites of both sexes and all ages (including John Rolfe) lay dead or dying were the Indian warriors finally forced to retreat. The surviving English struck back mercilessly at the Indians and turned back the threat for a time, although it was only after Opechancanough led another unsuccessful uprising in 1644 that the Powhatans finally ceased to threaten the eastern regions of the colony.

By then the Virginia Company in London was defunct. The company had poured virtually all its funds into its profitless Jamestown venture and in the aftermath of the 1622 Indian uprising faced imminent

aware, and Virginia, in addition to present-day Maryland—but for the powers it bestowed on him. He and his heirs were to hold their province as "true and absolute lords and proprietaries," and were to acknowledge the ultimate sovereignty of the king only by paying an annual fee to the crown. The Calverts could establish a government however they saw fit, adopt whatever methods they wished for distributing land, and even revive the medieval system of feudal dependency—awarding property to men who would become the vassals of the proprietor.

Since the Virginia Company (which still claimed its land rights in America) objected to the Calvert grant, Lord Baltimore remained at home to defend his interests at court. He appointed his brother Leonard Calvert governor and sent him with another brother to see to the settlement of the family's province. In March 1634, two ships—the *Ark* and the *Dove*—bearing 200 or 300 passengers entered the Potomac River and turned into one of its eastern tributaries. On a high and dry bluff, these first arrivals laid out the village of St. Mary's (named, diplomatically, for the queen). The neighboring Indians, already threatened by rival tribes in the region, befriended the settlers, provided them with temporary shelter, sold them land, and provided them with stocks of corn. The early Marylanders experienced no Indian assaults, no plagues, no starving time.

The Calverts had spent a large part of the family fortune in the development of their American possessions, and they needed to attract many thousands of settlers if their venture was to pay. As a result, they had to encourage the immigration of Protestants as well as their fellow English Catholics, who were both relatively few in number and generally reluctant to emigrate. The Protestant settlers (mostly Anglicans) outnumbered the Catholics from the start, and the Calverts quickly realized that Catholics would always be a minority in the colony. It seemed prudent to adopt a policy of religious toleration. To appease the non-Catholic majority, Lord Calvert appointed a Protestant as governor in 1648. A year later, he sent from England the draft of an "Act Concerning Religion," which assured freedom of worship to all Christians.

Nevertheless, politics in Maryland remained plagued for years by tensions between the Catholic minority (including the proprietor) and the Protestant majority. Zealous Jesuits and crusading Puritans frightened and antagonized their opponents with their efforts to establish the dominance of their own religion. There was frequent violence, and in 1655 a civil war temporarily unseated the proprietary government and replaced it with one dominated by Protestants. The English in Maryland were spared serious conflict with Indians, but they made up for that by inflicting decades of conflict and instability on themselves.

Despite the latitude provided by their charter, the Calverts established a government in Maryland that soon resembled that of other colonies and of England itself. At the insistence of the first settlers, the Calverts agreed in 1635 to the calling of a representative assembly—the House of Delegates—whose proceedings were based on the rules of Parliament. Within fifteen years, the colony had a bicameral legislature, with an upper house that consisted of the governor and his council.

In other respects, however, the distribution of power in Maryland differed sharply from that in other parts of English America. The proprietor retained absolute authority to distribute land as he wished, and Lord Baltimore initially granted large estates to his relatives and to other English aristocrats, so that a distinct upper class soon established itself in Maryland. By 1640, a severe labor shortage in the colony had forced a modification of the land grant procedure; and Maryland, like Virginia, adopted a "headright" system—a grant of 100 acres to each male settler, another 100 for his wife and each servant, and 50 for each of his children. But the great landlords of the colony's earliest years remained powerful even as the population grew larger and more diverse. Like Virginia, Maryland became a center of tobacco cultivation; and like Virginia, planters worked their land with the aid, first, of indentured servants imported from England and then, beginning late in the seventeenth century, with black slaves imported from Africa. Settlement and trade remained dispersed, centered on scattered large plantations, and few towns of any significance emerged.

Turbulent Virginia

By the mid-seventeenth century, the Virginia colony had survived its early disasters and was increasing both its population and the complexity and profitability of its economy. It was also growing more politically contentious, as emerging factions within the state began to compete for the favor of the government. Perhaps the most important dispute involved policy toward the natives. As settlement moved west and encroached still further on Indian lands, border conflicts grew increasingly frequent. Much of the tension within English Virginia in the late seventeenth century revolved around how to respond to those conflicts.

Virginia had been a royal colony, with its governor appointed by the king, ever since the collapse of the Virginia Company in 1624. One of those royal governors, Sir William Berkeley, dominated the politics of the colony for more than thirty years. He arrived in Virginia in 1642 at the age of thirty-six with an appointment from King Charles I; and with but one interruption he remained in control of the government until the 1670s.

Berkeley's policies were generally popular during the first years of his tenure. The governor helped to open up the interior of Virginia by sending out explorers who crossed the Blue Ridge Mountains. He directed a force that put down the 1644 Indian uprising, captured Opechancanough, and (against Berkeley's orders) shot and killed him. The defeated Indians agreed to a treaty ceding to England all the land between the York and the James rivers east of the fall line and prohibiting white settlement west of that line.

This attempt to prevent Indian territory—like many such attempts later in American history—was a failure from the start, largely because of the rapid growth of the Virginia population. Cromwell's victory in 1649 in the English civil war (see p. 46) and the flight of many of the defeated Cavaliers to the colony added significantly to what was already a substantial population increase from other sources. By 1650, Virginia's population of 16,000 was twice what it had been ten years before; by 1660, it had more than doubled again, to 40,000. As the choice lands along the tidewater became scarce, new arrivals and indentured servants completing their terms or escaping from their masters pressed westward into the piedmont. By 1652, English settlers had established three counties in the territory recently set aside for the Indians. Unsurprisingly, there were frequent clashes between Indians and whites.

When Cromwell seized power in England in 1649, Berkeley lost the governorship of Virginia; but King Charles II reappointed him after the Stuart Restoration in 1660. Once back in office, Berkeley, by the force of his personality and by his success in corrupting the council and the House of Burgesses, made himself practically an autocrat. When the first burgesses were elected in 1619, all men aged seventeen or older were entitled to vote. By 1670, the vote was restricted to landowners, and elections were rare. The same burgesses, loyal and subservient to the governor, remained in office year after year. Each county continued to have only two representatives, even though some of the new counties of the interior contained many more people than the old ones of the tidewater area. Thus the more recent settlers on the frontier were underrepresented or (if living in areas not yet formally organized as counties) not represented at all.

A pattern was emerging in Virginia that would repeat itself time and again in other parts of America. New settlements in the west (or the "back country," as it was often known) were growing larger and more prosperous, developing interests and political demands of their own. But more established elites near the coast continued to ignore the demands of the back country's citizens for representation and assistance.

Bacon's Rebellion

In 1676, back-country unrest combined with factional political rivalries to create a major conflict. Nathaniel Bacon, a young, handsome, ambitious graduate of Cambridge University in England, arrived in Virginia in 1673. His wealth and family background enabled him to purchase a good farm in the west and to obtain a seat on the governor's council. He established himself, in other words, as a member of the back-country gentry—an influential, propertied elite that was emerging in the western region of the state just as other elites had emerged earlier in the east.

The new back-country gentry was at odds in crucial ways with its tidewater counterpart. Isolated geographically from the colonial government, western aristocrats sensed themselves cut off from real political power. As part of a new, still half-formed frontier economy, their position was always precarious, and it became even more so as Virginia began to suffer serious economic difficulties in the 1670s. Above all, perhaps, the frontier elite was in constant danger of attack from the Indians, on whose lands (reserved to the tribes by treaty) they were encroaching. The result was a set of frustrations and resentments that came to a head in response to Berkeley's policies for dealing with the natives. Property owners in the back country had long chafed at the governor's attempts to hold the line of settlement steady so as to avoid antagonizing the Indians. It was, they believed, an effort by the eastern aristocracy to protect its dominance by restricting western expansion. (In reality, it was in part an effort by Berkeley to protect his own lucrative fur trade with the Indians.)

Bacon's rift with Berkeley was not a direct result of these regional tensions. It was at least in part a result of his own thwarted political and economic hopes. An exceptionally ambitious man, he chafed at his exclusion from the inner circle of the governor's council (the so-called Green Spring group, whose members enjoyed special access to patronage); Bacon resented, too, Berkeley's refusal to allow him a piece of the Indian fur trade. He was, in short, developing grievances that made him a natural leader of an opposition faction.

Bloody events thrust him into that role. Indians in western Virginia had long chafed at the continual movement of white settlers into their lands. In 1675, some Doeg Indians raided a western plantation and killed a white servant. Bands of local whites retaliated indiscriminately, attacking not only the small Doeg tribe but the powerful Susquehannock as well. The Indians responded with more raids on plantations and killed many more white settlers. As the fighting escalated, Bacon and other concerned landholders demanded that the governor send the militia out to pursue and destroy the Indian warriors. Berkeley, however, took a more cautious route and ordered the construction of several new forts along the western line of settlement. Western landowners were outraged, and Bacon responded to the controversy by offering to organize a volunteer army of back-country men who would do their own fighting.

Berkeley rejected the offer (and a resolution by the House of Burgesses calling on him to grant Bacon a commission). The governor saw Bacon as a potential rival, and he feared a needless slaughter of the natives, most of whom had played no role in the recent fighting. Bacon ignored him and launched a series of vicious but generally unsuccessful pursuits of the Indian challengers. When Berkeley heard of the unauthorized military effort, he dismissed Bacon from the governor's council and proclaimed him and his men to be rebels. At that point what had been an unauthorized assault on the Indians became a military challenge to the colonial government, a conflict known as Bacon's Rebellion. It was the largest and most powerful insurrection against established authority in the history of the colonies, one that would not be surpassed until the Revolution.

Twice, Bacon led his army east to Jamestown. The first time he won a temporary pardon from the governor; the second time, after the governor reneged on the agreement, he burned the city and drove the governor into exile. In the midst of widespread social turmoil throughout the colony, Bacon stood on the verge of taking command of Virginia. Instead, he died suddenly of dysentery; and Berkeley, his position bolstered by the arrival of British troops, soon managed to regain control. In 1677, the Indians (aware of their inability to defeat the white forces militarily) reluctantly signed a new treaty that opened new lands to white settlement.

Bacon's Rebellion was significant for several reasons. It was evidence of the continuing struggle to define the Indian and white spheres of influence in Virginia—of the unwillingness of English settlers to abide by earlier agreements with the natives and the unwillingness of the Indians to tolerate further encroachments into their territory. It revealed the bitterness of the competition among rival elites—and between easterners and westerners in particular—in the still half-formed society of the colonies.

But it also revealed something that Bacon himself had never intended to unleash: the potential for instability in the colony's large population of free, landless men. These men—most of them former indentured servants—had formed the bulk of Bacon's constituency during the rebellion. They were not frontier aristocrats but propertyless and unemployed people with no discernible prospects. Unable to find work or land in the well-populated east, they had gravitated to the back country. But without money or connections, they were seldom able to establish a secure stake there either and instead generally worked as transient laborers on farms and plantations. They were, moreover, living in a region with few European women and were thus unable to marry and begin families. As a result, they came to constitute a large, unstable, floating population eager above all for access to land. Bacon had for a time maintained his popularity among them by exploiting their hatred of Indians, but ultimately he found himself, without entirely meaning to, leading a movement that reflected their animosity toward the landed gentry (of which Bacon himself was a part). One result was that landed elites in both eastern and western Virginia began to recognize a common interest in quelling social unrest from below. That was one of several reasons for their turning increasingly to the African slave trade to fulfill their need for labor. Enslaved blacks might pose dangers too, but the events of 1676 suggested that the perils of importing a large white working class were even greater.

The Growth of New England

The Plymouth Company, which along with the London (later Virginia) Company had received a royal charter in 1606, never established a permanent settlement in America. It did, however, sponsor explorations of the territory to which it laid claim; and in the process, it gave the region a name. Captain John Smith, after his return from Jamestown, made an exploratory journey for the Plymouth merchants, wrote an enthusiastic pamphlet about the lands he had seen, and called them "New England."

Plymouth Plantation

The first enduring settlement in New England—the second in English America—resulted from the discontent of a congregation of Puritan Separatists in England. For years, Separatists had been periodically imprisoned and even executed for defying the government and the Church of England; some of them, as a result, began to contemplate leaving England altogether in search of freedom to worship as they wished. It was illegal to leave the realm without the consent of the king, but in 1608 a congregation of Separatists from the hamlet of Scrooby began emigrating quietly, a few at a time, to Leyden, Holland, to begin their lives anew. There they could meet and hold their services without interference. But as aliens, they were not allowed to join the Dutch guilds of craftsmen, and so they had to work long and hard at unskilled and poorly paid jobs. They were particularly troubled by the effects of the tolerant atmosphere of Dutch society, which soon seemed to pose as much of a threat to their dream of a close-knit Christian community as had the repression in England. They watched with alarm as their children began to speak Dutch, marry into Dutch families, and drift away from their families and their church. As a result, some of the Separatists decided to move again, this time across the Atlantic, where they hoped to create the kind of community they wanted without interference and where they could spread "the gospel of the Kingdom of Christ in those remote parts of the world."

Leaders of the Scrooby group obtained permission from the Virginia Company to settle as an independent community with land of their own in Virginia. Although they failed in their efforts to secure a formal guarantee of religious freedom from

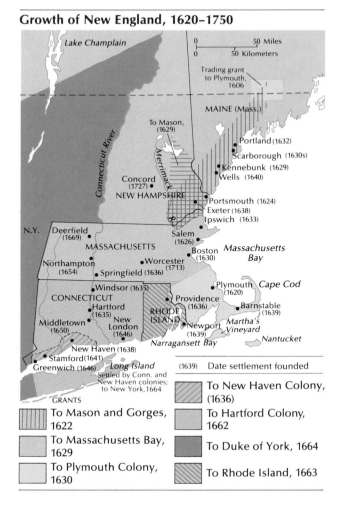

Growth of New England, 1620–1750

Lake Champlain

0   50 Miles
0   50 Kilometers

Trading grant to Plymouth, 1606

MAINE (Mass.)

Connecticut River

Merrimack

To Mason, (1629)

Portland (1632)
Scarborough (1630s)
Kennebunk (1629)
Wells (1640)

Concord (1727)
NEW HAMPSHIRE

Portsmouth (1624)
Exeter (1638)
Ipswich (1633)

N.Y.   Deerfield (1669)

Salem (1626)

MASSACHUSETTS

Boston (1630)   *Massachusetts Bay*

Northampton (1654)   Worcester (1713)
Springfield (1636)

Windsor (1635)
CONNECTICUT   Providence (1636)   Plymouth (1620)   *Cape Cod*
Hartford (1635)   RHODE ISLAND   Barnstable (1639)
Middletown (1650)   New London (1646)   Newport (1639)   *Martha's Vineyard*
    Narragansett Bay   Nantucket
New Haven (1638)
Stamford (1641)
Greenwich (1646)   *Long Island*
    Settled by Conn. and
    New Haven colonies;
    to New York, 1664
GRANTS

(1639)   Date settlement founded

	To Mason and Gorges, 1622		To New Haven Colony, (1636)
	To Massachusetts Bay, 1629		To Hartford Colony, 1662
	To Plymouth Colony, 1630		To Duke of York, 1664
			To Rhode Island, 1663

James I, they received informal assurances that he would "not molest them, provided they carried themselves peaceably." (This was a historic concession by the crown, for it opened English America to settlement not only by the Scrooby group, but by other dissenting Protestants.) The next step was to arrange financing. Several English merchants agreed to advance the necessary funds to the Separatists, on the condition that they agree to a communal plan of settlement like that of Jamestown, with the merchants to share in the profits at the end of seven years.

The migrating Puritans "knew they were pilgrims" even before they left Holland, their leader and historian, William Bradford, later wrote. Their departure for America (from Plymouth, on the English coast) was delayed, and it was not until September that the *Mayflower*, with thirty-five "saints" (Puritan Separatists) and sixty-seven "strangers" aboard, fi-

The White Population of New England, 1620–1700

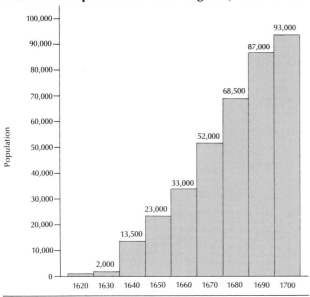

for a time at least, markedly different from the experiences of the early English settlers farther south. That was in part because the New England natives, decimated by smallpox, were significantly weaker than their southern neighbors. It was also, perhaps, because the Pilgrims were less actively hostile. In the end, the survival and growth of the colony depended crucially on the assistance of the natives. Important Indian friends—Squanto, Samoset, Massasoit, among others—showed them how to gather seafood and cultivate corn. Squanto, who had earlier been captured by an English explorer and taken to Europe, spoke English and was of particular help to the new settlers. After the first harvest, the settlers invited the Indians to join them in an October festival, the original Thanksgiving. They could not aspire to rich farms on the sandy and marshy soil, but they soon developed a profitable trade in fish and furs. From time to time new colonists arrived from England, and in a decade the population reached the modest total of 300.

The people of "Plymouth Plantation" were entitled to elect their own governor, and they chose the remarkable William Bradford again and again. As early as 1621, Bradford won them title to their land by securing a patent from the Council for New England (the successor to the old Plymouth Company, which had charter rights to the territory). But he never succeeded in his efforts to obtain a royal charter giving the Pilgrims clear rights of self-government. Nevertheless, Bradford governed for many years without any real interference. He terminated the communal labor plan, distributed land among the families, and thus, as he explained it, made "all hands very industrious." He and a group of fellow "undertakers" assumed the colony's debt to its original financiers in England and, with earnings from the fur trade, finally paid it off—even though the financiers had not lived up to their agreement to continue sending supplies.

The Pilgrims were always a poor community. As late as the 1640s, they had only one plow among them. They clung, however, to the belief that God had put them in the New World to live as a truly Christian community; and they were, on the whole, happy to be left alone to live their lives in what they considered godly ways. At times, they spoke of serving as a model for older Christians; Governor Bradford wrote in retrospect: "As one small candle may light a thousand, so the light here kindled hath shone to many, yea in some sort to our whole nation." But the Pilgrims were far less committed to grand designs, far less con-

nally put out to sea. By the time they sighted land in November, it was too late in the year to go on. Their original destination was probably the mouth of the Hudson River, in the northeast corner of the London Company's Virginia grant. But they found themselves instead on Cape Cod. After a few explorations of the region, they chose a site for their settlement in the area just north of the cape, an area John Smith had labeled "Plymouth" on his map.

Plymouth lay outside the London Company's territory, and the settlers realized that they would be without a government once ashore. In addition, some of the "strangers" on board ship began to display what some considered a lawless spirit; so one of the "saints" drew up an agreement, the Mayflower Compact, which forty-one of the passengers signed. The compact was like the church covenant by which the Separatists formed congregations, except that it established a civil government and professed allegiance to the king. Then, on December 21, 1620, the Pilgrims stepped ashore at Plymouth Rock.

They settled on cleared land that had once been an Indian village until, four years earlier, a smallpox epidemic (known as "the plague") had swept through the region and depopulated it. The Pilgrims' first winter was a difficult one; half the colonists perished from malnutrition, disease, and exposure. Those who survived, however, managed to keep the colony alive.

The Pilgrims' experience with the Indians was,

Boston Harbor
The founders of Boston (and of the Massachusetts Bay Colony, of which it was the capital) envisioned the town as a peaceful, harmonious, religious community. But they also hoped to create a thriving commercial center that would contribute to their own and the empire's prosperity. This early view of Boston harbor, showing the north battery, built in 1646, suggests the growing commercial orientation of the city even in its early years.   (Library of Congress)

cerned about how they were viewed by others, than were the Puritans who settled the larger and more ambitious English colonies to their north.

The Massachusetts Bay Experiment

Turbulent events in England in the 1620s (when combined with the example of the Plymouth colony) generated a strong interest in colonization among other groups of Puritans. A protracted and often bitter struggle was in progress between king and Parliament; and for a time, religious dissenters suffered severely from the results. James I had been creating serious tensions for years by his effort to assert the divine right of kings and by his harsh, repressive policies toward Puritans. The situation worsened after his death in 1625, when he was succeeded by his son, Charles I. Charles was even more aggressively autocratic than his father, and his efforts to restore Roman Catholicism to England and to destroy religious nonconformity launched the nation on the road that in the 1640s would lead to civil war. The Puritans were particular targets of Charles's wrath (many of them were imprisoned for their beliefs), and for

them the climate of England was becoming intolerable. The king's dissolution of Parliament in 1629 (it was not to be recalled until 1640) ensured that there would be no political redress.

In the midst of this political and social turmoil, a group of Puritan merchants began organizing a new enterprise designed to take advantage of opportunities in America. At first, their interest was largely an economic one. They obtained a grant of land in New England for most of the area now comprising Massachusetts and New Hampshire; they acquired a charter from the king (who was evidently unaware of their religious inclinations) allowing them to create the Massachusetts Bay Company and to establish a colony in the New World; and they bought equipment and supplies from a defunct fishing and trading company that had attempted (and failed) to establish a profitable enterprise in North America. In 1629, they were ready to dispatch a substantial group of settlers to New England.

Among the members of the Massachusetts Bay Company, however, were a number of Puritans who saw the enterprise as something more than a business venture. They began to consider the possibility of emigrating themselves, of creating in New England a refuge for Puritans. Members of this faction met secretly in Cambridge in the summer of 1629 and agreed to move en masse to America if the other members of the company would transfer control of the enterprise to them. When those investors who preferred to remain in England concurred and sold their stock to the prospective emigrants, no obstacle remained.

The new owners of the company elected as their governor John Winthrop, a gentleman of means, university-educated, with a deep piety and a forceful character. Winthrop had been instrumental in organa-

John Winthrop

Unlike some other English emigrants to America, John Winthrop did not travel to the New World to improve his economic circumstances. Born to a socially prominent family, he had studied at Trinity College, Cambridge, and had become a prosperous lawyer. However, his strong Puritan views, and the dismay with which he viewed the religious climate of early seventeenth-century England, motivated him to establish a new society in America. "The eyes of all people are upon us," he said in his famous sermon, "A Model of Christian Charity," which he delivered on the ship *Arabella* shortly before it arrived in New England. The new colony would be "a city upon a hill," an example of virtue and godliness to the rest of the world.   (American Antiquarian Society)

nizing the migration, and he commanded the expedition that sailed for New England in 1630: seventeen ships and 1,000 people (who were, unlike the earlier migrants to Virginia, mostly family groups). It was the largest single migration of its kind in the seventeenth century. Winthrop carried with him the charter of the Massachusetts Bay Company, which meant that the colonists would be responsible to no company officials in England, only to themselves.

Unlike the two previous English settlements in America—Jamestown and Plymouth—the Massachusetts migration quickly produced several different new settlements. Although the port of Boston, at the mouth of the Charles River, became the company's headquarters and the colony's capital, colonists moved in the course of the next decade into a number of other new towns in eastern Massachusetts: Charlestown, Newtown (later renamed Cambridge), Roxbury, Dorchester, Watertown, Ipswich, Concord, Sudbury, and others.

The Massachusetts Bay Company soon transformed itself into the Massachusetts colonial government. According to the terms of the original company charter, the "freemen" (the eight stockholders) were to meet as a general court to choose officers and adopt rules for the corporation. But this commercial definition of government, which concentrated authority in what was, in effect, a corporate board of directors, quickly gave way to a more genuinely political system. The definition of "freemen" changed to include all male citizens, not just the stockholders. John Winthrop dominated colonial politics just as he had dominated the original corporation, but after 1634 he and most other officers of the colony had to face election each year. By 1644, the general court had evolved into a bicameral legislature, with a lower House of Deputies and an upper chamber consisting of the governor and his council.

Unlike the Separatist founders of Plymouth, the Puritan founders of Massachusetts had come to America with no intention of breaking away from the Church of England. They only wanted, they claimed, to rescue the church from what they saw as the evil influence of Rome. Yet if they continued to feel any real attachment to the Anglican establishment, they gave little sign of it in their behavior. In every town, the community church had (in the words of the prominent minister John Cotton) "complete liberty to stand alone," without connection to any Anglican hierarchy and without adherence to Anglican ritual. Each congregation chose its own minister and regulated its own affairs. Thus arose in

Massachusetts—as well as in Plymouth—what came to be known as the Congregational church.

The Massachusetts Puritans were not grim or joyless, as many observers would later come to believe. But they were serious and pious people. They strove to lead useful, conscientious lives of thrift and hard work, and they honored material success as evidence of God's favor. "We here enjoy God and Jesus Christ," Winthrop wrote to his wife soon after his arrival; "is this not enough?" He and the other Massachusetts founders believed they were founding a holy commonwealth, a model—a "city upon a hill"—for the corrupt world to see and emulate. But if Massachusetts was to become a beacon to others, it had first to maintain its own purity and "holiness." And to that end, the preachers and the officers of the government worked closely together. Ministers had no formal political power, but they exerted great influence on church members, who alone could vote or hold office. The government in turn protected the ministers, taxed the people (members and nonmembers alike) to support the church, and enforced the law requiring attendance at services. In this Puritan oligarchy, dissidents had no more freedom of worship than the Puritans themselves had had in England.

Like other new settlements, the Massachusetts Bay colony had early difficulties. During their first winter (1629–1630), nearly 200 died and many others decided to leave. But more rapidly than Jamestown, the colony soon grew and prospered—in large part because the predominance of family groups enabled the population to reproduce itself much more quickly. The nearby Pilgrims and neighboring Indians helped with food and advice. Incoming settlers, many of them affluent, brought needed tools and other goods, which they exchanged for the cattle, corn, and other produce of the established colonists and the natives. The dominance of nuclear families in the colony (a sharp contrast to the early years at Jamestown) helped ensure a feeling of commitment to the community and a sense of order among the settlers. And the strong religious and political hierarchy ensured a measure of social stability.

Exodus from the Bay Colony

It did not take long for English settlement to begin moving outward from Massachusetts Bay to various parts of New England (and to other places in English America). Eventually, such migrations would occur as a result of the growing population pressures in the original settlements. At first, however, they were responses to other things. Some people migrated for a simple economic reason: the unproductiveness of the stony soil around Boston. Others left because of the oppressiveness of the theocratic government of Massachusetts. The Puritan authorities considered opposition to their church as much a threat to the community as heresy or treason. And as the population grew, more and more people arrived in Massachusetts who did not accept all the religious tenets of the colony's leaders or who were not Puritan "saints" at all and hence could not vote. Tolerance for independent thinkers was limited, and most had little choice but to conform or leave.

The Connecticut Valley, about 100 miles west of the edge of white settlement around Boston, began attracting English families as early as the 1630s, despite the presence of native tribes more powerful than those in eastern Massachusetts and despite claims to those lands by the Dutch. The Connecticut settlers were attracted by the valley's fertile lands and by its isolation from the religious character of Massachusetts Bay.

The valley appealed in particular to Thomas Hooker, a minister of Newtown (Cambridge), who defied the Massachusetts government in 1635 and led his congregation through the wilds to establish the town of Hartford. Four years later, the people of Hartford and of two other newly founded upriver towns, Windsor and Wethersfield, established a colonial government of their own and adopted a constitution known as the Fundamental Orders of Connecticut. This created a government similar to that of Massachusetts Bay but gave a larger proportion of the men the right to vote and hold office. (Women were barred from voting virtually everywhere.)

Another Connecticut colony, the project of a Puritan minister and a wealthy merchant from England, grew up around New Haven on the Connecticut coast. It reflected impatience not with the orthodoxy of Massachusetts Bay, but with what its founders considered the increasing religious laxity in Boston. The Fundamental Articles of New Haven (1639) established a Bible-based government even stricter than that of Massachusetts Bay. New Haven remained independent until 1662, when a royal charter officially sanctioned the Hartford colony and awarded it jurisdiction over the New Haven settlements.

Rhode Island had its origins in the religious and political dissent of Roger Williams, an engaging but controversial young minister who lived for a time in Salem, Massachusetts. Even John Winthrop, who considered Williams a heretic, called him a "sweet and amiable" man, and William Bradford described him as "a man godly and zealous, having many precious parts, but very unsettled in judgment." Williams was a confirmed Separatist who argued that the Massachusetts church should abandon even its nominal allegiance to the Church of England. At least equally troubling to colonial leaders, he was friendly with the neighboring Indians and proclaimed that the land the colonists were occupying belonged to the natives and not to the king or to the Massachusetts Bay Company. The colonial government considered Williams a dangerous man and voted to deport him, but he escaped before they could send him back to England. During the bitter winter of 1635–1636, he took refuge with Narragansett tribesmen; and the following spring he bought a tract of land from them, and with a few followers, created the town of Providence on it.

In time, other communities of dissidents arose in Rhode Island. Roger Williams (who, having paid for the land, considered himself the proprietor of the region) was advocating complete freedom of worship and was denying that government had any authority at all over religious practice. In 1644, he obtained a charter from Parliament empowering him to establish a single government for the various settlements around Providence. The new government was based on the Massachusetts pattern, but it did not restrict the vote to church members nor tax the people for church support. A royal charter of 1663 confirmed this arrangement and added a guarantee of "liberty in religious concernments." For a time, Rhode Island was the only colony in which all faiths (including Judaism) could worship without interference.

An even greater challenge to the established order in Massachusetts Bay emerged in the person of Anne Hutchinson, an intelligent and charismatic woman from a substantial Boston family. Hutchinson had come to Massachusetts with her husband in 1634 as part of a community led by the minister John Cotton. She shared Cotton's belief that the Holy Spirit dwelled within and guided every true believer. But she went further than Cotton in arguing that the faithful could communicate directly with God (as she claimed she herself had done) and that they could gain from Him assurance of grace and salvation—a challenge to the traditional doctrine of predestination.

Such teachings (known as the Antinomian heresy) were a serious threat to the spiritual authority of the established clergy. The belief that an individual could receive a revelation directly from God carried with it an implication that ministers were not essential to the task of discovering one's chance of salvation. Both the church and the government (which were in many ways the same thing) always insisted that faith was not open to differing personal interpretations. Hutchinson also affronted prevailing assumptions about the proper role of women in Puritan society. She was not a retiring, deferential wife and mother, but a powerful religious figure in her own right.

Hutchinson developed a large following among women (and ultimately also among men) in Boston. As her influence grew, and as she began to deliver open attacks on some members of the clergy, the Massachusetts hierarchy mobilized to stop her. Hutchinson's followers were numerous and influential enough to prevent Winthrop's reelection as governor in 1636, but the next year he returned to office and directed the orthodox ministers to charge her with heresy. In 1638, after a trial at which Winthrop himself presided and at which Hutchinson embarrassed her accusers by displaying a remarkable knowledge of theology, she was convicted of sedition and banished as "a woman not fit for our society." With her family and some of her followers, she moved to a point on Narragansett Bay not far from Providence. Later still, she moved south into New York, where in 1643 she and her family died during an Indian uprising.

The Hutchinson affair had an important impact on the settlement of the areas north of Massachusetts Bay. New Hampshire and Maine were established in 1629 when two English proprietors, Captain John Mason and Sir Ferdinando Gorges, divided a grant they had received from the Council for New England along the Piscataqua River and created two separate colonies. But despite lavish promotional efforts, especially by Gorges, few settlers moved into these northern regions until the religious disruptions in Massachusetts Bay. In 1639, John Wheelwright, a disciple of Anne Hutchinson, led some of his fellow dissenters to Exeter, New Hampshire. Other groups—of both dissenting and orthodox Puritans—soon followed. The Massachusetts Bay Company tried to extend its authority over this entire northern territory, but with only partial success. After a long legal battle in England, New Hampshire became a separate colony in 1679. Maine remained a part of Massachusetts until 1820.

Settlers and Natives

The first white settlers in New England generally maintained amicable relations with the natives; indeed the health and even survival of the colonies were to a large degree dependent on such relations in the early years. Indians provided the settlers with food and helped them adapt to the land. Not only did whites learn of such vital food crops as corn (which Indians had adapted from a Mexican strain to the colder, damper climate of the northern regions), beans, pumpkins, and potatoes from the natives; they also learned such crucial agricultural techniques as annual burning for fertilization and planting beans to replenish exhausted soil. The task of establishing many white settlements was much easier than it would otherwise have been because of the extensive lands Indians had already cleared (and either abandoned or sold).

Natives served as partners to white northerners in some of their most important trading activities (and particularly in the creation of the thriving North American fur trade). They served as an important market for such manufactured goods as iron pots, blankets, metal-tipped arrows, eventually guns and rifles, and (often tragically) alcohol. Indeed, commerce with the Indians was responsible for the creation of some of the first great fortunes in British North America and for the emergence of elite families who would exercise influence in the colonies (and later the nation) for many generations. Some white settlers attempted to educate the Indians and found a small but receptive audience for their efforts. Protestant missionaries evangelized among the natives. Their converts became known as "praying Indians" or "red Puritans." Some of them became at least partially assimilated into white society. The relationship between whites and Indians, in New England as throughout the areas of white settlement in the Americas, was one of constant interaction, one in which each group influenced the other in crucial ways.

But as in other areas of white settlement, there were also conflicts, and the early peaceful relations between whites and Indians did not last. That tensions soon developed was primarily a result of the white colonists' insatiable appetite for land and their steady encroachments into territory the natives considered their own. But the particular character of those conflicts—and the brutality with which whites assaulted their Indian foes—emerged as well out of Puritan attitudes toward the natives. At first, some white New Englanders looked at the Indians with a somewhat bemused admiration. Before long, however, they came to look on them primarily as heathen, and hence as a constant threat to the existence of a godly community in the New World. Some Puritans believed the solution to the Indian "problem" was to "civilize" the natives by converting them to Christianity and European ways; and some English missionaries had modest success in producing converts. One such missionary, John Eliot, even translated the Bible into an Indian language. Other Puritans, however, envisioned a harsher "solution": displacing or, if that failed, exterminating the natives.

The perception of an Indian menace seemed particularly severe to those colonial leaders concerned about religious dissent. That white settlers such as Roger Williams and Anne Hutchinson were challenging orthodoxy from within the Christian community made the existence of an alternative "pagan" culture nearby all the more troubling. And that dissenters such as Roger Williams advocated toleration of and respect for the natives only increased the perceived link between dissent and the natives.

In 1637, hostilities broke out between English settlers in the Connecticut Valley and the Pequot Indians of the region, a conflict (known as the Pequot War) that ended disastrously for the natives. White frontiersmen marched against a palisaded Pequot stronghold and set it afire. About 400 Indians died, burned to death in the flaming stockade or killed as they attempted to escape. Those who survived were hunted down, captured, and sold as slaves. The Pequot tribe was almost wiped out.

The bloodiest and most prolonged encounter between whites and Indians in the seventeenth century began in 1675, a conflict that whites would remember for generations as King Philip's War. As in Connecticut nearly forty years before, an Indian tribe—in this case the Wampanoags, under the leadership of a chieftain known to the white settlers as King Philip and among his own people as Metacomet—rose up to resist English encroachment on their lands. The Wampanoags had not always been hostile to the settlers; indeed, Metacomet's grandfather had once forged an alliance with the English. But by the 1670s,

ulating twenty of them and causing the deaths of over a thousand people (including at least one-sixteenth of the white males in the colony). The war greatly weakened both the society and economy of Massachusetts. But the white settlers gradually prevailed, beginning in 1676. Massachusetts leaders recruited guides and spies from rival tribes and from among the so-called "praying Indians" of the region—natives who had been converted to Christianity by missionaries and who had settled in or near the towns of the whites. Among these new allies was a group of Mohawks who ambushed Metacomet and shot and killed him, then bore his severed head to Boston to present to the colonial leaders. After that the fragile alliance that Metacomet had managed to forge among local tribes collapsed. Europeans were soon able to crush the uprising. Some Wampanoag leaders were executed; others were sold into slavery in the West Indies. The power of the Wampanoags and their allies was destroyed.

Yet these victories by the white colonists did not end the danger to their settlements. This was in part because other Indians in other tribes survived, capable of launching future wars. It was also because the New England settlers faced competition not only from the natives but also from the Dutch and the French, who claimed the territory on which some of the outlying settlements were established. The French, in particular, would pose a constant threat to the English through their alliance with the Algonquins. In later years, they would support hostile Indians in their attacks on the New England frontier.

The Restoration Colonies

By the end of the 1630s, then, English settlers had established the beginnings of what would eventually become six of the thirteen original states of the American republic: Virginia, Massachusetts, Maryland, Connecticut, Rhode Island, and New Hampshire. But for nearly thirty years after Lord Baltimore received the charter for Maryland in 1632, the English government launched no additional colonial ventures. It was preoccupied with troubles of its own at home.

The English Civil War

England's problems had begun during the rule of the unpopular James I. James attracted widespread oppo-

Metacomet, or King Philip
This eighteenth-century engraving by Paul Revere shows the Indian chieftain Metacomet, known to the English as King Philip of Mount Hope (the site of his tribe's principal stronghold). Metacomet, son of Massasoit, became chief of the Wampanoags in 1662 and inherited his tribe's resentment at having been forced from their lands along Narragansett Bay by European settlers. In 1675, after several years of tension between the Wampanoags and English authorities in Plymouth, he launched the first of many attacks on white settlements in eastern Massachusetts, sparking the prolonged conflict that became known as King Philip's War. (New York Public Library)

they had become convinced that only armed resistance could protect them from the movement of the English into their lands and (more immediately) from the efforts by a colonial government to impose English law on the natives. (A court in Plymouth had recently tried and hanged several Wampanoags for murdering a member of their own tribe.)

For three years, the natives inflicted terror on a string of Massachusetts towns, destroying or depop-

sition before he died in 1625, but he never came into open conflict with Parliament. His son, Charles I, was not so fortunate. After he dissolved Parliament in 1629 and began ruling as an absolute monarch, he steadily alienated a growing number of his subjects—and the members of the powerful Puritan community above all. Finally, desperately in need of money, Charles called Parliament back into session and asked it to levy new taxes. But he antagonized the members by dismissing them twice in two years; and in 1642, they organized a military force, thus commencing the English Civil War.

The conflict between the Cavaliers (the supporters of the king) and the Roundheads (the forces of Parliament, who were largely Puritans) lasted seven years. Finally, in 1649, the Roundheads defeated the king's forces, captured Charles himself, and—in an action that horrified not only much of continental Europe at the time but future generations of English men and women—beheaded the monarch. To replace him, they elevated the stern Roundhead leader Oliver Cromwell to the position of "protector," from which he ruled for the next nine years. When Cromwell died in 1658, the Protectorate fell upon hard times. His son and heir proved unable to maintain his authority, and two years later, King Charles II, son of the beheaded monarch, returned from exile and seized the throne.

Among the many results of the Stuart Restoration was the resumption of colonization in America. Charles II quickly began to reward faithful courtiers with grants of land in the New World; and in the twenty-five years of his reign, he issued charters for four additional colonies: Carolina, New York, New Jersey, and Pennsylvania. The new colonies were all proprietary ventures (modeled on Maryland rather than on Virginia and Massachusetts), thus exposing an important change in the nature of American settlement. No longer did private companies take an interest in launching colonies, realizing at last that there were no quick profits to be had in the New World. In their place were emerging ventures with different aims: not so much quick commercial success as permanent settlements that would provide proprietors with land and power.

The Carolinas

Carolina (a name derived from *Carolinus,* the Latinate form of "Charles") was, like Maryland, carved in part from the original Virginia grant. Charles II awarded the territory to a group of eight court favorites, all prominent politicians already active in colonial affairs. In successive charters issued in 1663 and 1665, the eight proprietors received joint title to a vast territory stretching south to the Florida peninsula and west to the Pacific Ocean. Like Lord Baltimore, they received almost kingly powers over their grant.

Also like him, they expected to profit as landlords and land speculators. They reserved tremendous estates for their own development, and they planned to sell or give away the rest in smaller tracts (using a headright system similar to those in Virginia and Maryland) and to collect annual payments as quitrents from the settlers. Although committed Anglicans themselves, they welcomed any settlers they could get, whatever their faith. Indeed, the charter of the colony guaranteed religious freedom to everyone who would worship as a Christian. The proprietors also promised a measure of political freedom; laws were to be made by a representative assembly. With these and other incentives, they hoped to attract settlers from the existing American colonies and thus to avoid the expense of financing expeditions from England.

Their initial efforts to profit from settlement in Carolina failed dismally. Governor Berkeley of Virginia, one of the proprietors, did manage to encourage a number of landless people from his own colony to settle in the area of Carolina just to the south, along Albemarle Sound. But the region was isolated by the Dismal Swamp and had no adequate harbor, and it grew slowly. Farther south, there was for a time virtually no growth at all. A few early colonizing ventures were quickly abandoned, and most of the original proprietors soon concluded that the Carolina venture could not succeed. One man, however, persisted—Anthony Ashley Cooper, soon to become the earl of Shaftesbury. Cooper convinced his partners that since settlers were not going to flock to Carolina from other parts of North America, the proprietors should finance expeditions to Carolina from England themselves. And in the spring of 1670, the first of these expeditions—a party of 300—set out from England. Only 100 people survived the difficult voyage; those who did established a settlement in the Port Royal area of the Carolina coast. Ten years later they founded a city at the junction of the Ashley and Cooper rivers, which in 1690 became the colonial capital. They called it Charles Town. (It was later renamed Charleston.)

The earl of Shaftesbury wanted a planned and

Charles Town in 1739

An English engraver produced this prospect of the harbor at Charles Town (now Charleston), South Carolina, as it looked six decades after the city was founded in 1680. It was by then the principal port of the southern colonies. The city's original waterfront (or battery), pictured here, looks much the same today as it did in the eighteenth century. (I.N. Phelps Stokes Collection of American Historical Prints, New York Public Library)

well-ordered community with a uniform pattern of settlement and a clearly defined social order. With the aid of the English philosopher John Locke, he drew up the Fundamental Constitution for Carolina in 1669, a document that was more a response to their analysis of problems in England than a reflection of realities in America. According to the Constitution, the Carolina territory was to be divided into counties of equal size, with each county divided into equal parcels. The largest number of parcels would be distributed among the proprietors themselves (who were to be known as "seigneurs"); a local aristocracy (consisting of lesser nobles known as "landgraves" or "caciques") would receive fewer parcels; and ordinary settlers ("leet-men") would receive less land still. At the bottom of this stratified society would be poor whites, who had no political rights, and black slaves, whose subjection would be complete. "Every freeman of Carolina," the Constitution stated, "shall have absolute power and authority over his Negro slaves, of what opinion or religion soever." Proprietors, nobles, and other landholders would have a voice in the colonial parliament in proportion to the size of their landholdings.

In fact, however, Carolina developed along lines quite different from the almost Utopian vision of Shaftesbury and Locke. For one thing, the colony was never really united in anything more than name. The northern and southern regions of the colony remained widely separated and were socially and economically distinct from one another. The northern settlers were mainly backwoods farmers, largely isolated from the outside world, scratching out a meager existence at subsistence agriculture. They developed no important aristocracy and for many years imported virtually no black slaves. In the south, fertile lands and the good harbor at Charles Town promoted a far more prosperous economy and a far more stratified, aristocratic society. There too, however, the carefully planned social order of the Fundamental Constitution largely failed to take root. Settlements grew up rapidly along the Ashley and Cooper rivers, and colonists established a flourishing trade in corn, lumber, cattle, pork, and (beginning in the 1690s) rice—which was to become the colony's principal commercial crop. Traders from the interior used Charles Town to market furs and hides they had acquired from their Indian trading partners; some also marketed Indian slaves, generally natives captured by rival tribes and sold to the white traders.

Southern Carolina very early developed close ties to the large (and now overpopulated) European colony on the island of Barbados. For many years, Barbados was Carolina's most important trading partner. And during the first ten years of settlement, most of the new settlers in Carolina were Barbadians, some of whom arrived with large groups of black workers and established themselves quickly as substantial landlords. African slavery had taken root on Barbados earlier than in any of the mainland colonies; and the white Caribbean migrants—tough, uncompromising profitseekers—established a similar slave-based plantation society in Carolina. (The proprietors, too, encouraged the importation of blacks; four of them had a financial interest in the African slave trade.)

For several decades, Carolina remained one of the most factious of all the English colonies in America. There were tensions between the small farmers of the Albemarle region in the north and the wealthy planters in the south. And there were conflicts between the rich Barbadians in southern Carolina and the smaller landowners around them. After Lord Shaftesbury's death, the proprietors proved unable to establish order, and in 1719, the colonists seized control of the colony from them. Ten years later, the king divided the region into two royal colonies, North and South Carolina.

New Netherland and New York

In 1664, one year after he issued the Carolina charter, Charles II granted to his brother James, the duke of York, all the territory lying between the Connecticut and Delaware rivers. Unlike other such grants, however, this one faced a major challenge from prior European claims. Some of the territory presumably belonged to the Massachusetts Bay Company by virtue of the sea-to-sea grant it had secured decades before. A far more serious challenge, however, lay in the Dutch claim to the entire area and in the existence of Dutch settlements at New Amsterdam and other strategic points.

The emerging conflict between the English and the Dutch in America was part of a larger struggle between the two nations in the seventeenth century over their commercial rivalry throughout the world. The English had particular reason for resenting the Dutch presence in America, where they served as a wedge between northern and southern English colonies and provided bases for Dutch smugglers evading English customs laws. In 1664, troop-carrying vessels of the English navy, under the command of Rich-

New Amsterdam
Shown here is the "Stadt Huys" (state house) in New Amsterdam, on Manhattan Island. New Netherland, of which New Amsterdam was the capital, was the principal Dutch possession in the New World until it was captured by the English in 1664 and renamed New York. Dutch influence in the colony remained strong long after control passed to England, as this 1679 drawing by the Dutch travelers Josef Dankers and Peter Stuyler suggests. (Long Island Historical Society)

ard Nicolls, put in at New Amsterdam and extracted a surrender from the arbitrary and unpopular Dutch governor, Peter Stuyvesant, who tried but failed to mobilize resistance to the invasion. Under the Articles of Capitulation, the colony surrendered to the British and received in return assurances that the Dutch settlers would not be displaced. Several years later, in 1673, the Dutch reconquered and briefly held their old provincial capital. But they lost it again, this time for good, in 1674.

The duke of York finally possessed New Netherland (which he renamed New York) both on paper and in fact; and he was free to rule virtually as an absolute monarch. But he recognized the problems inherent in governing a society with so diverse a population. New York contained not only Dutch and English, but Scandinavians, Germans, French, a large number of Africans (imported as slaves by the Dutch West India Company), and members of several different Indian tribes. There were, of course, several different religious faiths among these groups. James made no effort to impose his own Roman Catholicism on the colony. Like other proprietors before him, he delegated powers to a governor and a council. The Duke's Laws, which the first governor, Roger Nicolls, issued, provided for no representative assemblies. (The English Parliament had overthrown and executed James's father, Charles I, and the duke was unwilling to see a similar breeding ground for revolt established in his American lands.) The laws did, however, establish local governments and guarantee religious toleration.

These concessions failed to satisfy all New Yorkers. Many settlers complained about the inequality of property holding and political power. In addition to confirming the great Dutch "patroonships" already in existence (among them, Rensselaerswyck, a vast 700,000-acre empire near Albany), James granted large estates to some of his own political supporters in order to create a class of influential landowners loyal to him. Power in the colony thus remained widely dispersed—among wealthy English landlords, Dutch patroons (who remained for many years an unassimilated but powerful minority), fur traders (who forged important alliances with the Iroquois), and the duke's political appointees. Like Carolina, New York would for many years be a highly factious society.

By 1685, when the duke of York ascended the English throne as James II, New York contained about four times as many people (around 30,000) as when he had taken it over some twenty years before. Most of them still lived within the Hudson Valley,

close to the river itself, with the largest settlement at its mouth, in the town of New York (formerly New Amsterdam).

Originally, James's claims in America extended south of the Hudson to the Delaware valley and beyond. But shortly after receiving his charter, he gave a large portion of that land to a pair of political allies, both Carolina proprietors, Sir John Berkeley and Sir George Carteret. Carteret named the territory New Jersey, after the island in the English channel on which he had been born. The new proprietors soon found themselves embroiled in a series of political disputes with the leadership of New York, and partly as a result, the venture in New Jersey generated few profits for them. In 1674, Berkeley sold his half interest to two enterprising members of the Society of Friends, and the colony was divided into two jurisdictions, East and West Jersey. The squabbling (and profitlessness) of New Jersey continued, and in 1702, the two halves of the colony were again joined and became a single royal colony.

In one respect, at least, the European settlements in New Jersey resembled those in New York (from which much of the population had come). There was enormous ethnic and religious diversity, and there were relatively few efforts by the weak colonial government to impose strict control on the divergent groups in the population. But unlike New York, New Jersey developed no important class of large landowners; most of its residents remained small farmers. Nor did New Jersey (which, unlike New York, had no natural harbor) produce any single important city.

The Quaker Colonies

More than any other colony (except perhaps Massachusetts), Pennsylvania was born out of the efforts of dissenting English Protestants to find a home for their own distinctive social order. The Society of Friends originated in mid-seventeenth-century England and grew into an important force as a result of the preachings of George Fox, a Nottingham shoemaker, and Margaret Fell. Their followers came to be known as Quakers from Fox's admonition to them to "tremble at the name of the Lord." The essence of Fox's and Fell's teachings was the doctrine of the Inner Light, the illumination from God within each soul, which when rightly heeded could guide human beings along the paths of righteousness. Unlike the Puritans, Quakers rejected the concept of predestination and original sin. All people had divinity within themselves and need only learn to cultivate it; all could attain salvation. Also unlike the Puritans, Quakers granted women a position within the church generally equal to that of men. Women and men alike could become preachers and define church doctrine. A symbol of that sexual equality was the long-time partnership between Fox and Fell.

Of all the Protestant sectarians of the time, the Quakers were the most anarchistic and the most democratic. They had no church government except for periodic meetings, at which the congregations were represented on a local, regional, and national basis. They had no traditional church buildings, only meeting houses. They had no paid clergy, and in their worship they spoke up one by one as the spirit moved them. Disregarding distinctions of gender and class, they addressed one another with the terms "thee" and "thou," words commonly used in other parts of English society only in speaking to servants and social inferiors. They refused to take oaths. And, as confirmed pacifists, they would not take part in wars. The Quakers were unpopular enough as a result of these beliefs and practices, and they increased their unpopularity by occasionally breaking up other religious groups at worship. Many were jailed.

As a result, like the Puritans before them, the Quakers looked to America for asylum. A few of them went to New England. But there (except in Rhode Island), they were greeted with fines, whippings, and banishment; three men and a woman who refused to leave were actually put to death. Others migrated to northern Carolina, and there, as the fastest-growing religious community, they were soon influential in colonial politics. But most Quakers desired a colony of their own, and Fox himself visited America in 1671–72 to look over the land. As the representative of a despised sect, however, he could not get the necessary royal grant without the aid of someone influential at the court. Fortunately for his cause, his teachings had struck the hearts of a number of wealthy and prominent men, one of whom in particular made possible a large-scale effort to realize the Quaker dream.

William Penn—whose father was Sir William Penn, an admiral in the Royal Navy and a landlord of valuable Irish estates—received a gentleman's education at his father's expense but could not overcome his mystical inclinations despite his father's efforts to force him to do so. Converted to the doctrine of the Inner Light, the younger Penn took up evangelism, and although always moderate and soft-spoken, he was sent repeatedly to prison, where he wrote a powerful tract, *No Cross, No Crown,* one of what would eventually be several dozen religious books. With George Fox he visited the European continent and found Quakers there who, like Quakers in England, longed to emigrate to the New World.

Penn turned his attention first to New Jersey,

A Quaker Meeting

An anonymous artist painted this view of a Quaker meeting in approximately 1790. Because the Society of Friends (or Quakers) believed that all people were equal in the eyes of God, they appointed no ministers and imposed no structure on their religious services. Members of the congregation stood up to speak at will. (Museum of Fine Arts, Boston)

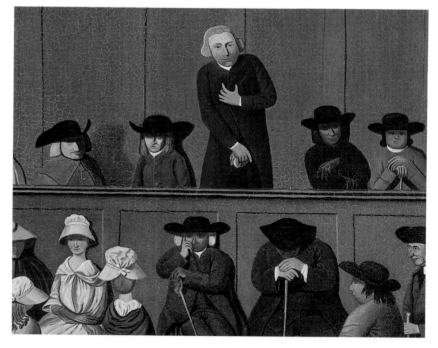

half of which (after 1674) belonged to two fellow Quakers and of which Penn himself became an owner and proprietor. But in 1681, after the death of his father, he received from the king an even more valuable grant of lands. Penn had inherited his father's Irish lands and also his father's claim to a large debt from the king. Charles II, who possessed more land than cash, paid the debt with a grant of territory between New York and Maryland—an area larger than England and Wales combined and which (unknown to him) contained more value in soil and minerals than any other province of English America. Within this fabulous estate Penn was to have the rights of both landlord and ruler; he was to make token acknowledgment of the feudal suzerainty of the king by the payment of two beaver skins a year. At the king's insistence, the territory was to be named Pennsylvania, after Penn's late father.

Like most other American proprietors, Penn intended to make money from land sales and quitrents and from private property to be worked for him. He promptly sold several large tracts to rich Quaker associates and one tract of 15,000 acres to a group of German immigrants. Through his informative and honest advertising—as in his pamphlet entitled *A Brief Account of the Province of Pennsylvania,* which was translated into several European languages—Penn made Pennsylvania the best-known and most cosmopolitan of all the colonies. Settlers flocked to the province from England and the continent, joining a substantial group of Swedes and Finns who were already there. But Penn and his descendants were to find almost hopeless the task of collecting quitrents, and the colony never became a great source of profit for them, (Indeed, Penn himself, near the end of his life, was imprisoned in England for debt and died in poverty in 1718.)

Penn, however, was much more than a mere real estate promoter, and he undertook in Pennsylvania what he called a holy experiment. Colonies, he said, were the "seeds of nations," and he proposed to plant in his realm the seeds of brotherly love. He advised a liberal Frame of Government with a representative assembly. He personally sailed to Pennsylvania in 1682 to oversee the laying out, between the Delaware and the Schuylkill rivers, of the city he appropriately named Philadelphia ("Brotherly Love"), which with its rectangular streets, like those of Charles Town, helped set the pattern for most later cities in America. Penn believed, as had Roger Williams, that the land belonged to the Indians, and he was careful to see that

they were reimbursed for it, as well as to see that they were not debauched by the fur traders' alcohol. Indians honored Penn as a rarity, an honest white man, and during his lifetime the colony had no major conflicts with the natives. More than any other English colony, Pennsylvania prospered from the outset, because of Penn's successful recruitment of emigrants, his thoughtful planning, and the region's mild climate and fertile soil.

But the colony was not without conflict. By the late 1690s, some residents of Pennsylvania were beginning to chafe at the nearly absolute power of the proprietor. Residents of the southern areas of the colony, in particular, complained that the government in Philadelphia was unresponsive to their needs. As a result, a substantial opposition emerged to challenge Penn. Pressure from these groups grew to the point that in 1701, shortly before he departed for England for the last time, Penn agreed to a Charter of Liberties for the colony. The charter established a representative assembly (consisting, alone among the English colonies, of only one house) and which greatly limited the authority of the proprietor. The charter also permitted "the lower counties" of the colony to establish their own representative assembly. The three counties did so in 1703 and as a result became, in effect, a separate colony: Delaware. Until the Revolution, however, it continued to have the same governor as Pennsylvania.

The Founding of Georgia

The establishment of the Restoration proprietary colonies expanded English settlement along the length of the Atlantic coast from New England to South Carolina. Although the population of each colony continued to grow, pushing the frontier of settlement steadily westward, for several decades there were no attempts to enlarge the English realm in America farther north or south. Not until 1733 did another new colony emerge: Georgia, the last English colony on the mainland of what would become the United States.

Georgia was unique in its origins. It was founded neither by a corporation (as Massachusetts and Virginia had been) nor by a wealthy proprietor (as in the case of Maryland, the Carolinas, Pennsylvania, and others). Its guiding purpose was neither the pursuit of profit nor the desire for a religious refuge. Georgia emerged from the work of a group of unpaid trustees led by General James Oglethorpe, a member of Par-

Indians in Colonial Georgia

The Yuchi were a small tribe who in the seventeenth and eighteenth centuries inhabited the northeast region of what is now Georgia (near the lands of their neighbors, the larger Creek and Cherokee tribes). A German immigrant to the region in the early years of Georgia's existence as an English colony painted this watercolor of a Yuchi celebration. The guns hanging at the rear of the hut at upper left suggest that the tribe was by then already trading with the white settlers. (Royal Library, Copenhagen)

liament and a hero of the most recent war with Spain. The founders of Georgia were not uninterested in economic success, but they were driven primarily by military and philanthropic motives. They wanted to erect a military barrier against the Spanish lands on the southern border of English America; and they wanted to provide a refuge for the impoverished, a place where English men and women without prospects at home could begin a new life.

The need for a military buffer between South Carolina and the Spanish settlements in Florida was growing urgent in the first years of the eighteenth century. There had been tensions between the English and the Spanish ever since the first settlement at Jamestown; and although in a treaty of 1676, Spain had recognized England's title to lands already occupied by English settlers, conflict between the two colonizing powers continued. In 1686, a force of Indians and Creoles from Florida, directed by Spanish agents, attacked and destroyed an outlying South Carolina settlement south of the treaty line. And when hostilities broke out again between Spain and England in 1701 (known in England as Queen Anne's War and on the continent as the War of the Spanish Succession), the fighting renewed in America as well. That war ended in 1713, but another European conflict with repercussions for the New World was continually expected.

Oglethorpe was, therefore, keenly aware of the military advantages of an English colony south of the Carolinas. Yet his interest in settlement rested even more on his philanthropic interests. As head of a parliamentary committee investigating English prisons, he had grown appalled by the plight of honest debtors rotting in confinement. Such prisoners, and other poor people in danger of succumbing to a similar fate, could, he believed, become the farmer-soldiers of the new colony in America.

A 1732 charter from King George II transferred the land between the Savannah and Altamaha rivers to the administration of Oglethorpe and his fellow trustees for a period of twenty-one years. Their colonization policies reflected the vital military purposes of the colony. Landholdings were limited in size so as to make the settlement compact and easily defended against Spanish and Indian attacks. Blacks—free or slave—were excluded; rum was prohibited; and trade with the Indians was strictly regulated to limit the possibility of wartime insurrection. Roman Catholics were excluded to forestall the danger of collusion with enemy coreligionists.

Oglethorpe himself led the first colonial expedition to Georgia, which built a fortified town at the mouth of the Savannah River in 1733 and later constructed additional forts south of the Altamaha. In the end, only a few debtors were released from jail and sent to Georgia; but hundreds of needy tradesmen and artisans from England and Scotland and many religious refugees from Switzerland and Germany were brought to the new colony at the expense of the trustees, who raised funds from charitable individuals as well as from Parliament.

The strict rules governing life in the new colony helped stifle its development in its early years. Settlers in Georgia needed a work force as much as those in other southern colonies, and almost from the start they began demanding the right to buy slaves. Some opposed the restrictions on the size of individual property holdings. Many resented the nearly absolute political power of Oglethorpe and the trustees. As a result, newcomers to the region generally preferred to settle in South Carolina, where there were far fewer restrictive laws.

Oglethorpe (whom some residents of Georgia began addressing rhetorically as "our perpetual dictator") at first bitterly resisted the demands of the settlers for social and political reform. But over time, he wearied of the conflict in the colony and grew frustrated at its failure to grow. He also suffered military disappointments; a 1740 assault on the Spanish outpost at St. Augustine, Florida, ended in failure. Oglethorpe, now disillusioned with his American venture, began to loosen his grip. Even before the 1740 defeat, the trustees had removed the limitation on individual landholdings. In 1750, they removed the ban on slavery; a year later they ended the prohibition of rum and returned control of the colony to the king, who immediately permitted the summoning of a representative assembly. Georgia continued to grow more slowly than the other southern colonies, but in other ways it now developed along lines roughly similar to those of South Carolina.

The Development of Empire

The English colonies in America had originated as quite separate projects, and for the most part they grew up independent of one another, with little thought that they belonged—or ought to belong—to a unified imperial system. Yet the growing commercial success of the colonial ventures was by the mid-seventeenth century producing pressure in England for a more rational, uniform structure to the empire.

The Drive for Reorganization

Reorganization, many claimed, would increase the profitability of the colonies and the power of the En-

glish government to supervise them. Above all, it would contribute to the success of the mercantile system, the foundation of the English economy. Colonies would provide a market for England's manufactured goods and a source of supply for raw materials it could not produce at home, thus promoting the principal goal of the mercantile system—increasing the total wealth of the nation. But for the new possessions truly to promote mercantilist goals, England would have to exclude foreigners (as Spain had done) from its colonial trade. According to mercantilist theory, any wealth flowing to another nation could come only at the expense of England itself. Hence the British government sought to monopolize trade relations with its colonies.

In theory, the mercantile system offered benefits to the colonies as well by providing them with a ready market for the raw materials they produced and a source for the manufactured goods they did not. But some colonial goods were not suitable for export to England. The mother country produced wheat, flour and fish itself and had no interest in obtaining them from America. Colonists also found it more profitable at times to deal with the Spanish, French, or Dutch even in goods that England did import. Thus, a considerable trade soon developed between the English colonies and non-English markets.

For a time, the English government made no serious efforts to restrict this challenge to the principles of mercantilism, but gradually it began passing laws to regulate colonial trade. During Oliver Cromwell's "Protectorate," in 1650 and 1651, Parliament passed laws to keep Dutch ships out of the English colonies. After the Restoration, the government of Charles II adopted three Navigation Acts. The first of them, in 1660, closed the colonies to all trade except that carried in English ships. This law also required certain items, among them tobacco, to be exported from the colonies only to England or to an English possession. The second act, in 1663, provided that all goods sent from Europe to the colonies had to pass through England on the way, and that they could be subject to English taxation in the process. The third act, in 1673, was a response to the widespread evasion of the new export controls by the colonial shippers, who frequently left port claiming to be heading for another English colony but who then sailed to a foreign port. It imposed duties on the coastal trade among the English colonies, and it provided for the appointment of customs officials to enforce the Navigation Acts. These acts, with later amendments and additions, were to form the legal basis of England's mercantile system in America for a century.

The Dominion of New England

Enforcement of the Navigation Acts required not only the stationing of customs officials in America, but the establishment of an agency in England to oversee colonial affairs. All the colonial governments (except Virginia, a "royal colony" since 1624 with a governor appointed by the king) had previously operated largely independently of the crown, with governors chosen by the proprietors or the colonists themselves and with increasingly powerful representative assemblies. Massachusetts, the leading commercial colony, seemed at times to consider itself something close to an independent republic; its merchants were particularly blatant in their violations of the Navigation Acts. Officials in London recognized, therefore, that to increase their control over their colonies they would have to create an instrument separate from the unreliable colonial governments.

In 1675, in the wake of a royal commission report detailing the extent of illegal trade in Massachusetts, the king authorized the formation of a new committee, the Lords of Trade, to make recommendations for imperial reform. Following their advice, he moved in 1679 to increase his control over Massachusetts by stripping the colony of its authority over New Hampshire and chartering a separate, royal colony there whose governor he would himself appoint. The king wanted to make Massachusetts a royal colony as well and began seeking legal grounds for revoking the colony's corporate charter. He found them, he believed, in the colony's defiance of English law. When the Lords of Trade ordered Massachusetts to enforce the Navigation Acts, the General Court replied that Parliament had no power to legislate for the colony. And when the Lords of Trade sent a customs official to Boston to supervise the enforcement of the acts, the General Court not only refused to recognize him but arrested the local agents he appointed. Finally the king began legal proceedings that led, in 1684, to revocation of the charter.

Charles II's brother and successor, James II, who succeeded to the throne in 1685, went much further. He created a single Dominion of New England, which combined the government of Massachusetts with the governments of the rest of the New England colonies and later with those of New York and New Jersey as well. He eliminated the existing assemblies within the new Dominion and appointed a single governor, Sir Edmund Andros, to supervise the entire region from Boston. Andros was an able administrator but a stern and tactless man; his rigid enforcement of the Navigation Acts and his brusque dismissal of the colonists' claims to the "rights of Englishmen" made him quickly and thoroughly unpopular.

The "Glorious Revolution"

James II was not only losing friends in America; he was making powerful enemies in England by attempting to exercise autocratic control over Parliament and the courts and by appointing his fellow Catholics to high office. By 1688, his popular support had all but vanished, and Parliament was emboldened to invite his Protestant daughter Mary and her husband, William of Orange, ruler of the Netherlands and Protestant champion of Europe, to assume the throne. James II (perhaps remembering what had happened to his father, Charles I) offered no resistance and fled to France. As a result of this bloodless coup, which the English called "the Glorious Revolution," William and Mary became joint sovereigns.

When Bostonians heard of the overthrow of James II, they moved quickly to unseat his unpopular viceroy in New England. Andros managed to escape an angry mob but was soon arrested and imprisoned. The new sovereigns in England chose not to contest the toppling of Andros and moved quickly to abolish the Dominion of New England and restore separate colonial governments. They did not, however, recreate them exactly as they had been. In 1691, they combined Massachusetts with Plymouth and made it a royal colony. The new charter restored the General Court, but it gave the crown the right to appoint the governor. It also replaced church membership with property ownership as the basis for voting and officeholding.

Andros had been governing New York through a lieutenant governor, Captain Francis Nicholson, who enjoyed the support of the wealthy merchants and fur traders of the province—the same groups who had dominated the colony for years. Other, less favored colonists—farmers, mechanics, small traders, and shopkeepers—had a long accumulation of grievances against both Nicholson and his allies.

The leadership of the New York dissidents fell to Jacob Leisler, a German immigrant and a prosperous merchant who had married into a prominent

---

SIGNIFICANT EVENTS

1607   Jamestown founded (p. 30)

1609   Pilgrims flee to Holland from England (p. 38)

1612   Tobacco production established in Virginia (p. 32)

1619   First African workers arrive in Virginia (p. 33)

        Virginia House of Burgesses meets for first time (p. 33)

1620   Pilgrims found Plymouth colony (p. 38)

1622   Powhatan Indians attack English colony in Virginia (p. 34)

1624   Dutch establish settlement on Manhattan Island (p. 23)

1629   New Hampshire and Maine established (p. 43)

1630   Puritans establish Massachusetts Bay colony at Boston (p. 41)

1634   First English settlements founded in Maryland (p. 34)

1635   Roger Williams founds settlement in Rhode Island (p. 43)

1636   Connecticut colony founded (p. 42)

1637   Anne Hutchinson expelled from Massachusetts Bay colony (p. 43)

        Pequot War fought (p. 44)

1642–1648   English Civil War (p. 46)

1649   Charles I executed (p. 46)

1660   English Restoration: Charles II becomes king (p. 46)

        First Navigation Act passed (p. 53)

1663   Carolina colony chartered (p. 46)

        Second Navigation Act passed (p. 53)

1664   English capture New Netherland (p. 48)

        New Jersey chartered (p. 49)

1673   Third Navigation Act passed (p. 53)

1675–1676   King Philip's War in New England (p. 44)

1676   Bacon's Rebellion in Virginia (p. 36)

1681   William Penn receives charter for Pennsylvania (p. 51)

1685   James II becomes king (p. 54)

1686   Dominion of New England established (p. 54)

1688   Glorious Revolution in England: William and Mary ascend throne (p. 54)

1689   Glorious Revolution in America: rebellion breaks out against Andros in New England; Leisler leads rebellion in New York (p. 54)

1732   Georgia chartered (p. 52)

Dutch family but had never won acceptance as one of the colony's ruling class. Much like Francis Bacon in Virginia, the ambitious Leisler chafed at his exclusion and eagerly grasped the opportunity to challenge the colonial elite. In May 1689, when news of the Glorious Revolution in England and the fall of Andros in Boston reached New York, Leisler raised a militia, captured the city fort, drove Nicholson into exile, and proclaimed himself the new head of government in New York. For two years, he tried in vain to stabilize his power in the colony amid fierce factional rivalry. In 1691, when William and Mary appointed a new governor, Leisler briefly resisted this challenge to his authority, and although he soon yielded, his hesitation allowed his many political enemies to charge him with treason. He and one of his sons-in-law were hanged, drawn, and quartered. Fierce rivalry between what became known as the "Leislerians" and the "anti-Leislerians" dominated the politics of the factious colony for many years thereafter.

In Maryland, many people erroneously assumed when they heard news of the Glorious Revolution that their proprietor, the Catholic Lord Baltimore who was living in England, had sided with the Catholic James II and opposed William and Mary. So in 1689, an old opponent of the proprietor's government, John Coode, started a new revolt as head of an organization calling itself "An Association in Arms for the Defense of the Protestant Religion, and for Asserting the Right of King William and Queen Mary to the Province of Maryland and All the English Dominions." The insurgents drove out Lord Baltimore's officials, and through an elected convention, chose a committee to run the government, and petitioned the crown for a charter as a royal colony. In 1691, William and Mary complied, stripping the proprietor of his authority. The colonial assembly established the Church of England as the colony's official religion and excluded Catholics from public office. Maryland became a proprietary colony again in 1715, but only after the fifth Lord Baltimore joined the Anglican church.

Thus the Glorious Revolution of 1688 in England touched off revolutions, mostly bloodless ones, in several colonies. Under the new king and queen, the representative assemblies that had been abolished were revived, and the scheme for colonial unification from above was abandoned. But the Glorious Revolution in America was not, as many Americans later came to believe, a clear demonstration of American

resolve to govern itself or a clear victory for colonial self-rule. In New York and Maryland, in particular, the uprisings had more to do with local factional and religious divisions than with any larger vision of the nature of the empire. And while the insurgencies did succeed in eliminating the short-lived Dominion of New England, their ultimate results were governments that actually increased the crown's potential authority. As the first century of English settlement in America came to its end, the colonists were becoming more a part of the imperial system than ever before.

SUGGESTED READINGS

General Histories. Charles M. Andrews, *The Colonial Period in American History*, 4 vols. (1934–1938); Clarence L. Ver Steeg, *The Formative Years, 1607–1763* (1964); John E. Pomfret and F. M. Shumway, *Founding the American Colonies, 1583–1660* (1970).

Jamestown. Philip L. Barbour, ed., *The Complete Works of Captain John Smith*, 3 vols. (1986); Bradford Smith, *Captain John Smith* (1953); Philip L. Barbour, *The Three Worlds of Captain John Smith* (1964); Alden T. Vaughn, *American Genesis* (1975).

The Chesapeake. Darret B. and Anita H. Rutman, *A Place in Time* (1984); Allan Kulikoff, *Tobacco and Slaves* (1986); Fredrick F. Siegel. *The Roots of Southern Distinctiveness* (1987); Suzanne Lebsock, *A Share of Honour* (1984); Aubrey Land et al., *Law, Society, and Politics in Early Maryland* (1977); T. H. Breen, *Tobacco Culture* (1985); Wesley Frank Craven, *The Dissolution of the Virginia Company* (1932), *The Southern Colonies in the Seventeenth Century* (1949), and *White, Red, and Black: The Seventeenth Century Virginian* (1971); Edmund S. Morgan, *American Slavery, American Freedom* (1975); Richard L. Morton, *Colonial Virginia*, 2 vols. (1960); Wilcomb E. Washburn, *The Governor and the Rebel* (1958); David W. Jordon, *Foundations of Representative Government: Maryland, 1632–1715* (1987); David B. Quinn, ed., *Early Maryland in a Wider World* (1982); Gloria Main, *Tobacco Colony: Life in Early Maryland, 1650–1720* (1982); Lois G. Carr and David W. Jordan, *Maryland's Revolution of Government, 1689–1692* (1974); Thad Tate and David L. Ammerman, eds., *The Chesapeake in the Seventeenth Century* (1979).

Plymouth and Massachusetts Bay. William Bradford, *Of Plymouth Plantation* (1952); George Langdon, *Pilgrim Colony* (1966); John Demos, *A Little Commonwealth* (1970); William Cronon, *Changes in the Land: Indians, Colonists, and the Ecology of New England* (1983); Samuel Eliot Morison, *Builders of the Bay Colony* (1930); Darrett Rutman, *Winthrop's Boston* (1965); R. E. Wall, *Massachusetts Bay: The Crucial Decade, 1640–1650* (1972); Edmund S. Morgan, *The*

Puritan Dilemma: The Story of John Winthrop; Alden T. Vaughn, *New England Frontier: Puritans and Indians* (1965); Bernard Bailyn, *The New England Merchants in the Seventeenth Century* (1955).

New England Puritanism. Perry Miller, *The New England Mind: The Seventeenth Century* (1939), *The New England Mind: From Colony to Province* (1953), *Orthodoxy in Massachusetts* (1933), and *Errand into the Wilderness* (1956); Edmund S. Morgan, *Visible Saints* (1963), *The Puritan Family* (1966), and *Roger Williams: The Church and the State* (1967); Kenneth Silverman, *The Life and Times of Cotton Mather* (1984); Charles Hambrick-Stowe, *The Practice of Piety* (1982); Philip F. Gura, *A Glimpse of Sion's Glory* (1984); Harry S. Stout, *The New England Soul* (1986); Norman Pettit, *The Heart Prepared: Grace and Conversion in Puritan Spiritual Life* (1989); Sacvan Bercovitch, *The American Jeremiad* (1978) and *The Puritan Origins of the American Self* (1975); Andrew Delbanco, *The Puritan Ordeal* (1989); David Hall, *The Faithful Shepherd* (1972) and *Worlds of Wonder, Days of Judgment* (1989); Robert Middlekauff, *The Mathers* (1971); Larzer Ziff, *Puritanism in America* (1973); Kai Erikson, *Wayward Puritans* (1966); W. K. B. Stoever, *A Faire and Easy Way to Heaven* (1978); J. V. James, *Colonial Rhode Island* (1975); M. J. A. Jones, *Congregational Commonwealth: Connecticut, 1636–1662* (1968); Paul R. Lucas, *Valley of Discord* (1976).

The Restoration Colonies. Christopher Hill, *The World Turned Upside Down* (1972); H. T. Merrens, *Colonial North Carolina* (1964); M. E. Sirmans, *Colonial South Carolina* (1966); Clarence L. Ver Steeg, *Origins of a Southern Mosaic* (1975); Robert Weir, *Colonial South Carolina* (1983); Roger Ekirch, *Poor Carolina* (1981); Peter H. Wood, *Black Majority* (1974); Oliver A. Rink, *Holland on Hudson* (1986); Thomas J. Archdeacon, *New York City, 1664–1710* (1976); Michael Kammen, *Colonial New York* (1975); Thomas J. Condon, *New York Beginnings* (1968); Van Cleaf Bachman, *Peltries or Plantations* (1969); George L. Smith, *Religion and Trade in New Netherland* (1973); Patricia Bonomi, *A Factious People* (1971); Barry Levy, *Quakers and the American*

Family (1988); Alan Tully, *William Penn's Legacy* (1977); Edwin B. Bronner, *William Penn's Holy Experiment* (1962); Mary Maples Dunn, *William Penn: Politics and Conscience* (1967); James T. Lemmon, *The Best Poor Man's Country* (1972); J. E. Pomfret, *The Province of East and West New Jersey, 1609–1702* (1956) and *The Province of East New Jersey* (1962); T. R. Reese, *Colonial Georgia: A Study in British Imperial Policy in the Eighteenth Century* (1963); K. Coleman, *Colonial Georgia* (1976).

The Development of Empire. Lawrence Gipson, *The British Empire Before the American Revolution*, 15 vols. (1936–1970); Stephen S. Webb, *The Governors-General* (1979) and *1676: The End of American Independence* (1984); Leonard Labaree, *Royal Government in America* (1964); Michael Kammen, *Empire and Interest* (1970); Thomas C. Barrow, *Trade and Empire* (1967); I. K. Steele, *The Politics of Colonial Policy* (1968); James Henretta, *Salutary Neglect* (1972); Michael Hall, *Edward Randolph and the American Colonies* (1960); Viola Barnes, *The Dominion of New England* (1923); Lawrence Harper, *The English Navigation Laws* (1939); David S. Lovejoy, *The Glorious Revolution in America* (1972); J. M. Sosin, *English America and the Revolution of 1688* (1982) and *English America and the Restoration Monarchy of Charles II* (1980).

Detail from *The Fishing Lady*, (c. 1750)
This embroidered sampler depicts scenes of upper-class life in colonial New England. The heavily
English style of the sampler reflects the continuing dominance of English culture in American life.
(*Museum of Fine Arts, Boston*)

CHAPTER 3

◩ ◮ ◪

Life in Provincial America

◩ ◮ ◪

As the extent of settlement in North America grew, and as the economies of the colonies began to flourish, several distinctive ways of life emerged. The new American societies differed considerably from the society that most had attempted to re-create in the New World—the society of England. They differed as well from one another.

There were many reasons for the divergence between the culture of the colonies and that of the homeland. Immigrants to the New World found a very different physical environment from the one they had left—a landscape both vaster and less tamed. The economy and the society of the American colonies evolved in response to the physical surroundings. They also found a very different population. English society had not been transplanted whole to the New World. English culture and society could not be re-created intact in America in part because large segments of English culture and society were not represented there. Even more important, some of the early colonists—and many more as time went on—were not English at all. Beginning with the Dutch settlements in New York, the area that would become the United States became a magnet for immigrants from many lands: Scotland, Ireland, the European continent. And beginning with the first importation of slaves into Virginia, English North America became the destination for thousands of forcibly transplanted Africans. Above all, perhaps, European and African settlers were interacting constantly with a native population that for many years outnumbered them. For all the efforts of the colonists to isolate themselves from Indian society and create a culture all their own, the European and Native American worlds could not remain entirely separate. Thus while English culture continued to predominate in the areas of white settlement, American society took its eventual shape from a wide range of influences.

Just as the colonies were becoming increasingly different from England, so were they different from one another. Not until the mid-eighteenth century did the colonists begin to call themselves "Americans." Indeed, the pattern of society in some areas of North America seemed to resemble that of others scarcely at all. The civilization of Puritan New England differed markedly from that of the mid-Atlantic colonies; it differed even more from the plantation economy of the South. And although Americans would ultimately discover that they had enough in common to join together to form a single nation, these regional differences continued to affect their society well beyond the colonial period.

The Colonial Population

Not until long after the beginning of European colonization did the European settlers in North America come to outnumber the native population. But after uncertain beginnings at Jamestown and Plymouth, the European population grew rapidly and substantially, through continued immigration and through

America in 1700

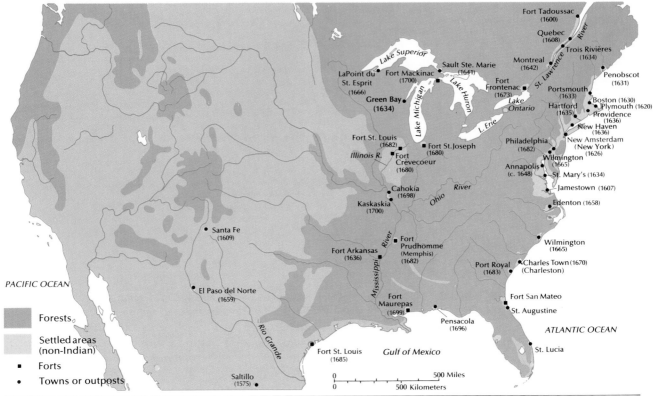

natural increase, until by the late seventeenth century whites and their black servants became the dominant population group along the Atlantic coast.

The Early Population

A few of the early settlers were members of the English upper classes—usually the younger sons of the lesser gentry, men who stood to inherit no land at home and aspired to establish estates for themselves in America. For the most part, however, the early colonial population was decidedly unaristocratic. It included some members of the emerging English middle class, businessmen who migrated to America for religious or commercial reasons or (like John Winthrop) both. But the dominant element was English laborers. Some came to the New World independently. The religious dissenters who formed the bulk of the population of early New England, for example, were mostly men and women of modest means who arranged their own passage, brought

their families with them, and established themselves immediately on their own land.

Others—for a time the majority in the Southern and later in the mid-Atlantic colonies—came as indentured servants. At least three-fourths of the immigrants to the Chesapeake in the seventeenth century arrived in that capacity. The system of temporary servitude in the New World developed out of existing practices in England. Young men and women bound themselves to a master for a fixed term of servitude (usually four to five years). In return they received passage to America, food, and shelter. Upon completion of their terms of service, male indentures were supposed to receive such benefits as clothing, tools, and occasionally land; in reality, however, many left service without anything approaching adequate preparation or resources to begin earning livings on their own. Roughly one-fourth of the indentures in the Chesapeake were women, most of whom worked as domestic servants and who expected to marry when their terms of servitude expired. Because men greatly outnumbered women in the region in the seventeenth century, those expectations were nearly always fulfilled.

Most indentured servants came to the colonies voluntarily, but some did not. Beginning as early as 1617, the English government occasionally dumped shiploads of convicts in America to be sold into servitude, although some criminals, according to Captain John Smith, "did chuse to be hanged ere they would go thither, and were." The government also transported prisoners taken in battles with the Scots and the Irish in the 1650s, as well as other groups deemed undesirable: orphans, vagrants, paupers, and those who were "lewd and dangerous." Still other involuntary immigrants were neither dangerous nor indigent but simply victims of kidnapping, or "impressment" by aggressive and unscrupulous investors and promoters.

It was not difficult to understand why the system of indentured servitude proved so appealing to those in a position to employ servants in colonial America—particularly once it became clear, as it quickly did, that the native population could not be transformed into a servile work force. The indenture system provided a means of coping with the severe labor shortage in the New World. And in the Chesapeake, the headright system (by which masters received additional land grants for every servant they imported) offered another incentive. For the servants themselves, the attractions were not always so clear. Those who came voluntarily often did so to escape troubles in England; others came in the hope of establishing themselves on land or in trades of their own when their terms of service expired. Yet the reality often differed sharply from the hope.

By the late seventeenth century, when the indentured servant population had become one of the largest elements of the population, serious problems were beginning to develop. Some former indentures managed to establish themselves successfully as farmers, tradespeople, or artisans. Others (mostly males) found themselves without land, without employment, without families, and without prospects; and there grew up in some areas a large floating population of young single men—such as those who supported Bacon's Rebellion—who traveled restlessly from place to place in search of work or land and served as a potential (and at times actual) source of social unrest, particularly in the Chesapeake. Even those free laborers who did find employment or land for themselves and settled down with families often did not stay put for very long. The phenomenon of families simply pulling up stakes and moving to an-

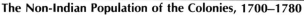

The Non-Indian Population of the Colonies, 1700–1780

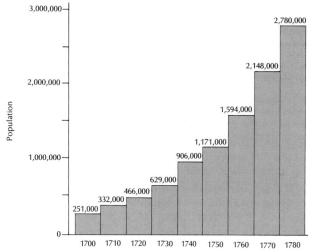

other, more promising location every several years was one of the most prominent characteristics of the colonial population.

Indentured servitude remained an important source of population growth well into the eighteenth century, but beginning in the 1670s the flow began to decline substantially. A decrease in the English birth rate and an improvement in economic conditions there reduced the pressures on many English men and women who might otherwise have considered emigrating. After 1700, those who did travel to America as indentured servants generally avoided the southern colonies, where working conditions were arduous and prospects for advancement were slim, and settled in the mid-Atlantic colonies, especially Pennsylvania and New York, where they could anticipate better opportunities. In the Chesapeake, landowners themselves began to find the indenture system less attractive, in part because they were facing increasing challenges and competition from former servants. That was one reason for the increasing centrality of black slavery in the Southern agricultural economy.

Birth and Death

At first, new arrivals in most colonies, whatever their background or status, could anticipate great hardship: inadequate food, frequent epidemics, and in an appallingly large number of cases, early death. Gradually, however, conditions of settlement improved enough to allow the population to begin to expand. By the end of the seventeenth century, the European population in the English colonies of North America had grown to over a quarter of a million.

Although immigration remained for a time the greatest source of population increase, the most important long-range factor in the growth of the colonial population was its ability to reproduce itself. Marked improvement in the reproduction rate began in New England and the mid-Atlantic colonies in the second half of the seventeenth century, and after the 1650s natural increase became the most important source of population growth there. The New England population more than quadrupled through reproduction alone in the second half of the seventeenth century. This was less a result of unusual fertility (families in England and in other colonies were probably equally fertile) than of exceptional longevity. Indeed, the life spans of residents of some areas of New England were nearly equal to those of people in the twentieth century. In the first generation of American-born colonists, according to one study, men who survived infancy lived to an average age of seventy-one, women to seventy. The next generation's life expectancy declined somewhat—to sixty-five for men who survived infancy—but remained at least ten years higher than the English equivalent and approximately twenty years higher than life expectancy in the South. Scholars disagree on the reasons for these remarkable life spans, but some of the factors that probably contributed to it include the cool climate and the relatively disease-free environment it produced, clean water (a stark contrast to England in these years), and the absence of large population centers that might breed epidemics.

Conditions improved much more slowly in the South. The mortality rates in the Chesapeake region did not begin to match those elsewhere until nearly a hundred years later. Throughout the seventeenth century, the average life expectancy for men in the region was just over forty years, and for women slightly less. One in four children died in infancy, and fully half died before the age of twenty. The high death rate among adults meant that only about a third of all marriages lasted more than ten years; thus those children who survived infancy often lost one or both of their parents before reaching maturity. Widows, widowers, and orphans formed a substantial proportion of the Chesapeake population. The continuing ravages of disease (particularly malaria) and the prevalence of salt-contaminated water kept the death rate high in the South; only after the settlers developed immunity to the local diseases (a slow process known as "seasoning") did life expectancy increase significantly. Population growth was substantial in the region, but this was largely a result of immigration.

Natural increases in the population whenever they occurred were in large part a result of a steady improvement in the sex ratio through the seventeenth century. In the early years of settlement, more than three-quarters of the white population of the Chesapeake consisted of men. And even in New England, which from the beginning had attracted more families (and thus more women) than the Southern colonies, 60 percent of the inhabitants were male in 1650. Gradually, however, more women began to arrive in the colonies; and increasing birth rates, which of course produced roughly equal numbers of males and females, contributed to shifting the sex ratio as well. Not until well into the eighteenth century did the ratio begin to match that in England (where women were a slight majority), but by the late seventeenth century, the proportion of males to females in all the colonies was becoming more balanced.

Women and Families in the Chesapeake

The importance of reproduction in the labor-scarce society of seventeenth-century America had significant effects on both the status and the life cycles of women. The high sex ratio meant that few women remained unmarried for long. The average European woman in America married for the first time at twenty or twenty-one years of age, considerably earlier than in England; in some areas of the Chesapeake, the average bride was three to four years younger.

In the Chesapeake, the most important factor in shaping the structure of families and the role of women remained, until at least the mid-eighteenth century, the extraordinarily high mortality rate. Under those circumstances, the traditional patriarchal family structure of England—by which husbands and fathers exercised firm, even dictatorial control over the lives of their wives and children—was difficult to maintain. Because so few families remained intact for long, rigid patterns of familial authority were constantly undermined. Sexual mores were also more flexible than in England or other parts of America.

Because of the large numbers of indentured servants who were forbidden to marry until their terms of service expired, premarital sexual relationships were frequent. Female servants who became pregnant before the expiration of their terms could expect harsh treatment: heavy fines, whippings if no one could pay the fines, an extra year or two of service added to her contract, and loss of her child after weaning. Bastard children were themselves bound out as indentures at a very early age. On the other hand, a pregnant woman whose term of service expired before the birth of her child or whose partner was able to buy her remaining time from her master might expect to marry quickly. Over a third of Chesapeake marriages occurred with the bride already pregnant.

Women in the Chesapeake could anticipate a life consumed with child bearing. The average wife experienced pregnancies every two years. Those who lived long enough bore an average of eight children apiece (up to five of whom typically died in infancy or early childhood). Since childbirth was one of the most frequent causes of female death, few women survived to see all their children grow to maturity.

For all the hardships women encountered in the seventeenth-century South, they also enjoyed more power and a greater level of freedom than women in other areas (or than Southern women in later years). Because men were plentiful and women scarce, females had considerable latitude in choosing husbands. (They also often had no fathers or other male relatives nearby trying to control their choices.) Because women generally married at a much younger age than men, they also tended to outlive their husbands (even though female life expectancy was somewhat shorter than male). Widows were generally left with several children and with responsibility for managing a farm or plantation, a circumstance of enormous hardship but one that also gave them significant economic power. Although the law required husbands to leave only a relatively small proportion to their widows, in fact men often willed them everything—evidence of the high regard with which husbands tended to regard their wives.

Widows seldom remained unmarried for long, however. Those who had no grown sons to work the tobacco farms and plantations had particular need for male assistance, and marriage was the surest way to secure it. Since many widows married men who were themselves widowers, complex combinations of households were frequent. With numerous stepchildren, half brothers, and half sisters living together in a single household, women often had to play the role of peacemaker—a role that may have enhanced further their authority within the family.

The high mortality rate in the seventeenth-century Chesapeake also created large numbers of orphans, many with no property and no extended family on which to rely. Much earlier than in England or in the northern American colonies, therefore, Maryland and Virginia created special courts and other institutions to protect and control orphaned children.

By the early eighteenth century, the demographic character of the Chesapeake was beginning to change, and with it the nature and structure of the typical family. Life expectancy was increasing, and indentured servitude was in decline. Hence natural reproduction was becoming the principal source of white population increase. The sex ratio was becoming more equal. One result of these changes was that life for white people in the region became less perilous and less arduous. Another result was that women lost some of the power that their small numbers had once given them. As families grew more stable, traditional patterns of male authority revived. By the mid-eighteenth century, Southern families were becoming highly patriarchal.

Women and Families in New England

In New England, where many more immigrants arrived with family members and where death rates declined far more quickly, family structure was much more stable than in the Chesapeake and hence much more traditional. Because the sex ratio was less imbalanced, most men could expect to marry. But women remained in the minority; as in the Chesapeake, they married young, began producing children early, and continued to do so well into their thirties. In contrast to the South, however, Northern children were more likely to survive (the average family raised six to eight children to maturity); and their families were more likely to remain intact. Fewer New England women became widows, and those who did generally lost their husbands later in life. Hence women were less often cast in roles independent of their husbands. Young women, moreover, had less control over the conditions of marriage, both because there were fewer unmarried men vying for them and because their fathers were more often alive and able to exercise control over their choice.

Among other things, increased longevity meant that, unlike the situation in the Chesapeake (where three-fourths of all children lost at least one parent before the age of twenty-one), New England parents usually lived to see their children and even their

A Boston Woman and Her Baby, c. 1674
This oil portrait by an unknown Boston artist is of Elizabeth Freake and her daughter Mary. The lives of most New England women in the seventeenth century were largely consumed by childbearing and child rearing, although women also performed other important functions in the home-centered economies of the time.   (Worcester Art Museum)

women became pregnant before marriage than in the South (although even in Puritan New England, the premarital pregnancy rate was not insubstantial—as high as 20 percent in some communities).

For New Englanders more than for residents of the Chesapeake, the status of women and family relationships were determined in part by religious belief. Whereas in the South, established churches were relatively weak, in New England the Puritan church was a powerful institutional presence. The Puritan belief that men and women were equal before God and hence equally capable of interpreting the Bible created possibilities for women to emerge as spiritual leaders. On the whole, however, religious authority was lodged in the hands of men, who used it in part to reinforce a highly patriarchal view of society. The case of Anne Hutchinson—a women who became an important religious figure only to be disciplined and expelled by the male church hierarchy—is an example of both the possibilities and the limits of female spiritual power.

Puritanism placed a high value on the family, which was not only the principal economic unit but the principal religious unit within every community. In one sense, then, Puritan women played important roles within the family because the position of wife and mother was highly valued in their culture. At the same time, however, Puritanism served to reinforce the idea of nearly absolute male authority and the assumption of female weakness and inferiority. Women were expected to be modest and submissive. (Such popular girls' names as Prudence, Patience, Chastity, and Comfort suggest something about Puritan expectations of female behavior.) A wife was expected to devote herself almost entirely to serving the needs of her husband; a women was to be judged by the degree to which "she looks well to the Wayes of her Household."

Women may have been subordinate to their husbands, but they were at least as important to the New England agricultural economy as the men. Not only did they bear and raise children who at relatively young ages became part of the work force, but they themselves were continuously engaged in tasks vital to the functioning of the farm—gardening, raising poultry, tending cattle, spinning, and weaving, as well as cooking, cleaning, and washing. Northern women also appear to have played an important role in influencing the spending of family resources. Homes in New England were larger, better built, and more comfortably furnished than those in the Southern colonies; and given the Puritan definition of

grandchildren grow to maturity. Still, the lives of most New England women were nearly as consumed by childbearing and child rearing as those of women in the Chesapeake. Even women who lived into their sixties spent the vast majority of their mature years with young children in the home.

The longer lives in New England also meant that parents continued to influence their children's lives far longer than did parents in the South. They were less likely than parents in England actually to "arrange" marriages for their children; but few sons and daughters could choose a spouse entirely independent of their parents' wishes. Men tended to rely on their fathers for land to cultivate—generally a prerequisite for beginning families of their own. Women needed dowries from their parents if they were to hope to attract desirable husbands. Stricter parental supervision of children meant, too, that fewer

Africans Bound for America
Shown here are the below-deck slave quarters of a Spanish vessel en route to the West Indies. A British warship captured the slaver, and a young English naval officer (Lt. Francis Meynell) made this watercolor sketch on the spot. The Africans seen in this picture appear somewhat more comfortable than prisoners on other slave ships, who were often chained and packed together so tightly that they had no room to stand or even sit.   (National Maritime Museum, London)

the home as the woman's sphere, it is reasonable to assume that wives and mothers were in large part responsible.

While family life in the Chesapeake colonies grew more patriarchal in the late seventeenth and early eighteenth centuries, New England families were growing somewhat less patriarchal. As settlement spread beyond the early Puritan centers, as the authority of the church began gradually to decline, and as sons began increasingly to chafe under the control of their fathers, family life became somewhat more fluid, and the rigid division of authority between generations and between the sexes that had characterized seventeenth-century communities became less universal. Only by the rigid standards of seventeenth-century New England, however, did the eighteenth-century family seem flexible. Patriarchal forms remained dominant, and the status of women remained intimately bound to their roles as wives and mothers.

The Beginnings of Slavery in British America

The demand for black servants to supplement the always scarce Southern labor supply existed almost from the first moments of settlement. The supply of African laborers, however, remained relatively restricted during much of the seventeenth century because of the nature of the Atlantic slave trade, which did not at first serve the English colonies in America. The Portuguese slave trade that had begun in the sixteenth century shipped captive men and women from the west coast of Africa to the new European colonies in South America and the Caribbean. Gradually, however, Dutch and French navigators joined the slave trade. A substantial commerce in slaves grew up within the Americas, particularly between the Caribbean islands and the Southern colonies of English America. By the late seventeenth century,

———————— WHY HISTORIANS DISAGREE ————————

"Facts" Versus Interpretations

Unlike some other fields of scholarship, history is not an exact science. We can establish with some certainty many of the basic "facts" of history—that the United States declared its independence in 1776, for example; or that the North won the Civil War; or that the first atomic bomb was detonated in 1945. But wide disagreement remains, and will always remain, about the *significance* of such facts. There are as many different ways of viewing a historical event as there are historians viewing it. In reading any work of history, therefore, it is important to ask not only what facts the author is presenting but how he or she is choosing and interpreting those facts.

Historians disagree with one another for many reasons. People of different backgrounds, for example, often bring different attitudes to their exploration of issues. A black historian might look at the American Revolution in terms of its significance for the members of his or her race and thus draw conclusions about it that would differ from those of a white historian. A Southerner might view Reconstruction in terms different from a Northerner. Social, religious, racial, ethnic, and gender differences among historians all contribute to the shaping of distinctive points of view.

Historians might disagree, too, as a result of the methods they use to explore their subjects. One scholar might choose to examine slavery by using psychological techniques; another might reach different conclusions by employing quantitative methods and making use of a computer. Because history is an unusually integrative discipline—that is, because it employs methods and ideas from many different fields of knowledge, ranging from science to the humanities, from economics to literary criticism—the historian has available an enormous range of techniques, each of which might produce its own distinctive results.

One of the greatest sources of disagreement among historians is personal ideology—a scholar's assumptions about the past, the present, politics, society. Historians who accept the teachings of Karl Marx and others that economics and social classes lie at the root of all historical processes will emphasize such matters in their examination of the past. Others might stress ideas, or the influence of particular individuals, or the workings of institutions and bureaucracies. A critic of capitalism, for example, might argue that American foreign policy after World War II was a reflection of economic imperialism. A critic of communism would be more likely to argue that the United States was merely responding to Soviet expansionism.

Perhaps most important, historical interpretations differ from one another according to the time in which they are written. It may not be true, as some have said, that "every generation writes its own history." But it is certainly true that no historian can entirely escape the influence of his or her own time. Hence, for example, historians writing in the relatively calm 1950s often emphasized very different issues and took very different approaches from those who wrote in the turbulent 1960s, particularly on such issues as race and foreign policy. A scholar writing in a time of general satisfaction with the nation's social and political system is likely to view the past very differently from one writing in a time of discontent. Historians in each generation, in other words, tend to emphasize those features of the past that seem most relevant to contemporary concerns.

All of this is not to say that present concerns dictate, or should dictate, historical views. Nor is it to say that all interpretations are equally valid. On some questions, historians do reach general agreement; some interpretations prove in time to be without merit, while others become widely accepted. What is most often the case, however, is that each interpretation brings something of value to our understanding of the past. The history of the world, like the life of an individual, has so many facets, such vast complexities, so much that is unknowable, that there will always be room for new approaches to understanding it. Like the blind man examining the elephant, in the fable, the historian can get hold of and describe only one part of the past at a time. The cumulative efforts of countless scholars examining different aspects of history contribute to a view of the past that grows fuller with every generation. But the challenge and the excitement of history lie in the knowledge that that view can never be complete.

the supply of black workers in North America was becoming plentiful.

As the commerce in slaves grew more extensive and more sophisticated, it also grew more horrible. Before it ended in the nineteenth century, it was responsible for the forced immigration of as many as 11 million Africans to North and South America and the Caribbean. (Until the late eighteenth century, the number of African immigrants to the Americas was higher than that of Europeans.) In the flourishing slave marts on the African coast, native chieftains made large numbers of blacks available by capturing members of enemy tribes in battle and bringing them—tied together in long lines, or "coffles"—out of the forests and to the ports. Then, after some haggling on the docks between the European traders and the African suppliers, the terrified victims were packed into the dark, filthy holds of ships for the horrors of the "middle passage"—the journey to America. For weeks, sometimes even months, the black prisoners were kept chained in the bowels of the slave ships, unable to stand, hardly able to breathe, supplied with minimal food and water. Women were often victims of rape and other sexual abuse. Those who died en route, and many did, were simply thrown overboard. Slave traders accepted such deaths as an inevitable result of the system. They tried to cram as many Africans as possible into their ships to ensure that enough would survive to yield a profit at journey's end. Upon arrival in the New World, slaves were auctioned off to white landowners and transported, frightened and bewildered, to their new homes.

The first black laborers arrived in English North America before 1620, and as English seamen began to establish themselves in the slave trade, the flow of Africans to the colonies gradually increased. But North America was always a much less important market for African slaves than other parts of the New World, especially the islands of the Caribbean and Brazil; fewer than 5 percent of the blacks imported to the Americas arrived in the English colonies. In the beginning, those blacks who did arrive in what became the United States came not directly from Africa, but from the West Indies. Not until the 1670s did traders start importing blacks directly from Africa to North America. Even then, however, the flow remained small for a time, mainly because a single group, the Royal African Company of England, maintained a monopoly on the trade and managed as a result to keep prices high and supplies low.

A turning point in the history of the black population in North America was 1697, the year that the Royal African Company's monopoly was finally broken. With the trade now opened to English and colonial merchants on a competitive basis, prices fell and the number of blacks arriving greatly increased. By the end of the century, about 25,000 slaves lived in America. That was approximately 10 percent of the population, but because blacks were so heavily concentrated in a few Southern colonies, they were already beginning to outnumber whites in some areas. The high sex ratio among African immigrants (there were perhaps twice as many men as women in most areas) retarded the natural increase of the black population. But in the Chesapeake at least, more new slaves were being born than were being imported from Africa. In South Carolina, by contrast, the arduous conditions of rice cultivation ensured that the black population would barely be able to sustain itself through natural increase until much later.

By 1760, the number of Africans in the colonies had increased tenfold since the turn of the century—to approximately a quarter of a million. A relatively small number (16,000 in 1763) lived in New England; there were slightly more in the middle colonies (29,000). The vast majority, however, continued to live in the South. By then the flow of free white laborers to that region had all but stopped, and blacks had become securely established as the basis of the Southern work force.

It was not entirely clear at first that the status of black laborers in America would be fundamentally different from that of white indentured servants. In the rugged conditions of the seventeenth-century South, it was often difficult for whites and blacks to maintain strictly separate roles. In some areas—South Carolina, for example, where the number of black arrivals swelled more quickly than anywhere else—whites and blacks lived and worked together for a time on terms of relative equality. Some blacks were treated much like white hired servants, and some were freed after a fixed term of servitude. A few blacks themselves became landowners, and some apparently owned slaves of their own.

Gradually, however, relations between the races evolved in such a way that by the early eighteenth century a rigid distinction had become established between black and white. (See "Where Historians Disagree," page 68.) White servants were necessarily freed after a term of servitude; their masters were required by contract to release them. There was no such necessity to free black workers, and the assumption slowly spread that blacks would remain in service permanently. Another incentive for making the

======= WHERE HISTORIANS DISAGREE =======

The Origins of Slavery

How did the institution of slavery establish itself in the New World? How did white people come to believe that Africans should be kept in bondage? Historians have offered a number of different interpretations.

The debate had its modern origins in an important 1950 article by Oscar and Mary Handlin ("Origins of the Southern Labor System," *William and Mary Quarterly*). They pointed out that in the seventeenth century many residents of the American colonies (and of England) lived in varying degrees of "unfreedom," that there was nothing unusual or new about a dependent labor force. What was new was the transformation of black servitude in America into a permanent system, based on race, with the condition of slavery passed from one generation to the next. The Handlins identified this transition from "servant" to "slave" more as a legal process by which colonial legislatures sought to increase the available labor force than as a response to racial prejudice. The leaders of the Chesapeake hoped to attract white laborers to the New World; to do so, they had to make clear the distinction between voluntary and involuntary servitude. Hence the institutionalization of slavery: It was an effort to persuade whites that their status would be higher than that of blacks.

Winthrop Jordan, in *White over Black* (1968), offered a different view of how slavery developed in America. Jordan emphasized that Europeans had long viewed people of color—and particularly black Africans—as inferior beings preeminently fit to serve whites. Slavery did not evolve slowly from a system of relative racial equality. Blacks and whites were viewed and treated differently from the beginning; and the institution that finally emerged was a natural reflection of the deep-seated racism that the white settlers had brought with them. David Brion Davis, similarly, argued in *The Problem of Slavery in Western Culture* (1966) and later works that American slavery emerged not so much from the legal or economic conditions of the colonies as from a deeply embedded set of cultural assumptions. Davis placed less emphasis than Jordan on racism, arguing that the notion of slavery was an integral part of Western culture and that African servitude in America was not so very different from other forms of slavery in other societies.

Several historians in the 1970s returned to an emphasis on the particular conditions within the American colonies that helped produce the slave system. But unlike the Handlins, they saw the legal process by which slavery emerged as secondary to other issues. Peter Wood, in *Black Majority* (1974), emphasized the economic benefits that the black labor force provided whites in colonial South Carolina. In the early years of settlement (the "frontier period") in South Carolina, blacks and whites often worked together. Black workers were relatively few in number, and differentiations in status were relatively vague. After the 1690s, however, whites discovered that African workers were better suited than Europeans to do the arduous work of rice cultivation, which was now coming to dominate the economy of the colony. Importation of black workers rapidly increased; and by the early eighteenth century, whites were becoming uneasy about the presence of a black majority in the colony. The hardening of the slave system, through legislation and in practice, reflected white fears of black resistance or even revolt.

Edmund S. Morgan, in *American Slavery, American Freedom* (1975), also argued that the labor system in the South was at first relatively flexible and later grew more rigid. In an examination of colonial Virginia, Morgan suggested that the early colonists did not at first intend to create a permanent system of human bondage. By the late seventeenth century, however, the flourishing tobacco economy had created a growing need for cheap labor. The existence of a large, dependent white labor force, which was difficult to recruit and even more difficult to control, was unappealing to the colonists. African workers could be recruited and controlled more easily. The creation of a rigid slave system in the eighteenth century was, therefore, less a result of historic racism than a response to economic and social needs. Racism emerged largely as a result of slavery; it was not the cause of slavery. Morgan went on to argue that the later development of democratic ideas in Virginia was made possible by the existence of slavery. A dependent white labor force would have made the idea of political equality difficult to sustain; but by making the dependent workers into slaves, outside the white political world, it was possible to believe that all white citizens were politically equal.

status of blacks rigid was that the children of slaves provided white landowners with a self-perpetuating labor force. White assumptions about the inferiority of the black race contributed further to the growing rigidity of the system; most whites considered them a lesser breed, capable of little more than manual labor. Indeed, many whites convinced themselves that they were actually helping the Africans by "civilizing" and Christianizing them; conversion to Christianity did not, however, entitle slaves to freedom. That slavery was developing in a society that was already multiracial also had an impact on its evolution. Whites had already defined themselves as a superior race in their relations with the native Indian population and used that self-definition to justify their harsh and often duplicitous dealings with the tribes. The idea of subordinating an inferior race was, therefore, already implanted in the European imagination by the time substantial numbers of Africans appeared in their midst.

Whites were willing to tolerate a certain ambiguity in the system when the number of blacks remained small; but by the early eighteenth century, once the slave trade increased and the black population began to grow, they moved quickly to clarify the status of Africans. The result was the evolution of a system of permanent servitude, a system made legal in the early eighteenth century when colonial assemblies began to pass "slave codes" limiting the rights of blacks and ensuring almost absolute authority to white masters. One factor, and one factor only, determined whether a person was subject to the slave codes: color. And while in the colonial societies of Spanish America, people of mixed race were granted a different (and higher) status than pure Africans, English America recognized no such distinctions. Any African ancestry was enough to classify a person as black.

Later Immigration

Perhaps the most distinctive and enduring feature of the American population was its polyglot character, its bringing together of peoples of many different races, ethnic groups, and nationalities. The forced importation of Africans was one important element of this multicultural peopling of the new land, but equally important was the arrival of substantial non-English groups from Europe. By the early eighteenth century, the flow of immigrants from England itself began to decline substantially. This decrease was a result not only of the improvement of economic con-

ditions there but also of new restrictions on emigration imposed by a government alarmed at the continuing exodus, which threatened to depopulate whole regions of the country. White immigration continued, however, as large numbers of French, Germans, Swiss, Irish, Scots, and Scandinavians contributed to the patchwork of the American population.

The earliest, although not the most numerous, of these immigrants were the French Calvinists, or Huguenots. The Edict of Nantes of 1598 had granted them liberties and privileges that enabled them to constitute practically a state within the state in Roman Catholic France. In 1685, however, the edict was revoked; and soon thereafter, singly and in groups, the Huguenots began seizing opportunities to leave the country. A total of about 300,000 left France in the following decades, and a small proportion of them traveled to the English colonies in North America.

Many German Protestants suffered similarly from the arbitrary religious policies of their rulers; and all Germans, Catholics as well as Protestants, suffered from the devastating wars between their principalities and King Louis XIV of France (the "Sun King"). The Rhineland of southwestern Germany, the area known as the Palatinate, experienced particular hardships. Its proximity to France exposed its people to slaughter and its farms to ruin at the hands of invaders. And the unusually cold winter of 1708–1709 provided a final blow to the precarious economy of the region. More than 12,000 Palatinate Germans sought refuge in England, and approximately 3,000 of them soon found their way to America. They arrived in New York and tried at first to make homes in the Mohawk Valley, only to be ousted by the powerful landlords of the region. Some of the Palatines moved farther up the Mohawk, out of reach of the patroons, but most made their way to Pennsylvania, where they received a warm welcome (and where they ultimately became known to English settlers as the "Pennsylvania Dutch," a corruption of their own German term for their nationality, "Deutsch"). After that, the Quaker colony became the usual destination of Germans, who sailed for America in growing numbers. (Among them were Moravians and Mennonites, with religious views similar to those of the Quakers.) Many German Protestants went to North Carolina as well, especially after the founding of New Bern in 1710 by a company of 600 German-speaking Swiss.

The most numerous of the newcomers were the so-called Scotch-Irish—Scotch Presbyterians who had settled in northern Ireland (in the county of Ul-

Dominant Immigrant Groups in Colonial America, c. 1760

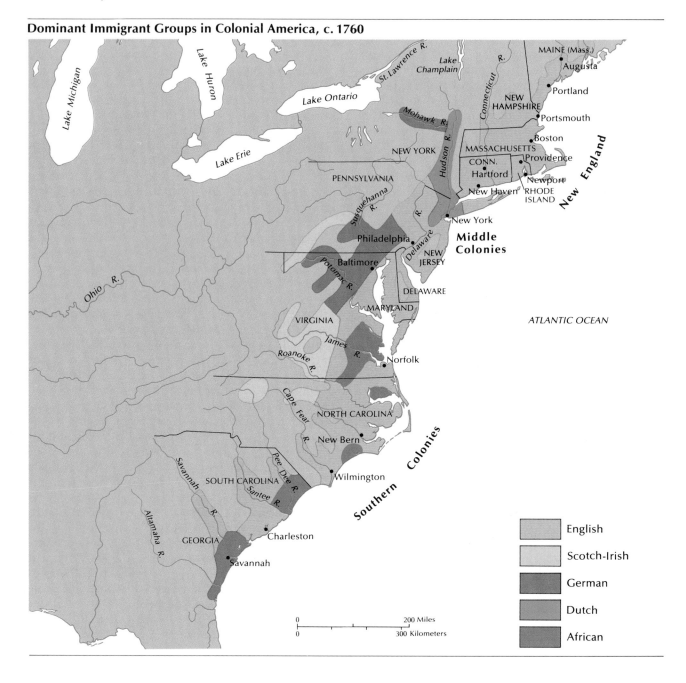

Legend:
- English
- Scotch-Irish
- German
- Dutch
- African

ster) in the early seventeenth century. The Ulster colonists had prospered for a time despite the handicap of barren soil and the need for constant struggle to suppress the Catholic natives. But in the first years of the eighteenth century, the English government prohibited Ulster from exporting to England the woolens and other products that had become the basis of the northern Irish economy; at the same time, the government virtually outlawed the practice of the

Presbyterian religion in Ulster and insisted on conformity with the Anglican church. After 1710, moreover, the long-term leases of many Scotch-Irish expired; English landlords doubled and even tripled the rents. Thousands of tenants embarked for America in successive waves of emigration.

Often coldly received at the colonial ports, most of the Scotch-Irish pushed out to the edges of European settlement. There they occupied land without much regard for who actually claimed to own it, whether absentee whites, Indians, or the colonial governments. They believed that "it was against the laws of God and nature that so much land should be idle while so many Christians wanted it to labor on and to raise bread." They were also as ruthless in their displacement and suppression of the Indians as they had been with the native Irish Catholics.

Immigrants from Scotland itself and from southern Ireland added other elements to the colonial population. Scottish Highlanders, some of them Roman Catholics who had been defeated in rebellions in 1715 and 1745, immigrated into several colonies, North Carolina above all. Presbyterian Lowlanders, faced in Scotland with high rents in the country and unemployment in the towns, left for America in large numbers shortly before the American Revolution. The Irish migrated steadily over a long period, and by the time of the Revolution they were almost as numerous as the Scots, although less conspicuous. Many of them had by then abandoned their Roman Catholic religion and with it much of their ethnic identity.

Continuing immigration and improving natural increase contributed to a rapid population growth of the colonies in the eighteenth century. In 1700, the colonial population totaled less than 250,000; by 1775, it was over 2 million—a nearly tenfold increase. Throughout the colonial period, the population nearly doubled every twenty-five years.

The Colonial Economy

Colonial Americans engaged almost from the beginning in a wide range of economic pursuits, but except for a few areas in the West where the small white populations subsisted largely on the fur and skin trade with the Indians, farming dominated all areas of European and African settlement throughout the seventeenth and eighteenth centuries. Beyond that basic similarity, however, the economies of the different regions varied markedly from one another; and even within colonies, different areas grew in different ways.

The Southern Economy

In the Chesapeake region, where tobacco early established itself as the basis of the economy, a strong demand for the crop in Europe enabled some planters to grow enormously wealthy and at times allowed

the region as a whole to prosper. But throughout the seventeenth and eighteenth centuries, tobacco growers experienced the same problem that would afflict American farmers repeatedly for centuries: periodic overproduction. Production of tobacco frequently exceeded demand, and as a result the price of the crop could suffer severe declines. The result was a boom-and-bust cycle in the Chesapeake economy, with the first major bust occurring in 1640, followed by varying degrees of recovery.

Most of the Chesapeake planters believed that the way to protect themselves from the instability of the market was to grow more tobacco. That only made the problem worse; it also helped change the nature of the Chesapeake economy as a whole. Those planters who could afford to do so expanded their landholdings, enlarged their fields, and acquired additional laborers. After 1700, tobacco plantations employing several dozen slaves or more were common.

South Carolina and Georgia were unsuitable for the growing of tobacco, and they relied instead on rice production. The low-lying coastline with its many tidal rivers made it possible to establish, through the construction of dams and dikes, rice paddies that could be flooded and then drained. Rice cultivation was arduous work—performed standing knee deep in the mud of malarial swamps, under a blazing sun, surrounded by insects—a task so difficult and unhealthful that white laborers generally refused to perform it. Hence the far greater dependence of planters in South Carolina and Georgia on slaves than their Northern counterparts. Yet it was not only because blacks could be compelled to perform these difficult tasks that whites found them so valuable. It was also because they were much better at the work than whites. They showed from the beginning a greater resistance than whites to malaria and other local diseases (although the impact of disease on black workers was by no means inconsiderable). And they proved more adept at performing the basic agricultural tasks required. That was in part because some of them had come from rice-producing regions of west Africa (a fact that has led some historians to conclude that blacks were responsible for introducing rice cultivation to America in the early seventeenth century). It was also because most Africans were more accustomed to the hot and humid climate of the rice-growing regions than were the Europeans.

In the early 1740s, another staple crop contributed to the South Carolina economy: indigo. Eliza Lucas, a young Antiguan woman who managed her

Selling Tobacco

This late-seventeenth-century label was used in the sale of American tobacco in England. The drawing depicts Virginia as a land of bright sunshine, energetic slaves, and prosperous, pipe-smoking planters. (American Heritage)

HENRY NUNNs
Beſt Virginia
CAMBRIDGE

family's American plantations, experimented with cultivating the West Indian plant (which was the source of a blue dye in great demand in Europe) in America and discovered that it could grow on the high ground of South Carolina that was unsuitable for rice planting, and that it was harvested during the season when the rice was still growing. It became an important complement to rice and a popular import in England.

Because of the South's early dependence on large-scale cash crops, the Southern colonies developed less of a commercial or industrial economy than the colonies of the North. The trading in tobacco and rice was handled largely by merchants based in London and, later, in the Northern colonies. Few cities of more than modest size developed in the South; no substantial local merchant communities emerged. A pattern was established that would characterize the Southern economy, and differentiate it from that of other regions, for more than two centuries.

The Northern Economy

The economies of the Northern colonies—the settlements stretching from Pennsylvania into Maine—were more varied than those of their Southern counterparts. In the North, as in the South, agriculture continued to dominate, but it was agriculture of a more diverse kind. In addition to farming, there gradually emerged an important commercial sector of the economy.

One reason that agriculture did not remain the exclusive economic pursuit of the North was that conditions for farming were less favorable than in the South. In most of New England, in particular, colder weather and hard rocky soil made it difficult for colonists to develop the kind of large-scale commercial farming system that Southerners were creating. Instead, most settlers cultivated relatively small areas of land, growing food, raising animals, and in general attempting to serve their own families' needs. Modest cash crops—livestock, apples, and corn—enabled New Englanders to trade for those things they could not grow or make for themselves. But most New Englanders did not produce a staple crop that could become a major export item.

Conditions for agriculture were far better in southern New England and the middle colonies, where the soil was fertile and the weather slightly more temperate. Farmers in New York, Pennsylvania, and the Connecticut River valley cultivated staple crops for sale both at home and abroad. The region was the chief supplier of wheat to much of New England and to parts of the South. Some areas of the region were, for various reasons, less productive than others. In New York, for example, the concentration of land ownership and the maintenance of great estates (some of them thousands and even hundreds of thousands of acres large) worked to discourage production. Few people were willing to work as tenants on large estates when they could get farms of their own in other colonies. In Pennsylvania, by contrast, German immigrants succeeded in greatly increasing production by applying the methods of intensive cultivation they had practiced in Europe. The sex ratio in the German communities was relatively even, and women commonly worked alongside the men in the fields—a practice that other immigrant groups on occasion found appalling.

From time to time, entrepreneurs in New England and the middle colonies (particularly New Jersey and Pennsylvania) attempted to augment their agricultural economy with industrial enterprises. Beginning with a failed effort to establish an ironworks in Saugus, Massachusetts, in the mid-seventeenth century, colonists embarked on innumerable industrial ventures. Many such ventures failed, but the colonists did manage to establish a wide range of industrial activities on a modest scale. At the simplest level, almost every colonist engaged in a certain amount of industry at home. Women, in particular, were active in spinning, weaving, making soap and candles, and other tasks basic to the life of the family. Men engaged in carpentry. Occasionally these home industries provided families with goods they could trade or sell. Beyond these private efforts, craftsmen and artisans established themselves in colonial towns as cobblers, blacksmiths, rifle makers, cabinetmakers, silversmiths, and printers. In some areas, entrepreneurs harnessed the water power of the many streams and rivers to run small mills—some for grinding grain, others for processing cloth, still others for milling lumber. And in several places, large-scale shipbuilding operations began to flourish.

The largest industrial enterprise anywhere in English North America was that of the German ironmaster Peter Hasenclever in northern New Jersey. Founded in 1764 with British capital, it employed several hundred laborers, many of them imported from ironworks in Germany. There were other, smaller ironmaking enterprises in every northern colony (with particular concentrations in Massachusetts, New Jersey, and Pennsylvania), and there were ironworks as well in several of the southern colonies. But these and other growing industries did not become the basis for the kind of explosive industrial growth that Great Britain experienced in the late eighteenth century. That was in part because of such restrictions as those imposed by the Iron Act of 1750, a measure passed by Parliament restricting colonists from engaging in metal processing (and stifling the development of a steel industry in America). Similar prohibitions applied to the manufacture of woolens (the Woolen Act of 1699) and hats (the Hat Act of 1732), although Americans often disregarded such legislation. The real obstacles to industrialization, however, were more basic: an inadequate labor supply, an inadequate domestic market, and an inadequate infrastructure of transportation facilities, energy supplies, and other necessities. Americans would not overcome such obstacles until the mid-nineteenth century.

More important than manufacturing to the economy of the Northern colonies were the so-called extractive industries—those that exploited the natural resources of the continent. The flourishing fur trade of the first decades of settlement did not survive for long; by the mid-seventeenth century, the supply of fur-bearing animals along the Atlantic seaboard had been nearly exhausted, and the interior fur trade was largely in the hands of the Algonquins and their French allies. For the next century and more, the colonists relied instead on lumbering, which took advantage of the vast forests of the New World; mining, which exploited iron and other mineral reserves throughout the colonies; and fishing, particularly in the waters off the New England coast. These extractive industries provided what manufacturing and agriculture often failed to give the Northern colonists: commodities that could be exported to England in exchange for manufactured goods. And they helped, therefore, to produce the most distinctive feature of the Northern economy—a thriving commercial class.

The Rise of Commerce

The inability of any one colony, or any one region, to attain genuine economic self-sufficiency required the development of commerce. But the form that commerce took reflected not only economic necessity but a wide array of arcane legal restrictions and the financial peculiarities of the seventeenth- and eighteenth-century world.

Perhaps the most remarkable feature of colonial commerce in the seventeenth century was that it was able to survive at all. American merchants faced such bewildering and intimidating obstacles, and lacked so many of the basic institutions of trade, that they managed to stay afloat only with great difficulty. There was, first, no commonly accepted medium of exchange. The colonies had almost no specie (gold or silver coins). They experimented at times with different forms of paper currency—tobacco certificates, for example, which were secured by tobacco stored in warehouses; or land certificates, secured by property. Such paper was not, however, acceptable as payment for any goods from abroad; and it was, in any case, ultimately outlawed by Parliament. For many years, colonial merchants had to rely on a haphazard system of barter or on crude money substitutes such as beaver skins.

A second obstacle was the near impossibility of rationalizing trade. In the fragmented, jerry-built commercial world of colonial America, no merchants could be certain that the goods on which their commerce relied would be produced in sufficient quantity, nor could they be certain of finding adequate markets for them. Few channels of information existed to inform traders of what they could expect in foreign ports; vessels sometimes stayed at sea for several years, journeying from one market to another, trading one commodity for another, attempting to find some way to turn a profit. Engaged in this chaotic commerce, moreover, were an enormous number of small, fiercely competitive companies, which made the problem of rationalizing the system even more acute.

Despite these and other problems, commerce in the colonies not only survived but grew. There was an elaborate coastal trade, through which the colonies did business with one another and with the West Indies, largely in such goods as rum, agricultural products, meat, and fish. The mainland colonies received sugar, molasses, and at times slaves from the Caribbean markets in return. There was as well an expanding international trade, which linked the North American colonies in an intricate network of commerce with England, continental Europe, and the west coast of Africa. This commerce has often been described, somewhat inaccurately, as the "triangular trade," suggesting a neat process by which merchants carried rum and other goods from New England to Africa, exchanged their merchandise for slaves, whom they then transported to the West Indies (hence the term "middle passage" for the dread journey—it was the second of the three legs of the voyage), and then exchanged the slaves for sugar and molasses, which they shipped back to New England to be distilled into rum. In fact, the system was almost never so simple. The "triangular" trade in rum, slaves, and sugar was in fact a maze of highly diverse trade routes: between the Northern and Southern colonies, America and England, America and Africa, the West Indies and Europe, and other combinations.

Out of this complex and highly risky trade emerged a group of adventurous entrepreneurs who by the mid-eighteenth century were beginning to constitute a distinct merchant class. Concentrated in the port cities of the North (Boston, New York, Philadelphia, and other, smaller, trading centers), they enjoyed protection from foreign competition within the English colonies; the British Navigation Acts had excluded all non-British ships from the colonial carrying trade. They had access to a market in England for such colonial products as furs, timber, and American-built ships. But that did not satisfy all their commercial needs. Many colonial products—fish, flour, wheat, and meat, all of which England could produce for itself—required markets altogether outside the British empire. Ignoring laws restricting colonial trade to England and its possessions, many merchants developed markets in the French, Spanish, and Dutch West Indies, where prices were often higher than in the British colonies. The profits from this commerce enabled the colonies to import the manufactured goods they needed from Europe.

In the course of the eighteenth century, the colonial commercial system began to stabilize. In some cities, the more successful merchants expanded their operations so greatly that they were able to dominate some sectors of trade and curb some of the destabilizing effects of competition. Merchants managed, as well, to make extensive contacts in the English commercial world, securing their positions in certain areas of transatlantic trade. But the commercial sector of the American economy remained open to newcomers, largely because it—and the society on which it was based—was expanding so rapidly.

Overseas Trade During the Colonial Period

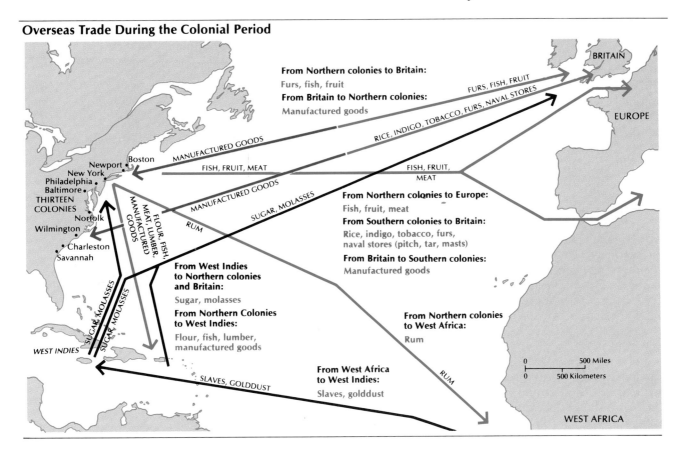

From Northern colonies to Britain:
Furs, fish, fruit

From Britain to Northern colonies:
Manufactured goods

From Northern colonies to Europe:
Fish, fruit, meat

From Southern colonies to Britain:
Rice, indigo, tobacco, furs,
naval stores (pitch, tar, masts)

From Britain to Southern colonies:
Manufactured goods

From West Indies
to Northern colonies
and Britain:
Sugar, molasses

From Northern Colonies
to West Indies:
Flour, fish, lumber,
manufactured goods

From Northern colonies
to West Africa:
Rum

From West Africa
to West Indies:
Slaves, golddust

Patterns of Society

It was not only in the composition of its population and the structure of its economy that the society of the colonies differed from that of England. It was also in the nature of its most basic social institutions.

Although there were sharp class distinctions in the colonies, the well-defined and deeply entrenched class system of England failed to reproduce itself in America. In England, where land was scarce and the population large, the relatively small proportion of the people who owned land had enormous power over the great majority who did not; the imbalance between land and population became a foundation of the English economy and the cornerstone of its class system. In America, of course, precisely the inverse was true. Land was abundant and people were scarce. Aristocracies emerged there, to be sure; but they tended to rely less on land ownership than on control of a substantial work force, and they were generally less secure and less powerful than their English coun-

terparts. Far more than in England, there were opportunities in America for social mobility—both up and down.

There emerged, too, new forms of community whose structure reflected less the British model than the realities of the American environment. These forms varied greatly from one region to another, but several basic—and distinctly American—types emerged.

The Plantation

The plantation system of the American South illustrated clearly both the differences between the colonial and English class systems and the way in which colonial communities evolved in response to local conditions. The first plantations emerged in the early settlements of Virginia and Maryland, in response to the establishment of tobacco as the economic basis of the Chesapeake. Some planters hoped to re-create in America the entrenched, landholding aristocracy of

England, and in a few cases—notably in the great Maryland estates granted by Lord Baltimore to his relatives and friends—a semblance of such an aristocracy did emerge. The Maryland plantation of Charles Carroll of Carrollton, reputedly the wealthiest man in the colonies, covered 40,000 acres and contained 285 slaves. And there were other plantations, in Maryland, Virginia, and the tobacco-growing regions of North Carolina, that eventually attained similar size.

On the whole, however, seventeenth-century colonial plantations were rough and relatively small estates. In the early days in Virginia, they were little more than crude clearings on the edges of settlement, where landowners and indentured servants worked side by side in conditions so horrible that death was an everyday occurrence. Even in later years, when the death rate declined and the landholdings became more established, plantation work forces seldom exceeded thirty people. Most landowners lived in rough cabins or houses, with their servants or slaves nearby. Relatively few lived in anything resembling aristocratic splendor.

The economy of the plantation, like all agricultural economies, was a precarious one. In good years, successful growers could earn great profits, expand their operations, and move closer to becoming true landed aristocrats. But since they could not control their markets, even the largest planters were constantly at risk. When prices for their crops fell—as tobacco prices did, for example, in the 1660s—they faced the prospect of ruin. The plantation economy created many new wealthy landowners, but it also destroyed many.

Because plantations were often far from cities and towns—which were, in any case, relatively few in the South—they tended to become self-contained communities. Residents lived in close proximity to one another in a cluster of buildings that included the "great house" of the planter himself (a house that was usually, although not always, far from great), the service buildings, the barns, and the cabins of the slaves. Wealthier planters often created something approaching a full town on their plantations, with a school (for white children only), a chapel, and a large population. Smaller planters lived more modestly, but still in a relatively self-sufficient world.

On the larger plantations, the presence of a substantial slave work force altered not only the economic, but the family, lives of the planter class. Plantation mistresses, unlike the wives of small farmers, could rely on servants to perform ordinary household chores and could thus devote more time to

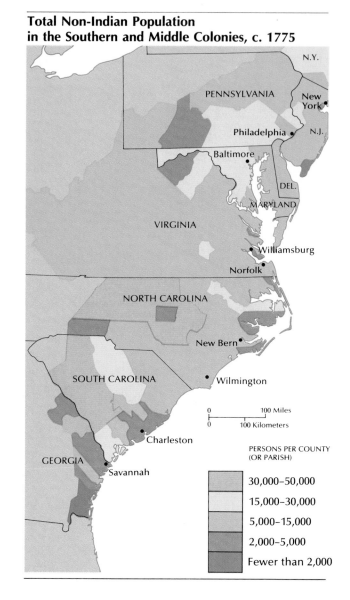

Total Non-Indian Population in the Southern and Middle Colonies, c. 1775

PERSONS PER COUNTY (OR PARISH)

30,000–50,000

15,000–30,000

5,000–15,000

2,000–5,000

Fewer than 2,000

their husbands and children than their counterparts in other parts of colonial society. But they also had to endure the frequent sexual liaisons between their husbands or sons and black women of the slave community. Southern women generally learned to pretend not to notice these relationships, but they were almost certainly a source of anxiety and resentment. Black women, naturally, had even greater cause to resent such liaisons.

Although the English class system did not reproduce itself among white Americans, Southern society was highly stratified in its own way. Even though the fortunes of planters could rise and fall quickly, at any given time there were always particularly wealthy landowners who exercised far greater social and economic influence than their less prosperous neighbors. Within a given area, a great landowner not only controlled the lives of those who worked his own plantation but the livelihood of independent farmers who could not effectively compete with him and thus depended on him to market their crops and supply them with credit. Some whites were unable to buy (or retain ownership) of their land and rented their farms from wealthy planters. Independent farmers, working small plots of land with few or no slaves to help them, formed the majority of the Southern agrarian population; it was the planters, however, who dominated the Southern agrarian economy. The result was an economy and a society growing more sharply stratified.

The black slaves, of course, lived very differently. On the smaller farms with only a handful of slaves, it was not always possible for a rigid separation to develop between whites and blacks. But over three-fourths of all blacks lived on plantations of at least ten slaves; nearly half lived in communities of fifty slaves or more. And in these larger establishments, they began to develop a society and culture of their own—influenced by their white masters, to be sure, but also partly independent of them.

Although whites seldom encouraged formal marriages among slaves, usually hoping only that they would produce children rapidly, blacks themselves developed a strong and elaborate family structure. Slaves attempted to construct nuclear families, and they managed at times to build stable households, even to work together growing their own food in gardens provided by their masters. But such efforts were in constant jeopardy. Any family member could be sold at any time to another planter, even to one in another colony. As a result, the black family evolved along lines in many ways different from its white counterpart. Blacks placed special emphasis on extended kinship networks. They even created surrogate "relatives" for blacks separated entirely from their own families. They adapted themselves, in short, to difficult conditions over which they had limited control.

Blacks also developed languages of their own. In South Carolina, for example, the early slaves communicated with one another in "Gullah," a hybrid of English and African tongues, that not only reinforced the blacks' sense of connection with their African ancestry but enabled them to engage in conversations

**Black Population:
Proportion of Total Population, c. 1775**

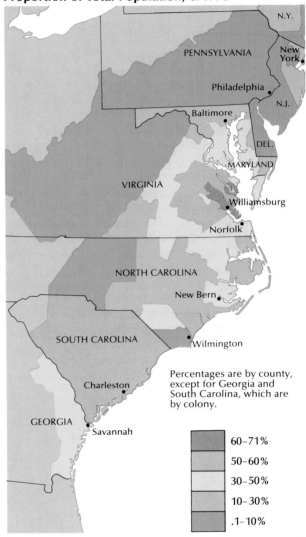

Percentages are by county, except for Georgia and South Carolina, which are by colony.

	60–71%
	50–60%
	30–50%
	10–30%
	.1–10%

their white masters could not understand. There emerged too a distinctive slave religion, which blended Christianity with African folklore and which became a central element in the emergence of an independent black culture.

Nevertheless, black society was subject to constant intrusions from and interaction with white society. Black house servants, for example, at times lived in what was, by black standards, great luxury; but they were also isolated from their own community and under constant surveillance from whites. Black women were subject to the usually unwanted sexual advances from owners and overseers and hence to bearing mulatto children, who were rarely recognized by their white fathers but who were generally accepted as members of the slave community. On some plantations, black workers were treated with kindness and even affection by their masters and mistresses and at times displayed genuine devotion in return. On others, they encountered physical brutality and occasionally even sadism, against which they were virtually powerless.

There were occasional acts of individual resistance by slaves against masters, and on at least two occasions during the colonial period there were actual slave rebellions. In the most important such revolt, the so-called Stono Rebellion in South Carolina in 1739, about 100 blacks rose up, seized weapons, killed several whites, and attempted to escape south to Florida. The uprising was quickly crushed and most participants executed. The most frequent form of resistance was simply running away, but that provided no real solution either. There was nowhere to go.

Most slaves, male and female, worked as field hands (with the women shouldering the additional burdens of cooking and child rearing). But on the larger plantations that aspired to genuine self-sufficiency, some slaves learned trades and crafts: blacksmithing, carpentry, shoemaking, spinning, weaving, sewing, midwifery, and others. These skilled craftsmen and craftswomen were at times hired out to other planters. Some set up their own establishments in towns or cities and shared their profits with their owners. On occasion, they were able to buy their freedom. There was a small but significant free black population living in Southern cities by the time of the Revolution.

As an economic unit, the Southern plantation was both efficient and productive and helped the agricultural output of the region to expand greatly in the course of the colonial period. As a social unit, it achieved stability at the cost of human freedom.

The Puritan Community

A very different form of community emerged in Puritan New England, but one that was also distinctively American. The characteristic social unit in New England was not the isolated farm, but the town. Each new settlement drew up a "covenant" among its members, binding all residents together in a religious and social commitment to unity and harmony. Some such settlements consisted of people who had immigrated to America together (occasionally of entire Puritan congregations who had traveled to the New World en masse). More often, they consisted of people who had come together during their voyage or after their arrival in America. These communities proved strong in part because their members had usually actively chosen to become a part of them.

The structure of the towns generally reflected the spirit of the covenant. Colonists laid out a village, with houses and a meeting house arranged around a central pasture, or "common." They also divided up the outlying fields and woodlands of the town among the residents; the size and location of a family's field depended on the family's numbers, wealth, and social station. But wherever their lands might lie, families generally lived with their neighbors close by, reinforcing the strong sense of community.

Once established, a town was generally able to run its own affairs, with little interference from the colonial government. Residents held a yearly "town meeting" to decide important questions and to choose a group of "selectmen," who governed until the next meeting. As a rule, all adult males were permitted to participate in the meeting. But important social distinctions remained, the most crucial of which was membership in the church. Only those residents who could give evidence of grace, of being among the elect (the "visible saints") assured of salvation, were admitted to full membership, although other residents of the town were required to attend church services.

The English system of primogeniture—the passing of all property to the firstborn son—was not recreated in New England. Instead, a father divided up the lands allotted to him among all his sons. His

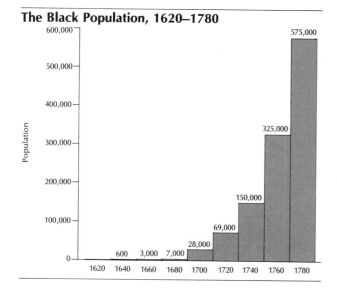

The Black Population, 1620–1780

Population (y-axis): 0 to 600,000

- 1620: 600
- 1640: 3,000
- 1660: 7,000
- 1680: 28,000
- 1700: 69,000
- 1720: 150,000
- 1740: 325,000
- 1760: 575,000
- 1780: 575,000

control of this inheritance was one of the most effective means of exercising power over the family. Often a son would reach his late twenties before his father would allow him to move into his own household and work his own land. Even then, sons would usually continue to live in close proximity to their fathers. Young women were generally more mobile than their brothers, since they did not stand to inherit land; their dowries and their inheritances consisted instead of movable objects (furniture, household goods, occasionally money or precious objects) and thus did not tie them to a particular place.

The early Puritan community, in short, was a tightly knit organism. The town as a whole was bound together by the initial covenant, by the centralized layout of the village, by the power of the church, and by the town meeting. The family was held together by the rigid patriarchal structure that limited opportunities for younger members (males in particular) to strike out on their own. Yet as the years passed and the communities grew, this communal structure experienced strains. This was partly because of the increasing commercialization of New England society, which introduced new forces and new tensions into the communities of the region. But it was also a result of other pressures that had been developing within even purely agricultural communities, pressures that were a result primarily of population growth.

As towns grew larger, residents tended to cultivate lands farther and farther from the community center and, by necessity, to live at increasing distances from the church. Often, groups of outlying residents would eventually apply for permission to build a church of their own, usually the first step toward creation of a wholly new town. Such applications were frequently the occasion for bitter quarrels between the original townspeople and those who proposed to break away.

The practice of distributing land through the patriarchal family structure contributed further tensions to the Puritan community. In the first generations, fathers generally controlled enough land to satisfy the needs of all their sons. After several generations, however, when such lands were being subdivided for the third or fourth time, there was often too little to go around, particularly in communities surrounded by other towns, with no room to expand outward. The result was that in many communities,

The New England Town: Sudbury, Massachusetts, 17th Century

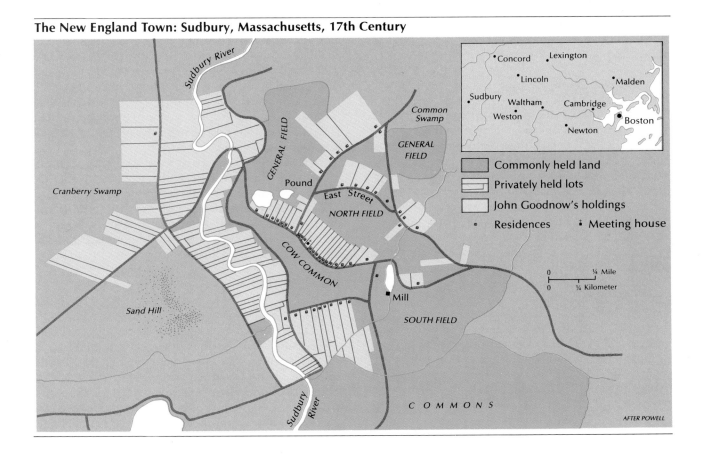

groups of younger residents were breaking off and moving elsewhere—at times far away—to form towns of their own.

Even within the family, economic necessity often worked to undermine the patriarchal model to which most Puritans, in theory at least, subscribed. It was not only the sons who needed their fathers (as a source of land and wealth); fathers needed their sons, as well as their wives and daughters, as a source of labor to keep the farm and the household functioning. Thus while in theory men had nearly dictatorial control over their wives and children, in reality relationships were more contractual, with patriarchal authority limited by economic necessity (and, of course, bonds of affection).

It would, however, be easy to exaggerate the degree to which the cohesiveness of the Puritan community declined in the late seventeenth century. Against the strict standards of the first years of settlement, and the even stricter standards of Puritan expectations, New England towns may have seemed to be unraveling. But measured against most contemporary communities in England or other parts of America, the Puritan town remained remarkably communal. The best evidence of the enduring importance of the covenant to New Englanders may be the amount of time and energy they devoted to worrying about and warning of its erosion.

The Witchcraft Phenomenon

The gap between the expectation of a cohesive, united community and the reality of an increasingly diverse and fluid one at times produced severe social and psychological strain. At the extreme, these tensions could produce bizarre and disastrous events. One example was the widespread hysteria in the 1680s and 1690s over supposed witchcraft (the human exercise of Satanic powers) in New England. The most famous outbreak (although by no means the only one) was in Salem, Massachusetts, where adolescent girls began to exhibit strange behavior and leveled accusations of witchcraft against several West Indian servants steeped in voodoo lore. The hysteria they produced spread throughout the town, and before it was over, hundreds of people (most of them women) were accused of witchcraft. As the crisis in Salem grew, accusations shifted from marginal women like the West Indians to more prominent and substantial people. Nineteen residents of Salem were put to death before the trials finally ended in 1692; the girls who had been the original accusers later recanted and admitted that their story had been fabricated.

In Salem, at least, the witchcraft crisis seems to have been in part a reflection of social strains peculiar to the community. The character of the accused and the accusers there suggests that it emerged out of tensions between those who were gravitating toward the new commercial economy of the town's thriving seaport and those who remained tied to the languishing agricultural economy of the community's western areas. Residents of the outlying areas of the town resented the favored position of their eastern neighbors. The accusations were usually made by the relatively isolated and unsuccessful members of the community against people associated with its more prosperous segments—perhaps reflections of a jealousy that could not be openly expressed in a "godly" community and which hence found other, more dangerous expressions.

But the Salem experience was not unique. Accusations of witchcraft spread through many New England towns in the early 1690s (and indeed had emerged regularly in Puritan society for many years before). Research into the background of accused witches reveals that most were middle-aged women, often widowed, with few or no children. Accused witches were, moreover, generally of low social position, were often involved in domestic conflicts, had frequently been accused of other crimes, and were considered abrasive by their neighbors. Puritan society had little tolerance for "independent" women, and that so many "witches" were women who were not securely lodged within a patriarchal family structure (and who seemed openly to defy the passive, submissive norms society had created for them) suggests that tensions over sexual roles played a substantial role in generating the crisis.

The witchcraft controversies were also a reflection of the highly religious character of these societies. New Englanders believed in the power of Satan and his ability to assert his power in the world. Belief in witchcraft was not a marginal superstition, rejected by the mainstream. It was a common feature of Puritan religious conviction.

Cities

To call the commercial centers that emerged along the Atlantic coast in the eighteenth century "cities" would be to strain today's definition of that word. Even the largest colonial community was scarcely bigger than a modern small town. Yet by the standards of the eighteenth century, cities did indeed exist in America. In the 1770s the two largest ports—Philadelphia and New York—had populations of

A Witchcraft Trial in Salem, 1692

Although most of those prosecuted for sorcery were women, this mid-nineteenth-century painting by T. H. Matteson depicts the witchcraft trial of a man, George Jacobs (seen kneeling at lower right). Jacobs had strongly opposed the witchcraft proceedings and had criticized the young women whose afflictions had helped create the hysteria in Salem. One of those women, Sarah Churchill, was a servant in Jacobs's home and said that she had seen his name written in the devil's book. Jacobs scornfully denied charges that he was a wizard. But when asked to recite the Lord's Prayer in the courtroom, he stumbled. He was convicted and hanged. (Essex Institute, Salem, Massachusetts)

28,000 and 25,000, respectively, which made them larger than most English urban centers. Boston (16,000), Charles Town (later Charleston), South Carolina (12,000), and Newport, Rhode Island (11,000), were also substantial communities by the standards of the day.

Colonial cities served as trading centers for the farmers of their regions and as marts for international trade. Their leaders were generally merchants who had acquired substantial estates. Although in most colonial communities, disparities of wealth were generally not very great, in cities they sometimes came to seem enormous. Wealthy merchants

and their families moved along crowded streets dressed in fine imported clothes, often riding in fancy carriages, coming in and out of large houses with staffs of servants. Moving beside them were the numerous minor tradesmen, workers, and indigents, dressed simply and living in crowded and often filthy conditions. It would be an exaggeration to claim that sharp class divisions emerged in the cities, but more than in any other area of colonial life (except of course in the relationship between masters and slaves) social distinctions were real and visible in urban areas.

There were other distinctive features of urban

Baltimore in 1752
Baltimore remained a small and relatively quiet port even two decades after its founding in 1729. Most Maryland to-bacco growers shipped their crops from their own wharves along the river and had little need for a central harbor.
(Maryland Historical Society, Baltimore)

life as well. Cities were the centers of much of what industry there was in the colonies, such as the distill-eries for turning imported molasses into exportable rum. They were the locations of the most advanced schools and sophisticated cultural activities and of shops where imported goods could be bought. In addition, they were communities with social prob-lems that were peculiarly urban: crime, vice, pollu-tion, traffic. Unlike smaller towns, cities were required to establish elaborate corporate govern-ments. They set up constables' offices and fire de-partments. They developed systems for supporting the urban poor, whose numbers grew steadily and became especially large in times of economic crisis.

Cities were also particularly vulnerable to fluc-tuations in trade. When a market for a particular prod-uct became glutted and prices fell, the effects on residents of a town—merchants and those whose live-lihoods derived from commerce—could be severe. In the countryside, the impact was generally more muted.

Finally, and of particular importance for the po-litical future of the colonies, cities became places where new ideas could circulate and be discussed.

Because there were printers, it was possible to have regular newspapers. Books and other publications form abroad introduced new intellectual influences. And the taverns and coffeehouses of cities provided forums in which people could gather and debate the issues of the day. It was hardly surprising that when the revolutionary crisis began to build in the 1760s and 1770s, it manifested itself in the cities.

The Colonial Mind

Two powerful forces were competing for the Amer-ican mind in the eighteenth century. One was the traditional intellectual and religious outlook of the sixteenth and seventeenth centuries, with its empha-sis on a personal God, intimately involved with the world, keeping watch over individual lives. The other was the new spirit of the Enlightenment, a movement that was sweeping both Europe and America and that stressed the importance of science and human reason. The old views made possible such phenomena as the belief in witchcraft, and they placed great value on a stern moral code in which intellect was less important than faith. The Enlightenment, by contrast, suggested that people had substantial control over their own lives and the course of their societies, that the world could be explained and therefore could be structured along rational scientific lines. Much of the intellectual climate of colonial America was shaped by the tension between these two impulses.

The Pattern of Religions

The American colonists brought their religions with them from abroad. But like so many other imported institutions, religion took on a new and distinctive pattern in the New World. In part, this was because of the sheer number of different faiths established in America. With the immigration of diverse sectarians from several countries, the colonies became an ecclesiastical patchwork. Toleration flourished to a degree unmatched in any European nation, not because Americans deliberately sought to produce it, but because conditions virtually required it.

The experience of the Church of England illustrated how difficult the establishment of a common religion would be in the colonies. By law, Anglicanism was established as the official faith in Virginia, Maryland, New York, the Carolinas, and Georgia. In these colonies everyone regardless of belief or affiliation was supposed to be taxed for the support of the church. Actually, except in Virginia and Maryland, the Church of England succeeded in maintaining its position as the established church only in certain localities. To strengthen Anglicanism, in America and elsewhere, the Church of England in 1701 set up the Society for the Propagation of the Gospel in Foreign Parts. Missionaries of the SPG founded a number of new Anglican communions in the colonies, especially in Massachusetts and Connecticut. But Anglicanism never succeeded in becoming the dominant religious force in America that some members of the SPG envisioned.

Even in areas where a single faith had once predominated, the forces of denominationalism soon began to be felt. In New England, for example, Puritans had originally believed themselves all to be part of a single faith: Calvinism. In the course of the eighteenth century, however, there was a growing tendency for different congregations to affiliate with different denominations. Some became Congregationalists; others identified themselves as Presbyte-

rians. In belief, these two groups were essentially the same, but they differed in ecclesiastical organization. Each Congregationalist church was virtually autonomous; the Presbyterians had a more highly centralized government, with a governing body of presbyters (made up of ministers and lay elders) for the churches of each district. In the early eighteenth century, many of the Puritan churches of Connecticut, and most of those founded in colonies to the south by emigrants from New England, adopted the Presbyterian form of government.

In parts of New York and New Jersey, Dutch settlers had established their own Calvinist denomination, Dutch Reformed, which survived long after the colonies became part of the British empire. The American Baptists (of whom Roger Williams is considered the first) were also originally Calvinistic in their theology. Then, in Rhode Island and in other colonies, a bewildering variety of Baptist sects sprang up. They had in common a belief that infant baptism did not suffice and that rebaptism, usually by total immersion, was necessary when believers reached maturity. Some Baptists remained Calvinists, believers in predestination; others came to believe in salvation by free will.

Protestants extended toleration to one another more readily than to Roman Catholics. To strict Puritans, the pope seemed no less than the Antichrist. They viewed their Catholic neighbors across the border in New France (Canada) not only as commercial and military rivals, but as agents of the devil bent on frustrating the divine mission of the wilderness Zion in New England. In most of the English colonies, however, Roman Catholics were far too small a minority to occasion serious conflict. They were most numerous in Maryland, and even there they numbered no more than 3,000. Ironically, they suffered their worst persecution in that colony, which had been founded as a refuge for them and had been distinguished by its Toleration Act of 1649. According to Maryland laws passed after 1691, after the overthrow of the original proprietors, Catholics not only were deprived of political rights but also were forbidden to hold religious services except in private houses.

Jews in provincial America totaled no more than about 2,000 at any time. The largest community lived in New York City. Smaller groups settled in Newport and Charleston, and there were scattered Jewish families in all the colonies. Nowhere could they vote and hold office. Only in Rhode Island could they practice their religion openly.

The Decline of Piety

By the beginning of the eighteenth century, some Americans were growing troubled by the apparent decline in religious piety in their society. In part, this was a result of the rise of denominationalism. With so many diverse sects existing side by side, some people were tempted to doubt whether any particular denomination, even their own, possessed a monopoly of truth and grace. More important, however, were other changes in colonial society. The movement of the population westward and the wide scattering of settlements had caused many communities to lose touch with organized religion. The rise of towns and the multiplication of material comforts led to an increasingly secular outlook in densely settled areas. The progress of science and free thought in Europe—and the importation of Enlightenment ideas to America—caused at least some colonists to adopt a rational and skeptical view of the world.

Concerns about declining piety surfaced as early as the 1660s in New England, where the Puritan oligarchy warned of a deterioration in the power of the church. As the first generation of American Puritans died, the number of church members rapidly declined, for few of the second generation seemed to harbor enough religious passion to demonstrate the "saving grace" that was a prerequisite for membership. The children of "saints" had generally been baptized and had attended church, but in the absence of a true "conversion experience," many had never become full members. When these people began to have children of their own, the clergy was faced with a dilemma. Should the infants of these unconverted churchgoers be baptized? In 1662, a conference of ministers attempted to solve the problem by instituting the Halfway Covenant, which gave these men and women of the third and later generations the right to be baptized but not the right to partake of communion or vote in church affairs.

As time passed, this carefully drawn distinction between full and half members was often forgotten, and in many communities the church came to include the families of all who could take part in colonial politics as voters and officeholders. Qualification for membership in the church, in other words, became largely secular. Orthodox Puritans, however, continued to oppose the transformation that was enveloping the erstwhile land of the saints. Sabbath after Sabbath, ministers preached sermons of despair (known as "jeremiads"), deploring the signs of waning piety. "Truly so it is," one minister lamented in 1674, "the very heart of New England is changed and exceedingly corrupted with the sins of the times." There was, he said, a growing spirit of profaneness, pride, worldliness, sensuality, gainsaying and rebellion, libertinism, carnality, formality, hypocrisy, "and a spiritual idolatry in the worship of God." Only in relative terms was religious piety actually declining in New England. By the standards of later eras (or by the standards of other societies of the seventeenth century), the Puritan faith, like the communal character of the New England town and the patriarchal character of the Puritan family, remained remarkably strong. But New Englanders measured their faith by their own standards, not by those of other times and places, and to them the "declension" of religious piety seemed a serious problem.

The Great Awakening

By the early eighteenth century, similar concerns were emerging in other regions and among members of other faiths. Everywhere, colonists were coming to believe, religious piety was in decline and opportunities for spiritual regeneration were dwindling. The result was the first great American revival.

It was known as the Great Awakening. Although the first stirrings (or "freshenings") began in some places early in the century, the Great Awakening was truly launched in the 1730s and reached its climax in the 1740s. Then, for a time, a new spirit of religious fervor seemed for thousands of Americans to have reversed the trend away from piety.

That the movement was not purely religious in origin is suggested by the identity of those who responded most frequently to it: residents of areas where social and economic tensions were greatest; women (who constituted the majority of converts) frustrated by their social and familial subjugation; younger sons of the third or fourth generation of settlers—those who stood to inherit the least land and who thus faced the most uncertain futures. The social origins of the revival were evident too in much of its rhetoric, which emphasized the potential for every person to break away from the constraints of the past and start anew in his or her relationship to God (and, implicitly, to the world). But social tensions were not alone responsible for the revival. At work, too, was a powerful desire among people of all backgrounds for an intense religious experience.

Wandering exhorters from England did much to stimulate the revivalistic spirit. John and Charles Wesley, the founders of Methodism (which had begun as a reform movement within the Church of

England) visited Georgia and other colonies in the 1730s with the intention of revitalizing religion and converting Indians and blacks. George Whitefield, a powerful open-air preacher and for a time an associate of the Wesleys, made several evangelizing tours through the colonies. Everywhere he went, Whitefield drew tremendous crowds.

But the Wesleys, Whitefield, and other evangelizers from abroad were less important to American revivalism in the long run than the colonial ministers attempting to restore religious fervor in America. Theodore Frelinghuysen, of the Dutch Reformed church, and Gilbert Tennent, a Presbyterian, were

George Whitefield

Whitefield succeeded John Wesley as leader of the Calvinistic Methodists in Oxford, England. Like Wesley, he was a major force in promoting religious revivalism in both England and America. He made his first missionary journey to the New World in 1738 and returned in the mid-1740s for a celebrated journey through the colonies that helped spark the Great Awakening. (National Portrait Gallery, London)

important native voices of evangelism. But the outstanding preacher of the Great Awakening was the New England Congregationalist Jonathan Edwards—a deeply orthodox Puritan but also one of the most original theologians in American history. From his pulpit in Northampton, Massachusetts, Edwards attacked the new doctrines of easy salvation for all. He preached anew the traditional Puritan ideas of the absolute sovereignty of God, the depravity of man, predestination, the necessity of experiencing a sense of election, and salvation by God's grace alone. His vivid descriptions of hell could terrify his listeners. Day after day agonized sinners crowded his parsonage to seek his aid; at least one committed suicide in despair at his inability to experience grace.

The Great Awakening spread over the colonies like a religious epidemic. It was most successful in frontier areas and was strongest of all in the Southern backcountry. The Awakening created a sharp division in the Presbyterian church between a large and rapidly growing group of revivalistic "New Light" Presbyterians and the traditional "Old Lights." New Methodist and Baptist sects attracted other converts.

The Great Awakening not only led to the division of existing congregations and the founding of new ones. It also affected areas of society outside the churches. Some of the revivalists denounced book learning as a snare and a delusion, a positive hindrance to salvation; and in some communities the result was a retreat from commitments to secular education. But other evangelists saw education as a means of furthering their own brand of religion and founded schools for the preparation of New Light ministers. Perhaps more important, by challenging the importance of formal church hierarchies and insisting that salvation could come only through individual grace, the revival implicitly challenged traditional sources of authority and traditional patterns of deference in colonial society. It injected a vaguely egalitarian spirit into a strongly hierarchical and deferential society.

Language and Letters

American literary and artistic life remained closely tied to its English origins. But distinctive features of colonial language and literature soon became evident. As early as the mid-seventeenth century, newcomers to the colonies noticed a gradual Americanization of the English language. New words originated in borrowings from the Indians (for example, *skunk, squash*), from the French (*prairie, portage*), and from the Dutch (*boss, cookie*). Americanisms also arose from the combining of words already in the English language (*bullfrog, snowplow*), from the formation of new adjectives based on existing nouns (*kinky, chunky*), from the adoption of unfamiliar uses for familiar words (*branch*, to mean "stream"), and from the retention of old English expressions that were being dropped in England. After 1700, English travelers in America began to notice a strangeness in accent as well as vocabulary, and in 1756 the great lexicographer Dr. Samuel Johnson mentioned the existence of an "American dialect." In fact, there were several American dialects and several American accents, reflecting the distances between and the social diversity among the various colonies.

Colonial America produced relatively little literature of real artistic importance, certainly nothing to compare with the literary output of England or Europe in the same years. Benjamin Franklin was one of the most significant of the colonial writers, although his work consisted largely of pragmatic, advisory essays—as suggested by such titles as *Advice to a Young Man on Choosing a Mistress* (1745), *Reflections on Courtship and Marriage* (1746), *Observations Concerning the Increase of Mankind* (1755), and *Advice to a Young Tradesman* (1762). The most prolific colonial literary figures, however, were such theologians as Cotton Mather and Jonathan Edwards.

Education

Many colonists placed a high value on education, despite the difficulties they confronted in gaining access to it. Some families tried to teach their children to read and write at home, although the heavy burden of work in most agricultural households limited the time available for schooling. In Massachusetts, a 1647 law required every town to support a public school, and while many communities failed to comply, a modest network of educational establishments emerged as a result. Elsewhere, the Quakers and other sects operated church schools. And in some communities, widows or unmarried women conducted "dame schools" by holding private classes in their homes. In cities, master craftsmen set up evening schools for their apprentices; at least a hundred such schools appeared between 1723 and 1770.

Only a relatively small number of children received education beyond the primary level; but white male Americans, at least, achieved a high degree of literacy. By the time of the Revolution, well over half of all white men could read and write, a rate substantially higher than in most European countries. The literacy rate for women lagged behind men until the nineteenth century; and while opportunities for further education were scarce for males, they were almost nonexistent for females. Nevertheless, colonial girls often received the same home-based education as boys in their early years, and their literacy rate too was substantially higher than their European counterparts.

Black slaves had virtually no access to education at all. Occasionally a master or mistress would teach slave children to read and write, but they had few real incentives to do so. Indeed, as the slave system became more firmly entrenched, strong social (and ul-

A "Dame School" Primer

More than the residents of any other region of North America (and far more than those of most of Europe), the New England colonists strove to educate their children and achieved perhaps the highest level of literacy in the world. Throughout the region, young children attended institutions known as "dame schools" (because the teachers were almost always women) and learned from primers like this one. Puritan education emphasized both basic skills (the alphabet and reading) and moral and religious precepts, as this sample page suggests. (American Antiquarian Society)

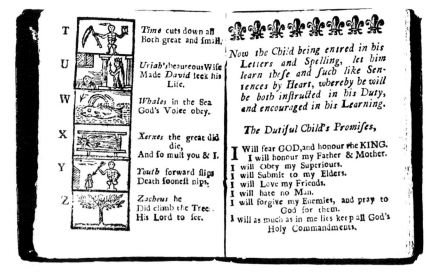

timately legal) sanctions developed to discourage any efforts to promote black literacy, lest it encourage slaves to question their stations. Indians, too, remained largely outside the white educational system —to a large degree by choice; most tribes preferred to educate their children in their own way. But some white missionaries and philanthropists established schools for Native Americans and helped create a small but significant population of Indians literate in spoken and written English.

Nowhere was the intermingling of the influences of traditional religiosity and the new spirit of the Enlightenment clearer than in the colleges and universities that grew up in colonial America. Of the six colleges in operation by 1763, all but two were founded by religious groups primarily for the training of preachers. Yet in almost all, the influences of the new scientific, rational approach to knowledge could be felt.

Harvard, the first American college, was established in 1636 by the General Court of Massachusetts at the behest of Puritan theologians, who wanted to create a traning center for ministers. Two years later, in 1638, instruction began in Cambridge. In that same year the college was named for a Charlestown minister, John Harvard, who had died and left his library and half his estate to the college. Decades later, in 1693, William and Mary College (named for the English king and queen) was established in Williamsburg, Virginia, by Anglicans; like Harvard, it was conceived as an academy to train clergymen. And in 1701, conservative Congregationalists, dissatisfied with the growing religious liberalism of Harvard, founded Yale (named for one of its first benefactors, Elihu Yale) in New Haven, Connecticut. Out of the Great Awakening emerged the College of New Jersey, founded in 1746 and known later as Princeton (after the town in which it was located). One of its first presidents was Jonathan Edwards.

Despite the religious basis of these colleges, students at most of them could derive something of a liberal education from the curricula, which included not only theology, but logic, ethics, physics, geometry, astronomy, rhetoric, Latin, Hebrew, and Greek. From the beginning, Harvard was intended not only to provide an educated ministry but also to "advance learning and perpetuate it to posterity." King's College, founded in New York in 1754 and later renamed Columbia, was even more devoted to the spread of secular knowledge. It had no theological faculty and was interdenominational from the start. The Academy and College of Philadelphia, which became the University of Pennsylvania, was

from its birth in 1755 a completely secular institution, founded by a group of laymen under the inspiration of Benjamin Franklin. It offered courses in utilitarian subjects—mechanics, chemistry, agriculture, government, commerce, and modern languages —as well as in the liberal arts.

By the mid-eighteenth century, the colonies were (in comparison with most European nations) well supplied with colleges; and from them emerged a group of men steeped in the ideas and principles of the Enlightenment. Some Americans continued to travel to England for a university education, and they brought home with them still more new theories and philosophies. After 1700, however, most colonial leaders received their entire education in America. But the advantages of higher education were not widely shared. Women and blacks were excluded from all colleges and universities. And among white men, only those from relatively affluent families could afford to attend.

The Allure of Science

The clearest indication of the spreading influence of the Englightenment in America was an increasing interest in scientific knowledge. Most of the early colleges established chairs in the natural sciences and introduced some of the advanced scientific theories of Europe, including Copernican astronomy and Newtonian physics, to their students. But the most vigorous promotion of science in these years occurred outside the colleges, through the private efforts of amateurs and the activities of scientific societies. Leading merchants, planters, and even theologians became corresponding members of the Royal Society of London, the leading English scientific organization. Benjamin Franklin, the most celebrated amateur scientist in America, won international fame through his experiments with electricity (and most notably through his 1752 demonstration, using a kite, that lightning and electricity were the same).

The high value that influential Americans were beginning to place on scientific knowledge was clearly demonstrated by the most daring and controversial scientific experiment of the eighteenth century: inoculation against smallpox. The Puritan theologian Cotton Mather had learned of experiments in England by which people had been deliberately infected with mild cases of smallpox in order to immunize them against the deadly disease. Despite strong opposition from many of his neighbors, he urged inoculation on his fellow Bostonians during an

The Magnetic Dispensary

In this 1790 painting, artist Samuel Collings caricatured the popular enthusiasm that Benjamin Franklin and others had produced for scientific experiments. The men and women shown here are rubbing iron rods with silk cloth to produce static electricity. A popular pastime was to place the charged rods over people's heads to watch their hair stand on end. (Library Company of Philadelphia)

epidemic in the 1720s. The results confirmed the effectiveness of the technique. Other theologians (including Jonathan Edwards) took up the cause, along with many physicians. By the mid-eighteenth century, inoculation had become a common medical procedure in America.

Concepts of Law and Politics

In law and politics, as in other parts of their lives, Americans in the seventeenth and eighteenth centuries believed that they were re-creating in the New World the practices and institutions of the Old. But as in other areas, they managed, without meaning to or even realizing it, to create something very different.

Changes in the law in America resulted in part

from the scarcity of English-trained lawyers, who were almost unknown in the colonies until after 1700. Not until a full generation after that did authorities in England try to impose the common law and the statutes of the realm upon the provinces. By then, it was already too late. Although the American legal system adopted most of the essential elements of the English system, including such ancient rights as trial by jury, significant differences had already become well established.

Pleading and court procedures were simplified in America, and punishments were made less severe. Instead of the gallows or prison, colonists more commonly resorted to the whipping post, the branding iron, the stocks, and (for "gossipy" women) the ducking stool. In a labor-scarce society, it was not in the interests of communities to execute or incarcerate

SIGNIFICANT EVENTS

1636 Harvard College founded in Massachusetts (p. 87)

1640 Instability in tobacco markets begins (p. 71)

1647 Massachusetts law requires a public school in every town (p. 86)

1662 Halfway Covenant established in New England (p. 84)

1650 Population of New England begins to grow by natural increase (p. 62)

1670s Flow of indentured servants declines; slave traders begin importing slaves directly from Africa to North America (p. 61)

1685 Edict of Nantes revoked in France; Huguenots begin migrating to North America (p. 69)

1690s Rice production becomes central to South Carolina economy (p. 71)

1691 Official toleration of Catholics ends in Maryland (p. 83)

1692 Witchcraft trials begin in Salem (p. 80)

1693 College of William and Mary founded in Virginia (p. 87)

1697 Royal African Company monopoly of slave trade broken; slave importations begin to increase (p. 68)

1701 Yale College founded in Connecticut (p. 87)

1708–1709 First major migration of Palatinate Germans to North America begins (p. 69)

1710 Major Scotch-Irish migrations to North America begin (p. 71)

1720 Cotton Mather initiates smallpox inoculations in Massachusetts (p. 87)

1734 Great Awakening begins in Massachusetts (p. 84)
John Peter Zenger tried in New York (p. 89)

1739 George Whitefield arrives in North America; Great Awakening intensifies (p. 85)

1739 Stono slave rebellion in South Carolina (p. 78)

1740s Indigo production begins in South Carolina (p. 71)

1746 College of New Jersey founded at Princeton (p. 87)

1754 King's College (later Columbia University) founded in New York (p. 87)

1764 Major ironworks established in New Jersey (p. 73)

potential workers. Crimes were redefined. In England, a printed attack on a public official, whether true or false, was considered libelous. In the colonies, at the 1734 trial of the New York publisher John Peter Zenger, who was powerfully defended by the Philadelphia lawyer Andrew Hamilton, the courts ruled that criticisms of the government were not libelous if factually true—a verdict that removed some restrictions on the freedom of the press. There was a subtle but decisive transformation in legal philosophy; colonists came to think of law as a reflection of the divine will or the natural order, not as an expression of the power of an earthly sovereign.

Even more significant for the future of the relationship between the colonies and England were important differences that were emerging between the American and British political systems. Because the royal government that was in theory the ultimate authority over the colonies was so far away, Americans created a group of institutions of their own that

gave them—in reality, if not in theory—a large measure of self-government. In most colonies, local communities grew accustomed to running their own affairs with minimal interference from higher authorities. Communities also expected to maintain strict control over their delegates to the colonial assemblies, and those assemblies came to exercise many of the powers that Parliament exercised in England (even though in theory Parliament remained the ultimate authority in America). Provincial governors had broad powers on paper, but in fact their influence was sharply limited. They lacked control over appointments and contracts; such influence resided largely in England or with local colonial leaders. They could never be certain of their tenure in office; because governorships were patronage appointments, a governor could be removed any time his patron in England lost favor. And in many cases, governors were not even familiar with the colonies they were meant to govern. Some governors were native-born Americans, but most were Englishmen who came to the colonies for the first time to assume their offices. The results of all this were that the focus of politics in the colonies became a local one, the provincial governments became accustomed to acting more or less independently of Parliament, and a set of assumptions and expectations about the rights of the colonists took hold in America that was not shared by policy makers in England. These differences caused few problems before the 1760s, because the British did little to exert the authority they believed they possessed. But when, beginning in 1763, the English government began attempting to tighten its control over the American colonies, a historic crisis resulted.

SUGGESTED READINGS

General Social Histories. James A. Henretta and Gregory Nobles, *The Evolution of American Society, 1700–1815,* rev. ed. (1987); Richard Hofstadter, *America at 1750: A Social Portrait* (1971); David Hackett Fischer, *Albion's Seed* (1989).

Population and Family. Robert V. Wells, *The Population of the British Colonies in America Before 1776* (1975); Philip Greven, *Four Generations* (1970) and *The Protestant Temperament: Patterns of Child-Rearing, Religious Experience, and the Self in Early America* (1977); John Putnam Demos, *Past, Present, and Personal: The Family and Life Course in American History* (1986); Edmund S. Morgan, *The Puritan Family* (1966); J. William Frost, *The Quaker Family in Colonial America* (1972); Christopher Jedrey, *The World of John Cleaveland: Family and Community in Eighteenth-Century New England* (1979); Joan M. Jensen, *Loosening the Bonds: Mid-Atlantic Farm Women, 1750–1850* (1986); Laura Thatcher Ulrich, *Good Wives: Image and Reality in the Lives of Women in Northern New England, 1650–1750* (1982); Roger Thompson, *Women in Stuart England and America* (1974); Lyle Koehler, *A Search for Power: 'The Weaker Sex' in Seventeenth-Century New England* (1982); Daniel Blake Smith, *Inside the Great House: Planter Family Life in Eighteenth Century Chesapeake Society* (1980); Judith Walzer Leavitt, *Brought to Bed: Child Bearing in America, 1750–1950* (1986).

Immigration. Bernard Bailyn, *The Peopling of British North America: An Introduction* (1986) and *Voyagers to the West: A Passage in the Peopling of America on the Eve of the Revolution* (1986); Albert B. Faust, *The German Element in the United States,* 2 vols. (1909); Ian C. C. Graham, *Colonists from Scotland: Emigration to North America, 1707–1783* (1956); James G. Leyburn, *The Scotch-Irish: A Social History* (1962); Frederic Klees, *The Pennsylvania Dutch* (1950); R. J. Dickson, *Ulster Immigration to the United States* (1966); Marcus L. Hanson, *The Atlantic Migration, 1607–1860* (1940); James Kettner, *The Development of American Citizenship* (1978).

Society and Slavery in the Colonial South. Edmund S. Morgan, *American Slavery, American Freedom* (1975); Peter Wood, *Black Majority* (1974); Winthrop Jordan, *White over Black* (1968); David Brion Davis, *The Problem of Slavery in Western Culture* (1966); Mechal Sobel, *The World They Made*

Together: Black and White Values in Eighteenth-Century Virginia (1987); David W. Galenson, *Traders, Planters, and Slaves: Market Behavior in Early English America* (1986); Rhys Isaac, *The Transformation of Virginia, 1740–1790* (1982); Jean E. Friedman, *The Enclosed Garden: Women and Community in the Evangelical South* (1985); Jack P. Greene, *Pursuits of Happiness* (1988); Allan Kulikoff, *Tobacco and Slaves* (1986); Philip D. Curtin, *The Atlantic Slave Trade* (1969); Daniel Littlefield, *Rice and Slaves: Ethnicity and the Slave Trade in Colonial South Carolina* (1981); David Eltis, *Economic Growth and the Ending of the Transatlantic Slave Trade* (1987); Jay Coughtry, *The Notorious Triangle: Rhode Island and the African Slave Trade, 1799–1807* (1981); Abbot E. Smith, *Colonists in Bondage* (1947); Gerald Mullin, *Flight and Rebellion* (1972); Eugene Genovese, *From Rebellion to Revolution* (1979); Gary B. Nash, *Red, White, and Black,* rev. ed. (1982); Charles Joyner, *Down by the Riverside: A South Carolina Slave Community* (1984); T. H. Breen and Stephen Innes, *'Myne Own Ground,' Race and Freedom on Virginia's Eastern Shore* (1980); T. H. Breen, *Tobacco Culture* (1985); Julia C. Spruill, *Women's Life and Work in the Southern Colonies* (1972); J. Leitch Wright, Jr., *Anglo-Spanish Rivalry in North America* (1971) and *The Only Land They Knew: The Tragic Story of the American Indians in the Old South* (1981).

Society and Town in Colonial New England. Kenneth Lockridge, *A New England Town* (1970); Michael Zuckerman, *Peaceable Kingdoms* (1970); Darrett Rutman, *Winthrop's Boston* (1965); Charles Grant, *Democracy in the Connecticut Frontier Town of Kent* (1961); Paul Boyer and Stephen Nissenbaum, *Salem Possessed* (1974); John Putnam Demos, *Entertaining Satan: Witchcraft and the Culture of Early New England* (1982); Carol Karlsen, *The Devil in the Shape of a Woman: Witchcraft in Colonial New England* (1987); E. M. Cook, Jr., *The Fathers of Towns* (1975); Sumner Chilton Powell, *Puritan Village* (1963); Richard Bushman, *From Puritan to Yankee* (1967); Robert Gross, *The Minutemen and Their World* (1976).

The Colonial Economy. Alice Hanson Jones, *Wealth of a Nation to Be* (1980); Jackson Turner Main, *The Social Structure of Revolutionary America* (1965); Stuart Bruchey, *Roots of American Economic Growth, 1607–1861* (1965); John J. McCusker and Russell R. Menard, *The Economy of British America, 1607–1787* (1985); Carl Bridenbaugh, *Myths and Realities: Societies of the Colonial South* (1963); Paul G. E.

Clemens, *The Atlantic Economy and Colonial Maryland's Eastern Shore: From Tobacco to Grain* (1980); Edmund S. Morgan, *Virginians at Home* (1952); Jacob M. Price, *France and the Chesapeake,* 2 vols. (1973), *The Tobacco Adventure to Russia* (1961), and *Capital and Credit in the British Overseas Trade: The View from the Chesapeake, 1700–1776* (1980); Harry R. Merrens, *Colonial North Carolina in the Eighteenth Century* (1964); Stephen Innes, *Labor in a New Land: Economy and Society in Seventeenth Century Springfield* (1983); Stephen Innes, ed., *Work and Labor in Early America* (1988); David W. Galenson, *White Servitude in Colonial America: An Economic Analysis* (1982); Sharon U. Salinger, *"To Serve Well and Faithfully": Labor and Indentured Servants in Pennsylvania, 1692–1800* (1987).

Cities and Commerce.   Carl Bridenbaugh, *Cities in the Wilderness* (1938) and *Cities in Revolt* (1955); Gary B. Nash, *The Urban Crucible* (1979) and *Forging Freedom: The Formation of Philadelphia's Black Community, 1720–1840* (1988); G. B. Warden, *Boston, 1687–1776* (1970); Stephanie G. Wolf, *Urban Village* (1976); Stuart Bruchey, *The Colonial Merchant* (1966); J. F. Shepherd and G. M. Walton, *The Economic Rise of Early America* (1979); James B. Hedges, *The Browns of Providence Plantation,* vol. 1 (1952); Frederick B. Tolles, *Meeting House and Counting House: The Quaker Merchants of Colonial Philadelphia, 1682–1763* (1948); Thomas M. Doerflinger, *A Vigorous Spirit of Enterprise: Merchants and Economic Development in Revolutionary Philadelphia* (1986); Bernard Bailyn, *The New England Merchants in the Seventeenth Century* (1955); Marcus Rediker, *Between the Devil and the Deep Sea: Merchant Seamen, Pirates, and the Anglo-American Maritime World, 1700–1750* (1987); Arthur Jensen, *The Maritime Commerce of Colonial Philadelphia* (1963); Randolph S. Klein, *Portrait of an Early American Family* (1975).

Colonial Religion.   For studies of Puritanism, see bibliography for chapter 2. Patricia U. Bonomi, *Under the Cope of Heaven: Religion, Society, and Politics in Colonial America* (1986); Sidney Ahlstrom, *A Religious History of the American People* (1972); W. W. Sweet, *Religion in Colonial America* (1942); Carl Bridenbaugh, *Mitre and Sceptre: Transatlantic Faiths, Ideas, Personalities, and Politics, 1689–1775* (1962); Sidney Mead, *The Lively Experiment: The Shaping of Christianity in America* (1963), J. T. Ellis, *Catholics in America* (1965); J. R. Marcus, *Early American Jewry* (1951); Janet Whitman, *John Woolman, American Quaker* (1942); William C. McLoughlin, *New England Dissent, 1630–1833,* 2 vols. (1971); Marilyn Westerkamp, *Triumph of Laity* (1988).

The Great Awakening.   Edwin S. Gaustad, *The Great Awakening in New England* (1957); J. M. Bumsted and John E. Van de Wetering, *What Must I Do to Be Saved? The Great Awakening in Colonial America* (1976); Alan Heimert, *Religion and the American Mind* (1966); Perry Miller, *Jonathan Edwards* (1949); Ola Winslow, *Jonathan Edwards* (1940); Patricia Tracy, *Jonathan Edwards: Pastor* (1980); Conrad Wright, *The Beginnings of Unitarianism in America* (1955); J. W. Davidson, *The Logic of Millennial Thought* (1977).

Education.   Lawrence A. Cremin, *American Education: The Colonial Experience, 1607–1783* (1970); Bernard Bailyn, *Education in the Forming of American Society* (1960); James Axtell, *The School upon a Hill: Education and Society in Colonial New England* (1974); Robert Middlekauff, *Ancients and Axioms* (1963); Samuel Eliot Morison, *The Founding of Harvard College* (1935); Jurgen Herbst, *From Crisis to Crisis* (1982); Kenneth Lockridge, *Literacy in Colonial New England* (1974).

Culture and the Enlightenment.   Louis B. Wright, *The Cultural Life of the American Colonies* (1957); Daniel J. Boorstin, *The Americans: The Colonial Experience* (1958); Richard Beale Davis, *Intellectual Life in the Colonial South,* 2 vols. (1978): Henry May, *The Enlightenment in America* (1976); Howard Mumford Jones, *O Strange New World* (1964); Jean-Christophe Agnew, *Worlds Apart: The Market and the Theater in Anglo-American Thought, 1550–1750* (1986); Brook Hindle, *The Pursuit of Science in Revolutionary America* (1956); Carl Van Doren, *Benjamin Franklin* (1941); V. W. Crane, *Benjamin Franklin and a Rising People* (1954); H. Leventhal, *In the Shadow of Enlightenment* (1976).

Law and Politics.   Bernard Bailyn, *The Origins of American Politics* (1968); Jack P. Greene, *The Quest for Power* (1963); J. R. Pole, *Political Representation in England and the Origins of the American Republic* (1966); Michael Kammen, *Spheres of Liberty: Changing Perceptions of Liberty in American Culture* (1986); Thomas Curry, *The First Freedoms: Church and State in America to the Passage of the First Amendment* (1986); Leonard W. Labaree, *Royal Government in America* (1930); Robert Zemsky, *Merchants, Farmers, and River Gods* (1971); Caroline Robbins, *The Eighteenth-Century Commonwealthman* (1959); J. G. A. Pocock, *The Machiavellian Moment* (1975); Robert Ferguson, *Law and Letters in American Culture* (1984); Marylynn Salmon, *Women and the Law of Property in Early America* (1986); Gerald W. Gawalt, *The Promise of Power: The Emergence of the Legal Profession in Massachusetts, 1760–1840* (1979); A. G. Roeber, *Faithful Magistrates and Republican Lawyers: Creators of Virginia Legal Culture, 1680–1810* (1981).

The Boston Massacre (1770), by Paul Revere
This is one of many engravings, by Revere and others, of the conflict between British troops and Boston laborers that became important propaganda documents for the Patriot cause in the 1770s. Among the victims of the massacre listed by Revere was Crispus Attucks, probably the first black man to die in the struggle for American independence. *(American Antiquarian Society)*

CHAPTER 4

◥◭◸

The Empire Under Strain

◥◭◸

As late as the 1750s, few Americans saw any reason to object to their membership in the British Empire. The imperial system provided them with many benefits: opportunities for trade and commerce, military protection, political stability. And those benefits were accompanied by few costs; for the most part, the English government left the colonies alone. While Britain did attempt to regulate the colonists' external trade, those regulations were usually so laxly administered that they could be easily circumvented. Some Americans predicted that the colonies would ultimately develop to a point where greater autonomy would become inevitable. But few expected such a change to occur soon.

By the mid-1770s, however, the relationship between the American colonies and their British rulers had become so strained, so poisoned, so characterized by suspicion and resentment that the once seemingly unbreakable bonds of empire were on the verge of dissolution. And in the spring of 1775, the first shots were fired in a war that would ultimately win America its independence. How had it happened? And why so quickly?

In one sense, it had not happened quickly at all. Ever since the first days of settlement in North America, the ideas and institutions of the colonies had been diverging from those in England in countless ways. Only because the relationship between America and Britain had been so casual had those differences failed to create serious tensions in the past. In another sense, however, the Revolutionary crisis emerged in response to important and relatively sudden changes in the administration of the empire. Beginning in 1763, the English government embarked on a series of new policies toward its colonies—policies dictated by changing international realities and new political circumstances within England itself— that brought the differences between the two societies into sharp focus. In the beginning, most Americans reacted to the changes with relative restraint. Gradually, however, as crisis followed crisis, a large group of Americans found themselves fundamentally disillusioned with the imperial relationship. By 1775, that relationship was, for all practical purposes, damaged beyond repair.

A Loosening of Ties

After England's Glorious Revolution of 1688 and the collapse of the Dominion of New England, the English government (or the British government after 1707, when Great Britain was created by the union of England and Scotland) made no serious or sustained effort to tighten its control over the colonies for over seventy years. During those years, it is true, an increasing number of colonies were brought under the direct control of the king. New Jersey in 1702, North and South Carolina in 1729, Georgia in 1754—all became royal colonies, bringing the total to eight; in all of them, the king had the power to appoint the governors and other colonial officials. During those

ENGLISH MONARCHS, 1702–1802	
Anne	1702–1714
George I	1714–1727
George II	1727–1760
George III	1760–1820

years, Parliament also passed new laws supplementing the original Navigation Acts and strengthening the mercantilist program—laws restricting colonial manufactures, prohibiting paper currency, and regulating trade. On the whole, however, the British government remained uncertain and divided about the extent to which it ought to interfere in colonial affairs. The colonies were left, within broad limits, to go their separate ways.

A Tradition of Neglect

In the fifty years after the Glorious Revolution, the British Parliament established a growing supremacy over the king. During the reigns of George I (1714–1727) and George II (1727–1760), both of whom were German-born and unaccustomed to English ways, the prime minister and his fellow cabinet ministers began to become the nation's real executives. They held their positions not by the king's favor but by their ability to control a majority in Parliament.

These parliamentary leaders were less inclined than the seventeenth-century monarchs had been to engage in experiments in imperial organization. They depended heavily on the support of the great merchants and landholders, most of whom feared that any such experiments would require large expenditures, would increase taxes, and would diminish the profit of the colonial trade. The first of the prime ministers, Robert Walpole, deliberately refrained from strict enforcement of the Navigation Acts, believing that relaxed trading restrictions would stimulate commerce.

Meanwhile, the day-to-day administration of colonial affairs remained decentralized and inefficient. There was no colonial office in London. The nearest equivalent was the Board of Trade and Plantations, established in 1696—a mere advisory body that had little role in any actual decisions. Real authority rested in the Privy Council (the central administrative agency for the government as a whole), the admiralty, and the treasury. But those agencies were responsible for administering laws at home as well as

overseas; none could concentrate on colonial affairs alone. To complicate matters further, there was considerable overlapping and confusion of authority among the departments.

Few of the London officials, moreover, had ever visited America; few knew very much about conditions there. What information they did gather came in large part from agents sent to England by the colonial assemblies to lobby for American interests; and these agents, naturally, did nothing to encourage interference with colonial affairs. (The best known of them, Benjamin Franklin, represented not only his own colony, Pennsylvania, but also Georgia, New Jersey, and Massachusetts.)

It was not only the incoherence of administrative authority in London and the ministerial policy of salutary neglect that weakened England's hold on the colonies. It was also the character of the royal officials in America—the governors and other officers of the royal colonies and (in all the colonies) the collectors of customs and naval officers. Some of these officeholders were able and intelligent men; most were not. Appointments were generally made as the result of bribery or favoritism, not in response to merit. Many appointees remained in England and, with part of their salaries, hired substitutes to take their places in America. Such deputies were generally poorly paid and faced great temptation to augment their incomes with bribes. Few resisted the temptation. Customs collectors, for example, routinely waived duties on goods when merchants paid them to do so. Even honest and well-paid officials usually found it expedient, if they wanted to get along with their neighbors, to yield to the colonists' resistance to trade restrictions.

Resistance to imperial authority centered in the colonial legislatures. By the 1750s the assemblies had established the right to levy taxes, make appropriations, approve appointments, and pass laws for their respective colonies. Their legislation was subject to veto by the governor or the Privy Council; but they had leverage over the governor through their control of the colonial budget, and they could circumvent the Privy Council by repassing disallowed laws in slightly altered form. The assemblies came to look upon themselves as little parliaments, each practically as sovereign within its colony as Parliament itself was in England. In 1754, the Board of Trade reported to the king, regarding the members of the New York assembly: they "have wrested from Your Majesty's governor the nomination of all offices of government, the custody and direction of the public military stores, the mustering and direction of troops raised for Your Majesty's service, and in short almost every other part of executive government."

Intercolonial Disunity

Despite their frequent resistance to the authority of London, the colonists continued to think of themselves as loyal English subjects. In many respects, in fact, they felt stronger ties to England than they did to one another. "Fire and water," an English traveler wrote, "are not more heterogeneous than the different colonies in North America." New Englanders and Virginians viewed each other as something close to foreigners. A Connecticut man denounced the merchants of New York for their "frauds and unfair practices," while a New Yorker condemned Connecticut because of the "low craft and cunning so incident to the people of that country." Only an accident of geography, it seemed, connected these disparate societies to each other.

Yet for all their differences, the colonies could scarcely avoid forging connections with one another. The growth of the colonial population, which produced an almost continuous line of settlement along the seacoast, brought the people of the various colonies into closer and closer contact. So did the gradual

An Appeal for Colonial Unity

This sketch, one of the first American editorial cartoons, appeared in Benjamin Franklin's Philadelphia newspaper, the *Pennsylvania Gazette,* on May 9, 1754. It was meant to illustrate the need for intercolonial unity and, in particular, for the adoption of Franklin's Albany Plan. (Library Company of Philadelphia)

construction of roads and the rise of intercolonial trade. The colonial postal service likewise helped increase communication. In 1691, it had operated only from Massachusetts to New York and Pennsylvania. In 1711, it was extended to New Hampshire in the north; in 1732, to Virginia in the south; and ultimately, all the way to Georgia.

Still, the colonists were loath to cooperate even when, in 1754, they faced a common threat from their old rivals, the French, and France's Indian allies. A conference of colonial leaders—with delegates from Pennsylvania, Maryland, New York, and New England—was meeting in Albany in that year to negotiate a treaty with the Iroquois. The delegates stayed on to talk about forming a colonial federation for defense against the Indians. Benjamin Franklin proposed, and the delegates tentatively approved, a plan by which Parliament would set up in America "one general government" for all the colonies, each of which would "retain its present constitution" except for certain powers to be granted to the general government—such as the authority to govern all relations with the Indians.

War with the French and Indians was already beginning when this Albany Plan was presented to the colonial assemblies. None approved it. Only the Massachusetts assembly even gave it serious attention. "Everyone cries, a union is necessary," Franklin wrote to the Massachusetts governor, "but when they come to the manner and form of the union, their weak noodles are perfectly distracted."

The Struggle for the Continent

In one sense, the war that raged in North America through the late 1750s and early 1760s was but one part of a larger struggle between England and France for dominance in world trade and naval power. The British victory in that struggle, known in Europe as the Seven Years' War, confirmed England's commercial supremacy and cemented its control of the settled regions of North America.

In another sense, however, the conflict was the final stage in a long struggle among the three principal powers in northeastern North America: the English, the French, and the Iroquois. For more than a century prior to the conflict—known in America as the French and Indian War—these three groups had maintained a precarious balance of power. The events of the 1750s upset that balance, produced a prolonged and open conflict, and established a precarious dominance for the English societies throughout the region.

The French and Indian War had additional significance for the English colonists in America. By bringing the Americans into closer contact with British authority than ever before, it raised to the surface some of the underlying tensions in the colonial relationship.

New France and the Iroquois Nation

The French and the English had coexisted relatively peacefully in North America for nearly a century. But by the 1750s, as both English and French settlements expanded, religious and commercial tensions began to produce new frictions and new conflicts.

The origins of the crisis lay in part in the expansion of the French presence in America in the late seventeenth century—part of Louis XIV's search for national unity and increased world power. The French finance minister, Jean Colbert, persuaded the king that he could best increase the nation's glory by creating a new, four-part empire. France itself would be the center, the source of capital and manufactured goods; its West Indian islands (especially Martinique and Guadeloupe) would be suppliers of sugar and other exotic products; posts along the African coast would support the slave trade; and the settlements in North America would be a market for exports from France and a granary for provisioning the West Indies. In response to Colbert's proposals, France began to devote new attention to the development of its North American territories, and French settlement rapidly expanded. The lucrative fur trade drew immigrant peasants ever deeper into the wilderness. Missionary zeal drew large numbers of Jesuits into the interior in search of potential converts. The bottomlands of the Mississippi River valley attracted farmers discouraged by the short growing season in Canada.

By the mid-seventeenth century, the French Empire in America comprised a vast territory. Louis Joliet and Father Jacques Marquette, French explorers of the 1670s, journeyed together by canoe from Green Bay on Lake Michigan as far south as the junction of the Arkansas and Mississippi rivers. (They were the first to confirm that the Mississippi flowed into the Gulf of Mexico, not—as most had believed—the Gulf of California.) A year later, René Robert Cavelier, Sieur de La Salle, began the explorations that finally, in 1682, took him to the delta of the Mississippi, where he claimed the surrounding country for France and named it Louisiana in the king's honor. Subsequent traders and missionaries wandered to the southwest as far as the Rio Grande, and the explorer Pierre Gaultier de Varennes, Sieur de La Vérendrye, pushed westward in 1743 from Lake Superior to a point within sight of the Rocky Mountains. The French had by then revealed the outlines of, and laid claim to, the whole continental interior.

To secure their hold on these enormous claims, they founded a string of widely separated communities, strategically located fortresses, and far-flung missions and trading posts. Fort Louisbourg, on Cape Breton Island, guarded the approach to the Gulf of St. Lawrence. Would-be feudal lords established large estates ("seigneuries") along the banks of the St. Lawrence River; and on a high bluff above the river stood the fortified city of Quebec, the center of the French Empire in America. Montreal to the south and Sault Sainte Marie and Detroit to the west marked the northern boundaries of French settlement. On the lower Mississippi emerged plantations much like those in the Southern colonies of English America, worked by black slaves and owned by "Creoles" (white immigrants of French descent). New Orleans, founded in 1718 to service the French plantation economy, soon was as big as some of the larger cities of the Atlantic seaboard; Biloxi and Mobile to the east completed the string of French settlement.

But the French were not, of course, alone in the continental interior. They encountered there a large and powerful Indian population, and their relations with the natives were crucial to the shaping of their empire. Both the French and the English were aware that the battle for control of North America would be determined in part by which group could best win the allegiance of native tribes—as trading partners and, at times, as military allies. The Indians, for their part, were principally concerned with protecting their independence, and what alignments they formed with the European societies growing up around them were generally marriages of convenience, determined by which group offered the most attractive terms. The English—with their more advanced commercial economy—could usually offer the Indians better and more plentiful goods. But the French offered something that was often more important: tolerance. Unlike the English settlers, who strove constantly to impose their own social norms on the Indians they encountered, the French settlers in the interior generally adjusted their own behavior to Indian patterns. French fur traders frequently married Indian women and adopted tribal ways; Jesuit missionaries interacted comfortably with the natives and converted them to Catholicism by the thousands without challenging most of their social customs. By the mid-eighteenth century, therefore, the French had far better and closer relations with most of the Indians of the interior than did the English.

The most powerful native group, however, had a rather different relationship with the French. The Iroquois Confederacy—the five Indian nations (Mohawk, Seneca, Cayuga, Onondaga, and Oneida) that had formed a defensive alliance in the fifteenth century—had been the most powerful native presence in the Ohio Valley and a large surrounding region since the 1640s, when they had fought—and won—a bitter war against the Hurons. With their major competitors now largely exterminated or driven from the region, the Iroquois formed an important commercial relationship with the English and Dutch along the eastern seaboard.

The Hurons had been the principal trading partners of the French in the early seventeenth century, and their disappearance pushed French traders farther into the interior in search of furs and native partners to help trap them. For nearly a century, however, neither the French nor the English raised any serious challenge to the Iroquois control in the Ohio Valley. The Iroquois maintained their autonomy in part by avoiding too close a relationship with either group. They traded successfully with both the English and the French and astutely played the two groups off against each other. As a result, they managed to maintain an uneasy balance of power in the Great Lakes region.

Anglo-French Conflicts

As long as England and France remained at peace in Europe, and as long as the precarious balance in the North American interior survived, English and French colonists coexisted without serious difficulty. But after the Glorious Revolution in England, the English throne passed to one of Louis XIV's principal enemies, William III, who was also the *stadholder* (chief magistrate) of the Netherlands and who had long opposed French expansionism. William's successor, Queen Anne (the daughter of James II), ascended the throne in 1702 and carried on the struggle

against France and its new ally, Spain. The result was a series of Anglo-French wars that continued intermittently in Europe for nearly eighty years.

The wars had important repercussions in America. King William's War (1689–1697) produced only a few, indecisive clashes between English and French in northern New England. Queen Anne's War, which began in 1701 and continued for nearly twelve years, generated more substantial conflicts: border fighting with the Spaniards in the south as well as with the French and their Indian allies in the north. The Treaty of Utrecht, which brought the conflict to a close in 1713, transferred substantial areas of French territory from the French to the English in North America, including Acadia (Nova Scotia) and Newfoundland.

Two decades later, European rivalries led to still more conflicts in America. Disputes over British trading rights in the Spanish colonies produced a war between England and Spain and led to clashes between the British in Georgia and the Spaniards in Florida. (It was in the context of this conflict that the last English colony in America, Georgia, was founded in 1733; see pp. 51–53.) The Anglo-Spanish conflict soon merged with a much larger European war, in which England and France lined up on opposite sides of a territorial dispute between Frederick the Great of Prussia and Maria Theresa of Austria. (France supported Prussia, in the hope of seizing the Austrian Netherlands; England supported Austria, to keep Holland from the French.) The English colonists in America were soon drawn into the struggle, which they called King George's War; and between 1744 and 1748 they engaged in a series of conflicts with the French. New Englanders captured the French bastion at Louisbourg on Cape Breton Island; but the peace treaty that finally ended the conflict forced them (in bitter disappointment) to abandon it.

In the aftermath of King George's War, relations among the English, French, and Iroquois in North America quickly deteriorated. The Iroquois (in what in retrospect appears a major blunder) began for the first time to grant trading concessions in the interior to English merchants. In the context of the already tense Anglo-French relationship in America, that decision set in motion a chain of events disastrous for the Iroquois Confederacy. The French, fearful that the English were using the concessions as a first step toward expansion into French lands (which to some extent they were), began in 1749 to construct new fortresses in the Ohio Valley. The English, interpreting the French activity as a threat to their western settlements, protested and began making military preparations and building fortresses of their own. The balance of power that the Iroquois had carefully and successfully maintained for so long rapidly disintegrated; and the five Indian nations had little choice now but to ally themselves with the British and assume an essentially passive role in the conflict that ensued.

For the next five years, tensions between the English and the French increased, until in the summer of 1754 the governor of Virginia sent a militia force (under the command of an inexperienced young colonel, George Washington) into the Ohio Valley to challenge French expansion. Washington built a crude stockade (Fort Necessity) not far from Fort Duquesne, the larger outpost the French were building on the site of what is now Pittsburgh. After the Virginians staged an unsuccessful attack on a French detachment, the French countered with an assault on Fort Necessity, trapping Washington and his soldiers inside. After a third of them died in the fighting, Washington surrendered.

The clash marked the beginning of the French and Indian (or, as Europeans knew it, Seven Years') War, the climactic event in the long Anglo-French struggle for empire.

The Great War for the Empire

The French and Indian War lasted nearly nine years, and it moved forward in three distinct phases. During the first of these phases, from the Fort Necessity debacle in 1754 until the expansion of the war to Europe in 1756, it was primarily a local, North American conflict. The English colonists managed the war largely on their own. The British provided modest assistance during this period, but they provided it so ineptly that it had little impact on the struggle. The British fleet failed to prevent the landing of large French reinforcements in Canada; and the newly appointed commander in chief of the British army in America, General Edward Braddock, failed miserably in a major effort in the summer of 1755 to retake the crucial site at the forks of the Ohio River where Washington had lost the battle at Fort Necessity. A French and Indian ambush a few miles from the fort left Braddock dead and what remained of his forces in disarray. The local colonial forces, meanwhile, were preoccupied with defending themselves against raids on their western settlements by the Indians of the Ohio Valley. Virtually all of them (except the Iroquois) were now allied with the French, having interpreted the defeat of the Virginians at Fort Duquesne as evidence of British weakness. Even the

Iroquois, who were nominally allied with the British, remained fearful of antagonizing the French. They engaged in few hostilities and launched no offensive into Canada, even though they had, under heavy English pressure, declared war on the French. By late 1755, many English settlers along the frontier had withdrawn to the east of the Allegheny Mountains to escape the hostilities.

The second phase of the struggle began in 1756, when the governments of France and England formally opened hostilities and a truly international conflict (the Seven Years' War) began. In Europe, the war was marked by a realignment within the complex system of alliances. France allied itself with its former enemy, Austria; and England joined France's former ally, Prussia. The fighting now spread to the West Indies, India, and Europe itself. But the principal struggle remained the one in North America, where so far England had suffered nothing but frustration and defeat.

Beginning in 1757, William Pitt, the English secretary of state (and future prime minister), began to transform the war effort in America by bringing it for the first time fully under British control. Pitt himself began planning military strategy for the North American conflict, appointing military commanders, and issuing orders to the colonists. Military recruitment had slowed dramatically in America after the defeat of Braddock, and to replenish the army British commanders began forcibly enlisting colonists (a practice known as "impressment"). Officers also began to seize supplies and equipment from local farmers and tradesmen and to compel colonists to offer shelter to British troops— all generally without compensation. The Americans, who had long ago become accustomed to running their own affairs and who had been fighting for over two years without much assistance or direction from the British, resented these new impositions and firmly resisted them—at times, as in a 1757 riot in New York City, violently. By early 1758, the friction between the British authorities and the colonists was threatening to bring the war effort to a halt.

Beginning in 1758, therefore, Pitt initiated the third and final phase of the war by relaxing many of the policies that Americans had found obnoxious. He agreed to reimburse the colonists for all supplies requisitioned by the army. He returned control over recruitment to the colonial assemblies (which resulted in an immediate and dramatic increase in enlistments). And he dispatched large numbers of additional troops to America.

Finally, the tide of battle began to turn in En-

The Seige of Louisbourg, 1758

The fortress of Louisbourg, on Cape Breton Island in Nova Scotia, was one of the principal French outposts in eastern Canada, during the French and Indian War. It took a British fleet of 157 ships nearly two months to force the French garrison to surrender. "We had not had our Batteries against the Town above a Week," wrote a British soldier after the victory, "tho we were ashore Seven Weeks; the Badness of the Country prevented our Approaches. It was necessary to make Roads for the Cannon, which was a great Labour, and some Loss of Men; but the spirits the Army was in is capable of doing any Thing." (New Brunswick Museum)

gland's favor. The French, who had always been outnumbered by the British colonists and who, after 1756, suffered from a series of poor harvests, were unable to sustain their early military successes. By mid-1758, the British regulars in America (who did the bulk of the actual fighting) and the colonial militias were seizing one French stronghold after another. Two brilliant English generals, Jeffrey Amherst and James Wolfe, captured the fortress at Louisbourg in July 1758; a few months later Fort Duquesne fell without a fight. The next year, at the end of a siege of Quebec, supposedly impregnable atop its towering cliff, the army of General James Wolfe struggled up a hidden ravine under cover of darkness, surprised the larger forces of the Marquis de Montcalm, and defeated them in a battle in which both commanders were slain. The dramatic fall of Quebec on September 13, 1759, marked the beginning of the end of the American phase of the war. A

year later, in September 1760, the French army formally surrendered to Amherst in Montreal.

Not all aspects of the struggle were as romantic as Wolfe's assault on Quebec. The British resorted at times to such brutal military expedients as population dispersal. In Nova Scotia, for example, they uprooted several thousand French inhabitants, whom they suspected of disloyalty, and scattered them throughout the English colonies. (Some of these Acadians eventually made their way to Louisiana, where they became the ancestors of the present-day Cajuns.) Elsewhere, English and colonial troops were inflicting worse atrocities on the Indian allies of the French—for example, offering "scalp bounties" to those who could bring back evidence of having killed a native. The French and their Indian allies retaliated, and hundreds of families along the English frontier perished in brutal raids on their settlements.

Peace finally came after the accession of George

III to the British throne and the resignation of Pitt, who, unlike the new king, wanted to continue hostilities. Pitt's aims were largely realized nevertheless in the Peace of Paris, signed in 1763. Under its terms, the French ceded to Great Britain some of their West Indian islands and most of their colonies in India. The French also transferred Canada and all other French territory east of the Mississippi, except New Orleans, to Great Britain. They ceded New Orleans and their claims west of the Mississippi to Spain, thus surrendering all title to the mainland of North America.

The French and Indian War had profound effects on the British Empire and the American colonies. It greatly expanded England's territorial claims in the New World. At the same time, it greatly enlarged Britain's debt; financing the vast war had been a major drain on the treasury. And it generated substantial resentment toward the Americans among English leaders. They were contemptuous of the colonists for what they considered American military ineptitude during the war; they were angry that the colonists had made so few financial contributions to a struggle waged largely for American benefit; they were particularly bitter that some colonial merchants had been selling food and other goods to the French in the West Indies throughout the conflict. All these factors combined to persuade many English leaders that a major reorganization of the empire, giving London increased authority over the colonies, would be necessary in the aftermath of the war.

The war had an equally profound but very different effect on the American colonists. It was an experience that forced them, for the first time, to act in concert against a common foe. The colonies were still far from united, but they had learned certain lessons in cooperation. The friction of 1756–1757 over British requisition and impressment policies, and the 1758 return of authority to the colonial assemblies, established an important precedent in the minds of the colonists; it seemed to confirm the illegitimacy of English interference in local affairs. And for thousands of Americans, those who served in the colonial armed forces, the war served as an important socializing experience. The provincial troops, unlike the British regiments, had generally viewed themselves as part of a "people's army." The relationship of soldiers to their units was, the soldiers believed, in some measure voluntary; their army was a communal, not a coercive or hierarchical organization. The contrast with the British regulars, whom the colonists widely resented for their arrogance and arbitrary use of power, was striking; and in later years,

the memory of that contrast helped to shape the American response to British imperial policies.

For the Indians of the Ohio Valley, the third major party in the French and Indian War, the British victory was disastrous. Those tribes that had allied themselves with the French had earned the enmity of the victorious English. The Iroquois Confederacy, which had allied itself with Britain, fared only slightly better. English officials saw the passivity of the Iroquois during the war (a result of their effort to hedge their bets and avoid antagonizing the French) as evidence of duplicity. In the aftermath of the peace settlement, the Iroquois alliance with the British quickly unraveled, and the Iroquois Confederacy itself began to crumble from within. The Six Nations would continue to contest the English for control of the Ohio Valley for another fifty years; but increasingly divided and increasingly outnumbered, they would seldom again be in a position to deal with their white rivals on terms of military or political equality.

The New Imperialism

With the treaty of 1763, England found itself truly at peace for the first time in more than fifty years. Undistracted by war, the British government could now turn its attention to the organization of its empire. And after the difficult experiences of the previous decade, many English leaders were convinced that the question of imperial organization could no longer be ignored.

In fact, they had virtually no choice; even if policymakers had wished to revert to the old colonial system with its half-hearted enforcement of the mercantilist program, they would have found it virtually impossible to do so. Saddled with enormous debts from the many years of fighting, England was desperately in need of new revenues from its empire. And responsible for vast new lands in the New World, the imperial government could not long avoid expanding its involvement in its colonies.

Burdens of Empire

The experience of the French and Indian War, however, suggested that such increased involvement would not be easy to establish. Not only had the colonists proved so resistant to British control that

The Thirteen Colonies in 1763

HUDSON'S BAY COMPANY

Lake Superior

QUEBEC

B R I T I S H   T E R R I T O R Y

MAINE
(Mass.)

St. Lawrence R.

Quebec

Montreal

□ Fort Michilimackinac

LaBaye •

Lake Michigan

Lake Huron

Fort
Frontenac •

Connecticut R.

Merrimac R.

N.H.

• Falmouth

□ Fort Niagara

Lake Ontario

Fort □ *Mohawk R.*
Stanwix

Albany •

NEW YORK

Hudson R.

★ Portsmouth
Gloucester

Bennington •

★ Boston
★ MASS.

Providence
★ Plymouth

Fort Detroit □

Lake Erie

Allegheny R.

PENNSYLVANIA

Kingston •

Hartford ★
CONN.   R.I.

Providence •

Newport

• St. Joseph

Maumee R.

Susquehanna R.

Delaware R.

New Haven •

Poughkeepsie •

Southampton

Mountains

★ New York

★ Perth Amboy
Trenton •
NEW JERSEY

Reading •

Illinois R.

Ohio R.

• Fort
Duquesne

Philadelphia ★   • Burlington

R.

New
Castle •
• Dover

DELAWARE

• Baltimore

• St. Louis

• Vincennes

Wabash R.

Ohio R.

Shenandoah R.

Potomac R.

Annapolis ★

MARYLAND

VIRGINIA

ATLANTIC   OCEAN

Richmond •

James R.   ★ Williamsburg

SPANISH
LOUISIANA

Mississippi R.

R.

Cumberland

Petersburg •   • Norfolk

Roanoke R.

• Edenton

Tennessee R.

NORTH CAROLINA

• Greensville

Cape Fear R.

New Bern
★   • Portsmouth

Fayetteville •

• Wilmington

DISPUTED TERRITORY
(Claimed by Spain and Britain)

Camden •

Columbia •

Santee R.

Appalachian

• Kingston

Savannah R.

• Augusta

SOUTH
CAROLINA

Ashley R.

Cooper R.

Charleston •

GEORGIA

Altamaha R.

NON-INDIAN
SETTLEMENT

| | Before 1700 |
| | 1700–1763 |

WEST FLORIDA

★ Savannah

• Mobile

★ Pensacola

EAST FLORIDA

0 ——— 150 Miles
0 ——— 200 Kilometers

• New Orleans

Gulf of Mexico

St. Augustine ★

Frontier line
in 1763

Proclamation Line
of 1763

★   Provincial capital

Pitt had been forced to relax his policies in 1758, but the colonial assemblies had continued after that to respond to British needs slowly and grudgingly. Unwilling to be taxed by Parliament to support the war effort, the colonists were generally reluctant to tax themselves as well. Defiance of imperial trade regulations and other British demands continued, and even increased, through the last years of the war.

The problems of managing the empire were compounded after 1763 by a basic shift in Britain's imperial design. In the past, the English had viewed their colonial empire primarily in terms of trade; they had opposed acquisition of territory for its own sake. But by the mid-eighteenth century, a growing number of English and American leaders (including both William Pitt and Benjamin Franklin) were beginning to argue that land itself was of value to the empire—because of the population it could support, the taxes it could produce, and the imperial splendor it would confer. The debate between the old commercial imperialists and the new territorial ones came to a head at the conclusion of the French and Indian War. The mercantilists wanted England to return Canada to France in exchange for Guadeloupe, the most commercially valuable of the French "sugar islands" in the West Indies. The territorialists, however, prevailed. The acquisition of the French territories in North America was a victory for, among others, Benjamin Franklin, who had long argued that the American people would need these vast spaces to accommodate their rapid and, he believed, limitless growth. But Franklin and his supporters in the colonies were soon to discover that the new acquisitions brought with them unexpected problems.

With the territorial annexations of 1763, the area of the British Empire was suddenly twice as great as it had been, and the problems of governing it thus became many times more complex. Almost immediately, England faced a series of sharply conflicting pressures as it attempted to devise a policy for governing the new lands. Some argued that the empire should restrain rapid settlement and development of the Western territories. To do otherwise would be to risk further costly conflicts with the Indians and might help encourage France to launch a new attack somewhere in America in an effort to recover some of its lost territories and prestige. And restricting settlement would keep the land available for hunting and trapping. Others wanted to see the new territories opened for immediate development; but they disagreed among themselves about who should control the Western lands. Colonial governments made fer-

vent, and often conflicting, claims of jurisdiction. Others argued that control should remain in England, that the territories should be considered entirely new colonies, unlinked to the existing settlements. There were, in short, a host of problems and pressures that the British could not ignore.

At the same time, the government in London was running out of options in its effort to find a way to deal with its staggering war debt. Landlords and merchants in England itself were objecting strenuously to increases in what they already considered excessively high taxes. The colonies, on the other hand, had contributed virtually nothing, the British believed, to the support of a war fought in large part for their benefit. The necessity of stationing significant numbers of British troops on the Indian border after 1763 was adding even more to the cost of defending the American settlements. And the halfhearted response of the colonial assemblies to the war effort had suggested that in its search for revenue, England could not rely on any cooperation from the colonial governments. Only a system of taxation administered by London, the leaders of the empire believed, could effectively meet England's needs.

At this crucial moment in Anglo-American relations, with the imperial system in desperate need of redefinition, the government of England was thrown into turmoil by the accession to the throne of a new king. George III assumed power in 1760 on the death of his grandfather. And he brought two particularly unfortunate qualities to the office. First, he was determined, unlike his two predecessors, to reassert the authority of the monarchy. Pushed by his ambitious mother, he removed from power the longstanding and relatively stable coalition of Whigs, who had (under Pitt and others) governed the empire for much of the century. In their place, he created a new coalition of his own through patronage and bribes and gained an uneasy control of Parliament. Yet the new ministries that emerged as a result of these changes were inherently unstable, each lasting in office an average of only about two years.

In addition to these dangerous political ambitions, the king had serious intellectual and psychological limitations. He suffered, apparently, from a rare mental disease that produced intermittent bouts of insanity. (Indeed, in the last years of his long reign he was, according to most accounts, a virtual lunatic, confined to the palace and unable to perform any official functions.) Yet even when George III was lucid and rational, which was most of the time in the 1760s and 1770s, he was painfully immature (he had

George III
This portrait by the Scottish artist Allan Ramsay shows the 22-year-old English king in his coronation robes as he ascended the throne in 1760. American patriots during the long revolutionary crisis came to consider George III a vicious and brutal tyrant. In reality, the king was a man of limited ability who tried desperately, stubbornly, and generally unsuccessfully to play a role for which he was fundamentally ill-suited. As early as 1780, he began to suffer intermittently from insanity. After 1810, he was blind and permanently deranged and spent the last decade of his sixty-year reign as an invalid, barred from all official business by the Regency Act of 1811. His son (later King George IV) served as regent in those years. (Colonial Williamsburg Foundation)

been only twenty-two when he ascended the throne) and insecure—striving constantly to prove his fitness for his position but time and again finding himself ill equipped to handle the challenges he seized for himself. The king's personality, therefore, contributed

both to the instability and to the intransigence of the British government during these critical years.

More immediately responsible for the problems that soon emerged with the colonies, however, was George Grenville, whom the king made prime minister in 1763. Grenville, a brother-in-law of William Pitt, did not share Pitt's sympathy with the American point of view. He agreed instead with the prevailing opinion within Britain that the colonists had been too long indulged and that they should be compelled to obey the laws and to pay a part of the cost of defending and administering the empire. He promptly began trying to impose a system upon what had been an unsystematic aggregation of colonial possessions in America.

The British and the Tribes

The Western problem was the most urgent. With the repulse of the French, frontiersmen from the English colonies had begun immediately to move over the mountains and into the upper Ohio Valley. Objecting to this intrusion, an alliance of Indian tribes, under the Ottawa chieftain Pontiac, struck back. To prevent an escalation of the fighting that might threaten western trade, the British government issued a ruling—the Proclamation of 1763—forbidding settlers to advance beyond a line drawn along the mountain divide between the Atlantic and the interior.

The Proclamation of 1763 was appealing to the British for several reasons. It would allow London, rather than the provincial governments and their land-hungry constituents, to control the westward movement of the white population. Hence, westward expansion would proceed in an orderly manner, and conflicts with the tribes, which were both militarily costly and dangerous to trade, might be limited. Slower Western settlement would also slow the population exodus from the coastal colonies, where England's most important markets and investments were. And it would reserve opportunities for land speculation and fur trading for English rather than colonial entrepreneurs.

Although Native Americans had few illusions about the Proclamation, which required them to cede still more land to the white settlers, many Indian groups supported the agreement as the best bargain available to them. The Cherokee, in particular, worked actively to hasten the drawing of the boundary, hoping to put an end to white encroachments for good. Relations between the Western tribes and the

British improved in at least some areas after the Proclamation, partly as a result of the work of the Indian superintendents the British appointed. John Stuart was in charge of Indian affairs in the Southern colonies and Sir William Johnson in the Northern ones. Both were sympathetic to Native American needs and lived among the tribes; Johnson married a Mohawk woman, Mary Brant, who was later to play an important role in the American Revolution.

Purchasing Tribal Lands

This document, signed with tribal symbols by representatives of the six Iroquois nations, was a product of the Treaty of Fort Stanwix in 1768. That treaty established a new border between Indian and colonial territory and, like most such agreements, wrested additional land from the tribes. The document shown here is, in effect, a receipt in which tribal leaders acknowledge receiving $10,000 from the Penn family in exchange for land in western Pennsylvania. The relatively favorable terms of this particular transaction between whites and Indians may have been a result of the involvement of Sir William Johnson, the general superintendent of Indian affairs in the northern colonies, who had developed good relations with the Iroquois.   (The Granger Collection)

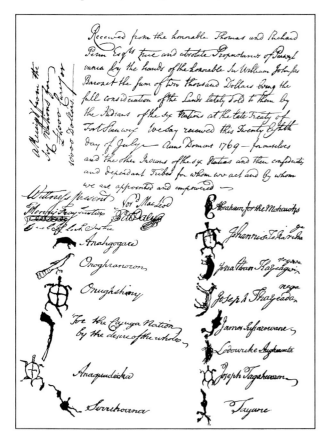

In the end, however, the Proclamation of 1763 failed to meet even the modest expectations of the Indians. It had some effect in limiting colonial land speculation in the West and in controlling the fur trade; but on the crucial point of the line of settlement, it was almost completely without impact. White settlers continued to swarm across the boundary and continued to claim lands farther and farther into the Ohio Valley. The British authorities tried repeatedly to establish limits to the expansion. In 1768, Stuart and Johnson negotiated new agreements with the Western tribes creating a supposedly permanent boundary (which, as always, increased the area of white settlement at the expense of the Indians). But these treaties (signed respectively at Hard Labor Creek, South Carolina, and Fort Stanwix, New York) also failed to stop the white advance. Within a few years, the 1768 agreements were replaced with new ones, which pushed the line of settlement still farther West.

The Colonial Response

The Grenville ministry soon moved to increase its authority in the colonies in more direct ways. Regular British troops, London announced, would now be stationed permanently in the provinces; and under the Mutiny Act of 1765 the colonists were required to assist in provisioning and maintaining the army. Ships of the British navy were assigned to patrol American waters and search for smugglers. The customs service was reorganized and enlarged. Royal officials were ordered to take up their colonial posts in person instead of sending substitutes. Colonial manufacturing was to be restricted, so that it would not compete with the rapidly expanding industry in Great Britain.

The Sugar Act of 1764, designed in part to eliminate the illegal sugar trade between the continental colonies and the French and Spanish West Indies, lowered the duty on molasses and raised the duty on sugar; and it established new vice-admiralty courts in America to try accused smugglers—thus depriving them of the benefit of sympathetic local juries. The Currency Act of 1764 required the colonial assemblies to stop issuing paper money (a widespread practice during the war) and to retire on schedule all the paper money already in circulation. Most momentous of all, the Stamp Act of 1765 imposed a tax on every printed document in the colonies: newspapers, almanacs, pamphlets, deeds, wills, licenses.

North America in 1763

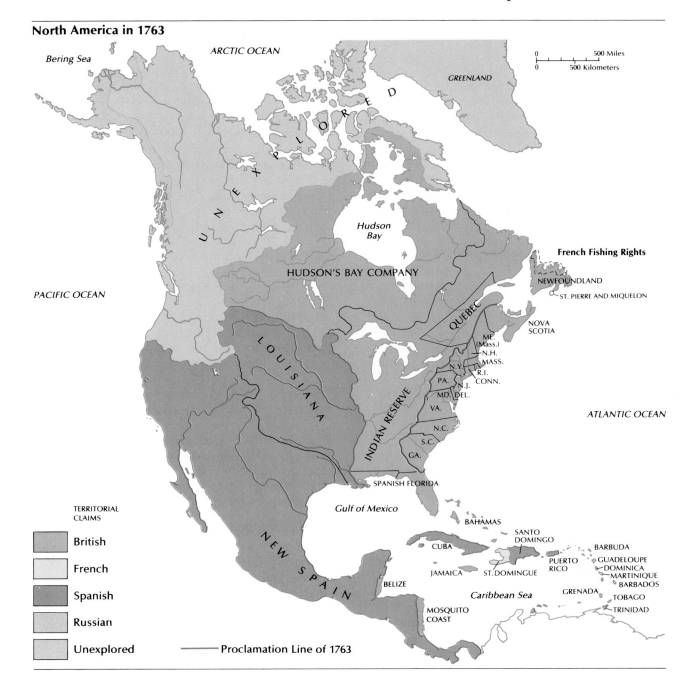

Bering Sea

ARCTIC OCEAN

GREENLAND

0   500 Miles

0   500 Kilometers

U N E X P L O R E D

Hudson Bay

HUDSON'S BAY COMPANY

French Fishing Rights

NEWFOUNDLAND

ST. PIERRE AND MIQUELON

PACIFIC OCEAN

QUEBEC

NOVA SCOTIA

ME. (Mass.)
N.H.
MASS.
N.Y.
R.I.
CONN.
PA.
N.J.
MD. DEL.
VA.

ATLANTIC OCEAN

L O U I S I A N A

I N D I A N   R E S E R V E

N.C.

S.C.

GA.

SPANISH FLORIDA

TERRITORIAL CLAIMS

Gulf of Mexico

BAHAMAS

SANTO DOMINGO

CUBA

BARBUDA

GUADELOUPE
DOMINICA
MARTINIQUE
BARBADOS

British

French

Spanish

PUERTO RICO

JAMAICA   ST. DOMINGUE

N E W   S P A I N

Russian

BELIZE

Caribbean Sea

GRENADA

TOBAGO

TRINIDAD

Unexplored   —— Proclamation Line of 1763

MOSQUITO COAST

The new imperial program was an effort to re-apply to the colonies the old principles of mercantilism. And in some ways, it proved highly effective. British officials were soon collecting more than ten times as much annual revenue in America as before 1763. But the new policies created many more problems than they solved.

The colonists may have resented the new imperial regulations, but they faced many obstacles to an effective effort to resist them. For one thing, Americans continued to harbor as many grievances against one another as against the authorities in London. In 1763, for example, a band of Pennsylvania frontiersmen known as the Paxton Boys descended on Philadelphia to demand relief from taxation and money to support their own defense needs; bloodshed was averted only by concessions from the colonial government.

In 1771, a small-scale civil war broke out as a result of the so-called Regulator movement in North Carolina. The Regulators were farmers of the Carolina upcountry who organized to oppose the high taxes that local sheriffs (appointed by the colonial governor) collected. The western counties were badly underrepresented in the colonial assembly, and the Regulators failed to win redress of their grievances there. Finally they armed themselves and began resisting tax collections by force. To suppress the revolt, Governor William Tryon raised an army of militiamen, mostly from the eastern counties, who defeated a band of 2,000 Regulators in the Battle of Alamance. Nine on each side were killed and many others wounded. Afterward, six Regulators were hanged for treason.

The bloodshed was exceptional, but bitter conflicts within the colonies were not. After 1763, however, the new policies of the British government began to create common grievances among virtually all colonists that to some degree counterbalanced these internal divisions. For under the Grenville program, as the Americans saw it, all people—in all classes, in all colonies—would suffer.

Northern merchants would suffer from restraints on their commerce, from the closing of the West to land speculation and fur trading, from the closing of opportunities for manufacturing, and from the increased burden of taxation. Southern planters, in debt to English merchants, would now have to pay additional taxes and would be unable to ease their debts by speculating in Western land. Professional men—ministers, lawyers, professors, and others—depended on merchants and planters for their livelihood and thus shared their concerns about the effects of English law. Small farmers, the largest group in the colonies, would suffer from increased taxes and from the abolition of paper money, which had been the source of most of their loans. Workers in towns faced the prospect of narrowing opportunities, particularly because of the restraints on manufacturing and paper money.

The new restrictions came, moreover, at the beginning of a postwar economic depression. The British government, by pouring money into the colonies to finance the fighting, had stimulated a wartime boom; that flow stopped after 1763. Now the authorities in London proposed to aggravate the problem by taking money *out* of the colonies. The imperial policies would, many colonists feared, doom them to permanent economic stagnation and a declining standard of living.

In reality, most Americans soon found ways to live with (or circumvent) the new British policies. The American economy was not, in fact, being destroyed. But economic anxieties were rising in the colonies nevertheless, and they created a growing sense of unease, particularly in the cities—the places most directly affected by British policies and the places where resistance first arose. The periodic economic slumps that were occurring with greater and greater frequency, the frightening depression of the early 1760s, the growth of a large group within the population who were unemployed or semiemployed, and who were in either case a destabilizing element in the community: all combined to produce a feeling in some colonial cities—and particularly in Boston, the city suffering the worst economic problems—that something was deeply amiss.

Whatever the economic consequences of George III's and Grenville's programs, the political consequences were—in the eyes of the colonists, at least—far worse. Nowhere else in the world did so large a proportion of the people take an active interest in public affairs; plus Americans were accustomed (and deeply attached) to a wide latitude in self-government. The keys to self-government, they believed, were the provincial assemblies; and the key to the power of the provincial assemblies was their long-established right to give or withhold appropriations for the costs of government within the colonies. By attempting to circumvent the colonial assemblies, raise extensive revenues directly from the public, and provide salaries directly and unconditionally to royal officials in America, the British government was challenging the basis of colonial political power: control over public finance.

Home rule, therefore, was not something new and different that the colonists were striving to attain. It was something old and familiar that they desired to keep. The movement to resist the new imperial policies, a movement for which many would ultimately fight and die, was thus at the same time democratic and conservative. It was a movement to conserve liberties Americans believed they already possessed.

Stirrings of Revolt

By the mid-1760s, therefore, a hardening of positions had begun in both England and America that would bring the colonies into increasing conflict with the mother country. The victorious war for empire had given the colonists a heightened sense of their own importance and a renewed commitment to protecting their political autonomy. It had given the British a strengthened belief in the need to tighten administration of the empire and a strong desire to use the colonies as a source of revenue. The result was a progression of events that, more rapidly than anyone could have imagined, destroyed the English empire in America.

The Stamp Act Crisis

Prime Minister Grenville could not have devised a better method for antagonizing and unifying the colonies than the Stamp Act of 1765 if he had tried. Unlike the Sugar Act of a year earlier, which affected few people other than the New England merchants whose trade it hampered, the new tax fell on all Americans, of whatever section, colony, or class. And it evoked particular opposition from some of the most powerful and strategically placed members of the population—people with substantial economic and political power, and people with particular influence over public opinion. Merchants and lawyers were obliged to buy stamps for ships' papers and legal documents. Tavern owners, often the political oracles of their neighborhoods, were required to buy stamps for their licenses. Printers—the most influential group in distributing information and ideas in colonial society—had to buy stamps for their newspapers and other publications.

The actual economic burdens of the Stamp Act were, in the end, relatively light. What made the law obnoxious to the colonists was not so much its immediate cost as the precedent it seemed to set. In the past, taxes and duties on colonial trade had always been interpreted as measures to regulate commerce, not raise money. Some Americans had even managed to persuade themselves that the Sugar Act, which was in fact designed primarily to raise money, was not fundamentally different from the traditional nature of imperial duties. The Stamp Act, however, could be interpreted in only one way. It was a direct attempt by England to raise revenue in the colonies without the consent of the colonial assemblies. If this new tax were allowed to pass without resistance, the door would be open for far more burdensome taxation in the future.

Few colonists believed that they could do anything more than grumble and buy the stamps—until the Virginia House of Burgesses sounded a "trumpet of sedition" that aroused Americans to action almost everywhere. The "trumpet" was sounded by a group of young Virginia aristocrats. They hoped, among other things, to challenge the power of tidewater planters who (in alliance with the royal governor) dominated Virginia politics. Foremost among the malcontents was Patrick Henry, who had already achieved fame through his fiery oratory and his defiance of British authority. Henry made a dramatic speech to the House in May 1765, concluding with a vague prediction that if present policies were not revised, George III, like earlier tyrants, might lose his head. There were shocked cries of "Treason!" and, according to one witness, an immediate apology from Henry (although many years later he was quoted as having made the defiant reply: "If *this* be treason, make the most of it"). Henry introduced a set of resolutions declaring that Americans possessed the same rights as the English, especially the right to be taxed only by their own representatives; that Virginians should pay no taxes except those voted by the Virginia assembly; and that anyone advocating the right of Parliament to tax Virginians should be deemed an enemy of the colony. The House of Burgesses defeated the most extreme of Henry's resolutions, but all of them were printed and circulated as the "Virginia Resolves" (creating an impression in other colonies that the people of Virginia were more militant than they actually were).

In Massachusetts at about the same time, James Otis persuaded his fellow members of the colonial assembly to call an intercolonial congress for concerted action against the new tax. In October 1765, the Stamp Act Congress, as it was called, met in New York with delegates from nine colonies and decided to petition the king and the two houses of Parliament. Their petition conceded that Americans owed to Parliament "all due subordination," but it denied that the colonies could rightfully be taxed except through their own provincial assemblies.

Meanwhile, in several colonial cities mobs began taking the law into their own hands. During the summer of 1765 serious riots broke out up and down the coast, the largest of them in Boston. Men belonging to the newly organized Sons of Liberty terrorized stamp agents and burned the stamps. The agents, themselves Americans, hastily resigned, and the sale of stamps in the continental colonies virtually ceased. In Boston, the mob attacked as well such pro-British "aristocrats" as the lieutenant governor, Thomas Hutchinson (who had privately opposed passage of the Stamp Act but who, as an officer of the crown, felt obliged to support it once it became law). Hutchinson's elegant house was pillaged and virtually destroyed.

The Stamp Act crisis brought the colonies to the

Patrick Henry and the Parson's Cause, 1763

A dispute over ministerial salaries in the 1750s and early 1760s, known as the "Parson's Cause," became the occasion for some of the earliest colonial challenges to British authority. In 1759 the Privy Council in England responded to appeals from Anglican ministers in Virginia and overturned a colonial law regulating (and limiting) their salaries. As a result, ministers were able to sue for back pay. In a 1763 trial in Hanover County, the young Virginia attorney Patrick Henry persuaded a jury to rule against the Rev. James Maury in one such suit on the grounds that the king and his government had exceeded their authority. This painting by George Cooke (c. 1830) portrays Henry addressing the court as a large crowd of onlookers presses at the doors. (Virginia Historical Society)

brink of war with the British government. But the crisis subsided, largely because England backed down. The authorities in London were not deterred by the legislative resolutions, the petitions, or the riots; what changed their attitude was economic pressure. Even before the Stamp Act, many New Englanders had stopped buying English goods to protest the Sugar Act of 1764. Now the colonial boycott spread, and the Sons of Liberty intimidated those colonists who were reluctant to participate in it. The merchants of England, feeling the loss of much of their colonial market, begged Parliament to repeal the Stamp Act, while stories of unemployment, poverty, and discontent arose from English seaports and manufacturing towns.

The Marquis of Rockingham, who succeeded Grenville as prime minister in July 1765, tried to appease both the English merchants and the American colonists; and he finally convinced the king that the Stamp Act should not survive. On March 18, 1766, it was repealed. Rockingham's opponents were strong and vociferous, and they insisted that unless the colonists were compelled to obey the Stamp Act, they would soon cease to obey any laws of Parliament. To satisfy them, Parliament passed on the same day the Declaratory Act, declaring parliamentary authority over the colonies "in all cases whatsoever." In their rejoicing over the repeal, most Americans paid little attention to this sweeping declaration of Parliament's power.

The Townshend Program

The Rockingham government's policy of appeasement was not as well received in England as it was in America. English landlords, a powerful political force, angrily protested that the government had "sacrificed the landed gentlemen to the interests of traders and colonists." They were fearful, in other words, that the retreat of the government from its policy of taxing the colonies would result in renewed taxes on them. The king finally bowed to their pressure and dismissed the Rockingham ministry. To replace it, he called upon the aging but still powerful William Pitt to form a government. Pitt had been a strong critic of the Stamp Act and had a reputation in America as a friend of the colonists (although some Americans had looked askance at his acceptance of a peerage in 1766). Once in office, however, Pitt (now Lord Chatham) was so hobbled by gout and at times so incapacitated by mental illness that the actual leadership of his administration fell to the chancellor of the exchequer, Charles Townshend—a brilliant, flamboyant, and at times reckless politician known to his contemporaries variously as "the Weathercock" and "Champagne Charlie."

Townshend had to deal almost immediately with the litany of imperial problems and colonial grievances left over from the Grenville ministry. With the Stamp Act repealed, the greatest American grievance involved the Mutiny (or Quartering) Act of 1765, which required the colonists to provide quarters and supplies for the British troops in America. The British considered this a reasonable requirement. The troops were stationed in North America to protect the colonists from Indian or French attack and to defend the frontiers; lodging the troops in coastal cities was simply a way to reduce the costs of supplying them. To the colonists, however, the law was another assault on their liberties. They did not so much object to quartering the troops or providing them with supplies; they had been doing that voluntarily ever since the last years of the French and Indian War. They resented that these contributions were now made mandatory, and they considered it another form of taxation without their consent. They responded with defiance. The Massachusetts Assembly refused to vote the mandated supplies to the troops. The New York Assembly soon did likewise, posing an even greater challenge to imperial authority, since the army headquarters were in New York City.

To enforce the law and to try again to raise revenues in the colonies, Townshend steered two measures through Parliament in 1767. First, the New York Assembly was disbanded until the colonists agreed to obey the Mutiny Act. (By singling out New York, Townshend thought he would avoid Grenville's mistake of arousing all the colonies at once.) Second, new taxes (known as the Townshend Duties) were levied on various goods imported to the colonies from England—lead, paint, paper, and tea. The colonists could not logically object to taxation of this kind, Townshend reasoned, because it met standards they themselves had accepted. Benjamin Franklin, as a colonial agent in London trying to prevent the passage of the Stamp Act, had long ago argued for the distinction between "internal" and "external" taxes and had denounced the stamp duties as internal taxation. Townshend himself had considered the distinction laughable; but he was now imposing duties on clearly external transactions.

Townshend's efforts to satisfy colonial grievances were, however, to no avail. The new duties were no more acceptable to Americans than the stamp tax. Although they were ostensibly external taxes, they would be paid by colonial merchants and, indirectly, by colonial consumers. Their purpose was the same as that of the Stamp Act: to raise revenue from the colonists without their consent. And the suspension of the New York Assembly, far from isolating New York, aroused the resentment of all the colonies. They considered this assault on the rights of one provincial government a precedent for the annihilation of the rights of all of them.

The Massachusetts Assembly took the lead in opposing the new measures by circulating a letter to all the colonial governments urging them to stand up against every tax, external or internal, imposed by Parliament. At first, the circular evoked little response in some of the legislatures (and ran into strong opposition in Pennsylvania's). Then Lord Hillsborough, secretary of state for the colonies, issued a circular letter of his own in which he warned that assemblies endorsing the Massachusetts letter would be dissolved. Massachusetts defiantly reaffirmed its support for the circular. (The vote in the Assembly was 92 to 17, and "ninety-two" became a patriotic rallying cry throughout British America.) The other colonies, including Pennsylvania, promptly rallied to the support of Massachusetts.

Besides persuading Parliament to levy import duties and suspend the New York Assembly, Townshend took steps to enforce commercial regulations in the colonies more effectively than ever. The most fateful of these steps was the establishment of a board of customs commissioners in America. Townshend hoped the new board would stop the rampant corruption in the colonial customs houses; and to some extent his hopes were fulfilled. The new commissioners virtually ended the smuggling in Boston, where they established their headquarters, although smugglers continued to carry on a busy trade in other colonial seaports.

The Boston merchants—accustomed, like all colonial merchants, to loose enforcement of the Navigation Acts and doubly aggrieved now that the new commission was diverting the lucrative smuggling trade elsewhere—were indignant; and they took the lead in organizing another boycott. In 1768, the merchants of Philadelphia and New York joined them in a nonimportation agreement, and later some Southern merchants and planters also agreed to cooperate. The colonists boycotted British goods subject to the Townshend Duties; and throughout the colonies, American homespun and other domestic products became suddenly fashionable, while English luxuries fell from favor.

Late in 1767, Charles Townshend died—before the consequences of his ill-conceived program had become fully apparent. The question of dealing with colonial resistance to the Townshend Duties fell, therefore, to the new prime minister, Lord North. Hoping to break the nonimportation agreement and divide the colonists, Lord North secured the repeal in March 1770 of all the Townshend Duties except the tea tax.

The Boston Massacre

Whatever pacifying effects the repeal of the Townshend Duties might have had was negated by an event in Massachusetts that occurred before news of the repeal reached America. The harassment of the new customs commissioners in Boston had grown so intense that the British government had placed four regiments of regular troops within the city. The presence of the "redcoats" was a constant affront to the colonists' sense of independence and a constant reminder of what they considered British oppression. Everywhere they went, Bostonians encountered British soldiers—often arrogant, and intrusive, sometimes coarse and provocative. There was particular tension between the redcoats and Boston laborers. Many British soldiers, poorly paid and poorly treated by the army, wanted jobs in their off-duty hours; and

they thus competed with local workers in an already tight market. Clashes between them were frequent.

On the night of March 5, 1770, a few days after a particularly intense skirmish between workers at a ship-rigging factory and British soldiers who were trying to find work there, a mob of dockworkers, "liberty boys," and others began pelting the sentries at the customs house with rocks and snowballs. Hastily, Captain Thomas Preston of the British regiment lined up several of his men in front of the building to protect it. There was some scuffling; one of the soldiers was knocked down; and in the midst of it all, apparently, several British soldiers fired into the crowd, killing five people (among them a mulatto sailor, Crispus Attucks).

This murky incident, almost certainly the result of panic and confusion, was quickly transformed by local resistance leaders into the "Boston Massacre"—a graphic symbol of British oppression and brutality. The victims became popular martyrs; the event became the subject of such lurid (and inaccurate) accounts as the widely circulated pamphlet *Innocent Blood Crying to God from the Streets of Boston*. A famous engraving by Paul Revere portrayed the massacre as a carefully organized, calculated assault on a peaceful crowd. The British soldiers, tried before a jury of Bostonians, were found guilty of no more than manslaughter and were given only a token punishment. Colonial pamphlets and newspapers, however, convinced many Americans that the soldiers were guilty of official murder. Year after year, resistance leaders marked the anniversary of the massacre with demonstrations and speeches.

The leading figure in fomenting public outrage over the Boston Massacre was Samuel Adams, the most effective radical in the colonies. Adams (a distant cousin of John Adams, second president of the United States) was born in 1722 and was thus somewhat older than other leaders of colonial protest. As a member of an earlier generation with strong ties to New England's Puritan past, he was particularly inclined to view public events in stern moral terms. A failure in business, he had occupied several political and governmental positions; but his real importance was as a publicist, a voice unflagging in expressing outrage at British oppression. England, he argued, had become a morass of sin and corruption; only in America did public virtue survive. He spoke frequently at Boston town meetings; and as one unpopular English policy followed another—the Townshend Duties, the placement of customs commissioners in Boston, the stationing of British troops in the city (with its violent

The British in Boston, 1768

British troops arrived in Boston on September 30, 1768, marched into the city, and pitched tents on the Boston common. The soldiers were charged with ensuring the safety of British customs officers, who three months earlier had been driven from the city by local residents and had appealed to England for protection. The presence of the troops became a continuing irritant in relations between the colonists and the British government. This 1770 engraving by Paul Revere shows troops embarking from British naval vessels at Long Wharf and marching "with insolent Parade" up King Street into the city. (Henry Francis du Pont Winterthur Museum)

results)—his message attracted increasing support. In 1772, he proposed the creation of a "committee of correspondence" in Boston to publicize the grievances against England throughout the colony, and he became its first head. Other colonies followed Massachusetts's lead, and a loose network of political organizations was soon established that kept the spirit of dissent alive through the 1770s.

The Philosophy of Revolt

A superficial calm settled on the colonies for approximately three years after the Boston Massacre. In reality, however, American political life remained restless and troubled. The crises of the 1760s had helped to arouse an ideological excitement in the colonies; the events of the early 1770s had produced instruments for publicizing colonial grievances; and gradually a political outlook took hold in America that would ultimately serve to justify revolt.

"The Revolution was effected before the war commenced," one of the greatest of the Revolutionary leaders, John Adams, afterward remarked. "The Revolution was in the minds and hearts of the people." Adams exaggerated. Few Americans were willing to consider complete independence from England until after the war had begun; and even those few (among them Samuel Adams) generally refrained from admitting that independence was their goal. But John Adams was certainly correct in arguing that well before the fighting began in 1775, a profound ideological shift had occurred in the way many Americans viewed the British government and their own.

The ideas that would support the Revolution emerged from many sources. Some were indigenous to America, drawn from religious (particularly Puritan) sources or from the political experiences of the colonies. But these native ideas were enriched and enlarged by the importation of powerful arguments from abroad. Of most importance, perhaps, were the "radical" ideas of those in Great Britain who stood in opposition to their government. Some were Scots, who viewed the English government as tyrannical. Others were embittered "country Whigs," who considered the existing system corrupt and oppressive. Drawing from some of the great philosophical minds of earlier generations—most notably John Locke—these English dissidents framed a powerful argument against their government; and while that argument had only limited appeal in England, it found a ready audience in the troubled colonies.

Central to this emerging ideology was a new concept of what government should be. Because humans were inherently corrupt and selfish, government was necessary to protect individuals from the evil in one another. But because any government was run by corruptible people, it needed safeguards against abuses of power.

In the eyes of most Englishmen and most Americans, the English constitution was the best system ever devised to meet these necessities. By distributing power among the three elements of society—the monarch, the aristocracy, and the common people—the English political system ensured that no individual or group could exercise authority unchecked by another. Yet by the mid-seventeenth century, dissidents in both England and America were becoming deeply concerned that this noble constitution was being eroded. The king and his ministers were exercising such corrupt and autocratic authority, they believed, that the elements of power were no longer in balance. The independence of the various elements of government was being undermined; a single center of power was emerging; and the system was thus threatening to become a dangerous tyranny.

Except among such disenchanted groups as the Scots and the "country Whigs," such arguments found little sympathy in England—largely because of the way in which most English people viewed their constitution. They revered it, but they considered it a flexible, constantly changing entity—an assortment of laws and customs that had evolved through many centuries and that remained elastic and vague. The English constitution was not a written document; nor was it a fixed set of unchangeable rules. It was a general sense of the "way things are done." Americans, by contrast, drew from their experience with colonial charters, in which the shape and powers of

government were permanently inscribed on paper; and they had difficulty accepting the idea of a flexible, changing set of basic principles. Many argued that the English constitution should itself be written down, to prevent fallible politicians from tampering with its essence.

Part of that essence, Americans believed, was their right to be taxed only with their own consent. When Townshend levied his "external" duties, the Philadelphia lawyer John Dickinson published a widely circulated pamphlet, *Letters of a Pennsylvania Farmer,* which argued that even external taxation was legal only when designed to regulate trade and not to raise a revenue. Gradually, most Americans ceased to accept even that distinction, and they finally took an

John Dickinson

This 1770 portrait by Charles Willson Peale shows the Pennsylvania lawyer and popular opponent of British mercantile policies. Dickinson was more moderate than many colonial agitators; but in his famous *Letters from a Farmer in Pennsylvania to the Inhabitants of the British Colonies,* published in 1768, he suggested that Americans might have to use force in resisting British oppression if conciliation failed. He was later a delegate to the Constitutional Convention of 1787. (Historical Society of Pennsylvania)

unqualified stand: "No taxation without representation." Whatever the nature of a tax—whether internal or external, whether designed to raise revenue or to control trade—it could not be levied without the consent of the colonists themselves.

This clamor about "representation" made little sense to the English. Only about 4 percent of the population of Great Britain was entitled to vote for members of Parliament, and some populous boroughs in England had no representatives at all. According to the prevailing English theory, such apparent inequities were of no importance. Members of Parliament did not represent individuals or particular geographical areas. Instead, each member represented the interests of the whole nation and indeed the whole empire, no matter where the member happened to come from. The unenfranchised boroughs of England, the whole of Ireland, and the colonies thousands of miles away—all were thus represented in the Parliament at London, even though they elected no representatives of their own.

This was the theory of "virtual" representation. But Americans, drawing from their experiences with their town meetings and their colonial assemblies, believed in "actual" representation. Every community was entitled to its own representative, elected by the people of that community and directly responsible to them. Since they had none of their own representatives in Parliament, it followed that they were not represented there. But even having representatives in Parliament, many believed, would not resolve the problem. For participation in the decisions of Parliament would in effect bind them to those decisions, even though they would be outnumbered and outvoted. More important, American members of Parliament would be so isolated from the people who had elected them that they would not be able to perform as true representatives. Thus most colonists reverted to the argument that they could be fairly represented only in their own colonial assemblies.

According to the emerging American view of the empire, these assemblies played the same role within the colonies—had the same powers, enjoyed the same rights—that Parliament did within England. The empire, the Americans argued, was a sort of federation of commonwealths, each with its own legislative body, all tied together by common loyalty to the king (a view that augured the structure of the British Commonwealth in the twentieth century). This concept allowed them to vent their anger not at the empire itself, but at the English Parliament, which was presumptuously exerting authority to which it was not entitled over the colonies. Not until very late did they begin to criticize the king himself. And not until the colonies were ready to declare their independence in 1776 were they ready to repudiate the English constitution.

What may have made the conflict between England and America ultimately insoluble was a fundamental difference of opinion over the nature of sovereignty. By arguing that Parliament had the right to legislate for England and for the empire as a whole, but that only the provincial assemblies could legislate for the individual colonies, Americans were in effect arguing for a division of sovereignty. Parliament would be sovereign in some matters; the assemblies would be sovereign in others. To the British, such an argument was untenable and absurd. Sovereignty, they believed, was by definition unitary. In any system of government there must be a single, ultimate authority. And since the empire was, in their view, a single, undivided unit, there could be only one authority within it: the English government of king and Parliament. Thus it was that the Anglo-American crisis ultimately presented the colonists with a stark choice. In the eyes of the English, there was, in effect, no middle ground between complete subordination and complete independence. Slowly, cautiously, Americans found themselves pushed toward independence.

That movement began with resistance, rather than with sentiment for open revolt. Opposition to British policies in the 1760s had not taken the form of repudiation of England but of refusal to obey certain unjust laws. During this stage of the crisis, the colonists justified their actions by citing the teachings of the Bible and the ideas of John Locke. To show that resistance against tyranny was lawful in God's sight, they pointed to such biblical events as the overthrow of a king of Israel who had burdened his people with unjust taxes. To show that resistance had justification in the philosophy of the Enlightenment, they pointed to Locke's *Two Treatises on Civil Government* (1690), in which he had attempted to justify the English revolution of 1688–1689 by which Parliament had won supremacy over the king. Locke argued that humans had originally lived in a state of nature and had enjoyed complete liberty; later, they had agreed to a "compact" and established a government to protect their "natural rights," especially their right to the ownership and enjoyment of private property. But the government was limited by the terms of the compact and by "natural law." It could not, for example, take property without the consent of the owners.

Americans took particular note of Locke's statement: "If any one shall claim a power to lay and levy taxes on the people by his own authority, and without such consent of the people, he thereby invades the fundamental law of property, and subverts the end of government."

The biblical and Lockean justifications for resistance included, however, a possible justification for actual rebellion as well. The Bible suggested that people had a right not only to resist but to overthrow unjust rulers. And Locke had argued that if a government should persist in exceeding its rightful powers, the people would be released not only from their obligation to obey particular laws but from their obligation to obey the government at all. They would have the right to dissolve the "compact" and make a new one, to establish another government. The right to resist was, in other words, only the first step. If resistance proved ineffective, if a government proved to be so thoroughly corrupt and tyrannical that it could not be reformed, then citizens were entitled to revolt against it. They had a "right of revolution."

By the early 1770s, the relationship between America and England had become poisoned by resentment and mutual suspicion. Americans had become convinced that a "conspiracy against liberty" existed within the British government. And they had articulated a philosophy that seemed to them to justify whatever measures might be necessary to protect themselves from that conspiracy. Only a small distance remained to be traversed before the colonies would move from resistance to revolution, before they would be ready to break their ties with the empire. That distance was crossed quickly, beginning in 1773, when a new set of British policies shattered forever the imperial relationship.

The Tea Excitement

The apparent calm in America in the first years of the 1770s masked a growing sense of frustration and resentment in response to the continued and increasingly heavy-handed enforcement of the Navigation Acts. The customs commissioners, who remained in America despite the repeal of the Townshend Acts, proved to be clumsy, intrusive, and arrogant officials, who harassed colonial merchants and seamen constantly with petty restrictions (and who also enriched themselves through graft and through illegal seizures of merchandise). The popular anger lying just beneath the surface was visible in occasional acts of rebellion. At one point, colonists seized a British revenue ship on the lower Delaware River. And in 1772, angry residents of Rhode Island boarded the British schooner *Gaspée,* set it afire, and sank it in Narragansett Bay. The British response to the *Gaspée* affair further inflamed American opinion. Instead of putting the accused attackers on trial in colonial courts, the British sent a special commission to America with power to send the defendants back to England for trial. Once again, the British were challenging America's right to exercise independent authority.

What finally revived the revolutionary fervor of the 1760s to its old strength, however, was a new act of Parliament—one that the English government had expected to be relatively uncontroversial. It involved the business of selling tea. In 1773, Britain's East India Company (which possessed an official monopoly on trade with the Far East) was sitting on large stocks of tea that it could not sell in England. It was on the verge of bankruptcy. In an effort to save it, the government passed the Tea Act of 1773, which gave the company the right to export its merchandise directly to the colonies without paying any of the regular taxes that were imposed on the colonial merchants, who had traditionally served as the middlemen in such transactions. With these privileges, the company could undersell American merchants and monopolize the colonial tea trade.

The act proved inflammatory for several reasons. First, it angered influential colonial merchants, who feared being replaced and bankrupted by a powerful monopoly. The East India Company's decision to grant franchises to certain American merchants for the sale of their tea created further resentments among those excluded from this lucrative trade. More important, however, the Tea Act revived American passions about the issue of taxation without representation. The law provided no new tax on tea. But the original Townshend duty on the commodity—the only one of the original duties that had not been repealed—survived. It was the East India Company's exemption from that duty that put the colonial merchants at such a grave disadvantage in competition with them. Lord North assumed that most colonists would welcome the new law because it would reduce the price of tea to consumers by removing the middlemen. But resistance leaders in America argued that it was another insidious example of the results of an unconstitutional tax. The colonists responded by boycotting tea.

The boycott was an important event in the history of colonial resistance. Unlike earlier protests, most of which had involved relatively small numbers of people, the boycott mobilized large segments of the population. It also helped link the colonies together in a common experience of mass popular protest. Particularly important to the movement were the activities of colonial women, who were among the principal consumers of tea and now became the leaders of the effort to boycott it.

Women had played a significant role in resistance activities from the beginning. Several women (most prominently Mercy Otis Warren) had been important in writing the dissident pamphlets that did so much to fan colonial resentments in the 1760s. Women had participated actively in anti-British riots

Mercy Otis Warren

John Singleton Copley painted this portrait of Mercy Otis Warren in 1763, when she was thirty-five years old and only beginning to become active as a writer and polemicist. In the 1770s, she was one of the leading critics of British rule in America and wrote, among other things, two satirical plays attacking the American Tories. In 1805, she published a celebrated three-volume history of the American Revolution. She died in 1814. (Museum of Fine Arts, Boston)

and crowd activities in the 1760s; they had formed an informal organization—the Daughters of Liberty—that occasionally mocked their male counterparts as insufficiently militant. The Sons of Liberty, they wrote in a 1768 poem, were "Supinely asleep, and depriv'd of their Sight . . . strip'd of their Freedom, and rob'd of their Right." Now, as the sentiment for a boycott grew, women mobilized as never before, determined (as the Daughters of Liberty had written) "that rather than Freedom, we'll part with our Tea."

In the last weeks of 1773, with strong popular support, leaders in various colonies made plans to prevent the East India Company from landing its cargoes in colonial ports. In Philadelphia and New York, determined colonists kept the tea from leaving the company's ships; and in Charleston, they stored it away in a public warehouse. In Boston, after failing to turn back the three ships in the harbor, local patriots staged a spectacular drama. On the evening of December 16, 1773, three companies of fifty men each, masquerading as Mohawks, passed through a tremendous crowd of spectators (which served to protect them from official interference), went aboard the three ships, broke open the tea chests, and heaved them into the harbor. As the electrifying news of the Boston "tea party" spread, other seaports followed the example and staged similar acts of resistance of their own.

When the Bostonians refused to pay for the property they had destroyed, George III and Lord North decided on a policy of coercion, to be applied only against Massachusetts—the chief center of resistance. In four acts of 1774, Parliament closed the port of Boston, drastically reduced the powers of self-government in the colony, permitted royal officers to be tried in other colonies or in England when accused of crimes, and provided for the quartering of troops in the colonists' barns and empty houses.

These Coercive Acts—or, as they were more widely known in America, Intolerable Acts—were followed by the Quebec Act, which was separate from them in origin and quite different in purpose. Its object was to provide a civil government for the French-speaking Roman Catholic inhabitants of Canada and the Illinois country. The law extended the boundaries of Quebec to include the French communities between the Ohio and Mississippi rivers. It also granted political rights to Roman Catholics and recognized the legality of the Roman Catholic church within the enlarged province. In many ways it was a liberal and much-needed piece of legislation. But to many in the thirteen colonies, the Quebec Act was a

Paying the Excise Man
This eighteenth-century satirical drawing by a British
artist depicts Bostonians forcing tea down the throat of a
customs official, whom they have tarred and feathered.
In the background, colonists are dumping tea into the
harbor (presumably a representation of the 1773 Boston
Tea Party); and on the tree at right is a symbol of the
Stamp Act, which the colonists had defied eight years
earlier.   (Metropolitan Musem of Art)

threat. They were already alarmed by rumors that
the Church of England was scheming to appoint a
bishop for America who would impose Anglican authority on all the various sects. And since the line
between the Church of England and the Church of
Rome had always seemed to Americans dangerously
thin, the passage of the Quebec Act convinced many
of them that a plot was afoot in London to subject
Americans to the tyranny of the pope. Those interested in Western lands, moreover, believed that the
act would hinder westward expansion.

The Coercive Acts, far from isolating Massachusetts, made it a martyr in the eyes of residents of
other colonies and sparked new resistance up and
down the coast. Colonial legislatures passed a series

of resolves supporting Massachusetts. Women's
groups throughout the colonies mobilized to extend
the boycotts of British goods and to create substitutes
for the tea, textiles, and other commodities they were
shunning. In Edenton, North Carolina, fifty-one
women signed an agreement in October 1774 declaring their "sincere adherence" to the anti-British resolutions of their provincial assembly and proclaiming
their duty to do "every thing as far as lies in our
power" to support the "publick good." Among other
things, the Edenton Proclamation was an example of
how colonial women, in the face of the mounting
political tension, were expanding their notion of their
appropriate role in public events.

Cooperation and War

Revolutions do not simply happen. They must be
organized and led. Beginning in 1765, colonial leaders developed a variety of organizations for converting popular discontent into action—organizations
that in time formed the basis for an independent government.

New Sources of Authority

The passage of authority from the royal government
to the colonists themselves began on the local level,
where the tradition of autonomy was already strong.
In colony after colony, local institutions responded to
the resistance movement by simply seizing authority
on their own. At times, entirely new, extralegal bodies emerged semispontaneously and began to perform
some of the functions of government. In Massachusetts in 1768, for example, Samual Adams called a
convention of delegates from the towns of the colony
to sit in place of the General Court, which the governor had dissolved. The Sons of Liberty, which Adams had helped to organize in Massachusetts and
which sprang up elsewhere as well, became another
source of power. Its members at times formed disciplined bands of vigilantes, who made certain that all
colonists respected the boycotts and other forms of
popular resistance. And in most colonies, committees of prominent citizens began meeting to perform
additional political functions.

The most famous and most effective of these
new groups were the committees of correspondence,

The First Battles of the Revolution

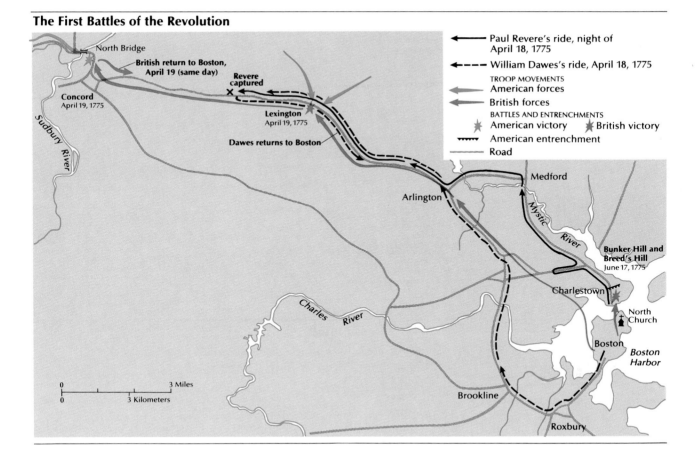

which Adams had inaugurated in Massachusetts in 1772. Virginia later established the first intercolonial committees of correspondence, which made possible continuous cooperation among the colonies. And Virginia took the greatest step of all toward united action in 1774 when, after the royal governor dissolved the assembly, a rump session met in the Raleigh Tavern at Williamsburg, declared that the Intolerable Acts menaced the liberties of every colony, and issued a call for a Continental Congress.

Variously elected by the assemblies and by extralegal meetings, delegates from all the thirteen colonies except Georgia were present when, in September 1774, the First Continental Congress convened in Philadelphia's Carpenters' Hall. They made five major decisions. First, in a very close vote, they rejected a plan (proposed by Joseph Galloway of Pennsylvania) for a colonial union under British authority (much like the earlier Albany Plan), with a legislative council made up of representatives from the colonial assemblies and a president-general to be appointed by the

king. Second, they endorsed a statement of grievances, whose tortured language reflected the conflicts among the delegates between moderates and extremists. The statement reflected the influence of the moderates by seeming to concede Parliament's right to regulate colonial trade by addressing the king as "Most Gracious Sovereign"; but it included a more extreme demand for the repeal of all oppressive legislation passed since 1763. Third, they approved a series of resolutions from a Suffolk County (Massachusetts) convention recommending, among other things, that military preparations be made for defense against possible attack by the British troops in Boston. Fourth, they agreed to nonimportation, nonexportation, and nonconsumption as means of stopping all trade with Great Britain, and they formed a "Continental Association" to see that these agreements were enforced. And fifth, the delegates agreed, on adjournment, to meet again the next spring, thus indicating that they conceived of the Continental Congress as a continuing organization.

The Retreat

From Concord to Lexington of the Army of Wild Irish Asses Defeated by the Brave American Militia

Mr Deacon Mr Loeings Mr Mulikens Mr Bonds Houses and Barn all Plunderd and Burnt on April 19.th

The British Retreat from Concord, 1775

This American cartoon satirizes the retreat of British forces from Concord after the battle there on April 19, 1775. Patriot forces are lined up on the left, and the retreating British forces (portrayed with dog heads, perhaps because many of the soldiers were "wild" Irish) straggles off at right—some fleeing in panic, others gloating over the booty they have plundered from the burning homes above. In its crude and exaggerated way, the cartoon depicts the success of Patriot forces at the Old North Bridge in Concord in repulsing a British contingent under the command of Lord Percy. As the redcoats retreated to Lexington and then to Boston, they continued to encounter fire from colonial forces, not arrayed in battle lines as shown here, but hidden along the road. One British soldier described the nightmarish withdrawal: "We were fired on from Houses and behind Trees . . . the Country was . . . full of Hills, Woods, stone Walls . . . which the Rebels did not fail to take advantage of." (John Carter Brown Library, Brown University)

Through their representatives in Philadelphia the colonies had, in effect, reaffirmed their autonomous status within the empire and declared economic war to maintain that position. The more optimistic of the Americans supposed that economic warfare alone would win a quick and bloodless victory, but the more pessimistic had their doubts. "I expect no redress, but, on the contrary, increased resentment and double vengeance," John Adams wrote to Patrick Henry; "we must fight." And Henry replied, "By God, I am of your opinion."

During the winter, the Parliament in London debated proposals for conciliating the colonists. Lord Chatham (William Pitt) urged the withdrawal of troops from America, and Edmund Burke called for the repeal of the Coercive Acts; but their efforts were in vain. Lord North finally won approval early in 1775 for a series of measures known as the Conciliatory Propositions, but they were in fact far less conciliatory than the approaches Burke or Chatham had urged. Parliament now proposed that the colonies, instead of being taxed directly by Parliament, would tax themselves at Parliament's demand. With this offer, Lord North hoped to divide the American moderates, whom he believed represented the views of the majority, from the extremist minority. But his offer was too little and too late. It did not reach America until after the first shots of war had been fired.

Lexington and Concord

For months, the farmers and townspeople of Massachusetts had been gathering arms and ammunition

SIGNIFICANT EVENTS

1713 Treaty of Utrecht concludes Queen Anne's War (p. 97)

1744–1748 King George's War (p. 97)

1754 Albany Plan for intercolonial cooperation rejected (p. 95)

Battle of Fort Duquesne begins French and Indian War (p. 98)

1756 Seven Years' War begins in Europe (p. 98)

1757 British policies provoke riots in New York (p. 98)

1758 Pitt returns authority to colonial assemblies (p. 98)

British capture Fort Duquesne (p. 99)

1759 British forces under Wolfe capture Quebec (p. 99)

1760 George III becomes king (p. 100)

French army surrenders to Amherst at Montreal (p. 99)

1763 Peace of Paris ends Seven Years' (and French and Indian) War (p. 100)

Grenville becomes prime minister (p. 103)

Paxton uprising in Pennsylvania (p. 105)

1764 Sugar Act passed (p. 104)

Currency Act passed (p. 104)

1765 Stamp Act crisis (p. 107)

Mutiny Act passed (p. 109)

1766 Stamp Act repealed (p. 108)

Declaratory Act passed (p. 108)

1767 Townshend Duties imposed (p. 109)

1768 Boston, New York, and Philadelphia merchants make nonimportation agreement (p. 110)

1770 Boston Massacre (p. 110)

Most Townshend Duties repealed (p. 110)

1771 Regulator movement quelled in North Carolina (p. 106)

1772 Committees of correspondence established in Boston (p. 116)

Gaspée incident in Rhode Island (p. 114)

1773 Tea Act passed (p. 114)

Bostonians stage tea party (p. 116)

1774 Intolerable Acts passed (p. 116)

First Continental Congress meets at Philadelphia (p. 117)

1775 Clashes at Lexington and Concord begin American Revolution (pp. 119–120)

and training as "minutemen," preparing to fight on a minute's notice. The Continental Congress had approved preparations for a defensive war, and the citizen-soldiers only waited for an aggressive move by the British regulars in Boston.

In Boston, General Thomas Gage, commanding the British garrison, knew of the warlike bustle throughout the countryside but considered his army too small to do anything until reinforcements should arrive. He resisted the advice of less cautious officers, who assured him that the Americans would never dare actually to fight, that they would back down quickly before any show of British force. Major John Pitcairn, for example, insisted that a single "small action" with the burning of a few towns would "set everything to rights."

When General Gage received orders to arrest the rebel leaders Sam Adams and John Hancock, known to be in the vicinity of Lexington, he still hesitated. But when he heard that the minutemen had stored a large supply of gunpowder in Concord (eighteen miles from Boston) he at last decided to act. On the

night of April 18, 1775, he sent a detachment of about 1,000 men out from Boston on the road to Lexington and Concord. He intended to surprise the colonials and seize the illegal supplies without bloodshed.

But patriots in Boston were watching the British movements closely; and during the night two horsemen, William Dawes and Paul Revere, were dispatched to warn the villages and farms. When the redcoats arrived in Lexington the next day, several dozen minutemen awaited them on the town common. Shots were fired and minutemen fell; eight of them were killed and ten more wounded. Advancing to Concord, the British discovered that the Americans had hastily removed most of the powder supply, but the redcoats burned what was left of it. All along the road from Concord back to Boston, the British were harassed by the continual gunfire of farmers hiding behind trees, rocks, and stone fences. By the end of the day, the British had lost almost three times as many men as the Americans.

The first shots—the "shots heard round the world," as Americans later called them—had been fired. But who had fired them first? According to one of the minutemen at Lexington, Major Pitcairn had shouted to the colonists on his arrival, "Disperse, ye rebels!" When this command was ignored, he had given the order to fire. British officers and soldiers told a different story. They claimed that the minutemen had fired first, that only after seeing the flash of American guns had they begun to shoot. Whatever the truth, the rebels succeeded in circulating their account well ahead of the British version, adorning it with horrible tales of British atrocities. The effect was to rally to the rebel cause thousands of colonists, North and South, who previously had had little en-

thusiasm for it. Now that the English had, as they believed, opened fire on American citizens, the issue was clearly drawn.

It was not immediately clear to the British, and even to many Americans, that the skirmishes at Lexington and Concord were the first battles of a war. Many saw them as simply another example of the tensions that had been afflicting Anglo-American relations for years. But whether they recognized it at the time or not, the British and the Americans had taken a decisive step. The War for Independence had begun.

SUGGESTED READINGS

General Histories. Robert Middlekauff, *The Glorious Cause: The American Revolution, 1763–1789* (1982); Edward Countryman, *The American Revolution* (1985); Alfred E. Young, Jr., ed., *The American Revolution* (1976); John C. Miller, *Origins of the American Revolution* (1957); Merrill Jensen, *The Founding of a Nation* (1968); Edmund S. Morgan, *The Birth of the Republic* (1956); J. R. Alden, *A History of the American Revolution* (1969); Charles M. Andrews, *The Colonial Background of the American Revolution* (1924, rev. 1931); Lawrence Henry Gipson, *The Coming of the Revolution, 1763–1775* (1954); Ian R. Christie and Benjamin W. Labaree, *Empire or Independence, 1760–1776* (1976); Ian R. Christie, *Crisis of Empire* (1966).

The British Imperial System. Lawrence Henry Gipson, *The British Empire Before the American Revolution*, 15 vols. (1936–1970); Robert C. Newbold, *The Albany Congress and Plan of Union of 1754* (1955); Richard Pares, *War and Trade in the West Indies, 1739–1763* (1936); Howard H. Peckham, *The Colonial Wars, 1689–1762* (1963); Alan Rogers, *Empire and Liberty* (1974); Lewis B. Namier, *England in the Age of the American Revolution*, rev. ed. (1961) and *The Structure of Politics at the Accession of George III*, rev. ed. (1961); John Brewer, *Party Ideology and Popular Politics at the Accession of George III* (1967); Bernard Donoughue, *British Politics and the American Revolution: The Path to War, 1773–1775* (1965); John Brooke, *King George III* (1972); Michael Kammen, *A Rope of Sand* (1968).

The French and the Indians. Fred Anderson, *A People's Army: Massachusetts Soldiers and Society in the Seven Years War* (1984); Thomas P. Abernethy, *Western Lands and the American Revolution* (1937); J. M. Sosin, *Whitehall and the Wilderness* (1961); David H. Corkran, *The Cherokee Frontier* (1962); R. S. Cotterill, *The Southern Indians* (1954); Howard H. Peckham, *Pontiac and the Indian Uprising* (1947); William Pencak, *War, Politics, and Revolution in Provincial Massachusetts* (1981); Francis Jennings, *Empire of Fortune* (1988), and *The Ambiguous Iroquois Empire* (1984).

Merchants and the Empire. Joseph Ernst, *Money and Politics in America, 1755–1775* (1973); Arthur M. Schlesinger, *The Colonial Merchants and the American Revolution* (1917); Oliver M. Dickinson, *The Navigation Acts and the American Revolution* (1951); Thomas Doerflinger, *A Vigorous Spirit of Enterprise: Merchants and Economic Development in Revolutionary Philadelphia* (1986).

American Resistance. David Ammerman, *In the Common Cause* (1974); Hiller B. Zobel, *The Boston Massacre* (1970); Edmund S. Morgan and Helen M. Morgan, *The Stamp Act Crisis* (1953); Benjamin W. Labaree, *The Boston Tea Party* (1964); John Shy, *Toward Lexington* (1965); Pauline Maier, *From Resistance to Revolution* (1972); Dirk Hoerder, *Crowd Action in Revolutionary Massachusetts* (1977); Paul A. Gilje, *The Road to Mobocracy: Popular Disorder in New York City, 1763–1834* (1987).

Revolutionary Ideology. Bernard Bailyn, *The Ideological Origins of the American Revolution* (1967); Ian R. Christie, *Wilkes, Wyvil, and Reform* (1962); George Rudé, *Wilkes and Liberty* (1962); Isaac Kramnick, *Bolingbroke and His Circle* (1968); Clinton Rossiter, *Seedtime of the Republic* (1953); Nathan Hatch, *The Sacred Cause of Liberty* (1977); Richard Merritt, *Symbols of American Community, 1735–1775* (1966); Gary B. Nash, *The Urban Crucible* (1979); Rhys Isaac, *The Transformation of Virginia, 1740–1790* (1982).

Revolutionary Politics. Carl Becker, *The History of Political Parties in the Province of New York* (1909); Richard D. Brown, *Revolutionary Politics in Massachusetts* (1970); David Lovejoy, *Rhode Island Politics and the American Revolution* (1958); L. R. Gerlach, *Prologue to Independence* (1976); Theodore Thayer, *Pennsylvania Politics and the Growth of Democracy* (1953); Ronald Hoffman, *A Spirit of Dissension* (1973); R. E. Brown and B. K. Brown, *Virginia, 1705–1786* (1964); Charles S. Sydnor, *Gentlemen Freeholders* (1952).

The Other Pilgrims

The story of the Pilgrims and the first Thanksgiving remains one of the oldest and best known in American history. Schoolchildren still learn about the Pilgrims' flight from religious persecution in England, their efforts to make a new home at Plymouth, and their first celebration with their Indian neighbors to give thanks for their survival, as one of the great symbolic events of the American past.

But there is another pilgrim story that is much less familiar. The colonists at Plymouth, like those up and down the Atlantic seaboard, did not travel alone. Along with themselves and their worldly goods, they brought to North America a host of other organisms, plants, and animals that were familiar to Europeans but completely unknown to the Indians. The colonization of America was as much a biological invasion as a cultural one, and its long-term result was a subtle but radical transformation of the American landscape.

Most devastating to the Indians were the Old World diseases. Among these were the childhood illnesses—chicken pox, measles, mumps—that were so common in Europe as to be an expected part of growing up. Others were more serious epidemics like smallpox or debilitating illnesses like tuberculosis. All had been absent from North America, which meant that the Indians' immune systems were not equipped with antibodies that could defend against them. The area around Plymouth had experienced a mysterious European epidemic just three years before the Pilgrims arrived. The illness had depopulated the area's Indian villages. Sixteen years later, equally large numbers of Indians fell victims to a devastating smallpox epidemic. In Plymouth as in most parts of North America, Indian communities experienced population declines of 50 to 90 percent as a result of these epidemics, which would continue for centuries.

The disappearance of so many Indians was itself a profound change in the American landscape, but Indians who survived the epidemics soon helped European colonists bring about many other changes. Among the most important ecologically was the fur trade. Indian demand for trade goods encouraged tribes to hunt native animals much more intensively than before. Animal populations declined as hunting pressure increased, so much so that areas like New England had lost most of their

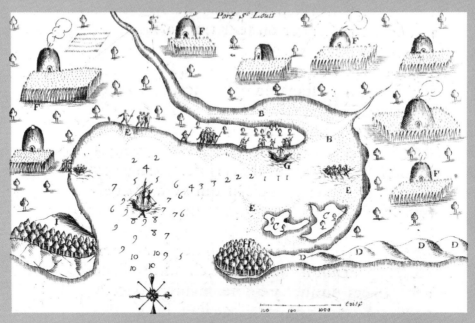

Champlain's Map of Plymouth Plantation, 1605
When Samuel de Champlain visited Plymouth, Massachusetts, in 1605, he drew this map of the bay showing numerous Indian settlements in the vicinity. The many cornfields suggest what a prosperous community this was. Fifteen years later, when the Pilgrims arrived, most of these Indians would be dead from European diseases. (Houghton Library, Harvard University)

large mammals within two centuries of the first settlements. By 1800, such animals as deer, moose, turkeys, and wolves had vanished from the lands around Plymouth, and they were fast disappearing elsewhere as well.

Their departure made room for the domesticated grazing animals that colonists brought with them. Cattle, sheep, hogs, and horses were among the most important members of colonial society, furnishing such diverse items as meat, leather, milk, cheese, textile fibers, and animal power for doing work. Most of these animals had been entirely absent from Indian America. Increasing their livestock became one of the colonists' overriding goals. As the herds expanded, so did the colonists' need for new land. It led them to cut down forests to create new pastures and to plant those pastures with imported European species like clover and bluegrass. Wherever the animals grazed, they encouraged the spread of European weeds that thrived on disturbed soils. Thus it was that dozens of plant migrants made their way to America and eventually became some of its most common inhabitants: dandelions, stinging nettles, chickweeds, mulleins, and others. The Indians went so far as to call plantain "Englishman's foot" because of the way it sprang up wherever the Europeans settled or grazed animals.

Cattle and horses were critical to colonial agriculture because they made it possible to plant crops using plows. Indians had depended for their farming on hoes, which required more human labor and limited the amount of land that one person or family could tend. Although some of the crops the colonists planted with their plows were in fact Indian—corn being the most important—many were brought across the Atlantic as seeds. Wheat, rye, barley, and oats soon appeared in colonists' fields and quickly spread wherever the colonists went. Scattered in plowed fields, such grains furnished colonists with bread and helped feed their animals.

But not all colonial crops involved plows. In their gardens, colonial women tended vegetables and herbs that were a mixture of Indian and European crops, using metal-edged hoes to do so. Cabbages, peas, and potatoes (a Caribbean plant reimported from Europe) lent variety to the colonial diet. Herbs added flavorings to otherwise bland meals, furnished medicines for healing, and supplied the color in homespun fabrics. In the orchards around their homesteads, colonists planted apples, pears, plums, cherries, and other fruit trees. From apples came one of the colonists' favorite beverages, cider, and from orchards generally came fresh fruit, preserves, and other sweeteners of colonial tables.

Everywhere, European migrants brought with them the species with which they were most familiar and on which they most depended for their livelihoods. To enable those plants and animals to thrive, colonists sought to re-create the ecological conditions under which they had lived on the other side of the Atlantic. Toward that end, they divided their lands into the familiar functional units of a peasant agricultural system: grain fields, pastures, hay meadows, woodlots, orchards, gardens, barnyards. They built fences to separate the places reserved for animals from the places where crops grew, lest the animals eat the crops. And so the fence—a con-

Domesticated Animals at Plymouth

Among the most important Eurasian species that colonists like the Pilgrims introduced to North America were domesticated grazing animals. Goats ate almost anything and supplied their owners with dairy products; horses, although rare at first, helped pull plows and wagons. Even more important to the colonists were cattle, pigs, and sheep. (Plimoth Plantation Photo)

struction almost entirely absent from Indian America—became for the colonists a symbol of "improvement," a sign that the landscapes of the New World were becoming more like those of the Old.

The changing landscape was in many ways a reproduction of the agricultural world they had left behind in England, and it was familiar precisely because it contained so many of the plants and animals that lay at the foundation of English society. When the Pilgrims celebrated their first November harvest, they were partly thanking their Indian neighbors for the corn and wild meat they had shared. But they gave thanks too for their own crops and animals, on which not just their survival but their sense of safety, familiarity, and home depended. Those other, nonhuman, pilgrims were in fact the foundation on which the whole of colonial society would be built. Without them, the English colonies would never have succeeded as they did.

WASHINGTON crossed here
Christmas-eve 1776, aided by Genl
Sullivan, Greene, lord Sterling, Mercer &c

***Washington Crossing the Delaware,* by Edward Hicks**
This idealized nineteenth-century depiction of a dramatic moment in the American Revolution
suggests how important memories of the war remained to Americans even a century later. Although
the original caption identifies the date of the crossing as Christmas Eve, 1776, the actual date was
Christmas Night. (*Bucks County Historical Society, Pennsylvania*)

CHAPTER 5

The American Revolution

Two struggles occurred simultaneously during the seven years of war that began in April of 1775. One was the military conflict with Great Britain. The second was a political conflict within America. The two struggles had profound effects on each other.

The military conflict was, by the standards of later wars, a relatively modest one. Battle deaths on the American side totaled fewer than 5,000. The technology of warfare was so crude that cannons and rifles were effective only at extraordinarily close range; and fighting of any kind was virtually out of the question in bad weather. Yet the war in America was, by the standards of its own day, an unusually savage conflict, pitting not only army against army, but at times the population at large against a powerful external force. This shift of the war from a traditional, conventional struggle to a new kind of conflict—a revolutionary war for liberation—made it possible for the United States finally to defeat the vastly more powerful British.

At the same time, Americans were wrestling with the great political questions that the conflict necessarily produced: first, whether to demand independence from Britain; then, how to structure the new nation they had proclaimed. Only the first of these questions had been resolved by the time of the British surrender at Yorktown in 1781. But by then the United States had already established itself—both in its own mind and in the mind of much of the rest of the world—as a nation with a special mission, a society dedicated to new, enlightened ideals. Thomas

Paine, himself an important figure in shaping the Revolution, reflected the opinion of many when he claimed that the American War for Independence had "contributed more to enlighten the world, and diffuse a spirit of freedom and liberality among mankind, than any human event . . . that ever preceded it."

The States United

Although many Americans had been expecting a military conflict with Britain for months, even years, the actual beginning of hostilities in 1775 found the colonies generally unprepared for the enormous challenges awaiting them. A still-unformed nation, with a population less than a third as large as the 9 million of Great Britain, and with vastly inferior economic and military resources, faced the task of mobilizing for war against the world's greatest armed power. And Americans faced that task deeply divided about what they were fighting for.

Defining American War Aims

Three weeks after the battles of Lexington and Concord, when the Second Continental Congress met in the State House in Philadelphia, the delegates (again from every colony except Georgia, which was not represented until the following autumn) agreed to support the war. But they disagreed about its purpose. At one extreme was a group led by the Adams cousins (John and Samuel), Richard Henry Lee of Virginia, and others, who already favored independence; at the other extreme was a group led by such moderates as John Dickinson of Pennsylvania, who hoped for an early reconciliation with Great Britain. Most of the delegates tried to find some middle ground between these positions. Their uncertainty was reflected in the nature of two very different declarations, which they adopted in quick succession. Although they dismissed Lord North's Conciliatory Propositions as insincere, they voted for one last appeal to the king: the so-called Olive Branch Petition. Then, on July 6, 1775, they adopted a Declaration of the Causes and Necessity of Taking Up Arms. It proclaimed that the British government had left the American people with only two alternatives, "unconditional submission to the tyranny of irritated ministers or resistance by force."

As the war began, most Americans believed they were fighting not for independence but for a redress of grievances within the British Empire. During the first year of fighting, however, many of them began to change their minds, for several reasons. First, the costs of the war—human and financial—were so high that the original war aims began to seem too modest to justify them. Second, what lingering affection they retained for the mother country greatly diminished when the British began trying to recruit Indians, black slaves, and foreign mercenaries (the hated "Hessians") against them. Third, and most important, they felt that they were being forced toward independence when the British government rejected the Olive Branch Petition and instead enacted the Prohibitory Act, which closed the colonies to all overseas trade and made no concessions to American demands except an offer to pardon repentant rebels. The British enforced the Prohibitory Act with a naval blockade of colonial ports.

The publication in January 1776 of an impassioned pamphlet crystallized these feelings. It was called, simply, *Common Sense*. Its author, unmentioned on the title page, was Thomas Paine, who had emigrated from England to America less than two years before (with letters of introduction from Benjamin Franklin, whom he had met in London). Long a failure in various trades, Paine now proved a brilliant success as a revolutionary propagandist. His pamphlet—reprinted month after month by the thousands, passed from hand to hand, debated and

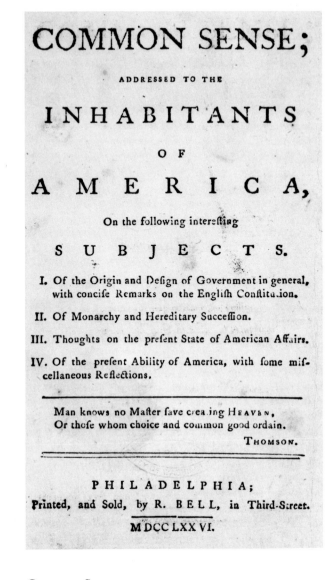

Common Sense

Shown here is the title page of the first edition of Thomas Paine's influential pamphlet, published anonymously in Philadelphia on January 10, 1776. Paine served in Washington's army during the campaigns in New Jersey and at the same time wrote a series of essays designed to arouse support for the Patriot cause. They were collectively titled *The Crisis* (the first of them contains the famous phrase "These are the times that try men's souls"). In later years Paine took an active part in the French Revolution, on behalf of which he published *The Rights of Man* (1791–1792). He also wrote *The Age of Reason* (1794–1796), which attacked conventional Christian beliefs and promoted his own "deist" philosophy. He returned to America in 1802 and spent the last years before his death in 1809 in poverty and obscurity. (Library of Congress)

discussed—helped change the American outlook toward the war. Paine's purpose was to expose the folly of continuing to believe reconciliation with Britain was possible. He wanted to turn the anger of Americans away from the specific parliamentary measures they were resisting and toward what he considered the root of the problem—the English constitution itself. It was not enough, he argued, for Americans to continue blaming their problems on particular ministers, or even on Parliament. It was the king, and the system that permitted him to rule, that was to blame. Thus it was simple common sense for Americans to break completely with a government that could produce so corrupt a monarch as George III, a government that could inflict such brutality on its own people, a government that could drag Americans into wars in which America had no interest. The island kingdom of England was no more fit to rule the American continent than a satellite was fit to rule the sun.

The Decision for Independence

Common Sense had an enormous influence on American thinking. It sold more than 100,000 copies in only a few months. To many of its readers it was a revelation. Although sentiment for independence was still far from unanimous, the first months of 1776 saw a rapid growth of support for the idea.

In the midst of all this, the Continental Congress (meeting again in Philadelphia) was moving slowly and tentatively toward a final break with England. It opened American ports to the ships of all nations except Great Britain, entered into communication with foreign powers, and recommended to the various colonies that they establish governments without the authority of the empire, as in fact most already were doing. Congress also appointed a committee to draft a formal declaration of independence. On July 2, 1776, it adopted a resolution: "That these United Colonies are, and, of right, ought to be, free and independent states; that they are absolved from all allegiance to the British crown, and that all political connexion between them and the state of Great Britain is, and ought to be, totally dissolved." Two days later, on July 4, Congress approved the Declaration of Independence itself, which provided the formal justifications for the actions the delegates had in fact taken two days earlier.

The Declaration was largely the work of Thomas Jefferson, a thirty-three-year-old Virginian,

although it was slightly revised by Benjamin Franklin and John Adams, his colleagues on the drafting committee. Congress made more drastic changes, striking out passages that condemned the British people and the slave trade. As Adams afterward observed, Jefferson said little in the document that was new. Its virtue lay in the eloquence with which it expressed beliefs already widespread in America.

The document was in two parts. In the first, Jefferson restated the familiar contract theory of John Locke: the theory that governments were formed to protect the rights of life, liberty, and property; Jefferson gave the theory a more idealistic tone by referring instead to the rights of "life, liberty and the pursuit of happiness." In the second part he listed the alleged crimes of the king, who, with the backing of Parliament, had violated his contract with the colonists and thus had forfeited all claim to their loyalty.

The Declaration's ringing endorsement of the idea that "all men are created equal" helped stimulate humanitarian movements of many kinds in the United States; abroad it helped inspire the French Revolution's own Declaration of the Rights of Man. More immediately, the Declaration—and its claim of American sovereignty—led to increased foreign aid for the struggling rebels and prepared the way for France's intervention on their side. It steeled American Patriots, as those opposing the British called themselves, to fight on, to reject the idea of a peace that stopped short of winning independence. And at the same time it created deep divisions within American society.

At the news of the Declaration of Independence, crowds in Philadelphia, Boston, and other places gathered to cheer, fire guns and cannons, and ring church bells. But there were many in America who did not rejoice. Some had disapproved of the war from the beginning. Others had been willing to support it only so long as its aims did not conflict with their basic loyalty to the king. Such people were a minority, but a large one. They called themselves Loyalists; they were known as Tories to the Whig or Patriot majority.

The Declaration of Independence simply confirmed what circumstances had already ensured: that the American people, at war with Great Britain, would have to devise a means of governing themselves and supporting their military struggle. To meet these new demands, new institutions emerged at both the local and the national levels.

The individual colonies now began to call themselves states—a reflection of their belief that each

Raising the Liberty Pole, 1776
In this nineteenth-century engraving by John C. McRae, Americans celebrate the Declaration of Independence in July 1776 by raising a flagpole decked with Patriot banners. In the background other enthusiasts take down a sign bearing a likeness of George III.   (Library of Congress)

province was now in some respects a separate and sovereign entity. And as states, they had to create new governments to replace the royal governments that independence had repudiated. By 1781, most states had produced written constitutions for themselves that established republican governments; some of these governments survived, with only minor changes, for decades to come.

At the national level, however, the process was more uncertain and less successful. For a time, Americans were uncertain whether they even wanted a real national government; the Continental Congress had never been considered more than a coordinating mechanism, and virtually everyone considered the individual colonies (now states) the real centers of authority. Yet fighting a war required a certain

amount of central direction, and Americans began almost immediately to try to reconcile these two contradictory assumptions.

No sooner had the Congress appointed a committee to draft a declaration of independence than it appointed another to draft a plan of union. And after much debate and many revisions, the Congress adopted the committee's plan in November 1777. The document (which was not formally ratified by the states until 1781) was known as the Articles of Confederation. It did little more than confirm the weak, decentralized system already in operation. The Continental Congress would survive as the chief coordinating agency of the war effort, but its powers over the individual states would be extraordinarily limited. Indeed, the Articles did not make it entirely clear that

Revolutionary Soldiers
Jean Baptiste de Verger, a French officer serving in America during the Revolution, kept a journal of his experiences illustrated with watercolors. Here he portrays four American soldiers carrying different kinds of arms: a black infantryman with a light rifle, a musketman, a rifleman, and an artilleryman.   (Brown University Library)

the Congress was to be a real government at all. The war was won as much in spite of as because of its efforts. (See pp. 149–157 for a fuller discussion of the structure of the new state and national governments.)

Mobilizing for War

Congress and the states faced overwhelming tasks in raising and organizing armies, providing the necessary supplies and equipment, and paying the costs of war. Supplies of most kinds were scarce at the outset, and shortages persisted to the end. America's numerous gunsmiths were not able to meet the wartime demand for guns and ammunition; nor were they able to produce heavy arms. Congress in 1777 established a government arsenal at Springfield, Massachusetts. Even so, Americans managed to manufac-

ture only a small fraction of the equipment they used. They supplemented their own manufactures with matériel that fell into their hands on the seizure of British forts, the surrender of British armies, and the capture of supply ships by American privateers. But they got most of their war materials from European nations, particularly from France.

One of the nation's severest problems was finding a way to finance the war. Congress lacked the authority and the states generally lacked the inclination to impose taxes on the public. Hard currency (gold and silver) was scarce in America, as it always had been; and when Congress requisitioned money from the states, none of them contributed more than a small part of its expected share. Congress had only limited success raising money by floating long-term loans at home, since few Americans could afford war bonds and those few usually preferred to invest in more profitable ventures, such as privateering. So it had no choice in the end but to issue paper money. Continental currency came from the printing presses in large and repeated batches. The states added sizable paper-currency issues of their own.

The result, predictably, was inflation. Prices rose to fant..stic heights, and the value of paper money fell proportionately. Many American farmers and merchants began to prefer doing business with the British, who could pay for goods in gold or silver coin. (That was one reason why George Washington's troops suffered from severe food shortages at Valley Forge in the winter of 1777–1778; many Philadelphia merchants would not sell to them.) Congress tried in vain to stem the inflationary spiral. It recommended price control regulations, but soon realized the futility of that approach. It tried to retire its paper currency by accepting it for payment of taxes at a fortieth of its face value and declaring it worthless for any other purpose. Ultimately, however, it was able to finance the war effort only by borrowing heavily from other nations.

Only a small proportion of eligible American men were willing to volunteer for the American armies once the first surge of patriotism ebbed after 1775. The states had to resort to persuasion and force, to bounties and the draft. Once recruited, militiamen remained under the control of their respective states. Congress very early recognized the disadvantages of this decentralized system and called for a Continental army with a single commander in chief. George Washington, a forty-three-year-old Virginia planter-aristocrat who had commanded colonial forces during the French and Indian War, possessed more experience than any other American-born officer available. He had also been an early advocate of independence. Above all, he was admired, respected, and trusted by nearly all Patriots. He was the unanimous choice of the delegates, and he took command in June 1775.

Congress had chosen well. Throughout the war, Washington kept faithfully at his task, despite difficulties and discouragements that would have daunted a lesser man. He had to deal with serious problems of morale among soldiers who consistently received short rations and low pay; open mutinies broke out in 1781 among the Pennsylvania and New Jersey troops. During the discouraging winter of Valley Forge, moreover, some congressmen and army officers apparently began conspiring (in the so-called Conway Cabal, named for Thomas Conway, one of its alleged leaders) to replace Washington as com-

mander in chief. And the Continental Congress, Washington's "employers," always seemed too little interested in supplying him with manpower and equipment and too much interested in interfering with his conduct of military operations

Washington was not without shortcomings as a military commander; indeed, he lost more battles than he won. Yet for all his faults and failures, he was indisputably a great war leader. With the aid of foreign military experts such as the Marquis de Lafayette from France and the Baron von Steuben from Prussia, he succeeded in building and holding together a force of fewer than 10,000 men (not counting the militias of the separate states) that ultimately prevailed against the mightiest power in the world. Even more important, perhaps, in a new nation still unsure of either its purposes or its structure, with a central government both weak and contentious, Washington was the indispensable man whose steadiness, courage, and dedication to his cause provided the army—and the people—with a symbol of stability around which they could rally. He was not the most brilliant of the country's early leaders. But in the crucial years of the war, at least, he was the most successful in holding the new nation together.

The War for Independence

On the surface, at least, all the advantages in the military struggle between America and Great Britain appeared to lie with the British. They possessed the greatest navy and the best-equipped army in the world. They had access to the resources of an empire. They had a coherent structure of command. The Americans, by contrast, were struggling to create an army and a government at the same time that they were trying to fight a war.

Yet the United States had advantages that were not at first apparent. Americans were fighting on their own ground, far from the center of British might. They were more committed to the conflict; the British people were only half-heartedly supporting the war. And beginning in 1777, the Americans had the benefit of substantial aid from abroad, after the American war had merged with a world contest in which Great Britain faced the strongest powers of Europe—most notably France—in a struggle for imperial supremacy.

But the American victory was not simply the

The Battle of Bunker Hill, 1775
British troops attack Patriot forces outside Boston on June 17, 1775, in the first great battle of the American Revolution. The British ultimately drove the Americans from their positions on Breed's Hill and Bunker Hill, but only after suffering enormous casualties. General Gage, the British commander, reported to his superiors in London after the battle: "These people show a spirit and conduct against us they never showed against the French." This anonymous painting reveals the array of British troops and naval support and also shows the bombardment and burning of Charles Town from artillery in Boston.   (National Gallery of Art, Washington)

result of these advantages, or even of the remarkable spirit and resourcefulness of the people and the army. It was a result, too, of a series of egregious blunders and miscalculations by the British in the early stages of the fighting, when England could (and probably should) have won. And it was, finally, a result of the transformation of the war—through three distinct phases—into a new kind of conflict that the British military, for all its strength, could not hope to win.

The First Phase: New England

For the first year of the fighting—from the spring of 1775 to the spring of 1776—the British remained un-

certain about whether or not they were actually engaged in a war. Many English authorities continued to believe that what was happening in America was a limited, local conflict and that British forces were simply attempting to quell pockets of rebellion in the contentious area around Boston. Gradually, however, the colonial forces took the offensive and proved to England that the war was not confined to Massachusetts, that the entire territory of the American colonies was becoming a battleground.

After the British withdrawal from Concord and Lexington in April 1775, American forces besieged the army of General Thomas Gage in Boston. The Patriots suffered severe casualties in the Battle of

The Revolution in the North, 1775–1776

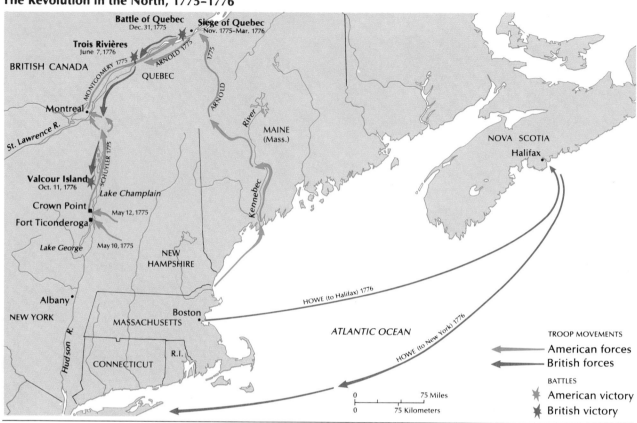

Bunker Hill (actually fought on Breed's Hill) on June 17, 1775, and were ultimately driven from their position there. But they inflicted far greater losses on the enemy (indeed, the heaviest casualties the British were to suffer in the entire war) and thereafter continued to tighten the siege. By the first months of 1776, the British finally concluded that Boston was not the best place from which to wage a continental war. Not only was it in the center of the most fervently anti-British region of the colonies; it was also tactically indefensible—a narrow neck of land, easily isolated and besieged. By late winter, in fact, Patriot forces had surrounded the city and had occupied strategic positions on the heights. And so, on March 17, 1776 (a date still celebrated in Boston as Evacuation Day), the redcoats departed Boston for Halifax with hundreds of Loyalist refugees. Within a year from the firing of the first shots, the enemy had been driven—temporarily—from American soil.

Elsewhere, the war was proceeding fitfully and inconclusively. To the south, at Moore's Creek

Bridge in North Carolina, a band of Patriots crushed an uprising of Loyalists on February 27, 1776, and thereby discouraged a British plan to invade the Southern states. The British had based those plans on the expectation of substantial aid from local Tories; they realized now that such aid might not be as effective as they had hoped. To the north, the Americans themselves undertook an invasion of Canada—hoping to remove the British threat and to win the Canadians to their cause. Benedict Arnold, the commander of a small American force, threatened Quebec in late 1775 and early 1776 after a winter march of incredible hardship. He was joined by Richard Montgomery, who combined his forces with Arnold's and took command of both. Montgomery was killed in the assault on the city; and although a wounded Arnold kept up the siege for a time, the Quebec campaign ended in frustration. A civilian commission sent to Canada by Congress and headed by the seventy-year-old Franklin met with no more success in its efforts to win the allegiance of the northern colonists. Canada was not to become the fourteenth state.

The British evacuation in 1776 was not, therefore, so much a victory for the Americans (although their accomplishments so far had been impressive) as a reflection of changing English assumptions about the war. By the spring of 1776, it had become clear to the British that the conflict was not a local phenomenon in the area around Boston. The American campaigns in Canada, the agitation in the South, and the growing evidence of colonial unity all suggested that England must be prepared to fight a much larger conflict. The departure of the British marked, therefore, a shift in strategy more than an admission of defeat.

The Second Phase: The Mid-Atlantic Region

The next phase of the war, which lasted from 1776 until early 1778, was when the British were in the best position to win. Indeed, had it not been for a series of blunders and misfortunes, they probably would have crushed the rebellion then. For during this period the struggle became, for the most part, a traditional, conventional war. And in that, the Americans were woefully overmatched.

The British regrouped quickly after their retreat from Boston. During the summer of 1776, in the weeks immediately following the Declaration of Independence, the waters around the city of New York became filled with the most formidable military force Great Britain had ever sent abroad. Hundreds of men-of-war and troopships and 32,000 disciplined soldiers arrived, under the command of the affable Sir William Howe. Howe felt no particular hostility toward the Americans. He hoped to awe them into submission rather than shoot them; and he believed that most of them, if given a chance, would show that they were loyal to the king. In a parley with commissioners from Congress, he offered them a choice between submission with royal pardon and a battle against overwhelming odds.

To oppose Howe's awesome array, Washington could muster only about 19,000 poorly armed and trained soldiers, including both Continentals and state troops; he had no navy at all. Yet without hesitation, the Americans rejected Howe's offer and chose continued war—which meant inevitably a succession of defeats. The British pushed the defenders off Long Island, compelled them to abandon Man-

hattan, and then drove them in slow retreat over the plains of New Jersey, across the Delaware River, and into Pennsylvania.

For eighteenth-century Europeans, warfare was a seasonal activity. The British settled down for the winter with occupation forces at various points in New Jersey and with an outpost of Hessians (German mercenaries) at Trenton on the Delaware. But Washington did not content himself with sitting still. On Christmas night 1776, he daringly recrossed the icy river, surprised and scattered the Hessians, and occupied the town. Then he advanced to Princeton and drove a force of redcoats from their base in the college there. But Washington was unable to hold either Princeton or Trenton, and he finally took refuge for the rest of the winter in the hills around Morristown. As the campaign of 1776 came to an end, the Americans could console themselves with the thought that they had won two minor victories, that their main army was still intact, and that the invaders were no nearer than before to the decisive triumph that Howe had so confidently anticipated. The heavy British advantages in men and supplies, however, remained.

For the campaigns of 1777 the British devised a strategy that, if Howe had stuck to it, might have cut the United States in two and prepared the way for final victory by Great Britain. Howe would move from New York up the Hudson to Albany, while another force, in a gigantic pincers movement, would come down from Canada to meet him. One of Howe's ambitious younger officers, the dashing John Burgoyne, secured command of this northern force and elaborated on the plan by preparing for a two-pronged attack along both the Mohawk and the upper Hudson approaches to Albany.

But after setting this plan in motion, Howe made a major (and many believed inexplicable) blunder and adopted a different plan for himself. He decided to launch an assault on the rebel capital Philadelphia—an assault that would, he hoped, discourage the Patriots, rally the Loyalists, and bring the war to a speedy conclusion. He removed the bulk of his forces from New York by sea, landed at the head of the Chesapeake Bay, brushed Washington aside at the Battle of Brandywine Creek on September 11, and proceeded north to Philadelphia, which he was able to occupy with little resistance. Meanwhile, Washington, after an unsuccessful October 4 attack at Germantown (just outside Philadelphia), went into winter quarters at Valley Forge. The Continental Congress, now dislodged from its capital, reassembled at York, Pennsylvania.

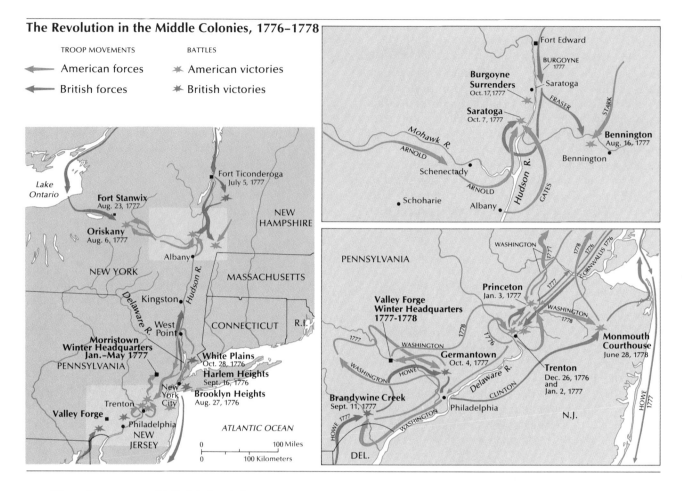

The Revolution in the Middle Colonies, 1776–1778

TROOP MOVEMENTS

⟵ American forces

⟵ British forces

BATTLES

✳ American victories

✳ British victories

Lake Ontario

Fort Stanwix
Aug. 23, 1777

Oriskany
Aug. 6, 1777

Fort Ticonderoga
July 5, 1777

NEW HAMPSHIRE

Albany

NEW YORK

Delaware R.

Kingston

Hudson R.

MASSACHUSETTS

West Point

CONNECTICUT   R.I.

Morristown
Winter Headquarters
Jan.–May 1777

PENNSYLVANIA

White Plains
Oct. 28, 1776

Harlem Heights
Sept. 16, 1776

New York City

Brooklyn Heights
Aug. 27, 1776

Trenton

Valley Forge

Philadelphia

NEW JERSEY

ATLANTIC OCEAN

0   100 Miles

0   100 Kilometers

Fort Edward

BURGOYNE 1777

Burgoyne Surrenders
Oct. 17, 1777

Saratoga

FRASER

STARK

Saratoga
Oct. 7, 1777

Mohawk R.

ARNOLD

Bennington
Aug. 16, 1777

Bennington

Schenectady

ARNOLD

Schoharie

Albany

Hudson R.

GATES

PENNSYLVANIA

WASHINGTON

1777

1778

1776

CORNWALLIS 1776

Princeton
Jan. 3, 1777

Valley Forge
Winter Headquarters
1777-1778

1777

WASHINGTON
1778

1778

WASHINGTON

1777

WASHINGTON

HOWE

Germantown
Oct. 4, 1777

Delaware R.

1776

CLINTON

Trenton
Dec. 26, 1776
and
Jan. 2, 1777

Monmouth
Courthouse
June 28, 1778

Brandywine Creek
Sept. 11, 1777

HOWE 1777

WASHINGTON

Philadelphia

N.J.

HOWE 1777

DEL.

Howe's move to Philadelphia left Burgoyne to carry out his twofold campaign in the north alone. He sent Colonel Barry St. Leger with a fast-moving force up the St. Lawrence River toward Lake Ontario and the headwaters of the Mohawk, while Burgoyne himself advanced directly down the upper Hudson Valley. He got off to a flying start. He seized Fort Ticonderoga easily and with it an enormous store of powder and supplies; that caused such consternation in Congress that the delegates removed General Philip Schuyler from command of American forces in the north and replaced him with Horatio Gates.

By the time Gates took command, Burgoyne had already experienced a sudden reversal of his military fortunes as a result of two staggering defeats. In one of them—at Oriskany, New York, on August 6—a Patriot band of German farmers led by Nicholas Herkimer held off a force of Indians and Tories commanded by St. Leger. That gave Benedict Arnold time to go to the relief of Fort Stanwix and close off the Mohawk Valley to St. Leger's advance.

In the other battle—at Bennington, Vermont, on August 16—New England militiamen under the Bunker Hill veteran John Stark severely mauled a detachment that Burgoyne had sent out to seek supplies. Short of materials, with all help cut off, Burgoyne fought several costly engagements and then withdrew to Saratoga, where Gates surrounded him. On October 17, 1777, Burgoyne ordered what was left of his army, nearly 5,000 men, to lay down their arms.

The campaign in upstate New York was not just a British defeat. It was a setback for the ambitious efforts of several Iroquois leaders, who hoped to involve Indian forces in the English military effort, believing that a British victory would help stem white encroachments on tribal lands.

Although the Iroquois Confederacy had declared its neutrality in the Revolutionary War in 1776, not all Native Americans were content to remain passive. Among those who worked to expand the Indian role in the war were a Mohawk brother and sister, Joseph and Mary Brant. Both were people of stature within the Mohawk nation: Joseph was a celebrated warrior; Mary was a magnetic woman and the widow of Sir William Johnson, the British superintendent of Indians, who had achieved wide popularity among the tribes. The Brants persuaded their own tribe to contribute to the British cause and attracted the support of the Seneca and Cayuga as well. They played an important role in Burgoyne's unsuccessful campaigns in the North. But the alliance was a sign of the growing divisions within the Iroquois Confederacy. Only three of the six nations of the Confederacy supported the British. The Oneida and the Tuscarora backed the Americans; the Onondaga split into several factions. The three-century-old Confederacy, weakened by the aftermath of the French and Indian War, continued to unravel.

The alliance had other unhappy consequences for the Iroquois. A year after Oriskany, Indians joined British troops in a series of raids on outlying white settlements in upstate New York. Months later, Patriot forces under the command of General John Sullivan harshly retaliated, wreaking such destruction on Indian settlements that large groups of Iroquois fled north into Canada to seek refuge. Many never returned.

To the Patriots, however, the New York campaign was a remarkable victory. News of it reverberated throughout the new nation and through Europe as well. The British surrender at Saratoga became a major turning point in the war—above all, perhaps, because it led directly to an alliance between the United States and France.

The British failure to win the war during this period, a period in which they had overwhelming advantages, was in large part a result of their own mistakes. And in assessing them, the role of William Howe looms large. Howe's problems were not entirely of his own making. He was hobbled in part by his instructions from his superiors in England: He was told to conciliate the Americans, and he was told, at the same time, to defeat them. His efforts to fulfill that contradictory mandate accounted for many of his problems. But it also seems clear that Howe himself was ill suited to serve as commander in a war of revolution. Time and again, he showed not only serious deficiencies in tactical and strategic judgment, but a lack of aggressive instincts. With the Continental army weakened and in disarray, Howe refrained from moving in for the final attack, although he had several opportunities. Instead, he repeatedly allowed Washington to retreat and regroup; and he permitted the American army to spend a long winter unmo-

lested in Valley Forge, where—weak and hungry—they might have been easy prey for British attack.

Some believed that Howe did not want to win the war, that he was secretly in sympathy with the American cause. His family had close ties to the colonies; and he himself was linked politically to those forces within the British government that opposed the war. Others pointed to personal weaknesses: Howe's apparent alcoholism, his romantic attachments (he spent the winter of 1777–1778 in Philadelphia with his mistress when many were urging him to move elsewhere). But the most important problem, it seems clear, was lack of judgment.

Whatever the reasons, the failure of the British to crush the Continental army in the mid-Atlantic states, combined with the stunning American victory at Saratoga (which was a direct result of Howe's strategic incompetence), transformed the war and ushered it into a new and final phase.

Securing Aid from Abroad

Central to this transformation of the war was American success in winning the indirect assistance of several European nations, and the direct support of France. Even before the Declaration of Independence, Congress drew up a plan for liberal commercial arrangements with other countries and prepared to send representatives to the capitals of Europe to negotiate treaties with the governments there. Such treaties would, of course, require European recognition of the United States as one of the sovereign nations of the world. "Militia diplomats," John Adams called the early American representatives abroad; and unlike the diplomatic regulars of Europe, they knew little of the formal art and etiquette of Old World diplomacy. Since transatlantic communication was slow and uncertain (it took from one to three months to cross the Atlantic), they had to interpret the instructions of Congress very freely and make crucial decisions entirely on their own.

Of all the possible foreign friends of the United States, the most promising and the most powerful was France, which was still smarting from its defeat at the hands of Great Britain in 1763. King Louis XVI of France, who had come to the throne in 1774, had an astute and determined foreign minister in the Count de Vergennes; and Vergennes quickly realized that France had a great deal to gain from the creation of an independent United States. If Britain were to lose that crucial part of its empire, the relative power of France would increase.

From the beginning, therefore, there was interest in an alliance on both the American and French sides; and diplomatic efforts began almost as soon as the first shots in the war were fired. For a time, however, France remained reluctant to provide the United States with what it most wanted: diplomatic recognition. Through a series of covert bargains, facilitated by the creation of a fictional trading firm and the use of secret agents on both sides (among them the famed French dramatist Caron de Beaumarchais), the Americans secured large quantities of much-needed supplies. But they wanted more.

After the Declaration of Independence, Benjamin Franklin himself went to France to lobby for further aid and for diplomatic recognition of the United States. A natural diplomat, Franklin became a popular hero among the French—aristocrats and common people alike. (He also became a particular favorite of many Parisian women.) But Vergennes was at first reluctant to accede to Franklin's requests; he wanted some evidence that the Americans had a real chance of winning before he would agree to open French intervention. The news that Vergennes and Franklin were waiting for—the news from Saratoga—arrived in London on December 2 and in Paris on December 4, 1777. In London, the reports of Burgoyne's surrender persuaded Lord North to launch a new peace offensive: an offer of complete home rule within the empire for Americans if they would quit the war. In Paris, Franklin learned of Lord North's intentions from a British spy and made certain that Vergennes heard of them as well. The news worried the foreign minister. He feared the Americans might accept the offer and thus destroy France's opportunity to weaken Britain's imperial power; and he realized that French assistance might help persuade the Americans to continue the struggle. On February 6, 1778, therefore, Vergennes signed a series of agreements with the American diplomats that signaled the formal recognition of the United States as a sovereign nation and laid the groundwork for greatly expanded French assistance to the American war effort.

The entrance of France into the conflict substantially altered the British approach to the war. It was now an international conflict involving England's traditional European rivals. In the course of the next two years, France, Spain, and the Netherlands all drifted into another general war with Great Britain in Europe. France and the Netherlands allied themselves openly with the United States; all three nations contributed indirectly to the ultimate American victory by complicating England's task and directly by offering financial and material assistance. But it was France that served as America's truly indispensable ally. Not only did it furnish the new nation with most of its money and munitions, but it also provided a navy and an expeditionary force that proved invaluable in the final, successful phase of the revolutionary conflict.

The Final Phase: The South

The last phase of the military struggle in America was fundamentally different from either of the first two. The British government had never been fully united behind the war in the first place; after the defeat at Saratoga and the intervention of the French, it imposed new limits on its commitment to the conflict. Instead of a full-scale military struggle against the American army, therefore, the British chose a different strategy. They would attempt to enlist the support of those elements of the American population—a majority, they continued to believe—who were still loyal to the crown; they would, in other words, work to undermine the Revolution from within. Since Loyalist sentiment was considered to be strongest in the Southern colonies, the main focus of the British effort shifted there; and it was thus in the South, for the most part, that the war was fought to its conclusion.

The new strategy was a dismal failure. British forces spent three years (from 1778 to 1781) moving through the South, fighting small battles and large, and attempting to neutralize (or to use the terminology of a later American war, "pacify") the territory through which they traveled. All such efforts ended in frustration. The British badly overestimated the extent of Loyalist sentiment. While it was true that in Georgia and the Carolinas there were numerous Tories, some of them disgruntled members of the Regulator movement, it was also true that Patriot sentiment was far stronger than the British believed. In Virginia, support for independence was as fervent as in Massachusetts. And even in the lower South, Loyalists often feared to offer aid to the British because they realized they might face reprisals from the Patriots around them. There were also severe logistical problems facing the British in the South. Patriot forces could move at will throughout the region, living off the resources of the countryside, blending in with the civilian population and leaving the British unable to distinguish friend from foe. The British, by contrast, suffered all the disadvantages of an army in hostile territory.

It was this phase of the conflict that made the war truly "revolutionary"—not only because it introduced a new kind of warfare, but because it had the effect of mobilizing and politicizing large groups of the population who had previously remained aloof from the struggle. With the war expanding into previously isolated communities, with many civilians forced to involve themselves whether they liked it or not, the political climate of the United States grew more heated than ever. And support for independence, far from being crushed as the British had hoped, greatly increased.

That was the backdrop against which the important military encounters of the last years of the war occurred. In the North, where significant numbers of British troops remained, the fighting settled into a relatively quiet stalemate. Sir Henry Clinton replaced the hapless William Howe in 1778 and moved what had been Howe's army from Philadelphia back to New York. There the British troops stayed for more than a year, with Washington using his army to keep watch around them. The American forces in New York did so little fighting in this period that Washington sent some troops west to strike back against hostile Indians who had been attacking white settlers. During that same winter, George Rogers Clark, with orders from the state of Virginia—not from either Washington or Congress—led a daring expedition over the mountains and captured settlements in the Illinois country from the British and their Indian allies.

During this period of relative calm, the American forces—and George Washington in particular—were shocked by the exposure of treason on the part of General Benedict Arnold. Arnold had been one of the early heroes of the war; but now, convinced that the American cause was hopeless, he conspired with British agents to betray the Patriot stronghold at West Point on the Hudson River. In the nick of time, the scheme was exposed and foiled; and Arnold fled to the safety of the British camp, where he spent the rest of the war.

But the decisive fighting took place in the South. The British did have some significant military successes during this period. On December 29, 1778, they captured Savannah, on the coast of Georgia; and on May 12, 1780, they took the port of Charleston, South Carolina. They inspired some Loyalists to take up arms and advance with them into the interior. But

although the British were able to win conventional battles, they were constantly harassed as they moved through the countryside by Patriot guerrillas led by such resourceful fighters as Thomas Sumter, Andrew Pickens, and Francis Marion, the "Swamp Fox." Penetrating to Camden, South Carolina, Lord Cornwallis (Clinton's choice as British commander in the South) met and crushed a combined force of militiamen and Continentals under Horatio Gates on August 16, 1780. Congress recalled Gates, and Washington gave the Southern command to Nathanael Greene, a former Quaker blacksmith from Rhode Island and probably the ablest of all the American generals of the time next to Washington himself.

Even before Greene arrived in the war theater, the tide of battle already had begun to turn against Cornwallis. At King's Mountain (near the North Carolina–South Carolina border) on October 7, 1780, a band of Patriot riflemen from the backwoods killed, wounded, or captured an entire force of 1,100 New York and South Carolina Tories, upon whom Cornwallis had depended as auxiliaries. Once Greene arrived, he confused and exasperated Cornwallis by dividing the American forces into fast-moving contingents while refraining from a showdown in open battle. One of the contingents inflicted what Cornwallis admitted was "a very unexpected and severe blow" at Cowpens on January 17, 1781. Finally, after receiving reinforcements, Greene combined all his forces and maneuvered to meet the British on ground of his own choosing, at Guilford Court House, North Carolina. After a hard-fought battle there on March 15, 1781, Greene was driven from the field; but Cornwallis had lost so many men that he decided at last to abandon the Carolina campaign.

Cornwallis withdrew to the port town of Wilmington, North Carolina, to receive supplies being sent to him by sea; later he moved north to carry on raids in the interior of Virginia. But Clinton, concerned for the army's safety, ordered him to take up a position on the peninsula between the York and James rivers and wait for water transport to New York or Charleston. So Cornwallis retreated to Yorktown and began to build fortifications there.

At that point, George Washington decided to try to trap Cornwallis at Yorktown. He coordinated his efforts with the Count de Rochambeau, commander of the French expeditionary force in America, and Admiral de Grasse, commander of a French fleet in American waters. Washington and Rochambeau marched a French-American army from New York to join Lafayette in Virginia, while de Grasse sailed

The Revolution in the South, 1778–1781

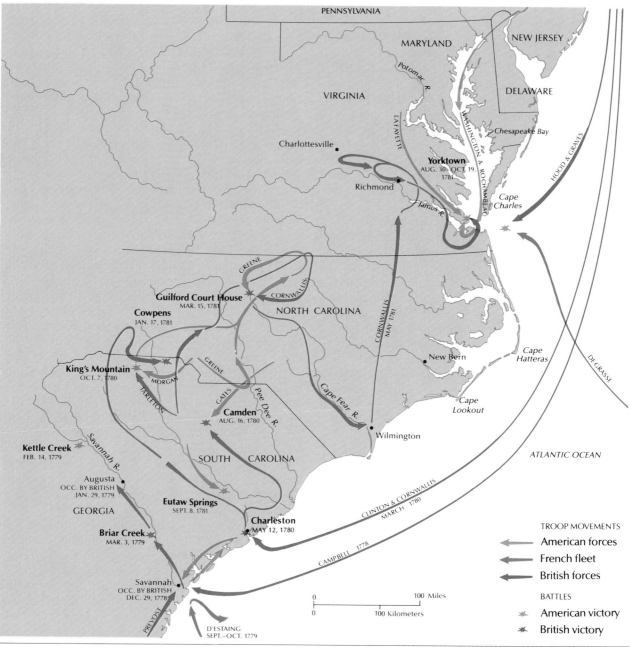

PENNSYLVANIA

MARYLAND

NEW JERSEY

DELAWARE

VIRGINIA

Potomac R.

Chesapeake Bay

Charlottesville

Yorktown
AUG. 30– OCT. 19, 1781

Richmond

James R.

Cape Charles

GREENE

CORNWALLIS

Guilford Court House
MAR. 15, 1781

NORTH CAROLINA

Cowpens
JAN. 17, 1781

MORGAN

GREENE

New Bern

Cape Hatteras

DE GRASSE

King's Mountain
OCT. 7, 1780

TARLETON

GATES

Pee Dee R.

Camden
AUG. 16, 1780

Cape Fear R.

Cape Lookout

Wilmington

Kettle Creek
FEB. 14, 1779

Savannah R.

SOUTH CAROLINA

ATLANTIC OCEAN

Augusta
OCC. BY BRITISH
JAN. 29, 1779

Eutaw Springs
SEPT. 8, 1781

GEORGIA

CLINTON & CORNWALLIS
MARCH 1780

Charleston
MAY 12, 1780

Briar Creek
MAR. 3, 1779

CAMPBELL 1778

Savannah
OCC. BY BRITISH
DEC. 29, 1778

PREVOST

D'ESTAING
SEPT.–OCT. 1779

| | 0 | 100 Miles |
| 0 | 100 Kilometers | |

TROOP MOVEMENTS
→ American forces
→ French fleet
→ British forces

BATTLES
✴ American victory
✴ British victory

with additional troops for the Chesapeake Bay and the York River. These joint operations, perfectly timed and executed, caught Cornwallis between land and sea. After a few shows of resistance, he asked for terms on October 17, 1781 (four years to the day after the capitulation of Burgoyne at Saratoga). Two days later, as a military band played the old tune "The World Turn'd Upside Down," he surrendered his whole army of more than 7,000.

Except for a few skirmishes, the fighting was now over; but the war was not yet won. British forces continued to hold the seaports of Savannah, Charleston, Wilmington, and New York. Before long, a British fleet met and defeated Admiral de

The Surrender of Cornwallis
The principal British army in America surrendered at Yorktown, Virginia, on October 19, 1781. Although not until 1783, after two years of difficult negotiations, did the British sign a treaty formally recognizing the independence of the United States, Yorktown marked the end of major hostilities. In this 1846 print by Nathaniel Currier, George Washington (on horseback in the foreground) accepts the sword of the British commander, Lord Cornwallis. The Marquis de Lafayette (mounted on a white horse to the right of Washington) looks on.   (Library of Congress)

Grasse's fleet in the West Indies, ending Washington's hopes for further French naval assistance. For more than a year, then, although there was no significant further combat between British and American forces, it remained possible that the war might resume and the struggle for independence might still be lost.

Winning the Peace

The victory at Yorktown had immediate repercussions in England. Cornwallis's defeat provoked outcries against continuing the war and raised demands for cultivating American friendship as an asset in international politics. Lord North resigned as prime minister; Lord Shelburne emerged from the political wreckage to succeed him; and British emissaries appeared in France to talk informally with the American diplomats there. Benjamin Franklin outlined for them what he called the "necessary" terms of peace, including independence and the establishment of the Mississippi as the western boundary of the United States. He also added several "desirable" terms, including the cession of Canada.

The three principal American diplomats—Franklin, John Jay, and John Adams—were under instructions to cooperate fully with France in their negotiations with England. But the French soon proved less reliable as diplomatic allies than they had as military supporters. Vergennes insisted that France

could not agree to any settlement of the war with England until its ally Spain had achieved its principal war aim: winning back Gibraltar from the British. There was, moreover, no real prospect of that happening soon. And the American diplomats began to fear that their alliance with France might keep them at war indefinitely. Disillusionment with the French increased when Jay learned that Vergennes's private secretary had gone on a secret mission to England; there were rumors that the French and Spanish were planning to bargain away American independence in a larger settlement with the British.

As a result, Franklin, Jay, and Adams soon ceased to keep Vergennes informed of their diplomatic efforts. They proceeded on their own and soon drew up a preliminary treaty with Great Britain. After the preliminary articles were signed on November 30, 1782, Franklin skillfully pacified Vergennes (who had, in any case, been kept informed of the American efforts by his own spies) and avoided an immediate rift in the French-American alliance.

The final treaty was signed September 3, 1783, when both Spain and France agreed to end hostilities. It included a number of provisions that Franklin, Jay, and Adams had opposed, some of which were to lead to serious friction with Great Britain and Spain in the years ahead. And it failed to include most of Franklin's "desirable" terms (including the cession of Canada to the United States). But the treaty did endorse the "necessary" terms Franklin had outlined; and it was, on the whole, remarkably favorable to the

---
WHERE HISTORIANS DISAGREE

The American Revolution

One of the oldest and most enduring controversies among American historians involves the nature of the American Revolution. Two broad schools of interpretation have emerged. One group of scholars has argued that the Revolution was primarily a political and intellectual event; that Americans in the 1770s were fighting to defend principles and ideals. Others have maintained that much of the motivation for the Revolution was social and economic; that Americans were inspired to fight because of economic interests and social aspirations. Although there is a wide range of views and approaches within each of these schools, the question of "ideas" versus "interests" remains the crucial divide in interpretation.

The emphasis on ideology as the cause of the Revolution reflects, to some extent, the view of those who were involved in the event itself. Early histories of the Revolution, written by participants and contemporaries, invariably emphasized the high ideals of the Founding Fathers. That approach continued in an almost unbroken line throughout the nineteenth century, culminating in the work of one of the first great American historians, George Bancroft, who wrote in 1876 that the Revolution "was most radical in its character, yet achieved with such benign tranquillity that even conservatism hesitated to censure." Its aim, he believed, was to "preserve liberty" against the threat of British tyranny.

In the early twentieth century, historians first began seriously to examine the social and economic forces that may have contributed to the Revolution. Influenced by the reform currents of the progressive era, during which the power of economic interests came under scorching criti-

cism, a number of scholars adopted the ideas of Carl Becker, who wrote in 1909—in a case study of New York—that not one but two questions were involved in the struggle. "The first was the question of home rule; the second was the question, if we may so put it, of who should rule at home." In addition to the fight against the British, in other words, there was also in progress a kind of civil war, a contest for power between radicals and conservatives that led to the "democratization of American politics and society." J. Franklin Jameson, expanding on Becker's views, argued in an influential book—*The American Revolution Considered as a Social Movement* (1926)—that the "stream of revolution, once started, could not be confined within narrow banks, but spread abroad upon the land. . . . Many economic desires, many social aspirations were set free by the political struggle, many aspects of society profoundly altered by the forces thus let loose."

Other "progressive" historians accepted the importance of economics as a cause of the Revolution but differed with Becker and Jameson over the form economic influences took. Arthur M. Schlesinger, for example, argued in an influential 1917 study that it was the colonial merchants who were chiefly responsible for arousing American resistance to the British; and that although they spoke of principles and ideals, their real motives were economic self-interest: freedom from the restrictive policies of British mercantilism. In the end, however, the Revolution could not be controlled by the merchants and became a far more broadly based social movement than they had anticipated or desired.

Economic interpretations of the Revolution pre-

United States in granting a clear-cut recognition of independence and a generous, though ambiguous cession of territory—from the southern boundary of Canada to the northern boundary of Florida and from the Atlantic to the Mississippi. With good reason the American people celebrated as the last of the British occupation forces embarked from New York and General Washington, at the head of his troops, rode triumphantly into the city.

War and Society

Historians have long debated whether the American Revolution was a social as well as a political revolution. Some have argued that the colonists were struggling not only over the question of home rule, but over "who should rule at home." Others claim that domestic social and economic concerns had little to

WHERE HISTORIANS DISAGREE

vailed for several decades; but the relatively conservative political climate of the 1950s helped produce new studies that reemphasized the role of ideology. Robert E. Brown, in *Middle-Class Democracy and the American Revolution in Massachusetts* (1955), contended that long before 1776, Massachusetts was "very close to a complete democracy" and that the internal social conflicts that some historians ascribed to the era simply did not exist. Edmund S. Morgan, like Brown, argued in 1956 that most Americans of the Revolutionary era shared the same basic political principles, that the rhetoric of the Revolution could not be dismissed as propaganda—as Schlesinger had claimed—but should be taken seriously as the motivating force behind the movement. The preeminent statement of the importance of ideas in the conflict came from Bernard Bailyn, in *The Ideological Origins of the American Revolution* (1967). After reading hundreds of Revolutionary pamphlets, Bailyn concluded that they "confirmed my rather old-fashioned view that the American Revolution was above all else an ideological, constitutional, political struggle and not primarily a controversy between social groups undertaken to force changes in the organization of the society or the economy."

By the time Bailyn's book was published, however, a new group of historians was already reviving a social and economic approach to the Revolution. Influenced by the New Left of the 1960s, they claimed that domestic tensions between classes contributed in crucial ways to the development of the Revolutionary movement. Historians such as Jesse Lemisch and Dirk Hoerder pointed to the actions of mobs in colonial cities as evidence of the social concerns of resisting Amer-

icans. Joseph Ernst reemphasized the significance of economic pressures on colonial merchants and tradesmen. Gary B. Nash, in *The Urban Crucible* (1979), emphasized the role of increasing economic tension and distress in colonial cities in creating a climate in which the Revolutionary movement could flourish. Edward Countryman, in *A People in Revolution* (1981) and *The American Revolution* (1985), also stressed the social and economic roots of the Revolution. And Rhys Isaac suggested in *The Transformation of Virginia, 1740–1790* (1982) that the religious and cultural changes in colonial life, and the relationship between those changes and class alignments, underlay the new political outlook that led to the Revolution.

The new socioeconomic interpretations of the Revolution do not usually maintain that the struggle was a class conflict. Participants in the Revolution did not often justify their positions, even to themselves, in purely, or even primarily, economic terms. What the new interpretations suggest is that the political ideas (the ideologies) of participants emerged at least in part out of social, cultural, and economic circumstances. Historians arguing along these lines have been careful to avoid the deterministic quality of some earlier economic interpretations; that is, they do not claim that a person's view of the Revolution was *determined* by his or her social or economic condition. They do maintain, however, that material circumstances must be a factor in any workable explanation of the conflict. "Everyone has economic interests," Gary Nash has written, "and everyone . . . has an ideology." Only by exploring the relationships between the two, he maintains, can historians hopefully to understand either.

do with the conflict. (See "Where Historians Disagree," above.) Whatever the motivations of Americans, however, there can be little doubt that the War for Independence had important effects on the nature of American society.

Loyalists and Minorities

Any war produces both winners and losers. The losers in the American Revolution included not only the

British but American Loyalists. Estimates differ as to how many Americans remained loyal to England during the Revolution, but it is clear that there were many—at least a fifth (and some estimate as much as a third) of the white population. Their motivations were varied. Some were officeholders in the imperial government, who stood to lose their positions as a result of the Revolution. Others were merchants whose trade was closely tied to the imperial system. (Most merchants, however, supported the Revolution.) Still others were people who lived in relative isolation and who thus had not been exposed to the wave of discontent that had turned so many Americans against Britain; they had simply retained their traditional loyalties. There were also cultural and ethnic minorities who feared that an independent America would not offer them sufficient protection. And there were those who, expecting the British to win the war, were simply currying favor with the anticipated victors.

What happened to these men and women during the war is a turbulent and at times tragic story. Hounded by Patriots in their communities, harassed by legislative and judicial actions, the position of many of them became intolerable. Up to 100,000 fled the country. Those who could afford to—for example, the hated Tory governor of Massachusetts, Thomas Hutchinson—fled to England, where many lived in difficult and lonely exile. Others of more modest means moved to Canada, establishing the first English-speaking community in the province of Quebec. Some returned to America after the war and, as the early passions and resentments faded, managed to reenter the life of the nation. Others remained abroad for the rest of their lives.

Most Loyalists were people of average means, but a substantial minority consisted of men and women of wealth. They left behind large estates and vacated important positions of social and economic leadership. Even some who remained in the country saw their property confiscated and their positions forfeited. The result was new opportunities for Patriots to acquire land and influence, a situation that produced important social changes in many communities. It would be an exaggeration, however, to claim that the departure of the Loyalists was responsible for anything approaching a social revolution. The Revolution did not create a general assault on the wealthy and powerful in America. When the war ended, those who had been wealthy at its beginning were, for the most part, still wealthy. Those who had wielded social and political influence (which often accompanied the possession of wealth) continued to wield it. Indeed, the distribution of wealth became more uneven in the aftermath of the war than it had been in the decades preceding it.

The war had a significant effect on other minorities as well, and on certain religious groups in particular. No sect suffered more than the Anglicans, many of whose members were Loyalists and all of whom were widely identified with England. In Virginia and Maryland, where the colonial governments had recognized Anglicanism as the official religion and had imposed a tax for its maintenance, the new Revolutionary regimes disestablished the church and thus eliminated the subsidy. In other states, Anglicans had benefited from aid from England, which also ceased with the outbreak of war. By the time the fighting ended, many Anglican parishes no longer even had clergymen, for there were few recruits to take the places of those who had died or who had left the country as Loyalist refugees. Since there had never been an American bishop or an intercolonial organization of the church, there was little institutional strength from which those Anglicans who remained could rebuild their church; and although Anglicanism survived in America, it was to remain permanently weakened from its losses during the Revolution. Also weakened were the Quakers in Pennsylvania and elsewhere, who won widespread unpopularity because of their pacifism. Their refusal to support the war destroyed much of the social and political prestige they had enjoyed, and the church was never to recover fully.

While the war was weakening the Anglicans and the Quakers, it was improving the position of the Roman Catholic church. On the advice of Charles Carroll of Carrollton, a Maryland statesman and Catholic lay leader, most American Catholics supported the Patriot cause during the war. The French alliance brought Catholic troops and chaplains to the country, and the gratitude with which most Americans greeted them did much to erode old hostilities toward Catholics, whom Americans had in the past often denounced as agents of the devil. The church did not greatly increase its numbers as a result of the Revolution, but it did strengthen itself considerably as an institution. Shortly after the peace treaty was signed, the Vatican provided the United States with its own Catholic hierarchy. (Until then, the American church had been controlled by the English bishops.) Father John Carroll (also of Maryland) was named head of Catholic missions in America in 1784 and, in 1789, the first American bishop. In 1808 he became archbishop of Baltimore. Hostility toward Catholics had not disappeared forever from American life, but the church had established a solid footing from which to withstand future assaults.

For the largest of America's minorities—the black population—the war had limited, but nevertheless profound, significance. For some, it meant freedom. Because so much of the fighting occurred in the South during the last years of the war, many slaves came into contact with the British army, which—in

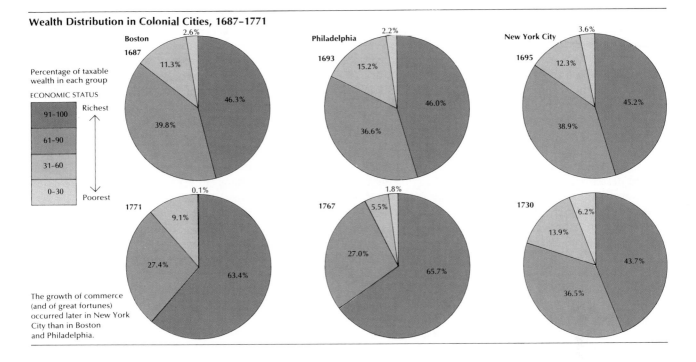

Wealth Distribution in Colonial Cities, 1687–1771

Percentage of taxable
wealth in each group

ECONOMIC STATUS

91–100	Richest
61–90	
31–60	
0–30	Poorest

Boston
1687
2.6%
11.3%
46.3%
39.8%

Philadelphia
1693
2.2%
15.2%
46.0%
36.6%

New York City
1695
3.6%
12.3%
45.2%
38.9%

1771
0.1%
9.1%
27.4%
63.4%

1767
1.8%
5.5%
27.0%
65.7%

1730
6.2%
13.9%
43.7%
36.5%

The growth of commerce
(and of great fortunes)
occurred later in New York
City than in Boston
and Philadelphia.

the interests of disrupting and weakening the American cause—emancipated thousands of them and took them out of the country. For other blacks, the Revolution meant exposure to the idea, although not the reality, of liberty. In the towns and cities of the South, where large groups of both free and enslaved blacks lived, the ideology of the Revolution had a pronounced effect. Although most blacks could not read, few could avoid exposure to the new and exciting ideas; and in many cases, they attempted to apply those ideas to themselves. The result was a series of incidents in several communities in which blacks engaged in open resistance to white control. In Charleston, South Carolina, Thomas Jeremiah, a free black, was executed after white authorities learned of elaborate plans for a slave uprising. It would be many years before blacks would be in a position to make more than sporadic efforts on behalf of their freedom; but the experience of the Revolution produced distinct stirrings of discontent.

That was one reason why Revolutionary sentiment was more restrained in South Carolina and Georgia than in other colonies. Blacks constituted a majority in South Carolina and almost half the population in Georgia, and whites in both places feared that revolution would foment slave rebellions. The same fears helped prevent English colonists in the Caribbean islands (who were far more greatly out-numbered by black slaves) from joining with the continental Americans in the revolt against Britain.

Native Americans and the Revolution

Indians viewed the American Revolution with considerable uncertainty. The American Patriots tried to persuade them to remain neutral in the conflict, which they described as a "family quarrel" between the colonists and Britain that had nothing to do with the tribes. The British too generally sought to maintain Indian neutrality, fearing that native allies would prove unreliable and uncontrollable. Most tribes ultimately chose to stay out of the war.

To some Indians, however, the Revolution threatened to replace a ruling group in which they had developed at least some measure of trust (the British) with one they considered generally hostile to them (the Patriots). The British had consistently sought to limit the expansion of white settlement into Indian land (even if unsuccessfully); the Americans had spearheaded the encroachments. Thus some Indians, among them those Iroquois who participated in the Burgoyne campaign in upper New York, chose to join the English cause. Still others took advantage of the conflict to launch attacks of their own.

In the western Carolinas and Virginia, the Cherokee, led by Chief Dragging Canoe, launched a series of attacks on outlying white settlements in the summer of 1776. Patriot militias responded with overwhelming force, ravaging Cherokee lands and forcing the chief and many of his followers to flee west across the Tennessee River. Those Cherokee who remained behind agreed to a new treaty by which they gave up still more land. Not all Indian military efforts were so unsuccessful. Some Iroquois, despite the setbacks at Oriskany, continued to wage war against Americans in the West and caused widespread destruction in large agricultural areas of New York and Pennsylvania—areas whose crops were of crucial importance to the Patriot cause. And although the retaliating American armies inflicted heavy losses on the Indians, the attacks continued throughout the war.

In the end, however, the Revolution generally weakened the position of Native Americans in several ways. The Patriot victory increased the white demand for Western lands; many American whites associated restrictions on settlement with British oppression and expected the new nation to remove the obstacles. At the same time, white attitudes toward the tribes, seldom friendly in the best of times, took a turn for the worse. Many whites deeply resented the assistance such nations as the Mohawk had given the British and insisted on treating them as conquered people. Others derived from the Revolution a paternalistic view of the tribes that was only slightly less dangerous to the Native Americans. Thomas Jefferson, for example, came to view the Indians as "noble savages," uncivilized in their present state but redeemable if they were willing to adapt to the norms of white society.

Among the Indians themselves, the Revolution both revealed and increased the deep divisions that made it difficult for them to form a common front to resist the growing power of whites. In 1774, for example, the Shawnee Indians in western Virginia had attempted to lead a widespread uprising against white settlers moving into the lands that would later become Kentucky. They attracted virtually no allies and (in a conflict known as Lord Dunmore's War) were defeated by the colonial militia and forced to cede still more land to white settlers. The Cherokee generated little support from surrounding tribes in their 1776 battles. And the Iroquois, whose power had been eroding since the end of the French and Indian War, were unable to act in unison in the Revolution; the nations that chose to support the British attracted little support from tribes outside the Confederacy

(many of whom resented the long Iroquois domination of the interior).

Nor did the conclusion of the Revolutionary War end the fighting between white Americans and Indians. Bands of Native Americans continued to launch raids against white settlers on the frontier. And white militias, often using such raids as pretexts, continued to attack Indian tribes who stood in the way of expansion. Perhaps the most vicious massacre of the era occurred in 1782, after the British surrender, when white militias slaughtered a peaceful band of Delaware Indians at Gnadenhuetten in Ohio. They claimed to be retaliating for the killing of a white family several days before, but few believed this band of Delaware (who were both Christian converts and pacifists) had played any role in the earlier attack. The white soldiers killed ninety-six people, including many women and children. Such massacres did not become the norm of Indian-white relations. But they did reveal how little the Revolution had done to settle the basic conflict between the two peoples.

Women's Rights and Women's Roles

The long Revolutionary War, which touched the lives of almost every region, naturally had a profound effect on American women. The departure of so many men to fight in the Patriot armies left wives, mothers, sisters, and daughters in charge of farms and businesses. Often, women handled these tasks with great success. But in many cases, inexperience, inflation, the unavailability of male labor, or the threat of enemy troops led to severe dislocations. Other women whose husbands or fathers were called away to war did not have even a farm or shop to fall back on. Cities and towns developed significant populations of impoverished women, who on occasion led popular protests against price increases. On a few occasions, hungry women rioted and looted for food. On several other occasions (in New Jersey and Staten Island), women launched attacks on occupying British troops, whom they were required to house and feed at considerable expense.

Not all women, however, stayed behind when the men went off to war. Sometimes simply by choice, more often out of economic necessity or because they had been driven from their homes by the enemy (and by the smallpox and dysentery the British army carried with it), women flocked in increasing numbers to the camps of the Patriot armies to join their male relatives. George Washington looked askance at these female "camp followers," convinced that they were disruptive and distracting (even though his own wife, Martha, spent the winter of 1778–1779 with him at Valley Forge). Other officers were even more hostile, voicing complaints that reflected a high level of anxiety over this seeming violation of traditional sex roles (and also, perhaps, the generally lower class backgrounds of the camp women). One described them in decidedly hostile terms: "their hair falling, their brows beady with the heat, their belongings slung over one shoulder, chattering and yelling in sluttish shrills as they went and spitting in the gutters." In fact, however, the women were of significant value to the new army, which had not yet developed an adequate system of supply and auxiliary services and which profited greatly from the presence of women who increased army morale and who provided a ready source of volunteers to do cooking, laundry, nursing, and other necessary tasks.

But female activity did not remain restricted to "women's" tasks. In the rough environment of the camps, traditional sex distinctions proved difficult to maintain. Considerable numbers of women became involved, at least intermittently, in combat—including the legendary "Molly Pitcher," so named because she carried pitchers of water to soldiers on the battlefield, who watched her husband fall during one encounter and immediately took his place at a field gun. A few women even disguised themselves as men so as to be able to fight.

After the war, of course, the soldiers and the female camp followers returned home. The experience of combat had little visible lasting impact on how society (or women themselves) defined female roles in peacetime. The Revolution did, however, call certain assumptions about women into question in other ways. The emphasis on liberty and the "rights of man" led some women to begin to question their position in society as well. "By the way," Abigail Adams wrote to her husband John Adams in 1776, "in the new code of laws which I suppose it will be necessary for you to make, I desire you would remember the ladies and be more generous and favorable to them than your ancestors. Do not put such unlimited power into the hands of the Husbands."

Adams was calling for a very modest expansion of women's rights: for new protections against abusive and tyrannical men. A few women, however, went further. Judith Sargent Murray, one of the leading essayists of the late eighteenth century, wrote in 1779 that women's minds were as good as those of men and that girls as well as boys therefore deserved

Abigail Adams
When this portrait was painted in the mid-1780s, Abigail Adams was living in London, where her husband, John Adams, was serving as the first American ambassador. Harboring strong political opinions, she was outspoken on public issues, and critics often charged John Adams with being "under the sovereignty of his wife." But she was generally more a fierce defender of her husband's policies than an active force in shaping them. During much of her married life, she lived apart from her husband, who spent many years traveling on diplomatic assignments. As a result, she became a tireless letter writer. Her correspondence survives today as one of the most important sources of information about her extraordinary family. (New York State Historical Association, Cooperstown)

access to education. Murray later served as one of the leading defenders of the works of the English feminist Mary Wollstonecraft, whose *Vindication of the Rights of Women* was published in America in 1792. After reading it, Murray rejoiced that "the Rights of Women" were beginning to be understood in the United States and that future generations of women would inaugurate "a new era in female history."

But in most respects the new era did not arrive. Some political leaders—among them Benjamin Franklin and Benjamin Rush—voiced support for the education of women and for other feminist reforms. Yale students in the 1780s debated the question, "Whether women ought to be admitted into the magistracy and government of empires and republics." And there was for a time wide discussion of the future role of women in the new republic. But few concrete reforms were enacted into law or translated into practice; and indeed, women lost certain protections and privileges under the new regime that they had enjoyed under the old.

In colonial society, under the doctrines of English common law, an unmarried woman had certain legal rights, but a married woman had virtually no rights at all. She could own no property and earn no independent wages; everything she owned and everything she earned belonged to her husband. She had no legal authority over her children; the father was, in the eyes of the law, the autocrat of the family. Because she had no property rights, she could not engage in any legal transactions (buying or selling, suing or being sued, writing wills). She could not vote. Nor could she obtain a divorce; that too was a right reserved almost exclusively to men. That was what Abigail Adams (who herself enjoyed a very happy marriage) meant when she appealed to her husband not to put "such unlimited power into the hands of the Husbands."

The Revolution did little to change any of these legal customs. In some states, it did become easier for women to obtain divorces. And in New Jersey, women obtained the right to vote (although that right was repealed in 1807). Otherwise, there were few advances and some setbacks—including the loss of the right of widows to regain their dowries from their husbands' estates. That change left many widows without any means of support and was one of the reasons for the increased agitation for female education: such women needed a way to support themselves.

The Revolution, in other words, far from challenging the patriarchal structure of American society actually confirmed and strengthened it. Not even many American women ever doubted that they should continue to occupy a sphere distinct from men, that their place remained in the family. Abigail Adams, in the same letter in which she asked her husband to "remember the Ladies," urged him to "regard us then as Beings placed by providence under your protection and in imitation of the Supreme Being make use of that power only for our happiness." Nevertheless, the revolutionary experience did contribute to an alteration of women's expectations

of their status within the family. In the past, they had often been little better than servants in their husbands' homes; men and women both had generally viewed the wife as a clear subordinate, performing functions in the family of far less importance than those of the husband. But the Revolution encouraged people of both sexes to reevaluate the contribution of women to the family and the society.

Part of this change was a result of the participation of women in the Revolutionary struggle itself. And part was a result of the reevaluation of American life during and after the Revolutionary struggle. As the republic searched for a cultural identity for itself, it began to place additional value on the role of women as mothers. The new nation was, many Americans liked to believe, producing a new kind of citizen, steeped in the principles of liberty. Mothers had a particularly important task, therefore, in instructing their children in the virtues that the republican citizenry was expected now to possess. Wives were still far from equal partners in marriage, but their ideas and interests were increasingly considered worthy of respect.

The War Economy

Inevitably, the Revolution produced important changes in the structure of the American economy. After more than a century of dependence on the British imperial system, American trade suddenly found itself on its own. No longer did it have the protection of the great British navy; on the contrary, English ships now attempted to drive American vessels from the seas. No longer did American merchants have access to the markets of the empire; those markets were now hostile ports—including, of course, the most important source of American trade: England itself.

Yet while the Revolution was responsible for much disruption in traditional economic patterns, it served in the long run to strengthen the American economy. Well before the war was over, American ships had learned to evade the British navy with light, fast, easily maneuverable vessels. Indeed, the Yankees began to prey on British commerce with hundreds of privateers. For many a shipowner, privateering proved to be more profitable than ordinary peacetime trade. More important in the long run, the end of imperial restrictions on American shipping opened up enormous new areas of trade to the nation. Colonial merchants had been violating

Banner of the Society of Pewterers
Members of the American Society of Pewterers carried this patriotic banner when they marched in a New York City parade in July 1788. Its inscription celebrates the adoption of the new federal Constitution and predicts a future of prosperity and freedom in "Columbia's Land." The banner also suggests the growing importance of American manufacturing, which had received an important boost during the Revolution when British imports became unavailable.   (New-York Historical Society)

British regulations for years, but the rules of empire had nevertheless served to inhibit American exploration of many markets. Now, enterprising merchants in New England and elsewhere began to develop new commerce in the Caribbean and South America. By the mid-1780s, American merchants were developing an important new pattern of trade with the Orient; and by the end of that decade, Yankee ships were regularly sailing from the eastern seaboard around Cape Horn to California, there exchanging manufactured goods for hides and furs, and then proceeding across the Pacific to barter for goods in China. There was also a substantial increase in trade among the American states.

When English imports to America were cut off—first by the prewar boycott, then by the war itself—there were desperate efforts throughout the states to stimulate domestic manufacturing of certain necessities. There was no great industrial expansion as a result, but there were several signs of the economic growth that was to come in the next century. Americans began to make their own cloth— "homespun," which became both patriotic and fashionable—to replace the now unobtainable British fabrics. It would be some time before a large domestic textile industry would emerge, but the nation was never again to rely exclusively on foreign sources for its cloth. There was, of course, pressure to build factories for the manufacture of guns and ammunition.

And there was a growing awareness that America need not forever be dependent on other nations for manufactured goods. Having broken politically with the British Empire, citizens of the new nation began to dream of breaking economically with it too—of developing a strong economy to rival that of the Old World.

The war stopped short of revolutionizing the American economy. Not until the nineteenth century would that begin to occur. But it did serve to release a wide range of entrepreneurial energies that, despite the temporary dislocations, encouraged growth and diversification.

The Creation of State Governments

At the same time that Americans were struggling to win their independence on the battlefield, they were also struggling to create new institutions of government for themselves, to replace the British system they had repudiated. The construction of these new political institutions occurred in several stages and continued over a period of more than fifteen years. Yet its most crucial phase occurred in the very first years after independence, during the war itself; and it occurred not at the national but at the state level.

The formation of state governments began early in 1776, even before the adoption of the Declaration of Independence. It was the most creative period of American political development; for in it was determined the basic structure of the republic, and in it were resolved many of the early problems of republican government. At first, the new state constitutions reflected primarily the fear of bloated executive power that had become so pronounced during the 1760s and early 1770s. Gradually, however, Americans began to become equally concerned about the instability of a government too responsive to the popular will. In a second phase of state constitution writing, therefore, they gave renewed attention to the idea of balance in government.

The Assumptions of Republicanism

If Americans agreed on nothing else when they began to build new governments for themselves, they agreed that those governments would be republican. To them, that meant a political system in which all power was derived from the people, rather than from some supreme authority (such as a king) standing above them. The success of any government, therefore, depended on the nature of its citizenry. If the population consisted of sturdy, independent property owners, then the republic could survive. If it consisted of a few powerful aristocrats and a great mass of dependent workers, then it would be in danger. From the beginning, therefore, the ideal of the small freeholder became basic to American political ideology.

Another crucial part of that ideology was the concept of equality. The Declaration of Independence had given voice to that idea in its most ringing phrase: "all men are created equal." It was a belief that stood in direct contrast to the old European assumption of an inherited aristocracy. Every citizen, Americans believed, was born in a position of equality with every other citizen. It would be the innate talents and energies of individuals that would determine their roles in society, not their position at birth. The republican vision did not, in other words, envision a society without social gradations. Some people would inevitably be wealthier and more powerful than others. But all people would have to earn their success. There would be no equality of condition, but there would be full equality of opportunity.

In reality, of course, these assumptions could not always be sustained. The United States was never able to become a nation in which all citizens were independent property holders. From the beginning, there was a sizable dependent labor force—the white members of which were allowed many of the privileges of citizenship, the black members of which were allowed virtually no rights at all. American women remained both politically and economically subordinate, with few opportunities for advancement independent of their husbands. Native Americans were systematically exploited and displaced by whites hungry for land and impatient with legalities. Nor was it possible to ensure full equality of opportunity. American society was more open and more fluid than that of most European nations; but it remained true that wealth and privilege were often passed from one generation to another. The conditions of a person's birth survived as a crucial determinant of success.

Nevertheless, in embracing the assumptions of republicanism, Americans were adopting a powerful, even revolutionary new ideology, one that would enable them to create a form of government never before seen in the world. Their experiment in statecraft became a model for many other countries and made the United States for a time the most admired and studied nation on earth.

The First State Constitutions

Two of the original thirteen states saw no need to produce new constitutions. Connecticut and Rhode Island already had corporate charters which provided them with governments that were republican in all but name; they simply deleted references to England and the king from their charters and adopted them as constitutions. The other eleven states, however, chose to create entirely new governments. In doing so, Americans at first devoted their greatest efforts to avoiding what they considered to be the problems of the British system they were repudiating.

The first and perhaps most basic decision was that the constitutions were to be written down. In England, the constitution was not a document but a vague understanding about the way society should be structured. Americans believed that the vagueness of that understanding had allowed the British government to become corrupted. To avoid a similar fate, they insisted that their own government rest on clearly stated and permanently inscribed laws, so that no individual or group could pervert them.

The second decision was that the power of the executive, which Americans believed had grown bloated and threatening in England (and even, at times, in the colonies), must be limited. Only one state went so far as to eliminate the executive altogether: Pennsylvania. But most states inserted provisions sharply limiting the power of the governor over appointments, reducing or eliminating his right to veto bills, and preventing him from dismissing or otherwise interfering with the legislature. Above all, every state forbade the governor or any other executive officer from holding a seat in the legislature, thus ensuring that the two branches of government would remain wholly separate, that the English parliamentary system would not be re-created in America. The constitutions also added provisions protecting the judiciary from executive control, although in most states the courts had not yet emerged as fully autonomous branches of government.

In limiting the executive and expanding the power of the legislature, the new constitutions were moving far in the direction of direct popular rule. They did not, however, move all the way. Only in Georgia and Pennsylvania did the legislature consist of one house. In all the other states, there was an upper and a lower chamber; and in most cases, the upper chamber was designed to represent the "higher orders" of society. In all states, there were property requirements for voters—in some states, only the modest amount that would qualify a person as a taxpayer, in other states somewhat greater requirements. Such requirements tended to have little impact, since property ownership was widespread among the white male population. But universal suffrage was not yet an accepted part of American government.

The initial phase of constitution writing proceeded rapidly. Ten of the states completed the process before the end of 1776. Only Georgia, New York, and Massachusetts delayed. Georgia and New York completed the task by the end of the following year, but Massachusetts did not finally adopt its version until 1780. By then, the construction of state governments had moved into a new phase.

Revising State Governments

By the late 1770s, Americans were already growing concerned about what they perceived as the excessive factiousness and instability of their new state governments. Legislatures were the scene of constant squabbling. Governors were unable to exercise sufficient power to provide any real leadership. It was proving extraordinarily difficult to get the new governments to accomplish anything at all. To many observers, the problem began to appear to be one of too much democracy. By placing so much power in the hands of the people (and of their elected representatives in the legislature), the state constitutions were inviting disorder and political turbulence.

As a result, most of the states began to revise their constitutions to cope with these problems. Massachusetts was the first to act on the new concerns. By waiting until 1780 before finally ratifying its first constitution, Massachusetts allowed these changing ideas to shape its government; and the state produced a constitution that was to serve as a model for the efforts of others.

Two changes in particular characterized the Massachusetts and later constitutions. The first was a change in the process of constitution writing itself. In the first phase, the documents had usually been written by state legislatures. As a result, they could easily be amended (or violated) by those same bodies. By 1780, sentiment was growing to find a way to protect the constitutions from the people who had written them, to make it difficult to change the documents once they were approved. The solution was the constitutional convention: a special assembly of the people that would meet only for the purpose of writing the constitution and that would never (except under extraordinary circumstances) meet again. The constitution would, therefore, be the product of the popular will; but once approved, it would be protected from the whims of public opinion and from the political moods of the legislature.

The second change was similarly a reflection of the new concerns about excessive popular power: a significant strengthening of the executive. In Massachusetts, the governor under the 1780 constitution became one of the strongest in any state. He was to be elected directly by the people; he was to have a fixed salary (in other words, he would not be dependent on the good will of the legislature each year for his wages); he would have expanded powers of appointment; and he would be able to veto legislation. Other states soon followed. Those states that had weak or nonexistent upper houses strengthened or created them. Most states increased the powers of the governor; and Pennsylvania, which had had no executive at all at first, now produced a strong one. By the late 1780s, almost every state had either revised its constitution or drawn up an entirely new one to make allowances for the belief in the need for stability.

Opportunity, Toleration, and Slavery

The new state governments—both under the first constitutions and under the later, revised ones—adopted a number of policies that increased opportunities for social and political mobility. In one way or another, they multiplied opportunities for land ownership and thus enlarged the voting population. For example, they eliminated the legal rights of primogeniture (the requirement that a father's estate be passed intact to his first son) and entail (whereby a man kept his estate intact from generation to generation by willing that it never be sold). In fact, neither practice had ever been widespread in America; but in a few places, the new laws did contribute to the erosion of landed aristocracies.

The new states also moved far in the direction of complete religious freedom. Most Americans continued to believe that religion should play some role in government; but they did not wish to give special privileges to any particular denomination. In some states, religious tests survived as a qualification for officeholding. (Atheists, and in a few places Catholics, were barred from office; but since there were few of either in most of the states in question, the requirements were largely meaningless.) More characteristic, however, was the erosion of the privileges that many churches had once enjoyed. New York and the Southern states, in which the Church of England had been tax-supported, soon saw to the complete disestablishment of the church; and the New England states stripped the Congregational church of many of its privileges. Boldest of all was Virginia, which in its Declaration of Rights announced the principle of complete toleration. And in 1786, Virginia enacted a Statute of Religious Liberty, written by Thomas Jefferson, which called for the complete separation of church and state.

More difficult to resolve was the question of slavery. The rhetoric of the Revolution—which emphasized the importance of liberty and the danger of enslavement—could not help but direct attention to America's own institution of bondage. And in some places, it cast the institution into disrepute. In areas where slavery was weak—in New England, where there had never been many slaves, and in Pennsylvania, where the Quakers were outspoken in their opposition to slavery—it was abolished. Pennsylvania

passed a general gradual-emancipation act in 1780; and the supreme court of Massachusetts ruled in 1783 that the ownership of slaves was impermissible under the state's bill of rights. Even in the South, there were some pressures to amend the institution (a result, in part, of the activities of the first antislavery society in America, founded in 1775). Every state but South Carolina and Georgia prohibited the further importation of slaves from abroad, and even South Carolina laid a temporary wartime ban on the slave trade. Virginia passed a law encouraging manumission (the freeing of slaves), and other states encountered growing political pressures to change the institution.

In the end, however, most of the pressures came to naught. Slavery survived in all the Southern and border states; and it would continue to survive for nearly a century more. The reasons were many. Racist assumptions about the natural inferiority of blacks persuaded many Americans that there was nothing incompatible in asserting innate human rights while denying those rights to blacks. And economic pressures made whites reluctant to free slaves. Many Southerners had enormous investments in their black laborers and were unwilling to consider losing them.

An equally important obstacle was that few Southerners—even such men as Washington and Jefferson, who expressed deep moral misgivings about slavery—could envision any alternative to it. If slavery were abolished, what would happen to the black people in America? Some argued that they should be sent back to Africa, but that was clearly unrealistic. The black population was too large; and many slaves were now so many generations removed from Africa that they felt but little identification with it and had no wish to return. Few whites believed that blacks could be integrated into American society as equals. Even those most opposed to slavery usually shared the general assumptions about the unfitness of blacks for citizenship. In maintaining slavery, Jefferson once remarked, Americans were holding a "wolf by the ears." However unappealing it was to hold on to, letting go promised to be even worse. Jefferson himself, for all his qualms, never let go. He continued to own slaves until he died; and unlike George Washington, he made no provision for their freedom on his death.

There was, finally, a more subtle obstacle to the elimination of slavery. The economy of the South depended, most Southerners believed, on a large, servile labor force. Yet the ideals of republicanism required a homogeneous population of independent, property-owning citizens. Were slavery to be abolished, the South would find itself with a substantial population of unpropertied free people; and whether that class were black or white, its existence would raise troubling implications for the future of democracy. The social tensions that would inevitably ensue would, Southerners feared, ultimately destroy the stability of society.

Thus, just as in the early years of settlement, so during the Revolution: Americans encountered only vague, philosophical pressures to abolish slavery but powerful social and economic pressures to maintain it. As a result, slavery survived.

The Search for a National Government

Americans were much quicker to agree on the proper shape of their state institutions than they were to decide on the form of their national government. At first, most believed that the central government should remain a relatively weak and unimportant force—indeed, it should remain something less than a government at all. Each state would be virtually a sovereign nation. National institutions would serve only as loose, coordinating mechanisms, with little independent authority. Such beliefs reflected the assumption that a republic operated best in a relatively limited, homogeneous area; that were a republican government to attempt to administer too large and diverse a nation, it would founder. It was in response to such ideas that the Articles of Confederation emerged.

The Confederation

No sooner did the Continental Congress appoint a committee to draft a declaration of independence in 1776 than it appointed another to draft a plan of union. After much debate and many revisions, the Congress adopted the committee's proposal in November 1777 as the Articles of Confederation.

The Articles provided for a national political structure very similar to the one already in operation. Congress was to survive as the central—indeed the only—institution of national authority. But its powers were to be somewhat expanded. It was to have

the authority to conduct wars and foreign relations, and to appropriate, borrow, and issue money. But it could not regulate trade, draft troops, or levy taxes directly on the people. For troops and taxes it would have to make requisitions of the states; it would, in effect, have to address formal requests to the state legislatures, which could and often did refuse them. There was to be no separate, single, strong executive (the "president of the United States" was to be merely the presiding officer at the sessions of Congress). Congress itself was to see to the execution of laws through an executive committee of thirteen, made up of one member from each state; through ad hoc and standing committees for specific functions; and through such administrative departments as it might choose to create. There were to be no Confederation courts, except for courts of admiralty; disputes among the states were to be settled by a complicated system of arbitration. States were to retain their individual sovereignty, each of the legislatures electing and paying the salaries of two to seven delegates to Congress, and each delegation, no matter how numerous, having only one vote. At least nine of the states (through their delegations) would have to approve any important measure, such as a treaty, before Congress could pass it; and all thirteen state legislatures would have to approve before the Articles could be ratified or amended.

Ratification was delayed by differences of opinion about the proposed plan. The small states insisted on equal state representation, but the larger states wanted representation to be based on population. More important, the states claiming Western lands wished to keep them, but the rest of the states demanded that all such territory be turned over to the Confederation government. The "landed" states founded their claims largely on colonial charters. The "landless" states, particularly Maryland, maintained that as the fruit of common sacrifices in war the Western lands had become the rightful property of all the states. At last New York gave up its rather hazy claim, and Virginia made a qualified offer to cede its lands to Congress. Then Maryland, the only state still holding out against ratification, approved the Articles of Confederation, and they went into effect in 1781. The Confederation thus came into being in time to conclude the war and make the peace. Until then, during the years of fighting from 1775 to 1781, the Second Continental Congress had served as the agency for directing and coordinating the war effort of the thirteen states.

In later years, it became popular to characterize

the performance of the Confederation, which existed from 1781 until 1789, as an almost total failure. Such judgments are not entirely fair. The Confederation did manage to solve some of the problems facing the new nation. It performed particularly effectively in organizing America's territories in the West. Yet the new government was far from a success. Lacking adequate powers to deal with interstate issues, lacking any effective mechanisms that would have permitted it to enforce its will on the states, and lacking sufficient stature in the eyes of the world to be able to negotiate effectively, it suffered a series of damaging setbacks.

Diplomatic Failures

Evidence of the low esteem in which the rest of the world held the Confederation was its difficulty in persuading Great Britain (and to a lesser extent Spain) to live up to the terms of the peace treaty of 1783. That treaty had recognized the independence of the United States and granted the new nation a vast domain—on paper. But Americans found it hard to exercise their full sovereignty in fact.

Even though the treaty had pledged the British to evacuate American soil, British forces continued to occupy a string of frontier posts along the Great Lakes within the United States. The Canadians and the British wanted to maintain points of contact with Indian tribes in the Northwest for the conduct of the fur trade and the continuance of defensive alliances with them. Nor did the British honor their agreement to make restitution to slaveowners whose slaves the British army had confiscated. The British justified these violations of the treaty by pointing to American violations. The United States had not honored its promise to make restitution to the Loyalists; and it had reneged on the agreement to honor debts to English creditors.

There were disputes as well over boundaries. The two countries argued over the northeastern boundary of the new nation. And the peace arrangements led also to a boundary dispute between the United States and Spain. Britain ceded Florida back to Spain in the 1783 settlement (it had acquired Florida in the 1763 treaty) but made no precise definition of the territory's northern boundary. The Spanish and the Americans disagreed sharply over that definition.

The peace with Great Britain failed in other ways to give Americans the benefits they desired and ex-pected. American merchants now had new opportunities for exploiting worldwide routes of trade, which before the war had been legally closed to them. But while commerce was expanding in new directions, most American trade continued in the prewar, imperial pattern. To earn the British funds needed to pay for British imports, Americans wanted full access to British markets; England, however, placed sharp postwar restrictions on that access.

In 1784, Congress sent John Adams as minister to London with instructions to get a commercial treaty and speed up the evacuation of the frontier posts; but that effort simply produced more humiliation for the Confederation. Taunted by the query whether he represented one nation or thirteen, Adams made no headway in England. And throughout the 1780s, the British government refused even to return the courtesy of sending a minister to the American capital.

In dealing with the Spanish government, the Confederation demonstrated similar weakness. Spain, unlike England, was willing to discuss its differences with the United States, and in 1785 its representative, Diego de Gardoqui, arrived in New York (where Congress had moved from Philadelphia) to negotiate with the secretary for foreign affairs, John Jay. After months of friendly conversations, Jay and Gardoqui initialed a treaty in 1786. It called for the Spanish government to grant Americans the right to trade with Spain but not with its colonies; it accepted the American interpretation of the Florida boundary; and (in a secret article) it called for a Spanish-American alliance to protect American soil from British encroachments. The United States would guarantee Spanish possessions in America and would agree to "forbear" (although not officially to abandon) its right to navigate the Mississippi for twenty years. But the treaty came to naught. Southern states were incensed at the idea of giving up their access to the Mississippi in exchange for trading privileges that would benefit only Northern merchants. Jay could not win ratification of the treaty by the necessary nine states.

The Confederation and the Northwest

The Confederation's most important accomplishment was its resolution of some of the potentially explosive controversies involving settlement and development of the Western lands—although even this achievement in the end served as evidence of the new government's essential impotence.

During and after the Revolution, unprecedented numbers of American settlers had moved into the trans-Appalachian lands that the British had attempted to reserve for the Indians. When the war began, only a few thousand whites had lived west of the Appalachian divide; by 1790 their numbers had increased to 120,000. The colonial governments and, for a time, the Continental Congress had long ignored these Western settlements. The Confederation now faced the daunting task of trying to include them in the political structure of the new nation. The West-

ern settlers were already often in conflict with the established centers of the East over Indian policies, trade provisions, and taxes. At times, in fact (as with the Paxton Boys uprising in Pennsylvania in 1763 and the Regulator movements in North Carolina in 1771), there had been overt hostilities between Eastern and Western peoples.

For a time, Congress faced the additional difficulty of competing with state governments for jurisdiction over the trans-Appalachian region. With Virginia's cession of its Western territory to Congress in 1781, the landed states began to yield their claims to the Confederation. Although not until 1802

State Claims to Western Lands and Cessions to National Government, 1782–1802

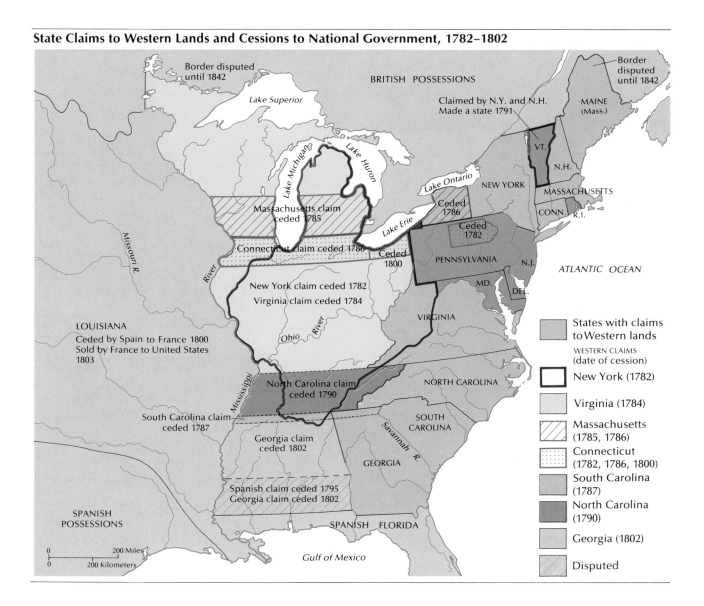

did the last of the states, Georgia, give up its claim, by 1784 the states had ceded enough land to the Confederation to permit Congress to begin making policy for the national domain.

Congress's first and most important decision was to create a process by which the Western territories would ultimately become states. The Ordinance of 1784, based on a proposal by Thomas Jefferson, divided the territory into ten self-governing districts, each of which could petition Congress for statehood when its population equaled the number of free inhabitants of the smallest existing state. Then, in the Ordinance of 1785, Congress devised a system for surveying and selling the Western lands—partly because the Confederation, desperately in need of money, was eager for the income land sales would provide. The territory north of the Ohio River was to be surveyed and marked off into neat rectangular townships, each six miles square and containing thirty-six one-square-mile sections. (This grid system established a pattern that would leave an indelible mark on the American landscape and, through it, the American economy. See "The American Environment," pp. 245–249.) In every township four sections were to be set aside for the United States; and the revenue from the sale of one was to support creation of a public school (the first example of federal aid to education). Sections were to be sold at auction for not less than one dollar an acre. Since there were 640 acres in a section, the prospective buyer of government land had to have at least $640— a very large sum by the standards of the day.

Despite protests from Jefferson and others that these terms favored land speculators at the expense of the actual settlers, Congress moved quickly to begin the sales. When the survey proved slower than expected, it disposed of several million unsurveyed acres to the Ohio and Scioto companies (land speculation businesses) by accepting as payment loan certificates that had been issued during the war to American soldiers. Those certificates were by now almost worthless, and most of the soldiers had long since sold them to speculators at a fraction of their original worth. By agreeing to accept them at face value, Congress provided a tremendous boon for the speculators. In addition, Virginia and Connecticut had reserved other large tracts of land at the time of cession for their Revolutionary War veterans. Thus, even before the government finished its surveys, much of the best Western land was already spoken for.

In 1787, after strenuous lobbying by the Ohio and Scioto companies and in response to their own

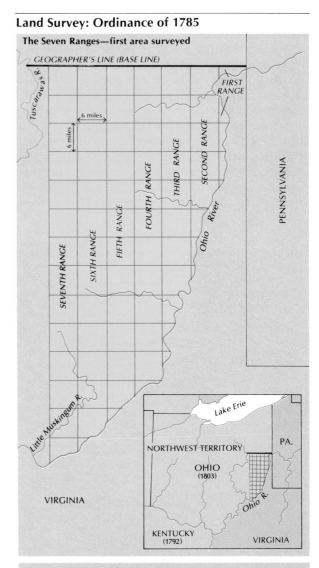

Land Survey: Ordinance of 1785

The Seven Ranges—first area surveyed

GEOGRAPHER'S LINE (BASE LINE)

FIRST RANGE
SECOND RANGE
THIRD RANGE
FOURTH RANGE
FIFTH RANGE
SIXTH RANGE
SEVENTH RANGE

Tuscarawas R.
6 miles
6 miles
Ohio River
PENNSYLVANIA
Little Muskingum R.

Lake Erie
NORTHWEST TERRITORY
PA.
OHIO (1803)
Ohio R.
VIRGINIA
KENTUCKY (1792)
VIRGINIA

One township (six miles square)

36	30	24	18	12	6
35	29*	23	17	11*	5
34	28	22	16	10	4
33	27	21	15	9	3
32	26*	20	14	8*	2
31	25	19	13	7	1

Section 16 reserved for school funds

*Four sections reserved for subsequent sale

6 miles

1 mile

A

B | C
   | D | E

One section = 640 acres (1 mile square)
A Half section = 320 acres
B Quarter section = 160 acres
C Half-quarter section = 80 acres
D & E Quarter-quarter section = 40 acres

concerns about the 1784 law, Congress passed yet another law governing Western settlement—legislation that became known as the "Northwest Ordinance." Instead of the ten territories the 1784 law had proposed establishing, the 1787 Ordinance created a single Northwest Territory, which might subsequently be divided into between three and five territories. (This was, in part, a response to the fear of the existing states that they would soon be heavily outnumbered by new states in the West.) It also specified the process by which each territory could become a state and established a population of 60,000 as a minimum for statehood. The law also guaranteed freedom of religion and the right to trial by jury in the Northwest. And it prohibited slavery throughout the territory.

The Western lands south of the Ohio River did not receive the same attention from Congress, and development of that region was more chaotic. There was rapid settlement in the region that became Kentucky and Tennessee beginning in the late 1770s; in the 1780s, speculators and settlers began trying to set up governments of their own without guidelines from Congress, and then to ask for recognition as states. The Confederation Congress was never able successfully to sort out and resolve the conflicting claims in that region. But in the Northwest territory, the Western land policies of the Confederation created a system that—on paper at least—brought a high degree of order and stability to the process of white settlement.

Indians and the Western Lands

In reality, however, that order and stability came slowly, and at great cost. That was because the lands the Confederation was taking from the states, neatly subdividing, and offering for sale consisted in large part of territory claimed by the Indians of the region. Congress tried to resolve that problem in 1784, 1785, and 1786 by persuading Iroquois, Choctaw, Chickasaw, and Cherokee leaders to sign several treaties ceding substantial Western lands in the North and South to the United States. But those agreements proved largely ineffective. Even the Indian nations that agreed to the treaties did so grudgingly. In 1786, the leadership of the Iroquois Confederacy repudiated the treaty it had signed two years earlier and threatened to attack the white settlements in the disputed lands (although by then the Six Nations were too weak to mount an effective resistance). Other

tribes had never agreed to the treaties affecting them. One of those, the Creeks, strenuously resisted white movement into their lands in Georgia and South Carolina for five years until 1790 when their leader, Alexander McGillivray (who had fought with the British during the Revolution), negotiated a treaty with the federal government settling the dispute for a time. Other tribes—among them the Miami, Shawnee, Delaware, Ottawa, and Chippewa—some of whom had once been represented in negotiations with whites by the Iroquois, formed new confederations of their own in an effort to strengthen their hand in dealings with the U.S. government.

Violence between whites and Indians on the Northwest frontier reached a crescendo in the early 1790s. The first governor of the new Northwest Territory, General Arthur St. Clair, tried and failed in 1789 to forge an agreement with the recalcitrant Miami, Shawnee, and Delaware, who were preventing the Ohio Company and others from extending white settlement north of the Ohio River. In 1790 and again in 1791, the Miami, led by the famed warrior Little Turtle, defeated United States forces in two major battles near what is now the western border of Ohio; in the second of those battles, on November 4, 1791, 630 white Americans died in fighting at the Wabash River (the greatest military victory Indians had ever or would ever achieve in their battles with whites). Efforts to negotiate a settlement foundered on the Miami insistence that no treaty was possible that did not forbid white settlement west of the Ohio River. Not until 1794, when General Anthony Wayne led another army into the Ohio Valley, did negotiations resume. Wayne led 4,000 soldiers into the region, moved cautiously toward the Maumee River, and built forts as he went. British officials in Canada, who were providing supplies to the Indians, themselves constructed a fort about twenty miles from the mouth of the river, well within the boundaries of the United States. In the summer of 1794, Wayne met and decisively defeated the Indians in a battle fought near the British fort: the Battle of Fallen Timbers, so named because it occurred at a place where trees had been blown over by a wind storm. The British garrison prudently stayed out of the fight.

A year later, the Miami signed the Treaty of Greenville, ceding substantial new lands to the United States in exchange for a formal acknowledgment of their claim to that portion of their territory they retained. This was the first recognition by the United States government of the sovereignty of Indian nations; in doing so, the U.S. was repudiating

Little Turtle
Little Turtle led the Miami confederacy in its wars with the United States in what is now Ohio and Indiana in the early 1790s. For a time he seemed almost invincible, but in 1794 Little Turtle was defeated in the Battle of Fallen Timbers. In this sketch (a rough copy of a painting attributed to Gilbert Stuart), Little Turtle wears a medal bearing the likeness of George Washington, awarded him by the United States after the signing of the Treaty of Greenville.   (The Bettmann Archive)

its earlier position and affirming that Indian lands could be ceded only by the tribes themselves. That hard-won assurance, however, proved a frail protection against the pressure for white expansion westward in later years.

The conflicts in the Ohio Valley in the aftermath of the Northwest Ordinance suggested the continuing tenuousness of the American claim to control of its Western territories. Large areas of the region remained highly unstable, and hence unreceptive to white settlement, until the first decades of the nineteenth century.

Debts, Taxes, and Daniel Shays

At the end of the Revolutionary war, foreign ships crowded into American seaports with cargoes of all kinds, and the American people bought extravagantly with cash or credit—satisfying a desire for foreign goods that had found few outlets during the Revolution. As a result, there was a rapid and substantial flow of hard currency out of the country. Consumer indebtedness to importing merchants increased greatly. And a postwar depression, which lasted from 1784 to 1787, was intensified. The depression increased the perennial American problem of an inadequate money supply, a problem that bore particularly heavily on debtors. It was in dealing with this increasingly serious problem of debts that Congress was perceived as having most seriously failed.

The Confederation itself had an enormous outstanding debt, and few means with which to pay it. It had borrowed money during the war that was now due to be repaid; it owed money to its Revolutionary soldiers; it had substantial debts abroad. Its powers of taxation, in the meantime, were limited. Because it could not impose taxes directly on the people, it had to make requisitions of the states, which the states often refused to meet. On the whole, Congress received only about one-sixth of the money it requisitioned—barely enough to meet the government's ordinary operating expenses. The nation was faced with the prospect of defaulting on its obligations, a possibility that threatened to destroy the fragile new government.

This alarming prospect brought to the fore a group of leaders who would play a crucial role in the shaping of the republic for several decades. Committed nationalists, they were seeking ways to increase the powers of the central government and to permit it to meet its financial obligations. Robert Morris, the head of the Confederation's treasury; Alexander Hamilton, his young protégé; James Madison of Virginia; and others were soon lobbying for a "continental impost"—a 5 percent duty on imported goods, to be levied by Congress and used to fund the debt. The impost would, the nationalists believed, not only preserve the financial integrity of the new nation; it would strengthen the national government by making it principally responsible for the nation's debts.

But their schemes met with substantial opposition. Many Americans feared that the impost plan was the first step toward the creation of a corrupt center of privilege, that it would concentrate too

SIGNIFICANT EVENTS

much financial power in the hands of Robert Morris and his allies in Philadelphia. The first effort to secure the impost, in 1781, received the approval of twelve state delegations in Congress; but it required unanimity, and Rhode Island's refusal to agree killed the plan. A second effort in 1783 also failed to win approval. Angry and discouraged, the nationalists largely withdrew from any active involvement in the Confederation. But some of them—most notably Alexander Hamilton—would return to fight virtually the same battles again in the first years of government under the Constitution.

In the absence of any effective action by Congress, the domestic debt problem remained in the hands of the states, which generally relied on increased taxation to deal with their financial difficulties. To the state creditors—that is, the bondholders—this was

sound, honest public finance, which protected their legitimate interests. But poor farmers, already burdened by debt and now burdened again by taxes on their lands, considered such policies unfair, even tyrannical. They demanded that the state governments issue paper currency to increase the money supply and make it easier for them to meet their obligations. Resentment ran especially high among farmers in New England, who felt that the states were extorting money from them to swell the coffers of wealthy bondholders in Boston and other towns. Debtors who failed to pay their taxes found their mortgages foreclosed and their property seized; sometimes they found themselves in jail.

Throughout the late 1780s, therefore, mobs of distressed farmers rioted periodically in various parts of New England. They caused the most serious trouble in Massachusetts. Dissidents in the Connecticut Valley and the Berkshire Hills, many of them Revolutionary veterans, rallied behind Daniel Shays, himself a former captain in the Continental army. Organizing and drilling his followers, Shays put forth a program of demands that included paper money, tax relief, a moratorium on debts, the removal of the state capital from Boston to the interior, and the abolition of imprisonment for debt. During the summer of 1786, the Shaysites concentrated on the immediate task of preventing the collection of debts, private or public, and went in armed bands from place to place to keep courts from sitting and to prevent sheriffs' sales of confiscated property. In Boston, members of the legislature, including Samuel Adams, denounced Shays and his men as rebels and traitors.

When winter came, the rebels advanced on Springfield hoping to seize weapons from the arsenal there. An army of state militiamen, financed by a loan from wealthy merchants who feared a new revolution, set out from Boston to confront them. In January 1787, this army met Shays's ragged troops, killed several of them, captured many more, and scattered the rest to the hills in a blinding snowstorm.

As a military enterprise, Shays's Rebellion was a fiasco. But it had important consequences for the future of the United States. In Massachusetts, it resulted in a few immediate gains for the discontented groups. Shays and his lieutenants, at first sentenced to death, were soon pardoned, and some concessions to Shays's earlier demands were granted in the way of tax relief and the postponement of debt payments. Far more significant, however, the rebellion added urgency to a movement already gathering support throughout the new nation—the movement to produce a new, national constitution.

SUGGESTED READINGS

General Histories. Robert Middlekauff, *The Glorious Cause: The American Revolution, 1763–1789* (1985); Edward Countryman, *The American Revolution* (1985); Alfred E. Young, Jr., ed., *The American Revolution* (1976); Merrill Jensen, *The Founding of a Nation, A History of the American Revolution, 1763–1789* (1968); Edmund S. Morgan, *The Birth of the Republic, 1763–1789* (1956); Michael Kammen, *A Season of Youth: The American Revolution and the Historical Imagination* (1978).

The Road to Independence. Carl Becker, *The Declaration of Independence* (1922); Morton White, *The Philosophy of the American Revolution* (1978); Gary Wills, *Inventing America* (1978); Eric Foner, *Tom Paine and Revolutionary America* (1976); David Hawke, *Paine* (1974); Peter Shaw, *The Character of John Adams* (1976) and *American Patriots and the Rituals of Revolution* (1981); John R. Howe, Jr., *The Changing Political Thought of John Adams* (1966); Edmund S. Morgan, *The Meaning of Independence* (1976).

The War. Willard Wallace, *Appeal to Arms* (1950); John R. Alden, *The American Revolution* (1964); Piers Mackesy, *The War for America* (1964); Don Higginbotham, *The American War for Independence* (1971) and *George Washington and the American Military Tradition* (1985); Howard H. Peckham, *The War for Independence* (1958); Christopher Ward, *The War of the Revolution*, 2 vols. (1952); John Shy, *A People Numerous and Armed* (1976); Charles Royster, *A Revolutionary People at War* (1979); G. W. Allen, *Naval History of the American Revolution*, 2 vols. (1913); Samuel Eliot Morison, *John Paul Jones* (1959); T. G. Frothingham, *Washington: Commander in Chief* (1930); Douglas Southall Freeman, *George Washington*, 7 vols. (1948–1957); James T. Flexner, *George Washington in the American Revolution* (1968); Charles Royster, *Light-Horse Harry Lee and the Legacy of the American Revolution* (1981); E. Wayne Carp, *To Starve the Army at Pleasure: Continental Army Administration and American Political Culture, 1775–1783* (1984).

Revolutionary Diplomacy. Samuel F. Bemis, *The Diplomacy of the American Revolution* (1935); Richard B. Morris, *The Peacemakers* (1965); Gerald Stourzh, *Benjamin Franklin and American Foreign Policy*, rev. ed. (1969); Jonathan R. Dull, *A Diplomatic History of the American Revolution* (1985); L. S. Kaplan, *Colonies into Nation: American Diplomacy, 1763–1801* (1972); Clarence L. Ver Steeg, *Robert Morris* (1954); E. J. Ferguson, *The Power of the Purse* (1961).

The Loyalists. Wallace Brown, *The King's Friends* (1965); Robert M. Calhoon, *The Loyalists in Revolutionary America* (1973); Mary Beth Norton, *The British Americans: The Loyalist Exiles in England 1774–1789* (1972); William H. Nelson, *The American Tory* (1962); Bernard Bailyn, *The Ordeal of Thomas Hutchinson* (1974); Paul H. Smith, *Loyalists and Redcoats* (1964); James W. St. G. Walker, *The Black Loyalists* (1976).

Women, Family, and the Revolution. Mary Beth Norton, *Liberty's Daughters* (1980); Linda K. Kerber, *Women of the Republic* (1980); Linda Grant DePauw, *Founding Mothers* (1975); Joan Jensen, *Loosening the Bonds: Mid-Atlantic Farm Women, 1750–1850* (1986); Joy Day Buel and Richard Buel, Jr., *The Way of Duty: A Woman and Her Family in Revolutionary America* (1984); Jay Fliegelman, *Prodigals and Pilgrims* (1982).

Indians and Blacks in the Revolution. James H. O'Donnell, III, *Southern Indians in the American Revolution* (1973); Barbara Graymont, *The Iroquois in the American Revolution* (1973); Isabel T. Kelsay, *Joseph Brant, 1743–1807* (1984);

Anthony F. C. Wallace, *The Death and Rebirth of the Seneca* (1969); Benjamin Quarles, *The Negro in the American Revolution* (1961); Duncan McLeod, *Slavery, Race and the American Revolution* (1974); Ira Berlin and Ronald Hoffman, eds., *Slavery in the Revolutionary Era* (1982); David Brion Davis, *The Problem of Slavery in the Age of Revolution* (1975); Edmund S. Morgan, *American Slavery, American Freedom* (1975); Arthur Zilversmit, *The First Emancipation* (1967).

Social Effects.   J. F. Jameson, *The American Revolution Considered as a Social Movement* (1962); Staughton Lynd, *Class Conflict, Slavery and the United States Constitution* (1968); Merrill Jensen, *The American Revolution Within America* (1974); Richard McCormick, *Experiment in Independence* (1950); Jackson Turner Main, *The Social Structure of Revolutionary America* (1965); Jerome J. Nadlehaft, *The Disorders of War: The Revolution in South Carolina* (1981); Robert Gross, *The Minutemen and Their World* (1976); Charles G. Steffen, *The Mechanics of Baltimore: Workers and Politics in the Age of Revolution, 1763–1812* (1984); Edward Countryman, *A People in Revolution* (1981).

State Governments.   Gordon S. Wood, *The Creation of the American Republic* (1969); Stephen E. Patterson, *Political Parties in Revolutionary Massachusetts* (1973); Irwin Polishook, *Rhode Island and the Union, 1774–1795* (1969); Willi Paul Adams, *The First American Constitutions* (1980); Jackson Turner Main, *Political Parties Before the Constitution* (1973), *The Sovereign States, 1775–1783* (1973), and *The Upper House in Revolutionary America, 1763–1788* (1967).

The Articles of Confederation.   John Fiske, *The Critical Period of American History, 1783–1789* (1883); Jack N. Rakove, *The Beginnings of National Politics* (1979); Merrill Jensen, *The New Nation* (1950) and *The Articles of Confederation,* rev. ed. (1959); H. James Henderson, *Party Politics in the Continental Congress* (1974); Jack Eblen, *The First and Second United States Empires* (1968); David Szatmary, *Shays' Rebellion: The Making of an Agrarian Insurrection* (1980); Andrew R. L. Cayton, *The Frontier Republic: Ideology and Politics in the Ohio Country, 1780–1825* (1986); Steven Watts, *The Republic Reborn: War and the Making of Liberal America, 1790–1800* (1987).

The Inauguration of George Washington, April 30, 1789
Washington took the oath of office as the first president of the United States under the new Constitution at Federal Hall in New York City, which was then the nation's capital city. *(The Granger Collection)*

CHAPTER 6

⬚ ⬚ ⬚

The Constitution and the New Republic

⬚ ⬚ ⬚

By the late 1780s, most Americans had grown deeply dissatisfied with the deficiencies of the Confederation. The national government was plagued with factiousness and instability. It was unable to deal effectively with the economic problems that affected the new nation. It had displayed a frightening powerlessness in the face of Shays's Rebellion and in the process had demonstrated the existence of a serious power vacuum; the national government did not have the authority to deal with rebellions, and the states did not have the resources to do so alone.

A decade earlier, Americans had deliberately avoided creating a genuine national government, fearing that it would encroach on the sovereignty of the individual states. Now they were ready to reconsider. Serious discussions began in 1786 about the construction of a new political system, and in 1787, the nation created for itself what the individual states had created for themselves years before: a written constitution and a government consisting of three independent branches.

The American Constitution derived most of its principles from the state documents that had preceded it. But it was also a remarkable achievement in its own right. Out of the contentious atmosphere of a fragile new nation, Americans fashioned a system of government that would survive for more than two centuries as one of the stablest and most successful in the world. William Gladstone, the great nineteenth-century British statesman, once called the Constitution the "most wonderful work ever struck off at a given time by the brain and purpose of man." And although Gladstone may have exaggerated, the American people in the years to come generally agreed. Indeed, to them the Constitution took on some of the characteristics of a sacred document, a holy mystery. Later generations viewed its framers as men almost godlike in their wisdom. They considered its provisions, set out in a brief 7,000 words, an unassailable "fundamental law," from which all public policies, all political principles, all solutions of controversies must spring.

Yet the adoption of the Constitution did not complete the creation of the republic. It only defined the terms in which debate over the future of government would continue. Americans may have agreed that the Constitution was a nearly perfect document, but they disagreed—at times fundamentally—on what that document meant. Some believed that the founders had intended the federal government to exercise broad powers beyond those specifically enumerated in the Constitution ("implied powers"). Others argued that the framers had intended to limit federal power to the precise areas specified in the Constitution ("expressed powers"), that all other authority would remain at the state level. Out of this disagreement emerged the first great political battles of the new nation.

Toward a New Government

So unpopular and ineffectual had the Confederation Congress become by the mid-1780s that it began to lead an almost waiflike existence. In 1783, its members timidly withdrew from Philadelphia to escape from the clamor of army veterans demanding their back pay. They took refuge for a while in Princeton, New Jersey, then moved on to Annapolis, and in 1785 settled in New York. Through all of this, the delegates were often conspicuous largely by their absence. Only with great difficulty was a quorum secured to permit ratification of the treaty with Great Britain ending the Revolutionary War. Eighteen members, representing only eight states, voted on the Confederation's most important piece of legislation, the Northwest Ordinance. In the meantime, a major public debate was beginning over the future of the Confederation.

Advocates of Centralization

Weak and unpopular though the Confederation was, it had for a time satisfied a great many—probably a majority—of the people. They did not want a strong or prestigious central government, and they were willing to tolerate the deficiencies of Congress in order to avoid the even greater problems they believed a more powerful national state would produce. They had fought the Revolutionary War to avert the danger of what they considered remote and tyrannical authority; now they desired to keep political power centered in the states, where it could be carefully and closely controlled.

Important groups in the population, however, were beginning to clamor for a national government capable of dealing with the new nation's many problems—particularly the economic problems that most directly afflicted them. Some military men, many of them members of the exclusive and hereditary Society of the Cincinnati (formed by Revolutionary army officers in 1783), were disgruntled at the refusal of Congress to fund their pensions. They began aspiring to influence and invigorate the national government; some even envisioned a form of military dictatorship and flirted briefly (in 1783, in the so-called Newburgh Conspiracy) with a direct challenge to Congress, until George Washington intervened and blocked the potential rebellion.

American manufacturers—the artisans and "mechanics"—wanted to replace the varying state tariffs with a uniformly high national duty. Merchants and shippers wanted to replace the thirteen different (and largely ineffective) state commercial policies with a single, national one. Land speculators wanted the "Indian menace" finally removed from their Western tracts. Creditors wanted to stop the states from issuing paper money. Investors in Confederation securities wanted the Confederation debt made good and the value of their securities enhanced. Large property owners in general looked for protection from the threat of mobs, a threat that seemed particularly menacing in light of such episodes as Shays's Rebellion.

By 1786, such demands had grown so powerful that the issue was no longer whether the Confederation should be changed but how drastic the changes should be. Even the defenders of the existing system reluctantly came to agree that the government needed strengthening at its weakest point—its lack of power to tax. The failure of Congress to approve Robert Morris's proposal for a continental impost discouraged those who believed that such strengthening could occur within the present system.

The most resourceful of the reformers was Alexander Hamilton, political genius, New York lawyer, one-time military aide to General Washington, and illegitimate son of a Scottish merchant in the West Indies. From the beginning, Hamilton had been dissatisfied with the Articles of Confederation. He now saw little to be gained by piecemeal amendments, and he called for a national convention to overhaul the entire document. To this end, he took advantage of a movement for interstate cooperation that began in 1785 when a group of Marylanders and Virginians met in Alexandria to settle differences between the two states.

One of the Virginians, James Madison, was as eager as Hamilton to see a stronger government. He induced the Virginia legislature to invite all the states to send delegates to a larger conference on commercial questions. This group met at Annapolis in 1786, but representatives from only five states appeared. Nevertheless, the delegates adopted a report drafted by Hamilton (who was representing New York) recommending that Congress call a convention of special delegates from all the states to gather in Philadelphia the next year and consider ways to "render the constitution of the Federal government adequate to the exigencies of the union."

At that moment, in 1786, there seemed little possibility that the Philadelphia convention would be any better attended or would accomplish any more than the meeting at Annapolis. Supporters of the idea believed that only by winning the support of George Washington could they hope to prevail. For a time, however, Washington showed little interest in joining the cause. Although he was one of the wealthiest

George Washington at Mount Vernon
Washington was in his first term as President in 1790 when an anonymous folk artist painted this view of his home at Mount Vernon, Virginia. Washington appears in uniform, along with members of his family, on the lawn. After he retired from office in 1797, Washington returned happily to his plantation and spent the two years before his death in 1799 "amusing myself in agricultural and rural pursuits." He also played host to an endless stream of visitors from throughout the country and Europe.   (National Gallery of Art, Washington)

men in the country, he was suffering from a common planter's malady: a temporary shortage of cash. So he was reluctant to undertake the trouble and expense of an extended visit to Philadelphia.

But then, early in 1787, the news of Shays's Rebellion spread throughout the nation, news that seemed to augur other, more dangerous insurrections elsewhere. Thomas Jefferson, then the American minister in Paris, was not alarmed. "I hold," he confided in a letter to James Madison, "that a little rebellion, now and then, is a good thing, and as necessary in the political world as storms in the physical." At Mount Vernon, however, Washington took the news less calmly. "There are combustibles in every State which a spark might set fire to," he exclaimed. "I feel infinitely more than I can express for the disorders which have arisen. Good God!" Some suggested that Washington make himself a military dictator; he refused even to consider the possibility. But after Congress issued its calls for a constitutional convention, he borrowed money for the journey and, in May, left Mount Vernon for Philadelphia.

A Divided Convention

Fifty-five men, representing all the states except Rhode Island, attended one or more sessions of the convention that sat in the Philadelphia State House from May to September 1787. They constituted a remarkable collection of talent, but they were far from the godlike creatures that later generations would at times describe. These "Founding Fathers," as they were to become known, were on the whole relatively young men. Many of them were in their twenties and thirties, and only one (Benjamin Franklin, then eighty-one years old) was genuinely aged. The average age was forty-four. They were men of practical experience in business, plantation management, and politics. And they were well educated by

The Signing of the Constitution, 1787
This mural by Albert Herter, depicting the final moments of the Constitutional Convention in Philadelphia, is in the Supreme Court chamber in the Wisconsin State Capitol. It shows George Washington seated behind the desk. In the right foreground are James Madison (holding his cloak) and Alexander Hamilton. Benjamin Franklin stands in the foreground at left.   (Brent Nicastro/Third Coast Stock Source)

the standards of their time; more than a third were college graduates. Most represented the great property interests of the country and, as such, feared what one of them called the "turbulence and follies" of democracy.

The convention's first decision (after unanimously choosing Washington to preside over its sessions) was to conduct its business in complete secrecy. There would be no official transcript of its deliberations; there would be no reports to the press. (In fact, if James Madison had not kept a private diary chronicling the proceedings, historians might know little about what happened in Philadelphia.) The second decision, of great importance, was that each state delegation would have a single vote (as in the Confederation Congress); but major decisions would not require unanimity, as they did in Congress, just a simple majority.

Almost all the delegates agreed that the United States needed a stronger central government. There were great differences of opinion, however, as to how much stronger the government should be, what specific powers it should have, and what its structure

should be. There were differences, in particular, over how power should be divided among the large and small states and over how economic interests in different sections of the country should be protected.

Among the states, Virginia was then much the largest in population. In Philadelphia, the Virginia delegates were also the best prepared for the work of the convention. And among the Virginians, James Madison (thirty-six years old) was the most important intellect. Even before the convention met, he had devised in some detail a plan for a new "national" government. Virginians controlled the agenda from the moment the convention began.

Edmund Randolph of Virginia opened the deliberations by proposing that "*a national* government ought to be established, consisting of a *supreme* Legislative, Executive, and Judiciary." For all its vagueness, this was a drastic proposal. It called for the creation of a government very different from the existing confederation. It is an indication of how committed the delegates were to fundamental reform that they approved this resolution after only perfunctory debate. That opened the way for Randolph to introduce the details of Madison's plan. The Virginia Plan (as it came to be known) proposed the abandonment of the Articles of Confederation and the creation of a wholly new government; it also proposed giving the larger influence within that new government to the richer and more populous states. It called for a national legislature consisting of two houses. In the lower house, the states would be represented in proportion to their population; thus the largest state (Virginia) would have about ten times as many representatives as the smallest (Delaware). Members of the upper house were to be elected by the lower house; thus some of the smaller states might at times have no members at all in the upper house.

The proposal aroused immediate opposition among delegates from Delaware, New Jersey, and other small states. But the opponents were at first uncertain how to proceed. For a while, some argued that Congress had called the convention "for the sole and express purpose of revising the Articles of Confederation," and that the states in commissioning their "deputies" had authorized them to do no more than revise the Articles. They challenged the convention's authority to consider such drastic changes. Eventually, however, William Paterson of New Jersey submitted a substantive alternative to the Virginia Plan, a proposal for a "federal" as opposed to a "national" government. The New Jersey Plan envisioned what was in effect simply a revision and strengthening of the Articles. It preserved the existing one-house legislature, in which each state had equal representation; but it gave the legislature expanded powers to tax and to regulate commerce. After a spirited debate, the majority of the delegates voted to table Paterson's proposal.

The Virginia Plan remained the basis for discussion. But its supporters now realized they would have to make concessions to the small states if the convention was ever to reach a general agreement. They soon conceded an important point by agreeing to permit the members of the upper house to be elected by the state legislatures rather than by the lower house of the national legislature. Thus each state would be sure of always having at least one member in the upper house. There remained, however, the question of how many members each state should have.

Questions also remained about the number of representatives each state should have in the lower house. If the number was to depend on population, were slaves to be counted as part of the population? Were slaves, in other words, to be considered per-

sons or property? The delegates from the states with large and apparently permanent slave populations—especially those from South Carolina—wanted to have it both ways. They argued that slaves should be considered persons in determining representation (although they never considered permitting slaves to vote). But they wanted slaves to be considered property if the new government were to levy taxes on each state on the basis of population. Representatives from states where slavery had disappeared or was expected to disappear argued that slaves should be included in calculating taxation but not representation. No one argued seriously for giving slaves citizenship.

Differences Compromised

The delegates bickered for weeks. By the end of June, as both temperature and tempers rose to uncomfortable heights, the convention seemed in danger of collapsing. Benjamin Franklin, who remained a calm voice of conciliation through the summer, warned that if they failed, the delegates would "become a reproach and by-word down to future ages. And what is worse, mankind may hereafter, from this unfortunate instance, despair of establishing governments by human wisdom, and leave it to chance, war and conquest." Partly because of Franklin's soothing presence, the delegates refused to give up.

Finally, on July 2, the convention agreed to create a "grand committee," with a single delegate from each state (and with Franklin as chairman), to resolve the disagreements. The committee returned with a proposal that became the basis of the "Great Compromise" and that finally resolved the difficult problem of representation. The committee proposed a legislature in which the states would be represented in the lower house on the basis of population, with each slave counted as three-fifths of a free person in determining the basis for both representation and direct taxation. (The three-fifths formula was based on the specious assumption that a slave was three-fifths as productive as a free worker and thus contributed only three-fifths as much wealth to the state.) And the committee proposed that in the upper house, the states should be represented equally with two members apiece. The proposal broke the deadlock. On July 16, 1787, the convention voted to accept it.

In the ensuing weeks, while several committees worked on the details of various parts of the emerging constitution, the convention as a whole agreed to other important compromises on the issue of tariffs and trade regulations and on the most explosive issue of all: slavery. The representatives of the Southern states feared that the power to regulate trade, if granted to the national government, might lead to export duties on their crops, commercial agreements (as in the recent Jay-Gardoqui treaty) that would sacrifice the interests of rice and tobacco growers, and interference with the slave trade. The South Carolinians proposed that a two-thirds vote in the legislature be required not only to approve commercial treaties but also to pass commercial laws. Although the convention rejected that proposal, it made some important concessions to the Southerners. The new legislature would not be permitted to tax exports; it would be forbidden to impose a duty of more than $10 a head on imported slaves; and it would have no authority to stop the slave trade for twenty years. To those delegates who viewed the continued existence of slavery as an affront to the principles of the new nation, this was a large and difficult concession. They agreed to it because they feared that without it the Constitution would fail.

Other differences of opinion the convention was unable to harmonize, and it disposed of them by evasion or omission—leaving important questions alive that would surface again in later years. One such question was whether the new courts or some special agency should be empowered to review and disallow acts of the legislature. The proposal for a "council of revision," a part of the original Virginia Plan, was dropped, and no provision was added to confer the power of judicial review explicitly on the courts. There was no bill of rights, restraining the powers of the national government in the way that bills of rights restrained the state governments. Madison opposed the idea, arguing that specifying rights that were reserved to the people would, in effect, *limit* those rights. Others, however, feared that without such protections the national government might abuse its new authority.

James Madison

Madison (seen here in a portrait by Gilbert Stuart) was often overshadowed by the more charismatic Thomas Jefferson; but he was at least as important a figure as his fellow Virginian in developing the political ideas that became the foundation of the American republic. Madison and Jefferson were political allies for over thirty years, but they were not always in complete agreement. During the debate over the federal Constitution, Jefferson favored the addition of a Bill of Rights. Madison, however, argued that a written declaration of rights should be avoided since any such declaration might be construed as *limiting* rights rather than guaranteeing them. His concerns found expression, finally, in the Ninth Amendment, which stated that "the enumeration in the Constitution of certain rights shall not be construed to deny or disparage others retained by the people." (Bowdoin College Museum of Art)

The Constitution of 1787

Many minds contributed to the creation of the American Constitution, and its terms were the result of many compromises. But the man who made the single greatest contribution to the new concept of government embodied in the document was James Madison, the most creative political thinker of his generation. It had been Madison who devised the

Virginia Plan, from which the final document ultimately emerged. And it was Madison who did most of the drafting of the Constitution itself. But Madison's most important achievement was in helping to resolve two important philosophical questions that had served as obstacles to the creation of an effective national government: the question of sovereignty and the question of limiting power.

The question of sovereignty had been one of the chief sources of friction between the American colonies and Great Britain. England had argued that sovereignty could not, by definition, be divided, that it must reside in a single place; and in British eyes, that place had been Parliament, where the authority of king, Lords, and Commons meshed to produce a stable center of power. Thus the colonial assemblies could have no independent power, because that would imply a division of sovereignty—in British eyes, a logical impossibility. Americans themselves were not entirely comfortable with the idea of divided sovereignty either, and their reservations had helped shape their first attempts to form a union. Under the Articles of Confederation, virtually all sovereignty resided in the individual states. Congress was simply a creature of the states, with no real sovereignty of its own (and thus without sufficient authority to fulfill its expected functions).

The creation of the federal Constitution had required at the start a resolution of questions associated with sovereignty. How could a national government exercise sovereignty concurrently with state governments? Where did ultimate sovereignty lie? The answer, Madison and his contemporaries decided, was that all power, at all levels of government, flowed ultimately from the people. Thus neither the federal government nor the state governments were truly sovereign. All of them derived their authority from below. The opening phrase of the Constitution (devised by Robert Morris) was "We the people of the United States of America"—an expression of the belief that the new government derived its power not from the states but from the public at large. The logical obstacle to the distribution of authority among different branches or different levels of government was thus removed.

The resolution of the problem of sovereignty made possible one of the distinctive features of the Constitution—its distribution of powers between the national and state governments. It was, Madison wrote at the time, "in strictness, neither a national nor a federal Constitution, but a composition of both." It had many features that were clearly national. The Constitution and the government it created were to be the "supreme law" of the land; no state would have the authority to defy it. The federal government was to have broad powers, including the power to tax, to regulate commerce, to control the currency, and to pass such laws as would be "necessary and proper" for carrying out its other responsibilities. Gone was the stipulation of the Articles that "each State shall retain every power, jurisdiction, and right not *expressly* delegated to the United States in

Congress assembled." On the other hand, the Constitution was "federal" in creating a government that accepted the existence of separate states and left certain important powers in their hands.

In addition to solving the question of sovereignty, the Constitution produced a distinctive solution to a problem that was particularly troubling to Americans: the problem of concentrated authority. Nothing so frightened the leaders of the new nation as the prospect of creating a tyrannical government. Nothing was so important to them as avoiding the problems that had, they believed, turned England into a despotic state. Indeed, that fear had been one of the chief obstacles to the creation of a national government at all.

Drawing from the ideas of the French philosopher Baron de Montesquieu, most Americans had long believed that the best way, perhaps the only way, to avoid tyranny was to keep government close to the people. That meant, according to Montesquieu, that a republic must remain confined to a relatively small area; a large nation would breed corruption and despotism because the rulers would be so distant from most of the people that there would be no way to control them. In the new American nation, these assumptions had led to the belief that the individual states must remain sovereign and that a strong national government would be dangerous.

Madison, however, helped break the grip of these assumptions by arguing that a large republic would be *less,* not more likely to produce tyranny, because it would contain so many different factions that no single group would ever be able to dominate it. (In this, he drew from—among other sources—the Scottish philosopher David Hume.) This idea of many centers of power "checking each other" and preventing any single, despotic authority from emerging not only made possible the idea of a large republic. It also helped shape the internal structure of the federal government. The Constitution's most distinctive feature was its "separation of powers" within the government, its creation of "checks and balances" among the legislative, executive, and judicial branches. (Here again, the new idea of sovereignty was crucial. Since ultimate authority resided in the people, there need be no single, ultimate center of authority within the government.)

It was a system designed to prevent any one person, any one faction, any one element of government from exercising excessive power. The array of forces within the government would constantly com-

——— WHERE HISTORIANS DISAGREE ———

The Background of the Constitution

The debate among historians about the motives of those who framed the American Constitution mirrors in many ways the debate about the causes of the American Revolution. To some scholars, the creation of the federal system was an effort to preserve the ideals of the Revolution by eliminating the disorder and contention that threatened the new nation. To others, supporters of the Constitution appear to have been men attempting to protect their own economic interests, even at the cost of betraying the principles of the Revolution.

The first and most influential exponent of the former view was John Fiske, whose book *The Critical Period of American History* (1888) painted a grim picture of political life under the Articles of Confederation. The nation was, Fiske argued, reeling under the impact of a business depression, the weakness and ineptitude of the national government, the threats to American territory from Great Britain and Spain, the inability of either the Congress or the state governments to make good their debts, the interstate jealousies and barriers to trade, the widespread use of inflation-producing paper money, and the lawlessness that culminated in Shays's Rebellion. Only the timely adoption of the Constitution, Fiske claimed, saved the young republic from disaster.

Fiske's view met with little dissent until 1913, when Charles A. Beard published a powerful challenge to it in *An Economic Interpretation of the Constitution of the United States*. According to Beard, the 1780s had been a "critical period" not for the nation as a whole but for certain conservative business interests who feared that the decentralized political structure of the republic imperiled their financial position. Such men, he claimed, wanted a government able to promote industry and trade, protect private property, and perhaps most of all, make good the public debt—much of which was owed to them. The Constitution was, Beard claimed, "an economic document drawn with superb skill by men whose property interests were immediately at stake" and who won its ratification over the opposition of a majority of the people. Were it not for their impatience and determination, he argued in a later book (1927), the Articles of Confederation might have formed a perfectly satisfactory, permanent form of government. The Beard view of the Constitution influenced more than a generation of historians. As late as the 1950s, for example, Merrill Jensen argued in *The New Nation* (1950) that the 1780s were not years of chaos and despair, but a time of hopeful striving and that only the economic interests of a small group of wealthy men can account for the creation of the Constitution.

But the 1950s also produced a series of powerful and persuasive challenges to the Beard thesis. Robert E. Brown, for example, argued in 1956 that "absolutely no correlation" could be shown between the wealth of the delegates to the Constitutional Convention and their position on the Constitution. Forrest McDonald, in *We the People* (1958), looked beyond the convention itself to the debate between the Federalists and the Antifederalists and concluded similarly that there was no

pete with (and often frustrate) one another. Congress would have two chambers—the Senate and the House of Representatives, each with members elected in a different way and for different terms—each checking the other, since both would have to agree before any law could be passed. The president would have the power to veto acts of Congress; and the executive's independence from the legislature would be assured by the special process by which a president would be elected. Electors would be chosen in whatever way the separate states might designate, and the sole duty of this electoral college would be to cast votes for president and vice president. If no one received an electoral majority, then the final selection among the leading candidates would be up to the House of Representatives, with each state casting a single vote. The federal courts would be protected from both the executive and the legislature. Justices would be appointed by the president and confirmed by the Senate, but once in office they would serve for life.

The "federal" structure of the government, which divided power between the states and the na-

WHERE HISTORIANS DISAGREE

consistent relationship between wealth and property on the one hand and support for the Constitution on the other. Instead, opinion on the new system was far more likely to reflect local and regional interests. Areas suffering social and economic distress were likely to support the Constitution; states that were stable and prosperous were likely to oppose it. There was no intercolonial class of monied interests operating in concert to produce the Constitution.

The cumulative effect of these attacks has been virtually to destroy Beard's argument; hardly any historians any longer accept his thesis without reservation. By the 1960s, however, a new group of scholars was beginning to revive an economic interpretation of the Constitution—one that differed from Beard's in important ways but that nevertheless emphasized social and economic factors as motives for supporting the federal system. Jackson Turner Main argued, in *The Antifederalists* (1961), that supporters of the Constitution, while not perhaps the united creditor class that Beard described, were nevertheless economically distinct from critics of the document. The Federalists, he argued, were "cosmopolitan commercialists," eager to advance the economic development of the nation; the Antifederalists, by contrast, were "agrarian localists," fearful of centralization. Gordon Wood's important study, *The Creation of the American Republic* (1969), de-emphasized economic grievances but nevertheless suggested that profound social divisions found reflection in the debate over the state constitutions in the 1770s and 1780s; and that those same divisions helped shape the argument over the federal Constitution. The Federalists, he suggested, were largely traditional aristocrats. They had become deeply concerned by the instability of life under the Articles of Confederation and were particularly alarmed by the decline in popular deference toward social elites. The creation of the Constitution was part of a larger search to create a legitimate political leadership based on the existent social hierarchy; it reflected the efforts of elites to contain what they considered the excesses of democracy.

Other historians have stressed not so much class divisions or economic interests as regional or generational differences. H. James Henderson argued in 1974, in *Party Politics in the Continental Congress*, that the debate over the Constitution was part of a larger argument over the integration of different regions into a single nation. Stanley Elkins and Eric McKitrick contended in a 1961 article ("The Founding Fathers," *Political Science Quarterly*) that the Federalists tended to be younger men than the Antifederalists and saw the development of a strong, united nation as the key to their own future. Pauline Maier, in *The Old Revolutionaries* (1980), offered portraits of early leaders of the resistance to Britain toward the end of their lives and argued that their passage from the scene made it possible for new ideas about the nature of the Revolution—ideas that found reflection in the Constitution—to emerge among the leaders of the next generation.

tion, and the system of "checks and balances," which divided power among various elements within the national government itself, was designed to protect the United States from the kind of despotism that Americans believed had emerged in England. But it was also designed to protect the nation from another kind of despotism, perhaps more menacing: the tyranny of the people. Fear of the "mob," of an "excess of democracy" was at least as important to the framers as fear of a single tyrant. Shays's Rebellion had been only one example, they believed, of what could happen if a nation did not defend itself against the unchecked exercise of popular will. Thus in the new government, only the members of the House of Representatives would be elected directly by the people. Senators, the president, federal judges—all would be insulated in varying degrees from the public.

But in Madison's view, at least, the new system provided an even more fundamental protection against unrestrained popular will. The competition among the many factions within the federal system would permit no faction to attain genuine dominance. Real authority, Madison believed, would come to be lodged in a small group of particularly talented and virtuous people, who would look out for the interests of society as a whole.

The Constitution did not satisfy everyone. Edmund Randolph, the governor of Virginia and the man who had originally introduced the Virginia Plan, was so unhappy about how far the final version had departed from the initial proposal that he refused to sign the document. Several delegates from the smaller states also withheld their approval. Most members of the convention, however, were willing to overlook their reservations. On September 17, 1787, thirty-nine delegates signed the Constitution, doubtless sharing the feelings that Benjamin Franklin expressed at the end: "Thus I consent, Sir, to this Constitution, *because I expect no better, and because I am not sure that it is not the best.*"

Adoption and Adaptation

The delegates at Philadelphia had greatly exceeded their instructions from Congress and the states. Instead of making simple revisions in the Articles of Confederation, they had produced a plan for a completely different form of government. They had reason to doubt, therefore, whether the Constitution would ever be ratified under the procedures laid down in the Articles of Confederation, which required unanimous approval of any alterations in the Articles by the state legislatures. So the convention changed the rules. The Constitution specified that the new government would come into existence among the ratifying states when only nine of the thirteen had ratified. It recommended to Congress that the Constitution be submitted to state *conventions,* called specifically to consider the document, rather than to the legislatures of the states.

Federalists and Antifederalists

The Congress in New York was completely overshadowed by the events in Philadelphia, and it passively accepted the convention's work and submitted it to the states for approval. All the state legislatures (with the exception of Rhode Island) elected delegates to ratifying conventions, most of which had begun meeting by early 1788. Even before the rati-

fying conventions adjourned, however, a great national debate on the new Constitution had begun—in the legislatures, in mass meetings, in the columns of newspapers, and in the daily conversations of many men and women. The debate was intense, but it was generally peaceful and deliberative. Occasionally, however, passions rose to the point that opposing factions came to blows. In at least one place—Albany, New York—such clashes resulted in injuries and death.

Although the preamble made reference to "We the people," the whole people of the United States did not become involved in the ratification process. Most women and blacks and some unpropertied white males had no voice at all in the process. And approximately three-fourths of the adult white males eligible to vote for delegates to the ratifying conventions failed to do so, mainly because of indifference. Of those who did vote, a large majority apparently favored ratification; but because the Constitution was such a complex document, embodying so many different ideas, its real standing among the people at large remained in doubt.

The friends of the Constitution had a number of advantages. They were the better-organized group, and they had the weight of fame and superior leadership on their side. They could point to the support of the two most eminent men in America, Franklin and Washington. (Washington, for example, had declared that the nation faced a choice between the Constitution and disunion.) And they seized control of an appealing label for themselves: "Federalists"—the term that opponents of centralization had once used to describe themselves—thus implying that they were less commited to a "nationalist" government than in fact they were. They called their critics "Antifederalists" and implied in the process that the opposition stood for nothing constructive, that it stood for chaos itself. The Constitution's opponents protested the name, and tried to call themselves "Federal Republicans" instead. But the pejorative "Antifederalist" label stuck.

The Federalists also had the support of the ablest political philosophers of their time: Alexander Hamilton, James Madison, and John Jay. Those three men, under the joint pseudonym "Publius," wrote a series of essays—widely published in newspapers throughout the nation—explaining the meaning and virtues of the Constitution. The essays were later issued as a book, and they are known today as *The Federalist Papers.* They constitute the single most authoritative commentary on the Constitution and perhaps the greatest American contribution to political theory.

The opponents of ratification produced no comparable writings, no "Antifederalist Papers." They tried to make a vigorous case for themselves in speeches, pamphlets, and newspaper propaganda; but much of the press simply ignored them. Perhaps inevitably, the Antifederalists resorted mainly to negative argument. They insisted that the Constitution was illegal—as indeed it was if judged by the terms of the Articles of Confederation. The new government, they claimed, would increase taxes, obliterate the states, wield dictatorial powers, favor the "well born" over the common people, and put an end to individual liberty. Above all, they protested, the Constitution lacked a bill of rights.

The Antifederalist concern about inclusion of a bill of rights revealed one of the most important sources of their opposition to the new Constitution: a basic mistrust of human nature and of the capacity of human beings to wield power. (They have, on occasion, been described as "men of little faith.") They echoed the early Revolutionary fears of corruption and tyranny, and they argued that any government that centralized authority in the hands of the powerful would inevitably produce despotism. The Federalists shared many of these fears, but they believed that the Constitution provided ample protection against tyranny. The Antifederalists did not. The idea of a bill of rights, therefore, reflected a belief that no government could be trusted not to infringe on the liberties of its citizens; only by enumerating the natural rights of the people could there be any certainty that those rights would be protected.

Despite the efforts of the Antifederalists, ratification proceeded reasonably smoothly during the winter of 1787–1788. The Delaware convention was the first to act and ratified the Constitution unanimously, as did New Jersey and Georgia. In the larger states of Pennsylvania and Massachusetts, the Antifederalists put up a more determined struggle but lost in the final vote. New Hampshire ratified the document in June 1788—the ninth state to do so. It was now theoretically possible for the Constitution to go into effect.

A new government could not hope to succeed, however, without the participation of Virginia and New York, whose conventions remained closely divided. But by the end of June, Virginia and then New York had consented to the Constitution by narrow margins. The New York convention yielded to expediency—even some of the most staunchly An-

tifederalist delegates feared that the state's commercial interests would suffer if, once the other states gathered under the "New Roof," New York were to remain outside. Massachusetts, Virginia, and New York all ratified, on the assumption—although not on the express condition—that certain desired amendments would be added to the Constitution, above all a bill of rights. Deciding to wait and see what became of these hopes for amendment, the North Carolina convention adjourned without taking action. Rhode Island did not even call a convention to consider ratification.

Completing the Structure

The first elections under the Constitution were held in the early months of 1789, and the results showed that the new government was to be in the hands of its friends. Almost all the newly elected congressmen and senators had favored ratification, and many had served as delegates to the Philadelphia convention.

There was never any real doubt about who would be the first president. George Washington had presided at the Constitutional Convention, and many who had favored ratification did so only because they expected him to preside over the new government as well. Washington received the votes of all the presidential electors, whom the states, either by legislative action or by popular election, had named. John Adams, a leading Federalist (although he had not been a member of the convention, being the American minister to London at the time), received the next highest number of electoral votes and became vice president.

Congressmen were so slow to reach New York (which was, for the time being, to remain the national capital) that not until April was a quorum on hand to make an official count of the electoral vote and send a messenger to notify General Washington of his election. After a journey from Mount Vernon marked by elaborate celebrations along the way, Washington was inaugurated on April 30.

The responsibilities facing the first president and the first Congress were in some ways greater than those facing any president or Congress to follow, for the Constitution left many important questions unanswered. What, for example, should be the rules of the two houses of Congress for the conduct of their business? What code of etiquette should govern the relations between the president on the one hand and Congress and the people on the other? Should the chief executive have a lofty title, such as "His Highness the President of the United States and Protector of Their Liberties"? (John Adams believed that he should.) What was the true meaning of the many ambiguous phrases in the Constitution? In answering these and other questions, Washington and his colleagues knew they were setting precedents that, in many cases, would give lasting direction to the development of the new government.

Thus the first Congress served in many ways almost as a continuation of the Constitutional Convention, as it acted to fill various gaps in the Constitution. Most conspicuous was the drafting of a bill of rights, which proponents of the Constitution had promised in order to conciliate the Antifederalists. By early 1789, even Madison had come to agree that some sort of bill of rights would be essential to legitimize the new government in the eyes of its opponents. Dozens of amendments had been proposed in the state ratifying conventions, and Congress (led by Madison, a member of the House of Representatives) undertook the task of sifting through them, reducing them to a manageable number, and sending them to the states for ratification. They approved twelve amendments on September 25, 1789; ten of them were ratified by the states by the end of 1791. (Thus what we know as the Bill of Rights is, in legal terms, simply the first ten amendments to the Constitution.)

Nine of those amendments placed limitations on Congress by forbidding it to infringe on certain basic rights: freedom of religion, speech, and the press; immunity from arbitrary arrest; trial by jury; and others. The Tenth Amendment reserved to the states all powers except those specifically withheld from them or delegated to the federal government.

In regard to the structure of the federal courts, the Constitution had only this to say: "The judicial power of the United States shall be vested in one Supreme Court, and in such inferior courts as the Congress may from time to time ordain and establish." Thus the convention had left to Congress the number of Supreme Court judges to be appointed and the kinds of lower courts to be organized. In the Judiciary Act of 1789, Congress provided for a Supreme Court of six members, with a chief justice and five associate justices; for thirteen district courts with one judge apiece; and for three circuit courts of appeal, each to consist of one of the district judges sitting with two of the Supreme Court justices. In the same act, Congress gave the Supreme Court the power to make the final decision in cases involving the constitutionality of state laws. If the Constitution was in fact to be the "supreme law of the land," the various state courts could not be left to decide for themselves whether the state legislatures were violating that supreme law.

As for executive departments, the Constitution referred indirectly to them but did not specify what or how many there should be. The first Congress created three such departments—state, treasury, and war—and also established the offices of the attorney general and postmaster general. In appointing department heads and other high officials, Washington selected men who were generally well disposed toward the Constitution and who as a group would provide a balanced representation of the different sections of the country. To the office of secretary of the treasury he appointed Alexander Hamilton of New York, who at age thirty-two was an acknowledged expert in public finance. For secretary of war he chose a Massachusetts Federalist, General Henry Knox. As attorney general he named Edmund Randolph of Virginia, sponsor of the plan on which the Constitution had been based. As secretary of state he chose another Virginian, Thomas Jefferson, who had been away from the country as minister to France (and thus, like Adams, had not been a delegate to the Constitutional Convention).

From time to time, Washington called on these four men for advice, usually as individuals; but the department heads did not yet operate as a "cabinet." Washington assumed at first that the Senate would serve as an advisory council, since according to the Constitution the Senate was to give its advice and consent for the appointment of high officials and for the ratification of treaties. With only twenty-two members in the beginning, the Senate was small enough so that Washington could expect to consult personally with it. He changed his mind, however, after he took the draft of a treaty to the senators for their advice. They demanded that he leave the document for them to inspect and change at their leisure; Washington refused and resolved never again to submit a treaty to the senators until its negotiation had been completed. Thus he set a precedent in treaty making that his successors have generally followed.

Federalists and Republicans

The resolution of these initial issues stopped far short, however, of resolving the disagreements about the nature of the new government. On the contrary, for the first twelve years under the Constitution, American politics was characterized by a level of acrimony seldom matched in any period since. The framers of the Constitution had dealt with many disagreements not by solving them but by papering them over with a series of vague compromises; as a result, the disagreements survived to plague the new government.

At the heart of the controversies of the 1790s was the same basic difference in philosophy that had lain at the heart of the debate over the Constitution. On one side stood a powerful group that believed America required a strong, *national* government: that the country's mission was to become a genuine nation-state, with centralized authority, a complex commercial economy, and a proud standing in world affairs. On the other side stood another group—a minority at first, but one that gained strength during the decade—that envisioned a far more modest central government. It would be stronger than that under the Confederation, to be sure; but it would remain a far weaker instrument than the European equivalents. Moreover, American society should not, this group believed, aspire to be highly commercial or urban. It should remain predominantly rural and agrarian. The centralizers became known as the Federalists and gravitated to the leadership of Alexander Hamilton. Their opponents acquired the name Republicans and gathered under the leadership of James Madison and Thomas Jefferson.

Hamilton and the Federalists

Control of the new government lay from the beginning largely in the hands of the Federalists. It remained there for twelve years. One reason was George Washington, who had always envisioned a strong national government and who during his eight years as president did little to hamper the efforts of those attempting to consolidate its power. Yet Washington's role in enacting the Federalist program was in many respects a passive one, a result of his concept of the office he held. The president, Washington believed, should not be directly involved in political controversies. He should be an almost Olympian figure, above the fray—a symbol of American nationhood. Washington thus avoided any personal involvement in the deliberations of Congress; he made few efforts to mediate among contending factions; he remained aloof.

As a result, the dominant figure in his administration became his talented secretary of the treasury,

Alexander Hamilton, a man who exerted more influence than anyone else on domestic and foreign policy both during his term of office and, to an almost equal extent, after his resignation in 1794. Of all the leading men of his time, Hamilton was one of the most aristocratic in personal tastes and political philosophy—ironically, perhaps, since his own origins had been humble. Far from embracing republican ideals of the virtue of the people, he believed that a stable and effective government required an elite ruling class; authority should be lodged in the hands of the "enlightened few." As a result, he hoped to adapt the British system of rule by the king and the aristocracy as closely as possible to the United States. The alternative, he was certain, would be continuing disorder.

The new government could best be strengthened, Hamilton believed, by attracting the support of the wealthy. And the best way to do that was to give them a stake in its success. Thus Hamilton first proposed that the existing public debt be "funded," that the miscellaneous, uncertain, depreciated certificates of indebtedness that the old Congress had issued during and since the Revolution—many of them now in the possession of wealthy speculators—be called in and exchanged for uniform, interest-bearing bonds, payable at definite dates. Next, he recommended that the Revolutionary state debts be "assumed," taken over by the United States, his object being to cause state as well as federal bondholders to look to the central government for eventual payment. Hamilton did not, in other words, envision paying off and thus eliminating the debt. He wanted instead to create a large and permanent national debt, new bonds being issued as old ones were paid off. The result, he believed, would be that creditors—the wealthy classes most likely to lend money to the government—would have a permanent stake in seeing the government survive.

Hamilton also planned the establishment of a national bank. At the time, there were only a few banks in the country, located principally in Boston, Philadelphia, and New York. A new, national bank would serve several purposes. It would provide loans and currency to businesses. It would give the government a safe place for the deposit of federal funds. It would facilitate the collection of taxes and the disbursement of the government's expenditures. It would keep up the price of government bonds through judicious bond purchases. The bank was to be chartered by the federal government, was to have a monopoly of the government's own banking business, and was to be controlled by directors of whom one-fifth would be appointed by the government.

The funding and assumption of debts, together with the payment of regular interest on them, would cost a great deal of money, and so Hamilton had to find adequate sources of revenue. He thought the government should depend mainly on two kinds of taxes (in addition to the receipts to be anticipated from the sales of public land). One of these was an excise to be paid by distillers of alcoholic liquors. This tax would hit most heavily the whiskey distillers of the back country, especially in Pennsylvania, Virginia, and North Carolina—small farmers who converted part of their corn and rye crop into whiskey.

The other tax on which Hamilton planned to rely was the tariff on imports. Such a tax would not only raise revenue but would also protect and encourage American manufacturing by raising the price of competing manufactured goods brought in from abroad. One of the first acts of the new Congress, in 1789, was the passage of a tariff law; but the level of duties under this law was extremely low. Hamilton advocated a higher and more decidedly protective tariff. In his famous "Report on Manufactures" of 1791, he laid out a grand scheme for stimulating the growth of industry in the United States and glowingly described the advantages that such growth would bring to the nation. Factories, he said, would make the nation more nearly self-sufficient in wartime, would increase prosperity by creating a home market for the produce of the farms, and would make possible the fuller utilization of all kinds of labor—including, as Hamilton envisioned it, women and children, who, unlike men, could be spared from farm work, he believed.

The Federalists, in short, offered more than a vision of how to ensure the stability of the new government. They offered a vision of the sort of nation America should become—a nation with a wealthy, enlightened ruling class; one possessing a vigorous, independent commercial economy with a thriving industrial sector; a country able to play a prominent role in world economic affairs.

Enacting the Federalist Program

Hamilton faced fervent opposition to many aspects of his program, and from 1789 to 1792 he and his supporters found themselves involved in continuous and often bitter debates. In the end, however, he won passage of almost all the measures he proposed.

Very few members of Congress objected to Hamilton's plan for funding the national debt; they agreed that the government must make its credit good. But many did oppose his proposal to fund the debt *at par,* that is, to exchange new bonds for old certificates of indebtedness on a dollar-for-dollar basis. The old certificates had been issued to merchants and farmers in payment for war supplies during the Revolution, or to officers and soldiers of the Revolutionary army in payment for their services. Many of these holders had been forced to sell their bonds during the hard times of the 1780s to speculators, who had bought them at a fraction of their face value.

Thus while almost everyone agreed that the government should pay what it owed, there was wide disagreement over *whom* it should pay the money to. Many congressmen believed that the original holders deserved some consideration, and James Madison, now a representative from Virginia, argued for a plan by which the new bonds would be divided between the original purchasers and the speculators. But Hamilton's allies insisted that such a plan was impracticable and that the honor of the government required a literal fulfillment of its earlier promises to pay. Congress finally passed the funding bill in the form that Hamilton desired.

His proposal that the federal government assume the state debts encountered even greater difficulty. Its opponents had a strong case, for if the federal government took over the state debts, the people of one state would have to pay federal taxes for servicing the debts of other states. Some states' debts were much larger than others; Massachusetts, for example, owed far more money than did Virginia. Naturally, Virginia's representatives in Congress balked at the assumption bill. Only by striking a bargain with the Virginians were Hamilton and his supporters able to win passage of the bill.

The deal involved the location of the national capital. The Virginians wanted to create a new capital near them in the South. Hamilton met with Thomas Jefferson (after Jefferson's return from France) and agreed over dinner to provide Northern support for placing the capital in the South in exchange for Virginia's votes for the assumption bill. The capital had moved from New York back to Philadelphia in 1790. But the new bargain called for the construction of a new capital city on the banks of the Potomac River, on land to be selected by Washington himself. The government would move its operations by the beginning of the new century.

Hamilton thus settled the thorny issue of assumption reasonably easily. It was his bank bill that sparked the first of many debates over the proper interpretation of the Constitution. Hamilton, of course, argued that establishment of a national bank was compatible with the intent of the Constitution, even though the document did not explicitly authorize it. But Madison, Jefferson, Randolph, and others argued that the Constitution should be construed in a strict sense and that Congress should exercise no powers that the document had not clearly assigned it. Both the House and the Senate finally agreed to Hamilton's bill; and although Washington initially displayed some uncertainty about its legality, he finally signed it. The Bank of the United States began operations in 1791, under a charter that granted it the right to continue for twenty years. Hamilton also had his way with the excise tax, although protests from farmers later forced revisions to reduce the burden on the smaller distillers. He failed to win passage of a tariff as highly protective as he had hoped for, but the tariff law of 1792 did raise the rates somewhat.

Once enacted, Hamilton's program had many of the effects he had intended and won the support of influential segments of the population. Public credit was quickly restored; the bonds of the United States were soon selling at home and abroad at prices even above their par value. Speculators (among them many members of Congress) reaped large profits as a result. Manufacturers profited from the tariffs, and merchants in the seaports benefited from the new banking system.

Others, however, found the Hamilton program less appealing. Small farmers in particular, who formed the vast majority of the population, complained that they had to bear a disproportionate burden of taxation. Not only did they owe property taxes to their state governments, but they bore the brunt of the excise tax and, indirectly, of the tariff. A feeling grew that the Federalist program served the interests not of the people but of small, wealthy elites. Out of this feeling an organized political opposition arose.

The Republican Opposition

The Constitution had made no reference to political parties, and the omission had been no oversight. Most of the framers—and George Washington in particular—believed that organized parties were evil and should be avoided. It was inevitable that men would disagree on particular issues, but most be-

lieved that such disagreements need not lead to the formation of permanent factions. "The public good is disregarded in the conflicts of rival parties," Madison had written in *The Federalist Papers* (in Number 10, perhaps the most influential of all the essays), "and . . . measures are too often decided, not according to the rules of justice and the rights of the minor party, but by the superior force of an interested and overbearing majority."

Yet not many years had passed after the ratification of the Constitution before Madison and others became convinced that Hamilton and his followers had become just such an "interested and overbearing majority." Not only had the Federalists enacted a program that many of these leaders opposed. More ominously, Hamilton himself had, in their eyes, worked to establish a national network of influence that embodied all the worst features of a party. The Federalists had used their control over appointments and the awarding of government franchises, and all the other powers of their offices, to reward their supporters and win additional allies. They had encouraged the formation of local associations—largely aristocratic in nature—to strengthen their standing in local communities. They were doing many of the same things, their opponents believed, that the corrupt British governments of the early eighteenth century had done.

Because the Federalists appeared to their critics to be creating such a menacing and tyrannical structure of power, there was no alternative but to organize a vigorous opposition. And the result was the emergence of an alternative political organization, which called itself the Republican party. (This first "Republican" party is not related to the modern Republican party, which was born much later, in the 1850s.) By the late 1790s, the Republicans were going to even greater lengths than the Federalists to create an apparatus of partisan influence. In every state they had formed committees, societies, and caucuses; Republican groups were corresponding with one another across state lines; they were banding together to influence state and local elections. And they were justifying their actions by claiming that they and they alone represented the true interests of the nation—that they were fighting to defend the people against a corrupt conspiracy by the Federalists. Just as Hamilton believed that the network of supporters he was creating represented the only legitimate interest group in the nation, so the Republicans believed that their party organization represented the best interests of the people. Neither side was willing to admit that

The Jeffersonian Idyll

American artists in the early nineteenth century were drawn to tranquil rural scenes, symbolic of the Jeffersonian vision of a nation of small, independent farmers. By 1822, when Francis Alexander painted this pastoral landscape, the simple agrarian republic it depicts was already being transformed by rapid economic growth.   (National Gallery of Art, Washington)

it was acting as a party; nor would either concede the right of the other to exist.

From the beginning, the preeminent figures among the Republicans were Thomas Jefferson and James Madison. Indeed, the two men were such intimate collaborators with such similar political philosophies that it is sometimes difficult to distinguish the contributions of one from those of the other. But Jefferson, as the more magnetic personality of the two, gradually emerged as the most prominent spokesman for the Republicans.

Jefferson, himself a farmer, believed that farmers were God's chosen people and that an ideal republic would consist of sturdy citizens, each tilling his own soil. He was an aristocrat by birth, but he had faith in the good intentions of the ordinary farmer-citizens and believed that they could, if properly educated, be trusted to govern themselves through the election of able and qualified men. Urban people, by contrast, posed a danger to the republic; Jefferson feared city mobs as "sores upon the body politic." Thus he opposed the development of extensive manufactures because they would lead to the growth of cities packed with propertyless workers. Jefferson envisioned, in short, a decentralized society, dominated by small

property owners engaged largely in agrarian activities. He did not scorn commercial activity; farmers would, he assumed, market their crops through national and even international trade. Nor did he oppose industrial activity; Americans should, he believed, develop a certain amount of manufacturing capacity. But Jefferson did believe that the nation should avoid a highly urbanized, industrial economy and that the abundance of land in America was the society's greatest economic resource.

As a member of President Washington's official circle, Jefferson differed so strongly with his colleague Hamilton on particular issues such as the Bank that he soon offered to resign. But Washington, eager to preserve at least the appearance of national unity, persuaded him to remain as secretary of state. Although the two secretaries continued to serve the same president, they worked increasingly against each other. Each began to organize a following in Congress as well as in the country at large.

On the surface, the debate between the Federalists and the Republicans mirrored the earlier battle between Federalists and Antifederalists. In fact, however, the Republicans attracted support from some of those who had been most fervent in their support of the Constitution—among them Madison. The new Republicans did not denounce the Constitution. On the contrary, they professed to be its special friends and champions and accused their opponents of violating it.

Although both parties had supporters in all parts of the country and among all classes, there were regional and economic differences. The Federalists were most numerous in the commercial centers of the Northeast and in such Southern seaports as Charleston; the Republicans were most numerous in the rural areas of the South and the West. The factions differed in their social philosophies as well—as their reactions to the progress of the French Revolution suggest. As that revolution grew increasingly radical in the 1790s, with its attacks on organized religion, the overthrow of the monarchy, and eventually the guillotining of the king and queen, the Federalists watched in horror. The Republicans, in contrast, applauded the democratic, antiaristocratic spirit they believed the French Revolution embodied. Some even imitated the French radicals (the Jacobins) by cutting their hair short, wearing pantaloons, and addressing one another as "Citizen" and "Citizeness."

When the time came for the nation's second presidential election in 1792, both Jefferson and Hamilton urged Washington to run for a second term. The president would have preferred to retire to his plantation at Mount Vernon, but he agreed to serve for another four years. Almost all Americans viewed Washington as a figure above the partisan battle, and as long as he was president the factional dispute remained relatively contained. But Washington was, in reality, far more in sympathy with the Federalists than with the Republicans. And during his presidency, Hamilton managed to remain the dominant figure in government.

Asserting National Sovereignty

The Federalists consolidated their position—and attracted wide public support for the new national government—by dealing effectively with two problems that the old Confederation had been unable fully to resolve. They helped stabilize the Western frontier, and they improved America's position in world affairs.

Securing the Frontier

Despite its success in winning passage of the Northwest Ordinance, the old Congress had been largely unable to tie the outlying Western areas of the country firmly to the government. Farmers in western Massachusetts had risen in revolt; settlers in Vermont, Kentucky, and Tennessee had toyed with the idea of separating from the Union. At first, the new government under the Constitution faced similar problems.

In 1794, farmers in western Pennsylvania raised a major challenge to federal authority when they refused to pay a whiskey excise tax and began terrorizing the tax collectors (much as colonists had done throughout America at the time of the Stamp Act). But the federal government did not leave settlement of the so-called Whiskey Rebellion to the authorities of Pennsylvania as Congress had left Shays's Rebellion to the authorities of Massachusetts. At Hamilton's urging, Washington took drastic steps. He called out the militias of three states; he raised an army of nearly 15,000, a larger force than he had commanded against the British during most of the Revolution; and he personally accompanied the army into Pennsylvania. At the approach of the militiamen, the farmers around Pittsburgh, where the rebellion centered, either ran for cover or stayed home and claimed to be law-abiding citizens. The rebellion quickly collapsed.

The federal government won the allegiance of the whiskey rebels through intimidation. It won the loyalties of other frontier people by accepting new states as members of the Union. The last of the original thirteen colonies joined the union once the Bill of Rights had been appended to the Constitution—North Carolina in 1789 and Rhode Island in 1790. Then Vermont, which had had its own state government since the Revolution, was accepted as the fourteenth state in 1791 after New York and New Hampshire finally agreed to give up their claims to sovereignty over it. Next came Kentucky, in 1792, when Virginia gave up its claim to that region. When North Carolina finally ceded its Western lands to the Union, Tennessee achieved territorial status and in 1796 became a state.

The new government faced a greater challenge, inherited from the Confederation, in the more distant areas of the Northwest and the Southwest, where Indians (occasionally in alliance with the British and Spanish) continued to challenge the republic's control of the territory it claimed. The ordinances of 1784–

Washington in Command, 1794

Washington remembered with horror how the ineffectual response of the Confederation government to Shays's Rebellion in 1786 had threatened the unity of the nation. When Pennsylvania farmers rose up in the Whiskey Rebellion in 1794, the President decided at once on a strong military response and personally took command of the army he ordered into the field. This painting, credited to Frederick Kemmelmeyer, shows Washington reviewing troops in Cumberland, Maryland, as they prepare to march against the insurgents. (Metropolitan Museum of Art)

1787, establishing the terms of white settlement in the West, had produced a series of border conflicts with Indian tribes resisting white settlement in their lands. The new government inherited these clashes, which continued with few interruptions for nearly a decade (see pp. 157–158). And although the United States eventually managed to defeat virtually every Indian challenge (if often at great cost), even the most optimistic observer recognized that the larger question of who was to control the lands of the West— white civilization or the Indian nations—remained unanswered.

These clashes revealed another issue the Constitution had done little to resolve: the place of the Indian nations within the new federal structure. Native Americans received few mentions in the Constitution. Article I excluded "Indians not taxed" from being counted in the population totals that determined the number of seats states would receive in the

House of Representatives; and it gave Congress the power to "regulate Commerce with foreign Nations, and among the several States, and with the Indian tribes." Article VI bound the new government to respect treaties negotiated by the Confederation; since most of those treaties had been with the tribes, this provision too had important implications for relations with the Indians. But none of this did very much to clarify the precise legal standing of Indians or Indian nations within the United States.

On the one hand, the Constitution seemed to recognize the existence of the tribes as legal entities. On the other hand, it made clear that they were not "foreign Nations" in the same sense that European countries were and at the same time that their members were not citizens of the United States. The tribes received no direct representation in the new government. Above all, the Constitution did not address the major issue that would govern relations between whites and Indians: land. Indian nations lived within the boundaries of the United States, yet they claimed (and the white government at times agreed) that they had some measure of sovereignty within their own land. But neither the Constitution nor common law offered any clear guide to the rights of a "nation within a nation" or to the precise nature of tribal sovereignty, which ultimately depended on control of land. Thus, the relationship between the tribes and the United States remained to be determined by a series of treaties, agreements, and judicial decisions in a process that has continued for two centuries.

Maintaining Neutrality

Not until 1791 did Great Britain send a minister to the United States, and then only because Madison and the Republicans were threatening to place special trade restrictions on British ships. That was only one symbol of the difficulty the new government had in establishing its legitimacy in the eyes of the British.

A crisis in Anglo-American relations emerged in 1793 when the new French government established after the revolution of 1789, after executing King Louis XVI, went to war with Great Britain and its allies. The new federal government was uncertain how to respond. Should the United States recognize the radical government of France by accepting a diplomatic representative from it? Was the United States obligated by the alliance of 1778 to go to war on the side of France? Washington (responding to advice from both Hamilton and Jefferson) recognized the French government and issued a proclamation in 1793 announcing the determination of the United States to remain at peace and (although it did not use the word) neutral. A year later, Congress passed a neutrality act forbidding American citizens to participate in the war and prohibiting the use of American soil as a base of operations for either side.

The first challenge to American neutrality came from France, when its first diplomatic representative, the youthful and brash Edmond Genêt, arrived in America. Instead of landing at Philadelphia and presenting himself immediately to the president, Genêt disembarked at Charleston. There he made plans for using American ports to outfit French warships, issued letters of marque and reprisal authorizing American shipowners to serve as French privateers, and commissioned the aging George Rogers Clark to undertake an overland expedition against the possessions of Spain, an ally of Great Britain and an enemy

of France. In all of this, Genêt was brazenly ignoring Washington's proclamation and flagrantly violating the Neutrality Act. His conduct infuriated Washington (who provided "Citizen Genêt," as he was known, with an icy reception in Philadelphia) and the Federalists; it also embarrassed all but the most ardent Francophiles among the Republicans. At last, Washington demanded that the French government recall him; but by then Genêt's party, the Girondins, was out of power in France and the still more extreme Jacobins were in control, so it would not have been safe for him to return. The president granted him political asylum in the United States, and he settled with his American wife on a Long Island farm. The neutrality policy had survived its first great test.

A second challenge, an even greater one, came from Great Britain. Early in 1794, the Royal Navy began seizing hundreds of American ships engaged in trade in the French West Indies. At the news of the seizures, opinion in the United States became as strongly anti-British as it had recently been anti-French. Anti-British feeling rose still higher at the report that the governor general of Canada had delivered a warlike speech to the Indians on the Northwestern frontier. Hamilton was deeply concerned. War would mean an end to imports from England, and most of the revenue for maintaining his financial system came from duties on those imports.

Jay's Treaty

Hamilton and the other Federalists believed, therefore, that this was no time for ordinary diplomacy. They could not, they knew, rely on the State Department in their quest for a settlement with Britain. Jefferson had resigned as secretary of state in 1793 to devote more time to his political activities; but his successor, Edmund Randolph, was even more ardently pro-French than Jefferson had been. Hence the Federalists persuaded Washington to name a special commissioner to England: the staunch New York Federalist, former secretary for foreign affairs under the old Confederation, and current chief justice of the Supreme Court, John Jay. Jay was instructed to secure compensation for the recent British assaults on American shipping, to demand withdrawal of British forces from the frontier posts, and to negotiate a commercial treaty that would not violate America's existing treaty with France, signed at the time of the alliance in 1778.

Jay negotiated a long and complex treaty in 1794,

and in the process he yielded more to Great Britain and obtained less for the United States than he had been instructed to do. But there was much to be said for the agreement. By settling the conflict with Britain, it gave the United States valuable time for peaceful development. It also provided for undisputed American sovereignty over the entire Northwest; and it produced a reasonably satisfactory commercial relationship with a nation whose trade was important to the United States. Nevertheless, when the terms were published, the treaty was bitterly denounced and Jay himself was burned in effigy in various parts of the country. The Republicans condemned the treaty virtually unanimously as a surrender to Britain and an assault on France. Even some Federalists were outraged. Opponents of the treaty went to extraordinary lengths to defeat it in the Senate; French agents aided them and cheered them on. The American minister to France, James Monroe, and even the secretary of state, Edmund Randolph, cooperated closely with the French in a desperate attempt to prevent ratification. But in the end the Senate, after making some amendments, consented to what was by then known as Jay's Treaty.

The treaty led directly to a settlement of America's important conflict with Spain. Fearing a joint Anglo-American challenge to Spanish possessions in North America, the Spanish government was now eager to appease the United States. Thus when Thomas Pinckney arrived in Spain as a special negotiator, he had no difficulty in gaining nearly everything that the United States had sought from the Spaniards for more than a decade. Under Pinckney's Treaty (signed in 1795), Spain recognized the right of Americans to navigate the Mississippi to its mouth and to deposit goods at New Orleans for reloading on ocean-going ships; agreed to fix the northern boundary of Florida where Americans always had insisted it should be, along the 31st parallel; and required Spanish authorities to prevent the Indians in Florida from raiding across the border.

The Downfall of the Federalists

The Federalists' impressive triumphs did not ensure their continued dominance in the national government. On the contrary, success seemed to produce problems of its own—problems that eventually led to their downfall.

Since almost everyone in the 1790s agreed that there was no place in a stable republic for an organized opposition, the emergence of the Republicans as powerful contenders for popular favor seemed to the Federalists a grave threat to national stability. When, beginning in the late 1790s, major international perils confronted the government as well, the temptation to move forcefully against the opposition became too great to resist. Facing what they believed was a stark choice between respecting individual liberties and preserving stability, the Federalists chose stability. The result was political disaster. After 1796, the Federalists never won another election. The popular respect for the institutions of the federal government, which they had worked so hard to produce among the people, survived. But the Federalists themselves gradually vanished as an effective political force.

The Election of 1796

As the time approached for the election of 1796, some friends of Washington urged him to run again. Already twice elected without a single vote cast against him in the electoral college, he could be counted on to hold the Federalist party together and carry it to a third great victory. But Washington, weary of the burdens of the office and disgusted with the partisan abuse that was now being heaped on him, was determined to retire to Mount Vernon. With Hamilton's assistance, he composed a long letter to the American people and had it published in a Philadelphia newspaper. The letter became known as Washington's "Farewell Address." Its reference to the "insidious wiles of foreign influence" was not just a warning against international entanglements; it was a denunciation of those Republicans who had been conspiring with the French to frustrate the Federalist diplomatic program.

There was no doubt that Jefferson would be the candidate of the Republicans in 1796, and he chose as his running mate the New York Republican leader, Aaron Burr. The Federalists faced a more difficult choice. Hamilton, the very personification of Federalism, was not "available" because his forthright views had created too many enemies. John Jay was too closely identified with his unpopular treaty. And Thomas Pinckney, although *his* treaty had been enthusiastically received, had the handicap of being a South Carolinian at a time when party leaders thought the next candidate should be a Northerner.

John Adams, who as vice president was directly associated with none of the Federalist measures, finally received the party's nomination for president at a caucus of the Federalists in Congress; Pinckney received the nomination for vice president.

The Federalists were still clearly the dominant party, and there was little doubt of their ability to win a majority of the presidential electors. But without Washington to mediate, they fell victim to fierce factional rivalries that almost led to their undoing. Hamilton and many other Federalists (especially in the South) were not reconciled to Adams's candidacy and continued to prefer Pinckney. And when, as ex-

John Adams

Adams was America's leading diplomat in 1783, when he posed for this portrait by John Singleton Copley. His own illustrious career marked the beginning of four generations of public distinction among members of his family. (Fogg Art Museum, Harvard University)

pected, the Federalists elected a majority of the presidential electors, some of these Pinckney supporters declined to vote for Adams; he managed to defeat Jefferson by only three electoral votes. Because a still larger number of Adams's supporters declined to vote for Pinckney, Jefferson finished second in the balloting and became vice president. (The Constitution provided for the candidate receiving the second highest number of electoral votes to become vice president—hence the awkward result of men from different parties serving in the nation's two highest offices. The Twelfth Amendment, adopted in 1804, reformed the electoral system to prevent such situations.)

Adams assumed the presidency, therefore, under inauspicious circumstances. He presided over a divided party, which faced a strong and resourceful Republican opposition committed to its extinction. And Adams himself was not the dominant figure in his own party; Hamilton remained the most influential Federalist, and Adams was never able to challenge him effectively. The new president was one of the country's most accomplished and talented statesman, but he had few skills as a politician. Austere, rigid, aloof, he showed no ability to conciliate differences, to solicit support, or to inspire enthusiasm. He was a man of enormous, indeed intimidating rectitude; and he seemed to assume that his own virtue and the correctness of his positions would alone be enough to sustain him. He was wrong.

The Quasi War with France

American relations with Great Britain and Spain improved as a result of Jay's and Pinckney's treaties. But the nation's relations with France, now under the government of the Directory, went from bad to worse. French vessels captured American ships on the high seas and at times imprisoned the crews. And when the South Carolina Federalist Charles Cotesworth Pinckney, brother of Thomas Pinckney, arrived in France to replace Monroe, the Directory refused to receive him as the official representative of the United States.

Some of the president's advisers, in particular Secretary of State Timothy Pickering (a rigid New Englander who detested France) favored war. Most (including Hamilton) recommended attempting to reach a peaceful settlement. Adams chose conciliation, and he appointed a bipartisan commission—consisting of Charles Pinckney, the recently rejected minister; John Marshall, a Virginia Federalist, later chief justice of the Supreme Court; and Elbridge Gerry, a Massachusetts Republican but a personal friend of the president—to negotiate with the Directory. When the three Americans arrived in France in 1797, three agents of the Directory's foreign minister, Prince Talleyrand, demanded a loan for France and a bribe for French officials before any negotiations could begin. Pinckney delivered the commission's response in a succinct and angry phrase: "No! No! Not a sixpence!"

When Adams received the commissioners' report, he sent a message to Congress in which he urged readiness for war, denounced the French for their insulting treatment of the United States, and vowed he would not appoint another minister to France until he knew the minister would be "received, respected and honored as the representative of a great, free, powerful and independent nation." The Republicans asked for proof of the president's charge that the United States had been insulted. And Adams responded by turning the commissioners' report over to Congress, after deleting the names of the three French agents and designating them only as Messrs. X, Y, and Z. When the report was published, the "XYZ Affair" provoked an even greater reaction than Adams had expected. There was widespread popular outrage at France's actions and strong popular support for the Federalists' response. For nearly two years, 1798 and 1799, the United States found itself engaged in an undeclared war with France.

Adams quickly persuaded Congress to cut off all trade with France, abrogate the treaties of 1778, and authorize public and private vessels of the United States to capture French armed ships on the high seas. In 1798, Congress created a Department of the Navy and appropriated money for the construction of new warships. The navy soon won a number of duels with French vessels and captured a total of eighty-five ships, including armed merchantmen.

The United States had not only abandoned neutrality in the war between Britain and France. It was now cooperating so closely with the British as to be virtually a cobelligerent. Adams declined an English offer to lend ships to the United States, preferring that the nation build up a navy of its own. But the British did provide the American navy with shot and shell, furnished officers to help with the training and direction of American crews, and offered signaling information so that British and American ships could communicate readily with one another.

The French, taking notice of all this, finally began to see the wisdom of an accommodation with the Americans. Adams sent a new three-man commission to Paris in 1800; and the new French government (headed now by "first consul" Napoleon Bonaparte) agreed to a treaty with the United States that canceled the old agreement of 1778 and established new commercial arrangements. Federalists in the Senate objected that the agreement failed to provide compensation for American maritime losses at the hands of the French, and they delayed ratification until after Adams had left office. But the "quasi war" nevertheless came to a reasonably peaceful end, and the United States at last freed itself from the entanglements and embarrassments of its "perpetual" alliance with France.

Repression and Protest

The outbreak of hostilities in 1798 had given the Federalists an advantage over the political opposition, and in the congressional elections of that year they increased their majorities in both houses of Congress. But their newfound popularity seemed to go to their heads, and they began to consider new ways to weaken and silence the Republicans. Their pretext was the supposed necessity of protecting the nation from dangerous foreign and subversive influences in the midst of the undeclared war. The result was some of the most controversial legislation in American history: the Alien and Sedition Acts.

The Alien Act was aimed at those critics of the administration who were foreign by birth (many of them Irish and French). It placed new obstacles in the way of foreigners who wished to become American citizens, and it strengthened the president's hand in dealing with aliens. Even more severe was the Sedition Act, which empowered the government to prosecute those who engaged in "sedition" against the government. In theory, only libelous or treasonous activities were subject to prosecution. But the law had the capacity to become a potent vehicle for stifling any opposition. The Republicans responded to the new laws with anger and dismay, interpreting them as part of a Federalist campaign to destroy them. The Alien and Sedition Acts became, as a result, the spark that finally ignited the political passions that had been building for nearly a decade.

John Adams signed the new laws, but he was reasonably cautious in implementing them. He did not act to deport any aliens, as he was empowered to

Building an American Navy

After the Revolutionary War the United States abandoned the warships it had accumulated in its struggle with Great Britain, and for fifteen years there was no American navy. But when undeclared hostilities broke out with France in 1798, the federal government created a Department of the Navy and began a major shipbuilding program. This engraving shows work on the frigate *Philadelphia* in a Pennsylvania shipyard. The ship was not completed in time to be used against the French, but it saw action in 1803 during the war against Tripoli. When pirates from Tripoli captured the ship, American sailors staged a daring raid and destroyed it.   (New-York Historical Society)

do; and he prevented the government from launching a massive crusade against the opposition. Nevertheless, the legislation did have a significant repressive effect, enough to justify the fears of the Republicans that they were tyrannical in intent. The Alien Act, together with the Naturalization Act passed at approximately the same time, discouraged immigration and encouraged some foreigners already in the country to leave. And the administration made use of the Sedition Act to arrest several dozen men; ten were convicted. Most of those prosecuted were Republi-

can newspaper editors whose only crime had been to criticize the Federalists in government.

The Republicans faced an important question as they attempted to decide how to oppose these laws, which they considered clear violations of the Constitution. What agency of government should decide the question of constitutionality? The Supreme Court had never attempted to invalidate an act of Congress; and the Republican leaders Jefferson and Madison concluded that the state legislatures should decide. They ably expressed their view in two sets of reso-

Congressional Pugilists, 1798
This cartoon was inspired by the celebrated fight on the floor of the House of Representatives between Matthew Lyon, a Republican representative from Vermont, and Roger Griswold, a Federalist from Connecticut. Griswold (at right) attacks Lyon with his cane, and Lyon retaliates with fire tongs. Other members of Congress seem to be enjoying the battle. (New York Public Library)

lutions in 1798-1799, one written (anonymously) by Jefferson and adopted by the Kentucky legislature (1798, 1799) and the other drafted by Madison and approved by the Virginia legislature (1798). The Virginia and Kentucky Resolutions, as they were known, used the arguments of John Locke, which had become so familiar during the pre-Revolutionary crisis. They asserted that the federal government had been formed by a "compact" or contract among the states. It was a limited government, possessing only certain delegated powers. Whenever it exercised any additional and undelegated powers, its acts were "unauthoritative, void, and of no force." The parties to the contract, the states, must decide for themselves when and whether the central government exceeded its powers. And "nullification" by the states was the "rightful remedy" whenever the general government went too far.

The Republicans failed to win wide support for their efforts on behalf of nullification; only Virginia and Kentucky voted to declare the congressional statutes void. They did, however, succeed in elevating their dispute with the Federalists to the level of a national crisis. By the late 1790s, the entire nation was as deeply and bitterly politicized as it would ever be in its history. The partisan divisions reached into every community. Friends and families became bitterly divided. State legislatures at times resembled battlegrounds; loud and angry debates were almost constant, and on several occasions there were rowdy fistfights and brawls in the legislative chambers. Even

the United States Congress was plagued with violent disagreements. In one celebrated incident in the chamber of the House of Representatives, Matthew Lyon, a Republican from Vermont, responded to an insult from Roger Griswold, a Federalist from Massachusetts, by spitting in Griswold's eye. Griswold attacked Lyon with his cane, Lyon fought back with a pair of fire tongs, and soon the two men were wrestling on the floor. Such incidents were not only embarrassing to Congress; they served as a disturbing reminder to the public at large of the rancor and instability that had afflicted the nation under the Articles of Confederation. By 1800, it seemed as though the nation was again on the verge of dissolving into chaos.

The "Revolution" of 1800

In this troubled atmosphere, Americans went about the task of electing a president in the fall of 1800. The presidential candidates were the same as four years earlier: Jefferson was the Republican nominee, with Aaron Burr again his running mate; Adams campaigned for reelection as a Federalist, with Charles Pinckney as the party's candidate for vice president.

The campaign of that year was probably the ugliest in American history. Adams and Jefferson themselves displayed reasonable dignity; but their supporters showed no such restraint. (It was during this campaign, for example, that the story of Jefferson's alleged romantic involvement with a black slave woman was first widely aired—a story whose truth scholars continue to debate.) In addition to personal invective, each side argued strenuously that its opponents threatened the very existence of the republic. The Federalists accused Jefferson of being a dangerous radical and his followers of being wild men who, if they should come to power, would bring on a reign of terror comparable to that of the French Revolution at its worst. The Republicans pictured Adams as a tyrant conspiring to become king; and they accused the Federalists of plotting to subvert human liberty and impose slavery on the people—accusations that mirrored the anti-British propaganda of the pre-Revolutionary years.

The election was close, and the crucial contest was in New York. There, Aaron Burr mobilized an organization of revolutionary war veterans, the Tammany Society, to serve as a Republican political machine. And through Tammany's efforts, the party carried the city by a large majority, and with it the state. Jefferson was, apparently, elected.

But an unexpected complication soon jeopardized the Republican victory. The Constitution called for each elector to "vote by ballot for two persons." The normal practice was for an elector to cast one vote for his party's presidential candidate and another for the vice presidential candidate. To avoid a tie, the Republicans had intended for one elector to refrain from voting for Burr. But the plan went awry. When the votes were counted, Jefferson and Burr each had 73. No candidate had a majority, and—in accordance with the Constitution—the House of Representatives was now empowered to choose between the two top candidates, between Jefferson and Burr. Each state delegation would cast a single vote.

The Federalists controlled a majority of the states' votes in the existing Congress (the new Congress, elected in 1800, did not convene until after the inauguration of the president), and they had the privilege of deciding which of their opponents was to be the next president. Some hoped to use the situation to salvage the election for the Federalists; others wanted to strike a bargain with Burr and elect him. The House met in February 1801 to resolve the election and balloted again and again without mustering a majority for either Jefferson or Burr. Finally, a week before the inauguration, several leading Federalists concluded that Burr (whom many suspected of having engineered the deadlock in the first place) was too unreliable to trust with the presidency. On the thirty-sixth ballot, Jefferson was elected.

As a result of the election of 1800, the Republicans captured not only the presidency but a majority of the seats in both houses of the next Congress as well. The only branch of the government left in Federalist hands was the judiciary, and Adams and his fellow partisans during their last months in office took steps to make their hold on the courts secure. By the Judiciary Act of 1801, passed by the lame duck Congress, the Federalists reduced the number of Supreme Court justiceships by one but at the same time greatly increased the number of federal judgeships as a whole. The act created a separate system of circuit courts of appeal, standing between the federal district courts and the Supreme Court, to replace the old circuit courts on which district judges and Supreme Court justices had served together; and it called for the creation of ten new district judgeships.

Adams quickly appointed Federalists to the newly created positions. Indeed, some claimed that he stayed up until midnight on his last day in office, March 3, 1801, to complete the signing of the judges' commissions; these officeholders became known as the "midnight appointments." Since federal judges held office for life, the Federalists assumed that Jefferson would be powerless as president to remove Adam's appointees.

Despite these last Federalist efforts, the Republicans viewed their victory as almost complete. The nation had, they believed, been saved from tyranny. A new era could now begin, one in which the true principles on which America had been founded would once again govern the land. The exuberance with which the victors viewed the future—and the importance they ascribed to the defeat of the Federalists—was clearly revealed by the phrase Jefferson himself later used to describe his election. He called it the "Revolution of 1800." It remained to be seen how revolutionary it would really be.

SUGGESTED READINGS

The Constitution.   Max Farrand (ed.), *Records of the Federal Convention of 1787,* 4 vols. (1911–1937); Max Ferrand, *The Framing of the Constitution of the United States* (1913); Michael Kammen, *A Machine that Would Go of Itself: The Constitution in American Culture* (1986); Charles A. Beard, *An Economic Interpretation of the Constitution of the United States* (1913); Forrest McDonald, *We the People: The Economic Origins of the Constitution* (1958), *E Pluribus Unum: The Formation of the American Republic, 1776–1790* (1965); and *Novus Ordo Seclorum: The Intellectual Origins of the Constitution* (1985); Robert E. Brown, *Charles Beard and the Constitution* (1956); Leonard Levy, *Constitutional Opinions: Aspects of the Bill of Rights* (1986) and *Original Intent and the Framers' Constitution* (1988); Thomas Curry, *The First Freedom: Church and State in America to the Passage of the First Amendment* (1986); William L. Miller, *The First Liberty: Religion and the American Republic* (1986); Richard B. Morris, *The Forging of the Union, 1781–1789* (1987); Clinton Rossiter, *1787: The Grand Convention* (1965); Christopher Collier and James Lincoln Collier, *Decision: Philadelphia: The Constitutional Convention of 1787* (1986); Douglas Adair, *Fame and the Founding Fathers* (1974); Jackson Turner Main, *The Anti-Federalists* (1961); Alpheus T. Mason, *The State Rights Debate* (1964); J. E. Cooke, ed., *The Federalist* (1961); Garry Wills, *Explaining America* (1981); Linda G. DePauw, *The Eleventh Pillar: New York State and the Federal Constitution* (1966); Gerald Stourzh, *Alexander Hamilton and the Idea of Republican Government* (1970); Robert A. Rutland, *The Ordeal of the Constitution* (1966); Michael Lienesch, *New Order of the Ages: Time, the Constitution, and the Making of Modern American Political*

Thought (1988); Edmund S. Morgan, *Inventing the People: The Rise of Popular Sovereignty in England and America* (1988).

The Federalist Era.   John C. Miller, *The Federalist Era, 1789–1801* (1960); Leonard D. White, *The Federalists* (1948); Forrest McDonald, *The Presidency of George Washington* (1974); Ralph Adams Brown, *The Presidency of John Adams* (1975); Stephen Kurtz, *The Presidency of John Adams* (1957); John R. Howe, *The Changing Political Thought of John Adams* (1966); Manning Dauer, *The Adams Federalists* (1953); Richard Kohn, *Eagle and Sword: The Federalists and the Creation of the Military Establishment in America, 1783–1802* (1975); Carl E. Prince, *The Federalists and the Origins of the U.S. Civil Service* (1978); Ralph Ketchum, *Presidents Above Party: The First American Presidency, 1789–1829* (1984); Leonard Levy, *Legacy of Suppression: Freedom of Speech and Press in Early American History,* rev. ed. (1985); James M. Smith, *Freedom's Fetters: The Alien and Sedition Laws and American Civil Liberties* (1956); Leland D. Baldwin, *The Whiskey Rebels* (1939); Thomas P. Slaughter, *The Whiskey Rebellion: Frontier Epilogue to the American Revolution* (1986); Irving Brant, *The Bill of Rights* (1965); John C. Miller, *Crisis in Freedom* (1951).

The Jeffersonian Republicans.   Charles A. Beard, *The Economic Origins of the Jeffersonian Opposition* (1915); Joseph Charles, *The Origins of the American Party System* (1956); Noble Cunningham, *The Jeffersonian Republicans* (1957); Merrill D. Peterson, *Thomas Jefferson and the New Nation* (1970); Richard Hofstadter, *The Idea of a Party System*

(1970); Norman K. Risjord, *Chesapeake Politics, 1781–1800* (1978); Alfred F. Young, *The Democratic-Republicans of New York* (1967); William N. Chambers, *Political Parties in a New Nation* (1963); Patricia Watlington, *The Partisan Spirit* (1972); John Zvesper, *Political Philosophy and Rhetoric: A Study of the Origins of American Party Politics* (1977); Richard W. Buel, Jr., *Securing the Revolution: Ideology in American Politics, 1789–1815* (1972); Joyce Appleby, *Capitalism and a New Social Order: The Republican Vision of the 1790s* (1984); Drew McCoy, *The Elusive Republic: Political Economy in Jeffersonian America* (1980) and *The Last of the Fathers: James Madison and the Republican Legacy* (1989).

Federalist Diplomacy. Felix Gilbert, *To the Farewell Address* (1961); Samuel F. Bemis, *Jay's Treaty* (1923) and *Pinckney's Treaty* (1926, rev. 1960); Alexander DeConde, *Entangling Alliance* (1958) and *The Quasi-War* (1966); Lawrence S. Kaplan, *Jefferson and France* (1967); Harry Ammon, *The Genêt Mission* (1973); Louis M. Sears, *George Washing-ton and the French Revolution* (1960); Bradford Perkins, *The First Rapprochement: England and the United States* (1967); Charles Ritcheson, *Aftermath of Revolution: British Policy Toward the United States, 1783–1795* (1969); Paul A. Varg, *Foreign Policies of the Founding Fathers* (1963).

The Founders. Douglas Southall Freeman, *George Washington*, 7 vols. (1948–1957); Garry Wills, *Cincinnatus: George Washington and the Enlightenment* (1984); Barry Schwartz, *George Washington: The Making of a Symbol* (1987); Esmond Wright, *Franklin of Philadelphia* (1986); Dumas Malone, *Jefferson and His Time*, 6 vols. (1948–1981); Merrill Peterson, *Thomas Jefferson and the New Nation* (1970); Irving Brant, *James Madison* (1950); James T. Flexner, *George Washington*, 4 vols. (1965–1972); Page Smith, *John Adams* (1962); John C. Miller, *Alexander Hamilton* (1959); Milton Lomask, *Aaron Burr*, 2 vols. (1979, 1982); Richard B. Morris, *Witnesses at the Creation: Hamilton, Madison, Jay, and the Constitution* (1985).

The Louisiana Purchase, 1803
Soldiers fire a salute as the French flag is lowered and the American flag raised in the main square of New Orleans, the principal European settlement in Louisiana. The ceremony marked transfer of formal possession of the vast territory from France to the United States. This 1903 painting by Thure De Thulstrup commemorated the centennial of the event. (*Louisiana Historical Society/Herb Orth, LIFE Magazine © 1957 Time, Inc.*)

CHAPTER 7

⧄ ⧄ ⧄

The Jeffersonian Era

⧄ ⧄ ⧄

Thomas Jefferson and his followers assumed control of the national government in 1801 as the champions of a distinctive vision of America. They envisioned a society of sturdy, independent farmers, happily free from the workshops, the industrial towns, and the city mobs of Europe. They favored a system of universal education that would introduce all Americans to the scientific rationalism of the Enlightenment. They promoted a cultural outlook that emphasized localism and republican simplicity. Above all, they proposed a federal government of sharply limited power, with most authority remaining at the level of the states.

Almost nothing worked out as they had planned, for during their years in power the young republic was developing in ways that made much of their vision obsolete. The American economy in the period of Republican ascendancy became steadily more diversified and complex. Growing cities, expanding commerce, and nascent industrialism made the ideal of a simple, agrarian society impossible to maintain. The quest for universal education foundered, and the nation's institutions of learning remained largely the preserve of privileged elites. American cultural life, far from reflecting localism and simplicity, was dominated by a vigorous and ambitious nationalism reminiscent of (and often encouraged by) the Federalists. And although American religion began, as the Jeffersonians had hoped, to confront and adjust to the spread of Enlightenment rationalism, the new skepticism did not survive unchallenged. A great wave of revivalism, beginning early in the century, ultimately almost submerged the new rational philosophy.

The Republicans did manage to translate some of their political ideals into reality. Jefferson dismantled much of the bureaucratic power structure that the Federalists had erected in the 1790s, and he helped to ensure that in many respects the federal government would remain a relatively unimportant force in American life. Yet at the same time, he frequently encountered situations that required him to exercise strong national authority. On occasion, he used his power more forcefully and arbitrarily than his Federalist predecessors.

The Republicans did not always like these nationalizing and modernizing trends, and on occasion they resisted them. For the most part, however, they had the sense to recognize what could not be changed. In adjusting to the new realities, they themselves began to become agents of the very transformation of American life they had once strenuously resisted.

The Rise of Cultural Nationalism

In many respects, American cultural life in the early nineteenth century seemed to reflect the Republican vision of the nation's future. Opportunities for education increased, the nation's literary and artistic life began to free itself from European influences, and American religion began to confront and adjust to the spread of Enlightenment rationalism. In other respects, however, the new culture was posing a serious challenge to Republican ideals.

Education and Professionalism

Central to the Republican vision of America was the concept of a virtuous and enlightened citizenry. An ignorant electorate, the Jeffersonians believed, could not be trusted to preserve democracy; education, therefore, was essential. Jefferson himself called emphatically for a national "crusade against ignorance." Republicans believed, therefore, in the creation of a nationwide system of public schools, in which all male citizens would receive free education.

Such hopes were not fulfilled. Although some states endorsed the principle of public education for all, none actually created a working system of free schools. A Massachusetts law of 1789 reaffirmed the colonial laws by which each town was obliged to support a school, but enforcement was so lax as to make it almost meaningless. Even in Boston, there were only seven public schools in 1790, most of them poorly housed. In Virginia, Jefferson had as wartime governor proposed a plan for universal elementary education and for advanced education for the gifted. Neither during nor after the war did the state legislature enact the proposal into law. As late as 1815, after more than a decade of Republican ascendancy in the nation's politics, not a single state had a comprehensive public school system.

Instead, schooling became primarily the responsibility of private institutions, most of which were open only to those who could afford to pay for them. In the South and in the Middle Atlantic states, where most schools were run by religious groups, almost

The One-Room School
Children of many different ages came together in the one-room school. While one group recited, the others studied their lessons. A single teacher—often a recent college graduate supporting himself while preparing for a career in law or politics—had to instruct and discipline the children, tend the fire, and perform various custodial chores. *(Library of Congress)*

every institution required tuition from the parents of prospective students. Poor farmers and workers, therefore, were usually excluded. In New England (and to a lesser extent elsewhere), there were a growing number of private academies available to the children of the relatively prosperous, but few schools for the less favored. Many of the new academies were modeled on those founded by the Phillips family at Andover, Massachusetts, in 1778, and at Exeter, New Hampshire, three years later. By 1815, there were thirty such private secondary schools in Massachusetts, thirty-seven in New York, and several dozen more scattered throughout the country. Many were frankly aristocratic in outlook, training their students to become members of the nation's elite.

Reformers who believed in the power of education to reform and redeem ignorant and "backward" people spurred a growing interest in Indian education. Because Jefferson and his followers liked to think of Native Americans as "noble savages" (uncivilized, but unlike blacks, not necessarily innately inferior), they hoped that schooling the Indians in white culture would tame and "uplift" the tribes. Although white governments did little to promote Indian education, missionaries and mission schools proliferated among the tribes.

The Republican enthusiasm for education did not always include a belief in the importance of schooling for women. Private secondary schools such as those in New England generally accepted only male students; even many public schools excluded females from the classroom. No less than other groups of their era, the Republicans clung to a patriarchal vision of society, which envisioned virtuous white males presiding benevolently over a world in which all other groups would be dependents.

Yet the late eighteenth and early nineteenth century did see some important advances in education for women. American females in the eighteenth century had received very little education of any kind, and the female illiteracy rate at the time of the revolution was very high—at least 50 percent. At the same time, Americans had begun to place a new value on the importance of the "republican mother" in training the new generation. That raised an important question. If mothers remained ignorant, how could they raise their children to be enlightened? Beginning as early as the 1770s and accelerating thereafter, such concerns led to the creation of a network of female academies throughout the nation (usually for the daughters of affluent families). In 1789, Massachusetts required that its public schools serve females as

well as males. Other states, although not all, soon followed.

There were, however, strict limits to this new belief in education for women. Most men, at least, assumed that female education should serve only to make women better wives and mothers. They had no need, therefore, for advanced or professional training; there was no reason for colleges and universities to make space for female students.

Those assumptions did not go entirely unchallenged. In 1784, Judith Sargent Murray published an essay defending the rights of women to education, and defending it in terms very different from those used by most men. Men and women were equal in intellect and equal in potential, Murray argued. Women, therefore, should have precisely the same educational opportunities as men. What was more, they should have opportunities to earn their own livings, to establish a role for themselves in society apart from their husbands and families. Murray's ideas became an inspiration to later generations of women, but during most of her own lifetime (1751–1820) they attracted relatively little support.

The new educational system, whether for men or for women, provided opportunities sharply restricted by wealth. There were some efforts to provide the poor with access to this system of private education or with separate schools of their own. Religious schools and private academies occasionally waived tuition for some who could not afford to pay it. In New York, the Free School Society provided a special institution for the poor. But such efforts fell far short of fulfilling Jefferson's vision of equal and universal education. The institutions available to the poor were not nearly numerous enough to accommodate everyone, and the education they offered was often clearly inferior to that provided more prosperous students. The New York Free School, for example, economized by adopting England's so-called Lancastrian method, by which teachers taught only a few bright student "monitors," who then drilled their fellow pupils in what they had learned.

There was a similar gap between the Republican ideal and the early eighteenth-century reality in the nature of American higher education. On the one hand, the number of colleges and universities in America grew substantially in the early years of the republic. At the outbreak of the Revolution there had been a total of nine colleges in all the colonies. By 1800, there were twenty-two, and the number continued to increase steadily thereafter. None of the new schools, however, was truly public. Even those established by state legislatures (in Georgia, North Carolina, Vermont, Ohio, and South Carolina, for example, all of which established universities between 1785 and 1805) relied on private contributions and on tuition fees to survive. Scarcely more than one man in a thousand (and no women at all) had access to any college education; and those few who did attend universities were almost without exception members of prosperous, propertied families.

The education that the colleges provided was, moreöver, exceedingly limited—narrow training in the classics and a few other areas and intensive work in theology. Indeed, the clergy was the only profession for which college training was generally required. There were a few institutions that attempted to provide their students with advanced training in other fields. The College of William and Mary in Virginia, the University of Pennsylvania, and Columbia College in New York all created law schools before 1800, but most lawyers continued to train for their profession simply by apprenticing themselves to practicing attorneys.

The University of Pennsylvania created the first American medical school early in the nineteenth century, under the leadership of Benjamin Rush. Most doctors, however, studied medicine by working with an established practitioner. Some American physicians believed in applying new scientific methods to medicine and struggled against age-old prejudices and superstitions. Efforts to teach anatomy, for example, encountered strong public hostility because of the dissection of cadavers that the study required. Municipal authorities had virtually no understanding of medical science and had almost no idea what to do in the face of the severe epidemics that so often swept their populations; only slowly did they respond to the warnings of Rush and others that lack of adequate sanitation programs were to blame for disease.

Individual patients often had more to fear from their doctors than from their illnesses. Even the leading advocates of scientific medicine often embraced useless and dangerous treatments. Benjamin Rush, for example, was an advocate of the new and supposedly scientific techniques of bleeding and purging, and very many of his patients died. George Washington's death in 1799 was probably less a result of the minor throat infection that had afflicted him than of the efforts of his physicians to cure him by bleeding and purging.

The medical profession also used its newfound commitment to "scientific" method to justify expanding its own control to kinds of care that had traditionally been outside its domain. Most childbirths, for example, had been attended by female midwives. In the early nineteenth century, physicians began to handle deliveries themselves and to work for restrictions on the role of midwives. Among the results of that change was a narrowing of opportunities for women (midwifery was an important female occupation) and a restriction of access to childbirth care for poor mothers (who could have afforded midwives, but who could not pay the higher physicians' fees).

Education and professional training in the early republic thus fell far short of the Jeffersonian vision. Indeed, efforts to promote education and increase professionalism often had the effect of strengthening existing elites rather than eroding them. Nevertheless, the ideal of equal educational opportunity survived, and in later decades it would become a vital force behind universal public education.

"The Rising Glory of America"

Many Americans in the Jeffersonian era may have repudiated the belief of the Federalists in political and economic centralization; but most embraced another form of nationalism with great fervor. Having won political independence from Europe, they aspired now to a form of cultural independence. And in the process, they dreamed of an American literary and artistic life that would rival the greatest achievements of Europe. As a "Poem on the Rising Glory of America" had foretold as early as 1772, Americans believed that their "happy land" was destined to become the "seat of empire" and the "final stage" of civilization, with "glorious works of high invention and of wond'rous art." The United States, one eighteenth-century writer proclaimed, would serve as "the last and greatest theatre for the improvement of mankind."

Such nationalism found expression, among other places, in early American schoolbooks. The Massachusetts geographer Jedidiah Morse, author of *Geography Made Easy* (1784), said the country must have its own textbooks so that the people would not be infected with the aristocratic ideas of England. The Connecticut schoolmaster and lawyer Noah Webster likewise contended that the American schoolboy should be educated as a patriot, his mind filled with nationalistic, American thoughts. "As soon as he opens his lips," Webster wrote, "he should rehearse the history of his own country; he should lisp the praise of liberty, and of those illustrious heroes and statesmen who have wrought a revolution in her favor."

Further to encourage a distinctive American culture and help unify the new nation, Webster insisted on a simplified and Americanized system of spelling —"honor" instead of "honour," for example. His *American Spelling Book,* first published in 1783 and commonly known as the "blue-backed speller," eventually sold over 100 million copies, to become the best-selling book (except for the Bible) in the entire history of American publishing. Webster also wrote grammars and other schoolbooks. His school dictionary, issued in 1806, was republished in many editions and was eventually enlarged to become (in 1828) *An American Dictionary of the English Language.* His speller and his dictionary established a national standard of words and usages. Although Webster's Federalist political views fell into disfavor in the early nineteenth century, his cultural nationalism remained popular and influential.

Those Americans who aspired to create a more elevated national literary life faced a number of obstacles. There was, to be sure, a large potential audience for a national literature—a reading public developed in large part by the wide circulation of newspapers and political pamphlets during the Revolution. But there were few opportunities for a would-be American author to get his work before the public. Printers preferred to publish popular works by English writers (for which they had to pay no royalties); magazine publishers filled their pages largely with items clipped from British periodicals. Ony those American writers willing to pay the cost and bear the risk of publishing their own works could compete for public attention.

Even so, a growing number of American authors strove to create a strong native literature so that, as the poet Joel Barlow wrote, "true ideas of glory may be implanted in the minds of men here, to take the place of the false and destructive ones that have degraded the species in other countries." Barlow himself, one of a group of Connecticut writers known as the "Hartford Wits," published an epic poem, *The Columbiad,* in 1807, in an effort to convey the special character of American civilization. The acclaim it received helped to encourage other native writers.

Among the most ambitious was the Philadelphia writer Charles Brockden Brown. Like many Americans, he was attracted to the new literary form of the novel, which had become popular in England in the late eighteenth century and had been successfully imported to America. But Brown sought to do more than simply imitate the English forms; he tried to use his novels to give voice to distinctively American themes, to convey the "soaring passions and intellectual energy" of the new nation. His obsession with originality led him to produce a body of work characterized by a fascination with horror and deviant behavior. Perhaps as a result, his novels failed to develop a large popular following.

Far more successful was Washinton Irving, a resident of New York who won wide acclaim for his satirical histories of early American life and his powerful fables of society in the New World. His popular folk tales, recounting the adventures of such American rustics as Ichabod Crane and Rip Van Winkle, made him the widely acknowledged leader of American literary life in the early eighteenth century and one of the few writers of that era whose works would continue to be read by later generations.

Perhaps the most influential works by American authors in the early republic were not poems, novels, or stories, but works of history that glorified the nation's past. Mercy Otis Warren, the influential pamphleteer and agitator during the 1770s, continued her literary efforts with a three-volume *History of the Revolution*, published in 1805 and emphasizing the heroism of the American struggle. Mason Weems, an Anglican clergyman, published a eulogistic *Life of Washington* in 1806, which became one of the best-selling books of the era. Weems had little interest in historical accuracy. He portrayed the aristocratic former president as a homespun man possessing simple republican virtues. (He also invented the story of the young Washington cutting down a cherry tree.) History, like literature, was serving as a vehicle for instilling a sense of nationalism in the American people.

Religion and Revivalism

The American Revolution had had a disastrous impact on traditional forms of religious practice. Not only had the Anglicans suffered for their alleged British sympathies and the Quakers for their pacifism, but the positions of almost all organized churches had in some ways declined. The detachment of religion from government in the years following independence weakened some established religions—notably Congregationalism in New England. The ideology of individual liberty and reason weakened others. By the 1790s, only a small proportion (perhaps as few as 10 percent) were members of formal churches, and ministers were complaining often about the "decay of vital piety." In fact, most Americans continued to hold strong religious beliefs (even if the widespread popular fervor of the Great Awakening of the 1730s had largely faded). What had declined was their commitment to organized churches and denominations.

Religious traditionalists were particularly alarmed about the emergence of new, "rational" religious doctrines—theologies that attempted to reconcile modern, scientific attitudes with Christian faith. They offered an approach to religion that sharply de-emphasized the role of God in the world and challenged much of conventional Christian orthodoxy. Some Americans, including Jefferson and Franklin, embraced "deism," which had originated among Enlightenment philosophers in France. Deists accepted the existence of God, but they considered Him a remote being who, after having created the universe, had withdrawn from direct involvement with the human race and its sins. Such views originated among a small group of highly educated people, but by 1800 deist ideas were reaching a much wider audience. Books and articles attacking religious "superstitions" were widely read and much discussed. Among the most influential was Thomas Paine's *The Age of Reason*, published between 1794 and 1796. Paine once declared that Christianity was the "strangest religion ever set up," for "it committed a murder upon Jesus in order to redeem mankind from the sin of eating an apple."

Religious skepticism also produced the philosophies of "universalism" and "unitarianism," which emerged at first as dissenting views within the New England Congregational church. Disciples of these new ideas rejected the traditional Calvinist belief in predestination, arguing that salvation was available to all. They rejected, too, the idea of the Trinity. Jesus was only a great religious teacher, they claimed, not the son of God. So wide was the gulf between these dissenters and the Congregationalist establishment that a permanent schism finally occurred. The Universalist church was founded as a separate denomination in Gloucester, Massachusetts, in 1779 (by James Murray, later the husband of Judith Sargent Murray), and the Unitarian church was established in Boston three years later.

Yet although many Americans believed that the spread of rationalism foretold the end of traditional, evangelistic religion in the new nation, nothing could have been further from the truth. Deism, universalism, and unitarianism in the end attracted more curiosity than commitment. They appeared more powerful than they actually were in part because those who clung to more traditional faiths were for a time confused and disorganized, unable to react effectively. Beginning in 1801, however, traditional religion staged a dramatic comeback in the form of a wave of revivalism known as the Second Great Awakening.

The origins of the awakening lay in the efforts of conservative theologians of the 1790s to fight the spread of religious rationalism, and in the efforts of church establishments to revitalize their organizations. Presbyterians strengthened their organization and expanded their efforts on the frontier, with conservatives in the church becoming increasingly militant in response to so-called New Light dissenters. Methodism, founded in England by John Wesley, spread to America in the 1770s and established itself as a formal church in 1784 under the leadership of Francis Asbury. Authoritarian and hierarchical in structure, the Methodists sent itinerant preachers throughout the nation to win recruits for the new church, which soon became the fastest-growing denomination in America. Almost as successful were the Baptists, who were themselves relatively new to America; they found an especially fervent following in the South.

By 1800, the revivalist energies of all these denominations were combining to create the greatest surge of evangelical fervor since the first Great Awakening sixty years before. Beginning among Presbyterians in several Eastern colleges (most notably at Yale, under the leadership of President Timothy Dwight), the new awakening soon spread throughout the country, reaching its greatest heights in the Western regions. In only a few years, a large proportion of the American people were mobilized by the movement, and membership in those churches embracing the revival—most prominently the Methodists, the Baptists, and the Presbyterians—was mushrooming. At Cane Ridge, Kentucky, in the summer of 1801, a group of evangelical ministers presided over the nation's first "camp meeting"—an extraordinary revival that lasted several days and impressed all who saw it with its size (some estimated that 25,000 people attended) and its fervor. Such events became common in subsequent years, as the Methodists in particular came to rely on them as a way to "harvest" new members. The Methodist circuit-riding preacher Peter Cartwright won national fame as he traveled from region to region exhorting his

Methodist Camp Meeting, 1837

Camp (or revival) meetings were popular among some evangelical Christians in America as early as 1800. By the 1820s, there were approximately 1,000 meetings a year, most of them in the South and the West. After one such meeting in 1806, a participant wrote: "Will I ever see anything more like the day of Judgment on this side of eternity—to see the people running, yes, running from every direction to the stand, weeping, shouting, and shouting for joy. . . . O! glorious day they went home singing and shouting." This lithograph, dated 1837, suggests the degree to which women predominated at many revivals. (The Granger Collection)

listeners to embrace the church. Even Cartwright, however, was often unprepared for the results of his efforts—a religious frenzy that manifested itself at times in convulsions, fits, rolling in the dirt, and the twitching "holy jerks."

The message of the Second Great Awakening was not entirely uniform, but its basic thrust was clear. Individuals must readmit God and Christ into their daily lives, must embrace a fervent, active piety, and must reject the skeptical rationalism that threatened traditional beliefs. Yet the wave of revivalism did not serve to restore the religion of the past. Few denominations any longer accepted the idea of predestination; and the belief that a person could affect his or her own destiny, rather than encouraging irreligion as many had feared, added intensity to the individual's search for salvation. The Awakening, in short, combined a more active piety with a belief in God as an active force in the world whose grace could be attained through faith and good works.

Nor did the Awakening work to reestablish old institutional forms of religion. Instead, it reinforced the spread of different sects and denominations and helped to create a general public acceptance of the idea that men and women could belong to different Protestant churches and still be committed to essentially the same Christian faith. Finally, the new evangelicalism—by spreading religious fervor into virtually every area of the nation, including remote regions where no formal church had ever existed—provided a vehicle for establishing a sense of order and social stability in communities still searching for an identity.

One of the striking features of the Awakening was the preponderance of women within it. Young women, in particular, were drawn to the revivalism, and female converts far outnumbered males. In some areas, church membership became overwhelmingly female as a result. One reason for this was that women were more numerous in certain regions than men. Adventurous young men often struck out on their own and moved West; women, for the most part, had no such options. Their marriage prospects thus diminished and their futures plagued with uncertainty, some women discovered in religion a foundation on which to build their lives. But even in areas where there was no shortage of men, women flocked to the revivals in enormous numbers, which suggests that they were responding as well to their changing economic roles. The movement of industrial work out of the home (where women had often contributed to the family economy through spinning and weaving) and into the factory—a process making rapid strides in the early nineteenth century (see pp. 260–261)—robbed older women, in particular, of one of their most important social roles. Younger, unmarried women with more mobility could follow the work out of the home and into the factory with less difficulty, but that movement, too, created personal and social strains. Religious enthusiasm helped compensate for the losses and adjustments these transitions produced; it also provided access to a new range of activities associated with the churches—charitable societies ministering to orphans and the poor, missionary organizations, and others—in which women came to play important roles.

Although revivalism was most widespread within white society, it penetrated the lives of other cultures as well. In some areas of the country, revivals were open to people of all races, and many blacks not only attended, but embraced the new religious fervor. Out of these revivals, in fact, emerged a substantial group of black preachers, who became important figures within the slave community. Some of them translated the apparently egalitarian religious message of the Awakening—that salvation was available to all—into a similarly egalitarian message for blacks in the present world. Out of black revival meetings in Virginia, for example, arose an elaborate plan in 1800 (devised by Gabriel Prosser, the brother of a black preacher) for a slave rebellion and attack on Richmond. The plan was discovered and the rebellion forestalled by whites, but revivalism continued in subsequent years to create racial unrest in the South. In the coming years, fears of such challenges to white supremacy led directly to a strengthening of the laws governing race relations.

The spirit of revivalism was particularly strong in these years among Native Americans, although its origins and the forms it took were very different from those of white or black society. The dislocations and military defeats Indians suffered in the aftermath of the American Revolution created a sense of crisis among many of the Eastern tribes in particular; as a result, the 1790s and early 1800s became an era of Indian religious fervor and of prophecy.

It was not the first such era. In the 1760s, the Delaware prophet Neolin had sparked a widespread revival in the Old Northwest with a message combining Christian and Indian imagery and bringing to Native American religion a vision of a personal God, intimately involved in the affairs of man. Neolin had also called for Indians to rise up in defense of their lands and had denounced the growth of trade and other relationships with white civilization. His exhortations had helped stimulate the Indian military efforts of 1763 and beyond.

The 1790s produced another age of Indian revivalism. Presbyterian and Baptist missionaries were active among the Southern tribes and sparked a great wave of conversions. But the most important revivalism came from the efforts of another great prophet: Handsome Lake, a Seneca whose seemingly miraculous "rebirth" after years of alcoholism helped give him a special stature within his tribe. Handsome Lake, like Neolin, called for a revival of traditional Indian ways. That meant repudiating the individualism of white society, which Handsome Lake argued had penetrated tribal life with alarming results, and restoring the communal quality of the Indian world.

(He claimed to have met Jesus, who instructed him to "tell your people they will become lost when they follow the ways of the white man.") Handsome Lake's message spread through the scattered Iroquois communities that had survived the military and political setbacks of previous decades and inspired many Indians to give up whiskey, gambling, and other destructive customs derived from white society.

But the revival did not, in fact, lead to a true restoration of traditional Iroquois culture. Instead, Handsome Lake encouraged Christian missionaries to become active within the tribes; and he urged Iroquois men to abandon their roles as hunters (partly because so much of their hunting land had been seized by whites) and become sedentary farmers instead. Iroquois women, who had traditionally done the farming, were to move into more domestic roles. When some women resisted the change, Handsome Lake denounced them as witches.

The Second Great Awakening also had important effects on those Americans who did not accept its teachings. The rational "freethinkers," whose skeptical philosophies had done so much to produce the revivals, were in many ways their victims. They did not disappear after 1800, but their influence rapidly declined, and for many years to come they remained a distinct and defensive minority within American Christianity. Instead, the dominant religious characteristic of the new nation would be a fervent evangelicalism, which would survive into the mid-nineteenth century and beyond.

Stirrings of Industrialism

It was not only culturally and religiously that the nation was developing in ways unforeseen by Jefferson and his followers. Economically, the United States was taking the first, tentative steps toward a transformation that would ultimately shatter forever the vision of a simple, agrarian republic.

The Industrial Revolution in England

While Americans were engaged in a revolution to win their independence, an even more important revolution was in progress in England: the emergence of modern industrialism. Historians differ over precisely when the industrial revolution began, but it is clear that by the end of the eighteenth century it was well under way. Its essence was relatively simple: power-driven machines were taking the place of hand-operated tools and were permitting manufacturing to become more rapid and extensive. But however simple the causes, the social and economic consequences of the transformation were complex and profound.

The factory system in England took root first in the manufacture of cotton thread and cloth. There, one invention followed another in quick succession. Improvements in weaving made necessary improvements in spinning; and these changes required new devices for carding (combing and straightening the fibers for the spinner). Water, wind, and animal power continued to be important in the textile industry; but far more important was the emergence of steam power—which began to proliferate after the appearance of James Watt's advanced steam engine (patented in 1769). Cumbersome and inefficient by modern standards, Watt's engine was nevertheless a major improvement over the earlier "atmospheric" engine of Thomas Newcomen. England's textile industry quickly became the most profitable in the world, and it helped encourage comparable advances in other fields of manufacturing as well.

At the same time, England's social system was undergoing a wrenching change. Hundreds of thousands of men and women were moving from rural areas into cities to work in factories; and there they experienced both the benefits and the costs of industrialization. The standard of living of the new working class, when objectively quantified, was significantly higher than that of the rural poor. Most of those who moved from farm to factory, in other words, experienced some improvement in their material circumstances. But the psychological costs of being suddenly uprooted from one way of life and thrust into another, fundamentally different one could outweigh the economic gains. There was little in the prior experience of most workers to prepare them for the nature of industrial labor: disciplined, routinized work on a fixed schedule, which stood in sharp contrast to the varying, seasonal work pattern of the rural economy. Nor were the factory workers often prepared for life in the new industrial towns and expanding cities. They experienced, too, a fundamental change in their relationship with their employers. Unlike the landlords and local aristocrats of rural England, factory owners and managers—the new class of industrial capitalists, many of them accumulating unprecedented wealth—were usually remote and inaccessible figures. They dealt with their workers impersonally, and the result was a growing schism between the two classes—each lacking access to or understanding of the other.

As a result, English life was being transformed at every level. The middle class was expanding and coming to dominate the economy, although not yet the culture or the nation's politics. Working men and women were beginning to think of themselves as a distinct class, with common goals and interests. And their simultaneous efforts to adjust to their new way of life and to resist its most damaging aspects made the late eighteenth and early nineteenth centuries a time of continuing social turbulence.

Not since the agrarian revolution thousands of years earlier, when humans had turned from hunting to farming for sustenance, had there been an economic change of a magnitude comparable to the industrial revolution. Centuries of traditions, of social patterns, of cultural and religious assumptions, were challenged and often shattered.

Technology in America

Nothing even remotely comparable to the English industrial revolution occurred in America in the first two decades of the nineteenth century. Indeed, it was opposition to the kind of economic growth occurring in England that had helped the Republicans defeat the Federalists in 1800; and Americans continued to view British industrialization with deep ambivalence. Yet even while they warned of the dangers of rapid economic change, Americans of the age of Jefferson were welcoming a series of technological advances that would ultimately help ensure that the United States too would be transformed.

Some of these technological advances were imported from England. The British government attempted to protect the nation's manufacturing preeminence by preventing the export of textile machinery or the emigration of skilled mechanics. But despite such efforts, a number of immigrants arrived in the United States with advanced knowledge of English technology, eager to introduce the new machines to America. Samuel Slater, for example, used the knowledge he had acquired before leaving England to build a spinning mill in Pawtucket, Rhode Island, for the Quaker merchant Moses Brown in 1790. It was generally recognized as the first modern factory in America.

More important than imported technology,

Slater's Mill

Samuel Slater served as an apprentice in England in the 1780s to Richard Arkwright, an inventor of machinery for the new cotton mills that were driving the English industrial revolution. Slater left for America in 1789 disguised as a farm boy, because English law prohibited anyone with knowledge of such technology from emigrating and taking the nation's industrial "secrets" abroad. In 1790 he designed the first successful cotton-spinning mill in the United States at Pawtucket, Rhode Island; and in 1815 he added facilities for weaving woolen cloth. This drawing shows the Pawtucket bridge, falls, and mill as they appeared sometime between 1810 and 1819.   (Rhode Island Historical Society)

however, was that of purely domestic origin. America in the early nineteenth century produced several important inventors of its own. Among them was Oliver Evans, of Delaware, who devised a number of ingenious new machines: an automated flour mill, a card-making machine, and others. He worked several important improvements in the steam engine, and in 1795 he published America's first textbook of mechanical engineering: *The Young Mill-Wright's and Miller's Guide*. In his own flour mill, which went into operation in 1787 (the year the Constitutional Convention first met), virtually all operations were mechanized. Only two men were required to operate the mill: one of them emptying a bag of wheat into the machinery, another putting the lid on the barrels of flour and rolling them away.

Even more influential for the future of the nation were the inventions of the Massachusetts-born, Yale-educated Eli Whitney, who revolutionized both cotton production and weapons manufacturing. The

growth of the textile industry in England had created an enormous demand for cotton, a demand that planters in the American South were finding it impossible to meet. Their greatest obstacle was the difficulty of separating seeds from cotton fiber—a process that was essential before cotton could be sold. There was one variety of cotton with smooth black seeds and long fibers that was easily cleaned; but this long-staple or Sea Island variety could be grown successfully only along the coast or on the offshore islands of Georgia and South Carolina. There was not nearly enough of it to satisfy demand. Another variety, short-staple cotton, could be grown in much of the South; but its sticky green seeds were extremely difficult to remove, and a skilled worker could clean no more than a few pounds a day by hand. Then, in 1793, Whitney, who was working at the time as a tutor on the Georgia plantation of General Nathanael Greene's widow, invented a machine that performed the arduous task quickly and efficiently. It was dubbed the cotton gin ("gin" being a derivative of "engine"); and it would soon transform the life of the South.

Mechanically, the gin was very simple. A toothed roller caught the fibers of the cotton boll and pulled them between the wires of a grating. The grating caught the seeds, and a revolving brush removed the lint from the roller's teeth. With the device, a single operator could clean as much cotton in a few hours as a group of workers had once needed a whole day to do. The results were profound. Soon cotton growing spread into the upland South; and within a decade, the total crop increased eightfold. Black slavery, which with the decline of tobacco production had seemed for a time to be a dwindling institution, was now restored to importance, expanded, and firmly fixed upon the South.

The cotton gin not only changed the economy of the South. It also helped transform the North. The large supply of domestically produced fiber served as a strong incentive to entrepreneurs in New England and elsewhere to develop a native textile industry. Few Northern states could hope to thrive on the basis of agriculture alone; by learning to process cotton, they could become industrially prosperous instead. The manufacturing preeminence of the North, which emerged with the development of the textile industry in the 1820s and 1830s, helped drive a wedge between the nation's two most populous regions and ultimately contributed to the coming of the Civil War. It also helped ensure the eventual Union victory.

Whitney also made a major contribution to the development of modern warfare, and with it a contribution to other industrial techniques. During the two years of undeclared war with France (1798 and 1799), Americans were deeply troubled by their lack of sufficient armaments for the expected hostilities. Production of muskets—each carefully handcrafted by a skilled gunsmith—was distressingly slow. Whitney responded by devising a machine to make each of the parts of a gun according to an exact pattern. Tasks could thus be divided among several workers, and one laborer could assemble a rifle out of parts made by several others. Before long, the same system was being applied to sewing machines, clocks, and many other complicated products.

The new technological advances were relatively isolated phenomena during the early years of the nineteenth century. Not until at least the 1840s did the nation begin to develop a true manufacturing economy. But the inventions of this period were crucial in making the eventual transformation possible.

Trade and Transportation

One of the prerequisites for industrialization is a transportation system that allows the efficient conveyance of raw materials to factories and of finished goods to markets. The United States had no such system in the early years of the republic, and thus it had no domestic market extensive enough to justify large-scale production. Yet even then efforts were under way that would ultimately remove the transportation obstacle.

There were several ways to solve the problem of the small American market. One was to develop markets overseas; and American merchants continued their efforts to do that. One of the first acts of the new Congress when it met in 1789 was to pass two tariff bills giving preference to American ships in American ports, helping to stimulate an expansion of shipping. More important, indeed the principal reason for the growth of American trade in this period, was the outbreak of war in Europe in the 1790s, allowing Yankee merchant vessels to take over most of the carrying trade between Europe and the Western Hemisphere. As early as 1793, the young republic had a merchant marine and a foreign trade larger than those of any country except England. In proportion to its population, the United States had more ships and international commerce than any country in the world. And the shipping business was growing fast. Between 1789 and 1810, the total tonnage of American vessels engaged in overseas traffic rose from less than 125,000 to nearly 1 million. Only 30 percent of the country's exports had been carried in American ships in 1789; over 90 percent was being so carried by 1810. The figures for imports increased even more dramatically, from 17.5 percent to 90 percent in the same period.

Another solution to the problem of limited markets was to develop new markets at home, by improving transportation between the states and into the interior. Progress was slower here than in international shipping, but some improvements were occurring nevertheless. In river transportation, a new era began with the development of the steamboat. Oliver Evans's high-pressure engine, lighter and more efficient than James Watt's, made steam more feasible for powering boats and, eventually, the locomotive, as well as mill machinery. Even before the high-pressure engine was available, a number of inventors experimented with steam-powered craft, and John Fitch exhibited to some of the delegates at the Constitutional Convention a forty-five-foot vessel with paddles operated by steam. The perfecting of

Launching the Ship *Fame,* 1802
This painting by the American artist George Ropes shows the launching of a new merchant ship, the *Fame,* at Salem, Massachusetts, in 1802 amid banners and fanfare. Salem was one of several booming American ports whose ships sailed the world trading in exotic goods from Europe and Asia. (Essex Institute, Salem, Massachusetts)

the steamboat was chiefly the work of the inventor Robert Fulton and the promoter Robert R. Livingston. Their *Clermont,* equipped with paddle wheels and an English-built engine, sailed up the Hudson in the summer of 1807, demonstrating the practicability of steam navigation (even though it took the ship thirty hours to go 150 miles). In 1811, a partner of Livingston, Nicholas J. Roosevelt (a remote ancestor of Theodore Roosevelt), introduced the steamboat to the West by sending the *New Orleans* from Pittsburgh down the Ohio and Mississippi. The next year, this vessel entered on a profitable career of service between New Orleans and Natchez.

Meanwhile, in land transportation, what was to become known as the turnpike era had begun. In 1792, a corporation constructed a toll road running the sixty miles from Philadelphia to Lancaster, with a hard-packed surface of crushed rock. This venture proved so successful that similar turnpikes (so named

from the kind of tollgate frequently used) were laid out from other cities to neighboring towns. Since the turnpikes were built and operated for private profit, construction costs had to be low enough and the prospective traffic heavy enough to ensure an early and ample return. Therefore these roads, radiating from Eastern cities, ran for comparatively short distances and through thickly settled areas. Similar highways would not be extended over the mountains until the state governments or the federal government began to participate in the financing of the projects.

Country and City

Despite all the changes and all the advances, America remained in the early nineteenth century an overwhelmingly rural and agrarian nation. Only 3 percent of the population lived in towns of more than

8,000 at the time of the second census in 1800. Ten percent lived west of the Appalachian Mountains, far from what urban centers there were. Much of the country remained a wilderness. Even the nation's largest cities could not begin to compare, either in size or in cultural sophistication, with such European capitals as London and Paris.

Yet here too there were signs of change. The leading American cities might not yet have become world capitals, but they were large and complex enough to rival the important secondary cities of Europe. Philadelphia, with 70,000 residents, and New York, with 60,000, were becoming major centers of commerce, of learning, and of a distinctively urban culture. So too were the next largest cities of the new nation: Baltimore (26,000 in 1800), Boston (24,000), and Charleston (20,000).

Much remained to be done before this small and still half-formed nation would become a complex modern society. It was still possible in the early nineteenth century to believe that those changes might not ever occur. But forces were already at work that, in time, would lastingly transform the United States.

And Thomas Jefferson, for all his commitment to the agrarian ideal, found himself as president obliged to confront and accommodate them.

Jefferson the President

Privately, Thomas Jefferson may well have considered his victory over John Adams in 1800 to be what he later termed it: a revolution "as real . . . as that of 1776." Publicly, however, he was restrained and conciliatory at the time, attempting to minimize the differences between the two parties and calm the passions that the bitter campaign had aroused. "We are all republicans, we are all federalists," he said in his inaugural address. And during his eight years in office, he did much to prove those words correct. There was no complete repudiation of Federalist policies, no true "revolution." Indeed, at times Jefferson seemed to outdo the Federalists at their own work—most notably in overseeing a remarkable expansion of the territory of the United States.

America in 1800

Forests

Settled areas (non-Indian)

• Cities, settlements, and other outposts

■ Forts

In some respects, however, the Jefferson presidency did indeed represent a fundamental change in the direction of the federal government. The new administration oversaw a drastic reduction in the powers of some national institutions, and it forestalled the development of new powers in areas where the Federalists would certainly have attempted to expand them. Neither the executive nor the legislative branch of government was willing or able to exercise decisive authority in most areas of national life by the end of the Jeffersonian era. Only the courts continued trying to assert federal power in the ways the Federalists had envisioned.

The Federal City

The relative unimportance of the federal government during the era of Jefferson was symbolized by the character of the newly founded national capital, the city of Washington. John Adams had moved to the new seat of government during the last year of his administration. And there were many at that time who envisioned that the raw, uncompleted town would soon emerge as a great and majestic city, a focus for the growing nationalism that the Federalists were promoting. The French architect Pierre L'Enfant had designed the capital on a grand scale, with broad avenues radiating from the uncompleted Capitol building, which was to adorn one of the area's highest hills. Washington was, many Americans believed, to become the Paris of the United States.

In reality, throughout Jefferson's presidency—indeed throughout most of the nineteenth century—Washington remained little more than a straggling, provincial village. Although the population increased steadily from the 3,200 counted in the 1800 census, it never rivaled that of New York, Philadelphia, and the other major cities of the nation. One problem was the climate: wet and cold in winter, hot and almost unbearably humid in summer, reflecting the marshy character of the site. Another problem, however, was that those in the federal government responsible for the development of the city did little to further its growth. The Republican administrations of the early nineteenth century oversaw the completion of several sections of the present-day Capitol building, of the White House, and of a few other government buildings. Otherwise, they allowed the city to remain a raw, inhospitable community, one whose muddy streets were at times almost impassable, one in which the Capitol and the White House were often cut off from each other by rising creeks and washed-away bridges.

Members of Congress viewed the city not as a home but as a place to visit briefly during sessions of the legislature and leave as quickly as possible. Few owned houses in Washington. Most lived in a cluster of simple boardinghouses in the vicinity of the Capitol. It was not unusual for a member of Congress to resign his seat in the midst of a session to return home if he had an opportunity to accept the more prestigious post of member of his state legislature. During the summers, the entire government in effect packed up and left town. The president, the cabinet, the Congress, and most other federal employees spent the hot summer months far from the uncomfortable capital.

President and Party Leader

From the outset, Jefferson acted in a spirit of democratic simplicity in keeping with the frontierlike character of the unfinished federal city. He was a wealthy and aristocratic planter by background, the owner of more than 100 slaves, and a man of rare cultivation and sophistication; but he conveyed to the public an image of plain, almost crude disdain for pretension. He walked like an ordinary citizen to and from his inauguration at the Capitol, instead of riding in a coach at the head of a procession. In the presidential mansion, which had not yet acquired the name the White House, he disregarded the courtly etiquette of his predecessors (in part, no doubt, because as a widower he had no first lady to take charge of social affairs). At state dinners, he let his guests scramble pell-mell for places at the table. He did not always bother to dress up, prompting the fastidious British ambassador to complain on one occasion of being received by the president in coat and pantaloons that were "indicative of utter slovenliness and indifference to appearances." Even when carefully dressed, the tall, freckle-faced, sandy-haired Jefferson did not offer an impressive physical appearance. He was shy. His posture was awkward. He walked with a shambling gait. And he was an ineffective public speaker.

Yet Jefferson managed nevertheless to impress most of those who knew him. He was a brilliant and charming conversationalist, a writer endowed with literary skills unmatched by any president before or since (with the possible exception of Lincoln), and undoubtedly one of the nation's most intelligent and creative men, with a wider range of interests and accomplishments than any public figure in American

Washington, D.C., in the Early Nineteenth Century

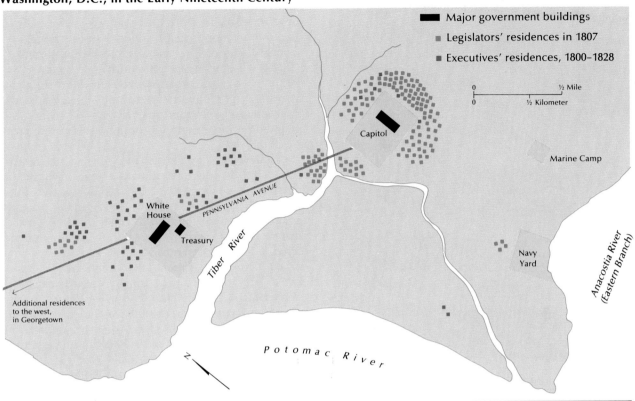

history. In addition to politics and diplomacy, he was an active architect, educator, inventor, scientific farmer, and philosopher-scientist. He diverted himself with such pastimes as sorting the bones of prehistoric animals or collecting volumes for one of the nation's greatest private libraries (which later became the basis of the original Library of Congress).

Jefferson was, above all, a shrewd and practical politician, equaled in that regard perhaps only by Lincoln and Franklin D. Roosevelt. On the one hand, he went to great lengths to eliminate the aura of majesty surrounding the presidency that he believed his predecessors had created. He decided, for example, to submit his messages to Congress not by delivering them in person, as Washington and Adams had done, but by sending them in writing, thus avoiding even the semblance of attempting to dictate to the legislature. (The precedent he established survived for more than a century, until the administration of Woodrow Wilson.) At the same time, however, Jefferson worked hard to exert influence as the leader of his party, giving direction to Republicans in Congress by quiet and sometimes even devious means.

To his cabinet he appointed members of his own party who shared his philosophy. His secretary of state was James Madison, a long-time friend and neighbor in Virginia whose collaboration with the president throughout Jefferson's administration was so close that it was often difficult to tell which of the two men was more responsible for government policy. His secretary of the treasury was Albert Gallatin, a Swiss-born politician with a French accent whose financial expertise made him the rival of Hamilton, but who was a staunch opponent of Hamilton's policies.

Although the Republicans had objected strenuously to the efforts of their Federalist predecessors to build a network of influence through patronage, Jefferson too used his powers of appointment as an effective political weapon. Like Washington before him, he believed that federal offices should be filled with men loyal to the principles and policies of the administration. True, he did not attempt a sudden and drastic removal of Federalist officeholders, possibly because of assurances to the contrary that had been given in his name when Federalist votes in Con-

Thomas Jefferson
This 1805 portrait by the noted American painter Rembrandt Peale shows Jefferson at the beginning of his second term as President. It also conveys (through the simplicity of dress and the slightly unkempt hair) the image of democratic simplicity that Jefferson liked to project as the champion of the "common man."
(New-York Historical Society)

gress were needed to break the tie with Burr. Yet at every convenient opportunity he replaced the holdovers from the Adams administration with his own trusted followers. By the end of his first term about half the government jobs, and by the end of his second term practically all of them, were held by loyal Republicans. The president punished Burr and the Burrites by withholding patronage from them; he never forgave the man whom he believed guilty of plotting to frustrate the intentions of the party and the ambitions of its rightful candidate.

The Twelfth Amendment, added to the Constitution in 1804 before the election of that year, ensured that a tie vote between the presidential and vice-presidential candidates of the same party could not occur again. The amendment recognized by implication the existence of political parties; it stipulated that the electors should vote for president and vice

president as separate and distinct candidates. Burr had no chance to run on the ticket with Jefferson a second time. In place of Burr, the congressional caucus of Republicans nominated his New York factional foe, George Clinton. The Federalist presidential nominee, Charles C. Pinckney, fared poorly against the popular Jefferson, who carried even the New England states (except Connecticut) and was reelected by the overwhelming electoral majority of 162 to 14. The Republican membership of both houses of Congress increased.

Jefferson's popularity faded during his second term, and he had to deal with a revolt within the party ranks. His brilliant but erratic relative John Randolph of Roanoke, the House leader, turned against him, accusing him of acting like a Federalist instead of a states' rights Republican. Randolph mustered a handful of anti-Jefferson factionalists, who called themselves "Quids." Randolph's most importance grievance stemmed from a controversy over Western land claims. The Georgia legislature, before ceding its territorial rights to the federal government, had made and then canceled a grant of millions of acres along the Mississippi to the Yazoo Land Companies. The fate of the so-called Yazoo claims remained a subject of debate for years. Jefferson favored a compromise settlement that would have satisfied both the state of Georgia and the Yazoo investors, many of whom were Northern Republicans whose support he needed. But Randolph insisted that the company's claims were fraudulent and charged the president with complicity in corruption. A number of members of Congress were investors in the land companies or supporters of their claims, and time and again Randolph would point his bony finger at one or another of these men and shriek contemptuously, "Yazoo!" He prevented the government from making any settlement of the question until both he and Jefferson were out of office. (See p. 266.)

Dollars and Ships

Jefferson's administration did take some steps toward dismantling the governmental structure that the Federalists had attempted to erect. Under Washington and Adams, the Republicans believed, the government had been needlessly extravagant. Yearly federal expenditures had nearly tripled between 1793 and 1800. The public debt had also risen, as Hamilton had intended. And an extensive system of internal taxa-

Jefferson the Architect
Thomas Jefferson drew this sketch of the front elevation of his house at Monticello, in Virginia. The upper portico specified here was never completed; and the octagonal structures on either end of the house are not shown. Jefferson drew elaborate plans for almost every part of Monticello and provided precise specifications down to the last detail. Among his other architectural accomplishments is the splendid central campus of the University of Virginia. (Massachusetts Historical Society)

tion, including the hated whiskey excise tax, had been erected.

The Jefferson administration moved deliberately to reverse the trend. In 1802, it persuaded Congress to abolish all internal taxes, leaving customs duties and the sale of Western lands as the only source of revenue for the government. At the same time, Secretary of the Treasury Gallatin carried out a plan for drastic retrenchment in government spending, scrimping as much as possible on expenditures for the normal operations of government, cutting the already small staffs of the executive departments to minuscule levels. Although Jefferson was unable entirely to retire the national debt as he had hoped, he did cut it almost in half (from $83 million to $45 million).

Jefferson also effected what he called a "chaste reformation" of the armed forces. The tiny army of 4,000 men he reduced to 2,500. The navy he pared down from twenty-five ships in commission to seven, cutting the number of officers and sailors accordingly. Anything but the smallest of standing armies, he argued, might menace civil liberties and civilian control of government. And a large navy, he feared, might be misused to promote overseas commerce, which Jefferson believed should remain secondary to agriculture.

Yet despite his claims that "Peace is our passion," Jefferson was not a pacifist. At the same time that he was reducing the size of the army and navy, he was helping to establish the United States Military Academy at West Point, founded in 1802. And when trouble began brewing overseas, he began again to build up the fleet.

Such trouble appeared first in the Mediterranean, off the coast of northern Africa. For years the Barbary states of North Africa—Morocco, Algiers, Tunis, and Tripoli (now part of Libya)—had made piracy a national enterprise. They demanded protection money from all nations whose ships sailed the Mediterranean. Even the ruler of the seas, Great Britain, gave regular contributions to the pirates. (England did not in fact particularly desire to eliminate a racket that hurt its naval rivals and maritime competitors more seriously than itself.) During the 1780s and 1790s the United States agreed to treaties providing for annual tribute to Morocco and the rest, and from time to time the Adams administration ransomed American sailors who had been captured and were being held as slaves. Jefferson was reluctant to continue this policy of appeasement. "Tribute or war is the usual alternative of these Barbary pirates," he said. "Why not build a navy and decide on war?"

The decision was not left to Jefferson. In 1801, the pasha of Tripoli, dissatisfied with the American response to his extortionate demands, had the flagpole of the American consulate chopped down—his way of declaring war. Jefferson concluded that, as president, he had a constitutional right to defend the United States without a war declaration by Congress; and he sent a naval squadron to relieve American ships already at the scene. Not until 1803, however, was the fleet, under commodores Edward Preble and Samuel Barron, strong enough to take effective action. In 1805, the pasha, by threatening to kill captive Americans, compelled Barron to agree to peace. The agreement ended the payment of tribute to Tripoli by America, but it exacted from the United States a substantial (and humiliating) ransom of $60,000 for the release of the prisoners.

Conflict with the Courts

Having won control of the executive and legislative branches of government, the Republicans looked with suspicion on the judiciary, which remained largely in the hands of Federalist judges. Soon after Jefferson's first inauguration, his followers in Congress launched an attack on this last preserve of the opposition. First, the legislators repealed the Judiciary Act of 1801, thus abolishing the new circuit courts and arranging instead for each of the Supreme Court justices to sit with a district judge on circuit duty. With their energies stretched thin, the Republicans believed, the jurists would be unable to become active or influential foes. Jefferson lacked authority to remove Adams's "midnight appointees" from their newly created jobs; but Congress had achieved the same objective by pulling their benches

The Barbary Wars
The first American naval force to combat the Barbary Coast pirates proved inadequate to defeat the forces of Tripoli, and in 1803 President Jefferson sent reinforcements. Among those joining the war in that year was Lieutenant Stephen Decatur, who was later to win fame as a naval commander in the War of 1812. He is shown here in hand-to-hand combat with Algerians attacking his ship. In 1804 he engineered a daring raid during which Americans destroyed the frigate *Philadelphia*, which had been captured by Tripoli. (Brown Brothers)

out from under them, despite Federalist protests that the repeal violated the constitutional provision that judges should hold office for life.

The debate over the Judiciary Act of 1801 led to one of the most important judicial decisions in the history of the nation. Federalists had long maintained that the Supreme Court had the authority to review acts of Congress and to nullify those that were in conflict with the Constitution. Hamilton had argued for such a power in *The Federalist Papers* (although the Constitution said nothing specifically to support him), and the Court itself had actually exercised the review power in 1796 when it upheld the validity of a law passed by the legislature. But the Court's authority would not be secure, it was clear, until it actually declared a congressional act unconstitutional.

In 1803, in the case of *Marbury* v. *Madison,* it did so. William Marbury, one of Adams's "midnight appointments," had been named a justice of the peace in the District of Columbia. But his commission, although duly signed and sealed, had not been delivered to him before Adams left office. Madison, who as Jefferson's secretary of state was responsible for transmitting appointments, then refused to hand over the commission. Marbury applied to the Supreme Court for an order (a writ of mandamus) directing Madison to perform his official duty. In a historic ruling, the Court found that Marbury had a right to his commission but that the Court had no authority to order Madison to deliver it. On the surface, therefore, the decision was a victory for the administration. But of far greater importance than the relatively insignificant matter of Marbury's commission was the Court's reasoning in the decision.

The original Judiciary Act of 1789 had given the Court the power to compel executive officials to act in such matters as the delivery of commissions, and it was on that basis that Marbury had filed his suit. But the Court ruled that Congress had exceeded its authority, that the Constitution had defined the powers of the judiciary, and that the legislature had no right to expand them. The relevant section of the 1789 act was, therefore, void. In seeming to deny its own authority, the Court was in fact radically enlarging it. The justices had repudiated a relatively minor power (the power to force the delivery of a commission) by asserting a vastly greater one (the power to nullify an act of Congress). The administration, recognizing the significance of the ruling, was alarmed. But since the Court had shrewdly encased this assertion of its power within a ruling favorable to the government, it was difficult for the Republicans to protest.

The chief justice of the United States at the time of the ruling was (as he would remain until 1835) John Marshall, one of the towering figures in the history of American law. A leading Federalist and prominent Virginia lawyer, he had served John Adams as secretary of state. (It had been Marshall, ironically, who had neglected to deliver Marbury's commission in the closing hours of the administration.) In 1801, just before leaving office, Adams had appointed him chief justice; and almost immediately Marshall established himself as the dominant figure on the Court, shaping virtually all its most important rulings—including, of course, *Marbury* v. *Madison.* Marshall had served with George Washington's army at Valley Forge during the Revolution, and he retained from the experience a vivid impression of a weak, divided, and inefficient government. Through a succession of Republican presidents, he battled to give the federal government unity and strength. And in so doing, he established the judiciary as a coequal branch of government with the executive and the legislature—a position that the founders of the republic had never clearly indicated it should occupy.

Jefferson recognized the threat that an assertive judiciary could pose to his policies, and even while the *Marbury* case was still pending he was preparing for a renewed assault on the last Federalist stronghold. If he could not remove the judges he considered obnoxious directly, perhaps he could do so indirectly through the process of impeachment. According to the Constitution, the House of Representatives was empowered to bring impeachment charges against any civil officer for "high crimes and misdemeanors," and the Senate sitting as a court was authorized to try the officer on the charges. Jefferson sent evidence to the House to show that one of the district judges, John Pickering of New Hampshire (who was suffering from severe mental illness), was unfit for his position. The House accordingly impeached him, the Senate found him guilty of high crimes and misdemeanors, and Pickering was removed from the bench.

Later the Republicans went after bigger game, a justice of the Supreme Court itself. Justice Samuel Chase, a rabidly partisan Federalist, had in the 1790s applied the Sedition Act with what the Republicans considered particular brutality; and he had delivered political speeches from the bench, insulting President Jefferson and denouncing the Jeffersonian doctrine of equal liberty and equal rights. In so doing, Chase was guilty of no high crime or misdemeanor in the constitutional sense, and he was only saying what thousands of Federalists believed. Some Republicans concluded, however, that impeachment should not be viewed merely as a criminal proceeding and that a judge could properly be impeached for political reasons—for obstructing the other branches of the government and disregarding the will of the people.

At Jefferson's own suggestion, the House of Representatives set up a committee to investigate Chase's conduct. Impeached by the House on the basis of the committee's findings, the justice was brought to trial before the Senate early in 1805. Jefferson did his best to secure a conviction, even temporarily cultivating the friendship of Aaron Burr, who as vice president presided over the trial. But Burr performed his duties with aloof impartiality, and John Randolph as the impeachment manager bungled the prosecution. A majority of the senators finally voted for conviction, but not the necessary two-thirds majority. Chase was acquitted. The decision set an important precedent. It helped establish that impeachment would not become a purely political weapon, that something more than partisan disagreement would have to underlie the process.

In one sense, the effort to impeach Chase was helpful to the Republicans despite the failure, for it pressured federal judges as a whole to be more discreet and less partisan in statements from the bench. Federalist jurists had reason to fear that were they to antagonize the Republicans and the public too greatly, future impeachment efforts might succeed. But in a larger sense, the Republican assault on the judiciary was a failure. Marshall remained secure in his position as chief justice. The duel between the Court and the president continued. And the judiciary survived as a powerful force within the government—more often than not on behalf of the centralizing, expansionary policies that the Republicans had been trying to reverse.

Doubling the National Domain

In the same year that Jefferson was elected president of the United States, Napoleon Bonaparte made himself ruler of France with the title of first consul; and in the year that Jefferson was reelected, Napoleon assumed the name and authority of emperor. The two men had little in common. Yet for a time they were of great assistance to each other in international politics—until Napoleon's ambitions moved from Europe to America and created conflict and estrangement.

Jefferson and Napoleon

Napoleon failed in a grandiose plan to seize India from the British Empire (although he succeeded in the conquest of Italy), and his imperial ambitions began to seek a new target. France, he recalled, had once possessed a vast empire in North America; and he began to dream of extending French power into the New World once again. The French possessions east of the Mississippi had been ceded to Great Britain in 1763 and were now, for the most part, incorporated within the United States. Those territories were lost to France forever. But the lands west of the Mississippi France had ceded to Spain, now a relatively weak neighbor; and those, Napoleon believed, could be recovered. In 1800 (on the day after the French agreed to the settlement with the United States, ending the quasi war), Napoleon reached a secret agreement with Spain (the treaty of San Ildefonso) to reacquire these North American possessions. Thus France once again held title to Louisiana, which included almost the whole of the Mississippi Valley to the west of the river, plus New Orleans to the east of the river near its mouth. Napoleon hoped that Louisiana would form the continental heartland of his proposed North American empire.

Other essential parts of his empire-to-be were the sugar-rich and strategically valuable West Indian islands that still belonged to France—Guadeloupe, Martinique, and above all Santo Domingo. Plans for the islands were threatened, however, by unrest among the Caribbean slaves. Blacks in Santo Domingo had been inspired by the French Revolution to rise in revolt and create a republic of their own, under the remarkable black leader, Toussaint L'Ouverture. Taking advantage of a truce in his war with England, Napoleon sent to the West Indies an army led by his brother-in-law Charles Leclerc, which crushed the insurrection and restored French authority.

Jefferson was for a time unaware of Napoleon's imperial ambitions in America, and he pursued a foreign policy that reflected his well-known admiration for France. He appointed as the American minister to Paris the ardently pro-French Robert R. Livingston. Continuing the peace policy of Adams, he worked to secure ratification of the Franco-American settlement of 1800 and began observing the terms of the treaty even before it was ratified. The Adams administration had joined with the British in recognizing and supporting the rebel regime of Toussaint in Santo Domingo; Jefferson assured the French minister in Washington that the American people, especially those of the slaveholding states, did not approve of the black revolutionary, who was setting a bad example for their own slaves. He even implied that the United States might join with France in putting down the rebellion (although nothing ever came of the suggestion).

Jefferson began to reappraise the whole subject of American relations with France when he heard rumors of the secret retrocession of Louisiana. "It completely reverses all the political relations of the U.S.," he wrote to Minister Livingston on April 18, 1802. Always before, America had looked to France as its "natural friend." But there was on the earth "one single spot" the possessor of which was "our natural and habitual enemy." That spot was New Orleans, the outlet through which the produce of the fast-growing Western regions of the United States was shipped to the markets of the world. If France should actually take and hold New Orleans, Jefferson said, then "we must marry ourselves to the British fleet and nation."

Jefferson was even more alarmed when, in the fall of 1802, he learned that the Spanish intendant at New Orleans (who still governed the city, since the French had not yet taken formal possession of the region) announced a disturbing new regulation. American shippers servicing the Mississippi River had for many years been accustomed to depositing their cargoes in New Orleans for transfer to ocean-going vessels. The intendant now forbade the practice, even though Spain had guaranteed Americans that right in the Pinckney Treaty of 1795. Without such a right, the lower Mississippi would be effectively closed to American shippers.

Westerners suspected that Napoleon himself had ordered the closing of the river for sinister purposes of his own, and they demanded that something be done to reopen it. Some of the more extreme among them clamored for war with France; and they were joined in that clamor by the Federalists of the Northeast, who were not greatly concerned about the specific problems of the Westerners but who believed that by encouraging Western discontent they could embarrass the Jefferson administration. The president faced a dilemma. If he yielded to the frontier clamor and sought satisfaction through force, he would run the risk of a major war with France. If, on the other hand, he ignored the Westerners' demands, he might lose their political support.

Jefferson, however, saw another way out of the dilemma: the purchase of New Orleans from Napoleon. Jefferson was not particularly interested in acquiring the lands of Louisiana to the west of the Mississippi. But he was eager to acquire the vital port city; and almost as soon as he heard the rumors of Napoleon's reacquisition of the Louisiana Territory, he instructed Livingston in Paris to negotiate for the purchase of New Orleans. Livingston on his own authority suggested to the French that they might be glad to be rid of the upper part of Louisiana as well.

Jefferson also persuaded Congress to appropriate funds for an expansion of the army and the construction of a river fleet, and he allowed the impression to emerge that American forces, despite his own desire for peace, might soon descend on New Orleans. At the same time, he dispatched a special envoy to work with Livingston in Paris: James Monroe, who had served as minister to France in the 1790s and was well remembered there, and who was popular among Westerners in the United States. Jefferson told Monroe that if he and Livingston could not reach satisfactory terms with the French, they should cross the Channel and begin discussions with the British government. No one ever had a chance to determine whether Jefferson was serious in his hints of an attack on New Orleans and an alliance with Great Britain or whether he was merely attempting to put pressure on the French. Because even before Monroe arrived in Paris, Napoleon suddenly decided to dispose of the entire Louisiana Territory.

Startling though this decision seemed to some of his advisers, Napoleon had good reasons for it. His plans for an American empire had already gone seriously awry, partly because of misfortunes best described in two words—*mosquitoes* and *ice*. Mosquitoes had brought yellow fever and death to General Leclerc and to thousands of the soldiers whom Napoleon had sent to reconquer Santo Domingo. Ice had locked in a Dutch harbor earlier than anticipated in the winter of 1802. That had delayed the departure of an expeditionary force that Napoleon wished to send to reinforce Leclerc's army and take possession of Louisiana. When the harbor thawed in the spring of 1803, it was too late to send the fleet to America. By then, Napoleon was preparing for a renewed war in Europe and feared that he would not be able to hold Louisiana if the British, with their superior naval power, should attempt to take it. He also realized that, quite apart from the British threat, there was danger from the United States itself. It would be virtually impossible to prevent the Americans, who were pushing steadily into the Mississippi Valley, from overrunning Louisiana sooner or later.

The Louisiana Purchase

Napoleon left the negotiations over Louisiana to his finance minister, Barbé-Marbois, rather than his foreign minister, Talleyrand (since Talleyrand was remembered and distrusted in America for the XYZ

Affair). Barbé-Marbois had lived for some time in the United States and had married an American woman; the delegates from the United States considered him trustworthy. Livingston and Monroe had to decide first whether they should even consider making a treaty for the purchase of the entire Louisiana Territory, since they had not been authorized by their government to do so. But they were reluctant to wait for new instructions from home; they feared Napoleon might withdraw his offer as suddenly as he had made it. And so, aware that Jefferson could always reject any treaty they negotiated, they decided to proceed. After some haggling over the price—Barbé-Marbois asked and got somewhat more than Napoleon's minimum—Livingston and Monroe signed the agreement on April 30, 1803.

By the terms of the treaty, the United States was to pay a total of 80 million francs ($15 million), directly or indirectly to the French government. The United States was also to grant certain exclusive commercial privileges to France in the port of New Orleans. Moreover, the United States was to incorporate the residents of Louisiana into the Union and grant them as soon as possible the same rights and privileges as other citizens—an implication that the new territories would soon be admitted as states. The boundaries were not clearly defined; the treaty simply specified that Louisiana would occupy the "same extent" as it had when owned by France and Spain. When Livingston and Monroe appealed to Talleyrand for his opinion about the boundary, he merely replied: "You have made a noble bargain for yourselves, and I suppose you will make the most of it."

In Washington, the president was both pleased and embarrassed when he received the treaty. He was glad to get such a "noble bargain"; but according to his oft-repeated views on the Constitution, the United States government lacked authority to accept it. Jefferson had always insisted that the federal government could rightfully exercise only those powers explicitly assigned to it, and nowhere did the Constitution say anything about the acquisition of new territory. But his advisers argued that his treaty-making power under the Constitution would justify the purchase of Louisiana. Finally the president gave in, trusting, as he said, "that the good sense of our country will correct the evil of loose construction when it shall produce ill effects."

Jefferson called Congress into special session. And despite objections to the treaty from a few die-hard Federalists from New England, the Senate promptly gave its consent and the House soon passed the necessary appropriation bill. Spain was then still administering Louisiana; the French had never taken actual possession. Finally, late in 1803, the French assumed formal control of Louisiana just long enough to turn the territory over to General James Wilkinson, the commissioner of the United States and the commander of a small occupation force. In New Orleans, beneath a bright December sun, the recently raised French tricolor was lowered and the American flag raised.

For the time being, the Louisiana Territory was given a semimilitary government with officials appointed by the president; later it was organized on the general pattern of the Northwest Territory, with the assumption that it would be divided into states. The first of these was admitted to the union as the state of Louisiana in 1812.

Exploring the West

Meanwhile, a series of bold explorations were revealing the geography of the far-flung new territory. In 1803, even before Napoleon's offer to sell Louisiana, Jefferson planned an expedition that was to cross the continent to the Pacific Ocean, gather geographical facts, and investigate prospects for trade with the Indians. Congress secretly provided the necessary funds, and Jefferson named as leader of the expedition his private secretary and Virginia neighbor, the thirty-two-year-old Meriwether Lewis, a veteran of Indian wars skilled in the ways of the wilderness. Lewis chose as a colleague the twenty-eight-year-old William Clark, who—like George Rogers Clark, his older brother—was an experienced frontiersman and Indian fighter.

Lewis and Clark, with a company of four dozen men, set up winter quarters in St. Louis at about the time the United States took formal possession of Louisiana. In the spring of 1804, they started up the Missouri River, and with the Shoshoni woman Sacajawea as their guide, her baby on her back, they eventually crossed the Rocky Mountains, descended the Snake and the Columbia rivers, and in the late autumn of 1805 camped on the Pacific coast. In September 1806, they were back in St. Louis with elaborate records of the geography and the Indian civilizations they had observed along the way. No longer were white Americans completely ignorant of the lands of the Far West.

While Lewis and Clark were on their epic jour-

UNDER MY WINGS EVERY THING PROSPERS

New Orleans in 1803
Because of its location near the mouth of the Mississippi River, New Orleans was the principal port of western North America in the early nineteenth century. Through it, Western farmers shipped their produce to markets in the East and Europe. This 1803 painting celebrates the American acquisition of the city from France as part of the Louisiana Purchase. (Chicago Historical Society)

ney, Jefferson dispatched other explorers to fill in the picture of the Louisiana Territory. The most important of these was Lieutenant Zebulon Montgomery Pike. Then only twenty-six years old, Pike led an expedition in the fall of 1805 from St. Louis up the Mississippi River in search of its source. He did not find it, but he learned a great deal about the upper Mississippi Valley. In the summer of 1806, Pike set out again and proceeded up the valley of the Arkansas river and into what later became Colorado, where he discovered, but failed in his attempt to climb, the peak that now bears his name. His account of his Western travels created an enduring (and inaccurate) impression among most Americans that the land between the Missouri and the Rockies was a desert that farmers could never cultivate and that ought to be left forever to the nomadic Indian tribes.

The Burr Conspiracy

In the long run, the Louisiana Purchase prepared the way for the growth of the United States as a great continental power. At first, however, the purchase provoked reactions that seemed to threaten the very existence of the Union.

Jefferson's triumphant reelection in 1804 suggested that most of the nation approved the new acquisition. But some New England Federalists raged against it. They realized that the more the West grew and the more new states joined the Union, the less power the Federalists and their region would retain. In Massachusetts, a group of the most extreme Federalists, known as the Essex Junto, concluded that the only recourse for New England was to secede from the Union and form a separate "Northern Confed-

Meriwether Lewis
In 1807, when the French painter Charles de Saint-Mémin produced this watercolor, Lewis had returned from his fabled expedition through the Far West with William Clark and had been named governor of the Louisiana Territory by President Jefferson. He had served earlier as a private secretary to Jefferson. (New-York Historical Society)

eracy." To justify their position, they cited states' rights arguments similar to those Jefferson had used only a few years earlier to justify his call for nullification of the Alien and Sedition Acts.

If a Northern Confederacy was to have any hope for lasting success as a separate nation, the Federalists believed, it would have to include New York and New Jersey as well as New England. But the leading Federalist in New York, Alexander Hamilton, refused to support the secessionist scheme. "Dismemberment of our empire," he wrote, "will be a clear sacrifice of great positive advantages without any counterbalancing good, administering no relief to our real disease, which is *democracy."* Hamilton feared that disorders like those of the French Revolution were about to sweep over the United States. If so, the country would need a military dictator, an American Napoleon, to bring order out of chaos—perhaps Hamilton himself, who by now clearly had no future in electoral politics.

Hamilton opposed the secessionists as well because their plans threatened to strengthen his greatest political rival in New York. Vice President Aaron Burr was another politician without prospects, at least within the party of Thomas Jefferson, who had never forgiven him for his role in the 1800 election deadlock. When Federalists approached Burr and offered him their support if he would run for governor in 1804, he agreed. There were rumors that he had agreed as well to support disunion plans and that he would, if elected, lead the state into secession along with New England. There was no evidence to support such rumors. Hamilton, however, accused Burr of plotting treason and made numerous private remarks, widely reported in the press, about Burr's "despicable" character. When Burr lost the election, he blamed his defeat on Hamilton's malevolence and demanded redress. "These things," he wrote, "must have an end." He challenged Hamilton to a duel.

Dueling had already fallen into some disrepute in America, but many people still considered it a legitimate institution for settling matters of "honor." Hamilton feared that refusing Burr's challenge would brand him a coward and damage his prospects of future glory. And so, on a July morning in 1804, the two men crossed the Hudson River and met at Weehawken, New Jersey. Hamilton was mortally wounded; he died the next day.

Burr fled New York to escape an indictment for murder and spent months traveling through the South. He returned to Washington to preside over the United States Senate the following winter and then, at the end of his term as vice president, faced a political outlook more hopeless than ever. He was ambitious, resourceful, and enormously charismatic. But he was largely discredited within the existing political organizations of his country. He was, in short, a man in search of a cause.

He found it, apparently, in the wilderness. Even before his duel with Hamilton, Burr had apparently dreamed of glorious exploits in the unsettled lands of the Southwest. (Hamilton had cherished some of the same ambitions, which may have been another rea-

Exploration of the Louisiana Purchase, 1803–1807

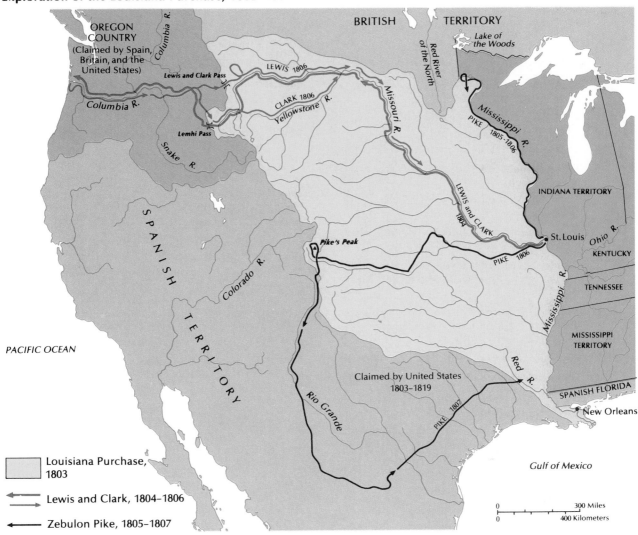

OREGON COUNTRY (Claimed by Spain, Britain, and the United States)

BRITISH TERRITORY

Lake of the Woods

Columbia R.

LEWIS 1806

Red River of the North

Lewis and Clark Pass

Columbia R.

CLARK 1806

Yellowstone R.

Missouri R.

Mississippi R.

PIKE 1805-1806

Lemhi Pass

Snake R.

S P A N I S H   T E R R I T O R Y

LEWIS and CLARK 1804

INDIANA TERRITORY

St. Louis   Ohio R.

KENTUCKY

Pike's Peak

PIKE 1806

Colorado R.

Mississippi R.

TENNESSEE

PACIFIC OCEAN

Claimed by United States 1803–1819

Rio Grande

Red R.

MISSISSIPPI TERRITORY

PIKE 1807

SPANISH FLORIDA

New Orleans

Gulf of Mexico

Louisiana Purchase, 1803

Lewis and Clark, 1804–1806

Zebulon Pike, 1805–1807

0   300 Miles
0   400 Kilometers

son for Burr's challenge to him.) Both before and after the duel, Burr corresponded with prominent men of the region, especially with General James Wilkinson, now governor of the Louisiana Territory.

Burr and Wilkinson hoped, it seems clear, to lead an expedition that would capture Mexico from the Spanish. "Mexico glitters in all our eyes," he wrote; "the word is all we wait for." But there were also rumors that they intended to separate the Southwest from the Union, which Burr would rule as an empire of his own. Historians disagree about Burr's real intentions, but there is little evidence that these rumors were true.

Whether true or not, many of Burr's opponents chose to believe the rumors—including, ultimately, Jefferson himself. In the fall of 1806, Burr led a group of armed followers down the Ohio River by boat. Disturbing reports of his activities flowed into Washington throughout the winter, the most alarming from Wilkinson, who, having suddenly turned against Burr, informed the president that treason was afoot, that an attack on New Orleans was imminent. Jefferson ordered the arrest of Burr and his men as traitors; eventually Burr was tracked down and brought to Richmond for trial.

Jefferson was not present in Richmond but, de-

SIGNIFICANT EVENTS

1769   James Watt patents steam engine (p. 199)

1778   Phillips Academy founded in Andover, Massachusetts (p. 193)

1779   Universalist church founded in Gloucester, Massachusetts (p. 196)

1781   Phillips Exeter Academy founded in New Hampshire (p. 193)

1782   Unitarian church founded in Boston (p. 196)

1784   Judith Sargent Murray publishes essay on rights of women (p.193)

American Methodist church formally established (p. 196)

1789   Massachusetts law requires public schools to admit female students (p. 193)

1790   Samuel Slater builds textile mill, first modern factory in America, in Pawtucket, Rhode Island (p. 199)

1792   Toll road constructed from Philadelphia to Lancaster, beginning the turnpike era (p. 202)

1793   Eli Whitney invents cotton gin (p. 200)

1794   First black churches in America established (p. 198)

1794–1796   Thomas Paine's *Age of Reason* attacks traditional religion (p. 196)

1800   United States capital moves to Washington, D.C. (p. 204)

1800   Gabriel Prosser's plans for slave rebellion in Virginia foiled (p. 198)

1801–1805   Conflict with Tripoli (p. 208)

1801   Second Great Awakening begins (p. 196)

John Marshall appointed chief justice of the Supreme Court (p. 209)

1802   Jefferson administration abolishes all internal federal taxes (p. 207)

United States Military Academy founded at West Point (p. 208)

1803   Louisiana Territory purchased from French (p. 208)

Supreme Court establishes power of judicial review in *Marbury* v. *Madison* (p. 209)

1804–1806   Lewis and Clark, and Zebulon Pike, explore Louisiana Territory (p. 212)

1804   Aaron Burr kills Alexander Hamilton in duel (p. 214)

Thomas Jefferson reelected president (p. 213)

1806   Burr conspiracy uncovered (p. 215)

1807   Fulton and Livingston launch the *Clermont,* first steamboat (p. 202)

Burr tried for conspiracy (p. 216)

1828   Webster's *American Dictionary of the English Language* published (p. 195)

termined to secure a conviction, carefully managed the government's case from Washington. The prosecution relied hopefully on its star witness, General Wilkinson—a disreputable character who had been in the pay of the Spaniards during the entire affair and had demanded extra money from them on the grounds that in heading off the Burr expedition, he had saved their territory from attack. Despite the administration's efforts to influence the trial, Chief Justice Marshall, presiding over the case on circuit duty, insisted that Burr receive a fair hearing—for both judicial and political reasons.

In the course of the trial, which continued from May through October 1807, Marshall applied literally the constitutional provision that no one shall be convicted of treason except on the testimony of at least two witnesses to the same "overt act." He excluded all evidence not bearing directly on such an act. Thus the jury had little choice but to acquit Burr, since not even one witness had actually seen him waging war against the United States or giving aid and comfort to its enemies. The trial had given the chief justice another chance to frustrate the president. And Marshall's strict, and extremely difficult, standards of proof established a precedent that made it almost impossible to convict anyone of treason against the United States.

Burr was free, but his political reputation was permanently destroyed. For several years, he lived in self-imposed exile in Europe. In 1812, he returned to America and established a successful legal practice in New York. He lived long enough to hail the Texas revolution of 1836 as the fruition of the movement to "liberate" Mexico that he had tried to launch.

The Burr conspiracy was in part the story of a single man's soaring ambitions and flamboyant personality. But it was also a symbol of the larger perils still facing the new nation. With a central government that remained deliberately weak, with vast tracts of land only nominally controlled by the United States, with ambitious political leaders will-ing, if necessary, to circumvent normal channels in their search for power, the United States remained an imperfectly realized nation. The legitimacy of the federal government was yet to be fully asserted.

SUGGESTED READINGS

General Histories.   Henry Adams, *History of the United States During the Administration of Jefferson and Adams,* 9 vols., (1889–1891); Marcus Cunliffe, *The Nation Takes Shape, 1789–1832* (1959); Charles Mayfield, *The New Nation* (1981); Marshall Smelser, *The Democratic Republicans, 1801–1815* (1968).

Society and Culture.   Joseph J. Ellis, *After the Revolution: Profiles of Early American Culture* (1979); Russel B. Nye, *The Cultural Life of the New Nation* (1960); Kenneth Silverman, *A Cultural History of the American Revolution* (1976); Lawrence A. Cremin, *American Education: The National Experience* (1981); Carl F. Kaestle, *The Evolution of an Urban School System* (1973); Harry Warfel, *Noah Webster, Schoolmaster to America* (1936); Priscilla F. Clement, *Welfare and the Poor in the Nineteenth-Century City* (1985); William W. Sweet, *Revivalism in America* (1944); William G. McLoughlin, *Revivals, Awakenings, and Reform* (1978); Sydney Ahlstrom, *A Religious History of the American People* (1972); Whitney R. Cross, *The Burned Over District* (1950); John Boles, *The Great Revival in the South* (1972); Cathy Davidson, *The Revolution and the Word* (1986); Terry D. Bilhartz, *Urban Religion and the Second Great Awakening* (1986); Jan Lewis, *The Pursuit of Happiness: Family and Values in Jefferson's Virginia* (1983); Richard Slotkin, *Regeneration Through Violence* (1973).

Economic Growth.   Stuart Bruchey, *The Roots of American Economic Growth* (1965); Thomas C. Cochran, *Frontiers of Change: Early Industrialization in America* (1981); Douglas C. North, *The Economic Growth of the United States, 1780–1860* (1961); W. Elliot Brownlee, *Dynamics of Ascent* (1979); Nathan Rosenberg, *Technology and American Economic Growth* (1972); Merritt Roe Smith, *Harpers Ferry Armory and the New Technology* (1977); Anthony F. C. Wallace, *Rockdale* (1978); Arthur H. Cole, *The American Wool Manufacture,* 2 vols. (1926); Caroline F. Ware, *Early New England Cotton Manufacture* (1931); C. M. Green, *Eli Whitney and the Birth of American Technology* (1956); W. J. Rorabaugh, *The Craft Apprentice: From Franklin to the Machine Age in America* (1986); Barbara M. Tucker, *Samuel Slater and the Origins of the American Textile Industry, 1790–1860* (1984); George R. Taylor, *The Transportation Revolution* (1951); James Henretta and Gregory Nobles, *The Evolution of American Society, 1700–1815,* rev. ed., 1987.

Politics and Government.   Morton Borden, *Parties and Politics in the Early Republic* (1967); Noble Cunningham, *The Jeffersonian Republicans in Power* (1963) and *The Process of Government Under Jefferson* (1978); Robert Dawidoff, *The Education of John Randolph* (1979); James S. Young, *The Washington Community* (1966); David Hackett Fischer, *The Revolution of American Conservatism* (1965); Linda Kerber, *Federalists in Dissent* (1970); James M. Banner, *To the Hartford Convention* (1967); Leonard White, *The Jeffersonians* (1951); Alexander Balinky, *Albert Gallatin: Fiscal Theories and Policy* (1958); Robert M. Johnstone, Jr., *Jefferson and the Presidency* (1978); Dumas Malone, *Jefferson the President: First Term* (1970) and *Jefferson the President: Second Term* (1974); Richard Ellis, *The Jeffersonian Crisis* (1971); Leonard Baker, *John Marshall: A Life in Law* (1974).

Jeffersonian Thought.   Adrienne Koch, *The Philosophy of Thomas Jefferson* (1943); Charles M. Wiltse, *The Jeffersonian Tradition in American Democracy* (1935); Merrill Peterson, *The Jeffersonian Image in the American Mind* (1960); Leonard W. Levy, *Jefferson and Civil Liberties: The Darker Side* (1963); Drew McCoy, *The Elusive Republic: Political Economy in Jeffersonian America* (1980).

Foreign Policy.   Irving Brant, *James Madison: Secretary of State* (1953); Bradford Perkins, *Prologue to War: England and the United States, 1805–1812* (1961); Alexander DeConde, *The Affair of Louisiana* (1976); Arthur P. Whitaker, *The Mississippi Question* (1934); George Dangerfield, *Chancellor Robert R. Livingston of New York* (1960); Harry Ammon, *James Monroe and the Quest for National Identity* (1971); Bernard deVoto, *Course of Empire* (1952); Bernard deVoto, ed., *The Journals of Lewis and Clark* (1953); Nathan Schachner, *Aaron Burr* (1937); Thomas P. Abernethy, *The Burr Conspiracy* (1954); Milton Lomask, *Aaron Burr,* 2 vols. (1979, 1982).

Indians and the West.   B. W. Sheehan, *Seeds of Extinction* (1973); Francis S. Philbrick, *The Rise of the New West* (1965); Ray Allen Billington, *Westward Expansion* (1967); Richard White, *The Roots of Dependency* (1983); James P. Ronda, *Lewis and Clarke Among the Indians* (1984); Charles Wilkinson, *American Indians, Time, and the Law,* rev. ed. (1982); Francis P. Prucha, *American Indian Policy in the Formative Years* (1962); Reginald Horsman, *Expansion and American Indian Policy, 1783–1812* (1962), and *Matthew Elliott, British Indian Agent* (1964); R. David Edmunds, *The Shawnee Prophet* (1983) and *Tecumseh and the Quest for Indian Leadership* (1984).

***New Harmony on the Wabash* (1830s), by Karl Bodmer**
The German artist Karl Bodmer painted this landscape of New Harmony, Indiana, sometime in the
1830s while accompanying Prince Maximilian of Wied on a journey through the then sparsely settled
American Northwest. (*Indiana Historical Society*)

CHAPTER 8

◪ ⧄ ◩

Free Seas
and
Fresh Lands

◪ ⧄ ◩

Two very different conflicts took shape in the early nineteenth century that would, together, draw the United States into a difficult and frustrating war. One was the continuing struggle in Europe (the Napoleonic Wars), which in 1803 escalated once again into a full-scale conflict. At first, the hostilities posed no direct danger to the United States and in many respects worked indirectly to benefit it—by enabling Americans to develop a profitable trade with belligerents on both sides. As the fighting continued, however, both the British and the French took steps to prevent the United States from trading with (and thus assisting) the other. Tensions between the Old and New Worlds rapidly grew.

The other conflict was an older one, on the North American continent itself. The ceaseless westward expansion of white settlement was now stretching to the Mississippi River and beyond, colliding once again with a native population committed to protecting its lands from intruders. In both the North and the South, the threatened tribes mobilized themselves—and began building new and effective alliances—to resist white encroachments. They began as well to forge connections with British forces in Canada and Spanish forces in Florida. The Indian conflict on land, therefore, became intertwined with the European conflict on the seas. Together they drew the United States into a war with Great Britain—the War of 1812.

That war was a less than glorious experience for the United States. America drifted into the conflict with Britain gradually, not in response to a single great event that might have galvanized public opinion behind it. And so the war provoked wide domestic opposition, especially from those whose economic fortunes were endangered by it. It also produced several humiliating defeats (including the British capture and burning of Washington) and only a few decisive American victories. It ended with a treaty that fell far short of guaranteeing the nation's war aims—a treaty that signaled, at best, a draw.

But the more important war, in the long run, was the conflict with the Indians. And in that, white America won a series of important, indeed decisive, victories. The most important Indian alliance in the West was destroyed. The most effective Indian leader was killed. Large new territories were opened for white settlement, and the way was paved for the ultimate removal of the tribes to the arid lands farther west. White Americans have long considered the conflict with Great Britain the real war, but the victories over the tribes had far more lasting effects on the nation than the inconclusive struggle with the British.

The war had other effects on the United States as well. It greatly stimulated American nationalism, helping to diminish for a time the tensions between North and South. And it stimulated manufacturing and economic growth, and thus accelerated progress toward industrialization. The conflict ultimately became another factor in consigning to oblivion the Jeffersonian vision of a small, decentralized, agrarian nation.

Causes of Conflict

Politicians at the time disagreed sharply over the causes of the War of 1812. Historians have continued to debate them ever since. Some have argued that the question of frontier lands and the conflicts with the Indians lay at the heart of the conflict. Others claim that the real issue was freedom of the seas. In fact, the two matters were closely related to each other. The war cannot be understood without considering both.

Neutral Rights

The early nineteenth century saw a dramatic expansion of American shipping in the Atlantic. Britain's naval superiority prevented France and Spain (constantly at war with the English) from carrying on more than a modest ocean trade. But the British merchant marine was preoccupied with commerce in Europe and Asia and devoted little energy to trade with America. Thus the United States stepped effectively into the void and developed one of the most important merchant marines in the world. Year after year, American shippers assumed a larger and larger proportion of the carrying trade between Europe and the West Indies.

In 1805, at the Battle of Trafalgar, a British fleet virtually destroyed what was left of the French navy. Napoleon continued in the following years to extend his domination over the continent of Europe by land; but Britain remained the undisputed master of the seas. Because France could no longer challenge the British navy, Napoleon was powerless to invade the British Isles. He needed, therefore, to find another way to bring England to terms—through economic, rather than naval, pressure. The result was what he called the Continental System. The British, he reasoned, were a nation of shopkeepers; they depended for their existence on buying and selling in the rest of the world, especially in Europe. If he could close the Continent to their trade, he thought, they ultimately would have to make concessions. Accordingly, he issued a series of decrees (one in Berlin in 1806 and another in Milan in 1807) barring British ships and neutral ships touching at British ports from landing their cargoes at any European port controlled by France or its allies.

The British government replied to Napoleon's decrees by establishing—through a series of "orders in council"—an unusual blockade of the European coast. The blockade did not explicitly bar imports to Napoleon's Europe; but it required that the goods be carried either in British vessels or in neutral vessels stopping at British ports—precisely what Napoleon's policies forbade.

Caught between Napoleon's Berlin and Milan decrees and Britain's orders in council, American vessels ran a double risk. If they sailed directly for the European continent, they took the chance of being captured by the British navy. If they sailed by way of a British port, they ran the risk of seizure by the French. Both of the warring powers were violating America's rights as a neutral nation. But most Americans considered the British, with their greater sea power, the worse offender. British ships pounced on Yankee merchantmen all over the ocean; the French could do so only in European ports. In particular, British vessels stopped American ships on the high seas and seized sailors off the decks, making them victims of "impressment."

Impressment

The British navy—with its floggings, its low pay, and its dirty and dangerous conditions on shipboard—was a "floating hell" to its sailors. They had to be "impressed" (forced) into the service, and at every good opportunity they deserted. By 1807, many of them had joined the American merchant marine or the American navy. To check this loss of vital manpower, the British claimed the right to stop and search American merchantmen (although not naval vessels) and reimpress deserters. They did not claim the right to take native-born Americans, but they did insist on the right to seize naturalized Americans born on British soil; according to the laws of England, a true-born subject could never give up allegiance to the king. In practice, the British often impressed native as well as naturalized Americans. Thousands of sailors claiming the protection of the United States government were thus kidnapped. To these hapless men, impressment was little better than slavery. To their American shipowning employers, it was at least a serious nuisance. And to millions of proud and patriotic Americans, even those living far from the ocean, it was an intolerable affront to the national honor.

In the summer of 1807, the British went to more provocative extremes in an incident involving not an ordinary merchantman, but a vessel of the American

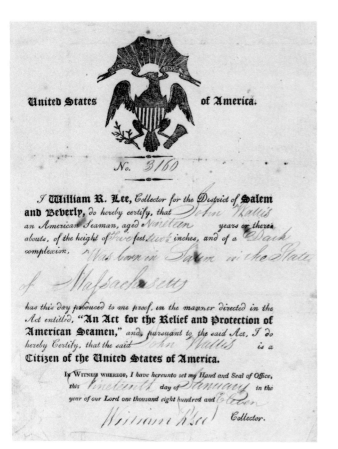

Protection from Impressment

To protect American sailors from British impressment, the federal government issued official certificates of United States citizenship—known as "protection papers." But British naval officers, aware that such documents were often forged, frequently ignored them. (Essex Institute, Salem, Massachusetts)

navy. Sailing from Norfolk, with several alleged deserters from the British navy among the crew, the American naval frigate *Chesapeake* was hailed by His Majesty's Ship *Leopard,* which had been lying in wait off Cape Henry, at the entrance to Chesapeake Bay. The American commander, Commodore James Barron, refused to allow the Chesapeake to be searched, so the *Leopard* opened fire. Barron was unprepared for action and was compelled to surrender. A boarding party from the *Leopard* dragged four men off the American frigate.

When news of the *Chesapeake-Leopard* incident reached America, a loud cry arose for a war of revenge. Even the "most temperate people and those

most attached to England," the British minister reported home, "say that they are bound as a people and that they must assert their honor on the first attack upon it." If Congress had been in session, the country might have stampeded into war. But, as the French minister in Washington informed Talleyrand, "the president does not want war" and "Mr. Madison [the secretary of state] dreads it now still more."

Instead of calling a special session of Congress and demanding a war declaration, Jefferson made a determined effort to maintain the peace. First, he issued an order expelling all British warships from American waters, to lessen the likelihood of future incidents. Then he sent instructions to his minister in England, James Monroe, to demand from the British government the complete renunciation of impressment. The British government was conciliatory—to a degree. It disavowed the action of the officer primarily responsible for the *Chesapeake-Leopard* affair, Admiral Berkeley, and recalled him. It offered to compensate the wounded and the families of those killed in the exchange. And it promised to return three of the captured sailors (one of the original four had been hanged). But the British cabinet refused to concede anything to Jefferson's main point; instead, the cabinet issued a proclamation reasserting the right of search to recover deserting seamen.

The impressment issue therefore prevented any permanent settlement of Anglo-American differences. Even after the British completed a financial settlement, the *Chesapeake* outrage remained an open sore in the relations between the two nations. That incident, and the larger impressment issue it symbolized, was probably the most important single cause of the War of 1812, even though the conflict did not begin for another five years.

"Peaceable Coercion"

Even at the height of the excitement over the *Chesapeake*, Jefferson made no preparations for war. He and Madison believed that the United States could bring Great Britain—and, if necessary, France—to terms through the use of economic pressure. Dependent as both nations were on the Yankee carrying trade, they would presumably mend their ways if threatened with the complete loss of it.

Thus when Congress met for its regular session

late in 1807, Jefferson hastily drafted a drastic measure. Madison revised it, and both the House and the Senate, dominated by Republicans, promptly enacted it into law. It was known as the Embargo, and it became one of the most controversial political issues of its time. The Embargo prohibited American ships from leaving the United States for any foreign port anywhere in the world. (If it had specified only British and French ports, Jefferson reasoned, it could have been evaded by means of false clearance papers.) Congress also passed a "force act" to give the government power to enforce the Embargo.

The law was widely evaded, but it was effective enough to have serious repercussions—in France, in Great Britain, and above all in the United States itself. Throughout the nation—except in the frontier areas of Vermont and New York, which soon doubled their overland exports to Canada—the Embargo created a serious depression. The planters of the South and the farmers of the West, although deprived of foreign markets for their crops, were willing to suffer in comparative silence, devoted Jeffersonian Republicans that most of them were. But the Federalist merchants and shipowners of the Northeast, who were hit hardest by the depression, made no secret of their rabid discontent.

The Northeastern merchants disliked impressment, disliked the British blockade of the European continent, and disliked Napoleon's Continental System. But they hated Jefferson's Embargo much more. Previously, in spite of the risks from Britain and France, they had managed to keep up their business and had earned excellent profits. Now they lost money every day that their ships idled at the wharves. Again, as at the time of the Louisiana Purchase, they concluded that Jefferson had violated the Constitution and had subverted the original purposes of the republic.

The election of 1808 came in the midst of the Embargo-induced depression. James Madison was safely elected to succeed Jefferson as president; but the Federalist candidate, Charles Pinckney, made the most of the Embargo's unpopularity and won a far larger proportion of the popular and electoral votes than he had in 1804. And although the Republicans continued to hold a majority in Congress, the Federalists gained a number of seats in both the House and the Senate. To Jefferson and Madison, the returns plainly indicated that the Embargo was a growing political liability. A few days before leaving office, Jefferson approved a bill terminating his experiment with what he called "peaceable coercion." But Madison made no basic change in the general policy of attempting to settle differences with Britain through economic rather than military means.

Madison was a stark contrast to his friend and predecessor, Thomas Jefferson. Small, wizened, with a scholarly frown that seemed perpetual, he had little personal charm and few political skills. His greatest political asset may have been his wife, Dolly, a native of North Carolina and a gracious, energetic, and popular woman. John C. Calhoun wrote of Madison at the time: "Our President tho a man of amiable manners and great talents has not I fear those commanding talents which are necessary to control those about him." Madison's presidency was marked, therefore, by frustration and contention. His diplomatic efforts to resolve the disputes with Europe came to naught; his preparations for war were inadequate; his administration was in constant confusion.

Dolly Madison

Dolly Payne was born in North Carolina, grew up a Quaker in Virginia, and in 1794 (a year after her first husband had died of yellow fever) married James Madison. He was forty-three; she was twenty-six. A woman of enormous charm and social grace, she became one of her husband's greatest political assets. She acted as hostess for President Jefferson, a widower, while her husband was serving as secretary of state; and she presided over a lively social life at the White House during her eight years as First Lady. (New-York Historical Society)

Just before Madison's inauguration, Congress passed a modified Embargo bill known as the Non-Intercourse Act, which reopened trade with all nations but Great Britain and France. A year later, in 1810, the Non-Intercourse Act expired and was replaced by another expedient, commonly called Macon's Bill No. 2. This measure reopened free commercial relations with the whole world, including Great Britain and France, but authorized the president to prohibit commerce with either belligerent if it should continue its violations after the other had stopped. Napoleon, in an effort to induce the United States to reimpose the Embargo against his enemy, announced that France would no longer interfere with American shipping. Madison fell for Napoleon's bait and announced that an embargo against Great Britain alone would automatically go into effect early in 1811 unless Britain renounced its restrictions on American shipping.

In time, the new Embargo, although less well enforced than the earlier, all-inclusive one had been, hurt the economy of England enough that the government repealed its blockade of Europe. But the repeal was too late to prevent war. The blockade was not the only American grievance against Britain. The others included impressment and the role of the British in the continuing conflicts with Indian tribes along America's Western frontier.

The "Indian Problem" and the British

Given the ruthlessness with which white settlers had dislodged Indian tribes to make room for expanding settlement, it was hardly surprising that ever since the Revolution most Indians had continued to look to England—which had historically attempted to limit Western expansion—for protection. The British in Canada, for their part, had relied on Indian friendship to keep up their fur trade, even within the territory of the United States, and to maintain potentially useful allies. At one point, in 1794, America had nearly gone to war with Great Britain because of its Indian policy, but Anthony Wayne's victory over the tribes at Fallen Timbers and the conclusion of Jay's Treaty dispelled the danger and brought on a period of comparative peace. Then, in 1807, the British assault on the *Chesapeake* and the war crisis that resulted aggravated the frontier conflict between Indians and settlers. The conflict elevated to prominence two important (and very different) leaders: William Henry Harrison and Tecumseh.

The Virginia-born Harrison, already at twenty-

six years of age a veteran Indian fighter, went to Washington as the congressional delegate from the Northwest Territory in 1799. He was a committed advocate of growth and development in the Western lands, and he was largely responsible for the passage in 1800 of the so-called Harrison Land Law, which enabled settlers to acquire farms from the public domain on much easier terms than before. Land in the Northwest Territory soon was selling fast. The growth of population led to a division of the area into the state of Ohio and the territories of Indiana, Michigan, and Illinois. By 1812, Ohio contained 250,000 people and was beginning to resemble an Eastern state. Paths had widened into roads; villages had sprung up and had in some cases grown into cities; forests had receded before the spreading cornfields. Michigan still had few settlers in 1812, but Illinois contained a scattered population of about 13,000, and Indiana 25,000. Harrison's vision of the rapid expansion of white settlement westward was well on its way to realization.

In 1801, Jefferson appointed Harrison governor of Indiana Territory. In that capacity, Harrison devoted himself to carrying out the president's now clearly defined approach to the "Indian problem." Jefferson offered the Indians a choice: they could convert themselves into settled farmers and become a part of white society, or they could migrate to the west of the Mississippi. In either case, they would have to give up their claims to their tribal lands in the Northwest.

But policies set in Washington were less important in defining relations between Indians and whites than events on the frontier itself, where white settlers continued to press for access to Indian lands and continued to violate the terms of the treaties the federal government had signed with the tribes of the region. White settlers were seizing land legally guaranteed to the tribes. They were also depleting the supplies of wild game on which Indian hunters depended. The legal system was little help; white juries almost always acquitted people accused of crimes against the Indians. Harrison himself, no champion of Indian rights, occasionally remarked unhappily on the way whites treated the natives. "A great many of the inhabitants of the Fronteers," he once wrote, "consider the murdering of Indians in the highest degree meritorious." Thus Jefferson's policy of assimilation, which Harrison was supposed to implement, seemed to many whites a benign alternative to continuing conflict between settlers and tribes.

To the Indians, however, Washington's policy seemed far from benign, especially given the bludgeon-like efficiency with which Harrison set out to implement it. He played off one tribe against another and used whatever tactics he felt would advance his aims. Through threats, bribes, and trickery, he concluded treaty after treaty with the separate tribes of the Northwest. By 1807, the United States claimed treaty rights to eastern Michigan, southern Indiana, and most of Illinois. Meanwhile, in the Southwest, white Americans were taking millions of acres from other tribes in the states of Georgia and Tennessee and in Mississippi Territory. Having been forced off their traditional hunting grounds, the Indians throughout the Mississippi Valley were growing increasingly resentful. But the separate tribes were helpless by themselves against the power of the United States. They might have passively accepted their fate if two complicating factors had not arisen.

One complication was the policy of the British authorities in Canada. For years they had neglected their Indian friends across the border to the south. Then came the *Chesapeake* incident and the surge of anti-British feeling throughout the United States. Now the British colonial authorities, expecting an American invasion of Canada, began to take desperate measures for their own defense. "Are the Indians to be employed in case of a rupture with the United States?" asked the lieutenant governor of upper Canada in a letter of December 1, 1807, to Sir James Craig, governor general of the entire province. The governor replied: "If we do not employ them, there cannot exist a moment's doubt that they will be employed against us." Craig at once took steps to renew friendship with the Indians and provide them with increased supplies.

Tecumseh and the Prophet

The second, and much more important, factor intensifying the border conflict was the rise of two remarkable native leaders. One was Tenskwatawa, a charismatic religious leader and orator known as the Prophet. He had experienced a mystical awakening in the process of recovering from alcoholism, and having freed himself from what he considered the evil effects of white culture, he began to speak to his people of the superior virtues of Indian civilization and the sinfulness and corruption of the white world. In the process, he inspired a religious revival that spread through numerous tribes and helped unite them. The Prophet increased his influence and convinced many of his followers that he had supernatural powers when he commanded the sun to be dark on the day of a solar eclipse. (He had learned of the eclipse in advance from Canadian traders.)

Like Neolin before him, and like Handsome Lake, his contemporary in the East, Tenskwatawa demonstrated the power of religious leaders to mobilize the tribes behind political and military objectives. The Prophet's headquarters at the confluence of Tippecanoe Creek and the Wabash River (known as Prophetstown) became a sacred place for people of many tribes and attracted thousands of Indians from throughout the Midwest. Out of their common religious experiences, they began to consider joint political and military efforts as well.

The prophet's brother Tecumseh—"the Shooting Star," chief of the Shawnees—emerged as the leader of these more secular efforts. Tecumseh understood, as few other Indian leaders had, that only through united action could the tribes hope to resist the steady advance of white civilization. Beginning in 1809, in the aftermath of the Treaty of Fort Wayne, by which tribes in Indiana ceded vast lands to the United States, he set out to unite all the tribes of the Mississippi Valley, north and south. Together, he promised, they would halt white expansion, recover the whole Northwest, and make the Ohio River the boundary between the United States and the Indian country. He maintained that Harrison and others, by negotiating treaties with individual tribes, had obtained no real title to land. The land belonged to all the tribes; none of them could rightfully cede any of it without the consent of the others. "The Great Spirit gave this great island to his red children. He placed the whites on the other side of the big water," Tecumseh told Harrison. "They were not contented with their own, but came to take ours from us. They have driven us from the sea to the lakes—we can go no farther."

In 1811, Tecumseh left Prophetstown and traveled down the Mississippi to visit the tribes of the South and persuade them to join the alliance. At about the same time, a great earthquake—with its center at New Madrid, Missouri—rumbled up and down the Mississippi Valley, causing much of the river to change its course. Many Indians saw this phenomenon as another sign that a new era was at hand.

During Tecumseh's absence, Governor Harrison saw a chance to destroy the growing influence of the two Indian leaders. With 1,000 soldiers he camped near Prophetstown; and on November 7, 1811, he provoked an armed conflict. Although the white forces suffered losses as heavy as those of the natives, Harrison succeeded in driving off the Indians and burning the town. The Battle of Tippecanoe (named for the creek near which it was fought) disillusioned

Tecumseh
Tecumseh's efforts to unite the tribes of the Mississippi Valley against further white encroachments on their lands led him ultimately into an alliance with the British after the Battle of Tippecanoe in 1811. In the War of 1812, he was commissioned a brigadier general by the British and fought against the United States in the Battle of the Thames. He is shown in this painting (by the daughter of an English officer stationed near Detroit) wearing British military trousers. (Fort Malden National Historic Park)

many of the Prophet's followers, for they had come to believe that his magic would protect them from the white man's bullets. Tecumseh returned to find the confederacy in disarray. But there were still many warriors eager for combat, and by the spring of 1812 they were active along the frontier, from Michigan to Mississippi, raiding white settlements and terrifying white settlers.

The bloodshed along the Western borders was largely a result of the Indians' own initiative, but Britain's agents in Canada had encouraged the uprising (using the Prophet as a "vile instrument," as Harrison put it) and had provided guns and supplies that enabled the Indians to do battle. To Harrison and most white residents of the regions, there seemed only one way to make the West safe for Americans. That was to drive the British out of Canada and annex that province to the United States—a goal that many Westerners had long cherished for other reasons as well.

The Lure of Florida

While frontiersmen in the North demanded the conquest of Canada, those in the South looked to the acquisition of Florida (an expanse of land including not only the present state of Florida, but the southern areas of what are now Alabama, Mississippi, and Louisiana as well). Spanish possession of that territory created perpetual nuisances for white Americans. Slaves escaped from the United States south

across the Florida border, and Indians in Florida launched frequent raids north into white settlements along the border. But white Southerners coveted Florida for other reasons, because without it they had no direct access to the Gulf of Mexico. Through the territory ran such rivers as the Alabama, the Apalachicola, and others that could provide residents of the Southwest with access to valuable ports on the Gulf. In 1810, American settlers in West Florida (the area presently part of Mississippi and Louisiana) took matters into their own hands. They seized the Spanish fort at Baton Rouge, and they sent a request to the federal government that the territory be annexed to the United States. President Madison unhesitatingly proclaimed its annexation and then began scheming to get the rest of Florida too. With Madison's connivance, George Mathews, a former governor of Georgia, attempted in 1811 to foment a revolt in East Florida. Spain protested, and Madison backed down; but the desire of Southern frontiersmen for all of Florida did not abate. That desire became yet another motivation for war with Britain. Spain was Britain's ally, and a war would give these frontiersmen an excuse for taking Spanish as well as British territory.

By 1812, therefore, war fever was raging on both the northern and southern frontiers. The white residents of these outlying regions were not numerous in comparison with the population of the country as a whole. For the most part, moreover, they were represented in Congress by only a few, nonvoting territorial delegates. Their demands, however, found substantial support in Washington among a group of determined young congressmen who soon earned the name of "war hawks."

The War Hawks

Three days before the Battle of Tippecanoe, a new Congress met in Washington for the session of 1811–1812. In the congressional elections of 1810, voters had indicated their impatience with the temporizing measures of both Republicans and Federalists by electing a large number of representatives eager for war with Britain. A new generation had arrived on the political scene—aggressive and impatient young men, the most influential of whom came from the new states in the West or from the back country of the old states in the South.

Two of their natural leaders, both recently elected to the House of Representatives, were Henry Clay and John C. Calhoun, men who would loom large in American politics for the next four decades. The tall, magnetic Clay, barely thirty-four when he arrived in Washington in 1811, was a Virginian by birth but had made Kentucky his home. He had already served briefly in the United States Senate in 1806 and 1807. Calhoun was only twenty-nine years old, the son of Scotch-Irish pioneers in the South Carolina hills. He was as striking in appearance as Clay but lacked the Kentuckian's personal magnetism. Calhoun's great strength was his powerful intellect and his equally powerful ambition.

When Congress organized itself in 1811, the war faction of young Republicans won control of both the House and the Senate. Clay was elected Speaker of the House, a position of influence then second only to that of the president, and he filled committees with those who believed as he did in the necessity of preparing for war. He appointed Calhoun to the crucial Committee on Foreign Affairs, and he began agitating immediately for the conquest of Canada. Madison, who still hoped to maintain the peace, was losing control of his government. On June 18, 1812, he gave in to the pressure and approved a declaration of war against Britain.

The War of 1812

Preoccupied with their struggle against Napoleon in Europe, the British were not eager for an open conflict with the United States. Even after the Americans declared war, Britain largely ignored them for a time. But in the fall of 1812, the course of battle—and of European history—changed. Napoleon launched a catastrophic campaign against Russia; before the winter was over his army was in disarray, his power in Europe was greatly diminished, and his empire was well on the way to its final defeat. With the threat from France diminishing, Britain was able by late 1813 to turn its military attention to America.

The Course of Battle

Thomas Jefferson believed that an American conquest of Canada, which so many Westerners were by 1812 demanding, would be a "mere matter of marching." It was not. American forces tried repeatedly to conquer the British territories to the north; all such efforts ended in frustration. In the summer of 1812, the elderly General William Hull, governor of Michigan Territory, led American forces into Canada by way of Detroit, as part of a planned three-pronged invasion. He was soon forced to retreat to Detroit, and in August he surrendered the fort there. Other invasion efforts also failed. In the meantime, Fort Dearborn (Chicago) fell before an Indian attack.

In the face of these disasters and defeats on land, the Madison administration and its supporters took what consolation they could from the news of American successes on the sea. American frigates engaged British warships in a series of duels and won some spectacular victories, one of the most renowned being the victory of the *Constitution* over the *Guerrière*. American privateers destroyed or captured one British merchant ship after another, occasionally braving the coastal waters of the British Isles and burning vessels within sight of the shore. But these acts of bravado soon provoked an angry and effective British counterattack. By 1813, the British navy was driving the American frigates to cover and imposing a close blockade on the United States.

While British sea power dominated the ocean, American fleets seized control of the Great Lakes. First, the Americans took command of Lake Ontario, enabling troops to cross over to York (Toronto), the capital of Canada. At York, on April 27, 1813, the invaders stumbled on a hidden land mine, the explosion of which killed more than fifty, including General Zebulon M. Pike. Some of the enraged survivors, without authorization, set fire to the capital's public buildings, which burned to the ground. After de-

The War of 1812

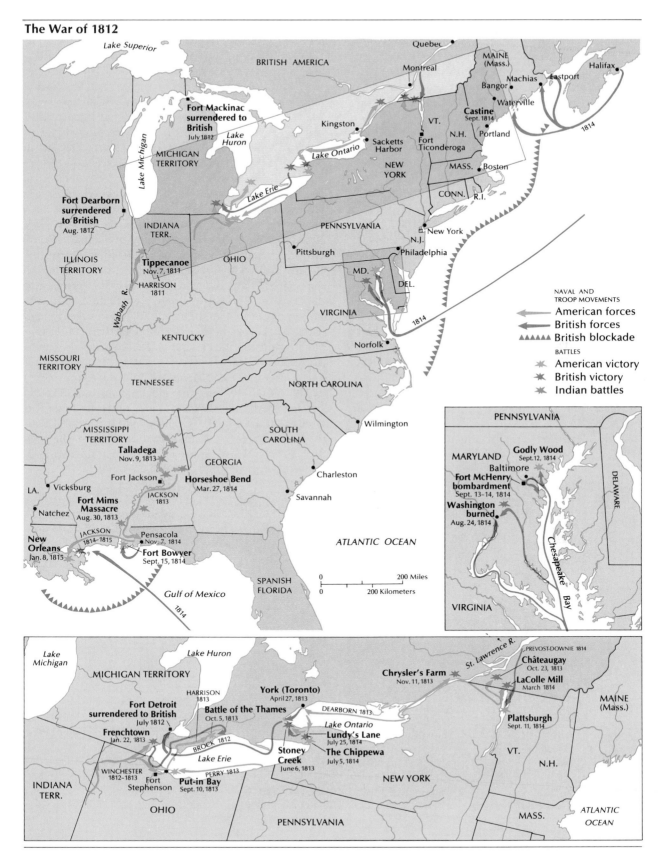

NAVAL AND TROOP MOVEMENTS
→ American forces
→ British forces
▲▲▲▲ British blockade

BATTLES
✹ American victory
✹ British victory
✹ Indian battles

stroying some ships and military stores, the Americans departed to their own lands across the lake.

American forces next seized control of Lake Erie, mainly through the work of the youthful Oliver Hazard Perry. Perry's fleet took up a position at Put-in Bay, near a group of islands off the mouth of the Maumee River. With the banner "Don't Give Up the Ship" flying on his flagship, he awaited the British fleet, whose intentions he had learned from a spy. When the fleet arrived on September 10, 1813, he dispersed it and established American dominance of the lake.

This made possible, at last, an American invasion of Canada by way of Detroit. The post had been hard to reach overland; but after Perry's victory at Put-in Bay, supplies as well as men could be quickly and easily transported by water. William Henry Harrison, who had replaced Hull in the Western command, now pushed up the river Thames into upper Canada and on October 5, 1813, won a victory chiefly notable for the death of Tecumseh, who had been commissioned a brigadier general in the British army. The Battle of the Thames resulted in no lasting occupation of Canada, but it weakened and disheartened the Indians of the Northwest and greatly diminished their ability to defend their claims to the region.

While Harrison was harrying the tribes of the Northwest, another white military leader was striking an even harder blow at the Creeks in the Southwest. The Creeks, aroused by Tecumseh on his Southern visit and supplied by the Spaniards in Florida, had attacked Fort Mims, on the Alabama River just north of the Florida border and had massacred the frontier families taking shelter within its stockade. Andrew Jackson, a wealthy Tennessee planter and a general in the state's militia, temporarily abandoned plans for an invasion of Florida and set off in pursuit of the Creeks instead. On March 27, 1814, in the Battle of Horseshoe Bend, Jackson's men took frightful vengeance on the Indians—slaughtering women and children along with warriors. Jackson's victory broke the resistance of the Creeks, who were already weakened by internal divisions. (Some Creeks even fought on Jackson's side at Horseshoe Bend.) The tribe agreed to cede most of its lands to the United States and retreated westward, farther into the interior. The battle also won Jackson a commission as major general in the United States Army, and in that capacity he led his men farther south into Florida and, on November 7, 1814, seized the Spanish fort at Pensacola.

Until 1814, the British had committed few forces of their own to the struggle on land and had restricted themselves largely to aiding the Indians. But after the Battles of the Thames and Horseshoe Bend, the Indians were no longer a major factor in the conflict, and the British approach to the war now shifted.

The Battle of Lake Erie
In the Battle of Lake Erie twenty-eight-year-old Captain Oliver Hazard Perry maneuvered a British fleet into a decisive engagement—one of the bloodiest naval battles of the war and a major triumph for the United States. After the battle Perry sent a message to General William Henry Harrison that read: "We have met the enemy and they are ours." The victory gave the United States control of Lake Erie and forced the British to evacuate their strongholds at Malden and Detroit. Perry is shown here standing at the stern of the launch, preparing to board the U.S.S. *Niagara* after his own ship had been destroyed by the British.
(New York State Historical Association, Cooperstown)

The surrender of Napoleon made it possible for England to transfer part of its European army to America to dispose of what they called the "dirty shirts," the unkempt Americans. And so in 1814, the British prepared to invade the United States from three approaches—Chesapeake Bay, Lake Champlain, and the mouth of the Mississippi.

An armada under Admiral Sir George Cockburn sailed up the Patuxent River from Chesapeake Bay and landed an army that marched a short distance overland to Bladensburg, on the outskirts of Washington. A much more numerous force of American militiamen opposed the British, but they had been hastily assembled and poorly trained. Unnerved by the repeated assaults of the well-disciplined redcoats, they finally broke formation and ran. The British marched into Washington on August 24, 1814, and put the government to flight. Then they set fire to several public buildings, including the White House, in retaliation for the earlier American burning of the Canadian capital at York. The sack of Washington marked the low point of American fortunes in the war.

Leaving Washington in partial ruins, the invading army proceeded up the bay toward Baltimore. But Baltimore, guarded by Fort McHenry, was ready. To block the approaching fleet, the American garrison had stretched a chain across the Patapsco River (the entry to Baltimore's harbor) and had sunk several boats, forcing the British to bombard the fort from a distance. Through the night of September 13, Francis Scott Key (a Washington lawyer who was on board one of the British ships on a mission to secure the release of an American prisoner) watched the bombardment. The next morning, "by the dawn's early light," he could see the flag on the fort still flying; he recorded his pride in the moment by scribbling a poem—"The Star-Spangled Banner"—on the back of an envelope. The British withdrew from Baltimore. Key's words were set to the tune of an old English drinking song and established lasting fame as an American patriotic anthem. (In 1931, it became the official national anthem.)

Meanwhile, another British invasion force was descending on northern New York. The British navy had gathered a fleet on Lake Champlain about the size of the American fleet drawn up in opposition; and they had an army nearby three times as large as the mixed force of American regulars and militia facing it. Despite the odds, however, the American defenders destroyed the invading fleet; the British army then retreated to Canada. This important victory—the

Battle of Plattsburgh, on September 11, 1814—secured the northern border of the United States.

Far to the south, the most serious threat of all soon materialized. In December 1814, a formidable array of battle-hardened British veterans, fresh from the duke of Wellington's peninsular campaign against the French in Spain, landed below New Orleans. On Christmas Day, Wellington's brother-in-law, Sir Edward Pakenham, arrived to take command. (Neither he nor anyone else in America knew that a treaty of peace between the British and American governments had been signed in faraway Belgium the day before.) Awaiting Pakenham's advance up the Mississippi was Andrew Jackson with a motley collection of Tennesseans, Kentuckians, Creoles, blacks, and pirates drawn up behind earthen breastworks. On January 8, 1815, the redcoats advanced on the American fortifications. For all their discipline and bravery, the exposed British forces were no match for Jackson's well-protected men. After the Americans had repulsed several waves of attackers, the British finally retreated, while an American band struck up "Hail, Columbia!" Left behind were 700 British dead, including Pakenham himself, 1,400 wounded, and 500 other prisoners. Jackson's losses: 8 killed, 13 wounded.

The Revolt of New England

With a few notable exceptions, such as the Battle of New Orleans, the military operations of the United States between 1812 and 1815 consisted of a series of bungled, humiliating failures. In retrospect, these frustrations seem unsurprising. The American government was woefully unprepared for the war at the outset, and it faced increasing popular opposition as the contest dragged on. In some areas, in fact, the opposition went to such extremes that it became almost a part of the British war effort. That was nowhere more true than in New England, where some Federalists celebrated British victories, deliberately sabotaged their own country's war effort, and even plotted disunion and a separate peace. Once again, the Federalists—who were beginning to regain some of their political strength because of dissatisfaction with Madison's handling of the war—destroyed their own prospects through extremism.

Until 1814, the British blockade of the American coast did not extend north of Newport, Rhode Island. The British government was deliberately cultivating the New England trade, and the merchants of

New England happily responded. Goods carried in Yankee ships helped to feed British troops in Canada as well as in Spain, and for a time many New England shipowners grew rich by trading with the enemy while denouncing Madison and the war (although eventually the business of the shipowners as a whole fell far below the level of the prosperous prewar years).

Although most of the money in the nation was concentrated in New England, the government was unable to sell more than a very few war bonds there. One Treasury bond issue, desperately needed to keep soldiers in the field, almost fell through because of the refusal of the New England banks to make loans. Secretary of the Treasury Albert Gallatin had to turn to his friend John Jacob Astor of New York and to two foreign-born bankers of Philadelphia for the necessary funds.

In Congress, the Republicans had continual trouble with the Federalist opposition. John C. Calhoun, leader of the administration forces, faced New England obstructionists in every effort to win approval of measures in support of the war. Foremost among the obstructionists was a young congressman from New Hampshire, Daniel Webster. Introducing resolution after resolution to embarrass the administration, Webster demanded to know the reasons for the war and intimated (correctly) that Napoleon had tricked the president into antagonizing England. Every measure to finance the fighting—by loans, taxes, tariffs, or a national bank—Webster and his Federalist allies vehemently denounced. At a time when voluntary enlistments were lagging and the army was seriously undermanned, he opposed a bill to encourage enlistments. In desperation, the administration proposed to draft men into the regular army from the state militias. (On several occasions, the governors of New England states had refused to allow their state militias to take orders from the president or to fight outside the country.) Webster declared that no such law could be enforced in his part of the country and thus helped doom the conscription bill to defeat.

As new states in the South and West, all strongly Republican, had joined the Union, the Federalists had become more and more hopelessly a minority party in the country as a whole. But they were still the majority party in New England. And some of them began to dream of creating a separate nation in that region, which they could dominate and in which they could escape the dictation of slaveholders and backwoodsmen. The talk of secession, heard before at the time of the Louisiana Purchase and again at the time

of Jefferson's Embargo, revived during the war and reached a climax in the winter of 1814–1815, when the republic appeared to be on the verge of ruin.

On December 15, 1814, while the British were beginning their invasion by way of New Orleans, delegates from the New England states met in Hartford, Connecticut, to consider the grievances of their section against the Madison administration. The would-be seceders were overruled by the comparatively moderate men, who were in the overwhelming majority at the Hartford Convention. The convention's report reasserted the right of nullification but only hinted at secession, observing that "the severance of the Union by one or more States, against the will of the rest, and especially in time of war, can be justified only by absolute necessity." But the report proposed seven amendments to the Constitution (presumably as the condition of New England's remaining in the Union)—amendments designed to protect New England from the growing influence of the South and the West.

Because the war was going badly and the government was becoming desperate, the New Englanders assumed that the Republicans would have to give in to the Hartford Convention terms. Soon after the convention adjourned, however, the news of Jackson's smashing victory at New Orleans reached the cities of the Northeast. A day or two later, reports arrived from abroad of a treaty of peace. "Peace is signed in the arms of victory!" the magazine *Niles's Register* exclaimed. In the euphoria of this presumed triumph, the Hartford Convention and the Federalist party came to seem futile, irrelevant, even treasonable.

The Peace Settlement

Peace talks between the United States and Britain had begun even before the first battles of the War of 1812 were fought. President Madison, who had never really wanted a declaration of war and who regretted "the necessity that had produced it," hoped for an early end to hostilities even after the war began.

The British government, eager to liquidate the minor war and concentrate upon the major one, against Napoleon, sent an admiral to Washington in the fall of 1812 with proposals for an armistice, but the negotiations failed because of Madison's continued insistence that the British renounce impressment and England's continued refusal to do so. Twice, Russia offered to mediate the conflict; twice the Brit-

The Battle of New Orleans

The Battle of New Orleans was the last major engagement and the greatest American victory on land of the War of 1812. General Andrew Jackson commanded about 4,500 troops and fended off superior British forces under the command of Sir Edward Pakenham (who was killed in the fighting). The artist Hyacinthe de Laclotte drew the sketch that became the basis of this painting while standing above the battlefield during the decisive engagement. The British suffered over 2,000 casualties in the battle, the Americans 21. But the American triumph was a hollow one. Unknown to the commanders in Louisiana, the Peace of Ghent, which brought an official end to the war, had been signed in Europe two weeks before.   (New Orleans Museum of Art)

ish declined. Finally, however, the British agreed to meet the Americans in direct negotiations on neutral ground. After prolonged delays, diplomats from the two countries met in Ghent, Belgium, on August 8, 1814. John Quincy Adams, Henry Clay, and Albert Gallatin led the American delegation.

Although both sides began the negotiations by making extravagant demands, the final treaty did very little except end the fighting itself. The Americans gave up their demand for a British renunciation of impressment and for the cession of Canada to the United States. The British abandoned their call for creation of an Indian buffer state in the Northwest and other territorial concessions. The agreement in the end did little more than restore the territorial boundaries that had existed before the war and refer other disputes to arbitration. Hastily drawn up, it was signed on Christmas Eve 1814.

Both sides had reason to accept this skimpy agreement. The British were exhausted and in debt from their prolonged conflict with Napoleon and eager to settle the lesser dispute in North America. The Americans realized that the defeat of Napoleon in Europe removed the incentive for the British to interfere with American commerce. Indeed, by the end of 1815, impressment had all but ceased.

Other settlements followed the Treaty of Ghent and contributed to a long-term improvement in Anglo-American relations. A commercial treaty in 1815 gave Americans the right to trade freely with England and the British Empire except for the West Indies. A fisheries convention in 1818 renewed the

6789

privileges of Americans to catch and dry fish at specified places along the shores of British North America. The Rush-Bagot agreement of 1817 provided for mutual disarmament on the Great Lakes. Gradually disarmament was extended to the land, and eventually (although not until 1872) the Canadian-American boundary became the longest "unguarded frontier" in the world.

For the other parties to the War of 1812, the Indian tribes east of the Mississippi, the Treaty of Ghent was of no lasting value. The United States agreed to restore to the tribes lands seized by white Americans in the fighting, but those provisions were never enforced. In the end, the war served as another disastrous blow to the capacity of Indians to resist white expansion. Tecumseh, their most important leader, was dead. The British, their most important allies, were gone from the Northwest. The alliance that Tecumseh and the Prophet had forged was in disarray. The end of the war served as a spur to white movement westward, and the Indians had lost much of their capacity to oppose the expansion.

No sooner had peace come in 1815 than Congress declared war again, this time against Algiers, which had taken advantage of the War of 1812 to loose its pirates once more against American shipping in the Mediterranean. Two American squadrons now proceeded to North African waters. One of the two, under the command of Stephen Decatur, captured a number of enemy ships, blockaded the coast of Algiers, and forced the dey (the Algerian ruler) to accept a treaty that not only ended the payment of tribute by the United States but required Algiers to pay reparations to America. Decatur then sailed on to Tunis and Tripoli and collected additional indemnities. This naval action in the Mediterranean did more to provide Americans with free access to the seas than the War of 1812 itself had done.

Postwar Expansion

With the international conflict settled, Americans could once again turn their attention to their internal affairs. The aftermath of the war made clear how far the nation had already moved from its agrarian origins. Commerce revived and expanded. Industry, which had made a few tentative beginnings in the first years of the century, advanced rapidly. Westward expansion, deterred for a time by the conflicts with the

Indians and the British, now accelerated dramatically. The period following the war, in short, was one of rapid growth—too rapid, as it turned out, for the boom was followed in 1819 by a disastrous bust. The collapse proved to be only a temporary obstacle to economic expansion, but it revealed clearly that the United States continued to lack some of the basic institutions necessary to sustain long-term growth.

Banking and Currency

The War of 1812 may have stimulated the growth of manufactures. But it also produced chaos in shipping and banking; and it exposed dramatically the inadequacy of the existing transportation system. The aftermath of the war, therefore, saw the emergence of a series of political issues connected with national economic development: reestablishing the Bank of the United States (the first Bank's charter had not been renewed when it expired in 1811), protecting the new industries, and providing a nationwide network of roads and waterways.

The wartime experience seemed to underline the need for another national bank. After the expiration of the first Bank's charter, a large number of state banks had sprung up. They issued vast quantities of bank notes but did not always bother to retain a large enough reserve of gold or silver to redeem the notes on demand. The notes passed from hand to hand more or less as money; but their actual value depended on the reputation of the bank that issued them. There was, therefore, a wide variety of notes, of widely differing value, in circulation at the same time. The result was a confusion that made honest business difficult and counterfeiting easy. In legal terms, bank notes were not genuine currency and thus did not technically violate the clause of the Constitution giving Congress the exclusive power to regulate the currency and forbidding the states to emit bills of credit. But the use of bank notes as money clearly challenged the spirit of that clause.

Congress struck at the currency problem not by prohibiting the bank notes but by chartering a second Bank of the United States in 1816. It was essentially the same institution as the one founded under Hamilton's leadership in 1791 except that it had more capital than its predecessor. The national bank could not forbid state banks from issuing notes; but its size and power gave it the ability to dominate the state banks. It could compel them to issue only sound notes or risk being forced out of business.

The United States Capitol in 1824
The slightly idealized view by the American artist Charles Burton shows the approach to the west front of the United States Capitol along Pennsylvania Avenue. The large, columned rotunda that today rises above the building was built in the 1860s to replace the simpler dome shown in this painting. Other later additions included the two wings containing the present chambers of the Senate and the House of Representatives. (Metropolitan Museum of Art)

Protecting Industry

American manufacturing had flourished during the war. The nation's principal import was manufactured goods; and with imports effectively blocked, manufacturers prospered. Goods were so scarce that, even with comparatively unskilled labor and poor management, new factories could be started with an assurance of quick profits.

The American textile industry had experienced a particularly dramatic growth. The first census of manufacturing, in 1810, revealed 269 cotton and 24 woolen mills in the country. But the Embargo of 1807 and the War of 1812 had spurred a tremendous expansion. Between 1807 and 1815, the total number of cotton spindles increased more than fifteenfold, from 8,000 to 130,000. Until 1814, the textile factories—most of them in New England—produced only yarn and thread; the weaving of cloth was left to families operating handlooms at home. Then the Boston merchant Francis Cabot Lowell, after examining textile machinery in England, developed a power loom better than its English counterpart. In 1813, Lowell organized the Boston Manufacturing Company and, at Waltham, Massachusetts, founded the first mill in America to carry on the processes of spinning and weaving under a single roof. Lowell's company was an important step in revolutionizing American manufacturing.

As the War of 1812 came to an end, however, the prospects for American industry suddenly dimmed. British ships swarmed into American ports and unloaded cargoes of manufactured goods to be sold at cut-rate prices, even below cost. As Lord

Balance of Trade: Exports and Imports of Goods and Services to and from All Countries, 1790–1820

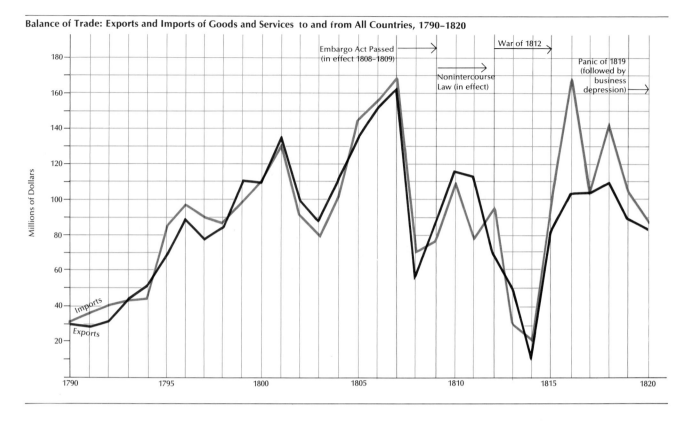

Brougham explained to Parliament, it was "well worth while to incur a loss upon the first exportation, in order, by the glut, to stifle in the cradle those rising manufactures in the United States, which war had forced into existence, contrary to the natural course of things." The "infant industries" cried out for protection against these tactics, arguing that they needed time to grow strong enough to withstand the foreign competition. In 1816, protectionists in Congress won passage of a tariff law that effectively limited competition from abroad on a broad range of items, among the most important of which was cotton cloth. There were objections from agricultural interests, who stood to pay higher prices for manufactured goods. But the nationalist dream of creating an important American industrial economy prevailed.

Transportation

The nation's most pressing economic need in the aftermath of the war, however, was for improvements in its transportation system. Without a better trans-

portation network, manufacturers would not have access to the raw materials they needed and would not be able to send their finished goods to markets. So an old debate resumed: Should the federal government help to finance roads and other "internal improvements"?

The idea of using government funds to finance road building was not a new one. When Ohio entered the Union in 1803, the federal government had agreed that part of the proceeds from the sale of public lands there should be used for building roads. And in 1807, Jefferson's secretary of the treasury, Albert Gallatin, had proposed that a national road, financed partly by the Ohio land sales, be built from the Potomac to the Ohio. Both Congress and the president had approved. The next year, Gallatin presented a comprehensive plan of internal improvements that required an appropriation of $20 million. Work on the new roads did not begin until 1811 (partly because of Jefferson's doubts about the constitutionality of such expenditures). Finally, however, construction of the National Road got under way at Cumberland, Maryland, on the Potomac; and by 1818, this highway—with a crushed stone surface and mas-

The National Road, 1827

This picture of heavy traffic along the National Turnpike suggests the rapid acceleration of commerce in the eastern United States in the 1820s and the pressure that economic growth was placing on existing means of transportation. The painting also shows the Fair View Inn, which stood three miles from Baltimore, Maryland.   (The Bettmann Archive)

sive stone bridges—was completed to Wheeling, Virginia, on the Ohio River. Meanwhile the state of Pennsylvania gave $100,000 to a private company that extended the Lancaster pike westward to Pittsburgh.

Over both of these roads moved a heavy traffic of stagecoaches, Conestoga wagons, private carriages, and other vehicles, as well as droves of cattle. Despite high tolls, freight rates across the mountains were now lower than ever before. They were not low enough to permit the long-distance hauling of such bulky loads as wheat or flour. But commodities with a high value in proportion to their weight, especially manufactures, moved from the Atlantic seaboard to the Ohio Valley in unprecedented quantities.

At the same time, on the rivers and the Great Lakes, steam-powered shipping was experiencing rapid expansion. The development of steamboat lines was already well under way before the War of 1812, thanks to the technological advances introduced by Robert Fulton and others. (See pp. 255–257.) The war had retarded expansion of the system for a time; but by 1816, river steamers were beginning to journey up and down the Mississippi to the Ohio River, and up the Ohio as far as Pittsburgh, for the first time. Within a few years, steamboats were carrying far more cargo on the Mississippi than all the earlier forms of river transport—flatboats, barges, and others—combined. They stimulated the agricultural

economy of the West and the South, by providing much readier access to markets at greatly reduced cost. And they enabled Eastern manufacturers to send their finished goods west much more readily.

But despite the progress with steamboats and turnpikes, there remained serious gaps in the transportation network of the country, as experience during the War of 1812 had shown. Once Atlantic shipping was cut off by the British blockade, the coastal roads became choked by the unaccustomed volume of north-south traffic. At the river ferries, long lines of wagons waited for a chance to cross. Oxcarts, pressed into emergency service, took six or seven weeks to go from Philadelphia to Charleston. In some areas there were serious shortages of goods normally carried by sea, and prices rose to new heights. Rice cost three times as much in New York as in Charleston, flour three times as much in Boston as in Richmond. There were military consequences, too. On the Northern and Western frontiers, the American campaigns were frustrated partly by the absence of good roads.

With this wartime experience in mind, President Madison in 1815 called the attention of Congress to the "great importance of establishing throughout our country the roads and canals which can be best executed under the national authority," and he suggested that a constitutional amendment would resolve any doubts about the authority of Congress to provide

Deck Life on the *Paragon,* 1811–1812

The *North River Steamboat Clermont,* launched in 1806 by the inventor Robert Fulton and propelled by an engine he had developed, traveled from Manhattan to Albany (about 150 miles) in thirty-two hours. That was neither the longest nor the fastest voyage to date, but the *Clermont* proved to be the first steam-powered vessel large and reliable enough to be commercially valuable. Within a few years Fulton and his partner Robert R. Livingston had several steamboats operating profitably around New York. The third vessel in their fleet, the *Paragon,* shown here in a painting by the Russian diplomat and artist Pavel Petrovich Svinin, could carry 150 people and contained an elegant dining salon fitted with bronze, mahogany, and mirrors. Svinin called it "a whole floating town," and Fulton told a friend that the *Paragon* "beats everything on the globe, for made as you and I are we cannot tell what is in the moon." (Metropolitan Museum of Art)

for the construction of canals and roads. Representative Calhoun promptly introduced a bill that would have used the funds owed the government by the Bank of the United States to finance internal improvements. "Let us, then, bind the republic together with a perfect system of roads and canals," Calhoun urged. "Let us conquer space."

Congress passed the internal improvements bill, but President Madison, on his last day in office (March 3, 1817), returned it with his veto. He supported the purpose of the bill, he explained, but he still believed that Congress lacked authority to fund the improvements without a constitutional amendment. And so on the issue of internal improvements, at least, the nationalists fell short of their goals. The

tremendous task of building the transportation network necessary for the growing American economy was left to the state governments and to private enterprise.

The Great Migration

One reason for the growing interest in internal improvements was the sudden and dramatic surge in westward expansion in the years following the War of 1812. "Old America seems to be breaking up and moving westward," wrote an English observer at the time. By the time of the census of 1820, white settlers had pushed well beyond the Mississippi River, and the population of the Western regions was increasing more rapidly than that of the nation as a whole. Almost one of every four white Americans lived west of the Appalachians in 1820; ten years before, only one in seven had resided there. There were several important reasons for this expansion. Population pressures and economic pressures pushed many Americans from the East; the availability of new lands and the decline of Indian resistance drew them to the West.

The pressures driving Americans out of the East came in part from the continued growth of the American population—both through natural increase and immigration. Between 1800 and 1820, the nation's population nearly doubled—from 5.3 million to 9.6 million. The growth of the nation's cities absorbed some of that increase; but most Americans were still farmers, and the agricultural lands of the East were by now largely occupied. Some of the farmland in the East, moreover, was exhausted. And in the South, the spread of the plantation system, and of a slave labor force, limited opportunities for new settlers.

Meanwhile, the West itself was becoming increasingly attractive. The War of 1812 had helped diminish one of the traditional obstacles to Western expansion: Indian opposition. And in the aftermath of the war, the federal government continued its policy of pushing the remaining tribes farther and farther west. A series of treaties in 1815 wrested still more land from the Indians. And in the meantime, the government was erecting a chain of stockaded forts along the Great Lakes and the upper Mississippi, to protect the frontier. It also created a "factor" system, by which government factors or agents supplied the Indians with goods at cost. This not only worked to drive Canadian traders out of the region; it also helped create a situation of dependency that made the Indians themselves easier to control.

The fertile lands now made secure for white settlement drew migrants from throughout the East to what was then known as the Old Northwest (now part of the Midwest). The Ohio and Monongahela Rivers were the main routes westward, until the completion of the Erie Canal in 1825. The pioneers reached the river by traveling along the turnpike to Pittsburgh or along the National Road to Wheeling, or by sailing down one of its tributaries—such as the Kanawha, the Cumberland, or the Tennessee. Once on the Ohio, they floated downstream on flatboats bearing all their possessions, then left the river (often at Cincinnati, which was becoming one of the

region's—and the nation's— principal cities) and pressed on overland with wagons, handcarts, packhorses, cattle, and hogs.

Once having arrived at their destination, preferably in the spring or early summer, the settlers built a lean-to or cabin, then hewed a clearing out of the forest and put in a crop of corn to supplement the wild game they caught and the domestic animals they had brought with them. It was a rough existence, often plagued by loneliness, poverty, dirt, and disease. Men, women, and children worked side by side in the fields—and at times had virtually no contact for weeks or months at a time with anyone outside their own families.

Life on the frontier was not, however, as solitary and individualistic as later myth suggested. Migrants often journeyed westward in groups, which at times became the basis of new communities where schools, churches, stores, and other community institutions were built. The labor shortage in the interior meant that neighbors developed systems of mutual aid, gathering periodically to raise a barn, clear land, harvest crops, or make quilts. Gradually, the settlers built a thriving farm economy based largely on family units of modest size and committed to the cultivation of grain and the raising of livestock.

Another common feature of life in the Northwest (and indeed in much of early nineteenth-century America) was mobility. Individuals and families were constantly on the move, settling for a few years in one place, then selling their land (often at a significant profit, given the rapidly rising price of farm properties in the region) and settling again somewhere else. When new areas for settlement opened farther to the west, it was often the people on the frontier—rather than those who remained in the East—who flocked to them first.

In the Southwest, the new agricultural economy emerged along different lines—just as the economy of the Old South had long been different from that of the Northeast. The principal attraction there was cotton. The cotton lands in the uplands of the Old South had lost much of their fertility through overplanting and erosion. But the market for cotton continued to grow, and so there was no lack of ambitious farmers seeking fresh soil in a climate suitable for the crop. In the Southwest, around the end of the Appalachian range, stretched a broad zone within which cotton could thrive—including what was to become known as the Black Belt of central Alabama and Mississippi, a vast prairie with a dark, productive soil of rotted limestone.

Agrarian Life in Illinois, 1833

Americans flocked to the open lands of the West in the 1830s in search of economic opportunity. Many found it, but some also discovered that life on the sparsely settled plains could be bleak, lonely, and perilous. This painting by the Swiss artist Carl Bodmer of a farm in Illinois suggests both the isolation of life in the West and the abundance of land available to settlers.   (Joslyn Art Museum, Omaha, Nebraska)

The advance of the Southern frontier meant the spread of cotton and slavery. Usually the first arrivals were ordinary frontier people like those farther north, small farmers who made rough clearings in the forest. Then came wealthier planters, who bought up the cleared or partially cleared land, while the original settlers moved farther west and started over again. The large planters made the westward journey in a style quite different from that of the first pioneers. Over the alternately dusty and muddy roads came great caravans consisting of herds of livestock, wagonloads of household goods, long lines of slaves, and—bringing up the rear—the planter's family riding in carriages. Success in the wilderness was by no means assured, even for the wealthiest settlers. But many planters soon expanded small clearings into vast fields white with cotton. They replaced the cabins of the pioneers with more sumptuous log dwell-

ings and ultimately with imposing mansions that demonstrated the rise of a newly rich class.

The rapid growth of the West resulted in the admission of four new states to the Union in the immediate aftermath of the War of 1812: Indiana in 1816, Mississippi in 1817, Illinois in 1818, and Alabama in 1819.

The Far West

Not many Americans were yet much interested in the Far Western areas of the continent. Except for New Englanders engaged in Pacific whaling or in the China trade, few Americans were familiar with the Oregon coast. Only fur traders and trappers had any knowledge of the land between the Missouri and the Pacific.

Before the War of 1812, John Jacob Astor's American Fur Company had established Astoria as a trading post at the mouth of the Columbia River in Oregon. But when war came, Astor sold his interests to the Northwestern Fur Company, a British concern operating out of Canada; and after the war he centered his own operations in the Great Lakes area, from which he eventually extended them westward to the Rockies. Other companies carried on operations up the Missouri and its tributaries and in the Rocky Mountains. At first, fur traders did most of their business by purchasing pelts from the Indians. But beginning with Andrew and William Ashley's Rocky Mountain Fur Company, founded in 1822, more and more traders dispatched white trappers into the wilderness to travel with the Indians in pursuit of furs.

The trappers or "mountain men" explored the Far West and gained an intimate knowledge of the region and its people; but although such men as Jedediah S. Smith ultimately became famous for their exploits, they did not write books or draw maps, and thus their knowledge did not spread widely. Public awareness of the region increased as a result of the explorations of Major Stephen H. Long. In 1819 and 1820, with instructions from the War Department to find the sources of the Red River, Long led nineteen soldiers on a journey up the Platte and South Platte rivers through what is now Nebraska and eastern Colorado (where he discovered the peak named for him), and then returned eastward along the Arkansas River through what is now Kansas.

Long's expedition failed to find the headwaters of the Red River. But Long wrote an influential report on his trip and assessed the region's potential for future settlement and development. "In regard to this extensive section of country between the Missouri River and the Rocky Mountains," he said, "we do not hesitate in giving the opinion that it is almost wholly unfit for cultivation, and of course uninhabitable by a people depending upon agriculture for their subsistence." On the published map of his expedition, he labeled the Great Plains the "Great American Desert" —giving increased currency to the idea earlier advanced by Pike and others that the land beyond the Missouri River was unfit for cultivation.

The "Era of Good Feelings"

The expansion of the economy, the growth of the West, the creation of new states—all reflected the rising spirit of nationalism that was permeating the United States in the years following the war. That spirit found reflection, for a time, in the course of American politics.

Ever since 1800, the presidency seemed to have been the special possession of Virginians, who had

Jim Butler, Mountain Man
Well before most Americans were interested in settling the lands of the Far West, a small group of solitary trappers and explorers—known in popular legend as "mountain men"—moved through the region in search of wealth and solitude. This pencil sketch by an unknown artist shows one of these early pioneers. (Gilcrease Institute of Art)

passed it from one to another in unvarying sequence. After two terms in office Jefferson named his secretary of state, James Madison, to succeed him; and after two more terms, Madison secured the presidential nomination for *his* secretary of state, James Monroe. Many in the North already were expressing their impatience with the so-called Virginia Dynasty, but the Republicans had no difficulty in electing their candidate in the listless campaign of 1816. Monroe received 183 ballots in the electoral college; his Federalist opponent, Rufus King of New York, only 34— from the states of Massachusetts, Connecticut, and Delaware.

Monroe was sixty-one years old when he became president, and he seemed in many respects a relic of an earlier age. Tall and dignified, he wore such old-fashioned garb as knee-length pantaloons and white-topped boots. In the course of his long and varied career, he had served as a soldier in the Revolution, as a diplomat, and most recently as a cabinet officer. He had once seemed an impulsive man, but he was now widely admired for his caution and patience.

Monroe entered office under what seemed to be remarkably favorable circumstances. With the decline of the Federalists, his party faced no serious opposition. With the conclusion of the War of 1812, the nation faced no important international threats. American politicians had dreamed since the first days of the republic of a time in which partisan divisions and factional disputes might come to an end, a time in which the nation might learn to exhibit the harmony and virtue that the founders had envisioned. The postwar years seemed, at last, to provide an opportunity; and Monroe attempted to use his office to realize that dream.

He made that clear, above all, in the selection of his cabinet. For secretary of state, the first and most important position, he chose the New Englander and former Federalist John Quincy Adams. Jefferson, Madison, and Monroe had all served as secretary of state before becoming president; Adams, therefore, immediately became the heir apparent, suggesting that the "Virginia Dynasty" would soon come to an end. Monroe offered the office of secretary of war to Henry Clay, but Clay turned him down and remained Speaker of the House. So he chose instead the forceful South Carolinian John C. Calhoun. In his other appointments as well, Monroe seemed to go out of his way to include both Northerners and Southerners, Federalists and Republicans—to harmonize the various interests and sections of the country in a government of national unity.

Soon after his inauguration, Monroe did what no other president since Washington had done: He made a goodwill tour through the country, eastward to New England, westward as far as Detroit. In New England, so recently the scene of rabid Federalist discontent, he was greeted everywhere with enthusiastic demonstrations. The *Columbian Centinel*, a Federalist newspaper in Boston, commenting on the "Presidential Jubilee" in that city, observed that an "era of good feelings" had arrived. This phrase soon spread throughout the country and became a popular label for the presidency of Monroe.

In 1817, there seemed every reason to expect the "era of good feelings" to be just that—a time of happy national unity. And on the surface, at least, those expectations were realized. In 1820, when Monroe was a candidate for reelection to the presidency, only one elector voted against him; and he did so to ensure that Washington would remain the only unanimously elected president. The Federalists did not even bother to put up an opposing candidate. For all practical purposes, the opposition party had now ceased to exist.

But beneath this surface calm, serious social and political divisions were emerging. Indeed, the years of Monroe's presidency became in the end a time of very bad feelings—a time in which the dream of a harmonious republic unsullied by party and faction was shattered forever.

John Quincy Adams and Florida

Whatever problems there were, however, did not seem to affect Monroe's secretary of state, John Quincy Adams. Like his father, the second president of the United States, Adams had spent much of his life in diplomatic service. He had represented the United States in Britain, Russia, the Netherlands, and Prussia. He had helped negotiate the Treaty of Ghent. And he had demonstrated in all his assignments a calmness and firmness that made him one of the great diplomats in American history.

He was also a committed nationalist; and when he assumed the office of secretary of state, he considered his most important task to be the promotion of American expansion. His first major challenge was Florida. The United States had already annexed West Florida, but most Americans still believed the nation should gain possession of the entire peninsula. Even the claim to West Florida was under dispute. Spain still claimed the whole of the province, East and

West, and actually occupied most of it. In 1817, Adams began negotiations with the Spanish minister, Luis de Onís, in hopes of resolving the dispute and gaining the entire colony for the United States.

In the meantime, however, events were taking their own course in Florida itself. Andrew Jackson, now in command of American troops along the Florida frontier, had orders from Secretary of War Calhoun to "adopt the necessary measures" to put a stop to the continuing raids on American territory by the Seminole Indians south of the Florida border. Jackson (with, he later claimed, tacit encouragement from Washington) used those orders as an excuse to invade Florida, seize the Spanish forts at St. Marks and Pensacola, and order the hanging of two British subjects on the charge of supplying the Indians and inciting them to hostilities.

Instead of condemning or disavowing Jackson's raid, Adams urged the government to assume complete responsibility for it, because he saw in it a chance to win an important advantage in his negotiations with Spain. The United States, he told the Spanish, had the right under international law to defend itself against threats from across its borders. Since Spain was unwilling or unable to curb those threats, America had simply done what was necessary. And he implied that the nation might consider even more drastic action in the future.

Jackson's raid had demonstrated to the Spanish that the United States could easily take Florida by force. Onís realized, therefore, that he had little choice but to come to terms with the Americans, although he was determined to make the most of a bad situation. Under the terms of the Adams-Onís Treaty of 1819, Spain ceded all of Florida to the United States. In return, the American government assumed $5 million in outstanding claims by its citizens against Spain. The United States also gave up its claims to Texas, and Spain its claims to territory north of the 42nd parallel from the Rockies to the Pacific. Thus a line was drawn from the Gulf of Mexico northwestward across the continent establishing the northern border of the Spanish Empire and transferring to the United States the Spanish title to the West Coast north of California. Adams and Onís had concluded something more than a Florida agreement; it was a "transcontinental treaty."

The Panic of 1819

But the Monroe administration had little time to revel in its diplomatic successes. At the same time that Adams was completing his negotiations with Onís, the nation was falling victim to a serious economic crisis that helped revive many of the political disputes that the "era of good feelings" had presumably settled.

In part, the Panic of 1819 was a delayed reaction to the War of 1812 and to the preceding years of warfare in Europe. Ever since 1793, the continual fighting had drawn manpower from European fields, disrupted European business and agriculture, and created an abnormally high foreign demand for the produce of American plantations and farms. The whole period was one of exceptionally high prices for American producers, and although some prices fell with the decline of trade in 1814, they recovered with the resumption of exports to Europe after the war.

The rising prices for farm products stimulated a land boom in the United States, particularly in the West. After the war, the government land offices did a bigger business than ever before, a level of business they would maintain for twenty years. In 1815, sales totaled about 1 million acres; in 1819, more than 5 million. Many settlers bought on credit; under the land laws of 1800 and 1804 they could pay as little as $80 down, and then, they hoped, raise the remaining three installments within four years from the proceeds of their farming. Speculators bought large tracts of choice land, hoping to resell it at a profit to incoming settlers. At the land-office auctions, bidding became so spirited that much of the public land sold for prices far above the minimum of $2 an acre, some in the Black Belt of Alabama and Mississippi going for $100 and more. Optimistic real estate promoters often paid still higher prices and then laid out town sites, even in swamps, hoping to make fortunes through the sale of city lots.

The availability of easy credit helped fuel the speculative boom. Until the refounding of the Bank of the United States in 1817, settlers and speculators could borrow readily from state banks and pay the government for the land with bank notes. Even after 1817, wildcat banks continued to provide easy credit for a few years. Indeed, the Bank of the United States itself at first offered easy loans. But in 1819, new management took over. Concerned that the Bank was endangering its stability by extending too much credit, the new governors called in loans and foreclosed mortgages, thus acquiring thousands of acres of mortgaged land in the West. They also gathered up state bank notes and presented them to the state banks for payment in cash. And since state banks often had too little cash on hand to meet the demand,

SIGNIFICANT EVENTS

1803   Napoleonic Wars escalate in Europe (p. 219)

1805   British defeat French at Trafalgar (p. 220)

1806–1807   Napoleon issues Berlin and Milan decrees (p. 220)

1807   *Chesapeake-Leopard* incident nearly precipitates war with Great Britain (p. 221)
Embargo Act passed (p. 222)
Congress approves construction of National Road (p. 234)

1808   Economy plunges into depression (p. 222)
Madison elected president (p. 222)

1809   Embargo Act repealed (p. 222)
Non-Intercourse Act passed (p. 223)

1810   Macon's Bill No. 2 reopens trade with Britain and France (p. 223)
United States annexes west Florida (p. 225)

1811   Harrison is victorious in Battle of Tippecanoe: destroys Tecumseh's Indian confederacy (p. 224)
First Bank of the United States closes after charter is not renewed (p. 232)

1812   United States declares war on Great Britain (June 14) (p. 226)
Madison reelected president (p. 240)

1813   British erect naval blockade (p. 226)
American forces burn York (Toronto), Canadian capital (p. 226)

1813   Perry defeats British fleet at Put-in Bay on Lake Erie (p. 228)
Harrison defeats British and Tecumseh at Battle of the Thames (p. 228)
Lowell establishes textile mill at Waltham, Massachusetts (p. 233)

1814   Jackson, at Battle of Horseshoe Bend, slaughters Creek Indians (p. 228)
British troops capture and burn Washington (p. 229)
Americans win Battle of Plattsburgh (p. 229)
Hartford Convention meets (p. 230)
Treaty of Ghent signed (p. 231)

1815   Jackson wins Battle of New Orleans (p. 229)
Naval war fought with Algiers (p. 232)

1816   Second Bank of the United States chartered (p. 232)
Monroe elected president (p. 240)

1818   Jackson invades Florida, ends first Seminole War (p. 241)
Rush-Bagot agreement signed (p. 232)

1819   Commercial panic destabilizes economy (p. 242)
Spain cedes Florida to United States in Adams-Onís Treaty (p. 241)

1820   Monroe reelected president (p. 240)

many were forced to close their doors. That started a financial panic, with depositors flooding even the comparatively sound state banks with notes to be cashed, forcing many of them out of business as well. Many Americans, particularly those in the West, blamed the Bank of the United States for the crisis—the beginning of a process that would ultimately make the Bank's existence one of the nation's most burning political issues.

Six years of depression followed. Prices for both manufactured goods and agricultural produce fell rapidly. Manufacturers demanded protection from foreign competition and ultimately secured passage of a new tariff in 1824. Farmers who had bought land on credit could no longer earn enough from sale of their crops to keep up their payments, and they too demanded relief. Congress responded with the land law of 1820 and the relief act of 1821. The new land law required new purchasers to buy their farms outright, without credit, but made land much cheaper than before. The relief act allowed existing landowners to pay off their debts at a reduced price and gave them more time to meet their installments.

The Panic of 1819 and the widespread distress that followed seemed to some Americans to confirm fears that rapid economic growth and territorial expansion would destabilize the nation and threaten its survival. But most Americans by 1820 were irrevocably committed to such growth and expansion. And public debate in the future would revolve less around the question of whether such growth was good or bad than around the question of how it should be encouraged and controlled. That debate, which the Panic of 1819 did much to encourage, created new factional divisions within the Republican party and ultimately brought the era of nonpartisanship—the "era of good feelings"—to an acrimonious end.

SUGGESTED READINGS

The War of 1812. J. C. A. Stagg, *Mr. Madison's War: Politics, Diplomacy, and Warfare in the Early American Republic, 1783–1830* (1983); Julius W. Pratt, *Expansionists of 1812* (1925); Reginald Horsman, *The Causes of the War of 1812* (1962) and *The War of 1812* (1969); Bradford Perkins, *Prologue to War: England and the United States, 1805–1812* (1961); A. L. Burt, *The United States, Great Britain, and British North America* (1940); Roger H. Brown, *The Republic in Peril: 1812* (1964); Harry L. Coles, *The War of 1812* (1965); F. F. Beirne, *The War of 1812* (1949); John Mahon, *The War of 1812* (1975); William Wood, *The War with the United States* (1915); Irving Brant, *James Madison: Commander-in-Chief* (1961); Robert V. Remini, *Andrew Jackson and the Course of American Empire* (1977); Alfred T. Mahan, *Sea Power in Its Relation to the War of 1812,* 2 vols. (1905); Samuel F. Bemis, *John Quincy Adams and the Foundations of American Foreign Policy* (1949); Bradford Perkins, *Castlereagh and Adams* (1964); R. David Edmunds, *The Shawnee Prophet* (1983) and *Tecumseh and the Quest for Indian Leadership* (1984).

Postwar Expansion. George Dangerfield, *The Awakening of American Nationalism* (1965) and *The Era of Good Feelings* (1952); Shaw Livermore, Jr., *The Twilight of Federalism* (1962); Bray Hammond, *Banks and Politics in America from the Revolution to the Civil War* (1957); Murray N. Rothbard, *The Panic of 1819* (1962).

The West. Francis S. Philbrick, *The Rise of the West, 1745–1830* (1965); Thomas P. Abernethy, *The South in the New Nation* (1961); Frederick Jackson Turner, *The Rise of the New West* (1906) and *The Frontier in American History* (1920); Ray Allen Billington, *The Far Western Frontier* (1965) and *Westward Expansion* (1974); John A. Hawgood, *America's Western Frontier* (1967); David J. Wishart, *The Fur Trade of the American West* (1979); Frederick Merk, *History of the Westward Movement* (1978); Dale Van Every, *The Final Challenge* (1964); Julie Roy Jeffrey, *Frontier Women: The Trans-Mississippi West* (1979); Glenda Riley, *The Female Frontier* (1988); Colin Calloway, *Crown and Calumet* (1987).

The Grid

🟦 🔺 🟦

Among the many environmental changes that people have wrought upon the American landscape is one so familiar that we inhabit it every day without ever recognizing its significance. Only when we board an airplane and see our world from above do we grasp the extraordinary transformations it entailed. Everywhere there are lines on the land, boundaries that divide one person's property from another's. In those lines is an intricate story of environmental change.

When European colonists first arrived in North America, one of their earliest tasks was to divide up the land around their settlements into tracts that individuals could own. The pattern of property boundaries they established is called a *cadastral system,* and different versions of such systems had profoundly different consequences for the way colonial lands and societies developed.

The Spanish, for instance, had given a few of their most prominent colonists in New Mexico, Texas, and California vast estates with the right to claim payments in labor or produce from the people who lived there. Such grants became a means of subjugating Indian inhabitants, but they also shaped the European society that developed upon them. Class differences were reinforced by the uneven distribution of land, and a semifeudal society resulted. A similar land system was imposed by the Dutch along the banks of the Hudson River in New York, though most of the tenants who lived there were European immigrants rather than Indians. In the agricultural landscape of New York, one of the landlord's most important ways of extracting rent payments was running the estate's grain mill, earning a share of the flour it ground. In the case of both the Spanish and the Dutch, the cadastral system encouraged and reinforced social hierarchy.

The French imposed a different system in places like Louisiana, Missouri, and Illinois. Because their transportation network depended almost entirely on rivers, they aligned their property boundaries so that each tract of land fronted on the water. Long narrow fields called *rotures* were the result. Colonists built their houses to face the river, with their land stretching out behind. Long fields had the added convenience that one could plow them without having to turn one's horses around very often. The system encouraged dispersed settlement with few village centers, leading to the relative weakness of local elites and the relative strength of the few

Metes and Bounds, North Carolina
The lack of a standardized survey system in the southern colonies produced crazy-quilt field patterns that persist to this day. The irregular fencelines and property boundaries one sees when flying over the southern landscape reflect the metes and bounds surveys that were made centuries ago. (Comstock)

major cities, especially Montreal and New Orleans, toward which the rivers flowed.

The English colonies had at least two major cadastral systems. One was the New England town system, in which a large tract of land was granted to a small group of proprietors, who then divided it up for the benefit of individual settlers. The New England town system was designed to encourage compact settlements, and so all original colonists were given house lots near the church and meeting house in the center of town. Each also received tracts of land for traditional agricultural uses, so that each possessed croplands, pastures, meadows, and woodlots widely scattered in different parts of the town. The system had the great advantage of fitting ownership patterns to different ecological uses, but it tended to break down with time.

In the South, land was surveyed according to a system called *metes and bounds*— which in practice amounted to virtually no system at all. People wanting to buy land went to the county courthouse and purchased a claim to a given number of acres. They then went more or less wherever they chose and marked out the allotted number of acres. To describe their tract, they walked its property boundary and

The Grid, Illinois
Starting at the point where the Ohio River crosses the Pennsylvania-Ohio border, government surveyors applied the Land Ordinance of 1785 to most parts of the United States. The uniform checkerboard pattern of the national grid is visible to any traveler who flies or drives across this terrain. (Comstock)

described its corners: a tree here, a rock there, a river on this side. The result was a crazy-quilt pattern of properties, many of them overlapping because their owners had not known a prior claim existed when they were surveyed. The Southern system was cheap and initially easy to administer, but it produced so many conflicts over who owned what land that claimants were often forced to litigate their rights for decades.

When the government of the United States met in the wake of the Revolution to settle various problems of the new nation, one of the most important was exactly this one: what cadastral system was most appropriate for the republic? After the states began to cede their western lands to the national government in 1781, the United States for the first time acquired what would henceforth be called *the public domain*. The issue of what to do with it would remain a major concern of American politics right down to the present day.

Clearly, a semifeudal system of large land estates like that of the Spanish or Dutch was inappropriate for a republic like the United States. Members of Congress were also eager to avoid the random irregularities and legal conflicts associated with

Southern metes and bounds. They therefore turned to a modified version of the New England town system. After a trial run with an act in 1784, they finally passed what would become one of the great founding laws of American history, the Land Ordinance of 1785. Measured in terms of the future shape of the American landscape, this act was in many ways even more important than the Constitution itself.

The Ordinance originally applied only to what was then called the Northwest Territory—present-day Ohio, Indiana, Michigan, Illinois, and Wisconsin—but it became a model for all subsequent land systems administered by the federal government. One of its most important features was its requirement that lands be surveyed *before* they could be purchased, thus circumventing the problems of the southern system. To make sure that surveyed tracts did not overlap, the authors of the ordinance turned to a familiar Enlightenment symbol of rationality and order: the Cartesian coordinate plane that René Descartes had offered as a foundation for his new mathematics. America would be a gridded landscape.

Lands west of the Ohio River were divided into townships 6 miles to a side, each containing 36 square miles, or "sections." Surveyors walked along each side of a section and located its four corners so that there need be no confusion about where one section ended and another began. Would-be owners located their property by identifying its township, its section number, and which corner of the section it was in. One family, for instance, might own a forty-acre farm in the northeast quarter of the southwest quarter of section 23 of the second township in the fourth range of townships in Ohio. Townships were sold in two ways: either as 36 square-mile units to large proprietors who broke them up and resold them as speculations; or as 1 square-mile sections to smaller landowners.

Congress had two main goals in this and subsequent land ordinances: to encourage development of the Western lands and to raise funds for the federal treasury. In the absence of an income tax, the government's main sources of revenue were the tariff and the sale of public lands. There was thus an inevitable tension between the government's desire to earn as much money as it could from land sales, and settlers' desire to purchase land as cheaply as possible. Debates about the public lands for the rest of the eighteenth and nineteenth centuries revolved around how generous to be to settlers of small means. How low should the price of land be? Should the government offer credit to would-be purchasers who lacked the capital to make a purchase with their own funds? What was the smallest unit in which it could be sold? How near to frontier settlements should auctions be held? Western settlers inevitably argued for the most liberal answers to each of these questions, urging upon the government lower prices, generous credit, small unit sales, and Western auctions. The end result was the Homestead Act of 1862, in which a settler could acquire 160 acres simply by filing a claim and paying a nominal entry fee.

The environmental effects of the 1785 Ordinance are almost impossible to exaggerate. The modern landscape of the West and Middle West would be unrecognizable without it. As one flies today from Pennsylvania to Ohio, one instantly recognizes the shift from random field shapes to the rigid north-south, east-west rectilinear patterns of the grid. Aside from modern interstate highways, most roads still follow the edges of the original section lines. Farmers still plow their fields within the boundaries set by the original surveyors and still preserve many of the old gnarled "witness trees" the surveyors used to mark section corners. American towns mimic the national grid in the rectangular layout of their streets and lots. We live in a rectilinear world.

The 1785 Ordinance accomplished its goals with great success. It surveyed the public domain according to a regular system, prevented unnecessary litigation over property rights, and speeded the development of Western lands. But it was not without problems. It encouraged a dispersed form of settlement—each farm family often a half mile or more from its neighbors—that undermined the very community ideals that the Ordinance's model, the New England town system, had sought to promote. It led people to arrange their fields and roads according to a rigid north-south, east-west alignment, no matter what the local topography. The result was roads that were hillier and harder to travel than they need have been, and fields that were more susceptible to erosion. Finally, when the surveyors eventually reached the arid West, where a dry climate made traditional Eastern farming impossible, the square mile units of the grid proved inappropriate both for livestock raising and for irrigation. Settlers had to work around the grid in order to find new systems for living successfully in the very different far Western environment.

Despite these social and environmental problems, however, the grid is here to stay. Once drawn, property boundaries can survive for centuries and even millennia after the society that originally drew them has disappeared. In writing the 1785 Ordinance as they did, members of Congress made an indelible mark on the American landscape.

Fourth of July Picnic at Weymouth Landing **(c. 1845), by Susan Merrett**
Celebrations of Independence Day, like this one in eastern Massachusetts, became major festive events
throughout the United States in the early nineteenth century, a sign of rising American nationalism.
(*Art Institute of Chicago*)

CHAPTER 9

🔆 🔆 🔆

A Resurgence
of Nationalism

🔆 🔆 🔆

Like a "fire bell in the night," as Thomas Jefferson put it, the issue of slavery arose only five years after the end of the War of 1812 to threaten the unity of the nation. The specific question was whether the territory of Missouri should be admitted to the Union as a free or as a slaveholding state. But the larger issue, one that would arise again and again to plague the republic, was the question of whether the vast new Western regions of the United States would ultimately be controlled by the North or by the South.

Yet the Missouri crisis, which was settled by a compromise in 1820, was significant at the time not only because it augured the sectional crises to come but because it stood in such sharp contrast to the rising American nationalism of the 1820s. Whatever forces might be working to pull the nation apart, far stronger ones were acting for the moment to draw it together. The American economy was experiencing remarkable growth. Ultimately the industrialization of the North would contribute to sectional tensions. But for the moment, at least, economic progress—which brought with it new systems of transportation and communication—seemed likelier to link the nation more closely together. The federal government, in the meantime, was acting in both domestic and foreign policy to assert a vigorous nationalism—through the judicial decisions of John Marshall's Supreme Court; through congressional legislation encouraging economic growth; and through James Monroe's foreign policy, which attempted to assert the nation's rising stature in the world.

Above all, perhaps, the United States was held together in the 1820s by a set of shared sentiments and ideals, the "mystic bonds of union," as Abraham Lincoln later described them. The memory of the Revolution, the veneration of the Constitution and its framers, the widely held sense that America had a special destiny in the world—all combined to obscure sectional differences and arouse a vibrant, even romantic, patriotism. Every year, Fourth of July celebrations reminded Americans of their common struggle for independence, as fife and drum corps and flamboyant orators appealed to patriotism and nationalism. When the Marquis de Lafayette, the French general who had aided the United States during the Revolution, traveled through the country in 1824, crowds without distinction of section or party cheered him in frenzied celebration.

And on July 4, 1826—the fiftieth anniversary of the adoption of the Declaration of Independence—there occurred an event which seemed to many to confirm that the United States was a nation specially chosen by God. On that special day, Americans were to learn, two of the greatest of the country's founders and former presidents—Thomas Jefferson, author of the Declaration, and John Adams, "its ablest advocate and defender" (as Jefferson had said)—died within hours of each other. Jefferson's last words, those at his bedside reported, were "Is it the Fourth?" And Adams comforted those around him moments before his death by saying, "Thomas Jefferson still survives."

Events would prove that the forces of nationalism were not, in the end, strong enough to overcome the emerging sectional differences. For the time being, however, they permitted the republic to enter an era of unprecedented expansion confident and united.

America's Economic Revolution

There had been signs for many years that the United States was about to enter a period of dramatic economic growth. In the 1820s and 1830s, that period finally began. Improvements in transportation and the expanding range of business activity created, for the first time, a national market economy. Each area of the country could concentrate on the production of a certain type of goods, relying on other areas to buy its surplus production and to supply it with those things it no longer produced itself. This regional specialization enabled much of the South, for example, to concentrate on growing its most lucrative crop: cotton. And it enabled the North to develop a new factory system—to begin an industrial revolution that would, in time, become even greater than the one that had begun in England some forty years before. By the mid-1820s, the nation's economy was growing more rapidly than its population.

Many factors combined to produce this dramatic transformation. The American population was increasing and spreading across a far greater expanse of territory, providing both a labor supply for the production of goods and a market for the sale of them. A "transportation revolution"—based on the construction of roads, canals, and eventually railroads—was giving merchants and manufacturers access to new markets and raw materials. New entrepreneurial techniques were making a rapid business expansion possible. And technological advances were helping to spur industry to new levels of activity. Equally important, perhaps, Americans in the 1820s embraced an ethic of growth that was based on a commitment to hard work, individual initiative, thrift, and ambition.

The Population, 1820–1840

During the 1820s and 1830s, as during much of American history, three trends of population were clear: rapid increase, migration to the West, and movement to towns and cities.

Americans continued to multiply almost as fast as they had in the colonial period. The population still doubled roughly every twenty-five years. The population had stood at only 4 million in 1790. By 1820, it had reached 10 million; by 1830, nearly 13 million; and by 1840, 17 million. The United States was growing much more rapidly in population than the British Isles or Europe. By 1860 it had moved ahead of the United Kingdom and had nearly overtaken Germany and France.

The black population increased more slowly than the white. After 1808, when the importation of slaves became illegal, the proportion of blacks to whites in the nation as a whole steadily declined. In 1820, there was one black to every four whites; in 1840, one to every five. The slower increase of the black population was a result of its comparatively high death rate, not of a low birth rate. Slave mothers had large families, but life was shorter for both slaves and free blacks than for whites—a result of the enforced poverty in which virtually all blacks lived.

Severe epidemics continued to take a heavy, if periodic, toll on the American population; among the worst was a devastating cholera plague that swept the country in 1832. Public health efforts gradually improved, and the number and ferocity of such outbreaks slowly declined, as did the mortality rate as a whole. But the population increase was a result not only of lengthened life but of a high birth rate. The very high birth rates of the eighteenth century declined somewhat in the first decades of the nineteenth; in 1800, the rate for white women was 7.14, while in 1840 it had dropped to 6.14. But even this reduced

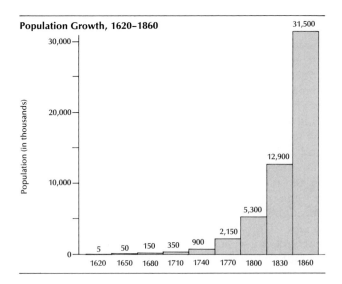

Population Growth, 1620–1860

The Family at Home, c. 1845
This painting by Henry F. Darby of a minister, his wife, and their six children is an indication of the size of many American families in the early nineteenth century. Unlike in colonial times, a woman in the 1840s could expect to see most of her children live to maturity. (Museum of Fine Arts, Boston)

rate, particularly when combined with longer life expectancy, produced very rapid population increases.

Since the time of independence, immigration had accounted for little of the nation's population growth. The long years of war in Europe, from 1793 to 1815, had kept the number of newcomers to America down to only a few thousand a year, and then the Panic of 1819 checked the immigrant tide that had risen after the restoration of peace. During the 1820s, arrivals from abroad averaged about 14,000 annually. Of the total population of nearly 13 million in 1830, the foreign-born numbered fewer than 500,000, most of them naturalized citizens. Soon, however, immigration began to grow once again. It reached a total of 60,000 for 1832 and nearly 80,000 for 1837.

Since the United States exported more goods than it imported, ships returning to America from Europe often had vacant space and took on immigrants to fill it. Competition among shipping lines reduced fares so that, by the 1830s, immigrants could get passage across the Atlantic for as little as $20 or $30. No longer did they need to sell their services to a temporary master in America in order to pay for the voyage. And so the system of indentured servitude, which had dwindled steadily after the Revolution, disappeared entirely after the Panic of 1819.

Until the 1830s, most of the new arrivals came from the same sources as had the bulk of the colonial population—from England and the northern (predominantly Protestant) counties of Ireland. In the

1830s, however, the number of immigrants arriving from the southern (Catholic) counties of Ireland began to grow, the beginning of a tremendous influx of Irish Catholics that was to occur over the next two decades. Generally, the newcomers—Irish as well as others—were welcome in the United States. They were a source of labor needed for building canals and railroads, manning ships and docks, and performing other heavy work essential to the expanding economic system. But the Irish, as Roman Catholics, excited Protestant prejudices in some communities. In 1834, an anti-Catholic mob set fire to a convent in Charlestown, Massachusetts. The next year, Samuel F. B. Morse (who is better remembered as a portrait painter and as the inventor of the telegraph) published his *Foreign Conspiracy,* which became something like a textbook for those crusading against what they imagined was a popish plot to gain control of the United States.

The Northwest and the Southwest continued to grow much more rapidly than the rest of the country. By 1830, more than a fourth of the American people lived west of the Appalachians; by 1850, nearly half. As a result, some of the seaboard states suffered a serious loss of human resources (as well as of the material goods that departing migrants took with them). Year after year the Carolinas, for example, lost nearly as many people through migration as they gained by natural increase, so that their populations remained almost static. The same was true of Vermont and New Hampshire. Many villages in these two states were completely depopulated, their houses and barns left to rot, as their people scattered over the country in search of a better life than the infertile granite hills afforded.

Not all the migrating villagers and farmers sought the unsettled frontier: some moved instead to the increasingly crowded population centers. Cities (defined as communities of 8,000 or more) grew faster than the nation as a whole. In 1820 there were more than twice as many cities, and in 1840 more than seven times as many, as there had been in 1790. While the vast majority of Americans continued to reside in the open country or in small towns, the number of city dwellers increased remarkably. In 1790, one person in thirty lived in a community of 8,000 or more; in 1820, one in twenty; and in 1840, one in twelve.

The rise of New York City was phenomenal. By 1810 it had surpassed Philadelphia as the largest city in America. New York steadily increased its lead in both population and trade. Its growth was based in

Sources of Immigration, 1820–1840

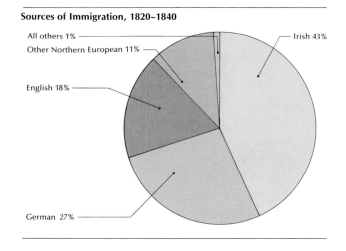

Total Immigration, 1820–1840

large part on its superior natural harbor. But it was also a result of several commercial and political decisions, by New Yorkers themselves and by others, following the War of 1812. After the war, the British chose New York as the chief place to "dump" their manufactured goods and thus helped make it the nation's leading center for imports. Liberal state laws regarding auction sales encouraged inland merchants to do their buying in New York. The first packet line, with regularly scheduled monthly sailings between England and the United States, made New York its American terminus in 1816. And the Erie Canal (completed in 1825) gave the city unrivaled access to the interior.

The Port of New York, 1828
This view of South Street in Manhattan shows the East River lined with docks. Other docks, similarly busy, lined the Hudson River on the opposite side of the island. The population of New York City was approaching 150,000 by 1828. (New York Public Library)

The Canal Age

The so-called turnpike era, which lasted from 1790 to about 1830, saw the construction of an important network of roads that did much to link the nation together and to open access to new markets and sources of materials. Roads alone, however, were not sufficient to provide the system of transportation necessary for a growing industrial society. And so, in the 1820s and 1830s, Americans began to construct other means of transportation as well. As in colonial times, they looked first to water routes.

The larger rivers, especially the Mississippi and the Ohio, became increasingly useful, as steamboats grew in number and improved in design. A special kind of steamboat evolved to meet the problems of navigation on the Mississippi and its tributaries.

These waters were shallow, with strong and difficult currents, shifting bars of sand and mud, and submerged logs and trees. So the boat needed a flat bottom, paddle wheels rather than screw propellers, and a powerful, high-pressure—and thus dangerously explosive—engine. (The river boats were, therefore, prone to deadly, spectacular accidents.) To accommodate as much cargo and as many passengers as possible, the boat was triple-decked, its superstructure rising high in the air. These river boats carried to New Orleans the corn and other crops of Northwestern farmers and the cotton and tobacco of Southwestern planters. From New Orleans, ocean-going ships took the cargoes on to Eastern ports.

But neither the farmers of the West nor the merchants of the East were completely satisfied with this pattern of trade. Farmers knew they would be able to

Canals in the Northeast, to 1860

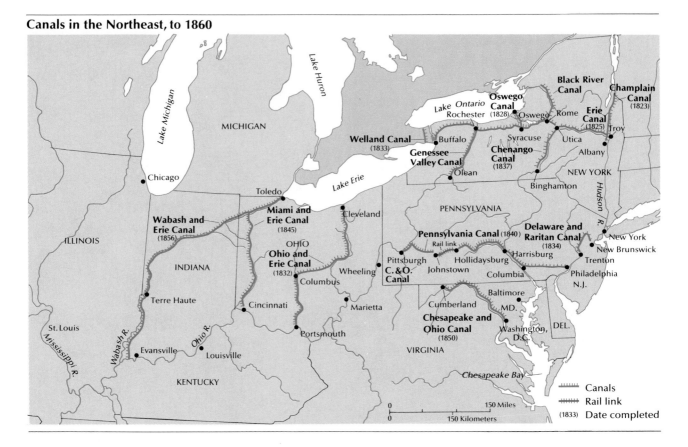

get better prices for their crops if they could ship them directly eastward to market, rather than by the roundabout river-sea route; and merchants knew they would be able to sell larger quantities of their manufactured goods if they could transport them more directly and economically to the West.

The highways across the mountains, such as the Philadelphia-Pittsburgh turnpike and the National Road, provided a partial solution to the problem. But the costs of hauling goods overland, although lower than before the roads were built, were too high for anything except the most compact and valuable merchandise. It took four horses a full day to pull a wagon weight of one ton twelve miles over an ordinary road; on a turnpike, four horses could haul one and a half tons eighteen miles in a day. But the same four horses could draw a boatload of a hundred tons twenty-four miles a day on a canal. Thus interest quickly grew in expanding the nation's water routes.

Canal building was a task too expensive for the existing institutions of private enterprise. Sectional jealousies and constitutional scruples prevented the federal government from financing the projects. So the job of digging extensive canals fell to the various states. New York was the first to act. It had the natural advantage of a comparatively level route between the Hudson River and Lake Erie through the only break in the Appalachian chain. Yet the engineering tasks were still imposing. The distance from the Hudson to Lake Erie was more than 350 miles, several times as long as any of the existing canals in America. There were high ridges to cross and a wilderness of woods and swamps to penetrate. For many years, New Yorkers debated whether the scheme was practical. The canal advocates finally won the debate after De Witt Clinton, a late but ardent convert to the cause, became governor in 1817. Digging began on July 4, 1817.

The building of the Erie Canal was by far the greatest construction project that Americans had ever undertaken. It was the work of self-made engineers. One of them had made a careful study of English canals, but he and his associates did more than merely copy what they had seen abroad. They devised ingenious arrangements of cables, pulleys, and gears for bringing down trees and uprooting stumps. Instead of the usual shovels and wheelbarrows, they used

The Erie Canal

This undated lithograph shows a barge (at lower right) departing from Lockport, New York, along the Erie Canal, drawn by a team of mules. It had just traversed the series of locks that, here as elsewhere, made it possible for canal traffic to negotiate sharp rises and falls in the terrain.   (The Bettmann Archive)

specially designed plows and scrapers for moving earth. To make watertight locks they produced cement from native limestone. The canal itself was of simple design: basically a ditch, forty feet wide and four feet deep, with towpaths along the banks for the horses or mules that were to draw the canal boats. (Steamboats were barred from the canals; the churning of a paddle wheel or propeller would cave in the earthen banks.) Cuts and fills, some of them enormous, enabled the canal to pass through hills and over valleys; stone aqueducts carried it across streams; and eighty-eight locks, of heavy masonry, with great wooden gates, took care of the necessary ascents and descents.

Not only was the Erie Canal an engineering triumph; it quickly proved a financial success as well. It opened for through traffic in October 1825, amid elaborate ceremonies and celebrations. Governor Clinton headed a parade of canal boats that made the trip from Buffalo to the Hudson and then downriver to New York City, where he emptied a keg of Erie water into the Atlantic to symbolize the wedding of the lake and the ocean. Traffic was soon so heavy that, within about seven years, the tolls had brought

in enough money to repay the entire cost of construction.

The profitability of the Erie encouraged the state to enlarge its canal system by building several branches. An important part of the system was the Champlain Canal, begun at about the same time as the Erie and completed in 1822, which connected Lake Champlain with the Hudson River. Some of the branches did not fully pay for themselves, but all provided valuable water connections between New York City and the larger towns of the state. The main line, by providing access to the Great Lakes, led beyond the state's borders, to the West.

The system of water transportation extended farther when the states of Ohio and Indiana, inspired by the success of the Erie Canal, provided water connections between Lake Erie and the Ohio River. In 1825, Ohio began the building of two canals, one between Portsmouth and Cleveland and the other between Cincinnati and Toledo, both of which were in use by 1833. In 1832, Indiana started the construction of a canal to connect Evansville with the Cincinnati-Toledo route. These canals made it possible to ship goods by inland waterways all the way from New York to New Orleans, although it was still necessary to transfer cargoes several times among canal, lake, and river craft. By way of the Great Lakes, it was possible to go by water from New York to Chicago. After the opening of the Erie Canal, shipping on the Great Lakes by sail and steam increased rapidly.

The consequences of the development of this transportation network were far-reaching. One of the immediate results was the stimulation of the settlement of the Northwest, not only because it had become easier for migrants to make the westward journey but also, and more important, because it had become easier for them, after establishing their farms, to ship their produce to markets. Towns boomed along the Erie and other canals. New York City benefited the most of all. Although much of the Western produce, especially corn, continued to go downriver to New Orleans, an increasing proportion of it (including most of the wheat of the Northwest) went to New York. And manufactured goods from throughout the East now moved in growing volume through New York and then via the comparatively direct and economical new routes to the West.

Rival cities along the Atlantic seaboard took alarm at the prospect of New York's acquiring so vast a hinterland, largely at their expense. If they were to hold their own, they knew that they too would have to find ways of tapping the Western market. Boston, its way to the Hudson River blocked by the Berkshire Mountains, did not try to connect itself to the West by canal. Its hinterland would remain confined largely to New England itself. Philadelphia and Baltimore had the still more formidable Allegheny Mountains to contend with, but they nevertheless made a serious effort at canal building. Beginning in 1834, Pennsylvania invested in a complicated and costly system of waterways and railways—with an arrangement of "inclined planes," stationary engines, and cable cars to take canal boats over the mountains—in an effort to connect Philadelphia with Pittsburgh. But the "Pennsylvania system" was a financial and technological failure. Baltimore planned a canal to ascend the Potomac Valley and tunnel through the mountains to the West. Work began on the grandly conceived Chesapeake and Ohio Canal in 1828, but only the stretch between Washington, D.C., and Cumberland, Maryland, was ever completed. In the South, Richmond and Charleston also aspired to build water routes to the Ohio Valley; Richmond, hoping to link the James and Kanawha rivers, eventually constructed a canal

that reached as far as Lynchburg but failed to traverse the Blue Ridge Mountains.

For none of these rivals of New York did canals provide a satisfactory way to the West. Some cities, however, saw their opportunity in a different and newer means of transportation. Even before the canal age had reached its height, the era of the railroad was already beginning.

The Early Railroads

Through most of the 1820s and 1830s, railroads played a secondary role in the nation's transportation system. But the emergence of the first rail lines was of great importance to the future of the American economy. These tentative beginnings led, by the time of the Civil War, to a great surge of railroad building, which linked the nation together as no previous system of transportation had ever done. Railroads eventually became the primary means of transportation for the United States and remained so until the creation of the interstate highway system in the mid-twentieth century.

It is difficult to identify the precise date of the invention of the railroad. It emerged from a combination of innovations, each of which had its own history. One of these innovations was the invention of railroad tracks: rails, wooden or iron, laid on a prepared roadbed to make a fairly straight and level track. Another was the employment of steam-powered locomotives. A third was the operation of trains as public carriers of passengers and freight.

For nearly 200 years before the nineteenth century opened, small railways—wheeled vehicles running along fixed tracks—with cars pulled by men and women or by animals had been used to haul coal from English mines; and in the early 1800s similar railways had appeared in the United States. But it took the development of steam power to make railroads viable as a general transportation method. By 1804, both English and American inventors had experimented with steam engines for propelling land vehicles as well as boats. In 1820, John Stevens ran a locomotive and cars around a circular track on his New Jersey estate. Finally, in 1825, the Stockton and Darlington Railroad in England began to operate with steam power over a short length of track. It became the first line to carry general traffic. All earlier rail lines had been operated by particular companies to service only their own needs.

This news quickly aroused the interest of American businessmen, especially in those seaboard cities that sought better communication with the West. The first to organize a railroad company was a group of New Yorkers, who in 1826 obtained a charter for the Mohawk and Hudson, and five years later began running trains along the sixteen miles between Schenectady and Albany. The first company to begin actual operations was the Baltimore and Ohio; the only living signer of the Declaration of Independence, Charles Carroll of Carrollton, dug a spadeful of earth in the ceremonies in Maryland to start the work on July 4, 1828; and a thirteen-mile stretch opened for business in 1830. Not only the seaboard but also the Mississippi Valley became the scene of railroad building. By 1836, a total of more than 1,000 miles of track had been laid in eleven states.

There did not yet exist what could properly be called a railroad system. Even the longest of the lines was comparatively short in the 1830s, and most of them served to connect water routes to one another and otherwise to supplement water transportation. Even when two lines did connect the tracks might differ in gauge (width), so that cars from the one line often could not fit onto the tracks of the other. Schedules were erratic, and since roadbeds and bridges were often of shoddy construction, wrecks were frequent.

In response to these deficiencies, railroad pioneers produced a series of important technological developments in the 1830s. Roadbeds were improved through the introduction of heavier iron rails attached to wooden ties resting on crushed rock—a system that enabled tracks better to withstand the shock of use. American manufacturers began to produce steam locomotives more flexible and powerful than the engines of the past, which had usually been imported from Europe. Passenger cars, originally mere stagecoaches, were redesigned after 1840 as elongated boxes with two rows of reversible seats and a center aisle—thus making room for more people.

Railroads and canals were soon competing bitterly with each other. For a time, the Chesapeake and Ohio Canal Company blocked the advance of the Baltimore and Ohio Railroad through the narrow gorge of the upper Potomac, and the state of New York prohibited railroads from hauling freight in competition with the Erie Canal and its branches. But railroads had the advantages of speed and year-round operation (canals had to close for the winter freeze) and could be located almost anywhere, regardless of terrain and the availability of water. Where free competition existed, railroads gradually prevailed. The future belonged to the towns and cities along the path of the "iron horse," not to those that continued to depend exclusively on waterways.

The Expansion of Business

The rapid expansion of business activity in the 1820s and 1830s was in part a result of the growth in population and improvements in the means of transportation. It was also, however, the result of daring,

Racing on the Railroad

Peter Cooper, who in later years was best known as a philanthropist and as the founder of the Cooper Union in New York City, was also a successful iron manufacturer. Cooper designed and built the first steam-powered locomotive in America in 1830 for the Baltimore and Ohio railroad. On August 28 of that year, he raced his locomotive (the "Tom Thumb") against a horse-drawn railroad car. This sketch depicts the moment when Cooper's engine overtook the horse-car. (Museum of the City of New York)

imagination, and ruthlessness on the part of new generations of businessmen and their employees. Two industries, one old and one new, illustrated the capacities of American enterprise. One was the whaling industry, which was reaching its heyday in the 1830s. From New Bedford and other New England ports, bold skippers and their crews, having driven most of the whales from the Atlantic, voyaged far into the Pacific in their hazardous tracking of the source of spermaceti for candles, whale oil for lamps, and whalebone for corset stays and other uses. Another example of Yankee enterprise was the ice industry. For years, Northeastern farmers had harvested winter ice from ponds and stored it for the summer; but the large-scale transportation and sale of ice as a commodity began in the 1830s. The New England ice harvest then found a ready market in Northern cities, on Southern plantations, and halfway around the world in India, where it was carried in fast-sailing ships; a voyage was considered highly successful if no more than half the cargo melted on the way.

Retail distribution of goods, whether of foreign or domestic origin, remained somewhat haphazard by the standards of later times; but it was becoming more systematic than it had ever been before. Stores specializing in groceries, dry goods, hardware, and other lines appeared in the larger cities. Smaller towns and villages depended on the general store. Storekeepers did much of their business by barter, taking country eggs and other produce in exchange for such things as pins and needles, sugar, and coffee. Many customers, living remote from any store, welcomed the occasional visits of peddlers, who came on foot or by horse.

The organization of business was undergoing a gradual change. Most businesses continued to be operated by individuals or partnerships operating on a limited scale. The dominating figures were the great merchant capitalists, who controlled much of the big business of the time. They owned their own ships. They organized certain industries on the putting-out system: providing materials to individual craftsmen, directing the work, and selling the finished product.

In larger enterprises, however, the individual merchant capitalist was giving way before the advance of the corporation. Corporations had the advantage of combining the resources of a large number of shareholders, and they began to develop particularly rapidly in the 1830s, when certain legal obstacles to their formation were removed. In the past, a corporation had had to obtain a charter, which at first could be granted only by a special act of the state legislature. By the 1830s, however, states were beginning to pass general incorporation laws. No longer did each corporation need to obtain specific legislative approval. A group could now secure a charter merely by paying a fee. Moreover, the laws began to grant the privilege of limited liability. This meant that individual stockholders risked losing the value of their own investment if a corporation should fail, but they were not liable (as they had been in the past) for the corporation's larger losses.

Corporations made possible the accumulation of larger and larger amounts of capital for manufacturing enterprises as well as for banks, turnpikes, and railroad companies. Some of this capital came from the profits of wealthy merchants who turned from shipping to newer ventures. Some came from the savings of people of only moderate means. Some came from tax collections, since state governments often bought shares in turnpike, canal, and railroad companies. A considerable part was supplied by foreign, especially English, investors.

But these sources provided too little capital to meet the demands of the ambitious schemes of some businesses, and they relied on an expansion of credit—some of it by dangerously unstable means. Credit mechanisms remained highly underdeveloped in the early nineteenth century. The government alone was permitted to issue currency, but it issued no paper—only gold and silver coins—and the amount of official currency in circulation was thus too small to support the demand for credit. Under pressure from corporate promoters, many banks issued large quantities of bank notes to provide capital for expanding business ventures. The notes rested on a bank's promise to redeem them in gold and silver on demand; but many institutions issued notes far in excess of their own reserves. As a result, bank failures were frequent and bank deposits often insecure.

The Rise of the Factory

All of these changes—increasing population, improved transportation, and the expansion of business activity—contributed to perhaps the most profound economic development in mid-nineteenth-century America: the rise of factory manufacturing. Although industry experienced its most spectacular surge of antebellum growth in the 1810s, it was in the 1820s and 1830s that the factory system established itself as an integral part of the national economy.

Before the War of 1812, most of what manufacturing there was in the United States took place within households or in small, individually operated workshops. Most goods were produced by hand; most were sold in local markets. Gradually, however, improved technology and increased opportunities for commerce stimulated the beginnings of a fundamental change. It came first in the New England textile industry. There, even before the war and the Embargo, some farsighted entrepreneurs were beginning to make use of the region's extensive waterpower and of the new machines (some imported from England, some developed at home) to bring textile operations together under a single roof. This factory system, as it was to be called, spread rapidly in the 1820s. Spinning and weaving in the home remained for a time the principal means of producing cloth, but factories were beginning to make serious inroads into the old process of production.

In the shoe industry as well, mass production through the specialization of tasks was expanding and was by the 1830s becoming an important force in the industry. Most of the work in shoe factories continued to be done by hand, but manufacturing in the newer establishments was increasingly divided among men and women who, in a careful division of labor, specialized in one or another of the various tasks involved in production. Private cobblers continued to produce shoes for individual customers; and the artisanal workshops, where groups of shoemakers worked under a single roof but did not divide up the tasks, remained the largest source of shoe manufacturing. But the future of the industry was more clearly suggested by factories producing large numbers of identical shoes in ungraded sizes and without distinction as to rights and lefts. As with textiles, the new shoe factories emerged first in eastern Massachusetts.

By the 1830s, factory production was spreading from textiles and shoes into other industries as well; and manufacturing was moving beyond Massachusetts and New England to become an important force throughout the American Northeast.

From the beginning, American industry relied heavily on technology for its growth. Because labor was scarce in the United States, at least in comparison to other industrializing countries, there was great incentive for entrepreneurs to improve the efficiency of their productive enterprises by introducing new labor-saving devices. Machine technology advanced more rapidly in the United States in the mid-nineteenth century than in any other country in the world.

Change was so rapid, in fact, that some manufacturers built their new machinery out of wood; by the time the wood wore out, they reasoned, improved technology would have made the machine obsolete. By the end of the 1830s, so advanced had American technology—particularly in textile manufacturing—become that industrialists in Britain and Europe were beginning to travel to the United States to learn new techniques, instead of the other way around.

Men and Women at Work

However advanced their technology, manufacturers still relied above all on a supply of labor. In later years, much of that supply would come from great waves of immigration from abroad. In the 1820s and 1830s, however, labor had to come primarily from the native population. Recruitment was not an easy task. Ninety percent of the American people still lived and worked on farms. City residents, although increasing in number, were relatively few, and the potential workers among them even fewer. Many urban laborers were skilled artisans who owned and managed their own shops as small businessmen; they were not likely to flock to factory jobs. The available unskilled workers were not numerous enough to form a reservoir from which the new industries could draw.

What did produce the beginnings of an industrial labor supply was the transformation of American agriculture in the nineteenth century. The opening of vast, fertile new farmlands in the Midwest, the improvement of transportation systems, the development of new farm machinery—all combined to increase food production dramatically. No longer did each region have to feed itself entirely from its own farms; it could import food from other regions. Thus in the Northeast, and especially in New England, where poor land had always placed harsh limits on farm productivity, the agricultural economy began slowly to decline, freeing up rural people to work in the factories.

Two systems of recruitment emerged to bring this new labor supply to the expanding textile mills. One, common in the mid-Atlantic states and in parts of New England, brought whole families from the farm to the mill. Parents and children, even some who were no more than four or five years old, worked together tending the looms. The second system, common in Massachusetts, enlisted young women— mostly the daughters of farmers—in their

Specialized Manufacturing Towns: Lowell, Massachusetts, 1832

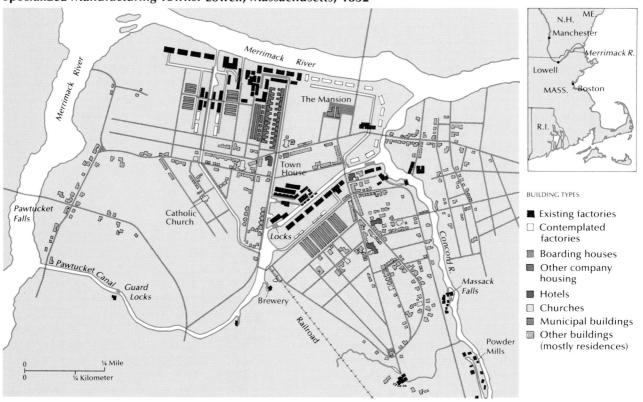

BUILDING TYPES

- ■ Existing factories
- □ Contemplated factories
- ▨ Boarding houses
- ▦ Other company housing
- ■ Hotels
- ▢ Churches
- ▦ Municipal buildings
- ▨ Other buildings (mostly residences)

late teens and early twenties. It was known as the Lowell or Waltham system, after the factory towns in which it first emerged. Many of these women worked for several years in the factories, saved their wages, and returned home to marry and raise children. Others married men they met in the factories or in town and remained part of the industrial world. But even they often stopped working in the mills and took up domestic roles instead.

Labor conditions in these early years of the factory system were significantly better than those in English industry, better too than they would ultimately become in the United States. The employment of young children entailed undeniable hardships. But the evils were fewer than in Europe, since working children in American factories usually remained under the supervision of their parents. In England, by contrast, asylum authorities often hired out orphans to factory employers who showed little solicitude for their welfare.

Even more distinctive from the European labor system was the lot of working women in the mills in Lowell and factory towns like it. In England, as a parliamentary investigation revealed, woman workers were employed in coal mines in unimaginably wretched conditions. Some had to crawl on their hands and knees, naked and filthy, through cramped, narrow tunnels, pulling heavy coal carts behind them. It was little wonder, then, that English visitors to America considered the Lowell mills a female paradise by contrast. The Lowell workers lived in clean boardinghouses and dormitories maintained for them by the factory owners. They were well fed and carefully supervised. Because many New Englanders considered the employment of women to be vaguely immoral, the factory owners placed great emphasis on maintaining an upright environment for their employees, enforcing strict curfews and requiring regular church attendance. Factory girls suspected of immoral conduct were quickly dismissed. Wages for the Lowell workers, modest as they were, were nevertheless generous by the standards of the time. The women even found time to write and publish a monthly magazine, the *Lowell Offering*.

Women at Work, 1834
This engraving shows women at work in a New England textile mill, processing cotton into cloth. It illustrates the growing importance of heavy machinery in the textile industry, which made factory labor increasingly noisy, hot, and dangerous. (The Granger Collection)

Yet even these relatively well-treated workers often found the transition from farm life to factory work difficult, even traumatic. Uprooted from everything familiar, forced to live among strangers in a regimented environment, many women suffered from loneliness and disorientation. Still more had difficulty adjusting to the nature of factory work—to the repetition of fixed tasks hour after hour, day after day. That the women had to labor from sunrise to sunset was not in itself always a burden; many of them had worked similarly long days on the farm. But that they now had to spend those days performing tedious, unvarying chores, and that their schedules did not change from week to week or season to season, made the adjustment to factory work a painful one.

Female mill workers suffered, moreover, from a special disadvantage. They were, like male workers, generally products of a farm economy in decline and were forced to find nonagricultural work by which to support themselves and contribute to the maintenance of their families. But unlike men, they had very few options. They had no access to construction work; they could not become sailors or dockworkers; it was considered unthinkable for women to travel the country alone, as many men did, in search of opportunities. Work in the mills was in many cases virtually the only option available to them.

The relative powerlessness of women workers was one reason for the gradual breakdown of the paternalistic factory system. In the competitive textile market as it developed in the 1830s and 1840s—a market prey to the booms and busts that afflicted the American economy as a whole—manufacturers found it difficult to maintain the high living standards and reasonably attractive working conditions with which they had begun. Wages declined; the hours of work lengthened; the conditions of the boardinghouses deteriorated as the buildings decayed and overcrowding increased. In 1834, mill girls in Lowell organized a union—the Factory Girls Association—which staged a strike to protest a 25 percent wage cut. Two years later, the association struck again—against a rent increase in the boardinghouses. Both strikes failed, and a recession in 1837 virtually destroyed the organization. Eight years later, led by the militant Sarah Bagley, the Lowell women created the Female Labor Reform Association and began agitating for a ten-hour day and for improvements in conditions in the mills. The new association not only made demands of management; it turned to state government and asked for legislative investigation of conditions in the mills. By then, however, the character of the factory work force was changing again. Textile manufacturers were turning to a less contentious labor supply: immigrants. The mill girls were gradually moving into other occupations: teaching, domestic service, or marriage.

The increasing supply of immigrant workers was a boon to manufacturers and other entrepreneurs. At last they had access to a cheap and plentiful source of labor. These new workers, because of their growing numbers and because of unfamiliarity with their new country, had even less leverage than the women they at times displaced; and thus they often encountered far worse working conditions. Construction gangs, made up increasingly of Irish immigrants, performed the heavy, unskilled work on turnpikes, canals, and railroads under often intolerable conditions. Because most of these workers had no marketable skills and because of native prejudice against them, they received wages so low—and received them so intermittently, since the work was seasonal and uncertain—that they generally did not earn enough to support their families in even minimal comfort. Many of them lived in flimsy, unhealthy shanties.

By the 1840s, the Irish workers (men and women) predominated in the New England textile mills as well; and their arrival accelerated the deterioration of working conditions there. There was far less social pressure on owners to provide a decent environment for Irish workers than for native women. Employers began paying piece rates rather than a daily wage and employed other devices to speed up production and exploit the labor force more efficiently. By the mid-1840s, the town of Lowell—once a model for foreign visitors of enlightened industrial development—had become a squalid slum. Similarly miserable working-class neighborhoods were emerging in other Northeastern cities.

It was not only the unskilled workers who suffered from the transition to the modern factory system. It was the skilled artisans whose trades the factories were displacing. Threatened with obsolescence, faced with increasing competition from industrial capitalists, craftsmen began early in the nineteenth century to form organizations—the first American labor unions—to protect their endangered positions. As early as the 1790s, printers and cordwainers took the lead. The cordwainers—makers of high-quality boots and shoes—suffered from the competition of merchant capitalists. These artisans sensed a loss of security and status with the development of mass-production methods, and so did members of other skilled trades: carpenters, joiners, masons, plasterers, hatters, and shipbuilders. In such cities as Philadelphia, Baltimore, Boston, and New York, the skilled workers of each craft formed societies for mutual aid. During the 1820s and 1830s, the craft societies began to combine on a city-wide basis and set up central organizations known as trade unions. Since, with the widening of the market, workers of one city competed with those at a distance, the next step was to federate the trade unions or to establish craft unions of national scope. In 1834,

delegates from six cities founded the National Trades' Union; and in 1836, the printers and the cordwainers set up their own national craft unions.

This early labor movement soon collapsed. Labor leaders struggled against the handicap of hostile laws and hostile courts. By the common law, as interpreted by judges in the industrial states, a combination among workers was viewed as, in itself, an illegal conspiracy. But adverse court decisions did not alone halt the rising unions. The death blow came from the Panic of 1837 and the ensuing depression.

Sectionalism and Nationalism

For a brief but alarming moment, the increasing differences between the nation's two leading sections threatened in 1819 and 1820 to damage the unity of the United States. But once a sectional crisis was averted with the Missouri Compromise, the forces of nationalism continued to assert themselves; and the federal government began to assume the role of promoter of economic growth.

The Missouri Compromise

When Missouri applied for admission to the Union as a state in 1819, slavery was already well established there. The French and Spanish inhabitants of the Louisiana Territory (including what became Missouri) had owned slaves, and in the Louisiana Purchase treaty of 1803 the American government promised to protect the property of the inhabitants. By 1819, approximately 60,000 people resided in Missouri Territory, of whom about 10,000 were slaves.

In that year, while Missouri's application for statehood was being considered in Congress, Representative James Tallmadge, Jr., of New York, proposed an amendment that would prohibit the further introduction of slaves into Missouri and provide for the gradual emancipation of those already there. The Tallmadge Amendment provoked a controversy that was to rage for the next two years.

Although the issue arose suddenly, the sectional jealousies that produced it had long been accumulating. Already the concept of a balance of power between the Northern and Southern states was well developed. From the beginning, partly by chance and partly by design, new states had come into the Union more or less in pairs, one from the North, another from the South. With the admission of Alabama in 1819, the Union contained an equal number of free and slave states, eleven of each. If Missouri were to be admitted as a slave state, not only would the existing sectional balance be upset but a precedent would be established that in the future would increase the political power of the South still further.

This concern about the balance of power among the states was not yet accompanied by a widespread or fervent opposition to slavery itself. There were groups, in both the North and the South, opposed to slavery on moral grounds and committed to its destruction. On the eve of the dispute over Missouri, for example, the Manumission Society of New York was busy with attempts to rescue runaway slaves; and Quakers were conducting a campaign to strengthen the laws against the African slave trade and to protect free blacks from kidnappers who sold them into slavery. But most Northern opponents of slavery were affluent philanthropists and reformers associated with the Federalist party; and for many of them, humanitarian concerns were secondary to political ones.

The Missouri controversy provided the opportunity for which Federalist leaders such as Rufus King had long waited: the opportunity to attempt a revival and reinvigoration of their party. By appealing to the Northern people on the issue of slavery extension, the Federalists hoped to win many of the Northern Republicans away from their allegiance to the Republican party's Southern leadership. In New York, the De Witt Clinton faction of the Republicans, who had joined with the Federalists in opposition to the War of 1812 and were outspoken in their hostility to "Virginia influence" and "Southern rule," were more than willing to cooperate with the Federalists again. The cry against slavery in Missouri, Thomas Jefferson wrote, was "a mere party trick." He explained: "King is ready to risk the union for any chance of restoring his party to power and wriggling himself to the head of it, nor is Clinton without his hopes nor scrupulous as to the means of fulfilling them."

The Missouri question was soon complicated by the application of Maine for admission as a state. Massachusetts had earlier consented to the separation of this northern part of the commonwealth, but only on the condition that Maine be granted statehood before March 4, 1820. The Speaker of the House, Henry Clay, now informed Northerners that if they refused to consent to Missouri's becoming a slave state, Southerners would deny the application of Maine. Despite the warning, the Northern majority

in the House continued to insist on the principle of the Tallmadge Amendment; but in the Senate, a few Northerners sided with the Southerners and prevented its passage.

The Maine question, however, ultimately produced a way out of the impasse. The Senate finally agreed to combine the Maine and Missouri proposals into a single bill. Maine would be admitted as a free state, Missouri as a slave state. Then, to make the package more acceptable to the House, Senator Jesse B. Thomas of Illinois proposed an amendment prohibiting slavery in all the rest of the Louisiana Purchase territory north of the southern boundary of Missouri (latitude 36° 30′). The Senate adopted the Thomas Amendment, and Speaker Clay, with great difficulty, guided the amended Maine-Missouri bill through the House.

Nationalists in both North and South hailed the Missouri Compromise as a happy resolution of a danger to the Union. Others, however, were less optimistic. Thomas Jefferson, for example, saw in the controversy a "speck on our horizon" which might ultimately "burst on us as a tornado." And he added, "The line of division lately marked out between the different portions of our confederacy is such as will never, I fear, be obliterated." (That was one reason why Jefferson, in his last years, devoted so much attention to the construction of the University of Virginia—an institution that would, he hoped, confirm Southern students in the values of their own region and protect them against the taint of "anti-Missourianism" that he believed pervaded the Northern universities.) The Missouri Compromise revealed, in short, a strong undercurrent of sectionalism that competed with—although at the moment failed to derail—the powerful tides of nationalism.

Marshall and the Court

John Marshall served as chief justice of the United States for almost thirty-five years, from 1801 to 1835. He was a man of practical and penetrating mind, of persuasive and winning personality, and of strong will; and he dominated the Court as no one else before or since. During his years as chief justice, Republican presidents filled vacancies with Republican justices, one after another; and yet Marshall continued to carry a majority with him in most of the Court's decisions. The members of the Court boarded together, without their families, during the winter months when the Court was in session, and

The Missouri Compromise, 1820

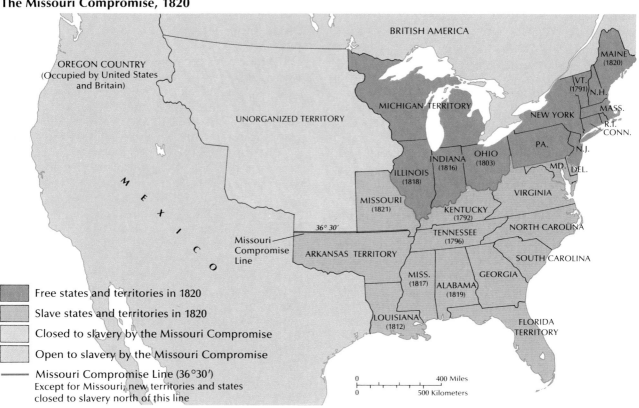

Free states and territories in 1820

Slave states and territories in 1820

Closed to slavery by the Missouri Compromise

Open to slavery by the Missouri Compromise

——— Missouri Compromise Line (36°30′)
Except for Missouri, new territories and states closed to slavery north of this line

Marshall had abundant opportunity to influence his younger associates.

But Marshall's achievements went beyond the narrow one of influencing his colleagues. He effectively molded the development of the Constitution itself. The net result of the hundreds of opinions delivered by the Marshall Court was to strengthen the judicial branch at the expense of the other two branches of the government; increase the power of the United States and lessen that of the states themselves; and advance the interests of the propertied classes, especially those engaged in commerce.

No state, the Constitution says, shall pass any law "impairing the obligation of contracts." The first Supreme Court case involving this provision was that of *Fletcher* v. *Peck* (1810), which arose out of the notorious Yazoo land frauds (see p. 206). The Court had to decide whether the Georgia legislature of 1796 could rightfully repeal the act of the previous legislature granting lands under shady circumstances to the Yazoo Land Companies. In the unanimous decision, Marshall held that a land grant was a contract

and therefore, regardless of any corruption involved, the repeal was invalid. This was the first time the Supreme Court had voided a state law on the ground that it conflicted with a provision of the United States Constitution, although the Court had previously declared state laws unconstitutional because they were inconsistent with federal laws or treaties.

Dartmouth College v. *Woodward* (1819) expanded further the meaning of the contract clause. The case had originated in a quarrel between the trustees and the president of the college, and it became a major political issue in New Hampshire when the Republicans championed the president and the Federalists took the side of the trustees. Having gained control of the state government, the Republicans undertook to revise Dartmouth's charter (granted by King George III in 1769) so as to convert the private college into a state university. When the case came before the Supreme Court in Washington, Daniel Webster, a Dartmouth graduate, represented the trustees in opposing the charter revision. The Court, he reminded the judges, had decided in *Fletcher* v. *Peck* that "a *grant* is a con-

John Marshall

Marshall became Chief Justice of the United States Supreme Court in 1801 after establishing himself as one of the leaders of the Federalist party. He served as Chief Justice for thirty-five years, longer than anyone else in American history. And despite the frequent opposition of a series of Republican presidents, he used his position to make the judiciary a vigorous instrument for asserting and strengthening American nationalism. (Boston Athenaeum)

tract." The Dartmouth charter, he went on, "is embraced within the very terms of that decision," since "a grant of corporate powers and privileges is as much a *contract* as a grant of land." Then, according to legend, he brought tears to the eyes of the justices with an irrelevant peroration that concluded: "It is, sir, as I have said, a small college. And yet there are those who love it." A year later, the Court gave its decision in

favor of Webster and the trustees. The ruling had a significant bearing on the development of business corporations. It proclaimed that corporation charters were contracts and that contracts were inviolable; this doctrine placed important restrictions on the ability of state governments to control corporations.

The *Dartmouth College* case raised another important constitutional question as well. Did the Supreme Court have the power to override the decisions of state courts? The Judiciary Act of 1789 and the *Dartmouth College* decision itself both seemed to have established that the Court did have that right. But some advocates of states' rights, notably in the South, continued to argue otherwise. In *Cohens* v. *Virginia* (1821), Marshall provided a ringing reaffirmation of the constitutionality of federal review of state court decisions. The states no longer were sovereign in all respects, he wrote, since they had given up part of their sovereignty in ratifying the Constitution. The state courts, he insisted, must submit to federal jurisdiction; otherwise the government would be prostrated "at the feet of every state in the Union."

Meanwhile, in *McCulloch* v. *Maryland* (1819), Marshall had confirmed the "implied powers" of Congress by upholding the constitutionality of the Bank of the United States. The Bank, with headquarters in Philadelphia and branches in various cities throughout the country, had become so unpopular in the South and the West that several of the states tried to drive the branches out of business by outright prohibition or by prohibitory taxes. Maryland, for example, laid a heavy tax on the Baltimore branch of the Bank. This case presented two constitutional questions to the Supreme Court: Could Congress charter a bank? And if so, could one of the states thus tax it? As one of the Bank's attorneys, Webster first repeated the arguments used originally by Hamilton to prove that the establishment of such an institution came within the "necessary and proper" clause. Then, to dispose of the tax issue, Webster added an ingenious argument of his own. The power to tax, he said, involved a "power to destroy," and if the states could tax the Bank at all, they could tax it to death. Since the Bank with its branches was an agency of the federal government, the power to tax it was the power to destroy the United States itself. Marshall adopted Webster's words in deciding for the Bank.

The case of *Gibbons* v. *Ogden* (1824) raised the question of the powers of Congress, as against the powers of the states, in regulating interstate commerce. The state of New York had granted Robert Fulton and Robert Livingston's steamboat company the exclusive right to carry passengers on the Hudson River to New York City. From this monopoly, Aaron Ogden obtained the business of navigation across the river between New York and New Jersey. Thomas Gibbons, with a license granted under an act of Congress, went into competition with Ogden, who brought suit against him and was sustained by the New York courts. When Gibbons appealed to the Supreme Court, the justices faced the twofold question whether "commerce" included navigation and whether Congress alone or Congress and the states together could regulate interstate commerce. Marshall replied that "commerce" was a broad term embracing navigation as well as the buying and selling of goods. Although he did not say that the states had no authority whatever regarding interstate commerce, he asserted that the power of Congress to regulate such commerce was "complete in itself" and might be "exercised to its utmost extent." He concluded that the state-granted monopoly was void.

The decision, the last of Marshall's great pronouncements, was the first conspicuous one in which the Marshall Court appeared to be on the popular side. Most people, then as always, hated monopolies, and he had declared this particular monopoly unconstitutional. But the lasting significance of *Gibbons* v. *Ogden* was that it freed internal transportation from restraints by the states and thus prepared the way for the unfettered economic development of the nation by private capitalism.

More immediately, however, the decision had the effect of helping to head off a movement that was under way to weaken the Supreme Court. For some time, such Virginia Republicans as Thomas Jefferson, Spencer Roane, and John Taylor had argued against the views of their fellow Virginian John Marshall. In *Construction Construed and Constitutions Vindicated,* published in 1820, Taylor argued that Marshall and his colleagues were not merely interpreting but were actually changing the nature of the Constitution, which should properly be changed only by the amending process. In Congress some critics of the Court, mostly from the South and the West, proposed various means of curbing what they called judicial tyranny. A Kentucky senator suggested making the Senate, not the Court, the agency to decide the constitutionality of state laws and to settle interstate disputes. Other senators and congressmen introduced bills to increase the membership of the Court (from seven to ten) and to require more than a mere majority to declare a state law unconstitutional.

Still others argued for "codification," that is, for making legislative statutes the basis of the law, rather than the common-law precedents that judges used. Such a reform, codifiers argued, would limit the power of the judiciary and prevent "judge-made" law. The Court reformers did not succeed, however, in passing any of their various panaceas; and after the *Gibbons* v. *Ogden* decision, the hostility to the judicial branch of the government gradually died down.

The decisions of the Marshall Court had a profound cumulative influence on the future development both of American government and of the American economy. They established the primacy of the federal government over the states in exercising control over the economy. They opened the way for an increased federal role in promoting economic growth. And they created or affirmed protection for corporations and other private economic institutions from local government interference, hence facilitating the growth of the new industrial capitalist economy. They were, in short, highly nationalistic decisions, designed to promote the growth of a strong, unified, and economically developed United States.

The Court and the Tribes

The nationalist inclinations of the Marshall Court were visible as well in a series of decisions concerning the legal status of Indian tribes within the United States. But these decisions not only affirmed the supremacy of the United States; they carved out a distinctive position for Native Americans within the constitutional structure.

The first of the crucial Indian decisions was in the case of *Johnson* v. *McIntosh* (1823). Leaders of the Illinois and Pinakeshaw tribes had sold parcels of their land to a group of white settlers (including Johnson), but had later signed a treaty with the federal government ceding to the United States territory that included those same parcels. The government proceeded to grant homestead rights to new white settlers (among them McIntosh) on the land claimed by Johnson. The Court was asked to decide which claim had precedence. Marshall's ruling, not surprisingly, favored the United States. But in explaining it, he laid out the beginnings of a definition of the place of Indians within the nation. The tribes had a basic right to their tribal lands, he said, that preceded all other American law. Individual American citizens could not buy or take land from the tribes; only the federal government could do that.

Eight years later, in *Cherokee Nation* v. *Georgia,* the Marshall Court refused to hear a case filed by the Cherokee Nation against a Georgia law abolishing their tribal legislature and courts. The Cherokee argued that because the tribe was a "foreign nation," the Supreme Court (which had constitutional responsibility for mediating disputes between the states and foreign nations) had jurisdiction. Marshall disagreed. The tribes were not foreign nations, he said. They did, however, have a special status within the nation. "The conditions of the Indians in relation to the United States is perhaps unlike that of any two people in existence," he wrote. "Their relation to the United States resembles that of a ward to his guardian." This was the origin of what became known as the "trust relationship," by which the United States claimed broad powers over the tribes but accepted substantial responsibility for protecting their welfare.

Most important was the Court's 1832 decision in *Worcester* v. *Georgia.* The Georgia state government had passed a law requiring any U.S. citizen desiring to enter Cherokee territory to obtain permission from the governor. Two missionaries (one of them named Worcester) sued, claiming the state was encroaching on the federal government's constitutionally mandated role to regulate trade with the tribes. Marshall invalidated the Georgia law, another important step in consolidating federal authority over the states. In doing so, he defined further the nature of the Indian nations. The tribes, he explained, were sovereign entities in much the same way Georgia was a sovereign entity, "distinct political communities, having territorial boundaries within which their authority is exclusive." In defending the power of the federal government, he was also affirming, indeed expanding, the constitutional nation of tribal authority.

The Marshall decisions, therefore, did what the Constitution itself had not done: They defined a place for Indian tribes within the American political system. The tribes had basic property rights. They were sovereign entities not subject to the authority of state governments. But the federal government, like a "guardian" to its "ward," had ultimate authority over tribal affairs—even if that authority was, according to the Court, limited by the government's obligation to protect Indian welfare. These provisions were not usually enough to defend Indians from the steady westward march of white civilization. But they were the basis of what legal protections they have had.

The Latin American Revolution

Just as the Supreme Court was asserting American nationalism in the shaping of the country's economic life, so the Monroe administration was expressing nationalism in the shaping of foreign policy. As in earlier and later years, the central concern of the United States was its position in relation to Europe. But in defining that position, Americans were forced in the 1820s to develop a policy toward Latin America, which was suddenly winning its independence.

To most citizens of the United States, South and Central America had long seemed to constitute a "dark continent." After the War of 1812, however, they suddenly emerged into the light, and Americans looking southward beheld a gigantic spectacle: the Spanish Empire struggling in its death throes, a whole continent in revolt, new nations in the making with a future no one could foresee.

Already a profitable trade had developed between the ports of the United States and those of the Rio de la Plata (Argentina), Chile, and above all Cuba. Americans exported flour and other staples and received in return sugar, gold, and silver. Great Britain remained the principal trading nation in Latin America, but American commerce was growing steadily. Many believed that trade would increase much faster once the United States established regular diplomatic and commercial relations with the countries in revolt.

In 1815, the United States proclaimed its neutrality in the wars between Spain and its rebellious colonies. This neutrality was in itself advantageous to the rebels, since it implied a partial recognition of their status as nations. It meant, for example, that their warships would be treated as bona-fide belligerent vessels, not as pirate ships. Moreover, even though the neutrality law was revised and strengthened in 1817 and 1818, it still permitted the revolutionists to obtain unarmed ships and supplies from the United States. In short, the United States was not a strict and impartial neutral but a nonbelligerent whose policy, though cautious, was intended to help the insurgents and actually did.

Secretary of State John Quincy Adams and President James Monroe hesitated at first to take the risky step of recognition unless Great Britain would agree to do so at the same time. In 1818 and 1819, the United States made two bids for British cooperation, and both were rejected. Finally, the nationalist impulses so strong in the United States of the 1820s prevailed. In 1822, President Monroe decided to proceed alone. He informed Congress that five nations—La Plata, Chile, Peru, Colombia, and Mexico—were ready for recognition, and he requested an appropriation to send ministers to them. The United States would be the first country formally to recognize the new governments, in defiance of the rest of the world.

The Monroe Doctrine

In 1823, Monroe stood forth as an even bolder champion of America against Europe and an even more forthright champion of American nationalism. Presenting to Congress his annual message on the state of the Union, he announced a policy that would ultimately be known (beginning some thirty years later) as the "Monroe Doctrine." One part of this policy had to do with the role of Europe in America. "The American continents," Monroe declared, ". . . are henceforth not to be considered as subjects for future colonization by any European powers." Furthermore, "we should consider any attempt on their part to extend their system to any portion of this hemisphere as dangerous to our peace and safety." And the United States would consider any "interposition" against the sovereignty of existing American nations as an unfriendly act. A second aspect of the pronouncement had to do with the role of the United States in Europe. "Our policy in regard to Europe," said Monroe, ". . . is not to interfere in the internal concerns of any of its powers."

How did the president happen to make these statements at the time he did? What specific dangers, if any, did he have in mind? Against what powers in particular was his warning directed? To answer these questions, it is useful to consider first the relations of the United States with the European powers as of 1823, and then the process by which the Monroe administration reached its decision to announce the new "doctrine."

After Napoleon's defeat, the powers of Europe combined in a "concert" to uphold the "legitimacy" of established governments and to prevent the overthrow of existing regimes from within or without. When Great Britain withdrew, the concert became a quadruple alliance, with Russia and France the strongest of its four members. In 1823, after assisting in the suppression of other revolts in Europe, the four allies authorized France to intervene in Spain to restore the Bourbon dynasty that revolutionists had over-

James Monroe

This portrait of the fifth president of the United States, by Rembrandt Peale, was painted in the White House during Monroe's presidency. Peale was best known for his idealized portraits of George Washington, painted after Washington's death. (James Monroe Museum and Memorial Library)

thrown. Some observers in England and the Americas wondered whether the allies next would back France in an attempt to retake by force the lost Spanish Empire in America. In fact, such concerns were almost certainly groundless. France was still a relatively weak power, not yet recovered from the long and exhausting Napoleonic Wars. It did, to be sure, try to promote the establishment of friendly kingdoms in Latin America by means of intrigue, but it dared not challenge British sea power with an expedition to subvert the new governments by force.

In the minds of most Americans, and certainly in the mind of their secretary of state, Great Britain seemed an even more serious threat to American interests. Adams was much concerned about supposed

British designs on Cuba. Like Jefferson and others before him, Adams feared the transfer of Cuba from a weak power such as Spain, its present ruler, to a strong power such as Great Britain. He thought Cuba eventually should belong to the United States; for the "Pearl of the Antilles" had great economic and strategic value and, because of its location, was virtually a part of the American coastline. Adams did not desire to seize the island; he wanted only to keep it in Spanish hands until, by a kind of political gravitation, it should fall naturally to the United States. Despite his worries over the supposed British threat to Cuba, he and other American leaders were pleased to see the rift between Great Britain and the concert of Europe. He was willing to cooperate with Britain, but only to the extent that its policies and his own coincided.

Those policies did not always coincide, however, as the British demonstrated when they rejected the American overtures for joint recognition of Latin American independence in 1818 and 1819. The Americans demonstrated the same thing by their reaction to a British proposal for a joint statement in 1823. That summer, the British secretary for foreign affairs, George Canning, suggested to the American minister in London, Richard Rush, that Great Britain and the United States should combine in announcing to the world their opposition to any European movement against Latin America. But Canning's refusal to join the United States in recognizing the Latin American nations forestalled agreement. And in the fall, after receiving assurances from France that it had no plans to intervene militarily in Latin America, the British abandoned the proposal altogether.

Even before Canning changed his mind about cooperation with the United States, Monroe and Adams were developing grave reservations about a joint pronouncement. Adams, in particular, argued that the American government should act alone instead of following along like a "cock-boat in the wake of a British man-of-war." Canning's loss of interest, therefore, only strengthened an already growing inclination within the administration to make its own pronouncement.

Although Canning's overture led to Monroe's announcement, the message was directed against all the powers of Europe, including Great Britain, which seemed at least as likely as Russia to undertake further colonizing ventures in America. Monroe and Adams hoped the message would rally the people of Latin America to look to their own security. They also hoped it would stir the people of the United States. America was mired in a business depression, divided by sectional politics, and apathetic toward the rather lackluster administration of Monroe. In the rumors of European aggression against the Western Hemisphere lay a chance for the president to arouse and unite the people with an appeal to national pride. The Monroe Doctrine was, then, in one sense a culmination of the growing spirit of unity and nationalism that had been emerging in the United States for over a decade. But it was also an expression of concern about the forces that were already gathering to threaten that spirit.

The Revival of Opposition

For a time during the "era of good feelings," it seemed that the dream of the founders of the republic—of a nation free of party strife—had been realized. After 1816, the Federalist party offered no presidential candidate. Soon it ceased to exist as a national political force. Presidential politics was now conducted wholly within the Republican party, which considered itself not a party at all but an organization representing the whole of the population.

Yet the policies of the federal government during and after the War of 1812, and particularly the nationalizing policies of the 1820s, continued to spark opposition. At first, criticism remained contained within the existing one-party structure. But by the late 1820s, partisan divisions were emerging once again. In some respects, the division mirrored the schism that had produced the first party system in the 1790s. The Republicans had in many ways come to resemble the early Federalist regimes in their promotion of economic growth and centralization. And the opposition, like the opposition in the 1790s, stood opposed to the federal government's expanding role in the economy. There was, however, a crucial difference. At the beginning of the century, the opponents of centralization had also often been opponents of economic growth. Now, in the 1820s, the controversy involved not whether but how the nation should continue to expand.

The "Corrupt Bargain"

From 1796 to 1816, presidential candidates had been nominated by caucuses of the members of each of the two parties in Congress. In 1820, when the Federalists declined to oppose his candidacy, Monroe ran unopposed as the Republican nominee without the necessity of a caucus nomination. If the caucus system had prevailed in 1824, the nominee of the Republicans in Congress would have run unopposed again. But it did not prevail. Several men aspired to the presidency, and they and their followers were unwilling to let a small group of congressmen and senators determine which one of them was to win the prize.

In 1824, therefore, "King Caucus" was overthrown. Fewer than a third of the Republicans in Congress even bothered to attend the gathering. The caucus did go through the motions of nominating a candidate: William H. Crawford of Georgia, the secretary of the treasury. Other candidates received nominations from state legislatures and endorsements from irregular mass meetings throughout the country.

John Quincy Adams, secretary of state for two terms, had made a distinguished record in the conduct of foreign affairs, and he held the office that had become the traditional stepping stone to the presidency. But as he himself ruefully realized, he was a man of cold and forbidding manners, not a candidate with strong popular appeal. Crawford, in contrast, was an impressive giant of a man who had the backing not only of the congressional caucus but also of the extreme states' rights faction of the Republican party. In midcampaign, however, he was stricken by a paralyzing illness.

Challenging the two cabinet contenders was Henry Clay, the Speaker of the House. The tall, black-haired, genial Kentuckian had a personality that gained him a devoted following. He also stood for a definite and coherent program, which he called the "American System." His plan, attractive to citizens just recovering from a business depression, was to create a great home market for factory and farm producers by raising the tariff to stimulate industry, maintaining the national bank to facilitate credit and exchange, and spending federal funds on internal improvements to provide transportation between the cities and the farms.

Andrew Jackson, the fourth major candidate, offered no such clear-cut program. Although Jackson had served briefly as a representative in Congress and was a member of the United States Senate, he had no significant legislative record. Nevertheless, he had the advantages of a military hero's reputation and a campaign shrewdly managed by the Tennessee politician friends who had put him forward as a candidate. To some of his contemporaries he seemed a crude, hot-tempered frontiersman and Indian fighter. Actually, although he had arisen from a humble background as an orphan in the Carolinas, he had become a well-to-do planter who lived in an elegant mansion ("The Hermitage") near Nashville.

Once the returns were counted, there was no doubt that the next vice president was to be John C. Calhoun, of South Carolina, who ran on both the Adams and the Jackson tickets. But there was considerable doubt as to who the next president would be. Jackson received a plurality, although not a majority, of the popular vote. In the electoral college too he came out ahead, with 99 votes to Adams's 84, Crawford's 41, and Clay's 37. Again, however, he lacked a majority. So, in accordance with the Twelfth Amendment, the final decision was left to the House of Representatives, which was to choose among the three candidates with the highest electoral vote. Clay was out of the running.

But while Clay could not be elected president in 1824, he was in a strong position to determine who would be. As Speaker, he had indirect influence throughout the House of Representatives. And as a candidate for the presidency whose electors had won in three states—Kentucky, Ohio, and Missouri—he was in a position to influence those state delegations directly.

Before Congress made its decision, supporters of Jackson, Crawford, and Adams approached Clay on behalf of their respective candidates. Jackson's followers insisted that Jackson, with his popular and electoral pluralities, was really the people's choice and that Congress had no rightful alternative but to ratify the people's will. But Jackson was Clay's most dangerous rival for the political affections of the West; and Jackson, moreover, had demonstrated no support for Clay's nationalistic legislative program. Crawford was out of the question, for he was now a paralytic, incapable of discharging the duties of the presidency. Adams was no friend of Clay and had clashed with him repeatedly when both were peace delegates at Ghent and afterward. But alone among the candidates, Adams was an ardent nationalist and a likely supporter of the American System. Thus Clay finally gave his support to Adams, and the House elected him.

The Jacksonians were angry enough at this, but they became far angrier when the new president announced that Clay was to be his secretary of state. The State Department was the well-established route to the presidency, and Adams thus appeared to be naming Clay as his own successor. To the Jacksonians, it seemed clear that Clay and Adams must have agreed to make each other president—Adams now, Clay next; and they claimed to be horrified by this "corrupt bargain." Very likely there had been some sort of understanding; and though there was nothing corrupt, or even unusual, about it, it proved to be politically costly for both Adams and Clay.

Soon after Adams's inauguration as president, Jackson resigned from the Senate to accept a renomination for the presidency from the Tennessee legislature and to begin a three-year campaign for election in 1828. Politics now overshadowed all else. Throughout his term in the White House, Adams and his policies were to be thoroughly frustrated by the political bitterness arising from the "corrupt bargain."

John Quincy Adams
This photograph of the former president was taken shortly before his death in 1848—almost twenty years after he had left the White House—when he was serving as a congressman from Massachusetts. During his years as president, he was—as he had been throughout his life—an intensely disciplined and hard-working man. He rose at four in the morning and made a long entry in his diary for the previous day. He wrote so much that his right hand at times became paralyzed with writer's cramp, so he taught himself to write with his left hand as well. (Brown Brothers)

The Second President Adams

In his inaugural address and in his first message to Congress, John Quincy Adams gave voice to his own nationalistic vision of the powers and duties of the federal government. He recommended "laws promoting the improvement of agriculture, commerce, and manufactures, the cultivation of the mechanic and of the elegant arts, the advancement of literature, and the progress of the sciences, ornamental and profound." He had no chance of getting an appropriation from Congress for most of these goals. All he actually did get was a few million dollars to improve rivers and harbors and to extend the National Road westward from Wheeling. Still, this was more than Congress had appropriated for internal improvements under all his predecessors together.

Even in the field of diplomacy, where Adams had more experience than any other president before or since, he failed in the major efforts of his administration. Yielding to Secretary of State Clay's wish for cooperation with the Latin American governments, Adams appointed two delegates to attend an international conference that the Venezuelan liberator, Simón Bolivar, had called to meet at Panama in 1826. Objections arose in Congress for two reasons. One was that Southerners opposed the idea of white Americans mingling in Panama with black delegates from Haiti, a country whose independence the United States refused to recognize. The other reason for obstruction was simply politics—the determination of Jacksonians to discredit the administration. They charged that Adams aimed to sacrifice American interests and involve the nation in an entangling alliance. While the Jacksonians filibustered, Congress delayed the Panama mission so long that by the time it was finally approved it was too late. One of the American delegates died on the way to the conference; the other arrived after it was over. Adams had hoped to offset British influence, which prevailed in Latin America, by having the United States play an active role at the conference. Those hopes were dashed.

Adams was also the loser in a contest with the state of Georgia, which wished to remove the remaining Creek and Cherokee Indians from the state so as to gain additional soil for cotton planters. The United States government, in a 1791 treaty, had guaranteed the Creeks possession of the land they then occupied. But in 1825, white Georgians had extracted a new treaty from William McIntosh, the son of a white father and an Indian mother who had become the leader of one faction in the tribe. McIntosh had long been an advocate of Indian cooperation with the United States. He was, for example, one of the Creeks who had fought with Andrew Jackson against his fellow tribesmen in the War of 1812, and he had long called on the Creeks to cede their tribal lands in Georgia and Alabama to the United States and move West. The 1825 treaty was a culmination of his efforts.

Adams believed the new treaty had no legal force. He was almost certainly correct. McIntosh did not represent the wishes of the tribe; indeed, the tribal council voted to execute him shortly after the signing of the agreement. Adams refused to enforce the treaty, thereby setting up a direct conflict between the president and the leaders of the state. The governor of Georgia defied the president and went ahead with plans for Indian removal. The conflict was finally resolved in 1827, when the Creeks succumbed

to pressure and agreed to still another treaty, in which they again yielded their land, thus undercutting Adams's position. The affair was memorable in one sense: Adams became one of the few major American public figures firmly to oppose the continuing displacement of the Indians. At the time, however, it was as a political embarrassment to him.

Even more damaging to the administration was its support for a new tariff on imported goods in 1828. This measure originated in the demands of Massachusetts and Rhode Island woolen manufacturers, who complained that the British were dumping woolens on the American market at prices with which the domestic mill owners could not compete. The New Englanders were frustrated at first by Southern opposition in Congress, but eventually they combined with the middle and Western states to create political pressures that could not be resisted.

But the 1828 bill, the result of these efforts, contained provisions attractive to the West that antagonized its original New England supporters. It established high duties not only on woolens, as the New Englanders had wanted, but also on a number of other items, such as flax, hemp, iron, lead, molasses, and raw wool, some of which the West produced and for which they wanted protection from foreign rivals. That distressed New England manufacturers; the benefits of protecting their manufactured goods from foreign competition now had to be weighed against the prospects of having to pay more for raw materials. Indeed, a story arose that the bill had taken its shape from a Jacksonian plot to embarrass and discredit Adams. The bill related to "manufactures of no sort or kind but the manufacture of a president of the United States," John Randolph said. The bill would present Adams with a dilemma, for he would lose friends whether he signed or vetoed it. To sign the bill would lose him support in both the South and the Northeast. To veto it would lose him support from the farmers and manufacturers of the West.

When Congress considered the bill item by item, Southerners voted against proposals to reduce the tariff rates, in the hope that some of its outrageous duties would so antagonize New Englanders that they would help defeat it. But when it came to a final test, Daniel Webster voted for it despite its duties on raw materials, and he carried with him enough New England votes to enable the bill to pass. Adams signed it. The tactics of the Southerners had backfired, and they were left cursing the bill as the "tariff of abominations."

Choctaws in Louisiana
The Choctaws were among the many Mississippi Valley tribes to experience forced relocation at the hands of the United States in the 1830s. Originally located in central Mississippi, the tribe marched through Louisiana and Arkansas and into Indian Territory (now Oklahoma) beginning in 1830. Some members of the tribe remained behind at various points along the way, living alongside the white community and adopting many of its ways. The French artist Alfred Boisseau painted this scene of a group of them walking along a bayou in Louisiana in 1845. (New Orleans Museum of Art)

Jackson Triumphant

By 1828, the schism within the Republican party was complete. Once again, as in 1800, two parties offered candidates in the presidential election. On one side stood the supporters of John Quincy Adams, who called themselves the National Republicans. They supported the economic nationalism of the preceding years. Opposing them were the followers of Andrew Jackson, who took the name Democratic Republicans. They argued for a dispersal of public authority, an assault on privilege, and a widening of opportunity. Adams attracted the support of most of the remaining Federalists (among whose number he had once counted himself); Jackson appealed to a broad coalition that stood opposed to the "economic" aristocracy.

Issues seemed to count for little in the campaign of 1828. There was much talk of the "corrupt bargain" and frequent rhetorical references to the "tariff of abominations." But while Adams's position on the tariff was a matter of record (he had signed the bill), nobody knew where Jackson stood. Again, as in 1824, personalities became a more important factor than policies. Indeed, the tone of the campaign was such as to suggest that two criminals were running for the highest office in the land.

The Jacksonians charged that Adams as president had been guilty of gross waste and extravagance and had used public funds to buy gambling devices (a chess set and a billiard table) for the White House. But that was not the worst of Adams's alleged crimes. While Adams had been minister to Russia, the Jacksonians falsely claimed, he had tried to procure a beautiful American girl for the sinful pleasures of the czar.

Adams's supporters directed even worse accusa-

SIGNIFICANT EVENTS

1817–1825   Erie Canal constructed (p. 256)

1819   Supreme Court hears *Dartmouth College* and *McCulloch* v. *Maryland* (pp. 266, 267)

1820   Missouri Compromise enacted (p. 265)

Monroe reelected president without opposition (p. 272)

1823   Monroe Doctrine proclaimed (p. 270)

1824   John Quincy Adams wins disputed presidential election (p. 272)

Supreme Court rules in *Gibbons* v. *Ogden* (p. 267)

1826   Thomas Jefferson and John Adams die on July 4 (p. 251)

1827   Creek Indians cede lands to Georgia (p. 274)

1828   "Tariff of abominations" passed (p. 274)

Andrew Jackson elected president (p. 276)

1830   Baltimore & Ohio becomes first American railroad to begin operations (p. 259)

1830s   Major immigration from southern (Catholic) Ireland begins (p. 254)

Factory system spreads in textile and shoe industries (p. 261)

First craft unions founded (p. 264)

1832   Cholera plague (p. 252)

1834   Woman workers at Lowell mills stage strike (p. 263)

1845   Female Labor Reform Association established at Lowell (p. 263)

tions at Jackson. He was, they claimed in speeches, handbills, and pamphlets, a murderer and an adulterer. A "coffin handbill" listed, within coffin-shaped outlines, the names of militiamen whom Jackson was said to have shot in cold blood during the War of 1812. (The men had been deserters who were executed after due sentence by a court-martial.) It was also rumored that Jackson had knowingly lived in sin with the wife of another man. Actually, he had married the woman, his beloved Rachel, at a time when the pair apparently believed her first husband had divorced her.

Jackson's victory was decisive, if sectional. He won 56 percent of the popular vote and an electoral majority of 178 votes to Adams's 83. But the Jacksonians made few inroads into the National Republican strongholds of the Northeast. Adams swept virtually all of New England, and he showed significant strength in the mid-Atlantic region. Nevertheless, the Jacksonians considered their victory complete, and they hailed it as an event as important as the victory of Jefferson in 1800. Once again, the forces of privilege had been ejected from Washington. Once again, a champion of democracy would occupy the White House and restore liberty to the society and the economy. America had entered, many claimed, the "era of the common man." And Andrew Jackson, the people's champion, departed for Washington determined to transform the federal government.

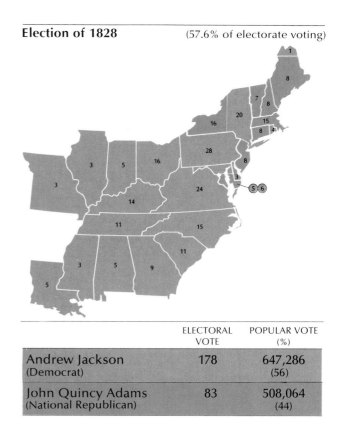

Election of 1828   (57.6% of electorate voting)

	ELECTORAL VOTE	POPULAR VOTE (%)
Andrew Jackson (Democrat)	178	647,286 (56)
John Quincy Adams (National Republican)	83	508,064 (44)

SUGGESTED READINGS

The Economic Revolution: General Histories. See Suggested Readings for Chapter 7. W. Elliot Brownlee, *Dynamics of Ascent* (1974); Stuart Bruchey, *The Growth of the Modern American Economy* (1975).

Transportation. George R. Taylor, *The Transportation Revolution* (1951); Nathan Miller, *The Enterprise of a Free People* (1962); R. E. Shaw, *Erie Water West* (1966); Harry N. Scheiber, *Ohio Canal Era* (1969); Albert Fishlow, *American Railroads and the Transformation of the Ante-Bellum Economy* (1965).

Business and Technology. E. P. Douglas, *The Coming of Age of American Business* (1971); Thomas C. Cochran and William Miller, *The Age of Enterprise* (1942); Thomas C. Cochran, *Business in American Life* (1972); Richard D. Brown, *Modernization: The Transformation of American Life, 1600–1865* (1976); Diane Lindstrom, *Economic Development in the Philadelphia Region, 1810–1850* (1978); Merritt Roe Smith, *Harpers Ferry Armory and the New Technology* (1977); David J. Jeremy, *Transatlantic Industrial Revolution: The Diffusion of Textile Technologies Between Britain and America, 1780–1830* (1981); H. J. Habbakuk, *American and British Technology in the Nineteenth Century* (1962); Nathan Rosenberg, *Technology and American Economic Growth* (1972).

Factories and the Working Class. Arthur H. Cole, *The American Wool Manufacture,* 2 vols. (1926); Caroline Ware, *The Early New England Cotton Manufacture* (1931); Barbara M. Tucker, *Samuel Slater and the Origins of the American Textile Industry, 1790–1860* (1985); Thomas Dublin, *Women at Work* (1979); Alan Dawley, *Class and Community* (1977); Alice Kessler-Harris, *Out to Work: A History of Wage-Earning Women in the United States* (1982); Mary Blewett, *Men, Women, and Work* (1988); Christine Stansell, *City of Women: Sex and Class in New York, 1789–1860* (1986); Bruce Laurie, *Working People of Philadelphia* (1980); Susan E. Hirsch, *Roots of the American Working Class: The Industrialization of Crafts in Newark, 1800–1860* (1978); Steven J. Ross, *Workers on the Edge: Work, Leisure, and Politics in Industrializing Cincinnati, 1788–1890* (1985); Sean Wilentz,
Chants Democratic: New York City and the Rise of the American Working Class, 1788–1850 (1984).

Political Affairs. George Dangerfield: *The Awakening of American Nationalism* (1965) and *The Era of Good Feelings* (1952); Glover Moore, *The Missouri Compromise* (1953); Paul C. Nagle, *One Nation Indivisible: The Union in American Thought, 1815–1828* (1965); Glyndon Van Deusen, *The Life of Henry Clay* (1937); Harry Ammon, *James Monroe: The Quest for National Identity* (1971); Charles M. Wiltse, *John C. Calhoun: American Nationalist* (1944); Wesley Frank Craven, *The Legend of the Founding Fathers* (1956); Shaw Livermore, *The Twilight of Federalism* (1962); Samuel F. Bemis, *John Quincy Adams and the Union* (1956); Robert V. Remini, *The Election of Andrew Jackson* (1963); Norman K. Risjord, *The Old Republicans: Southern Conservatism in the Age of Jefferson* (1965).

The Courts. Albert J. Beveridge, *The Life of John Marshall,* 4 vols. (1916–1919); Leonard Baker, *John Marshall: A Life in Law* (1974); Francis N. Stites, *John Marshall: Defender of the Constitution* (1981); Richard E. Ellis, *The Jeffersonian Crisis: Courts and Politics in the Young Republic* (1971); R. Kent Newmyer, *The Supreme Court Under Marshall and Taney* (1968); Charles G. Haines, *The Role of the Supreme Court in American Government and Politics, 1789–1835* (1970); D. O. Dewey, *Marshall Versus Jefferson: The Political Background of* Marbury v. Madison (1970); Alexander M. Bickel, *Justice Joseph Story and the Rise of the Supreme Court* (1971); James McClellan, *Joseph Story and the American Constitution* (1971).

The Monroe Doctrine. Arthur P. Whitaker, *The United States and the Independence of Latin America* (1941); Dexter Perkins, *The Monroe Doctrine* (1927) and *Hands Off: A History of the Monroe Doctrine* (1941); Ernest R. May, *The Making of the Monroe Doctrine* (1975); Samuel F. Bemis, *John Quincy Adams and the Foundations of American Foreign Policy* (1940); Bradford Perkins, *Castlereagh and Adams: England and the United States, 1812–1823* (1964); Frank Thistlethwaite, *The Anglo-American Connection in the Early Nineteenth Century* (1959).

Detail from *The Verdict of the People* (1855), by George Caleb Bingham
This scene of an election day gathering is peopled almost entirely by white men. Women and blacks
had no vote, but among white males political rights expanded substantially in the 1830s and 1840s.
(*Boatmen's National Bank, St. Louis*)

CHAPTER 10

❦❦❦

Democracy in America

❦❦❦

When the French aristocrat Alexis de Tocqueville visited the United States in 1831, one feature of American society struck him as "fundamental": the "general equality of condition among the people." Unlike older societies, in which privilege and wealth were passed from generation to generation within an entrenched upper class, America had no rigid distinctions of rank. "The government of democracy," he wrote in his classic study *Democracy in America* (1835–1840), "brings the notion of political rights to the level of the humblest citizens, just as the dissemination of wealth brings the notion of property within the reach of all the members of the community."

Yet Tocqueville also wondered how long the fluidity of American society could survive in the face of the growth of manufacturing and the rise of the factory system. Industrialism, he feared, would create a large class of dependent workers and a small group of new aristocrats. For, as he explained it, "at the very moment at which the science of manufactures lowers the class of workmen, it raises the class of masters."

Americans, too, pondered the future of their democracy in these years of economic and territorial expansion. Some feared that the nation's rapid growth would produce social chaos and insisted that the country's first priority must be to establish order and a clear system of authority. Others argued that the greatest danger facing the nation was privilege and that society's goal should be to eliminate the favored status of powerful elites and make opportunity more widely available. The advocates of this latter vision seized control of the federal government in 1829 with the inauguration of Andrew Jackson.

Jackson and his followers were not egalitarians. They did nothing to challenge the existence of slavery; they supervised one of the most vicious assaults on American Indians in the nation's history; and they accepted the necessity of economic inequality and social gradation. Jackson himself was a frontier aristocrat, and most of those who served him were themselves people of wealth and standing. They were not, however, usually aristocrats by birth. They had, they believed, risen to prominence on the basis of their own talents and energies; and their goal in public life was to ensure that others like themselves would have the opportunity to do the same.

The "democratization" of government over which Andrew Jackson presided was permeated with the rhetoric of equality and aroused the excitement of working people. To the national leaders who promoted that democratization, however, its purpose was less to aid the farmers and laborers who were Jackson's greatest champions than to challenge the power of Eastern elites for the sake of the rising entrepreneurs of the South and the West.

The Advent of Mass Politics

On March 4, 1829, an unprecedented throng—thousands of Americans from all regions of the country, including farmers, laborers, and others of humble

Jackson's Inaugural Levee, 1829

Even in the relatively rustic days of the early republic, presidential inaugurations often took place amid almost monarchical grandeur. But when Andrew Jackson entered office in 1829, having won election as the champion of democratic simplicity, he avoided formal trappings and threw the White House open to the public. Frontier settlers and common people of all kinds had flocked to Washington to witness the inauguration of their hero, and the result was an invasion of the White House by an enormous and—in the view of some conservative observers—cretinous horde. Jackson's critics described the inaugural levee as the triumph of "King Mob." (Library of Congress)

rank—crowded before the Capitol in Washington, D.C., to witness the inauguration of Andrew Jackson. After the ceremonies, the boisterous crowd poured down Pennsylvania Avenue, following their hero to the White House. And there, at a public reception open to all, they filled the state rooms to overflowing, trampling one another, soiling the carpets, ruining the elegantly upholstered sofas and chairs in their eagerness to shake the new president's hand. "It was a proud day for the people," wrote Amos Kendall, one of Jackson's closest political associates. "General Jackson is *their own* President." To other observers, however, the scene was less appealing. Justice of the Supreme Court Joseph Story, a friend and colleague of John Marshall, looked on the inaugural levee, as it was called, and remarked with disgust: "The reign of King 'Mob' seems triumphant."

In a sense, both Kendall and Story were correct. For if what some have called the "age of Jackson" did not mark the elevation of all Americans to prosperity and equality, it did mark a transformation of American politics that extended power widely to new groups. Formerly the preserve of a relatively small group of property owners, politics now became the province of virtually all the nation's white male citizens (few Jacksonians were willing to contemplate the participation of women or blacks in the electoral process). In a political sense at least, the era well earned its title "the age of the common man."

President of the Common Man

Unlike Thomas Jefferson, Jackson was no democratic philosopher. Nevertheless, in his own plain, straightforward way, he too expressed a distinct theory of democracy. Government, he insisted, should offer "equal protection and equal benefits" to all the people. It should provide special favors to no one. Once in office, he set about to dismantle those institutions and policies that he believed worked to protect special privileges and restrict opportunity.

His first target was the personnel procedures of the federal government. For a generation, ever since the downfall of the Federalists in 1800, there had been no change of party in the national administration. Officeholders in Washington, therefore, had stayed on year after year, many of them growing gray and some of them growing corrupt. "Office is considered as a species of property," Jackson told Congress in a bitter denunciation of the entrenched "class" of permanent officeholders, "and government rather as a means of promoting individual interests than as an instrument created solely for the service of the people." Official duties, he believed, could be made "so plain and simple that men of intelligence may readily qualify themselves for their performance." Offices belonged to the people, he argued, not to the entrenched officeholders. Or, as one of his henchmen, William L. Marcy of New York, more cynically put it, "To the victors belong the spoils."

In actual practice, Jackson did not do nearly as much as his partisan critics claimed to remove existing government employees and replace them with appointees of his own. During the entire eight years of his presidency he removed a total of no more than one-fifth of the federal officeholders; and many of them he removed for cause, such as misuse of government funds. Proportionally, Jackson dismissed no more of the jobholders than Jefferson had done. Nevertheless, by embracing the philosophy of the "spoils system," a system already well entrenched in a number of state governments, the Jackson administration fixed it firmly upon American politics.

Eventually the Jacksonians adopted another instrument of democratic politics: the national nominating convention. Jackson supporters had long resented the process by which presidential candidates were selected by congressional caucus, a process that they believed was designed to restrict access to the office to those favored by entrenched elites. Jackson himself had achieved office without resort to the caucus; and in 1832, to renominate him for the presidency, his followers staged the first national convention of a major party. Although in later generations the party convention would be seen by many as the source of corruption and political exclusivity, in the 1830s it was viewed as a great triumph of the people. Power in the party would, through the convention, arise directly from the populace, circumventing established political institutions.

Despite the rhetoric, however, the acceptance of the spoils system and the creation of the political convention exposed not only the extent but the limits of Jacksonian political democracy. Both served to limit the power of entrenched elites—permanent officeholders and the exclusive party caucus. Yet neither really transferred power to the common people. Appointments to office almost always went to prominent political allies of the president and his associates. Delegates to national conventions were less often common men than members of local party elites. Political opportunity within the party was expanding, but within limits.

The Expanding Electorate

In other ways, however, Jacksonian politics did indeed transfer power to the population at large. For it was in this era that a true mass electorate emerged. The expansion of the franchise began in Ohio and other new states of the West, which, on joining the Union, adopted constitutions that guaranteed all adult white males the right to vote and permitted all voters the right to hold public office. Older states, concerned about the loss of their population to the West, began slowly and haltingly to grant additional political rights to their people so as to encourage them to stay. Even before the War of 1812 a few of the Eastern states had permitted white men to vote whether or not they owned property or paid a tax. Eventually, all the states (although some of them not until after the Civil War) changed their constitutions in the direction of increased democracy.

Change provoked resistance, and at times the democratic trend fell short of the aims of the more radical reformers, as when Massachusetts held its constitutional convention in 1820. Reform-minded delegates complained that in the Massachusetts government the rich were better represented than the poor, both because of the restrictions on voting and officeholding and because of the peculiar system of property representation in the state senate. But Daniel Webster, one of the conservative delegates, opposed democratic changes on the grounds that "power *naturally* and *necessarily* follows property" and that "property as such should have its weight and influence in political arrangement." Webster and the rest of the conservatives could not prevent the reform of senate representation, nor could they prevent elimination of the property requirement for voting. But, to the dismay of the radicals, the new constitution required that every voter be a taxpayer and that the governor be the owner of considerable real estate.

More often, however, it was the forces of democratization that prevailed in the states. In the New York convention of 1821, for example, conservatives led by Chancellor James Kent insisted that a taxpaying requirement for suffrage was not enough and that, at least in the election of state senators, the property qualification should be retained. Kent argued that society "is an association for the protection of property as well as of life" and that "the individual who contributes only one cent to the common stock ought not to have the same power and influence in directing the property concerns of the partnership as he who contributes his thousands." But reformers, citing the Declaration of Independence, maintained that life, liberty, and the pursuit of happiness, not property, were the main concerns of society and government. The property qualification was abolished.

The wave of state reforms was generally peaceful, but in Rhode Island democratization efforts created considerable instability. The Rhode Island constitution in the 1830s was still the old colonial charter, little changed; and under its terms, more than half the adult males of the state were disqualified as voters. The conservative legislature, representing this restricted electorate, consistently blocked all efforts at reform. In 1840, the lawyer and activist Thomas L. Dorr and a group of his followers formed a "People's party," held a convention, drafted a new constitution, and submitted it to a popular vote. It was overwhelmingly approved. The existing legislature, however, refused to accept the Dorr constitution and submitted one of its own to the voters; it was narrowly voted down. The Dorrites, in the meantime, had begun to set up a new government, under their own constitution, with Dorr as governor; and so, in 1842, two governments were laying claims to legitimacy in Rhode Island. The old state government ꞏproclaimed that Dorr and his followers were rebels and began to imprison them. The Dorrites, in the meantime, made a brief and ineffectual effort to capture the state arsenal. The Dorr Rebellion, as it was known, quickly failed, and Dorr himself surrendered and was briefly imprisoned. But the episode helped spur the old guard finally to draft a new constitution, which greatly expanded the suffrage.

In the South, democratization moved more slowly. Reformers in several states criticized the overrepresentation of the tidewater areas and the underrepresentation of the back country in the legislatures. The Virginia constitutional convention, which met in 1829, granted some slight concessions to the western counties, but not enough to satisfy the resi-

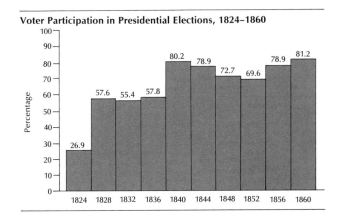

Voter Participation in Presidential Elections, 1824–1860

dents of the area. Elsewhere in the Southeast the planters and politicians of the older counties continued to dominate the state governments.

Other limitations on democratization survived as well. With few exceptions, free blacks could not vote anywhere in the South and hardly anywhere in the North. Pennsylvania at one time allowed black suffrage, but in 1838 it amended the state constitution to prohibit it. Women could vote in neither the North nor the South, regardless of the amount of property they might own. Everywhere the ballot was open, not secret, and often it was cast as a spoken vote rather than a written one. The lack of secrecy meant that voters could be, and often were, bribed or intimidated.

Despite the persisting limitations, however, the number of voters increased far more rapidly than did the population as a whole. Indeed, one of the most striking political trends of the early nineteenth century was the change in the method of choosing presidential electors and the dramatic increase in popular participation in the process. In 1800, the legislature had chosen the presidential electors in ten of the states, and the people in only six. By 1828, electors were chosen by popular vote in every state but South Carolina, which had no popular presidential elections until after the Civil War. In the presidential election of 1824, fewer than 27 percent of adult white males had voted. In the election of 1828, the figure rose to about 58 percent. In 1840, 80 percent of white men cast their ballots. The multiplication of voters was only in part the result of a widening of the electorate. It was in greater measure the result of a heightening of interest in politics and a strengthening of party organization.

The Legitimation of Party

Even at the peak of the first party system in 1800, virtually no one had been willing to accept the *idea* of a party system. There was wide agreement that parties were evils to be avoided, that the nation should strive for a broad consensus in which permanent factional lines would not exist. But in the 1820s and 1830s, those assumptions gave way to a new view: that permanent, institutionalized parties were a desirable part of the political process, that indeed they were essential to democracy.

Like so many other American political developments, the elevation of the idea of party occurred first at the state level, most prominently in New York. There a dissident political faction under the leadership of Martin Van Buren (known as the "Bucktails" or the "Albany Regency") began in the years after the War of 1812 to challenge the political oligarchy—led by the aristocratic governor, De Witt Clinton—that had dominated the state for years. In itself, the challenge was nothing new; factional rivalries occurred in virtually every state. What was new was the way in which Van Buren and his followers posed their challenge. Refuting the traditional view of a political party as undemocratic, they argued that only an institutionalized party, based in the populace at large, could ensure genuine democracy. The alternative was the sort of oligarchy that Clinton had created. In this new kind of party, ideological commitments would be less important than loyalty to the party itself. Preservation of the party as an institution—through the use of favors, rewards, and patronage—would be the principal goal of the leadership. Above all, for a party to survive, it must have a permanent opposition. Competing parties would give each political faction a sense of purpose and would force politicians to remain continually attuned to the will of the people. The opposing parties would check and balance each other in much the same way that the different branches of government checked and balanced one another.

By the late 1820s, this new idea of party was emerging in other states beyond New York—in Pennsylvania, for example, where the spoils system was introduced well before it was transplanted to the federal government. The election of Jackson in 1828, the result of a popular movement apparently removed from the usual political elites, seemed further to legitimize the idea of party. And finally, in the 1830s, a fully formed two-party system began to operate at the national level, with each party committed to its own existence as an institution and willing to accept the legitimacy of its opposition. "Parties of some sort must exist," said a New York newspaper. "'Tis in the nature and genius of our government."

"Our Federal Union"

True to the new concept of party, Andrew Jackson had won election on the basis of no clearly articulated program. His followers—who soon began to call themselves Democrats (no longer Democratic Republicans), thus giving a permanent name to what would become the nation's oldest political party—had interests so diverse that a statement of precise aims would have alienated many of them at the outset. Yet Jackson entered office with certain strong convictions about the purposes of government and about the nature of the presidency. He believed that the federal government should work on behalf of common people, eliminating the privileges of established elites. In general, that meant reducing the functions of government, since a concentration of power in Washington would, he believed, almost inevitably produce a restriction of opportunity to those favored few with political connections. But Jackson believed, too, in forceful presidential leadership. And although he spoke frequently of the importance of states' rights, he was strongly committed to the preservation of the Union. Thus at the same time that Jackson was contemplating an economic program to reduce the power of the national government, he was forced to assert the supremacy of the Union in the face of a potent challenge. For he had no sooner entered office than his own vice president—John C. Calhoun—began to assert a dangerous new constitutional theory: nullification.

Calhoun and Nullification

Calhoun was forty-six years old in 1828, a man with a distinguished past and what seemed to be a promising future. He had been a congressional leader during the War of 1812; he had served for eight years as head of the War Department (compiling a record as one of the few great secretaries of war); he had been vice president in John Quincy Adams's administration. And now, he was running for another term as vice president, this time with Andrew Jackson. Presumably he could look forward to the presidency itself.

But the tariff question confronted Calhoun with a dilemma. Once he had been a forthright protectionist, coming out strongly for the tariff of 1816. But since that time many South Carolinians had changed their minds on the subject. Carolina cotton planters were disturbed because their state's economy appeared to be stagnating. One reason was the ex-

Charleston, 1831

The little-known South Carolina artist S. Bernard painted this view of Charleston's East Battery in 1831. Then as now, residents and visitors liked to stroll along the battery and watch the activity in the city's busy harbor. But Charleston in the 1830s was a less important commercial center than it had been a few decades earlier. By then, overseas traders were increasingly avoiding Southern ports and doing more and more business in New York. (Yale University Art Gallery)

haustion of the South Carolina soil, which could not compete effectively with the newly opened fertile lands of the Southwest. But most Carolinians blamed their trouble on the "tariff of abominations" of 1828, which they argued raised the prices they had to pay for the manufactured goods they could not produce for themselves. Some exasperated Carolinians were ready to consider a drastic remedy—secession. This was a challenge Calhoun had to meet in order to maintain his leadership in the state and make a future for himself in national politics.

Quietly he worked out a theory to justify state resistance to the tariff law—action that would stop short of secession. Following lines laid down by Madison and Jefferson in their Virginia and Kentucky Resolutions of 1798–1799 Calhoun began with the assumption that sovereignty, the ultimate source of power, lay in the states, which were separate political communities. The Supreme Court was not competent to judge whether acts of Congress were constitutional, since the Court, like the Congress, was a creation of the states. If Congress enacted a law of doubtful constitutionality— say, a protective tariff— a state could "interpose" to frustrate the law. That is, the people of the state could hold a convention, which could declare the federal law null and void within the state. The law would remain inoperative until three-fourths of the whole number of states ratified an amendment to the Constitution specifically assigning Congress the power in question. The nullifying state would then submit to the will of the nation; or, if unwilling to do that, it could secede from the Union. The legislature of South Carolina published Calhoun's first statement of his theory in 1828, anonymously, in a document entitled *The South Carolina Exposition and Protest*. This paper condemned the "tariff of abominations" as unconstitutional, unfair, and unendurable—a law fit to be nullified.

Calhoun's real hope, however, was that the theory of nullification would never be put to the test, that it would simply pressure the federal government to respond to South Carolina's grievances. He hoped in particular that Jackson as president would persuade Congress to make drastic reductions in tariff rates.

But Calhoun did not, he soon discovered, have as much influence in the new administration as he had hoped. He had a powerful rival for Jackson's favor in Martin Van Buren.

The Rise of Van Buren

Van Buren was about the same age as Calhoun and equally ambitious. But he was very different in background and personality. Born of Dutch ancestry in the village of Kinderhook, near Albany, New York, he advanced himself through skillful maneuvering to the position of United States senator, a position he held from 1820 to 1828. He also made himself the party boss of his state by organizing and leading the Albany Regency, the Democratic machine of New York. He supported Crawford for president in 1824, but he afterward became one of the most ardent of Jacksonians, helping to carry his state for Jackson in 1828 while getting himself elected governor. By this time he had a reputation as a political wizard. Short and slight, with reddish-gold sideburns and a quiet manner, he was known by such nicknames as "the Sage of Kinderhook," "the Little Magician," and "the Red Fox." Never giving or taking offense, he was in temperament just the opposite of the choleric Jackson. But the two were soon to become the closest of friends. Van Buren promptly resigned the governorship and went to Washington in 1829 when Jackson called him to head the new cabinet as secretary of state.

Except for Van Buren, Jackson's cabinet contained no one of more than ordinary talent. It was assembled largely to represent and harmonize the sectional and factional interests within the party. Jackson relied instead on an unofficial circle of political allies who came to be known as the "Kitchen Cabinet." Noteworthy in this group were several newspaper editors, among them Isaac Hill, from New Hampshire, and Amos Kendall and Francis P. Blair, from Kentucky. But the most important of all was Van Buren, a member of both the official and the unofficial cabinets. Jackson and Van Buren grew closer still through a curious quarrel over a woman and etiquette, which helped drive a wedge between the president and Calhoun.

Peggy O'Neale was the attractive and vivacious daughter of a Washington tavern keeper with whom both Andrew Jackson and his friend John H. Eaton had taken lodgings while serving as senators from Tennessee. Peggy was married at a young age to a navy purser and was the mother of two children; but rumors began to circulate in Washington in the mid-

Martin Van Buren
As leader of the so-called Albany Regency in New York in the 1820s, Van Buren helped create one of the first modern party organizations in the United States. Later, as Andrew Jackson's secretary of state and (after 1832) vice president, he helped bring party politics to the national level. So it was perhaps ironic that in 1840, when he ran for reelection to the presidency, he should lose to William Henry Harrison, whose Whig party made effective use of many of the techniques of mass politics that Van Buren himself had pioneered.   (Library of Congress)

1820s that she and Senator Eaton had become "familiar." In 1828, Peggy's husband died. She and Eaton were soon married. Only weeks after the wedding, Jackson named his friend Eaton secretary of war and thus made the new Mrs. Eaton a cabinet wife. The rest of the administration wives, led by Mrs. Calhoun, refused to receive her. Jackson was furious. His own wife, Rachel, now dead, had been slandered by his political enemies. He was confident that Peggy Eaton too was an innocent victim of politics. He demanded that his secretaries and associates treat her with respect and accept her into their social world. Calhoun, however, bowed to his wife's adamant demands and refused, thus taking sides against the president. Van Buren, who was a widower, befriended the Eatons and thus ingratiated himself with Jackson.

By 1831, partly as a result of the repercussions of the Peggy Eaton affair, Jackson had settled on Van Buren as his choice to succeed him in the White House. Calhoun's dreams of the presidency had all but vanished.

The Webster-Hayne Debate

At the height of the Eaton affair, a great debate emerged on the nature of the Constitution that dramatically revealed the gulf between Jackson and Cal-

houn. The debate received its most dramatic and public expression in the United States Senate in January 1830. The controversy grew out of a seemingly routine Senate discussion of federal policy toward the public lands in the West. In the midst of the discussion, a senator from Connecticut suggested that all land sales and surveys be temporarily discontinued. Senator Thomas Hart Benton of Missouri, the Jacksonian leader in the Senate and a sturdy defender of the West, charged that the proposal to stop land sales was intended to keep New England workers from going West and would serve to choke off the growth and prosperity of the frontier.

Robert Y. Hayne, a young and eloquent senator from South Carolina, took up the argument after Benton. Hayne and other Southerners had no direct interest in the Western lands. But they hoped to win Western support for their drive to lower the tariff, and so they were willing to back the Westerners on

The Webster-Hayne Debate
This scene from the famous Webster-Hayne debate in 1830 shows Webster replying to South Carolina Senator Robert Hayne's defense of states' rights. Webster's speeches during the debate were read, admired, and often memorized and repeated throughout the North for years. This painting, by G. P. A. Healy, hangs today in Faneuil Hall in Boston, where Webster once spoke.   (Frick Art Reference Library)

this issue. Hayne suggested in his speech before the Senate that the South and the West were both victims of the tyranny of the Northeast, and he hinted that the two regions might well combine in self-defense against that tyranny.

Daniel Webster, now a senator from Massachusetts, had once been an advocate of states' rights and himself an opponent of tariffs—in the waning days of the Federalist party. But like Calhoun, he had changed his position with the changing interests of his section. The day after Hayne's speech, Webster took the floor. Ignoring Benton, he directed his remarks to Hayne and, through him, to Calhoun in the vice president's chair. He reviewed much of the history of the republic, with occasional disregard for historical facts, to prove that New England always had been the friend of the West. Referring to the tariff of 1816, he said that New England was not responsible for the protectionist policy but had accepted it after other sections had fixed it upon the nation. Then, changing the subject, he spoke gravely of disunionists and disunionism in South Carolina.

Webster was, in effect, challenging Hayne to a debate not on the original grounds of the public lands and the tariff but on the issue of states' rights versus national power. Hayne, coached by Calhoun, responded with a defense of the theory of nullification. Webster listened and then spent two full afternoons delivering his remarkable second reply to Hayne, a speech that Northerners quoted and revered for years to come. "I go for the Constitution as it is, and for the Union as it is," he proclaimed, in a description of the "true principles" of the Constitution. "It is, Sir, the people's Constitution, the people's government, made for the people, made by the people, and answerable to the people." He concluded with the ringing appeal: "Liberty *and* Union, now and for ever, one and inseparable!"

Calhoun's followers were sure that Hayne had the better of the argument. The important question at the moment, however, was what President Jackson thought. The answer soon became clear at the annual banquet in honor of Thomas Jefferson, whom the Democrats considered the founder of their party. As was customary at such affairs, the guests settled down after dinner to hear a series of toasts. The president, urged on by Van Buren, had arrived with a prepared toast, which he had written down, underscoring certain words. When his turn came to speak, he stood up and proclaimed: "Our *Federal* Union—*It must be preserved.*" While he spoke he looked sternly and directly at Calhoun. The diminutive Van Buren,

who stood on his chair to see better from the far end of the table, thought he saw Calhoun's hand shake and a trickle of wine run down the outside of his glass. Calhoun responded to the president's toast with his own: "The Union—next to our liberty most dear. May we always remember that it can only be preserved by distributing evenly the benefits and the burthens of the Union." Both in the Congress and in the executive branch, sharp lines had been drawn.

The Nullification Crisis

For more than two years, the sectional tensions aroused by the Webster-Hayne debate and the nullification doctrine continued without producing a direct confrontation between the federal government and the South. In 1832, however, the state of South Carolina precipitated a crisis. Having waited four years for Congress to repeal the "tariff of abominations," South Carolinians watched with anger as Congress enacted a new tariff that year which offered them virtually no relief. Some of the more militant South Carolinians were now ready for revolt. Had it not been for Calhoun, they might have attempted to withdraw the state from the Union. Having lost the confidence of Jackson, Calhoun was now an open advocate of nullification; and in the aftermath of the 1832 tariff, he persuaded extremists in South Carolina to adopt that doctrine—not secession—as their remedy. The question of whether to nullify the tariff act was the leading issue in the state elections of 1832, and the result was a ringing victory for the nullifiers (although opponents of nullification—the Unionists—constituted a sizable minority; a referendum question on the issue passed 23,000 to 17,000).

Without delay, the newly elected legislature called for the election of delegates to a state convention. And the convention, once assembled, voted to declare null and void the tariffs of 1828 and 1832 and to forbid the collection of duties within the state. The legislature then passed laws to enforce the ordinance and make preparations for military defense. The nullifiers needed strong leaders, they believed, to take command at home and to present the South Carolina case in Washington. They elected Hayne governor of the state; and they chose Calhoun to replace Hayne as senator. Calhoun resigned the vice presidency to defend his state's position in the Senate.

Jackson was outraged. Privately, he threatened to hang Calhoun. Publicly, he insisted that nullification was treason and that its adherents were traitors. Cooperating closely with the Unionists of South Carolina, he took steps to strengthen the federal forts in the state, ordering General Winfield Scott to Charleston with a warship and several revenue cutters.

When Congress convened early in 1833, the president asked for new and specific authority with which to handle the crisis. His followers introduced a "force bill" authorizing him to use the army and navy to see that acts of Congress were obeyed. Violence seemed a real possibility early in 1833, as Calhoun took his place in the Senate. He introduced a set of resolutions on the "constitutional compact" and then spoke out in opposition to the force bill.

Webster's reply to Calhoun on February 16, 1833, dealt directly with the constitutional issues at stake. The Constitution, Webster argued, was no mere compact among sovereign states. It was an "executed contract," an agreement to set up a permanent government, supreme within its allotted sphere and acting directly upon the people as a whole. Webster dismissed secession as a revolutionary but not a constitutional right, then denounced nullification as no right at all. The nullifiers, he said, rejected "the first great principle of all republican liberty; that is, that the majority must govern." They pretended to be concerned about minority rights, but they did not practice what they preached. "Look to South Carolina, at the present moment. How far are the rights of minorities there respected?" Obviously the nullificationist majority was proceeding with a "relentless disregard" for the rights of the Unionist minority— "a minority embracing, as the gentleman himself will admit, a large portion of the worth and respectability of the state."

Calhoun was in a predicament. Not a single state had come to South Carolina's support. It was itself divided, and it could not hope to prevail if a showdown with the federal government should come. If the nullifiers meekly yielded, however, Calhoun would be politically ruined. He was saved by the timely intervention of the "Great Pacificator," Henry Clay, newly elected to the Senate. Clay devised a compromise by which the tariff would be lowered year after year, until in 1842 it would reach approximately the same level as in 1816. The compromise and the force bill were passed on the same day, March 1, 1833. Webster consistently opposed any concessions to the nullifiers, but Jackson was satisfied. He signed the new tariff measure as well as the force bill.

In South Carolina, the convention reassembled and repealed its ordinance of nullification as applied to the tariffs of 1828 and 1832. But unwilling to allow Congress to have the last word, the convention adopted a new ordinance nullifying the force act. Both the force act itself and the nullification of it were, however, purely symbolic. The original tariff, toward which the force act was directed, had already been repealed. Calhoun and his followers claimed a victory for nullification, which had, they insisted, forced the revision of the tariff. But the episode taught Calhoun and his allies an important lesson: No state could assert and maintain its rights by independent action. Calhoun continued in the following years to talk of states' rights and nullification. But he devoted himself primarily to building up a sense of Southern solidarity so that when another trial should come, the whole section might be prepared to act as a unit in resisting federal authority.

Jackson and States' Rights

Despite his ringing defense of the authority of the federal government in the nullification crisis, Andrew Jackson was not an opponent of the rights of the states. On the contrary, some of his most important decisions as president reflected his view that, as he had declared in his inaugural address, none but "constitutional" undertakings should be pursued by the federal government. Thus throughout his administration, he frequently vetoed laws that he considered to exceed the powers originally granted to Congress by the states.

The Maysville Road Bill of 1830 prompted the most significant of Jackson's vetoes. The bill authorized the government to buy stock in a private company so as to provide a federal subsidy for the construction of a turnpike from Maysville to Lexington, within the state of Kentucky. The Maysville pike was a segment of a projected highway that was to form a great southwestern branch of the National Road. Nevertheless, since the pike itself was an intrastate and not an interstate project, Jackson doubted whether Congress constitutionally could give aid to it. Earlier (in 1822) President Monroe had declared in a veto message that the federal government should support only those improvements that were of general rather than local importance. Now, with Van Buren's assistance, Jackson prepared a veto message based on similar grounds. He also urged economy, denounced the selfish "scramble for appropriations," and stressed the desirability of paying off the national debt. Although Jackson also refused to sign other appropriation bills, he did not object to every proposal for federal spending to build roads or improve rivers and harbors. During his two terms such expenditures continued to mount, far exceeding even those of the John Quincy Adams administration.

The Maysville veto was not popular in the West, where better transportation was a never-ending demand. Others of Jackson's policies, however, met with wholehearted approval in both the South and the West—most prominently, his use of federal powers to remove all Indian tribes from the areas of white settlement.

The Removal of the Indians

There had never been any doubt about Andrew Jackson's attitude toward the Indian tribes that continued to live in the Eastern states and territories of the United States. He wanted them to move West, beyond the Mississippi, out of the way of expanding white settlement. Jackson's antipathy toward the Indians had a special intensity because of his own earlier experiences leading military campaigns against tribes along the Southern border. But in most respects, his views were little different from those of most other white Americans.

In the eighteenth century, many whites had considered the Indians "noble savages," peoples without real civilization but with an inherent dignity that made civilization possible among them. By the first decades of the nineteenth century, this vaguely philanthropic attitude (the attitude of, among others, Thomas Jefferson) was giving away to a new and more hostile one, particularly among the whites in the Western states and territories whom Jackson came to represent. Whites were coming to view Native Americans simply as "savages," not only uncivilized but uncivilizable. That was one reason for the commitment to Indian removal: the belief that whites should not be expected to live in close proximity to the "savage" Indians; that Indian cultures and societies were unworthy of respect.

White Westerners favored removal as well, because they feared that continued contact between the expanding white settlements and the Indians would produce endless conflict and violence. Most of all, however, they favored Indian removal because of their own insatiable desire for land. The tribes possessed valuable acreage in the path of expanding white settlement. Whites wanted that territory.

The federal government had already taken substantial strides toward removing the Indians from the East by the time Jackson entered the White House. But substantial tribal enclaves remained. In the Old Northwest, the long process of expelling the woodland Indians culminated in a last battle in 1831–1832, between an alliance of Sauk (or Sac) and Fox Indians under the fabled and now aged warrior Black Hawk and white settlers in Illinois. An earlier treaty had ceded tribal lands in Illinois to the United States; but Black Hawk and his followers refused to recognize the legality of the agreement, which had been signed by a rival tribal faction. Hungry and resentful, a thousand of them crossed the river and reoccupied vacant lands in Illinois. White settlers in the region feared that the resettlement was the beginning of a substantial invasion, and they assembled the Illinois state militia and federal troops to repel the "invaders." The Black Hawk War, as it became known, was notable chiefly for the viciousness of the white military efforts. White leaders in western Illinois vowed to exterminate the "bandit collection of Indians" and attacked them even when Black Hawk attempted to

Black Hawk and Whirling Thunder
After his defeat by white settlers in Illinois in 1832, the famed Sauk warrior Black Hawk and his son, Whirling Thunder, were captured and sent on a tour by Andrew Jackson, displayed to the public as trophies of war. They showed such dignity through the ordeal that the public quickly began to sympathize with them. This portrait, by John Wesley Jarvis, was painted on the tour's final stop, in New York City. Black Hawk wears the European-style suit, while Whirling Thunder wears native costume to emphasize his commitment to his tribal roots. Soon thereafter, Black Hawk returned to his tribe, wrote a celebrated autobiography, and died in 1838. (The Bettmann Archive)

surrender. The Sauks and Foxes, defeated and starving, retreated across the Mississippi into Iowa. White troops (and some bands of Sioux whom they encouraged to join the chase) pursued them as they fled and slaughtered most of them. Black Hawk himself was captured and sent on a tour of the East, where Andrew Jackson was one of many curious whites who arranged to meet him. (Abraham Lincoln served as a captain of the militia, but saw no action, in the Black Hawk War; Jefferson Davis was a lieutenant in the regular army.)

More troubling to the government in the 1830s were the remaining Indian tribes of the South. In western Georgia, Alabama, Mississippi, and Florida lived what were known as the "Five Civilized Tribes"—the Cherokee, Creek, Seminole, Chickasaw, and Choctaw—most of whom had established settled agricultural societies with successful economies. The Cherokees in Georgia had formed a particularly stable and sophisticated culture, with its own written language and a formal constitution (adopted in 1827) which created an independent Cherokee Nation. They were, therefore, even more closely tied to their lands than many of the more nomadic tribes to the north. Even some whites argued that the Cherokees, unlike other tribes, should be allowed to retain their eastern lands, since they had become such a "civilized" society and had, under pressure from missionaries and government agents, given up many of their traditional ways. Cherokee men had once been chiefly hunters and had left farming mainly to women. Now the men gave up most of their hunting and (like white men) took over the farming themselves; Cherokee women, also like their white counterparts, restricted themselves largely to domestic tasks.

The federal government, to which the Constitution had delegated the power to negotiate with the Indian tribes, had worked steadily through the first decades of the nineteenth century to negotiate treaties with the Southern Indians that would remove them to the West and open their lands for white settlement. But the negotiating process often did not proceed fast enough to satisfy the region's whites. The state of Georgia's independent effort to dislodge the Creek Indians, over the objection of President Adams, was one example of this impatience. (See p. 274.) That same impatience became evident early in Jackson's administration, when the legislatures in Georgia, Alabama, and Mississippi began extending their laws over the tribes remaining in their states. They received assistance in these efforts from Congress, which in 1830 passed the Removal Act (with Jackson's approval) which appropriated funds for negotiating treaties with the Southern tribes and relocating them to the West. The president quickly despatched federal officials to negotiate nearly a hundred new treaties with the remaining tribes. Thus, the Southern tribes faced a combination of pressures from both the state and federal governments. Most tribes were too weak to resist white pressures, and they ceded their lands in return for only token payments. Some, however, resisted.

In Georgia, the Cherokees tried to stop the white encroachments by appealing to the Supreme Court. The Court's decision in *Cherokee Nation* v. *Georgia* and *Worcester* v. *Georgia* (see p. 269) seemed at least partially to vindicate the tribe. But Jackson's longtime hostility toward the Indians and longtime commitment to their removal had little sympathy for the Cherokees and little patience with the Court. Eager to retain the support of Southerners and Westerners in the increasingly bitter partisan battles in which his administration was becoming engaged, the president had vigorously supported (and even actively encouraged) Georgia's efforts to remove the Cherokees before the Court decision. His reaction to Marshall's rulings reflected his belief that the justices were using the issue to express their hostility to the larger aims of his presidency. When the chief justice announced the decision in *Worcester* v. *Georgia,* Jackson reportedly responded with contempt. "John Marshall has made his decision," he is said to have stated. "Now let him enforce it." The decision was not enforced.

In 1835, the government extracted a treaty from a minority faction of the Cherokees, none of them a chosen representative of the Cherokee Nation, which ceded to Georgia the tribe's land in that state in return for $5 million and a reservation west of the Mississippi. The great majority of the 17,000 Cherokees did not recognize the treaty as legitimate and refused to leave their homes. But Jackson was not to be thwarted. He sent an army of 7,000 under General Winfield Scott to round them up and drive them westward at bayonet point.

About 1,000 fled across the state line to North Carolina, where eventually the federal government provided a reservation for them in the Smoky Mountains which survives today. But most of the rest made the long, forced trek to Oklahoma beginning in the winter of 1838. Along the way a Kentuckian observed: "Even aged females, apparently nearly ready to drop in the grave, were travelling with heavy burdens attached to their backs, sometimes on frozen ground and sometimes on muddy streets, with no covering for their feet." Thousands, perhaps a quarter or more of the émigrés, perished before reaching

The Expulsion of Indians from the South, 1830–1835

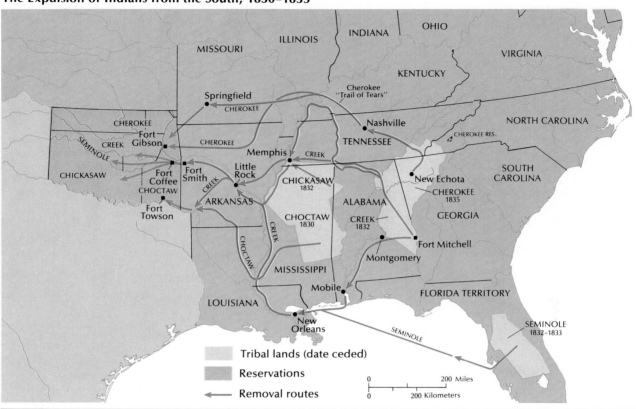

Tribal lands (date ceded)

Reservations

← Removal routes

0   200 Miles

0   200 Kilometers

their unwanted destination. In the harsh new reservations in which they were now forced to live, the survivors never forgot the hard journey. They called their route "The Trail Where They Cried," the Trail of Tears.

The Cherokees were not alone in experiencing the hardships of the Trail of Tears. Between 1830 and 1838, virtually all the "Five Civilized Tribes" were expelled from the Southern states and forced to relocate in the "Indian Territory" (formally created by the Indian Intercourse Act of 1834) in what later became Oklahoma. The new territory seemed safely removed from existing white settlements and embraced land that most whites considered undesirable. It had the additional advantage, the government believed, of being bordered on the west by what explorers such as Lewis and Clark and Stephen H. Long had christened the "Great American Desert," land deemed unfit for habitation. It seemed unlikely that whites would ever seek to settle along the western borders of the Indian Territory; and thus the danger of whites surrounding the reservation and producing further conflict could be avoided. The Choctaws of

Mississippi and western Alabama were the first to make the trek, beginning in 1830. The army moved out the Creeks of eastern Alabama and western Georgia in 1836. The Chickasaw in northern Mississippi began the long march westward a year later, and the Cherokees, finally, a year after that.

Only the Seminoles in Florida managed to resist the pressures, and even their success was limited. Like other tribes, the Seminoles had agreed under pressure to a settlement (the 1832–1833 treaties of Payne's Landing) by which they ceded their lands and agreed to move to Indian Territory within three years. Most did move West, but a substantial minority, under the leadership of the chieftain Osceola, refused to leave and staged an uprising beginning in 1835 to defend their lands. (Joining the Indians in their struggle was a group of runaway black slaves, who had been living with the tribe.) The Seminole War dragged on for years. Jackson sent troops to Florida, but the Seminoles with their black associates were masters of guerrilla warfare in the jungly Everglades. Even after Osceola had been treacherously captured under a flag of truce and had died in prison; even after white

The Trail of Tears
This twentieth-century painting by Robert Lindneux shows the forced evacuation of 18,000 Cherokee Indians from their ancestral lands in Georgia beginning in 1838. An epidemic of smallpox, along with starvation and exposure, cost thousands of Indians their lives. Here the Cherokees, guarded by soldiers carrying guns and bayonets, cross the Missouri River on their way to their new and unfamiliar homes in what is now Oklahoma.
(Woolaroc Museum, Bartlesville, Oklahoma)

troops engaged in a systematic campaign of extermination against the resisting Indians and their black allies; even after 1,500 white soldiers had died and the federal government had spent $20 million on the struggle—even then, followers of Osceola remained in Florida. Finally, in 1842, the government abandoned the war. By then, many of the Seminoles had been either killed or forced westward. But the relocation of the Seminoles, unlike the relocation of most of the other tribes, was never complete.

By the end of the 1830s, virtually all the important Indian societies east of the Mississippi (with such exceptions as the Seminoles and a few Cherokee) had been largely removed to the West. The tribes had ceded over 100 million acres of Eastern land to the federal government; they had received in return about $68 million and 32 million acres in the far less hospitable lands west of the Mississippi between the Missouri and Red rivers. There they lived, divided by tribe into a series of sharply defined reservations, in a territory surrounded by a string of United States forts to keep them in (and to keep most whites out), in a region whose climate and topography bore little relation to anything they had known before. Eventually, even this forlorn enclave would face encroachments from white civilization.

Jackson and the Bank War

How far Jackson was willing to go to destroy the power of what he considered institutions of elite power became clear in one of the most celebrated episodes of his presidency: the war against the Bank of the United States. His opponents in this case, he believed, were the same Eastern aristocrats he had battled throughout his political career. So he approached his battle with them with special fervor.

The Bank of the United States was a private corporation chartered by the federal government, which owned one-fifth of the Bank's stock. The Bank was a monopoly, with the exclusive right to hold the government's deposits. With its headquarters in Philadelphia and its branches in twenty-nine other cities, it also did a tremendous business in general banking, totaling about $70 million a year. Its services were important to the national economy because of the credit it provided for profit-making enterprises; because of its bank notes, which circulated throughout the country as a dependable medium of exchange; and because of the restraining effect that its policies had on the less well managed banks chartered by the various states. Nevertheless, Andrew Jackson was determined to destroy it.

Biddle's Institution

Nicholas Biddle, president of the Bank from 1823 on, had done much to put the institution on a sound and prosperous basis. A member of an aristocratic Philadelphia family, he personally owned a large proportion of the Bank's stock, so much of it that together with two other large stockholders he controlled the Bank. A banker, not a politician, he had no desire to mix in politics. But he finally concluded it was necessary to do so in self-defense when, with the encouragement of Jackson, popular opposition to the Bank rose to a threatening pitch.

Opposition came from two very different groups: "soft money" people and "hard money" people. Advocates of soft money consisted largely of state bankers and their allies. They objected to the Bank of the United States because it restrained the state banks from issuing notes freely. The other set of critics, the hard-money people, believed that coin was the only safe currency, and they condemned all banks of issue—that is, all banks issuing bank notes—whether chartered by the states or (as in the case of the Bank of the United States) by the federal government. The soft-money advocates were believers in rapid economic growth, speculation, the "main chance." The hard-money forces tended to cling to older ideas of "public virtue" and to look with suspicion on reckless expansion and speculation.

Jackson himself supported the hard-money position. Many years before, he had been involved in grandiose land and mercantile speculations based on paper credit. His business had been ruined, and he himself had fallen deeply into debt as a result of the Panic of 1797. Thereafter he was suspicious of all banks. Once he became president, he expressed that suspicion by suggesting that the charter of the Bank of the United States, which was due to expire in 1836, should not be renewed.

To preserve the institution, Biddle began to grant banking favors to influential men in the hope of winning them to his side. At first he sought to cultivate Jackson's supporters, with some success. Then he turned more and more to Jackson's opponents. He extended loans on easy terms to several prominent newspaper editors, to a number of important state politicians, and to more than fifty congressmen and senators. In particular, he relied on Senators Clay and Webster, the latter of whom was connected with the Bank in various ways—as legal counsel, director of the Boston branch, frequent and heavy borrower, and Biddle's personal friend.

Clay, Webster, and other advisers persuaded Biddle to apply to Congress for a recharter bill in 1832, four years ahead of the expiration date. After investigating the Bank and its business, Congress passed the recharter bill. Jackson at once vetoed it, sending it back to Congress with a stirring message in which he denounced the Bank as unconstitutional, undemocratic, and un-American. The Bank's supporters in Congress failed to obtain the two-thirds majority necessary to override the veto. And the

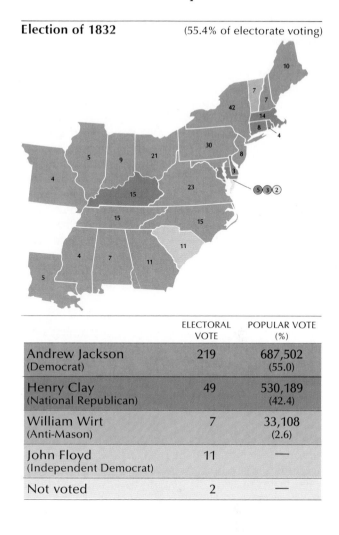

Election of 1832   (55.4% of electorate voting)

	ELECTORAL VOTE	POPULAR VOTE (%)
Andrew Jackson (Democrat)	219	687,502 (55.0)
Henry Clay (National Republican)	49	530,189 (42.4)
William Wirt (Anti-Mason)	7	33,108 (2.6)
John Floyd (Independent Democrat)	11	—
Not voted	2	—

Bank question emerged as the paramount issue of the coming election, just as Clay had hoped.

In 1832, Clay ran as the unanimous choice of the National Republicans, who had held a nominating convention in Baltimore late in the previous year. Jackson, with Van Buren as his running mate, sought reelection as the candidate of the Democrats. Still another candidate was in the field, representing a third party for the first time in American history. He was William Wirt, the nominee of the Anti-Mason party. (See p. 297.) The legislature of South Carolina gave that state's electoral vote in protest to a man who was not even a candidate, John Floyd, one of Calhoun's Virginia followers. Despite this varied opposition, Jackson won reelection overwhelmingly. He received 55 percent of the popular vote and 219 electoral votes (more than four times as many as Clay).

The "Monster" Destroyed

Jackson, at least, interpreted his reelection as a mandate to continue his war on the bank. As soon as the nullification crisis was resolved, he determined to strike a decisive blow at the "monster." He could not abolish the institution before the expiration of its charter, but he could reduce its power in the meantime. He resolved to remove the government's deposits from the Bank. Under the law establishing the Bank, the secretary of the treasury had to give the actual order to remove them. The incumbent secretary, who believed that such an action would destabilize the financial system, refused to give the order. Jackson removed him and appointed a replacement. When the new secretary similarly procrastinated, Jackson named a third: Roger B. Taney, the attorney general, a close friend and ally of the president. Taney was eager to cooperate.

With Taney at the head of the Treasury Department, the process of removing the government's deposits began immediately. The government stopped putting new funds in the Bank. At the same time, it continued paying bills by drawing on its existing deposits in the Bank, which steadily dwindled. Meanwhile the government opened accounts with a number of state banks, depositing its incoming receipts with them. These banks, including one in Baltimore with which Taney himself was associated, were chosen presumably on the basis of their financial soundness but also, often, on the basis of their political leanings. Jackson's enemies called them his "pet banks." By 1836 there were eighty-nine of them.

The proud and poetic Biddle, "Czar Nicholas" to Jacksonians, was not a man to give in without a fight. "This worthy President," he wrote sarcastically, "thinks that because he has scalped Indians and imprisoned Judges, he is to have his way with the Bank. He is mistaken." When the administration began to transfer funds directly from the Bank of the United States to the pet banks (as opposed to the earlier practice of simply depositing new funds in those banks), Biddle struck back. The loss of these government deposits, amounting to several millions, made it necessary, he claimed, to call in loans and raise interest rates, since the government deposits had served as the basis for much of the Bank's credit. He realized that by making borrowing more difficult, he was bound to hurt business and cause unemployment; but he consoled himself with the belief that a short depression would help to bring about a recharter of the Bank. "Nothing but the evidence of suf-

fering," he told the head of the Boston branch, would "produce any effect in Congress."

During the winter of 1833–1834, with interest high and money scarce, there was suffering indeed, as many businesses failed and thousands of workers lost their jobs. All over the country, friends of the Bank organized meetings to adopt petitions begging for relief from Congress, petitions that delegates then brought in person to Washington and that pro-Bank senators or representatives introduced with appropriately gloomy speeches. But Jacksonians denied responsibility. When distressed citizens appealed to the president he answered, "Go to Biddle."

The banker finally carried his contraction of credit too far to suit even his own friends, and some of them did go to Biddle. A group of New York and Boston merchants protested (as one of them reported) that the business community "ought not and would not sustain him in further pressure, which he very well knew was not necessary for the safety of the bank, and in which his whole object was to coerce a charter." To appease the business community, Biddle at last reversed himself and began to grant credit in abundance and on reasonable terms. His hopes of winning a recharter of the Bank died in the process.

The "Bank War" was over, and Jackson had won it. But with the passing of the Bank of the United States, on the expiration of its charter in 1836, the country lost a valuable financial institution. Economic troubles lay ahead.

The Taney Court

The discouraging aftermath of the Bank War did not weaken Jackson's commitment to "democratizing" the nation's political and economic life. On the contrary, he continued to move forcefully against what he perceived to be institutions of aristocratic privilege and excessive federal power. And in 1835, he moved against the most powerful institution of economic nationalism of all: the Supreme Court. When John Marshall died in 1835, the president appointed as the new chief justice his trusted ally in the Bank War, Roger B. Taney—a man fervently committed to Jacksonian democracy.

Taney never dominated the Court in the way Marshall had managed to do, nor did he preside over a sharp break in constitutional interpretation. But he did help produce a marked change in emphasis. Taney and the majority of his colleagues were moderate agrarian liberals; in general, they tended to sup-

"The Downfall of Mother Bank"

This 1832 Democratic cartoon celebrates Andrew Jackson's destruction of the Bank of the United States. The president is shown here driving away the Bank's corrupt supporters by ordering the withdrawal of government deposits. (New-York Historical Society)

port the right of the people, acting through state legislatures, to regulate private property rights and the activities of corporations. Although they stopped far short of accepting Calhoun's extreme states' rights philosophy, the justices were modifying Marshall's vigorous nationalism.

Perhaps the clearest indication of the new judicial mood was the celebrated case of *Charles River Bridge* v. *Warren Bridge* of 1837. The case involved a dispute between two Massachusetts companies over the right to build a bridge across the Charles River between Boston and Cambridge. One company had a longstanding charter from the state to operate a toll bridge for a specified number of years, a charter that the firm claimed guaranteed it a monopoly of the bridge traffic. The second company had applied to the legislature for authorization to construct a second, competing bridge that would—since it would

be toll-free—greatly reduce the value of the first company's charter. The first company contended that in granting the second charter the legislature was engaging in a breach of contract.

The Marshall Court, in the *Dartmouth College* case and other decisions, had ruled clearly that states had no right to abrogate contracts. But now Taney, speaking for the Democratic majority on the Court, supported the right of Massachusetts to award the second charter. Although he advanced elaborate legal precedents to support the decision, the ruling reflected less the influence of the law than the influence of Jacksonian social theory. The object of government, Taney maintained, was to promote the general happiness, an object that took precedence over the rights of property. A state, therefore, had the right to amend or abrogate a contract if such action was necessary to advance the well-being of the community.

In the *Charles River Bridge* case, he maintained, such abrogation had been clearly necessary. The original bridge company, by exercising a monopoly, was benefiting from unjustifiable privilege. (It did not help the first company that its members were largely Boston aristocrats and that it was closely associated with elite Harvard College; the challenging company, by contrast, was composed largely of newer, aspiring entrepreneurs—the sort of people with whom Jackson and his allies instinctively identified.) The decision was another indication of one of the cornerstones of Jacksonian philosophy. The key to democracy was an expansion of economic opportunity, which would not occur if older corporations could maintain monopolies and choke off competition from newer companies.

The Emergence of the Second Party System

Jackson's forceful—some claimed tyrannical—tactics in crushing first the nullification movement and then the Bank of the United States helped galvanize a growing opposition coalition that by the mid-1830s was ready to assert itself in national politics. It began as a gathering of national political leaders opposed to Jackson's use of power. Denouncing the president as "King Andrew I," they began to refer to themselves as Whigs, after the party in England that traditionally worked to limit the power of the king. As the new party began to develop as a national organization with constituencies in every state, its appeal became more diffuse. Nevertheless, both in philosophy and in the character of its adherents, the Whig party offered a discernible contrast to the party of Jackson.

The partisan competition of the 1820s and 1830s produced what has come to be known as the "second party system." The first party system—the system that began in the 1790s between the Federalists and the Republicans—had begun to collapse early in the nineteenth century. By 1816, the Federalist party was virtually extinct, and nothing had emerged to replace it. Political battles revolved for a time not around parties, but around shifting and usually temporary factional alignments. But in the 1820s, divisions began to emerge that seemed more lasting—divisions that ultimately produced a new two-party system consisting of Whigs and Democrats.

Party Philosophies

Even before the election of Jackson in 1828, those who would ultimately form the Democratic party had stood for a certain general approach to government and society; and during the years of the Jackson administration, that approach began to take the form of something similar to a philosophy. To the Democrats, America's future was to be one of steadily expanding opportunities. To that end, the federal government should be limited in power, the rights of states should be protected, and the nation should work to eliminate all social and economic arrangements that served to entrench privilege and stifle the common man. Jacksonians tended to romanticize the "honest workers," the "simple farmers," and the "forthright businessmen" who stood, they believed, in sharp contrast to the corrupt, monopolistic, aristocratic forces of established wealth. As Jackson himself said in his farewell address, the society of America should be one in which "the planter, the farmer, the mechanic, and the laborer, all know that their success depends on their own industry and economy," in which no one's opportunity would be stifled by artificial privilege.

There was no necessary connection between this philosophy of a fluid, open society and opposition to economic development; and indeed, many Jacksonians believed wholeheartedly in the necessity of material progress. Yet in practice, Democrats were far more likely than others to look with suspicion on proposals for stimulating modern commercial and industrial growth. They tended to associate such growth with the creation of menacing institutions of power—the Bank of the United States, for example; and they often spoke yearningly of a simpler era in which no such concentrations of privilege had existed. Both in Washington and in state governments, Democratic legislators, much more often than their Whig counterparts, opposed such modernizing institutions as chartered banks and corporations, state-supported internal improvements, even public schools. Rather than economic development and consolidation, Democrats favored territorial expansion, which would, they believed, widen opportunities for aspiring Americans. And among the most radical members of the party—the so-called Locofocos, mainly workingmen and small businessmen and professionals in the Northeast—sentiment was strong for a vigorous, ultimately perhaps even violent, assault on monopoly and privilege far in advance of anything Jackson himself ever contemplated.

The political philosophy that became known as

Whiggery, by contrast, looked far more favorably on expanding the power of the federal government, encouraging industrial and commercial development, and knitting the country together into a consolidated economic system. While Democrats often looked with suspicion on such technological advances as railroads, telegraphs, and manufacturing machinery, Whigs embraced such material progress enthusiastically. And where Democrats advocated rapid geographic expansion, Whigs urged a more prudent, cautious movement into the West, fearful that too rapid territorial growth would produce instability. Their vision of America was of a nation embracing the industrial future, of a nation rising to world greatness as a commercial and manufacturing power. And although Whigs insisted that their vision would result in increasing opportunities for all Americans, they tended to attribute particular value to the enterprising, modernizing forces in their society—the entrepreneurs and institutions that most effectively promoted economic growth. Thus while Democrats were inclined to oppose legislation establishing banks, corporations, and other modernizing institutions, Whigs generally favored such measures.

Party Constituencies

To some extent, the constituencies of the two major parties were reflections of these diffuse philosophies. The Whigs were strongest among the more substantial merchants and manufacturers of the Northeast; the wealthier planters of the South (those who favored commercial development and the strengthening of ties with the North); and the ambitious farmers and rising commercial class of the West—usually migrants from the Northeast—who advocated internal improvements, expanding trade, and rapid economic progress. The Democrats drew more support from the smaller merchants and the workingmen of the Northeast; from those Southern planters who looked with some suspicion on Northern industrial growth; and from those Westerners—usually with Southern roots—who favored a predominantly agrarian economy and opposed the development of powerful economic institutions in their region. Whigs, in short, tended to be wealthier than Democrats, tended to have more aristocratic backgrounds, and tended to be more commercially ambitious.

But party divisions were not always so simple. For one thing, although Democrats tended to be people of more modest means than Whigs, they did not

include those most conspicuously excluded from economic opportunity. Some of the poorest residents of the Northeast—unskilled laborers, recent Protestant immigrants, and others—gravitated toward the Whigs. To them, the Democrats, often representatives of the lower middle class that stood one rung above them on the social ladder, seemed more menacing and hostile than the Whigs.

Furthermore, Whigs and Democrats alike were more interested in winning elections than in maintaining philosophical purity. And both parties made adjustments from region to region in order to attract the largest possible number of voters, so that often the original ideology of the party appeared to be almost lost. In New York, for example, the Whigs—under the leadership of party boss Thurlow Weed—developed a large popular following by turning the Democrats' own tactics against their opponents. Their vehicle was a movement known as Anti-Masonry. The so-called Anti-Mason party had emerged in the 1820s in response to widespread resentment against the secret and exclusive, hence supposedly undemocratic, Society of Freemasons. Such resentments rose to new heights when, in 1826, a former Mason, William Morgan, mysteriously disappeared from his home in Batavia, New York, shortly before he was scheduled to publish a book purporting to expose the secrets of Freemasonry. The assumption was widespread that Morgan had been abducted and murdered by the vengeful Masons. Weed and other opponents of Jackson seized on the Anti-Mason frenzy to launch spirited attacks on Jackson and Van Buren (both Freemasons), implying that the Democrats were connected with the anti democratic conspiracy. The excitement soon spread to other states—most notably Pennsylvania; and in 1831, some Anti-Masons broke with the Whigs and held their own national convention in Harrisburg to nominate a presidential candidate—William Wirt—for the next year's campaign.

By embracing Anti-Masonry, Whigs discovered a vehicle that permitted them to portray themselves to the public as opponents of aristocracy and exclusivity. They were, in other words, attacking the Democrats with the Democrats' own issues. Both parties, therefore, were adopting the rhetoric of democracy and equality; and the specific issues that divided them in their legislative battles were often obscured in actual campaigns.

Religious and ethnic divisions also played an important role in determining the constituencies of the two parties. Irish Catholics, one of the largest of

—————— WHERE HISTORIANS DISAGREE ——————

Jacksonian Democracy

Andrew Jackson was not only one of the most powerful political figures of the nineteenth century; he also became the symbol of a political philosophy and a social spirit that seemed to be gaining strength in America in the 1820s and 1830s. Historians have taken a particular interest, therefore, both in Jackson and in the set of social and political ideas he has come to represent. And they have disagreed markedly both about the man himself and about the social and ideological movement that has come to be known as "Jacksonian Democracy." As with many other issues on which historians differ, their views of Jackson have often reflected the political climate of their own day.

In the late nineteenth century, when the historical profession was dominated by aristocratic Easterners with Whiggish political views, studies of Jackson were largely hostile. Conservative biographers such as James Parton (*Life of Andrew Jackson,* 1860) denounced the Jacksonians as "barbarians" who had turned government over to the "rabble." By embracing the spoils system, such historians argued, Jackson had paved the way for the rampant corruption in government of later years. By destroying the Bank of the United States, he had struck a heavy blow against American financial stability.

By the early twentieth century, the writing of history, and with it the historical view of the Jacksonians, had begun to experience an important transformation. Under the influence of Frederick Jackson Turner, historians began to emphasize the role of the West in American life and to see in the frontier a healthy, democratic influence on the nation. Turner and his disciples, most of them Westerners or Southerners themselves, rejected the view of Whiggish historians that the Jacksonians had been ill-bred rabble. Instead, they argued, Democrats of Jackson's time had been freedom-loving frontiersmen of the West, challenging the conservative aristocracy of the East, which was attempting to restrict opportunity. Jackson himself, they claimed, was much like the progressives

of their own time: a true democrat who strove to make government responsive to the will of the people rather than to the desires of special interests. Dissenters such as Thomas P. Abernethy (*From Frontier to Plantation in Tennessee,* 1932) argued that Jackson had himself been a frontier aristocrat and had opposed the democratic trend in his own state. For the most part, however, the view of Jacksonianism as "frontier democracy" (as Turner had argued in his famous essay "The Significance of the Frontier in American History," 1893) prevailed through the first half of the twentieth century.

A new era in Jacksonian scholarship began in 1945 with the publication of the celebrated study by Arthur M. Schlesinger, Jr., *The Age of Jackson.* Like Turner and others, Schlesinger admired Jackson for bringing a healthy democratic influence to American politics and saw the Jacksonian era as one of steadily expanding political opportunity. He did not, however, share the view of earlier historians that the roots of Jacksonianism lay in the West. Instead, Schlesinger claimed, the conflict between Democrats and Whigs was a conflict "not of sections, but of classes." Jacksonian Democracy was an effort "to control the power of the capitalist groups, mainly Eastern, for the benefit of noncapitalist groups, farmers and laboring men, East, West, and South." Emphasizing the role of the urban working classes in the Jacksonian coalition, he saw in the 1830s an early version of modern reform efforts to "restrain the power of the business community."

Other historians have accepted Schlesinger's view that classes were more important than sections, but they have disagreed with him about which class Jackson represented. Richard Hofstadter's influential essay in *The American Political Tradition* (1948) portrayed Jackson as the spokesman of rising entrepreneurs—aspiring businessmen who saw the road to opportunity blocked by the monopolistic power of the Eastern aristocracy. Thus the Jacksonians were opposed to special priv-

WHERE HISTORIANS DISAGREE

ileges only to the extent those privileges blocked their own road to success. They were less sympathetic to the aspirations of those below them—workers and small farmers. Bray Hammond, in *Banks and Politics in America from the Revolution to the Civil War* (1957), argued similarly that the Jacksonian cause was "one of enterpriser against capitalist, of banker against regulation, and of Wall Street against Chestnut"—that is, of the rising bankers of New York City against the established bankers of the Philadelphia-based Bank of the United States.

Still another view of Jacksonianism emerged in the 1950s from historians concerned with the ideological origins of the movement. Marvin Meyers, in *The Jacksonian Persuasion* (1957), emphasized the appeal of the Jeffersonian heritage to the Jacksonians. Jackson and his followers looked with mistrust on the new industrial society emerging around them and yearned instead for a restoration of the agrarian, republican virtues of an earlier time. In destroying the Bank, limiting federal economic activities, and emphasizing states' rights, they were attempting to restore a simpler, more decentralized world. Ironically, their actions contributed instead to the expansion of unregulated capitalism.

Lee Benson, in *The Concept of Jacksonian Democracy* (1961), a study of political parties in New York, used new quantitative techniques to challenge virtually all previous interpretations of Jacksonianism. There was no consistent difference—in class, occupation, or region—between the Jacksonians and anti-Jacksonians, Benson argued. Both parties contained big as well as small businessmen, farmers, and city workers. Nor were there any significant ideological differences. Both parties used the same "agrarian" rhetoric; both were in favor of greater equality of opportunity and greater political democracy. Local and cultural factors—religion and ethnicity, for example—were the crucial determinants of party divisions, not economic interests or ideology. Because the

movement toward democracy was much broader than the Democratic party, he suggested, the "age of Jackson" should be renamed the "age of egalitarianism."

Other historians have continued Benson's de-emphasis of party divisions in the Jacksonian period and have cited instead social and economic developments that transcended partisan concerns. Edward T. Pessen, in *Jacksonian America* (1969), portrayed the mid-nineteenth century as a time of widespread and increasing social and economic inequality but suggested that party divisions did not reflect the broader stratification of American society. Richard McCormick (1966) and Glyndon Van Deusen (1963) similarly emphasized the pragmatism of Jackson and the Democrats and de-emphasized clear ideological or social party divisions.

More recent historians have begun to turn the discussion of early nineteenth-century politics back to the question of class. Among the new studies is Sean Wilentz's *Chants Democratic* (1984), which traces the emergence in New York City of an industrial work force with an increasingly powerful class identity. The grievances of such people, he argues, were important in reshaping the way Americans defined the concept of republicanism. "Republicanism" is a concept that has attracted the interest of many scholars in recent years. It describes an ideology, stretching back to the eighteenth century and forward into the twentieth, that many historians believe has been central to American history: the belief that citizens in a republic should have unobstructed opportunities to advance toward ownership of their own land or their own enterprises. Workers in New York, Wilentz argues, waged an attack on the emerging system of laissez-faire capitalism and the wage system, which together threatened to choke off their chances for advancement. The degree to which the new industrial system threatened republican ideals helped create a radical tradition in American public life that found reflection, for a time, in at least some parts of the Jacksonian constituency.

the recent immigrant groups, tended to support the Democrats, who appeared to reflect their own vague aversion to commercial development and entrepreneurial progress. And not only Irish but German Catholics found the Democrats more willing than the Whigs to respect and protect their cultural values and habits. Catholics resented such Whiggish reform movements as temperance, public education, and enforced Sabbath observance, seeing them as attempts to impose Protestant moral standards on them.

Evangelical Protestants gravitated toward the Whigs for the same reasons that Catholics opposed the new party. Such Protestants embraced a religious and cultural outlook that encouraged constant development and improvement. They envisioned a society progressing steadily toward unity and order, and they looked on the new immigrant communities as a threat to that progress—as groups that needed to be disciplined and taught "American" ways. They liked to claim that immigrants supported the Democratic party because the Democrats engaged in shameless vote buying and other frauds. But their own cultural outlook was more to blame for their failure to attract support from such groups. In many communities, these and other local ethnic, religious, and cultural tensions were far more influential in determining party alignments than any concrete political or economic proposals.

Party Leadership

If presidential politics were indicative of popular favor, it would be fair to say that the Whigs, in the more than twenty years of their existence as a party, enjoyed relatively little public support. Only in 1840 and 1848 were Whig candidates able to capture the White House, and in each of those elections the winning contestant was a popular military hero. Yet when elections at every level—congressional, state, and local, as well as presidential—are considered, the balance between the two parties appears much more even.

The Democrats maintained their edge over the Whigs at the level of national leadership largely because of the popularity of a single man. Throughout the 1830s, the Democratic party was the party of Andrew Jackson—beloved war hero, champion of the people, a political figure of such magnetism that no opponent could hope to match him. The Whigs, on the other hand, rallied behind three national leaders—each a powerful and charismatic figure in his own right, but each, too, a man with significant political

limitations. Henry Clay, Daniel Webster, and John C. Calhoun all brought their own formidable constituencies into the Whig coalition. (All also brought their own intense ambitions for the presidency.) But none was ever able to forge a truly national constituency capable of winning a presidential election.

The glamorous Clay, "Harry of the West," won many supporters throughout the country through his support for internal improvements and economic development—the American System. But his image as a devious political operator and his regional identification with the West proved an insuperable liability. He ran for president three times and never won. Daniel Webster, the greatest orator of his era, gained

Daniel Webster

"The great god Webster," as he was occasionally known, was the most passionately admired public figure of his age. Crowds of up to 100,000 turned out at times for his speeches, even though many of them, in an age before amplification, presumably could not even hear him. Yet Webster inspired contempt as well as admiration among his contemporaries. His shady connections with influential businessmen tarnished his reputation among many Americans. So did his consuming (and unfulfilled) ambition for the presidency and his often embarrassing affection for brandy.   (Library of Congress)

fame and respect for his passionate speeches in defense of the Constitution and the Union. Some of his admirers, of whom a large number were wealthy businessmen, considered him a greater man than any president. But Webster's close connection with the Bank of the United States and the protective tariff, his reliance on rich men for financial support, and his unfortunate and often embarrassing fondness for brandy—all prevented him from developing enough of a national constituency to win him the office he so desperately wanted.

John C. Calhoun, the third member of what became known as the Great Triumvirate, was equally controversial. He never considered himself a true Whig, and his identification with the nullification controversy in effect disqualified him from national leadership in any case. Yet he sided with Clay and Webster on the issue of the national bank. And he shared with them a strong animosity toward Andrew Jackson. Calhoun did not embrace the belief of most Southern Whigs in the importance of commercial development. He did, however, produce reasons of his own for advocating an alliance between the upper classes of the two regions. In his *South Carolina Exposition and Protest* of 1828 and in later writings, he presented a critique of modern capitalism that in its frank predictions of class struggle resembled much of what Karl Marx and Friedrich Engels would say in later decades—although Calhoun drew from those predictions very different prescriptions for social action than Marx and Engels would produce. Capitalist society would, Calhoun predicted, inevitably become divided into two classes: "capitalists" and "operatives." The former, he argued, would expropriate and impoverish the latter; and unless steps were taken to prevent it, a revolutionary struggle would ensue. "There is and always has been in an advanced stage of wealth and civilization," he insisted in 1837, "a conflict between labor and capital." Northern businessmen had a common interest with Southern planters, therefore, in working to prevent the revolutionary danger by protecting their position against threats from below. Such views found scant sympathy among Northern Whigs. Webster, for example, admitted that "in the old countries of Europe there is a clear and well-defined line between capital and labor"; but he declared that there was no line so "broad, marked, and visible" in the United States.

The Whigs, in other words, were able to marshal an imposing array of national leaders, each with his own powerful constituency. Yet for many years they were unable to find a way to merge those constituencies into a single winning combination. The result was that the Democrats for a time, as in the election of 1836, appeared far more dominant than they actually were.

The Crowded Campaign of 1836

The importance of incumbency in the age of party politics became abundantly clear in 1836. Despite the growing power of the Whigs, Jackson and the Democrats continued to control federal appointments and contracts; and they made liberal use of their patronage powers to bolster the fortunes of their candidates. The party also benefited from Jackson's continuing popularity and from its elaborate party organization. With little debate, the party convention nominated Jackson's personal favorite, Martin Van Buren, as its candidate for president.

The Whigs in 1836 could boast no such unity and discipline. Indeed, they could not even agree on a single candidate. Their strategy, masterminded by Biddle, was to run several candidates, each of them supposedly strong in one part of the country. Webster would represent them in New England; Hugh Lawson White of Tennessee would seek the votes of the South; and the former Indian fighter and hero of the War of 1812 from Ohio, William Henry Harrison, would attract support in the middle states and in the West. As Biddle advised: "This disease is to be treated as a local disorder—apply local remedies—if General Harrison will run better than anybody else in Pennsylvania, by all means unite upon him." None of the three candidates could expect to get a majority in the electoral college, but separately they might draw enough votes from Van Buren to prevent his getting a majority. The decision would then rest, as in 1824–1825, with the House of Representatives, where the Whigs might be better able to elect one of their candidates. But the three Whigs proved to be no match for the one Democrat. When the returns were in, Van Buren had 170 electoral votes to 124 for all his opponents.

Post-Jacksonian Politics

Andrew Jackson retired from public life in 1837, the most beloved political figure of his age. He left the presidency in the hands of a friend and ally dedicated to continuing his policies and sustaining the political party he had helped to create. But Martin Van Buren was a different man from his predecessor, and also far less fortunate. Never was he able to establish the great personal popularity that had sustained Jackson during the bleaker moments of his presidency. And unlike Jackson, Van Buren was plagued throughout his administration with economic difficulties that contributed to the strengthening of the Whigs. For the next eight years, party politics would be highly competitive and often deeply embittered.

Economic Dilemmas

Van Buren's success in the 1836 election was a result in part of a nationwide economic boom that was reaching its height in that year. Canal and railroad builders were at a peak of activity. Prices were rising as people indulged in an orgy of spending and speculating. Money was plentiful—most of it manufactured by the banks, which multiplied their loans and notes with little regard to their reserves of cash. By 1837, bank loans outstanding amounted to five times as much as in 1830. Never had the nation seemed so prosperous.

Land as usual was a favorite target of speculation, especially the land sold by the federal government. After congressional legislation in 1821 had abolished installment buying and set the minimum price at $1.25 an acre, sales of public lands had slowed. They averaged 300,000 to 400,000 acres a year in the late 1820s and early 1830s. Then the business suddenly boomed. Between 1835 and 1837 nearly 40 million acres were disposed of, and the expression "doing a land-office business" came into use to describe fast selling of any kind. Nearly three-fourths of the land being sold went to speculators, who acquired large tracts in the hope of reselling at a profit. Speculators generally borrowed from the banks to make payment at the land offices.

For the moment, the government enjoyed great profits from the booming business. Receipts from land sales, which had averaged less than $2.4 million annually for the ten years preceding 1835, rose to more than $24 million in 1836. These land sales, when combined with the revenues the government received from the compromise tariff of 1833, created a series of substantial federal budget surpluses and made possible a steady reduction of the national debt (something Jackson had always advocated). Finally, from 1835 to 1837, the government for the first and only time in its history was out of debt, with a substantial surplus in the Treasury.

The question for Congress and the administration was how to get rid of the Treasury surplus. Tampering with the tariff was out of the question; few people wanted to reopen that touchy subject so soon after the compromise that had put it to rest. Instead, support began to build for returning the federal surplus to the states. In 1836, Congress passed and Jackson signed a distribution act, which required the federal government to pay whatever surplus had accumulated by the end of the year (estimated at $40 million) to the states in four quarterly installments as a loan without security or interest. Each state would receive a share proportional to its representation in Congress. No one seriously expected the "loan" to be repaid. As the states began to receive their shares, they promptly spent the money, mainly to encourage the construction of highways, railroads, and canals. The distribution of the surplus thus gave further stimulus to the economic boom. At the same time the withdrawal of federal funds strained the pet banks, for they had to call in a large part of their own loans in order to make the transfer of funds to the state governments.

Congress did nothing to check the speculative fever, with which many congressmen themselves were badly infected. Webster, for one, was buying up thousands of acres in the West. But Jackson was concerned. Although money continued to pour into the Treasury from the land offices, most of it was paper of dubious value. The government was selling good land and was receiving in return a miscellaneous collection of state bank notes, none of them worth any more than the credit of the issuing bank. Jackson finally decided to act. In 1836, he issued the "specie circular," which announced that in the future only hard money or the notes of specie-paying banks (that is, notes backed by gold or silver) would be accepted in payment for public lands.

Jackson had been correct in fearing that the speculative fever was reaching dangerous proportions and that the banking system was seriously unstable. He was wrong, however, in thinking his specie circular would forestall further difficulties. Van Buren had been president less than three months when panic struck. The banks of New York, followed by those of the rest of the country, suddenly suspended specie payments (that is, they stopped paying gold and silver on demand for their bank notes and other obligations). During the next few years, hundreds of banks failed, and so did hundreds of other business firms. As unemployment grew, bread riots occurred in some of the larger cities. Prices fell, especially the price of land. Webster was only one of a great many who all at once found themselves "land poor." Many railroad and canal schemes were abandoned; several of the debt-burdened state governments ceased to pay interest on their bonds, and a few repudiated their debts, at least temporarily. The depression, the worst the American people had ever experienced, lasted for five years and proved catastrophic for Van Buren and the Democrats.

The Whigs blamed Jackson for the depression. It had come, they said, because of his destruction of the national bank and his mismanagement of public finance. But the Whigs were also in part to blame. The distribution of the Treasury surplus had been a Whig measure, although Jackson had signed it. (With the onset of the panic, the distribution was halted before the entire surplus had been transferred to the states.) Distribution, by weakening the pet banks, helped to bring on the crash. So did Jackson's specie circular, which started a general run on the banks as land buyers rushed to trade in their bank notes for specie with which to make land-office payments. Distribution of the surplus and the specie circular only precipitated the depression, however; they did not cause it.

While the Bank of the United States, if continued, could have lessened the overexpansion of credit, a period of financial stringency doubtless would have come sooner or later. For this was an international depression, affecting England and Western Europe as well. English investors faced a financial crisis at home, and they began to withdraw funds from America; that accounted for part of the strain on American banks. Then a succession of crop failures on American farms not only reduced the purchasing power of farmers but also required the import of foodstuffs; and payment for these imports drew additional money out of the country.

The Panic of 1837 had significant consequences beyond its immediate financial impact. Hard times increased social, sectional, and economic tensions. In the economically troubled cities, fears were rising that a real and dangerous class conflict was taking shape in America. Southern planters suffered heavy losses and became confirmed in their conviction that national policies worked to their disadvantage. The decline of business profits in the North intensified the belief of manufacturers that the compromise of 1833 must be undone and the tariff raised. Defaults on interest payments and outright repudiation of state bonds, many of them held by the English, added to difficulties in relations between the United States and Great Britain. And these accumulated grievances soon translated into dissatisfaction with the administration. Thus in 1840, the predominance of the Democrats came temporarily to an end.

The Van Buren Program

The modern concept that government can successfully fight depressions, and that it has an obligation to do so, did not exist in Van Buren's time. The only tradition of government intervention in economic matters was the Federalist–National Republican–Whig program of aid to business, to which Democrats were fiercely opposed. Consequently, Van Buren recommended few direct antidepression measures. He persuaded Congress to authorize the borrowing of $10 million to meet expenses during the emergency. He also urged that the government accept only specie for taxes and other payments.

In formulating a program of permanent legislation, the administration clearly reflected the wishes of the dominant farmer-labor segment of the party. The president urged Congress to reduce the price of public lands, and he recommended passage of a general "preemption" bill giving settlers already in an area the right to buy 160 acres at a set minimum price before land in that area was opened for public sale. A bill graduating land prices downward passed the Senate three times but was blocked in the House. A similar fate befell the preemption bill.

Stymied by legislative opposition, Van Buren resorted to executive action to please his urban followers. By presidential order he established a ten-hour workday on all federal projects. For the first time in the nation's history, the government thus took direct action to aid the rising labor class.

The most important measure in the president's program, and the most controversial, was his proposal for a new fiscal system. With the Bank of the United States destroyed and with Jackson's expedient of pet banks discredited, some kind of new system was urgently needed. Van Buren's fiscal ideas demonstrated both his ingenuity and his commitment to Democratic principles. The plan he suggested, known as the "independent treasury" or "subtreasury" system, was simplicity itself. Government funds would be placed in an independent treasury at Washington and in subtreasuries in specified cities throughout the country. Whenever the government had to pay out money, its own agents would handle the funds. No bank or banks would have the government's money or name to use as a basis for speculation. The government and the banks would be "divorced."

Van Buren placed the independent treasury proposal before Congress in a special session he called in 1837. It encountered the immediate and bitter opposition of most Whigs and of many conservative Democrats. Twice a bill to establish an independent

"The Times," 1837

This savage caricature of the economic troubles besetting the United States in 1837 illustrates, among other things, popular resentment of the hard-money orthodoxies of the time. A sign on the Custom House reads: "All bonds must be paid in Specie." Next door, the bank announces: "No specie payments made here." Women and children are shown begging in the street, while unemployed workers stand shoeless in front of signs advertising loans and "grand schemes." (New-York Historical Society)

treasury passed the Senate only to fail in the House. Not until 1840, the last year of Van Buren's presidency, did the administration succeed in driving the measure through both houses of Congress.

The Log Cabin Campaign

As the campaign of 1840 approached, the Whigs scented victory. The effects of the depression still gripped the country, and the Democrats, the party in power, were thus vulnerable to attack. The Whigs now realized that a party representing the upper-income groups must, if it expected to win, pose as a party of the people.

The Whigs also realized that they would have to achieve more unity and a stronger organization than they had demonstrated in 1836. They would have to settle on one candidate who could appeal to all segments of the party and to all sections of the country. Obviously, the easiest way to coordinate the party was through the new mechanism of the national nominating convention, already used by the Democrats. Accordingly, the Whigs held their first convention in Harrisburg, Pennsylvania, in December 1839. Their veteran leader, Henry Clay, expected the nomination; but the party bosses decided otherwise. Clay had too definite a record; he had been defeated too many times; he had too many enemies. Passing him over, the convention nominated William Henry Harrison of

Ohio, and for vice president, John Tyler of Virginia.

William Henry Harrison was a descendant of the Virginia aristocracy, but he had spent all his adult life in the Northwest, where he first went as a young army officer in General Wayne's campaign against the Indians. (See p. 157.) Although he had little experience in government, he was a renowned Indian fighter (like Jackson) and a popular national figure.

The Democrats, meeting in national convention at Baltimore, nominated Van Buren, pointed proudly to their record (especially the independent treasury), and condemned all the works of the Whigs (especially the Bank of the United States). Demonstrating that their party was, in some respects, no more united than the Whigs, the Democrats failed to nominate a vice-presidential candidate, declaring vaguely that they would leave the choice of that office to the wisdom of the voters.

The campaign of 1840 displayed in full the effects of an established party system on American politics and, in so doing, established a new pattern for presidential contests. The Whigs—who had emerged as a party largely because of their opposition to Andrew Jackson's common-man democracy, who in most regions represented the more affluent elements of the population, who stood for government policies that would aid business—were in the 1840 campaign almost indistinguishable from their opponents. Democrats and Whigs used the same techniques of mass voter appeal; the same evocation of simple, rustic values; the same identification with the common people. What mattered now was not the philosophical purity of the party but its ability to win votes.

Thus it was that the eager Whigs depicted themselves as the party of the people, the party able to save the nation from depression; and thus it was that they used against Martin Van Buren the same tactics that the Democrats had so often used against them. They accused the president of being an aloof aristocrat who used cologne, drank champagne, ate off gold plates, and otherwise engaged in undemocratic and un-American practices. In retaliation, a Democratic newspaper unwisely sneered that Harrison was a simple soul who would be glad to retire to a log cabin if provided with a pension and plenty of hard cider. In a country where many people lived or had lived in log cabins, this was an unwise line of attack; and the Whigs took full advantage. Yes, their candidate was a simple man of the people, they proclaimed, and he loved log cabins and cider. (Actually he was a man of substance and lived in a large and well-appointed house.)

A Whig Banner, 1840
This campaign banner sustains the popular fiction, popularized by the leaders of the Whig party, that their presidential candidate, William Henry Harrison, had been born in a log cabin and was a devotee of hard cider. In fact, Harrison was from a prosperous Virginia family, had attended college, and had studied law before entering the army. Nevertheless, the rustic image assigned to him in 1840 was an effective tool in ridding the Whig party of its elitist image. (New-York Historical Society)

Thereafter, the log cabin was an established symbol at every Whig meeting, and hard cider an established beverage. Against such techniques and the lingering effects of the depression the Democrats could not win. When the votes were counted in November, Harrison had 234 electoral votes to 60 for Van Buren. But the Whig victory was not as sweeping as it seemed; of the popular vote, Harrison had 1,275,000 to Van Buren's 1,128,000, a majority of less than 150,000.

The Frustration of the Whigs

Despite their decisive victory, the Whigs were to find the next four years frustrating and divisive ones. In large part, that was because their appealing new president, "Old Tippecanoe," William Henry Harrison, never had a chance to demonstrate what sort of leader he might become. Sixty-eight years old in 1841, he had appeared to be in good health. But the strain of the campaign, of the inauguration (after which he rode bareheaded through the streets of Washington to the White House in bitter cold), and of the pressing demands of grasping job seekers apparently became too much for him. Shortly after taking office, he contracted a cold, which soon turned into pneumonia. Harrison died on April 4, 1841, exactly one month after he had been inaugurated.

Harrison was the first president to die in office, and there was momentary uncertainty as to what should happen next. The Constitution clearly stated that the "Powers and Duties" of the highest office would "devolve on the Vice President" in the event of a president's death. But there were some who believed that the "Powers and Duties" were not the same thing as the office, that the vice president could become only an "acting president," that his authority might in some way be compromised. This potentially critical constitutional problem was resolved by Vice President Tyler, who calmly took the oath of office as president and left no doubt that he considered himself a legitimate chief executive. The question of the legal status of a vice president who succeeded to the presidency was never raised again.

More troubling to the leaders of the Whig party than such constitutional questions was that with Harrison gone, control of government had fallen to a man with whom they had much weaker ties. Harrison in his brief weeks in office had generally deferred to Henry Clay and Daniel Webster, confirming the predictions of those who had foretold that the Whig chieftains would be the real powers in government. Webster had become secretary of state; four of Clay's allies had taken other positions in the cabinet. Under Tyler, things were to change.

Tyler was a member of an aristocratic Virginian family. Originally a Democrat, he had left the party in reaction to what he considered Jackson's excessively egalitarian program and his imperious methods. One reason the Whigs had included him on their ticket was to attract the votes of similarly disenchanted conservative Democrats. But while Tyler had certain attitudes in common with the Whig leadership, there were still signs of his Democratic past in his approach to public policy. Clay apparently had the impression that the new president would support the restoration of a national bank and other Whig projects, but Tyler soon indicated otherwise. A break occurred between the president and Clay that was never to heal.

There were, to be sure, some elements of Clay's ambitious program that Tyler was willing to accept. The president signed a bill abolishing the independent treasury system. He agreed to a bill raising tariff rates to nearly the same level as 1832 (although he displayed little enthusiasm for the proposal). And he approved a measure—the Preemption Act of 1841—to increase the appeal of the Whigs to Western settlers and farmers. The bill was virtually identical to the one the Whigs had defeated when Van Buren proposed it. This "log cabin bill," as the Whigs called it, was promoted as a measure to relieve the suffering caused by the depression and to prove the party's devotion to the welfare of the common man.

Although Tyler supported Whig measures designed to appeal to Democratic voters, he was less willing to cooperate with the party leadership in pursuing the heart of the Whig program—the creation of a national financial system similar to the Bank of the United States. Tyler favored a national bank, but one very different from that proposed by Clay. His was to be a "states' rights national bank," one that would confine its operations to the District of Columbia and establish branches in the states only with the consent of those states. Twice he vetoed bills that would have set up what the Whigs tried to disguise as a "fiscal corporation."

Lacking a sufficient majority to override the veto, the Whigs fumed at the president, who added to their anger by vetoing a number of internal improvement bills. In an unprecedented action, a conference of congressional Whigs read Tyler out of the party. All the cabinet members resigned except Webster. To fill their places, the president appointed five men of his own stripe—former Democrats. When the office of secretary of state became vacant in 1844, Tyler appointed John C. Calhoun, who had now rejoined the Democratic party that he had left in the 1830s.

A portentous new political alignment was taking shape. Tyler and a small band of conservative Southern Whigs who followed him were preparing to rejoin the Democrats. Into the common man's party of Jackson and Van Buren was arriving a group of men with decidedly aristocratic political ideas, who thought that government had an obligation to protect and even expand the institution of slavery, and who believed in states' rights with a single-minded, almost fanatical devotion.

Whig Diplomacy

In the midst of these domestic controversies, a series of incidents brought Great Britain and the United States to the brink of war in the late 1830s.

SIGNIFICANT EVENTS

1820–1840 State constitutions revised (pp. 281–282)

1823 Nicholas Biddle becomes president of Bank of the United States (p. 292)

1826 William Morgan disappearance inflames Anti-Masonry (p. 297)

1828 Calhoun's *South Carolina Exposition and Protest* outlines nullification doctrine (p. 284)

1829 Andrew Jackson inaugurated (p. 279)

1830 Webster and Hayne debate (p. 286)
Jackson vetoes Maysville Road bill (p. 288)
Indian Removal Act passed (p. 290)

1830–1838 Indians expelled from Southeast (pp. 290–291)

1831 Anti-Mason party established (p. 297)
Supreme Court rules in *Cherokee Nation* v. *Georgia* (p. 290)

1832 Democrats hold first national party convention (p. 281)
Jackson vetoes bill to recharter Bank of the United States (p. 293)
Jackson reelected president (p. 293)

1833 Jackson and Taney remove federal deposits from Bank of the United States (p. 294)
Commercial panic disrupts economy (p. 294)

1832–1833 Nullification crisis erupts (p. 287)

1834 Indian Trade and Intercourse Act renewed (p. 291)

1835 Roger Taney succeeds Marshall as Chief Justice of the Supreme Court (p. 294)
Federal debt retired (p. 302)

1835–1840 Tocqueville publishes *Democracy in America* (p. 279)

1835–1842 Seminole War (pp. 291–292)

1836 Jackson issues "specie circular" (p. 302)
Martin Van Buren elected president (p. 301)

1837 Supreme Court rules in *Charles River Bridge* case (p. 295)

1837–1844 Commercial panic and depression (p. 302)

1838 "Aroostook War" fought in Maine and Canada (p. 307)

1839 Whigs hold their first national convention (p. 304)

1840 William Henry Harrison elected president (p. 305)
Independent Treasury Act passed (p. 304)

1841 Harrison dies; John Tyler succeeds (p. 306)

1842 Dorr Rebellion hastens reform in Rhode Island (p. 282)
Webster-Ashburton Treaty signed (p. 308)

One such incident occurred in upstate New York. In 1837, a rebellion against the British colonial government broke out in the eastern provinces of Canada; many Americans applauded the rebels and furnished them with material aid. The rebels chartered a small American steamship, the *Caroline,* to carry supplies across the Niagara River from New York. One night while the ship was moored at a wharf on the American side, Canadian authorities sent over a force that took possession of the *Caroline* and burned it. In the melée one American was killed. Excitement flared on both sides of the border. President Van Buren issued a proclamation asking Americans to abide by the neutrality laws, and he sent General Winfield Scott to the border to act as a pacifier. The State Department demanded an apology and reparations from Great Britain, but the British government neither disavowed the attack nor offered compensation for it.

While the *Caroline* affair simmered, another troublesome issue began to plague Anglo-American relations: the issue of the boundary between Canada and Maine. The Treaty of 1783 had left the boundary ill defined, and all subsequent attempts to fix it by mutual agreement and by arbitration had failed. In 1838, groups of Americans and Canadians, mostly lumberjacks, began to move into the Aroostook River region in the disputed area. A head-smashing brawl between the two groups—the "Aroostook War"—threatened more trouble between England and America.

Eventually a Canadian named Alexander McLeod was arrested in New York and charged with the murder of the American who had died in the *Caroline* incident. The British government reacted with majestic rage, contending that McLeod could not be accused of murder because he had acted under official orders. The foreign secretary, the bellicose Lord Palmerston, demanded McLeod's release and threatened that his execution would bring "immediate and frightful" war. Webster as secretary of state did not think McLeod was worth a war but could do nothing to release him. The prisoner was under New York jurisdiction and had to be tried in the state courts, a peculiarity of American jurisprudence that the British did not seem to understand. Fortunately for the cause of peace—and for himself—McLeod was acquitted.

Festering points of disagreement still remained. In an attempt to stamp out the African slave trade, Great Britain had long sought the right to search American merchant ships suspected of carrying black cargoes. This was a sensitive subject to the American government, which remembered well the events that had precipitated the War of 1812. The United States had steadfastly refused the British request. As a result, slavers of other nations frequently sought to avoid capture by hoisting the American flag. Complicating the issue was the domestic slave trade, in which slaves were carried by sea from one American port to another. Sometimes the ships in this trade were blown off their course to the British West Indies, where the authorities, acting under English law, freed the slaves. In 1841, an American brig, the *Creole*, sailed from Virginia for New Orleans with more than 100 slaves aboard. En route the slaves mutinied, took possession of the ship, and took it to the Bahamas. Here British officials declared the bondsmen free. Although Webster protested, England refused to return the slaves. Many Americans, especially Southerners, were infuriated.

At this critical juncture a new government came to power in Great Britain, one that was more disposed to conciliate the United States and to settle the outstanding differences between the two countries. The new ministry sent to America an emissary, Lord Ashburton, to negotiate an agreement on the Maine boundary and other matters. Ashburton liked Americans, and Webster admired the English. To avoid war, both were willing to compromise. The result of their deliberations was the Webster-Ashburton Treaty of August 9, 1842.

By the terms of this arrangement, the United States received about seven-twelfths of the disputed area. Minor rectifications were made in other areas, and the boundary was now established as far west as the Rocky Mountains. It was agreed that both Great Britain and the United States would maintain naval squadrons off the African coast, the American ships being charged with chasing slavers using the American flag.

Through the exchange of notes that were not part of the treaty, Webster and Ashburton also eased the memory of the *Caroline* and *Creole* affairs. Ashburton expressed "regret" for the raid on the *Caroline*, and he pledged that in the future there would be no "officious interference" with American ships forced by "violence or accident" to enter British ports. Webster used secret funds to inspire newspaper propaganda favorable to his arrangements with Ashburton, and the treaty proved quite popular. War talk faded, and Anglo-American relations suddenly looked better than they had for many years.

During the Tyler administration, the United States established diplomatic relations with China. In 1842, Britain forced China to open certain ports to foreign trade. Eager to share the new privileges, American mercantile interests persuaded Tyler and Congress to send a commissioner—Caleb Cushing—to China to negotiate a treaty giving the United States some part in the China trade. In the Treaty of Wang Hya, concluded in 1844, Cushing secured most-favored-nation provisions giving Americans the same privileges as the English. He also won for Americans the right of "extraterritoriality"—the right of Americans accused of crimes in China to be tried by American, not Chinese, officials. In the next ten years, American trade with China steadily increased.

In their diplomatic efforts, at least, the Whigs were able to secure some important successes. But by the end of the Tyler administration, the party could look back on few other victories. Having elected a president in 1840, they had watched as the policies of the administration (and the political allegiances of its principal figures, including the president himself) became steadily more Democratic. And in the election of 1844, the Whigs lost even their nominal control of the White House. They were to win only one more national election in their history—in 1848—before a great sectional crisis arose that would shatter their party and, for a time, the Union.

SUGGESTED READINGS

General History. Glyndon Van Deusen, *The Jacksonian Era* (1959); John Mayfield, *The New Nation, 1800–1845* (1981); James C. Curtis, *Andrew Jackson and the Search for Vindication* (1976); Edward Pessen, *Jacksonian America*, rev. ed. (1979).

Democracy. Alexis de Tocqueville, *Democracy in America*, 2 vols. (1835); Moisie Ostrogorskii, *Democracy and the Organization of Political Parties*, 2 vols. (1902); Chilton Williamson, *American Suffrage from Property to Democracy, 1760–1860* (1960); Louis Hartz, *The Liberal Tradition in*

America (1955); Michael Kammen, *Spheres of Liberty: Changing Perceptions of Liberty in American Culture* (1986); Marvin E. Gettleman, *The Dorr Rebellion* (1973); Patrick T. Conley, *Democracy in Decline* (1977).

Jacksonian Society.   Edward Pessen, *Riches, Class, and Power Before the Civil War* (1973); Douglas T. Miller, *Jacksonian Aristocracy* (1967); Sean Wilentz, *Chants Democratic: New York City and the Rise of the American Working Class, 1788–1850* (1984); Mary Ryan, *Cradle of the Middle Class: The Family in Oneida County, New York, 1790–1865* (1981); Christine Stansell, *City of Women: Sex and Class in New York, 1789–1860* (1986); Nancy Hewitt, *Women's Activism and Social Change: Rochester, New York, 1822–1872* (1984); Carroll Smith-Rosenberg, *Religion and the Rise of the City* (1971).

Jacksonian Politics.   Arthur M. Schlesinger, Jr., *The Age of Jackson* (1945); Marvin Meyers, *The Jacksonian Persuasion* (1960); Richard Hofstadter, *The American Political Tradition* (1948); John William Ward, *Andrew Jackson: Symbol for an Age* (1955); Lee Benson, *The Concept of Jacksonian Democracy* (1961); Leonard White, *The Jacksonians: A Study in Administrative History* (1954); Richard B. Latner, *The Presidency of Andrew Jackson: White House Politics, 1829–1837* (1979); Richard B. McCormick, *The Second American Party System: Party Formation in the Jacksonian Era* (1966); Ronald P. Formisano, *The Birth of Mass Political Parties: Michigan, 1827–1861* (1971); Harry L. Watson, *Jacksonian Politics and Community Conflict: The Emergence of the Second Party System in Cumberland County, North Carolina* (1981); C. B. Swisher, *Roger B. Taney* (1936); Morton Horwitz, *The Transformation of American Law, 1780–1860* (1977).

Andrew Jackson.   Robert V. Remini, *Andrew Jackson and the Course of American Empire: 1767–1821* (1977), *Andrew Jackson and the Course of American Freedom: 1822–1832* (1981), *Andrew Jackson and the Course of American Democracy* (1984), and *Andrew Jackson* (1966); Marquis James, *Andrew Jackson*, 2 vols. (1933–1937); James Parton, *Life of Andrew Jackson*, 3 vols. (1860).

Nullification.   William V. Freehling, *Prelude to Civil War: The Nullification Controversy in South Carolina* (1966); Charles S. Sydnor, *The Development of Southern Sectionalism 1819–1848* (1948); Merrill D. Peterson, *Olive Branch and Sword: The Compromise of 1833* (1983).

Indian Policies.   Ronald N. Satz, *American Indian Policy in the Jacksonian Era* (1975); Michael Rogin, *Fathers and Children: Andrew Jackson and the Destruction of American Indians* (1975); Grant Foreman, *Indian Removal: The Emigration of the Five Civilized Tribes* (1932) and *Indians and Pioneers: The Story of the American Southwest Before 1830* (1936); Arthur H. DeRosier, Jr., *The Removal of the Choctaw Indians* (1970); Theda Perdue, *Slavery and the Evolution of Cherokee Society, 1540–1866* (1979); Daniel F. Littlefield, Jr., *Africans and Seminoles: From Removal to Emancipation* (1976) and *Africans*

and Creeks: From the Colonial Period to the Civil War (1979); Thurman Wilkins, *Cherokee Tragedy* (1970); Michael D. Green, *The Politics of Indian Removal: Cherokee Government and Society in Crisis* (1982); Richard White, *The Roots of Dependency* (1983); Angie Debo, *A History of the Indians of the United States* (1970), *The Road to Disappearance: A History of the Creek Indians* (1941), and *And Still the Waters Run: The Betrayal of the Five Civilized Tribes* (1973); Wilcomb E. Washburn, *The Indian in America* (1975); William Brandon, *The Last Americans* (1974); B.W. Sheehan, *Seeds of Extinction: Jeffersonian Philanthropy and the American Indian* (1973); Francis P. Prucha, *American Indian Policy in the Formative Years* (1962); Cecil Elby, *"That Disgraceful Affair"* (1973).

The Bank War.   Robert V. Remini, *Andrew Jackson and the Bank War* (1967); Bray Hammond, *Banks and Politics in America from the Revolution to the Civil War* (1957); Peter Temin, *The Jacksonian Economy* (1969); J. M. McFaul, *The Politics of Jacksonian Finance* (1972); William G. Shade, *Banks or No Banks: The Money Issue in Western Politics, 1832–1865* (1972); J. A. Wilburn, *Biddle's Bank* (1967); T. P. Govan, *Nicholas Biddle; Nationalist and Public Banker* (1959); Reginald C. McGrane, *The Panic of 1837* (1924); J. R. Sharp, *The Jacksonians Versus the Banks* (1970).

Post-Jacksonian Politics.   Robert V. Remini, *Martin Van Buren and the Making of the Democratic Party* (1959); James C. Curtis, *The Fox at Bay: Martin Van Buren and the Presidency* (1970); John Niven, *Martin Van Buren: The Romantic Age of American Politics* (1983); Paul Goodman, *Toward a Christian Republic: Anti-Masonry and the Great Transition in New England, 1826–1836* (1988); E. M. Carroll, *Origins of the Whig Party* (1925); Daniel Walker Howe, *The Political Culture of the American Whigs* (1979); Thomas Brown, *Politics and Statesmanship: Essays on the American Whig Party* (1985); Claude M. Fuess, *Daniel Webster*, 2 vols. (1930); Richard N. Current, *Daniel Webster and the Rise of National Conservatism* (1955); Irving Bartlett, *Daniel Webster* (1978); Norman D. Brown, *Daniel Webster and the Politics of Availability* (1969); Sydney Nathans, *Daniel Webster and Jacksonian Democracy* (1973); Robert Dalzell, *Daniel Webster and the Trial of American Nationalism* (1973); Maurice C. Baxter, *One and Inseparable: Daniel Webster and the Union* (1984); Clement Eaton, *Henry Clay and the Art of American Politics* (1957); George R. Poage, *Henry Clay and the Whig Party* (1936); Merrill D. Peterson, *The Great Triumvirate: Webster, Clay, and Calhoun* (1987); Thomas H. O'Connor, *Lords of the Loom: The Cotton Whigs and the Coming of the Civil War* (1968); William Preston Vaughn, *The Anti-Masonic Party in the United States, 1826–1843* (1983); Oscar D. Lambert, *Presidential Politics in the United States, 1841–1844* (1936); R. G. Gunderson, *The Log Cabin Campaign* (1957). Oliver P. Chitwood, *John Tyler: Champion of the Old South* (1939); Howard Jones, *To the Webster-Ashburton Treaty* (1977); A. B. Corey, *The Crisis of 1830–1842 in Canadian-American Relations* (1941); John B. Brebner, *North Atlantic Triangle* (1945).

***Steamboats at the Sugar Levee, New Orleans* (1853), by Hippolyte Valentin Sebron**
New Orleans was the principal market city of the lower South in the 1850s—the beneficiary, as this
painting suggests, of the booming cotton economy that was transforming the region in those years.
(*Tulane University*)

CHAPTER 11

❧ ✦ ❧

The North and the South: Diverging Societies

❧ ✦ ❧

Americans in the mid-nineteenth century liked to believe that theirs was a nation specially ordained by God, that their Union represented a beacon of liberty and stability that would serve as a model to the rest of the world. In fact, however, the United States in these years was in many respects not truly a nation at all—at least not in the way nations would be defined in later times. It was, rather, a highly decentralized confederation of states, many of which had little in common with one another. Those states remained together in part because the union was so loose, and the central authority of the nation so weak, that the differences among them did not often have to be confronted.

When the United States began to move in the direction of greater national unity, as it did in the 1840s, it encountered a series of major obstacles. And one obstacle, in particular, became so powerful that it soon threatened to tear the nation apart: sectionalism. The rivalry of one part of the country with another was not, of course, new to the mid-nineteenth century. There had been sectional differences as early as the seventeenth century among the colonies of the South, the mid-Atlantic, and New England.

By the 1840s and 1850s, however, sectionalism had changed both in its nature and in its intensity. In many respects, there were now four quite distinct regions: the Northeast, with a growing industrial and commercial economy and an increasing density of population; the Northwest, a rapidly expanding agricultural region; the Southeast, with a settled plantation system and (in some areas) declining economic

fortunes as well; and the Southwest, a booming frontierlike region with an expanding cotton economy. As the sectional crisis grew more intense, however, many Americans came to view their nation as divided into two sections, each with a distinctive and relatively homogeneous culture: the North and the South.

The most obvious aspect of this division was a basic difference in the labor systems of the sections. The South was not only maintaining but, as its plantation economy expanded into new areas of the Southwest, intensifying its commitment to slavery as its primary source of labor. The Northeast and the Northwest were committed to a free-labor economy. But slavery was only part of a larger difference between the sections. In the North, a modern, diversified economy was developing, with an important manufacturing sector, a flourishing commercial life, and an expanding range of urban services and activities. Between the North and the Northwest, moreover, close economic and cultural ties were developing. And the South, as a result, was becoming—or at least sensed itself becoming—isolated, left behind. Dependent on the North for manufactured goods, for commercial services, for many of the most basic necessities of life; cut off from the flourishing agricultural regions of the Northwest; committed to a way of life that much of the rest of the nation considered obsolete: the South was coming to seem a colonial appendage of the powerful regions to the north. In the 1840s and 1850s, this schism between Northern and Southern societies greatly intensified. Ultimately, it produced tensions and conflicts that contributed to the disruption of the Union.

The Developing North

The most conspicuous change in American life in the 1840s and 1850s was the rapid development of the economy and society of the Northeast. Industrialization, which had begun slowly in the years immediately following the War of 1812 and had gathered force in the 1820s and 1830s, now burst forth as a major factor in the Northern economy. Urban centers, in the past relatively few and relatively small, now grew rapidly. Class divisions became more visible and pronounced. New industrial capitalists and financiers accumulated fortunes only rarely seen in earlier times; a growing urban middle class became an ever more important factor in American society; and a rapidly expanding industrial labor force created a distinct working class. The Northeast, and its new economic ally the Northwest, were developing a complex, modern society, one that would greatly increase the differences that had always existed between that region and the South.

Northeastern Industry

Between 1840 and 1860, American industry experienced a steady and, in some fields, spectacular growth. In 1840, the total value of manufactured goods produced in the United States stood at $483 million; ten years later the figure had climbed to over $1 billion; and in 1860 it reached close to $2 billion. For the first time, the value of manufactured goods was approximately equal to that of agricultural products.

Of the approximately 140,000 manufacturing establishments in the country in 1860, 74,000 were located in the Northeast. They included, moreover, most of the larger enterprises. Although the Northeast had only a little more than half the mills and factories of the nation, it produced more than two-thirds of the manufactured goods. Of the 1,311,000 workers in manufacturing in the United States, about 938,000 were employed in the mills and factories of New England and the middle states.

Even the most highly developed industries still showed qualities of immaturity and were far from the production levels they would later attain. Cotton manufacturers, for example, produced goods of coarse grade; fine items continued to be imported from England. The woolens industry suffered from a limited supply of domestic raw wool and could not even produce enough coarse goods to satisfy the home market. American industry exported little; it was unable to meet fully the demands of American consumers. But technology and industrial ingenuity were preparing the way for future American industrial primacy.

The machine tools used in the factories of the Northeast—such as the turret lathe, the grinding machine, and the universal milling machine—were by the 1840s already better than those in European factories. The principle of interchangeable parts, first applied decades earlier in gun factories by Eli Whitney and Simeon North, was by the 1840s being introduced into many other industries. Coal was replacing wood as an industrial fuel, particularly in the smelting of iron. Coal was also being used to generate power in steam engines, which were replacing the water power that had in the past driven most of the factory machinery in the Northeast. The production of coal, most of it mined in the Pittsburgh area of western Pennsylvania, leaped from 50,000 tons in 1820 to 14 million tons in 1860. The new power source made it possible to locate mills away from running streams and thus permitted industry to expand still more widely.

The great technical advances in American industry owed much to American inventors. Patent records give some indication of the extent of Yankee ingenuity in these years. In 1830, the number of inventions patented was 544; in 1850, the figure rose to 993; and in 1860, it stood at 4,778. Several industries provide particularly vivid examples of how a technological innovation could produce a major economic change. In 1839, Charles Goodyear, a New England hardware merchant, discovered a method of vulcanizing rubber; his process had been put to 500 uses by 1860 and had succeeded in establishing a major American rubber industry. In 1846, Elias Howe of Massachusetts constructed a sewing machine; Isaac Singer made improvements on it, and the Howe-Singer machine was soon employed in the manufacture of ready-to-wear clothing. A few years later, during the Civil War, it would supply the Northern troops with uniforms.

In an earlier period, the dominant economic figures in the Northeast had been the merchant capitalists—entrepreneurs who engaged in foreign or domestic trade, who invested their surplus capital in banks, and who sometimes financed small-scale domestic manufacturers. The merchant capitalists remained figures of importance in the 1840s. In such cities as New York, Philadelphia, and Boston, important and influential mercantile groups operated shipping lines to Southern ports—carrying away cotton, rice, and sugar—or dispatched fleets of trading vessels to the ports of Europe and the Orient. Many of these vessels were the famous clippers, the most beautiful and the fastest sailing ships afloat. In their heyday in the late 1840s and early 1850s, the clippers were capable of averaging 300 miles a day, which compared favorably with the best time then being made by steamships.

Nevertheless, merchant capitalism was entering a state of decline by the middle of the century. Although the value of American exports, still largely agricultural, increased from $124 million in 1840 to $334 million in 1860, American merchants in the 1850s saw much of their carrying trade fall into the hands of British competitors, who enjoyed the advantages of steam-driven iron ships and government subsidies.

Foreign competition was not, however, the principal cause of the decline of the merchant capitalist. It was the rise of the factory system in the United States. Merchants now saw greater opportunities for profit in manufacturing than in trade. They reduced their mercantile investments and became owners and operators of factories or invested their money in factories operated by others. Indeed, one reason that industries developed soonest in the Northeast was that an affluent merchant class already existed there and had the money and the will to finance them.

As in the past, many business concerns continued to be owned by individuals, by families, or by small groups of partners. But by the 1840s, particularly in the textile industry, the corporate form of organization was spreading rapidly. In their overseas ventures, merchants had been accustomed to diversifying their risks by buying shares in a number of vessels and voyages. They employed the same device when they moved their capital from trade to manufacturing. They tended to purchase shares in several textile companies. Ownership of American enterprise, in other words, was moving away from individuals and families and toward its highly dispersed modern form: many stockholders, each owning a relatively small proportion of the total. The discovery

of new and more flexible forms of financing was, along with the technological innovations of the era, a crucial factor in the advancement of industrialization.

Whatever the form of business organization, and there continued to be many different forms, industrial capitalists soon became the new ruling class, the aristocrats of the Northeast. And just as they had sought and secured economic dominance, they reached for and often achieved political influence. In local or national politics, the capitalists liked to be represented by highly literate lawyers who could articulate their prejudices and philosophy. Their ideal of a representative was Daniel Webster of Massachusetts, whom the business leaders of the section, at considerable financial cost to themselves, supported for years in the United States Senate.

Transportation and Communications

The new industrial economy could not have developed without an adequate transportation system. New forms of transportation were essential for moving raw materials to the factories and for moving finished goods out. And they were essential, above all, in forging ties between the industrial Northeast and the growing agricultural regions of the Northwest—an alliance that became crucial not only to the growth of the American economy but also to the sectional tensions that would soon rise to threaten the Union.

In the 1830s, most of the goods exchanged between the two sections were carried on the Erie Canal. But after 1840, railroads gradually supplanted canals and all other modes of transport. The railroads enabled the Western farmers to ship their products cheaply and quickly to Eastern markets and thus helped to force many Eastern farmers out of business.

In 1840, the total railroad trackage of the country was only 2,818 miles; by the end of the decade, the trackage figure had risen to 9,021 miles. But an unparalleled burst of railroad construction occurred in the 1850s. The amount of trackage tripled between 1850 and 1860. The Northeast developed the most comprehensive and efficient system, with twice as much trackage per square mile as the Northwest and four times as much as the South. Railroads were reaching even west of the Mississippi, which at several points was spanned by iron bridges. One line ran from Hannibal to St. Joseph on the Missouri River, and another was being built from St. Louis to Kansas City.

The First Railroad Station
Mount Clare Station in Baltimore, Maryland, was the first railroad passenger depot in the world. Constructed in 1829 by the Baltimore and Ohio Railroad, it inaugurated passenger service between Baltimore and Washington, D.C., on August 25, 1835. The open cars and small steam engine suggest the limits of railroad technology in the 1830s. (Baltimore and Ohio Railroad/The Bettmann Archive)

In the South, such towns as Charleston, Atlanta, Savannah, and Norfolk had direct connections with Memphis, and thus with the Northwest; and Richmond was connected, via the Virginia Central, with the Memphis and Charleston railroad. In addition, several independent lines furnished a continuous connection between the Ohio River and New Orleans. Much of the South, however, remained unconnected to the national railroad system. Most lines in the region were short, local ones. The absence of a major railroad system became another factor isolating the South from the rest of the nation.

A new feature in railroad development—one that would profoundly affect the nature of sectional alignments—was the trend toward the consolidation of short lines into trunk lines. By 1853, four major railroad trunk lines had surmounted the Appalachian barrier to connect the Northeast with the Northwest. Two, the New York Central and the New York and Erie, gave New York City access to the Lake Erie ports. The Pennsylvania road linked Philadelphia and Pittsburgh, and the Baltimore and Ohio connected Baltimore with the Ohio River at Wheeling. From the terminals of these lines, other railroads into the interior touched the Mississippi River at eight points. Chicago became the rail center of the West, served by fifteen lines and more than a hundred daily trains. The appearance of the great trunk lines tended to divert traffic from the main water routes—the Erie Canal and the Mississippi River. By lessening the dependence of the West on the Mississippi, the railroads helped weaken further the connection between the Northwest and the South.

Capital to finance the railroad boom came from various sources. Private American investors provided part of the necessary funding, and railroad companies borrowed large sums from abroad. But local governments—states, counties, cities, towns—also often contributed capital, because they were eager to have railroads to serve their needs. This support took the form of loans, stock subscriptions, subsidies, and donations of land for rights of way. The railroads obtained additional assistance from the federal government in the shape of public land grants. In 1850, Senator Stephen A. Douglas of Illinois and other railroad-minded politicians persuaded Congress to grant federal lands to the state of Illinois to aid the Illinois Central, which was building toward the Gulf of Mexico; Illinois then transferred the land to the railroad company as an incentive to build lines in the state. Other states and their railroad promoters demanded the same privileges; and by 1860, Congress had allotted over 30 million acres to eleven states.

Facilitating the operation of the railroads was another important technological innovation: the magnetic telegraph. Its lines extended along the tracks, connecting one station with another and aiding the scheduling and routing of the trains. But the telegraph had an importance to the nation's economic development all its own. It permitted instant communication between distant cities, tying the nation together as never before. And yet, ironically, it also helped reinforce the schism between the two sections. As with railroads, telegraph lines were far more extensive in the North than in the South; and they helped similarly to link the North to the Northwest (and thus to separate the Northwest further from the South).

The telegraph had burst into American life in 1844, when Samuel F. B. Morse, after several years of experimentation, succeeded in transmitting from Baltimore to Washington the news of James K. Polk's nomination for the presidency. The Morse telegraph seemed, because of the relatively low cost of constructing wire systems, the ideal answer to the problems of long-distance communication. By 1860, more than 50,000 miles of wire connected most parts of the country; and a year later, the Pacific telegraph, with 3,595 miles of wire, was opened between New York and San Francisco. By then, nearly all of the independent lines had been absorbed into one organization, the Western Union Telegraph Company.

New forms of journalism also served to draw communities together into a common communications system, as well as to reveal more clearly to different regions their differences from one another. In 1846, Richard Hoe invented the steam cylinder rotary press, making it possible to print newspapers rapidly and cheaply. The development of the telegraph, together with the introduction of the rotary press, made possible much speedier collection and distribution of news than ever before. In 1846, the Associated Press was organized for the purpose of cooperative news gathering by wire; no longer did publishers have to depend on an exchange of newspapers for out-of-town reports. Major metropolitan newspapers began to appear in the larger cities of the Northeast. Horace Greeley's *Tribune*, James Gordon

Bennett's *Herald,* and Henry J. Raymond's *Times* were all published in New York; but all gave serious attention to national and even international events and had substantial circulations beyond the city. Southern newspapers, by contrast, tended to have smaller budgets and reported largely local news. Few had any impact outside their immediate communities. The combined circulation of the *Tribune* and the *Herald* exceeded that of all the daily newspapers published in the South put together.

In the long run, journalism would become an important unifying factor in American life. In the 1840s and 1850s, however, the rise of the new journalism helped to feed the fires of sectional discord. Most of the major magazines and newspapers were in the North, reinforcing the South's sense of subjugation. Above all, the news revolution—along with the revolutions in transportation and communications that accompanied it—contributed to a growing awareness within each section of how the other section lived and of the deep differences that had grown up between the North and the South—differences that would ultimately seem irreconcilable.

The Growth of the Railroads, 1850–1860

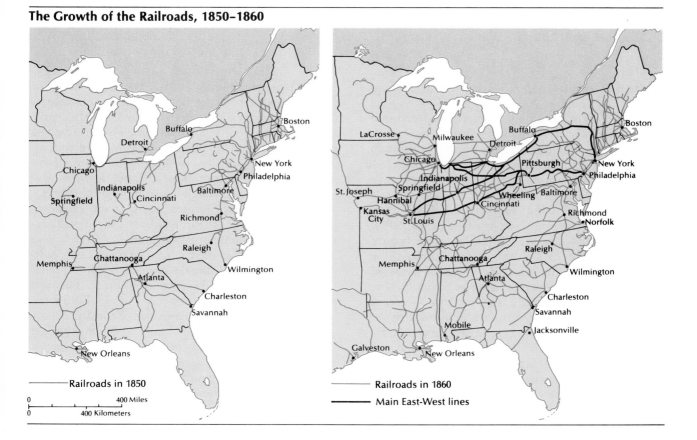

Population Density of the United States, 1820

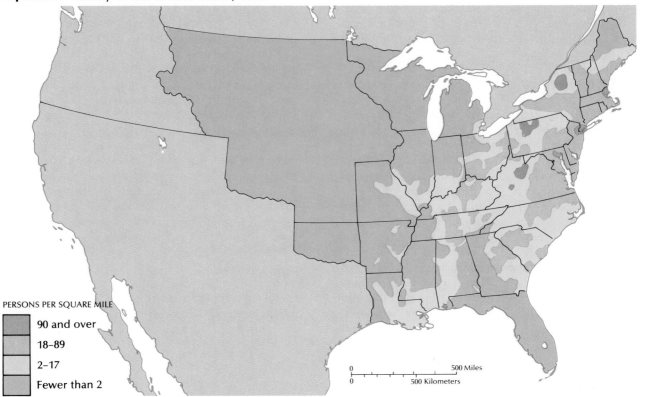

PERSONS PER SQUARE MILE

90 and over

18–89

2–17

Fewer than 2

500 Miles

500 Kilometers

Cities and Immigrants

One of the most profound changes in the nature of Northeastern society in the antebellum period was in the character and distribution of the population, above all the growing size of cities. Between 1840 and 1860, the population of New York, for example, rose from 312,000 to 805,000. (New York's population numbered 1.2 million in 1860 if Brooklyn, which was then a separate municipality, is included.) Philadelphia's population grew over the same twenty-year period from 220,000 to 565,000; Boston's from 93,000 to 177,000. By 1860, 26 percent of the population of the free states was living in towns or cities (places of 2,500 people or more), up from 14 percent in 1840; that percentage was even higher for the industrializing states of the Northeast. (In the South, by contrast, the increase of urban residents was only from 6 percent in 1840 to 10 percent in 1860.)

The enlarged urban population was in part simply a reflection of the growth of the national population as a whole, which rose by more than a third—from 23 million to over 31 million—in the decade of the 1850s alone. But it was also a result of the flow of people into the cities from two sources in particular. The first and for a time larger source was the native farming classes of the Northeast, whose members were being forced off their lands by Western competition. The second and at least equally important source was immigration from Europe. Between 1830 and 1840, only a relatively small number of foreigners had moved to the United States, about 500,000 in all. Beginning in 1840, however, the floodgates opened. The number of immigrants arriving in 1840—84,000—was the highest for any one year so far in the century. But in the ensuing years, even that number would come to seem insignificant. Between 1840 and 1850, more than 1.5 million Europeans moved to America; in the last years of the decade, the average number arriving annually was almost 300,000. Of the 23 million people in the United States in 1850, 2,210,000 (approximately 10 percent) were foreign-born. Still greater numbers arrived in the 1850s—over 2.5 million. Almost half the population of New York City in the 1850s consisted of recent immigrants. In St. Louis, Chicago, and Milwaukee,

Population Density of the United States, 1860

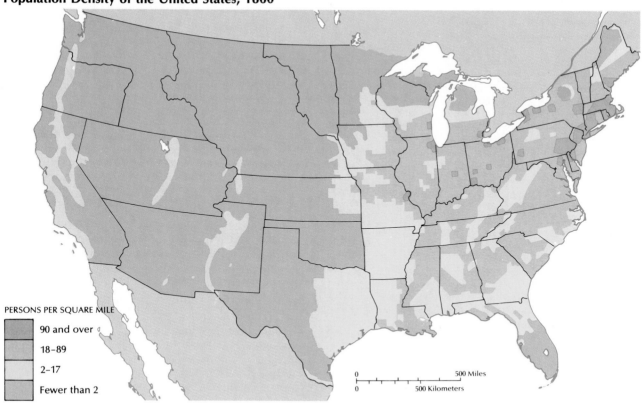

PERSONS PER SQUARE MILE
- 90 and over
- 18–89
- 2–17
- Fewer than 2

0   500 Miles
0   500 Kilometers

the foreign-born outnumbered those of native birth. Few immigrants settled in the South. Only 500,000 lived in the slave states in 1860, and a third of these were concentrated in Missouri.

The newcomers came from many different countries and regions: England, France, Italy, Scandinavia, Poland, and Holland. But the overwhelming majority came from Ireland and Germany. In 1850, the Irish constituted approximately 45 percent and the Germans over 20 percent of the foreign-born in America. By 1860, there were more than 1.5 million Irish-born and approximately 1 million German-born people in the United States. Several factors accounted for the prevalence of immigrants from Ireland and Germany: widespread poverty caused by the economic dislocations of the industrial revolution, famines resulting from the failure of the potato and other crops, dislike of English rule by the Irish, and the collapse of the liberal revolution of 1848 in Germany.

Irish and German patterns of settlement in America were very different from one another. The great majority of the Irish settled in the Eastern cities, where they swelled the ranks of unskilled labor. Germans generally moved on to the Northwest, where they became farmers or went into business in the Western towns. One reason for the difference was wealth. German immigrants generally arrived with at least some money; the Irish had practically none. Another important reason was gender. Most German immigrants were members of family groups or were single men, for whom movement to the agricultural frontier was both possible and attractive. The largest number of Irish immigrants consisted of single women, for whom movement west was much less plausible. They were more likely to stay in the Eastern cities, where factory and domestic work was available.

The Rise of Nativism

The new foreign-born population almost immediately became a major factor in American political life. Wisconsin, after its admission to the Union in 1848, permitted aliens to become voters as soon as they had declared their intention of seeking citizenship and had resided in the state for a year. Other states followed

Sources of Immigration, 1840–1860

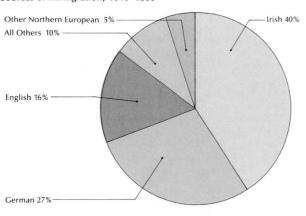

Other Northern European 5%
All Others 10%
Irish 40%
English 16%
German 27%

Total Immigration, 1840–1860

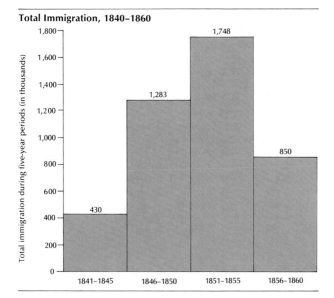

Total immigration during five-year periods (in thousands)

1841–1845	1846–1850	1851–1855	1856–1860
430	1,283	1,748	850

from the native work force. Protestants took note of the Irish Catholics' aptitude for politics and claimed that the church of Rome was attaining an undue power in American government. Whig politicians were outraged because so many of the newcomers voted Democratic. Many Americans of older stock feared that immigrants would inject new and radical philosophies into national thought.

Out of these tensions and prejudices emerged a number of secret societies to combat the "alien menace." Most of them originated in the Northeast. Some later spread to the West and even to the South. The first of these, the Native American Association, began agitating against immigration in 1837. In 1845, nativists held a convention in Philadelphia and formed the Native American party. But anti-immigrant sentiment crested in the 1850s. Many of the nativist groups combined in 1850 to form the Supreme Order of the Star-Spangled Banner. It endorsed a list of demands that included banning Catholics or aliens from holding public office, more restrictive naturalization laws, and literacy tests for voting. The order adopted a strict code of secrecy, which included the secret password, used in lodges across the country, "I know nothing." Ultimately, members of the movement became known as the "Know-Nothings."

Gradually, the Know-Nothings turned their attention to party politics, and after the election of 1852 they created a new political organization that they called the American party. In the East, the new organization scored an immediate and astonishing success in the elections of 1854: The Know-Nothings cast a large vote in Pennsylvania and New York and won control of the state government in Massachusetts. Elsewhere, the progress of the Know-Nothings was more modest. Western members of the party, because of the presence of many German voters in the area, found it expedient to proclaim that they were not opposed to naturalized Protestants. After 1854, however, the strength of the Know-Nothings declined; and the party's most lasting impact was its contribution to the collapse of the second party system and the creation of new national political alignments. (See pp. 392–393.)

Labor in the Northeast

The increasing migration of farmers into the cities, and the great rise in immigration from abroad, became another essential factor in the promotion of industrialization. It provided a labor force.

In the early years of industrial growth, the work

Wisconsin's lead in liberalizing voting laws, and in most places the polling officials were even more generous than the law allowed. Many politicians saw in the immigrant population a source of important potential support; and they eagerly courted the new arrivals for their ballots. Others, however, viewed the growing foreign population with alarm. Among the results of their fears were the first important organized nativist movements in American history.

The emerging nativism took many forms. Some nativists argued that the immigrants were mentally and physically defective, that they bred urban slums, that they corrupted politics by selling their votes. Others complained that because the aliens were willing to work for low wages, they were stealing jobs

"Americans Shall Rule America"

Thomas Swann, a Maryland railroad magnate, was elected mayor of Baltimore in 1856 as the candidate of the American (or "Know-Nothing") party after a campaign characterized by widespread violence and disorder. This cartoon lambasting the American party's activities in Baltimore conveys the opponents' image of the Know-Nothings as a party of drunken hooligans. (Maryland Historical Society)

force of the Northeastern factories had remained both small and for the most part impermanent. Because mills had been relatively few, manufacturers had made do with a modest, largely female labor supply—for example, the mill girls of Waltham and Lowell, who generally worked only temporarily in the factories before marrying or returning home. (See pp. 262–263.) By the 1840s, however, the need for factory workers was such that a large, permanent laboring class was beginning to emerge, drawn from the new urban population.

It had also been easy in the early years for mill owners to treat their workers with a paternal solicitude that at times softened the conditions of living and working in a new and alien environment. But with the expansion of industry, such niceties were quickly forgotten. No longer did workers live in neat boardinghouses or dormitories carefully maintained and patrolled by their employers. Instead, they were generally left to their own devices, to find whatever accommodations they could in the squalid factory towns that were rapidly growing up. No longer were the conditions of factory labor monitored so as to reduce the hardship of the workers. Instead, factories were becoming large, noisy, unsanitary, and often dangerous places to work; the average workday was extending to twelve, often fourteen hours; and wages

were declining, so that even skilled male workers could hope to earn only from $4 to $10 per week, while unskilled laborers were likely to earn only about $1 to $6 per week. Women and children, whatever their skills, also earned less than most men. Conditions were still not as bad as in most factory towns in England and Europe; but neither were American factories the models of cleanliness, efficiency, and human concern that many people had once believed them to be.

Workers faced with the arduous conditions of the new factory complexes made a number of efforts to improve their lot. They tried, with little success, to persuade state legislatures to pass laws setting a maximum workday. Two states—New Hampshire in 1847 and Pennsylvania in 1848—actually passed ten-hour laws, limiting the workday unless the workers agreed to an "express contract" calling for more time on the job. Such measures were virtually without impact, however, because employers could simply require prospective employees to sign the "express contract" as a condition of hiring. Three states—Massachusetts, New Hampshire, and Pennsylvania—passed laws regulating child labor. But again, the results were minimal. The laws simply limited the workday to ten hours for children unless their parents agreed to something longer; employers had little dif-

New England Textile Workers
Women continued to constitute the majority of the work force in the cotton mills of New England even after the carefully monitored life of the "Lowell girls" became a thing of the past—as this 1868 engraving by Winslow Homer suggests. About 58 percent of the textile industry work force was female in the 1860s. Approximately 7 percent were children under twelve (shown here carrying their lunch pails alongside the adults). (Library of Congress)

ficulty persuading parents to consent to additional hours.

Perhaps the greatest legal victory of industrial workers came in Massachusetts in 1842, when the supreme court of the state, in *Commonwealth* v. *Hunt*, declared that unions were lawful organizations and that the strike was a lawful weapon. Other state courts gradually accepted the principles of the Massachusetts decision. But the union movement of the 1840s and 1850s remained, on the whole, generally feeble and ineffective. Partly because many workers were reluctant to think of themselves as members of a permanent laboring force, resistance to organization remained strong. And those unions that did manage to establish a foothold in industry were usually not strong enough to stage strikes, and even less frequently strong enough to win them.

What organization there was among workers usually occurred at the local level and among limited groups of skilled workers. These early unions often had more in common with preindustrial guilds than with modern labor organizations. Their primary purpose was in most cases to protect the favored position of their members in the labor force by restricting admission to the skilled trades. As early as the 1830s, a few local craft unions had begun to associate with one another to form national organizations. (See p. 264.) More such associations emerged in the 1850s, among them the National Typographical Union, founded in 1852, followed by the Stone Cutters in 1853, the Hat Finishers in 1854, and the Molders and the Machinists, both in 1859.

Virtually all the early craft unions excluded women, even though female workers were numerous in almost every industry. As a result, women themselves were establishing women's protective unions by the 1850s, often with the support of middle-class female reformers. Like the male craft unions, the female protective unions had little power in dealing with employers. They did, however, serve an important role as mutual aid societies for women workers.

Despite these modest efforts at organization and protest, what was most notable about the American working class in the 1840s and 1850s was its relative passivity. In England, workers were becoming a powerful, united, and often violent economic and political force. They were creating widespread social turmoil and helping to transform the nation's political structure. In America, nothing of the sort happened.

Many factors combined to inhibit the growth of effective labor resistance. Among the most important was the flood of immigrant laborers into the country. The newcomers were usually willing to work for lower wages than native workers; and because they were so numerous, manufacturers had little difficulty replacing disgruntled or striking workers with eager immigrants. Ethnic divisions and tensions—both between natives and immigrants, and among the various immigrant groups themselves—often caused working-class resentments to be channeled into internal bickering rather than complaints against employers. There was, too, the sheer strength of the industrial capitalists, who had not only economic but political and social power and could usually triumph over even the most militant challenges. But a full understanding of the nature of the working-class response to industrialism requires an examination of the emerging social and economic structure of antebellum America.

Wealth and Mobility

The commercial and industrial growth of the United States greatly increased national wealth in the 1840s and 1850s. It elevated, too, the average income of the American people. But what evidence there is—and it is admittedly sketchy—suggests that this increasing wealth was not being widely distributed. Some groups of the population, of course, shared hardly at all in the economic growth: slaves, Indians, landless farmers, and many of the unskilled workers on the fringes of the manufacturing system. But even among the rest of the population, disparities of income were becoming so marked as to be impossible

to ignore. Wealth had always been unequally distributed in the United States, to be sure. Even in the era of the Revolution, according to some estimates, 45 percent of the wealth was concentrated in the hands of about 10 percent of the population. But by the mid-nineteenth century, that concentration had become far more pronounced. In Boston in 1845, for example, 4 percent of the citizens are estimated to have owned more than 65 percent of the wealth; in Philadelphia in 1860, 1 percent of the population possessed more than half the wealth. Among the American people at large in 1860, 5 percent of the families possessed more than 50 percent of the wealth.

On the surface, such figures would seem likely to have encouraged a far greater level of class conflict than actually occurred. But a number of factors operated to quell resentments. There was, first, the fact that however much the *relative* economic position of American workers may have been declining, the *absolute* living standard of most laborers was improving. Life, in material terms at least, was usually better for factory workers than it had been on the farms or in the European societies from which they had migrated. They ate better, they were often better clothed and housed, and they had greater access to consumer goods.

There was also a significant amount of mobility within the working class, which helped to limit discontent. Opportunities for *social* mobility, for working one's way up the economic ladder, were limited; but opportunities did exist. A few workers did manage to move from poverty to riches by dint of work, ingenuity, and luck—a very small number, but enough to support the dreams of those who watched them. And a much larger number of workers managed to move at least one notch up the ladder—for example, becoming in the course of a lifetime a skilled, rather than an unskilled, laborer. Such people could envision their children and grandchildren moving up even further.

More important than social mobility was *geographical* mobility, which was even more extensive in the United States than in Europe, where it was considerable. America had a huge expanse of unsettled land in the West, much of it being opened for settlement for the first time in the 1840s and 1850s. To some workers, therefore, the dream of saving money to move out to the frontier could become a reality—thus creating what the historian Frederick Jackson Turner called a "safety valve" for discontent. For most workers, however, the expense and expertise required for a move to the agricultural frontier made such a step impossible. Far more frequent was the movement of laborers from one industrial town to another. Restless, questing, these "people in motion," as some scholars have described them, were often the victims of layoffs, looking for better opportunities elsewhere. Their search may seldom have led to a marked improvement in their circumstances; but the rootlessness of this large segment of the work force—perhaps the most distressed segment—made effective organization and protest far more difficult.

There was, finally, another "safety valve" for working-class discontent: politics. Economic opportunity may not have greatly expanded in the nineteenth century, but opportunities to participate in politics did. And to many working people, access to the ballot seemed to offer a way to help guide their society and to feel like a significant part of their communities.

Women and the "Cult of Domesticity"

The new industrializing society of the Northern regions of the United States produced profound changes in the nature and function of the family. At the heart of the transformation was the shift of income-earning work out of the home and into the shop, mill, or factory. In the early decades of the nineteenth century (and for many years before that), the family itself had been the principal unit of economic activity. Family farms, family shops, and family industries were the norm throughout most of the United States. Men, women, and children worked together, sharing tasks and jointly earning the income that sustained the family.

Among the farming population, which continued to constitute the majority of the American people, the family generally remained a unit of joint economic activity. But even here, important changes were in progress. As farming spread to the fertile lands of the Northwest and as the size and profitability of farms expanded, agricultural work became more commercialized. Farm owners in need of labor began to rely less on their families (which were often not large enough to satisfy the demand) and more on hired male workers. These farmhands performed many of the tasks that on smaller farms had once been the jobs of the women and children of the family. As a result, farm women tended to work increasingly at domestic tasks—cooking, sewing, gardening, and dairying—a development that tended to remove them from the principal income-producing activities of the farm.

Farm women in the new agricultural regions of the Northwest tended, therefore, to enjoy lower economic status than their earlier counterparts in the East.

In the industrial economy of the rapidly growing cities, there was a more significant erosion of the traditional economic function of the family. The urban household itself became less important as a center of production. Instead, most income earners left home each day to work elsewhere. A sharp distinction began to emerge between the public world of the workplace—the world of commerce and industry—and the private world of the family—a world now dominated by housekeeping, child rearing, and other primarily domestic concerns.

The emerging distinction between the public and private worlds, between the workplace and the home, was accompanied by the emergence of increasingly sharp distinctions between the social roles of men and women—distinctions that affected not only factory workers and farmers, but members of the growing middle class as well. There had, of course, always been important differences between the male and female spheres in American society. Women had long been denied many legal and political rights enjoyed by men; it was widely assumed that within the family the husband and father ruled, that the wife and mother bowed to his demands and desires. It had long been practically impossible for most women to obtain divorces, although divorces initiated by men were often easier to arrange. (Men were also far more likely than women to win custody of children in case of a divorce.) In most states, husbands retained almost absolute authority over both the property and persons of their wives; wife beating was illegal in only a few areas. And women traditionally had very little access to the worlds of business or politics. Indeed, women generally were forbidden by custom to speak in public before mixed audiences.

Women traditionally also had far less access to education than men, a situation that survived into the mid-nineteenth century. Although they were encouraged to attend school at the elementary level, they were strongly discouraged—and in most cases effectively barred—from pursuing higher education. Oberlin in Ohio became the first college in America to accept woman students; it permitted four to enroll in 1837, despite criticism that coeducation would become a rash experiment approximating free love. Oberlin authorities were confident that "the mutual influence of the sexes upon each other is decidedly happy in the cultivation of both mind & manners." But few other institutions shared their views. Coeducation remained extraordinarily rare until long after the Civil War; and only a very few women's colleges—such as Mount Holyoke, founded in Massachusetts by Mary Lyon in 1837—emerged.

But however unequal the positions of men and women in the preindustrial era, those positions had generally been defined within the context of a household in which all members played crucial roles in the generation of family income. In the middle-class family of the new industrial society, however, the husband was assumed to be the principal, usually the only, income producer. The wife was now expected to remain in the home and to engage in largely domestic activities.

The result was an important shift in the middle-class concept of the woman's place within the family and of the family's place within the larger society. Women in the mid-nineteenth century came to be seen as guardians of the "domestic virtues." Their role as mothers, entrusted with the nurturing of the young, seemed more central to the family than it had in the past. And their role as wives—as companions and helpers to their husbands—grew more important as well. Middle-class women, no longer producers, now became more important as consumers. They learned to place a high value on keeping a clean, comfortable, and well-appointed home; on entertaining; on dressing elegantly and stylishly.

Occupying their own, separate sphere, women began to develop a distinctive female culture. Friendships among women became increasingly intense; women began to form their own social networks (and, ultimately, to form female clubs and associations that were of great importance to the advancement of various reforms). A distinctive feminine literature began to emerge to meet the demands of middle-class women. There were romantic novels (many of them by female writers), which focused on the private sphere that women now inhabited. There were women's magazines, of which the most prominent was *Godey's Lady's Book,* edited after 1837 by Sarah Hale, who had earlier founded a women's magazine of her own. The magazine scrupulously avoided dealing with public controversies or political issues and focused instead on fashions, shopping and homemaking advice, and other purely domestic concerns. Politics and religion were inappropriate for the magazine, Hale explained in 1841, because "other subjects are more important for our sex and more proper for our sphere."

By the standards of a later era, the increasing isolation of women from the public world seems to be a form of oppression and discrimination. And it is true that few men considered women fit for business, politics, or the professions. On the other hand, most middle-class men—and many middle-class women as well—considered the new female sphere a vehicle for expressing special qualities that made women in some ways superior to men. Women were to be the custodians of morality and benevolence, just as the home—shaped by the influence of women—was to be a refuge from the harsh, competitive world of the marketplace. It was the responsibility of women to provide religious and moral instruction to their children and to counterbalance the acquisitive, secular impulses of their husbands. Thus the "cult of domesticity," as some scholars have called it, brought both benefits and costs to middle-class women. It allowed them to live lives of greater material comfort than in the past, and it placed a higher value on their "female virtues" and on their roles as wife and mother. At the same time, it left women increasingly detached from the public world, with fewer outlets for their interests and energies.

The costs of that detachment were particularly clear among unmarried women of the middle class. By the 1840s, the ideology of domesticity had grown so powerful that few genteel women would any longer consider working (as many had in the past) in shops or mills (and few employers would consider hiring them). But unmarried women nevertheless required some income-producing activity. They had few choices. They could become teachers or nurses, professions that seemed to call for the same female qualities that made women important within the home; and both those professions began in the 1840s and 1850s to attract large numbers of women. Otherwise, unmarried females were largely dependent on the generosity of relatives.

Except for teaching and nursing, work by women outside the household gradually came to be seen as a lower-class preserve. Working-class women could not afford to stay home and cultivate the "domestic virtues." They had to produce income for their families. They continued to work in factories and mills, but under conditions far worse than those that the original, more "respectable" woman workers had enjoyed. They also frequently found employment in middle-class homes. Domestic service became one of the most frequent sources of female employment. In other words, now that production had moved outside the household, women who needed to earn money had to move outside their own households to do so.

Accompanying (and perhaps in part caused by) the changing economic function of the family was a decline in the birth rate. In 1800, the average American woman could be expected to give birth to approximately seven children during her childbearing years. By 1860, women bore an average of five children apiece. The birth rate fell most quickly in urban areas and among middle-class women. Mid-nineteenth-century Americans had access to some birth control devices, which undoubtedly contributed in part to the change. There was also a significant rise in abortions, which remained legal in some states until after the Civil War and which, according to some estimates, may have terminated as many as 20 percent of all pregnancies in the 1850s. But the most important cause of the declining birth rate was almost certainly a change in sexual behavior—including increased abstinence.

The deliberate effort among middle-class men and women to limit family size was a reflection of a much larger shift in the nature of society in the mid-nineteenth-century North. In a world in which the economy was becoming increasingly organized, in which production was moving out of the home, in which individuals were coming to expect more from the world, in which more emphasis was being placed on calculations about the future, the idea of making careful decisions about bearing children was of particular appeal. It expressed the increasingly secular, rationalized, and progressive orientation of the rapidly developing American North.

Northeastern Agriculture

The story of agriculture in the Northeast after 1840 is one of decline and transformation. The reason for the decline was simple: the farmers of the section could no longer compete with the new and richer soil of the Northwest. Centers of production were gradually shifting westward for many of the farm goods that had in the past been most important to Northeastern agriculture: wheat, corn, grapes, cattle, sheep, and hogs. In 1840, the leading wheat-growing states were New York, Pennsylvania, Ohio, and Virginia; in 1860, they were Illinois, Indiana, Wisconsin, Ohio, and Michigan. In the case of corn, Illinois, Ohio, and Missouri supplanted New York, Pennsylvania, and Virginia. In 1840, the most important cattle-raising areas in the country were New York, Pennsylvania, and New England; but by the 1850s, the leading cat-

tle states were Illinois, Indiana, Ohio, and Iowa in the West, and Texas in the South.

Some Eastern farmers responded to these changes by moving west themselves and establishing new farms. Still others moved to mill towns and became laborers. Some farmers, however, remained on the land and managed to hold their own against, at times even to surpass, the Northwest in certain lines of agriculture. As the Eastern urban centers increased in population, many farmers turned to the task of supplying food to the city masses; they engaged profitably in truck gardening (vegetables) or fruit raising. New York, for example, led all other states in apple production. The rise of cities also stimulated the rise of dairy farming. The profits to be derived from supplying milk, butter, and cheese to local markets attracted many farmers in central New York, southeastern Pennsylvania, and various parts of New England. Approximately half the dairy products of the country were produced in the East; most of the rest came from the West, where Ohio was the leading dairy state. Partly because of the expansion of the dairy industry, the Northeast led other sections in the production of hay. New York was the leading hay state in the nation, and large crops were grown in Pennsylvania and New England. The Northeast also exceeded other areas in producing potatoes.

Nevertheless, while agriculture in the region remained an important part of the economy, it was steadily becoming less important relative both to the agriculture of the Northwest and to the industrial growth of the Northeast itself. As a result, the rural population in many parts of the Northeast continued to decline.

The Old Northwest

Life was different in the states of what was known as the Northwest—now the Midwest—in the mid-nineteenth century. There was some industry in this region, more than in the South; and in the two decades before the Civil War, the section experienced steady industrial growth. By 1860, it had 36,785 manufacturing establishments employing 209,909 workers. Along the southern shore of Lake Erie was a flourishing industrial and commercial area of which Cleveland was the center. Another manufacturing region was in the Ohio River valley, with the meat-packing city of Cincinnati as its nucleus. Farther west, the rising city of Chicago, destined to become the great metropolis of the section, was emerging as the national

Pastoral America, 1848
This painting by the American artist Edward Hicks suggests the degree to which Americans continued to admire the "Peaceable Kingdom" (the name of another, more famous Hicks work) of the agrarian world. Hicks entitled this work *An Indian Summer view of the Farm w. Stock of James C. Cornell of Northampton Bucks county Pennsylvania. That took the Premium in the Agricultural Society, October the 12, 1848.* It portrays the diversified farming of a prosperous Pennsylvania family, shown here in the foreground with their cattle, sheep, and workhorses. In the background stretches a field ready for plowing and another ready for harvesting.   (National Gallery of Art, Washington)

center of the agricultural machinery and meat-packing industries. The most important industrial products of the West were farm machinery, flour, meat, distilled whiskey, and leather and wooden goods.

On the whole, however, industry was far less important in the Northwest than in the Northeast. Large portions of the region—most of the upper third of the Great Lakes states—continued to be populated largely by Indians until after the Civil War. In those areas, hunting and fishing, along with some sedentary agriculture, remained the principal economic activities. But the tribes did not become fully integrated into the new commercialized economy that was emerging elsewhere in the Northwest.

For the white (and occasionally black) settlers who populated the lands that had by now been largely wrested from the natives, the Northwest was primarily an agricultural region. Its rich and plentiful lands made farming there a lucrative and expanding activity, in contrast to the Northeast, where agriculture was in decline. Thus the typical citizen of the Northwest was not the industrial worker or poor, marginal farmer, but the owner of a reasonably prosperous family farm. The average size of Western farms was 200 acres, the great majority of them owned by the people who worked them.

In concentrating on corn, wheat, cattle, sheep, and hogs, the Western farmer was motivated by sound economic reasons. As the Northeast became more industrial and urban, it enlarged the domestic market for farm goods. At the same time, England and certain European nations, undergoing the same process, started to import larger amounts of food. This growing worldwide demand for farm products resulted in steadily rising farm prices. For the farmers, the 1840s and early 1850s were years of increasing prosperity.

The expansion of agricultural markets had profound effects on sectional alignments in the United States. The Northwest sold by far the greatest part of its products to the residents of the Northeast; only the surplus remaining after domestic needs were satisfied was exported abroad. The new well-being of Western farmers, then, was sustained in large part by Eastern purchasing power. Eastern industry, in turn, found an important market for its products in the prospering West. Between the two sections a strong economic relationship was emerging that was profitable to both—and that was increasing the isolation of the South within the Union.

To meet the increasing demand for its farm products, the Northwest worked strenuously, and often frantically, to increase its productive capacities. One way it did so was by taking advantage of the large areas of still unoccupied land and enlarging the area under cultivation during the 1840s. By 1850, the growing Western population had settled the prairie regions east of the Mississippi and was pushing beyond the river. But another way the Northwest increased production was by adopting agricultural techniques designed to produce the largest possible crop in the shortest possible time. The average Western farmer engaged, therefore, in wasteful, exploitive methods of farming that often resulted in rapid exhaustion of the region's rich soil.

Northwestern farmers were discovering less destructive techniques. New varieties of seed, notably Mediterranean wheat, which was hardier than the native type, were introduced in some areas; better breeds of animals, such as hogs and sheep from England and Spain, were imported to take the place of native stock. Of greater importance were the improvements that Americans continued to introduce in farm machines and tools. During the 1840s, more efficient grain drills, harrows, mowers, and hay rakes were placed in wide use. The cast-iron plow, devised earlier, continued to be popular because its parts could be replaced when broken. An even better implement appeared in 1847, when John Deere established at Moline, Illinois, a factory to manufacture plows with steel moldboards, which were more durable than those made of iron.

Two new machines heralded a coming revolution in grain production. The most important was the automatic reaper, invented by Cyrus H. McCormick of Virginia. The reaper took the place of sickle, cradle, and hand labor and enabled a crew of six or seven men to harvest in a day as much wheat (or any other small grain) as fifteen men could harvest using the older methods. McCormick, who had patented his device in 1834, established a factory at Chicago, in the heart of the grain belt, in 1847. By 1860, more than 100,000 reapers were in use on Western farms. Almost as important to the grain grower was the thresher—a machine that separated the grain from the wheat stalks. Threshers appeared in large numbers after 1840. Before that time, grain was generally flailed by hand (seven bushels a day was a good average for a farm) or trodden by farm animals (twenty bushels a day on the average). A threshing machine could thresh twenty-five bushels or more in an hour. Most of the threshers were manufactured at the Jerome I. Case factory in Racine, Wisconsin.

The Northwest was the most self-consciously democratic section of the country. But its democracy was of a relatively conservative type—capitalistic, property conscious, middle-class. Abraham Lincoln, an Illinois Whig, voiced the economic opinions of many of the people of his section. "I take it that it is best for all to leave each man free to acquire property as fast as he can," said Lincoln. "Some will get wealthy. I don't believe in a law to prevent a man from getting rich; it would do more harm than good. . . . When one starts poor, as most do in the race of life, free society is such that he knows he can better his condition; he knows that there is no fixed condition of labor for his whole life."

The Expanding South

The South, like the North, experienced dramatic growth in the middle years of the nineteenth century. Southerners fanned out into the new territories of the Southwest and established new communities, new states, and new markets. The Southern agricultural economy grew increasingly productive and increasingly prosperous. Trade in such staples as sugar, rice, tobacco, and above all cotton made the South a major force in international commerce and created substantial wealth within the region. Southern society, Southern culture, Southern politics—all were affected by these important demographic and economic changes. The South in the 1850s was a very different

The New Orleans Cotton Exchange
Edgar Degas, the great French artist, painted this scene of cotton traders examining samples in the New Orleans cotton exchange in 1873. By this time the cotton trade was producing less impressive profits than those that made it the driving force of the booming Southern economy of the 1850s. Degas' mother came from a Creole family of cotton brokers in New Orleans; and two of the artist's brothers (depicted here reading a newspaper and leaning against a window) joined the business in America. (Giraudon/Art Resource)

place from the South of the first years of the century.

Yet for all the expansion and all the changes, the South experienced a much less fundamental transformation in these years than did the North. It had begun the nineteenth century a primarily agricultural region; it remained overwhelmingly agrarian in 1860. It began the century with few important cities and little industry; and so it remained sixty years later. In 1800, the economy of the South had been dominated by a plantation system dependent on slave labor; by 1860, that system had only strengthened its grip on

the region. As one historian has written, "The South *grew,* but it did not *develop.*" And as a result, it became increasingly unlike the North and increasingly sensitive to what it considered to be threats to its distinctive way of life.

The Rise of King Cotton

The most important economic development in the South of the mid-nineteenth century was the shift of

Slavery and Cotton: The South in 1820 and 1860

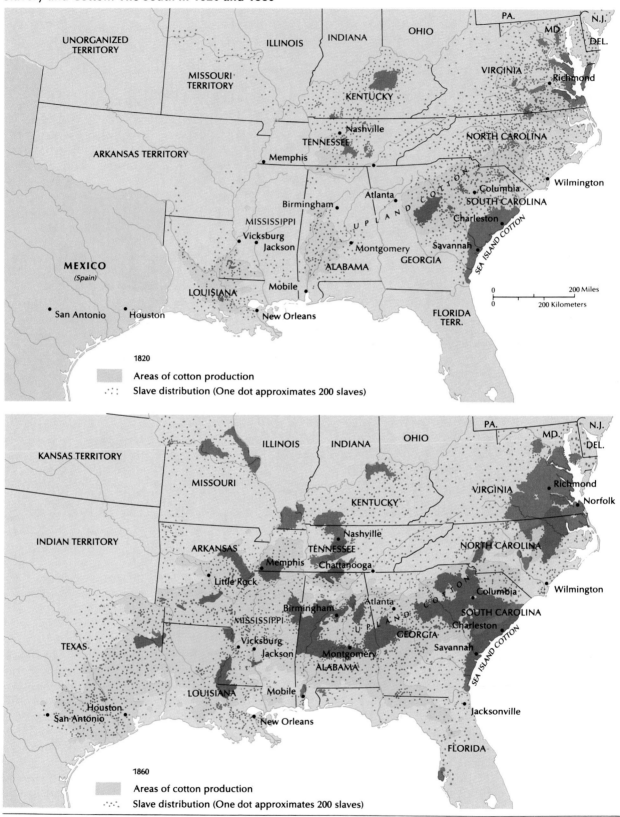

1820

Areas of cotton production

::: Slave distribution (One dot approximates 200 slaves)

1860

Areas of cotton production

::: Slave distribution (One dot approximates 200 slaves)

economic power from the "upper South," the original Southern states along the Atlantic coast, to the "lower South," the expanding agricultural regions in the new states of the Southwest. That shift reflected above all the growing dominance of cotton in the Southern economy.

Much of the upper South continued in the nineteenth century to rely, as it always had, on the cultivation of tobacco. But the market for that crop was notoriously unstable, subject to recurrent depressions, including a prolonged one that began in the 1820s and extended into the 1850s. And tobacco rapidly exhausted the land on which it was grown, which made it difficult for most growers to remain in business in the same place for very long. By the 1830s, therefore, many farmers in the old tobacco-growing regions of Virginia, Maryland, and North Carolina were shifting to other crops—notably wheat—while the center of tobacco cultivation was moving westward, into the piedmont area.

The southern regions of the coastal South—South Carolina, Georgia, and parts of Florida—continued to rely on rice production, a more stable and lucrative crop. But rice demanded substantial irrigation and needed an exceptionally long growing season (nine months), so cultivation of that staple remained restricted to a relatively small area. Sugar growers, similarly, enjoyed a reasonably profitable market for their crop; but sugar cultivation, too, required special conditions and a long growing time and thus did not spread much beyond a small area in southern Louisiana and eastern Texas. Long-staple (Sea Island) cotton was another lucrative crop; but like rice and sugar, it could be grown only in a limited area—the coastal regions of the Southeast.

The decline of the tobacco economy in the upper South, and the inherent limits of the sugar, rice, and long-staple cotton economies farther south might have forced the region to shift its attention to other, nonagricultural pursuits in the nineteenth century had it not been for the growing importance of a new product, which soon overshadowed all else: short-staple cotton. This was a hardier and coarser strain of cotton, which could be grown effectively in a variety of climates and in a variety of soils. It was more difficult to process than the long-staple variety; its seeds were far more difficult to remove from the fiber. But the invention of the cotton gin (see pp. 200–201) had largely solved that problem, and by the 1820s cotton production was spreading rapidly. From the western areas of South Carolina and Georgia, production moved steadily—first into Alabama and Mississippi, then into northern Louisiana, Texas, and Arkansas. By the 1850s, cotton had come to be the linchpin of the Southern economy. In 1820, the South had produced only about 500,000 bales of cotton. By 1850, it was producing nearly 3 million bales a year, and by 1860 nearly 5 million. There were periodic fluctuations in cotton prices, resulting generally from overproduction; periods of boom were frequently followed by abrupt busts. But the cotton economy continued to grow, even if in fits and starts. By the time of the Civil War, cotton constituted nearly two-thirds of the total export trade of the United States and was bringing in nearly $200 million a year. The annual value of the rice crop, in contrast, was $2 million. It was little wonder that Southern politicians now proclaimed: "Cotton is king!"

Settlement of the cotton kingdom bore certain resemblances to the rush of gold seekers to a new frontier. The prospect of tremendous profits quickly drew settlers by the thousands. Some who came were wealthy planters from the older states who transferred their assets and slaves to a cotton plantation. Most were small slaveholders or slaveless farmers who intended to become planters. A similar shift occurred in the slave population. In the period 1820–1860, the number of slaves in Alabama leaped from 41,000 to 435,000, and in Mississippi from 32,000 to 436,000. In the same period, the increase in Virginia was only from 425,000 to 490,000. It has been estimated that between 1840 and 1860, 410,000 slaves moved from the upper South to the cotton states—either accompanying masters who were themselves migrating to the Southwest, or (more often) sold to planters already there. Indeed, the sale of slaves to the Southwest became an important economic activity in the upper South and helped the troubled planters of that region to compensate for the declining value of their crops.

Southern Trade and Industry

In the face of this booming agricultural expansion, other forms of economic activity developed slowly in the South. The business classes of the region—the manufacturers and merchants—were not without importance. There was growing activity in flour milling and in textile and iron manufacturing, particularly in the upper South. The Tredegar Iron Works in Richmond, for example, compared favorably with the best iron mills in the Northeast. But industry remained an insignificant force in comparison with the agricultural economy. The total value of Southern textile manufactures in 1860 was $4.5 million—a threefold increase over the value of those goods twenty years before, but only about 2 percent of the value of the cotton exported that year.

To the degree that the South developed a non-farm commercial sector, it was largely to serve the needs of the plantation economy. Particularly important were the brokers, or factors, who marketed the planters' crops. These merchants were centered in such towns as New Orleans, Charleston, Mobile, and Savannah, where they worked to find buyers for cotton and other crops and where they purchased needed goods for the planters they served. The South had only a very rudimentary financial system, and the factors often also served the planters as bankers, providing them with credit. Planters frequently accumulated substantial debts, particularly during periods when cotton prices were in decline; and the Southern merchant-bankers thus became figures of considerable influence and importance in the region. There were also substantial groups of professional people in the South—lawyers, editors, doctors, and others; they too, however, were closely tied to and dependent on the plantation economy.

However important these manufacturers, merchants, and professionals might have been to Southern society, they were relatively unimportant in comparison with the manufacturers, merchants, and professionals of the North, on whom Southerners were coming more and more (and increasingly unhappily) to depend. Perceptive Southerners recognized the economic subordination of their region. "From the rattle with which the nurse tickles the ear of the child born in the South to the shroud that covers the cold form of the dead, everything comes to us from the North," exclaimed the Arkansas journalist Albert Pike.

Perhaps the most prominent advocate of Southern economic independence was James B. D. De Bow, a resident of New Orleans. He published a magazine advocating Southern commercial and agricultural expansion: *De Bow's Review,* which survived from its founding in 1846 until 1880. De Bow made his journal into a tireless advocate of Southern economic independence from the North, warning constantly of the dangers of the "colonial" relationship between the sections. One writer noted in the pages of his magazine: "I think it would be safe to estimate the amount which is lost to us annually by our vassalage to the North at $100,000,000. Great God!" Yet *De Bow's Review* was itself clear evidence of the dependency of the South on the North. It was printed in New York, because no New Orleans printer had facilities adequate to the task; it was filled with ad-

vertisements from Northern manufacturing firms; and its circulation was always modest in comparison with those of Northern publications. In Charleston, for example, it sold an average of 173 copies per issue; *Harper's Magazine* of New York regularly sold 1,500 copies to Carolinians.

Despite this awareness of the region's "colonial dependency," the South made few serious efforts to develop an economy that might challenge that dependency. An important question about antebellum Southern history, therefore, is why the region did so little to develop a larger industrial and commercial economy of its own.

Part of the reason was the great profitability of the region's agricultural system, and particularly of cotton production. Another reason was that wealthy Southerners had so much capital invested in their land and in their slaves that they had little left for other investments. Some historians have suggested that the Southern climate—with its long, hot, steamy summers—was less suitable for industrial development than the climate of the North. Still others have gone so far as to claim that Southern work habits impeded industrialization; some white Southerners appeared—at least to many Northern observers—not to work very hard, to lack the strong work ethic that fueled Northern economic development.

But the Southern failure to create a flourishing commercial or industrial economy was also in part the result of a set of values distinctive to the South that discouraged the growth of cities and industry. White Southerners liked to think of themselves as representatives of a special way of life: one based on traditional values of chivalry, leisure, and elegance. Southerners were, they argued, "cavaliers"—people happily free from the base, acquisitive instincts of Northerners, people more concerned with a refined and gracious way of life than with rapid growth and development. But appealing as the "cavalier" image was to Southern whites, it conformed to the reality of Southern society in strictly limited ways.

Plantation Society

Only a minority of Southern whites owned slaves. In 1850, when the total white population of the South was over 6 million, the number of slaveholders was only 347,525. In 1860, when the white population was just above 8 million, the number of slaveholders had risen to only 383,637. These figures are somewhat misleading, since each slaveholder was nor-

The Olivier Plantation (1861), by Adrian Persac
Persac was a land surveyor who often made paintings of the properties he surveyed, among them this idyllic scene of a plantation near New Iberia, Louisiana. One year after the painting was completed, the plantation was destroyed amid the chaos the Civil War brought to the area.   (Louisiana State Museum)

mally the head of a family averaging five members. But even with all members of slaveowning families included in the figures, those owning slaves still amounted to perhaps no more than one quarter of the white population. And of the minority of whites holding slaves, only a small proportion owned them in substantial numbers.

How, then, did the South come to be seen—both by the outside world and by many Southerners themselves—as a society dominated by great plantations and wealthy landowning planters? In large part, it was because the planter aristocracy—the cotton magnates, the sugar, rice, and tobacco nabobs, the whites who owned at least forty or fifty slaves and 800 or more acres—exercised power and influence far in excess of their numbers. They stood at the apex of society, determining the political, economic, and even social life of their region. Enriched by vast annual incomes, dwelling in palatial homes, surrounded by broad acres and many black servants, they became a class to which all others paid a certain deference.

Southerners liked to compare their planter class to the old upper classes of England and Europe: true aristocracies long entrenched. In fact, however, the Southern upper class was in most cases not at all similar to the landed aristocracies of the Old World.

In some areas of the upper South—the tidewater region of Virginia, for example—the great aristocrats were sometimes people whose families had occupied positions of wealth and power for generations. In most of the South, however, a longstanding landed aristocracy, though central to the "cavalier" image, was largely a myth. Even the most important planters in the cotton-growing areas of the region were, typically, new to their wealth and power. As late as the 1850s, the great landowners in the lower South were still often first-generation settlers, who had arrived with only modest resources, who had struggled for many years to clear land and develop a plantation in what was at first a rugged frontier, and who had only relatively recently begun to live in the comfort and luxury for which they were now famous. Large areas of the "Old South" (as Americans later called the South of the pre–Civil War era) had been settled and cultivated for less than two decades at the time of the Civil War. Nor was the world of the planter nearly as leisured and genteel as the "cavalier" myth would suggest. Growing staple crops was a business—often a big and highly profitable business—which was in its own way just as competitive and just as risky as the industrial enterprises of the North. Planters had to supervise their operations carefully if they hoped to make a profit. They were, in many respects, just as much competitive capitalists as the industrialists of the North whose life styles they claimed to hold in contempt.

Indeed, it may have been the newness and precariousness of the plantation way of life, and the differences between the reality of that life and the image of it, that made many Southern planters determined to portray themselves as genteel aristocrats. Having struggled so hard to reach and maintain their position, they were all the more determined to defend it. Perhaps that was why the defense of slavery and of the South's "rights" was stronger in the new, booming regions of the lower South and weaker in the more established and less flourishing areas of the tidewater.

Wealthy Southern whites sustained their image of themselves as aristocrats in many ways. They adopted an elaborate code of "chivalry," which obligated white men to defend their "honor" (often through dueling). They avoided such "coarse" occupations as trade and commerce; those who did not become planters often gravitated toward the military, a "suitable" career for men raised in a culture in which medieval knights (as portrayed in the novels of Walter Scott) were a powerful and popular image. Above all, perhaps, the aristocratic ideal found reflection in the definition of a special role for Southern white women.

The Southern Lady

In some respects, affluent white women in the South occupied roles very similar to those occupied by middle-class white women in the North. Their lives were expected to be centered in the home, where they would serve as companions to (and hostesses

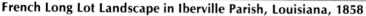

French Long Lot Landscape in Iberville Parish, Louisiana, 1858

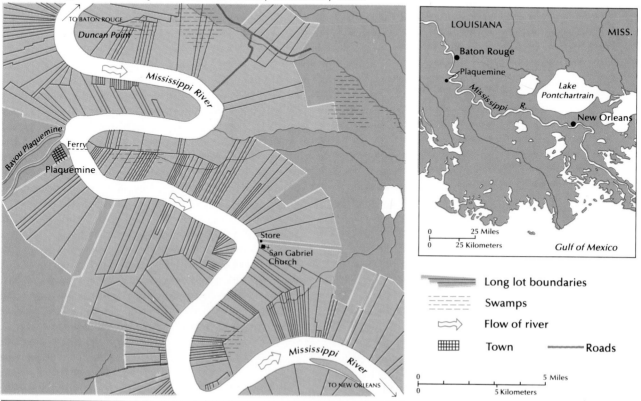

for) their husbands and as nurturing mothers for their children. Even less frequently than in the North did "genteel" Southern white women engage in public activities or find income-producing employment.

But the life of the "Southern lady" was also in many ways very different from that of her Northern counterpart. For one thing, the cult of honor in the region meant that Southern white men gave particular importance to the "defense" of women. In practice, this generally meant that white men were even more dominant and white women even more subordinate in Southern culture than they were in the North. George Fitzhugh, one of the South's most important social theorists, wrote in the 1850s: "Women, like children, have but one right, and that is the right to protection. The right to protection involves the obligation to obey."

More important in determining the role of Southern white women, however, were the social realities in which they lived. The vast majority of females in the region lived on farms, relatively isolated from people outside their own families, with virtually no access to the "public world" and thus few opportunities to look beyond their roles as wives

and mothers. For many white women, living on farms of modest size meant a fuller engagement in the economic life of the family than was becoming typical for middle-class women in the North. These women engaged in spinning, weaving, and other production; they participated in agricultural tasks; they helped supervise the slave work force. On the larger plantations, however, even these limited roles were often considered unsuitable for white women; and the "plantation mistress" became, in some cases, more an ornament for her husband than a meaningful part of the economy or the society.

Southern white women also had far less access to education than their Northern counterparts. Nearly a quarter of all white women over twenty were completely illiterate; relatively few women had more than a rudimentary exposure to schooling. Even wealthy planters were not much interested in extensive schooling for their daughters. The few female "academies" in the South were designed largely to train women to be suitable wives.

Southern white women had other special burdens as well. The Southern white birth rate remained nearly 20 percent higher than that of the nation as a

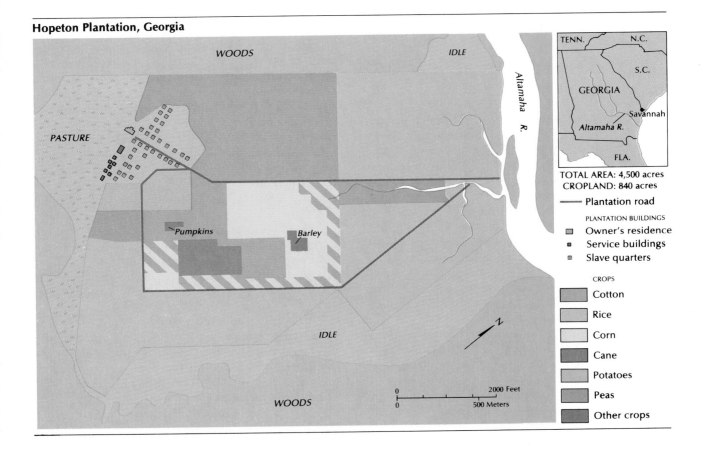

Hopeton Plantation, Georgia

WOODS

IDLE

Altamaha R.

PASTURE

Pumpkins

Barley

IDLE

WOODS

TENN.   N.C.

S.C.

GEORGIA

Savannah

Altamaha R.

FLA.

TOTAL AREA: 4,500 acres
CROPLAND: 840 acres

—— Plantation road

PLANTATION BUILDINGS
▫ Owner's residence
▪ Service buildings
▫ Slave quarters

CROPS
Cotton
Rice
Corn
Cane
Potatoes
Peas
Other crops

2000 Feet
500 Meters

whole, and infant mortality in the region remained higher than elsewhere; nearly half the children born in the South in 1860 died before they reached five years of age. And the slave labor system created particular problems. Male slaveowners had frequent sexual relationships with the female slaves on their plantations; the children of those unions became part of the plantation labor force and served as a constant reminder to white women of their husbands' infidelity. Black women (and men) were obviously the most important victims of such practices. But white women suffered too. They deeply resented their husbands' liaisons with slaves, and yet the social code under which they lived generally prevented them from venting their anger (except toward slave women, whom plantation mistresses often treated very harshly), or even openly acknowledging that the relationships existed at all.

A few Southern white women rebelled against their roles and against the prevailing assumptions of their region. Some became outspoken abolitionists and joined Northerners in the crusade to abolish slavery. (See pp. 361–362.) Some agitated for other reforms within the South itself. Most white women, however, found few outlets for whatever discontent they felt with their lot. Instead, they generally convinced themselves of the benefits of their position and—like Southern white men—defended the special virtues of the Southern way of life.

The Plain Folk

The typical white Southerner was not a great planter and slaveholder, but a modest yeoman farmer. Some owned a few slaves, with whom they worked and lived far more closely than did the larger planters. Most (in fact, two-thirds of all white families) owned no slaves at all. These "plain folk," most of whom owned their own land, devoted themselves largely to subsistence farming. During the 1850s, the number of nonslaveholding landowners increased much faster than the number of slaveholding landowners. While there were occasional examples of poor farmers moving into the ranks of the planter class, such cases were rare. Most yeomen knew that they had little prospect of substantially bettering their lot.

One reason was the Southern educational system, which provided poor whites with few opportunities to learn and thus limited their chances of advancement. For the sons of wealthy planters, however, the system provided ample opportunities to gain an education. In 1860 there were 260 Southern colleges and universities, public and private, with 25,000 students enrolled in them, or more than half the total number of students in the United States. The lower South had 11,000 students in its institutions of higher learning, while New England, with approximately the same population, could boast only 3,748. College was within the reach of only the upper class, however. And below the college level, where the white lower classes more often looked, the schools of the South were not only fewer but also inferior to those of the Northeast (although not much worse than the crude schools of the Northwest). The South had more than 500,000 white illiterates, or over half of the country's total.

That a majority of the South's white population consisted of modest farmers largely excluded from the dominant plantation society raises important questions about the antebellum South. Why did the plain folk have so little power in the public world of the Old South? Why did they not oppose the aristocratic social system in which they shared so little? Why did they not resent the system of slavery, from which they generally did not benefit? There is no single answer to such questions.

Some nonslaveowning whites did oppose the slaveholding oligarchy, but for the most part in limited ways and in a relatively few, isolated areas. These were the Southern highlanders, the "hill people," who lived in the Appalachian ranges east of the Mississippi and in the Ozarks to the west of the river. Of all Southern whites, they were the most set apart from the mainstream of the region's life. They practiced a crude form of subsistence agriculture, owned practically no slaves, and had a proud sense of seclusion. They held to old ways and old ideals, which included the ideal of loyalty to the nation as a whole. Such whites frequently expressed animosity toward the planter aristocracy of the other regions of the South and misgivings about (although seldom moral objections to) the system of slavery. The mountain region was the only part of the South to defy the trend toward sectional conformity; and it was the only part to resist the movement toward secession when it finally developed. Even during the Civil War itself, many refused to support the Confederacy; some went so far as to fight for the Union.

Far greater in number, however, were the nonslaveowning whites who lived in the midst of the plantation system. Many, perhaps most of them, accepted that system because they were tied to it in important ways. Small farmers depended on the local plantation aristocracy for many things: for access to cotton gins, for markets for their modest crops and their livestock, for financial assistance in time of need.

In many areas, there were also extensive networks of kinship linking lower- and upper-class whites. The poorest resident of a county might easily be a cousin of the richest aristocrat. Taken together, these mutual ties—a system of vaguely paternal relationships—helped mute what might otherwise have been pronounced class tensions.

There were other white Southerners, however, who did not share in the plantation economy in even these limited ways and yet continued to accept its premises. These were the members of that tragic and degraded class—numbering perhaps a half-million in 1850—known variously as "crackers," "sand hillers," or "poor white trash." Occupying the infertile lands of the pine barrens, the red hills, and the swamps, they lived in miserable cabins amid almost unbelievable squalor. Their degradation resulted partly from dietary deficiencies and disease. These poor whites resorted at times to eating clay; and they were afflicted by pellagra, hookworm, and malaria. Held in contempt by both the planters and the small farmers of the South, they formed a true underclass. In some material respects, their plight was worse than that of the black slaves (who themselves often looked down on the poor whites).

Even among these Southerners—the true outcasts of white society in the region—there was no real opposition to the plantation system or slavery. In part, undoubtedly, this was because these men and women were so benumbed by poverty that they had little strength to protest. But it resulted also from perhaps the single greatest unifying factor among the Southern white population—the one force that was most responsible for reducing tensions among the various classes. That force was race. However poor and miserable white Southerners might be, they could still consider themselves members of a ruling race; they could still look down on the black population of the region and feel a bond with their fellow whites born of a determination to maintain their racial supremacy. As Frederick Law Olmsted, a Northerner who visited the South and chronicled Southern society in the 1850s, wrote: "From childhood, the one thing in their condition which has made life valuable to the mass of whites has been that the niggers are yet their inferiors."

The "Peculiar Institution"

White Southerners often referred to slavery as the "peculiar institution." By that, they meant not that the institution was odd but that it was distinctive, special.

The description was an apt one, for American slavery was indeed distinctive. The South in the mid-nineteenth century was the only area in the entire Western world—except for Brazil and Cuba— where slavery still existed; and Southern slavery differed even from its Caribbean and Latin American counterparts. Slavery, more than any other single factor, isolated the South from the rest of American society. And as that isolation increased, so did the commitment of Southerners to defend the institution. William Harper, a prominent South Carolina politician in the 1840s, wrote: "The judgment is made up. We can have no hearing before the tribunal of the civilized world. Yet, on this very account, it is more important that we, the inhabitants of the slave-holding States, insulated as we are by this institution, and cut off, in some degree, from the communion and sympathies of the world by which we are surrounded, . . . and exposed continually to their animadversions and attacks, should thoroughly understand this subject, and our strength and weakness in relation to it."

Within the South itself, the institution of slavery had paradoxical results. On the one hand, it isolated blacks from whites, drawing a sharp and inviolable line between the races. As a result, blacks under slavery began to develop a society and culture of their own, one that was in many ways unrelated to the white civilization around them. On the other hand, slavery created a unique bond between blacks and whites—masters and slaves—in the South. The two races may have maintained separate spheres, but each sphere was deeply influenced by, indeed dependent on, the other.

Varieties of Slavery

Slavery was an institution established and regulated in detail by law. The slave codes of the Southern states forbade slaves to hold property, to leave their masters' premises without permission, to be out after dark, to congregate with other slaves except at church, to carry firearms, or to strike a white person even in self-defense. The codes prohibited whites from teaching slaves to read or write, and they denied to slaves the right to testify in court against white people. They contained no provisions to legalize slave marriages or divorces. If an owner killed a slave while punishing him, the act was generally not considered a crime. Slaves, however, faced the death penalty for killing or even resisting a white person and for inciting to revolt. The codes also contained extraordinarily rigid provisions for defining a per-

Slave Ownership in the South and Border States, 1860

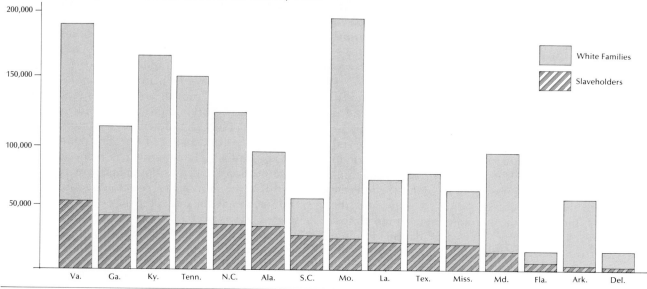

son's race. Anyone with even a trace of African ancestry was considered black. And anyone thought to possess any such trace was presumed to be black unless he or she could prove otherwise.

These and dozens of other restrictions and impositions indicate that the slaves lived under a uniformly harsh and dismal regime. Had the laws been rigidly enforced, that might have been the case. In fact, however, they were applied unevenly. Sometimes slaves did acquire property, were taught to read and write, and did assemble with other slaves, in spite of laws to the contrary. Although major slave offenses were generally referred to the courts (and thus to the jurisdiction of the slave codes), most transgressions were handled by masters, who inflicted widely varying punishments. In other words, despite the rigid provisions of law, there was in reality considerable variety within the slave system. Some blacks lived in almost prisonlike conditions, rigidly and harshly controlled by their masters. Many (probably most) others enjoyed a certain flexibility and (at least in comparison to the regimen prescribed by law) a striking degree of autonomy.

The nature of the the relationship between masters and slaves depended in part on the size of the plantation. Thus the typical master had a different image of slavery from that of the typical slave. Most masters possessed very few slaves, and their experience with (and image of) slavery was therefore shaped by the special nature of slavery on the small farm. Small farmers generally supervised their workers di-

rectly and often worked closely alongside them. On such farms, blacks and whites developed a form of intimacy unknown on larger plantations. The paternal relationship between such masters and their slaves could, like relationships between fathers and children, be warm and in many ways benevolent. It could also be tyrannical and cruel. In general, the evidence suggests, blacks themselves preferred to live on larger plantations, where they had more opportunities for privacy and for a social world of their own.

Although the majority of slaveowners were small farmers, the majority of slaves lived on plantations of medium or large size, with sizable slave work forces. There the relationship between master and slave was usually far less intimate. Substantial planters often hired overseers and even assistant overseers to represent them. "Head drivers," trusted and responsible slaves often assisted by several subdrivers, acted under the overseer as foremen. Larger planters generally used one of two methods of assigning slave labor. One was the task system, most widely used in rice culture, under which slaves were assigned a particular task in the morning, for example, hoeing one acre; after completing the job, they were free for the rest of the day. The other, far more common, was the gang system, employed on the cotton, sugar, and tobacco plantations, under which slaves were simply divided into groups, each of them directed by a driver, and worked for as many hours as the overseer considered a reasonable workday.

Slaves were generally provided with at least

Returning from the Cotton Field
In this photograph, South Carolina field workers return after a day of picking cotton, some of their harvest carried in bundles on their heads. A black slave driver leads the way. (New-York Historical Society)

enough necessities to enable them to live and work. They were furnished with an adequate if rough diet, consisting mainly of corn meal, salt pork, and molasses. Many were allowed to raise gardens for their own use and were issued fresh meat on special occasions. They received issues of cheap clothing and shoes. They lived in rude cabins, called slave quarters, usually clustered together in a complex near the master's house. The plantation mistress or a doctor retained by the owner provided some medical care; but slave women themselves—as "healers" and midwives, or simply as mothers—were the more important source.

Slaves worked hard, beginning with light tasks as children, and their workdays were longest at harvest time. Slave women worked particularly hard. They generally shared the labor in the fields with the men, and they assumed as well the crucial chores traditionally reserved for women—cooking, cleaning, and child rearing. Because slave families were often divided, with husbands and fathers frequently living on neighboring plantations (or, at times, sold to plantation owners far away), black women often found themselves acting in effect as single parents. Within the slave family, therefore, women acquired a special authority.

Some historians have argued that the material conditions of slavery were, in fact, superior to those of Northern industrial workers. Whether or not that is true (and the evidence for this conclusion is at least debatable), the conditions of American slavery were undoubtedly less severe than those of slavery in the Caribbean and South America. There the slave supply was constantly replenished well into the nineteenth century by the African slave trade, giving owners less incentive to protect their existing laborers. Working and living conditions there were arduous, and masters at times literally worked their slaves to death. In the United States, in contrast, there were strong economic incentives to maintain a healthyslave population. One result of this was that America

Growth of Slave Labor, 1800–1860

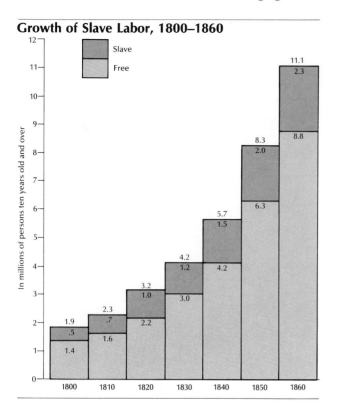

became the only country where a slave population actually increased through natural reproduction.

One example of the solicitude with which masters often treated their slaves was the frequent practice of using hired labor, when available, for the most unhealthy or dangerous tasks. A traveler in Louisiana noted, for example, that Irishmen were employed to clear malarial swamps and to handle cotton bales at the bottom of chutes extending from the river bluff down to a boat landing. If an Irishman died of disease or ,was killed in an accident, the master could hire another for a dollar a day or less. But he would lose an investment of perhaps $1,000 or more if he lost a prime field hand. Still, cruel masters might forget their pocketbooks in the heat of anger. And slaves were often left to the discipline of overseers, who had no pecuniary stake in their well-being; overseers were paid in proportion to the amount of work they could get out of the slaves they supervised.

Household servants had a somewhat easier life—physically at least—than did field hands. On a small plantation, the same slaves might do both field work and house work; but on a large one, there would generally be a separate domestic staff: nursemaids, housemaids, cooks, butlers, coachmen. These people lived close to the master and his family, eating the leftovers from the family table and in some cases even sleeping in the "big house." Between the blacks and whites of such households affectionate, almost familial relationships might develop. More often, however, house servants resented their isolation from their fellow slaves and the lack of privacy that came with living in such close proximity to the family of the master. Female household servants were especially vulnerable to sexual abuse by their masters. When emancipation came after the Civil War, it was often the house servants who were the first to leave the plantations of their former owners.

Slavery in the cities differed significantly from slavery in the country. On the relatively isolated plantations, slaves had little contact with free blacks and lower-class whites, and masters maintained a fairly direct and effective control; a deep and unbridgeable chasm yawned between slavery and freedom. In the city, however, a master often could not supervise his slaves closely and at the same time use them profitably. Even if they slept at night in carefully watched backyard barracks, they went about by day on errands of various kinds. Others—particularly skilled workers such as blacksmiths or carpenters—were hired out; and after hours they often fended for themselves, neither their owners nor their employers bothering to supervise them. Thus urban slaves gained numerous opportunities to mingle with free blacks and with whites. In the cities, the line between slavery and freedom remained, but it became less and less distinct.

Indeed, white Southerners generally considered slavery to be incompatible with city life; and as Southern cities grew, the number of slaves in them declined, relatively if not absolutely. The reasons were social rather than economic. Fearing conspiracies and insurrections, urban slaveowners sold off much of their male property to the countryside. The cities were left with an excess of black women while they continued to have an excess of white men (a situation that helped to account for the birth of many mulattoes). While slavery in the cities declined, segregation of blacks both free and slave increased. Segregation was a means of social control intended to make up for the loosening of the discipline of slavery itself.

The Slave Market
The transatlantic slave trade was abolished long before 1852, the year of this painting. Slave auctions such as this one, therefore, almost always involved blacks being sold from one plantation to another. Younger men and women, capable of hard field work, were in particular demand and were thus especially likely to be separated from their families by sale. (Chicago Historical Society)

The Slave Trade

The transfer of slaves from one part of the South to another was one of the most important demographic consequences of the development of the Southwest. Sometimes slaves moved to the new cotton lands in the company of their original owners, who were migrating themselves. More often, however, the transfer occurred through the medium of professional slave traders. Traders transported slaves over long distances on trains or on river or ocean steamers. On shorter journeys, the slaves moved on foot, trudging in coffles of hundreds along dusty highways. Eventually they arrived at some central market such as

Natchez, New Orleans, Mobile, or Galveston, where purchasers collected to bid for them. At the auction, the bidders checked the slaves like livestock, watching them as they were made to walk or trot, inspecting their teeth, feeling their arms and legs, looking for signs of infirmity or age. It paid to be careful, for traders were known to deceive buyers by blacking gray hair, oiling withered skin, and concealing physical defects in other ways. A sound young field hand would fetch a price that, during the 1840s and 1850s, varied from $500 to $1,700, depending mainly on fluctuations in the price of cotton. An attractive woman, desirable as a concubine, might bring much more.

The domestic slave trade was essential to the growth and prosperity of the whole system. It was also one of its most horrible aspects. The trade dehumanized all who were involved in it. It separated children from parents, and parents from each other. Even families kept together by scrupulous masters might be broken up in the division of the estate after the master's death. Planters condoned the trade and eased their consciences by holding the traders in contempt and assigning them a low social position.

The foreign slave trade was as bad or worse. Although federal law had prohibited the importation of slaves from 1808 on, they continued to be smuggled in as late as the 1850s. The numbers can only be guessed at. There were not enough such imports to satisfy all planters, and the Southern commercial conventions, which met annually to consider means of making the South economically independent, began to discuss the legal reopening of the trade. "If it is right to buy slaves in Virginia and carry them to New Orleans," William L. Yancey of Alabama asked his fellow delegates at the 1858 meeting, "why is it not right to buy them in Cuba, Brazil, or Africa and carry them there?" The convention that year voted to recommend the repeal of all laws against slave imports. Only the delegates from the states of the upper South, which profited from the domestic trade, opposed the foreign competition.

Slave Resistance

Few issues have sparked as much debate among historians as the effects of slavery on the blacks themselves. (See "Where Historians Disagree," pp. 342–343.) Slaveowners, and many white Americans for generations to come, liked to argue that the slaves were generally content, "happy with their lot." That may well have been true in some cases. But it is clear that the vast majority of Southern blacks were not content with being slaves, that they yearned for freedom even though most realized there was little they could do to secure it. Evidence for that conclusion comes, if from nowhere else, from the reaction of slaves when emancipation finally came. Virtually all Southern blacks reacted to freedom with joy and celebration; relatively few chose to remain in the service of the whites who had owned them before the Civil

War (although most blacks, of course, remained for many years subservient to whites in one way or another).

Rather than contented acceptance, the dominant response of blacks to slavery was a complex one: a combination of adaptation and resistance. At the extremes, slavery could produce two opposite reactions—each of which served as the basis for a powerful stereotype in white society. One extreme was what became known as the "Sambo"—the shuffling, grinning, head-scratching, deferential slave who acted out the role that he recognized the white world expected of him. More often than not, the "Sambo" pattern of behavior was a charade, a façade assumed in the presence of whites. The other extreme was the slave rebel—the black who could not bring himself or herself to either acceptance or accommodation but harbored an unquenchable spirit of rebelliousness.

Actual slave revolts were extremely rare, but the knowledge that they were possible struck terror into the hearts of white Southerners everywhere. In 1800, Gabriel Prosser gathered 1,000 rebellious slaves outside Richmond, but two blacks gave the plot away, and the Virginia militia was called out in time to head it off. Prosser and 35 others were executed. In 1822, the Charleston free black Denmark Vesey and his followers—rumored to total 9,000—made preparations for revolt; but again the word leaked out, and retribution followed. In 1831, Nat Turner, a slave preacher, led a band of blacks who armed themselves with guns and axes and, on a summer night, went from house to house in Southampton County, Virginia. They slaughtered sixty white men, women, and children before being overpowered by state and federal troops. More than a hundred blacks were put to death in the aftermath. Nat Turner's was the only actual slave insurrection in the nineteenth-century South, but slave conspiracies and threats of renewed violence continued throughout the section as long as slavery lasted.

For the most part, however, resistance to slavery took other, less drastic forms. In some cases, slaves worked "within the system" to free themselves from it—earning money with which they managed to buy their own and their families' freedom. One example was Elizabeth Keckley, a slave woman who bought freedom for herself and her son with proceeds from sewing. She later became a seamstress and personal servant and companion to Mary Lincoln in the White

Harriet Tubman with Escaped Slaves
Harriet Tubman (c. 1820–1913) was born into slavery in Maryland. In 1849, when her master died, she escaped to Philadelphia to avoid being sold out of state. Over the next ten years, she assisted first members of her own family and then
up to 300 other slaves to escape from Maryland to freedom. During the Civil War, she served alternately as a nurse and
as a spy for Union forces in South Carolina. She is shown here, on the left, with some of·the slaves she had helped to
free.   (Smith College)

House. Some slaves had the good fortune to be set
free by their master's will after his death—for example, the more than 400 slaves belonging to John Randolph of Roanoke, freed in 1833. From the 1830s on,
however, state laws made it more and more difficult,
and in some cases practically impossible, for an
owner to manumit (set free) his slaves. The laws,
when permitting manumission, often required the removal of the freed slaves from the state. Slaveowners
objected to the very presence of free blacks, who by
their existence set a disturbing example for the slaves.

By 1860, there nevertheless were about 250,000
free blacks in the slaveholding states, more than half
of them in Virginia and Maryland. A few (generally
on the northern fringes of the slaveholding regions)
attained wealth and prominence. Some owned slaves
themselves, usually relatives whom they had bought
in order to ensure their ultimate emancipation. Most,
however, lived in abject poverty, under conditions
worse than those afflicting blacks in the North. Law
or custom closed many occupations to them, forbade
them to assemble without white supervision, and
placed numerous other restraints on them. They were
only quasi-free, and yet they had all the burdens of
freedom: the necessity to support themselves, to find
housing, to pay taxes. Yet great as were the hardships of freedom, blacks usually preferred them to
slavery.

—————— WHERE HISTORIANS DISAGREE ——————

The Nature of Plantation Slavery

Few subjects have produced so rich a historical literature, or so lively a scholarly debate, as the nature of American slavery. Even more vividly than other historical controversies, the argument over slavery illustrates the extent to which historians are influenced by the times in which they write. Popular attitudes about race have always found reflection in historical examinations of slavery.

The first accounts of slavery, written before the Civil War by contemporaries of the institution, were usually stark expressions of the political beliefs of their authors. Southern chroniclers emphasized the benevolent features of the system, the paternalism with which masters cared for their slaves (a contrast, they implied, to the brutal impersonality of Northern factory owners and their "wage slaves"), and the carefree, happy demeanor of the slaves themselves. From Northern writers (many of them abolitionists) came a picture of slavery as a brutal, savage institution that dehumanized all who were touched by it. Theodore Dwight Weld's *American Slavery as It Is* (1839), for many years a widely cited book, depicted a system so cruel and savage that the book inspired many of its readers to embrace abolitionism. That, of course, was Weld's intent.

By the end of the nineteenth century, however, the political climate had changed. White Americans were now eager for sectional reconciliation, and in both North and South, there was emerging—in popular literature, in folktales and myths, and increasingly in scholarship—a romantic vision of the Old South as a graceful and serene civilization. It was a receptive climate for the publication in 1918 of the most influential study of slavery of the time (and for many years thereafter): Ulrich B. Phillips's *American Negro Slavery*. Phillips portrayed slavery as an essentially benign institution, in which kindly masters looked after submissive, childlike, and generally contented blacks. Black people, he suggested, were for the most part lazy and irresponsible, and the occasional harshness of the slave system was simply a necessary part of supervising a backward labor force. For nearly thirty years, Phillips's apologia for the Southern slaveowner remained the authoritative work on the subject.

In the 1940s, as concern about racial injustice began increasingly to engage the attention of white Americans, new approaches to slavery started to emerge. As early as 1941, Melville J. Herskovits was challenging one of Phillips's principal assumptions: that slaves had retained little if any of their African cultural inheritance. In fact, Herskovits argued, many Africanisms survived in slave culture for generations. Two years later, Herbert Aptheker attacked another of Phillips's claims: that slaves were submissive and content. "Discontent and rebelliousness," he wrote in *American Negro Slave Revolts,* "were not only exceedingly common, but, indeed, characteristic of American Negro slaves."

But the more influential challenge to Phillips came in the 1950s from historians who claimed that he had neglected the brutality of the system and the damage it did to those who lived under it. Kenneth Stampp's *The Peculiar Institution* (1956), the first comprehensive study of slavery since Phillips, emphasized the harshness of the system—not only its physical brutality but its psychological impact on men and women kept in a virtual prison with little room to develop their own social and cultural patterns. An even more devastating portrait of slavery came from Stanley Elkins. In *Slavery* (1959), he argued that many slaves had, indeed, displayed childlike, submissive, "Sambo" personalities, as Phillips had suggested. But such personalities, he argued, were evidence of the terrible damage the institution had inflicted on them. Comparing the slave system to Nazi concentration camps in World War II, he cited the effects on the individual of enforced "adjustment to absolute power" and the tragic distortions of character that resulted.

Stampp and Elkins reflected the general belief of white liberals in the 1950s and early 1960s that their society bore a large measure of guilt for the

WHERE HISTORIANS DISAGREE

injustices it had inflicted on blacks, that whites must work to undo the damage they had done in the past. By the early 1970s, however, racial attitudes had changed again, with the emergence of the "black power" ideology and the conviction among many blacks and some whites that blacks themselves should determine their own future. The new emphasis on black pride and achievement, therefore, helped produce a new view of the black past, emphasizing the cultural and social accomplishments of blacks under slavery. John Blassingame, in *The Slave Community* (1973), echoed the approach of Herskovits thirty years before in arguing that "the most remarkable aspect of the whole process of enslavement is the extent to which the American-born slaves were able to retain their ancestors' culture." Herbert Gutman, in *The Black Family in Slavery and Freedom, 1750–1925* (1976), provided voluminous evidence to support his claim that the black family, far from being weakened and destroyed by the slave system, survived with remarkable strength, although with some significant differences from the prevailing form of the white family. The slave community, Gutman claimed, was so successful in preserving and developing its own culture that the master class was unable, despite its great legal power, to affect it in any significant way.

This emphasis on the ability of blacks to maintain their own culture and society under slavery, and on their remarkable achievements within the system, formed the basis of two studies in 1974 that claimed to present comprehensive new portraits of the entire system. *Time on the Cross: The Economics of American Negro Slavery,* by Robert Fogel and Stanley Engerman, used quantitative methods to show not only that slaves were skilled and efficient workers, not only that the black family was strong and healthy, but also that the institution of slavery was a prosperous one that (in material terms, at least) benefited masters and slaves alike. Slave workers, Fogel and Engerman claimed, were generally better off than Northern industrial workers. Slaves often rose to managerial

positions on plantations. Whippings were few, and families were rarely broken up. The findings of *Time on the Cross* soon came under harsh attack—both from those who were offended by what they considered an apology for slavery, and more important, from historians who claimed to have discovered crucial flaws in Fogel and Engerman's methods. More influential in the long run was Eugene Genovese's *Roll, Jordan, Roll: The World the Slaves Made.* Genovese revived the idea of "paternalism" as the central element of the slave system. But in his view, paternalism was not an expression of white generosity; it was a powerful instrument of control. And it worked in two directions, enabling blacks to make demands of whites as well as the other way around. Moreover, within this paternal system, Genovese claimed, blacks retained a large cultural "space" of their own within which they developed their own family life, traditions, social patterns, and above all religion. Indeed, slaves had by the mid-nineteenth century developed a sense of themselves as part of a separate black "nation"—a nation tied to white society in important ways, but nevertheless powerful and distinct.

Although no comparably sweeping new interpretations of slavery have emerged in the last decade and a half, historians have continued to examine the institution and have, in the process, opened new avenues of exploration. Among the most important is the study of black women. Elizabeth Fox-Genovese is one of several historians who have portrayed the world of black women as in many ways distinctive, defined by their dual roles as members of the plantation work force and anchors of the black family. In *Within the Plantation Household* (1988), Fox-Genovese rejects the contention of some other historians that slave women formed special bonds, born of shared female experiences, with the plantation mistresses. But she agrees that a full understanding of the nature of plantation slavery must include a consideration of the role of gender as well as of race.

SIGNIFICANT EVENTS

1808 Importation of slaves to United States banned (p. 340)

1831 Nat Turner slave rebellion breaks out in Virginia (p. 340)

1834 Cyrus McCormick patents mechanical reaper (p. 326)

1837 Oberlin becomes first men's college to accept woman students (p. 322)

Mount Holyoke Seminary for women founded (p. 323)

1842 Massachusetts supreme court, in *Commonwealth* v. *Hunt,* declares unions and strikes legal (p. 320)

1844 Samuel F. B. Morse sends first telegraphic message (p. 314)

1845 Irish potato famine begins, spurring major emigration to America (p. 317)

1846 Rotary press invented, making possible rapid printing of newspapers (p. 315)

Associated Press organized (p. 315)

1848 Failed revolution in Germany spurs emigration to America (p. 317)

1849 Rise in cotton prices spurs production boom (p. 329)

1852 American party (Know-Nothings) formed (p. 318)

Some blacks attempted to resist slavery by escaping from it, by running away. A small number managed to escape to the North or to Canada, especially after sympathetic whites began organizing the so-called underground railroad to assist them in flight. But the odds against a successful escape, particularly from the Deep South, were almost impossibly great. The hazards of distance and the slaves' ignorance of geography were serious obstacles. So were the white "slave patrols," which stopped wandering blacks on sight throughout the South demanding to see travel permits. Without such a permit, slaves were presumed to be runaways and were taken captive. For blacks who attempted to escape through the woods, slave patrols often employed bloodhounds. Despite all the obstacles to success, however, blacks continued to run away from their masters in large numbers. Some did so repeatedly, undeterred by the whippings and other penalties inflicted on them when captured.

But perhaps the most important method of resistance was simply a pattern of everyday behavior by which blacks defied their masters. That whites so often considered blacks to be lazy and shiftless suggests one means of resistance: refusal to work hard. Slaves might also steal from their masters or from neighboring whites. They might perform isolated acts of sabotage: losing or breaking tools (Southern planters gradually began to buy unusually heavy hoes because so many of the lighter ones got broken) or performing tasks improperly. In extreme cases, blacks might make themselves useless by cutting off their fingers or even committing suicide. Or, despite

the terrible consequences, they might on occasion turn on their masters and kill them. The extremes, however, were rare. For the most part, blacks resisted by building into their normal patterns of behavior subtle methods of rebellion.

Slave Religion and the Black Family

But resistance was only part of the slave response to slavery. The other was an elaborate process of adaptation—a process that did not imply contentment with bondage but a recognition that there was no realistic alternative. One of the ways blacks adapted was by developing a rich and complex culture, one that enabled them to sustain a sense of racial pride and unity. In many areas, they retained a language of their own, sometimes incorporating African speech patterns into English. They developed a distinctive music, establishing in the process what was perhaps the most impressive of all American musical traditions. The most important features of black culture, however, were the development of two powerful institutions: religion and the family.

A separate slave religion was not supposed to exist. Almost all blacks were Christians, and their masters expected them to worship under the supervision of white ministers—often in the same chapels as whites. Indeed, autonomous black churches were banned by law. Nevertheless, blacks throughout the South developed their own version of Christianity, at times incorporating such African practices as voodoo, but more often simply bending religion to the special circumstances of bondage. Natural leaders emerging within the slave community rose to the rank of preacher; and when necessary, blacks would hold services in secret, often at night.

Black religion was more emotional than its white counterparts, and it reflected the influence of African customs and practices. Slave prayer meetings routinely involved fervent chanting, spontaneous exclamations from the congregation, and ecstatic conversion experiences. Black religion was also more joyful and affirming than that of many white denominations. And above all, black religion emphasized the dream of freedom and deliverance. In their prayers and songs and sermons, black Christians talked and sang of the day when the Lord would "call us home," "deliver us to freedom," "take us to the Promised Land." And while their white masters generally chose to interpret such language merely as the expression of hopes for life after death, blacks themselves used the images of Christian salvation to express their own dream of freedom in the present world.

The slave family was the other crucial institution of black culture in the South. Like religion, it suffered from certain legal restrictions—most notably the lack of legal marriage. Nevertheless, the nuclear family consistently emerged as the dominant kinship model among blacks. Such families did not always operate according to white customs. Black women generally began bearing children at younger ages than most whites, often as early as age fourteen or fifteen. Slave communities did not condemn premarital pregnancy in the way white society did, and black couples would often begin living together before marrying. It was customary, however, for couples to marry soon after conceiving a child. Family ties were no less strong than those of whites, and many slave marriages lasted throughout the course of long lifetimes.

When marriages did not survive, it was often because of circumstances over which blacks had no control. Up to a third of all black families were broken up by the slave trade. And that accounted for some of the other distinctive characteristics of the black family, which adapted itself to the cruel realities of its own uncertain future. Networks of kinship—which grew to include not only spouses and their children, but aunts, uncles, grandparents, even distant cousins—remained strong and important and often served to compensate for the breakup of nuclear families. A slave suddenly moved to a new area, far from his or her family, might create "fictional" kinship ties and become "adopted" by a family in the new community. Even so, the impulse to maintain contact with a spouse and children remained strong long after the breakup of a family. One of the most frequent causes of flight from the plantation was a slave's desire to find a husband, wife, or child who had been sent elsewhere. It was not only by breaking up families through sale that whites intruded on black family life. Black women, usually powerless to resist the sexual advances of their masters, often bore the children of whites—children whom the whites seldom recognized as their own and who were consigned to slavery from birth.

In addition to establishing social and cultural institutions of their own, slaves adapted themselves to slavery by forming complex relationships with their masters. However much blacks resented their lack of freedom, they often found it difficult to maintain an entirely hostile attitude toward their owners. Not only were they dependent on whites for the material means of existence—food, clothing, and shelter; they also often derived from their masters a sense of security and protection. There was, in short, a paternal relationship between slave and master—sometimes harsh, sometimes kindly, but almost invariably important. That paternalism, in fact, became (even if not always consciously) a vital instrument of white control. By creating a sense of mutual dependence, whites helped reduce resistance to an institution that, in essence, was designed solely for the benefit of the ruling race.

SUGGESTED READINGS

The Northern Economy. See Suggested Readings for Chapters 7 and 9. Thomas C. Cochran, *Frontiers of Change: Early Industrialization in America* (1981); David A. Hounshell, *From the American System to Mass Production, 1800–1932: The Development of Manufacturing Technology in the United States* (1985); Paul W. Gates, *The Farmer's Age* (1960); Peter Temin, *Iron and Steel in Nineteenth-Century America* (1964); Alfred D. Chandler, Jr., *The Visible Hand: The Managerial Revolution in American Business* (1977); James Norris, *R.G. Dun & Co., 1841–1900* (1978); Joseph E.

Walker, *Hopewell: A Social and Economic History of an Iron-making Community* (1966); Robert W. Fogel, *Railroads and American Economic Growth* (1964); Carter Goodrich, *Government Promotion of Canals and Railroads, 1800–1890* (1960); John F. Stover, *The Life and Decline of the American Railroad* (1970) and *Iron Road to the West: American Railroads in the 1850s* (1978); R. L. Thompson, *Wiring a Continent* (1947).

Immigration. John Bodnar, *The Transplanted: A History of Immigrants in America* (1985); Marcus Hansen, *The Immi-*

grant in *American History* (1940) and *The Atlantic Migration, 1607–1860* (1940); Maldwyn A. Jones, *American Immigration* (1960); Oscar Handlin, *The Uprooted* (1951, rev. 1973) and *Boston's Immigrants* (1941); Charlotte Erickson, *Invisible Immigrants* (1972); Philip Taylor, *The Distant Magnet* (1971); Robert Ernst, *Immigrant Life in New York City, 1825–1863* (1949); Kathleen N. Conzen, *Immigrant Milwaukee: 1836–1860* (1976); Carl Wittke, *We Who Built America*, rev. ed. (1964), *Refugees of Revolution: The German Forty-Eighters in America* (1952), and *The Irish in America* (1956); Hasia Diner, *Erin's Daughters in America* (1983); Harold Runblom and Hans Norman, *From Sweden to America* (1976); Theodore C. Blegen, *Norwegian Migration to America*, 2 vols. (1931–1940); Stuart C. Miller, *The Unwelcome Immigrant* (1969); Rowland T. Berthoff, *British Immigrants in Industrial America, 1790–1950* (1953); Jay P. Dolan, *The Immigrant Church: New York's Irish and German Catholics* (1975); Ray Billington, *The Protestant Crusade, 1800–1860* (1938); I. M. Leonard and R. D. Parmet, *American Nativism, 1830–1860* (1971); T. J. Curran, *Xenophobia and Immigration* (1975); Allan Nevins, *The Ordeal of the Union*, 2 vols. (1947).

Northern Labor, Society, and Culture. Susan E. Hirsch, *Roots of the American Working Class: The Industrialization of Crafts in Newark, 1800–1860* (1978); W. J. Rorabaugh, *The Craft Apprentice: From Franklin to the Machine Age* (1986); Bruce Laurie, *Working People of Philadelphia* (1980); Norman Ware, *The Industrial Worker, 1840–1860* (1924); Henry Pelling, *American Labor* (1960); Hannah Josephson, *The Golden Threads* (1949); David Thelen, *Paths of Resistance: Tradition and Dignity in Industrializing Missouri* (1986); Mary Ryan, *Cradle of the Middle Class: The Family in Oneida County, New York, 1790–1865* (1981); Christine Stansell, *City of Women: Sex and Class in New York, 1789–1860* (1986); Carroll Smith-Rosenberg, *Disorderly Conduct: Visions of Gender in Victorian America* (1985); Alan Dawley, *Class and Community: The Industrial Revolution in Lynn* (1976); Michael Frisch, *Town into City: Springfield, Massachusetts, and the Meaning of Community, 1840–1880* (1972); Peter Knights, *The Plain People of Boston, 1830–1860* (1971); Don Doyle, *The Social Order of a Frontier Community: Jacksonville, Illinois, 1825–1870* (1978); Stuart Blumin, *The Urban Threshold: Growth and Change in a Nineteenth-Century Community* (1976); Sam Bass Warner, Jr., *The Urban Wilderness* (1972); Richard C. Wade, *The Urban Frontier, 1790–1830* (1957); Raymond A. Mohl, *Poverty in New York, 1783–1825* (1971); Edward Pessen, *Riches, Classes, and Power Before the Civil War* (1973); Stephan Thernstrom, *Poverty and Progress* (1964); Frank Luther Mott, *American Journalism* (1950); Glyndon Van Deusen, *Horace Greeley* (1953).

The Southern Mind. W. J. Cash, *The Mind of the South* (1941); Avery Craven, *The Growth of Southern Nationalism* (1953); John McCardell, *The Idea of a Southern Nation* (1979); Charles S. Sydnor, *The Development of Southern Sectionalism, 1819–1848* (1948); Clement Eaton, *Freedom of Thought in the Old South* (1940) and *The Growth of Southern Nationalism, 1848–1861* (1961); William R. Taylor, *Cavalier and Yankee: The Old South and American National Character* (1961); Rollin G. Osterweis, *Romanticism and Nationalism in the Old South* (1949); John Hope Franklin, *The Militant South* (1956); Drew Gilpin Faust, *A Sacred Circle: The Dilemma of the Intellectual in the Old South* (1977) and *James Henry Hammond and the Old South: A Design for Mastery* (1982); Bertram Wyatt-Brown, *Southern Honor: Ethics and Behavior in the Old South* (1982) and *Yankee Saints and Southern Sinners* (1985); Edward L. Ayers, *Vengeance and Justice* (1984); Donald G. Mathews, *Religion in the Old South* (1977); Ann C. Loveland, *Southern Evangelicals and the Social Order, 1800–1860* (1980); Frank Freidel, *Francis Lieber* (1947).

The Plantation Economy. Gavin Wright, *The Political Economy of the Cotton South: Households, Markets, and Wealth in the Nineteenth Century* (1978); Lewis C. Gray, *History of Agriculture in the Southern United States to 1860*, 2 vols. (1933); Ulrich B. Phillips, *Life and Labor in the Old South* (1929); R. R. Russel, *Economic Aspects of Southern Sectionalism, 1840–1861* (1924); Frank L. Owsley, *Plain Folk of the Old South* (1949); Ralph A. Wooster, *Politicians, Planters, and Plain Folk* (1975); J. William Harris, *Plain Folk and Gentry in a Slave Society* (1985); Peter Kolchin, *Unfree Labor: American Slavery and Russian Serfdom* (1987).

The Planters. Robert Manson Myers (ed.), *The Children of Pride* (1972); Mary D. Robertson (ed.), *Lucy Breckinridge of Grove Hill* (1979); Carol Bleser, *The Hammonds of Redcliffe* (1981); Frances Ann Kemble, *Journal of a Residence on a Georgian Plantation in 1838–1839* (1863); Eugene Genovese, *The Political Economy of Slavery* (1965) and *The World the Slaveholders Made* (1969); James Oakes, *The Ruling Race: A History of American Slaveholders* (1982); Kenneth S. Greenberg, *Masters and Statesmen: The Political Culture of American Slavery* (1985).

Southern White Women. Anne Firor Scott, *The Southern Lady* (1970); Catherine Clinton, *The Plantation Mistress: Woman's World in the Old South* (1982); Mary Boykin Chesnut, *A Diary from Dixie* (1981, ed. by C. Vann Woodward); Suzanne Lebsock, *The Free Women of Petersburg: Status and Culture in a Southern Town* (1984); Jane Turner Censer, *North Carolina Planters and Their Children, 1800–1860* (1984); Elizabeth Fox-Genovese, *Within the Plantation Household* (1988).

Slavery. Kenneth Stampp, *The Peculiar Institution* (1955); Stanley Elkins, *Slavery* (1959); Herbert Aptheker, *American Negro Slave Revolts* (1943); Melville J. Herskovits, *The Myth of the Negro Past* (1941); John Blassingame, *The Slave Community* (1973); Eugene Genovese, *Roll, Jordan, Roll: The World the Slaves Made* (1974); Herbert Gutman, *The Black Family in Slavery and Freedom* (1976); Judith Chase, *Afro-American Art and Craft* (1971); Dena Epstein, *Sinful Tunes and Spirituals* (1977); Lawrence W. Levine, *Black Culture and Black Consciousness: Afro-American Folk Thought from Slavery to Freedom* (1977); Michael P. Johnson and James L. Roark, *Black Masters* (1984); G. P. Rawick, *From Sundown* to Sunup: The Making of the Black Community (1973); Leslie Howard Owens, *This Species of Property* (1976); Robert Fogel and Stanley Engerman, *Time on the Cross*, 2 vols. (1974); Herbert Gutman, *Slavery and the Numbers Game* (1975); P. A. David et al., *Reckoning with Slavery* (1976); Barbara Jean Fields, *Slavery and Freedom on the Middle Ground* (1985); Jacqueline Jones, *Labor of Love, Labor of Sorrow* (1985); Deborah G. White, *Ar'n't I a Woman?* (1985); Robert Starobin, *Industrial Slavery in the Old South* (1970); Richard C. Wade, *Slavery in the Cities* (1964); Stephen B. Oates, *The Fires of Jubilee* (1974); Robert Starobin, *Denmark Vesey* (1970); Carl Degler, *Neither Black nor White* (1971); Joel Williamson, *New People: Miscegenation and Mulattoes in the United States* (1980); Ira Berlin, *Slaves Without Masters* (1974); Leon Litwack, *North of Slavery* (1961); Orlando Patterson, *Slavery and Social Death: A Comparative Study* (1982); David Brion Davis, *Slavery and Human Progress* (1984).

Girls' Evening School (c. 1840), **Anonymous**
Schooling for women, which expanded significantly in the mid-nineteenth century, included training in domestic arts (as indicated by the sewing table at right), as well as in reading, writing, and other basic skills. (*Museum of Fine Arts, Boston*)

CHAPTER 12

◩ ◉ ◪

An Age of Reforms

◩ ◉ ◪

The United States in the mid-nineteenth century was a society in transition. The nation was growing rapidly in geographical extent, in the size and diversity of its population, and in the dimensions and complexity of its economy. And like any people faced with such rapid and fundamental alterations in their surroundings, Americans reacted with ambiguity. On the one hand, they were excited by the new possibilities that economic growth was providing. On the other hand, they were painfully aware of the dislocations that it was creating: the challenges to traditional values and institutions, the social instability, the uncertainty about the future.

One result of these conflicting attitudes was the emergence of a bewildering array of movements intended to adapt society to its new realities, to "reform" the nation. These reform efforts took so many different shapes that generalizations about them are difficult, but in general they reflected one of two basic impulses, and at times elements of both. Many of these movements rested on an optimistic faith in human nature, a belief that within every individual resided a spirit that was basically good and that society should attempt to unleash. This assumption—which spawned in both Europe and America a movement known, in its artistic aspects at least, as romanticism—stood in marked contrast to the traditional Calvinist assumption that human impulses and instincts were evil and needed to be repressed. Instead, reformers now argued, individuals should strive to give full expression to the inner spirit, should work to unleash their capacity to experience joy and to do good.

A second impulse, which appeared directly to contradict the first but in practice often existed alongside it, was a desire for order and control. With their society changing so rapidly, with their traditional values and institutions being challenged and eroded, many Americans yearned above all for a restoration of stability and discipline to their nation. Often, this impulse embodied a conservative nostalgia for better, simpler times. But it also inspired efforts to create new institutions of social control, suited to the realities of the new age.

The reforms that flowed from these two impulses came in many guises and mobilized many different groups. Reformers were far more numerous and influential in the North and Northwest than in the South, but reform activity could be found in all areas of the nation. In the course of the 1840s, however, one issue—slavery—came to overshadow all others. And one group of reformers—the abolitionists—became the most visible of all. At that point, the reform impulse, which at first had been a force that tended to unify the sections, became another wedge between the North and the South.

Culture and Liberation

"In the four quarters of the globe," wrote the English wit Sydney Smith in 1820, "who reads an American book? or goes to an American play? or looks at an

American picture or statue?'' The answer, he assumed, was obvious—no one.

American intellectuals were painfully aware of the low regard in which their culture was held by Europeans; and they continued in the middle decades of the century to work for a liberation of their nation's culture—for the creation of an American artistic life independent of Europe, one that would express their own nation's special virtues. At the same time, however, the nation's cultural leaders were beginning to strive for another kind of liberation, one that would gradually come almost to overshadow their self-conscious nationalism. That impulse, which was—ironically—largely an import from Europe, was the spirit of romanticism. In literature, in philosophy, in art, even in politics and economics, American intellectuals were committing themselves to the liberation of the human spirit.

A Literary Flowering

The effort to create a distinctively American literature, which Washington Irving and others had advanced in the first decades of the century, bore important fruit in the 1820s with the emergence of the first great American novelist: James Fenimore Cooper. The author of over thirty novels in the space of three decades, Cooper was known to his contemporaries as a master of adventure and suspense. What most distinguished his work, however, was its evocation of the American frontier. Cooper had grown up in central New York, at a time when the wilderness was not far away; and he retained throughout his life a fascination with man's relationship to nature and with the challenges (and dangers) of America's expansion westward. His most important novels—the "Leatherstocking Tales," among them *The Last of the Mohicans* (1826) and *The Deerslayer* (1841)—explored the American frontiersman's experience with Indians, pioneers, violence, and the law.

Cooper's novels were a continuation, in many ways a culmination, of the early nineteenth-century effort to produce a truly American literature. But they also served as a link to the concerns of later intellectuals. For in the "Leatherstocking Tales" could be seen not only a celebration of the American spirit and landscape but an evocation, through the character of Natty Bumppo, of the ideal of the independent individual, with a natural inner goodness. There was also evidence of the second impulse that would motivate American reform: the fear of disorder. In portraying other characters, who exemplified the vicious, grasping nature of some of the nation's Western settlers, Cooper was suggesting a need for social discipline even in the wilderness.

Emerging on the heels of Cooper was another group of important American writers who displayed even more clearly the grip of romanticism on the nation's intellectual life. Walt Whitman, the self-proclaimed poet of American democracy, was the son of a Long Island carpenter and lived for many years roaming the country doing odd jobs. Finally, in 1855, he hired a printer and published a first, thin volume of work: *Leaves of Grass*. His poems were an unrestrained celebration of democracy, of the liberation of the individual, and of the pleasures of the flesh as well as of the spirit. In these poems, as well as in a large body of other work spanning nearly forty more years until his death in 1892, Whitman not only helped liberate verse from traditional, restrictive conventions but helped express the questing spirit of individualism that characterized his age.

The new literary concern with the unleashing of human emotions did not always produce optimistic and exuberant works. Herman Melville is a case in point. Born in New York in 1819, Melville ran away to sea as a youth and spent years sailing the world (including the South Seas) before returning home to become the greatest American writer of his era. The most important of his novels was *Moby Dick,* published in 1851. His portrayal of Ahab, the powerful, driven captain of a whaling vessel, was a story of courage and of the strength of individual will; but it was also a tragedy of pride and revenge. Ahab's maniacal search for Moby Dick, a great white whale that had maimed him, suggested how the search for personal fulfillment and triumph could not only liberate but destroy. The result of Ahab's great quest was the annihilation of Ahab himself.

Similarly bleak were the works of one of the few Southern writers of the time to embrace the search for the essence of the human spirit: Edgar Allan Poe. In the course of his short and unhappy life (he died in 1849 at the age of forty), Poe produced stories and poems that were primarily sad and macabre. His first book, *Tamerlane and Other Poems* (1827), received little recognition. But later works, including his most famous poem, "The Raven" (1845), established him as a major, if controversial, literary figure. Poe evoked images of individuals rising above the narrow confines of intellect and exploring the deeper world of the spirit and the emotions. Yet that world, he seemed to say, was one of pain and horror. Other American writers were contemptuous of Poe's work and his message, but he was ultimately to have a profound effect on European poets such as Baudelaire.

Poe, however, was something of an exception in the world of Southern literature. The South experienced a literary flowering of its own in the mid-nineteenth century, and it produced writers and artists who were, like their Northern counterparts, concerned with defining the nature of American society and of the American nation. But Southerners tended to produce very different images of what that society was and should be.

Southern novelists of the 1830s (among them Beverly Tucker, William Alexander Caruthers, and John Pendleton Kennedy), some of them writers of great talent, many of them residents of Richmond, produced historical romances or romantic eulogies of the plantation system of the upper South. In the 1840s, the Southern literary capital moved to Charleston, home of the most distinguished of the region's men of letters: William Gilmore Simms. For a time, his work expressed a broad nationalism that transcended his regional background; but by the 1840s he had become a strong defender of Southern institutions—especially slavery—against the encroachments of the North. There was, he believed, a unique quality to Southern life that it was the duty of intellectuals to defend.

One group of Southern writers, however, produced works that were more distinctively American and less committed to a glorification of the peculiarities of Southern life. These were the writers of the frontier, who depicted the society of the backwoods rural areas. Augustus B. Longstreet, Joseph G. Baldwin, Johnson J. Hooper, and others focused not on aristocratic "cavaliers," but on ordinary people and poor whites. Instead of romanticizing their subjects, they were deliberately and sometimes painfully realistic. And they seasoned their sketches with a robust, vulgar humor that was something new in American literature. These Southern realists established a tradition of American regional humor that was ultimately to find a supreme exponent in Mark Twain.

The Transcendentalists

One of the outstanding expressions of the romantic impulse in America came from a group of New England writers and philosophers known as the transcendentalists. Borrowing heavily from German philosophers such as Kant, Hegel, and Schelling, and from the English writers Coleridge and Carlyle, the transcendentalists embraced a theory of the individual that rested on a distinction (first suggested by Kant) between what they called "reason" and "understanding." Reason, as they defined it, was the highest human faculty; it was the individual's innate capacity to grasp beauty and truth by giving full expression to the instincts and emotions. Understanding, by contrast, was the use of intellect in the narrow, artificial ways imposed by society; it involved the repression of instinct and the victory of externally imposed learning. Every person's goal, therefore, should be liberation from the confines of "understanding" and cultivation of "reason." Each individual should strive to "transcend" the limits of the intellect and allow the emotions, the "soul," to create an "original relation to the Universe."

Transcendentalist philosophy emerged first among a small group of intellectuals centered in Concord, Massachusetts. Their leader and most eloquent voice was Ralph Waldo Emerson. A Unitarian minister in his youth, Emerson left the church in 1832 to devote himself entirely to writing and teaching the elements of transcendentalism. He produced a significant body of poetry, but he was most renowned for his essays and lectures. In "Nature" (1836), one of his best-known essays, Emerson wrote that in the quest for self-fulfillment, individuals should work for a communion with the natural world: "in the woods, we return to reason and faith. . . . Standing on the bare ground,—my head bathed by the blithe air, and uplifted into infinite space,—all mean egotism vanishes. . . . I am part and particle of God." In other essays, he was even more explicit in advocating a commitment of the individual to the full exploration of inner capacities. "Nothing is at last sacred," he wrote in "Self-Reliance" (1841), perhaps his most famous essay, "but the integrity of your own mind." The quest for self-reliance, he explained, was really a search for communion with the unity of the universe, the wholeness of God, the great spiritual force that he described as the "Oversoul." Each person's innate capacity to become, through his or her private ef-

Ralph Waldo Emerson
Along with Margaret Fuller and Henry David Thoreau, Emerson helped make Concord, Massachusetts, the center of American transcendentalism. He derived many of his ideas about the mystical union between human beings and nature from the works of the English poets Thomas Carlyle, Samuel Taylor Coleridge, and William Wordsworth. (The Bettmann Archive)

forts, a part of this essence was perhaps the classic expression of the romantic belief in the "divinity" of the individual.

Almost as influential as Emerson was another leading Concord transcendentalist, Henry David Thoreau. Thoreau went even further than his friend Emerson in repudiating the repressive forces of society, which produced, he said, "lives of quiet desperation." Each individual should work for self-realization by resisting pressures to conform to society's expectations and responding instead to their own instincts. Thoreau's own effort to free himself—immortalized in his most famous book, *Walden* (1854)—led him to build a small cabin in the Concord woods on the edge of Walden Pond, where he lived alone for two years as simply as he could. "I went to the woods," he explained, "because I wished to live deliberately, to front only the essential facts of life, and see if I could not learn what it had to teach, and not, when I came to die, discover that I had not lived." Thoreau's rejection of what he considered the artificial constraints of society extended as well to his relationship with government. In 1846, he went to jail (briefly) rather than agree to pay a poll tax. He would not, he insisted, give financial support to a government that permitted the existence of slavery. In his 1849 essay "Resistance to Civil Government," he explained his refusal by claiming that the individual's personal morality had the first claim on his or her actions, that a government which required violation of that morality had no legitimate authority. The proper response was "civil disobedience," or "passive resistance"—a public refusal to obey unjust laws.

Visions of Utopia

Although transcendentalism was above all an individualistic philosophy, it helped spawn the most famous of all nineteenth-century experiments in communal living: Brook Farm. The dream of the Boston transcendentalist George Ripley, Brook Farm was established as an experimental community in

West Roxbury, Massachusetts, in 1841. There, according to Ripley, individuals would gather to create a new form of social organization, one that would permit every member of the community full opportunity for self-realization. All residents would share equally in the labor of the community so that all could share too in the leisure; for it was leisure that was the first necessity for cultivation of the self. (Ripley was one of the first Americans to attribute positive connotations to the idea of leisure; most of his contemporaries equated it with laziness and sloth.) Participation in manual labor served another purpose as well: It helped individuals bridge the gap between the world of the intellect and the world of the flesh, thus aiding them to become whole people. The obvious tension between the ideal of individual freedom and the demands of a communal society took their toll on Brook Farm. Increasingly, individualism gave way to a form of socialism. Many residents became disenchanted and left; when a fire destroyed the central building of the community in 1847, the experiment dissolved.

Among the original residents of Brook Farm was the writer Nathaniel Hawthorne, who expressed his disillusionment with the experiment and, to some extent, with transcendentalism in a series of notable novels. In *The Blithedale Romance* (1852), he wrote scathingly of Brook Farm itself, portraying the disastrous consequences of the experiment on the individuals who submitted to it. In other novels—most notably *The Scarlet Letter* (1850) and *The House of Seven Gables* (1851)—he wrote equally passionately about the price individuals pay for cutting themselves off from society. Egotism, he claimed (in an indirect challenge to the transcendentalist faith in the self), was the "serpent" that lay at the heart of human misery.

The failure of Brook Farm did not, however, prevent the formation of other experimental communities. Some borrowed, as Ripley had done, from the ideas of the French philosopher Charles Fourier, whose ideas of socialist communities organized as cooperative "phalanxes" received wide attention in America. Others drew from the ideas of the Scottish industrialist and philanthropist Robert Owen. Owen himself founded an experimental community in Indiana in 1825, which he named New Harmony. It was to be a "Village of Cooperation," in which every resident worked and lived in total equality. The community was an economic failure, but the vision that

had inspired it continued to enchant Americans. Dozens of other "Owenite" experiments began in other locations in the ensuing years.

Redefining Sexual Roles

One of the principal concerns of many of the new utopian communities (and of the new social philosophies on which they rested) was the relationship between men and women. In transcendentalism and other movements of this period can be seen expressions of a kind of feminism that would not gain a secure foothold in American society until the late twentieth century. Margaret Fuller, a leading transcendentalist, suggested the important relationship between the discovery of the "self" that was so central to antebellum reform and the questioning of sexual roles: "Many women are considering within themselves what they need and what they have not," she wrote in 1845. "I would have Woman lay aside all thought, such as she habitually cherishes, of being taught and led by men."

A redefinition of sexual roles was crucial to one of the most enduring of the utopian colonies of the nineteenth century: the Oneida Community, established in 1848 in upstate New York by John Humphrey Noyes. The Oneida "Perfectionists," as residents of the community called themselves, rejected traditional notions of family and marriage. All residents, Noyes declared, were "married" to all other residents; there were to be no permanent conjugal ties. But Oneida was not, as its horrified critics often claimed, an experiment in unrestrained "free love." It was a place where the community carefully monitored sexual behavior; where women were to be protected from unwanted childbearing; in which children were raised communally, often seeing little of their own parents. The Oneidans took special pride in what they considered the liberation of their women from the demands of male "lust" and from the traditional bonds of family.

The Shakers, even more than the Oneidans, made a redefinition of traditional sexual roles central to their society. Founded by "Mother" Ann Lee in the 1770s, the society of the Shakers survived throughout the nineteenth century and into the twentieth. (A small remnant survives today.) But the Shakers attracted a particularly large following in the antebellum period and established more than twenty

Shakers Near Lebanon, Pennsylvania

The Shakers always welcomed visitors to their strikingly simple farms and shops and to their distinctive worship services. Outsiders were often astonished by the singing, shaking, shouting, and ecstatic movement these otherwise dignified and restrained men and women displayed during their ritualistic dances. The lithographer Nathaniel Currier produced this view of a Shaker service in about 1838 and gave evidence of the contempt with which many Americans viewed the sect. The dancers (separated by sex, as befitted the celibate Shaker community) look awkward and even grotesque here, although in reality—according to most accounts—they moved with rhythm and grace. The elegance of a visitor (at left) stands in sharp contrast to the simple attire and spare surroundings of the Shakers themselves.   (New York Public Library)

communities throughout the Northeast and Northwest in the 1840s. They derived their name from a unique religious ritual—a sort of dance, in which members of a congregation would "shake" themselves free of sin while performing a loud chant.

The most distinctive feature of Shakerism, however, was its commitment to complete celibacy—which meant, of course, that no one could be born to Shakerism; all Shakers had voluntarily to choose the faith. Shaker communities attracted about 6,000 members in the 1840s, more women than men, and they lived in communities in which contacts between men and women were very limited. They openly endorsed the idea of sexual equality; they even embraced the idea of a God who was not clearly male or female. Within the Shaker society as a whole, it was women who exercised the most power. Mother Ann Lee was succeeded as leader of the movement by Mother Lucy Wright. Shakerism, one observer wrote in the 1840s, was a refuge from the "perversions of marriage" and "the gross abuses which drag it down."

The Shakers were not, however, motivated only by a desire to escape the burdens of traditional sexual roles. They were trying as well to create a society separated and protected from the chaos and disorder that they believed had come to characterize American life as a whole. They were less interested in personal freedom than in social discipline. And in that, they were much like other dissenting religious sects and other utopian communities of their time. Another example was the Amana Community, founded by German immigrants in 1843, which moved to Iowa in 1855; the Amanas attempted to realize Christian ideals by creating an ordered, socialist society.

The Mormons

Among the most important efforts to create a new and more ordered society within the old was that of the Church of Jesus Christ of Latter Day Saints—the Mormons. Mormonism began in upstate New York as a result of the efforts of Joseph Smith, a young, energetic, but economically unsuccessful man, who had spent most of his twenty-four years moving restlessly through New England and the Northeast. Then, in 1830, he published a remarkable document—the Book of Mormon—which was, he claimed, a translation of a set of golden plates he had found in the hills of New York, revealed to him by an angel of God. The Book of Mormon told the story of an ancient civilization in America, whose now vanished kingdom could become a model for a new holy community in the United States.

Gathering a small group of believers around him, Smith began in 1831 an effort to find a sanctuary for his new community of "saints," an effort that would continue, unhappily, for more than twenty years. Time and again, the Mormons attempted to establish their "New Jerusalem." Time and again, they met with persecution from surrounding communities suspicious of their radical religious doctrines—which included polygamy (the right of men to take several wives), a rigid form of social organization, and most damaging of all, an intense secrecy, which gave rise to wild rumors among their critics of conspiracy and depravity.

Driven from their original settlements in Independence, Missouri, and Kirtland, Ohio, the Mormons moved on to the new town of Nauvoo, Illinois, which in the early 1840s became an imposing and economically successful community. In 1844, however, Joseph Smith was arrested, charged with treason (for conspiring against the government to win foreign support for a new Mormon colony in the Southwest), and imprisoned in Carthage, Illinois. There an angry mob attacked the jail, forced Smith from his cell, and shot and killed him. The Mormons now abandoned Nauvoo and, under the leadership of Smith's successor, Brigham Young, traveled across the desert—a society of 12,000 people, in one of the largest group migrations in American history—and established a new community in Utah, the present Salt Lake City. There, at last, the Mormons were able to create a permanent settlement. And although they were not long to remain as isolated from the rest of American society as they were at the beginning, never again were they to be dislodged.

Like other experiments in social organization of the era, Mormonism reflected a belief in human perfectibility. God had once been a man, the church taught; and thus every man or woman could aspire to become—as Joseph Smith had done—a god. But unlike other new communities, the Mormons did not embrace the doctrine of individual liberty. Instead, they created a highly organized, centrally directed, almost militarized social structure, a refuge against the disorder and uncertainty of the secular world. They placed particular emphasis on the structure of the family. The original Mormons were, for the most part, men and women who felt displaced in their rapidly changing society—economically marginal people left behind by the material growth and social progress of their era. In the new religion, they found security and order.

Remaking Society

The simultaneous efforts to liberate the individual and impose order on a changing world did not simply produce efforts to escape from society and create alternatives to it. They also helped to create a wide range of new movements to remake society—movements in which, to a striking degree, women formed the real rank and file and often the leadership as well. By the 1830s, such movements had taken the form of organized reform societies. "In no country in the world," Tocqueville had observed, "has the principle of association been more successfully used, or more unsparingly applied to a multitude of different objects, than in America. . . . for there is no end which the human will, seconded by the collective exertions of individuals, despairs of attaining."

The new organizations did indeed work on behalf of a wide range of goals: temperance; education; peace; the care of the poor, the handicapped, and the mentally ill; the treatment of criminals; the rights of women; and many more. Few eras in American history have witnessed as wide a range of reform efforts. And few eras have exposed more clearly the simultaneous attraction of Americans to the ideas of personal liberty and social order.

Revivalism, Morality, and Order

The philosophy of reform arose from two distinct sources. One was the optimistic vision of those who, like the transcendentalists, rejected Calvinist doctrines and preached the divinity of the individual. These included not only Emerson, Thoreau, and their followers, but a much larger group of Americans who embraced the doctrines of Unitarianism and Universalism and absorbed European romanticism.

The second, and in many respects more important, source was Protestant revivalism—the movement that had begun with the Second Great Awakening early in the century and had, by the 1820s, evolved into a powerful force for social reform. Although the New Light revivalists were theologically far removed from the transcendentalists and Unitarians, they had come to share the optimistic belief that every individual was capable of salvation. According to Charles Grandison Finney, a Presbyterian minister who became the most influential revival evangelist of the 1820s and 1830s, traditional Calvinist doctrines of predestination and individual human helplessness were both obsolete and destructive. Each person, he preached, contained within himself or herself the capacity to experience spiritual rebirth and achieve salvation. A revival need not depend on a miracle from God; it could be created by individual effort.

Finney enjoyed particular success in upstate New York, where he helped launch a series of passionate revivals in towns along the Erie Canal—a region so prone to religious awakenings that it was known as the "burned-over district." It was no coincidence that the new revivalism should prove so powerful there, for this region of New York was experiencing—largely as a result of the construction of the canal—a major economic transformation. And with that transformation had come changes in the social fabric so profound that many men and women felt baffled and disoriented. (It was in roughly this same area of New York that Joseph Smith first organized the Mormon church.)

Finney's doctrine of personal regeneration appealed strongly to those who felt threatened by change. In Rochester, New York, the site of his greatest success, he staged a series of emotionally wrenching religious meetings that aroused a large segment of the community. He had particular success in mobilizing women, on whom he tended to concentrate his efforts—both because women found the liberating message of revivalism particularly appealing and because, Finney discovered, they provided him with access to their male relatives. Gradually, he developed a large following among the relatively prosperous citizens of the region, who were enjoying the economic benefits of the new commercial growth but who were also uneasy about some of the social changes accompanying it (among them the introduction into their community of a new, undisciplined pool of transient laborers). For them, revivalism became not only a means of personal salvation but a mandate for the reform (and control) of the larger society. In particular, Finney's revivalism became a call for a crusade against personal immorality. "The church," he maintained, "must take right ground on the subject of Temperance, the Moral Reform, and all the subjects of practical morality which come up for decision from time to time."

Evangelical Protestantism added major strength, therefore, to one of the most influential reform movements of the era: the crusade against drunkenness. No social vice, argued some reformers (including, for example, many of Finney's converts in cities such as Rochester), was more responsible for crime, disorder, and poverty than the excessive use of alcohol. Women, who were particularly active in the temperance movement, claimed that alcoholism placed a particular burden on them: men spent money needed by their families on alcohol, and drunken husbands often beat and abused their wives. Although advocates of temperance had been active since the late eighteenth century, the new reformers gave the movement an energy and influence it had never known. In 1826, the American Society for the Promotion of Temperance emerged as a coordinating agency among various groups; it attempted to use many of the techniques of revivalism in preaching abstinence. Then, in 1840, six reformed drunkards in Baltimore organized the Washington Temperance Society and began to draw large crowds to hear their impassioned and intriguing confessions of past sins. By then, temperance advocates had grown dramati-

The Drunkard's Progress
This 1846 lithograph by Nathaniel Currier shows what temperance advocates argued was the inevitable consequence of alcohol consumption. Beginning with an apparently innocent "glass with a friend," the young man rises step by step to the summit of drunken revelry, then declines to desperation and suicide while his abandoned wife and child grieve. (Library of Congress)

cally in numbers; more than a million people had signed a formal pledge to forgo hard liquor.

As the movement gained in strength, it also became divided in purpose. Some temperance advocates now urged that abstinence include not only liquor but beer and wine; not everyone agreed. Some began to demand state legislation to restrict the sale and consumption of alcohol (Maine passed such a law in 1851); but others insisted that temperance must rely on the conscience of the individual. Whatever their disagreements, however, most temperance advocates shared similar motives. By promoting abstinence, reformers were attempting to promote individual moral self-improvement. They were also trying to impose discipline on society.

The latter impulse was reflected particularly clearly in the battle over prohibition laws, which pitted established Protestants against new Catholic immigrants. The arrival of the immigrants was profoundly disturbing to established residents of many communities; and the restriction of alcohol seemed to them a way to curb the disorder that they believed the new population was creating.

Education and Rehabilitation

One of the outstanding reform movements of the mid-nineteenth century was the effort to produce a system of universal public education. As of 1830, no state could yet boast such a system, although some—such as Massachusetts—had supported a limited version for many years. Now, however, interest in public education grew rapidly—a reflection of the new belief in the innate capacity of every person and of society's obligation to tap that capacity; but a reflection, too, of the desire to expose students to stable social values as a way to resist instability.

The greatest of the educational reformers was Horace Mann, the first secretary of the Massachusetts

Board of Education, which was established in 1837. To Mann and his followers, education was the only way to "counterwork this tendency to the domination of capital and the servility of labor." It was also the only way to protect democracy, for an educated electorate was essential to the workings of a free political system. Mann reorganized the Massachusetts school system, lengthened the academic year (to six months), doubled teachers' salaries (although he did nothing to eliminate the large disparities between the salaries of male and female teachers), enriched the curriculum, and introduced new methods of professional training for teachers. Other states experienced similar expansion and development: building new schools, creating teachers' colleges, and offering vast new groups of children access to education. Henry Barnard helped produce a new educational system in Connecticut and Rhode Island. Pennsylvania passed a law in 1835 appropriating state funds for the support of universal education. Governor William Seward of New York extended public support of schools throughout the state in the early 1840s. By the 1850s, the principle of tax-supported elementary schools had been accepted in all the states; and all, despite continuing opposition from certain groups, were making at least a start toward putting the principle into practice.

Yet the quality of the new education continued to vary widely. In some places—Massachusetts, for example, where Mann established the first American state-supported teachers' college in 1839 and where the first professional association of teachers was created in 1845—educators were usually capable men and women, often highly trained, and with an emerging sense of themselves as career professionals. In other areas, however, teachers were often barely literate, and funding for education was so limited as to restrict opportunities severely. In the newly settled regions of the West, where the population was highly dispersed, many children had no access to schools at all. In the South, the entire black population was barred from education (although approximately 10 percent of the slaves managed to achieve literacy anyway); and only about a third of all white children of school age were actually enrolled in schools in 1860. In the North, the percentage was 72 percent; but even there, many students attended classes only briefly and casually.

The interest in education (and, implicitly, in the unleashing of individual talents that could result from

The Emerson School, Boston, 1850
This daguerreotype (or early photograph) shows a classroom in a Boston school named for Ralph Waldo Emerson, who years before had been a student there. A stern male teacher oversees a class of young women, who not many years before had been considered unfit subjects for advanced education.   (Metropolitan Museum of Art)

it) was visible too in the growing movement to educate American Indians in the antebellum period. Some reformers held racist assumptions about the unredeemability of nonwhite peoples; but even many who accepted that idea about blacks continued to believe that Indians could be "civilized" if only they could be taught the ways of the white world. Efforts by missionaries and others to educate Indians and encourage them to assimilate were particularly prominent in such areas of the Far West as Oregon, where substantial numbers of whites were beginning to settle in the 1840s but where conflicts with the natives had not yet become acute. Nevertheless, the great majority of Native Americans remained outside the reach of educational reform, either by choice or by circumstance or both.

Despite limitations and inequities, the achievements of the school reformers were impressive by any standard. By the beginning of the Civil War, the United States had one of the highest literacy rates of any nation of the world: 94 percent of the population of the North and 83 percent of the white population of the South (58 percent of the total population).

The conflicting impulses that underlay the movement for school reform were visible in some of the different educational institutions that emerged. In New England, for example, the transcendentalist Bronson Alcott established an experimental school in Concord that reflected his strong belief in the importance of complete self-realization. He urged children to learn from their own inner wisdom, not from the imposition of values by the larger society. Children were to teach themselves, rather than relying on teachers. A similar emphasis on the potential of the individual sparked the creation of new institutions to help the handicapped, institutions that formed part of a great network of charitable activities known as the Benevolent Empire. Among them was the Perkins School for the Blind in Boston, the first such school in America. Nothing better exemplified the romantic impulse of the era than the belief of those who founded Perkins that even society's least-favored members—the blind and otherwise handicapped—could be helped to discover an inner strength and wisdom. One teacher at the school expressed such attitudes when he described to the visiting English writer Charles Dickens the case of a blind, deaf, and speechless young woman who had been taught to communicate with the world. Although the "darkness and the silence of the tomb were around her," the teacher explained, "the immortal spirit which had been implanted within her could not die, nor be maimed nor mutilated." Gradually, she had learned to deal with the world around her, even to sew and knit, and most importantly, to speak through sign language. No longer was she a "dog or parrot." She was "an immortal spirit, eagerly seizing upon a new link of union with other spirits!"

More typical of educational reform, however, were efforts to use schools to impose a set of social values on children—the values that reformers believed were appropriate for their new, industrializing society. These values included thrift, order, discipline, punctuality, and respect for authority. Horace Mann, for example, spoke frequently of the role of public schools in extending democracy and expanding individual opportunity. But he spoke, too, of their role in creating social order. "The unrestrained passions of men are not only homicidal, but suicidal," he said in words that directly contradicted the emphasis of Alcott and other transcendentalists on instinct and emotion. "Train up a child in the way he should go, and when he is old he will not depart from it."

Similar impulses helped create another powerful movement of reform: the creation of "asylums," as they were now called for the first time, for criminals and for the mentally ill. On the one hand, in advocating prison and hospital reform, Americans were reacting against one of society's most glaring ills. Criminals of all kinds, debtors unable to pay their debts, the mentally ill, even senile paupers—all were crowded together indiscriminately into prisons and jails, which in some cases were literally holes; one jail in Connecticut was an abandoned mine shaft. Beginning in the 1820s, numerous states replaced these antiquated facilities with new penitentiaries and mental institutions designed to provide a proper environment for inmates. New York built the first penitentiary at Auburn in 1821; in Massachusetts, the reformer Dorothea Dix began a national movement for new methods of treating the mentally ill. Imprisonment of debtors and paupers was gradually eliminated, as were such traditional practices as public hangings.

But the creation of "asylums" for social deviants was not simply an effort to curb the abuses of the old system. It was also an attempt to reform and rehabilitate the inmates. New forms of rigid prison discipline were designed to rid criminals of the "laxness" that had presumably led them astray. Solitary confinement and the imposition of silence on work crews (both instituted in Pennsylvania and New York in the 1820s) were meant to give prisoners opportunities to meditate on their wrongdoings. Some reformers argued that the discipline of the asylum could serve as a model for other potentially disordered environments—for example, factories and schools. But penitentiaries and many mental hospitals soon fell victim to overcrowding, and the original reform ideal was gradually lost. Most prisons ultimately degenerated into little more than warehouses for criminals, with scant emphasis on rehabilitation. The idea, in its early stages, had envisioned far more.

A Pennsylvania Asylum

In 1843 the United States had only thirteen mental hospitals. Most communities locked the mentally ill in jails with common criminals and often confined them to the worst quarters. By the 1880s, largely as a result of the work of the Massachusetts reformer Dorothea Dix, who worked tirelessly prodding states to build new facilities, there were more than 120 asylums for the insane—including this one in Berks County, Pennsylvania, which also served as an almshouse for the poor.   (Historical Society of Berks County, Reading, Pennsylvania)

The "asylum" movement was not, however, restricted only to criminals and people otherwise considered "unfit." The idea that a properly structured institution could prevent moral failure or rescue individuals from failure and despair helped spawn the creation of new orphanages designed as educational institutions. Such institutions, reformers believed, would provide an environment in which children who might otherwise be drawn into criminality could be trained to be useful citizens. Similar institutions emerged to provide homes for "friendless" women—women without families or homes, but otherwise respectable, for whom the institutions might provide an opportunity for rehabilitation. (Such homes were in part an effort to prevent such women from turning to prostitution.)

Some of these same impulses underlay the emergence in the 1840s and 1850s of a new "reform" approach to the problems of Native Americans: the idea of the reservation. For several decades, the dominant thrust of U.S. policy toward the Indians in areas of white settlement had been relocation. The principal motive behind relocation had always been a simple one: getting the tribes out of the way of white civilization. But among some whites there had also been another, if secondary, intent: to move the Indians to a place where they would be protected from whites and allowed to develop to a point where assimilation might be possible. Even Andrew Jackson, whose animus toward Indians was legendary, once described the removals as part of the nation's "moral duty . . . to protect and if possible to preserve and perpetuate the scattered remnants of the Indian race."

It was a small step from the idea of relocation to the idea of the reservation: the idea of creating an enclosed region in which Indians would live in isolation from white society. Again, the reservations served white economic purposes above all—moving Native Americans out of good lands that white settlers wanted. But they also were meant to serve a reform purpose. Just as prisons, asylums, and orphanages would provide society with an opportunity to train and uplift misfits and unfortunates within white society, so the reservations might provide a way to undertake what one official called "the great work of regenerating the Indian race." Indians on reservations, reformers argued, would learn the ways of civilization in a protected setting and would progress toward (in the words of an Indian commissioner of the time) "a point at which they will be able to compete with a white population, and to sustain themselves under any probable circumstances of contact or connexion with it."

The Rise of Feminism

The reform ferment of the antebellum period had a particular meaning for American women. They played central roles in a wide range of reform movements and a particularly important role in the movement on behalf of the abolition of slavery. In the process, they expressed their awareness of the problems that women themselves faced in a male-dominated society. The result was the creation of the first important American feminist movement, one that laid the groundwork for more than a century of agitation for women's rights.

Women in the 1830s and 1840s suffered not only all the traditional restrictions imposed on members of their sex by society but a new set of barriers that had emerged from the transformation of the family. (See pp. 322–324.) Those women who began to involve themselves in reform movements in the 1820s and 1830s came to look on such restrictions with rising resentment. Some began to defy them. Sarah and Angelina Grimké, sisters born in South Carolina who had become active and outspoken abolitionists, ignored attacks by men who claimed that their activities were inappropriate for their sex. "Men and women were CREATED EQUAL," they argued. "They are both moral and accountable beings, and whatever is right for man to do, is right for women to do." Other reformers—Catharine Beecher, Harriet Beecher Stowe (her sister), Lucretia Mott, Elizabeth Cady Stanton, and Dorothea Dix—similarly pressed at the boundaries of "acceptable" female behavior, chafing at the restrictions placed on them by men.

Finally, in 1840, the patience of several women snapped. A group of American female delegates arrived at a world antislavery convention in London, only to be turned away by the men who controlled the proceedings. Angered at the rejection, several of the delegates—notably Lucretia Mott and Elizabeth Cady Stanton—became convinced that their first duty as reformers should now be to elevate the status of women. Over the next several years, Mott, Stanton, and others began drawing pointed parallels between the plight of women and the plight of slaves; and in 1848, they organized in Seneca Falls, New York, a convention to discuss the question of women's rights. Out of the meeting emerged a "Declaration of Sentiments and Resolutions" (patterned on the Declaration of Independence), which stated that "all men and women are created equal," that women no less than men are endowed with certain inalienable rights. Their most prominent demand was for the right to vote, thus launching a movement for woman suffrage that would survive until the battle was finally won in 1920. But the document was in many ways more important for its rejection of the whole notion that men and women should be assigned separate "spheres" in society.

It should not be surprising, perhaps, that many of the women involved in these feminist efforts were Quakers. Quakerism had long embraced the ideal of sexual equality and had tolerated, indeed encouraged, the emergence of women as preachers and community leaders. Women taught to expect the absence of sex-based restrictions in their own communities naturally resented the restrictions they encountered when they moved outside them. Quakers had also been among the leaders of the antislavery movement, and Quaker women had played a leading role within those efforts. Not all Quakers went so far as to advocate full sexual equality in American society; but enough Quaker women coalesced around such demands to cause a schism in the yearly meeting of Friends in Genesee, New York, in 1848. That dissident faction formed the core of the group that organized the Seneca Falls convention. Of the women who drafted the Declaration of Sentiments there, all but Elizabeth Cady Stanton were Quakers.

Progress toward feminist goals was limited in the antebellum years, but certain individual women did manage to break the social barriers to advancement. Elizabeth Blackwell, born in England, gained acceptance and fame as a physician. Her sister-in-law Antoinette Brown Blackwell became the first ordained woman minister in the United States; and another sister-in-law, Lucy Stone, took the revolutionary step of retaining her maiden name after marriage. She became a successful and influential lecturer on women's rights. Emma Willard, founder of the Troy Female Seminary in 1821, and Catharine Beecher, who founded the Hartford Female Seminary in 1823, worked on behalf of women's education. Some women expressed their feminist sentiments even in their choice of costume—by wearing a distinctive style of dress (introduced in the 1850s) that combined a short skirt with full length pantalettes—an outfit that allowed freedom of movement without loss of modesty. Introduced by the famous actress Fanny Kemble, it came to be called the "bloomer" costume, after one of its advocates, Amelia Bloomer. (It provoked so much controversy that feminists finally abandoned it, believing that the furor was drawing attention away from their more important demands.)

Yet there was an irony in this rise of interest in the rights of women. Feminists benefited greatly from their association with other reform movements, most notably abolitionism; but at the same time, they suffered as a result. For the demands of women were usually assigned—even by some women themselves—a secondary position to what many considered the far greater issue of the rights of slaves.

The Crusade Against Slavery

The antislavery movement was not new to the mid-nineteenth century. There had been efforts even before the Revolution to limit, and even eliminate, the institution, efforts that had helped remove slavery from most of the North by the end of the eighteenth century. There were powerful antislavery movements in England and Europe that cried out forcefully against human bondage. But American antislavery sentiment remained relatively muted in the first decades after independence. Not until 1830 did it begin to gather the force that would ultimately enable it to overshadow virtually all other efforts at social reform.

Early Opposition to Slavery

In the early years of the nineteenth century, those who opposed slavery were, for the most part, a calm and genteel lot, expressing moral disapproval but engaging in few overt activities. To the extent that there was an organized antislavery movement, it centered on the concept of colonization—the effort to encourage the resettlement of American blacks in Africa or the Caribbean. In 1817, a group of prominent white Virginians organized the American Colonization Society (ACS), which worked carefully to challenge slavery without challenging property rights or Southern sensibilities. The ACS proposed a gradual manumission of slaves, with masters receiving compensation (through funds raised by private charity or appropriated by state legislatures). The liberated blacks were then to be transported out of the country and helped to establish a new society of their own. The ACS was not without impact. It received some funding from private donors, some from Congress, some from the legislatures of Virginia and Maryland. And it arranged the shipment of several groups of blacks out of the country, some of them to the west coast of Africa, where in 1830 they established the nation of Liberia (which became an independent black republic in 1846, with its capital, Monrovia, named for the American president who had presided over the initial settlement). But the ACS was in the end a negligible force. Neither private nor public funding was nearly enough to carry out the vast projects its supporters envisioned. In the space of a decade, they managed to "colonize" fewer slaves than were born in the United States in a month. Nothing, in fact, would have been enough; there were far too many blacks in America in the nineteenth century to be transported to Africa by any conceivable program. And the ACS met resistance, in any case, from blacks themselves, many of whom were now three or more generations removed from Africa and had no wish to move to an alien land. (The Massachusetts free black Paul Cuffe had met similar resistance from members of his race in the early 1800s when he proposed a colonization scheme of his own.)

By 1830, in other words, the early antislavery movement was rapidly losing strength. Colonization was proving not to be a viable method of attacking the institution, particularly since the cotton boom in the Deep South was increasing the commitment of planters to their "peculiar" labor system. Those opposed to slavery had reached what appeared to be a dead end.

Garrison and Abolitionism

It was at this crucial juncture, with the antislavery movement seemingly on the verge of collapse, that a new figure emerged to transform it into a dramatically different phenomenon. He was William Lloyd Garrison. Born in Massachusetts in 1805, Garrison was in the 1820s an assistant to the New Jersey Quaker Benjamin Lundy, who published the leading antislavery newspaper of the time—the *Genius of Universal Emancipation*—in Baltimore. Garrison shared Lundy's abhorrence of slavery, but he soon grew impatient with his employer's moderate tone and mild proposals for reform. In 1831, therefore, he returned to Boston to found his own weekly newspaper, the *Liberator*.

Garrison's philosophy was so simple as to be genuinely revolutionary. Opponents of slavery, he said, should view the institution from the point of view of the black man, not the white slaveowner. They should not, as earlier reformers had done, talk

William Lloyd Garrison

Garrison was the first member of the antislavery movement to call publicly for "immediate and complete emancipation" of blacks. That was in 1831, and for the next three decades he remained a stern and uncompromising enemy of slavery. After the Civil War, however, Garrison displayed little interest in the plight of the blacks he had tried to emancipate. In the last years before his death in 1879, he worked on behalf of woman suffrage, Indian rights, and the prohibition of alcohol. (Wichita State University Library, Wichita, Kansas)

about the evil influence of slavery on white society; they should talk about the damage the system did to blacks. And they should, therefore, reject "gradualism" and demand the immediate, unconditional, universal abolition of slavery. Garrison spoke with particular scorn about the advocates of colonization. They were not emancipationists, he argued; on the contrary, their real aim was to strengthen slavery by ridding the country of those blacks who were already free. The true aim of foes of slavery, he insisted, must be to extend to blacks all the rights of American citizenship. As startling as the drastic nature of his proposals was the relentless, uncompromising tone with which he promoted them. "I am aware," he wrote in the very first issue of the *Liberator,* "that many object to the severity of my language; but is there not cause for severity? I *will* be as harsh as truth, and as uncompromising as justice. . . . I am in earnest—I will not equivocate—I will not excuse—I will not retreat a single inch—AND I WILL BE HEARD."

Garrison soon attracted a large group of followers throughout the North, enough to enable him to found the New England Antislavery Society in 1832 and a year later, after a convention in Philadelphia, the American Antislavery Society. Membership in the new organizations mushroomed. By 1835, there were more than 400 societies; by 1838, there were 1,350, with more than 250,000 members. Antislavery sentiment was developing a strength and assertiveness greater than at any point in the nation's history.

This success was in part a result of the similarity between abolitionism and other reform movements of the era. Like reformers in other areas, abolitionists were calling for an unleashing of the individual human spirit, the elimination of artificial social barriers to fulfillment. Who, after all, was more in need of assistance in realizing individual potential than the enslaved blacks? Theodore Dwight Weld, a prominent abolitionist (and husband of Angelina Grimké), expressed this belief in an 1833 letter to Garrison. Slavery was a sin, Weld wrote, because "no condition of birth, no shade of color, no mere misfortune of circumstances can annul the birthright charter, which God has bequeathed to every being upon whom he has stamped his own image, by making him a *free moral agent.*"

Black Abolitionists

Abolitionism had a particular appeal, needless to say, to the free black population of the North, which in 1850 numbered about 250,000, mostly concentrated in cities. These free blacks lived in conditions of poverty and oppression often far worse than their slave counterparts in the South. An English traveler who had visited both sections of the country wrote in 1854 that he was "utterly at a loss to imagine the source of that prejudice which subsists against [the black man] in the Northern states, a prejudice unknown in the South, where the relations between the Africans and

the European [white American] are so much more intimate." This confirmed an earlier observation by Tocqueville that "the prejudice which repels the Negroes seems to increase in proportion as they are emancipated." Northern blacks were often victimized by mob violence; they had virtually no access to education; they could vote in only a few states; and they were barred from all but the most menial of occupations. Most worked either as domestic servants or, as sailors in the American merchant marine, and their wages were such that they lived, for the most part, in squalor. Some were kidnapped by whites and forced back into slavery.

For all their problems, however, Northern blacks were aware of, and fiercely proud of, their freedom. And they remained acutely sensitive to the plight of those members of their race who remained in bondage, aware that their own position in society would remain precarious as long as slavery existed. Many in the 1830s came to support Garrison. But there were also important black leaders who expressed the aspirations of their race. One of the most militant was David Walker, a resident of Boston, who in 1829 published a harsh pamphlet: *Walker's Appeal . . . to the Colored Citizens.* In it he declared: "America is more our country than it is the whites'—we have enriched it with our *blood and tears.*" He warned: "The whites want slaves, and want us for their slaves, but some of them will curse the day they ever saw us." Slaves should, he declared, cut their masters' throats, should "kill, or be killed!"

Most black critics of slavery, however, were less violent in their rhetoric. The greatest of them all— one of the most electrifying orators of his time, black or white—was Frederick Douglass. Born a slave in Maryland, Douglass escaped to Massachusetts in 1838, became an outspoken leader of antislavery sentiment, and spent two years lecturing in England, where he was lionized by members of that country's vigorous antislavery movement. On his return to the United States in 1847, Douglass purchased his freedom from his Maryland owner and founded an antislavery newspaper, the *North Star,* in Rochester, New York. He achieved wide renown as well for his autobiography, *Narrative of the Life of Frederick Douglass* (1845), in which he presented a damning picture of slavery. Douglass demanded for blacks not only freedom but full social and economic equality. Black abolitionists had been active for years; they had held their first national convention in 1830. But with Douglass's leadership, they became a far more influential

Frederick Douglass

Frederick Douglass was the most prominent black American of the nineteenth century. Born in Maryland to an unknown white father and a slave mother, he escaped from slavery into the North in 1838. He quickly became a leader in the abolitionist movement—lecturing widely, editing a newspaper (*The North Star*), and in 1845 publishing his own autobiography, which became an important document in advancing the antislavery cause. Douglass was particularly popular among antislavery groups in England, where he spent two years in the 1840s. (UPI/Bettmann Newsphotos)

force; and they began, too, to forge alliances with white antislavery leaders such as Garrison.

Antiabolitionism

The rise of abolitionism was a powerful force, but it provoked a powerful opposition as well. Almost all white Southerners, of course, looked on the movement with fear and loathing. But so too did many Northern whites. Indeed, even in the North, abolitionists were never more than a small, dissenting minority. To its critics, the abolitionist crusade was a

dangerous and frightening threat to the existing social system. It would, warned some whites (including many substantial businessmen), produce a destructive war between the sections. It might, others feared, lead to a great influx of free blacks into the North. And whatever the long-range consequences, this strident, outspoken movement seemed to many Northern whites a sign of the disorienting social changes that their society was experiencing. It was yet another threat to stability and order.

The result was an escalating wave of violence directed against abolitionists in the 1830s. When Prudence Crandall attempted to admit several black girls to her private school in Connecticut, local citizens had her arrested, threw filth into her well, and forced her to close down the school. A mob in Philadelphia attacked the abolitionist headquarters, the "Temple of Liberty," in 1834, burned it to the ground, and began a bloody race riot. Another mob seized Garrison on the streets of Boston in 1835 and threatened to hang him. He was saved from death only by being locked in jail. Elijah Lovejoy, the editor of an abolitionist newspaper in Alton, Illinois, was victimized repeatedly by mob violence. Three times angry whites invaded his offices and smashed his presses. Three times Lovejoy installed new machines and began publishing again. When a mob attacked his office a fourth time, late in 1837, he tried to defend his press. The attackers set fire to the building and, as Lovejoy fled, shot and killed him.

That so many men and women continued to embrace abolitionism in the face of such vicious opposition from within their own communities suggests much about the nature of the movement. Abolitionists were not people who made their political commitments lightly or casually. They were strong-willed, passionate crusaders, displaying enormous courage and moral strength, and displaying too at times a level of fervency that many of their contemporaries (and some later historians) found disturbing. Abolitionists were widely attacked, even by some who shared their aversion to slavery, as wild-eyed fanatics bent on social revolution. The antiabolitionist mobs, in other words, were only the most violent expression of a sentiment that many other white Americans shared.

Abolitionism Divided

By the mid-1830s, the abolitionist crusade had become impossible to ignore. It had also begun to ex-

135,000 SETS, 270,000 VOLUMES SOLD.

UNCLE TOM'S CABIN

FOR SALE HERE.

AN EDITION FOR THE MILLION, COMPLETE IN 1 Vol., PRICE 37 1-2 CENTS.
"   "   IN GERMAN, IN 1 Vol., PRICE 50 CENTS.
"   "   IN 2 Vols., CLOTH, 6 PLATES, PRICE $1.50.
SUPERB ILLUSTRATED EDITION, IN 1 Vol., WITH 153 ENGRAVINGS,
PRICES FROM $2.50 TO $5.00.

The Greatest Book of the Age.

Uncle Tom's Cabin

This poster (advertising, among other things, a German edition of Harriet Beecher Stowe's novel) did not exaggerate when it described *Uncle Tom's Cabin* as "The Greatest Book of the Age." There were, to be sure, greater literary accomplishments; but no American book of the nineteenth century had so profound a political impact. Abraham Lincoln, who was introduced to Stowe in the White House, reportedly said to her: "So you are the little lady who has brought this great war." Stowe was a wife and mother in Brunswick, Maine, when she began writing the novel in 1851. It was, she claimed, a response to a "vision" that came to her while she was taking Communion; but the greater inspiration was probably several abolitionist works she had recently read describing the horrors of the slave system.   (The Bettmann Archive)

perience serious internal strains and divisions. One reason was the violence of the antiabolitionists, which persuaded some members of the movement that a more moderate approach was necessary. Another reason was the growing radicalism of William Lloyd Garrison, who shocked even many of his own allies (including Frederick Douglass) by attacking not only slavery but the government itself. The Constitution,

he said, was "a covenant with death and an agreement with hell." The nation's churches, he claimed, were bulwarks of slavery. In 1840, finally, Garrison precipitated a formal division within the American Antislavery Society by insisting that women, who had always been central to the organization's work, be permitted to participate in the movement on terms of full equality. He continued after 1840 to arouse controversy with new and even more radical stands: an extreme pacifism that rejected even defensive wars; opposition to all forms of coercion—not just slavery but prisons and asylums; and finally, in 1843, a call for Northern disunion from the South. The nation could, he suggested, purge itself of the sin of slavery by expelling the slave states from the Union.

From 1840 on, therefore, abolitionism moved in many channels and spoke with many different voices. The Garrisonians remained influential, with their uncompromising moral stance. Others operated in more moderate ways, arguing that abolition could be accomplished only as the result of a long, patient, peaceful struggle—"immediate abolition gradually accomplished," as they called it. At first, they depended on "moral suasion." They would appeal to the conscience of the slaveholders and convince them that their institution was sinful. When that produced no results, they turned to political action, seeking to induce the Northern states and the federal government to aid the cause wherever possible. They joined the Garrisonians in helping runaway slaves find refuge in the North or in Canada through the so-called underground railroad (although their efforts were never as highly organized as the term suggests). After the Supreme Court (in *Prigg* v. *Pennsylvania,* 1842) ruled that states need not aid in enforcing the 1793 law requiring the return of fugitive slaves to their owners, abolitionists secured the passage of "personal liberty laws" in several Northern states. These laws forbade state officials to assist in the capture and return of runaways. Above all, the antislavery societies petitioned Congress to abolish slavery in places where the federal government had jurisdiction—in the territories and in the District of Columbia—and to prohibit the interstate slave trade. But political abolitionism had severe limits. Few members of the movement believed that Congress could constitutionally interfere with a "domestic" institution such as slavery within the individual states themselves.

While the abolitionists engaged in pressure politics, they never formed a political party with an abolition platform. Antislavery sentiment underlay the

SIGNIFICANT EVENTS

1817 American Colonization Society founded (p. 362)

1821 New York constructs first penitentiary (p. 359)

1823 Catharine Beecher founds Hartford Female Seminary (p. 362)

1825 Robert Owen founds New Harmony community in Indiana (p. 353)

1826 James Fenimore Cooper publishes *The Last of the Mohicans* (p. 350)

American Society for the Promotion of Temperance founded (p. 356)

1829 David Walker publishes *Appeal . . . to the Colored Citizens* (p. 364)

1830 Joseph Smith publishes the Book of Mormon (p. 355)

1831 William Lloyd Garrison begins publishing *The Liberator* (p. 364)

1833 American Antislavery Society founded (p. 364)

1837 Horace Mann becomes first secretary of Massachusetts Board of Education (p. 357)

Elijah Lovejoy killed by antiabolitionist mob in Illinois (p. 365)

1840 Garrison demands admission of women into American Antislavery Society, precipitating schism (p. 366)

1840 Liberty party formed (pp. 366–367)

1841 Brook Farm founded in Roxbury, Massachusetts (p. 352)

1843 Amana Community founded (p. 355)

1844 Joseph Smith killed (p. 355)

1845 Frederick Douglass publishes autobiography (p. 364)

1847 Brook Farm dissolved (p. 353)

Mormons found Salt Lake City (p. 355)

1848 Women's rights convention held at Seneca Falls, New York (p. 361)

Oneida Community founded in New York (p. 353)

1850 Nathaniel Hawthorne publishes *The Scarlet Letter* (p. 353)

1851 Herman Melville publishes *Moby Dick* (p. 350)

1852 Harriet Beecher Stowe publishes *Uncle Tom's Cabin* (p. 367)

1854 Henry David Thoreau publishes *Walden* (p. 352)

1855 Walt Whitman publishes *Leaves of Grass* (p. 350)

formation in 1840 of the Liberty party, which offered the Kentucky antislavery leader James G. Birney as its presidential candidate. But this party, and its successors, never campaigned for outright abolition (an illustration of the important fact that "antislavery" and "abolitionism" were not always the same thing). They stood instead for "free soil," for keeping slavery out of the territories. Some free-soilers were concerned about the welfare of blacks; others were people who cared nothing about slavery but simply wanted to keep the West a country for whites. Garrison dismissed free-soilism as "white-manism." But the free-soil position would ultimately do what abolitionism never could accomplish: attract the support of large numbers, even a majority, of the white population of the North. (See pp. 394–395.)

The frustrations of political abolitionism drove some critics of slavery to embrace more drastic measures. A few began to advocate violence; it was a group of prominent abolitionists in New England, for example, who funneled money and arms to John Brown for his bloody uprisings in Kansas and Virginia. (See pp. 393, 400–401.) Others attempted to arouse widespread public anger through propaganda. Abolitionist descriptions of slavery (for example, Theodore Dwight Weld and Angelina Grimké's *American Slavery as It Is: Testimony of a Thousand Witnesses* of 1839) presented what the authors claimed were careful, factual pictures of slavery but what were in fact highly polemical, often wildly distorted images.

The most powerful of all abolitionist propaganda, however, was a work of fiction: Harriet Beecher Stowe's *Uncle Tom's Cabin*. It appeared first, in 1851–1852, as a serial in an antislavery weekly. Then, in 1852, it was published as a book. It rocked the nation. It sold more than 300,000 copies within a year of publication and was later issued again and again to become one of the most remarkable best sellers in American history. And it succeeded, as a result, in bringing the message of abolitionism to an enormous new audience—not only those who read the book but those who watched dramatizations of its story by countless theater companies throughout the nation. The novel's emotional portrayal of good, kindly blacks victimized by a cruel system; of the loyal, trusting Uncle Tom; of the vicious overseer Simon Legree (described as a New Englander so as to prevent the book from seeming to be an attack on Southern whites); of the escape of the beautiful Eliza; of the heart-rending death of Little Eva: all became a part of American popular legend. Reviled through-

out the South, Stowe became a hero to many in the North. And in both regions, her novel helped to inflame sectional tensions to a new level of passion. Few books in American history have had so great an impact on the course of public events.

Even divided, therefore, abolitionism remained a powerful influence on the life of the nation. Only a relatively small number of people before the Civil War ever accepted the abolitionist position that slavery must be entirely eliminated in a single stroke. But the crusade that Garrison had launched, and that thousands of committed men and women kept alive for three decades, was a constant, visible reminder of how deeply the institution of slavery was dividing America.

SUGGESTED READINGS

Antebellum Literature. Vernon L. Parrington, *The Romantic Revolution in America, 1800–1860* (1927); F. O. Matthiessen, *American Renaissance* (1941); David Reynolds, *Beneath the American Renaissance: The Subversive Imagination in the Age of Emerson and Melville* (1988); Leo Marx, *The Machine and the Garden* (1964); Henry F. May, *The Enlightenment in America* (1976); Van Wyck Brooks, *The Flowering of New England, 1815–1865* (1936); Neil Harris, *Humbug: The Art of P. T. Barnum* (1973); Mary Kelley, *The Limits of Sisterhood* (1988).

Social Philosophies and Utopias. Ann Rose, *Transcendentalism as a Social Movement* (1981); P. F. Boller, Jr., *American Transcendentalism, 1830–1860: An Intellectual Inquiry* (1974); Gay Wilson Allen, *Waldo Emerson* (1981); Arthur M. Schlesinger, Jr., *Orestes A. Brownson: A Pilgrim's Progress* (1939); Henry Steele Commager, *Theodore Parker* (1936); Richard Lebeaux, *Young Man Thoreau* (1977); Perry Miller, *The Transcendentalists* (1950) and *The Life of the Mind in America: From the Revolution to the Civil War* (1966); Arthur Bestor, *Backwoods Utopias: The Sectarian and Owenite Phases of Communitarian Socialism in America, 1663–1829* (1950); M. L. Carden, *Oneida: Utopian Community to Modern Corporation* (1971); Raymond Muncy, *Sex and Marriage in Utopian Communities* (1973); Priscilla Brewer, *Shaker Communities and Shaker Lives* (1986); R. D. Thomas, *The Man Who Would Be Perfect: John Humphrey Noyes and the Utopian Impulse* (1977); Fawn Brodie, *No Man Knows My Name: The Life of Joseph Smith* (1945); Klaus J. Hansen, *Quest for Empire* (1967); Wallace Stegner, *The Gathering of Zion* (1964).

Antebellum Reforms. Alice Felt Tyler, *Freedom's Ferment* (1944); Ronald G. Walters, *American Reformers, 1815–1860* (1978); William G. McLoughlin, *Revivals, Awakenings, and Reform* (1978); Whitney R. Cross, *The Burned-Over District* (1950); Paul Johnson, *A Shopkeeper's Millennium* (1978);

Timothy L. Smith, *Revivalism and Social Reform in Mid-Nineteenth Century America* (1957); William W. Sweet, *Revivalism in America* (1949); Charles A. Johnson, *The Frontier Camp Meeting* (1955); C. C. Cole, Jr., *The Social Ideas of the Northern Evangelists, 1826–1860* (1954); W. J. Rorabaugh, *The Alcoholic Republic* (1979); Ian R. Tyrrell, *Sobering Up: From Temperance to Prohibition in Antebellum America, 1800–1860* (1979); David Rothman, *The Discovery of the Asylum* (1971); Estelle Freedman, *Their Sister's Keepers: Women's Prison Reform in America, 1830–1930* (1981).

Education. Michael Katz, *The Irony of Early School Reform* (1968); Lawrence A. Cremin, *American Education: The National Experience* (1980); Stanley K. Schultz, *The Culture Factory: Boston's Public Schools, 1789–1860* (1973); Paul Monroe, *The Founding of the American Public School System* (1949); Carl Bode, *The American Lyceum* (1956); Jonathan Messerli, *Horace Mann* (1972); Robert Trennert, *Alternatives to Extinction: Federal Indian Policy and the Beginning of the Reservation System* (1975).

Feminism. Barbara J. Berg, *The Remembered Gate: Origins of American Feminism. The Woman and the City* (1977); Ellen C. Du Bois, *Feminism and Suffrage: The Emergence of an Independent Woman's Movement in America, 1848–1860* (1978); Nancy Cott, *The Bonds of Womanhood: "Woman's Sphere" in New England, 1780–1835* (1977); Nancy A. Hewitt, *Women's Activism and Social Change: Rochester, New York, 1822–1872* (1988); Ann Douglas, *The Feminization of American Culture* (1977); Margaret H. Bacon, *Mothers of Feminism: The Story of Quaker Women in America* (1986); Lois Banner, *Elizabeth Cady Stanton* (1980); Kathleen Barry, *Susan B. Anthony* (1988); Kathryn K. Sklar, *Catharine Beecher: A Study in American Domesticity* (1973); William L. O'Neill, *Everyone Was Brave: The Rise and Fall of Feminism in the United States* (1970); Eleanor Flexner, *Century of Struggle,* rev. ed. (1975); Barbara Leslie Epstein,

The Politics of Domesticity: Women, Evangelism, and Temperance in Nineteenth-Century America (1981).

Antislavery and Abolitionism. Louis Filler, *The Crusade Against Slavery* (1960); Gerald Sorin, *Abolitionism* (1972); M. L. Dillon, *The Abolitionists* (1974); Blanche G. Hersh, *Slavery of Sex: Feminist Abolitionists in America* (1978); John McKivigan, *The War Against Proslavery Religion* (1984); Alan Kraut, ed., *Crusaders and Compromisers* (1983); J. B. Stewart, *Holy Warriors* (1976); Peter F. Walker, *Moral Choices: Memory, Desire, and Imagination in Nineteenth Century Abolition* (1978); Lawrence J. Friedman, *Gregarious Saints: Self and Community in American Abolitionism* (1982); Lewis Perry and Michael Fellman, eds., *Antislavery Reconsidered: New Perspectives on the Abolitionists* (1979); Aileen Kraditor, *Means and Ends in American Abolitionism: Garrison and His Critics on Strategy and Tactics, 1834–1850* (1967);

G. H. Barnes, *The Antislavery Impulse* (1933); Gerda Lerner, *The Grimké Sisters of South Carolina: Rebels Against Slavery* (1967); John L. Thomas, *The Liberator* (1963); James Brewer Stewart, *Wendell Phillips* (1987); Bertram Wyatt-Brown, *Lewis Tappan and the Evangelical War Against Slavery* (1969); Robert Abzug, *Theodore Dwight Weld* (1980); Irving Bartlett, *Wendell Phillips* (1962); Betty Fladeland, *James Gillespie Birney* (1955); Martin Duberman (ed.), *The Anti-Slavery Vanguard* (1965); Benjamin Quarles, *Black Abolitionists* (1969); William H. Pease and Jane H. Pease, *They Would Be Free* (1974); Arna Bontemps, *Free at Last: The Life of Frederick Douglass* (1971); Nathan Huggins, *Slave and Citizen* (1980); Leonard Richards, *Gentlemen of Property and Standing* (1970); George Fredrickson, *The Black Image in the White Mind: The Debate on Afro-American Character and Destiny, 1817–1914* (1971).

The Lincoln–Douglas Debates, Illinois, 1858
The still clean-shaven Abraham Lincoln lost in his 1858 bid to replace Stephen Douglas as United States senator from Illinois, but he gained wide national recognition for his performance in the debates between the two candidates during the campaign. This contemporary illustration, obviously drawn by a Lincoln admirer, shows banners which suggest how popular Lincoln had already become. (*The Granger Collection*)

CHAPTER 13

🙰 🙰 🙰

The Impending Crisis

🙰 🙰 🙰

Until the 1840s, the sectional tensions between North and South had remained relatively contained. On two occasions, serious crises had emerged that had threatened the Union; but neither had been permitted to develop very far. The first was resolved in 1819 by the Missouri Compromise. The second, the nullification crisis of the 1830s, was not so much resolved as allowed quietly to die.

Throughout these early decades, the nation generally avoided confronting its sectional differences. This was in part because the Union was so loose and the federal government so weak and unobtrusive that open conflicts seldom arose; and in part because people of all sections had certain shared sentiments (memories of the Revolutionary past, respect for the Constitution, dreams of national glory) and certain common institutions (the vigorous two-party system, an increasingly interdependent economy) that held them together. Had no new sectional issues arisen, it is possible that the United States would have avoided a civil war, that the two sections might have resolved their differences peaceably over time.

But new issues did arise, and almost without exception they centered around the question of slavery. From the North came the strident and increasingly powerful abolitionist movement, which kept the issue alive in the public mind and greatly increased sectional animosities. And from the West, more important, came a series of controversies that would ultimately destroy the fragile Union. For ironically, the vigorous nationalism that was in some ways helping to keep the United States together was also producing a desire for territorial expansion that would tear the nation apart. As America annexed extensive new lands—including Texas, the Southwest, California, the Oregon Country—the question continually arose: What would be the status of slavery in the territories?

Only the most fervent abolitionists believed that anything could be done to eliminate slavery in the states where it already existed; but a powerful coalition of Northerners began to insist that slavery be banned from new territorial acquisitions. White Southerners, in the meantime, began to argue that slavery extension was essential to protect the future status of their region in the nation. Unless the Southern economic system expanded, they came to believe, it would be consigned to a helpless minority position.

By the late 1840s, these differences had grown to create a dangerous and enduring crisis. Twice—first in 1850 and again in 1854—national leaders attempted to settle the issue by means of a great compromise. But after each such effort, the sectional question arose again in more virulent form, until finally, in 1861, the American people took up arms against one another.

Expansion and War

In the course of the 1840s, more than a million square miles of new territory came under the control of the United States—the greatest wave of expansion since the Louisiana Purchase nearly forty years before. By the end of the decade, the nation possessed nearly all

371

the territory of the present-day United States—everything except Alaska, Hawaii, and a few relatively small areas acquired later through border adjustments.

What accounted for this great new wave of expansion after a lull of nearly four decades? In part, it was a result of simple growth—growth of population and growth in the economy—which created pressures to extend the borders westward. In part, too, it was a result of American fears that European nations might somehow extend their influence into the Western lands. But neither of these factors was alone sufficient to explain the new thrust westward. America had not yet even approached developing all the lands it already held; and the threat of European intervention on the continent was limited to a few areas. What gave the decisive push to the nation's quest for new territory was a set of ideas—an ideology that acquired the name "Manifest Destiny."

Manifest Destiny

Manifest Destiny emerged out of a combination of the vigorous nationalism of the 1830s and the reform sentiment of the same era, for it reflected both national pride and an idealistic vision of social perfection. It was the idea that America was destined by God to expand its boundaries over a vast area—an area not clearly defined but certainly including much of the continent of North America. The motive for this expansion, advocates of Manifest Destiny maintained, was not a selfish desire for economic gain but an altruistic attempt to extend American liberty to new realms. John L. O'Sullivan, the influential Democratic editor who gave the movement its name, wrote in 1845 that the American claim to new territory

> . . . is by the right of our manifest destiny to overspread and to possess the whole of the continent which Providence has given us for the development of the great experiment of liberty and federative self government entrusted to us. It is a right such as that of the tree to the space of air and earth suitable for the full expansion of its principle and destiny of growth.

By the 1840s, the idea of Manifest Destiny had spread throughout the nation, publicized by the new "penny press," which made newspapers available to a far greater proportion of the population than ever before, and fanned by the rhetoric of nationalist politicians. The sentiment was strongest in the North

Expanding Settlement, 1810–1850

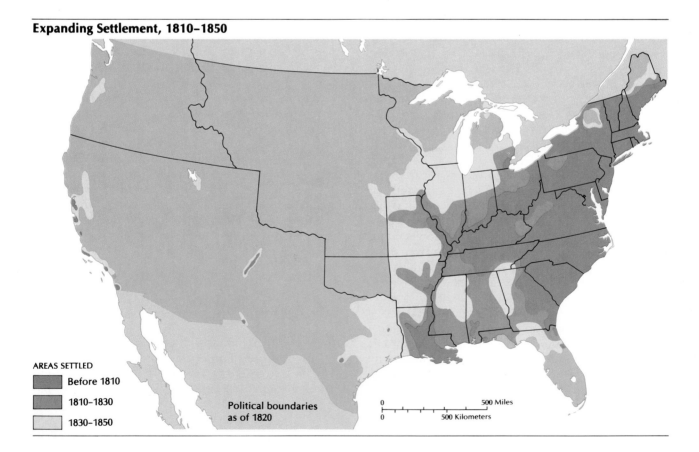

AREAS SETTLED
- Before 1810
- 1810–1830
- 1830–1850

Political boundaries
as of 1820

0 ——— 500 Miles
0 ——— 500 Kilometers

and West, but there were advocates in the South as well.

Devotees of Manifest Destiny disagreed among themselves, however, as to how far and by what means the nation should expand. Some had relatively limited territorial goals; others envisioned a vast new American "empire of liberty" extending north into Canada and south into Mexico, and including islands in the Caribbean and in the Pacific. A few visionaries dreamed of the United States becoming a federation of much of the entire world. There was disagreement too over whether the nation could be justified in using force to achieve its goals. Democratic politicians such as O'Sullivan implied that it could. Others, especially among the Whigs, believed that only peaceful methods should be used to acquire new territory. Daniel Webster, for example, said: "I have always wished that this country should exhibit to the nations of the earth the example of a great, rich, and powerful republic which is not possessed by a spirit of aggrandizement." America should, in other words, encourage other areas to join the nation through the strength of its example, not through force.

And there were other politicians—men such as Henry Clay—who were hesitant about any further expansion at all. They feared, correctly as it turned out, that the acquisition of new territories would reopen the painful controversy over slavery and threaten the stability of the Union. Their voices, however, were all but drowned out in the enthusiasm over expansion in the 1840s, which began with the issues of Texas and Oregon.

The Question of Texas

Southwest of the United States stretched the northern provinces of Mexico—Texas, New Mexico, and Upper California—once parts of Spain's colonial empire in North America but, since 1822, states in the independent republic of Mexico. Under Spanish rule, the provinces had been subject to only the lightest supervision from the government of the viceroyalty in Mexico, and only a few thousand whites had settled in them. The same conditions prevailed under the Mexican republic, which lacked the power and the population to govern and settle such distant areas. The United States had once claimed Texas as a part of the Louisiana Purchase, but it had renounced the claim in 1819. Twice thereafter, however, in the presidencies of John Quincy Adams and Andrew Jackson, the United States had offered to buy Texas, only to meet with indignant Mexican refusals.

But the Mexican government itself soon invited difficulties in Texas. In the early 1820s it encouraged American immigration by offering land grants to Stephen Austin and other men who promised to colonize the land. The motive of the Mexicans was to build up the economy of Texas, and hence their own tax revenues, by increasing the population with foreigners. But the experiment was to result in the loss of Texas to the United States. Thousands of Americans, attracted by reports of the rich soil in Texas, took advantage of Mexico's welcome. The great majority came from the Southern states, sometimes bringing slaves with them. By 1835, approximately 35,000 Americans were living in Texas.

Promoting the West

Cyrus McCormick was one of many American businessmen with an interest in the peopling of the American West. The reaper he invented was crucial to the cultivation of the new agricultural regions; and the rapid settlement of those regions was, in turn, essential to the health of his company. In this idealized poster, the McCormick Reaper Company presents a romantic image of vast, fertile lands awaiting settlement, an image that drew many settlers westward. (Chicago Historical Society)

"WESTWARD THE COURSE OF EMPIRE TAKES ITS WAY" WITH McCORMICK REAPERS IN THE VAN.

Almost from the beginning, there was friction between the new settlers and the Mexicans. Finally the Mexican government, realizing that its power over Texas was being challenged by the settlers, moved to exert control. A new law reduced the powers of the various states of the Mexican republic, a measure that white Texans took to be aimed specifically at them. In 1836, the American settlers defiantly proclaimed the independence of Texas.

The Mexican dictator, Antonio de Santa Anna, advanced into Texas with a large army. Even with the aid of volunteers, money, and supplies from private groups in the United States, the Texans were having difficulty in organizing a resistance. Their garrison at the Alamo mission in San Antonio was exterminated after a famous, if futile, defense by a group of Texas "patriots," a group that included, among others, the renowned frontiersman Davy Crockett; another garrison at Goliad suffered substantially the same fate when the Mexicans murdered most of the force after it had surrendered. But General Sam Houston, emerging as the national hero of Texas, kept a small army together, and at the Battle of San Jacinto (April 23, 1836, near present-day Houston), he defeated the Mexican army and took Santa Anna prisoner. Although the Mexican government later refused to recognize officially the captured dictator's vague promises to withdraw Mexican authority from Texas, it made no further attempt to subdue the province. Texas had won its independence.

The new republic desired to join the United States and through its new president, Sam Houston, immediately asked for recognition, to be followed by annexation. Many Northerners opposed the annexation of a large new slave territory. Others were opposed to incorporating a region that would add to Southern votes in Congress and in the electoral college. President Jackson, although he favored annexation in principle, feared that annexation might cause an ugly sectional controversy and even lead to a war with Mexico. He did not, therefore, propose annexation and did not even extend recognition to Texas until just before he left office in 1837. His successor, Martin Van Buren, also refrained, for similar reasons, from pressing the issue.

Spurned by the United States, Texas sought recognition, support, and money in Europe. Texan leaders talked about creating a vast southwestern nation, stretching to the Pacific, which would be a rival to the United States. It was the kind of talk that Europe, particularly England (which already saw in the United States a potential rival in world trade and naval influence), was pleased to hear. An independent Texas would be a counterbalance to the United States and a barrier to further American expansion; it would supply cotton for European industry and provide a market for European exports. England and France hastened to recognize and conclude trade treaties with Texas. Observing all this, and also eager to increase Southern power, President Tyler persuaded Texas to apply again, and Secretary of State Calhoun submitted an annexation treaty to the Senate in April 1844. Unfortunately for Texas, Calhoun presented annexation as if its only purpose were to extend and protect slavery. The treaty was soundly defeated.

By now, however, the annexation of Texas had become one of the major goals of advocates of Manifest Destiny. And the rejection of the treaty of annexation only spurred them to greater efforts toward their goal. The Texas question would soon become the central issue in the election of 1844.

The Question of Oregon

American interest in what was known as the Oregon Country, like the interest in Texas, had a long history. And like Texas, Oregon became in the 1840s a major political issue. The ownership of the territory had long been in dispute, but its boundaries were clearly defined—on the north the latitude line of 54°40', on the east the crest of the Rocky Mountains, on the south the 42nd parallel, and on the west the Pacific. Its half-million square miles included the present states of Oregon, Washington, and Idaho, parts of Montana and Wyoming, and half of British Columbia.

At various times in the past, the Oregon Country had been claimed by Spain, Russia, France, England, and the United States. By the 1820s, Spain, Russia, and France had withdrawn and surrendered their rights to Britain or to the United States or to both. For years after that, both nations claimed sovereignty over the region. Each could assert title on the basis of the activities of its explorers, maritime traders, and fur traders. The English had one solid advantage: They were in actual possession of a part of the area. In 1821, the powerful British fur trading organization, the Hudson's Bay Company, under the leadership of its factor, John McLoughlin, established a post at Fort Vancouver, north of the Columbia River.

Several times the English government proposed

the Columbia as a suitable line for dividing Oregon: Great Britain would retain possession of the regions to the north of the river, the United States would control the land to the south of it. The United States, also showing a desire to compromise, countered by suggesting the 49th parallel. This difference in official views prevented a settlement of the Oregon question in the treaty of 1818, which ended the War of 1812. Unable to agree on a demarcation line, the diplomats of the two powers provided in the treaty that citizens of each were to have equal access to Oregon for ten years. This arrangement, called joint occupation, was renewed in 1827 for an indefinite period, with either nation empowered to end it on a year's notice.

The first real American interest in Oregon came as a result of the activities of missionaries, notably Jason Lee, Marcus Whitman, and Father Pierre Jean de Smet, who had established religious and educational missions among the Oregon tribes at the request of the Indians. All the missionaries located their posts east or south of the Columbia River, mostly in the fertile Willamette Valley. They described their work in reports and letters that were published in the United States in influential religious journals and widely reprinted in secular newspapers. These reports dwelt as much on the rich soil and lovely climate of Oregon as on the spiritual condition of the Indians.

The Westward Migration

Throughout the 1840s, 1850s, and 1860s, hundreds of thousands of Americans moved to the far Western regions of the continent, settling in regions that had previously been inhabited almost entirely by Indians and a few white missionaries. Many were white planters from the southern states, who generally settled in Texas (often bringing substantial numbers of slaves with them). But the largest number came from the Old Northwest (what we now know as the Midwest)—white men and women, and a few blacks, who undertook arduous journeys in search of new opportunities. Most traveled in family groups, until the early 1850s, when the great gold rush attracted many single men. (See p. 386.) Most were reasonably young people. Most had experienced earlier, if usually shorter, migrations in the past.

All were in search of a new life, but they harbored many different visions of what the new life would bring. Some (particularly after the discovery of gold in California in 1849) hoped for quick and vast wealth. Others wanted land for farming or speculation and hoped to take advantage of the vast public lands the federal government was selling at modest prices. Still others hoped to succeed as merchants, serving the new white communities developing in the West. Some (among them the Mormons) were on religious missions or were attempting to escape hardships or oppression in the East.

The West Coast could be reached by sailing around Cape Horn. But the sea journey cost nearly three times as much as an overland trip and was, in any case, an option only for those who lived near the coast. The great majority of migrants traveled along the great overland trails. People heading west generally gathered in one of several major depots in Iowa and Missouri: Independence, St. Joseph, or Council Bluffs. There, migrants generally joined a wagon train, often led by hired guides, and set off—their belongings piled in covered wagons, livestock trailing behind.

The major route west was the two-thousand-mile-long Oregon Trail, which stretched from Independence across the Great Plains and through the South Pass of the Rocky Mountains. From there, migrants moved north into Oregon or south (along the California trail) to the northern California coast. Other migrations moved along the Santa Fe trail, which extended southwest from Independence into New Mexico.

However they traveled, overland migrants faced substantial dangers and hardships. The mountain and desert terrain in the later portions of the trip were particularly difficult. There was great pressure to get through the passes of the Rockies before the snows began, not always an easy task given the very slow pace of most wagon trains (about fifteen miles a day). Most journeys lasted five or six months (from May to November). There was danger of disease; many groups were decimated by cholera. And there were encounters with Indians.

In reality, Indians were usually more helpful than dangerous to the white migrants. They often served as guides through difficult terrain or aided travelers in crossing streams or herding livestock. They maintained an extensive trade with the white travelers in horses, clothing, and fresh food. In the minds of many white migrants, however, the Indians seemed a constant threat. Occasional Indian attacks on isolated travelers and small wagon trains fed the fear; the practice of some Plains Indians of charging tribute to those whites passing through their lands fed resentment. In the end, whites may have inflicted more violence on the Indians during these overland journeys than the Indians did on them. Indeed, what records there are suggest that more than half of those who died in fighting between whites and Indians along the overland trails were Indians. In any case, the number of deaths in such conflicts was relatively small in relation to the size of the migrations; fewer than 1000 whites and Indians combined died in such conflicts between 1840 and 1860.

Even when migrants avoided disaster (as most did), the strains of the long journey caused significant changes in ordinary life. Traditional sex roles soon gave way to pressing necessities, and women began performing such traditionally "male" tasks as driving cattle and loading wagons. And despite the traditional image of westward migrants as rugged individualists, travelers found the journey an intensely collective experience. Indeed, one of the most frequent causes of disaster for travelers was the breakdown of the necessarily communal character of the migratory companies. Those who made the journey successfully generally learned the value of cooperation.

Polk and Expansion

By the mid-1840s, there were already substantial numbers of Americans living in settlements up and down the Pacific Coast—more than 5,000 in Oregon, south of the Columbia River. These new settlers were demanding that the United States government take possession of the disputed territory, cries that were echoed by supporters of Manifest Destiny in the East. Such demands soon made themselves felt in national politics.

The election of 1844 was widely expected to be a contest between two old foes: Henry Clay, the anticipated presidential candidate of the Whigs (President Tyler having been driven out of the party), and former president Martin Van Buren, assumed to be the favorite for the Democratic nomination. Both men wished to avoid taking a stand on the heated issue of the annexation of Texas, because whatever stand they took was certain to lose them some votes. Consequently, they issued separate statements on the question so similar in tone as to suggest that they had consulted with one another in advance: Both favored annexation, but only with the consent of Mexico. Since such consent was unlikely at best, the statements had little or no meaning.

Sentiment for expansion was relatively mild within the Whig party, and Clay had no difficulty

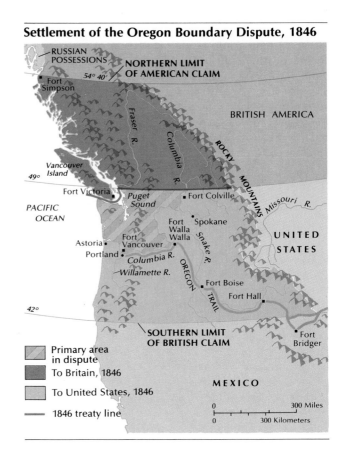

Settlement of the Oregon Boundary Dispute, 1846

securing the nomination despite his noncommittal position. The Whig platform discreetly omitted any reference to Texas. Among the Democrats, however, sentiment for annexation had grown to major proportions, particularly among party members in the South. They were enraged by Van Buren's equivocal stand on Texas, and their opposition destroyed the former president's chance of regaining the White House. Instead, the Democratic convention nominated James K. Polk.

Polk's supporters had skillfully exploited their candidate's backing for the annexation of Texas to generate votes for him at the convention. And in doing so, they won a victory for the first "dark horse" to win the presidential nomination of his party. Polk was not as obscure as his Whig critics suggested when they asked sarcastically during the campaign, "Who is James K. Polk?" Neither, however, was he a genuinely major figure within his party. Born in North Carolina, he had in his mid-twenties moved to Tennessee (following the pattern of the man who would become his political mentor, Andrew Jackson). For fourteen years, beginning in

Western Trails to 1860

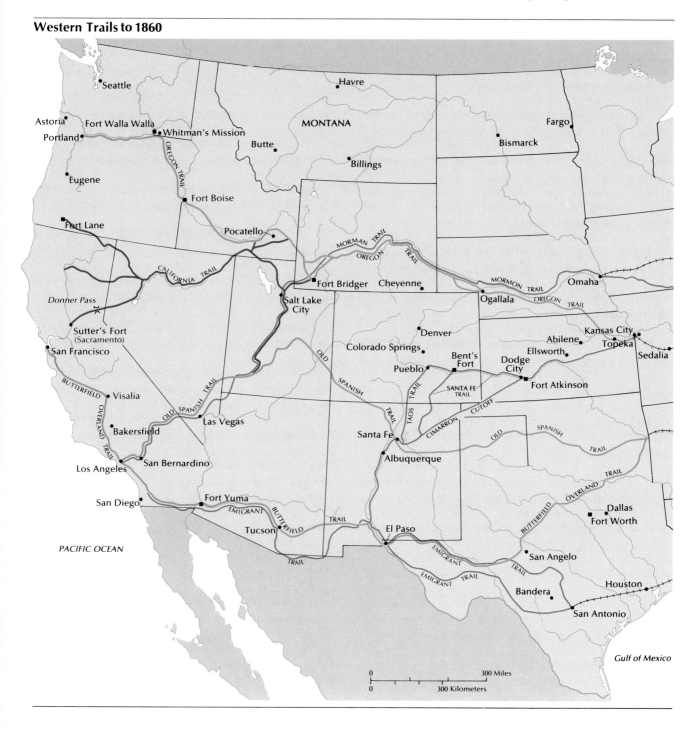

1825, he had served in the U.S. House of Representatives, four of them as its Speaker. Most recently, he had been governor of Tennessee. But in 1844, he had been out of public office—and for the most part out of the public mind—for three years. Hence his nomination was unexpected.

The sentiment that had made his victory possible could be seen in the key resolution of the Democratic platform: "that the re-occupation of Oregon and the re-annexation of Texas at the earliest practicable period are great American measures." The words "*re*-occupation" and "*re*-annexation" were intended to imply that in taking Oregon and Texas, the United States would only be confirming its claim to territories that had already belonged to it. By combining the Oregon and Texas questions, the Democrats hoped to appeal to both Northern and Southern expansionists.

Too late, Clay realized that he had mishandled the expansion issue. In midcampaign he announced that under certain circumstances he might be for the acquisition of Texas. His tardy straddling probably cost him more votes than it gained. Polk carried the election by 170 electoral votes to 105, although his popular majority was less than 40,000. The Liberty party, running James G. Birney a second time, polled 62,000 votes (as compared with 7,000 in 1840), mainly from antislavery Whigs who had turned against Clay.

The new president was an ordinary-looking man: short, thin, and grim of expression, with public manners that matched his appearance. But Polk was both intelligent and energetic, and he entered office with a clear idea of what he wished to accomplish and a firm grasp of the means necessary to attain it. Perhaps no president in American history was as successful in fulfilling his stated goals as James K. Polk.

One of those goals was achieved for him even before he took office. John Tyler, who remained in the White House until March 1845, interpreted the election returns as a mandate for annexation of Texas. He proposed to Congress that the territory be accepted into the Union by a joint resolution of both houses, a device that would eliminate the necessity of obtaining a two-thirds majority in the Senate for a treaty. In February 1845, Congress complied. There were conditions. Texas could be subdivided into no more than four additional states (in fact, it was never subdivided at all); it would retain responsibility for paying the debts that it had acquired as an independent nation (although it was permitted to retain its public lands as well, rather than ceding them to the federal government); and it had to submit to the

United States any boundary disputes in which it became involved. After the inauguration of Polk, Texas accepted the conditions; and in December 1845, it became a state.

Polk himself resolved the perplexing question of Oregon, although not without difficulty and not to the thorough satisfaction of his supporters. In his inaugural address, the new president seemed to reassert American title to all of the Oregon Country. In reality, however, he was willing to compromise—to effect a division on the line of the 49th parallel. The British minister in Washington was less conciliatory. He rejected Polk's offer without even referring it to London.

Abruptly, Polk took a more militant attitude. Saying America should look John Bull "straight in the eye" and hinting at war, he asserted again the American claim to all of Oregon. In his annual message to Congress in December 1845, he asked for approval to give notice to England that joint occupation was to end in a year. Citing the Monroe Doctrine (which had been largely forgotten during the previous twenty years), he insisted that the United States would permit no further European colonization. Congress, despite the dissent of some Whigs, complied with the president's request.

There was loose talk of war on both sides of the Atlantic—talk that in the United States often took the form of the bellicose slogan "Fifty-four forty or fight!" Neither nation, however, genuinely wished to resort to force. Finally, the British government offered to divide Oregon at the 49th parallel—that is, to accept Polk's original proposal. The president pretended to believe that the offer should be rejected, but with little resistance he allowed himself to be persuaded by the cabinet to submit the proposal to the Senate for advice. The result was that responsibility for the decision now shifted, no doubt to the president's great relief, from the White House to the Capitol. The Senate accepted the proposed agreement, and on June 15, 1846, a treaty was signed fixing the boundary at the 49th parallel, where it remains today. The United States had secured the larger and better part of the Oregon Country. It had certainly obtained all that it could reasonably have expected to get without war.

The Southwest and California

One of the reasons the Senate and the president had agreed so readily to the British proposal for settling the Oregon question was that new tensions were emerging in the Southwest—tensions that threatened to lead (and ultimately did lead) to a war with Mexico. The moment the United States admitted Texas to statehood in 1845, the Mexican government broke diplomatic relations with Washington. To make matters worse, a dispute now developed over the boundary between Texas and Mexico (which was now the southern boundary of the United States). The Texans claimed that the Rio Grande constituted the western and southern border, an assertion that included much of what is now New Mexico within Texas. Mexico, still refusing formally to concede the loss of Texas, nevertheless argued that the border had always been the Nueces River, well to the north of the Rio Grande. Polk recognized the Texas claim, and in the summer of 1845 he sent a small army under General Zachary Taylor to the Nueces line—to protect Texas, he claimed, against a possible Mexican invasion.

The semiprimitive economy of New Mexico, part of the area in dispute, supported a scanty population. The trade center of the region was the small metropolis of Santa Fe, 300 miles from the nearest settlements to the south and more than 1,000 miles from Mexico City and Vera Cruz, the economic centers on which New Mexico had relied during Spanish rule. This geographical isolation from Mexico helped produce a social and cultural isolation as well; for after Mexico had won its independence, the new government did for New Mexico much the same thing it did for Texas—it invited American traders into the region. The Mexicans hoped that the new trade with the United States would enhance the development of their province. It did. But it also, although on a more limited scale than in Texas, started a process by which New Mexico began to become more American than Mexican.

Soon a flourishing commerce—inaugurated in 1821 by William Becknell—developed between Santa Fe and Independence, Missouri, with long caravans moving back and forth along the Santa Fe Trail, carrying manufactured goods west and bringing back gold, silver, furs, and mules. The Santa Fe trade, as it was called, increased the American presence in New Mexico, and it signaled to advocates of expansion another direction for their efforts.

Americans were similarly increasing their interest in an even more distant province of Mexico: California. In this vast region lived perhaps 7,000 Mexicans, descendants of Spanish colonists, who engaged in agricultural pursuits, chiefly ranching, and carried on a skimpy trade with the outside world. Gradually, however, Americans began to arrive: first maritime traders and captains of Pacific whaling ships, who stopped to barter goods or buy supplies; then merchants, who established stores, imported merchandise, and developed a profitable trade with the Mexicans and Indians. Some of these new settlers began to dream of bringing California into the United States. Thomas O. Larkin, for example, set up a business in Monterey in 1832, quickly became a leading citizen of the region, and in 1844 accepted an appointment as American consul, with instructions to arouse sentiment among the Californians for annexation.

As reports spread of the rich soil and mild climate, immigrants began to enter California from the east by land. These were pioneering farmers, men of the type that were penetrating Texas and Oregon in search of greener pastures. By 1845, there were 700 Americans in California, most of them concentrated in the valley of the Sacramento River. The overlord of this region was John A. Sutter, once of Germany and Switzerland, who had moved to California in 1839 and had become a Mexican citizen. His headquarters at Sutter's Fort was the center of a magnificent domain where the owner ranched thousands of cattle and horses and maintained a network of small manufacturing shops to supply his armed retainers.

President Polk feared that Great Britain would try to acquire or dominate California as well as Texas— a suspicion that was given credence by the activities of British diplomatic agents in the province. His dreams of expansion thus began to extend beyond the Democratic platform. He was determined to acquire for his country New Mexico and California and possibly other parts of northern Mexico.

At the same time that he sent Taylor to the Nueces, Polk also sent secret instructions to the commander of the Pacific naval squadron to seize the California ports if he heard that Mexico had declared war. A little later, Consul Larkin was informed that, if the people wanted to revolt and join the United States, they would be received as brethren. Still later, an exploring expedition led by Captain John C. Frémont, of the army's corps of topographical engineers, entered California. The Mexican authorities, alarmed by the size of the party and its military character, ordered Frémont to leave. He complied, but moved only over the Oregon border.

After appearing to prepare for war, Polk resolved on a last effort to achieve his objectives by diplomacy. He dispatched to Mexico a special minister, John Slidell, a Louisiana politician, with instructions to settle with American money all the questions in dispute between the two nations. If Mexico would acknowledge the Rio Grande boundary for Texas,

Sutter's Fort

John Sutter, who migrated to the United States from Switzerland in 1834, settled in northern California several years later and persuaded the Mexican governor to grant him a large piece of land in the Sacramento River valley (the site of the California state capital today). There, with the help of Indian labor, he built a fortified town, surrounded by eighteen-foot walls, to protect against unfriendly Indians and established himself as one of the leading ranchers of the region. When gold was discovered on his property in 1848, his own workers quickly deserted him to join the search for instant wealth; his livestock was stolen; and his land was occupied by squatters. Four years later Sutter declared bankruptcy. (Library of Congress)

the United States would assume the damage claims, amounting to several millions, which Americans held against Mexico. If Mexico would cede New Mexico, the United States would pay $5 million. And for California, the United States would pay up to $25 million. Slidell soon notified his government that his mission had failed. Immediately after receiving Slidell's report, on January 13, 1846, Polk ordered Taylor's army to move across the Nueces to the Rio Grande.

If Polk was hoping for trouble, he was disappointed for months. Finally, in May, he decided to ask Congress to declare war on the grounds that Mexico had refused to honor its financial obligations and had insulted the United States by rejecting the Slidell mission. While Polk was working on a war message, the news arrived from Taylor that Mexican troops had crossed the Rio Grande and attacked a unit of American soldiers. Polk now revised his message. He declared: "Mexico has passed the boundary of the United States . . . and shed American blood upon the American soil. . . . War exists by the act of Mexico herself." Congress accepted Polk's interpretation of events and on May 13, 1846, declared war by votes of 40 to 2 in the Senate and 174 to 14 in the House.

The Mexican War

The war was never popular in the United States. Whig critics charged from the beginning that Polk had deliberately maneuvered the country into the conflict, that the border incident that had precipitated the declaration had been staged. Many argued that the hostilities with Mexico were draining resources and attention away from the far more important issue of Oregon; when the United States finally reached its agreement with Britain, opponents claimed that Polk had settled for less than he should have because he was preoccupied with Mexico. This opposition, limited at first to a relatively few Whigs in Congress, increased and intensified as the war continued and as the public became aware of the level of casualties and of the expense. Whigs in Congress generally supported military appropriation bills, not wishing to face accusations of obstructing the war effort. But they became ever bolder and more bitter in denouncing "Mr. Polk's war" as an aggressive and unnecessary conflict.

The president himself, in the meantime, was finding it more difficult than he had thought to achieve his goals. Although American forces were generally successful in their campaigns against the

Frémont at Fort Laramie

In 1842, Captain John C. Frémont, who was already an accomplished explorer, led the first successful scientific expedition by white Americans into the Rocky Mountains. His guide was the trapper Christopher "Kit" Carson (who later served as a Union general in the Civil War). This expedition was one of many exploratory journeys that brought Frémont fame as "the Pathfinder" and that made him into an important political figure. He was a U.S. senator from California and, in 1856, the Republican nominee for President. His party is shown here camped outside Fort Laramie in Wyoming Territory, displaying the flag that Frémont planted virtually everywhere he went.   (The Granger Collection)

Mexicans, final victory did not come nearly as quickly as Polk had hoped. In the opening phases of the war, the president assumed the planning of grand strategy, a practice that he continued almost to the end of the war. His basic idea was to seize key areas on the Mexican frontier and then force the Mexicans to make peace on American terms. Accordingly, he ordered Taylor to cross the Rio Grande and occupy northeastern Mexico, taking as his first objective the city of Monterrey. Polk seems to have had a vague idea that from Monterrey Taylor could advance southward, if necessary, and menace Mexico City. Taylor, known as "Old Rough and Ready," beloved by his soldiers for his courage and easy informality but ignorant of many of the technical aspects of war, attacked Monterrey in September 1846. After a hard fight he captured it, but at the price of agreeing to let the garrison evacuate without pursuit. Although the country hailed Taylor as a hero, Polk concluded that he did not possess the ability to lead an offensive

against Mexico City. Also, Polk began to realize that an advance south through the mountains would involve impossible problems of supply.

Polk launched two other offensives against New Mexico and California. In the summer of 1846, a small army under Colonel Stephen W. Kearny made the long march to Santa Fe and occupied the town with no opposition. Kearny sent part of his army (Missouri volunteers under Colonel A. W. Doniphan) south to join Taylor, and ordered other troops under his command to remain in the province and defend it. Then, under instructions from Polk, Kearny proceeded with a few hundred soldiers to California to take charge of operations there. In California a combined revolt and war was being staged by the settlers, Frémont's exploring party, and the American navy. The settlers had proclaimed California an independent nation in the "Bear Flag Revolution." Frémont had returned from Oregon to lead the rebels, and the navy had landed forces and an-

Scott's Army in Mexico City
General Winfield Scott leads an American army into the capital of Mexico in September 1847, the culminating triumph of the Mexican War. George W. Kendall of the New Orleans *Picayune* was one of the first war correspondents to accompany an army on its campaigns and was with Scott throughout the assault on the city. This print appeared in a history of the war that Kendall published several years later. (Library of Congress)

nexed California to the United States. When Kearny arrived, the Americans were fighting under the direction of Commodore R. F. Stockton of the navy. With some difficulty, Kearny brought the disparate American elements under his command, and by the autumn of 1846 he had completed the conquest of California.

In addition to northeastern Mexico, the United States now had possession of the two provinces for which it had gone to war. In a sense, the original objectives of the war had been achieved. Mexico, however, refused to recognize realities and would not agree to a peace or cede the conquered territory. At this point, Polk turned to General Winfield Scott, the commanding general of the army and its finest soldier, for help. Together, the two men devised a plan to force peace on the Mexicans—and, perhaps, gain even more new territory for the United States. Scott was to assemble an army at Tampico made up partly of troops from Taylor's army and partly of other forces. The navy would transport this new army down the coast to Vera Cruz, which the Americans would seize and make into a base. From Vera Cruz, Scott would move west along the National Highway to Mexico City. Late in 1846, Scott went to Mexico to organize his forces. Taylor, about half of whose army was transferred to Scott's command, was instructed to stand on the defensive.

While Scott was assembling his army off the coast, General Santa Anna, the Mexican dictator, decided to take advantage of the division of American forces by marching northward, crushing Taylor, and then returning to deal with Scott. With an army much larger than Taylor's, Santa Anna attacked the Americans at Buena Vista in February 1847. But he could

not break the American line and had to return to defend Mexico City.

In the meantime, Scott had taken Vera Cruz by siege and was moving inland, in one of the most brilliant campaigns in American military annals. With an army that never numbered more than 14,000, he advanced 260 miles into enemy territory, conserved the lives of his soldiers by using flanking movements instead of frontal assaults, and finally achieved his objective without losing a battle. At Cerro Gordo, in the mountains, he inflicted a smashing reverse on the Mexicans. He met no further resistance until he was within a few miles of Mexico City. After capturing the fortress of Chapultepec in a hard fight, the Americans occupied the enemy capital. A new Mexican government came into power, one that recognized defeat and was willing to make a peace treaty.

President Polk was now growing thoroughly unclear about his objectives. He continued to encourage those who demanded that the United States annex much of Mexico itself. At the same time, concerned about the approaching presidential election, he was growing anxious to get the war finished quickly. Along with the invading army, Polk had sent a special presidential agent authorized to negotiate a settlement with Mexico. The agent—Nicholas Trist, one of those obscure figures who occasionally have a major impact on history—concluded a treaty with the new Mexican government on February 2, 1848: the Treaty of Guadalupe Hidalgo. Mexico agreed to cede California and New Mexico to the United States and acknowledge the Rio Grande as the boundary of Texas. In return, the United States promised to assume the claims of its citizens against

The Mexican War, 1846–1848

Mexico and pay the Mexicans $15 million. When the treaty reached Washington, Polk faced a dilemma. Trist had obtained for the United States most of Polk's original demands, but he had stopped short of the more expansive dreams the president had come to harbor of acquiring more territory in Mexico. Polk angrily claimed that Trist had violated his instructions; he soon realized, however, that he had no choice but to accept the treaty. Some ardent expansionists were demanding that he hold out for annexation of—in a phrase widely bandied about at the time—"All Mexico!" Antislavery leaders, in the meantime, were charging that the demands for acquisition of Mexico were part of a Southern scheme to extend slavery to new realms (although other antislavery people, convinced that slavery could never be established in Mexico, were among those arguing for taking the whole country). To silence this bitter and potentially destructive debate, Polk submitted the Trist treaty to the Senate, which approved it by a vote of 38 to 14. The war was over, and America had gained a vast new territory. But it had also acquired a new set of troubling and divisive issues.

A New Sectional Crisis

James Polk tried during his presidency to be a leader whose policies transcended sectional issues. Thus he responded to the expansionist demands of both Northerners and Southerners. And he pursued economic policies designed similarly to strengthen the Democratic party as an organization with strong national support. He persuaded Congress, for example, to reestablish the independent treasury system—the Van Buren plan of 1840 to stabilize the nation's banks without resorting to another Bank of the United States. The Tyler administration had dismantled the system two years earlier, and Polk now delighted Democrats throughout the country by restoring it. He also delighted the South by fulfilling his campaign pledge to lower tariff rates—through the tariff of 1846, which achieved support as well from Northwestern Democrats.

Yet Polk was not to find it so easy to conciliate the sections. Although he acquired territory both in the Northwest and in the Southwest, Northerners continued to accuse him of having made Oregon a second priority so as to favor the expansionists of the South. The tariff bill, moreover, not only alienated manufacturers and merchants in the Northeast. It encouraged those Northwesterners who had supported it to believe that the president should, in return for their backing, now support internal improvements in their region. When Polk vetoed two bills providing federal funds for construction of roads and other improvements in the West, arguing that the national government had no authority to fund such projects, Westerners charged again that the administration was sacrificing their interests to those of the South.

The Sectional Debate

Sectional tensions were already rising, therefore, when a much more dangerous issue emerged. In August 1846, while the war was still in progress, Polk had asked Congress to provide him with $2 million that he could use to purchase peace with Mexico. When the appropriation was introduced in the House, David Wilmot of Pennsylvania, an antislavery Democrat from a high-tariff state, moved an amendment that slavery should be prohibited in any territory secured from Mexico. The so-called Wilmot Proviso passed the House but failed in the Senate. It would be called up again, debated, and voted on repeatedly for years.

Diametrically opposed to the Wilmot Proviso was the formula of the Southern extremists. They contended that the states jointly owned the territories and that the citizens of each state possessed equal rights in them, including the right to move to them with their property, particularly slave property. According to this view, Congress had no power to prohibit the movement of slavery into the public domain or to regulate it in any way except by extending protection. Neither could a territorial legislature, which was a creature of Congress, take any action to ban slavery.

Two compromise plans were presented. One, which President Polk supported, proposed to run the Missouri Compromise line of 36°30′ through the new territories to the Pacific coast, banning slavery north of the line and permitting it south of the line. The other, first prominently supported by Lewis Cass, Democratic senator from Michigan, was originally called "squatter sovereignty." Some years later, when taken up by Stephen A. Douglas, an Illinois senator of the same party, it was given the more dignified title of "popular sovereignty." According to this formula, the question of slavery in each territory should be left to the people there, acting through the medium of their territorial legislature.

Congress and the country debated the various formulas, but at the end of Polk's administration a decision had still not been reached. No territorial government had been provided for California or New Mexico (New Mexico included most of present New Mexico and Arizona, all of Utah and Nevada, and parts of Colorado and Wyoming). Even the organization of Oregon, so far north that slavery seemed unlikely ever to enter it, was held up by the controversy. Southern members of Congress, hoping to gain some advantage in the regions farther south, blocked a territorial bill for Oregon until August 1848, when a free-soil government was finally authorized.

The debate was partially stilled by the presiden-

American Expansion into the Southwest, 1845–1853

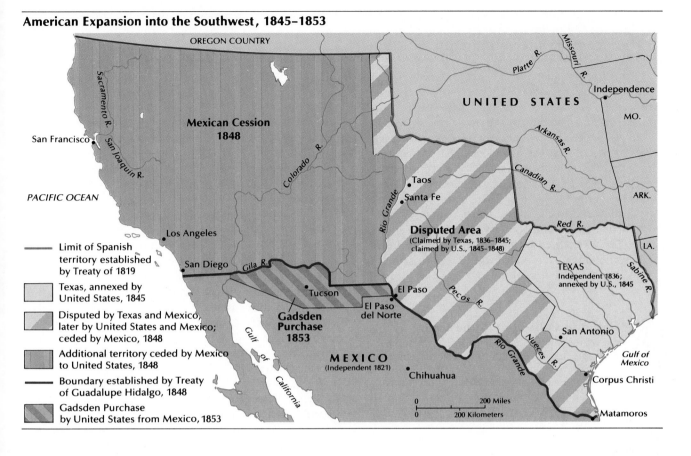

Legend:
- Limit of Spanish territory established by Treaty of 1819
- Texas, annexed by United States, 1845
- Disputed by Texas and Mexico, later by United States and Mexico; ceded by Mexico, 1848
- Additional territory ceded by Mexico to United States, 1848
- Boundary established by Treaty of Guadalupe Hidalgo, 1848
- Gadsden Purchase by United States from Mexico, 1853

tial campaign of 1848. Both the Democrats and the Whigs tried to avoid provocative references to the slavery question. When Polk declined to run for a second term, the Democrats nominated as their candidate Lewis Cass of Michigan, an elderly, honest, dull party wheel horse—and, according to most accounts (and portraits), a man of stunning physical unattractiveness. Although the platform was purposely vague, it could be interpreted as an endorsement of squatter sovereignty. The Whigs adopted no platform and presented as their candidate a military hero with no political record, General Zachary Taylor of Louisiana.

Ardent abolitionists and even moderates who merely opposed the expansion of slavery found it difficult to swallow either Cass or Taylor. The situation was ripe for the appearance of a powerful third party. The potential sources for such a group were the existing Liberty party and the antislavery Whigs and Democrats. Late in the campaign, third-party promoters held a national convention, adopted a platform endorsing the Wilmot Proviso, free homesteads

(free land for migrants to the West), and a higher tariff, and nominated former president Van Buren for the presidency. Thus was launched the Free Soil party—a major step toward what would ultimately be a dissolution of the existing party system and its replacement with another.

Taylor won a narrow victory. Although Van Buren failed to carry a single state, he polled an impressive 291,000 votes (10 percent of the total), and the Free-Soilers elected ten members to Congress. It is probable that Van Buren pulled enough Democratic votes away from Cass, particularly in New York, to throw the election to Taylor.

Taylor and the Territories

Zachary Taylor was the first man to be elected president with no previous political training or experience. He was also the first professional soldier to occupy the White House. (He was not, of course, the first general. Washington, Jackson, and Harrison had all attained that rank during their military service.) Taylor was a Southerner and a slaveholder, but from his long years in the army he had acquired a national outlook.

Almost immediately, the new president encountered problems connected with the territories recently acquired from Mexico. Congress had failed to provide a civil government for the new possessions, and the regions were being administered by military officials responsible to the president. There was particular pressure to establish a new government in California, for that territory was experiencing a remarkable boom. In January 1848, gold was accidentally discovered in the Sacramento Valley. As word of the strike spread, inhabitants of California and the whole Far West, fired by hopes of becoming immediate millionaires, stampeded to the area to stake out claims. By the end of summer the news had reached the Eastern states and Europe. Then the gold rush really started.

From the United States and throughout the world, thousands of "forty-niners" poured into California. By land and by sea, disdaining hunger, thirst, disease, and even death, the seekers after gold came—more than 80,000 of them in 1849 alone. By the end of that year, California had a population of approximately 100,000, more than enough to entitle it to statehood.

President Taylor believed that statehood would serve as the solution not only to the inadequacy of the military government in California but to the whole issue of slavery in the territories. Let California and New Mexico both frame state constitutions and apply for admission to the Union, he declared. Once they had become states, no one could deny their right to dispose of slavery as they wished. So Taylor directed military officials in the territories to expedite statehood movements.

California promptly ratified a constitution in which slavery was prohibited. When Congress assembled in December 1849, Taylor proudly described his efforts. He recommended that California be admitted as a free state and that New Mexico, when it was ready, be permitted to come in with complete freedom to decide the status of slavery as it wished. But Congress was not about to accept the president's program.

Complicating the situation was the emergence of side issues generated by the conflict over slavery in the territories. One such issue concerned slavery in the District of Columbia. Antislavery people, charging that human servitude in the capital was a national disgrace, demanded that it be abolished there. Southerners angrily replied that the institution could not be touched without the consent of Maryland, which had originally donated the land.

Another disturbing issue was the question of fugitive slaves. Northern personal liberty laws, forbidding courts and police officers to assist in the return of runaways, provoked Southerners to call for a new, more stringent *national* fugitive slave law.

A third issue related to the boundary between Texas and New Mexico. Texas claimed the portion of New Mexico east of the Rio Grande, although the federal government during the Mexican War had assigned this region to New Mexico. To Texans, it seemed that Washington was trying to steal part of their territory. They also resented the government's refusal to assume the Texas war debt. Southern extremists supported the pretensions of Texas, while

Gold Mining in California in the 1850s

This photograph shows a sluice, used in placer mining. A "placer" was a deposit of sand, dirt, or clay—often in the bed of a stream—that contained fine particles of gold, which could be mined by washing. The "sluice" was a wooden trough into which miners shoveled the earth and then ran a steady stream of water over it. Heavy particles (such as gold) would sink to the bottom, where they were caught by cleats (known as "riffles"). Placer mining was one of the simplest and cheapest methods of extracting gold from the land, but it seldom produced large strikes.   (The Bettmann Archive)

Northerners, eager to cut down the size of a slave state, upheld New Mexico.

But the biggest obstacle in the way of the president's program was the South—angered and frightened by the possibility that two new free states would be added to the Northern majority. Only in the Senate did the South still maintain equality. The number of free and slave states was equal in 1849—fifteen of each. But now the admission of California would upset the balance, with New Mexico, Oregon, and Utah still to come.

Responsible Southern leaders declared that if California was to be admitted, and if slavery was to be prohibited in the territories, the time had come for the South to secede from the Union. At the suggestion of Mississippi, a call went out for a Southern-rights convention to meet in June 1850 at Nashville, Tennessee, to consider whether the South should resort to the ultimate act of secession. In the North excitement ran equally high. Every Northern state legislature but one adopted resolutions demanding that slavery be barred from the territories. Public meetings all through the free states called for the passage of the Wilmot Proviso and the abolition of slavery in the District of Columbia. Such was the crisis that confronted Congress and the country as the tense year of 1850 opened.

The Compromise of 1850

Moderates and lovers of the Union turned their thoughts, during the winter of 1849–1850, to the framing of a great congressional compromise that would satisfy both sections and restore tranquillity. The venerable statesman from Kentucky, Henry Clay, headed the forces of conciliation. In Clay's view, no compromise would have any lasting effect unless it settled all the issues in dispute between the sections. Accordingly, he took a number of separate measures, which had been proposed before, combined them into one set of resolutions, and on January 29, 1850, presented them to the Senate. He recommended (1) that California be admitted as a free state; (2) that, in the rest of the Mexican cession, territorial governments be formed without restrictions as to slavery; (3) that Texas yield in its boundary dispute with New Mexico and be compensated by the federal government's taking over its public debt; (4) that the slave trade, but not slavery itself, be abolished in the District of Columbia; and (5) that a new and more effective fugitive slave law be passed.

These resolutions launched a debate that raged for seven months—both in Congress and throughout the nation. The debate occurred in two phases, the differences between which revealed much about how American politics was changing in the 1850s.

In the first phase of the debate, the dominant voices in Congress were those of old men—national leaders who still remembered Jefferson, Adams, and other founders—who argued for or against the compromise on the basis of broad ideals. Clay himself, seventy-three years old in 1850, was the most prominent of these spokesmen. He opened the oratorical tournament with a defense of his measures and a broad plea to both North and South to be mutually conciliatory. It was the Union, he claimed, and the shared sentiments of nationalism that had emerged from America's glorious past, that should be the primary concern of the lawmakers.

Early in March, another of the older leaders—John C. Calhoun, sixty-eight years old and so ill that he had to sit grimly in his seat while a colleague read his speech for him—made his contribution to the debate. Almost ignoring Clay's proposals, he devoted his argument to what to him was the larger, in fact the only subject: the minority status of the South; and he asked more for his section than any realistic observer believed could be given. Like Clay, however, Calhoun spoke emotionally of the bonds holding the nation together. Because of Northern aggressions, the cords that bound the Union were snapping. What could save it? The North, he insisted, must admit that the South possessed equal rights in the territories, must agree to observe the laws concerning fugitive slaves, must cease attacking slavery, and must accept an amendment to the Constitution guaranteeing a balance of power between the sections. The amendment would provide for the election of dual presidents, one from the North and one from the South, each possessing a veto power. In short, nothing would satisfy Calhoun but a comprehensive, permanent solution to the sectional problem. His proposal, however, would have required an abject surrender by the North.

After Calhoun came the third of the elder statesmen, the sixty-eight-year-old Daniel Webster. His "Seventh of March Address" was probably the greatest forensic effort of his long oratorical career. Still nourishing White House ambitions, he now sought to calm angry passions and to rally Northern moderates to support Clay's compromise.

After six months of debate, however—six months dominated by ringing appeals to the memory of the founders, to nationalism, to idealism—the effort to win approval of the compromise failed. In July, Congress defeated the Clay proposal. And with that, the controversy moved into its second phase, in which a very different cast of characters would predominate. Clay, ill and tired, left Washington to spend the summer resting in the mountains. He would return, but never with his old vigor; he died in 1852. Calhoun had died even before the vote in July. And Webster in the course of the summer accepted a new appointment as secretary of state, thus removing himself from the Senate and from the debate.

In place of these leaders, a new, younger group now emerged as the dominant voices. There was William H. Seward of New York, forty-nine years old, a wily political operator who staunchly opposed the proposed compromise. The ideals of Union were to him clearly less important than the issue of eliminating slavery. Emerging as the new voice of the South was Jefferson Davis of Mississippi, forty-two years old, a representative not of the old aristocratic South of Calhoun but of the new, cotton South—a hard, frontierlike country that was growing rapidly and prospering. To him, and to those he represented, the slavery issue was not only one of principles and ideals but also one of economic self-interest.

Most important of all, there was Stephen A. Douglas, the thirty-seven-year-old senator from Illinois. More than any of the others, Douglas represented the new generation of politicians coming to dominate national life. A Westerner from a rapidly growing frontier state, a man unpolished in manner, he was an open spokesman for the economic needs of his section—and especially for the new railroads. His was a career devoted not to any broad national goals, as Clay's, Webster's, and even Calhoun's had often been, but one devoted frankly to sectional gain and personal self-promotion.

The new leaders of the Senate were able, where the old leaders were not, to arrive at a compromise in 1850. In part, they were aided by a shift in popular sentiment. The country was entering a period of prosperity—the result of an expanding foreign trade, the flow of gold from California, and a boom in railroad construction—reminiscent of the flush days of the 1830s. Conservative economic interests everywhere wanted to end the sectional dispute and concentrate on internal expansion. Even in the South, excitement seemed to be abating. The Nashville convention met in June, adopted a few tame resolutions, and then quietly adjourned to await final action by Congress.

Progress toward the compromise was also furthered by the removal of the most powerful obstacle to it: the president. Zachary Taylor had been unyielding in his stand that the admission of California and possibly New Mexico must come first, that only then could other measures be discussed. Taylor had threatened not only to veto any measure that diverged from this proposal but to use force against the South (even to lead the troops in person) if they attempted to secede. But on July 9, Taylor suddenly died—the victim of a violent stomach disorder following an attack of heat prostration. He was succeeded by his vice president, Millard Fillmore of New York—a handsome and dignified man of no particular ability, but one who understood the political importance of flexibility. He ranged himself on the side of the compromise and used his powers of persuasion to swing Northern Whigs into line.

The new leaders benefited, however, not just from the shift in sentiment and the change in presidents, but also from their own pragmatic tactics. Douglas's first step, after the departure of Clay, was to break up the "omnibus bill" that Clay had envisioned as a great, organic solution to the sectional crisis and introduce instead a series of separate measures to be voted on one by one. Thus representatives of different sections could support those elements of the compromise favorable to them and could abstain from voting on or could vote against those they opposed. Douglas also gained support by avoiding the grand appeals to patriotism of Clay and Webster and resorting instead to complicated backroom maneuverings and deals—linking the compromise to such nonideological matters as the sale of government bonds and the construction of railroads. As a result of his efforts, by mid-September all the components of the compromise had been enacted by both houses of Congress and signed by the president.

The outcome was a great victory for Douglas and the forces of conciliation; but it was a clouded victory. For the passage of the Compromise of 1850, unlike the creation of the Missouri Compromise thirty years before, had not resulted from any widespread agreement on common national ideals. It was, rather, a victory largely of self-interest that had not resolved the underlying problems. Nevertheless, leaders in Congress hailed the event as a great triumph; and Millard Fillmore, signing the measure, called it a just settlement of the sectional problem, "in its character final and irrevocable."

It was one thing to pass the compromise through Congress and another to persuade the country to ac-

Slave and Free Territories According to the Compromise of 1850

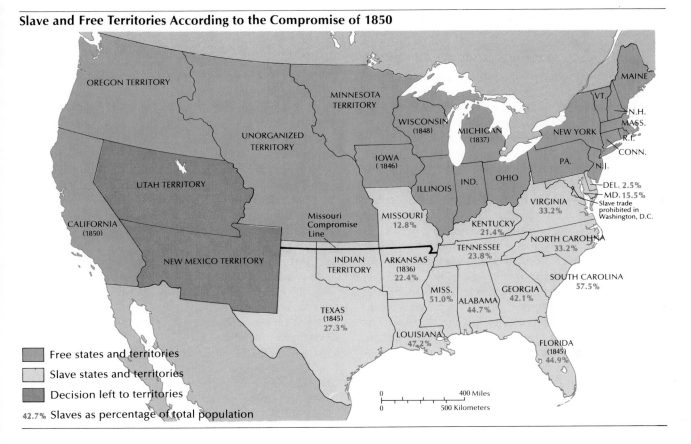

- ■ Free states and territories
- □ Slave states and territories
- ■ Decision left to territories
- **42.7%** Slaves as percentage of total population

cept it. In the North, the most objectionable of the measures was the Fugitive Slave Act. By this law, blacks accused of being runaways were denied trial by jury and the right to testify in their own behalf. Their status was to be decided by a federal judge or by a special commissioner appointed by the federal circuit courts. They could be remanded to slavery simply on the evidence of affidavits presented by those who claimed to be their owners.

But the Fugitive Slave Act was the only part of the compromise that most Southerners could ungrudgingly approve. The Nashville convention met again in November 1850 (with only about a third of the original delegates present) and condemned the compromise. Eventually the South brought itself to accept the settlement, but only after much agonizing, and then only conditionally. Epitomizing such feelings was the "Georgia Platform," which declared that Georgia would acquiesce in the compromise—but that if the North disregarded the Fugitive Slave Act or attempted to abolish slavery in the District of Columbia or denied admission to a state because it wished to have slavery, then Georgia would consider

the compact broken and would protect its rights even to the point of seceding from the union.

The Crises of the 1850s

For a few years after the Compromise of 1850, the sectional conflict seemed briefly to be forgotten, and much of the nation concentrated on enjoying prosperity and growth. But the tensions between North and South remained, and the crisis continued to smolder until—in 1854—it once more burst into flames.

The Uneasy Truce

How difficult it would be for the nation to put aside its sectional differences became clear almost immediately. For while the major parties attempted to display an unswerving devotion to the Compromise of 1850, events in the nation began to make their efforts seem unrealistic and even irrelevant.

Both major parties endorsed the Compromise in their platforms in 1852—the Democrats pledging fervently to avoid all attempts in any "shape or color" to renew agitation over slavery, the Whigs making the same promise in somewhat milder language. Both parties, similarly, nominated presidential candidates who were moderates on the sectional issue and were unlikely to arouse passionate opposition in either North or South. The Democrats chose the obscure New Hampshire politician Franklin Pierce (although not until after wrangling through forty-nine ballots, with the convention deadlocked among the three leading contenders—Lewis Cass, Stephen Douglas, and James Buchanan of Pennsylvania). The Whigs chose as their nominee the military hero General Winfield Scott, a man whose political views were so undefined that no one even knew whether or not he approved of the Compromise of 1850.

Yet the gingerly way in which party leaders dealt with the sectional question could not prevent its divisive influence from intruding on the election. The Whigs, in particular, suffered from their attempts to straddle the issue. Already plagued by the defections of those antislavery Northerners who had formed the Free Soil party in 1846, they alienated still more party members—the "Conscience" Whigs—by refusing to take an open stand against slavery now. Partly as a result of these divisions, Scott was the last presidential candidate the Whigs were ever to nominate. In the meantime, the Free Soil party was gaining in numbers and influence in the North; its presidential candidate, John P. Hale, repudiated the Compromise of 1850.

The divisions among the Whigs, and the vagueness of the party's support of the compromise, helped produce a victory for the Democrats in 1852. The new president, Franklin Pierce, was forty-nine years old when inaugurated the following March—the youngest person to serve in the office to that date. A charming, amiable man of no great distinction, he attempted to maintain party—and national— harmony by avoiding divisive issues. But those issues arose despite him.

Partly, they arose because there remained active political forces in the North—most notably the abolitionist organizations—who had never supported the Compromise of 1850 and who continued to work actively for the elimination of slavery. Partly, too, they arose because of the presence of eloquent and combative antislavery leaders in Congress—Senator Charles Sumner of Massachusetts, elected in 1850; Congressman Joshua R. Giddings of Ohio; and oth-

ers. Their denunciations of the South and its institution resounded from a national forum. Most of all, however, the sectional tensions continued because of Northern response to the Fugitive Slave Act. Always strong, that opposition intensified after 1850 when Southerners began appearing in Northern states to pursue fugitives or to claim as slaves blacks who had been living for years in Northern communities. So fervently did many opponents of slavery resent such efforts that mobs formed in city after city to prevent enforcement of the law. In 1851, a crowd in Boston took a runaway named Shadrach from a federal marshal and sent him on his way to Canada; in Syracuse, New York, later in the same year, another crowd rescued a slave named Jerry McHenry. In 1854, a Boston mob led by respectable and prominent citizens attempted, unsuccessfully, to seize the escaped slave Anthony Burns from federal officers.

Northern states tried to undermine the Fugitive Slave Act through legal means as well. Several states passed new personal liberty laws, designed to interpose state authority between the accused fugitive and the federal government. In Wisconsin and Massachusetts, such laws directed state courts to grant all fugitives a judicial hearing (heavily weighted in the fugitives' favor) before they could be deported from the state. The supreme court of Wisconsin, in *Ableman* v. *Booth* (1957), went so far as to declare the federal Fugitive Slave Act void and to ignore the U.S. Supreme Court when it overruled the Wisconsin ruling.

White Southerners watched all this with growing anger and alarm. The Fugitive Slave Act had been the one element of the Compromise of 1850 they had considered a victory. Now they had to watch while the North, through the extralegal device of mobs and through legal efforts of dubious constitutionality, made that victory meaningless.

"Young America"

The Pierce administration tried to avoid taking a position on most domestic issues likely to produce controversy. And in foreign policy as well, the Democrats tried to revive a sense of cross-sectional nationalism. Here, too, however, their efforts created more problems than they resolved.

Spearheading the revival of nationalist diplomacy was a group of Democrats who organized what they called the Young America movement. Aware of the great liberal and nationalist revolutions of 1848 in Europe, these adventurous Democrats were stirred by the vision of a republican Europe with governments based on the model of the United States. They continued to dream as well of expanding American commerce in the Pacific and of extending the sweep of Manifest Destiny with new acquisitions in the Western Hemisphere. The sentiments they aroused had a profound effect on the nation's foreign policy.

Those sentiments were first felt in the second half of the Whig administration, under the new president, Millard Fillmore, and his new secretary of state, Daniel Webster. One example of their approach to international relations was Webster's defiance of the powerful government of Austria by supporting the effort of Hungary to win its independence. The Fillmore administration also sponsored an expedition into the Pacific under Commodore Matthew C. Perry, who began efforts to open Japan—for nearly two centuries all but totally closed to the West—to American trade. Perry's efforts resulted in 1854 in a treaty giving Americans access to two Japanese ports.

Few Americans in either section objected to these displays of nationalism. But efforts by both the Fillmore and Pierce administrations to extend the nation's domain in its own hemisphere produced new problems. First Fillmore and then Pierce sanctioned a series of ill-considered and ultimately unsuccessful attempts to wrest Cuba from the Spanish Empire. Frustrated in efforts to acquire the island through open diplomacy, Pierce turned to more devious means—authorizing his minister to Spain, the impetuous Pierre Soulé, to try to "detach" Cuba from the empire by subterfuge. Soulé's clumsy efforts only widened the gap between Spain and the United States, particularly when he collaborated with several other American diplomats in Europe (John Y. Mason, minister to France, and James Buchanan, minister to Great Britain) to produce a preposterous document, the so-called Ostend Manifesto. In it, Soulé and the others declared that all parties—Spain, Cuba, and the United States—would benefit from the annexation of Cuba by America. What was more, if disturbances there became a threat to American security, the United States would be justified "by every law human and divine" in "wresting" the island from Spain. The document was meant to be confidential, but its contents soon became public, enraging many antislavery Northerners, who charged the administration with conspiring to bring a new slave state into the Union even at the risk of war.

The South, for its part, opposed all efforts to acquire new territory that would not support a slave system. The kingdom of Hawaii agreed to join the United States in 1854, but the treaty had no chance in the Senate because it contained a clause prohibiting slavery in the islands. A powerful movement to annex Canada to the United States—a movement that had the support of many Canadians eager for access to American markets—similarly foundered, at least in part because of slavery. Southerners eager to prevent the addition of free territory to the Union supported an 1854 treaty providing trade reciprocity between the two nations—a treaty that undercut pressures for annexation.

The Kansas-Nebraska Controversy

Controversy over the return of fugitive slaves and the efforts to extend American dominion abroad kept sectional tensions alive in the early 1850s. But what fully revived the crisis between North and South was the same issue that had produced it in the first place: slavery in the territories. By the 1850s, the line of frontier settlement had moved west to the great bend of the Missouri River. Beyond the boundaries of Minnesota, Iowa, and Missouri stretched a great expanse of plains, which most Americans had always believed was unfit for cultivation (it was widely known as the Great American Desert) and which the nation had thus assigned to the Indian tribes it had dislodged from the more fertile lands to the east. Now it was becoming apparent that large sections of this region were, in fact, suitable for farming. In the states of the Old Northwest, therefore, pressure began to build for efforts to extend settlement westward once again. Prospective settlers urged the government to open the area to them, provide territorial governments, and—despite the solemn assurance the United States had earlier given the Indians of the sanctity of their reservations—to dislodge the tribes so as to make room for white settlers. There was relatively little opposition from any segment of white society to the violation of Indian rights proposed by these demands. But the interest in further settlement raised two issues that did prove highly divisive and that gradually became entwined with each other: railroads and slavery.

As the nation expanded westward, the problem of communication between the older states and the so-called trans-Mississippi West (those areas west of the Mississippi River) became more and more critical. As a result, the idea of building a transcontinental railroad gradually gained favor both in and out of Congress. The problem, however, was where to place it—in particular, where to locate the railroad's eastern terminus. Northerners favored Chicago, the growing capital of the free states of the Northwest. Southerners supported St. Louis, Memphis, or New Orleans—all located in slave states. The transcontinental railroad, in other words, was—like nearly everything else in the 1850s—becoming entangled in sectionalism. It had become a prize that both North and South were struggling to secure.

One argument against a southern route had been removed through the foresight of Pierce's secretary of war, Jefferson Davis, a Mississippian. Surveys had indicated that a road with a southern terminus would probably have to pass through an area south of the Gila River, in Mexican territory. At Davis's suggestion, Pierce appointed James Gadsden, a Southern railroad builder, to negotiate with Mexico for the sale of this region. In 1853 Gadsden persuaded the Mexican government to dispose of a strip of land that today comprises a part of Arizona and New Mexico, the so-called Gadsden Purchase; the United States paid Mexico $10 million for the land.

Particularly interested in a transcontinental railroad was Senator Stephen A. Douglas, and his interest influenced him to introduce in Congress a fateful legislative act, one that accomplished the final destruction of the Compromise of 1850. As a senator from Illinois, a resident of Chicago, and above all, the acknowledged leader of the Northwestern Democrats, Douglas naturally wanted the transcontinental railroad for his own city and section. He realized too the potency of the principal argument against the northern route: that west of the Mississippi it would run largely through unsettled Indian country. In January 1854, as chairman of the Committee on Territories, he acted to forestall this argument. He introduced a bill to organize a huge new territory, to be known as Nebraska, west of Iowa and Missouri.

Douglas seemed to realize that this bill would encounter the opposition of the South, partly because it would prepare the way for a new free state, the proposed territory being in the Louisiana Purchase area north of the 36°30′ line of the Missouri Compromise and hence closed to slavery. In an effort to make the measure acceptable to Southerners, Douglas inserted a provision that the status of slavery in the territory would be determined by the territorial legislature—that is, according to popular sovereignty. Theoretically, at least, this would open the region to slavery. The concession was not enough to satisfy extreme Southern Democrats, particularly those from Missouri, who feared that their state

would be surrounded by free territory. They demanded more, and Douglas had to give more to get their support. He agreed to two additions to his bill: a clause specifically repealing the antislavery provision of the Missouri Compromise, and another creating two territories, Nebraska and Kansas, instead of one. Presumably Kansas would become a slave state. In its final form the measure was known as the Kansas-Nebraska Act.

Douglas persuaded President Pierce to endorse his bill, and so it became an official Democratic measure. But even with the backing of the administration, it encountered stiff opposition and did not become a law until May 1854. Nearly all the Southern members of Congress, whether Whigs or Democrats, supported the bill, and nearly all the Northern Whigs opposed it. The Northern Democrats in the House split evenly.

Of greater importance than the opposition to the Kansas-Nebraska Act in Congress was the reaction against it in the Northern states. The effort to repeal the Missouri Compromise—a measure that many Northerners believed had a special sanctity, almost as if it were a part of the Constitution—was particularly alarming. The whole North seemed to blaze with fury at this latest demonstration of the power of the slavocracy, and much of the fury was directed at Douglas, who, in the eyes of many Northerners, had acted as a tool of the slaveholders. No other piece of legislation in congressional history produced so many immediate, sweeping, and ominous changes as the Kansas-Nebraska Act. It destroyed the Whig party in the South except in the border states. At the same time, as many Southern Whigs became Democrats, it increased Southern influence in the Democratic party. It destroyed the popular basis of Whiggery in the North, with the result that by 1856 the national Whig party had disappeared and a conservative, nationalistic influence in American politics had been removed. It divided the Northern Democrats and drove many of them from the party. Most important of all, it called into being a new party that was frankly sectional in composition and creed.

People in both the major parties who opposed Douglas's bill began to call themselves Anti-Nebraska Democrats and Anti-Nebraska Whigs. In 1854, they formed a new party and began to call themselves "Republicans." The party had its beginnings in a series of spontaneous popular meetings throughout the Northwest, and the movement soon spread to the East. In the elections of 1854, the Republicans, often cooperating with the Know-

Nothings, elected a majority to the U.S. House of Representatives and won control of a number of Northern state governments.

At first, the Republican party was a one-idea organization: It simply opposed the expansion of slavery into the territories. Its original members were mostly former Whigs and Free-Soilers but also included a substantial number of former Democrats. In part, it represented the democratic idealism of the North. But it also represented the agricultural and business interests of the section. Soon the party gained additional support from advocates of federal aid to economic activity—advocates of high tariffs, homesteads, and internal improvements—who blamed the South for blocking such aid and thus hindering Northern development. When the Know-Nothing organization broke up, the Republicans absorbed most of its members. Thus the new party inherited the taint of nativism that once had clung to the Whigs. Like the Whigs, the Republicans repelled the Roman Catholics among the German, Irish, and other foreign-born groups. Yet the Republicans succeeded in attracting Protestants among German and Scandinavian, as well as British, immigrants.

"Bleeding Kansas"

The pulsing popular excitement aroused in the North by the Kansas-Nebraska Act was sustained by events during the next two years in Kansas. Almost immediately, settlers moved into this territory. Those from the North were encouraged by press and pulpit and the powerful organs of abolitionist propaganda. Often they received financial help from such organizations as the New England Emigrant Aid Company. Those from the South often received financial contributions from the communities they left.

In the spring of 1855, elections were held for a territorial legislature. Thousands of Missourians, some traveling in armed bands, moved into Kansas and voted. Although there were probably only some 1,500 legal votes in the territory, more than 6,000 votes were counted. With such conditions prevailing, the proslavery forces elected a majority to the legislature, which proceeded immediately to enact a series of laws legalizing slavery. The outraged free-staters, convinced that they could not get fair treatment from the Pierce administration, resolved on extralegal action. Without asking permission from Congress or the territorial governor, they elected delegates to a constitutional convention that met at Topeka and

adopted a constitution excluding slavery. They then chose a governor and legislature and petitioned Congress for statehood. Pierce called their movement unlawful and akin to treason. The full weight of the government, he announced, would be thrown behind the proslavery territorial legislature.

A few months later a proslavery federal marshal assembled a huge posse, consisting mostly of Missourians, to arrest the free-state leaders in Lawrence. The posse not only made the arrests but sacked the town. Several free-staters died in the melee. Retribution came immediately. Among the more extreme opponents of slavery in Kansas was a fierce, fanatical man named John Brown, who considered himself an instrument of God's will to destroy slavery. Brown estimated that five antislavery people had been murdered, and he decided that it was his sacred duty to take revenge. He gathered six followers, and in one night murdered five proslavery settlers, leaving their mutilated bodies to discourage other supporters of slavery from entering Kansas. The episode was known as the Pottawatomie Massacre; and its result was more civil strife in Kansas—irregular, guerrilla warfare conducted by armed bands, some of them more interested in land claims or loot than in ideologies.

In both North and South, the belief was widespread that the aggressive designs of the other section were epitomized by (and responsible for) what was happening in Kansas. Whether or not such beliefs were entirely correct is less important than that they became passionately held articles of faith in both sections. Thus "Bleeding Kansas" became a symbol of the sectional controversy.

Another symbol soon appeared, in the United States Senate. In May 1856, Charles Sumner of Massachusetts rose to discuss the problems of the strife-torn territory. He entitled his speech "The Crime Against Kansas." Handsome, eloquent, humorless, and passionately doctrinaire, Sumner embodied the most extreme element of the political antislavery movement. And in his speech, delivered with the righteous eloquence for which he was becoming famous, he bemoaned the fate of "bleeding Kansas" and fiercely denounced the Pierce administration, the South, and the institution of slavery. He singled out for particular attention his colleague in the Senate Andrew P. Butler of South Carolina, an outspoken defender of slavery. It was an age in which orators were accustomed to indulging in personal invective; but in his discussion of Butler, Sumner far exceeded the normal bounds. The South Carolinian was, Sumner claimed, the "Don Quixote" of slavery, having "chosen a mistress . . . who, though ugly to others, is always lovely to him, though polluted in the sight of the world, is chaste in his sight . . . the harlot slavery."

The pointedly sexual references and the general viciousness of the speech enraged Butler's nephew, Preston Brooks, a member of the U.S. House of Representatives from South Carolina. Brooks resolved to punish Sumner for his insults by a method approved by the Southern gentleman's code—a public, physical chastisement. Several days after the speech, Brooks approached Sumner at his desk in the Senate chamber during a recess, raised a heavy cane, and began beating him repeatedly on the head and shoulders. Sumner, trapped behind his desk, rose in agony with such strength that he tore the table from the bolts holding it to the floor, then collapsed, bleeding and unconscious. So severe were his injuries that he was unable to return to the Senate for four years, during which time his state refused to replace him. He became a potent symbol throughout the North—a martyr to the barbarism of the South.

Preston Brooks became a symbol too. Censured by the House, he resigned his seat, returned to South Carolina, and stood successfully for reelection. He had the virtually unanimous support of his state. Brooks's assault had made him a Southern hero. And as a result, he, like Sumner, served as evidence of how deep the antagonism between North and South had become.

The Free-Soil Ideology

What had happened to produce such deep hostility between the two sections? There were, obviously, important differences between the North and the South; but many of these differences had always existed. There were real issues—above all the question of slavery in the territories—dividing them; but these issues alone are not a sufficient explanation. Despite the passions generated by the conflict in Kansas, neither the North nor the South really seemed to believe that there was ever a genuine prospect of slavery becoming established there. At the height of the struggle between pro- and antislavery forces in the territory, there were almost no blacks in Kansas at all. Similarly, few of the remaining territories seemed likely ever to support flourishing slave systems. And despite the fervor of the abolitionists, relatively few

Northerners were yet willing to advocate an end to slavery where it presently existed.

Slavery and other issues attained such destructive importance among most Americans in part because they served as symbols for a set of other concerns on both sides. As the nation expanded and political power grew more dispersed, the North and the South each became concerned with ensuring that its vision of America's future would be the dominant one. And those visions were becoming—partly as a result of internal developments within the sections themselves, partly because of each region's conceptions (and misconceptions) of what was happening outside it—increasingly distinct and increasingly rigid.

In the North, assumptions about the proper structure of society came to center on the belief in "free soil" and "free labor." The abolitionists generated some support for their argument that slavery was a moral evil and must be eliminated. Theirs, however, was never the dominant voice of the North. Instead, an increasing number of Northerners, gradually becoming a majority, came to believe that the existence of slavery was dangerous not because of what it did to blacks but because of what it threatened to do to whites. At the heart of American democracy, they believed, was the right of all citizens to own property, to control their own labor, and to have access to opportunities for advancement. The ideal society, in other words, was one of small-scale capitalism, with everyone entitled to a stake and with the chance of upward mobility available to all.

According to this vision, the South was the antithesis of democracy. It was a closed, static society, in which the slave system preserved an entrenched aristocracy and the common whites had no opportunity to improve themselves. More than that, the South was a backward society—decadent, lazy, dilapidated. While the North was growing and prospering, displaying thrift, industry, and a commitment to progress, the South was stagnating, rejecting the Northern values of individualism and growth. The South was, Northern free-laborites further maintained, engaged in a conspiracy to extend slavery throughout the nation and thus to destroy the openness of Northern capitalism and replace it with the closed, aristocratic system of the South. This "slave power conspiracy," as it came to be known, threatened the future of every white laborer and property owner in the North. The only solution was to fight the spread of slavery and work for the day when the nation's democratic (i.e., free-labor) ideals extended to all sections of the country—the day of the victory of what Northerners called "Freedom National."

This was the ideology that lay at the heart of the new Republican party. There were abolitionists and others in the organization who sincerely believed in the rights of blacks to freedom and citizenship. Far more important, however, were those who cared less about the plight of blacks than about the threat that slavery posed to white labor and to individual opportunity. This ideology also strengthened the commitment of Republicans to the Union. Since the idea of continued growth and progress was central to the free-labor vision, the prospect of dismemberment of the nation—a diminution of America's size and economic power—was unthinkable.

The Proslavery Argument

In the South, in the meantime, a very different ideology was emerging—one that was entirely incompatible with the free-labor ideology in the North. It was a set of ideas that emerged out of a rapid hardening of position among Southern whites on the issue of slavery.

As late as the early 1830s, there had been a substantial number of Southern whites who had harbored deep reservations about slavery. Between 1829 and 1832, for example, a Virginia constitutional convention, and then the state legislature, responding to demands from nonslaveholders in the western part of the state, had seriously considered ending slavery through compensated emancipation. They had chosen not to do so in large part because of the tremendous expense it would have entailed. There had been, moreover, many antislavery societies in the South—more there in 1827 than there were in the North, most of them in the border states. And there were prominent Southern politicians who spoke openly in opposition to slavery—among them Cassius M. Clay of Kentucky.

By the mid-1830s, however, this ambivalence about slavery was beginning to be replaced by a militant defense of the system. In part, the change was a result of events within the South itself. The Nat Turner uprising terrified whites throughout the region. They had always been uneasy, always mindful of the horrors of the successful slave uprising in Santo Domingo in the 1790s. Now they were reminded again of their insecurity, and they were especially horrified because there had been long-trusted house servants among Turner's followers who, ax in hand,

had suddenly turned on their masters' sleeping families. Many slaveowners blamed Garrison and the abolitionists for the revolt, and they grew more determined than ever to make slavery secure against all dangers. There was, too, an economic incentive to defend the system. With the expansion of the cotton economy into the Deep South, slavery—which had begun to seem unprofitable in many areas of the original South—now became lucrative once again.

But the change was also a result of events in the North, and particularly of the growth of the abolitionist movement, with its strident attacks on Southern society. Harriet Beecher Stowe's *Uncle Tom's Cabin* was perhaps the most glaring example of such an attack, a book that enraged the South and increased its resentment of the North. But other abolitionist writings had been antagonizing white Southerners for years.

In response to these pressures, a growing number of white Southerners began to elaborate an intellectual defense of slavery. It began as early as 1832, when Professor Thomas R. Dew of the College of William and Mary published a pamphlet outlining the slavery case. In subsequent years, many others added their contributions to the cause; and in 1852, the defense was summed up in an anthology that gave the philosophy its name: *The Pro-Slavery Argument*.

The essence of the argument, as John C. Calhoun boasted in 1837, was that Southerners should cease apologizing for slavery as a necessary evil and defend it as "a good—a positive good." Slavery was, according to such theorists, good for the slaves because they were inferior creatures. They needed the guidance of white masters, and they were better off—better fed, clothed, and housed, and more secure—than Northern factory workers. It was good for Southern society because it was the only way the two races could live together in peace. It was good for the country as a whole because the Southern economy, dependent on slavery, was the key to the prosperity of the nation. And it was good in itself because it was sanctioned by the Bible—did not the Hebrews of the Old Testament own bondsmen, and did not the New Testament apostle Paul advise, "Servants, obey your masters"?

Above all, Southern apologists argued, slavery was good because it served as the basis for the Southern way of life—a way of life superior to any other in the United States, perhaps in the world. White Southerners looking at the North saw a society that they believed was losing touch with tra-

Antiabolitionist Violence
This 1838 woodcut depicts the antiabolitionist riot in Alton, Illinois, in which Elijah P. Lovejoy, publisher of an abolitionist newspaper, was slain on November 7, 1837. The death of Lovejoy aroused the antislavery movement throughout the United States. (Library of Congress)

ditional American values and replacing them with a spirit of greed, debauchery, and destructiveness. "The masses of the North are venal, corrupt, covetous, mean and selfish," wrote one Southerner. Others wrote with horror of the exploitation of the factory system, the growth of crowded, pestilential cities filled with unruly immigrants. The South, in contrast, was a stable, orderly society, operating at a slow and human pace. It had a labor system that avoided the feuds between capital and labor plaguing the North, a system that protected the welfare of its workers, a system that allowed the aristocracy to enjoy a refined and accomplished cultural life. It was, in short, as nearly perfect as any human civilization could become, an ideal social order in which all elements of the population were secure and content. Proslavery theoreticians—and many white Southerners, slaveowners and nonslaveowners alike, who were coming to accept their arguments—were creating a dream world as a defense against the growing criticism from the North. It was, as one historian has described it, an "affirmation of Southern perfection."

Some proslavery propagandists went so far as to argue that slavery was such a good thing that it should be extended to include white workers in the North as well as black laborers in the South. George Fitzhugh of Virginia—in *Sociology for the South, or the Failure of Free Society* (1854), *Cannibals All* (1857), and other writings—claimed that all society lived on forced labor and that in the South masters at least acknowledged responsibility for those whose labor they were exploiting. Slavery, therefore, was the only workable form of socialism—a system that all societies should adopt as the sole cure for class conflict and the other ills of competitive society. (Such arguments fueled the fears of those Northern free-labor advocates who argued that the South was plotting to extend slavery everywhere, even into the factory system.)

By the 1850s, Southern leaders had not only committed themselves to a militant proslavery ideology. They had also become convinced that they should silence advocates of freedom. Southern critics of slavery found it advisable to leave the region, among them Hinton Rowan Helper, whose *Impending Crisis of the South* (1857) contended that slavery hurt the welfare of the nonslaveholder and made the whole region backward. Beginning in 1835 (when a Charleston mob destroyed sacks containing abolitionist literature in the city post office), Southern postmasters generally refused to deliver antislavery mail. Southern state legislatures passed resolutions demanding that Northern states suppress the "incendiary" agitation of the abolitionists. Southern representatives even managed for a time to force Congress to honor a "gag rule" (adopted in 1836), according to which all antislavery petitions would be tabled without being read. Only the spirited protests of such Northerners as John Quincy Adams led to the repeal of the gag rule in 1844. Southern defenders of slavery, in other words, were not only becoming more militant about its virtues; they were becoming less tolerant of criticism of it—further encouraging those Northerners who warned of the "slave power conspiracy" against their liberties.

Buchanan and Depression

It was in this unpromising climate—with the country convulsed by the Brooks assault and the continuing violence in Kansas, and with each section becoming increasingly militant in support of its own ideology— that the presidential campaign of 1856 began. The Democrats adopted a platform that endorsed the Kansas-Nebraska Act and defended popular sovereignty. The leaders wanted a candidate who had not made many enemies and who was not closely associated with the explosive question of "Bleeding Kansas." So the nomination went to James Buchanan of Pennsylvania, a reliable party stalwart who as minister to England had been safely out of the country during the recent troubles, although he was a signer of the highly controversial Ostend Manifesto.

The Republicans, engaging in their first presidential contest, faced the campaign with confidence. They denounced the Kansas-Nebraska Act and the expansion of slavery but also approved a program of internal improvements, thus combining the idealism of antislavery with the economic aspirations of the North. Just as eager as the Democrats to present a safe candidate, the Republicans nominated John C. Frémont, who had made a national reputation as an explorer of the Far West and who had no political record.

The Native American, or Know-Nothing, party was beginning to break apart on the inevitable rock of sectionalism. At its convention, many Northern delegates withdrew because the platform was not sufficiently firm in opposing the expansion of slavery. The remaining delegates nominated former president Millard Fillmore. His candidacy was endorsed by the sad remnant of another party, the few remaining Whigs who could not bring themselves to support either Buchanan or Frémont.

The campaign was the most frenzied since the tempestuous election of 1840. It generated excitement largely as a result of the fervor of the Republicans, who shouted for "Free Soil, Free Speech, Free Men, and Frémont"; who depicted "Bleeding Kansas" as a sacrifice to the evil ambitions of the slavocracy; and who charged that the South, using Northern dupes such as Buchanan as its tools, was plotting to extend slavery into every part of the country.

The returns suggested that the prevailing mood of the country was still relatively conservative but that opinion was relatively narrowly divided. Buchanan, the winning candidate, polled 1,833,000 popular votes to 1,340,000 for Frémont and 872,000 for Fillmore. A slight shift of votes in Pennsylvania and Illinois, however, would have thrown those states into the Republican column and elected Frémont. More significant, perhaps, was that Frémont, who attracted virtually no votes at all in the South, nevertheless received a third of all votes cast. In the North, he had outpolled all other candidates.

The election of Buchanan was a disaster for the nation. He had been in public life for more than forty years at the time of his inauguration, and he was at age sixty-five the oldest president, except for William Henry Harrison, ever to have taken office. Whether because of his age and physical infirmities or because of a more fundamental weakness of character, he became a painfully timid and indecisive president in a time when the nation cried out as perhaps never before for strong, effective leadership.

In the year Buchanan took over, a financial panic struck the country, followed by several years of stringent depression. Europe had shown an unusual demand for American food during the Crimean War of 1854–1856. When that demand fell off, agricultural prices declined. The depression sharpened sectional differences. The South was not hit as hard as the North (since the region depended less on food crops), and Southern leaders thus found what they believed was confirmation for their claim that their economic system was superior to that of the free states. Smarting under previous Northern criticisms of Southern society, they loudly boasted of their superiority to the North.

In the North, the depression strengthened the Republican party. Distressed economic groups— manufacturers and farmers—came to believe that the hard times were the result of the unsound policies of Southern-controlled Democratic administrations. These groups thought that prosperity could be restored by a high tariff (the tariff had been lowered again in 1857), a homestead act, and internal improvements—all measures the South opposed. In short, the frustrated economic interests of the North were being drawn into an alliance with the antislavery elements and thus into the Republican party.

The Dred Scott Decision

The Supreme Court of the United States now projected itself into the sectional controversy with one of the most controversial decisions in its history—its ruling in the case of *Dred Scott* v. *Sanford,* handed down two days after Buchanan was inaugurated.

Dred Scott was a Missouri slave, once the property of an army surgeon who on military pilgrimages had carried Scott to Illinois, a free state, and to the Wisconsin Territory, where slavery was forbidden by the Missouri Compromise. Scott was persuaded by some abolitionists to bring suit in the Missouri courts for his freedom on the ground that residence in a free territory had made him a free man. The state supreme court decided against him. Meanwhile, the surgeon had died and his widow had married an abolitionist; and ownership of Scott had been transferred to her brother, J. F. A. Sanford, who lived in New York. Now Scott's lawyers could get the case into the federal courts on the ground that the suit lay between citizens of different states. Regardless of the final decision, Scott would be freed; his abolitionist owners would not keep him a slave. The case was intended less to determine Scott's future than to secure a federal decision on the status of slavery in the territories.

Of the nine justices of the Supreme Court, seven were Democrats (five of them from the South), one was a Whig, and one was a Republican. The Court was so divided that it was unable to issue a single ruling on the case and issued separate decisions on each of the major issues it raised. Each of the justices, moreover, wrote a separate opinion. The thrust of the rulings, however, was a defeat for Dred Scott and an affirmation of the South's argument that the Constitution guaranteed the existence of slavery. Chief Justice Roger Taney, who wrote one of the majority opinions, declared that Scott was not a citizen of Missouri or of the United States and hence could not bring a suit in the federal courts. According to Taney, no black could qualify as a citizen. So far as the Constitution was concerned, he added, blacks had no rights that white men were bound to respect. Having said this, Taney could simply have declined jurisdiction over the case. Instead, he went on to argue that Scott's sojourn in the North had not affected his status as a slave. Slaves were property, said Taney, and the Fifth Amendment prohibited Congress from taking property without "due process of law." Consequently, Congress possessed no authority to pass a law depriving persons of their slave property in the territories. The Missouri Compromise, therefore, had always been null and void.

The ruling did nothing to challenge the right of an individual state to prohibit slavery within its borders, but the statement that the federal government was powerless to act on the issue was a drastic and startling one. Few judicial opinions have stirred as much popular excitement. Southern whites were elated: The highest tribunal in the land had sanctioned the extreme Southern argument. On behalf of abolitionists, black and white, Frederick Douglass declared: "This very attempt to blot out forever the hopes of an enslaved people may be one necessary link in the chain of events preparatory to the complete overthrow of the whole slave system." Republicans claimed that the decision deserved as much consideration as any pronouncement by a group of political hacks "in any Washington bar room." They threatened that when they secured control of the national government, they would reverse the decision—by altering the personnel of the Court and "packing" it with new members.

Deadlock over Kansas

President Buchanan endorsed the decision and concluded that the best solution for the troubles over Kansas was to force the admission of that territory as a slave state. The existing proslavery territorial legislature called an election for delegates to a constitutional convention. The free-state residents refused to participate. As a result, the proslavery forces won control of the convention, which met in 1857 at Lecompton and framed a constitution establishing slavery. When an election for a new territorial legislature was called, the antislavery groups turned out to vote and won a majority. Promptly the legislature moved to submit the Lecompton constitution to the voters. The document was rejected by more than 10,000 votes.

Although both sides had resorted to fraud and violence, the Kansas picture was clear enough. The majority of the people in the territory did not want to see slavery established. Buchanan, however, ignored the evidence. He urged Congress to admit Kansas under the Lecompton constitution, and he tried to force the party to back his proposal. Stephen A. Douglas and other Western Democrats refused to accept this perversion of popular sovereignty. Openly breaking with the administration, Douglas denounced the Lecompton proposition. And although Buchanan's plan passed the Senate, Western Democrats helped to block it in the House. Partly to avert further division in the party, a compromise measure, the English bill (proposed by Indiana Democrat William English) won approval from Congress in

April 1858. It provided that the Lecompton constitution should be submitted to the people of Kansas for a third time. If the document was approved, Kansas was to be admitted and given a federal land grant; if it was disapproved, statehood would be postponed until the population reached 93,600, the legal ratio for a representative in Congress. Again, and for the last time, the Kansas voters decisively rejected the Lecompton constitution. Not until the closing months of Buchanan's administration in 1861, when a number of Southern states had withdrawn from the Union, would Kansas enter the Union—as a free state.

The Emergence of Lincoln

The congressional elections of 1858 were of greater interest and importance than most nonpresidential contests. Not only did they have an immediate and powerful influence on the course of the sectional controversy, but they projected into the national spotlight the man who was to be the dominating figure in the tragic years just ahead.

The senatorial election in Illinois attracted attention throughout the nation. Stephen A. Douglas, the most prominent Northern Democrat, was a candidate for reelection; and he was fighting for his political life. Since Douglas, or his successor, would be chosen by a legislature that was yet to be elected, the control of that body became a matter of paramount importance. To punish Douglas for his resistance to the Lecompton constitution, the Buchanan administration entered Democratic candidates opposed to him in many legislative districts. But Douglas's greatest worry was that he faced Abraham Lincoln, the ablest campaigner in the Republican party.

Lincoln had been the leading Whig in Illinois. He was now the leading Republican in the state, although hardly a national figure. His reputation still could not compare with that of the famous Douglas. Lincoln challenged the senator to a series of seven debates. Douglas accepted, and the two candidates argued their cases before huge crowds. The Lincoln-Douglas debates were widely reported by the nation's press, and before their termination the Republican who had dared to challenge the "Little Giant of Democracy" was a man of national prominence.

Douglas, in the course of defending popular sovereignty, accused the Republicans of promoting a war of sections, of wishing to interfere with slavery in the South, and of advocating social equality of the races. Lincoln denied these charges (properly, since neither he nor his party had ever advocated any of these things). He, in turn, accused the Democrats and Douglas of conspiring to extend slavery into the territories and possibly, by means of another Supreme Court decision, into the free states as well (a charge that was equally unfounded). Lincoln was particularly effective in making it appear that Douglas did not regard slavery as morally wrong. He quoted Douglas as saying he did not care whether slavery was "voted up, or voted down."

Lincoln was opposed to slavery—on moral, political, and economic grounds. He believed that it contradicted the American ideal of democracy. Let the idea be established that blacks were not created with an equal right to earn their bread, he said, and the next step would be to deny the right to certain groups of whites, such as immigrant laborers. His solicitude for the economic well-being of the white masses—his commitment to the ideology of free labor—helped to impel Lincoln to oppose the introduction of slavery into the territories. He maintained that the national lands should be preserved as places for poor white people to go to better their condition.

Lincoln was not an abolitionist. He opposed slavery, to be sure, but he had great difficulty envisioning an alternative to it in the areas where it already existed. He shared, moreover, the prevailing view among Northern whites that the black race was not prepared (and perhaps never would be) to live on equal terms with whites. He expressed interest at times in the colonization movement—the effort to "return" blacks to Africa. But he seemed to realize that this would never be a viable solution to the problem. "We have," he once said, "a due regard to the actual presence of [slavery] amongst us and the difficulties of getting rid of it in any satisfactory way and all the constitutional obligations thrown about it." He and his party would "arrest the further spread of it," that is, prevent its expansion into the territories; he would not directly challenge it where it already existed.

Yet the implications of Lincoln's argument were more sweeping than this relatively moderate formula suggests, for both he and other Republicans believed that by restricting slavery to the South, they would be consigning slavery to its "ultimate extinction." As he said in the most famous speech of the campaign:

A house divided against itself cannot stand. I believe this government cannot endure permanently half slave and half free. I do not expect the Union to be dissolved—I do not expect the house to fall—but I do expect it will cease to be divided. It will become all one thing, or all the other.

In the debate at Freeport, Lincoln asked Douglas: Can the people of a territory exclude slavery from its limits prior to the formation of a state constitution? Or in other words, is popular sovereignty still a legal formula despite the *Dred Scott* decision? The question was a deadly trap, for no matter how Douglas answered it, he would lose something. If he disavowed popular sovereignty, he would undoubtedly be defeated for reelection and his political career would be ended. But if he reaffirmed his formula, Southern Democrats would be offended, the party split deepened, and his chances of securing the Democratic nomination in 1860 damaged if not destroyed.

Douglas met the issue boldly. The people of a territory, he said, could, by lawful means, shut out slavery prior to the formation of a state constitution. Slavery could not exist a day without the support of "local police regulations": territorial laws recognizing the right of slave ownership. The mere failure of a legislature to enact such laws would have the practical effect of keeping slaveholders out. Thus despite the *Dred Scott* decision, a territory could exclude slavery. Douglas's reply became known as the Freeport Doctrine or, in the South, as the Freeport Heresy. It satisfied his followers sufficiently to win him reelection to the Senate, but throughout the North it aroused little enthusiasm.

Elsewhere, the elections went heavily against the Democrats, who lost ground in almost every Northern state. The administration retained control of the Senate but lost its majority in the House, where the Republicans gained a plurality. In the congressional sessions of 1858 and 1859, every demand of the Republicans and Northern Democrats was blocked by Southern votes or by presidential vetoes. The defeated measures included a tariff increase, a homestead bill, a Pacific railroad, and federal land grants to states for the endowment of agricultural colleges. The 1859 session was also marked by an uproarious struggle over the election of a Speaker of the House.

The controversies in Congress, however, were almost entirely overshadowed by another event in the fall of 1859: an event that enraged and horrified the entire South and greatly hastened the rush toward disunion.

John Brown's Raid

John Brown, the antislavery zealot whose bloody actions in Kansas had done so much to inflame the crisis there, made an even greater contribution to sectional conflict through a grim and spectacular episode that had major national implications. Still convinced that he was God's instrument to destroy slavery, he decided to transfer his activities from Kansas to the South itself. With encouragement and financial aid from some Eastern abolitionists, he made plans to seize a mountain fortress in Virginia from which he could make raids to liberate slaves. He would arm the freedmen, set up a black republic, and eventually force the South to concede emancipation. Because he needed guns, he chose Harpers Ferry, where a United States arsenal was located, as his base of operations. In October, at the head of eighteen followers, he descended on the town and captured the arsenal. Almost immediately he was attacked by citizens and

John Brown

Even in this formal photographic portrait (taken in 1859, the last year of his life), John Brown conveys the fierce sense of righteousness that fueled his extraordinary activities in the fight against slavery. (Library of Congress)

local militia companies, who were shortly reinforced by a detachment of U.S. Marines sent to the scene by the national government. With ten of his men killed, Brown had to surrender. He was promptly tried in a Virginia court for treason against the state, found guilty, and sentenced to death by hanging. Six of his followers met a similar fate.

Probably no other event had so much influence as the Harpers Ferry raid in convincing Southerners that their section was unsafe in the Union. Despite all their praise of slavery, one great fear always secretly gnawed at their hearts: the possibility of a general slave insurrection. Southerners now jumped to the conclusion that the Republicans were responsible for Brown's raid. This was, of course, untrue; prominent Republicans such as Lincoln and Seward condemned Brown as a criminal. But Southerners were more impressed by the words of such abolitionists as Wendell Phillips and Ralph Waldo Emerson, who now glorified Brown as a new saint. His execution made him a martyr to thousands of Northerners.

The Election of Lincoln

The election of 1860, judged by its consequences, was the most momentous in American history.

The Democrats gathered in convention in April at Charleston, South Carolina; and most of the Southern delegates arrived determined to adopt a platform providing for federal protection of slavery in the territories—that is, an official endorsement of the principles of the *Dred Scott* decision. The Western Democrats, arriving with bitter memories of how Southern influence had blocked their legislative demands in the recent Congress, resented the rule-or-ruin attitude of the Southerners. The Westerners hoped, however, to negotiate a face-saving statement on slavery so as to hold the party together. They vaguely endorsed popular sovereignty and proposed that all questions involving slavery in the territories be left up to the Supreme Court. By now, however, passions in the South had risen to a point where compromise was no longer possible. When the convention adopted the Western platform, the delegations from eight states of the lower South withdrew from the hall. The remaining delegates then proceeded to the selection of a candidate. Stephen A. Douglas led on every ballot, but he could not muster the two-thirds majority (of the original number of delegates) required by party rules. Finally the managers adjourned

the convention to meet again in Baltimore in June. At the Baltimore session, most of the Southerners reappeared, only to walk out again. Other Southerners, meanwhile, had assembled at Richmond. The decimated convention at Baltimore nominated Douglas. The Southern bolters at Baltimore joined the Democrats in Richmond to nominate John C. Breckinridge of Kentucky. Sectionalism had at last splintered the Democratic party.

The Republicans held their convention in Chicago in May. Although the divisions developing in the Democratic ranks seemed to spell a Republican triumph, the party managers took no chances. They were determined that the party, in both its platform and its candidate, should appear to the voters to represent conservatism, stability, and moderation rather than radical idealism. No longer was the Republican party a one-idea organization composed of crusaders against slavery. It now attempted to embrace every major interest group in the North that believed the South, the champion of slavery, was blocking its legitimate economic aspirations.

The platform endorsed such measures as a high tariff, internal improvements, a homestead bill, and a Pacific railroad to be built with federal financial assistance. On the slavery issue, the platform affirmed

Election of 1860 (81.2% of electorate voting)

	ELECTORAL VOTE	POPULAR VOTE (%)
Abraham Lincoln (Republican)	180	1,865,593 (39.8)
J. C. Breckinridge (Southern Democratic)	72	848,356 (18.1)
John Bell (Constitutional Union)	39	592,906 (12.6)
Stephen A. Douglas (Northern Democratic)	12	1,382,713 (29.5)

SIGNIFICANT EVENTS

the right of each state to control its own institutions. The Republicans were saying, in other words, that they did not intend to interfere with slavery in the South. But they also claimed that neither Congress nor territorial legislatures could legalize slavery in the territories. They would, in short, still oppose the expansion of slavery.

The leading contender for the nomination was Senator William H. Seward of New York, who faced competition from a number of favorite-son candidates. But Seward's prominence and his long, controversial political record damaged his chances. Passing him and other aspirants over, the convention nominated on the third ballot Abraham Lincoln, who was prominent enough to be respectable but obscure enough to have few foes, radical enough to please the antislavery faction in the party but conservative enough to satisfy the ex-Whigs. The vice-presidential nomination went to Hannibal Hamlin of Maine, a former Democrat.

As if three parties were not enough, a fourth entered the lists—the Constitutional Union party. Although posing as a new organization, it was really the last surviving remnant of the oldest conservative tradition in the country; its leaders were elder statesmen, and most of its members were former Whigs. Meeting in Baltimore in May, this party nominated John Bell of Tennessee and Edward Everett of Massachusetts. Its platform favored the Constitution, the Union, and enforcement of the laws; it avoided taking a clear stand on the issue of slavery.

In the North, the Republicans conducted a campaign reminiscent of the exciting Harrison-Van Buren contest of 1840, with parades, symbols, and mass meetings. For the most part, they stressed the economic promises in their platform and subordinated the slavery issue. Lincoln, following the customary practice of presidential candidates, made no speeches. Lesser party luminaries addressed rallies and party meetings. Unlike previous candidates, Lincoln refused to issue any written statements of his views, claiming that anything he said would be seized on by Southerners and misrepresented. In the November election, Lincoln won a majority of the electoral votes and the presidency, but only about two-fifths of the popular votes. The Republicans had elected a president, but they had failed to secure a majority in Congress; and of course they did not control the Supreme Court.

Nevertheless, the election of Lincoln served as the final signal to many Southerners that their position in the Union was hopeless. Throughout the campaign, various Southern leaders had warned that if the Republicans should win, they would secede from the Union. Within a few weeks of Lincoln's victory, this process of disunion began—a process that would quickly lead to a prolonged and bloody war between two groups of Americans, both heirs of more than a century of struggling toward nationhood, each now convinced that it shared no common ground with the other.

SUGGESTED READINGS

Westward Expansion. Ray Allen Billington, *Westward Expansion*, rev. ed. (1974) and *The Far Western Frontier, 1830–1860* (1956); John D. Unruh, *The Plains Across: The Overland Emigrants and the Trans-Mississippi West, 1840–1860* (1979); John M. Faragher, *Women and Men on the Overland Trail* (1979); Frederick Merk, *History of the Westward Movement* (1978), *Manifest Destiny and Mission in American History* (1963), *Fruits of Propaganda in the Tyler Administration* (1971), *Slavery and the Annexation of Texas* (1972), *The Oregon Question* (1967), and *The Monroe Doctrine and American Expansionism, 1843–1849* (1966); Albert K. Weinberg, *Manifest Destiny* (1935); William H. Goetzmann, *Exploration and Empire* (1966); Henry Nash Smith, *Virgin Land* (1950); Norman A. Graebner, *Empire of the Pacific* (1955); E. C. Barker, *Mexico and Texas, 1821–1835* (1928); William C. Binkley, *The Texas Revolution* (1952); Francis Parkman, *The Oregon Trail* (1849); R. L. Duffus, *The Santa Fe Trail* (1930); R. G. Cleland, *From Wilderness to Empire: A History of California, 1542–1900* (1944); R. W. Paul, *California Gold* (1947); J. S. Holliday, *Thbe World Rushed In* (1981); O. O. Winther, *The Great Northwest*, rev. ed. (1950).

Expansion and the Mexican War. David J. Weber, *The Mexican Frontier, 1821–1846: The American Southwest under Mexico* (1982); Charles G. Sellers, *James K. Polk: Continentalist, 1843–1846* (1966); J. S. Reeves, *American Diplomacy Under Tyler and Polk* (1907); David M. Pletcher, *The Diplomacy of Annexation: Texas, Oregon, and the Mexican War* (1973); G. M. Brack, *Mexico Views Manifest Destiny, 1821–1846* (1975); K. Jack Bauer, *The Mexican-American War, 1846–1848* (1974); John H. Schroeder, *Mr. Polk's War: American Opposition and Dissent* (1973); Otis A. Singletary, *The Mexican War* (1960); S. V. Conner and O. B. Faulk, *North America Divided* (1971); Holman Hamilton, *Zachary Taylor, Soldier of the Republic* (1941); C. W. Elliott, *Winfield Scott* (1937); Samuel F. Bemis (ed.), *American Secretaries of State*, vols. 5 and 6 (1928); Basil Rauch, *American Interest in Cuba, 1848–1855* (1948); Robert E. May, *The Southern Dream of a Caribbean Empire, 1854–1861* (1973); Robert W Johnson, *To the Halls of Montezuma: The Mexican War in the American Imagination* (1985).

The Sectional Crisis: General Studies. Allan Nevins, *The Ordeal of the Union*, 2 vols. (1947) and *The Emergence of Lincoln*, 2 vols. (1950); Michael Holt, *The Political Crisis of the 1850s* (1978); Roy F. Nichols, *The Disruption of American Democracy* (1948); Avery Craven, *The Coming of the Civil War* (1942); David Potter, *The Impending Crisis, 1848–1861* (1976); William J. Cooper, *The South and the Politics of Slavery, 1828–1856* (1978) and *Liberty and Slavery* (1983); James G. Randall and David Donald, *The Civil War and Reconstruction*, rev. ed. (1969); Richard H. Sewell, *A House Divided: Sectionalism and the Civil War, 1848–1865* (1988); James M. McPherson, *Ordeal by Fire* (1981) and *Battle Cry of Freedom* (1988).

The Compromise of 1850. Holman Hamilton, *Prologue to Conflict: The Crisis and Compromise of 1850* (1964); Chaplain W. Morrison, *Democratic Politics and Sectionalism: The Wilmot Proviso Controversy* (1973); Kinley J. Bauer, *Cotton Versus Conscience: Massachusetts Whig Politics and Southern Expansion, 1843–1858* (1967); Robert W. Johannsen, *Stephen A. Douglas* (1973); Charles M. Wiltse, *John C. Calhoun: Sectionalist, 1840–1850* (1951); Holman Hamilton, *Zachary Taylor: Soldier in the White House* (1951); Richard N. Current, *Daniel Webster and the Rise of National Conservatism* (1955); Robert F. Dalzell, Jr., *Daniel Webster and the Trial of American Nationalism, 1843–1852* (1973).

Sectional Crises in the 1850s. Gerald Wolff, *The Kansas-Nebraska Bill* (1977); James C. Malin, *The Nebraska Question* (1953); Paul W. Gates, *Fifty Million Acres: Conflict over Kansas Land Policy, 1854–1890* (1954); Stephen Oates, *To Purge This Land with Blood: A Biography of John Brown* (1970); R. O. Boyer, *The Legend of John Brown* (1973); Truman Nelson, *The Old Man: John Brown at Harpers Ferry* (1973); J. C. Furnas, *The Road to Harpers Ferry* (1959); Benjamin Quarles, *Allies for Freedom* (1974); Eric Foner, *Free Soil, Free Labor, Free Men* (1970), and *Politics and Ideology in the Age of the Civil War* (1980); William E. Gienapp, *The Origins of the Republican Party, 1852–1856* (1987); David Donald, *Charles Sumner and the Coming of the Civil War* (1960); Dale Baum, *The Civil War Party System: The Case of Massachusetts, 1848–1876* (1984); William Jenkins, *Pro-Slavery Thought in the Old South* (1935); Harvey Wish, *George Fitzhugh: Propagandist of the Old South* (1943); Don E. Fehrenbacher, *The Dred Scott Case* (1978).

The Emergence of Lincoln. Richard N. Current, *The Lincoln Nobody Knows* (1958); David Donald, *Lincoln Reconsidered* (1956); Don E. Fehrenbacher, *Prelude to Greatness: Lincoln in the 1850's* (1962); George B. Forgie, *Patricide in the House Divided* (1979).

The Flow of Water

No element of the North American landscape was more basic to the development of the young republic than water. The earliest settlements on the Eastern seaboard were all at the ocean's edge, where they had ready access to transatlantic trade. Each major city in the new nation—Boston, New York, Philadelphia, Baltimore, Charleston, New Orleans—began life as a port. The interior trade of the continent concentrated almost entirely along natural watercourses. Water was the catalyst that made trade and settlement possible.

It is thus not surprising that some of the earliest large-scale manipulations of the American landscape had to do with redirecting the flow of water. Until the 1820s, most crops raised west of theAppalachians traveled to market by floating downstream toward New Orleans, whether on the Ohio, the Mississippi, or the Missouri River. The great wave of canal building that swept the nation in the 1820s and 1830s was designed to divert that southward flow of commerce north toward the Great Lakes and east to the port towns on the Atlantic coast. The most dramatic success was of course the Erie Canal, which enabled New York City to capture the trade of the Great Lakes and Ohio Valley. The emergence of New York as the greatest metropolis on the continent occurred at the same time that settlement exploded on the shores of the Great Lakes, and both were encouraged by the canal. The canal also contributed to the decline of agriculture in New England, as farmers on marginal land found themselves unable to compete with abundant grain crops from the Western prairies.

In addition to rearranging the American agricultural landscape, canals had unexpected ecological consequences. The Erie Canal introduced to Lake Ontario the sea lamprey, a parasitic fish that attaches itself to other fish and weakens or kills them by sucking their blood. It had never before inhabited the Great Lakes, but it now began to put pressure on the lake's native whitefish, trout, and salmon. A complex redistribution of the lake's fish population was the long-term result, with many species declining and even disappearing. When Canada's Welland Canal finally opened water access around Niagara Falls, the lamprey moved into the upper Great Lakes, and the same story repeated itself there.

If canals created an artificial system of waterways, dams created an equally

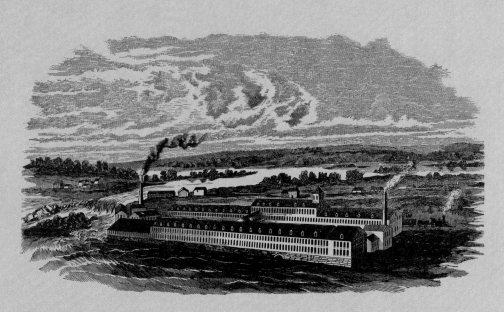

Water-Powered Factory on the Green River, Massachusetts
American factories in the early nineteenth century depended much more on water than on steam. They were typically located near major falls or rapids on large rivers, so that canals could divert water through wheels and turbines beneath the factory, supplying power to the machinery within. (The Bettmann Archive)

artificial system of power that altered traditional ways of consuming energy in the American economy. The industrial revolution came to the United States not with the steam engine but with the water wheel. Falling water had been used since earliest colonial times to grind flour and saw lumber, so that mills were some of the earliest town sites in the interior countryside. But large-scale exploitation of water power did not occur until New England capitalists used British technology to mechanize the production of textiles. The best known of the New England textile towns is probably Lowell, Massachusetts, which is justly renowned in American history for the new labor system it introduced in its factories. But Lowell's success would have been impossible had the city not harnessed the potential energy of the Merrimack River to drive its factories.

The implications of this new use of water were dramatic. Formerly, the energy that had driven the American economy had been biologically limited by the strength of horses and human workers. Now, an even larger share of that energy came from inanimate sources, first rivers, and later coal-powered steam. Power could be concentrated into an ever-expanding network of tools and machines, with dramatic implications for technological change and industrial productivity. At the same time, the natural flow of rivers was brought under human control, with disastrous results for certain fish species, like the salmon, which had formerly swum upstream to spawn. As dams blocked major rivers of the East Coast, salmon disappeared from most of their former homes.

The typical industrial town of the water-power era had certain features that are evident even today. It was always located beside a natural waterfall or rapids where a river dropped quickly from a higher to a lower elevation. A dam upstream from the town diverted water into a complicated network of canals and underground conduits. These delivered it to the factories, which straddled the natural drop in elevation. As the water flowed beneath the buildings, it turned large waterwheels and turbines. Long leather belts transmitted the resulting energy to driveshafts running the length of the factory. Unlike modern factories, which have horizontal

The Great New York Fire of December 16, 1835
One of the most devastating fires in New York City's history destroyed hundreds of buildings on December 16, 1835. Without an effective municipal water supply, firefighters had to bring water to the scene in tank carts and hand-pump it onto the flames. The fire encouraged New York citizens to support construction of the Croton Aqueduct. (The Bettmann Archive)

The Croton Aqueduct Brings Water to New York City, 1842
When the Croton Aqueduct was completed, bringing water from the upper Hudson Valley to the southern tip of Manhattan, the residents of New York City staged an immense celebration. A new fountain was built in honor of the event, and the aqueduct continues to supply the city with water today. (The Research Library, The New York Public Library)

one-story layouts because they use smaller and more flexible electric motors, waterpower factories had vertical plans, rising several stories to prevent friction from dissipating the power in their driveshafts. Energy was transmitted from the central shafts to individual machines by hundreds of long leather belts spinning at high speeds. There were no guards to protect workers from these exposed belts, and so injuries—lost fingers, broken bones, amputated limbs, and even deaths—were an almost daily occurrence.

Water-power towns lived and died with water. In winter, when rivers froze with ice, factories sometimes had to shut down for lack of power. (The same was true of canals: The canal economy regularly went into hibernation during the winter months, with trade coming nearly to a standstill between December and April.) Worse, water-power towns were regularly subject to flooding during storms and spring runoffs, and could suffer devastating destruction from the very source that ordinarily sustained them. This was one reason that the housing in such towns was often arranged so that the workers lived nearest the factories, in flimsy structures erected on the floodplain, while managers and owners lived on the hillsides in more expensive houses that were less exposed to flooding.

The final elements of the new water landscape of nineteenth-century America were in the cities. Although rarely located at water-power sites like the factory towns, the great port cities of the East Coast were no less eager to manipulate the water around them. To increase their supply of drinking water and to protect themselves from frequent fires, they constructed great reservoir systems like New York's Croton Aqueduct, completed in 1842, which brought water from dozens of miles away. A little later, they introduced sewers to dispose of dangerous urban wastes downstream from drinking supplies. As a result, the water-borne epidemics of cholera that had devastated the United States in 1832, 1849, and 1866 had nearly vanished by the end of the century.

Ports, canals, dams, factories, reservoirs, sewers: These are today such familiar features of the American landscape that we scarcely even notice them. At the time they were constructed, however, they constituted a revolution in the way Americans traveled, worked, drank, bathed, and protected themselves from disease. Controlling the flow of water was among the greatest environmental and technological changes of the nineteenth century.

Watching the Bombardment of Fort Sumter, Charleston, April 1861
This contemporary engraving shows residents of Charleston, most of them women, watching with
obvious distress as Confederate forces bombard the Union citadel, Fort Sumter. The shelling marked
the beginning of the Civil War. (*The Granger Collection*)

CHAPTER 14

⧄⧄⧄

The Civil War

⧄⧄⧄

By the end of 1860, the cords that had once bound the Union together appeared to have snapped. The almost mystical veneration of the Constitution and its framers was no longer working to unite the nation; residents of the North and South—particularly after the controversial *Dred Scott* decision— now differed fundamentally over what the Constitution said and what the framers had meant. The romantic vision of America's great national destiny had ceased to be a unifying force; the two sections now defined that destiny in different and apparently irreconcilable terms. The stable two-party system could not dampen sectional conflict any longer; that system had collapsed in the 1850s, to be replaced by a new one that accentuated rather than muted regional controversy. Above all, the federal government was no longer the remote, unthreatening presence it once had been; the need to resolve the status of the territories had made it necessary for Washington to deal with sectional issues in a direct and forceful way. And thus, beginning in 1860, the divisive forces that had always existed within the United States were no longer counterbalanced by unifying forces. As a result, the Union began to dissolve.

To the South, the war that resulted from that dissolution was a legitimate struggle for independence, a conflict no less glorious than the American Revolution of nine decades before. Ultimately, they would call it the "War Between the States," as if to imply that it had reflected a constitutional exercise of states' rights. To the North, however, the conflict was nothing more than a criminal insurrection— illegal, unjustifiable, even treasonous. And the Union government, therefore, assigned to the struggle an official name that attributed far less dignity to the Southern cause: the "War of the Rebellion."

Despite the differences in outlook between the sections, however, both sides encountered very similar experiences. Both were forced to mobilize a high proportion of their resources for victory; both were required to confront problems of production and organization never before encountered in a modern society; and by the end, both found themselves fighting a war that had resulted from supposedly fundamental regional differences in markedly similar ways.

The Secession Crisis

Almost as soon as the news of Abraham Lincoln's election reached the South, the militant leaders of the region—the champions of the new concept of Southern "nationalism," men known both to their contemporaries and to history as the "fire-eaters"— began to demand an end to the Union. The Southern states, they argued, should withdraw from the federal system and form a new nation of their own; and their vehicle should be a device that had, they claimed, firm legal grounding in the Constitution: secession.

411

The Process of Secession

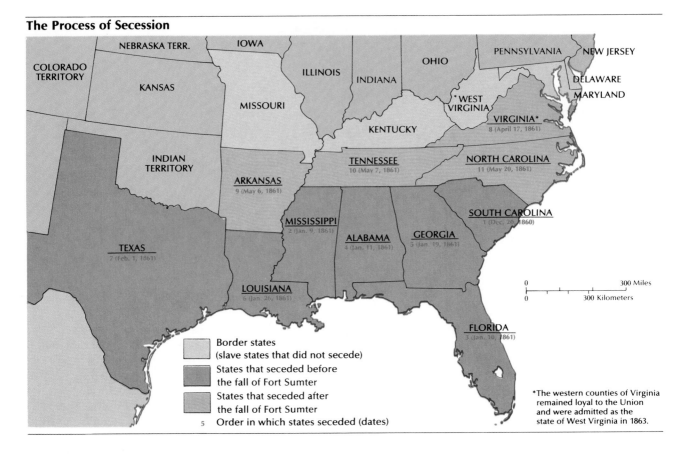

Border states
(slave states that did not secede)

States that seceded before
the fall of Fort Sumter

States that seceded after
the fall of Fort Sumter

5 Order in which states seceded (dates)

*The western counties of Virginia
remained loyal to the Union
and were admitted as the
state of West Virginia in 1863.

The Withdrawal of the South

The concept of secession was rooted in the political
philosophy the South had developed over the course
of several decades to protect its minority status in the
nation. According to this doctrine, the Union was an
association of sovereign states. The individual states
had once joined the Union; they could, whenever
they wished, dissolve their connections with it and
resume their status as separate sovereignties. It was a
momentous act to leave the Union, supporters of
secession believed. But it was a lawful act.

The Constitution did not, of course, specify a
method by which a state could secede; but most of
the Southern states came to agree that the proper
course was to follow the same procedures they had
used when they originally ratified the federal Constitution. The governor would call an election for delegates to a special state convention, which could then
pass an ordinance of secession. South Carolina, long

the hotbed of Southern separatism, was the first to do
so. Its convention took the state out of the Union on
December 20, 1860, by a unanimous vote. Even before Lincoln assumed the presidency, six other Southern states—Mississippi (January 9, 1861), Florida
(January 10), Alabama (January 11), Georgia (January
19), Louisiana (January 26), and Texas (February 1)—
had left the Union. In February 1861, representatives
of the seven seceded states met at Montgomery, Alabama, and formed a new, Southern nation—the
Confederate States of America.

Many Northerners reacted at first with confusion and indecision, no one more so than President
James Buchanan. In a message to Congress in December 1860, Buchanan declared that no state had the
right to secede from the Union. At the same time,
he questioned whether the federal government had
the authority to force a state back into the Union.
Buchanan's real goal at this point, however, was not
to resolve these difficult questions. He simply wanted

to avoid an open conflict and to maintain the symbolic authority of the national government until his successor could take office.

Among the first acts of the seceding states was to take possession of federal property—forts, arsenals, offices—within their boundaries. But they did not at first have sufficient military power to seize two important offshore forts: Fort Sumter, on an island in the harbor of Charleston, South Carolina, garrisoned by a small force under Major Robert Anderson; and Fort Pickens in the harbor of Pensacola, Florida. South Carolina sent commissioners to Washington to ask for the surrender of Sumter; but Buchanan, fearful though he was of provoking a clash, refused to yield the fort. In January 1861, he decided to reinforce it. He ordered an unarmed merchant ship, the *Star of the West,* to proceed to Fort Sumter with additional troops and supplies. When the vessel attempted to enter the harbor, it encountered fire from Confederate guns on shore and turned back. The first shots between the North and the South had been fired. Even so, neither section was ready to admit that a war had begun. And in Washington, attention turned once more to efforts to resolve the controversy through compromise.

The Failure of Compromise

As the situation in South Carolina deteriorated, President Buchanan urged Congress to try again to find a peaceful solution to the crisis. The Senate and the House appointed committees to study various plans of adjustment; and gradually—in the Senate at least—attention began to center on a proposal submitted by Senator John J. Crittenden of Kentucky. The Crittenden Compromise, as it was known, called for a series of constitutional amendments. One would have guaranteed the permanence of slavery in the states; others were designed to satisfy Southern demands on such matters as fugitive slaves and slavery in the District of Columbia. But the heart of Crittenden's plan dealt with slavery in the territories. He proposed to reestablish the Missouri Compromise line of 36°30' in all the territory that the United States then held or thereafter acquired. Slavery was to be prohibited north of the line and permitted south of it. Southern members of a Senate committee appointed to draft the compromise indicated they would accept this territorial division if the Republicans would. The

Republicans, after conferring with President-elect Lincoln in Illinois, voted against the proposal. Lincoln maintained that the restoration of the Missouri Compromise line would encourage the South to embark on imperialist adventures in Latin America. It also, of course, would have represented an abandonment by the Republicans of their most basic position: that slavery could not be allowed to expand.

There was one notable attempt outside Congress to produce a compromise. The legislature of Virginia called for a national peace conference at Washington. Representatives from twenty-one of the thirty-four states assembled early in February and produced a series of proposals that closely resembled the Crittenden scheme. The convention submitted the plan to the Senate, but the proposal received almost no support.

And so nothing had been resolved when Abraham Lincoln arrived in Washington for his inauguration—sneaking into the city in disguise by train in darkness, to avoid assassination as he passed through the slave state of Maryland en route. The country was now divided into two hostile nations, waiting for what was coming to seem an inevitable war.

In his eloquent inaugural address, Lincoln laid down several basic principles. The Union, he said, was older than the Constitution; hence no state could of its own volition leave the Union. The ordinances of secession were illegal, and acts of violence to support secession were insurrectionary or revolutionary. Of most immediate significance, given the ongoing struggle over Fort Sumter, Lincoln declared that he would enforce the laws and would "hold, occupy, and possess" federal property in the seceded states.

Conditions at Fort Sumter quickly forced Lincoln to translate his words into action. Major Anderson was running short of supplies; unless he received fresh provisions, the fort would have to be evacuated. Lincoln was convinced that if he surrendered Sumter, the South (and perhaps also the North) would never believe that he meant to sustain the Union. After much deliberation, therefore, he dispatched a naval relief expedition to the fort. At the same time, he carefully informed the authorities in South Carolina that ships were on the way, with supplies, and that there would be no attempt to send troops or munitions to the fort unless the supply ships met with resistance. The new Confederate government now faced a dilemma. If it permitted the expedition to land, it would appear to be bowing tamely to federal authority and would lose credibility among its own people. If it fired on the ships or the fort, it would appear (to the North, at least) to be the aggressor. After hours of anguished discussion, the government in Montgomery decided that to appear cowardly would be worse than to appear belligerent. It ordered General P. G. T. Beauregard, commander of Confederate forces at Charleston, to demand Anderson's surrender and, if the demand was refused, to attack the fort. Beauregard made the demand; Anderson rejected it. The Confederates then bombarded the fort for two days, April 12–13, 1861. On April 14, Anderson surrendered. The Civil War had begun.

In both the North and the South, events moved quickly. Lincoln immediately requested an expansion of the regular army and called for the states to raise their own forces to contribute to the struggle for the Union. In the South, four more slave states seceded and joined the Confederacy: Virginia (April 17, 1861), Arkansas (May 6), Tennessee (June 8), and North Carolina (May 20). The mountain counties in northwestern Virginia refused to accept the decision of their state, established their own "loyal" government, and in 1863 secured admission to the Union as the new state of West Virginia. The four remaining slave states, Maryland, Delaware, Kentucky, and Missouri, cast their lot with the Union, although not without considerable controversy (and in large part because of heavy pressure from Washington). These border states were crucial to the Union's hopes, and Lincoln kept a close watch on their actions. In two of them, Maryland and Missouri, he used military force to ensure that secessionists would have no opportunity to prevail.

The Question of Inevitability

Was the outbreak of war inevitable? Was there anything that Lincoln (or those before him) could have done to settle the sectional conflict peaceably? Those questions have preoccupied historians for more than a century without resolution. (See "Where Historians Disagree," pp. 416–417.)

In one sense, of course, the war was not inevitable. If the nation had not acquired new Western lands in the 1840s, if Douglas had not presented the Kansas-Nebraska Act to Congress in 1854, if the Supreme Court had chosen not to rule on the *Dred Scott* case, if John Brown had not raided Harpers Ferry, if Lincoln had not rejected the Crittenden Compro-

mise, or if the North had agreed (as some urged) to let the Southern states leave in peace—if any number of things that did happen had not happened, then there might not have been a war. Even after Lincoln's election, even after the secession of the South, it would have been technically possible for the nation to avoid armed conflict.

The real question, however, is not what hypothetical situations might have reversed the trend toward war but whether the preponderance of forces in the nation were acting to hold the nation together or to drive it apart. And by 1861, it seems clear that in both the North and the South, sectional antagonisms—whether justified or not—had risen to such a point that the existing terms of union had become untenable. People in both regions of the country had come to believe that two distinct and incompatible civilizations had developed in the United States and that those civilizations were incapable of living together in peace. Ralph Waldo Emerson, speaking for much of the North, said at the time: "I do not see how a barbarous community and a civilized community can constitute one state." And a slaveowner, expressing the sentiments of much of the South, said shortly after the election of Lincoln: "These [Northern] people hate us, annoy us, and would have us assassinated by our slaves if they dared. They are a different people from us, whether better or worse, and there is no love between us. Why then continue together?"

That the North and the South had come to believe these things may have made secession and war virtually inevitable. Whether these things were actually true—whether the North and the South were really as different and incompatible as they thought—is another question, one that the preparations for and conduct of the war help to answer.

The Opposing Sides

A comparison of the combatants on the eve of war reveals that in one crucial area, at least, there were indeed basic differences between the sections. All the great material factors were on the side of the North.

These advantages, important from the beginning, became more significant as the conflict continued and the superior economy of the North mobilized for war production. The North had a larger manpower reservoir from which to draw its armed forces. There were twenty-three states still in the Union, with a population of approximately 22 million. There were only eleven Confederate states, with a population of about 9 million, of whom 3.5 million were slaves.

The North had an even greater advantage in its levels of industrial production. Southern industry, particularly in those areas necessary for the conduct of a war, was almost nonexistent; the North already possessed an advanced industrial system. In the first year of the war, before Northern factories had converted to war production, both sides had to purchase large amounts of supplies, particularly arms, from Europe. After 1862, however, the North was able to manufacture practically all of its own war materials.

The South, on the other hand, had to rely on Europe throughout the war. It tried desperately to expand its own industrial facilities. The brilliant Confederate chief of ordnance, Josiah Gorgas, accomplished wonders in building arsenals and in supplying the armies with weapons and munitions. Nevertheless, both the quantity and the quality of Confederate firearms were inferior to those of the North. The Southern economic system was also unable to provide its soldiers with the other necessities of modern war: clothes, boots, blankets, medical supplies, and the like. The Northern armies (and Northern society in general) had more of everything after 1862 than the armies or the society of the South; and that was one reason why Confederate morale began rapidly to deteriorate by the end of 1863.

In addition, the transportation system of the North was superior in every respect to that of the South. The North had more and better means of inland water transportation (steamboats, barges), more surfaced roads, more wagons and animals. Above all, the North had approximately 20,000 miles of railroads, while the Confederacy, which comprised at least as large a land area, had only 10,000 miles. The trackage figures, however, do not tell the whole story of Southern railroad inferiority. There were important gaps between key points in the South, which required supplies to make detours over long distances or to be carried between rail lines by wagon. As the war continued, the Confederate railroad system steadily deteriorated, and by the last year and a half of the struggle it had almost collapsed.

The enormous imbalance in the material forces of the two sides suggests that the South had absolutely no chance to win the war. But in the beginning, at least, the material strengths of the North were not as decisive as they appear. The South was, for the most part, fighting a defensive war on its own land and thus had the advantage of local support and

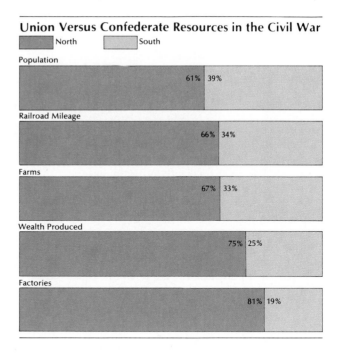

Union Versus Confederate Resources in the Civil War

North ■ South ▢

Population
61% / 39%

Railroad Mileage
66% / 34%

Farms
67% / 33%

Wealth Produced
75% / 25%

Factories
81% / 19%

familiarity with the territory. The South also had an advantage among its own white population: It claimed to be fighting for something concrete, something easy to understand. White southerners liked to say that they simply wanted to be independent, to be left alone; they had no aggressive designs on the North.

The North, on the other hand, faced a more difficult task, both militarily and politically. Its armies were fighting largely within the South. They had to maintain long lines of communications, deal with hostile local populations, and rely on the South's own inadequate transportation system. The Northern public, moreover, was far less united in support of the war than that of the white South. Union war aims were more difficult to define, especially since many Northerners so disliked the South that they saw no reason to fight to keep the Union together. As late as 1864, Northern sentiment often wavered. Thus a major Southern victory at any one of several crucial moments might have proved decisive by breaking the North's will to continue the struggle.

There was, moreover, one additional factor that many Southerners at first thought would virtually guarantee them a victory: cotton. The rapidly growing textile industries of England and France were, the South believed, dependent on their cotton. They would have no choice but to intervene in the conflict

WHERE HISTORIANS DISAGREE

The Causes of the Civil War

Debate over the causes of the Civil War began even before the war itself. In 1858, Senator William H. Seward of New York took note of the two competing explanations of the sectional tensions that were then inflaming the nation. On one side, he claimed, stood those who believed the sectional hostility to be "accidental, unnecessary, the work of interested or fanatical agitators." Opposing them stood those (like Seward himself) who believed there to be "an irrepressible conflict between opposing and enduring forces." Although he did not realize it at the time, Seward was drawing the outlines of a debate that would survive among historians for more than a century to come.

The "irrepressible conflict" argument was the first to dominate historical discussion. In the first decades after the fighting, histories of the Civil War generally reflected the views of Northerners who had themselves participated in the conflict. To them, the war appeared to be a stark moral conflict in which the South was clearly to blame, a conflict that arose inevitably as a result of the threatening immorality of slave society. Henry Wilson's *History of the Rise and Fall of the Slave Power* (1872–1877) was (as the title suggests) a particularly vivid version of this moral interpretation of the war, which argued that Northerners had fought to preserve the Union and a system of free labor against the aggressive designs of the South.

A more temperate interpretation, but one that reached generally the same conclusions, emerged in the 1890s, when the first serious histories of the war began to appear. Preeminent among them was the seven-volume *History of the United States from the Compromise of 1850 . . .* (1893–1900) by James Ford Rhodes. Like Wilson and others, Rhodes identified slavery as the central, indeed virtually the only, cause of the war. "If the Negro had not been brought to America," he wrote, "the Civil War could not have occurred." And because the North and South had reached positions on the issue of slavery that were both irreconcilable and unalterable, the conflict had become "inevitable."

Although Rhodes placed his greatest emphasis on the moral conflict over slavery, he suggested that the struggle also reflected fundamental differences between the Northern and Southern economic systems. Not until the 1920s, however, did the idea of the war as an irrepressible *economic* rather than *moral* conflict receive full expression, from Charles and Mary Beard in *The Rise of American Civilization* (2 vols., 1927). Slavery, the Beards claimed, was not so much a social or cultural institution as an economic one, a labor system. There were, they insisted, "inherent antagonisms" between Northern industrialists and Southern planters. Each group sought to control the federal government so as to protect its own economic interests. Both groups used arguments over slavery and states' rights only as smoke screens.

The economic determinism of the Beards influenced a generation of historians in important ways, but ultimately most of those who believed the Civil War to have been "irrepressible" returned to an emphasis on social and cultural factors. Allan Nevins argued as much in his great work, *The Ordeal of the Union* (8 vols., 1947–1971). The North and the South, he wrote, "were rapidly becoming separate peoples." At the root of these cultural differences was the "problem of slavery," but the "fundamental assumptions, tastes, and cultural aims" of the two regions were diverging in other ways as well.

More recent proponents of the "irrepressible conflict" argument have taken different views of the Northern and Southern positions on the conflict but have been equally insistent on the role of culture and ideology in creating them. Eric Foner, in *Free Soil, Free Labor, Free Men* (1970) and other writings, emphasized the importance of the "free-labor ideology" to Northern opponents of slavery. The moral concerns of the abolitionists were not the dominant sentiments in the North, he claimed. Instead, most Northerners (including Abraham Lincoln) opposed slavery largely because they feared it might spread to the North and threaten the position of free white laborers. Convinced that Northern society was superior to that

WHERE HISTORIANS DISAGREE

of the South, increasingly persuaded of the South's intentions to extend the "slave power" beyond its existing borders, Northerners were embracing a viewpoint that made conflict inevitable. Eugene Genovese, writing of Southern slaveholders in *The Political Economy of Slavery* (1965), emphasized their conviction that the slave system provided a far more humane society than industrial labor, that the South had constructed "a special civilization built on the relation of master to slave." Just as Northerners were becoming convinced of a Southern threat to their economic system, so Southerners believed that the North had aggressive and hostile designs on the Southern way of life. Like Foner, therefore, Genovese saw in the cultural outlook of the section the source of an all but inevitable conflict.

Historians who argue that the conflict emerged naturally, even inevitably, out of a fundamental divergence between the sections have, therefore, disagreed markedly over whether moral, cultural, social, ideological, or economic issues were the primary causes of the Civil War. But they have been in general accord that the conflict between North and South was deeply embedded in the nature of the two societies, that the crisis that ultimately emerged was irrepressible. Other historians, however, have questioned that assumption and have argued that the Civil War could have been avoided, that the differences between North and South were not important enough to have necessitated war. Like proponents of the "irrepressible conflict" school, advocates of the war as a "repressible conflict" emerged first in the nineteenth century. President James Buchanan, for example, believed that extremist agitators were to blame for the conflict, and many Southerners writing of the war in the late nineteenth century claimed that only the fanaticism of the Republican party could account for the conflict.

The idea of the war as avoidable did not gain wide recognition among historians until the 1920s and 1930s, when a group known as the "revisionists" began to offer new accounts of the origins of the conflict. One of the leading revisionists was James G. Randall, who saw in the social and economic systems of the North and the South no differences so fundamental as to require a war. Slavery, he suggested, was an essentially benign institution; it was, in any case, already "crumbling in the presence of nineteenth century tendencies." Only the political ineptitude of a "blundering generation" of leaders could account for the Civil War, he claimed. Avery Craven, another leading revisionist, placed more emphasis on the issue of slavery than had Randall. But in *The Coming of the Civil War* (1942) he too argued that slave laborers were not much worse off than Northern industrial workers, that the institution was already on the road to "ultimate extinction," and that war could, therefore, have been averted had skillful and responsible leaders worked to produce compromise.

More recent students of the war have kept elements of the revisionist interpretation alive by emphasizing the role of political agitation in the coming of the war. David Herbert Donald, for example, argued in 1960 that the politicians of the 1850s were not unusually inept, but that they were operating in a society in which traditional restraints were being eroded in the face of the rapid extension of democracy. Thus the sober, statesmanlike solution of differences was particularly difficult. Michael Holt, in *The Political Crisis of the 1850s* (1978), similarly emphasized the actions of politicians, rather than the irreconcilable differences between sections, in explaining the conflict, although he avoided placing blame on any one group. "Much of the story of the coming of the Civil War," he wrote, "is the story of the successful efforts of Democratic politicians in the South and Republican politicians in the North to keep the sectional conflict at the center of the political debate."

Like the proponents of the "irrepressible conflict" interpretation, the "revisionist" historians have differed among themselves in important ways. But the explanation of the Civil War has continued, even a century later, to divide roughly into the same two schools of thought that William Seward identified in 1858.

War by Railroad
Union soldiers pose beside a mortar mounted on a railroad car in July 1864, during the siege of Petersburg, Virginia. Six days after this photograph was taken, Union forces exploded a huge mine in a futile effort to take the city. After that, Grant dug in for a nine-month siege. Petersburg did not fall until April 2, 1865, only a week before the end of the war.   (National Archives)

on the side of the Confederacy and force the North to acquiesce in the South's independence.

The Mobilization of the North

For the North, the war years were a time of political and social discord, of frustration, and of the inevitable suffering that accompanies battle. Yet they were also a period of prosperity and expansion. The war provided a major stimulus to both industry and agriculture. Not only did the rising productivity of the North contribute to its ultimate victory; it also ensured that the region would be more highly developed at the end of the war than at the start.

Economic Measures

The expanding Northern economy received a powerful stimulant during the war from the economic legislation of the now dominant Republican party. With Southern opposition removed, the Republicans proceeded to enact an aggressively nationalistic program to promote economic development.

The Homestead Act and the Morrill Land Grant Act, both passed in 1862, were measures that the West had long sought. The Homestead Act entitled any citizen, or anyone who intended to become a citizen, to claim 160 acres of public land and to pur-

chase it for a small fee after living on it for five years. The Morrill Act gave every state 30,000 acres of public land for each of its congressional representatives. The states were to use the proceeds from the sale of that acreage to finance public education in agriculture, engineering, and military science. This provided a basis for the development of many new state colleges and universities, the so-called land-grant institutions.

A few days before President Buchanan left office, Congress passed the Morrill Tariff Act, which moderately increased duties and brought the rates up to approximately what they had been before 1846. Later measures, in 1862 and 1864, were even more frankly protective. By the end of the war, customs duties were, on average, the highest in the nation's history, and more than double the prewar rate.

Business achieved other victories in promoting railroads and immigration. One of the great dreams of those who believed in industrial growth was a railroad link between the Atlantic and Pacific coasts. Two laws, passed in 1862 and 1864, paved the way to realization of that dream. Congress created two new federally chartered corporations: the Union Pacific Railroad Company, which was to build westward from Omaha, and the Central Pacific, which was to build eastward from California. The two companies were to meet somewhere in the middle and complete the link. The government would provide free public lands and generous loans to the companies.

Immigration from Europe fell off in the first

years of the war, partly because of the unsettled conditions in America. That decrease, coupled with the military's demand for manpower, threatened to produce a serious labor shortage. Business leaders, with the support of the president, persuaded Congress to pass new legislation to encourage immigration: a contract labor law, enacted in 1864, which authorized employers to import laborers and collect the costs of transportation from future wages.

Perhaps the most important measure affecting the business and financial worlds was the National Bank Act, enacted in 1863 and amended in 1864. The act created a national banking system, which survived without serious modification until 1913. Under the new system, existing state banks or newly formed corporations were entitled to apply for federal charters and become national banks. To qualify for such charters, an institution had to possess a minimum amount of capital and had to invest one-third of that capital in government securities. In return, it would receive U.S. Treasury notes that it could issue as currency. In addition, Congress (in 1865) placed a tax on all state bank notes, which forced state notes out of existence and induced reluctant state banks to seek federal charters. At the outbreak of the war, 1,500 banks chartered by twenty-nine states had been issuing bank notes. The new system eliminated much of the chaos and uncertainty in the nation's currency and created a uniform system of national bank notes.

But reforming the currency did not alone solve one of the North's principal problems: financing the war. The government raised funds in three ways. It levied taxes, it borrowed money, and it issued paper currency.

Not until 1862, when war expenses began rapidly to mount, did Congress face the necessity of raising substantial new taxes. It passed the Internal Revenue Act, which placed duties on practically all goods and most occupations. For the first time, in 1861, the government levied an income tax: a duty of 3 percent on incomes above $800. Later, the rates were increased to 5 percent on incomes between $600 and $5,000 and 10 percent on incomes above $5,000. Through the various war taxes, the hand of the government was coming to rest on most individuals in the country. The United States was in the process of acquiring a national internal revenue system—in fact, a national tax system—one of the many nationalizing effects of the war. Even so, taxation raised only a small proportion of the funds necessary for financing

the war—$667 million in all (including tariff revenues); and strong popular resistance prevented the government from raising the rates. Other methods, therefore, became increasingly important.

The most significant of these was borrowing from the American public. In America's previous wars, the government had sold bonds only to banks and to a few wealthy investors. Now, however, the Treasury employed the services of Jay Cooke, a Philadelphia banker, to persuade ordinary citizens to buy bonds. Through high-pressure propaganda techniques, Cooke disposed of $400 million worth of bonds—the first example of mass financing of a war in American history. In all, the United States borrowed $2.6 billion.

The most controversial method of financing (and the least productive of revenue) was the printing of paper currency, or "greenbacks." The new currency paid no interest and was not supported by a specie reserve (gold or silver). Holders of greenbacks had only the good faith of the government (and its ability to win the war) to rely on. The value of the greenbacks fluctuated, therefore, according to the fortunes of the Northern armies. Early in 1864, with the war effort bogged down, a greenback dollar, in relation to a gold dollar, was worth only 39 cents. Even at the close of the war, its value had advanced to only 67 cents. The uncertain value of greenbacks made it difficult for the government to use them to pay many of its expenses. The Treasury issued only $450 million worth of paper currency in all. That was, however, enough to produce serious problems of inflation in the later years of the war.

Raising the Union Armies

When hostilities began, there were only about 16,000 troops in the regular army of the United States, many of them scattered throughout the West to keep order between whites and Indians along the frontier. Lincoln realized, therefore, that the Union would have to rely heavily on state militias. Shortly after assuming office, he called 75,000 militiamen into service for three months, the usual period of service set for state troops by existing militia laws. The president quickly recognized that the war would last longer than three months; and (without clear legal sanction) he called up 42,000 state volunteers for national service for three years and authorized an increase of 23,000 in the regular army. When Congress convened in July 1861, it passed legislation that not only endorsed Lincoln's

Sending the Boys Off to War
In this painting by Thomas Nast, New York's Seventh Regiment parades down Broadway in April 1861, to the cheers of exuberant, patriotic throngs, shortly before departing to fight in what most people then assumed would be a brief war. Thomas Nast is better known for his famous political cartoons of the 1870s.
(Seventh Regiment Armory, New York City)

previous acts but called for enlisting 500,000 volunteers to serve for three years.

For a time, this voluntary system brought out enough men to fill the armies. But after the first flush of enthusiasm had subsided, enlistments declined. Finally, in March 1863, Congress enacted the first national draft law in its history. (The Confederacy had begun conscription almost a year earlier.) Few exemptions were permitted: only high national and state officials, ministers, and men who were the sole support of dependent families. But a drafted man could escape service by hiring someone to go in his place or by paying the government a fee of $300.

Supporters of the law hoped that the threat of conscription would spur voluntary enlistments. Each state was assigned a quota of men to be raised. If a state could fill its quota, it would escape the draft completely; if it did not, the draft would make up the difference. Although only about 46,000 men were ever actually conscripted, the draft greatly increased voluntary enlistments. Approximately 1.5 million men served in the Union armies. (The Confederate armies had the services of about 900,000.)

To a people accustomed to a government that hardly touched their daily lives, conscription seemed a strange and ominous thing. Opposition to the law was widespread, particularly from laborers, immigrants, and Democrats opposed to the war (known as "Peace Democrats"). In places it erupted into violence. Demonstrators against the draft rioted in New York City for four days in July 1863, killed perhaps 1,000 people, mostly blacks, and burned down homes and businesses, again mostly those of free blacks. (Some Northern opponents of the war believed that blacks were responsible for the conflict.) Only the arrival of federal troops managed to subdue the rioters. Some Democratic governors (Horatio Seymour of New York among them) supported the war but contended that the national government had no constitutional power to conscript; they openly challenged the Lincoln administration on the issue.

Political Challenges

When Abraham Lincoln arrived in Washington early in 1861, most national leaders considered him a minor politician from the prairies. Lincoln's folksy, unpretentious demeanor helped strengthen some in their conviction that he was unfit for his position. But the new president had few doubts about his own abilities, as he demonstrated when he selected his cabinet. He assembled a group of men representing every faction of the Republican party and every segment of Northern opinion—men of extraordinary prestige and political influence, as difficult a set of prima donnas as any president had ever attempted to manage. Three of the secretaries, William Seward, Salmon P. Chase, and Edwin Stanton, were men of great ability; no one was more certain of that than they themselves. Seward and Chase were convinced that they, not Lincoln, should be president. For a time early in the administration, Seward tried to dominate Lincoln. He failed and ultimately became the president's loyal supporter. Chase never ceased trying to outshine the president and promote his own political prospects.

Lincoln demonstrated confidence as well by his bold exercise of the war powers of his office. In order to accomplish his purposes, he ignored certain parts of the Constitution. It would be foolish, he explained, to lose the whole by being afraid to disregard a part. He called for troops to repress the rebellion without asking Congress for a declaration of war. He increased the size of the regular army without legislative authority to do so. He unilaterally proclaimed a naval blockade of the South.

Lincoln's greatest political problems, however, came not from legal obstacles, but from widespread popular opposition to the war. The opposition came principally from two sources: from Southern sympathizers in the slave states that had remained in the Union, and from the peace wing of the Democratic party. Many Democrats did support the war and even accepted office from the administration. But Peace Democrats (or, as their enemies called them, "Copperheads") feared that agriculture and the Northwest were being subordinated to industry and the East, and that Republican nationalism was threatening states' rights. Some Peace Democrats called for a truce in the fighting and proposed a national convention to amend the Constitution in ways that would satisfy Southern demands. Some advocated the formation of an independent Western confederacy. Some joined such secret societies as the Knights of the Golden Circle and the Sons of Liberty, which many people believed conspired to aid the Southern rebels.

Lincoln used extraordinary methods to suppress opposition to the war. He ordered military arrests and suspended the right of habeas corpus. Suspected offenders could, therefore, be arrested and held without trial. Those who were tried appeared before military courts, where they would not have the benefit of sympathetic local juries. At first, Lincoln used these methods only in particularly sensitive areas, such as the border states; but in 1862, he proclaimed that all persons who discouraged enlistments or engaged in disloyal practices would be subject to martial law. In all, more than 13,000 persons were arrested and imprisoned for varying periods. The most prominent Copperhead in the country—

HANGING A NEGRO IN CLARKSON STREET.

The New York City Draft Riot, 1863

Opposition to the Civil War draft was widespread in the North and in July 1863 produced a violent four-day uprising in New York City in which as many as 1,000 people died. The riot began on July 13 with a march by 4,000 men, mostly poor Irish laborers, who were protesting the provisions by which some wealthy people could be exempted from conscription. "Rich man's war, poor man's fight," the demonstrators cried. Many New Yorkers also feared that the war would drive black workers north to compete for their jobs. The demonstration turned violent when officials began drawing names for the draft. The crowd burned the draft building and then split into factions. Some rioters attacked symbols of wealth: exclusive shops and mansions. Others terrorized black neighborhoods and lynched scores of residents. This contemporary engraving depicts one such lynching. Only by transferring five regiments to the city from Gettysburg (less than two weeks after the great battle there) was the government able to restore order. (The Granger Collection)

Clement L. Vallandigham, a member of Congress from Ohio—was seized by military authorities and exiled to the Confederacy. Lincoln defied all efforts to curb his authority to suppress opposition. He even defied the Supreme Court. When Chief Justice Taney issued a writ (*Ex parte Merryman*) requiring him to release an imprisoned Maryland secessionist leader, Lincoln simply ignored it. (After the war, in 1866, the Supreme Court held, in *Ex parte Milligan,* that military trials in areas where the civil courts were capable of functioning were unconstitutional.)

Early in the war, and particularly after the election of 1862, in which the Republicans suffered heavy losses, leaders of the party began working to create a broad coalition of all the groups that supported the war. In particular, they tried to attract the War Democrats. They called the new organization the Union party; but it was, in reality, little more than the Republican party and a small fringe of War Democrats. It encountered its major political test in the presidential election of 1864.

The Union convention met in June 1864 and nominated Lincoln for another term as president and Andrew Johnson of Tennessee, a War Democrat who had opposed his state's decision to secede, for the vice presidency. In August, the Democratic convention nominated George B. McClellan, a celebrated former Union general who had been relieved of his command by Lincoln. The peace faction won approval of a plank in the party platform denouncing the war as a failure and calling for a truce and a settlement with the South. McClellan repudiated the plank, but the Democrats stood before the country as the peace party—ready to profit from the growing war weariness of the nation and from the dismal state of the Union's military position. At this crucial moment, however, several Northern military victories, particularly the capture of Atlanta, Georgia, early in September, rejuvenated Northern morale and gave promise of Republican success in November.

The election was a smashing electoral triumph for Lincoln, who won 212 votes to McClellan's 21 and carried every state except Kentucky, New Jersey, and Delaware. Lincoln's popular majority, however, was uncomfortably small, 2,214,000 to 1,805,000, an advantage of only 400,000. A slight shift of popular votes in some of the more populous states would have changed the result. Had Union victories not occurred when they did, and had Lincoln not made special arrangements to allow Union troops to vote (presumably for him), the Democrats might have won and the future course of the nation might have been altered considerably.

The Politics of Emancipation

Lincoln had faced a challenge in 1864 not only from the Democrats but from members of his own Republican party, who almost succeeded in blocking his renomination. For the Republicans, no less than the Democrats, were plagued with factional divisions between two groups known as the Radicals and the Conservatives. On most questions, including economic matters, the two groups were in fundamental agreement. But they differed markedly on slavery. Radicals wanted to seize the opportunity presented by the war to abolish slavery—immediately and decisively. They had the benefit of influential and articulate congressional leaders: Representative Thaddeus Stevens of Pennsylvania, master of the party machine in the House; Senator Charles Sumner of Massachusetts; and Senator Benjamin F. Wade of Ohio. The Conservatives opposed slavery too, but they wanted to eliminate it in what they thought would be a less disruptive way—slowly and gradually. In the beginning, at least, they had the support of the president. Lincoln feared that too rapid an effort to abolish slavery would divide Northern opinion and so antagonize the border states, whose allegiance to the Union was already precarious, that it would become impossible to prevent them from seceding.

Nevertheless, legal attacks on slavery gathered steady momentum throughout the early years of the war. Lincoln made several attempts to persuade the loyal slave states to agree to a program of compensated gradual emancipation, but without notable success. Congress passed the Confiscation Act in August 1861, declaring free all slaves used for "insurrectionary" purposes. Subsequent laws in the spring of 1862 abolished slavery, with compensation to owners, in the District of Columbia and in the Western territories. In the summer of 1862, the Radicals decided that Northern opinion had reached a point where they could move still further. In July, they pushed through Congress the second Confiscation Act, a bold attempt to accomplish emancipation by legislative action. It declared free the slaves of persons aiding and supporting the insurrection, and authorized the president to employ blacks, including freed slaves, as soldiers.

As the war progressed, the country seemed slowly to accept emancipation as a central war aim; nothing less, many believed, would justify the enormous sacrifices of the prolonged and costly struggle. As a result, the Radicals gained increasing influence within the Republican party—a development that did not go unnoticed by the astute master of politics in the White House, who decided to seize the leadership of the rising antislavery sentiment himself.

On September 22, 1862, after the Union victory at the Battle of Antietam, the president issued a preliminary Emancipation Proclamation; and on the first day of 1863, he signed a final Emancipation Proclamation, which declared forever free the slaves in most areas of the Confederacy. He exempted from the edict those areas already under Union control: the state of Tennessee, western Virginia, and southern Louisiana. And the proclamation did not apply to the border slave states, which had never seceded from the Union. Since these areas were not enemy territory, the president reasoned that they were not subject to his war powers.

The proclamation freed immediately only a few slaves. But it clearly and irrevocably established that this was a war being fought not only to preserve the Union but also to eliminate slavery. Eventually, as federal armies occupied much of the South, the proclamation became a practical reality and led directly to the freeing of thousands of slaves. About 186,000 of these emancipated blacks served as soldiers, sailors, and laborers for the Union forces. And even in areas not directly affected by the proclamation, the antislavery impulse was gaining strength. By the end of the war, slavery had been abolished in two Union slave states, Maryland and Missouri, and in three "reconstructed" or occupied Confederate states, Tennessee, Arkansas, and Louisiana. The final step came early in 1865, when Congress approved the Thirteenth Amendment, which freed all slaves everywhere and abolished slavery as an institution. The required number of states ratified the amendment shortly after the end of the war. After more than two centuries, legalized slavery ceased to exist in the United States.

The War and Society

The Civil War did not, as many people once believed, transform the North from an agrarian to an industrial society. Industrialization was already far advanced when the war began; and in some respects, the war itself did not so much encourage as retard further growth—by diverting labor and resources to military purposes.

On the whole, however, the war served to advance the Northern industrial economy. That was in part a result of the new dominance of the Republican party and its promotion of nationalistic economic legislation. But it was also because the war itself required expansion in certain sectors. Coal production increased by nearly 20 percent during the war. Railroad facilities improved—mainly through the adoption of a standard gauge (track width). The loss of farm labor to the military forced many farmers to increase the mechanization of agriculture.

Not all the effects of the war were so progressive. Industrial workers experienced a substantial loss of purchasing power, as their wages failed to rise fast enough to keep pace with the substantial wartime inflation. Prices in the North rose by more than 70 percent during the war, while wages rose only about 40 percent. (Inflation was, however, a far less serious problem than in the South; see next section.) The liberalization of immigration laws began to introduce new competition into the labor market and helped keep wages low. The increasing mechanization of production threatened many skilled workers with the loss of their jobs. One result was a substantial increase in union membership in many industries and the creation of a group of national unions for coal miners, railroad engineers, and other workers. Employers reacted by establishing blacklists of union members and using brutal methods to prevent organization and suppress strikes.

Women found themselves, either by choice or by necessity, thrust into new and often unfamiliar roles. They took over positions vacated by men as teachers, retail sales clerks, office workers, and mill and factory hands. They were responding not only to the needs of employers for additional labor, but to their own, often desperate need for money. With husbands and fathers away in the army, many women were left destitute—particularly since military pay was small and erratic.

Above all, women became nurses. Nursing had previously been a primarily male occupation (although women had been entering the profession since the 1840s); in the course of the war, women became increasingly dominant within the field. In the process, they redefined the image of nursing. Gradually, society came to think of it as a profession less dependent on medical expertise than on a spirit of benevolence and self-sacrifice, a spirit that women were considered to possess in particular abundance. By the end of the century, nursing had become an almost entirely female profession.

The U.S. Sanitary Commission, an organization of civilian volunteers, mobilized large numbers of female nurses to serve in field hospitals. The federal government appointed the reformer Dorothea Dix to serve under the surgeon general and help mobilize a women's nursing corps. Female nurses not only cared for patients but performed other tasks considered appropriate for women: cooking, cleaning, and laundering.

The U.S. Sanitary Commission
Mathew Brady took this photograph of female nurses and Union soldiers standing before an infirmary at Brandy Station, Virginia, near Petersburg, in 1864. The infirmary was run by the U.S. Sanitary Commission, the government-supported nursing corps that became indispensable to the medical care of wounded soldiers during the Civil War. (The Bettmann Archive)

For many women, especially those who had become committed in the prewar years to feminist causes, the war seemed to be an enormously important and liberating experience. Clara Barton, who was active during the war in collecting and distributing medical supplies and who later became an important figure in the nursing professsion, said in 1888: "At the war's end, woman was at least fifty years in advance of the normal position which continued peace would have assigned her." That was a considerable exaggeration. But it captured the degree to which many women looked back on the war as a crucial moment in the redefinition of female roles and in the awakening of a sense of independence and new possibilities.

The Mobilization of the South

The first seven Southern states to secede left the Union as individual sovereignties. But they intended from the first to join together in a common confederation, which they hoped the states of the upper South would eventually join. Accordingly, representatives of the seceded states assembled at Montgomery, Alabama, early in February 1861, to create a Southern nation. When Virginia seceded, the government moved to Richmond—partly out of deference to Virginia,

partly because Richmond was one of the few Southern cities large enough to house the government.

Southerners were acutely aware, and boastfully proud, of the differences between their new nation and the nation they had left. Those differences were real. But there were also important similarities between the Union and the Confederacy, which became particularly clear as they mobilized for war: similarities in their political systems, in the methods they used for financing the war and conscripting troops, and in the way they fought.

The Confederate Government

The Confederate constitution was in most respects identical to the Constitution of the United States, but it contained a number of provisions designed to satisfy particular Southern demands. It expressly recognized the sovereignty of the individual states (although it made no mention of the right of secession). It gave the president an "item veto"—the power to veto part of a bill without rejecting the whole thing. And it specifically sanctioned slavery and made its abolition (even by one of the states) practically impossible.

Besides framing a constitution and passing temporary laws, the Montgomery convention named a provisional president and a provisional vice president: Jefferson Davis of Mississippi and Alexander H. Stephens of Georgia. Later, in a general election, the same two men were chosen, without opposition, for regular six-year terms. Davis had been a firm but not extreme advocate of Southern rights in the former Union; he was a moderate but not an extreme secessionist. Stephens had been the chief among those who had contended that secession was unnecessary. Indeed the Confederate government, like the Union government, was dominated throughout the war by men of the center. Just as Radical Republicans never managed to dominate the Lincoln administration, so in the Confederacy the extremist fire-eaters found themselves generally excluded from power.

Jefferson Davis embodied the spirit of the nation he had been called to lead. His family, which was of Southern yeoman stock, had moved from Kentucky, where he was born, to the new lush cotton lands of Mississippi, where they became rich planters almost overnight. Davis was a first-generation aristocrat. So also were most of the members of his government. The Confederacy was run largely by the cotton nabobs of the newer lower (or "Western") South, not by the old aristocracy of the seaboard states.

Lincoln's task was to preserve a nation. Davis's was the more difficult task of making one. Lincoln succeeded; Davis failed. He was a reasonably good administrator and served as his own secretary of war. He dominated his administration completely, encountering little interference from the generally tame members of his unstable cabinet. But Davis rarely provided genuinely national leadership. He spent too much time on routine items, on what one observer called "little trash." Moreover, he demonstrated a punctiliousness about legal and constitutional niceties that was inappropriate to the task of ensuring the survival of a new nation. Lincoln, without clear constitutional sanction, suspended habeas corpus; Davis asked his Congress for permission to do so and received only part of what he asked. One shrewd Confederate official (R. G. H. Kean) wrote: "All the revolutionary vigor is with the enemy. . . . With us timidity—hair splitting."

Outside the administration—in the Congress and among the public at large—opposition and dissent were widespread. Some white Southerners opposed secession and war altogether, particularly people in poorer areas where slaveholding was limited. In the "backcountry" and "upcountry" regions of many Southern states, men and women refused to support the new Confederate government, refused to serve in the Southern army, and at times abetted the Union. Some white Southerners even enlisted in the Union army. Most white Southerners, however,

supported the war in principle. But just as in the North, disenchanted citizens spoke openly and bitterly about the disappointing progress of the fighting, the incompetence of the president and the government, and the problems of the economy.

The Confederacy had been established on the ideal of the unity and homogeneity of the South; it was that ideal, in fact, that underlay the decision of the founders that there should be no party system in the new nation, that the white public should form a single united group. (A similar impulse supported the effort to create the Union party in the North in 1864.) But the quest for unity was in many ways no more successful in the Confederacy than in the Union. And the absence of a party system meant that disagreements often became far more destructive than they did within the government of the United States.

Money and Manpower

In contrast to the burgeoning prosperity of the wartime North, the South in the war years experienced shortages, suffering, and sacrifice. The Southern economy, despite a frantic expansion of industrial facilities, was unable to supply the needs of its armies and civilian population.

The officials in charge of financing the Confederacy's war effort faced several difficult challenges. They had to create a national revenue system capable of supporting a major war effort, and they had to do so in a society whose people were unaccustomed to bearing large tax burdens. Southern banking houses, except in New Orleans, were fewer and smaller than those of the North. Because excess capital in the South was usually invested in slaves and land, liquid assets were in short supply. The Confederacy's only specie was that seized from the U.S. mints located in the South, and it amounted to only about $1 million.

The Confederate Congress, like its counterpart in the North, was reluctant to enact rigorous wartime taxes. At first, it attempted to requisition funds from the individual states—most of which were unwilling to impose taxes on their citizens and paid their shares by issuing bonds or their own notes. Moving more boldly in 1863, Congress passed a bill that included license levies and an income tax. A unique feature was the "tax in kind." Farmers and planters had to contribute one-tenth of their produce to the government. But taxation in the end provided the Confederacy with modest revenue; it was the source of only about 1 percent of the government's total income.

The borrowing record of the Confederacy was little better than its tax program. Eventually, the government issued bonds in such large amounts that people doubted its ability to redeem them. The Confederacy also attempted to borrow money in Europe by pledging cotton stored in the South for future delivery. None of these efforts produced more than minimal results; and thus the Confederacy had to rely primarily on the least stable, most destructive form of financing: paper currency.

The Confederacy began issuing paper money and Treasury notes (the equivalent of the Northern greenbacks) in 1861. Once started, the process could not be stopped. By 1864, the staggering total of $1 billion had been issued, more than twice what the Northern government issued. And unlike the Union, the Confederacy did not establish a uniform currency system; thus states and cities issued their own notes. The result was a rapid depreciation of the value of Confederate money—inflation, of a kind far worse than anything the North experienced. Prices skyrocketed to astronomical heights, with predictable effects on the new nation's morale.

Like the United States, the Confederate States first raised armies by calling for volunteers. And as in the North, by the end of 1861 voluntary enlistments had begun to decline. By the beginning of 1862, the Confederacy was threatened by a manpower crisis. The government met the situation decisively. At Davis's recommendation, Congress in April enacted a Conscription Act, which declared that all able-bodied white males between the ages of eighteen and thirty-five were liable to military service for three years. A man who was drafted could escape his summons if he furnished a substitute. The prices for substitutes eventually went as high as $10,000 in Confederate currency. The purpose of the provision was to exempt men in charge of agricultural and industrial production. It aroused such bitter opposition from poorer whites, however, that it was repealed in 1863. But that was not the only feature of the draft that angered the common people of the region. A particular target of resentment was the provision exempting one white man on each plantation with twenty or more slaves. Angrily denounced as the "twenty-nigger law," it caused ordinary men to say: "It's a rich man's war but a poor man's fight."

Despite the opposition, conscription seemed for a time to work. At the end of 1862, an estimated 500,000 soldiers were in the Confederate army. In

Confederate Volunteers

Young Southern soldiers posed for this photograph in 1861, shortly before the first Battle of Bull Run. The Civil War was the first major military conflict in the age of photography, and it launched the careers of many of America's early photographers. (Cook Collection, Valentine Museum)

addition, the Confederate army recruited slave men and women to perform such services as cooking, laundry, and manual labor, hence freeing additional white manpower for fighting. (Only late in the war, when the military situation was becoming desperate, was there any effort to involve slaves in combat.) After 1862, conscription provided fewer and fewer men, and the armed forces steadily decreased in size. That was partly because federal armies seized large areas of the South and deprived the Confederacy of access to the manpower in the occupied regions. But it was also because of declining enthusiasm for the war within the areas the Confederacy continued to control. Military reverses in the summer of 1863 convinced many Southerners that the war was lost, causing a kind of passive resistance to the draft as men sought to avoid it by hiding in the hills and woods.

As 1864 opened, the government faced a critical manpower shortage. In a desperate move, Congress lowered the age limit for drafted men to seventeen and raised it to fifty, reaching out, it was said, toward the cradle and the grave. But the measure produced few new recruits in a nation now suffering from intense war weariness and becoming certain that defeat was inevitable. In 1864–1865, there were 100,000 desertions. An observant Confederate diarist, Mary Boykin Chesnut, wrote in her journal in March 1865: "I am sure our army is silently dispersing. Men are moving the wrong way, all the time. They slip by with no songs and no shouts now. They have given the thing up." In a frantic final attempt to raise men, Congress in 1865 authorized the drafting of 300,000 slaves. The war ended before this incongruous experiment could be attempted.

Both in financing the war and in raising men to fight it, the South used methods in many ways indistinguishable from those being used by the North. Only the results were different. As the war continued, the disparity between the resources—both economic and human—available to the two nations became increasingly clear. The North, despite many difficulties, managed to finance its war effort reasonably successfully and to raise enough men to fill its armies. The South suffered constantly, and increasingly, from shortages of both money and men.

States' Rights Versus Centralization

Many Southerners criticized the Davis administration's handling of the war. Many opposed the draft. But except for isolated pockets of Union sentiment in some of the mountain areas (see above, pp. 334, 425), there was at first very little opposition in the Confederacy to the war itself. Southerners were, however, bitterly divided over how the war should be conducted.

The greatest dividing force was, ironically enough, the principle of states' rights—the foundation of Southern political philosophy, for which the South claimed to have left the Union. States' rights had become such a cult with many Southerners that they resisted virtually all efforts to exert national authority, even those necessary to win the war. The most adamant opponents of centralization were a group of quixotic men who counted Vice President Alexander Stephens as their leader. They supported the war, but they were unwilling to sacrifice one iota of state sovereignty to win it. If victory had to be gained at the expense of states' rights, they preferred defeat. As the pressures of centralization grew,

Stephens and his followers became increasingly attracted to the idea of a negotiated peace with the North and even implied at times that Southern independence need not be a precondition of such a peace.

The states' righters obstructed the national government's conduct of the war in many ways. They were particularly critical of Davis's efforts to impose martial law and suspend habeas corpus, and they placed crippling restrictions on his ability to use such powers. They obstructed conscription at many points. Recalcitrant governors such as Joseph Brown of Georgia and Zebulon M. Vance of North Carolina at times attempted to keep their own states' troops entirely separate from the Confederate forces. Brown at one point had a substantial surplus of uniforms, which were badly needed by undersupplied Southern soldiers; nevertheless, he refused to allow them to be used for any but Georgia troops.

Despite the opposition, however, the Confederate government did make substantial strides in centralizing power in the South. The Confederate bureaucracy grew rapidly and by war's end was even larger than the bureaucracy in Washington. Davis imposed not only a manpower draft but a food draft—soldiers of the Confederate armies were empowered to seize crops from farms in their path in order to feed themselves. The government impressed slaves, often over the objections of their owners, to work as laborers on military projects. The Confederacy seized control of the railroads and shipping; it imposed regulations on industry; it limited corporate profits. States' rights sentiment was a significant handicap; but the South nevertheless took dramatic steps in the direction of centralization—becoming in the process increasingly like the region whose institutions it was fighting to escape.

Social Effects of the War

The war worked to transform Southern society in many of the same ways that it was changing the society of the North. The forced expansion of industry caused a substantial swelling of the region's previously modest urban population. Atlanta, Mobile, Richmond, and other cities experienced major growth; the population of Richmond more than doubled during the war.

The wartime experience was particularly significant for Southern women. Because so many men left their farms and plantations to fight, the task of keeping families together and maintaining agricultural production fell increasingly to women. Slaveowners' wives often became responsible for managing large slave work forces; the wives of more modest farmers learned to plow fields and harvest crops. Substantial numbers of females worked in government agencies in Richmond. Even larger numbers chose nursing, both in hospitals and in temporary facilities set up to care for wounded soldiers. Others became schoolteachers.

The long-range results of the war for Southern women are more difficult to measure but equally profound. The experience of the 1860s almost certainly forced many women to question the prevailing Southern assumption that females were unsuited for certain activities, that they were not fit to participate actively in the public sphere. A more concrete legacy was the decimation of the male population and the creation of a major sexual imbalance in the region. After the war, there were many thousands more women in the South than men. In Georgia, for example, women outnumbered men by 36,000 in 1870; in North Carolina by 25,000. The result, of course, was a large number of unmarried (or widowed) women who, both during and after the war, had no choice but to find employment—thus, by necessity rather than choice, expanding the number of acceptable roles for women in Southern society.

Perhaps the principal social effect of the war on the South, however, was widespread suffering and privation. Particularly once the effects of the Northern naval blockade began to be felt, the South experienced massive shortages of almost everything. The region was overwhelmingly agricultural; but since it had concentrated so single-mindedly for so long on producing cotton and other export crops, it did not grow enough food to meet its own needs. And despite the efforts of women to keep farms functioning, the departure of male workers seriously diminished the region's ability to keep up what food production there had been. Doctors were conscripted in large numbers to serve the needs of the military, leaving many communities without any medical care. Craftsmen such as blacksmiths and carpenters were in short supply.

Many Southerners responded to the scarcity of crucial goods by hoarding them or by selling them at exorbitant prices on the black market. Such practices were encouraged further by the nation's disastrous inflation—prices rose more than 7,000 percent in the course of the war—which made many reluctant to exchange any goods for money that they had reason to believe would soon be worthless.

As the war continued, the shortages, the inflation, and the suffering created increasing instability in Southern society. There were major food riots in cities in Georgia, North Carolina, and Alabama in 1863, as well as a large demonstration in Richmond that soon turned violent. Resistance to conscription, food impressment, and taxation increased throughout the nation. And in the meantime, increasing numbers of Southerners were becoming aware that the privations of war were not equally shared by people of different classes. The traditional deference toward the great planters of the region was eroding.

Strategy and Diplomacy

In the realm of military planning, the objectives of the Union were positive and those of the Confederacy negative. To achieve a victory, the Union had to conquer the rebels and reduce them to subjection, to obedience to federal law. The Confederacy had only to stave off defeat.

In the realm of diplomacy with European powers, the situation was reversed. The objectives of the Confederacy were positive, those of the Union negative. The Confederacy hoped to persuade foreign governments to step into the war and help make their independence a reality. The Union aimed only to preserve the status quo: to prevent foreign recognition and intervention.

The Commanders—North and South

Abraham Lincoln, a civilian all his life, had had no military education and no military experience except for a brief militia interlude. Yet he became a great war president and a great commander in chief—superior to Jefferson Davis, who was a trained soldier. Lincoln made himself a fine strategist, often showing keener insight than his generals. He recognized that numbers and resources were on his side, and he moved immediately to mobilize the maximum strength of Northern resources. He urged his generals to keep up a constant pressure on the whole defensive line of the Confederacy until a weak spot was found and a breakthrough could be made. At an early date, he realized that the proper objective of his armies was the destruction of the Confederate armies and not the occupation of Southern territory.

During the first three years of the war, Lincoln performed many functions that in a modern command system would be assumed by the chief of the general staff or the joint chiefs of staff. He formulated policy, devised strategic plans, and even directed tactical movements. Some of his decisions were wise, some wrong; but the general effect of his "interference" with the military machine was fortunate for the North.

At the beginning, Lincoln was inclined to take the advice of General Winfield Scott, the aging hero of the Mexican War who became the president's first chief of staff. The old general, however, was unable to adjust his thinking to the requirements of mass war. He retired from service on November 1, 1861, and Lincoln replaced him as general in chief with the young George B. McClellan, who was also the commander of the federal field army in the East, the Army of the Potomac. McClellan was a proud, even arrogant man who utterly lacked the abilities needed either to formulate strategy or to command an army. The one grand strategic design he submitted was defective because it envisioned operations in only one theater of the war, his own, and because it made places instead of enemy armies its objective. When McClellan took the field in March 1862, Lincoln removed him as general in chief and replaced him (four months later) with General Henry W. Halleck. The foremost American student of the art of war, Halleck had won an undeserved reputation as a successful general in the West. Now he cast himself in the role of an adviser instead of a decision maker. Again, Lincoln himself was forced to form and direct military strategy, a task that he performed until March 1864, when the nation finally achieved a modern command system.

In that system, Ulysses S. Grant, who had emerged as the North's greatest general, was named general in chief. Charged with directing the movements of all Union armies, Grant, because he disliked the political atmosphere of Washington, established his headquarters with the Army of the Potomac but did not technically become commander of that army. Grant proved to be the man for whom Lincoln had been searching. He could think of the war in overall terms and devise strategy for the war as a whole. Because Lincoln trusted Grant, he gave the general a relatively free hand. Grant, however, always submitted the broad outlines of his plans to the president for approval before putting them into action. By the new arrangement, Halleck became "chief of staff," acting as a channel of communication between Lincoln and

Ulysses S. Grant

One observer said of Grant (seen here posing for a photograph during the Wilderness campaign of 1864): "He habitually wears an expression as if he had determined to drive his head through a brick wall, and was about to do it." It was an apt metaphor for Grant's military philosophy, which relied on constant, unrelenting assault. One result was that Grant was willing to fight when other Northern generals held back. Another was that Grant presided over some of the worst carnage of the Civil War. (Library of Congress)

Grant and between Grant and the departmental commanders.

Lincoln's active command role underlines one of the most important changes occurring with the advent of modern warfare: the emergence of the civilian in strategic planning. As war became larger and more technological, strategy became a problem of directing the whole resources of a nation. It was too vast a problem for any one set of leaders, especially for the military.

The most dramatic example of civilian intervention in military affairs was the Committee on the Conduct of the War, a joint investigative committee of both houses of Congress and the most powerful agency that the legislative branch has ever created to secure for itself a voice in formulating war policies. Established in December 1861, under the chairmanship of Senator Benjamin F. Wade of Ohio, it became the spearhead of the Radical attack on Lincoln's war program. The Radicals believed that many of the Northern generals were not animated by a sufficiently ruthless desire for victory. In one sense, they were right. Some generals were for a time unable to abandon the eighteenth-century concept of war as a kind of game—as chessboard maneuvers conducted in leisurely fashion and without heavy casualties. But the Radicals ascribed the generals' hesitancy to a secret sympathy for slavery, which the professionals were supposed to have imbibed at West Point. The generals whom the committee favored—most of them incompetent amateurs—would have been no improvement; and the committee's efforts often seriously interfered with the conduct of the war. But the Radicals did help—even if not always in ways they had intended—to infuse a hard, relentless purpose into the conduct of the war.

Southern command arrangements centered on President Davis, and under his leadership the Confederacy failed to achieve a modern command system. Early in 1862, Davis assigned General Robert E. Lee to duty at Richmond, where, "under the direction of the President," he was "charged" with the conduct of the Confederate armies. Davis, however, had no intention of sharing control of strategy with anyone. Thus Lee, who had a brilliant military mind, acted only as Davis's adviser, furnishing counsel when called on. After serving a few months, Lee went into the field, and Davis did not appoint another adviser until February 1864. Then he selected Braxton Bragg, whom he had been forced to remove from field command after Bragg was defeated in the West. Bragg had real strategic ability, but he understood the political weakness of his position and restricted his function to providing technical advice.

In February 1865, the Confederate Congress, in a move directed at Davis, created the position of general in chief, which was intended for Lee. Davis named Lee to the post but took care to announce that legally he himself was still commander in chief. Lee accepted the job on the basis offered by the president:

Robert E. Lee
Lee provided a sharp contrast to his Northern counterpart, Ulysses S. Grant. Grant was slightly built, slouching, disheveled, and gruff. Lee was tall, dignified, and elegant in both dress and manner. He admired George Washington above all other men, and he attempted to emulate him in his conduct both of the war and of his life. Although he commanded a losing cause, he remained a national hero—not only in the South but also in much of the North in later years. (Cook Collection, Valentine Museum)

as a loyal subordinate instead of the dictator some people wanted him to be. The war ended before the new command experiment could be fully tested.

Below the level of highest command, the war was conducted—in both North and South—by men of markedly similar backgrounds. Much of the professional military leadership on both sides was a product of the national military academies of the United States—the army academy at West Point and the naval academy at Annapolis, Maryland. Union and Confederate officers, in other words, had been trained along similar lines; many were intimately acquainted, even friendly, with their counterparts on the other side. The amateurs who played an important role in both armies were also in many respects similar. These were the commanders of volunteer regiments—usually the acknowledged economic or social leaders of their communities, who appointed themselves officers and rounded up troops to lead. Although occasionally this system produced officers of real ability, it more often led to disorganization and frustration.

The Role of Sea Power

The Union had a considerable advantage in the area of sea power, where it had an overwhelming preponderance of strength. Lincoln made the most of it. The Union navy had two principal functions. One was to enforce the blockade of the Southern coast that the president proclaimed at the beginning of the war, on April 19, 1861. The other was to assist the Union armies in combined land-and-water operations.

In the Western theater of war—the vast region between the Appalachian Mountains and the Mississippi River—the larger rivers were navigable by large vessels. The Union navy helped the armies to conquer this area by transporting supplies and troops for them and joining them in attacking Confederate strong points. In defending themselves against the Union gunboats on the rivers, the Confederates had to depend mainly on land fortifications because of their lack of naval power. These fixed defenses proved no match for the mobile land-and-water forces of the Union.

At first, the blockade of the South was too large a task for the Union navy; and even after the navy had grown to its maximum size, it was unable to seal off completely the long shoreline of the Confederacy. Although large ocean-going ships could generally be kept away, small blockade runners continued to carry goods into and out of some Southern ports. Gradually the federal forces tightened the blockade by occupying stretches of the coast and seizing one port after another. They seized the last remaining important port—Wilmington, North Carolina—early in 1865. Fewer and fewer blockade runners got through, and the blockade increasingly hurt the South's economy.

In bold and ingenious attempts to break the blockade, the Confederates introduced some new weapons, among them an ironclad warship. They constructed this ship by plating with iron a former United States frigate, the *Merrimac,* which the Yankees had scuttled in Norfolk harbor when Virginia seceded. On March 8, 1862, the refitted *Merrimac,* renamed the *Virginia,* steamed out from Norfolk to attack the blockading squadron of wooden ships in nearby Hampton Roads. It destroyed two of the ships and scattered the rest—an event that caused jubilation in Richmond and consternation in Washington. But the federal government had already placed orders for the construction of several ironclads of its own (designed by Swedish immigrant engineer John Ericsson). One of these, the *Monitor,* arrived at Virginia on the night of March 8, shortly after the *Virginia's* dramatic foray. When the *Virginia* emerged on the following day to hunt for more victims, it encountered the *Monitor,* and the first battle between ironclad ships ensued. Neither vessel was able to penetrate the other's armor, but the *Monitor* put an end to the raids of the *Virginia.*

The Confederates later experimented with other new kinds of craft in the effort to pierce the blockade. One was a torpedo boat, which carried the torpedo on a long pole projecting in front. Another was a small, cigar-shaped, hand-powered submarine, the first ever to be used in war. In 1864, in Charleston harbor, such a submarine, pulling its mine behind it on a cable, dived under a blockading vessel, exploded the mine against the hull—and then was dragged to the bottom by the sinking ship. But such efforts, however ingenious, fell far short of breaking or even weakening the blockade.

After more than a year of these unsuccessful efforts, the South generally ceased trying to break the blockade and used its navy instead primarily to defend its ports. But the Confederacy never stopped hoping for a new way to challenge the blockade. The government tried, for example, to build or buy fast ships to prey on the Northern merchant marine on the high seas. The hope was that the Union would detach ships from the blockade to pursue the commerce raiders. The Confederates also hoped to purchase from abroad a specially built "ram" with which to smash the wooden blockading ships. As a result of these efforts, the naval war became an important element in the relations of both the Union and the Confederacy with the powers of Europe.

Europe and the Disunited States

Judah P. Benjamin, who occupied the Confederate foreign office for the greater part of the war, was a clever and intelligent man, but he lacked strong convictions and confined most of his energy to routine administrative tasks. William Seward, on the other hand, learned his job well after some initial blunders and went on to become one of the outstanding American secretaries of state. Of perhaps equal importance, the United States was represented in the key diplomatic post at London by a distinguished minister, Charles Francis Adams, who seemed to have inherited the diplomatic brilliance of his father, John Quincy Adams, and his grandfather, John Adams.

In the relationship of Europe to the Civil War, the key nations were Great Britain and France. They had acted together against Russia in the Crimean War and were united by an entente, one of the understandings of which was that questions concerning the United States fell within the sphere of British influence. Napoleon III, therefore, would not act in American affairs without the concurrence of Britain.

At the beginning of the war, the sympathies of the ruling classes of England and France lay largely with the Confederacy. But important English liberals such as John Bright and Richard Cobden saw the war as a struggle between free and slave labor, and they urged their followers to support the Union cause. The politically conscious but largely unenfranchised workers in Britain expressed their sympathy for the North frequently and unmistakably—in mass meetings, in resolutions, and, through the medium of Bright and other leaders, in Parliament itself. After Lincoln issued the Emancipation Proclamation, these groups intensified their activities on behalf of the Union cause.

Southern leaders regarded cotton as their best diplomatic weapon. England and France needed Southern cotton to keep their textile industries functioning; they would intervene on behalf of the Confederacy so as not to lose their supply. But this King Cotton diplomacy never worked as its champions had envisioned. In 1861, English manufacturers had a surplus of both raw cotton and finished goods on hand; thus the immediate effect of the blockade was merely to enable textile manufacturers to dispose of their remaining goods at high prices. Thereafter, the supply became increasingly short, and many mills were forced to close. But even then, both England and France managed to avoid a complete shutdown of their textile industries by importing supplies from new sources, notably Egypt and India. Most important of all, the workers, the people most seriously affected by the shortage, did not clamor to have the blockade broken. Even the 500,000 English textile workers thrown out of jobs continued to support the North.

The result of all this was that no European nation extended diplomatic recognition to the Confederacy. Although several times England and France considered offering to mediate the conflict, they never moved to intervene in the war. Neither could afford to do so unless the Confederacy seemed on the point of winning; and the South never came close enough to victory to convince its potential allies to support it. Even so, several crises emerged during the war that almost produced hostilities between the United States and Great Britain.

Immediately after the outbreak of war, Great Britain issued a proclamation of neutrality, which implicitly gave the Confederacy the status of a belligerent. France and other nations followed suit. The Northern government, which officially insisted that the war was not a war but a domestic insurrection, bitterly resented England's action. But the British government had proceeded in conformity with accepted rules of neutrality and in accordance with the realities of the situation. The United States was fighting a *war*, a fact that Lincoln himself had recognized in his proclamation establishing a blockade. Thereafter three crises or near crises developed, any one of which could have resulted in war between the two countries.

The first crisis, and the most dangerous one—the so-called *Trent* affair—occurred late in 1861. The Confederate commissioners to England and France, James M. Mason and John Slidell, had slipped through the then ineffective Union blockade to Havana, Cuba, where they boarded an English steamer, the *Trent,* for England. Hovering in Cuban waters was an American frigate, the *San Jacinto,* commanded by Captain Charles Wilkes, an impetuous officer who knew that the Southern diplomats were on the *Trent.* Acting without authorization from his government, Wilkes stopped the British vessel, arrested the commissioners, and bore them off in triumph to Boston. The British government drafted a demand for the release of the prisoners, reparation, and an apology. Lincoln and Seward, well aware that war with England would be suicidal, spun out the negotiations until American public opinion had cooled off, then returned the commissioners with an indirect apology.

The second issue—a case involving Confederate ships known as commerce destroyers—generated a long-lasting diplomatic problem. Lacking the resources to construct the vessels, the Confederacy contracted to have them built and equipped in British shipyards. British companies sold six ships to the

Confederacy, of which the most famous were the *Alabama,* the *Florida,* and the *Shenandoah.* The British government liked to claim that these were private transactions of which they had no prior knowledge. In fact, they knew exactly what was going on; Charles Francis Adams was informing them of it constantly and indignantly. The United States protested that this sale of military equipment to a belligerent violated the laws of neutrality. The protests formed the basis, after the war, for damage claims that the United States served on Great Britain. (See below, p. 466.)

The third incident—the affair of the Laird rams—could have developed into a crisis but did not because the British government suddenly decided to mend its ways. In 1863, the Confederacy placed an order with the Laird shipyards in England for two powerful ironclads with pointed prows for ramming and sinking Union vessels and thus breaking the blockade. Adams was instructed to inform the British that if the rams, or any other ships destined for the Confederacy, left port, there would be danger of war. Even before Adams delivered his message, the British government acted to detain the rams and to prevent the Confederacy from obtaining any other ships.

If Napoleon III had had his way, France and England would have intervened on behalf of the Confederacy at an early date. Unable to persuade Britain to act, he had to content himself with expressing sympathy for the Southern cause and permitting the Confederates to order commerce destroyers from French shipyards. The emperor's primary motive for desiring an independent South was his ambition to establish French colonial power in the Western Hemisphere. A divided America would be less able to block his plans. He seized the opportunity of the war to set up a French-dominated empire in Mexico.

Napoleon's Mexican venture was a clear violation of the Monroe Doctrine, perhaps the most serious one that had ever occurred. The United States viewed it in such a light, but for fear of provoking France into recognizing the Confederacy, it could do no more than register a protest. Only after the Civil War ended did the United States feel strong enough to put pressure on France to get out of Mexico. By then, the French venture was already in trouble in Mexico itself. In 1866, Napoleon withdrew his troops from Mexico; and the following year, the emperor he had installed there was captured and shot by insurrectionists led by a former (and future) Mexican president, Benito Juarez.

Campaigns and Battles

In the absence of direct intervention by the European powers, the two contestants in America were left to settle their conflict between themselves. They did so in four long years of bloody combat that produced more carnage than any war in American history, before or since. More than 600,000 Americans died in the course of the Civil War, far more than the 115,000 who perished in World War I or the 318,000 who died in World War II. And in proportion to the total population, the losses suffered in the 1860s were even higher. There were nearly 2,000 deaths for every 100,000 of population during the Civil War. In World War I, the comparable figure was only 109; in World War II, 241.

It was not only battle itself that produced the remarkable death toll. It was disease, to which the miserable conditions in which both armies had to live made soldiers highly vulnerable, and for which only the most primitive medical knowledge or facilities were available. Even minor battle injuries, moreover, could lead to death through infection or other complications because of inadequate health care. Despite the efforts of such volunteer organizations as the American Sanitary Commission, military medicine on both sides remained primitive. Not until World War I would scientific knowledge reach the point where disease would claim fewer victims than battle.

And the combat itself in the Civil War was of frightful intensity. After the Battle of Antietam, according to observers, one could have walked all the way across the vast battlefield atop the bodies of the fallen soldiers; the ground was almost entirely covered with the dead. Nearly 5,000 soldiers had been killed in a single day's fighting.

Despite the gruesome cost, the Civil War has become perhaps the most romanticized, the most intently studied, of all American wars. In large part, that is because the conflict produced—in addition to hideous fatalities—a series of military campaigns of classic strategic interest and a series of military leaders who displayed unusual daring and charisma.

The Opening Clashes, 1861

The year 1861 witnessed several small battles that accomplished large results and one big battle that had no important outcome. The small engagements occurred in Missouri and in western Virginia, the mountainous region that shortly would become the state of West Virginia.

In Missouri, the contending forces were headed by Governor Claiborne Jackson and other state officials, who wanted to take the state out of the Union, and by Nathaniel Lyon, commanding a small regular army force at St. Louis. Lyon led his column into southern Missouri, where he was defeated and killed by a superior Confederate force at the Battle of Wilson's Creek (August 10). He had, however, seriously blunted the striking power of the Confederates, and Union forces were able to hold most of the state.

Crossing the Ohio River into western Virginia came a Union force that had been assembled in Ohio under the command of George B. McClellan. McClellan succeeded by the end of the year in "liberating" the mountain people, who created their own state government loyal to the Union. Although possession of the region placed the Union forces on the flank of Virginia, they could not, because of the transportation obstacles presented by the mountains, use it as a base from which to move eastward. The occupation of western Virginia was, however, an important propaganda victory for the North: A Union-sympathizing area in the Confederacy had been wrenched from Southern control.

The one big battle of the year was fought in Virginia in the area between the two capitals. Just south of Washington was a Union army of over 30,000 under the command of General Irvin McDowell. A Confederate army of over 20,000 under P. G. T. Beauregard was based at Manassas in northern Virginia, about thirty miles southwest of Washington. If McDowell's army could knock out Beauregard's, Union leaders believed, the war might be ended immediately. In mid-July, McDowell marched his inexperienced troops toward Manassas. His movement was well advertised to the Confederates by Northern newspapers and Southern spies.

Beauregard retired behind Bull Run, a small stream north of Manassas, and called for reinforcements. They reached him the day before the battle, making the two armies approximately equal in size. In the First Battle of Bull Run, or First Battle of Manassas (July 21), McDowell's attack almost succeeded. But the Confederates stopped a last strong Union assault, then began a counterattack. A sudden wave of panic struck the Union troops, wearied after hours of hot, hard fighting. They retreated across the Bull Run Creek in a rout. Unable to reorganize his troops north of the stream, McDowell had to order a

retreat to Washington—a chaotic withdrawal complicated by the presence along the route of many civilians, who had ridden down from the capital, picnic baskets in hand, to watch the battle from nearby hills. The Confederates, as disorganized by victory as the Union forces were by defeat, and lacking supplies and transportation, were in no condition to undertake a forward movement.

Lincoln replaced McDowell with General McClellan, the victor of the fighting in western Virginia, and took measures to increase the army. Both sides girded themselves now for a real war.

The Western Theater

After the battle at Manassas, military operations in the East settled into a long and frustrating stalemate. The first decisive operations in 1862 occurred, therefore, in the Western theater. Here the Union forces were trying to secure control of the Mississippi River, which would enable them to divide the Confederacy and provide them with easy transportation into its heart. Most of their offensives were combined land- and-water operations, as Union forces moved on the river itself or along its banks. Northern soldiers advanced on the southern Mississippi from both the north and south, moving down from Kentucky and up from the Gulf of Mexico toward New Orleans.

In April, a Union squadron of ironclads and wooden vessels commanded by David G. Farragut (destined to be the first American awarded the rank of admiral) appeared in the Gulf. Smashing past the weak Confederate forts near the mouth of the river, Farragut ran up to New Orleans, which had been left virtually defenseless because the Confederate high command had expected the attack to come from the north. Farragut forced the civil authorities to surrender the city on April 25—the first major Union victory (even if one that occurred virtually without bloodshed) and an important turning point in the war. Throughout the rest of the war, Union forces controlled New Orleans and southern Louisiana. They thus closed off the mouth of the great river to Confederate trade, grasped the South's largest city and greatest banking center, and secured a base for future operations.

All Confederate troops in the West were under the command of one general, Albert Sidney Johnston, who had permitted a fatal weakness to appear in his long line of defense. The center of that line lay in Ten-

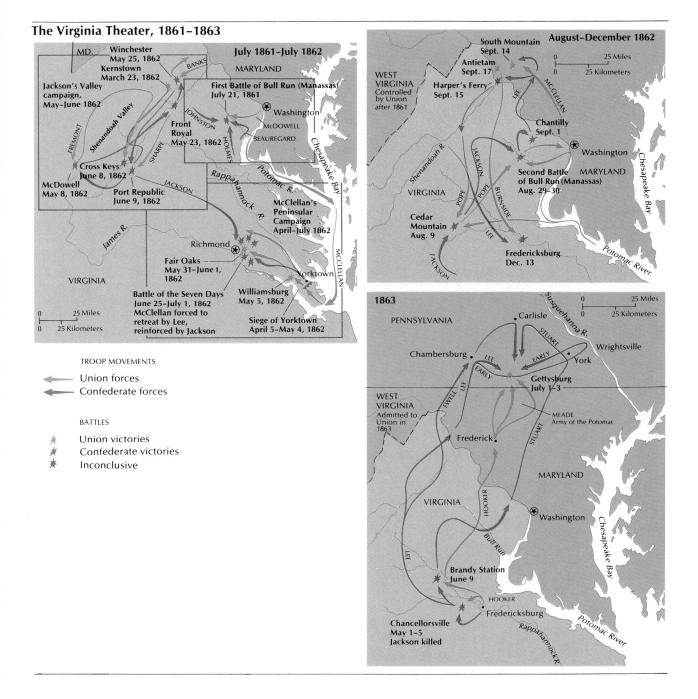

The Virginia Theater, 1861–1863

July 1861–July 1862

MD.

Winchester
May 25, 1862

Kernstown
March 23, 1862

MARYLAND

Jackson's Valley
campaign,
May–June 1862

BANKS

First Battle of Bull Run (Manassas)
July 21, 1861

Shenandoah Valley

FREMONT

JOHNSTON

Washington

Front
Royal
May 23, 1862

McDOWELL

SHARPE

HOLMES

BEAUREGARD

Cross Keys
June 8, 1862

McDowell
May 8, 1862

JACKSON

Port Republic
June 9, 1862

Rappahannock R.

Potomac R.

Chesapeake Bay

McClellan's
Peninsular
Campaign
April–July 1862

James R.

Richmond

Fair Oaks
May 31–June 1,
1862

Yorktown

MCCLELLAN

VIRGINIA

0   25 Miles
0   25 Kilometers

Battle of the Seven Days
June 25–July 1, 1862
McClellan forced to
retreat by Lee,
reinforced by Jackson

Williamsburg
May 5, 1862

Siege of Yorktown
April 5–May 4, 1862

TROOP MOVEMENTS

← Union forces
← Confederate forces

BATTLES

✳ Union victories
✳ Confederate victories
✳ Inconclusive

August–December 1862

South Mountain
Sept. 14

Antietam
Sept. 17

WEST
VIRGINIA
Controlled
by Union
after 1861

Harper's Ferry
Sept. 15

LEE

MCCLELLAN

0   25 Miles
0   25 Kilometers

Chantilly
Sept. 1

Washington

Shenandoah R.

JACKSON

POPE

POPE

BURNSIDE

Second Battle
of Bull Run (Manassas)
Aug. 29–30

MARYLAND

Chesapeake Bay

VIRGINIA

Cedar
Mountain
Aug. 9

LEE

JACKSON

Fredericksburg
Dec. 13

Potomac River

1863

PENNSYLVANIA

Susquehanna R.

Carlisle

Wrightsville

Chambersburg

LEE

STUART

EARLY

EARLY

York

EWELL

LEE

Gettysburg
July 1–3

WEST
VIRGINIA
Admitted to
Union in
1863

STUART

MEADE
Army of the Potomac

Frederick

0   25 Miles
0   25 Kilometers

MARYLAND

VIRGINIA

HOOKER

Washington

LEE

Bull Run

Chesapeake Bay

Brandy Station
June 9

HOOKER

Fredericksburg

Rappahannock R.

Potomac River

Chancellorsville
May 1–5
Jackson killed

nessee, at Fort Henry on the Tennessee River and Fort Donelson on the Cumberland—and the forts were located well to the south of (and hence behind) the main Southern flanks. If the Union forces, with the aid of naval power, could capture these outposts, they would be between the two Confederate flanks and in a position to destroy either.

This was exactly what the Union forces did in February 1862. Ulysses S. Grant proceeded to attack Fort Henry, whose defenders, awed by the ironclad river boats accompanying the Union army, surrendered with almost no resistance (February 6). Grant then marched to Donelson, while his naval auxiliary moved to the Cumberland River. At Donelson, the

Confederates put up a fight; but eventually the garrison of 20,000 had to capitulate (February 16). Grant, by the simple process of cracking the Confederate center and placing himself astride the river communications, had inflicted a near disaster on the Confederacy. As a result of his movement, the Confederates were forced out of Kentucky and had to yield half of Tennessee.

With about 40,000 men, Grant now advanced south along the Tennessee River to seize control of railroad lines that were vital to the Confederacy. He landed his army at Pittsburg Landing, and marched to nearby Shiloh, where a force almost equal to his and commanded by Albert Sidney Johnston and P. G. T. Beauregard caught him with a surprise attack. In the ensuing Battle of Shiloh (April 6–7), the Southerners drove Grant back to the river in the first day's fighting (during which Johnston was killed). The next day, reinforced by 25,000 newly arrived troops, Grant took the offensive and recovered the lost ground. Beauregard then withdrew. After the narrow victory at Shiloh, Union forces managed to occupy Corinth, Mississippi, which was the hub of several important railroads, and established control of the banks of the Mississippi River as far south as Memphis.

The Confederate army in Mississippi, now under the command of Braxton Bragg, moved north to Chattanooga, to be in a position to launch an offensive and win back the lost territory. The Confederates still controlled the eastern half of Tennessee; Bragg's task was to recover the rest of the state and, if possible, to carry the war into Kentucky. Opposing him was a Union army under Don Carlos Buell, whose assignment was to capture Chattanooga. Bragg chose not to risk an engagement near there and decided instead to draw Buell away from Tennessee by going north. When the two armies met, in central Kentucky, they fought an indecisive battle at Perryville (October 8). Bragg then turned back to Tennessee, and Buell followed him slowly—so slowly that Lincoln finally removed him from command and replaced him with William S. Rosecrans. Bragg and Rosecrans met finally in the Battle of Murfreesboro, or Stone's River (December 31–January 2). Again Bragg withdrew to the south, his campaign a failure.

In the course of the year, the Union forces had made considerable progress toward the achievement of their objectives in the West. But the major conflict remained in the East; and they were having much less success with their land campaigns there.

The Virginia Front, 1862

In the Eastern theater in 1862, Union operations were directed by young George B. McClellan, commander of the Army of the Potomac and the most controversial general of the war. McClellan was a superb trainer of men, but he never seemed ready to commit his troops to decisive battle. Opportunities for important engagements came and went, and McClellan continually failed to take advantage of them—claiming always that his preparations were not yet complete or that the moment was not quite right.

During the winter of 1861–1862, McClellan had concentrated on training his army of 150,000 men near Washington. He finally settled on a plan of operations for the spring campaign designed to capture the Confederate capital at Richmond. Instead of heading overland directly toward Richmond, he decided on a roundabout route. He would have the navy transport his troops south down the Potomac to the peninsula between the York and the James rivers. Then he would move up the peninsula and approach Richmond from the east.

McClellan began his Peninsular campaign with about 100,000 men. President Lincoln held back another 30,000—McDowell's corps—to protect the Union capital, although McClellan insisted that Washington would be safe as long as he was threatening Richmond. As he neared Richmond, he finally persuaded Lincoln to send him the additional men. But before he could do so, the Confederates took steps to divert him. A Confederate army under Thomas J. ("Stonewall") Jackson marched rapidly northward in the Shenandoah Valley as if to cross the upper Potomac and attack Washington from above. Alarmed, Lincoln dispatched McDowell's corps to head off Jackson. In his brilliant Valley campaign (May 4–June 9), Jackson defeated two separate Union armies and slipped away before McDowell could catch him.

Meanwhile, just outside Richmond, Confederate troops under Joseph E. Johnston attacked McClellan's army, but in the two-day Battle of Fair Oaks, or Seven Pines (May 31–June 1), could not budge it. Johnston, badly wounded, was replaced by Robert E. Lee, who was to prove a masterly commander in leading the Army of Northern Virginia throughout the rest of the war. Lee recalled Jackson from the valley and, with a combined force of 85,000 (as compared with McClellan's 100,000), launched a new offensive, which resulted in a series of engage-

The War in the West, 1861-1863

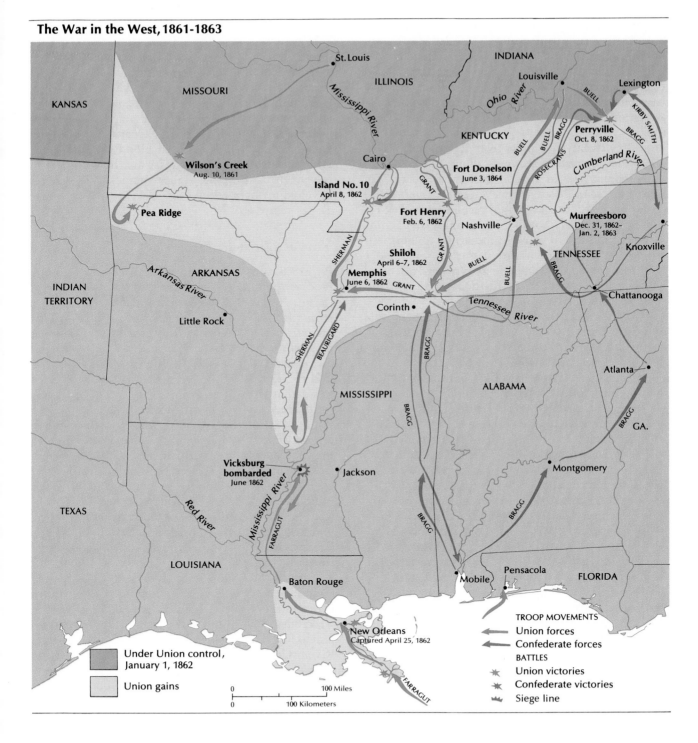

Wilson's Creek
Aug. 10, 1861

Pea Ridge

Island No. 10
April 8, 1862

Fort Henry
Feb. 6, 1862

Fort Donelson
June 3, 1864

Perryville
Oct. 8, 1862

Murfreesboro
Dec. 31, 1862–
Jan. 2, 1863

Shiloh
April 6–7, 1862

Memphis
June 6, 1862

**Vicksburg
bombarded**
June 1862

KANSAS

MISSOURI

St. Louis

ILLINOIS

INDIANA

Louisville

Lexington

KENTUCKY

Cairo

Nashville

Knoxville

TENNESSEE

Chattanooga

Atlanta

GA.

ARKANSAS

Little Rock

INDIAN
TERRITORY

Corinth

MISSISSIPPI

ALABAMA

Jackson

Montgomery

TEXAS

LOUISIANA

Baton Rouge

Mobile

Pensacola

FLORIDA

New Orleans
Captured April 25, 1862

Mississippi River

Ohio River

Cumberland River

Tennessee River

Arkansas River

Red River

BUELL

BRAGG

KIRBY SMITH

ROSECRANS

GRANT

SHERMAN

BEAUREGARD

FARRAGUT

TROOP MOVEMENTS
← Union forces
← Confederate forces

BATTLES
✳ Union victories
✳ Confederate victories
⚔ Siege line

Under Union control,
January 1, 1862

Union gains

0   100 Miles

0   100 Kilometers

ments known as the Battle of the Seven Days (June 25–July 1). Lee intended to cut McClellan off from his base on the York River and then to destroy McClellan's isolated army. Instead, McClellan managed to fight his way across the peninsula and set up a new base on the James. There, with naval support, the Army of the Potomac was safe. But so was Richmond.

Only twenty-five miles from Richmond, with a secure line of water communications, the Army of the Potomac was in a good position to renew the campaign. McClellan, however, time and again found reasons for delay. And Lincoln, instead of replacing McClellan with a more aggressive commander, decided to remove the army to northern Virginia and combine it with a smaller force under John Pope. Lincoln wished to start a new offensive on the direct Washington-to-Richmond overland route that he himself preferred.

As the Army of the Potomac left the peninsula by water, Lee moved the Army of Northern Virginia northward to strike Pope before McClellan could join him. Pope, who was as rash as McClellan was cautious, attacked the approaching Confederates without waiting for the arrival of all of McClellan's troops. In the ensuing Second Battle of Bull Run, or Second Battle of Manassas (August 29–30), Lee threw back the assault and routed Pope's army, which fled to Washington. Removing Pope from command, Lincoln put McClellan in charge of all the federal forces around the city.

Lee soon went on the offensive again, heading north through western Maryland. With some misgivings, Lincoln let McClellan move out to meet Lee. McClellan had the good luck to come into possession of a copy of Lee's orders, which revealed to him that the Confederate army was divided. A part of it, under Stonewall Jackson, had gone to capture Harpers Ferry. McClellan should have attacked quickly, before the Confederates could recombine. Instead, he gave Lee time to pull most of his forces together behind Antietam Creek, near the town of Sharpsburg. Here, in the bloodiest engagement of the war (September 17), McClellan with 87,000 men repeatedly assaulted Lee, who had 50,000. Late in the day—after appalling casualties on both sides—it seemed that the Confederate line might break, but the rest of Jackson's troops arrived from Harpers Ferry to fill the gap. Even then, McClellan might have broken through with one more effort. Instead, he allowed Lee to retreat into Virginia. Technically, Antietam was a Union victory; but in reality, it represented

another opportunity squandered. In November, Lincoln finally removed McClellan from command for good.

McClellan's replacement, Ambrose E. Burnside, was a short-lived mediocrity. He chose to drive at Richmond by crossing the Rappahannock at Fredericksburg, the strongest defensive point on the river. There (December 13) he flung his army at Lee's defenses in repeated attacks, all bloody, all hopeless. After losing a large part of his army, he withdrew to the north bank of the Rappahannock. He was relieved at his own request.

Year of Decision, 1863

As 1863 opened, Burnside's successor, Joseph Hooker (popularly known as "Fighting Joe"), was at the head of the Army of the Potomac, which, 120,000 strong, still lay north of the Rappahannock, opposite Fredericksburg. With part of the army, Hooker crossed the river upstream from Fredericksburg and threatened the town and Lee's army. But at the last minute, apparently, he lost his nerve and drew back to a defensive position in a desolate area of brush and scrub trees known as the Wilderness. Here, in the Battle of Chancellorsville (May 1–5), with only half as many men as Hooker had, Lee daringly divided the Confederate forces for a dual assault. He sent Jackson to hit the Union right while he himself charged the front. Hooker barely managed to extricate his army. Again Lee had frustrated Union objectives, but he had not won the decisive victory he was hoping for. And he had lost his ablest officer, Jackson, who was fatally wounded at the close of the battle.

While the Union forces were suffering repeated frustrations in the East, they continued to do much better in the West. Ulysses S. Grant kept driving at Vicksburg, Mississippi, one of the Confederates' two remaining strongholds on the southern Mississippi River. Coming downriver with naval support, he struck several unsuccessful blows at the Confederate defenses. The terrain in front of Vicksburg was difficult, with rough country on the north and low, marshy ground on the west. Finally, in May, Grant had the navy run supply boats past the river batteries to a point below Vicksburg. He moved his army safely southward by land, down the Louisiana side of the river and out of range of Vicksburg's powerful guns. Then, once he was south of the city, he transported his troops back across the river. Here the terrain was much more suitable for maneuvering. Moving swiftly to the east, Grant twice defeated Confederates trying to stop him. Then he turned back to the west and approached Vicksburg from the rear. After attempting to take the town by storm, he settled into a prolonged siege. Six weeks later, on July 4, Vicksburg—whose residents were by then literally starving—surrendered. Almost immediately, the other Confederate strong point on the river, Port Hudson, Louisiana, also surrendered—to a Union force that had moved north from New Orleans.

At last the Union had achieved one of its basic military aims: control of the whole length of the Mississippi. The Confederacy was split in two—Louisiana, Arkansas, and Texas were now cut off from the other seceded states. The victories on the Mississippi were one of the great turning points of the war.

The siege of Vicksburg had other effects on the Confederate war effort. Early in the siege, the Confederate government had begun considering various plans for relieving the town. Lee proposed an invasion of Pennsylvania, which would, he argued, remove the pressure on Vicksburg. If he could win a sudden victory on Northern soil, he said, England and France would probably come to the Confederacy's aid, and the Union might even quit the war before Vicksburg fell.

Lee started the northern campaign in June. He moved west to the Shenandoah Valley and then north through Maryland and into Pennsylvania. Hooker moved his troops west, to keep parallel with the Confederates' movement and to remain between Lee and Washington. Then, in mid-campaign, he was replaced by George C. Meade, a solid if unimaginative soldier. Units of Lee's and Meade's armies finally encountered one another at the small town of Gettysburg. There, on July 1–3, 1863, they fought the most celebrated battle of the war.

Meade's army established a strong, well-protected position on the hills south of the town. Lee, combative by nature and confident of his men, decided to attack even though his army was at a tactical disadvantage and was outnumbered 75,000 to 90,000. His first assault failed to reach the main line of the Union forces on Cemetery Ridge, so, a day later, he ordered a second and larger effort. In what is remembered as Pickett's Charge, a force of 15,000 Confederate soldiers advanced for almost a mile over open country that was being swept by hostile fire. Only about 5,000 made it up the ridge, and this remnant finally had to surrender or retreat. Lee was compelled to withdraw from Get-

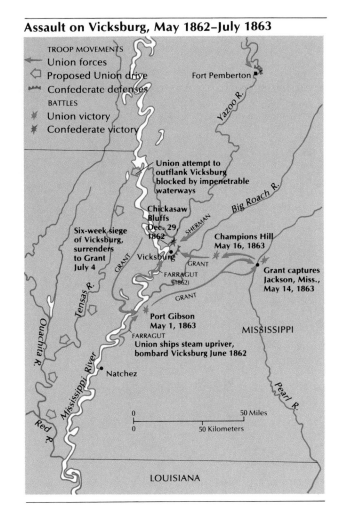

Assault on Vicksburg, May 1862–July 1863

TROOP MOVEMENTS
← Union forces
⬦ Proposed Union drive
⌇ Confederate defenses
BATTLES
✳ Union victory
✳ Confederate victory

Fort Pemberton
Yazoo R.
Union attempt to outflank Vicksburg blocked by impenetrable waterways
Big Roach R.
Chickasaw Bluffs Dec. 29 1862
SHERMAN
Six-week siege of Vicksburg, surrenders to Grant July 4
Champions Hill May 16, 1863
Vicksburg
GRANT
GRANT
FARRAGUT (1862)
Grant captures Jackson, Miss., May 14, 1863
GRANT
Port Gibson May 1, 1863
MISSISSIPPI
FARRAGUT
Union ships steam upriver, bombard Vicksburg June 1862
Tensas R.
Ouachita R.
Mississippi River
Natchez
Pearl R.
Red R.
0   50 Miles
0   50 Kilometers
LOUISIANA

tysburg, having lost nearly a third of his army. Meade failed to prevent the return of the Confederates to Virginia; but the Southern army had been so weakened that Lee never again attempted a large-scale invasion of the North. The Confederate retreat from Gettysburg, which began on the same day as the surrender at Vicksburg (July 4), was another great turning point in the war.

Before the end of the year, there was a third important turning point, this one in Tennessee. The Union army under Rosecrans occupied Chattanooga (September 9) after Bragg and the Confederates had evacuated the town. Rosecrans then went, unwisely, in pursuit of Bragg. Just across the Georgia line, Bragg, with reinforcements from Lee's army, was lying in wait. He fell upon Rosecrans in the Battle of Chickamauga (September 19–20), one of the few battles in which the Confederates enjoyed a numerical

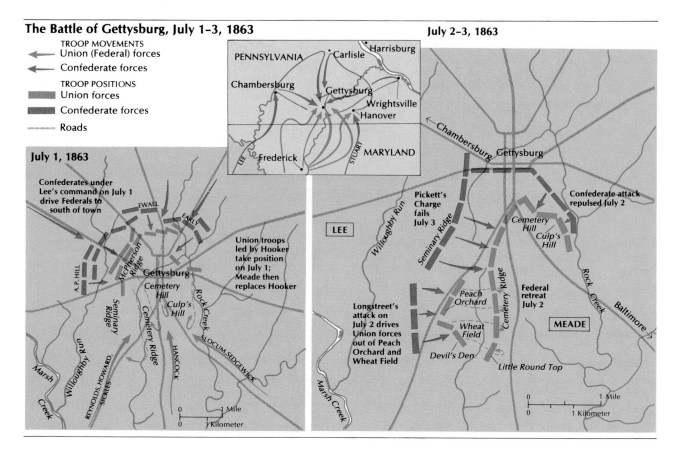

The Battle of Gettysburg, July 1–3, 1863

TROOP MOVEMENTS
← Union (Federal) forces
← Confederate forces

TROOP POSITIONS
▬ Union forces
▬ Confederate forces

▪▪▪ Roads

July 1, 1863

Confederates under Lee's command on July 1 drive Federals to south of town

Union troops led by Hooker take position on July 1; Meade then replaces Hooker

July 2–3, 1863

Pickett's Charge fails July 3

Confederate attack repulsed July 2

Longstreet's attack on July 2 drives Union forces out of Peach Orchard and Wheat Field

Federal retreat July 2

superiority (70,000 to 56,000). The Union right broke and ran, although the left, under George H. Thomas (who became known as "the Rock of Chickamauga"), continued to fight. Finally Thomas, along with the rest of the beaten army, sought refuge behind the Chattanooga defenses.

Soon the Union army in Chattanooga was under siege. Bragg held the heights nearby and controlled the roads and the Tennessee River, thus cutting off almost all fresh supplies. Finally Grant came to the rescue. In the Battle of Chattanooga (November 23–25), the reinforced Union army drove the Confederates back into Georgia. Northern troops then proceeded to occupy most of eastern Tennessee.

The Union forces had achieved a second important objective: control of the Tennessee River. At Chattanooga they were in a position to split the Confederacy again—what was left of it. No longer could the Southerners hope to gain their independence by some great military victory. They could hope to win only by holding on and exhausting the Northern will to fight.

The Last Stage, 1864–1865

Grant, who was now general in chief of all the Union armies, planned two grand offensives for 1864. In Virginia, the Army of the Potomac (which Meade continued to command but which Grant accompanied and actually directed) was to advance toward Richmond and force Lee into a decisive battle. In Georgia, the Western army, under William T. Sherman, was to advance east toward Atlanta and destroy the opposing Confederate force, now under the command of Joseph E. Johnston.

The twofold campaign began when the Army of the Potomac, 115,000 strong, crossed the Rappahannock and Rapidan rivers and plunged into the rough, wooded Wilderness area. Lee, with about 75,000 men, was determined to avoid a showdown unless he saw a chance to deal a decisive blow. In the Battle of the Wilderness (May 5–7), Lee stopped Grant, but only for the moment. Instead of withdrawing to rest and reorganize, as his predecessors had done after every battle, Grant resumed his march in the general direction of Richmond. Lee intercepted him a second time in the Battle of Spotsylvania Court House and engaged him in a bloody five-day struggle, which cost the Union armies 12,000 men; the heavy Confederate casualty figures were never released. Despite the enormous losses, Grant still refused to stop his advance. He moved now to the southeast, and Lee continued to keep between him and the Confederate capital. Just a few miles northeast of Richmond, at Cold Harbor (June 1–3), Grant made a desperate attack and was repulsed. In the whole month-long Wilderness campaign Grant had lost a total of 55,000 men (killed, wounded, and captured) to Lee's 31,000. Still the decisive victory eluded him.

"I propose to fight it out on this line if it takes all summer," Grant had declared during the Battle of Spotsylvania; but he now tried a different tack. He slipped away with his army, bypassed Richmond, and headed for Petersburg, a railroad center directly south of the capital. If he could seize Petersburg, he could cut off the capital's communications and force Lee to fight for them. But Grant's initial assault on Petersburg failed. Both sides settled down to a siege,

with trenches stretching for miles from Richmond to and around Petersburg. Grant kept trying to extend his left around Lee's right so as to get at the railroads that served as Lee's lifeline. But success was not to come until after nine months of struggle.

In Georgia, meanwhile, Sherman had been facing less resistance than Grant in Virginia. Sherman had 90,000 men and faced Confederate forces under Johnston of 60,000. Johnston was unwilling to risk the destruction of his army through a direct engagement with Sherman's superior force; and so, as Sherman advanced, he tried to delay him by maneuvering. Johnston stopped long enough to fight only one real battle—Kennesaw Mountain, northwest of Atlanta (June 27). Despite an impressive victory there, Johnston was unable to stop the Union advance toward Atlanta. Realizing that Sherman would soon reach the city, President Davis replaced Johnston with the combative John B. Hood. Twice Hood daringly attacked; he accomplished nothing except seriously to weaken his own army. Sherman took Atlanta on September 2. (News of the victory electrified the North and helped unite the previously

Virginia Campaigns, 1864–1865

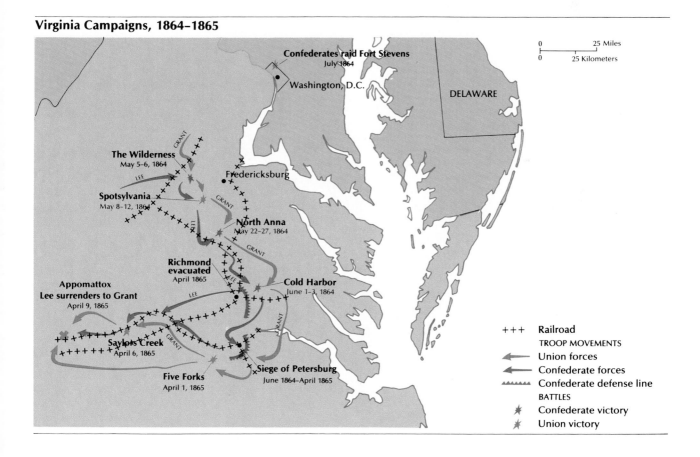

Sherman's Capture of Atlanta

General William T. Sherman's capture of Atlanta in 1864 came after a siege of more than six weeks, in which Confederate forces under General John B. Hood fought vainly against a much larger Union army. When Hood withdrew from the city and Union troops took possession of it, Sherman ordered the remaining residents to evacuate. Hood protested that the civilians in Atlanta had already suffered enough, but Sherman replied, "You might as well appeal against the thunderstorms as against the terrible hardship of war." Then, as he had done at other stops along his "March to the Sea," he burned much of the city to ensure that it would no longer be available as a transportation and supply center for the Confederacy. This lithograph by Currier and Ives shows Union troops entering Atlanta on September 2, 1864. (The Bettmann Archive)

Sherman's March to the Sea, 1863–1865

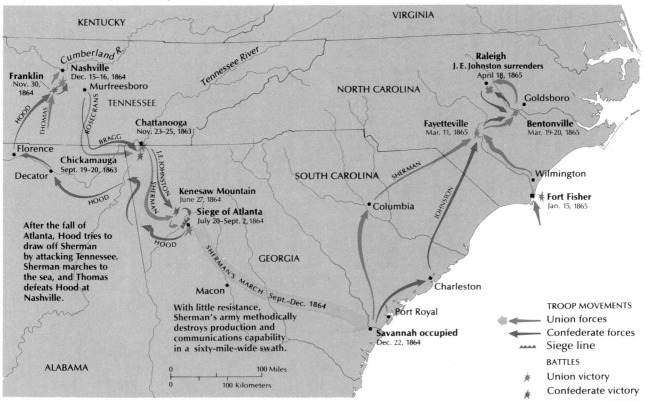

After the fall of Atlanta, Hood tries to draw off Sherman by attacking Tennessee. Sherman marches to the sea, and Thomas defeats Hood at Nashville.

With little resistance, Sherman's army methodically destroys production and communications capability in a sixty-mile-wide swath.

TROOP MOVEMENTS
Union forces
Confederate forces
Siege line
BATTLES
Union victory
Confederate victory

SIGNIFICANT EVENTS

1860 South Carolina secedes from Union (p. 412)

1861 Ten more Southern states secede (pp. 412, 414)

Confederate States of America formed (p. 424)

Jefferson Davis named president of Confederacy (p. 424)

Conflict at Fort Sumter, South Carolina (April 12–14), begins Civil War (p. 414)

George B. McClellan appointed commander of Army of the Potomac (p. 429)

Union blockades Confederate coast (p. 431)

Trent affair imperils U.S. relations with Britain (p. 432)

First Battle of Bull Run (July 21) (p. 434)

1862 Battle of Shiloh (April 6–7) (p. 436)

Union forces capture New Orleans (May 1) (p. 434)

Second Battle of Bull Run (August 29–30) (p. 438)

Battle of Antietam (September 17) (p. 438)

Battle of Fredericksburg (December 13) (p. 438)

McClellan removed from command (p. 438)

Robert E. Lee named commander of Confederate armies (p. 430)

Homestead Act and Morrill Land Grant Act passed (p. 418)

Union Pacific Railroad chartered (p. 418)

Confederacy enacts military draft (p. 426)

1862 Republicans experience heavy losses in congressional elections (p. 422)

1863 Lincoln issues Emancipation Proclamation (January 1) (p. 422)

Battle of Chancellorsville (May 1–5) (p. 438)

Battle of Gettysburg (July 1–3) (p. 439)

Vicksburg surrenders (July 4) (p. 439)

Battle of Chattanooga (November 23–25) (p. 440)

Union enacts military draft (p. 420)

Antidraft riots break out in New York City (p. 420)

South experiences food riots (p. 428)

West Virginia admitted to Union (p. 416)

1864 Battle of the Wilderness (May 5–7) (p. 440)

Petersburg, Virginia, besieged (p. 441)

Sherman captures Atlanta (September 2) (p. 441)

Sherman's "march to the sea" begins (p. 443)

Lincoln reelected president (p. 422)

Central Pacific Railroad chartered (p. 418)

1865 Lee surrenders to Grant at Appomattox (April 9) (p. 444)

Thirteenth Amendment, abolishing slavery, ratified (p. 423)

---

divided Republican party behind President Lincoln.)

Hood now schemed to draw Sherman out of Atlanta by moving back up through Tennessee and threatening an invasion of the North. Sherman refused to follow—he had other plans—but he sent reinforcements under George H. Thomas and John M. Schofield to help defend Nashville. Hood caught up with Schofield's force and, in the Battle of Franklin (November 30), further weakened his own army by ordering senseless charges against Schofield's well-protected positions. Then, in the Battle of Nashville (December 15–16, 1864), Thomas not only put Hood's army to flight but practically disintegrated it.

Meanwhile Sherman had started on a march from Atlanta to the sea. Living off the land, destroying supplies it could not use, his army cut a sixty-mile-wide swath of desolation across Georgia. "War

is hell," Sherman maintained. By that he meant not so much that war is terrible, and to be avoided, as that it should be made as horrible and costly as possible for the opponent. He sought not only to deprive the Confederate army of war materials and railroad communications but also to bring the war home to the Southern people and break their will to fight. By December 20, he had reached Savannah, which surrendered two days later and was offered to President Lincoln as a Christmas gift (and which, almost alone among the areas he conquered, he did not destroy; the city was, he claimed, too beautiful to burn). Early in 1865, Sherman turned northward and carried his destruction through South Carolina. On his entire march, he was virtually unopposed until he was well inside North Carolina, where a small force under Johnston could do no more than cause a brief delay.

In April 1865, Grant's Army of the Potomac—still engaged in the prolonged siege at Petersburg—finally captured a vital railroad junction southwest of the town. Lee could no longer hope to defend Richmond. With the remnant of his army, now reduced to about 25,000, Lee began moving west in the forlorn hope of finding a way to avoid Union forces to his south so that he could move toward North Carolina and link up with Johnston. But the Union army pursued him and blocked his escape route. Realizing that further bloodshed was futile, Lee arranged to meet Grant at a courthouse in the small town of Appomattox, Virginia. There, on April 9, he surrendered what was left of his forces. Nine days later, near Durham, North Carolina, Johnston surrendered to Sherman. Other Confederate forces lay down their arms over the next several weeks in Alabama, Texas, and elsewhere. In military terms, at least, the long war was now largely over. Jefferson Davis remained defiant and refused to accept defeat. He fled south from Richmond and was finally captured in Georgia. A few Southern diehards continued to fight, but even their resistance collapsed before long. Well before the last shot was fired, the painful process of trying to reunite the shattered nation had begun.

SUGGESTED READINGS

General Studies. James M McPherson, *Battle Cry of Freedom* (1988) and *Ordeal by Fire*, rev. ed. (1985); James G. Randall and David Donald, *The Civil War and Reconstruction*, rev. ed. (1969); Allan Nevins, *The War for the Union*, 4 vols. (1959–1971); Shelby Foote, *The Civil War: A Narrative*, 3 vols. (1958–1974); Bruce Catton, *This Hallowed Ground* (1956).

The Secession Crisis. Ralph A Wooster, *The Secession Conventions of the South* (1962); David Potter, *Lincoln and His Party in the Secession Crisis* (1942); William L. Barney, *The Road to Secession* (1972) and *The Secessionist Impulse: Alabama and Mississippi in 1860* (1974); Kenneth M. Stampp, *And the War Came* (1950); Richard N. Current, *Lincoln and the First Shot* (1963); Steven A. Channing, *Crisis of Fear* (1970); Michael P. Johnson, *Toward a Patriarchal Republic* (1977).

Lincoln. Benjamin Thomas, *Abraham Lincoln* (1952); Stephen B. Oates, *With Malice Toward None* (1979); James G. Randall, *Lincoln the President*, 4 vols. (1945–1955), the final volume completed by Richard N. Current; Carl Sandburg, *Abraham Lincoln*, 6 vols. (1929–1939); T. Harry Williams, *Lincoln and the Radicals* (1941) and *Lincoln and His Generals* (1952); William B. Hesseltine, *Lincoln and the War Governors* (1948); Robert V. Bruce, *Lincoln and the Tools of War* (1956); Harry J. Carman and Reinhard Luthin, *Lincoln and the Patronage* (1943); LaWanda Cox, *Lincoln and Black Freedom* (1981).

Politics and Society in the North. David Donald, *Charles Sumner and the Rights of Man* (1970); Benjamin P. Thomas and Harold M. Hyman, *Stanton* (1962); Glyndon Van Deusen, *William Henry Seward* (1967); Martin Duberman, *Charles Francis Adams* (1961); James G. Randall, *Constitutional Problems Under Lincoln* (1926); Robert P. Sharkey, *Money, Class, and Party* (1959); Wood Gray, *The Hidden Civil War* (1942); Frank Klement, *The Copperheads in the Middle West* (1960); George Fredrickson, *The Inner Civil War* (1965); Daniel Aaron, *The Unwritten War* (1973); Edmund Wilson, *Patriotic Gore* (1962); John P. Bugardt, ed.,

Civil War Nurse (1980); Susan M. Reverby, *Ordered to Care: The Dilemma of American Nursing, 1850–1945* (1987).

Blacks and Emancipation. Ira Berlin, Leslie Rowland, et al., eds., *Freedom: A Documentary History of Emancipation, 1861–1867, Series II: The Black Military Experience* (1982); Clarence L. Mohr, *On the Threshold of Freedom: Masters and Slaves in Civil War Georgia* (1986); Benjamin Quarles, *Lincoln and the Negro* (1962) and *The Negro in the Civil War* (1953); James M. McPherson, *The Struggle for Equality* (1964) and *The Negro's Civil War* (1965); Peter Kolchin, *First Freedom* (1972); John W. Blassingame, *Black New Orleans* (1973); Dudley T. Cornish, *The Sable Arm* (1966).

The Confederacy. Emory Thomas, *The Confederate Nation* (1979) and *The Confederate State of Richmond* (1971); Clement Eaton, *A History of the Southern Confederacy* (1954); Charles P. Roland, *The Confederacy* (1960); E. Merton Coulter, *The Confederate States of America* (1950); Clement Eaton, *Jefferson Davis* (1978); Hudson Strode, *Jefferson Davis*, 3 vols. (1955–1964); Thomas B. Alexander and Richard E. Beringer, *The Anatomy of the Confederate Congress* (1972); W. Buck Yearns, *The Confederate Congress* (1960); Emory Thomas, *The Confederacy as a Revolutionary Experience* (1971); Frank L. Owsley, *State Rights in the Confederacy* (1952); Bell I. Wiley, *The Life of Johnny Reb* (1943) and *The Plain People of the Confederacy* (1943); Paul D. Escott, *After Secession* (1978), *Slavery Remembered* (1979), and *Many Excellent People* (1985); James L. Roark, *Masters Without Slaves* (1977); Georgia Lee Tatum, *Disloyalty in the Confederacy* (1934); Ella Lonn, *Desertion During the Civil War* (1928); C. Vann Woodward, ed., *Mary Chestnut's Civil War* (1982).

Diplomacy. David P. Crook, *Diplomacy During The American Civil War* (1975) and *The North, the South, and the Powers, 1861–1865* (1974); Frank L. Owsley and Harriet Owsley, *King Cotton Diplomacy*, rev. ed. (1959); Gordon H. Warren, *Fountain of Discontent: The Trent Affair and Freedom of the Seas* (1981); Stuart L. Bernath, *Squall Across the*

Atlantic: American Civil War Prize Cases and Diplomacy (1970).

Military Histories. Douglas Southall Freeman, *Robert E. Lee,* 4 vols. (1934–1935); Thomas L. Connelly, *The Marble Man* (1977); John Carpenter, *Ulysses S. Grant* (1976); William McFeely, *Grant* (1981); Bruce Catton, *Mr. Lincoln's Army* (1951), *Glory Road* (1952), *A Stillness at Appomattox* (1954), *America Goes to War* (1958), *Banners at Shenandoah* (1956), and *Grant Moves South* (1960); Bell Wiley, *The Life of Billy Yank* (1952); Kenneth P. Williams, *Lincoln Finds a General,* 4 vols. (1949–1952); Richard S. West, Jr., *Mr. Lincoln's Navy* (1957); C. E. MacCartney, *Mr. Lincoln's Admirals* (1956); John Niven, *Gideon Welles, Lincoln's Secretary of the Navy* (1973); William N. Still, Jr., *Iron Afloat: The Story of the Confederate Armorclads* (1971) and *Confederate Shipbuilding* (1969); T. Harry Williams, *McClellan, Sherman, and Grant* (1962) and *P. G. T. Beauregard, Napoleon in Gray* (1955); Burke Davis, *Sherman's March* (1980); Thomas L. Livermore, *Numbers and Losses in the Civil War in America* (1957); Herman Hattaway and Archer Jones, *How the North Won* (1983); Archer Jones et al., *Why the South Lost the Civil War* (1986).

The Locomotive's Magic Wand

The railroad worked a revolution in the nineteenth-century American landscape. The story of the railroad's construction is among the most familiar narratives of American history. For contemporary observers, the locomotive was the great icon of the age, a "magic wand" that transformed city and country alike. Most saw in it the central symbol of American progress. The writer Caroline Kirkland was typical in describing the railroad as "the resistless chariot of civilization with scythed axles mowing down ignorance and prejudice as it whirls along," driving "the shadows of the past . . . into the dim woods." Among the "shadows" that fled before it were some of the most familiar features of American ecosystems.

The basic achievement of the railroad, in the most abstract economic terms, was to reduce the cost of space by accelerating the speed at which one could move across it. In the 1830s, traveling from New York to Chicago by lake and canal took roughly three weeks. By railroad in the 1850s, it took less than two days. The difference was even more impressive for roads. Whereas a team of horses was doing well to haul a wagonload of grain a dozen miles in a day, a railroad could transport the same grain *hundreds* of miles in the same time. No less important, the railroad liberated America's rural economy from the forced hibernation of winter. While roads and canals sat idle under winter ice, locomotives kept hauling goods to market no matter how cold the weather. As a result, the entire economy became more productive.

This was why the railroad seemed such a symbol of progress. Wherever it went, farms and towns sprang up in response to the new opportunities it brought. The pace of Western development increased dramatically as settlers followed the railroads out onto the Midwestern prairies in increasing numbers. As they plowed up the sod to raise grain, they dismantled the tallgrass prairie, so much so that it had almost disappeared by the end of the century. The same fate befell the white pine forests of northern Michigan, Wisconsin, and Minnesota. Sawed into lumber and shipped south on Lake Michigan or the Mississippi River, pine trees were delivered by rail to prairie farmers who used them for fences and houses. By 1900, the pines

446

Early Railroad Construction Crew
For many nineteenth-century Americans, the appearance of railroad surveyors and construction crews seemed to herald a new era. The locomotive symbolized progress, bringing in its wake a sudden growth of farms, factories, and towns. (The Bettmann Archive)

had nearly vanished from their former homes, and midwestern lumber companies were moving their operations elsewhere.

Farther west, an equally dramatic fate befell the great bison herds which had been the mainstay of Great Plains Indian life for generations. With the coming of the Union Pacific in the North and the Kansas Pacific in the South, bison were slaughtered at an almost unimaginable rate. A single hunting party could gun down hundreds in a day for their skins, while tourists could shoot from the windows of their trains without even stopping to inspect their kills. Within half a decade of the arrival of the railroads, over 4 million bison died on the Southern plains alone. By 1883, the last major herd had vanished from the Plains. An animal that had numbered in the tens of millions less than a quarter-century before now teetered on the brink of extinction. It was no accident that the last major battles between Plains Indians and the U.S. Army took place at exactly the same time. In addition to facilitating the movement of soldiers in such conflicts, the railroad had helped destroy the ecological foundation of the Indian economy.

The railroad also introduced the herds of livestock that soon replaced the bison. The drives that brought longhorn steers from Texas to the Kansas cattle towns did so for only one reason: to reach the railroad. As livestock expanded into the grass-lands where bison had once grazed, it was the railroad that permitted them to be shipped to market. The result was a newly integrated regional economy that fundamentally altered the environments that sustained it. By the late nineteenth century, the old shortgrass prairies of the high plains were raising range-fed cattle, their native bison having almost entirely disappeared. The tallgrass prairies of Iowa and Illinois had been converted to corn production. Their native bluestem grasses had been plowed under, and much of the grain they now raised was used in feedlots where Western cattle were fattened for final sale. Whether raised in Texas, Montana, or Illinois, cattle eventually made their way to Chicago's great Union Stockyard. There they were slaughtered and shipped to the Eastern markets where they were finally eaten.

Without the railroad, none of this would have occurred when and how it did. By the end of the century, the new technology had linked together the different regional environments of the continent with great urban markets. No matter where they lived, no matter what the time of year, Americans relied on the railroad to satisfy their basic needs with products from distant places: Minnesota flour, Texas beef, and Washington lumber all reached their customers via the iron horse. The widespread availability of such products liberated Americans from the constraints of local resources and created a truly national market. These benefits had been earned at the cost of immense ecological changes, but these were rarely evident to customers living hundreds of miles from landscapes they never saw. Had they seen the ties between their own lives and the slaughtered bison herds, vanished prairies, and disappearing forests, they would almost certainly have joined Caroline Kirkland in regarding them as reasonable costs of civilized progress.

Just how thoroughly the railroads altered the landscape of the United States can be suggested by one further change. Until the 1880s, every community in America had its own "local" time. People set their clocks according to the rules of astronomy: noon was the moment when the sun stood highest in the midday sky. When it was noon in Chicago, it was 11:50 A.M. in St. Louis, 11:27 A.M. in Omaha, and 12:18 P.M. in Detroit, with every possible variation in between. For the railroad companies, trying to keep track of hundreds of different times was a nightmare, since a train leaving a station at one local time arrived at its destination at an entirely different local time. Such scheduling problems could even cause train wrecks. And so, on November 18, 1883 the major railraod companies carved up the continent into four uniform time zones and declared that they intended to ignore all local times. Henceforth, for railroad purposes, every community in a time zone would have the same time. The U.S. government did not finally ratify this change until 1918, but most communities adopted railroad "standard" time very quickly. The magic wand of the locomotive had managed to change not just the many natural environments of North America, but time itself.

448

A Reconstruction-Era Tribute to the Election of Blacks to Congress
From left to right: Sen. Hiram R. Revels, Rep. Benjamin S. Turner, the Reverend Richard Allen, Frederick Douglass, Representative Josiah T. Walls, Representative Joseph H. Rainy, and writer William Wells Brown. (*Library of Congress*)

CHAPTER 15

Reconstructing the Nation

Few periods in the history of the United States have produced as much bitterness or created such enduring controversy as the era of Reconstruction—the years following the Civil War during which Americans attempted to reunite their shattered nation. Those who lived through the experience viewed it in sharply different ways. To white Southerners, Reconstruction was a vicious and destructive experience—a period of low, unscrupulous politics, a time when vindictive Northerners inflicted humiliation and revenge on the prostrate South and unnecessarily delayed a genuine reunion of the sections. Northern defenders of Reconstruction, in contrast, argued that their policies were the only way to prevent unrepentant Confederates from restoring Southern society as it had been before the war; without forceful federal intervention, there would be no way to forestall the reemergence of a backward aristocracy and the continued subjugation of blacks—no way, in other words, to prevent the same sectional problems that had produced the Civil War in the first place.

To most black Americans at the time, and to many people of all races since, Reconstruction was notable for other reasons. Not a vicious tyranny, as white Southerners charged, nor a drastic and necessary reform, as many Northerners claimed, it was, rather, an essentially moderate, even conservative program that fell far short of providing the newly freed slaves with the protection they needed. Reconstruction, in other words, was significant less for what it did than for what it failed to do. And when it came to an end, finally, in 1877—as a result of exhaustion and disillusionment among the white leaders of both sections, and of a series of complex bargains in the aftermath of the election of 1876—black Americans found themselves once again abandoned. They had received their freedom; and they had, with the help of federal protection, won some important other legal and constitutional guarantees during Reconstruction. But they had won no commitment from white society, or from the federal government, to enforce most of those guarantees. After 1877 nothing would save black people from being consigned to a system of economic peonage and legal subordination. The nation's racial problem, which had done so much to produce the Civil War, was left unresolved—to arise again and again in future generations.

The Problems of Peacemaking

In 1865, when the Confederacy finally surrendered to the North, no one in Washington knew quite what to do in response. Abraham Lincoln could not negotiate a treaty with the defeated government; he continued to insist that that government had no legal right to exist. Yet neither could he simply readmit the Southern states into the Union as if nothing had happened. The South had been devastated by the war—socially, economically, and politically. And there was now an

Charleston, 1865
Not until 1864 did substantial fighting and destruction begin to take place in the urban South. But in the last year of the war, several major cities (and many towns and smaller communities) experienced devastation at the hands of the Northern armies—among them Richmond, Atlanta, and (as seen here) Charleston. (Library of Congress)

enormous population of freed slaves, many of them wandering bewildered through the shattered land. Clearly the federal government had to act.

The Aftermath of War

In the North, the wartime prosperity continued into the postwar years; but Northerners who visited the South were appalled when they gazed on the desolation left in the wake of the war—gutted towns, wrecked plantations, neglected fields, collapsed bridges, and ruined railroads. Much of the personal property of white Southerners had been lost with the lost cause. Confederate bonds and currency were now worthless, and capital that had been invested in them was gone forever. With the emancipation of the slaves, Southern whites were deprived of property worth an estimated $2 billion. Southern blacks were left with no property at all.

Matching the shattered economy of the South was the disorganization of its social system. In the months that followed the end of the war, thousands of soldiers drifted back to their homes; but 258,000 had died in the war, and additional thousands returned wounded or sick. Many families approached the difficult task of rebuilding, therefore, without the help of adult males. Many white Southerners faced the prospect of starvation and homelessness.

If conditions were bad for Southern whites, they were generally far worse for Southern blacks—the 4 million men and women now emerging from the bondage that had held them and their ancestors for up to two and a half centuries. Many of these people, too, had seen service of one kind or another during the war. Some had served as body servants for Confederate officers or as teamsters and laborers for the Confederate armies. Nearly 200,000 had fought as combat troops in the Union ranks, and more than 38,000 had given their lives for the Union cause.

Countless other blacks, who had never worn a uniform or drawn army pay, had assisted the Union forces as spies or scouts. Still others had run off from the plantations and flocked to the Union lines in search of freedom and protection, often to be put to work for the Union armies. As soon as the war ended, many thousands more left the plantations in search of a new life in freedom. Old and young, many of them feeble and ill, they trudged to the nearest town or city or roamed the countryside, camping at night on the bare ground. Few had any possessions except the clothes they wore.

In 1865, in short, Southern society was in disarray. Blacks and whites, men and women faced a future of great uncertainty, in which traditional institutions and assumptions no longer seemed suitable. Nevertheless, people of both races had, even in 1865, distinct and very different ideas about how to respond to the new postwar world.

Many white Southerners hoped to restore their society to its antebellum form. Slavery, of course, had already been abolished in much of the South by the Emancipation Proclamation. The Thirteenth Amendment, which declared slavery unconstitutional, passed Congress on February 1, 1865; the amendment became law on December 18, 1865. But many white planters were determined to retain the essence of slavery even if its legal basis was now destroyed. Some planters continued to detain their black workers. In some cases, the former slaves simply did not learn that slavery had been abolished. But in other cases, they fell victim to efforts by white Southerners to re-create slavery in another form. Most planters agreed with a former Confederate leader who was saying (in June 1865) that slavery had been "the best system of labor that could be devised for the Negro race" and that the wise thing to do now would be to "provide a substitute for it."

Blacks, of course, had a very different vision of the postwar South. They wanted, above all, to know and feel their freedom and to be assured that they were not again to lose it. In the short run, they wanted protection from the threat of starvation. Beyond that, they wanted economic independence; and since the vast majority had always worked as farmers, that meant ownership of land. Blacks also longed for schooling—for their children if not for themselves. Finally, many blacks demanded political rights. "The only salvation for us besides the power of the Government is in the *possession of the ballot*," a convention of the black people of Virginia resolved in the summer of 1865. "All we ask is an *equal chance*."

In the immediate aftermath of the war, the federal government made modest efforts to help the emancipated slaves achieve their dreams of freedom. The government kept troops (many of them black) in the South to preserve order and protect the freedmen. In March 1865, Congress established the Bureau of Freedmen, Refugees, and Abandoned Lands (known as the Freedmen's Bureau) as an agency of the army. The bureau was empowered to provide former slaves with food, transportation, assistance in getting jobs and fair wages, and schools, and also to settle them on abandoned or confiscated lands. Under the able direction of General Oliver O. Howard, the bureau distributed 20 million rations. Missionaries and teachers, who had been sent to the South by Freedmen's Aid Societies and other private and church groups in the North, cooperated with the bureau in setting up schools for the former slaves. There were efforts as well to settle blacks on lands of their own. (The Freedmen's Bureau also offered considerable assistance to poor whites, many of whom were similarly destitute and homeless after the war.) But the Freedmen's Bureau was only a temporary expedient, not a permanent solution. Congress had given it authority to operate for only one year; and it was, in any case, far too small to deal by itself with the enormous problems facing Southern society. The real nature of Reconstruction, therefore, remained to be determined. It would be up to the federal government to determine whether the hopes of Southern whites or those of Southern blacks would prevail.

Issues of Reconstruction

At the time, it was by no means clear how the leaders of the North envisioned the future. The question of what kind of society should exist in the South and what kind of future blacks should enjoy there was tied to questions about the political and economic future of the North. The result was a prolonged debate about the proper course.

The terms by which the Southern states rejoined the Union had important implications for both major political parties. For the Democrats, a rapid readmission of the former Confederate states on easy terms was enormously appealing. To the Republicans, the prospect was alarming. The Republican victories in 1860 and 1864 had been a result, in large part, of the division of the Democratic party and the removal of the South from the electorate. The return of the South would, leaders of both parties believed, reunite the

Democrats and reduce the Republicans to minority status—especially since the South's representation in Congress would increase as a result of the abolition of slavery and with it the "three-fifths" clause of the Constitution, by which only three-fifths of the slave population had been counted in determining the number of members a state could send to the House of Representatives. The black population of the South would now be counted in full.

These political questions overlapped, of course, with important economic questions. The Republican party had taken advantage of the absence of the South from Congress to pass a program of nationalistic economic legislation—railroad subsidies, protective tariffs, and other measures of benefit to Northern business leaders and industrialists. Should the Democratic party regain power with heavy dependence on Southern support, these programs would be in jeopardy. Complicating these practical questions were emotional concerns of considerable importance: the widespread Northern belief that the South should be punished in some way for its rebellion and for the suffering and sacrifice that rebellion had cost; and the belief among many Northerners that the South should be transformed, made over in the North's image—its backward, feudal, undemocratic society civilized and modernized.

Even among the Republicans in Congress, there was considerable disagreement about the proper approach to Reconstruction—disagreements that reflected the same factional division (between the party's Conservatives and Radicals) that had created disputes during the war over emancipation. The Conservatives advocated a mild peace and the rapid restoration of the defeated states to the Union; they insisted that the South accept the abolition of slavery; but beyond that they did not propose to interfere with race relations or to alter the social system of the region. The Radicals, directed by such leaders as Thaddeus Stevens of Pennsylvania and Charles Sumner of Massachusetts, stood for a harder peace. Their most militant spokesmen urged that the civil and military chieftains of the late Confederacy be subjected to severe punishment, that large numbers of Southern whites be disfranchised, that the legal rights of blacks be protected, and that the property of rich Southerners who had aided the Confederacy be confiscated and distributed among the freedmen. Some Radicals favored granting suffrage to the former slaves, as a matter of right or as a means of creating a Republican electorate in the South. Other Radicals hesitated to state a position for fear of alienating public opinion—few Northern states permitted blacks to vote.

Between the Radicals and the Conservatives stood a faction of uncommitted Republicans, the Moderates. They rejected the punitive goals of the Radicals; but they supported measures to extract at least some concessions from the South on the matter of black rights. It would be this group, ultimately, that would determine the fate of the Reconstruction process.

Lincoln's Plan

Even before the war ended, President Lincoln formulated a Reconstruction plan that reflected his own sympathies for the Moderate and Conservative wings of his party. Lincoln believed there were a considerable number of actual or potential Unionists in the South—most of them former Whigs—who could be encouraged to join the Republican party and thus prevent the readmission of the South from strengthening the Democrats. More immediately, the Southern Unionists could serve as the nucleus for creating new, loyal state governments in the South. Lincoln was not uninterested in the fate of the freedmen; but he wanted to restore the Union as soon as possible and was willing, therefore, to defer considering questions about race relations.

Lincoln announced his plan in December 1863. It offered a general amnesty to all white Southerners—with the temporary exception of high civil and military officials of the Confederacy—who would take an oath pledging future loyalty to the government and acceptance of the wartime measures eliminating slavery. Whenever 10 percent of the number of voters in 1860 took the oath in any state, those loyal voters could proceed to set up a state government. Lincoln also hoped to extend the suffrage to at least a few blacks—to those who were educated, owned property, and had served in the Union army. In three Southern states—Louisiana, Arkansas, and Tennessee, all under Union occupation—loyal governments were reestablished under the Lincoln formula in 1864.

The Radical Republicans were astonished at the mildness of Lincoln's program, and they persuaded Congress to repudiate the new governments. Congress refused to seat representatives from the three "reconstructed" states and refused to count the electoral vote of those states in the election of 1864. But the Radicals could not simply reject Lincoln's plan;

they needed an alternative plan of their own. And for the moment, they were uncertain about what form that plan should take.

Their first effort to resolve that question was the Wade-Davis bill, passed by Congress in July 1864. By its provisions, the president would appoint for each conquered state a provisional governor who would take a census of all adult white males. If a majority of that group took an oath of allegiance to the Union, the governor was to call an election for a state constitutional convention. The privilege of voting for delegates to this meeting would be limited to those who would swear that they had never borne arms against the United States, the so-called ironclad oath. The state convention would be required to include provisions in the new constitution abolishing slavery, disfranchising Confederate civil and military leaders, and repudiating debts accumulated by the state governments during the war. After these conditions had been met, Congress would readmit the state to the Union.

The Wade-Davis bill was more drastic in almost every respect than the Lincoln plan. Instead of requiring 10 percent of prior voters to swear loyalty to the Union, the Radical plan called for a majority of all adult white males to do so. Instead of assuming, as Lincoln did, that the Southern states had never left the Union, it insisted that the states had in effect forfeited their rights as members of the republic and were thus subject to the dictates of Congress. Like the president's proposal, however, the Wade-Davis bill left up to the states the question of political rights for blacks.

Congress passed the bill a few days before it adjourned in 1864, and Lincoln disposed of it with a pocket veto. His action enraged the authors of the measure, Benjamin F. Wade and Henry Winter Davis, who issued a blistering denunciation of the veto, the Wade-Davis Manifesto, warning the president not to interfere with the powers of Congress to control Reconstruction. Lincoln could not ignore the bitterness and the strength of the Radical opposition. Practical as always, he realized that he would have to bow to at least some of the Radical demands; and so he began to move toward a new approach to Reconstruction.

The Death of Lincoln

What plan he might have produced no one can say. On the night of April 14, 1865, Lincoln and his wife attended a play at Ford's Theater in Washington. As they sat in the presidential box, John Wilkes Booth,

Abraham Lincoln and His Son Tad
During the last difficult months of the Civil War, Lincoln often found relief from the strains of his office in the company of his young son, Thomas (known as "Tad"), shown here with his father in an 1864 photograph by Mathew Brady. Much has been written about Lincoln's turbulent family life. His wife, Mary Todd Lincoln, was apparently a moody and difficult woman; but the marriage seems generally to have been a happy one. The Lincolns did, however, experience a series of heartbreaking bereavements as three of their four sons died in childhood. Their second child, Edward, died in 1850 at the age of three; their third, "Willie," died of fever in 1862 at the age of eleven; Tad outlived his father by only a few years and died in 1871 at the age of eighteen. Robert Todd Lincoln, the president's eldest son, lived a long and successful life, during which he served as secretary of war, American minister to England, and president of the Pullman Railroad Car Company. (Library of Congress)

an unsuccessful actor obsessed with aiding the Southern cause, entered the box from the rear and shot Lincoln in the head. Then he leaped to the stage (breaking his leg in the process), shouted "Sic semper tyrannis!" ("Thus always to tyrants!"—the motto of the state of Virginia), and disappeared into the night. The president was carried unconscious to a house across the street, where early the next morning—surrounded by family, friends, and political associates (including a tearful Charles Sumner)—he died.

The circumstances of Lincoln's death—the heroic war leader, the Great Emancipator, struck down in the hour of victory—earned him immediate martyrdom. It also produced wild fears and antagonisms throughout the North. There were widespread accusations that Booth had acted as part of a great conspiracy—accusations that contained some truth. Booth did indeed have associates, one of whom shot and wounded Secretary of State Seward the night of the assassination, another of whom set out to murder Vice President Johnson but abandoned the scheme at the last moment. Booth himself escaped on horseback into the Maryland countryside, where, on April 26, he was cornered by Union troops and shot to death in a blazing barn. Eight other conspirators were convicted by a military tribunal of participating in the conspiracy (at least two of them on the basis of virtually no evidence). Four were hanged.

To many Northerners, however, the murder of the president seemed evidence of an even greater conspiracy—one masterminded and directed by the unrepentant leaders of the defeated South. (There was never any conclusive evidence to support this—and many another—theory of the assassination; but questions continued to be raised about the event well into the twentieth century.) Militant Republicans exploited such suspicions relentlessly in the ensuing months, ensuring that Lincoln's death would help doom his plans for a relatively generous peace.

Johnson and "Restoration"

The Conservative leadership in the controversy over Reconstruction fell to Lincoln's successor, Andrew Johnson. Of all the men who have accidentally inherited the presidency, Johnson was undoubtedly the most unfortunate. A Southerner and former slaveholder, he became president as a bloody war against the South was drawing to a close. A Democrat before he had been placed on the Union ticket with Lincoln in 1864, he became the head of a Republican administration at a time when partisan passions, held in some restraint during the war, were about to rule the government. As if these handicaps of background were not enough, Johnson himself was an intemperate and tactless man, filled with resentments and insecurities.

Johnson revealed his plan of Reconstruction—or "Restoration," as he preferred to call it—soon after he took office, and he proceeded to implement it during the summer of 1865 when Congress was not in session. In some ways Johnson's scheme resembled Lincoln's; in many other respects, it reflected the more drastic demands of the Radicals. Like his predecessor, Johnson assumed that the seceded states had never left the Union; and, also like Lincoln, he offered amnesty for past conduct to all who would take an oath of allegiance. High-ranking Confederate officials and any white Southerner with land worth $20,000 or more would have to apply to the president for individual pardons. (Himself a self-made man, Johnson harbored deep resentments toward the old Southern aristocracy and apparently relished the prospect of these Confederate leaders humbling themselves before him to ask for amnesty.) For each state, the president appointed a provisional governor, who was to invite the qualified voters to elect delegates to a constitutional convention. Johnson did not specify that a minimum number of voters had to take the oath, as had the Lincoln and Wade-Davis proposals, but the implication was plain that he would require a majority. As conditions of readmittance, a state had to revoke the ordinance of secession, abolish slavery and ratify the Thirteenth Amendment, and repudiate the Confederate and state war debts—essentially the same stipulations that had been laid down in the Wade-Davis bill. The final procedure before restoration was for a state to elect a state government and send representatives to Congress.

By the end of 1865, all the states not previously reorganized under Lincoln's plan had complied with Johnson's requirements. All of the seceded states, therefore, had been reconstructed and were ready to resume their places in the Union—if Congress chose to recognize them when it met in December 1865. But the Radicals were determined not to recognize the Johnson governments, just as they had previously refused to recognize the Lincoln regimes. In that determination they had the support of much of the Northern public.

Many Northerners were disturbed by the seeming reluctance of some members of the Southern conventions to abolish slavery and by the refusal of all the conventions to grant suffrage to even a few blacks. They were astounded that states claiming to be "loyal" should elect as state officials and representatives to Congress prominent leaders of the recent Confederacy. Particularly hard to accept was Georgia's choice of Alexander H. Stephens, former vice president of the Confederacy, as a United States senator.

Radical Reconstruction

This initial phase of Reconstruction—often known as "presidential Reconstruction"—lasted only until Congress reconvened in December 1865. At that point, Republican leaders looked over Andrew Johnson's handiwork and expressed their displeasure. Congress immediately refused to seat the senators and representatives of the states the president had "restored." Instead, Radical leaders insisted, Congress needed to learn more about conditions in the postwar South. There must be assurances that the former Confederates had accepted their defeat and that emancipated blacks and loyal whites would be protected. Accordingly, Congress set up the new Joint Committee on Reconstruction to investigate conditions in the South and to advise Congress in laying down a Reconstruction policy of its own. The period of "congressional" or "Radical" Reconstruction had begun.

The Response to the Black Codes

During the next few months, the Radicals advanced toward a more severe program than their first plan—the Wade-Davis bill of 1864, which had left to the states the question of what rights the freed slaves should have. Johnson, unlike Lincoln, refused to compromise; and his intransigence helped the Radicals gain the support of many Moderate Republicans. The president insisted that Congress had no right even to consider a policy for the South until his own plan had been accepted and the Southern congressmen and senators had been admitted.

In the meantime, Northerners were learning more about what was happening in the defeated South; and what they learned persuaded many of them—including most of the important leaders in Congress—that far more drastic measures were necessary than the president had contemplated. For throughout the South in 1865 and early 1866, state legislatures were enacting sets of laws known as the Black Codes. These measures were the white South's solution to the problem of the free black laborer, and they were modeled in many ways on the codes that had regulated free blacks in the prewar South. As such, they created a new set of devices to guarantee white supremacy. Economically, the codes were intended to regulate the labor of a race that, in the opinion of whites, would not work except under some kind of compulsion. Although there were variations from state to state, all codes authorized local officials to apprehend unemployed blacks, fine them for vagrancy, and hire them out to private employers to satisfy the fine. Some of the codes tried to force blacks to work on plantations by forbidding them to own or lease farms or to take other jobs except as domestic servants. Socially, the codes were designed to invest blacks with a legal status outside slavery, but one that ensured that they would remain clearly subordinate to whites. To the white South, the Black Codes were a realistic approach to a great social problem. To the North, and to most blacks, they seemed to herald a return to slavery in all but name.

An appropriate agency for offsetting the Black Codes was the Freedmen's Bureau, but its scheduled year of existence was about to expire. In February 1866, Congress passed a bill to prolong the life of the bureau and to widen its powers. For settling labor disputes, it could now establish special courts, which could disallow work agreements forced on freedmen under the Black Codes. Johnson vetoed the bill, denouncing it as unconstitutional. Efforts to override him fell just short of the necessary two-thirds majority.

In April, Congress struck again at the Black Codes by passing the Civil Rights Act, which declared blacks to be U.S. citizens and empowered the federal government to intervene in state affairs when necessary to protect the rights of citizens. Johnson vetoed this bill, too. With Moderates and Radicals acting together, Congress promptly overrode the veto. Then Congress repassed the Freedmen's Bureau Act and overrode a second presidential veto of that law.

The Fourteenth Amendment

Emboldened by their evidently growing support in Congress, the Radicals acted again. The Joint Committee on Reconstruction submitted to Congress, in April 1866, a proposed amendment to the Constitution, the Fourteenth, which constituted the second Radical plan of Reconstruction. The amendment was adopted by Congress and sent to the states for approval in the early summer. It became one of the most important of all the provisions in the Constitution.

Section 1 of the amendment declared that all persons born or naturalized in the United States were citizens of the United States and of the state of their residence—the first official, national definition of cit-

The Memphis Race Riot, 1866
Angry whites (shown here shooting down blacks) rampaged through the black neighborhoods of Memphis, Tennessee, during the first three days of May 1866, burning homes, schools, and churches and leaving 46 people dead. Some claimed the riot was a response to strict new regulations protecting blacks that had been imposed on Tennessee by General George Stoneman, the military commander of the district; others argued that it was an attempt by whites to intimidate and control a black population that was trying to exercise its new freedom. Such riots were among the events that persuaded Radical Republicans in Congress to press for a harsher policy of reconstruction.   (The Granger Collection)

izenship. Next came a statement that no state could abridge the rights of citizens of the United States or deprive any person of life, liberty, or property without due process of law or deny to any person within its jurisdiction the equal protection of the laws. Section 2 provided that if a state denied the suffrage to any of its adult male inhabitants, its representation in the House of Representatives and the electoral college would suffer a proportionate reduction. (This was the first time the Constitution made reference to gender, and the wording clearly reflected the prevailing view in Congress and elsewhere that the franchise was properly restricted to men.) Section 3 prohibited persons who had previously taken an oath to support the Constitution and later had aided the Confederacy (in other words, former Southern members of Congress and other former officials) from holding any state or federal office—until Congress by a two-thirds vote of each house should remove their disability.

The Southern legislatures knew that if they ratified the amendment their states would be readmitted and Reconstruction probably would end. But they could not bring themselves to approve the measure, mainly because of Section 3, which put a stigma on their late leaders. Johnson himself advised Southerners to defeat the amendment. Only Tennessee, of the former Confederate states, ratified it, thus winning readmittance. The other ten, joined by Kentucky and Delaware, voted it down. The amendment thus failed to receive the required approval of three-fourths of the states and was defeated—but only temporarily. When the time was more propitious, the Radicals would bring it up again. Meanwhile, its rejection by the South strengthened the Radical cause.

The Northern public gave striking evidence of its support for the Radical program in the elections of 1866. The Radicals could point to recent events in the South—bloody race riots in New Orleans and other Southern cities in which blacks were the victims—as further evidence of the inadequacy of Johnson's policy. Johnson attempted to derail the Radical cause by campaigning for Conservative candidates; but he did his own cause more harm than good by the intemperate, brawling (and, some believed, drunken) speeches he made on a stumping tour (a "swing around the circle," as it was called) from Washington to Chicago and back. The voters returned to Congress an overwhelming majority of Republicans, most of them Radicals. In the Senate, there were to be 42 Republicans to 11 Democrats; in the House, 143 Republicans to 49 Democrats. Now the Republicans could enact any kind of Reconstruction plan they could themselves agree on. Confidently they looked forward to the struggle with Johnson that would ensue when Congress assembled in December 1866—and to their final victory over the president.

The Congressional Plan

After compromising differences among themselves and with the Moderates, the Radicals formulated their third plan of Reconstruction in three bills that passed Congress in the early months of 1867. All three were vetoed by Johnson and repassed. Together, they constituted a single program. Finally, nearly two years after the end of the war, the federal government had established a consistent plan for Reconstruction.

That two-year delay had important effects on the way the South would react to the program. In 1865, with the South reeling from its defeat and nearly prostrate, the federal government could probably have imposed on the region an even more radical plan than it ultimately did, without provoking immediate resistance. But by 1867, the South had begun to recover from the humiliation of defeat and had begun to reconstruct itself under the reasonably generous terms Lincoln and Johnson had extended. By then, therefore, measures that might once have seemed moderate had come to seem radical; and the congressional reconstruction plan created deep resentments and continuing resistance.

The congressional plan was based squarely on the principle that the seceded states had forfeited their political identity. The Lincoln-Johnson governments were declared to have no legal standing, and the ten seceded states (Tennessee was now out of the Reconstruction process) were combined into five military districts. Each district was to have a military commander, supported by troops, who was to prepare his provinces for readmission as states. To this end, he was to institute a registration of voters, which was to include all adult black males and those white males who were not disqualified by participation in the rebellion.

After the registration was completed in each province, the commanding general was to call the voters to elect a convention to prepare a new state constitution, which had to include provisions for black suffrage. If this document was ratified by the voters, elections for a state government could be held. Finally, if Congress approved the constitution, if the state legislature ratified the Fourteenth Amendment, and if this amendment was adopted by the required number of states and became a part of the Constitution—then the state was to be restored to the Union.

By 1868, seven of the former Confederate states (Arkansas, North Carolina, South Carolina, Louisiana, Alabama, Georgia, and Florida) had complied with the process of restoration outlined in the Reconstruction Acts—including ratification of the Fourteenth Amendment, which now became part of the Constitution. These states were readmitted to the Union. Delaying tactics by whites held up the return of Virginia and Texas until 1869 and Mississippi until 1870. And by then, Congress had added an additional requirement for readmission, which constituted the fourth and final congressional plan of Reconstruction. They had to ratify another constitutional amendment, the Fifteenth, which forbade the states and the federal government to deny the suffrage to any citizen on account of "race, color, or previous condition of servitude." (Again, Congress made no effort to advance female suffrage.)

Sponsors of the Fifteenth Amendment were motivated by both idealistic and practical considerations. They wished to be consistent in extending to blacks in the North a right they had already given to them elsewhere. The great majority of the Northern states still denied the suffrage to blacks when the Reconstruction Acts granted it to blacks in the Southern states. At the same time the amendment would put into the Constitution, where it would be safe from congressional repeal, a provision that would serve as a basis of Republican strength in the South. Sponsors of the amendment also saw it as a vehicle for protecting the party's precarious future in the North. A warning of trouble ahead had appeared in the state elections of 1867 in Pennsylvania, Ohio, and Indiana, all of which went Democratic that year. "We must establish the doctrine of national jurisdiction over all the states in matters of the franchise," the Radical leader Thaddeus Stevens now concluded. "We must thus bridle Pennsylvania, Ohio, Indiana et cetera, or the South *being in*, we shall drift into Democracy." In several of the Northern states the black vote, although proportionally small, would be large enough to decide close elections in favor of the Republicans. A number of Northern and border states refused to approve the Fifteenth Amendment, and it was adopted only with the support of the four Southern states that had to ratify it in order to be readmitted to the Union.

The Radicals saw themselves as architects of a revolution, and they did not intend to let the executive or the judiciary get in their way. They were prepared, if necessary, to establish a kind of congressional dictatorship.

To stop the president from interfering with their designs, Congress in 1867 passed two remarkable laws. One, the Tenure of Office Act, forbade the president to remove civil officials, including members of his cabinet, without the consent of the Senate. The principal purpose of the law was to protect the job of Secretary of War Edwin M. Stanton, who was cooperating with the Radicals. The other law, the Command of the Army Act, prohibited the president from issuing military orders except through the commanding general of the army (General Grant), whose headquarters were to be in Washington and who could not be relieved or assigned elsewhere without the consent of the Senate.

The congressional Radicals also took action to curb the Supreme Court from interfering with their

Political Reconstruction, 1866–1877

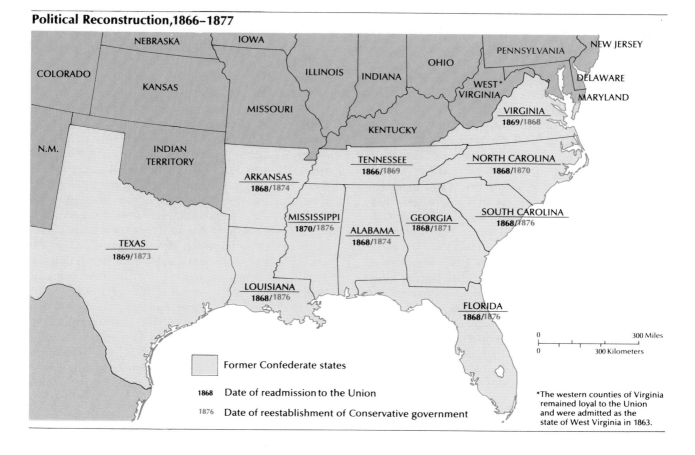

Former Confederate states

1868   Date of readmission to the Union

1876   Date of reestablishment of Conservative government

*The western counties of Virginia remained loyal to the Union and were admitted as the state of West Virginia in 1863.

plans. The Court, under Chief Justice Salmon P. Chase, had in 1866 declared in *Ex parte Milligan* that military tribunals were unconstitutional in places where civil courts were functioning. Although the decision was applied to a case originating in the war, it seemed to threaten the system of military government that the Radicals were planning for the South. Radicals in Congress immediately proposed legislation to require a two-thirds majority of the justices to overrule a law of Congress, to deny the Court jurisdiction in Reconstruction cases, to reduce its membership to three, and even to abolish it. The justices apparently took the hint. Over the next two years, the Court refused to accept jurisdiction in any cases involving questions of jurisdiction in the South.

The Impeachment of the President

The most aggressive move of Congress against another branch of government was the effort of the Radicals to remove Andrew Johnson from office. Although the president had long since ceased to be a serious obstacle to the passage of Radical legislation,

he was still the official charged with administering the Reconstruction programs; and as such, the Radicals believed, he was a serious impediment to their plans. Early in 1867, therefore, they began searching for evidence that Johnson had committed crimes or misdemeanors in office, the only legal grounds for impeachment; but they could find nothing on which to base charges. Then he gave them what was, in their view, a plausible reason for action by deliberately violating the Tenure of Office Act—in hopes of bringing a test case of the law before the courts. Johnson suspended Secretary of War Stanton, who had worked with the Radicals against the president, and named General Grant as his successor. When the Senate refused to concur in the suspension, Grant relinquished the office to Stanton. Johnson then dismissed Stanton.

In the House of Representatives the elated Radicals presented to the Senate eleven charges against the president. The first nine accusations dealt with the violation of the Tenure of Office Act. The tenth and eleventh charged Johnson with making speeches calculated to bring Congress into disrespect and with not faithfully enforcing the various Reconstruction

Thaddeus Stevens

Stern, uncompromising, and severe, Thaddeus Stevens of Pennsylvania was the incarnation of the North's vindictive designs, according to many Southerners during (and long after) Reconstruction. Others admired him as one of the few white leaders who remained firmly committed to racial equality. He served in the House of Representatives from 1849 to 1853 and again, more prominently, from 1859 until his death in 1868. He spent much of the last year of his life organizing and managing the impeachment trial of Andrew Johnson. (Library of Congress)

Acts. The trial before the Senate lasted for two months—from March 25 to May 26, 1868. Johnson's lawyers maintained that he was justified in technically violating a law in order to force a test case. And they argued that the measure did not apply to Stanton anyway: It gave tenure to cabinet members for the term of the president by whom they had been appointed, and Stanton had been appointed by Lincoln. The House managers of the impeachment stressed the theme that Johnson had opposed the will of Congress and was thus guilty of high crimes and misdemeanors. They put heavy pressure on all the Republican senators, but the moderates (who were themselves already losing faith to the Radical program and were thus growing reluctant to oppose

Johnson's effort to thwart it) vacillated. Seven Republicans joined the twelve Democrats to vote for acquittal. On three of the charges the vote was identical, 35 to 19, one short of the required two-thirds majority. After that, the Radicals dropped the impeachment campaign.

The South in Reconstruction

When white Southerners spoke bitterly in later years of the effects of Reconstruction, they referred most frequently to the governments Congress imposed on them—governments that were, they claimed, both incompetent and corrupt, that saddled the region with enormous debts, and that trampled on the rights of citizens. When black Southerners and their defenders condemned Reconstruction, in contrast, they spoke of its failure to guarantee to freedmen even the most elemental rights of citizenship—a failure that resulted in a new and cruel system of economic subordination. Controversy has raged for more than a century over which viewpoint is more nearly correct. (See "Where Historians Disagree," pp. 462–463.) Most students of Reconstruction tend now to agree, however, that the complaints of Southern whites, although in some respects accurate, greatly exaggerated the real nature of the postwar governments; while the complaints of blacks, although occasionally overstated, were largely justified.

The Reconstruction Governments

In the ten states of the South that were reorganized under the congressional plan, approximately one-fourth of the white males were at first excluded from voting or holding office. The voter registration of 1867 enrolled a total of 703,000 black and 627,000 white voters. The black voters constituted a majority in half the states—Alabama, Florida, South Carolina, Mississippi, and Louisiana—although only in the last three of these states did blacks outnumber whites in the population as a whole. But once new constitutions had been framed and new governments launched, most of them permitted nearly all whites to vote (although for several years the Fourteenth Amendment continued to keep the leading ex-Confederates from holding office). This meant that in most of the Southern states the Republicans could maintain control only with the support of a great many Southern whites.

—————— WHERE HISTORIANS DISAGREE ——————

Reconstruction

Debate over the nature of Reconstruction—not only among historians, but among the public at large—has created so much controversy over the decades that one scholar, writing in 1959, described the issue as a "dark and bloody ground." Among historians, the passions of the debate have to some extent subsided since then; but in the popular mind, Reconstruction continues to raise "dark and bloody" images.

For many years, a relatively uniform and highly critical view of Reconstruction prevailed among historians, a reflection of broad currents in popular thought. By the late nineteenth century, most white Americans in both the North and the South had come to believe that few real differences any longer divided the sections, that the nation should strive for a genuine reconciliation. And most white Americans believed as well in the superiority of their race, in the inherent unfitness of blacks for political or social equality. In this spirit was born the first major historical interpretation of Reconstruction, through the work of William A. Dunning. In his *Reconstruction, Political and Economic* (1907), Dunning portrayed Reconstruction as a corrupt outrage perpetrated on the prostrate South by a vicious and vindictive cabal of Northern Republican Radicals. Reconstruction governments were based on "bayonet rule." Unscrupulous and self-aggrandizing carpetbaggers flooded the South to profit from the misery of the defeated region. Ignorant, illiterate blacks were thrust into positions of power for which they were entirely unfit. The Reconstruction experiment, a moral abomination from its first moments, survived only because of the determination of the Republican party to keep itself in power. (Some later writers, notably Howard K. Beale, added an economic motive—to protect Northern business interests.) Dunning and his many students (who together formed what became known as the "Dunning school") compiled state-by-state evidence to show that the legacy of Reconstruction was corruption, ruinous taxation, and astronomical increases in the public debt.

The Dunning school not only shaped the views of several generations of historians. It also reflected and helped to shape the views of much of the public. Popular depictions of Reconstruction for years to come (as the book and movie *Gone with the Wind* suggested) portrayed the era as one of tragic exploitation of the South by the North. Even today, many white Southerners and many others continue to accept the basic premises of the Dunning interpretation. Among historians, however, the old view of Reconstruction has gradually lost all credibility.

W. E. B. Du Bois, the great black scholar, was among the first to challenge the Dunning view in a 1910 article and, later, in a 1935 book, *Black Reconstruction*. To him, Reconstruction politics in the Southern states had been an effort on the part of the masses, black and white, to create a more democratic society. The misdeeds of the Reconstruction governments had, he claimed, been greatly exaggerated and their achievements overlooked. The governments had been expensive, he insisted, because they had tried to provide public education and other public services on a scale never before attempted in the South. But Du Bois's use of Marxist theory in his work caused many historians who did not share his philosophy to dismiss his argument; and it remained for a group of less radical, white historians to shatter the Dunning image of Reconstruction.

In the 1940s, historians such as C. Vann Woodward, David Herbert Donald, Thomas B. Alexander, and others began to reexamine the record of the Reconstruction governments in the South and to suggest that their record was not nearly as bad as most historians had previously assumed. They looked, too, at the Radical Republicans in Congress and suggested that they had not been moti-

WHERE HISTORIANS DISAGREE

vated by vindictiveness and partisanship alone. By the early 1960s, a new view of Reconstruction was emerging from these efforts, a view whose appeal to historians grew stronger with the emergence of the "Second Reconstruction," the civil rights movement. The revisionist approach was summarized by John Hope Franklin in *Reconstruction After the Civil War* (1961) and Kenneth Stampp in *The Era of Reconstruction* (1965), which claimed that the postwar Republicans had been engaged in a genuine, if flawed, effort to solve the problem of race in the South by providing much-needed protection to the freedmen. The Reconstruction governments, for all their faults, had been bold experiments in interracial politics. The congressional Radicals were not saints, but they had displayed a genuine concern for the rights of slaves. And Andrew Johnson was not a martyred defender of the Constitution, but an inept, racist politician who resisted reasonable compromise and brought the government to a crisis. There had been no such thing as "bayonet rule" or "Negro rule" in the South. Blacks had played only a small part in Reconstruction governments and had generally acquitted themselves well. The Reconstruction regimes had, in fact, brought important progress to the South, establishing the region's first public school system and other important social changes. Corruption in the South had been no worse than corruption in the North at that time. What was tragic about Reconstruction, the revisionist view claimed, was not what it did to Southern whites but what it did not do for Southern blacks. By stopping short of the reforms necessary to ensure blacks genuine equality, Reconstruction had consigned them to more than a century of injustice and discrimination.

By the 1970s, then, the Dunning view of Reconstruction had all but disappeared from serious scholarly discussion. Instead, historians seemed to agree that Reconstruction had, in fact, changed the South relatively little; and they began to debate why Reconstruction fell as short as it did of guaranteeing racial justice. Some scholars have claimed that conservative obstacles to change were so great that the Radicals, despite their good intentions, simply could not overcome them. Others have argued that the Radicals themselves were not sufficiently committed to the principle of racial justice, that they abandoned the cause quickly when it became clear to them that the battle would not easily be won.

In recent years, however, scholars have begun to question the revisionist view—not in an effort to revive the old Dunning interpretation, but in an attempt to draw attention to those things Reconstruction in fact achieved. Leon Litwack's *Been in the Storm So Long* (1979) reveals that former slaves used the relative latitude they enjoyed under Reconstruction to build a certain independence for themselves within Southern society. They strengthened their churches; they reunited their families; they refused to work in the "gang labor" system of the plantations and forced the creation of a new labor system in which they had more control over their own lives. Eric Foner, in *Nothing but Freedom* (1983) and *Reconstruction: America's Unfinished Revolution* (1988), compares the aftermath of slavery in the United States with similar experiences in the Caribbean and concludes that what is striking about the American experience in this context is not how little was accomplished, but how far the former slaves moved toward freedom and independence in a short time. Reconstruction permitted blacks a certain amount of legal and political power in the South; and even though they held that power only temporarily, they used it for a time to strengthen their economic and social positions and win a position of limited but genuine independence. Reconstruction brought them, if not equality, something that emancipation alone had not guaranteed: freedom.

The Burdened South

This Reconstruction-era cartoon expresses the South's sense of its oppression at the hands of Northern Republicans. President Grant (whose hat bears Abraham Lincoln's initials) rides in comfort in a giant carpetbag, guarded by bayonet-wielding soldiers, as the South staggers under the burden in chains. More evidence of destruction and military occupation is visible in the background. (Culver Pictures)

These Southern white Republicans, whom their opponents derisively called "scalawags," consisted in part of former Whigs who, after the breakup of the Whig organization in the 1850s, had acted with the Southern Democrats but had never felt completely at home with them. Some of the scalawag leaders were wealthy (or once wealthy) planters or businessmen. Other Southern whites who supported the Republican party were farmers living in areas where slavery had been unimportant or nonexistent. These men, many of them wartime Unionists, favored the Republican program of internal improvements, which would help them get their crops to market.

White men from the North also served as Republican leaders in the South. Opponents of Reconstruction referred to them pejoratively as "carpetbaggers," thus giving the impression that they were penniless adventurers who had arrived with all their possessions in a carpetbag (then a common kind of cheap suitcase covered with carpeting material) in order to take advantage of the black vote for their own power and profit. In fact, the majority of the so-called carpetbaggers were veterans of the Union army who looked on the South as a new frontier, more promising than the West, and at the war's end had settled in it as hopeful planters or business or professional men.

The most numerous Republicans in the South were the black freedmen, the vast majority of whom had no formal education and no previous experience in public affairs. Among the black leaders, however, were well-educated men, most of whom had never been slaves and many of whom had grown up in the North or abroad. These blacks quickly became politically self-conscious. In various states, they held their own conventions to chart their future course. One such "colored convention," as Southern whites called them, assembled in Alabama in 1867 and announced: "We claim exactly *the same rights, privileges and immunities as are enjoyed by white men*—we ask nothing more and will be content with nothing less." Blacks were also organized, often with the assistance of Freedmen's Bureau agents and other Northern whites, in chapters of the Union League, which had been founded originally as a Republican electioneering agency in the North during the war. In addition, black churches helped give unity and political self-confidence to the former slaves. After emancipation, blacks withdrew from the white churches and formed their own—institutions based on the elaborate religious practices they had developed (occasionally surreptitiously) under slavery. "The colored preachers are *the great power* in controlling and uniting the colored vote," a white carpetbagger observed in 1868.

Blacks served as delegates to the conventions that, under the congressional plan, drew up new state constitutions in the South. Then, in the reconstructed states, blacks were elected to public offices of practically every kind. Altogether (between 1869 and 1901) twenty blacks were sent to the House of Representatives in Washington. Two went to the Senate, both of them from Mississippi. In 1870, Hiram R. Revels, an ordained minister and a former North Carolina free black who had been educated at Knox College in Illinois, took the Senate seat that Jefferson Davis once had occupied. In 1874, Blanche K. Bruce, who had escaped from slavery in Virginia and studied in the North, became a senator.

Yet while Southern whites complained loudly (both at the time and for generations to come) about "Negro rule" during Reconstruction, no such thing ever truly existed in any of the states. No black man was ever elected governor of a Southern state, although Lieutenant Governor P. B. S. Pinchback, a black man, briefly occupied the governor's chair in Louisiana. Blacks never controlled any of the state legislatures, although for a time they held a majority in the lower house of South Carolina. In the South as a whole, the number of black officeholders was less than proportionate to the number of blacks in the population.

The record of the Reconstruction governments is many-sided. The financial programs they instituted were a compound of blatant corruption and well-designed, if sometimes impractical, social legislation. The corruption and extravagance are familiar aspects of the Reconstruction story. Officeholders in many states enriched themselves through graft and other illicit activities. State budgets expanded to hitherto unknown totals, and state debts soared to previously undreamed-of heights. In South Carolina, for example, the public debt increased from $7 million to $29 million in eight years.

But these facts are misleading when considered alone. In large measure, the corruption in the South was part of a national phenomenon, with the same social force—an expanding capitalism eager to secure quick results—acting as the corrupting agent in all sections of the country. Corruption did not decline in Southern state governments once Reconstruction came to an end; in many states, in fact, it increased.

And the state expenditures of the Reconstruction years seem huge only in comparison with the tight budgets of the conservative governments of the pre-war era; they do not appear large when measured against the sums appropriated by later legislatures. The expenditures, moreover, represented an effort to provide the Southern states with services they desperately needed and that no governments had ever attempted to provide in the antebellum period: public education, public works programs, poor relief, and other costly new commitments. There was, to be sure, graft and extravagance in Reconstruction governments; there were also positive and permanent accomplishments.

Education

Perhaps the most important of those accomplishments was a dramatic improvement in Southern

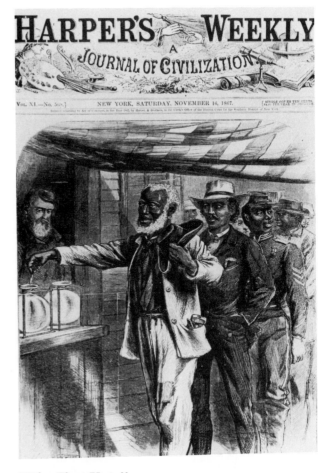

"The First Vote"

This cover illustration from an 1867 issue of *Harper's Weekly* shows freedmen exercising the right recently guaranteed them by the Fifteenth Amendment. Before the development of the technology that permitted the printing of photographs, woodcuts such as this one—usually based on drawings made on the scene by an artist and then transferred to wood blocks by skilled engravers—brought a sense of immediacy to the reporting of the news. (New-York Historical Society)

education—an improvement that benefited both whites and blacks. In the first years of Reconstruction, much of the impetus for educational reform in the South came from outside groups—from the Freedmen's Bureau, from Northern private philanthropic organizations, from many Northern white women who traveled to the South to teach in freedmen's schools—and from blacks themselves. Over the opposition of many Southern whites, who feared that education would give blacks "false notions of equality," these reformers established a large network of schools for former slaves—4,000 schools by 1870, staffed by 9,000 teachers (half of them black), and teaching 200,000 students (about 12 percent of the total school-age population of the freedmen). In the course of the 1870s, moreover, the Reconstruction governments of the states assumed the initiative and began to build a comprehensive public school system in the South. By 1876, more than half of all white children and about 40 percent of all black children were being educated in Southern schools. Several black "academies" were also beginning to operate—institutions that were, perhaps, not yet genuine colleges but that were offering more advanced education to freedmen than the public schools provided. Gradually, these academies grew into an important network of black colleges and universities, which would form the basis of black higher education in the South for many decades. Among the early institutions, for example, were schools that later became Fisk and Atlanta universities and Morehouse College.

Already, however, Southern education was becoming divided into two separate systems—one black and one white. Early efforts to integrate the schools of the region were a dismal failure. The Freedmen's Bureau schools, for example, were open to students of all races, but almost no whites attended them. New Orleans set up an integrated school system under the Reconstruction government; again, whites almost universally stayed away. The one federal effort to mandate school integration—the Civil Rights Act of 1875—had its provisions for educational desegregation removed before it was passed. As soon as the Republican governments of Reconstruction were replaced, the new Southern Democratic regimes quickly abandoned all efforts to promote integration.

Land Ownership

The most ambitious goal of the Freedmen's Bureau, and of some Republican Radicals in Congress, was to make Reconstruction the occasion for a fundamental reform of land ownership in the South. The effort failed. In the last years of the war and the first years of Reconstruction, the Freedmen's Bureau did oversee the redistribution of substantial amounts of land to freedmen in some areas—notably the Sea Islands off South Carolina and Georgia, and areas of Mississippi that had once belonged to the Davis family. By June 1865, the bureau had settled nearly 10,000 black families on their own land—most of it drawn from abandoned plantations. Blacks throughout the South were growing excited at the prospect of achieving a real economic stake in their region—the vision of "forty acres and a mule." By the end of that year, however, the experiment was already collapsing. Southern plantation owners were returning and demanding the restoration of their property. Andrew Johnson was supporting their demands. Despite the resistance of General Oliver O. Howard and other officials of the Freedmen's Bureau, most of the confiscated land was eventually returned to the original white owners. Congress, moreover, never exhibited much stomach for the idea of land redistribution. Despite the pleas of such Radicals as Thaddeus Stevens, very few Northern Republicans believed that the federal government had the right to confiscate property. Land reform did not become a lasting part of Reconstruction.

Nevertheless, there was a substantial change in the distribution of land ownership in the South in the postwar years—a result of many factors. Among whites, there was a striking decline in ownership of land. Whereas before the war more than 80 percent of Southern whites had lived on their own land, by the end of Reconstruction that proportion had dropped to about 67 percent. Some whites had fallen into debt and been forced to sell; some had fallen victim to increased taxes; some had chosen to leave the marginal lands they had owned to move to more fertile areas, where they rented. Among blacks, during the same period, the proportion who owned land rose from virtually none to more than 20 percent. Black landowners acquired their property through hard work, through luck, and at times through the assistance of such agencies as the Freedman's Bank, established in 1865 by antislavery whites in an effort to promote land ownership among blacks. (The bank failed in 1874, after internal corruption and a nationwide financial panic had destroyed its reserves.)

Despite these impressive achievements, however, the vast majority of blacks (and a growing minority of whites) did not own their own land during Reconstruction, and some of those who acquired land in the 1860s had lost it by the 1890s. These nonlandowners worked for others, through a great variety of systems. Many black agricultural laborers—perhaps 25 percent of the total—simply worked for wages. Most, however, became tenants of white landowners—that is, they acquired control of their own plots of land, working them on their own and paying their landlord either a fixed rent or a share of their crop (hence the term "sharecropping"). The new system represented a breakdown of the traditional plantation system, in which blacks had lived together and worked together under the direction of

After Slavery
Although many freed slaves remained agricultural laborers after Emancipation, a considerable number moved off the land in search of new occupations and new homes. For many, that meant living for some time without stable employment or a permanent home. This photograph from the late 1860s shows a group of former slaves at a county almshouse in the South. (The Bettmann Archive)

a master. As tenants and sharecroppers, blacks enjoyed at least a physical independence from their landlords and had the sense of working their own land, even if in most cases they could never hope to buy it. (See Chapter 16 for a fuller discussion of the new Southern economy.)

Incomes and Credit

The economic effect of Reconstruction on the freedmen, to the extent that it can be gauged, was mixed. In some respects, the postwar years were a period of remarkable economic progress for blacks. If the food, clothing, shelter, and other material benefits they had received under slavery are considered as income, then prewar blacks had earned about a 22 percent share of the profits of the plantation system. By the end of Reconstruction, they were earning 56 percent of the return on investment in Southern agriculture. Measured another way, the per capita income of blacks rose 46 percent between 1857 and 1879, while the per capita income of whites declined 35 percent. This represented one of the most significant redistributions of income in American history.

Nevertheless, the economic status of blacks did not improve as much as these figures suggest. For one thing, while their share of the profits was increasing, the total profits of Southern agriculture were declining—a result of the dislocations of the war and of a reduction in the world market for cotton. For another thing, while blacks were earning a

greater return on their labor than they had under slavery, they were working less. Women and children were less likely to labor in the fields than in the past. Adult men tended to work shorter days. In all, the black labor force worked about one-third fewer hours during Reconstruction than it had been compelled to do under slavery—a reduction that brought the working schedule of blacks roughly into accord with that of white farm laborers. The income redistribution of the postwar years raised both the absolute and the relative economic status of blacks in the South substantially. It did not, however, lift many blacks out of poverty. Black per capita income rose from about one quarter of white per capita income to about one-half in the first few years after the war. But after this initial increase, it rose hardly at all.

For blacks and poor whites alike, whatever gains there might have been as a result of land and income redistribution were often overshadowed by the ravages of another economic burden: the crop lien system. In the postwar South, the traditional credit structure—based on "factors" (see p. 330) and banks—was unable to reassert its former control. In its stead emerged a new system of credit, centered in large part on local country stores—some of them owned by planters, others owned by independent merchants. Blacks and whites, landowners and tenants: all depended on these stores for such necessities as food, clothing, seed, farm implements, and the like. And since the agricultural sector does not enjoy the same steady cash flow as other sectors of the economy,

The Southern Plantation Before and After Emancipation: Barrow Plantation, Oglethorpe County, Georgia

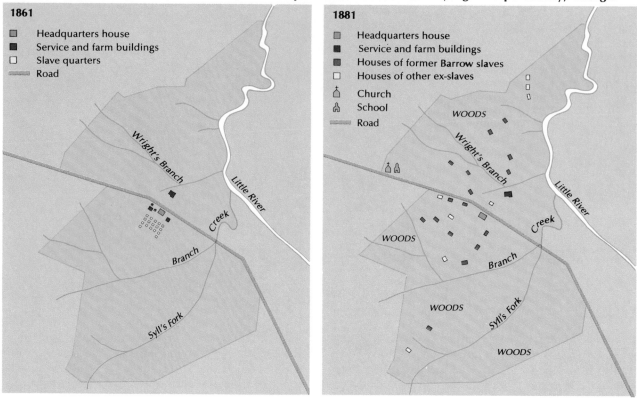

Southern farmers often had to rely on credit from these merchants in order to purchase what they needed. The credit came at high cost. Interest rates were, in effect, as high as 50 or 60 percent. Suppliers held liens (claims) on the crops of debtor farmers as collateral on the loans. If a farmer suffered a few bad years in a row, as often happened in the troubled agricultural markets of the 1870s, he could become trapped in a cycle of debt from which he could never escape.

This burdensome credit system had a number of effects on the South. One was that some blacks who had acquired land during the early years of Reconstruction gradually lost it as they fell into debt. (So, to a lesser extent, did white small landowners.) Another was that Southern farmers became utterly dependent on cash crops—and most of all on cotton—because only such marketable commodities seemed to offer any possibility of escape from debt. Thus Southern agriculture, never sufficiently diversified even in the best of times, became more one-dimensional than ever. Before the war, the South had grown most of its own food. By the end of Reconstruction, the region was importing a large propor-

tion—in some areas more than 50 percent—of what it needed to feed itself. The relentless planting of cotton, moreover, was contributing to an exhaustion of the soil. The crop lien system, in other words, was not only helping to impoverish small farmers; it was also contributing to a general decline in the Southern agricultural economy.

The Black Family in Freedom

One of the most striking features of the black response to Reconstruction was the concerted effort to build or rebuild family structures and to protect them from the interference they had experienced under slavery. A major reason for the rapid departure of so many blacks from the plantations on which they had spent their lives was the desire to find lost relatives and reunite families. Thousands of blacks wandered through the South looking for husbands, wives, children, or other relatives from whom they had been separated. Sometimes they found their loved ones, often by relying on an informal information network that quickly grew up in the black community or through advertising in newspapers. Sometimes, the search was in vain.

Former slaves were adamant in insisting that under the new economic system of the South they would acquire control over their own family lives. They rushed to have marriages, previously without legal standing, sanctified by church and law. At times, blacks held mass marriage ceremonies—sixty or seventy couples taking their vows simultaneously. Black families resisted living in the former slave quarters and moved instead to small cabins scattered widely across the countryside, where they could enjoy at least some privacy. It was often those blacks who had lived in closest proximity to whites—former house servants, for example—who were most determined to separate themselves from white society and create a home in which they would be able to control their own private lives.

Within the black family, the definition of male and female roles quickly came to resemble that within white families. Black men often forbade their wives and children to work in the fields. Such work, they believed, was a badge of slavery. Black women often chose to forgo such work themselves. Instead, women increasingly performed primarily domestic tasks—cooking, cleaning, gardening, raising children, attending to the needs of their husbands. Some black husbands refused to allow their wives to work as servants in white homes. "When I married my wife I married her to wait on me," one freedman told a former master who was attempting to hire his wife as a servant. "She got all she can do right here for me and the children."

But the effort to adapt the ideal of "domesticity" to the black family encountered at least some resistance. Not all black women wished to emulate the roles of their white counterparts—particularly those black women who, as former house servants, had observed the lives of white women closely. More important, however, economic necessity often required black women to engage in income-producing activities: working as domestic servants, taking in laundry, or helping their husbands in the field. By the end of Reconstruction, fully half of all black women over the age of sixteen were engaged in paid labor of some sort. And unlike among whites, most black female income earners were married.

The Grant Administration

Exhausted by the political turmoil of the Johnson administration, American voters in 1868 yearned for a strong, stable figure to guide them through the troubled years of Reconstruction. They did not find one. Instead, they turned trustingly to General Ulysses S. Grant, the conquering hero of the war and, by 1868, a widely revered national idol. Grant had been an inspired general, but he was a disastrous president. During his two terms in office, he faced problems that would have taxed the abilities of a master of statecraft. Grant, whatever his qualities, was no such leader. He was, rather, a generally dull and unimaginative man with few political skills and little real vision.

The Soldier President

Grant could have had the nomination of either party in 1868. But as he watched the congressional Radicals triumph over President Johnson, he concluded that the Radical Reconstruction policy expressed the real wishes of the people; so he was receptive when Radical leaders approached him with offers of the Republican nomination. Virtually without opposition, he received the endorsement of the party convention. The Democrats nominated former governor Horace Seymour of New York. The campaign was a bitter one, and Grant's triumph was by no means overwhelming. Grant carried twenty-six states and Seymour only eight. But Grant received only 3,013,000 popular votes to Seymour's 2,703,000, a scant majority of 310,000. This majority was a result of black votes in the reconstructed states of the South.

Ulysses S. Grant entered the White House with no political experience of any kind. After graduating from West Point with no particular distinction, Grant had entered the regular army, from which after years of service he had resigned under something of a cloud. In civilian life he undertook several dismal ventures that barely yielded him a living. His career before 1861 could be characterized as forty years of failure. Then came the Civil War, and Grant found at last the one setting, the one vocation for which he was supremely equipped—combat. The glory of his Civil War record, and virtually nothing else, had made him an attractive presidential candidate.

In choosing his official family, Grant proceeded as if he were creating a military staff. He sent several appointments to the Senate for confirmation without asking the recipients if they would serve; they first heard the news in the papers. Hamilton Fish, whom Grant appointed secretary of state, had been out of politics for twenty years when he heard the news that his name had been submitted to the Senate. He wired Grant that he could not accept, but he ultimately agreed to serve. Fish proved to be one of Grant's few truly distinguished appointees. Most of his later appointments went to men who were at best average and at worst incompetent or corrupt or both. Increasingly, Grant came to rely on the machine leaders in the party—the group most ardently devoted to the spoils system.

Diplomatic Successes

The Grant administration and the Johnson administration achieved their greatest success in foreign affairs. These were the accomplishments not of the presidents themselves, who displayed little aptitude for diplomacy, but of two outstanding secretaries of state: William H. Seward, who had served Lincoln during the Civil War and remained in office until 1869; and Hamilton Fish, who served throughout the two terms of the Grant administration.

An ardent expansionist and advocate of a vigorous foreign policy, Seward acted with as much daring as the demands of Reconstruction politics and the Republican hatred of President Johnson would permit. When Russia let it be known that it would like to sell Alaska to the United States, Seward readily agreed to pay the asking price of $7.2 million. Only by strenuous efforts was he able to induce the Senate to ratify the treaty and the House to appropriate the money (1867–1868). Critics jeered that the secretary had bought a useless frozen wasteland—"Seward's Icebox" some critics called it. But Alaska was an important fishing center in the North Pacific, and it was potentially rich in such resources as gold (and, as the nation would discover much later, oil). Seward was not content with expansion in continental North America. In 1867, he engineered the annexation of the tiny Midway Islands west of Hawaii.

In contrast with its sometimes shambling course in domestic politics, the performance of the Grant administration in the area of foreign affairs was, under the direction of Hamilton Fish, generally decisive and firm. A number of delicate and potentially dangerous situations confronted Fish from the beginning, but the most serious one arose out of a burning American grievance against England that had originated during the Civil War. Many Americans believed that the British government had violated the laws of neutrality by permitting Confederate ships, the *Alabama* and others, to be built and armed in English shipyards and let loose to prey on Northern commerce. American demands that England pay for the damages committed by these vessels became known as the *"Alabama* claims."

Seward tried earnestly to settle the *Alabama* claims before leaving office, but to no avail. The one successful effort to negotiate a settlement—the Johnson-Clarendon Convention of 1869, which would have submitted claims on both sides to arbitration—was rejected by the U.S. Senate shortly after Johnson left office because it contained no British apology. The debate featured a speech by Charles Sumner, chairman of the Committee on Foreign Relations, arguing that Britain's conduct had prolonged the war by two years. Therefore, Sumner insisted, England owed the United States for "direct damages" committed by the ships and "indirect damages" for the cost of the war for two years—which would have reached the staggering total of $2 billion.

England naturally would have nothing to do with any arrangement involving indirect claims, and settlement of the problem was temporarily stalled. Secretary Fish, however, continued to work for a solution, and finally, in 1871, the two countries agreed to the Treaty of Washington, providing for international arbitration of the issue and other pending controversies. In the treaty, Britain expressed regret for the escape of the *Alabama* and agreed to a set of rules governing neutral obligations that in effect conceded the case to the United States. This meant that the arbitrators would have only to fix the sum to be paid by Britain. They awarded $15.5 million to the United States.

The Defection of the Liberals

On both international and domestic matters, a wide breach soon developed between President Grant and a number of prominent Republicans, among them the famous Radical Charles Sumner. Sumner's extravagant demand for damages from Great Britain embarrassed Secretary Fish. Sumner also blocked a treaty for the annexation of Santo Domingo (now the Dominican Republic), a project in which Grant took a deep, even monomaniacal personal interest. The angry president got revenge by inducing his Senate friends to remove Sumner from the chairmanship of the Committee on Foreign Relations.

Among the principal political controversies of these years was the spoils system of presidential appointments, which Grant had used even more blatantly than most of his predecessors to reward party machine politicians. Sumner and other Republican leaders joined with reformers to agitate for a new civil service system to limit the president's appointive powers. Such scholarly journalists as E. L. Godkin of *The Nation* and George William Curtis of *Harper's Weekly* argued that the government should base its appointments not on services to the party but on fitness for office as determined by competitive examinations, as the British government already was doing. Grant reluctantly agreed to establish a civil service commission, which Congress authorized in 1871, to devise a system of hiring based on merit. This agency, under the direction of Curtis, proposed a set of rules that seemed to meet with Grant's approval. But Grant was not really much interested in reform, and even if he had been he could not have persuaded his followers to accept a new system that would undermine the very basis of party loyalty—patronage. Congress declined to renew the commission's appropriation, and the commission disbanded.

Nevertheless, controversy over civil-service reform remained one of the leading political issues of the next three decades. The debate involved more than simply an argument over patronage and corruption. It reflected, too, basic differences of opinion over who was fit to serve in public life. Middle-class reformers were saying, implicitly, that only educated, middle-class people (the "best men") should be permitted access to government office. Those opposing them—not simply party leaders but immigrant and labor groups, some farmers, and others—argued that the establishment of an elite corps of civil servants would exclude these groups from participation in government and restrict power to the upper classes.

Republican critics of the president also denounced him for his support of Radical Reconstruction. Grant continued to station federal troops in the South, and on many occasions he sent them to support Republican governments that were on the point of collapse. To growing numbers in the North this seemed like dangerous militarism, and they were more and more disgusted by the stories of governmental corruption and extravagance in the South. Some Republicans were beginning to suspect that there was corruption not only in the Southern state governments but also in the federal government. Still others criticized Grant because he had declined to speak out in favor of a reduction of the tariff.

Thus before the end of Grant's first term, members of his own party had begun to oppose him for a variety of reasons, all of which added up to what the critics called "Grantism." In 1872, hoping to prevent Grant's reelection, his opponents bolted the party. Referring to themselves as Liberal Republicans, they nominated their own presidential and vice presidential candidates. Horace Greeley, veteran editor and publisher of the New York *Tribune*, headed their ticket. The Democratic convention, seeing in Greeley's candidacy (and in the alliance with the Liberals it would achieve) the only chance to unseat Grant and the Republicans, endorsed Greeley with no great enthusiasm. Despite Greeley's recent attacks on Radical Reconstruction, many Southerners, remembering his own Radical past, chose to stay home on election day. Grant polled 286 electoral votes and 3,597,000 popular votes to Greeley's 66 and 2,834,000. Greeley had carried only two Southern and four border states. Three weeks later, apparently crushed by his defeat, Greeley died.

The Grant Scandals

During the campaign, the first of a series of political scandals had come to light. It originated with the Crédit Mobilier construction company, which had helped build the Union Pacific Railroad. The Crédit Mobilier was, in fact, controlled by a few Union Pacific stockholders who had awarded huge and fraudulent contracts to the construction company, thus milking the Union Pacific, a company of which they owned only a minor share, of money that in part came from government subsidies. To avert a congressional inquiry into the deal, the directors in effect gave Crédit Mobilier stock to key members of Congress. A congressional investigation in 1872 revealed that some highly placed Republicans—including Schuyler Colfax, now Grant's vice president—had accepted stock.

One dreary episode followed another in Grant's second term. Benjamin H. Bristow, Grant's third Treasury secretary, discovered that some of his officials and a group of distillers operating as a "whiskey ring" were cheating the government out of taxes by means of false reports. Among those involved was the president's private secretary, Orville E. Babcock. Grant defended Babcock, appointed him to another office, and eased Bristow out of the cabinet. Then a House investigation revealed that William W. Belknap, secretary of war, had accepted bribes to retain an Indian-post trader in office. Belknap resigned with Grant's blessing before the Senate could act on impeachment charges brought by the House.

The Grant Scandals

Grant's last years in office were plagued by revelations of scandals at various levels of the government. Although the president himself was never shown to have been directly involved, his reputation suffered nevertheless. This cartoon from *Puck* magazine shows Grant providing support for various corrupt members of his administration. (Historical Pictures Service)

Other, lesser scandals added to the growing impression that "Grantism" had brought rampant corruption to government.

The Greenback Question

Meanwhile, the Grant administration and the nation at large suffered another blow: the Panic of 1873. It began with the failure of a leading investment banking firm, Jay Cooke and Company, which had invested too heavily in postwar railroad building.

Depressions had come before with almost rhythmic regularity—in 1819, 1837, and 1857—but this was the worst one yet. It lasted four years.

Debtors pressured the government to follow an inflationary policy, which would have made it easier for them to pay their debts. But President Grant and most Republicans preferred what they called a "sound" currency—based solidly on gold reserves—which was to the advantage of the banks, moneylenders, and other creditors. The money question had confronted Grant and the Republicans in Congress from the beginning of his administration. The question was twofold: How should the war bonds be paid? And what should be the permanent place of greenbacks in the national currency? Representatives of the debtor interests argued that the bonds should be redeemed in greenbacks, thus increasing the amount of currency in circulation. The president favored payment in gold, and the Republican Congress moved speedily to promise redemption in "coin or its equivalent"; but refunding of the debt was to stretch out over a number of years.

The question of what to do about the greenbacks, however, remained unresolved. When Grant entered the White House, approximately $356 million of greenbacks were circulating. And in 1873, when the Supreme Court reversed an earlier decision and, in *Knox* v. *Lee*, affirmed the legality of greenbacks, the Treasury moved to increase the amount in circulation in response to the panic. For the same reason Congress, in the following year, voted to raise the total further. Grant, responding to pressures from Eastern financial interests, vetoed the measure—over the loud objections of many members of his own party.

With the greenback issue becoming more and more heated and divisive, and with an election year approaching, Republican leaders in Congress began searching for some way to settle the controversy. Their solution—introduced initially by Senator John Sherman of Ohio—was the Specie Resumption Act of 1875. This law provided that after January 1, 1879, the government would redeem greenback dollars at par with gold; that is, the present greenbacks, whose value constantly fluctuated, could be exchanged for new paper currency, whose value would be firmly pegged to the price of gold. The law protected the interests of the creditor classes, who had worried that debts would be repaid in debased paper currency. In theory, the new law protected the interests of debtor groups as well, by calling for an increase in the amount of specie-backed currency in circulation. In fact, however, "resumption" did not satisfy those who had been clamoring for an increase in greenbacks, because the gold-based money supply was never able to expand as much as they believed was necessary.

Thus the greenback issue survived after 1875, and the question of the proper composition of the currency emerged as one of the most controversial and enduring issues in American politics. Creditors and established financial interests continued to insist on a sound currency based on gold. Debtor groups—farmers, laborers, and some manufacturers—and debtor regions—the South and the West—continued to clamor for a currency based not on gold reserves but on the productive capacity of the nation. Otherwise, they claimed, they would continue to be strangled by an overvalued dollar circulating in insufficient quantities.

The question of greenbacks and the many other currency controversies that followed also became symbols of much deeper concerns. Agrarian dissidents and others came to see in the maintenance of the gold standard a conspiracy by entrenched financiers to keep farmers in economic bondage. Southerners and Westerners saw in the currency policies evidence of their subordination to the Northeast. Because in accepting the gold standard the United States was following the example of Great Britain and other European nations, many Americans came to view the policy as part of a dire international plot to enslave the American people. The greenbackers, as they were called, expressed their displeasure in 1875 by forming their own political organization: the National Greenback party. Active in the next three presidential elections, it failed to gain widespread support. But it did keep the money issue alive. And in the 1880s, the greenback forces began to merge with another, more powerful group of currency reformers—those who favored silver as the basis of currency—to help produce a political movement that would ultimately attain enormous strength.

The Abandonment of Reconstruction

As the North grew increasingly preoccupied with its own political and economic problems, interest in Reconstruction began to wane. The Grant administration continued to protect Republican governments in the South, but less because of any interest in ensuring the position of freedmen than because of a desire to prevent the reemergence of a strong Democratic party in the region. But even the presence of federal troops was not enough to prevent white Southerners from overturning many of the Republican governments that they believed had been so ruthlessly thrust upon them. In a few states, the Democrats (or Conservatives) returned to power almost as soon as civilian government was restored. In Virginia, North Carolina, and Georgia, Republican rule came to an end before or by 1871. In other states, the Democrats gradually regained control over several years. Texas was "redeemed"—as Southerners liked to call the restoration of Democratic rule—in 1873; Alabama and Arkansas in 1874; and Mississippi in 1876. For three other states—South Carolina, Louisiana, and Florida—the end of Reconstruction had to wait for the withdrawal of the last federal troops in 1876, a withdrawal that was the result of a long process of political bargaining and compromise at the national level.

The Southern States "Redeemed"

In the states where whites constituted a majority—the states of the upper South—overthrow of Republican control was a relatively simple matter. The whites had only to organize and win the elections. Restoration of suffrage to those whites who had been deprived of it helped them in their task. Presidential and congressional pardons returned the vote to numerous individuals; and in 1872, Congress passed the Amnesty Act, which restored political rights to 150,000 ex-Confederates and left only 500 excluded from political life.

In other states, where blacks were in the majority or the populations of the two races were almost equal, the whites resorted to intimidation and violence. Secret societies, complete with hooded robes and elaborate rituals, appeared in many parts of the South: the Ku Klux Klan, the Knights of the White Camellia, and others. They were frankly terroristic and attempted to frighten or physically prevent blacks from voting or otherwise exercising the normal rights of citizenship. Moving quickly to stamp out these societies, Congress passed two bills (1870 and 1871), which white Southerners called "force acts," and the Ku Klux Klan Act (also in 1871). These measures authorized the president to use military force and martial law in areas where the secret societies were active. Only rarely, however, did the laws have a significant impact.

More potent than the secret orders were open semimilitary organizations in the South that operated as rifle clubs under such names as Red Shirts and White Leagues. The first such society was founded in Mississippi, and the idea soon spread to other states; their tactics were called the Mississippi Plan. The plan called for whites in each community to organize and arm, and to be prepared, if necessary, to use force to win elections. But the heart of the scheme was in the phrase "drawing the color line." By one method or another, legal or illegal, every white man was to be forced to join the Democratic party or leave the community. By similar methods, every black male was to be excluded from political activity. In a few states, blacks were to be permitted to vote—if they voted Democratic.

Perhaps an even stronger influence than the techniques practiced by the armed bands was the simple weapon of economic pressure. The war had freed the slaves, but they were still laborers—hired workers or tenants—dependent on whites for their livelihood. Whites quickly discovered ways to use this dependence to increase their power over blacks. Planters refused to rent land to Republican blacks; storekeepers refused to extend them credit; employers refused to give them work. Without a secure economic base of their own—something Reconstruction had done nothing to give them—blacks were powerless to resist these pressures.

Southern blacks were, in the meantime, losing the support of many of their former supporters in the North, even of many humanitarian reformers who had worked for emancipation and equal rights. After the adoption of the Fifteenth Amendment in 1870, most reformers convinced themselves that their long campaign in behalf of black people at last was over; that with the vote, blacks ought to be able to take care of themselves. The party split of 1872, in part a response to the perceived corruption in Southern Reconstruction governments, weakened the Republicans in the South still further. Former Radical leaders such as Charles Sumner and Horace Greeley now began calling themselves Liberals, cooperating with the Democrats and outdoing even the Democrats in denunciations of what they viewed as black-and-carpetbag misgovernment. Within the South itself, many white Republicans joined the Liberals and moved into the Democratic party. Friction between black Republicans and those whites who remained in the party grew because of a well-justified feeling on the part of the blacks that they were not receiving a fair share of the power and the jobs.

The depression that began in 1873 aggravated political discontent in both the North and the South. In the congressional elections of 1874, the Democrats gained a majority of the seats in the House of Representatives, thus denying the Republicans control of the whole Congress for the first time since 1861. And President Grant, in view of the changing temper of the North, no longer was willing to use military force to prop up the Republican regimes that were still standing in the South. In 1875, when the Mississippi governor, Adelbert Ames (originally from Maine), appealed to Washington for troops to protect blacks from the terrorism of the Democrats, he received in reply a telegram that quoted Grant as saying: "The whole public are tired out with these annual autumnal outbreaks in the South, and the great majority are now ready to condemn any interference on the part of the government."

After the Democrats gained political control of Mississippi, only three states were left in the hands of the Republicans—South Carolina, Louisiana, and Florida. In the elections of 1876, again using terrorist tactics, the Democrats claimed victory in all three. But the Republicans claimed victory as well, and they were able to continue holding office because federal troops happened to be on the scene. If the troops were to be withdrawn, the last of the Republican regimes would fall. Resolution of the conflict would depend on the presidential election of 1876, which was itself in dispute because of the electoral controversies in the South.

The Compromise of 1877

Ulysses S. Grant was eager to run for another term in 1876, but the majority of the Republican leaders refused to consider him. They were impressed by the recent upsurge of Democratic strength and fearful that a third-term campaign and the rampant scandals with which Grant was by now associated would create controversy. Accordingly, they searched for a candidate who was not associated with the problems of the past eight years and could entice the Liberals back into the fold and unite the party until after the election. Senator James G. Blaine of Maine offered himself, but he had recently been involved in an allegedly crooked railroad deal. The Republican convention settled instead on Rutherford B. Hayes, a former Union army officer and congressman, three times governor of Ohio, and a champion of civil-service reform.

No personal rivalries divided the Democrats. Only one aspirant commanded serious attention: Governor Samuel J. Tilden of New York, whose name had become synonymous with governmental reform. A corporation lawyer and a millionaire, Tilden had long been a power in the Democratic organization of his state, but he had not hesitated to turn against the corrupt Tweed Ring of New York City's Tammany Hall and aid in its overthrow. His fight against Tweed brought him national fame and the governorship, in which position he increased his reputation for honest administration.

The campaign was an unusually bitter one, but there were in fact almost no differences of principle between the candidates. Hayes supported withdrawal of troops from the South and civil-service reform, and his record for probity was equal to Tilden's. Tilden vaguely supported a tariff reduction, but on other economic issues he was at least as conservative as his rival. He supported the gold standard—"sound money"—and he believed that government had no business interfering with economic interests. He looked on himself as a modern counterpart of Thomas Jefferson.

The November election produced an apparent Democratic victory. Tilden carried the South and several large Northern states, and his popular vote was 4,301,000 to 4,036,000 for Hayes. But the situation was complicated by the disputed returns from Louisiana, South Carolina, and Florida, whose total electoral vote was 19. Both parties claimed to have won these states, and double sets of returns were presented to Congress. Adding to the confusion was a contested vote in Oregon, where one of the three successful Republican electors was declared ineligible because he held a federal office. The Democrats contended that the place should go to the Democratic elector with the highest number of votes; but the Republicans insisted that according to state law, the remaining electors were to select someone to fill the vacancy. The disputed returns threw the outcome of the election into doubt. As tension and excitement gripped the country, two clear facts emerged from the welter of conflicting claims. Tilden had undisputed claim to 184 electoral votes, only one short of the majority. The 20 votes in controversy would determine who would be president, and Hayes needed all of them to secure the office.

With surprise and consternation, the nation now learned that no method existed to determine the va-

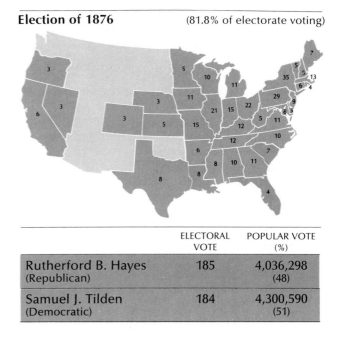

Election of 1876   (81.8% of electorate voting)

	ELECTORAL VOTE	POPULAR VOTE (%)
Rutherford B. Hayes (Republican)	185	4,036,298 (48)
Samuel J. Tilden (Democratic)	184	4,300,590 (51)

lidity of disputed returns. The Constitution stated: "The President of the Senate shall, in the presence of the Senate and House of Representatives, open all the certificates and the votes shall then be counted." The question was, how and by whom? The Senate was Republican and so, of course, was its president; the House was Democratic. Constitutional ambiguity and congressional division rendered a fair and satisfactory solution of the crisis impossible. If the president of the Senate counted the votes, Hayes would be the victor. If the Senate and House judged the returns separately, they would reach opposite decisions and checkmate each other. And if the houses voted jointly, the Democrats, with a numerical majority, would decide the result. Resort to any one of these lines of action promised to divide the country and possibly result in chaos.

Not until the last days of January 1877 did Congress act to break the deadlock by creating a special electoral commission to pass on all the disputed votes. The commission was to be composed of five senators, five representatives, and five justices of the Supreme Court. The congressional delegation would consist of five Republicans and five Democrats. The Court delegation, as established by the legislation creating the commission, would consist of two Republicans, two Democrats, and an independent. But before the commission could meet, the designated independent was elected to the Senate and resigned his seat on the Court. His place on the commission fell to a more partisan Republican. The commission sat throughout February and reached decisions by a straight party vote of 8 to 7, awarding every disputed vote to Hayes. Congress accepted the final verdict of the commission on March 2, only two days before the inauguration of the new president.

Ratification of the commission's findings, however, required a series of elaborate compromises among leaders of both parties. Behind the dealing, and partially directing it, were powerful economic forces with a stake in the outcome. Republican leaders, hoping to end a Democratic filibuster in the Senate, met secretly with Southern Democratic leaders to work out terms by which they would support the election of Hayes. According to the traditional account, certain Republicans and Southern Democrats met at Washington's Wormley Hotel, and the Republicans pledged that Hayes, after becoming president, would withdraw the troops from the South. Since withdrawal would mean the downfall of the last carpetbag governments, the Southerners, convinced they were getting as much from Hayes as they could get from Tilden, agreed to abandon the filibuster.

Actually, the story behind the "Compromise of 1877" is somewhat more complex. Hayes was on record before the election as favoring withdrawal of the troops, and in any event the Democrats in the House could have forced withdrawal simply by cutting off appropriations for the army in the Reconstruction process. The real agreement, the one that won the Southern Democrats over, was reached before the Wormley meeting. As the price of their cooperation, the Southern Democrats (among them some old Whigs) exacted several pledges from the Republicans: the appointment of at least one Southerner to the Hayes cabinet, control of federal patronage in their areas, generous internal improvements, federal aid for the Texas and Pacific Railroad, and, finally, withdrawal of the troops. Many of the Conservatives who controlled the Democratic parties of the redeemed Southern states were interested in industrializing the South, and they believed that the Republican program of federal aid to business would be more beneficial for their region than the archaic states' rights policy of the Democrats.

In his inaugural address, Hayes spoke primarily about the Southern problem. While he was careful to say that the rights of blacks must be preserved, he announced that the most pressing need of the South was the restoration of "wise, honest, and peaceful local self-government"—a signal that he planned to withdraw the troops and let whites take over control of the state governments. Hayes knew that this would lend weight to charges that he was paying off the South for acquiescing in his election and would strengthen those critics who referred to him as "his Fraudulency." But in fact, the political crisis surrounding the election had already created such bitterness there was probably nothing Hayes could have done to mollify his critics.

The president hoped to build up a "new Republican" party in the South composed of whatever conservative white groups could be weaned away from the Democrats and committed to some acceptance of black rights. But his efforts, which included a tour of Southern cities and even the decoration of a memorial to the Confederate war dead, failed. Although many white Southern leaders sympathized with the economic credo of the Republicans, they could not advise their people to support the party that had imposed Reconstruction. Nor were white Southerners pleased by Hayes's bestowal of federal offices on carpetbaggers or by his vetoes of Democratic attempts to repeal the force acts. The "solid South," although not yet fully formed, was beginning to take shape. Neither Hayes nor any other Republican could reverse the trend—particularly since no one was willing to use federal power to protect black voting rights, which alone held promise of giving the Republicans lasting strength in the region. The withdrawal of the troops was a signal that the national government was giving up its attempt to control Southern politics and to determine the place of blacks in Southern society.

The Legacy of Reconstruction

The record of the Reconstruction years is not one of complete failure, as many have charged. That slavery would be abolished was clear well before the end of the war; but Reconstruction worked other changes upon Southern society as well. There was a significant redistribution of income, from which blacks benefited. There was a more limited but not unimportant redistribution of land ownership, which enabled some former slaves to acquire property for the first time. There was both a relative and an absolute improvement in the economic circumstances of most blacks.

Nor was Reconstruction as disastrous an experience for Southern whites as most believed at the time. The region had emerged from a prolonged and bloody war defeated and devastated; and yet within a decade, the white South had regained control of its own institutions and, to a great extent, restored its traditional ruling class to power. No harsh punishments were meted out to former Confederate leaders. No drastic program of economic reform was imposed on the region. Few lasting political changes other than the abolition of slavery were forced on the South. Not many conquered nations fare as well.

Yet for all that, Americans of the twentieth century cannot help but look back on Reconstruction as a tragic era. For in those years the United States made its first serious effort to resolve its oldest and deepest social problem—the problem of race. And it largely failed in the effort. What was more, the experience so disappointed, disillusioned, and embittered white Americans that it would be many years before they would make the effort again.

Why did this great assault on racial injustice—an assault that had emerged over a period of more than fifty years—end so badly? In part, of course, it was because of the weaknesses and errors of the people who directed it. But in greater part, it was because the resolution of the racial problem required a far more fundamental reform of society than Americans of the time were willing to make. One after another, attempts to produce solutions ran up against conservative obstacles so deeply embedded in the nation's life that they could not be dislodged. Veneration of the Constitution sharply limited the willingness of national leaders to infringe on the rights of states and individuals in creating social change. A profound respect for private property and free enterprise prevented any real assault on economic privilege in the South, ensuring that blacks would not win title to the land and wealth they believed they deserved. Above all, perhaps, a pervasive belief among many of even the most liberal whites that the black race was inherently inferior served as an obstacle to the full equality of the freedmen. Given the context within which Americans of the 1860s and 1870s were working, what is surprising, perhaps, is not that Reconstruction did so little, but that it did even as much as it did. The era was tragic not just because it was a failure—the failure may have been inevitable from the beginning—but also because it revealed how great the barriers were to racial justice in the United States.

Given the odds confronting them, therefore, black Americans had reason for pride in the limited gains they were able to make during Reconstruction. And the nation at large had reason for gratitude that, if nothing else, the postwar era produced two great charters of freedom—the Fourteenth and Fifteenth amendments to the Constitution—which, although largely ignored at the time, would one day serve as the basis for a "Second Reconstruction," one that would renew the drive to bring freedom and equality to all Americans.

SIGNIFICANT EVENTS

1863 Lincoln announces preliminary Reconstruction plan (p. 454)

1864 Louisiana, Arkansas, Tennessee readmitted to Union under Lincoln plan (p. 454)

Wade-Davis bill passed (p. 455)

1865 Lincoln assassinated; Andrew Johnson becomes president (April 14) (p. 456)

Johnson readmits rest of Confederate states to Union under Lincoln plan (p. 456)

Black Codes enacted in South (p. 457)

Freedmen's Bureau established (p. 453)

Congress reconvenes (December) and refuses to admit Southern representatives; creates Joint Committee on Reconstruction (p. 457)

1866 Freedmen's Bureau Act renewed (p. 457)

Congress approves Fourteenth Amendment; most Southern states reject it (pp. 457–458)

Republicans gain in congressional elections (p. 458)

Ex parte Milligan challenges Radicals' Reconstruction plans (p. 460)

Ku Klux Klan formed in South (p. 473)

1867 Military Reconstruction Act (and two supplementary acts) outlines congressional plan of Reconstruction (p. 458)

Tenure of Office Act and Command of the Army Act restrict presidential power (p. 459)

Southern states establish Reconstruction governments under congressional plan (p. 459)

Alaska purchased (p. 470)

1868 Most Southern states readmitted to Congress under congressional plan (p. 459)

Andrew Johnson impeached but not convicted (pp. 460–461)

Fourteenth Amendment ratified (p. 458)

Ulysses S. Grant elected president (p. 469)

1869 Congress passes Fifteenth Amendment (p. 459)

First "redeemer" governments elected in South (p. 473)

1870 Last Southern states readmitted to Congress (p. 459)

"Force acts" passed (p. 473)

1871 *Alabama* claims settled (p. 470)

1872 Liberal Republicans defect (p. 471)

Grant reelected president (p. 471)

1873 Commercial and financial panic disrupts economy (p. 472)

1875 Specie Resumption Act passed (p. 472)

"Whiskey ring" scandal discredits Grant administration (p. 471)

1877 Rutherford B. Hayes elected president after disputed election (p. 475)

Last federal troops withdrawn from South after Compromise of 1877 (p. 476)

Last Southern states "redeemed" (p. 476)

SUGGESTED READINGS

General Studies. Eric Foner, *Reconstruction: America's Unfinished Revolution, 1863–1877* (1988); Kenneth Stampp, *The Era of Reconstruction* (1965); John Hope Franklin, *Reconstruction After the Civil War* (1961); William A. Dunning, *Reconstruction, Political and Economic, 1865–1877* (1907); W. E. B. Du Bois, *Black Reconstruction* (1935); E. Merton Coulter, *The South During Reconstruction* (1947); Rembert Patrick, *The Reconstruction of the Nation* (1967).

Early Reconstruction. Herman Belz, *Reconstructing the Union* (1969); William B. Hesseltine, *Lincoln's Plan of Reconstruction* (1960); Willie Lee Rose, *Rehearsal for Reconstruction: The Port Royal Experiment* (1964); Louis S. Gerteis, *From Contraband to Freedman* (1973); Richard H. Abbott, *The First Southern Strategy* (1986).

Congressional Reconstruction. William R. Brock, *An American Crisis* (1963); Howard K. Beale, *The Critical Year: A Study of Andrew Johnson and Reconstruction* (1930); Eric McKitrick, *Andrew Johnson and Reconstruction* (1960); Michael Les Benedict, *A Compromise of Principle: Congressional Republicans and Reconstruction, 1863–1869* and *The Impeachment and Trial of Andrew Johnson* (1973); Hans L. Trefousse, *The Radical Republicans* (1963) and *The Impeachment of a President* (1975); David Donald, *The Politics of Reconstruction* (1965); La Wanda Cox and John H. Cox, *Politics, Principles, and Prejudice, 1865–1867* (1963); Richard N. Current, *Old Thad Stevens* (1942); Fawn Brodie, *Thaddeus Stevens* (1959); David Donald, *Charles Sumner and the Rights of Man* (1970); Harold Hyman, *A More Perfect Union* (1973); Stanley Kutler, *The Judicial Power and Reconstruction Politics* (1968); Mark W. Summers, *Railroads, Reconstruction, and the Gospel of Prosperity* (1984); Charles Fairman, *Reconstruction and Reunion* (1971); Herman Belz, *A New Birth of Freedom* (1976) and *Emancipation and Equal Rights* (1978); William Gilette, *The Right to Vote* (1965).

The South in Reconstruction. Dan T. Carter, *When the War Was Over: The Failure of Self-Reconstruction in the South, 1865–1867* (1985); Michael Perman, *Reunion Without Compromise* (1973) and *The Road to Redemption: Southern Politics, 1869–1879* (1984); Joel G. Taylor, *Louisiana Reconstructed* (1974); Vernon Wharton, *The Negro in Mississippi, 1865–1890* (1965); Peyton McCrary, *Abraham Lincoln and Recon-*

struction (1978); Joel Williamson, *After Slavery: The Negro in South Carolina During Reconstruction* (1965); Thomas Holt, *Black over White* (1977); Roberta Alexander, *North Carolina Faces the Freedmen: Race Relations During Presidential Reconstruction, 1865–1867* (1985); C. Peter Ripley, *Slaves and Freedmen in Civil War Louisiana* (1976); Barbara Fields, *Slavery and Freedom on the Middle Ground* (1985); Michael Wayne, *The Reshaping of Plantation Society: The Natchez District* (1983); William Gillette, *Retreat from Reconstruction* (1980); James D. Anderson, *The Education of Blacks in the South* (1989); Roger Ransom and Richard Sutch, *One Kind of Freedom* (1977); Robert Higgs, *Competition and Coercion* (1977); Crandall A. Shifflett, *Patronage and Poverty in the Tabacco South: Louisa County, Virginia, 1860–1900* (1982); Leon Litwack, *Been in the Storm So Long* (1979); Eric Foner, *Nothing but Freedom: Emancipation and Its Legacy* (1983); Peter Kolchin, *First Freedom* (1972); Allen Trelease, *White Terror* (1967); William S. McFeely, *Yankee Stepfather: General O. O. Howard and the Freedmen* (1968); George Bentley, *A History of the Freedmen's Bureau* (1955); Otto Olsen, *Carpetbagger's Crusade: Albion Winegar Tourgée* (1965); L. N. Powell, *New Masters: Northern Planters During the Civil War and Reconstruction* (1980); William Harris, *Day of the Carpetbagger* (1979); Elizabeth Jacoway, *Yankee Missionaries in the South* (1979); Richard N. Current, *Those Terrible Carpetbaggers* (1988); William C. Harris, *The Day of the Carpetbagger: Republican Reconstruction in Mississippi, 1867–1875* (1979); Sarah Wiggins, *The Scalawag in Alabama Politics, 1865–1881* (1977); Jacqueline Jones, *Soldiers of Light and Love* (1980) and *Labor of Love, Labor of Sorrow: Black Women, Work, and the Family from Slavery to the Present* (1985); James Sefton, *The United States Army and Reconstruction* (1967).

The Grant Administration. William McFeely, *Grant* (1981); Margaret S. Thompson, *The "Spider Web": Congress and Lobbying in the Age of Grant* (1985); Allan Nevins, *Hamilton Fish* (1936); William B. Hesseltine, *U. S. Grant, Politician* (1935); David Loth, *Public Plunder* (1938); John G. Sproat, *"The Best Men"* (1968); Ari Hoogenboom, *Outlawing the Spoils* (1961); Irwin Unger, *The Greenback Era* (1964); C. Vann Woodward, *Reunion and Reaction* (1951); K. I. Polakoff, *The Politics of Inertia* (1973); Edwin C. Rozwenc (ed.), *Reconstruction in the South*, rev. ed. (1952).

Held Up by Buffalo (c. 1880), by N. H. Trotter
Once among the most numerous creatures in North America, the buffalo became almost extinct as a result of their indiscriminate slaughter by white settlers and travelers, who often fired at herds from moving trains simply for the sport of it. (*Smithsonian Institution*)

CHAPTER 16

❖ ❖ ❖

The New South and the Last West

❖ ❖ ❖

Much of the United States in the years following Reconstruction was preoccupied with the expansion and development of an already advanced urban-industrial society. In two regions of America, however, the experience was quite different. In the South, the first region of the country to have been settled by Europeans, and in the West, the last such region, the late nineteenth century was a time of new beginnings. For many residents of both regions, it was also a period of decline relative to the rest of the nation—a decline that would ultimately produce major social and political upheavals.

The South, recovering from a disastrous war and confronting once again the reality of an economy far less developed than that of the North, faced several choices in the years after Reconstruction. It could attempt to transform itself into a modern, industrial region able to compete effectively with its former enemy. Or it could attempt to rebuild its agrarian economy and restore some semblance of the once stable old order that many white Southerners had so valued in their civilization before the Civil War. In fact, the South attempted to do both. Substantial groups of white Southerners set out to promote the modern economic development of their region, to imitate Northern ways—to build what they liked to call a New South. Their efforts were not without result. But despite substantial progress in certain areas, the South remained at the end of the century what it had been since the end of the Civil War: an impoverished, primarily agricultural region, far behind the North in the development of commerce and

industry. The failure was a result in part of economic obstacles over which the region had little control; but it was a result, too, of the determination of the vast majority of white Southerners to protect the supremacy of their race—a determination that often came to overshadow all efforts at reform.

For the new West—the areas beyond the Mississippi River, most of which had remained unsettled or sparsely settled by white Americans in the years before the Civil War—the late nineteenth century was a time of dramatic growth and development. White settlers (and some blacks) now poured into the region—a region larger than all the previously settled area of America combined. They established there a new civilization of farms, ranches, mining operations, and more. It was a civilization that had much in common with the older regions of the United States, but one that took on a distinctive character of its own. The conquest of the West by white Americans was in part the story of a courageous struggle against imposing natural obstacles. It was also the story of a brutal assault against the Indian tribes of the region, who were once again disrupted and displaced by the onward march of white society.

The South in Transition

The Compromise of 1877—the agreement between Southern Democrats and Northern Republicans that helped settle the disputed election of 1876—was supposed to be the first step toward developing a stable, permanent Republican party in the South. In that respect, at least, it failed. In the years following the end of Reconstruction, white Southerners began to establish the Democratic party as the only viable political organization for the region's whites. They also created a social system that, for all its differences from the system of the antebellum period, concentrated most political and economic power in the hands of a powerful white aristocracy. This white leadership systematically excluded black Southerners from any significant access to power or influence in the region.

The "Redeemers"

By the end of 1877—after the last withdrawal of federal troops—every Southern state government had been "redeemed." That is, political power had been restored to white Democrats. Many white Southerners rejoiced at the restoration of what they liked to call "home rule." But in reality, political power in the region was soon more restricted than at any time since the Civil War. Once again, the South fell under the control of a powerful, conservative oligarchy, whose members were known variously as the "Redeemers" or the "Bourbons."

This post-Reconstruction ruling class was in some areas of the South much the same as the ruling class of the antebellum period. In Alabama, for example, the old planter elite—despite challenges from new merchant and industrial forces—retained much of its former power and continued largely to dominate the state for decades. In other areas, however, the Redeemers constituted a genuinely new class. Merchants, industrialists, railroad developers, financiers—some of them former planters, some of them Northern immigrants who had become absorbed into the region's life, some of them ambitious, upwardly mobile white Southerners from the region's lower social tiers—combined a commitment to "home rule" and social conservatism with a commitment to economic development.

Whatever their differences, the various Bourbon governments of the New South behaved in many respects quite similarly. Although one of the most heated conservative criticisms of the Reconstruction governments had been that they had fostered widespread corruption, the Redeemer regimes were, if anything, even more awash in graft, fraud, and waste. (In this, they were little different from governments in every region of the country.) Virtually all the new Democratic regimes, moreover, adopted policies of lowered taxation, reduced spending, and drastically diminished state services. The carpetbag

governments of Reconstruction, they complained, had saddled the South with huge debts. (In fact, some of the debt predated the Civil War.) It was the duty of the new leaders, therefore, to put the region back on a sound financial footing. Many of the most valuable accomplishments of Reconstruction were now dismantled. In one state after another, for example, state support for public school systems was reduced or eliminated. "Schools are not a necessity," commented a governor of Virginia.

The rule of the Bourbon oligarchies was not unchallenged. By the late 1870s, powerful dissenting groups were protesting the cuts in services. Even more, they were denouncing the commitment of their present governments to paying off the prewar and Reconstruction debts in full, at the original (usually high) rates of interest. In Virginia, for example, a vigorous "Readjuster" movement emerged, demanding that the state revise its debt payment procedures so as to make more money available for state services. In 1879, the Readjusters won control of the legislature; and in the next few years they captured the governorship and a U. S. Senate seat. In other states, similar protests emerged. There were demands for greenbacks and for other economic reforms, as well as for debt readjustments. (A few such independent movements included significant numbers of blacks in their ranks, but all consisted primarily of lower-income whites.) For a moment, at least, it seemed as though Southern politics was to become genuinely competitive. But the dissident uprising proved only temporary. By the mid-1880s, conservative Southerners—largely by exploiting racial prejudice—had effectively destroyed the Readjusters and other such movements. It would be several years before a new challenge to the power of the Bourbons would arise.

Industrialization and "the New South"

The fondest dream of some Southern leaders in the post-Reconstruction era was to see their region become the home of a vigorous industrial economy. The South had lost the war, many now argued, because its economy had been unable to compete with the modernized manufacturing capacity of the North. The region's task, therefore, must now be to "out-Yankee the Yankees." Influential spokesmen—most prominent among them Henry Grady, editor of the *Atlanta Constitution*—espoused a "New South creed." Grady and other promoters of a New South seldom challenged the longstanding commitment of white supremacy of most white Southerners. They did, however, advocate other important changes in Southern values. Above all, they promoted the virtues of thrift, industry, and progress—the same qualities that prewar Southerners had so often denounced in Northern society. "We have sown towns and cities in the place of theories," Grady boasted to a New England audience in the 1880s, "and put business above politics. . . . We have fallen in love with work."

But even the most fervent advocates of the New South creed were generally unwilling to break entirely with the Southern past. That was evident in, among other things, the popular literature of the region. At the same time that white Southern writers were extolling the virtues of industrialization in newspaper editorials and speeches, they were painting nostalgic portraits of the Old South in their literature. Few Southerners advocated a literal return to the old ways, but most whites eagerly embraced romantic talk of the "lost cause." And they responded warmly to the local-color fiction of such writers as Joel Chandler Harris, whose folk tales—the most famous being *Uncle Remus* (1880)—presented the slave society of the antebellum years as a harmonious world, marked by engaging dialect and by close emotional bonds between the races. Thomas Nelson Page similarly extolled the old Virginia aristocracy. The whites of the New South, in short, faced their future with one foot still in the past.

Even so, Southern industry expanded dramatically in the years after Reconstruction and became a more important part of the region's economy than ever before. Most visible was the growth in textile manufacturing. In the past, Southern cotton had usually been shipped out of the region to manufacturers in the North or in Europe. Now textile factories appeared in the South itself—drawn to the region from New England by the abundance of water power, the ready supply of cheap labor, the low taxes, and the accommodating conservative governments. The number of spindles in the region increased 900 percent in the last twenty years of the century. The tobacco processing industry, similarly, established an important foothold in the region, largely through the work of James B. Duke of North Carolina, whose American Tobacco Company became for a time a virtual monopoly in the processing of raw tobacco into marketable smoking materials. In the lower South, and particularly in Alabama, the iron (and, later, steel) industry grew rapidly. The city of Birmingham grew within a decade from modest beginnings to become a major center of pig iron processing. The Southern iron and steel industry represented by 1890 nearly a fifth of the nation's total capacity.

And the South made important progress as well toward remedying one of its greatest economic problems: its obsolete transportation system. Railroad development increased substantially in the post-Reconstruction years—at a rate far greater than that of the nation at large. Between 1880 and 1890, the total miles of track in the region more than doubled. And the South took a giant step toward integrating its transportation system with that of the rest of the country when, in 1886, it changed the gauge (width) of its trackage to correspond with the standards of the North. No longer would it be necessary for cargoes heading into the South to be transferred from one train to another at the borders of the region.

Yet Southern industry developed within strict limits, and its effects on the region were never even remotely comparable to the effects of industrialization on the North. The Southern share of national manufacturing doubled in the last twenty years of the century, to 10 percent of the total. But that percentage was the same the South had claimed in 1860; the region had, in other words, done no more than regain what it had lost during the war and its aftermath. The region's per capita income increased 21 percent in the same period. But at the end of the century, average income in the South was only 40 percent of that in the North; in 1860 it had been more than 60 percent. And even in those areas where development had been most rapid—textiles, iron, railroads—much, if not most, of the capital had come from the North. The South, in effect, was developing a colonial economy.

The growth of industry in the South required the region to recruit a substantial industrial work force for the first time. From the beginning, a high percentage of the factory workers (and an especially high percentage of textile workers) were women. Heavy male casualties in the Civil War had helped create a large population of unmarried women who desperately needed employment. Factories also hired entire families, who were often moving into towns from failed farms, and put women and children to work alongside husbands and fathers. Hours were long (often as much as twelve hours a day) and wages were low—far below the Northern equivalent; indeed one of the greatest attractions of the South to industrialists was that employers were able to pay workers there as little as one-half what Northern workers received.

Life in most mill towns was rigidly controlled by the owners and managers of the factories. They rigorously suppressed any attempts at protest or union organization. Company stores sold goods to workers at inflated prices and issued credit at exorbitant rates, and mill owners ensured that no competitors were able to establish themselves in the community. At the same time, however, the conditions of the mill town helped create a strong sense of community and solidarity among workers (even if it was only infrequently translated into militancy).

Some industries, textiles for example, offered virtually no opportunities to black workers. Others—tobacco, iron, and lumber, among others—did provide some employment for blacks but usually only the least desirable and lowest-paid positions. Some mill towns, therefore, were places where black and white culture often came into close contact. In the tobacco towns of North Carolina and the steel towns of Alabama, black and white workers lived in close proximity—a situation that contributed less to racial harmony than to the growing determination of white leaders to find new ways to defend white supremacy.

At times, industrialization proceeded on the basis of no wage-paying employment at all. Through the notorious "convict-lease" system, Southern states leased gangs of convicted criminals to private interests as a cheap labor supply. The system not only exposed the convicts to brutal and often fatal mistreatment without pay (the leasing fees went to the states, not the workers); it also denied employment in railroad construction and other projects to the free labor force.

The Crop-Lien System

Despite significant growth in Southern industry, the region remained primarily agricultural throughout the late nineteenth century. The most important economic reality in the post-Reconstruction South, therefore, was the impoverished state of agriculture. The 1870s and 1880s saw an acceleration of the process that had begun in the immediate postwar years: the imposition of systems of tenantry and debt peonage on much of the region; the reliance on a few cash crops rather than on a diversified agricultural system; and increasing absentee ownership of valuable farmlands (many of them purchased by merchants and industrialists, who paid little attention to whether the land was being properly used). During Reconstruction, perhaps a third or more of the farmers in the South were tenants; by 1990 the figure had increased to 70 percent. It was remarkable, perhaps, that despite all this more than 121,000 blacks owned their own land in 1890. But that figure still represented a tiny percentage of the black population as a whole.

At the center of the Southern agricultural system was the crop-lien system, which had emerged in the aftermath of the Civil War. (See pp. 466–467.) The collapse of antebellum financial institutions and the increasing scarcity of banks and currency in the South meant that credit—always important to farmers, with their seasonal production—was very difficult to obtain. Control of credit, therefore, generally fell into the hands of "furnishing merchants": the owners of the local stores from which farmers bought their tools, seed, and other necessities. Few farmers ever had enough money to pay cash for what they needed, so they bought their supplies on credit, backed by a guarantee to the merchant of a share of their crop (or a "lien") when it was harvested.

Furnishing merchants seldom had competitors (and indeed often went to considerable lengths to ensure they retained a monopoly). At times, the merchants were also the most important landowners in their communities, which gave them even more power over the economic life of the area. As a result, farmers buying from the local merchants had little choice but to pay the highly inflated prices the stores charged for goods bought on credit (as much as 40 percent above the cash price). They also paid interest, which was also often set at very high levels. By the time farmers harvested their crops, they were often so deeply in debt that they had to turn over the entire harvest to the merchant. Even that was generally not enough. Thus year after year, their indebtedness grew. Farmers who owned their own land often lost it as merchants seized it for payment of unpaid liens. Farmers who were already tenants found themselves increasingly under the control of merchants and landlords, whom they had little hope of ever paying off completely.

The crop-lien system was one of several factors contributing to a social and economic transformation of the Southern back country: the piney woods and mountain regions where cotton and slavery had always been rare and where farmers lived ruggedly independent lives. Subsistence agriculture had long been the norm in these areas; but as their indebtedness grew, many farmers now had to grow cash crops such as cotton instead of the food crops they had traditionally cultivated in order to make enough money to pay their debts. But the social and economic transformation of the back country was a result of other factors as well.

Many back-country residents had traditionally subsisted by raising livestock, which had roamed freely across the landscape. In the 1870s, as commercial agriculture began to intrude into these regions, many communities began to pass "fence laws," which required farmers to fence in their animals (as opposed to fencing off their crops, as had once been the custom). There were widespread protests against the new laws, and at times violent efforts to resist them. But the existence of the open range (which had once been as much a part of life in the back-country South as it was in the American West) could not survive the spread of commercial agriculture. In-

The Crop-Lien System: The South in 1880

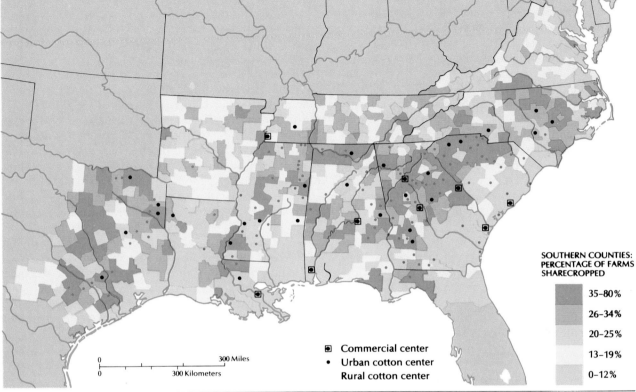

SOUTHERN COUNTIES:
PERCENTAGE OF FARMS
SHARECROPPED

35–80%
26–34%
20–25%
13–19%
0–12%

300 Miles
300 Kilometers

◙ Commercial center
• Urban cotton center
  Rural cotton center

creasingly, therefore, opportunities for families to live largely self-sufficiently were declining at the same time as opportunities for profiting within the market remained slim. The people of the back country, perhaps even more than other groups for whom agriculture had always been a business, felt the pain of losing their economic independence. They would be among the most important constituents for the populist protests of the 1880s and 1890s.

The crop-lien system was particularly devastating to Southern blacks, few of whom owned their own land to begin with. Already dependent on landowners as tenants and sharecroppers, they were especially vulnerable to the economic tyranny of the furnishing merchant. These economic difficulties were compounded by social and legal discrimination, which in the post-Reconstruction era began to take new forms and to inspire new responses.

Blacks and the New South

The "New South creed" was not the property of whites alone. Many blacks became enchanted by the vision of progress and self-improvement as well.

Some blacks succeeded in elevating themselves into a distinct middle class—one economically inferior to the white middle class, but nevertheless significant. These were former slaves (and, as the decades passed, their offspring) who managed to acquire property, establish small businesses, or enter professions. A few blacks accumulated substantial fortunes by establishing banks and insurance companies for their race. One of those was Maggie Lena, a black woman who became the first female bank president in the United States when she founded the St. Luke Penny Savings Bank in Richmond in 1903. Most middle-class blacks experienced more modest gains by becoming doctors, lawyers, nurses, or teachers serving members of their own race.

A cardinal tenet of this rising group of blacks was that education was vital to the future of their race. With the support of Northern missionary societies and, to a far lesser extent, a few Southern state governments, they expanded the network of black colleges and institutes that had taken root during Reconstruction into an important educational system. The chief spokesman for this commitment to education, and ultimately the major spokesman for his race as a whole, was Booker T. Washington, founder and president of the Tuskegee Institute in Alabama. Born into slavery, Washington had worked his own way out of poverty by virtue of having acquired an education (at Virginia's famous Hampton Institute). Once established, he urged other blacks to follow the same road to self-improvement.

Washington's message was both cautious and hopeful. The "great leap from slavery to freedom," he warned, should not permit blacks to forget how to work with their hands. They should attend school, learn skills, and establish a solid footing in agriculture and the trades. Industrial, not classical, education should be their goal. Blacks should, moreover, refine their speech, improve their dress, and adopt habits of thrift and personal cleanliness; they should, in short, adopt the standards of the white middle class. Only thus, he claimed, could they win the respect of the white population, the prerequisite for any larger social gains. In a famous speech in Georgia in 1895, Washington outlined a philosophy of race relations that became widely known as the Atlanta Compromise. "The wisest among my race understand," he said, "that the agitation of questions of social equality is the extremest folly." Blacks should, rather, engage in "severe and constant struggle" for economic gains; for, as he explained, "no race that has anything to contribute to the markets of the world is long in any degree ostracized." If blacks were ever to win the rights and privileges of citizenship, they must first show that they were "prepared for the exercise of these privileges."

In the context of his time, Washington's message was not as timid and conservative as it would later sound. As the first black leader since Frederick Douglass to acquire a wide audience among members of his race, he offered a powerful challenge to those whites who strove to discourage blacks from acquiring an education or winning any economic gains. He helped to awaken the interest of a new generation to the possibilities for self-advancement.

But Washington's message was comforting to Southern whites as well. For in it was an implicit promise that blacks would not challenge the system of segregation that they were then in the process of erecting.

The Birth of Jim Crow

Most white Southerners had never accepted the idea of blacks as equal citizens of their region. That the former slaves acquired any legal and political rights at all after emancipation was in large part the result of

federal support. That support all but vanished after 1877. Federal troops were no longer available to police the polls and prevent whites from excluding black voters. Congress was no longer taking an interest in the condition of the former slaves. And the courts were signaling a retreat as well. In a series of decisions in the 1880s and 1890s, the Supreme Court effectively stripped the Fourteenth and Fifteenth amendments of much of their significance. In deciding the so-called civil-rights cases of 1883, the Court ruled that the Fourteenth Amendment prohibited state governments from discriminating against people because of race but did not restrict private organizations or individuals from doing so. Thus railroads, hotels, theaters, and the like could legally practice segregation. Eventually, the Court also validated state legislation that discriminated against blacks. In *Plessy* v. *Ferguson* (1896), a case involving a law that required separate seating arrangements for the races on railroads, the Court held that separate accommodations did not deprive blacks of equal rights if the accommodations were equal, a decision that survived for years as part of the legal basis of segregated schools. In *Cumming* v. *County Board of Education* (1899), the Court went even further: Laws establishing separate schools for whites, the justices ruled, were valid even if they provided no comparable schools for blacks.

Even before these decisions, white Southerners were at work ensuring their supremacy and, gradually, their separation from contact with the black race to the extent possible. This movement from subordination to segregation was clearly illustrated in the case of black voting rights. In some states—particularly those such as South Carolina and the Deep South cotton states, where blacks constituted close to a majority of the population—disfranchisement began almost as soon as Reconstruction ended. South Carolina, for example, effectively reduced the black vote beginning early in the 1880s by introducing a complicated system of ballot boxes that illiterate voters could not decipher. Georgia required payment of a poll tax, which blacks generally could not afford. In some areas, however, black voting continued for some time after Reconstruction—largely because conservative whites believed they could use the black electorate to maintain their own power. Bourbon leaders often paid or intimidated blacks to vote for their candidates; thus they managed to beat down the attempts of poor white farmers to take control of the Democratic party.

The relative laxness of these franchise restrictions enabled blacks to continue through the 1880s and much of the 1890s to exercise some political influence—far less than that to which their numbers entitled them but more than they would later have. Until the end of the century, Republican candidates in some Southern states continued to receive as much as 40 percent of the vote—most of it from black voters. At least one Southern black served in every session of Congress until 1901. By the late 1890s, however, franchise restrictions were becoming much more rigid. During those years, some small white farmers began to demand complete black disfranchisement—both because of racial animosity and because they objected to the black vote being used against them by the Bourbons. Many members of the conservative elite, at the same time, began to fear that poor whites might unite politically with poor blacks to challenge them. They too began to support further franchise restrictions. The prospect of whites competing for the black vote—of blacks conceivably becoming the balance of power in the region—frightened whites at all economic levels. The time had come, they believed, to close ranks if white supremacy was to be maintained.

In devising laws to disfranchise blacks males (black females, like white women, had never voted), the Southern states had to find ways to evade the intent of the Fifteenth Amendment. That measure had not *guaranteed* suffrage to blacks; it had simply prohibited states from denying anyone the right to vote because of color. The Southern problem, then, was to exclude blacks from the franchise without seeming to base the exclusion on race. Two devices emerged before 1900 to accomplish this goal. One was the poll tax or some form of property qualification; few blacks were prosperous enough to meet such requirements. Another was the "literacy" or "understanding" test, which required voters to demonstrate the ability to read and to interpret the Constitution. The laws permitted local registrars to administer impossibly difficult reading tests to would-be voters or to rule that their interpretation of the Constitution was inadequate.

Such restrictions affected poor white voters as well as blacks. By the late 1890s, the black vote had decreased by 62 percent, the white vote by 26 percent. One result was that some states passed so-called grandfather laws, which permitted men who could not meet the literacy and property qualifications to be enfranchised if their ancestors had voted before Reconstruction began, thus barring the descendants of slaves from the polls while allowing poor whites access to them. In other states, however, the ruling elites were quite content to see poor whites, a potential source of opposition to their power, barred from voting.

The Supreme Court proved as compliant in ruling on the disfranchising laws as it was in dealing with the civil-rights cases. The Court eventually voided the grandfather laws, but it validated the literacy tests (in the 1898 case of *Williams* v. *Mississippi*) and displayed a general willingness to let the Southern states define their own suffrage standards as long as evasions of the Fifteenth Amendment were not too glaring.

Laws restricting the franchise and segregating schools were only part of a network of state statutes—known as the Jim Crow laws—that had by the first years of the twentieth century established an elaborate system of segregation reaching into almost every area of Southern life. Blacks and whites could not ride together in the same railroad cars, sit in the same waiting rooms, use the same washrooms, eat in the same restaurants, or sit in the same theaters. Blacks were denied access to parks, beaches, and picnic areas; they were barred from many hospitals. Much of the new legal structure did no more than confirm what had already been widespread social practice in the South since well before the end of Reconstruction. But the Jim Crow laws also served to strip many blacks of the social, economic, and political gains they had made in the more fluid atmosphere of the late nineteenth century. They served, too, as a means for whites to retain control of social relations between the races in the newly growing cities and towns of the South, where traditional patterns of deference and subjugation were more difficult to preserve than in the countryside. What had been maintained by custom in the rural South was to be maintained by law in the urban South.

More than legal efforts were involved in this process. The 1890s witnessed a dramatic increase in a phenomenon that had been a part of Southern life for many years: white violence against blacks, which (along with the Jim Crow laws) served to inhibit black agitation for equal rights. The worst such violence—lynching of blacks by white mobs, either because the victims were accused of crimes or because they had seemed somehow to violate their proper station—reached appalling levels. In the nation as a whole in the 1890s, there was an average of 187 lynchings each year, more than 80 percent of them in the South and the vast majority of those inflicted on blacks.

The most celebrated lynchings occurred in cities and towns, where large, well-organized mobs—occasionally with the tacit cooperation of local authorities—seized black prisoners from the jails and hung them in great public rituals. Such public lynchings were often highly orchestrated and planned well in advance. They attracted large audiences from surrounding regions. Entire families traveled many miles to witness the spectacles.

— WHERE HISTORIANS DISAGREE —

The Origins of Segregation

Not until after World War II, when the emergence of the civil rights movement forced white Americans to confront the issue of racial segregation, did historians pay much attention to the origins of the institution. Most had assumed that the separation of the races had emerged naturally and even inevitably out of the abolition of slavery. It had been a response to the failure of Reconstruction, the weakness and poverty of the black community, and the pervasiveness of white racism. It was, in effect, the way things had always been.

The first major challenge to these assumptions, indeed the first serious scholarly effort to explain the origins of segregation, was C. Vann Woodward's *The Strange Career of Jim Crow,* published in 1956. It is a book that was not only important in reshaping scholarship, but one that had a significant political impact as well. As a Southern liberal, Woodward was eager to refute assumptions that segregation was part of an unchanging and unchangeable Southern tradition. He wanted to convince scholars that the history of the South had been one of sharp discontinuities; and he wanted to convince a larger public that the racial institutions they considered part of a long, unbroken tradition were in fact the product of a particular set of historical circumstances.

In the aftermath of emancipation, and indeed for two decades after Reconstruction, Woodward argued, race relations in the South had remained relatively fluid. Blacks and whites did not often interact as equals, certainly, but black Southerners enjoyed a degree of latitude in social and even political affairs that they would subsequently lose. Blacks and whites often rode together in the same railroad cars, ate in the same restaurants, used the same public facilities. Blacks voted in significant numbers. Blacks and whites considered a number of different visions of how the races should live together, and as late as 1890 it was not at all clear which of those visions would prevail. By the end of the nineteenth century, however, a great wave of racist legislation—the Jim Crow laws, which established the basis of segregation—had hardened race relations and destroyed the gentler alternatives that many whites and blacks had considered viable only a few years before. The principal reason, Woodward argued, was the populist political insurgency of the 1890s, which mobilized blacks and whites alike and which frightened many white Southerners into thinking that blacks might soon be a major political power in the region. Southern conservatives, in particular, used the issue of white supremacy to attack the populists and to prevent blacks from forming an alliance with them. The result was disenfranchisement and segregation.

Woodward's argument suggested that laws were important in shaping social behavior—that laws had made segregation and, by implication, other laws could unmake it. Not all historians agree. A more pessimistic picture of segregation emerged in 1965 from Joel Williamson's study of South Carolina, *After Slavery*. Williamson argued that the laws of the 1890s did not mean very much, that they simply ratified a set of conditions that had been firmly established by the end of Reconstruction. As early as the mid-1870s, Williamson claimed, the races had already begun to live in two separate societies. Blacks had constructed their own churches, schools, businesses, and neighbor-

But such great public lynchings were relatively rare. Much more frequent, and more dangerous to blacks because less visible or predictable, were lynchings performed by small vigilante mobs, often composed of friends or relatives of the victim of a crime. Those involved in lynchings often saw their actions as a legitimate form of law enforcement; and indeed, some victims of lynchings had in fact committed crimes. But lynchings were also a means by which whites controlled the black population through terror and intimidation. Thus, some lynch mobs killed blacks whose only "crime" had been presumptuousness. Others chose as victims outsiders in the community, whose presence threatened to disturb the normal pattern of race relations. Whatever the circumstances, the victims of lynch mobs were denied the protection of the laws and the opportunity to prove their innocence.

The rise of lynching shocked the conscience of many white Americans in a way that other forms of racial injustice did not. Almost from the start there was a substantial antilynching movement. Ida B.

WHERE HISTORIANS DISAGREE

hoods; whites had begun to exclude blacks from white institutions. The separation was partly a result of pressure and coercion from whites, partly a result of the desire of blacks to develop their own, independent culture. Whatever the reasons, however, segregation was largely in place by the end of the 1870s, continuing in a different form a pattern of racial separation established under slavery. The laws of the 1890s did little more than codify an already established system.

Scholars writing more recently have revised or challenged both these interpretations by attempting to link the rise of legal segregation to changing social and economic circumstances in the South. Howard Rabinowitz's *Race Relations in the Urban South* (1978) links the rise of segregation to the new challenge of devising a form of race relations suitable to life in the growing Southern cities, into which rural blacks were moving in substantial numbers. The creation of separate public facilities—schools, parks, waiting rooms, etc.—was not so much an effort to drive blacks out of white facilities; they had never had access to those facilities, and few whites had ever been willing to consider granting them access. It was, rather, an attempt to create for a black community that virtually all whites agreed must remain essentially separate a set of facilities where none had previously existed. Without segregation, in other words, urban blacks would have had no schools or parks at all. The alternative to segregation, Rabinowitz suggests, was not integration, but exclusion.

In the early 1980s, a number of scholars began examining segregation anew in light of the rising American interest in South Africa, whose system of *apartheid* seemed to some historians similar in many ways to the now largely dismantled Jim Crow system in the South. John Cell's *The Highest Stage of White Supremacy* (1982) used the comparison to construct a revised explanation of how segregation emerged in the American South. Like Rabinowitz, he considered the increasing urbanization of the region the principal factor. But he ascribed different motives to those whites who promoted the rise of Jim Crow. The segregation laws, Cell argues, were a continuation of an unchanging determination by Southern whites to retain control over the black population. What had shifted was not their commitment to white supremacy but the things necessary to preserve it. The emergence of large black communities in urban areas and of a significant black labor force in factories presented a new challenge to white Southerners. They could not control these new communities in the same informal ways they had been able to control rural blacks, who were more directly dependent on white landowners and merchants than their urban counterparts. In the city, blacks and whites were in more direct competition than they had been in the countryside. There was more danger of social mixing. The city, therefore, required different, and more rigidly institutionalized, systems of control. The Jim Crow laws were a response not just to an enduring commitment to white supremacy, but to a new reality that required white supremacy to move to its "highest stage," where it would have a rigid legal and institutional basis.

Wells-Barnett, a black journalist, launched what became a substantial international antilynching movement with a series of impassioned articles in 1892 after the lynching of three of her friends in Memphis, her home town. The movement gradually gathered strength in the first years of the twentieth century, attracting substantial support from whites in both the North and South (particularly from white women). Its goal was a federal antilynching law, which would allow the national government to do what state and local governments in the South were generally unwilling to do: punish those responsible for lynchings.

But the substantial white opposition to lynchings in the South stood as an exception to the general support for suppression of the black race. Indeed, just as in the antebellum period, the shared commitment to white supremacy helped dilute the class animosities between poorer whites and the Bourbon oligarchies that might otherwise have emerged. Economic issues tended to take a subordinate role to race in Southern politics, distracting the gaze of the region from the glaring social inequalities that afflicted blacks and whites alike. Even when such issues did arise—as they did in the 1890s—the racial question

A Lynch Mob, 1893

A large, almost festive crowd gathers to watch the lynching of a black man accused of the murder of a three-year-old white girl. Lynchings remained frequent in the South until as late as the 1930s, but they reached their peak in the 1890s and the first years of the twentieth century. Lynchings such as this one—publicized well in advance and attracting whole families who traveled great distances to see them—were relatively infrequent. Most lynchings were the work of smaller groups, operating with less visibility. (Library of Congress)

ultimately proved an effective vehicle for dampening their impact. The commitment to racial supremacy, in short, was a burden for poor whites as well as for blacks.

The Origins of Black Protest

Black Americans faced enormous obstacles—legal, economic, social, and political—in challenging their oppressed status. Thus it was not surprising, perhaps, that so many embraced the message of Booker T. Washington in the late nineteenth century: a message that urged them to "put down your bucket where you are," to work for immediate self-

improvement rather than long-range social change. Not all blacks, however, were content with this approach. And by the turn of the century a powerful challenge was emerging—to the philosophy of Washington and, more important, to the entire structure of race relations. The chief spokesman for this new approach was W. E. B. Du Bois.

Du Bois, unlike Washington, had never known slavery. Born in Massachusetts, educated at Fisk University in Atlanta and at Harvard, he grew to maturity with a far more expansive view than Washington of the goals of his race and the responsibilities of white society to eliminate prejudice and injustice. In *The Souls of Black Folk* (1903), he launched an open attack on the philosophy of the Atlanta Compromise, accusing Washington of encouraging white efforts to impose segregation and of unnecessarily limiting the aspirations of his race. "Is it possible and probable," he asked,

> that nine millions of men can make effective progress in economic lines if they are deprived of political rights, made a servile caste, and allowed only the most meagre chance for developing their exceptional men? If history and reason give any distinct answer to these questions, it is an emphatic *No*.

Rather than content themselves with education at the trade and agricultural schools, Du Bois advocated, talented blacks should accept nothing less than a full university education. They should aspire to the professions. They should, above all, fight for the immediate restoration of their civil rights, not simply wait for them to be granted as a reward for patient striving.

In 1905, Du Bois and a group of his supporters met at Niagara Falls (on the Canadian side of the border; no hotel on the American side of the Falls would have them), and launched what became known as the Niagara Movement. Four years later, after a race riot in Springfield, Illinois, they joined with white progressives sympathetic to their cause to form the National Association for the Advancement of Colored People (NAACP). Whites held most of the offices; but Du Bois, its director of publicity and research, was the guiding spirit. In the ensuing years, the new organization led the drive for equal rights, using as its principal weapon lawsuits in the federal courts.

Within less than a decade, the NAACP had begun to win some important victories. In *Guinn* v. *United States* (1915), the Supreme Court supported their position that the grandfather clause in an Oklahoma law was unconstitutional. (The statute denied the vote to any citizen whose ancestors had not been enfranchised in 1860.) In *Buchanan* v. *Worley* (1917), the Court struck down a Louisville, Kentucky, law requiring residential segregation. Disfranchisement and segregation would survive through other methods for many decades to come, but the NAACP had established a pattern of black resistance that would ultimately bear important fruits. It had also established itself, particularly after Booker T. Washington's death in 1915, as one of the nation's leading black organizations, a position it would maintain for many years.

The NAACP was not a radical, or even an egalitarian, organization. It relied, rather, on the efforts of the most intelligent and educated members of the

W. E. B. Du Bois
Although Du Bois, unlike Booker T. Washington, never developed a large popular following, he was the acknowledged leader of the black elite in the late nineteenth and early twentieth centuries. He was the first black man ever to earn a doctorate at Harvard University, and he published a number of distinguished works of history during his long career. He also served for more than twenty years as editor of *The Crisis,* the newspaper of the NAACP. He died in 1963, at the age of ninety-five, having lived long enough to see the emergence of a powerful civil rights movement dedicated to achieving many of the goals for which he had fought throughout his life. This pastel portrait was drawn around 1925 by Winhold Reiss.   (National Portrait Gallery)

black race, the "talented tenth" as Du Bois called them. And it stressed not so much the elevation of all blacks from poverty and oppression as the opportunity for exceptional blacks to gain positions of full equality. Ultimately, its members believed, such efforts would redound to the benefit of all blacks. By creating a trained elite, blacks would, in effect, be creating a leadership group capable of fighting for the rights of the race as a whole.

The Conquest of the Far West

By the time of the Civil War, the western rim of English-speaking settlement had already moved far beyond what it had been even twenty years before. White civilization had crossed the Mississippi and established a permanent foothold in the next tier of states—Minnesota, Iowa, Missouri, and Arkansas—as well as in the eastern parts of Nebraska, Kansas, and Texas. But vast regions remained largely empty of white settlement. Much of the West was the province of nomadic Indian tribes, of wild animals, and of a few scattered immigrants from the East (most of them white, but some—in regions as scattered as Montana, Kansas, and Nebraska—black).

Even in 1860, however, there were clear signs that white Americans would not much longer be content to leave these vast Western territories to the Indians. For one thing, important white settlements had already been established on the Pacific coast, in California and Oregon. For another, ambitious men and women continued to press for access to new lands in the West; as one region began to fill up with settlers, such people demanded the right to move on to the next. And so, in the decades following the Civil War, Americans continued their great migration into the interior of their country until the line of European settlement stretched unbroken to the Pacific.

Delayed Settlement

When the westward-pushing pioneers entered the Great Plains, they saw an environment utterly different from the fertile prairies behind them. They saw a land distinguished by its level surface, its lack of timber, and its deficiency in rainfall. Early explorers had dubbed this region "the Great American Desert," and in the 1840s settlers had hastened through it on their way to California and Oregon. Its forbidding reputation was largely responsible for the fact that the edge of white settlement, after crossing the Mississippi, had jumped 1,500 miles to the Pacific coast.

By the 1860s, however, whites had begun to move into the unsettled parts of the West. They were attracted by gold and silver deposits, by the short-grass pasture for cattle and sheep, and finally by the plains' sod and the mountain meadowland that seemed suitable for farming or ranching.

The completion of the great transcontinental railroad lines helped encourage settlement. These roads and their feeders moved settlers and supplies into the vast interior spaces and furnished access to outside markets. The railroad companies themselves had an incentive, of course, to promote migration into the West; settlement of the region would provide markets for the lines they were building. So the companies actively solicited settlers by a number of devices, including selling their lands to migrants at low prices.

The land policy of the federal government also worked to encourage settlement. The Homestead Act of 1862 permitted settlers to buy a plot of 160 acres for a small fee if they occupied and improved it for five years. The Homestead Act had been intended as a democratic measure. It would bestow a free farm on any American who needed one; it would serve as a form of government relief to raise the living standards of the masses. But in practice the act proved a disappointment. Some 400,000 homesteaders became landowners, but a much larger number ultimately abandoned their lands in the face of the bleak life on the windswept plains.

The Homestead Act had rested on a number of false premises. The framers of the act assumed that mere possession of land was enough to sustain farm life; they ignored the increasing mechanization of agriculture and the rising costs of operation. They had made their calculations, moreover, on the basis of Eastern agricultural experiences that were inapplicable to the region west of the Mississippi. A unit of 160 acres was too small for the grazing and grain farming of the Great Plains.

Responding to Western pressures, Congress acted to increase allotments. The Timber Culture Act (1873) permitted homesteaders to receive grants of 160 additional acres if they planted 40 acres of trees on them. The Desert Land Act (1877) provided that claimants could buy 640 acres at $1.25 an acre provided they irrigated part of their holdings within three years. The Timber and Stone Act (1878), presumably applying to nonarable land, authorized sales at $2.50 an acre. These laws ultimately made it possible for individuals to acquire as much as 1,280 acres of land at little cost. Some enterprising settlers got much more. Fraud ran rampant in the administration of the acts. Lumber, mining, and cattle companies, by employing "dummy" registrants and using other illegal devices, seized millions of acres of the public domain.

Political organization followed on the heels of settlement. After the admission of Kansas as a state in 1861, the remaining territories of Washington, New Mexico, Utah, and Nebraska were divided into smaller and more convenient units. By the close of the 1860s, territorial governments were in operation in the new provinces of Nevada, Colorado, Dakota, Arizona, Idaho, Montana, and Wyoming. Statehood

Mining Towns, 1848–1883

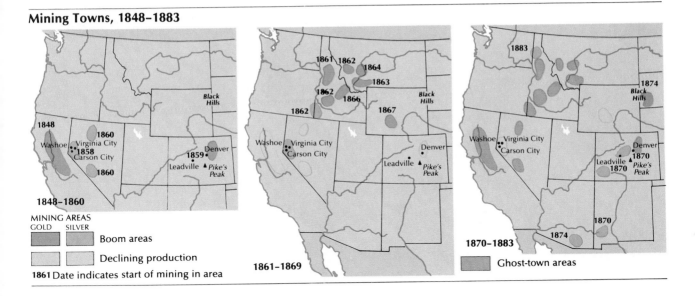

rapidly followed. Nevada became a state in 1864, Nebraska in 1867, and Colorado in 1876. In 1889, North and South Dakota, Montana, and Washington won admission; Wyoming and Idaho entered the next year. Utah was denied statehood until its Mormon leaders convinced the government in 1896 that polygamy (the practice of men taking several wives) had been abandoned. At the turn of the century, only three territories remained outside the fold: Arizona and New Mexico, excluded because of their scanty population, their politics (they were predominantly Democratic), and their refusal to accept admission as a single state; and Oklahoma (formerly Indian Territory), which was opened to white settlement and granted territorial status in 1889–1890.

The Arrival of the Miners

The first economic boom in the Far West came in mining, and the first part of the area to be extensively settled was the mineral-rich region of mountains and plateaus, where white settlers hoped to make quick fortunes by finding precious metals. The life span of the mining frontier was brief. It burst into being around 1860, flourished until the 1890s, and then abruptly declined.

News of a gold or silver strike would start a stampede reminiscent of the California gold rush of 1849. Then came several stages of settlement. Individual prospectors would exploit the first ores largely by hand, with pan and placer mining. After the shallower deposits had been depleted by these methods,

corporations moved in to engage in lode or quartz mining. Then, as those deposits dwindled, commercial mining either disappeared or continued on a restricted basis, and ranchers and farmers moved in and established a more permanent economy.

The first great mineral strikes occurred just before the Civil War. In 1858, gold was discovered in the Pike's Peak district of what would soon be the territory of Colorado; and the following year, a mob of 50,000 prospectors stormed in from California, the Mississippi Valley, and the East. Denver and other mining camps blossomed into "cities" overnight. Almost as rapidly as it had developed, the boom ended. Eventually, corporations, notably the Guggenheim interests, revived some of the glories and profits of the gold boom, and the discovery of silver near Leadville supplied a new source of mineral wealth.

While the Colorado rush of 1859 was in progress, news of another strike drew miners to Nevada. Gold had been found in the Washoe district, but the most valuable ore in the great Comstock Lode and other veins was silver. The first prospectors to reach the Washoe fields came from California; and from the beginning, Californians dominated the settlement and development of Nevada. In a remote desert without railroad transportation, the territory produced no supplies of its own, and everything—from food and machinery to whiskey and prostitutes—had to be shipped in from California to Virginia City, Carson City, and other roaring camp towns. When the placer deposits ran out, California capital bought the claims of the pioneer prospectors and installed quartz mining. For a brief span the outside owners reaped tre-

Colorado Boom Town

After a prospector discovered silver nearby in 1890, miners flocked to the town of Creede, Colorado. For a time in the early 1890s, 150 to 300 people arrived there daily. Although the town was located in a canyon so narrow that there was room for only one street, buildings sprouted rapidly to serve the growing community. Like other such boom towns, however, Creede's prosperity was short-lived. In 1893 the price of silver collapsed; and by the end of the century, Creede was almost deserted.   (Henry Ford Museum)

mendous profits; from 1860 to 1880 the Nevada lodes yielded bullion worth $306 million.

There were no more important mineral discoveries until 1874, when gold was found in the Black Hills of southwestern Dakota Territory. Prospectors swarmed into the area, then (and for years to come) accessible only by stagecoach. For a short time the boom flared. Then came the inevitable fading of resources. Corporations took over from the miners, and one gigantic company, the Homestake, came to dominate the fields. Population declined, and the Dakotas, like other boom areas of the mineral empire, waited for the approach of agricultural settlement.

Although it was the gold and silver discoveries that generated the most popular excitement, it was other, less glamorous natural resources that in the long run proved the most important to the development of the West. The great Anaconda copper mine that William Clark launched in 1881 marked the beginning of an industry that would remain important to Montana for many decades. In other areas, mining operations had significant success with lead, tin,

quartz, and zinc. Such efforts generally proved more profitable in the long run than the usually short-lived gold and silver extraction.

Life in the camp towns of the mineral empire had a hectic tempo and a gaudy flavor not to be found in any other part of the Far West. A speculative spirit, a mood of heady optimism, gripped everyone and dominated every phase of community activity. The conditions of mine life—the presence of precious minerals, the vagueness of claim boundaries, the cargoes of gold being shipped out—attracted outlaws and "bad men," operating as individuals or gangs. When the situation became intolerable in a community, those members interested in order set up their own law and enforced it through a vigilance committee, an agency used earlier in California. Sometimes criminals themselves secured control of the committee, and sometimes the vigilantes continued to operate as private "law" enforcers after the creation of regular governments. Additional evidence of the fluid character of these communities was the presence within them of people of many races: Indians,

Mexicans, blacks, and Chinese, as well as whites. Nonwhites almost always encountered prejudice and discrimination in these communities; social and legal pressure usually prevented them from owning land or holding lucrative jobs. But they did perform essential tasks in the mines and the camps, and they became an integral part of the region's economy.

Men greatly outnumbered women in the mining towns; and younger men, in particular, had difficulty finding female companions of comparable age. Those women who did gravitate to the new communities often came with their husbands, and their activities were generally (although not always) confined to the same kinds of domestic tasks that Eastern women performed. Single women, or women whose husbands were earning no money, did choose (or find it necessary) to work for wages at times, as cooks, laundresses, and tavern keepers. And in the sexually imbalanced mining communities, there was always a ready market for prostitutes.

The Cattle Kingdom

A second important element of the boom economy in the Far West was cattle ranching. The open range—the unclaimed grasslands of the public domain—provided a huge area on the Great Plains where cattlemen could graze their herds free of charge and unrestricted by the boundaries of private farms. The railroads gave birth to the range-cattle industry by giving it access to markets. Then the same railroads destroyed it by bringing farmers to the plains.

The Western cattle industry was Mexican and Texan by ancestry. Long before citizens of the United States invaded the Southwest, Mexican ranchers had developed the techniques that the cattlemen and cowboys of the Great Plains later employed: branding (a device known in all frontier areas where stock was common), roundups, roping, and the equipment of the herder—his lariat, saddle, leather chaps, and spurs. Americans in Texas adopted these methods and carried them to the northernmost ranges of the cattle kingdom. Texas also had the largest herds of cattle in the country; the animals were descended from imported Spanish stock—the famous wiry, hardy longhorns—and allowed to run wild or semi-wild. From Texas, too, came the horses that enabled the caretakers of the herds (the cowboys) to control them—small, muscular broncos or mustangs ideally adapted to the requirements of the cow country.

At the end of the Civil War, an estimated 5 million cattle roamed the Texas ranges, and Northern markets were offering fat prices for steers in any condition. Early in 1866, some Texas cattle ranchers began driving their combined herds, some 260,000 head, north to Sedalia, Missouri, on the Missouri Pacific Railroad. Traveling over rough country and beset by outlaws, Indians, and property-conscious farmers, the caravan suffered heavy losses, and only a fraction of the animals arrived in Sedalia. But the drive was an important experiment. It proved that cattle could be driven to distant markets and pastured along the trail, and that they would even gain weight during the journey. This first of the "long drives" prepared the way for the cattle kingdom.

With the precedent of the long drive established, the next step was to find an easier route through more accessible country. Special market facilities grew up at Abilene, Kansas, on the Kansas Pacific Railroad, and for years this town reigned as the railhead of the cattle kingdom. Between 1867 and 1871, cattlemen drove 1,460,000 head up the Chisholm Trail to Abilene—a town that, when filled with rampaging cowboys at the end of a drive, rivaled the mining towns in rowdiness. But by the mid-1870s, agricultural development in western Kansas was eating away at the open range land. At the same time, the supply of animals was increasing. Cattlemen therefore had to develop other trails and other market outlets. Dodge City and Wichita in Kansas, Ogallala and Sidney in Nebraska, Cheyenne and Laramie in Wyoming, and Miles City and Glendive in Montana all began to rival Abilene as major centers of stockherding.

A long drive was a spectacular experience. It began with the spring, or calf, roundup. The cattlemen of a district met with their cowboys at a specified place to round up the stock of the owners from the open range. As the cattle were driven in, the calves were branded with the marks of their mothers. Stray calves with no identifying symbols, "mavericks," were divided on a pro-rata basis. Then the cows and calves were turned loose to pasture, while the yearling steers (year-old males) were readied for the drive to the north. The combined herds, usually numbering from 2,000 to 5,000 head, moved out. Cowboys representing each of the major ranchers accompanied them.

Among the cowboys, the majority (in the early years) were veterans of the Confederate army. The next largest group consisted of blacks, who were more numerous than white Northerners or Mexicans and other foreigners. They were usually assigned such jobs as wrangler (herdsman) or cook. (In other contexts, black men played a role in the West not only as cowboys but also as explorers, trappers, miners, outlaws, and cavalrymen.)

The Cattle Kingdom, c. 1866–1887

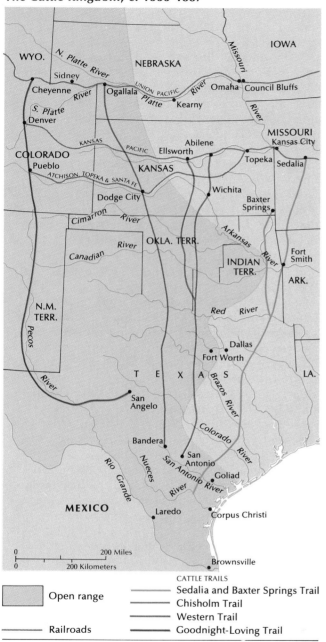

Open range

Railroads

CATTLE TRAILS

Sedalia and Baxter Springs Trail
Chisholm Trail
Western Trail
Goodnight-Loving Trail

Every cattleman had to have a permanent base from which to operate, and so the ranch emerged. A ranch consisted of the employer's dwelling, quarters for employees, and a tract of grazing land. In the early years of the cattle kingdom, most ranches were relatively small, since so much of the grazing occurred in the vast, open areas that cattlemen shared.

But as farmers and sheepmen encroached on the open plains, ranches became larger and more clearly defined; cattlemen gradually had to learn to raise their stock on their own land.

There had always been an element of risk and speculation in the open-range cattle business. At any time, "Texas fever"—a disease transmitted to cattle by parasite-carrying ticks—might decimate a herd. Rustlers and Indians frequently seized large numbers of animals. But as settlement of the plains increased, these traditional risks combined with new forms of competition. Sheepmen from California and Oregon brought their flocks onto the range to compete for grass. Farmers ("nesters") from the East threw fences around their claims, blocking trails and breaking up the open range. A series of "range wars"—between sheepmen and cattlemen, between ranchers and farmers—erupted out of the tensions between these competing groups. Some of the wars resulted in significant loss of life and extensive property damage.

Accounts of the lofty profits to be made in the cattle business—it was said that an investment of $5,000 would return $45,000 in four years—tempted Eastern, English, and Scottish capital to the plains. Increasingly, the structure of the cattle economy became corporate in form; in one year, twenty corporations with a combined capital of $12 million were chartered in Wyoming. The inevitable result of this frenzied extension was that the ranges, already severed and shrunk by the railroads and the farmers, were becoming overstocked. There was not enough grass to support the crowding herds or sustain the long drives. Finally nature intervened with a destructive finishing blow. Two severe winters, in 1885–1886 and 1886–1887, with a searing summer between them, stung and scorched the plains. Hundreds of thousands of cattle died, streams and grass dried up, princely ranches and costly investments disappeared in a season.

The open-range industry never recovered; the long drive disappeared for good. But the established cattle ranches—with fenced-in grazing land and stocks of hay for winter feed—survived and grew and prospered, eventually producing more beef than ever.

Although the cattle industry was overwhelmingly male in its early years, there were always a few women involved in ranching and driving. (The fabled Annie Oakley serves as evidence of the occasional participation of women in this largely masculine world.) As ranching became more sedentary, the presence of women greatly expanded. By

1890, there were more than 250,000 women who owned ranches or farms in the Western States. Indeed, the region provided women with many opportunities that were closed to them in the East—including the opportunity to participate in politics. Wyoming was the first state in the Union to guarantee woman suffrage; and throughout the West, women established themselves as an important political presence (and occasionally as significant office-holders).

The Romance of the West

The unsettled West had always occupied a special place in the American imagination. But the vast regions of this "last frontier" had a particularly strong romantic appeal. Some of the reasons were obvious. The Great Plains, the Rocky Mountains, the basin and plateau region beyond the Rockies, and the Sierra Nevada-Cascade ranges beyond that—all constituted a landscape of such brilliant diversity, such spectacular grandeur, so different from anything white Americans had encountered before, it was little wonder that newcomers looked on it with reverence and wonder. Painters of the new "Rocky Mountain School"—of whom the best known was Albert Bierstadt—celebrated the new West in grandiose canvases. They emphasized the ruggedness and dramatic variety of the region, exhibiting the same awe toward the land that earlier regional painters had displayed toward the Hudson River Valley and other areas.

Even more appealing than the landscape, perhaps, was the rugged, free-spirited life style that many Americans associated with the frontier—a life style that stood in sharp contrast to the increasingly stable and ordered world of the East. Particular public interest attached to the figure of the cowboy, who was transformed remarkably quickly into a powerful and enduring figure of myth. Admiring Americans seldom thought about the drearier aspects of the cowboy's life: the tedium, the loneliness, the physical discomforts, the relatively few opportunities for advancement. Instead, in Western novels such as Owen Wister's *The Virginian* (1902), they romanticized his freedom from traditional social constraints, his affinity with nature, even his supposed propensity for violence. The cowboy became one of the last and most powerful symbols of what had long been an important ideal in the American mind—the ideal of the natural man. That symbol survived for more than a century—in popular literature, in song, and later in film and on television.

Yet it was not simply the particular qualities of the new West that made it so important to the nation's imagination. It was also the fact that Americans considered it the *last* frontier. Since the earliest moments of European settlement in America, the image of uncharted territory to the west had always been a comforting and inspiring one. Now, with the last of that unsettled land being slowly absorbed into the nation's civilization, that image exercised a stronger pull than ever. Mark Twain, one of the greatest American writers of the nineteenth century, gave voice to this romantic vision of the frontier in a series of brilliant novels and memoirs. In some of his writing—notably *Roughing It* (1872)—he wrote of the Far West itself, and of his own experience as a newspaper reporter in Nevada during the mining boom. His greatest works, however, dealt with life on an earlier frontier: the Mississippi Valley of his boyhood. In *The Adventures of Tom Sawyer* (1876) and *The Adventures of Huckleberry Finn* (1885), he produced characters who repudiated the constraints of organized society and attempted to escape from it into a more natural world. For Huck Finn, the vehicle of escape might be a small raft on the Mississippi; but the yearning for freedom reflected the larger vision of the West as the last refuge from civilization.

One of the clearest and most influential statements of this romantic vision of the frontier came not from an artist but from the historian Frederick Jackson Turner, of the University of Wisconsin. In 1893, Turner delivered a memorable paper to a meeting of the American Historical Association entitled "The Significance of the Frontier in American History." In it, he took note of the findings of the 1890 census that the unsettled area of the West had been "so broken into by isolated bodies of settlement" that a continuous frontier line could no longer be drawn. And he argued that the passing of that line ended an era in the nation's history. For, as Turner explained it, "the existence of an area of free land, its continuous recession, and the advance of settlement westward, explain American development." This experience of expansion into the frontier, by stimulating individualism, nationalism, and democracy, had made Americans the distinctive people that they were. "Now," Turner concluded ominously, "four centuries from the discovery of America, at the end of a hundred years of life under the Constitution, the frontier has gone and with its going has closed the first period of American history."

In fact, Turner's forebodings were premature. A vast public domain still existed in the 1890s, and during the forty years thereafter the government was to give away many more acres than it had given as homesteads in the past. But Turner did express a growing and generally accurate sense that much of the best farming and grazing land was now taken, that in the future it would be far more difficult for individuals to acquire land for little or nothing.

In the "passing of the frontier," perhaps the greatest loss to the American people was a psychological one. As long as the country had remained open at one end, there had seemed to be constantly revitalizing opportunities in American life. Now there was a vague and ominous sense of being hemmed in. The psychological loss was all the greater because of what historian Henry Nash Smith, in *Virgin Land* (1950), called the "myth of the garden": the once widely held belief that the West was a kind of potential Garden of Eden where life could be begun anew and the ideals of democracy could be realized. The setting for utopia, once the New World as a whole, had shrunk to the West of the United States. And now even that West seemed to be vanishing.

The Dispersal of the Tribes

White Americans liked to think of the Far West as a vast unpeopled land awaiting settlement. In fact, the West already had a large population of Indians. Some were members of Eastern tribes—Cherokee, Creek, Winnebago, and others—who had been forcibly resettled west of the Mississippi in "Indian Territory" (later Oklahoma) before the Civil War. But most were members of tribes indigenous to the West.

The Western tribes had developed a number of patterns of civilization. The Pueblo of the Southwest had long lived largely as farmers and had established permanent settlements. They continued to occupy lands guaranteed them by the Spanish before the annexation of the Western territories by the United States. They grew corn; they built towns and cities of adobe houses; they practiced elaborate forms of irrigation. Other tribes in that region—the Navajo and Apache of western Texas and eastern New Mexico—lived more nomadically and combined hunting with farming and sheep herding, moving their settlements from place to place. The most numerous Indian groups in the West, however, consisted of the plains

Indians—the Sioux, the Blackfoot, the Cheyenne, the Kiowa, the Apache, the Comanche, the Crow, and others—who occupied large parts of what became Minnesota, the Dakotas, Nebraska, Idaho, and Montana.

Unlike many of the Eastern tribes—the woodland Indians whom white Americans had dispersed in earlier years—the plains Indians were powerful and often militant warriors. They fought a prolonged and at times successful battle to defend their lands against the encroachments of white settlement, a battle in which, according to some estimates, the Indians inflicted the greater casualties on their enemy. In the end, however, the tribes could not effectively resist the superior numbers and technology of the white invaders. Defeated and broken, they were finally forced to accept what meager lands the white man was willing to give them and to adapt themselves to an approximation of the sedentary, agrarian culture of their conquerors.

The Plains Indians

The plains Indians lived a largely nomadic life. In some areas, they engaged in forms of sedentary farming; but the semiarid, treeless plains encouraged the development of a culture based on hunting. Riding small but powerful horses, descendants of Spanish stock, the tribes moved through the spacious grasslands. Permanent settlements were rare. When a band halted, it constructed tepees as temporary dwellings; when it departed, it left the landscape almost completely undisturbed, a reflection of the deep reverence for nature that was central to Indian culture and religion.

The magnet that drew the hunters and guided their routes was the buffalo, or bison. This huge grazing animal provided the economic basis for the plains Indians' way of life. Its flesh was their principal source of food, and its skin supplied materials for clothing, shoes, tepees, blankets, robes, and utensils. "Buffalo chips," dried manure, provided fuel; buffalo bones were carved into knives and arrow tips; buffalo tendons formed the strings of bows. One observer accurately described the role of the buffalo in Indian society as "a galloping department store."

The culture of the plains Indians reflected their nomadic lifestyles and their intimate relationship with nature. Tribes (which sometimes numbered several thousand) were generally subdivided into "bands" of up to 500 men and women, each with its own governing council. Within each band, tasks were generally divided by sex. Women performed largely domestic and artistic roles: raising children, cooking, gathering roots and berries, preparing hides, and creating many of the impressive art works of tribal culture. They also tended fields and gardens in those places where bands remained settled long enough to raise crops. Men worked largely as hunters and traders and supervised the religious and military life of the band.

The plains Indians were proud and aggressive warriors, schooled in warfare from their frequent (and usually brief) skirmishes with rival tribes. Each tribe sustained a distinct warrior class, whose members competed with one another to develop reputations for fierceness and bravery. These warriors proved to be the most formidable foes white settlers had yet encountered. But they also suffered from several serious weaknesses that in the end made it impossible for them to prevail.

Perhaps the most crippling was the inability of the various tribes (and often even of the bands within tribes) to unite against white aggression. This was a problem that had plagued Native Americans in the East for centuries and had contributed to their ultimate undoing. The Western tribes were culturally ill-disposed toward political or military centralization and suffered similarly. Not only were they seldom able to draw together a coalition of Indians large enough to counter white power; they were also frequently distracted from their battles with whites by conflicts among the tribes themselves. And at times, tribal warriors faced white forces supplemented by guides and even fighters from other, usually rival, tribes.

White Policies Toward the Tribes

The Western tribes were also victimized by the incompetence and duplicity of those white officials charged with protecting them. It was the traditional policy of the federal government to regard the tribes simultaneously as independent nations and as wards of the president in Washington, and to negotiate agreements with them in the shape of treaties that were solemnly ratified by the Senate. This concept of Indian sovereignty had been responsible for the attempt of the government before 1860 to erect a permanent frontier between whites and Indians, to reserve the region west of the bend of the Missouri river as permanent Indian country. Seldom, how-

ever, did treaties or agreements with the tribes survive the pressure of white settlers eager for access to Indian lands. The history of relations between the United States and the Native Americans was, therefore, one of nearly endless broken promises.

By the early 1850s, the idea of establishing one great territory in which all the tribes could live gave way, in the face of white demands for access to lands on the "One Big Reservation," to a new reservations policy, known as "concentration." In 1851, each tribe was assigned its own defined treaty, confirmed by separate treaties (treaties often illegitimately negotiated with unauthorized "representatives" chosen by whites). The new arrangement had many benefits for whites and few for the Indians. It divided the tribes from one another and made them easier to defeat. It allowed the government to force tribes into scattered locations and to take over the most desirable lands for white settlement. But it did not survive as the basis of Indian policy for long.

In 1867, in the aftermath of a series of bloody conflicts, Congress established an Indian Peace Commission, composed of soldiers and civilians, to recommend a new and presumably permanent Indian policy. The commission decided that the earlier "concentration" policy should be replaced by a new one. All the plains tribes would be relocated in two large reservations—one in Indian Territory (Oklahoma), the other in the Dakotas. At a series of meetings with the tribes, government agents cajoled, bribed, and tricked the Arapaho, Cheyenne, Sioux, and others into agreeing to treaties establishing the new reservations.

But this "solution" proved no more satisfactory than the previous ones. Part of the problem was the way in which the government administered the reservations it had established. White management of Indian matters was entrusted to the Bureau of Indian Affairs, located in the Department of the Interior. The bureau was responsible for distributing land, making payments, and supervising the shipment of supplies. Its record was appalling. The bureau's agents in the West, products of political patronage, were often men of extraordinary incompetence and dishonesty. But even the most honest and diligent agents were generally ill-prepared for their jobs, had no understanding of tribal ways, and had little chance of success. The poor administration of the reservations was one reason for the constant conflicts between the tribes and the whites who were surrounding them.

But the problem was also a result of what was,

in effect, economic warfare by whites: the relentless slaughtering of the buffalo herds that supported the tribes' way of life. Even in the 1850s, whites had been killing buffalo at a rapid rate to provide food and supplies for the large bands of migrants traveling to the gold rush in California. After the Civil War the white demand for buffalo hides became a national phenomenon—partly for economic reasons and partly as a fad. (Everyone east of the Missouri seemed to want a buffalo robe from the romantic West.) Gangs of professional hunters swarmed over the plains to shoot the huge animals. Some hunters killed merely for the sport of the chase, although the lumbering victims did not present much of a challenge. Railroad companies hired riflemen (such as Buffalo Bill Cody) and arranged large shooting expeditions to kill large numbers of buffalo, hoping to thin the herds, which were obstructions to railroad traffic. The southern herd was virtually exterminated by 1875, and within a few years the smaller northern herd had met the same fate. In 1865, there had been at least 15 million buffalo; a decade later, fewer than a thousand of the great beasts survived. The army and the agents of the Bureau of Indian Affairs condoned and even encouraged the killing. By destroying the buffalo herds, whites were destroying the Indians' source of food and supplies and their ability to resist the white advance. They were also contributing to a climate in which Indian warriors felt the need to fight to preserve their way of life.

Indian Resistance

There was almost incessant fighting between whites and Indians on the frontier from the 1850s to the 1880s, as Indians struggled against the growing threats to their civilizations. Indian warriors, usually traveling in raiding parties of thirty to forty men, regularly attacked wagon trains, stagecoaches, and isolated ranches, often in retaliation for earlier attacks on them by whites. As the United States Army became more deeply involved in the fighting, the tribes began to focus more of their attacks on white soldiers.

At times, this small-scale fighting escalated into something resembling a war. During the Civil War, the eastern Sioux in Minnesota, cramped on an inadequate reservation and exploited by corrupt white agents, suddenly rebelled against the restrictions imposed on them by the government's policies. Led by Little Crow, they killed more than 700 whites before being subdued by a force of regulars and militiamen.

Thirty-eight of the Indians were hanged, and the tribe was exiled to the Dakotas.

At the same time, trouble flared in eastern Colorado, where the Arapaho and Cheyenne were coming into conflict with white miners settling in the region. Bands of Indians attacked stagecoach lines and settlements in an effort to regain territory they believed was theirs. In response to these incidents, whites called up a large territorial militia, and the army issued dire threats. The governor urged all friendly Indians to congregate at army posts before retribution fell on the hostiles. One Arapaho and Cheyenne band under Black Kettle, apparently in response to the invitation, camped near Fort Lyon on Sand Creek. Some members of the party were warriors, but Black Kettle believed he was under official protection and exhibited no hostile intention. Nevertheless, Colonel J. M. Chivington, apparently encouraged by the army commander of the district, led a volunteer militia force—much of it consisting of unemployed miners, many of whom were apparently drunk—to the unsuspecting camp and massacred perhaps 200 men, women, and children.

Some of the Arapaho and Cheyenne had another tragic experience before being forcibly settled on their reserve. Black Kettle, who had escaped the Sand Creek massacre, and his Cheyennes, some of whom were now at war with the whites, were caught on the Washita River, near the Texas border, by Colonel George A. Custer; white troops killed the chief and slaughtered his people.

At the end of the Civil War in the East, white troops stepped up their wars against the western Indians on several fronts. The most serious and sustained conflict was in Montana, where the army attempted to build a road, the Bozeman Trail, from Fort Laramie, Wyoming, to the new mining centers. The western Sioux resented this intrusion into the heart of their buffalo range, and led by one of their great chiefs, Red Cloud, they so harried the soldiers and the construction party—among other things, burning the forts that were supposed to guard the route—that the road could not be used.

The treaties of 1867 brought a temporary lull in the conflicts. But new forces soon shattered the peace again. In the early 1870s, more waves of white settlers, mostly miners, began to penetrate some of the lands in Dakota territory supposedly guaranteed to the tribes in 1867. At the same time, the federal government, responding to the recommendations of a commission, decided that it would no longer recognize the tribes as independent entities and would no longer negotiate with tribal chiefs. It was a step in-

The Battle of the Little Big Horn: An Indian View

This 1898 watercolor by one of the Indian participants portrays the aftermath of the Battle of the Little Big Horn, June 25–26, 1876, in which an army unit under the command of General George Armstrong Custer was surrounded and wiped out by Sioux and Cheyenne warriors. This grisly painting shows Indians on horseback riding over the corpses of Custer and his men. Custer can be seen lying at left center, dressed in yellow buckskin with his hat beside him. The four standing men at center are Sitting Bull, Rain-in-the-Face, Crazy Horse, and Kicking Bear (the artist). At lower right, Indian women begin preparations for a ceremony to honor the returning warriors. (Southwest Museum, Pasadena, California)

tended to undermine the collective nature of Indian life and to force the Indians to assimilate into white culture—a goal cherished by many white reformers, who believed that only through assimilation could the Indians achieve genuine "civilization."

Indian resistance flared anew, this time with even greater strength. In the northern plains, the Sioux, in response to the entrance of miners into the Black Hills and in anger at the corrupt behavior of white agents, rose up in 1875 and left their reservation. When white officials ordered them to return, bands of warriors gathered in Montana and united under two great leaders: Crazy Horse and Sitting Bull.

Three army columns set out to round them up and force them back onto the reservation. With the expedition, as colonel of the famous Seventh Cavalry, was the colorful and controversial George A. Custer, golden-haired romantic and glory seeker. At the Battle of the Little Bighorn in 1876—perhaps the most famous of all conflicts between whites and Indians—the tribal warriors surprised Custer and part

of his regiment, surrounded them, and killed every man. Custer has been accused of rashness, but he seems to have encountered something that no white man would likely have predicted. The chiefs had gathered together between 2,500 and 4,000 warriors, one of the largest Indian armies ever assembled at one time in the United States.

But the Indians did not have the political organization or the supplies to keep their troops united. Soon the warriors drifted off in bands to elude pursuit or search for food, and the army ran them down singly and returned them to Dakota. The power of the Sioux was soon broken. The proud leaders, Crazy Horse and Sitting Bull, accepted defeat and the monotony of life on reservations. Both were later killed by reservation police after being tricked or taunted into a last pathetic show of resistance.

In 1877, one of the most dramatic episodes in Indian history occurred in Idaho. Here the Nez Percé, a small and relatively peaceful tribe, refused to accept white demands that they move to a smaller reservation. When troops converged on them, their able leader, Chief Joseph, attempted to lead the band into Canada. Most Nez Percé did not follow Joseph and instead moved west to Washington state. But those who did became part of a remarkable chase. Joseph moved with 200 men and 350 women, children, and old people. Pursued by four columns, he covered 1,321 miles in seventy-five days, repelling or evading the army time and again, until he was finally caught just short of the Canadian border. Like so many other defeated Native Americans, these Nez Percé were shipped to the Indian Territory in Oklahoma, where most of them soon died of disease and malnutrition (although Joseph himself lived until 1908).

The last Indians to maintain organized resistance against the whites were the Apaches, who fought intermittently from the 1860s to the late 1880s. The two ablest chiefs of this fierce tribe were Mangas Colorados and Cochise. Mangas was murdered during the Civil War by white soldiers who tricked him into surrendering, and in 1872 Cochise agreed to peace in exchange for a reservation that included some of the tribe's traditional land. But Cochise died in 1874, and his successor, Geronimo—unwilling to bow to white pressures to assimilate—fought on for more than a decade longer, establishing bases in the mountains of Arizona and Mexico and leading warriors in intermittent raids against white outposts. With each raid, however, the number of warring Apaches dwindled, as some warriors died and others drifted away to the reservation. By 1886, Geronimo's plight was hopeless. His band consisted of only about thirty people, including women and children, while his white pursuers numbered perhaps five thousand. Geronimo recognized the odds and surrendered, an event that marked the end of formal warfare between Indians and whites.

The Apache wars were the most violent of all the Indian conflicts, perhaps because the tribes were now the most desperate. But as usual, it was the whites who committed the most flagrant and vicious atrocities. In 1871, for example, a mob of white miners invaded an Apache camp, slaughtered over a hundred Indians, and captured children, whom they sold as slaves to rival tribes. On other occasions, white troops murdered Indians who responded to invitations to peace conferences, once killing them with poisoned food.

Nor did the atrocities end with the conclusion of the Apache wars. Another tragic encounter occurred in 1890 as a result of a religious revival among the tribes—a revival that itself symbolized the catastrophic effects of the white assaults on Indian civili-

zation. The western Indians were by now aware that their culture and their glories were irrevocably fading; some were also near starvation because corrupt government agents had reduced their food rations. As other tribes had so often done in trying times in the past, many of these Indians turned to a prophet who led them into a religious revival. This time the prophet was Wovoka, a Paiute who inspired an ecstatic spiritual awakening that began in Nevada and spread quickly to the plains. The new revival emphasized the coming of a messiah, but its most conspicuous feature was a mass, emotional "Ghost Dance," which supposedly inspired mystical visions among its participants. White agents on the Sioux reservation watched the dances in bewilderment and fear; some believed they might be the preliminary to hostilities and called for troops to stop the ceremonies.

Some of the Indians fled to the Badlands to join other ghost dancers under the leadership of chief Big Foot. When the Seventh Cavalry (which had once been Custer's regiment) caught up with them at Wounded Knee, South Dakota, fighting broke out in which about 40 white soldiers and more than 200 of the Indians, including women and children, died. What precipitated the conflict is a matter of dispute. An Indian may well have fired the first shot, but the battle soon turned into a one-sided massacre, as the white soldiers turned their new machine guns on the Indians and mowed them down in the snow.

The Dawes Act

Even before the Ghost Dance and the Wounded Knee tragedy, the federal government had moved to destroy forever the tribal structure that had always been the cornerstone of Indian culture. Reversing its policy of nearly fifty years of creating reservations in which the tribes would be isolated from white society, Congress abolished the practice by which tribes owned reservation lands communally. Some supporters of the new policy believed they were acting for the good of the Indians. But the action was frankly designed to force Indians to become landowners and farmers, to abandon their collective society and culture and become part of white civilization. The Dawes Severalty Act of 1887 (usually known simply as the Dawes Act) provided for the gradual elimination of tribal ownership of land and the allotment of tracts to individual owners: 160 acres to the head of a family, 80 acres to a single adult or orphan, 40 acres to each dependent child. Adult owners were given United States citizenship, but un-

Burial at Wounded Knee
Soldiers bury some of the Sioux Indians killed at Wounded Knee. This mass grave held over 100 bodies, many of them women and children. The Wounded Knee massacre was the last major episode in a year-long effort by whites to suppress the Sioux religious revival known as the Ghost Dance.
(Amon Carter Museum)

like other citizens, they could not gain full title to their property for twenty-five years (supposedly to prevent them from selling the land to speculators). The act applied to most of the western tribes, although the Pueblo, who continued to occupy lands long ago guaranteed them, were exceptions.

In applying the Dawes Act, the Bureau of Indian Affairs moved relentlessly to promote the idea of assimilation that lay behind it. Not only did they try to move Indian families onto their own plots of land; they also took Indian children away from their families and sent them to boarding schools run by whites, where they believed the young people could be educated to abandon tribal ways. They also moved to stop Indian religious rituals and encouraged the spread of Christianity and the creation of Christian churches on the reservations.

Few Indians were prepared for this wrenching change from their traditional collective society to bourgeois individualism. In any case, white administration of the program was so corrupt and inept that ultimately the government simply abandoned it. Much of the reservation land, therefore, was never distributed to individual owners. Congress attempted to speed the transition with the Burke Act of 1906, but Indians continued to resist forced assimilation.

Neither then nor later could legislation provide a satisfactory solution to the problem of the Indians, largely because there was no entirely happy solution to be had. The interests of the Indians were not compatible with those of the expanding white civilization. Whites successfully settled the American West only at the expense of the region's indigenous people.

The Rise and Decline of the Western Farmer

The arrival of the miners, the empire building of the cattle ranchers, the dispersal of the Indian tribes—all served as a prelude to the decisive phase of white settlement of the Far West. Even before the Civil War, farmers had begun moving into the plains region, challenging the dominance of the ranchers and the Indians and occasionally coming into conflict with both. By the 1870s, what was once a trickle had become a deluge. Farmers poured into the plains and beyond, enclosed land that had once been hunting territory for Indians and grazing territory for cattle, and established a new agricultural region.

For a time in the late 1870s and early 1880s, the new Western farmers flourished—enjoying the fruits of an agricultural economic boom comparable in many ways to the booms that Eastern industry periodically enjoyed. Beginning in the mid-1880s, however, the boom turned to bust. American agriculture—not only in the new West but in the older Middle West and the South as well—was producing more than it ever had. But partly as a result, farmers were simultaneously suffering from declining prices for their goods. Both economically and

Completing the Transcontinental Railroad
Officials of the Union Pacific and Central Pacific companies shake hands and exchange bottles of champagne at Promontory Point, Utah, on May 10, 1869, after the last spike has been driven to join the two lines and complete the nation's first transcontinental railroad. The Union Pacific line began in Nebraska at the end of existing railroad connections to the East; the Central Pacific built its line eastward from California.   (Union Pacific Railroad Museum Collection)

psychologically, the agricultural economy began a long, steady decline—often in absolute terms, almost always in relation to the rest of the nation. Those who tried to improve their lot by moving west found that the frontier no longer provided them with a way out.

Farming on the Plains

Some farmers had drifted into the Great Plains region during its first stages of development, but the great rush of settlement came in the late 1870s. In the course of the next decade, the relentless advance of the farming frontier would gradually convert the plains country to an agricultural economy.

Many factors combined to produce this surge of Western settlement, but the most important was undoubtedly the railroads. Before the Civil War, the Great Plains had been virtually inaccessible to all but the most hardy pioneers, who could reach it only through an arduous journey by wagon. But beginning in the 1860s, a great new network of railroad lines started to develop that would, by the 1870s, open access to huge new areas of settlement. The first step toward this new access was the construction of the great "transcontinental" lines. An 1862 act of Congress (amended in 1864) chartered two railroad corporations, the Union Pacific and the Central Pacific. The Union Pacific was to build westward from Omaha, Nebraska, the Central Pacific eastward from

Sacramento, California, until they met. To provide the new companies with the necessary financial incentive, Congress made use of a practice that would become of vital importance to the future of the West: the land grant. For each mile of track a company laid, it would receive—in addition to the right of way for the track bed itself—twenty square miles of land in alternate sections (laid out in a checkerboard pattern) along the right of way.

The building of the transcontinental line was itself a dramatic and monumental achievement. Thousands of immigrant workers—mostly Irish on the eastern route, Chinese on the western—labored in what were at times unimaginably difficult conditions to penetrate mountain ranges, cross deserts, ward off Indians, and—finally—connect the two lines at Promontory Point in Utah in the spring of 1869. But while this first transcontinental line captured the greatest share of the public imagination, it was the construction of the great network of subsidiary lines in the following years that proved of greatest importance to the West. By the end of the century, five transcontinental lines were in operation; and from them were springing more and more spurs, penetrating much of the Great Plains. State governments, imitating Washington, induced railroad development by offering direct financial aid, favorable loans, and more than 50 million acres of land (on top of the 130 million acres the federal government had already offered). In some cases, government aid actually exceeded the cost of construction. Although operated by private corporations, the railroads were essentially public projects.

The construction of the railroad lines helped spur agricultural settlement in several ways. For one thing, it made access to the Great Plains easier—first enabling the farmers to reach the new lands, and later enabling them to ship their crops to market and to receive goods and supplies in return. For another, the railroad companies themselves now had great incentive to promote settlement—both to provide themselves with customers for their services and to increase the value of their vast land holdings. Thus the railroads embarked on a great advertising campaign to lure settlers into the new region, distributing posters and brochures throughout the East and Midwest with glowing descriptions of the "great fertility," "nutritious grasses," and "numerous streams" to be found in the plains. More than that, the companies set rates so low for settlers that almost anyone could afford the trip West. And it sold much of its land at very low prices, usually between $2 and $5 an acre (which, since the railroads had gotten the land for nothing, was still a significant profit). Some railroad companies even provided liberal credit to prospective settlers to encourage them to move West.

Contributing further to the great surge of white agricultural expansion was a temporary change in the climate. For several years in succession, beginning in the 1870s, rainfall in the plains states was well above average. White Americans now rejected the old idea that the region was the Great American Desert. Some even claimed that cultivation of the plains actually encouraged rainfall. Confident that they faced an era of indefinite prosperity, the new farmers scoffed at those who warned that the climate might change again. They scoffed too at the old cattle ranchers who warned that the light soil of the plains should not be deprived of its protective turf by cultivation.

Even under the most favorable conditions, farming on the plains presented problems not encountered in any previously settled region. First and most critical was the problem of fencing. Farmers had to enclose their land, if for no other reason than to protect it from the herds of the cattlemen. But traditional wood or stone fences were impossible on the plains; the materials were expensive to import and were, in any case, ineffective as barriers to cattle. In the mid-1870s, however, two Illinois farmers, Joseph H. Glidden and I. L. Ellwood, solved this problem by developing and marketing barbed wire. Produced in large quantities—40,000 tons a year—it sold cheaply, became standard equipment on the plains, and revolutionized fencing practices all over the country.

The second problem, a serious one even when rainfall was above average, was water. That problem became particularly acute after 1887, when a series of dry seasons began. Lands that had come to seem fertile and well watered now began to turn back into semidesert. Farmers devised one technique after another to deal with the problem, but none was fully satisfactory. One solution was the use of deep wells pumped by steel windmills, which ensured a steady water supply for stock. Another was dryland farming—a system of tillage designed to conserve moisture in the soil by covering it with a dust blanket—and the planting of drought-resistant crops. But these techniques were of limited usefulness. In many areas of the plains, commercial agriculture could not continue without large-scale irrigation, which in turn required government assistance. The federal government hoped state governments would take the lead in financing these expensive projects; and in the Carey Act of 1894, it transferred several million acres of public land to various states, on the understanding that the states would reclaim them through irrigation and then sell them. The states, however, made little progress, largely because the problems of reclamation cut across state boundaries. Irrigation, therefore, remained limited through most of the plains; and the majority of farmers had to deal with the water shortage as best they could on their own.

Farming on the plains, therefore, was always expensive and often risky. The uncertainty of rainfall and the danger of grasshopper plagues and tornadoes made every farm year a speculative experiment. Costs of operation were high, partly because many supplies had to be imported into the region from distant points, but mainly because of the nature of plains farming. In all the farm areas of the country, machines were playing a larger part in the agricultural process, and they were especially vital on the plains, where grain farming was conducted on large land units. Farm machinery made it possible for farmers with limited labor supplies to cultivate expansive landholdings. But machinery required a major capital investment, which not all prospective farmers could easily afford. The necessity of making that investment helped to create one of the central realities of life on Western farms: debt.

The Great Plains were not, as some have claimed, a refuge for the urban poor or a safety valve for proletarian unrest. The people who moved into the region were mostly people who had previously been farmers elsewhere; they came from agricultural areas in the Middle West, the East, and Europe. In the booming years of the early 1880s, with land values rising, the new farmers had no problem obtaining extensive and easy credit and had every reason to believe they would soon be able to retire their debts. But the arid years of the late 1880s—years in which crop prices were falling at the same time as production was becoming more expensive—changed that prospect with grim suddenness. Thousands of farmers found it impossible any longer to keep up payments on their loans and were forced to abandon their farms. What followed was a reversal of the frontier movement—settlers departing the Great Plains in large numbers, sometimes turning once-flourishing communities into desolate ghost towns. Those who remained continued to suffer from falling prices (wheat, which had sold for $1.60 a bushel at the end of the Civil War, dropped to 49 cents in the 1890s) and persistent indebtedness.

Changes in Agriculture

Americans had always liked to romanticize farm life. According to popular myth, the farmer was a sturdy yeoman—simple, honest, happy, dwelling close to nature, independent, self-reliant. The myth may once have had some basis in fact, but by the late nineteenth century it no longer reflected the reality of agricultural life. The simple, self-sufficient yeoman of myth had become a commercial farmer—attempting to do in the agricultural economy what industrialists were doing in the manufacturing economy.

Commercial farmers were not self-sufficient and made no effort to become so. They specialized in cash crops and sold them in national or world markets. They ceased making their own household supplies and growing their own food and bought them instead at town or village stores. This kind of farming, when it was successful, raised the farmers' living standards. But it also made them dependent on other people and on impersonal factors they could not control: bankers and interest rates, railroads and freight rates, national and European markets, world supply and demand. In short, farmers had become businessmen—but with a difference. Unlike the capitalists of the industrial order, they could not regulate their production or influence the prices of what they sold.

The period between 1865 and 1900 witnessed a tremendous expansion of agricultural facilities, not only in the United States but all over the world: in Brazil and Argentina in South America, in Canada, in Australia and New Zealand, and in Russia. World production increased at the same time as modern means of communication and transportation—the telephone, telegraph, cable, steam navigation, railroads—were welding the producing nations into one international market. American commercial farmers, constantly opening new lands, now produced more than the domestic market could absorb and had to depend on the world market to absorb their surplus. Cotton farmers depended on export sales for 70 percent of their annual income, and wheat farmers for 30 to 40 percent; other producers exported smaller proportions of their crops but enough, in most cases, for the exports to make the difference between a year of profit and one of loss.

But world prices were highly unpredictable. Starting in the 1880s, almost every sector of the farm economy began suffering from the effects of worldwide overproduction. And international prices soon declined to a point that made it difficult for even the most efficient farmers to make a profit. Despite the surface similarities between the growth of commercial agriculture and the growth of industry, the results were starkly different. Between 1860 and 1910, the number of farm families rose from 1.5 million to over 6 million. But whereas in 1860 agriculture had represented 50 percent of the total wealth of the country, by the early 1900s it represented only 20 percent. Where farmers had received 30 percent of the national income in 1860, they received only 18 percent by 1910. By the 1890s, 27 percent of the owned farms in the country were mortgaged, and by 1910, 33 percent. In 1880, 25 percent of all farms had been operated by tenants; by 1910, the proportion had grown to 37 percent. Commercial farming did, it is true, make some people fabulously wealthy. But the farm economy as a whole was suffering a significant decline relative to the rest of the nation.

The Farmers' Grievances

Farmers were painfully aware that something was wrong. Neither they nor anyone else yet understood, however, the full implications of national and world overproduction. Instead, they concentrated their attention and anger on more immediate, more comprehensible—and no less real—problems: inequitable freight rates, high interest charges, and an inadequate currency.

The farmers' first and most burning grievance was against the railroads. In all sections of the country, and especially in the states west of the Mississippi, farmers depended on the railroads to carry crops to the markets. In many cases, the roads

SIGNIFICANT EVENTS

1851 "Concentration" policy devised for Western tribes (p. 501)

1859 Colorado gold rush launches Western mining bonanza (p. 495)

1864 Nevada admitted to Union (p. 495)

1865–1867 Sioux War (p. 502)

1866 "Long drives" launch Western cattle bonanza (p. 497)

1867 Nebraska admitted to Union (p. 495)

Indian Peace Commission establishes "Indian Territory" (later Oklahoma) (p. 501)

1869 Union Pacific, first transcontinental railroad, completed (p. 506)

1873 Barbed wire invented (p. 507)

Comstock Lode silver deposits discovered in Nevada (p. 495)

Timber Culture Act passed (p. 494)

1874 Gold rush begins in Black Hills, Dakota Territory (p. 496)

1875 Sioux uprising begins (p. 503)

1876 Battle of the Little Bighorn (p. 503)

Colorado admitted to Union (p. 495)

Nez Percé Indians resist relocation (p. 503)

1879 Readjusters win control of Virginia legislature (p. 484)

1880 Joel Chandler Harris publishes *Uncle Remus* (p. 485)

1883 Supreme Court upholds segregation in private institutions (p. 488)

1885–1887 Harsh winters help destroy open-range cattle raising (p. 498)

1885 Mark Twain publishes *Huckleberry Finn* (p. 499)

1886 Geronimo captured (p. 504)

1887 Dawes Act passed (p. 504)

Prolonged drought in Great Plains begins (p. 507)

1889 North Dakota, South Dakota, Montana, Washington admitted to Union (p. 495)

Oklahoma (formerly "Indian Territory") opened to white settlement (p. 495)

1890s "Jim Crow" laws passed throughout South (p. 488)

Lynchings increase in South (p. 484)

1890 Battle of Wounded Knee (p. 504)

Wyoming and Idaho admitted to Union (p. 495)

1891 Hamlin Garland publishes *Main-Traveled Roads* (p. 510)

1893 Frederick Jackson Turner proposes "Turner thesis" (p. 499)

1895 Booker T. Washington outlines Atlanta Compromise (p. 488)

1896 *Plessy* v. *Ferguson* upholds "separate but equal" racial facilities (p. 488)

Utah admitted to Union (p. 495)

1898 *Williams* v. *Mississippi* validates literacy tests for voting (p. 489)

1905 NAACP founded (p. 493)

---

charged higher rates for farm than for other shipments, and higher rates in the South and West than in the Northeast. Freight rates sometimes consumed so much of the current price that farmers refused to ship their crops and either let them rot or used them as fuel. Railroads also controlled elevator and warehouse facilities in buying centers and charged arbitrary storage rates.

In the farmers' list of villains, the sources that controlled credit—banks, loan companies, insurance corporations—ranked second only to the railroads. Commercial farming was by its nature expensive, and ambitious producers needed credit to purchase machines or enlarge holdings. Although lenders had been eager to advance loans during the boom period of rising land values, they had insisted on high interest rates. Since sources of credit in the West and South were few, farmers had had to take loans on whatever terms they could get, often at interest rates of from 10 to 25 percent. Farmers who had borrowed in the flush times had to pay their loans back in later years, when prices were dropping and currency was becoming scarce. With good reason, the farmers fought for an increase in the volume of currency.

A third grievance concerned prices: both the prices farmers received for their products and the prices they paid for goods they bought. Farmers disposed of their products in a competitive world market over which they had no control and of which they had no advance knowledge. A farmer could plant a large crop at a moment when prices were high and find that by the time of the harvest the price had declined. There were no storage facilities in which farmers could hold their crops and wait for the price to go back up. They had few options, and their fortunes rose and fell in response to unpredictable forces. Naturally, they attempted to find some explanation for their plight; and they tended increasingly to blame their troubles on particular villains: speculators in distant cities, international bankers, regional and local middlemen. Many farmers became convinced (often with some reason) that such people were combining to fix prices so as to benefit themselves at the expense of the growers.

Many farmers also came to believe (again, not without reason) that manufacturers in the East were conspiring to keep the prices of farm goods low and the prices of industrial goods high. Farmers sold their crops in a competitive world market; but they bought manufactured goods in a domestic market protected by tariffs and dominated by trusts and corporations. According to government reports, more than 100 articles purchased by farmers—farm machinery, tools, sewing machines, blankets, staple foods, clothing, plowshares, and others—were protected. On these necessary items, the tariff added from 33 to 60 percent to the purchase price.

The Agrarian Malaise

Adding to these economic grievances, and in many ways a direct result of them, was a less tangible but deeply felt resentment. In part, it was an outgrowth of the isolation of farm life in these days before paved roads, automobiles, telephones, and radios. Farm families in some parts of the country—particularly in the prairie and plains regions, where large farms were scattered over vast areas—were virtually cut off from the outside world and human companionship. During the winter months and spells of bad weather, the loneliness and boredom could become nearly unbearable.

In addition to the isolation, there was often a general drabness and dullness to farm existence. Many farmers lacked access to adequate education for their children, to proper medical facilities, to recreational or cultural activities, to virtually anything that might give them a sense of being valued members of a community. Older farmers felt the sting of watching their children leave the farm for the city. They felt the humiliation of being ridiculed as "hayseeds" by the new urban culture that was coming to dominate American life. There was, in short, a general feeling of obsolescence, of being left behind by a society that no longer placed much value on the virtues of rural life.

This emerging agrarian malaise found reflection in the growing discontent of many farmers, a discontent that would help to create a great national political movement in the 1890s. It found reflection, too, in the literature that emerged from rural America. Writers in the late nineteenth century might romanticize the rugged life of the cowboy and the Western miner. For the farmer, however, the image was different. Hamlin Garland, perhaps the most celebrated writer to deal with the nature of agrarian life in this period, reflected the growing disillusionment in a series of novels and short stories. In the past, Garland wrote in the introduction to *Jason Edwards* (1891), the agrarian frontier had seemed to be "the Golden West, the land of wealth and freedom and happiness. All of the associations called up by the spoken word, the West, were fabulous, mythic, hopeful." Now, however, the bright promise had faded. In this novel and in other works (including his most famous achievement, a collection of stories entitled *Main-Traveled Roads*, also published in 1891), he showed how the trials of rural life were crushing the human spirit. "So this is the reality of the dream!" a character in *Jason Edwards* exclaims. "A shanty on a barren plain, hot and lone as a desert. My God!" Once, sturdy yeoman farmers had viewed themselves as the backbone of American life. Now, they were becoming painfully aware that their position was declining in relation to the rising urban-industrial society to the east.

SUGGESTED READINGS

The New South.   C. Vann Woodward, *Origins of the New South* (1951), *The Burden of Southern History* (rev., 1968), *American Counterpoint* (1971), *Thinking Back* (1986), and *The Future of the Past* (1989); Jonathan Wiener, *Social Origins of the New South: Alabama, 1860–1885* (1978); Paul Buck, *The Road to Reunion* (1937); Paul Gaston, *The New South Creed* (1970); W. J. Cash, *The Mind of the South* (1941); Orville Vernon Burton, *In My Father's House* (1985); Orville Vernon Burton and Robert C. McMath, Jr., eds., *Toward a New South?* (1982); J. Morgan Kousser and James M. McPherson, eds., *Region, Race, and Reconstruction* (1982).

Southern Politics.   C. Vann Woodward, *Reunion and Reaction* (1951) and *Tom Watson: Agrarian Rebel* (1938); Stanley P. Hirshson, *Farewell to the Bloody Shirt: Northern Republicans and the Southern Negro* (1962); Kenneth E. Davison, *The Presidency of Rutherford B. Hayes* (1972); Vincent P. DeSantis, *Republicans Face the Southern Question: The New De-*

parture Years, 1877–1897 (1959); J. Morgan Kousser, *The Shaping of Southern Politics: Suffrage Restriction and the Establishment of the One-Party South, 1880–1910* (1974); Paul Lewinson, *Race, Class, and Party* (1932); V. O. Key, Jr., *Southern Politics and the Nation* (1949); Francis B. Simkins, *Pitchfork Ben Tillman* (1944); Joseph F. Wall, *Henry Watterson: Reconstructed Rebel* (1956); Sheldon Hackney, *Populism to Progressivism in Alabama* (1959); David Potter, *The South and the Concurrent Majority* (1972); Carl Degler, *The Other South: Southern Dissenters in the Nineteenth Century* (1974).

Race, Economics, and Social Structure. Gavin Wright, *Old South, New South* (1986); Melvin Greenhut and W. Tate Whitman (eds.), *Essays in Southern Economic Development* (1964); Jacquelyn Dowd Hall et al., *Like a Family: The Making of a Southern Cotton Mill World* (1987); David Carlton, *Mill and Town in South Carolina, 1880–1920* (1982); Melton A. McLaurin, *Paternalism and Protest: Southern Cotton Mill Workers and Organized Labor* (1971); Altina L. Waller, *Feud: Hatfields, McCoys, and Social Changes: Appalachia, 1860–1900* (1988); Steven Hahn, *The Roots of Southern Populism: Yeoman Farmers and the Transformation of the Georgia Upcountry* (1983); Steven Hahn and Jonathan Prude, eds., *The Countryside in the Age of Capitalist Transformation* (1985); Roger Ransom and Richard Sutch, *One Kind of Freedom* (1977); C. Vann Woodward, *The Strange Career of Jim Crow* (rev., 1974); Howard Rabinowitz, *Race Relations in the Urban South, 1865–1890* (1978); Cynthia Neverdon-Morton, *Afro-American Women of the South and the Advancement of the Race, 1895–1925* (1989); James M. McPherson, *The Abolitionist Legacy: From Reconstruction to the NAACP* (1975); Robert Higgs, *Competition and Coercion: Blacks in the American Economy, 1865–1914* (1977); Joel Williamson, *After Slavery* (1965), *The Crucible of Race: Black-White Relations in the American South Since Emancipation* (1985), and *A Rage for Order* (1986), an abridgment of *The Crucible of Race;* Louis R. Harlan, *Booker T. Washington: The Making of a Black Leader, 1856–1901* (1972) and *Booker T. Washington: The Wizard of Tuskegee: 1901–1915* (1983); August Meier, *Negro Thought in America* (1963); Francis Broderick, *W. E. B. DuBois* (1959); Elliott M. Rudwick, *W. E. B. DuBois: Propagandist of Negro Protest* (rev., 1969).

Westward Expansion. Ray A. Billington and Martin Ridge, *Westward Expansion*, 5th ed. (1982); Robert V. Hine, *The American West*, 2nd ed. (1984); Frederick Merk, *History of the Westward Movement* (1978); Patricia Limerick, *The Legacy of Conquest: The Unbroken Past of the American West* (1987); Richard Slotkin, *The Fatal Envioronment: The Myth of the Frontier in the Age of Industrialization* (1985); Rodman W. Paul and Richard W. Etulain, *The Frontier and the American West* (1977); Thomas D. Clark, *Frontier America* (rev. 1969); Howard R. Lamar, *The Far Southwest, 1846–1912* (1966); Henry Nash Smith, *Virgin Land* (1950); Frederick Jackson Turner, *The Frontier in American History* (1920); Ray A. Billington, *Frederick Jackson Turner* (1973).

Miners and Cattlemen. Rodman W. Paul, *Mining Frontiers of the Far West, 1848–1880* (1963) and *The Far West and the Great Plains in Transition, 1859–1900* (1988); William S.

Greever, *Bonanza West: Western Mining Rushes* (1963); Duane A. Smith, *Rocky Mountain Mining Camps* (1967); Lewis Atherton, *The Cattle Kings* (1961); Ernest E. Osgood, *The Day of the Cattleman* (1929); Edward E. Dale, *The Range Cattle Industry*, rev. ed. (1969); J. M. Skaggs, *The Cattle Trailing Industry* (1973); Robert K. Dykstra, *The Cattle Towns* (1968); Andy Adams, *The Log of a Cowboy* (1927); Joe B. Frantz and Julian Choate, *The American Cowboy: The Myth and the Reality* (1955); L. Steckmesser, *The Western Hero in History and Legend* (1965); Odie B. Faulk, *Tombstone: Myth and Reality* (1972); Earl Pomeroy, *The Pacific Slope* (1965); Gunther Barth, *Instant Cities* (1975).

Indians. Wilcomb E. Washburn, *The Indian in America* (1975) and *Red Man's Land/White Man's Law* (1971); Ralph K. Andrist, *The Long Death: The Last Days of the Plains Indians* (1964); Francis P. Prucha, *American Indian Policy in Crisis* (1976) and *The Great White Father: The United States Government and the American Indians* (1984); William T. Hagan, *The Indian Rights Association: The Herbert Welsh Years, 1882–1904* (1985); Robert M. Utley, *Last Days of the Sioux Nation* (1963), *Frontiersmen in Blue: The United States Army and the Indian, 1848–1865* (1967), *Frontier Regulars: The United States Army and the Indian* (1973), and *The Indian Frontier of the American West, 1846–1890* (1984); Dee Brown, *Bury My Heart at Wounded Knee: An Indian History of the American West* (1970); Thomas W. Dunlay, *Wolves for the Blue Soldiers* (1982); Margert Coel, *Chief Left Hand: Southern Arapaho* (1981); Loretta Fowler, *Arapahoe Politics, 1851–1978: Symbols in Crisis of Authority* (1982); John Powell, *People of the Sacred Mountain: A History of the Northern Cheyenne Chiefs and Warrior Societies, 1830–1879*, 2 vols. (1981); Angie Debo, *Geronimo* (1976); Mari Sandoz, *Crazy Horse* (1961); James C. Olson, *Red Cloud and the Sioux Problem* (1965); Donald J. Berthrong, *The Southern Cheyennes* (1963); Frederick E. Hoxie, *A Final Promise: The Campaign to Assimilate the Indians, 1880–1920* (1984); Robert Mardock, *Reformers and the American Indian* (1971); Robert F. Berkhofer, Jr., *The White Man's Indian* (1978); Richard White, *The Roots of Dependency* (1983).

Western Women. Julie Jeffrey, *Frontier Women: The Trans-Mississippi West, 1840–1880* (1979); Sandra L. Myres, *Westering Women and the Frontier Experience, 1880–1915* (1982); Polly Welts Kaufman, *Women Teachers on the Frontier* (1984); Joanna L. Stratton, *Pioneer Women: Voices from the Kanas Frontier* (1981); John Mack Faragher, *Women and Men on the Overland Trail* (1979); Glenda Riley, *Women and Indians on the Frontier, 1825–1915* (1984); Susan Armitage and Elizabeth Jameson, eds., *The Women's West* (1987); Ruth Moynihan, *Rebel for Rights: Abigail Scott Dunaway* (1983).

Western Agriculture. Walter Prescott Webb, *The Great Plains* (1931); Fred A Shannon, *The Farmer's Last Frontier, 1860–1897* (1945); Gilbert C. Fite, *The Farmer's Frontier* (1966); Paul W. Gates, *History of Public Land Development* (1968); Everett Dick, *The Sod-House Frontier* (1937); Allan Bogue, *From Prairie to Corn Belt* (1963); John Mack Faragher, *Sugar Creek: Life on the Illinois Paririe* (1986). See also bibliography for Chapter 19.

Detail from *Forging the Shaft* (1874–1877), by John Ferguson Weir
Weir's father taught drawing and painting at the U.S. Military Academy at West Point, and Weir
himself directed the Yale School of Fine Arts for more than four decades. One of his patrons was the
owner of this foundry and ironworks at Cold Spring, New York, which made guns for the soldiers
at nearby West Point. (*Metropolitan Museum of Art*)

CHAPTER 17

Industrial Supremacy

"With a stride that astonished statisticians, the conquering hosts of business enterprise swept over the continent; twenty-five years after the death of Lincoln, America had become, in the quantity and value of her products, the first manufacturing nation of the world. What England had accomplished in a hundred years, the United States had achieved in half the time." So wrote the historians Charles and Mary Beard in the 1920s, expressing the amazement many Americans felt when they considered the remarkable expansion of their economy in the late nineteenth century.

In fact, America's rise to industrial supremacy was not as sudden as such observers believed. The nation had been building a manufacturing economy since early in the nineteenth century; industry was well established before the Civil War. But Americans were clearly correct in observing that the accomplishments of the last three decades of the nineteenth century overshadowed all the earlier progress. Those years witnessed nothing less than the transformation of the nation.

Many factors contributed to this dramatic industrial growth. The United States had an abundance of basic raw materials and energy sources, especially coal, iron, timber, petroleum, and water power. There was a large and growing supply of labor, the result of two great migrations: the movement of American farmers into the cities and the movement of European peasants across the ocean to the nation's industrial centers. American industry benefited as well from a remarkable technological inventiveness—widely heralded as "Yankee ingenuity"—which created the necessary machinery for industrial growth.

A talented, ambitious, and often ruthless group of entrepreneurs—known by some as "captains of industry" and by others as "robber barons"—developed new financial and administrative structures capable of organizing large-scale production and distributing manufactured goods to a national market. And the market itself was growing as a result of population growth, the new railroad network, and a host of new marketing techniques. Finally, the federal government worked to promote economic growth. Although it resisted most pressures to interfere with the prerogatives of capitalists, it worked to promote corporate growth. It made public resources available for private exploitation on generous terms; it erected protective tariff barriers against foreign competition; it established a new banking and currency system; and it provided direct subsidies of land and money.

The remarkable growth that resulted from these factors did much to increase the wealth and improve the lives of many Americans. But such benefits were far from equally shared. While the industrial titans and a growing middle class were enjoying a prosperity without precedent in the nation's history, workers, farmers, and others were experiencing an often painful ordeal that slowly edged the United States toward a great economic and political crisis.

Sources of Industrial Growth

Virtually all the forces that contributed to American economic growth were in operation in some form before the Civil War. But there were other forces at work in those years to inhibit economic development. Perhaps most important, conservative Southern planters, exercising great political power, had served as an obstacle to governmental policies favoring Northern capitalists. The years of war and Reconstruction removed that obstacle, as well as others. And in the 1870s and 1880s, the forces of economic progress took on renewed strength.

Industrial Technology

No one factor can be called the most important prerequisite of industrial growth. Indeed, industrialization depends above all on the working together of many forces at once. But one of the most important of such forces, certainly, is the emergence of new technologies and the discovery of new materials and productive processes. In the last decades of the nineteenth century, inventions appeared at a dizzying pace. In the entire history of the United States up to 1860, only 36,000 patents had been granted. For the period from 1860 to 1890, the figure was 440,000. Comparable technological advances were occurring in Europe in these same years, and Americans benefited from those as well.

Many of the postwar inventions and discoveries were in the field of communication. In 1866, Cyrus W. Field succeeded in laying a transatlantic telegraph cable to Europe. During the next decade, Alexander Graham Bell developed the first commercially useful telephone; and by the 1890s, the American Telephone and Telegraph Company, which handled his interests, had installed nearly half a million instruments in American cities. Other inventions that speeded the pace of business organization were the typewriter (by Christopher L. Sholes in 1868), the cash register (by James Ritty in 1879), and the calculating or adding machine (by William S. Burroughs in 1891).

The technological innovation that probably had the most revolutionary effect on industry and on the lives of the urban masses was the introduction in the 1870s of electricity as a source of light and power. Among the several men who pioneered this development were Charles F. Brush, who devised the arc lamp for street illumination, and Thomas A. Edison,

who invented, among many other electrical devices, the incandescent lamp (or light bulb), which could be used for both street and home lighting. Edison and others designed improved generators and built large power plants to furnish electricity to whole cities. Before the turn of the century, 2,774 power stations were in operation, and some 2 million electric lights were in use in the country. Electric power was by then becoming commonplace in street railway systems, in the elevators of urban skyscrapers, and in factories.

Another important technological breakthrough was the development of steel. A process by which iron could be transformed into steel—a much more durable and versatile material—had been discovered simultaneously in the 1850s by an Englishman, Henry Bessemer, and an American, William Kelly. (The process consisted of blowing air through molten iron to burn out the impurities.) After the Civil War, the new process transformed the metal industry; and in 1868, another method of making steel—the open-hearth process, introduced from Europe by the New Jersey ironmaster Abram S. Hewitt—made an appearance as well. Together, these techniques made possible the production of steel in great quantities and in large dimensions, thus facilitating use of the metal for the production of locomotives, steel rails, and ultimately, heavy girders for the construction of tall buildings.

The steel industry emerged first, unsurprisingly, where the iron industry already existed, in western Pennsylvania and eastern Ohio—a region where iron ore and coal were abundant. Pittsburgh quickly became the center of the steel world. But the rapid growth of the industry soon stimulated the development of new sources of ore in other areas. The mines of the upper peninsula of Michigan were furnishing more than half the supply by the 1870s. Beginning in the 1890s, the extensive Mesabi range in Minnesota developed into the greatest ore-producing region in the world. Another rich source was discovered around Birmingham, Alabama. Eventually new centers of production emerged closer to the new sources of ore and coal: Cleveland and Lorain in Ohio; Detroit, Chicago, and Birmingham.

The petroleum industry emerged in the late nineteenth century largely in response to the steel industry's need for lubrication for its machines. (Not until later did oil become important primarily for its potential as a fuel.) Many Americans had been aware for some time of the existence of petroleum reserves in western Pennsylvania, where oil often seeped to the surface of streams and springs. At first, however, no one was quite sure what it was or what to do with it. (Some charlatans bottled it and sold it as a patent medicine.) In 1855, however, the Pennsylvania businessman George H. Bissell sent a sample of oil to Professor Benjamin Silliman of Yale for analysis. Silliman told him that the substance could be used for lighting purposes and that it would also yield such products as paraffin, naphtha, and lubricating oil.

Convinced now that oil had commercial possibilities, Bissell raised money to begin drilling; and in 1859, Edwin L. Drake, one of Bissell's employees, established the first oil well near Titusville, Pennsylvania, which was soon producing 500 barrels of oil a month. Skeptics called the well "Drake's folly," but demand for petroleum grew quickly enough to precipitate an oil rush. Promoters began to develop other fields in Pennsylvania, Ohio, and West Virginia. By the 1870s, nearly 40 million barrels of petroleum had been produced; oil had advanced to fourth place among the nation's exports; and annual production was approaching 20 million barrels.

New technologies and materials similarly transformed other industries. The refrigerated freight car made possible the expansion of the great meatpacking organizations of Gustavus Swift, Philip Armour, and others. New ways of milling flour made possible the emergence of large milling companies in the Midwest (and particularly in Minnesota). New methods of canning foods and condensing milk helped establish the prepared-foods industry under the leadership of Gail Borden and others.

By the beginning of the twentieth century, the new technology was leading to even greater advances. There were early experiments in communication by radio conducted by the Italian inventor Guglielmo Marconi in the 1890s. There were the first steps toward the development of the airplane—the famous flight by the Wright brothers at Kitty Hawk, North Carolina, in 1903. But of more immediate importance was the development of the automobile. In the 1870s, designers in France, Germany, and Austria—inspired by the success of railroad engines—were already beginning to develop engines that might drive independently controlled vehicles. They achieved early successes with an "internal combustion engine," which used the expanding power of burning gas to drive pistons; and with this new engine, they created the first automobiles—essentially traditional carriages fitted with their own source of power to replace the horse.

Meanwhile, in the United States, inventors such

Drake and His Oil Well, c. 1866
Edwin L. Drake became the first American to tap petroleum at its source by drilling when he constructed an oil well (derided by many at the time as "Drake's Folly") at Titusville, Pennsylvania, in 1859. Drake got the idea by watching salt-well drilling operations around Syracuse, New York, and Pittsburgh; using similar techniques, he struck oil at Titusville on August 27, 1859, at a depth of sixty-nine feet. He is shown here, at right, wearing a top hat, in front of his well.   (The Bettmann Archive)

as Charles and Frank Duryea, Elwood Haynes, Ransom Olds, and Henry Ford were designing their own automobiles. The Duryeas built and operated the first gasoline-driven motor vehicle in America in 1903. (Earlier American cars had used other, cruder fuels.) Three years later, Ford produced the first of the famous cars that would bear his name. In 1898, the first automobile advertisement appeared in *Scientific Amer-*

ican, under the headline: "Dispense With a Horse." The first automobile showroom opened in New York in 1901. By 1900, automobile companies were turning out more than 4,000 cars a year. A decade later—when manufacturers were finally able to streamline operations so as to bring the cost down, and when American roads began to be improved to make extensive automobile traffic possible—the industry had become a major force in the economy, and the automobile was beginning to reshape American social and cultural life. In 1895, there had been only four automobiles on the American highways. By 1917, there were nearly 5 million.

The Science of Production

Central to the growth of the automobile and other industries were advances in the science of production. Convinced that a modern economy required modernization of the manufacturing process, industrialists by the turn of the century were turning in growing numbers to the new principles of "scientific management." The leading force behind the new science was Frederick Winslow Taylor.

Taylor's ideas were controversial during his lifetime, and they have remained controversial ever since. Taylor himself, and his many admirers, argued that scientific management was an essential prerequisite to an efficient, modern economy. It was a way to manage human labor to make it compatible with the demands of the machine age. But scientific management had another purpose as well, which made it far less appealing to many workers. It was a way to increase the employer's control of the workplace, to make working people less independent.

Taylor's first experiments were targeted not at machine operators but at manual laborers. Among other things, he urged employers to reorganize the production process by subdividing tasks. This would be a way to speed up production; it would also make workers more interchangeable and thus diminish a manager's dependence on any particular employee. But Taylor's ideas found their greatest influence in industries where machinery was becoming central to production. The new technology, Taylor argued, would be of little use unless workers could be trained to operate the machinery efficiently and effectively. If properly managed, he argued, fewer and fewer workers could perform simple tasks at much greater speed, greatly increasing productive efficiency. They would also be easier to control if they could be made part of

a scientifically designed process of production rather than left in control of the process themselves. Not until well into the new century—indeed not until the 1920s—did the influence of what became known as "Taylorism" reach its peak. Even then, relatively few manufacturers made literal use of his methods. But the impulse behind Taylorism—the attempt to bring to the performance of workers the same scientific standards that industrialists were bringing to the creation of new technologies—was affecting industry much earlier than that.

Manufacturers also began placing greater emphasis on industrial research. In part because of the phenomenal success of Thomas Edison's famous industrial laboratory in Menlo Park, New Jersey, dozens of corporations were, by the early years of the twentieth century, establishing laboratories of their own. By 1913, Bell Telephone, Du Pont, General Electric, Eastman Kodak, and about fifty other companies were budgeting hundreds of thousands of dollars each year for research by their own engineers and scientists.

Out of all the new methods and machines emerged the greatest triumph of production technology: mass production and, above all, the moving assembly line, which Henry Ford introduced in his automobile plants in 1914. This revolutionary technique cut the time for assembling a chassis from twelve and a half hours to one and a half hours. It enabled Ford to raise the wages and reduce the hours of his workers while cutting the base price of his Model T from $950 to $290. It served as an example for many other industries.

Railroad Expansion

The principal agent of industrial development in the late nineteenth century was the expansion of another transportation system: the railroads. Railroads promoted economic growth in many ways. As the nation's principal method of transportation, they made possible the expansion of genuinely national commerce by giving industrialists quick and relatively inexpensive access to distant markets and distant sources of raw materials. As the nation's largest businesses, the railroads created new forms of corporate organization that served as models for other industries. And as America's biggest investors, they stimulated economic growth through their own enormous expenditures on construction and equipment.

Railroads, 1870–1890

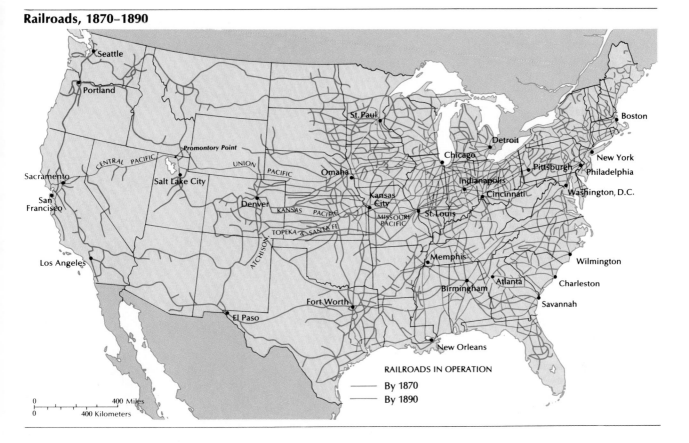

Even before the Civil War, railroads had been the most important single economic interest in the United States. In the years that followed, their importance grew still further. Every decade, the total railroad trackage increased dramatically: from 30,000 miles in 1860, to 52,000 miles in 1870, to 93,000 in 1880, to 163,000 in 1890, and to 193,000 at the turn of the century. Along with the extension of lines came improvements in technology that made railroad travel safer and more efficient: steel rails, heavier locomotives and cars, uniform track gauge, wider roadbeds, and perhaps most important, new braking systems (first introduced by George Westinghouse) that reduced the danger of derailments and pileups.

Government subsidies—those by the federal government to support the transcontinental lines and those by state and local governments to encourage subsidiary routes—were vital to these vast undertakings, which required far more capital than private entrepreneurs could raise by themselves. Equally important, perhaps, was the emergence of great railroad corporations—the first large economic combinations—which brought a vast proportion of the na-

tion's rails under the control of a very few men. Among the earliest such combinations was the Pennsylvania Railroad. It was one of the first companies to combine a large number of short lines under the direction of a single management. It also introduced a new system of administration by trained managers, who attempted to run the company according to the principles of the emerging science of business administration. Profits still went to the stockholders; but the actual running of the company was lodged in the hands of people who were not necessarily owners.

Other railroad combinations, however, saw owners continue to play a central role in management through the last decades of the nineteenth century: the vast New York Central empire of Cornelius Vanderbilt (a former steamship owner widely known as "the Commodore"), for example; or the Erie Railroad, controlled by the unscrupulous speculators Daniel Drew, Jay Gould, and James Fisk, whose self-serving exploitation of the company ultimately led to disaster. Indeed, these and other railroad tycoons—among them James J. Hill and Collis P. Huntington—became symbols to much of the nation of great economic power concentrated in a single individual. But railroad development was less significant for the individual barons it created than for its contribution to the growth of a new institution: the modern corporation.

The Corporation

There had been corporations in America since colonial times: organizations chartered by governments and charged with running such public facilities as bridges, roads, and banks. (See p. 260.) But the corporation in the modern sense of the word emerged as a major economic force only after the Civil War. By then, railroad magnates and other industrialists were realizing that many of the great ventures they envisioned could not be financed by any single person, no matter how wealthy, nor even by any single group of partners.

Under the laws of incorporation passed in many states in the 1830s and 1840s, business organizations could raise money by selling stock to members of the public; and in the decades after the Civil War, one industry after another adopted this practice of financing its undertakings. More important, perhaps, affluent Americans began to consider the purchase of stock to be a good investment even if they were not themselves involved in the business whose stock they were purchasing. The phenomenon of people investing in businesses with which they had no direct connection was almost entirely new. What made the practice appealing was that investors had only "limited liability"—that is, investors risked only the amount of their investments; they were not liable for any debts the corporation might accumulate beyond that point. Thus, it was now possible for entrepreneurs to gather vast sums of capital and undertake great projects.

The new type of corporation quickly spread beyond the railroad industry to other areas of the economy. In steel, the central figure was Andrew Carnegie, a Scottish immigrant who had worked his way up in the railroad industry. In 1873, he opened his own steelworks in Pittsburgh; and in the following decades, he expanded his company to a place of dominance in the industry. His methods were much like those of other rising industrial titans. From the railroads, he obtained rebates on his shipments so that he could cut his costs and hence his prices. He bought out rival concerns that could not meet his competition. He set up—in collaboration with his able associate Henry Clay Frick—a

Andrew Carnegie
Carnegie was one of a relatively small number of the great industrialists of the late nineteenth century who genuinely rose "from rags to riches." Born in Scotland, he came to the United States in 1848, at the age of thirteen, and soon found work as a messenger in a Pittsburgh telegraph office. His skill in learning to transcribe telegraphic messages (he became one of the first telegraphers in the country able to take messages by sound) brought him to the attention of a Pennsylvania Railroad official; and before he was twenty, he had begun his ascent to the highest ranks of industry. After the Civil War, he shifted his attention to the growing iron industry; in 1873 he invested all his assets in the development of the first American steel mills. Two decades later he was one of the wealthiest men in the world. In 1901 he abruptly resigned from the industrial world and spent the remaining years of his life as a philanthropist. By the time of his death in 1919, he had given away some $350 million. (Culver Pictures)

carefully integrated system that enabled him to control the processing of steel from mine to market. His company bought up coal mines and leased part of the Mesabi range, operated a fleet of ore ships on the Great Lakes, and acquired railroads. He financed his undertakings not only out of his own profits but out of the sale of stock. Then, in 1901, he sold out to the banker J. Pierpont Morgan, who merged the Carnegie interests with others to create the giant United States Steel Corporation—a $1.4 billion enterprise that controlled almost two-thirds of the nation's steel production.

A similar process, although usually on a more modest scale, was at work in other industries. Gustavus Swift developed a relatively small meat-packing company into a great national corporation, in part because of profits earned during the Civil War, in part because of his success in attracting investors in the years after the war. Isaac Singer had patented a sewing machine in 1851 and created—in I. M. Singer and Company—one of the first modern manufacturing corporations.

It was not simply the accumulation of capital that characterized the new organizations. It was also a new approach to management. Large, national business enterprises needed more systematic administrative structures than the limited, local ventures of the past. As a result, corporate leaders introduced a set of managerial techniques—the genesis of modern business administration—that relied on the division of responsibilities, a carefully designed hierarchy of control, modern cost-accounting procedures, and perhaps above all a new breed of business executive: the "middle manager," who formed a layer of command between workers and owners. Beginning in the railroad corporations, these new management techniques moved quickly into virtually every area of large-scale industry.

Efficient administrative capabilities helped make possible another major feature of the modern corporation: consolidation. Railroad companies attempting to create a national network of lines had quickly discovered that combination—the joining of small local enterprises into huge national organizations—enabled them to move more quickly and efficiently toward their goals. Other industries attempting to take advantage of the expanding national markets for manufactured goods did likewise, creating giant industrial organizations.

Businessmen created these huge organizations through two primary methods. The first was "horizontal integration"—the combining of a number of firms engaged in the same enterprise into a single corporation. The consolidation of many different railroad lines into one company was an example. The second method, which became prevalent in the 1890s, was "vertical integration"—the taking over of the businesses on which a company relied for its primary function. Carnegie Steel, which came to control not only steel mills, but mines, railroads, and other enterprises, was an example of vertical integration.

The most celebrated corporate empire of the late nineteenth century was Standard Oil. The greatest consolidationist of the time, John D. Rockefeller, pieced it together by using both methods. Beginning at the age of nineteen, when he became a partner in a Cleveland produce commission that earned great profits during the Civil War, Rockefeller displayed remarkable talents. Farsighted, acquisitive, and skilled at organization, he decided that his own economic future lay with the oil industry; and shortly after the Civil War, he launched a refining company in Cleveland (which he believed was destined to become a national center of the industry). From the beginning, he sought to eliminate his competition—especially the many small-scale companies that he believed were ruining the petroleum industry by introducing destabilizing competition. Allying himself with other wealthy capitalists, he proceeded methodically to buy out other refineries. In 1870, he formed the Standard Oil Company of Ohio, which in a few years had acquired twenty of the twenty-five refineries in Cleveland, as well as plants in Pittsburgh, Philadelphia, New York, and Baltimore.

So far, Rockefeller had expanded only horizontally. But soon he began expanding vertically as well. He built his own barrel factories and terminal warehouses and a network of pipelines that gave him control over most of the facilities for transporting petroleum. Standard Oil also owned its own freight cars and developed its own marketing organization, thus avoiding commissions to middlemen. By the 1880s, Rockefeller had established such dominance within the petroleum industry that to much of the nation he served as the leading symbol of monopoly.

Rockefeller and other industrialists saw consolidation as a way to cope with what many believed was the greatest curse of the modern economy: cutthroat competition. Businessmen insisted that they believed fervently in free enterprise and a competitive marketplace—but such beliefs often lasted only until they themselves were exposed to competition. Then they realized that the existence of too many competing firms in a single industry could spell instability and ruin for all, that a successful enterprise was one that could eliminate or absorb its competitors.

As the movement toward combination accelerated, new vehicles emerged to facilitate it. Again the railroads moved first. They began with so-called pool arrangements—informal agreements among various companies to stabilize rates and divide markets (arrangements that would, in later years, be known as cartels). But the pools ultimately proved unworkable, especially after the economic panic of the 1890s began to wreak havoc on the railroads and other corporations. If even a few firms in an industry were unwilling to cooperate (as was almost always the case), the pool arrangements could not survive.

The failure of the pools raised demands for new, more rigorous techniques of consolidation—resting less on cooperation than on centralized control. At first, the most successful such technique was the creation of the "trust"—pioneered by Standard Oil in the early 1880s. Over time, the word *trust* became in popular discourse a term for any great economic combination. But the trust was in fact a particular kind of organization, one that soon became a common vehicle for consolidating railroads and other industries as well. Under a trust agreement, stockholders in individual corporations transferred their stocks to a small group of trustees (in the case of the Standard Oil trust, to men chosen and dominated by Rockefeller) in exchange for shares in the trust itself. Owners of trust certificates often had no direct control over the decisions of the trustees; they simply received a share of the profits of the combination. Thus while John D. Rockefeller officially owned only a few refinery companies, he managed through the mechanism of the trust to extend his reach over a vast range of enterprises.

An even greater master of the trust was J. P. Morgan. In theory, Morgan was simply a bank president. In reality, he dominated scores of industrial organizations. Morgan's bank took control of one after another failing railroad line, reorganized it, and stabilized its operations. In the 1880s, he played a major role in saving the New York Central Railroad from collapse. Other railroads soon looked to Morgan (and such other banking firms as Kuhn Loeb and Company) for assistance. In the decades that followed, a similar system extended into other industries as well.

A third form of consolidation, closely related to the trust, began to emerge in the 1890s. In 1889, the state of New Jersey—followed later by many other states—changed its laws of incorporation to permit companies actually to buy up other companies. That made the cumbersome vehicle of the trust unnecessary and permitted actual mergers. Rockefeller quickly relocated Standard Oil in New Jersey and created there what became known as a "holding company"—a central corporate body that would formally buy up the stock of various members of the Standard Oil trust and establish direct, formal ownership of the corporations in the trust. Many other corporations followed suit.

Corporate organization in the late nineteenth century moved, therefore, through several stages on the way to establishing the modern system of business consolidation. It began with efforts to control competition and reduce instability by creating loose, informal pool arrangements, or *cartels*. It then moved to the more effective, but still awkward, *trust* arrangement. And then, in the 1890s, it took the final step of creating formal corporate structures controlling vast enterprises—*holding companies*. As a result, by the end of the nineteenth century 1 percent of the corporations in America were able to control more than 33 percent of the manufacturing. A congressional investigation disclosed in 1913 that Rockefeller and Morgan controlled between them companies valued at more than $22 billion. What was emerging, in other words, was a system of economic organization that lodged enormous power in the hands of a very few men—the great bankers of New York, industrial titans such as Rockefeller (who himself gained control of a major bank), and others.

Whether or not the ruthless concentration of economic power was the only way (or the best way) to promote industrial expansion became a major source of debate in America in the late nineteenth century and beyond. But it is clear that the industrial giants of the era were reponsible for substantial economic growth. They were integrating operations, cutting costs, creating a great industrial infrastructure, stimulating new markets. They were opening the way to large-scale mass production. Perhaps without realizing it, they were building the foundations of a great economic society. They were also creating the basis for some of the greatest public controversies of their era.

Capitalism and Its Critics

The rise of big business depended not only on technology, transportation, and organization, but on an ideology of growth and progress. Industrialists and financiers in the last decades of the nineteenth century developed a complex and wide-ranging rationale for their methods and power. And while this new set of ideas was in large part meant simply to justify what already existed, it also became a positive force, spurring others to greater efforts.

The new business philosophy was not without its critics. Farmers and workers were the most strident opponents, seeing in the growth of the great new corporate power centers a threat to their traditional notions of a republican society in which wealth and authority were widely distributed. The new economy, they argued, was eroding the opportunities for individuals to advance in society; it was stifling mobility. Middle-class critics pointed to the corruption that the new industrial titans seemed to produce, not only in their own enterprises but in local, state, and national politics as well. Even many businessmen were critical of the system and charged that the large corporations were not yet sufficiently modernized, that their methods were wasteful and inefficient.

The growing criticisms presented the captains of industry with a challenge. They not only had to build the new corporate economy. They had to legitimize it. They had to find a way to convince the public (and themselves) that the new structures they were creating were compatible with the ideology of individualism and equal opportunity that were so central to American life. Their efforts were never entirely successful. Critics continued to assail corporate power and to attract widespread popular support for their positions. But the philosophy of big business had a powerful impact nevertheless—not only among industrialists themselves, but among large groups of the American population.

The "Self-Made Man"

An important part of the emerging philosophy of capitalism rested squarely on the older ideology of individualism. The new industrial economy, its defenders argued, was not shrinking opportunities for individual advancement. It was expanding those opportunities. It was providing every individual with a chance to succeed and attain great wealth.

There was an element of truth in such claims, but only a small element. Before the Civil War there had been few millionaires in America; by 1892 there were more than 4,000 of them. Most of the new business tycoons had begun their careers from comfortable and privileged positions on the economic scale. But some—enough to invest the entire group with the aura of the American success story—had emerged from obscurity to riches. Andrew Carnegie had worked as a bobbin boy in a Pittsburgh cotton mill; James J. Hill had been a frontier clerk; John D. Rockefeller had started out as a clerk in a Cleveland commission house; and E. H. Harriman had begun as a broker's office boy. A few millionaires, in other words, were in fact what nearly all claimed to be: "self-made men."

And yet their rise to power and prominence was not always a result simply of hard work and ingenuity. It was also a result of ruthlessness and, at times, rampant corruption. Cornelius Vanderbilt expressed the attitude of many of his fellow tycoons with the belligerent question: "Can't I do what I want with my own?" So did his son William, in a much-quoted statement: "The public be damned." Once, when the elder Vanderbilt's lawyers warned him that a move he contemplated was illegal, he bellowed: "What do I care about the law? Hain't I got the power?" Not all tycoons were as openly contemptuous of the public and the laws as the Vanderbilts at times seemed to be. But many displayed a similar belief that their own activities were somehow exempt from normal restraints.

Industrialists showed little restraint, certainly, in their efforts to get what they wanted from the political system. They made large financial contributions to politicians and to political parties. They presented gifts of stock and cash to public officials in exchange for support. And more often than not, state and local governments responded to these tactics by doing the industrialists' bidding. Cynics said that Standard Oil did everything to the Ohio legislature except refine it. On one occasion a member of the Pennsylvania legislature was reported to have said: "Mr. Speaker, I move we adjourn unless the Pennsylvania Railroad has some more business for us to transact." During the notorious "Erie War" of 1868, in which Cornelius Vanderbilt did battle against Jay Gould and Jim Fisk for control of the Erie Railroad, both sides in the dispute offered lavish bribes to members of the New York State legislature to support measures favorable to their cause. The market price of legislators during the fight was $15,000 a head. One influential and enterprising leader collected $75,000 from Vanderbilt and $100,000 from Gould. The corruption was not all on one side. Politicians were not innocent victims. Many of them openly demanded bribes and in effect blackmailed businessmen.

"Modern Colossus of (Rail) Roads"
Cornelius Vanderbilt, known as the "Commodore," accumulated one of America's great fortunes by consolidating several large railroad companies under his control in the 1860s. His name became a synonym not only for enormous wealth, but also (in the eyes of many Americans) for excessive corporate power—as suggested in this cartoon, showing him standing astride his empire and manipulating its parts.   (Culver Pictures)

The average industrialist of the late nineteenth century was not, however, a Rockefeller or a Vanderbilt, but a more modest entrepreneur engaged in highly risky ventures in an unstable economy. For every successful millionaire, there were dozens of aspiring businessmen whose efforts failed in the face of overexpansion or vicious competition. Some industries fell under the control of a single firm or a small group of large firms. But far more industries remained fragmented, with many small companies struggling to carve out a stable position for themselves in an uncertain environment. The annals of

business did indeed include real stories of individuals rising from rags to riches. They also included stories of people moving from riches back to rags.

Survival of the Fittest

Most tycoons liked to claim that they had attained their wealth and power through hard work, acquisitiveness, and thrift—the traditional virtues of Protestant America. Those who succeeded, they argued, deserved their success. "God gave me my money," explained John D. Rockefeller, expressing the assumption that riches were a reward for worthiness. On the other hand, those who failed had earned their failure—through their own laziness, stupidity, or carelessness. "Let us remember," said a prominent Protestant minister, "that there is not a poor person in the United States who was not made poor by his own shortcomings."

Such assumptions became the basis of a social theory popularized by a number of leading intellectuals of the late nineteenth century: Social Darwinism, the application to human society of Charles Darwin's laws of evolution and natural selection among species. Just as only the fittest survived in the process of evolution, so in human society only the fittest individuals survived and flourished in the marketplace.

The English philosopher Herbert Spencer was the first and most important proponent of this theory. Struggle, Spencer argued, was a normal human activity, especially in economic life. The weak failed; the strong endured and became stronger. Society benefited from the elimination of the unfit and the survival of the strong and talented. In the end, the competitive process would lead to what Spencer called "the ultimate and inevitable development of the ideal man."

Spencer's books were very popular in America in the 1870s and 1880s. And his teachings found prominent supporters among American intellectuals, most notably William Graham Sumner of Yale, who promoted related ideas in a series of celebrated lectures, in magazine and journal articles, and finally in a famous 1906 book, *Folkways*. Sumner's philosophy did not always accord with Spencer's. But on one crucial point, he agreed fully with the ideas of Social Darwinism. Individuals, he argued, must have absolute freedom to struggle, to compete, to gratify their instinct for self-interest. The struggle for survival should be allowed to work itself out and should not be curbed by laws or the state.

The great financial titans themselves seized on the theories of Spencer and Sumner to justify their positions. "The growth of a large business is merely the survival of the fittest," Rockefeller proclaimed. "This is not an evil tendency in business. It is merely the working out of the law of nature and a law of God." Carnegie, who became the leading exponent of Social Darwinism among American industrialists, later described his reaction on first reading Spencer: "I remember that light came as in flood and all was clear."

Social Darwinism appealed to businessmen because it seemed to legitimize their success and confirm their virtues. It appealed to them because it placed their activities within the context of traditional American ideas of freedom and individualism. Above all, it appealed to them because it justified their tactics. Social Darwinists insisted that all attempts by labor to raise wages by forming unions and all endeavors by government to regulate economic activities would fail, because economic life was controlled by a natural law, the law of competition. And Social Darwinism coincided with another "law" that seemed to justify business practices and business dominance: the law of supply and demand as defined by Adam Smith and the classical economists. The economic system, they argued, was like a great and delicate machine functioning by natural and automatic rules, by the "invisible hand" of market forces. The greatest among these rules, the law of supply and demand, determined all economic values—prices, wages, rents, interest rates—at a level that was just to all concerned. Supply and demand worked because human beings were essentially economic creatures who understood and pursued their own interests, and because they operated in a free market where competition was open to all.

The ideas of Social Darwinism and classical economics provided an appealing ideology to justify business success and business tactics. It was not, however, an ideology that had very much to do with the realities of the corporate economy. At the same time that businessmen were celebrating the virtues of competition and the free market, they were making active efforts to protect themselves from competition and to replace the natural workings of the marketplace with control by great combinations. Vicious competitive battle—the thing that Spencer and Sumner celebrated and called a source of healthy progress—was in fact the very thing that American businessmen most feared and tried to eliminate.

Gospel of Wealth

Some businessmen attempted to temper the harsh philosophy of Social Darwinism with a more gentle, if in some ways equally self-serving idea: the "gospel of wealth." People of great wealth had not only great power but great responsibilities. It was their duty to use their riches to advance social progress. Carnegie himself elaborated on the idea in his 1901 book *The Gospel of Wealth.* People of wealth, he wrote, should consider all revenues in excess of their own needs as "trust funds" that they should administer for the good of the community; the person of wealth was "the mere trustee and agent for his poorer brethren." Carnegie did not believe in giving aid directly to the poor; he feared that such charity would encourage a sense of dependency. He preferred to contribute to institutions, notably libraries, that presumably would help the poor to help themselves. Carnegie was only one of many great industrialists who devoted large parts of their fortunes to philanthropic works.

The notion of private wealth as a public blessing existed alongside another popular concept: the notion of great wealth as something available to all. Russell H. Conwell, a Baptist minister, became the most prominent spokesman for the idea by delivering one lecture, "Acres of Diamonds," more than 6,000 times between 1880 and 1900. Conwell told a series of stories, which he claimed were true, of individuals who had found opportunities for extraordinary wealth in their own backyards. One such story involved a modest farmer who discovered a vast diamond mine in his own fields in the course of working his land. "I say to you," he told his audiences, "that you have 'acres of diamonds' beneath you right here . . . that the men and women sitting here have within their reach opportunities to get largely wealthy. . . . I say that you ought to get rich, and it is your duty to get rich." Most of the millionaires in the country, Conwell claimed (inaccurately), had begun on the lowest rung of the economic ladder and had worked their way to success. Every industrious individual had the chance to do likewise.

Perhaps the most famous promoter of the success story was Horatio Alger. Alger was originally a minister in a small town in Massachusetts but was driven from his pulpit as a result of a sexual scandal. He moved to New York, where he began writing his celebrated novels—more than 100 in all, which together sold more than 20 million copies. The titles varied: *Andy Grant's Pluck, Ragged Dick, Tom the Bootblack, Sink or Swim.* But the story and the message were invariably the same. A poor boy from a small town went to the big city to seek his fortune. By work, perseverance, and luck, he became rich.

Alternative Visions

Alongside the celebrations of competition, the justifications for great wealth, and the legitimation of the existing order stood a group of alternative philosophies, many of which openly challenged the premises of Social Darwinism and the gospel of wealth.

One such philosophy emerged from the work of Lester Frank Ward, author of a number of notable books, beginning with *Dynamic Sociology,* published in 1883. Ward was just as much a Darwinist as Sumner and Spencer, but he drew very different conclusions about the implications of Darwinism for human society. Civilization, he argued, was not governed by the abstract laws of natural selection. It was controlled by human intelligence, which was capable of shaping society as it wished. The chief goal of modern society, therefore, should not be unrestrained freedom of action for every individual. It should be the pursuit of the general good through cooperative action. The best instrument for the attainment of that goal was government. In contrast to Sumner, who believed that state intervention to remodel the environment was futile, Ward thought that an active government engaged in positive planning was society's best hope. Ward's ideas coincided with those of a growing number of American thinkers who believed that "survival of the fittest" was a ruthless and inefficient system for achieving social progress. He helped promote the idea that institutions should be "functional," that they should work actively to meet social needs, that human welfare should not be left to the impersonal workings of the capitalist economy. The people, through their government, could intervene in the economy and adjust it to serve their needs.

Other Americans skeptical of the laissez-faire ideas of the Social Darwinists adopted more drastic approaches to reform. Relatively few Americans embraced genuinely radical challenges to the existing order; but some dissenters did raise fundamental questions about the viability of capitalism. Some of these dissenters found a home in the Socialist Labor party, founded in the 1870s and led for many years by Daniel De Leon, an immigrant from the West Indies. Other party leaders were recent immigrants from eastern Europe. Although De Leon attracted a modest following in the industrial cities, the party

never succeeded in polling more than 82,000 votes. De Leon's theoretical and dogmatic approach appealed to intellectuals more than to workers, and a dissident faction of his party, eager to forge ties with organized labor, broke away and in 1901 formed the more enduring American Socialist party.

Other radicals gained a wider following. One of the most influential was Henry George. His angrily eloquent *Progress and Poverty,* published in 1879, was an immediate success; reprinted in successive editions, it became one of the ten best-selling nonfiction works in American publishing history. George tried to explain why poverty existed amidst the wealth created by modern industry. "This association of poverty with progress is the great enigma of our times," he wrote. "So long as all the increased wealth which modern progress brings goes but to build up great fortunes, to increase luxury and make sharper the contrast between the House of Have and the House of Want, progress is not real and cannot be permanent."

George blamed these social problems on the ability of a few monopolists to grow wealthy as a result of rising land values. An increase in the value of land, he claimed, was a result not of any effort by the owner, but of the growth of society around the land. This "unearned increment," this increase in the value of land resulting from increased demand rather than active improvement of the property by the owner, was rightfully the property of the community. And so George proposed a "single tax," to replace all other taxes, which would return the increment to the people. The tax, he argued, would destroy monopolies, distribute wealth more equally, and eliminate poverty. Single-tax societies sprang up in many cities; and in 1886, George, with the support of labor and the socialists, narrowly missed being elected mayor of New York.

Rivaling George in popularity was Edward Bellamy, whose utopian novel *Looking Backward,* published in 1888, sold more than 1 million copies. It described the experiences of a young Bostonian who in 1887 went into a hypnotic sleep from which he awakened in the year 2000. He emerged from his trance to find a new social order, based on universal membership in a workers' army, where want, politics, and vice were unknown, and where everyone was happy and fulfilled. The new society had emerged from a peaceful, evolutionary process. The large trusts of the late nineteenth century had continued to grow in size and to combine with one another until ultimately they formed a single, great trust, con-

The Hatch Family, 1871
This family portrait by Eastman Johnson was commissioned by Alfrederick Smith Hatch, a prominent Wall Street broker. The family is shown gathered in the regal library of their home on Park Avenue. The painting includes portraits of Hatch himself (seated at right), his wife (leaning against the mantle), the couple's ten children, Hatch's father, and Mrs. Hatch's mother. The relatively informal poses of many family members may reflect the influence of group photographs, which were becoming common in the 1870s. (Metropolitan Museum of Art)

trolled by the government, which absorbed all the businesses of all the citizens and distributed the abundance of the industrial economy equally among all the people. All aspects of life were organized with military efficiency. Society had become a great machine, "so logical in its principles and direct and simple in its workings" that it almost ran itself. "Fraternal cooperation" had replaced competition. Class divisions had disappeared. He labeled the philosophy motivating this vision "nationalism." *Looking Backward* had a remarkable impact. It inspired the formation of more than 160 Nationalist Clubs to propagate Bellamy's ideas. Bellamy himself devoted the remainder of his life to championing his brand of socialism.

The Problems of Monopoly

Relatively few Americans shared the views of those who questioned the entire structure of modern cap-

italism. But a growing number of people were by the end of the century becoming deeply concerned about a particular, glaring aspect of capitalism: the growth of monopoly.

From the beginning, large segments of the population had looked on the proliferation of business combinations with mistrust and hostility. The popular description of such men as Rockefeller, Carnegie, and Morgan as "robber barons" suggests the attitude of much of the public. So do the reports of the numerous conferences, commissions, and study groups that pointed with alarm to the effects of consolidation on the marketplace. The United States Industrial Commission reported in 1902 that "in most cases the combination has exerted an appreciable power over prices, and in practically all cases it has increased the margin between raw materials and finished products." Combinations were, in other words, the cause of artificially inflated prices; the influence of the free market was being restricted by the monopolistic practices of a few men. By the end of the century, a wide range of groups had begun to assail monopoly and economic concentration. Laborers, farmers, consumers, small manufacturers, conservative bankers and financiers, advocates of radical change—all joined the attack.

Defenders and opponents of combination alike looked with alarm at another problem of the modern economy: its disturbing pattern of instability. Although industrial output and agricultural production were expanding rapidly, other areas of the economy could not always keep pace. The nation's banks and financial institutions were neither strong enough nor efficient enough to meet adequately the new demands for their services. The increasingly important stock market was riddled with corruption. Above all, the market for goods was not growing as rapidly as the supply.

The result was one of the most troubling and distinctive features of modern industrial economy: a cycle of booms and busts that plagued American life throughout the late nineteenth and early twentieth centuries. Beginning in 1873, the economy fluctuated erratically, with severe recessions creating havoc every five or six years, each recession worse than the previous one, until finally, in 1893, the system seemed on the verge of total collapse.

One reason for the economic instability was that the new industries were not passing on enough of their profits to their workers to create an adequate market for the goods they were producing. This growing disparity in the distribution of wealth was producing not only an imbalance between supply and demand but a deep popular resentment. The standard of living may have been rising for virtually everyone, but the gap between rich and poor was visibly widening into an enormous chasm.

According to one estimate early in the century, 1 percent of the families in America controlled nearly 88 percent of the nation's assets. A small but conspicuous new class had emerged whose wealth almost defied description, whose fortunes were so vast that great feats of imagination were often required to enable them to be spent. Andrew Carnegie earned $23 million from his steel company in 1900 alone, and that was only part of his income (in an era in which there was as yet no income tax). John D. Rockefeller's personal wealth was estimated at one time to exceed $1 billion.

Some of the wealthy—Carnegie, for example— lived relatively modestly and donated large sums to philanthropic causes. Others, however, lived in a conspicuous luxury that earned the resentment of much of the nation. Like a clan of feudal barons, the Vanderbilts maintained, in addition to many country estates, seven garish mansions on seven blocks of New York City's Fifth Avenue. Other wealthy New Yorkers lavished vast sums on parties. The most notorious, a ball on which Mrs. Bradley Martin spent $368,000, created such a furor that she and her husband fled to England to escape public abuse.

Observing these flagrant displays of wealth were the four-fifths of the American people who lived modestly, and at least 10 million people who lived below the commonly accepted poverty line. To those in difficult economic circumstances, the sense of relative deprivation could be as frustrating and embittering as the poverty itself.

The Ordeal of the Worker

For the American worker, the experience of industrialization after the Civil War was similar in many ways to the experience before it. It was a mixed blessing. On the one hand, the average standard of living for laborers—in quantitative terms at least— rose significantly during the last decades of the nineteenth century. On the other hand, workers continued to suffer from the wide disparities in distribution of the nation's new wealth; from working conditions that were often arduous and unsafe; and from the intangible problems of adjusting to the impersonal character of work in the factory. Yet for workers, the late nineteenth century was also different from any previous era, if for no other reason than that their numbers were now much larger and the dimensions of both the promise and the problems of industrialization far greater.

The Immigrant Work Force

The dramatic expansion in the industrial work force, which was both a cause and a result of economic growth, arose out of a massive migration into industrial cities—immigration of two sorts. The first was the continuing flow of rural Americans into factory towns and cities—people disillusioned with or bankrupted by life on the farm and eager for new economic and social opportunities. The second was the great wave of immigration from abroad (primarily from Europe, but also from Asia, Canada, and other areas) in the decades following the Civil War—an influx that all but overshadowed the previous periods of immigration. The 25 million immigrants who arrived in the United States between 1865 and 1915 were more than four times the number who had arrived in the fifty years before. The greatest wave of new arrivals came after 1890; by the end of the first decade of the new century, immigrants were debarking in America at the rate of more than 1 million each year.

In the 1870s and 1880s, most of the immigrants came from the nation's traditional sources: England, Ireland, and northern Europe. Skilled artisans continued to emigrate from Great Britain to take advantage of the expanding opportunities in America. Economic troubles in European industry in the 1880s induced factory workers from Sweden, Germany, and England to move to the United States. And the declining agricultural economy of northern Europe (and of Ireland, in particular) pressured still others to journey to America. By the end of the century, however, the major sources of immigrants had shifted, with large numbers of southern and eastern Europeans (Italians, Poles, Russians, Greeks, Slavs, and others) pouring into the country and into the industrial work force.

The new immigrants were coming to America in part to escape the poverty and oppression of their homelands. But they were coming as well because they felt the pull of the United States—a pull based in part on realistic expectations of the opportunities available, and in part on distorted and artificial promises. Railroads, in order to dispose of their Western landholdings, painted an alluring picture of America in advertisements overseas. Industrial employers actively recruited workers under the Labor Contract Law, which—until its repeal in 1885—permitted them to pay for the passage of workers in advance and deduct the amount later from their wages. Even after the repeal of the law, employers continued to encourage the immigration of unskilled laborers, often with the assistance of foreign-born labor brokers, such as the Greek and Italian *padrones* who recruited work gangs of their fellow nationals.

The arrival of these new ethnic groups became a complicating factor in the already complicated dynamics of the working class. In addition to the traditional concerns about wages, working conditions,

The Statue of Liberty in Paris
The head of the Statue of Liberty sits in a Paris courtyard in 1883, awaiting shipment to the United States. The idea for the statue originated with the French politician Edouard Laboulaye, who proposed it in 1875 to commemorate the French and American revolutions. Frederic Bartholdi designed the 152-foot-high sculpture (originally known as "Liberty Enlightening the World"). It was presented as a gift to the United States in 1884 and dedicated in 1886. The millions of immigrants who entered the country through New York harbor in the late nineteenth and early twentieth centuries saw the statue as a symbolic promise of economic and political liberty.
(Library of Congress)

and the declining need for skilled artisans in the face of modern technology, there were now also serious ethnic tensions. Americans of old stock, as well as ethnics who had arrived a decade or so before, often looked on the new immigrants with fear and hostility. Industries that had traditionally been dominated by one national group now began to replace them with members of others—who could be hired at lower wages than the earlier workers. Poles, Greeks, and French Canadians began to displace the British and Irish workers in the textile factories of New En-

Occupational Distribution, 1880 and 1920

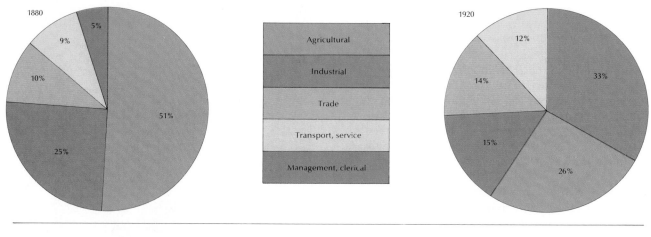

gland. Italians, Slavs, and Poles began to emerge as a major source of labor for the mining industry, which had traditionally been the province of native workers or northern European immigrants. Within industries, moreover, workers tended to cluster in particular occupations (and thus, often, at particular income levels) by ethnic group. In industry, at least, the idea of the "melting pot"—of Americans of different ethnic backgrounds melding together into one common culture—was of limited applicability.

Wages and Working Conditions

The average standard of living for workers may have been rising in the years after the Civil War; but for many laborers, the return for their labor remained pitifully small. It appeared even smaller in relation to the vast fortunes the industrial titans were accumulating—even in comparison with the rising incomes of the middle class. At the turn of the century, the average income of the American worker was $400–$500 a year—below the $600 figure that many believed was the minimum required to maintain a reasonable level of comfort. Nor did most workers enjoy any real job security. The boom-and-bust cycle of the economy made laborers in all industries vulnerable; and in some areas, workers were particularly susceptible to losing their jobs because of technological advances or because of the cyclical or seasonal nature of their work. Even those who were spared unemployment could find their wages suddenly and substantially cut in hard times. Few work-

ers, in other words, were ever very far from the prospect of poverty.

But American laborers faced a wide array of other hardships as well. There was, first, the difficult adjustment to the nature of modern industrial labor: the performance of routine, repetitive tasks, often requiring little skill, on a strict and monotonous schedule. In 1900, most workers labored at least ten hours a day (twelve hours a day in the steel industry), six days a week. To rural men and women, accustomed to flexible, seasonal work patterns, the new routine could be harsh and disorienting. To skilled artisans whose once-valued tasks were now performed by machines, the new system was impersonal and demeaning. Factory workers were employed, moreover, in plants free from effective government regulation or inspection. The result was workplaces that were often appallingly unsafe or unhealthy. Industrial accidents were frequent and severe. Compensation to the victims, either from their employers or from the government, was limited.

Women and Children at Work

The reduction of skilled work in factories induced many employers to increase greatly the use of women and children, whom they could hire for lower wages than adult males. By 1900, 20 percent of all manufacturing workers were women; and 20 percent of all women (well over 5 million) were wage earners. Women worked in all areas of industry, even in some of the most arduous jobs—for example, as machinists, railroad workers, and stokers. Most women, however, worked in a few industries where unskilled and semiskilled machine labor (as opposed to heavy manual labor) prevailed. The textile industry remained the largest single industrial employer of women. (Domestic service remained the most common female occupation overall.)

Women worked for wages as low as $6 to $8 a week, well below the minimum necessary for survival (and well below the wages paid to men working the same jobs). Advocates of a minimum wage law for women created a sensation when they brought several women to a hearing in Chicago to testify that low wages and desperate poverty had driven them to prostitution. (It was not, however, sensational enough for the Illinois legislature, which promptly defeated the bill.)

Child labor, which had always existed in the United States, had by 1900 become a national scandal. At least 1.7 million children under sixteen years of age were employed in factories and fields, more than twice the number so employed thirty years before; 10 percent of all girls aged ten to fifteen, and 20 percent of all boys, held jobs. Under the pressure of outraged public opinion, thirty-eight state legislatures passed child labor laws in the late nineteenth century; but these laws were painfully insufficient. Sixty percent of child workers were employed in agriculture, which was typically exempt from the laws; and such children often worked twelve-hour days picking or hoeing in the fields. The laws were hardly more effective for children employed in factories; they set a minimum age of twelve years and a maximum workday of ten hours, but employers often ignored even these minimal standards. In the cotton mills of the South, children working at the looms all night were kept awake by having cold water thrown in their faces. In canneries, little girls cut fruits and vegetables sixteen hours a day. Exhausted children were particularly susceptible to injury while working at dangerous machines, and they were maimed and even killed in industrial accidents at an alarming rate.

Yet as much as the appalling conditions of many woman and child workers troubled the national conscience, conditions for men were at least equally dangerous. In mills and mines, and on the railroads, the American accident rate was higher than that of any industrial nation in the world. As late as 1907, an average of twelve railroad men a week died on the job. In factories, thousands of workers faced such occupational diseases as lead or phosphorus poisoning, against which few employers took precautions.

Emerging Unionization

Labor attempted to fight back against such conditions by adopting some of the same tactics their employers had used so effectively: creating large combinations. In the last three decades of the nineteenth century, American workers engaged in a series of escalating struggles to form and win recognition for labor unions. By the end of the century, however, their efforts had met with little success.

There had been craft unions in America, representing small groups of skilled workers, for many years; and their number increased significantly during and after the Civil War. Alone, however, the unions could not hope to exert significant power in the economy; and in the 1860s some labor leaders began to search for ways to combine the energies of labor organizations. The first attempt to federate separate unions into a single national organization came in 1866, when William H. Sylvis founded the National Labor Union—a polyglot association, claiming 640,000 members, that included a variety of reform groups having little direct relationship with labor. After the Panic of 1873 the National Labor Union disintegrated and disappeared.

The individual unions experienced stormy times in other ways during the hard years of the 1870s. With their bargaining power weakened by depression conditions, they faced antagonistic employers eager to destroy them and a hostile public unsympathetic to their demand for job security. When labor disputes with employers turned bitter and violent, as they occasionally did, the public instinctively blamed the workers (or the "radicals" and "anarchists" they believed were influencing the workers) for the trouble, rarely the employers. Particularly alarming to middle-class Americans was the emergence of the "Molly Maguires" in the anthracite coal region of Pennsylvania. The Mollies operated within the Ancient Order of Hibernians (an Irish fraternal society) and occasionally used terrorist tactics. They attempted to intimidate the coal operators through violence and occasionally murder; and they added to the growing perception that labor activism was motivated by dangerous radicals. Much of the violence attributed to the Molly Maguires, however, was deliberately instigated by informers and agents employed by the mine owners, who wanted a pretext for ruthless measures suppressing unionization.

But excitement over the Molly Maguires was nothing compared to the near hysteria that gripped the country during the railroad strike of 1877. The

Child Labor and Child Luxury

Many working-class children of the early twentieth century found employment as "breaker boys," picking pieces of slate out of piles of coal at Pennsylvania mines. The coal dust was often so thick that they could hardly see one another, as the Lewis Hine photograph at left suggests. The children of wealthy industrialists would have found such lives almost unimaginable. Below, the children of American railroad executive George Jay Gould (son of Jay Gould) ride through a Paris park in "voiturettes," miniature automobiles manufactured in France.   (Left, International Museum of Photography/George Eastman House; below, Culver Pictures)

trouble started when the principal Eastern railroads announced a 10 percent slash in wages. Immediately, railroad workers, whether organized or not, went out on strike. Rail service was disrupted from Baltimore to St. Louis, equipment was destroyed, and rioting mobs roamed the streets of Pittsburgh and other cities. As the strike continued, it began to take on many of the features of an open class war. State militias were called out against the strikers; and finally, in July, the president agreed to a request by the governor of West Virginia and ordered federal troops to suppress the disorders there. Clashes between workers and soldiers were frequent and often vicious. In Baltimore, eleven demonstrators died and forty were wounded in a conflict between workers and militiamen. In Philadelphia, state militia opened fire on thousands of workers and their families attempting to block the railroad crossings; twenty died. Similar (if less bloody) encounters occurred throughout the industrial United States (including a general strike in St. Louis). In all, over 100 people died before the strike finally collapsed several weeks after it had begun.

The great railroad strike was America's first major labor conflict and a vivid illustration of a new reality in the American economic system. With business becoming national in its scope, disputes between labor and capital could no longer be localized but could affect the entire nation. It was an illustration as well of the depth of resentment among many American workers and of the lengths to which they were prepared to go to express that resentment. And it was, finally, an indication of the serious weaknesses afflicting the labor movement, which still lacked an institutional base adequate to sustain its efforts. The failure of the strike seriously weakened the railroad unions and damaged the reputation of labor organizations in other industries as well.

The Knights of Labor

The first major effort to create a genuinely national labor organization was the founding in 1869 of the Noble Order of the Knights of Labor, under the leadership of Uriah S. Stephens. Instead of attempting to create a federation of preexisting unions, as the National Labor Union had done, the Knights recruited individual members directly from the working class. Membership was open to all who "toiled," and the definition of a toiler was extremely broad: The only excluded groups were lawyers, bankers, liquor dealers, and professional gamblers. The Knights' definition of producer included all workers, most business

and professional people, and virtually all women—whether they worked in factories, as domestic servants, or in their own homes. Members met in local "assemblies"; an assembly might consist of the workers in a particular trade or a local union, or simply all the members of the Knights in a particular city or district. Presiding laxly over the entire order was an agency known as the general assembly.

Much of the program of the Knights was as vague as the organization. Although they championed an eight-hour day and the abolition of child labor, the leaders were more interested in long-range reform of the economy than in the immediate objectives of wages and hours that appealed to the trade unions. Indeed, leaders of the Knights hoped to replace the "wage system" with a new "cooperative system," in which workers would themselves control a large part of the economy.

For several years, the Knights remained a secret fraternal organization and engaged in no public activities. But in the 1870s, it moved out into the open. Under the leadership of Terence V. Powderly, who was elected "grand master workman" in 1879, the order entered a spectacular period of expansion. By 1886, it claimed a total membership of over 700,000. Important factors contributing to the increase in numerical strength were a business recession in 1884 that threw many workers out of jobs and a renewal of industrial strife that induced unorganized laborers as well as some trade unions to affiliate with the Knights. Not only did the membership grow, but the order now included many militant elements that the moderate leadership could not always control. Against Powderly's wishes, local unions or assemblies associated with the Knights launched a series of strikes. In 1885, striking railway workers forced the Missouri Pacific, a link in the Gould system, to restore wage cuts and recognize their union. But the victory was a temporary one. In the following year, a strike on another Gould road, the Texas and Pacific, was crushed, and the power of the unions in the Gould system was broken. By 1890, the membership of the Knights had shrunk to 100,000. A few years later, the organization disappeared altogether.

The AFL

Even before the Knights had entered their period of decline, a rival organization based on a very different organizational concept had appeared. In 1881, representatives of a number of craft unions formed the Federation of Organized Trade and Labor Unions of the United States and Canada. Five years later, this

Samuel Gompers

Gompers migrated to the United States from England as a boy and began work at the age of thirteen as a cigar maker, rising to become head of his local union. When the American Federation of Labor was organized in 1886, Gompers became its first president, a position he held (with only a single, one-year interruption) until 1924. Gompers helped the AFL to become the premier labor organization in the United States; he also helped commit the organization to a narrow, craft-oriented view of unionism that excluded an increasing proportion of workers as mass-production industries rose to prominence. He is shown here during a union-organizing drive in West Virginia. (George Meany Memorial Archives)

body took the name it has borne ever since, the American Federation of Labor (AFL). Under the direction of its president and guiding spirit, Samuel Gompers, the Federation soon became the most important labor group in the country. As its name implies, it was a federation or association of national trade unions, each of which enjoyed essential autonomy within the larger organization. Rejecting the Knights' idea of one big union for everybody, the

Federation was built on the principle of the organization of skilled workers into craft unions. Unlike the Knights, the AFL was generally hostile to organizing unskilled workers, who did not fit within the structure of the craft unions. The AFL also resisted organizing women (many of whom, of course, were unskilled workers, but some of whom worked in AFL-represented crafts); the Knights, in their openness to all, had included substantial numbers of woman members.

The program of the Federation differed as markedly from that of the Knights as did its organizational arrangements. Gompers and his associates accepted the basic premises of capitalism; their purpose was simply to secure for labor a greater share of capitalism's material rewards. Repudiating all notions of fundamental alteration of the existing system or long-range reform measures or a separate labor party, the AFL concentrated on labor's immediate objectives: wages, hours, and working conditions. While it hoped to attain its ends by collective bargaining, the Federation was ready to employ the strike if necessary.

As one of its first objectives, the Federation called for a national eight-hour day—a goal that remained central (and elusive) to the labor movement for more than four decades. The AFL set May 1, 1886, as the date by which the goal was to be achieved, and it decided to stage a general strike to achieve it if necessary. On the target day, strikes and demonstrations for a shorter workday took place all over the country. Although the national officers of the Knights of Labor had refused to cooperate in the movement, some local units joined in the demonstrations. So did a few unions that were dominated by European radicals who wanted to destroy "class government" by terroristic methods. The most sensational demonstrations occurred in Chicago, which was a labor stronghold and a center of radicalism.

A strike was already in progress in Chicago at the time, at the McCormick Harvester Company; and when the police harassed the strikers, labor and radical leaders called a protest meeting at the Haymarket Square. During the meeting, the police appeared and commanded those present to disperse. Someone—the person's identity was never determined—threw a bomb that resulted in the death of seven policemen and injury to sixty-seven others. The police, who on the previous day had killed four strikers, fired into the crowd and killed four more people. News of the Haymarket affair struck fear into Chicago and the business community of the nation. Blinded by hysteria, conservative, property-conscious Americans demanded a victim or victims—to demonstrate to labor that it must cease its course of violence. Chicago officials finally rounded up eight anarchists and charged them with the murder of the policemen, on the grounds that they had incited the individual who hurled the bomb. In one of the most injudicious trials in American history, all were found guilty. One was sentenced to prison and seven to death. Of the seven, one cheated his sentence by committing suicide, four were executed, and two had their sentences commuted to life imprisonment.

Neither the AFL nor the Knights of Labor had anything to do with the Haymarket bombing or even with the conflicts leading up to it. Yet both organizations found themselves saddled with much of the blame for the episode. The Knights, in particular, never recovered from the widespread vilification they encountered in the aftermath of the bombing. To most middle-class Americans, however, the significance of Haymarket was larger than the guilt or innocence of particular labor organizations. It was a sign, they believed, of how widespread the chaos of their society had become, a sign of the proliferation of radicalism. "Anarchism," most of whose adherents were relatively peaceful visionaries dreaming of a new social order, became in the public mind a code word for terrorism and violence. For the next thirty years, the specter of anarchism remained one of the most frightening concepts in the American imagination.

The Homestead Strike

Some of the most violent strikes in American labor history occurred in the economically troubled 1890s. Two of the strikes, the one at the Homestead plant of the Carnegie Steel Company in Pennsylvania and the one against the Pullman Palace Car Company in the Chicago area, took place in companies controlled by men who prided themselves on being among the most advanced of American employers: Andrew Carnegie, who had written magazine articles defending the rights of labor, and George M. Pullman, who had built a "model town" to house his employees.

The Amalgamated Association of Iron and Steel Workers, which was affiliated with the American Federation of Labor, was the most powerful trade union in the country. Its members were skilled workers, in great demand by employers and thus able to exercise significant power in the workplace. Employers sometimes called these skilled workers "little shopfloor autocrats," and in some plants the workers had won substantial control over the conditions under which they labored. The union had a rulebook with 56 pages of what it called "legislation," designed to limit the power of employers.

In the mid-1880s, however, the steel industry was changing in ways that threatened the power of the union. Demand for skilled workers was in decline as new production methods and new, large-scale corporate organizations streamlined the steelmaking process. The union was unable to establish a foothold in most of the Carnegie plants, which were coming to dominate the industry. In only one of the three major steel mills in the Carnegie system—the Homestead plant near Pittsburgh—was the union a force. By 1890, Carnegie and his chief lieutenant, Henry Clay Frick, had decided that the Amalgamated "had to go," even at Homestead. Over the next two years, they worked to undermine the union by announcing a series of wage cuts at Homestead. At first, the union acquiesced, aware that it was not strong enough to wage a successful strike. But in 1892, the company refused even to discuss its decisions with the Amalgamated, in effect denying the union's right to exert any influence at all on corporate policy. Carnegie was in Scotland, and the direction of the company was in the hands of Frick, who was determined to break the union once and for all.

Trouble began when management announced a new wage scale that would have meant pay cuts for a small minority of the workers. Frick gave the union two days to accept the proposal; and when the union refused and called instead for a strike, he abruptly shut down the plant and asked the Pinkerton Detective Agency to furnish 300 guards to enable the company to resume operations on its own terms—by hiring nonunion workers. (The Pinkerton Agency was in reality a strikebreaking concern.)

The hated Pinkertons, whose mere presence was often enough to incite workers to violence, approached the plant on barges in an adjacent river. Warned of their coming, the strikers met them at the docks with guns and dynamite, and a pitched battle broke out on July 6, 1892. After several hours of fighting, which brought death to three guards and ten strikers and severe injuries to many participants on both sides, the Pinkertons surrendered and were escorted roughly out of town. The company and local law officials then asked for militia protection. The Pennsylvania governor responded by sending the state's entire National Guard contingent, some 8,000 troops, to Homestead. Public opinion, at first sympathetic to the strikers, turned against them when a radical made an attempt to assassinate Frick. Production resumed, with strikebreakers now protected by troops. Slowly workers drifted back to their jobs; and finally—four months after the strike began—the

Breaking the Homestead Strike, 1892
State militiamen enter Homestead, Pennsylvania, to put an end to the Amalgamated union's violent strike by opening the Carnegie-owned steel plant to strikebreaking workers. This double photograph forms a "stereograph," which when viewed through a special lens (a "stereoscope") gave the impression of a three-dimensional scene. Stereographs were a new and popular entertainment in the 1890s; and this one suggests how quickly the Homestead Strike became a part of national folklore.   (Carnegie Library of Pittsburgh)

Amalgamated surrendered. Carnegie, hearing the news in Europe, sent a wire to Frick: "Life is worth living again."

The story of the Amalgamated in the aftermath of the Homestead strike was a dismal one. By 1900, every major steel plant in the Northeast had broken with the union, which now had virtually no power to resist. Its membership shrank from a high of 24,000 in 1891 (two-thirds of all eligible steelworkers) to fewer than 7,000 a decade later.

The Pullman Strike

A dispute of greater magnitude and equal bitterness, although involving less loss of life, was the Pullman strike in 1894. The Pullman Palace Car Company constructed sleeping and parlor cars, which it leased to most of the nation's railroads. It manufactured and repaired the cars at a plant near Chicago. There the company had built the 600-acre town of Pullman and rented dwellings to the employees. George M. Pullman, inventor of the sleeping car and owner of the

company, liked to exhibit his town as a model solution of the industrial problem and to refer to the workers as his "children."

Nearly all of the workers were members of a militant labor organization, the American Railway Union, recently organized by Eugene V. Debs. Debs had once been active in the Railroad Brotherhoods, an older railworkers' union affiliated with the AFL. But he had become impatient with the union's lack of interest in the lot of unskilled workers and had formed his own union, which soon attained a membership of 150,000, mainly in the Middle West.

The strike at Pullman began during the winter of 1893–1894, when the company slashed wages by an average of 25 percent. The company explained its action by citing its own lost revenues in the depression; but the cuts were more drastic than the workers could accept. Several of them who served on a committee to protest the cuts were discharged. At the same time, Pullman refused to reduce rents in its model town, even though the charges there were 20 to 25 percent higher than for comparable accommodations in surrounding areas. The strikers appealed to the Railway

SIGNIFICANT EVENTS

1851 I.M. Singer and Company, one of first modern corporations, founded (p. 519)

1859 First oil well drilled in Pennsylvania (p. 515)

1866 William H. Sylvis founds National Labor Union (p. 529)

First transatlantic cable laid (p. 514)

1868 Open-hearth steelmaking begins in America (p. 514)

1869 Knights of Labor founded (p. 531)

1870 John D. Rockefeller founds Standard Oil (p. 519)

1873 Carnegie Steel founded (p. 518)

Commercial and financial panic disrupts economy (p. 526)

1876 Alexander Graham Bell invents telephone (p. 514)

1877 Railroad workers strike nationwide (p. 531)

1879 Thomas A. Edison invents electric light bulb (p. 514)

Henry George publishes *Progress and Poverty* (p. 524)

1881 American Federation of Labor founded (p. 531)

1882 Rockefeller creates first trust (p. 520)

1886 Haymarket bombing blamed on anarchists (p. 532)

1888 Edward Bellamy publishes *Looking Backward* (p. 524)

1892 Workers strike Homestead plant (p. 533)

1893 Depression begins (p. 526)

1894 Workers strike Pullman Company (p. 534)

1901 J. P. Morgan creates United States Steel Corporation (p. 519)

American Socialist party founded (p. 524)

1903 Women's Trade Union League founded (p. 536)

Wright brothers make first successful flight at Kitty Hawk, North Carolina (p. 515)

1906 Henry Ford produces his first automobiles (p. 515)

William Graham Sumner publishes *Folkways* (p. 522)

1914 Ford introduces assembly line in his factories (p. 516)

Union for support, and that organization voted to refuse to handle Pullman cars and equipment.

The General Managers' Association, representing twenty-four Chicago railroads, prepared to fight the boycott. Switchmen who refused to handle Pullman cars were discharged. Whenever this happened, the union instructed its members to quit work. Within a few days thousands of railroad workers in twenty-seven states and territories were on strike, and transportation from Chicago to the Pacific coast was paralyzed.

Ordinarily, state governors responded readily to appeals from strike-threatened business; but the governor of Illinois, John P. Altgeld, was different—a man with demonstrated sympathies for workers and their grievances. Altgeld had criticized the trials of the Haymarket anarchists as unfair and irregular, and he had pardoned the convicted men who were still in prison when he took office. He had made it clear he would not call out the militia to protect employers now. Bypassing Altgeld, the railroad operators asked the federal government to send regular army troops to Illinois. At the same time, federal postal officials and marshals were bombarding Washington with

complaints that the strike was preventing the movement of mail on the trains. President Grover Cleveland, a man with a punctilious regard for the letter of the law, responded favorably to such requests. His attorney general, Richard Olney, a former railroad lawyer and a bitter foe of labor, was even more eager to accommodate the employers. Cleveland and Olney decided that the government could employ the army to keep the mails moving; and in July 1894, the president, over Altgeld's objections, ordered 2,000 troops to the Chicago area.

At Olney's suggestion, government lawyers obtained from a federal court an order restraining Debs and other union officials from interfering with the interstate transportation of the mails. This "blanket injunction" was so broad that it practically forbade Debs and his associates to continue the strike. They ignored the injunction and were arrested, tried for contempt of court (without a jury), and sentenced to six months in prison. With federal troops protecting the hiring of new workers and with the union leaders in a federal jail, the strike quickly collapsed.

It left a bitter heritage. It convinced many laborers that the government was not a neutral arbiter representing the common interest but a supporter of one side alone. Debs emerged from prison a martyr in the eyes of workers, a convert to Marxian socialism, and a dedicated enemy of capital.

Sources of Labor Weakness

The last decades of the nineteenth century were years in which labor, despite its organizing efforts, made few real gains. Industrial wages rose, but not enough to keep up with the rising cost of living. Labor leaders won a few legislative victories—the abolition by Congress in 1885 of the Contract Labor Law; the establishment by Congress in 1868 of an eight-hour day on public works projects and in 1892 of the same workday for government employees; and a host of state laws governing hours of labor and safety standards. But most such laws were not enforced. Labor organizations emerged and staged strikes and protests, but the end of the century found most workers with less political power and less control of the workplace than they had had forty years before. Historians have explained this failure in numerous ways.

One explanation stresses the nature of the labor unions themselves, which never succeeded in organizing more than a small percentage of the industrial work force. Only about 4 percent of all American workers (fewer than 1 million) were union members in 1900. What members there were came largely from a few sectors of the economy where skilled labor remained important. The great mass of unskilled laborers, who were emerging as the core of the industrial work force, were not represented by any union. The AFL, the most important labor organization in the country, was particularly weak. It excluded many potential members—women, blacks, recent immigrants, and others—who might have contributed to its strength. Women responded in 1903 by forming their own organization, the Women's Trade Union League, but the WTUL agitated primarily for legislation to protect woman workers, not for the general organization and mobilization of labor. Divisions within the work force contributed to this weakness. Tensions among different ethnic and racial groups kept laborers divided and frustrated many efforts to mobilize against employers.

A second source of labor weakness was the shifting nature of the work force. Many immigrant workers came to America intending to remain only briefly, to earn some money and return home. Although some of these workers ultimately did stay in the United States permanently, the assumption that they had no long-range future in the country eroded their willingness to organize. Other workers—natives and immigrants alike—were in constant motion, moving from one job to another, one town to another, seldom in one place long enough to establish any sort of stake or exert any real power. A study of Newburyport, Massachusetts, over a thirty-year period shows that 90 percent of the workers there vanished from the town records in those years, many of them presumably because they moved elsewhere.

Even workers who stayed put often did not remain in the same job for long. The rags-to-riches stories of the Horatio Alger novels had few counterparts in reality. But a certain amount of real social mobility did exist, and it served to undercut worker militancy. The gains were small, but they were often enough to keep hope alive and to limit discontent.

Above all, perhaps, workers made few gains in the late nineteenth century because of the strength of the forces arrayed against them. They faced corporate organizations of vast wealth and power, which were generally determined to crush any efforts by workers to challenge their prerogatives. Moreover, as the Homestead and Pullman strikes suggest, the corporations had the support of government—local, state, and federal—which was willing to send in troops to "preserve order" and crush labor uprisings on demand. The corporations also managed to control and intimidate their employees through an elaborate system of infiltration and espionage within working-class communities.

Despite the creation of new organizations, despite a wave of strikes and protests that in the 1880s and 1890s reached startling proportions, workers in the late nineteenth century failed on the whole to create successful organizations or to protect their interests in the way the large corporations managed to do. In the battle for power within the emerging industrial economy, the workers steadily lost ground as big business entrenched itself.

SUGGESTED READINGS

General Histories.   John A. Garraty, *The New Commonwealth* (1968); Edward C. Kirkland, *Industry Comes of Age: Business, Labor, and Public Policy, 1860–1897* (1961); Samuel P. Hays, *The Response to Industrialism, 1885–1914* (1957); Ray Ginger, *The Age of Excess* (1963); Carl Degler, *The Age of the Economic Revolution* (1977); Daniel Boorstin, *The Americans: The Democratic Experience* (1973); Thomas C. Cochran and William Miller, *The Age of Enterprise* (1942);

Robert Higgs, *The Transformation of the American Economy, 1865–1914* (1971); Robert Wiebe, *The Search for Order, 1877–1920* (1968).

Technology. Roger Burlingame, *Engines of Democracy: Inventions and Society in Mature America* (1940) and *Henry Ford* (1957); Lewis Mumford, *Technics and Civilization* (1934); George Daniels, *Science and Society in America* (1971); Nathan Rosenberg, *Technology and American Economic Growth* (1972); Elting E. Morison, *Men, Machines, and Modern Times* (1966); Judith McGaw, *Most Wonderful Machine: Mechanization and Social Change in Berkshire Paper Making, 1801–1885* (1988); Robert W. Bruce, *Bell* (1973), Frank E. Hill, *Ford* (1954); Allan Nevins, *Ford*, 3 vols. (1954–1962); Peter Temin, *Steel in Nineteenth Century America* (1964); Frederick A. White, *American Industrial Research Laboratories* (1961); Robert Conot, *A Streak of Luck* (1979); Richard N. Current, *The Typewriter and the Men Who Made It* (1954).

Railroads. George R. Taylor and I. D. Neu, *The American Railroad Network, 1861–1890* (1956); John F. Stover, *The Life and Decline of the American Railroad* (1970) and *The Railroads of the South, 1865–1900* (1955); Richard C. Overton, *Burlington West* (1941) and *Gulf to Rockies* (1953); Edward C. Kirkland, *Men, Cities, and Transportation*, 2 vols. (1948); Thomas C. Cochran, *Railroad Leaders* (1953); Edward G. Campbell, *The Reorganization of the American Railroad System* (1938); Gabriel Kolko, *Railroads and Regulation, 1877–1916* (1965); Lee Benson, *Merchants, Farmers, and Railroads* (1955); George H. Miller, *Railroads and the Granger Laws* (1971); Robert Fogel, *Railroads and American Economic Growth* (1964); Anthony F. C. Wallace, *St. Clair: A Nineteenth-Century Coal Town's Experience with a Disaster-Prone Industry* (1987).

The Corporation. Alfred D. Chandler, Jr., *Strategy and Structure: Chapters in the History of the American Industrial Enterprise* (1962); *Pierre S. DuPont and the Making of the Modern Corporation* (1971), and *The Visible Hand: The Managerial Revolution in American Business* (1977); Glenn Porter, *The Rise of Big Business* (1973); Glenn Porter and Harold C. Livesay, *Merchants and Manufacturers* (1971); Norma R. Lamoreaux, *The Great Merger Movement in American Business, 1895–1904* (1985); Matthew Josephson, *The Robber Barons* (1934); Maury Klein, *The Life and Legend of Jay Gould* (1986); Harold C. Livesay, *Andrew Carnegie and the Rise of Big Business* (1975); Allan Nevins, *Study in Power: John D. Rockefeller*, 2 vols. (1953); David F. Hawkes, *John D.: The Founding Father of the Rockefellers* (1980); Joseph Wall, *Andrew Carnegie* (1970); Bernard Weisberger, *The Dream Maker* (1979).

Ideologies. Edward C. Kirkland, *Dream and Thought in the Business Community, 1860–1900* (1956); Sidney Fine, *Laissez Faire and the General Welfare State: A Study of Conflict in American Thought, 1865–1901* (1956); Irvin G. Wylie, *The Self-Made Man in America* (1954); Daniel T. Rodgers, *The Work Ethic in Industrial America, 1850–1920* (1978); David Thelen, *Paths of Resistance: Tradition and Dignity in Industrializing Missouri* (1986); Louis Galambos, *The Public Image of Big Business in America, 1880–1940* (1975); Richard Hofstadter, *Social Darwinism in American Thought* (rev., ed., 1955); Robert G. McCloskey, *American Conservatism in the Age of Enterprise* (1951); Samuel Chugerman, *Lester F. Ward: The American Aristotle* (1939); Arthur E. Morgan, *Edward Bellamy* (1944); Charles A. Baker, *Henry George* (1955); John L. Thomas, *Alternative America: Henry George, Edward Bellamy, Henry Demarest Lloyd, and the Adversary Tradition* (1983); T. J. Jackson Lears, *No Place of Grace: Antimodernism and the Transformation of American Culture, 1880–1920* (1981).

Labor. Melvyn Dubofsky, *Industrialism and the American Worker, 1865–1920* (1975); Henry Pelling, *American Labor* (1960); Herbert G. Gutman, *Work, Culture, and Society in Industrializing America* (1976); David Montgomery, *Beyond Equality* (1975), *Workers' Control in America: Studies in the History of Work, Technology, and Labor Struggles* (1979), and *The Fall of the House of Labor* (1987); Richard J. Oestreicher, *Solidarity and Fragmentation: Working People and Class Consciousness: Detroit, 1875–1900* (1986); Brian Greenberg, *Worker and Community: Response to Industrialization in a Nineteenth-Century American City, Albany, New York, 1850–1884* (1985); Daniel Nelson, *Managers and Workers: Origins of the New Factory System in the United States, 1880–1920* (1975); Stuart Kaufman, *Samuel Gompers and the Origins of the American Federation of Labor* (1978); Philip Taft, *The A.F. of L. in the Time of Gompers*, 2 vols. (1957–1959); Samuel Gompers, *Seventy Years of Life and Labor*, 2 vols. (1975); Stanley Buder, *Pullman* (1967); Henry David, *The Haymarket Affair* (1936); P. K. Edwards, *Strikes in the United States, 1881–1974* (1981); Sheldon Stromquist, *A Generation of Boomers: The Pattern of Railroad Labor Conflict in Nineteenth-Century America* (1987); Steven J. Ross, *Workers on the Edge: Work, Leisure, and Politics in Industrializing Cincinnati, 1788–1890* (1985); Roy Rosenzweig, *"Eight Hours for What We Will": Workers and Leisure in an Industrial City, 1870–1920* (1983); Alexander Keyssar, *Out of Work: The First Century of Unemployment in Massachusetts* (1986).

Women. Susan E. Kennedy, *If All We Did Was to Weep at Home* (1979); Barbara Wertheimer, *We Were There: The Story of Working Women in America* (1977); Patricia Cooper, *Once a Cigar Maker: Men, Women, and Work Culture in American Cigar Factories, 1900–1919*; Mary Blewett, *Men, Women, and Work Culture: Class, Gender, and Protest in the New England Shoe Industry* (1988); Tamara Hareven, *Family Time and Industrial Time: The Relationship Between the Family and Work in a New England Industrial Community* (1982); Alice Kessler-Harris, *Out to Work: A History of Wage-Earning Women in the United States* (1982); Susan Levine, *Labor's True Women: Carpet Weavers, Industrialization, and Labor Reform in the Gilded Age* (1984).

The Left. J. H. M. Laslett, *Labor and the Left* (1970); Nick Salvatore, *Eugene V. Debs: Citizen and Socialist* (1982); Mari Jo Buhle, *Women and American Socialism, 1870–1920* (1981); Melvyn Dubofsky, *We Shall Be All: A History of the Industrial Workers of the World* (1969); Gerald N. Grob, *Workers and Utopia* (1961).

Snow in New York (1902), by Robert Henri
Henri was one of the leaders of the rebellion among American artists against formal, academic painting. He was influenced by the impressionists, but he also broke with tradition by portraying ordinary scenes of urban life. (*National Gallery of Art, Washington. Chester Dale Collection*)

CHAPTER 18

The Age of the City

The progress of industrialization and the rapid expansion of commerce changed the face of American society in countless ways. Nowhere, however, were the effects of these changes more visible than in the cities. It was there that most of the factories and corporate offices were located, there that the new economic system had its seat. And from the city there emerged a new set of social and cultural values that would ultimately extend to all areas of the country. The United States was becoming an urban nation in the late nineteenth century.

The change did not come easily. The rapid growth of the urban population placed an enormous strain on the capacities of most metropolitan communities. Roads, sewers, transportation facilities, housing, social services—all proved inadequate to the new demands being placed on them. Urban political systems fell victim to corruption and ineptitude. And American sensibilities often rebelled at the new and intimidating pace of urban life. Indeed, the crisis of the cities seemed to many Americans a symbol of all the many problems confronting a society in the throes of rapid and destabilizing change. Sociologist Charles Horton Cooley wrote: "Our cities, especially, are full of the disintegrated material of the old order looking for a place in the new."

Yet for all the problems, the city continued its rise to dominance in American society—in part because of economic developments over which individuals seemed to have little control, in part because the diversity and excitement of urban life proved alluring to increasing numbers of Americans. Traditional rural values changed slowly in response to the influence of the urban environment, but change they did. By the end of the nineteenth century, the city was clearly emerging as the central focus of American economic, social, and cultural life.

The New Urban Growth

The great folk movement from the countryside to the city was occurring simultaneously throughout much of the Western world, as industrialization and the factory system changed the face of Europe as well as the United States. From countries or regions that were industrializing slowly or not at all, people moved to other countries or other regions that were industrializing rapidly. Rural people from both America and Europe made their way in especially large numbers to the business and industrial centers of the United States.

The City's Lure

"We cannot all live in cities, yet nearly all seem determined to do so," Horace Greeley wrote soon after the Civil War. " 'Hot and cold water,' baker's bread, gas, the theatre, and the streetcars . . . indicate the tendency of modern taste." The city attracted people because of the many conveniences it offered years

America in 1900

before such things reached the village or the farm. It drew people because of its institutions of entertainment and culture—its theaters and amusements, its libraries and museums, its superior schools and colleges. It attracted people, above all, because it offered more opportunities for employment and higher wages than the countryside afforded. The lure of the city persisted despite the disappointments and hardships it presented to those who moved there.

In the half-century from 1860 to 1910, the rural population of the United States almost doubled, but the urban population increased seven times. In 1860, approximately one-sixth of the American people lived in towns of 8,000 or larger; by 1900, one-third of the people lived in such places. The number of cities with more than 50,000 inhabitants was 16 in 1860 and 109 in 1910. And in 1920, the census revealed that for the first time, a majority of the American people lived in "urban" areas—defined as communities of 2,500 people or more. The population of the New York urban area (the city and its environs) grew from less than 1 million in 1860 to more than 3 million in 1900. Even more spectacular

was the growth of Chicago, which had 100,000 inhabitants in 1860 and more than a million at the end of the century. Towns and cities were getting bigger and more numerous in all sections of the country.

Natural increase accounted for only a small part of the urban growth. Urban families experienced a high rate of infant mortality, a declining fertility rate, and a high death rate from disease. Without immigration, cities would have grown relatively slowly.

The Migrations

Domestic migration accounted for a substantial portion of city growth. The late nineteenth century was an age of unprecedented geographical mobility, as Americans left declining agricultural regions at a dramatic rate. During the 1880s, a decade in which the nation's population was growing by 25 percent, the total number of inhabitants was decreasing in two-fifths of Pennsylvania's total area, three-fifths of Connecticut's, more than half of Ohio's and Illinois's, and five-sixths of New York's. The decrease occurred almost entirely in farming regions. Many of those who left were moving to the newly developing agricultural lands of the West. But almost as many were moving to the cities of the East and the Midwest. Migration to the city was not always direct. Many people moved first to a nearby village, then to a larger town, and only then to the city itself.

The 1880s saw as well the beginnings of a population change that would, in the early twentieth century, become one of the most important migrations in American history: the movement of blacks from the rural South to industrial cities. The poverty, debt, violence, and oppression blacks encountered in the late-nineteenth-century South accounted for the movement more than did opportunities in the industrial North, for blacks arriving in the cities found relatively few opportunities open to them. Factory jobs for blacks were rare and professional opportunities almost nonexistent. Instead, urban blacks tended to work as cooks, janitors, domestic servants, and in other service occupations. Since many such jobs were considered women's work, black women often outnumbered black men in the cities.

By the end of the nineteenth century, there were substantial black communities (10,000 people or more) in over thirty cities—many of them in the South, but some (Washington, Baltimore, Chicago, New York) in the border states or the North. Nearly 80 percent of black Americans outside the South lived in cities. The real Great Migration of blacks to the cities began during World War I, but the migrations of the 1880s and 1890s paved the way for the much larger population movement to come.

The most important source of urban population growth in the late nineteenth century, however, was the arrival of great numbers of new immigrants from abroad. Some came to the United States from Canada, Latin America, and—particularly on the West Coast—China and Japan. But by far the greatest number came from Europe. This immigration—both because of its sheer numbers and because of the new variety of its national origins—did much to transform the nature of the industrial work force. (See pp. 526–528.) It helped to transform the character of the nation's cities as well, particularly after 1880, when the flow of new arrivals began to include large numbers of people from Southern and Eastern Europe. By the 1890s, more than half of all immigrants came from these new regions, as opposed to fewer than 2 percent in the 1860s.

In earlier stages of immigration, most new arrivals had headed west. Most Germans, for example, had moved to the farming regions of the Midwest. Those who had chosen urban life had generally settled not on the East Coast, but in such Midwestern cities as St. Louis, Cincinnati, and Milwaukee. Nearly all the Scandinavians had moved to farms in the Middle West or on the Great Plains. Immigrants who settled in cities were often relatively well educated and upwardly mobile people—businessmen, professionals, and skilled workers—although significant minorities of some immigrant groups became unskilled urban workers. (The Irish presented a significant exception to the general pattern. Even before the Civil War, they had tended to congregate in Eastern cities as unskilled workers, although by the late nineteenth century many had begun to achieve new and enhanced social and economic levels.)

The new immigrants of the late nineteenth century, by contrast, settled overwhelmingly in industrial cities, where they occupied largely unskilled jobs. They lacked the capital to buy land and begin farming in the West. They needed immediate employment. And only the city—with its factories, stockyards, railroads, and other industries—could provide it. The city had another appeal for them as well. As strangers in an alien land, they could find refuge in the city by living in communities with their fellow nationals.

The Ethnic City

The result was a radical transformation of life in the nation's large cities. By 1890, most of the population of the major urban areas consisted of immigrants: 87 percent in Chicago, 80 percent in New York, 84 percent in Milwaukee and Detroit. (London, the largest industrial city in Europe, had by contrast a population that was 94 percent native.) Equally striking was the diversity of the new immigrant populations. In other countries experiencing heavy immigration in this period, most of the new arrivals were coming from one or two sources. Argentina, for example, was experiencing a great influx of Europeans in this era, but almost all of them were coming from Italy or Spain. In the United States, no single national group dominated the new immigrant population. In the last four decades of the nineteenth century, 8 percent of the new arrivals came from Italy, 28 percent from Germany, 11 percent from Scandinavia, 7 percent from Austria and Hungary, 5 percent from Russia, 18 percent from Great Britain, and 15 percent from Ireland. Immigrants also arrived from Poland,

Population Growth, 1860–1900

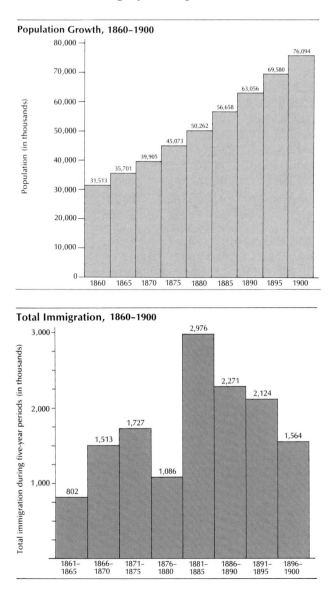

Immigration's Contribution to Population Growth, 1860–1920

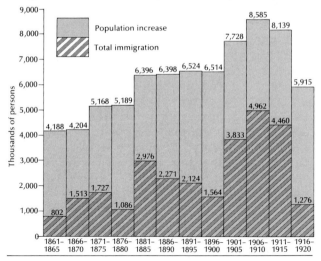

Total Immigration, 1860–1900

Sources of Immigration, 1860–1900

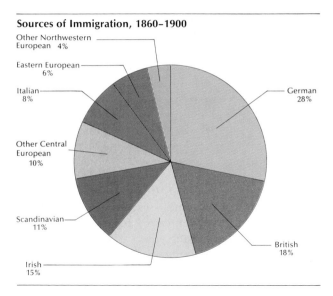

Greece, Canada, Japan, China, Holland, Mexico, and other nations. In some towns, a dozen different ethnic groups might find themselves living in close proximity to one another. No country had ever gathered its population from so wide a range of sources in so short a period of time.

Most of the new European immigrants were people from rural backgrounds, and the adjustment to city life was often a painful one. To help ease the transition, national groups usually formed close-knit ethnic communities within the cities: Italian, Polish, Jewish, Slavic, and other neighborhoods (often known as "immigrant ghettoes") that attempted to

re-create in the New World many of the features of the Old. It was impossible, of course, to reproduce in the modern city the social fabric of the farm villages from which many immigrants came—the seasonal work patterns, the intimate communal ties passed on from generation to generation, the strength of family life based on common economic activities. But the ethnic neighborhoods did provide immigrants with a sense of belonging to a coherent community.

Some ethnic neighborhoods consisted of people who had migrated to America from the same province, town, or village. Even when the population was more diverse, however, the community offered

Evolving Ethnic and Class Segregation in Milwaukee, 1850–1890

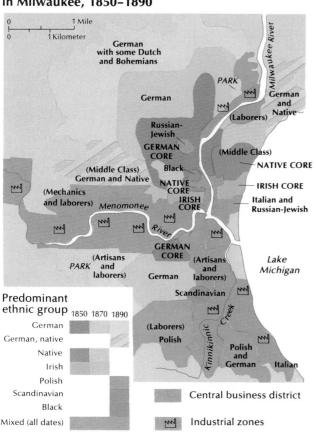

advanced economically more rapidly than others (for example, the Irish). Why that was so is a matter of considerable controversy. But one explanation is that, by huddling together in ethnic neighborhoods, immigrant groups tended to reinforce the cultural values of their previous societies. When those values were particularly well suited to economic advancement—as was, for example, the high value that Jews placed on education—then this ethnic identification helped members of a group to improve their lots. When other values predominated—maintenance of community solidarity, strengthening of family ties, preservation of order—progress could be less rapid.

Assimilation and Exclusion

Yet it would be easy to overstate the differences among the various immigrant communities, because virtually all groups had certain things in common. Most immigrants, of course, shared the experience of living in cities (and of adapting from a rural past to an urban present). Most were young; the majority of newcomers were between fifteen and forty-five years old. And in virtually all immigrant communities, the strength of ethnic ties had to compete against another powerful force: the desire for assimilation.

Many of the new arrivals had come to America with romantic visions of the New World. And however disillusioning they might find their first contact with the United States, they usually retained the dream of becoming true "Americans." Even many first-generation immigrants worked hard to rid themselves of all vestiges of their old cultures, to become thoroughly Americanized. Second-generation immigrants were even more likely to attempt to break with the old ways, to assimilate themselves completely into what they considered genuine American culture. Some even looked with contempt on parents and grandparents who continued to value traditional ethnic habits and values. The tension between the desire to become assimilated and the strength of ethnic ties was one that countless immigrants and their children wrestled with for years.

Assimilation was not, of course, entirely a matter of choice. Native-born Americans encouraged it, both deliberately and inadvertently, in countless ways. Public schools taught children in English, and employers often insisted that workers speak English on the job. Stores sold more American than European foods and other products, forcing immigrants to adapt their diets, clothing, and lifestyles to the

newcomers much that was familiar. They could find newspapers and theaters in their native languages, stores selling their native foods, church and fraternal organizations that provided links with their national pasts. And they could move through large areas of the city surrounded by their fellow nationals, an experience that helped cushion them against the loneliness of being in a new land. The immigrants also maintained close ties with their native countries. They kept in contact with relatives who had remained behind. Some (perhaps as many as a third in the early years) returned to Europe after a relatively short time; others attempted to help bring the rest of their families to America.

The cultural cohesiveness of the ethnic communities clearly eased the pain of separation from the immigrants' native lands. Whether it helped immigrants to become absorbed into the economic life of America is a more difficult question to answer. It is clear that some ethnic groups (Jews and Germans in particular)

realities of the market. Church leaders were often native-born Americans or older, more assimilated immigrants who encouraged their parishioners to adopt American ways. Some even reformed their theology and liturgy to make it more compatible with the norms of the new country. Reform Judaism, for example, was an effort by Jewish leaders to make their faith less "foreign" to the dominant culture of a largely Christian nation.

The arrival of these vast numbers of new immigrants, and the conspicuousness with which many of them clung to old ways and created culturally distinctive communities, provoked fear and resentment among many native Americans in much the same way earlier arrivals had done. Some people reacted against the immigrants out of generalized fears and prejudices, seeing in their "foreign-ness" the source of all the disorder and corruption of the urban world. "These people," a Chicago newspaper wrote shortly after the Haymarket bombing of 1886, "are not American, but the very scum and offal of Europe . . . Europe's human and inhuman rubbish." Others had economic concerns. Native laborers, fighting to raise their incomes and improve their working conditions, were often incensed by the willingness of the immigrants to accept lower wages and to take over the jobs of strikers.

The rising nativism provoked a series of political responses. Henry Bowers, a self-educated lawyer obsessed with a hatred of Catholics and foreigners, founded in 1887 the American Protective Association, a group committed to stopping the immigrant tide. By 1894, membership in the organization reportedly reached 500,000, with chapters throughout the Northeast and Midwest. That same year, a more genteel organization—the Immigration Restriction League—was founded in Boston by five Harvard alumni. It was dedicated to the belief that immigrants should be screened, through literacy tests and other standards designed to separate the desirable from the undesirable. The League avoided the crude theories of conspiracy and the rabid xenophobia of the American Protective Association; its more sophisticated nativism was ultimately far more effective in winning public support for restriction.

Even before the rise of these new organizations, politicians were struggling to find some answer to the "immigration question." Congress acted in 1882 to exclude the Chinese, who had been arriving in large numbers on the West Coast and who, among other things, made up a significant portion of the work force

building the Western railroads. In the same year, Congress passed a general immigration law, which denied entry to certain "undesirables"—convicts, paupers, the mentally incompetent—and which placed a tax of 50 cents on every person admitted. Later legislation of the 1890s enlarged the list of those barred from immigrating and increased the tax. These measures reflected a rising fear that continuing unlimited immigration would exhaust the resources of the nation and endanger its social institutions.

But the laws kept out only a small number of aliens and fell far short of fulfilling the hopes of either the American Protective Association or the Immigration Restriction League. That was because many native-born Americans, far from fearing immigration, welcomed it. A few argued that the newcomers enriched the nation by bringing new talents and energies and by introducing new elements to American culture. But most defenders of immigration used an economic argument: Immigration was providing a rapidly growing economy with a cheap and plentiful labor supply. America's industrial (and indeed agricultural) development would be impossible without it. Powerful business interests continued to oppose restrictions, and they found significant support within the government. Congress passed a literacy law in 1897, but President Grover Cleveland vetoed it.

The Urban Landscape

The city was a place of remarkable contrasts. It had homes of almost unimaginable size and grandeur, and hovels of indescribable squalor. It had conveniences unknown to earlier generations, and problems that seemed beyond the capacity of society to solve. Both the attractions and the problems were a result of one central fact: the stunning pace with which cities were growing. The expansion of the urban population helped to spur important new technological and industrial developments. But the rapid growth also produced misgovernment, poverty, traffic jams, overcrowding, filth, epidemics, and great fires. The pace of growth was simply too fast for planning and building to keep pace. "The problem in America," one municipal reformer said, "has been to make a great city in a few years out of nothing."

One of the greatest problems of this precipitous growth was that of finding housing for the thousands of new residents who were pouring into the cities every day. For the wealthy, housing was seldom a worry. The availability of cheap labor and the increasing accessibility of tools and materials reduced the cost of building in the late nineteenth century and permitted anyone with even a moderate income to afford a house. The richest urban residents often lived in palatial mansions in the heart of the city. Others of the rich, and many of the moderately well-to-do, took advantage of the less expensive land on the edges of the city and settled in new suburbs. Chicago, for example, boasted in the 1870s nearly one hundred residential suburbs connected with the city by railroad and offering the joys of "pure air, peacefulness, quietude, and natural scenery." Boston, too, saw the development of some of the earliest "streetcar suburbs"—Dorchester, Brookline, and others—which catered to both the wealthy and the middle class. New Yorkers of moderate means settled in the new suburb of Harlem, on the northern fringes of Manhattan, and commuted downtown by trolley or riverboat.

Most urban residents, however, could not afford to move to the suburbs or own their own housing. Instead, they stayed in the city centers and rented. And because demand was so high and space so scarce, they had little power with which to control building standards. Landowners, to maximize their rental incomes, tried to squeeze as many residents as possible into the smallest available space. In Manhattan, for example, the average population density in 1894 was 143 people per acre—a rate higher than that of some of the most crowded cities of Europe (Paris had 127 per acre, Berlin 101) and far higher than any other American city at the time or since. In some neighborhoods—the lower East Side, for example—the density was more than 700 people per acre, among the highest in the world.

In all the nation's major cities, poor residents jammed into decaying or makeshift housing. In the cities of the South—Charleston, New Orleans, Richmond—poor blacks crammed into abandoned, crumbling slave quarters. In Boston, they moved into cheap three-story wooden houses ("triple deckers"), many of them crumbling fire hazards. In Baltimore and Philadelphia, they crowded into narrow brick row houses. And in New York and many other cities, they lived in tenements.

More than a million poor New Yorkers were jammed into tenements—a term that had originally referred simply to a multiple-family rental building, but that had by the late nineteenth century come to be applied to slum dwellings only. The first tene-

A New York Tenement, 1910
This photograph of a woman and her children in a rear tenement bedroom was meant to illustrate the crowding and squalor of urban immigrant life. The photographer was Lewis Hine, who from 1907 to 1914 worked for a government committee investigating child labor and whose efforts to expose social conditions helped spur legislative action. He was also a pioneer in industrial photography and created some of the classic early images of factory production.   (George Eastman House)

ments, built in 1850, had been hailed as a great improvement in housing for the poor. "It is built with the design of supplying the laboring people with cheap lodgings," a local newspaper commented, "and will have many advantages over the cellars and other miserable abodes which too many are forced to inhabit." But tenements themselves became miserable abodes. The typical structure was three to five stories high, with many windowless rooms, little or no plumbing or central heating, and perhaps a row of privies in the basement. A New York state law of 1879 required a window in every bedroom of tenements built thereafter, but developers generally complied by providing openings onto dank and sunless airshafts.

Streetcar Suburbs in Nineteenth-Century New Orleans

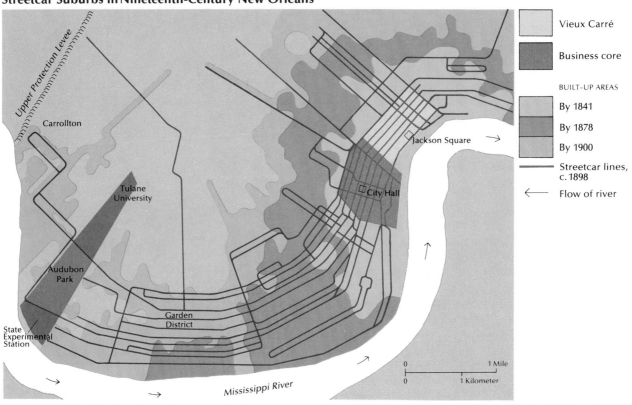

Jacob Riis, a Danish immigrant and New York newspaper reporter, shocked many middle-class Americans with his sensational (and some would say sensationalized) descriptions of tenement life in his 1890 book *How the Other Half Lives.* Slum dwellings, he said, were almost universally sunless, practically airless, and "poisoned" by "summer stenches." "The hall is dark and you might stumble over the children pitching pennies back there." But the solution reformers often adopted was to raze slum dwellings without building any new housing to replace them.

Urban growth posed monumental challenges to the transportation systems of the nation's cities. Old downtown streets were often too narrow for the heavy traffic that was beginning to move over them. Some were paved with cobblestones, but most lacked a hard surface and resembled either a sea of mud or a cloud of dust, depending on the weather. In the last decades of the century, more and more streets were paved, usually with wooden blocks, bricks, or asphalt; but paving could not keep up with the laying out of new thoroughfares. By 1890, Chicago had surfaced only about 600 of its more than 2,000 miles of streets.

It was not simply the conditions of the streets, however, that impeded urban transportation. It was the numbers of people who needed to move everyday from one part of the city to another—back and forth between their homes and their workplaces, churches, stores, and schools. Private vehicles could not answer the need; the solution lay in the development of mass transportation. Streetcars drawn on tracks by horses had been introduced into some cities even before the Civil War. New York had 16 lines by 1866, using 800 cars and nearly 8,000 horses. But the horsecars, while faster than the omnibuses and other smaller vehicles that had served as public transportation in the past, were still not fast enough. As a result, cities embarked on new efforts to improve their mass transit. New York in 1870 opened its first elevated railway, whose steam-powered trains moved rapidly above the city streets on massive iron structures; but the trains inflicted noise, filth, and often dangerously hot embers on the pedestrians below.

New York, Chicago, San Francisco, and other cities experimented with cable cars, towed by continuously moving underground cables. Richmond, Virginia, introduced the first electric trolley line in 1888, and by 1895 such systems were operating in 850 towns and cities, with a total of 10,000 miles of track. Boston in 1897 opened the first American subway when it put a mile and a half of its trolley lines underground. At the same time, cities were developing new techniques of road building and, in urban areas built around bodies of water, bridge building. One of the great technological marvels of the 1880s was the completion of the Brooklyn Bridge in New York—a dramatic steel-cable suspension span designed by John A. Roebling.

Cities were growing upward as well as outward, a result of the convergence of technological discoveries and the need for new space in the increasingly crowded downtown areas. The first modern "skyscraper"—by later standards a relatively modest building, ten stories high, constructed in Chicago in 1884—inaugurated a new era in urban architecture. Once builders perfected the technique of constructing tall buildings with cast iron and then steel beams, and once other inventors produced the electric elevator to make possible quick and safe vertical movement, no obstacle remained to even higher buildings. The greatest figure in the early development of the skyscraper was the Chicago architect Louis Sullivan, who introduced many of the modern, functional elements to the genre—large windows, sheer lines, limited ornamentation—in an attempt to emphasize the soaring height of the building as its most distinctive feature. Sullivan's students, among them Frank Lloyd Wright, expanded the influence of these innovations still further and applied them to low buildings as well as tall ones.

Strains of Urban Life

The increasing congestion of the city and the slow development of new services to cope with that congestion produced a number of serious health and safety hazards. One was fires. In one major city after another, major conflagrations in the late nineteenth century swept through downtowns, destroying blocks of buildings (many of them still constructed of wood) and forcing the almost total reconstruction of large areas. Chicago suffered its "great fire" in 1871, and Boston a disastrous fire the same year. Other cities—Baltimore, for example, and San Francisco, where a tremendous earthquake produced a catastrophic fire in 1906—experienced similar disasters. The great fires were terrible experiences for those who lived through (or died in) them. But they

Chicago, 1910
The stunning urban growth of the late nineteenth and early twentieth centuries taxed American cities up to, and often beyond, their limits. This view of Dearborn Avenue in Chicago, looking south, illustrates one of the problems of the industrial city: chronic congestion. Horse-drawn vehicles jostle with electric streetcars and swarms of pedestrians. (Chicago Historical Society)

were also important events in the development of the cities involved. Not only did they induce new strategies to prevent or limit future fires—the construction of fireproof buildings, the development of professional fire departments, and more—they also forced cities to rebuild at a time when new technological and architectural innovations were available. Some of the modern, high-rise downtowns of American cities arose out of the rubble of great fires.

An even greater hazard than fire was disease, especially in poor neighborhoods with inadequate sanitation facilities. But while slums suffered the worst from disease, entire cities were vulnerable. An epidemic that began in a poor neighborhood could (and often did) spread easily into other neighborhoods as well. Even though public health officials were acquainted with the germ theory of disease by the late nineteenth century, few municipal officials recognized the relationship of improper sewage disposal and water contamination to such epidemic diseases as typhoid fever and cholera. As late as the turn of the century, most city dwellers relied on private vaults and cesspools for the disposal of human wastes. Flush toilets and public sewer systems began to appear in the 1870s, but for many years they failed to solve the problem—largely because such systems emptied their sewage into open ditches within the city limits or into streams nearby, often polluting the city's own water supply in the process.

Above all, perhaps, the rapid growth of the city spawned widespread and often desperate poverty. Despite the rapid growth of urban economies, the sheer number of new residents ensured that many people would be unable to earn enough for a decent subsistence. Even in families where many members worked, the combined earnings were often not enough to pay for adequate food or housing.

Public agencies and private philanthropic organizations offered very limited relief. It would be many years before government at any level—local, state, or federal—would assume any substantial responsibility for welfare work. And philanthropic organizations were dominated by middle-class people, who tended to believe that too much assistance would breed dependency and that poverty was the fault of the poor themselves—a result of laziness or alcoholism or other kinds of irresponsibility. Most tried to restrict aid to the "deserving poor"—those who truly could not help themselves (at least according to the standards of the organizations themselves, which

conducted elaborate "investigations" to separate the "deserving" from the "undeserving"). Other charitable societies—for example, the Salvation Army, which began operating in America in 1879, one year after it was founded in London—concentrated more on religious revivalism than on the relief of the homeless and hungry. Tensions often arose between native Protestant philanthropists and Catholic immigrants over religious doctrine and standards of morality. Middle-class faith in the idea of self-improvement led to a widespread inattention to the structural roots of urban poverty.

Poverty and crowding naturally bred crime and violence. Much of the criminality in urban areas was relatively petty: pickpockets, con artists, swindlers, and petty thieves, often simply trying to survive by stealing. But there were also far more dangerous crimes. The American murder rate rose rapidly in the late nineteenth century (even as such rates were declining in Europe), from 25 murders for every million people in 1880 to over 100 by the end of the century. That reflected in part a very high level of violence in nonurban areas: the American South, where lynching and homicide were particularly high; and the West, where the rootlessness and instability of frontier communities (cow towns, mining camps, and the like) created much violence. But the cities contributed their share to the increase in crime as well. Native-born Americans liked to believe that the crime was a result of the violent proclivities of immigrant groups, and they cited the rise of gangs and criminal organizations in various ethnic communities. But even in the cities, native-born Americans were as likely to commit crimes as were immigrants.

The rising crime rates encouraged many cities to develop larger and more professional police forces and to build station houses in every neighborhood. But police forces themselves could spawn corruption and brutality, particularly since jobs on them were often filled through political patronage. Some members of the middle class, fearful of urban insurrections, felt the need for even more substantial forms of protection. Urban national guard groups built imposing armories on the outskirts of middle-class neighborhoods and stored large supplies of weapons and ammunition in preparation for uprisings that, in fact, virtually never occurred.

Rural Americans and Europeans alike reacted to the city with marked ambivalence. It was a place of strong allure and great excitement. Yet it was also a place of alienating impersonality, of a new feeling of anonymity, of a different kind of work with which the individual could feel only limited identification. To many, moreover, it was a place of poverty and sin. Theodore Dreiser's novel *Sister Carrie* (1900) exposed one troubling aspect of urban life: the plight of single women (like Dreiser's heroine, Carrie) who moved from the countryside into the city and found themselves without any means of support. Carrie first took an exhausting and ill-paying job in a Chicago shoe factory, then drifted into a life of "sin," exploited by predatory men. The novel was so shocking to contemporary sensibilities that Dreiser's publisher printed only 1,000 copies to fulfill his contract and refused to promote the book. But many women were experiencing in reality the dilemmas Carrie experienced in fiction. Living in conditions of extreme poverty and hardship, some drifted into prostitution—which, degrading and dangerous as it was, also produced a livelihood and a sense of community for desperate people.

The Machine and the Boss

New arrivals to the cities, and foreign immigrants in particular, faced severe obstacles. Many could not speak English. Few knew how to deal with the laws and customs of the new land. Large numbers found themselves indigent for long periods after their arrival before they could find work. There was, in short, an enormous demand for institutions to help immigrants adjust to American urban life. In the absence of sufficient help from government or middle-class philanthropic institutions, immigrants turned to other sources of assistance. Many ethnic communities created self-help organizations, which provided limited assistance to members in need. But for many residents of the inner cities, the principal source of assistance was the political machine.

The urban machine was one of America's most distinctive political institutions. It owed its existence to the power vacuum that the chaotic growth of cities (and the very limited growth of governments) had created. It was also a product of the potential voting power of large immigrant communities. Any politician who could mobilize that power stood to gain enormous influence or public office. And so there emerged a group of urban "bosses," many themselves of foreign birth or parentage. A large number of them were Irish, largely because they had the advantage of English as a native language and also because some had previous political experience from the long Irish struggle against the English at home.

The principal function of the political boss was a simple one: to win votes for his organization. To do so, he engaged in a wide array of activities. To win the loyalty of his constituents, a boss might provide them with occasional relief—a basket of groceries or a bag of coal. He might step in to save those arrested for petty crimes from jail. When he could, he found jobs for the unemployed. Above all, he rewarded many of his followers with patronage: with jobs in city government or in such city agencies as the police (which the machine's elected officials often controlled); with jobs building or operating the new transit systems; and with opportunities to rise in the political organization itself.

Yet machines were not simply mechanisms for maintaining political power. They were also vehicles for making money. Machine politicians enriched themselves and their allies through various forms of graft and corruption. Some of it might be fairly open—what George Washington Plunkitt of New York's Tammany Hall called "honest graft." For example, a politician might discover in advance where a new road or streetcar line was to be built, buy an interest in the land near it, and profit when the city had to buy the land from him or when property values rose as a result of the construction. But there was also a great deal of covert graft. A politician awarded contracts for the construction of streets, sewers, public buildings, and other projects to contractors (usually at prices well above the real cost) on condition that he himself receive a portion of the contract money—that is, a "kickback." In addition to awarding contracts, a municipal official could sell franchises for the operation of such public utilities as street railways, waterworks, and electric light and power systems.

Perhaps the most famously corrupt city boss was William M. Tweed, boss of New York City's Tammany Hall in the 1860s and 1870s. Tweed's notorious "ring" once spent over $1 million of city funds to build a modest courthouse originally budgeted at $250,000. And at times, apparently, Tammany officials raided the public treasury in even more direct and blatant ways. Tweed's excesses finally landed him in jail in 1872. But corruption remained part of machine politics in virtually every city. Middle-class

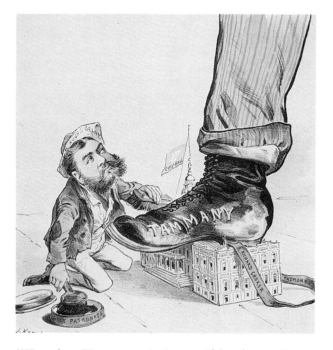

"Keeping Tammany's Boots Shined," c. 1887
This lithograph by cartoonist Joseph Keppler shows the heavy foot of New York City's Tammany Hall sitting atop City Hall, while Hugh Grant, a Tammany sheriff later elected mayor, applies the patronage polish that was the organization's lifeblood. The strap dangling from the boot bears the name of Richard Croker, who emerged as one of Tammany's principal leaders after the fall of Boss Tweed and who served as the undisputed chief of the organization from 1886 until 1901.   (The Bettmann Archive)

critics cited corruption as the principal characteristic of the machine, but other goals and achievements were at least as important. Political organizations were responsible for modernizing city infrastructures, for expanding the role of government, and for creating stability in a political and social climate that otherwise would have lacked a center. Above all, they were expert at the arts of winning elections and retaining the loyalties of voters.

New York's Tammany Hall was perhaps the most prominent example. Tammany leaders after Tweed—John Kelley, Richard Croker, and Charles Francis Murphy—created a well-ordered hierarchy in which district and ward leaders exercised substantial autonomy. Loyalty to the organization itself became the ultimate value, survival of the organization the overriding goal. "A well-organized political club,"

Richard Croker once remarked, "is made for the purpose of aggressive warfare. It must move, and it must always move forward against its enemies. . . . If it is encumbered by useless baggage or half-hearted or traitorous camp followers, it cuts them off and goes ahead." Machine leaders also forged important economic relationships with local businesses—especially streetcar and utilities companies, dependent on government contracts and franchises. Tammany after Tweed was less exuberant in its excesses, but more politically successful and more efficiently profitable.

Several factors made the continuation of boss rule possible. One, of course, was the power of immigrant voters, who were less concerned with political morality than with obtaining desperately needed services. The machines provided services; reformers usually did not. Another was the link between the political organizations and wealthy, prominent citizens who profited from their dealings with bosses and resisted efforts to overthrow them. Still another was the structural weakness of city governments. Within the municipal government, no single official usually had decisive power of responsibility. Instead, authority was generally divided among many officeholders— the mayor, the aldermen, and others—and was limited by the state legislature, which often had the ultimate authority over municipal affairs. The boss, by virtue of his control over his machine, formed an "invisible government" that provided an alternative to the inadequacy of the regular government. He might not hold an official position himself. (The real leaders of Tammany Hall, for example, seldom held public office.) But through his organization, on which the politicians of his party depended for election, he often controlled a majority of those who were in office.

The size and structure of machines varied considerably from city to city. Tammany Hall was an enormous, relentlessly hierarchical organization. Boston, by contrast, was the home of numerous competing machines, each the personal fiefdom of a single boss. Some bosses had no machines at all, but simply loose networks of personal loyalties that they could call upon for political advancement. Others operated autonomous neighborhood organizations—one reason why saloonkeepers, who owned the principal gathering places in many immigrant communities— assumed a special political importance.

But machine politicians did have certain things in common whatever the particular circumstances of their organizations. They were almost always garrulous and sociable men, eager to meet people and to collect friends. They were inveterate guests at weddings, funerals, and neighborhood parties, and frequent hosts of open houses, barbecues, and other gatherings of their own. They were accessible to their followers as much as possible, eager to distribute the favors and kindnesses that cemented loyalties. They were also often eager for recognition from the larger, middle-class culture. Some tried to earn respect by making substantial contributions to hospitals, parks, and libraries. Others (such as Tammany's Richard Croker) tried to buy respectability; Croker purchased horse farms in New York and Ireland and attempted to make a name in the aristocratic racing world.

The urban machine was not without competition. Reform groups frequently mobilized public outrage at the corruption of the bosses and often succeeded in driving machine politicians from office. Tammany, for example, saw its candidates for mayor and other high city offices lose almost as often as they won in the last decades of the nineteenth century. But the reform organizations typically lacked the permanence of the machine; and more often than not, their power faded after a few years. Only basic, permanent, structural change in the institutions of government, many critics of the machine were by 1900 beginning to argue, could effectively rescue the city from "boss rule."

Society and Culture in Urbanizing America

For urban middle-class Americans, who were increasing rapidly in numbers, wealth, and influence, the last decades of the nineteenth century were a time of dramatic advances. Indeed, it was in those years that a distinctive middle-class culture began to exert a powerful influence over the whole of American life. Other groups in society, however, viewed the changes of the period with less enthusiasm. Immigrants, blacks, factory workers, and others experienced some economic gains, but they also became more aware of the enormous gap separating them from the more affluent middle class. Most Americans continued to live on farms or in small communities;

as late as 1900, only 40 percent of the population was located in towns or cities of 2,500 inhabitants or more. And to them, the rise of the city, and the growing dominance of urban culture in American life as a whole, often seemed threatening.

Even those who viewed the changes in American society with ambivalence, however, often found themselves drawn to the new culture in various ways. They purchased the new products of the industrial economy; they shopped in the new chain stores or mail-order houses; they observed or participated in organized sports and leisure activities. Whether they liked it or not, Americans were encountering the birth of a new mass culture.

The industrial era also had an important impact on what is often known as "high culture": on the ideas and activities of intellectuals, artists, and educators. It became a time of greatly expanding educational opportunities, at least for some portions of the population; a time of revolutionary new scientific discoveries; and a time in which traditional spiritual beliefs found themselves severely tested.

The Rise of Mass Consumption

The rise of American industry could not have occurred without the growth of markets for the goods being produced. Although many Americans could not afford to buy the products of their factories, a mass market for industrial goods did emerge. Much of it consisted of members of the middle class, whose own increasing wealth allowed them to purchase more goods than they once had. But much of it, too, consisted of less affluent people who became consumers less because they were making more money than because mass production and mass distribution were making consumer goods less expensive.

Incomes were rising for almost everyone in the industrial era, although at highly uneven rates. The most conspicuous result of the new economy was the creation of vast fortunes; but perhaps the most important result for society as a whole was the growth and increasing prosperity of the middle class. The salaries of clerks, accountants, and other "white collar" workers rose by an average of a third between 1890 and 1910—and in some parts of the middle class much higher. Doctors, lawyers, and other professionals, for example, experienced a particularly dramatic increase in both the prestige and the profitability of their professions. Working-class incomes rose too in those years, although from a much lower base and often less rapidly than the cost of living. Iron and steel workers, for example, saw their hourly wages increase by a third between 1890 and 1910. Industries with large female work forces—shoes, textiles, and paper—saw more modest increases, as did almost all industries in the South. Family incomes for working-class people increased, too, because women and children so often worked to supplement the husband and father's earnings, or because families took in boarders or did laundry for the neighborhood.

As important as rising incomes, however, was the development of affordable products and the creation of new merchandising techniques, which made many consumer goods available to a mass market for the first time. A good example of such changes was the emergence of ready-made clothing as the basis of the American wardrobe. In the early nineteenth century, most Americans had made their own clothing—usually from cloth they bought from merchants, at times from fabrics they spun and wove themselves. The invention of the sewing machine and the spur that the Civil War (and its demand for uniforms) gave to the manufacture of clothing created an enormous industry devoted to producing ready-made garments. By the end of the century, virtually all Americans bought their clothing from stores; and partly as a result, much larger numbers of people were becoming concerned with questions of style. Interest in women's fashion, for example, had once been a luxury reserved for the relatively affluent. Now middle-class and even working-class women could strive to develop a distinctive style of dress.

Another example was the way Americans bought and prepared food. The development and mass production of tin cans in the 1880s created a large new industry devoted to packaging and selling canned food and (as a result of the techniques discovered by Gail Borden in the 1850s) condensed milk. Refrigerated railroad cars were making it possible for perishables—meats, vegetables, dairy products, and other foodstuffs—to be transported over long distances without spoiling. The growth of artificially frozen ice made possible the proliferation of iceboxes in homes that in the past had not been able to afford them. For most Americans, the changes meant improved diets, better health, and ultimately longer lives. Life expectancy rose six years in the first two decades of the twentieth century.

Changes in marketing also served to alter the way Americans consumed. Small local stores began to face competition from national "chain stores." The Atlantic and Pacific Tea Company (the A & P) began to establish a national network of grocery stores beginning in the 1870s. F. W. Woolworth's created a chain of dry goods stores. Sears Roebuck established a large market for its mail-order merchandise by distributing each year an enormous catalogue from which even people in remote rural areas could order new products.

In larger cities, the emergence of the great department stores helped to transform buying habits and to turn shopping into a more alluring and glamorous activity. Marshall Field in Chicago created one of the first American department stores—a place deliberately designed to create a sense of wonder and excitement. (Such stores had made earlier appearances in European cities.) Similar emporia emerged in New York, Brooklyn, Boston, Philadelphia, and other cities: Macy's, Abraham and Straus, Jordan Marsh, Wanamaker's.

The rise of mass consumption had particularly dramatic effects on American women, who were generally the primary consumers within family units. Women's clothing styles changed much more rapidly and dramatically than those of men. Women generally bought and prepared food for families, so the availability of new food products not only changed the way everyone ate, but the way women shopped and cooked. Canning and refrigeration meant greater variety in the diet. It also meant that food did not always have to be purchased on the day it was eaten. The consumer economy produced new employment opportunities for women as sales clerks in department stores and as waitresses in the rapidly proliferating restaurants. And it spawned the creation of a new movement in which women were to play a vital role: the consumer protection movement, which for many decades was one of the most important forces for reform in American society and politics. The National Consumers League, formed in the 1890s under the leadership of Florence Kelley, attempted to mobilize the power of women as consumers to force retailers and manufacturers to improve wages and working conditions. Other consumer organizations would lobby for improvements in the price, quality, and safety of products offered to purchasers.

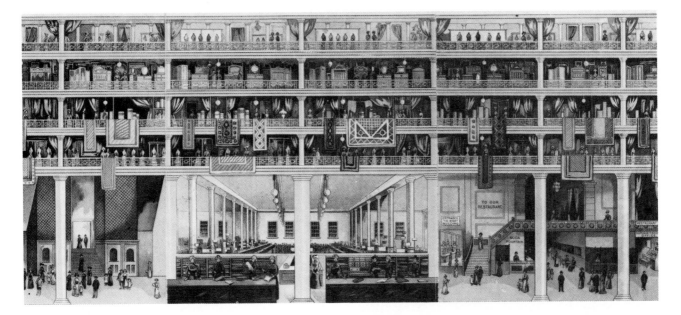

The Department Store, c. 1892
This detail from an advertisement shows an interior cross section of the Abraham and Straus department store in Brooklyn, New York. Early department stores boasted not just of the amount and variety of their merchandise but also of the magical qualities of the consumer world they created.   (New-York Historical Society)

Leisure and Sport

Not only was American society becoming more attracted to consuming. It was also becoming more concerned with finding uses for leisure time, which for most people was rapidly increasing. Members of the urban middle and professional classes, in particular, found themselves with large blocks of time in which they were not at work—evenings, weekends, even vacations. Factory workers in many industries found their hours declining (from an average of nearly seventy hours a week in 1860 to under sixty in 1900) and thus also had more time to engage in leisure activities. Even farmers found that the mechanization of agriculture gave them more free time to enjoy nonoccupational pastimes. Many Americans, in other words, were coming to live lives that were neatly compartmentalized, with clear distinctions between work and leisure that had not existed in the past. The change produced a search for new forms of recreation and entertainment.

Among the most important responses to this search was the rise of organized spectator sports. And the most popular of all the organized sports was baseball, which by the end of the century was well on its way to becoming the "national pastime." A game very similar to baseball—known as "rounders" and derived from cricket—had enjoyed limited popularity in Great Britain in the early nineteenth century. Versions of the game began to appear in America in the early 1830s, well before Abner Doubleday (who is erroneously believed to have invented the sport) laid out a diamond-shaped field in West Point, New York, in 1839 and attempted to standardize the rules.

By the end of the Civil War, interest in the game had grown rapidly. More than 200 teams or clubs existed, some of which toured the country playing rivals; they belonged to a national association of "Baseball Players" that had proclaimed a set of standard rules. These teams were amateur or semiprofessional. But as the game grew in popularity, it offered opportunities for profit, and the first salaried team, the Cincinnati Red Stockings, appeared in 1869. Other cities soon fielded professional teams, and in 1876 the National League (which still exists) was organized, chiefly by Albert Spalding. Soon a rival league appeared, the American Association. Compe-

Baseball in Chicago
The Boston Red Sox play the Chicago White Sox in August 1904, a year after the Red Sox had won the first World Series between the American and National League champions. An interleague squabble led to the cancellation of the World Series in 1904, but it resumed in 1905 and has experienced no interruption since. Professional baseball was already drawing large crowds in the early 1900s. Over 8,000 attended this game in Chicago. (Library of Congress)

tition between the two was intense, and in 1883 they played a postseason contest, an ancestor of the World Series. The American Association eventually collapsed, but in 1901 the American League was organized. And in 1903, the first modern World Series was played, in which the Boston Red Sox beat the Pittsburgh Pirates. By then, baseball had become an important business and a great national preoccupation (at least among men), attracting paying crowds at times as large as 50,000, building substantial "ball parks" in which to play the games, and engaging the interest of many Americans through extensive reports of the contests in newspapers and magazines.

Baseball was from the beginning a sport that had great appeal to working-class males. Baseball players tended to be people from modest backgrounds. Baseball crowds were drawn to a great degree from

among male urban laborers. The second most popular game, football, appealed for a time to a more elite segment of the male population, in part because it originated in colleges and universities. At first football was a game played informally by rival student groups at the same school. Then, in 1869, the first intercollegiate game in America occurred between Princeton and Rutgers, with twenty-five men on each team. Soon other Eastern schools fielded teams, and the game began to become entrenched as part of collegiate life. Early intercollegiate football bore only an indirect relation to the modern game; it was far more similar to what is now known as rugby. By the late 1870s, however, the game was becoming standardized and was taking on the outlines of its modern form.

As college football grew in popularity, it spread to other sections of the country, notably to the Middle Western state universities, destined soon to replace the Eastern schools as the great powers of the game. It also began to exhibit the taints of professionalism that have marked it ever since. Some schools used "ringers," tramp athletes who were not even registered as students. In an effort to eliminate such abuses, Amos Alonzo Stagg, athletic director and coach at the University of Chicago, led in forming the Western Conference, or Big Ten, in 1896, which established rules governing eligibility. Football also became known for an appalling level of violence on the field; eighteen college students died of football-related injuries and over a hundred were seriously hurt in 1905. The carnage prompted a White House conference on organized sports convened by President Theodore Roosevelt. As a result of its deliberations, a new intercollegiate association (which, in 1910, became known as the National College Athletic Association, the NCAA) revised the rules of the game in an effort to make it safer and more honest.

A wide range of other sports also emerged, both as entertainment for spectators and as recreation for large groups of participants. Basketball was invented in 1891 at Springfield, Massachusetts, by Dr. James A. Naismith, a Canadian working as athletic director for a local college. Boxing, which had long been a disreputable activity concentrated primarily among the urban lower classes, became by the 1880s a more popular and in some places more reputable sport, particularly after the adoption of the Marquis of Queensberry rules (by which fighters were required to wear padded gloves and to fight in rounds limited to three minutes) and the emergence of the first modern boxing hero, John L. Sullivan, who became heavyweight champion of the world in 1882. Nevertheless, boxing remained illegal in some states until after World War I.

The major spectator sports of the era were activities open almost exclusively to men. But a number of nonspectator sports were emerging in which women became important participants. Golf and tennis seldom attracted crowds in the late nineteenth century, but both experienced a rapid increase in popularity among relatively wealthy men and women—usually the only people who could afford to join the exclusive clubs where facilities for the sports were available. Bicycling and croquet also enjoyed widespread popularity in the 1890s among women as well as men. Women's colleges were beginning to introduce their students to more strenuous sports as well—track, crew, swimming, and (beginning in the late 1890s) basketball—challenging the once prevalent notion that vigorous exercise was dangerous to women.

Leisure and Popular Culture

Other forms of popular entertainment developed in the cities in response to the large potential markets there. In small theaters in ethnic communities, immigrants gathered to listen to the music of their homelands and hear comedians making light of their experiences in the New World. Popular plays with simple morals—often set in such exotic locations as the Old South or the West—provided an escape from the often difficult realities of urban life. Urban theaters also created one of the most distinctively American entertainment forms: the musical comedy, which evolved gradually from the comic operettas of European theater. George M. Cohan, an Irish vaudeville entertainer, became the first great creator of musical comedies in the early twentieth century, and he wrote a series of patriotic songs—"Yankee Doodle Dandy," "Over There," and "You're a Grand Old Flag"—that remained popular many decades later.

Vaudeville, too, became a distinctively American medium (even though it was adapted from French models) and remained the most popular urban entertainment in the first decades of the twentieth century. Even small community theaters or owners of modest saloons could afford to offer their customers vaudeville, which consisted of stringing together a variety of acts (musicians, comedians, magicians, jugglers, and others) and was, at least in the beginning, very inexpensive to produce. But as the economic potential of the medium grew, a few promoters began to stage more elaborate spectacles. Florenz Ziegfeld of New York, the most famous vaudeville producer of his day, staged elaborate pageants (the Ziegfeld Follies) filled with lavishly costumed female dancers (known as Ziegfeld Girls). He also helped create some of the great female stars of the era, among them Fanny Brice and Lillian Russell.

Vaudeville was also one of the few entertainment media open to blacks, who brought to this larger stage elements of the minstrel shows that they had developed for black audiences in the late nineteenth century. Some minstrel singers (including perhaps the most famous, Al Jolson) were whites wearing heavy makeup (or "blackface"). But most were black. People of both races, however, performed music based on the gospel and folk tunes of the plantation and on the jazz and ragtime of black urban communities. People of both races also tailored their acts to prevailing white prejudices, ridiculing blacks by acting out demeaning stereotypes.

Although the cities remained the principal home of these new entertainment media, smaller communities had at least some access to them as well. Traveling vaudeville troupes and minstrel shows penetrated many remote communities. Circuses, such as those run by P. T. Barnum and James Bailey, took advantage of the railroad system to move from town to town and perform under large tents that they carried with them. Wild West shows, showing off the alleged feats of cowboys and gunslingers and often displaying Indians as exotic curiosities, developed wide followings as well.

But the most important form of mass entertainment (until the invention of radio and television), and the one that reached most widely across the nation, was the movies. Thomas Edison and others had created the technology of the motion picture in the 1880s, and shortly thereafter short films became available to individual viewers watching peepshows in pool halls, penny arcades, and amusement parks. Soon, larger projectors made it possible to project the images onto big screens, which permitted substantial audiences to see films in theaters. By 1900, Americans were becoming attracted in large numbers to these early movies—usually plotless films of trains or waterfalls or other spectacles designed mainly to show off the technology. The great D. W. Griffith carried the motion picture into a new era with his silent epics—*The Birth of a Nation* (1915), *Intolerance* (1916), and others—which introduced serious plots and elaborate productions to filmmaking.

Motion pictures attracted a truly mass audience, composed of men and women, workers and members of the middle class, young and old. It was perhaps the first truly mass entertainment medium—one that reached all areas of the country and all levels of the population. The great film actors (Charlie Chaplin, Lillian Gish, Mary Pickford, Tom Mix, and others) became idols to millions of Americans.

Not all popular entertainment, however, involved public events. Many Americans amused themselves by reading popular novels and poetry. The so-called dime novels, cheaply bound and widely circulated, became popular after the Civil War, with sensational tales of the Wild West, suspenseful detective stories, sagas of scientific adventure (such as the Tom Swift stories), and novels of "moral uplift" (among them those of Horatio Alger). In addition to adventure stories, publishers distributed sentimental novels of romance, which developed a large audience among women, as did books about animals and about young children growing up. Louisa May Alcott's *Little Women,* most of whose readers were women, sold more than 2 million copies.

Mass Communications

The new urban industrial society required new vehicles for transmitting news and information. And so American publishing and journalism experienced an important change in the decades following the Civil War. Between 1870 and 1910, the circulation of daily newspapers increased nearly ninefold (from under 3 million to more than 24 million), a rate three times as great as the rate of population increase. And while standards varied widely from one paper to another, American journalism began to develop the beginnings of a professional identity. Salaries of reporters greatly increased; many newspapers began separating the reporting of news from the expression of opinion; and newspapers themselves became important businesses.

One striking change was the emergence of national press services, which made use of telegraphic communication to supply papers throughout the country with news and features and which contributed as a result to the standardization of the product. Such services furnished the same news to all their subscribing papers, and syndicates provided their customers with identical features, columns, editorials,

and pictures. By the turn of the century important newspaper chains had emerged, of which the most powerful was William Randolph Hearst's. By 1914, Hearst controlled nine newspapers and two magazines. He also helped popularize a new form of journalism (first introduced by his rival, the publisher Joseph Pulitzer) known as "yellow journalism"—a deliberately sensational, even lurid, style of reporting presented in bold graphics, designed to reach a genuinely mass audience. Yellow journalism reveled in scandal and spectacular exposés (some of them fraudulent, but some of them revealing real problems and helping to produce reforms). They also gave heavy attention to sports, popular entertainment, and fashion.

Another major change occurred in the nature of American magazines. In the past, mostly weekly and monthly periodicals had been literary journals. Now, beginning in the 1880s, there appeared a new kind of magazine, designed to appeal to the masses and achieve a mass circulation. One of the important pioneers of the popular magazine was Edward W. Bok, who took over the *Ladies' Home Journal* in 1899 and, by employing writers who aimed their material at a mass female audience, built the circulation of the journal to over 700,000. By the end of the century, there was a large array of popular magazines, priced at 5 to 15 cents, some of them with circulations of up to a million.

What made these new mass circulation publications possible was the growing importance of advertising in American commercial life. New industries needed above all to create new markets, and advertising was, many believed, the best way to do so. Not only did the amount of advertising increase in the decades after the Civil War, but the nature of the advertisements changed as well. Instead of small-type announcements, listing products and prices, merchants began to use pictures and bold headlines and enticing slogans. They attempted to make advertising a vehicle not just for alerting the public to the existence of a product, but also for stimulating a demand for that product among people who might otherwise not have had any interest in buying it.

High Culture in the Urban Age

In addition to the important changes in popular culture that accompanied the rise of cities and industry, there were profound changes in the realm of "high culture"—in the ideas and activities of intellectuals. Even the idea of a distinction between "highbrow" and "lowbrow" culture was new to the industrial era. In the early nineteenth century, most cultural activities attracted people of widely varying backgrounds and targeted people of all classes. Productions of Shakespeare, for example, were popular entertainments aimed at working-class people as much as at the educated elites. By the late nineteenth century, however, elites were developing an important, autonomous cultural and intellectual life, often quite separate from the popular amusements of the urban masses.

The Literature of Urban America

Foreign observers and even some American intellectuals in the late nineteenth century often viewed the culture of the United States with contempt, as they had since the first days of the Republic. "There is little to nourish and delight the sense of beauty there," wrote the English critic Matthew Arnold in 1888. Mark Twain, a more knowledgeable critic, expressed an equally dismissive view of American culture in 1873, when, in collaboration with Charles Dudley Warner, he published a novel satirizing the new urban-industrial society. The book's title suggests its message: *The Gilded Age*. To Twain, Warner, and others, American life, despite its glittering surface, was essentially acquisitive and corrupt, with little cultural depth.

Whatever the quality of culture and society in late nineteenth-century America, however, it was clear that the growth of industry and the rise of the city were having profound effects on them. Some writers and artists—the local-color writers of the South, for example, and even Mark Twain, in such novels as *Huckleberry Finn*—responded to the new civilization by evoking an older, more natural world. But others grappled directly with the modern order, exposing its problems and offering solutions.

One of the strongest impulses in late nineteenth- and early twentieth-century American literature was the quest for the re-creation of social reality. Some of the nation's most serious writers began to probe the oppression and suffering that they believed the urban-industrial society had created. The trend toward urban realism found an early voice in Stephen Crane, who—although best known for his novel of the Civil

War, *The Red Badge of Courage* (1895)—was the author of a powerful indictment of the plight of the working class. With *Maggie: A Girl of the Streets* (1893), Crane created a sensation through his glum descriptions of urban poverty and slum life. Theodore Dreiser was even more influential in encouraging writers to abandon the genteel traditions of earlier times and turn to the social dislocations of the present, both in *Sister Carrie* and in other, later novels—*The Financier* (1912), *The Titan* (1914), and others—which explored the injustices of the American economic system.

Many of Dreiser's contemporaries joined him in chronicling the oppression of America's poor. Frank Norris published *The Octopus* in 1901, an account of a struggle between oppressed wheat ranchers and powerful railroad interests in California. Another novel, *The Pit* (1903), attacked exploitation in the grain markets of Chicago. Upton Sinclair's *The Jungle* (1906) exposed abuses in the American meat-packing industry and helped to inspire legislative action to deal with the problem. Kate Chopin, a Southern writer who explored the oppressive features of traditional marriage, encountered widespread public abuse after publication of her shocking novel *The Awakening* in 1899. It described a young wife and mother who abandoned her family in search of personal fulfillment. It was formally banned in some communities.

One of the greatest and certainly one of the most prolific of the literary realists was William Dean Howells. Unlike the writers who focused on extremes of poverty and injustice, Howells described the common and the average, exposing the shallowness and corruption in ordinary American life styles. In *The Rise of Silas Lapham* (1884), he offered an unflattering portrait of the self-made businessman. His later novels, written during the more turbulent years of the 1890s and the early twentieth century, dealt more explicitly with social problems and injustices.

Other critics of American society responded to the new civilization not by attacking it but by withdrawing from it. Some, such as Henry Adams, effected an intellectual withdrawal. His great autobiography, *The Education of Henry Adams* (1906), portrayed a man disillusioned with and unable to relate to his society, even though he continued to live in it. Others retreated physically from the United States. Henry James, one of the preeminent writers of the era, lived the major part of his adult life in England and

Europe and produced a series of complex, coldly realistic novels—*The American* (1877), *Portrait of a Lady* (1881), *The Ambassadors* (1903), and many others—that showed the impact of Europe on Americans and his own ambivalence about the merits of the two civilizations.

Art in the Age of the City

American art through most of the nineteenth century had been undernourished and overshadowed by Europe. Most major American artists received their education overseas, painted in a European style (although many chose American subjects), and exhibited—if they exhibited at all—in foreign galleries. By 1900, however, important changes were under way. Now, nearly every major American city had a museum or gallery of at least modest proportions in which native artists could display their work and in which European masterpieces, many of them purchased by the great industrial titans, could be seen. And a number of American artists, although they continued to study and even at times to live in Europe, broke from the Old World traditions and experimented with new styles. John La Farge, for example, made use of light and color in ways that anticipated the French impressionists. Winslow

Homer, perhaps the greatest American artist of the era, was vigorously and almost blatantly American in his paintings of New England maritime life and other native subjects. James McNeil Whistler was one of the first Western artists to appreciate the beauty of Japanese color prints and to introduce Oriental concepts into American and European art.

By the first years of the new century, however, some American artists were turning even more decisively from the traditional academic style (a style perhaps best exemplified in America by the brilliant portraitist John Singer Sargent). Instead, younger painters were exploring the same grim aspects of modern life that were becoming the subject of American literature. Influenced by the work of the French impressionists but shaped, too, by the tenor of American urban life, members of the so-called Ashcan School produced work startling in its naturalism and stark in its portrayal of the social realities of the era. John Sloan, for example, attempted to capture the dreariness of American urban slums in his paintings; George Bellows caught the vigor and violence of his time in paintings and drawings of prize fights; Edward Hopper chose as his theme the starkness (and

Caprice in Purple and Gold, No. 2

James McNeill Whistler painted this formal study in 1864, an example of the academic style against which the Ashcan artists were rebelling. Whistler was one of the few American artists of the late nineteenth century to win serious attention from the artistic establishment of Europe. In this painting, he shows the growing influence of the Far East on European and American art. (Freer Gallery, Smithsonian Institution)

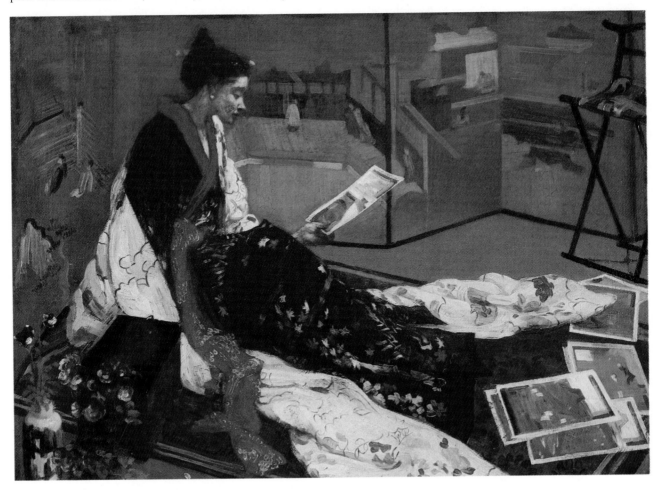

often the loneliness) of the modern city. Ultimately, some of these young artists would move beyond the Ashcan revolt to explore the fields of expressionism and abstraction; they showed their interest in new forms when, in 1913, they helped stage the famous "Armory Show" in New York City, which displayed the works of the French postimpressionists and some American moderns. For a time, however, their work closely paralleled that of the naturalist writers of the era.

The Impact of Darwinism

The single most profound intellectual development in the late nineteenth century was the widespread acceptance of the theory of evolution. The doctrine was associated most prominently with the English scientist Charles Darwin, although it was in fact the culmination of many years of theorizing by many men. It argued that the human species had evolved to its present state from earlier forms of life (and most immediately simian creatures similar to apes) through a process of "natural selection."

Darwinism challenged almost every tenet of traditional American faith. If the evolutionists were right, then man was not necessarily innately endowed by God with a higher nature. He was only a biological organism, another form (even if the highest form) of animal life. History, Darwinism suggested, was not the working out of a divine plan, as many Americans had believed. It was a random process dominated by the fiercest or luckiest competitors.

The theory of evolution met widespread resistance at first from educators, theologians, and even many scientists. By the end of the century, however, the evolutionists had converted most members of the urban professional and educated classes to their point of view. Even most middle-class Protestant religious leaders had accepted the doctrine, making significant alterations in theology to accommodate it. Evolution had become enshrined as an irrefutable theory in schools and universities; virtually no serious scientist any longer questioned its basic validity.

Unseen by most urban Americans at the time, however, the rise of Darwinism was contributing to a deep schism between the new, cosmopolitan culture of the city—which was receptive to new ideas such as evolution—and the most traditional, provincial culture of the rural areas—which remained wedded to fundamentalist religious beliefs and older values. Urban Americans smugly assumed that Dar-

winism had become as basic a scientific truth as the idea that the earth revolved around the sun, that challenges to it were now restricted to only a few superstitious people. In fact, opposition to the theory of evolution remained strong and deep among vast numbers of Americans. Indeed, the late nineteenth century saw not only the rise of a new, liberal Protestantism more in tune with new scientific discoveries. It also saw the beginning of an organized Protestant fundamentalism, which would gain in strength in the ensuing decades and would make its presence felt politically in the 1920s and again in the 1980s.

Out of the controversy over Darwinism emerged a wide range of new intellectual currents. There was the Social Darwinism of William Graham Sumner and others, which industrialists used so enthusiastically to justify their favored position in American life. But there were also more sophisticated philosophies, among them the doctrine that became known as "pragmatism," which seemed to many to be peculiarly the product of Americans and peculiarly suited to the nation's changing material civilization. William James, a Harvard psychologist (and brother of the novelist Henry James), was the most prominent publicist of the new theory, although earlier intellectuals such as Charles S. Peirce and later ones such as John Dewey were at least equally important in its development and dissemination. According to the pragmatists, who accepted the idea of organic evolution, modern society should rely for guidance not on inherited ideals and moral principles but on the test of scientific inquiry. No idea or institution was valid, they claimed, unless it worked. Even religious beliefs, James insisted, were subject to the test of experience. If faith helped an individual understand his or her world, then it was valid for that person; if it did not, then it was not. "The ultimate test for us of what a truth means," James wrote, "is the conduct it dictates or inspires."

An expanding network of social scientists soon brought this same concern for scientific inquiry into areas of thought long dominated by traditional orthodoxies. New economists, such as Richard T. Ely and Simon Patten, challenged old economic assumptions and argued for a more active and pragmatic use of the discipline. Sociologists such as Edward A. Ross and Lester Frank Ward urged the adaptation of scientific method to the solution of social and political problems. Historians such as Frederick Jackson Turner and Charles Beard challenged prevailing assumptions by arguing that economic factors more than spiritual ideals had been the governing force in historical development. John Dewey, for many decades one of the most influential of all American intellectuals, proposed a new approach to education that placed less emphasis on the rote learning of traditional knowledge and more on a flexible, democratic approach to schooling, one that enabled students to acquire knowledge that would help them deal with the realities of their society. The scientific method, he believed, would be the governing principle of this new, "instrumental" education. The relativistic implications of Darwinism also promoted the growth of anthropology and encouraged some scholars to begin examining other cultures—most significantly, perhaps, the culture of American Indians—in new ways. Slowly, small groups of white Americans began to look at Indian society as a coherent culture with its own norms and values that were worthy of respect and preservation, even though they were different from those of white society. It would be many years, however, before those assumptions received wide attention in the United States or had any important impact on policy.

Toward Universal Schooling

A society that was coming to depend increasingly on specialized skills and scientific knowledge was, of course, a society with a fundamental need for effective systems of education. The late nineteenth century, therefore, was a time of rapid expansion and reform of American schools and universities.

Most influential, perhaps, was the spread of universal free public education. That had long been an ideal of American society, but only after the Civil War did it truly begin to become a reality. In 1860, for example, there were only 100 public high schools in the entire United States. By 1900, the number had reached 6,000. And by 1914, that number had doubled—and along with it the number of students attending the high schools. Even more spectacular was the expansion of elementary and grade-school education. By 1900, compulsory attendance laws were in effect in thirty-one states and territories. Most of this expansion occurred in urban areas. Regions with few major cities—such as the South and parts of the Middle West—trailed far behind the urban-industrial areas in providing public education to their citizens. And in the South in particular, educational facilities were largely unavailable to blacks.

The drive to broaden educational opportunities

had an impact on white relations with the Indian tribes. Just as Northern missionaries and philanthropists had long been interested in the education of black Americans and had contributed to the creation of black schools and colleges in the South (see pp. 465–466), so educational reformers sought to provide educational opportunities to the tribes as well, in an effort to "civilize" them and help them adapt to white society. In the 1870s, reformers recruited small groups of Indians to attend Hampton Institute (a primarily black college) and in 1879 organized the Carlisle Indian Industrial School in Pennsylvania, which served for decades as the principal government institution of Indian education. Like many black colleges, Carlisle emphasized the kind of practical "industrial" education that Booker T. Washington had urged on blacks. Beginning in 1889, the Bureau of Indian Affairs (under the direction of Thomas Jefferson Morgan, a professional educator) began aggressive efforts to improve education. The Bureau supervised the creation of day schools on the reservations for young children and of boarding schools (such as Carlisle) for older ones. Ultimately, however, these reform efforts failed. That was partly because the funding and commitment needed to make them genuinely effective quickly faded. It was also because the venture itself—the effort to remove Indians from their traditional surroundings and transform them into members of white society—was unpopular with its intended beneficiaries. Native Americans, like most other Americans, wanted education. But they wanted an education that reflected the nature and values of their own culture.

Although opportunities for education above the high-school level did not expand to nearly the same degree as those below it, colleges and universities were proliferating rapidly in the late nineteenth century. They benefited particularly from great new resources made available by the national government. The federal government, by the Morrill Land Grant Act of the Civil War era, had donated land to states for the establishment of colleges to teach, among other things, agriculture and the mechanical arts. After 1865, particularly in the South and West, states began to take advantage of the law to strengthen existing institutions or to found new ones. In all, sixty-nine "land-grant" institutions came into existence in the last decades of the century—among them the state university systems of California, Illinois, Minnesota, and Wisconsin.

Supplementing the resources of the government were the millions of dollars contributed by business and financial tycoons who endowed private institutions. The motives of the magnates were various: they were influenced by the gospel of wealth; they believed that education would blunt class differences; they realized that the demands of an industrial society called for specialized knowledge; or they were simply vain. Men such as Rockefeller and Carnegie gave generously to such schools as Harvard, Chicago, Northwestern, Syracuse, Yale, Princeton, and Columbia. Other philanthropists founded new universities or reorganized older ones and thereby perpetuated their family names—Vanderbilt, Johns Hopkins, Cornell, Duke, Tulane, and Stanford.

Charles E. Eliot, who became president of Harvard in 1869 at the age of thirty-five and who remained in that position for forty years, pioneered a break with the traditional curriculum. The usual course of studies at American universities emphasized classical and humanistic courses, and each institution prescribed a rigid program of required courses. Under Eliot's leadership Harvard dropped most of its required courses in favor of an elective system and increased its course offerings to stress the physical and social sciences, the fine arts, and modern languages. Soon other institutions in all sections of the country were following Harvard's lead.

Eliot also renovated the Harvard medical and law schools, raising the requirements and lengthening the residence period, and again the Harvard model affected other schools. Improved technical training in other professions accompanied the advances in medicine and law. Both state and private universities hastened to establish schools of architec-

ture, engineering, education, journalism, and business. The leading center for graduate study, based on the German system with the Ph.D. degree as its highest award, was Johns Hopkins University (founded in 1876). In 1875, there were only 399 graduate students in the United States. By 1900, the number had risen to more than 5,000.

Education for Women

The post–Civil War era saw, too, an important expansion of educational opportunities for women, although such opportunities continued to lag far behind those available to men and were almost without exception denied to black women. More than half of all high school graduates in the late nineteenth century were girls, and some such students naturally looked for opportunities to extend their education further.

Some were able to do so by attending existing universities. At the end of the Civil War, only three American colleges (one of them Oberlin) were coeducational. But in the years after the war, many of the land-grant colleges and universities in the Middle West began to admit women along with men, in large part because of their inability to attract enough male students to fill up their space. And some private universities (notably Cornell and Wesleyan) began admitting small numbers of women in the belief that they were promoting a new sexual egalitarianism.

But the idea of coeducation did not prevail as the foundation of women's education in this era. Instead, most women hoping for schooling beyond the sec-

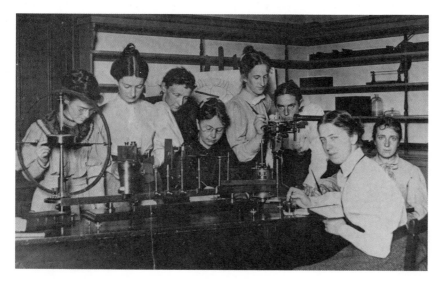

Wellesley College Students in Physics Class

Wellesley College, founded in 1870, was the first women's college in America to have scientific laboratories, including the physics lab shown here. Wellesley was one of a number of institutions founded shortly after the Civil War to give young women access to advanced education. Most graduates of women's colleges went on to lead conventional lives as wives and mothers. Some, however, used college to prepare for careers outside the home. Administrators at Bryn Mawr, a women's college near Philadelphia, are reported to have remarked: "Our failures marry." (Wellesley College Archives)

SIGNIFICANT EVENTS

1836 Mount Holyoke College founded as seminary for women (p. 563)

1839 Abner Doubleday establishes standardized rules for baseball (p. 553)

1865 Vassar College founded (p. 563)

1869 Princeton and Rutgers play first intercollegiate football game (p. 554)

1870 New York City opens elevated railroads (p. 546)

Wellesley College founded (p. 563)

1871 Great fires destroy much of Chicago and Boston (p. 547)

Smith College founded (p. 563)

1872 Tammany's Boss Tweed convicted of corruption (p. 549)

1876 Baseball's National League founded (p. 554)

Johns Hopkins University creates first modern graduate school (p. 562)

1879 Carlisle Indian Industrial School founded in Pennsylvania (p. 561)

1882 Congress restricts Chinese immigration (p. 544)

1884 First "skyscraper" built in Chicago (p. 547)

William Dean Howells publishes *The Rise of Silas Lapham* (p. 557)

1887 American Protective Association founded (p. 544)

1890 Jacob Riis publishes *How the Other Half Lives* (p. 546)

1891 James Naismith invents basketball (p. 554)

1894 Immigration Restriction League founded (p. 544)

1895 Stephen Crane publishes *The Red Badge of Courage* (p. 557)

1897 Boston opens first subway in America (p. 547)

1899 Kate Chopin publishes *The Awakening* (p. 557)

1900 Theodore Dreiser publishes *Sister Carrie* (pp. 549, 557)

1901 Baseball's American League founded (p. 554)

1903 Boston Red Sox win first World Series (p. 554)

Henry James publishes *The Ambassadors* (p. 558)

1906 Earthquake and fire destroy much of San Francisco (p. 547)

Upton Sinclair publishes *The Jungle* (p. 557)

1910 National College Athletic Association founded to regulate collegiate football (p. 554)

1913 Ashcan School artists stage Armory Show in New York City (p. 559)

---

ondary level turned to the growing network of women's colleges, most of them developed as the result of donations from philanthropists. A few female colleges had struggled to establish themselves early in the century. Mount Holyoke, for example, opened its doors to eighty students in 1836 as a "seminary" for women. It did not become a full-fledged college until the 1880s. By then, however, many new female institutions had emerged: Vassar, Wellesley, Smith, Bryn Mawr, Wells, and Goucher. Some of the larger private universities created on their campuses separate colleges for women (such as Barnard at Columbia and Radcliffe at Harvard). Proponents of women's colleges saw the institutions as places where female students could find the greatest outlets for their own skills and creativity, where they would not be treated as "second-class citizens" by predominantly male student bodies and faculties.

The new women's colleges confronted a complex task. On the one hand, they were committed to providing their students with wide opportunities to expand their intellectual and even professional horizons. On the other hand, they felt the need to defend themselves against charges that higher education was not, as many men and even some women believed, too "arduous" for women's presumably frail and delicate physical capacities. At times, the administrators of women's colleges displayed a firm determination to prove that their students were capable of doing the same demanding work as men. At the same time, however, they often included special programs of physical activity, to strengthen their students for the "ordeal" of education. And many women's colleges included as well training for their students in traditional women's roles.

The female college was among the first examples of an important phenomenon in the history of modern American women: the emergence of a distinctive women's community. Most faculty members and many administrators were women (usually unmarried). And the life of the college produced a spirit of sorority and commitment among educated women that had important effects in later years, as women became the leaders of many reform activities. Most female college graduates ultimately married, but they married at a more advanced age than their noncollege counterparts. A significant minority, perhaps over 25 percent, did not marry at all, but devoted themselves to careers. Leaders of Bryn Mawr college remarked at times that "Our failures marry." And while that was surely an exaggeration, the growth of female higher education clearly became for some women a liberating experience, persuading them that they had roles to perform in society other than as wives and mothers.

SUGGESTED READINGS

General Histories.   Howard Chudacoff, *The Evolution of American Urban Society,* rev. ed. (1981); Blake McKelvey, *The Urbanization of America* (1963); Constance M. Green, *The Rise of Urban America* (1965); Charles N. Glaab and Andrew T. Brown, *A History of Urban America* (1967); Arthur M. Schlesinger, *The Rise of the City, 1878–1898* (1933); Sam Bass Warner, Jr., *The Urban Wilderness* (1972) and *Streetcar Suburbs* (1962); Jon C. Teaford, *City and Suburb: The Political Fragmentation of Urban America* (1979) and *The Twentieth-Century American City: Problem, Promise, and Reality* (1986); Lewis Mumford, *The Culture of the Cities* (1938) and *The City in History* (1961).

Mobility and Race.   Stephan Thernstrom, *Poverty and Progress* (1964) and *The Other Bostonians* (1973); Michael Frisch, *Town into City* (1972); Richard Sennett, *Families Against the City* (1970; Clyde Griffen and Sally Griffen, *Natives and Newcomers* (1977); Howard Chudacoff, *Mobile Americans* (1972); Stephan Thernstrom and Richard Sennett (eds.), *Nineteenth Century Cities* (1969); Gilbert Osofsky, *Harlem: The Making of a Ghetto* (1966); Allan H. Spear, *Black Chicago* (1967); Kenneth L. Kusmer, *A Ghetto Takes Shape* (1976); David M. Katzman, *Before the Ghetto* (1966); Olivier Zunz, *The Changing Face of Inequality: Urbanization, Industrial Development, and Immigrants in Detroit, 1880–1920* (1982).

Immigration.   John Bodnar, *The Transplanted: A History of Immigrants in America* (1985) and *Immigration and Industrialization* (1977); Oscar Handlin, *The Uprooted,* rev. ed. (1973); Thomas Kessner, *The Golden Door: Italian and Jewish Immigrant Mobility* (1977); Josef Barton, *Peasants and Strangers: Italians, Rumanians, and Slovaks in an American City* (1975); Virginia Yans-McLaughlin, *Family and Community: Italian Immigrants in Buffalo, 1880–1930* (1977); Philip Taylor, *The Distant Magnet: European Emigration to the U.S.A.* (1971); Marcus Hansen, *The Immigrant in American History* (1940); Maldwyn A. Jones, *American Immigration* (1960); David Ward, *Cities and Immigrants* (1965); Barbara Solomon, *Ancestors and Immigrants* (1965); Elizabeth Ewen, *Immigrant Women in the Land of Dollars: Life and Culture on the Lower East Side, 1890–1925* (1985); Ewa Morawska, *For Bread and Butter: The Life-Worlds of East Central Europeans in Johnstown, Pennsylvania, 1890–1940*

(1985); Jack Chen, *The Chinese of America* (1980); Francis L. K. Hsu, *The Challenge of the American Dream: The Chinese in the United States* (1971); Moses Rischin, *The Promised City: New York's Jews* (1962); Humbert S. Nelli, *The Italians of Chicago* (1970; John W. Briggs, *An Italian Passage* (1978); John B. Duff, *The Irish in the United States* (1971); Mario T. Garcia, *Desert Immigrants: The Mexicans of El Paso, 1880–1920* (1981); Matt S. Maier and Feliciano Rivera, *The Chicanos: A History of Mexican-Americans* (1972); Harry Kitano, *Japanese-Americans: The Evolution of a Subculture* (1969); Victor Greene, *For God and Country: The Rise of Polish and Lithuanian Ethnic Consciousness in America* (1975); Edward R. Kantowicz, *Polish-American Politics in Chicago* (1975); Nathan Glazer and Daniel P. Moynihan, *Beyond the Melting Pot* (1963); Leonard Dinnerstein and David Reimers, *Ethnic Americans: A History of Immigration and Assimilation* (1975); Milton M. Gordon, *Assimilation in American Life* (1964); Thomas Sowell, *Ethnic America* (1981); Robert D. Cross, *The Church and the City* (1967): John Higham, *Strangers in the Land* (1955) and *Send These to Me* (1975).

Urban Poverty and Reform.   Robert H. Bremner, *From the Depths* (1956); James T. Patterson, *America's Struggle Against Poverty* (1981); Thomas L. Philpott, *The Slum and the Ghetto* (1978); Jacob Riis, *How the Other Half Lives* (1890), *Children of the Poor* (1892), and *The Battle with the Slum* (1902); Allen F. Davis, *Spearheads for Reform* (1967); Marvin Lazerson, *Origins of the Urban School* (1971); Stephan F. Brumberg, *Going to America, Going to School* (1986); Selwyn K. Troen, *The Public and the Schools* (1975); David B. Tyack, *The One Best System: A History of American Urban Education* (1974); Barbara Gutmann Rosencrantz, *Public Health and the State* (1972); James H. Cassedy, *Charles V. Chapin and the Public Health Movement* (1962); James F. Richardson, *The New York Police* (1970).

Urban Politics.   John M. Allswang, *Bosses, Machines and Urban Voters* (1977); Alexander B. Callow, *The Tweed Ring* (1966); Seymour Mandelbaum, *Boss Tweed's New York* (1965); Lyle Dorsett, *The Pendergast Machine* (1968); Zane Miller, *Boss Cox's Cincinnati* (1968); John Sproat, *The Best Men* (1968).

Social Thought and Urban Culture.   Lawrence Levine, *Highbrow/Lowbrow: The Emergence of a Cultural Hierarchy in*

America (1988); Morton White, *Social Thought in America* (1949); D. W. Marcell, *Progress and Pragmatism* (1974); Charles Forcey, *The Crossroads of Liberalism* (1961); Lawrence Cremin, *The Transformation of the School* (1961); Frank Luther Mott, *American Journalism,* rev. ed. (1962); Larzer Ziff, *The American 1890s: Life and Times of a Lost Generation* (1966); Jay Martin, *Harvests of Change* (1967); Susan Porter Benson, *Counter Cultures: Saleswomen, Managers, and Customers in American Department Stores, 1890–1940* (1986); Godfrey M. Lebhar, *Chain Stores in America* (1962); John F. Kasson, *Amusing the Million: Coney Island at the Turn of the Century* (1978); Kathy Peiss, *Cheap Amusements: Working Women and Leisure in Turn-of-the-Century New York* (1986); Gunther Barth, *City People* (1980); Allen Guttmann, *A Whole New Ball Game: An Interpretation of American Sports* (1988); Donald R. Mrozek, *Sport and American Mentality, 1880–1910* (1983); Harvey Green, *Fit for America: Fitness, Sport, and American Society* (1986); John A. Lucas and Ronald Smith, *Saga of American Sport* (1978); Dale Somers, *The Rise of Sports in New Orleans* (1972); Eliot Gorn, *The Manly Art: Bare-Knuckle Prize Fighting in America* (1986); Lewis Mumford, *The Brown Decades* (1931); T. J. Jackson Lears, *No Place of Grace: Antimodernism and the Transformation of American Culture, 1880–1920* (1981); T. J. Jackson Lears and Richard Wightman Fox, eds., *The Culture of Consumption* (1983); Christopher Tunnard and H. H. Reed, *American Skyline* (1955).

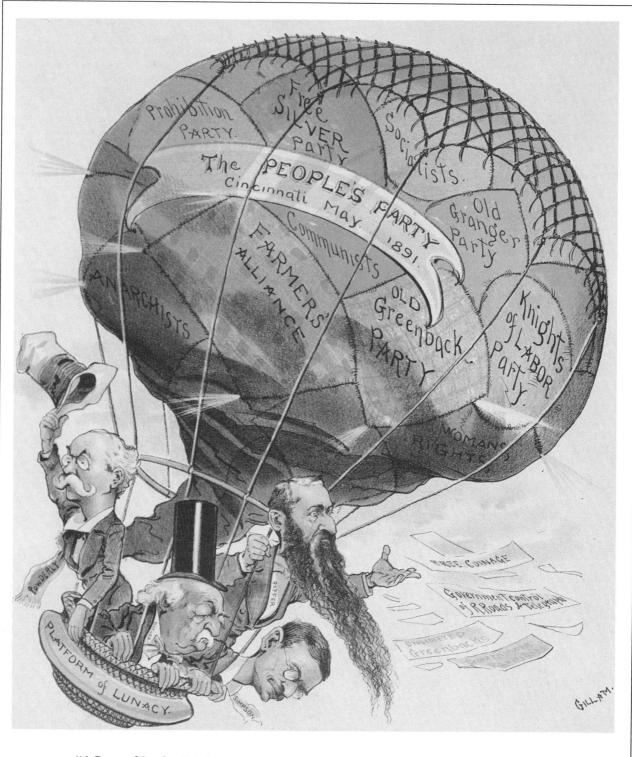

"A Party of Patches," *Judge* **Magazine, June 6, 1891**
This political cartoon suggests the contempt and fear with which many Easterners, in particular,
viewed the emergence of the People's party in 1891. (*Kansas State Historical Society, Topeka*)

CHAPTER 19

◣◈◿

From Stalemate
to Crisis

◣◈◿

The enormous social, economic, and cultural changes America was experiencing in the late nineteenth century strained not only the nation's traditional social arrangements but its political institutions as well. Growth and change brought both progress and disorder. And it was to government, gradually, that Americans would begin to look for leadership in their search for stability.

Yet American government during much of this period was ill equipped to deal with the new challenges confronting it. In the face of unprecedented dilemmas, it responded with apparent passivity and confusion. Its leaders, for the most part, seemed political mediocrities. The issues with which it was concerned were generally of minor relevance to the problems at hand. Rather than taking active leadership of the nation's dramatic transformation, the American political system for nearly two decades after the end of Reconstruction was locked in a rigid stalemate—watching the remarkable changes that were occurring in the nation and doing little to affect them.

Many observers pointed to the doldrums of the American party system as the major cause of this inaction. For in many respects the two parties had by the 1880s come to seem almost identical. "Tenets and policies, points of political doctrine and points of political practice have all but vanished," wrote the English historian James Bryce in 1888. "All has been lost, except office or the hope of it." And indeed there was much in the behavior of both the Democrats and the Republicans to support that view. Both parties strove to avoid taking positions on the great issues of the day: the rise of monopoly, the conflict between labor and management, the decline of the agrarian economy, and the defects of a financial system that produced a major collapse every twenty years or so. They tried, rather, to obscure such issues. And politicians often did appear more concerned, as Bryce had lamented, with government jobs than governmental principles.

But the torpor of the party system was more a symptom than the cause of the political stalemate of the late nineteenth century. The retreat from ideology may have been more pronounced during this period than usual, but seldom do American parties take sharply defined stands on major issues. The real problem in American politics in the 1880s and 1890s was that social and economic conditions were changing more rapidly than were ideas about public policy. Most people recognized that there were problems; few people had any idea what to do about them. Consequently, there was little in American political life to counteract the influence of conservative assumptions and powerful private interests.

The result was a political system in which problems and grievances could fester and grow without any natural outlet. And it was not surprising, under the circumstances, that by the 1890s the United States was heading into a grave national crisis. Difficulties emerged on all sides. An economic depression, the worst in American history to that point, produced widespread suffering and instability. American labor grew militant and at times violent. Above all, perhaps, American farmers—building on years of slow, determined political effort—raised a powerful challenge to the established order through what became known as the Populist revolt. By the mid-1890s, many people were beginning to fear that the nation faced revolution or collapse. Virtually everyone was forced to recognize that American society, for all its progress, faced serious maladjustments.

The Politics of Equilibrium

To modern eyes, the nature of the American political system in the late nineteenth century appears in many ways paradoxical. The two political parties enjoyed during those years a strength and stability that neither was ever to know again. And yet the federal government, which the two parties were struggling to control, was doing little of real importance. The enormous popular enthusiasm for party politics seemed to have had little to do with the very modest substantive actions of government.

What explains this apparent paradox is the nature of popular politics in the late nineteenth century. Americans in those years generally engaged in political activity not because of an interest in particular issues but because of broad regional, ethnic, or religious sentiments. Party loyalty had less to do with positions on public policy than with the way Americans defined themselves culturally.

The Party System

The most striking feature of the late-nineteenth-century party system was its remarkable stability. From the end of Reconstruction until the late 1890s, the electorate was divided almost precisely evenly between the Republicans and the Democrats; and loyalties fluctuated almost not at all. Sixteen states were solidly and consistently Republican, and fourteen states (most of them in the South) were solidly and consistently Democratic. Only five states were usually in doubt, and it was in them that national elections were commonly decided. The Republican party captured the presidency in all but two of the elections of the era, but those victories are misleading as an indication of Republican strength. In the five presidential elections beginning in 1876, the average popular vote margin separating the Democratic and

Republican candidates was 1.5 percent. In three of those elections, the margin was .5 percent or less; and in two of those three (1876 and 1888) the victorious candidate actually polled fewer popular votes than his opponent but won in the electoral college. The congressional balance was similarly stable. Between 1875 and 1895, the Republicans generally controlled the Senate and the Democrats generally controlled the House; in any given election, the number of seats that shifted from one party to the other was very small.

As striking as the balance between the parties was the intensity of public loyalty to them. In most of the country, Americans viewed their party affiliations with a passion and enthusiasm that is difficult for later generations to understand. Voter turnout in presidential elections between 1860 and 1900 averaged over 78 percent of all eligible voters. Even in nonpresidential years, from 60 to 80 percent of the voters turned out to cast ballots for congressional candidates. Large groups of potential voters were disfranchised in these years: women in most states; most blacks and many poor whites in the South. But for adult white males outside the South, there were virtually no franchise restrictions. The remarkable turnout represented a genuinely mass-based politics.

In fact, party politics in the late nineteenth century occupied a central position in American culture, comparable in some ways to the role that spectator sports and mass popular entertainment play today. Political campaigns were often the most important public events in the lives of communities. Political organizations served important social and cultural functions. Political identification was almost as important to most individuals as identification with a church or an ethnic group. Partisanship was an intense, emotional force, widely admired and often identified with patriotism.

What explains this remarkable loyalty to the two political parties? It was not, certainly, that the parties took distinct positions on important public issues. Both parties were solidly probusiness; and while the Republicans were somewhat more prominently identified with the protective tariff and other policies favored by the corporations, the Democrats often supported such measures as well. Both parties were firmly opposed to economic radicalism. Both were committed to a "sound currency" and to the existing financial system. Neither supported any positive programs to aid such troubled economic groups as farmers and workers.

What determined party loyalties was less concrete issues than cultural factors. Region was perhaps the most important of these factors. To white Southerners, loyalty to the Democratic party was a matter of unquestioned faith. The party had been the vehicle for their victory over the hated Reconstruction policies of the Republicans, and it remained the vehicle for the preservation of white supremacy. To many old-stock Northerners, white and black, Republican loyalties were equally intense for the opposite reason. The Grand Old Party had been the party of Lincoln; it had freed the slaves and preserved the Union; it was a bulwark against the forces of slavery and treason.

Religious and ethnic differences also helped determine party loyalties. The Democratic party attracted most Catholic voters, most recent immigrants, and most of the poorer workers; those three groups, of course, often overlapped. The Republican party appealed to Northern Protestants and citizens of old stock. Among the few substantive issues on which the parties took clearly different stands were matters concerning immigrants. The Republicans tended to be more nativist and to support measures restricting immigration. (The American Protective Association was commonly associated with the GOP, a fact the Democrats lost no opportunity to point out—and exaggerate.) Republicans tended as well to favor temperance legislation—laws to restrict the sale of alcoholic beverages. Catholics and immigrants viewed such proposals as an assault on their urban life style and opposed them, and the Democratic party followed their lead.

In the end, then, party identification was usually more a reflection of a wide range of vague cultural inclinations and prejudices than a calculation of economic interest. Individuals might choose to affiliate with a particular party because their parents had done so; or because it was the party of their region, their church, or their ethnic group. And they would typically cling to their party loyalties with great persistence and passion.

Presidents and Patronage

One reason the two parties managed to avoid substantive issues was that the federal government (and for the most part state and local governments as well) did very little, and was expected to do very little. Thus, there were few concrete issues over which to disagree. The leaders of both parties, therefore, were generally less concerned with policy than with office—with winning elections and controlling patronage.

Both parties were dominated by powerful bosses and machines chiefly concerned with controlling and dispensing jobs. The Democrats relied on the important city organizations (such as New York's Tammany Hall), which enabled them to mobilize the voting power of immigrants. The Republicans tended to depend on strong statewide organizations. Roscoe Conkling of New York—tall, handsome, and flamboyant—ruled New York Republicans and exercised considerable power in the United States Senate. To him, politics was a game for professionals, not for amateur "carpet knights." And it was a rough game: "Parties are not built by deportment, or by ladies' magazines, or gush," he once said. Matt Quay of Pennsylvania at times all but dominated not only his own state's Republicans but the national party as well. When Benjamin Harrison won the presidency in 1888, the candidate ascribed his victory to providence. Quay knew better. "Providence hadn't a damn thing to do with it," he announced. He wondered if the candidate knew how many men had violated laws to make him president.

The power of party bosses had an important effect on the power of the presidency, which remained an office of great symbolic importance but one whose occupants in these years found themselves unable to do very much except distribute government appointments. Indeed, filling jobs was almost all a president had time to do. He had to make almost 100,000 appointments (most of them in the post office, the only really large government agency); and to do that, he had to rely on a tiny staff working in a few rooms in the White House. James Garfield, who became president in 1881, once complained, "I have heretofore been treating of the fundamental principles of government, and here I am considering all day whether A or B should be appointed to this or that office."

Even in making appointments, however, presidents enjoyed only limited latitude. They generally had to tread carefully to avoid offending the various factions within their own parties. Rutherford B. Hayes, the victor in the disputed election of 1876 and a man who spent his entire four years in office under a cloud, discovered this unhappy state of affairs early in his presidency. While Democrats ridiculed him unmercifully as "His Fraudulency," he encountered formidable difficulties within his own party. By the end of his administration, two groups—the Stalwarts, led by Roscoe Conkling of New York, and the Half-Breeds, captained by James G. Blaine of Maine—

President and Mrs. Rutherford B. Hayes
Hayes was one of a series of generally undistinguished
late-nineteenth-century presidents whose subordination
to the fiercely competitive party system left them with
little room for independent leadership. This photograph
captures the dignity and sobriety that Hayes and his wife
sought to convey to the public. His wife was a temperance advocate and refused to serve alcoholic beverages in
the White House, thereby earning the nickname "Lem-
onade Lucy." Hayes attracted less whimsical labels. Because of the disputed 1876 election that had elevated him
to the presidency, critics referred to him throughout his
term as "His Fraudulency." (Library of Congress)

Breeds favored reform. In fact, neither group was
much interested in real political change; each simply
wanted a larger share of the patronage pie. Hayes
tried ineffectually to satisfy both groups and also to
award offices on the basis of merit; he succeeded only
in antagonizing virtually everyone.

Hayes's fondest dream was the institution of a
civil-service system, which would insulate many
government jobs from the quadrennial patronage
scramble. But he had little luck with Congress, or
even within the executive branch, in promoting his
ideas. He was unable even to win support for a renewal of the weak civil service commission created
under Grant.

The battle over patronage overshadowed all else
during Hayes's unhappy presidency. And his early
announcement that he would not seek reelection only
weakened him further. He had virtually no power in
Congress. The Democrats controlled the House
throughout his presidency, and the Senate during the
last two years of his term. And the Senate Republicans, led by Roscoe Conkling, fervently opposed his
efforts to defy the machines in making appointments.
Hayes's presidency was a study in frustration.

The Republicans managed to retain the presidency in 1880 despite Hayes's unhappy experience—
in part because of rising prosperity and in part because
they managed to agree on a ticket that made it possible for the Stalwarts and the Half-Breeds briefly to
paper over their differences. After a long convention
deadlock between the Stalwart candidate, former
president Grant, and the Half-Breed hopes, James G.
Blaine and John Sherman, the Republicans finally
nominated a "dark horse," James A. Garfield, a veteran congressman from Ohio. Garfield was known
as a Half-Breed; to conciliate the Stalwarts, the convention thus gave the vice-presidential nomination to
Chester A. Arthur, a Conkling henchman who had
become the focus of considerable controversy when
he was dismissed from a post in the New York customs house by Hayes. To oppose Garfield, the Democrats nominated General Winfield Scott Hancock, a
minor Civil War commander with no national following. Hancock's relative anonymity, combined
with a number of serious Democratic blunders during the campaign, produced a decisive victory for
Garfield, whose electoral majority was 214 to 155.
(His popular vote margin, however, was very thin.
He polled only about 10,000 more votes than his
rival.) The Republicans also captured both houses of
Congress.

Garfield entered the White House as a seemingly

were competing for control of the Republican party
and threatening to split it.

The dispute between the Stalwarts and the Half-
Breeds, which consumed so much political energy
and attention, was characteristic of the political
battles of the era. It had virtually no substantive foundation. Rhetorically, the Stalwarts favored traditional, professional machine politics while the Half-

perfect example of the American success legend. Born in a log cabin in Ohio, he had spent his youth and early manhood as a manual laborer, once working as a mule driver on the Ohio Canal—giving rise to a popular Republican campaign slogan, "from the towpath to the White House." He had worked his way through college, become a teacher, studied law, and been admitted to the bar. In 1863, he was elected to the House of Representatives, where he served with increasing (although never enormous) distinction until he became the Republican standard-bearer.

Garfield began his term in office by provoking some of the same fights that had plagued Hayes—attempting to defy Conkling and the Stalwarts in his appointments and showing support for civil-service reform. He soon found himself embroiled in an ugly public quarrel with both Conkling and Thomas Platt, the other senator from New York and another important Stalwart leader. But before it could be resolved, Garfield found himself victimized by the spoils system in a more terrible sense. On July 2, 1881, only four months after his inauguration, Garfield was shot twice while standing in the Washington railroad station by a gunman who shouted, "I am a Stalwart and Arthur is president now!" The assassin, Charles J. Guiteau, held a grudge because Garfield had refused to give him a government job. (Despite his apparent insanity, Guiteau was ultimately hanged.) Garfield lingered for nearly three months—receiving medical treatment that actually worsened what was originally an only moderately serious condition. At his death, people concerned about the menace of machine politics were doubly grieved. Even some Republicans echoed the sentiment of the man who groaned: "Chet Arthur president of the United States! Good God!"

Chester A. Arthur had spent a political lifetime as a devoted, skilled, and open spoilsman and a close ally of Roscoe Conkling. But on becoming president, he tried—like Hayes and Garfield before him—to follow an independent course and even to promote reform. He was undoubtedly influenced by the horrible circumstances that had brought him to the presidency and by his realization that the Garfield assassination had to some degree discredited the traditional spoils system.

The revelation of the "new" Arthur dismayed most of the party bosses. He kept most of Garfield's appointees in office. He also prodded Congress to pass a civil-service law. An astute politician, he realized that sentiment for reform was running high and that civil-service legislation was likely to pass whether he supported it or not. In 1883, finally, Congress passed the first national civil-service measure, the Pendleton Act. Under its terms, a limited number of federal jobs would be "classified"; applicants for them would be chosen on the basis of competitive written examinations. The law also barred the common practice of forcing officeholders to contribute to political campaigns. A bipartisan Civil Service Commission would administer the act.

At first only about 14,000 of some 100,000 offices were placed on the classified list. But the act gave future presidents the authority to increase the number of civil-service positions by executive order. Every chief executive thereafter extended the list, even if usually to prevent his own appointees from being removed by his successor. By this piecemeal and partisan process, the government finally achieved by the 1940s a system in which the majority of the people working for it were under the merit system.

The Return of the Democrats

The unsavory election of 1884 in many ways epitomized the way in which national political contests in the late nineteenth century focused on personality and factionalism rather than issues. The Republicans refused to nominate Arthur (who was in any case already suffering from an illness that would kill him two years later) and chose instead their most popular and controversial figure, Senator James G. Blaine of Maine—known to his adoring admirers as "the plumed knight" but to thousands of other Americans as a symbol of seamy party politics. To Republican Stalwarts, Blaine was anathema; Conkling, asked if he intended to campaign for Blaine, snapped that he did not engage in criminal activities. An independent reform faction, known derisively by their critics as the "mugwumps," announced they were prepared to bolt the party and support an honest Democrat. Rising to the bait, the Democrats nominated Grover Cleveland, the reform governor of New York. In fact, however, there was virtually no difference between Blaine and Cleveland on any substantive issue.

The campaign became an exercise in personal invective. At torchlit rallies, Democrats chanted: *Blaine! Blaine! James G. Blaine! Continental liar from the state of Maine!* The Republicans, unable to find any evidence of corruption in Cleveland's brief political career as mayor of Buffalo and governor of New York, seized instead on a personal scandal. Cleveland had been accused of fathering an illegitimate child as

Tammany Hall
Tammany Hall was the name of the building in Manhattan (shown here decorated for the 1868 Democratic National Convention) that served for a time as headquarters and meeting place for the political machine of the same name. The organization dominated the Democratic party of New York City in the late nineteenth and early twentieth centuries. Tammany faced frequent and at times successful challenges from reformers and others, who accused it (accurately) of fostering graft and corruption in city elections. But it also inspired intense loyalty from its own, largely Irish constituency because of the services it provided the community and because of the patronage opportunities it offered.   (New-York Historical Society)

a young man; and although his paternity had never been proved, he had agreed to support the infant. Republicans roared out at their rallies: *Ma! Ma! Where's my pa? Going to the White House. Ha! Ha! Ha!*

What may have decided the election, however, was the last-minute introduction of a religious controversy. In the closing days of the campaign, a delegation of Protestant ministers called on Blaine in New York City; and their spokesman, Dr. Samuel Burchard, referred to the Democrats as the party of "rum, Romanism, and rebellion." Blaine (whose mother was a Catholic) seemed not to notice Burchard's indiscretion; and soon the Democrats were spreading the news through New York and other Eastern cities that Blaine had tolerated a slander on the Catholic church. His denial came too late to counteract the charge. New York (with its large numbers of Catholic voters) was the pivotal state in what turned out to be an extremely close election. Cleveland won 219 electoral votes to Blaine's 182; the popular vote showed 4,875,000 for Cleveland and 4,852,000 for Blaine—a Democratic plurality of only 23,000.

Grover Cleveland—short, corpulent, brusque—was not a particularly appealing figure. He was rigid, self-righteous, and haughty. He did not evoke either public or private affection. He did, however, inspire respect. In his brief public career, he had fought politicians, grafters, pressure groups, and Tammany Hall. He had become famous as the "veto mayor" and the "veto governor," as an official who was not afraid to say no. He was the perfect embodiment of an era in which few Americans believed the federal government could, or should, do very much; in which most believed that the main function of politics was to stay out of the way of the expansion of business.

Cleveland hoped to use his presidency to streamline the federal government, to make it more businesslike. He was essentially uninterested in such issues as the currency and the tariff or the problems of farmers and workers. There was no proper role for government, he believed, in dealing with such problems. And he gave voice to that conviction when he explained his veto of an appropriation of $10,000 for drought-stricken farmers. The lesson must never be forgotten, he explained, that "though the people support the Government, the Government should not support the people." His administration was characterized from beginning to end by an unwavering commitment to economy in government.

Like his predecessors, Cleveland had to spend a large proportion of his time dealing with patronage. After years in the wilderness Democrats were hungry for office, and they expected the president to throw the Republican "rascals" out—immediately and in wholesale lots. Instead, the president compromised in a manner that did not completely satisfy either his own party or his mugwump followers. He placed an additional 12,000 offices on the classified list; but of the jobs not under civil service, he removed two-thirds of the incumbents and replaced them with Democrats.

Cleveland did introduce one major economic issue into the political arena. He had always been mildly dubious about the wisdom of high tariffs. And he concluded finally that the existing high rates were responsible for the annual surplus in federal revenues, which was tempting Congress to pass the "reckless" and "extravagant" legislation he so frequently vetoed. In December 1887, therefore, he asked Congress to reduce the tariff rates. Southern and Western Democrats, who already supported tariff reductions, responded enthusiastically to the president's request and pushed through the House a bill incorporating Cleveland's recommendations and providing for moderate reductions. In the Senate, however, the Republican leaders were defiant. Instead of enacting the House measure, they passed a bill of their own actually raising rates. A deadlock resulted, and the tariff became an issue in the election of 1888.

The Democrats renominated Cleveland and supported tariff reductions in their platform. The Republicans settled on former senator Benjamin Harrison of Indiana, who was relatively obscure but formidably respectable (the grandson of President William Henry Harrison); and in their platform they endorsed protection for American producers and generous pensions for Union veterans. The campaign was the first since the Civil War in which an issue of substance was an important factor, the first to involve a clear question of economic difference between the parties. It was also one of the most viciously corrupt (and one of the closest) elections in American history. Harrison won an electoral majority of 233 to 168, but Cleveland's popular vote exceeded Harrison's by 100,000.

Emerging Issues

Unlike William Henry Harrison, who had died only a month after assuming the presidency forty-eight years earlier, Benjamin Harrison lived out his full term of office. Yet his record as president was little more substantial than his grandfather's.

One reason for Harrison's failure was the intellectual drabness of the members of his administration—beginning with the president himself and extending through his cabinet. Another was Harrison's unwillingness to make any effort to influence the Congress. And yet during Harrison's dreary administration, public opinion was finally beginning to force the government to confront some of the pressing social and economic issues of the day. Most notably, perhaps, sentiment was rising in favor of legislation to curb the power of trusts.

By the mid-1880s, some fifteen Western and Southern states had adopted laws prohibiting combinations that restrained competition. But corporations found it easy to escape limitations by incorporating in states that offered special privileges. (New Jersey and Delaware were particularly notorious examples.) Any form of state regulation, moreover, was liable to be rejected by the Supreme Court. If antitrust legislation was to be effective, it would have to come from the national government. In 1888, both parties had made vague promises in their platforms to curb monopolies.

With little debate and by almost unanimous votes in both houses of Congress, the Sherman Antitrust Act became law in July 1890. Congress's only basis for national action against the trusts lay in its constitutional power to regulate interstate commerce; and that power determined the provisions of the new law, which declared illegal any "contract, combination in the form of trust or otherwise, or conspiracy in restraint of trade or commerce." The Sherman Act has been the basis for nearly a century of federal antitrust activity. At the time, however, relatively few members of Congress expected (or wanted) the new law to have any real effect on the structure of the economy. As one senator explained, his colleagues merely wanted to get up "some bill headed 'A bill to Punish Trusts' with which to go to the country" and get themselves reelected.

For over a decade after its passage, the Sherman Act had virtually no impact. Before 1901, the Justice Department instituted only fourteen suits under the law against business combinations, and it obtained almost no convictions. The courts were uniformly hostile to the law and proceeded to weaken it. In *United States* v. *E. C. Knight Co.* (1895), a case in which the government charged that a single trust controlled 98 percent of the manufacture of refined sugar in the country, the Supreme Court rejected the government's case by drawing a curious distinction between

"America Bound on the Rock of Monopoly"

This 1880s cartoon uses the Greek myth of Prometheus to illustrate the problem of monopoly in the United States, a problem that was rapidly becoming a highly charged national political issue. Prometheus (America) is bound to the rock of monopoly by the chains of "defective laws," his vital organs being devoured by predatory monopolists. The serpent of "congressmen used by monopolists" seems about to strike. Agonizingly far away, atop the slowly crawling snail of "legislative action," sits the sleeping "people's rights." (The Bettmann Archive)

W. Aldrich of Rhode Island framed the highest protective measure yet offered to a Congress. It became law in October 1890 as the McKinley Tariff Act. But Republican leaders apparently misinterpreted public sentiment, as the 1890 congressional elections seemed to prove.

Seldom has a party in power suffered such a stunning reversal as befell the Republicans in 1890. Their once substantial majority in the Senate was slashed to 8, and in the House they retained only 88 seats to 235 for the Democrats. Popular revulsion against the McKinley duties, pictured by the Democrats as raising the living costs of the masses, was an undoubted factor in the Republican debacle; McKinley himself was among those who went down to defeat. Nor were the Republicans able to recover in the course of the next two years. In the presidential election of 1892, Benjamin Harrison was again the Republican nominee and Grover Cleveland the Democratic. Once more the platforms of the two parties were almost identical except for the tariff, with the Republicans upholding protection and the Democrats pledging reduction. Only a new third party, the People's party, with James B. Weaver as its candidate, advocated economic reform. (See below, p. 579.) Cleveland amassed 277 electoral and 5,557,000 popular votes, compared to Harrison's 145 and 5,176,000 votes. Weaver ran far behind. For the first time since 1878, the Democrats won a majority of both houses of Congress.

Despite Cleveland's negative record, a large proportion of the people who had voted for him expected him to devise some original approach to the new problems troubling America. His inaugural address rudely disillusioned them, as he reaffirmed his devotion to laissez faire in words that had become familiar: "The lessons of paternalism ought to be unlearned." The policies of Cleveland's second term, therefore, were much like those of his first—devoted to minimal government and hostile to active state measures to deal with social or economic problems. As in his first term, he called on Congress to lower the existing tariff rates. Again, he won passage of a moderate downward revision in the House in 1894, only to see the bill gutted in the Senate. Cleveland denounced the result but allowed it to become law without his signature. The Wilson-Gorman Tariff, as the new law was known, provided a moderate (10 percent) reduction in the general tariff rate. But it offered special protection to sugar refiners and virtually every other important trust.

The bill threw one small crust to reformers: a mi-

manufacturing and commerce. The sugar trust was engaged in manufacturing, not in interstate commerce, the Court declared; and so, despite its obviously monopolistic characteristics, it was not illegal.

The Republicans were more interested, however, in the issue they believed had won them the 1888 election: the tariff. William McKinley of Ohio, a rising party luminary and chairman of the House Ways and Means Committee, and Senator Nelson

Shackled by the Tariff

This 1894 cartoon by the political satirist Louis Dalrymple portrays an unhappy Uncle Sam bound hands and feet by the McKinley Tariff and by what tariff opponents considered a closely related evil, monopoly. Members of the Senate are portrayed as tools of the various industries and special interests protected by the tariff. The caption, "A Senate for Revenue Only," is a parody of the anti-tariff rallying cry, "A tariff for revenue only," meaning that duties should be designed only to raise money for the government, not to stop imports of particular goods to protect domestic industries. (The Granger Collection)

nuscule tax on incomes (a 2 percent levy on incomes over $4,000), a concession to agrarian interests. But the Supreme Court, in *Pollock* v. *The Farmer's Loan and Trust Co.* (1895), declared the income tax unconstitutional. Only a constitutional amendment would permit the government to levy such a tax. (The nation approved such an amendment—the Sixteenth—in 1913.)

In addition to the questions of trusts and tariffs, the federal government began in the 1880s to encounter public pressure for action on another major issue: railroad regulation. For years, Congress had so studiously ignored all public clamor for regulation that proponents of reform had looked instead to the states. Farm organizations in the Midwest (most notably the Grangers—see below, pp. 576–577) succeeded in persuading several state legislatures to pass regulatory legislation in the early 1870s.

The railroad corporations contested the Granger Laws in court, arguing that the statutes preempted Congress's exclusive power to regulate interstate commerce and that they acted to deprive corporations of their property without the "due process" guaranteed under the Fourteenth Amendment. At first, however, the challenges had no effect. The Supreme Court, in *Munn* v. *Illinois* (1877), rejected such arguments, ruling that a state could under some circumstances regulate interstate commerce affecting it, in the absence of national regulation, and that a corporation was not a "person" within the meaning of the Constitution.

These initial Granger victories, however, proved short-lived once new justices friendly to an expanded notion of property rights were appointed to the Supreme Court. The so-called *Wabash* case of 1886 (*Wabash, St. Louis, and Pacific Railway Co.* v. *Illinois*) was the first indication of the new judicial view of state regulation. The Court held that an Illinois statute regulating freight rates was an unconstitutional attempt to control interstate commerce and infringed on the exclusive power of Congress. Later, the Courts limited the powers of the states to regulate commerce even within their own boundaries (in *Chicago, Milwaukee and St. Paul Railroad* v. *Minnesota,* 1890, and later rulings).

If there was to be any meaningful regulation of the railroads, it was now clear, it could come only from the federal government. And Congress, subjected to increasing pressure, grudgingly and inadequately responded in 1887 with the Interstate Commerce Act. This act prohibited discrimination in rates between long and short hauls and other unpopular railroad practices. It required railroads to publish their rate schedules and file them with the government. It provided that all fees for interstate rail transportation were to be "reasonable and just"—but failed to furnish a standard or method to determine the justness of a rate. A five-person agency, the Interstate Commerce Commission, was to administer the act, although the commissioners did not have enforcement powers.

For almost twenty years after its passage, the Interstate Commerce Act—haphazardly enforced and narrowly interpreted by the courts—was without practical effect; it did not accomplish widespread rate reduction or eliminate discrimination. No wonder an attorney general of the United States advised a railroad president not to ask for repeal of the act: "It satisfies the popular clamor for government supervision of the railroads at the same time that that supervision is almost entirely nominal."

The agitation over the tariff, the trusts, and the railroads was a sign that the dramatic growth of the American economy—and the emergence of powerful new institutions as a result—was creating problems that much of the public considered too important and dangerous to ignore. But the federal government's response to that agitation reflected the continuing weakness of the American state. The government still lacked institutions adequate to perform any significant role in American economic life. And American politics still lacked an ideology sufficient to justify any major expansion of government responsibilities. The effort to create such institutions and to produce such an ideology would occupy much of American public life in the coming decades. And it became visible first in a dramatic dissident movement that shattered the political equilibrium that the nation had experienced for the previous twenty years.

The Agrarian Revolt

No group watched the dismal performance of the federal government in the 1880s with more dismay than American farmers. Isolated from the urban-industrial society that was beginning to dominate national life, suffering from a long, painful economic decline, afflicted with a sense of obsolescence, rural Americans were keenly aware of the problems of the modern economy and particularly eager for government assistance in dealing with them. The result was the emergence of one of the most powerful movements of political protest in American history: what became known as Populism.

The Grangers

American farmers were, according to popular myth, the most individualistic of citizens, the least likely to join together in a cooperative economic or political movement. In reality, however, farmers had been making efforts to organize for many decades. There

"The Grange Awakening the Sleepers"
This 1873 cartoon suggests the way the Grange embraced many of the same concerns that the Farmers' Alliances and their People's party later expressed. A farmer is attempting to arouse passive citizens (lying in place of the "sleepers," or cross ties on railroad tracks), who are about to be crushed by a train. The cars bear the names of the costs of the railroads' domination of the agrarian economy. (Culver Pictures)

had been occasional cooperative movements in the first decades of the nineteenth century; but the first major farm organization appeared in the 1860s, less as a movement of protest than as a social and self-help association. The depression of 1873 turned it into an agency of political change.

The Grange had its origins shortly after the Civil War in a tour through the South by a minor Agriculture Department official, Oliver H. Kelley. Kelley was appalled by what he considered the isolation and drabness of rural life, and in 1867 he left the government and, with other department employees, founded the National Grange of the Patrons of Husbandry, to which Kelley devoted years of labor as secretary and from which emerged a network of local organizations. At first, the Granges defined their purposes modestly. They attempted to bring farmers together to learn new scientific agricultural techniques—to keep farming "in step with the music of the age." The Granges also hoped to create a feeling of community, to relieve the loneliness of rural life. An elaborate system of initiation and ritual and a strict code of secrecy lent to the organization many of the trappings of urban fraternal organizations.

At first the Grange grew slowly. But when the depression of 1873 caused a major decline in farm prices, membership rapidly increased. By 1875, the Grange claimed over 800,000 members and 20,000 local lodges; it had chapters in almost every state but was strongest, naturally, in the great staple-producing regions of the South and the Midwest.

As membership grew, the lodges in the Midwest began to focus less on the social benefits of organization and more on the economic possibilities. They attempted to organize marketing cooperatives to allow farmers to circumvent the hated middlemen. And they urged cooperative political action to curb the monopolistic practices of the railroads and warehouses. Throughout the midlands on Independence Day 1873, embittered farmers assembled to hear Granger orators read "The Farmers' Declaration of Independence," which proclaimed that the time had come for farmers, "suffering from long continued systems of oppression and abuse, to rouse themselves from an apathetic indifference to their own interests." The declaration also vowed that farmers would use "all lawful and peaceful means to free [themselves] from the tyranny of monopoly."

The Grangers launched the first major cooperative movement in the United States, although successful collective societies had existed earlier in England and other countries. They set up cooperative stores, creameries, elevators, warehouses, insurance companies, and factories that produced machines, stoves, and other items. Some 400 enterprises were in operation at the height of the movement, and some of them forged lucrative relationships with existing businesses. One corporation emerged specifically to meet the needs of the Grangers: Montgomery Ward and Company, founded in 1872, the first mail-order business. Eventually, however, most of the Grange enterprises failed, both because of the inexperience of their operators and because of the opposition of the middlemen whose businesses they were challenging.

The Grangers worked as well to elect state legislators pledged to their program. Usually they operated through the existing parties, although occasionally they ran candidates under such independent party labels as "Antimonopoly" and "Reform." At their peak, they managed to gain control of the

legislatures in most of the Midwestern states. Their purpose, openly and angrily announced, was to subject the railroads to government controls.

The Granger Laws of the early 1870s, by which many states imposed strict regulations on railroad rates and practices (see above, p. 555), seemed for a time to vindicate the predictions of those farmers who claimed that their new organization foretold a permanent change in the political status of agriculture. But the new regulations were soon destroyed by the courts. That defeat, combined with the political inexperience of many Grange leaders and above all the return of prosperity in the late 1870s, produced a dramatic decline in the power of the association. Some of the Granger cooperatives survived as effective economic vehicles for many years; but the movement as a whole dwindled rapidly. By 1880, its membership had shrunk to 100,000.

The Alliances

The successor to the Granges as the leading vehicle of agrarian protest began to emerge even before the Granger movement had faded. As early as 1875, farmers in parts of the South (most notably in Texas) were banding together in so-called Farmers' Alliances. Under the leadership of the Texan C. W. Macune and others, the Southern Alliance grew rapidly in the 1880s and by the end of the decade could boast more than 4 million members. In the meantime, a comparable movement was under way in the plains states and in the Midwest. This Northwestern Alliance never achieved the size or militancy of its Southern counterpart, but it too became a significant force. As the movement grew, the two Alliances developed an ever closer association with each other.

Like the Granges, the Alliances were in large part a response to local conditions and began by working for primarily local objectives; but they defined those objectives far more broadly. In addition to forming cooperatives and other marketing mechanisms, the Alliances also established stores, banks, processing plants, and other facilities for their members—to free them from dependence on the hated "furnishing merchants" who bound so many farmers into a miserable system of indebtedness. Alliance leaders were concerned, first and foremost, with immediate economic problems and particular local political struggles. Many, however, embraced as well a larger vision of a restored community, in which individuals could once again control their own

Mary Ellen Lease

Although critics insisted that stump speaking was an unsuitable activity for women, Mary Lease was one of the fieriest and most popular of the Populist orators. In 1890 alone, she delivered 160 speeches. Although she is perhaps best remembered for her admonition to Kansas farmers to "raise less corn and more hell," she was outspoken on a wide range of issues, including the troubles in Ireland and women's rights.   (Historical Pictures Service)

economic future. Essential to such communities, they argued, was cooperation—not a rigid collectivism that would suppress individuality, but a sense of mutual, neighborly responsibility that would enable farmers to resist the oppressive outside forces that threatened to enslave them. Alliance lecturers traveled throughout rural areas exhorting farmers to a new awareness of their political and economic plight. They lambasted the tendency in modern society for more and more power to be concentrated in the hands of a few great corporations and financial institutions.

The Alliances were notable, too, for the prominent role women played within them. From the beginning, women were full voting members in most local Alliances. Many held offices and served as lecturers. A few, most notably Mary Ellen Lease, went on to become fiery populist orators. Most others emphasized issues of particular concern to women, especially temperance. Like women in urban areas concerned about the impact of drinking on family life, agrarian women argued that sobriety was a key to stability in rural society.

Although the Alliances quickly became far more widespread than the Granges had ever been, they suffered from similar problems. Their cooperatives did not always work well, partly because the market forces operating against them were sometimes too strong to be overcome, partly because the cooperatives themselves were often mismanaged. Some came under the control of unscrupulous local entrepreneurs, who made them as exploitive as the old system of reliance on railroads and local stores. The enormous numerical strength and ideological fervor of the Alliance movement, combined with its economic failure, helped push it into a new phase at the end of the 1880s: the creation of a national political organization.

The first step came in 1889, when the Southern and Northwestern Alliances, despite continuing differences between them, agreed to a loose merger. But the decisive moment came in 1890, when the Alliances staged a national convention at Ocala, Florida, and issued the so-called Ocala Demands. Although Alliance members were not yet formally proclaiming the existence of a new party, the demands were nothing less than a party platform.

The Alliances played an active role in the 1890 off-year elections and surprised both conservatives and themselves with their success. The farm forces won partial or complete control of the legislatures in twelve states, eight in the South and four in the West. They elected six governors, three senators, and approximately fifty congressmen. The magnitude of the triumph was not perhaps as great as it seemed at first glance. Over forty of the successful Alliance candidates for Congress were loyal members of the Democratic party, who benefited—often passively—from the Alliance endorsements. Nevertheless, the dissident farmers drew enough encouragement from the results to contemplate further political action and—as it gradually became clear that neither of the two major parties was likely to respond to their demands—to form a party of their own.

Sentiment for a third party was strongest among the members of the Northwestern Alliance. But several Southern leaders—among them Tom Watson of Georgia, the only Southern congressman elected in 1890 openly to identify with the Alliance, and Leonidas L. Polk of North Carolina, perhaps the ablest mind in the movement—were similarly becoming convinced of the need for a new political organization. Plans for a third party were discussed at meetings in

Cincinnati in May 1891 and St. Louis in February 1892—meetings attended by many Northern Alliance members, a smaller but still significant number of Southern Alliance leaders, and representatives of the fading Knights of Labor (see above, p. 531), whom some farm leaders hoped to bring into the coalition. Then, in July 1892, 1,300 excited and exultant delegates poured into Omaha, Nebraska, to proclaim formally the creation of the new party, approve an official set of principles, and nominate candidates for the presidency and vice presidency. By common consent, the party already had a name, one first used by the Kansas agrarians: the People's party. The movement was more commonly referred to, however, by the Latin version of that name: Populism.

The election of 1892 dispelled whatever doubts may have remained as to the potential power of the new movement. The Populist presidential candidate—James B. Weaver of Iowa, a former Greenbacker who received the nomination after the sudden death of the early favorite, Leonidas Polk—polled more than 1 million votes, 8.5 percent of the total, and carried six mountain and plains states for 22 electoral votes. Nearly 1,500 Populist candidates won election to seats in state legislatures. The party elected three governors, five senators, and ten congressmen. It could also claim the support of many Republicans and Democrats in Congress who had been elected by appealing to Populist sentiment.

The Populist Constituency

There is no decisive evidence of precisely how many Populists there were, where they came from, or what characteristics they shared. Some generalizations, however, are possible. First, Populism was stronger in some regions than others. Its greatest influence was in an arc of states extending from the Dakotas southward through Nebraska and Kansas; in a string of Southern states stretching from Texas through northern Louisiana, Alabama, and Mississippi, and into Georgia and the Carolinas; and in the Rocky Mountain states. It was weakest in those areas where the Granges had been most successful, because that was where agriculture had managed to achieve its greatest security and stability.

Populism was also more appealing to certain kinds of farmers than to others. Unsurprisingly, it was most often small farmers with little long-range economic security who flocked to the movement—people whose operations were only minimally mechanized, if at all, who relied on one crop, and who had access only to limited and unsatisfactory mechanisms of credit. Large, diversified, efficient producers were not likely to flock to the Populist banner. The status of small farmers differed, of course, from region to region. In the Midwest, the Populists were usually family farmers struggling to hold onto their land (or to get it back if they had lost it). In the South, there were many modest landowners too, but in addition there were significant numbers of sharecroppers and tenant farmers. Whatever their differences, however, most Populists had at least one thing in common: They were engaged in a type of farming that was becoming less viable in the face of new, mechanized, diversified, and consolidated commercial agriculture.

There is evidence, too, that Populists tended to be not only economically but culturally marginal, that the movement appealed above all to geographically isolated farmers who felt cut off from the mainstream of national life and resented their isolation. Populism gave such people an outlet for their grievances; it also provided them with a social experience, a sense of belonging to a community, that they had previously lacked.

The Populist constituency was as notable for the groups it failed to attract as for those it attracted. There were energetic and continuing efforts to include labor within the coalition. Representatives of the Knights of Labor attended early organizational meetings; the new party added a labor plank to its platform—calling for shorter hours for workers and restrictions on immigration, and denouncing the use of private detective agencies as strikebreakers in labor disputes. Populist spokesmen attempted to generate enthusiasm for the movement within the working class; and Populist publications spoke of the natural connection between oppressed farmers and oppressed industrial workers. But it was all to little avail. One problem was that the labor organizations themselves were too weak to be able to deliver any substantial support. Another problem was a consistent failure to define clearly enough the areas of common interest between the two groups.

In the South in particular, white Populists also considered the desirability of attracting blacks, whose numbers and poverty made them possibly valuable allies. And indeed there was an important black component to the movement—a network of "Colored Alliances" that by 1890 numbered over one and a quarter million members. Many Midwestern Alliancemen advocated a full merger of the Colored Alliances with the national movement. Even some

—— WHERE HISTORIANS DISAGREE ——

Populism

American history offers few examples of successful popular movements operating outside the two major parties. Perhaps that is why Populism, which in its brief, meteoric life became one of the few such phenomena to gain real national influence, has attracted particular attention from historians. It has also produced deep disagreements among them. Scholars have differed on many grounds in their interpretations of Populism, but at the heart of most such disagreements have been disparate views of the value of popular, insurgent politics. Some historians have harbored a basic mistrust of such mass uprisings and have, therefore, viewed the Populists with suspicion and hostility. Others have viewed such insurgency approvingly, as evidence of a healthy resistance to oppression and exploitation; and to them, the Populists have appeared as essentially admirable, democratic activists.

This latter view underlay the first, and for many years the only, general history of Populism: John D. Hicks's *The Populist Revolt* (1931). Rejecting the popular view of the Populists as misguided and unruly radicals, Hicks described them as people reacting rationally and progressively to economic misfortune. Hicks was writing in an era in which the ideas of Frederick Jackson Turner were dominating historical studies, and he brought to his analysis of Populism a strong emphasis on regionalism. Populists, he argued, were part of the democratic West, resisting the pressures from the more aristocratic East. (He explained Southern Populism, somewhat awkwardly, by describing the South as an "economic frontier" region—not newly settled like the West, but prey to many of the same pressures and misfortunes.) The Populists, Hicks suggested, were aware of the harsh, even brutal, impact of Eastern industrial growth on rural society, and they were proposing reforms that would limit the oppressive power of the new financial titans and restore a measure of control to the farmers themselves. Populism was, he wrote, "the last phase of a long and perhaps a losing struggle—the struggle to save agricultural America from the devouring jaws of industrial America." A losing struggle, perhaps, but not a vain one; for many of the reforms the Populists advocated, Hicks implied, became the basis of later progressive legislation.

This generally approving view of Populism prevailed among historians for more than two decades. But in the early 1950s—when the memory of European fascism and the uneasiness about contemporary communism combined to create a general hostility among scholars toward mass popular politics—a harsh new view of the Populist movement appeared in a work by one of the nation's leading historians. Richard Hofstadter, in *The Age of Reform* (1955), admitted that Populism embraced some progressive ideas and advocated some sensible reforms. But the bulk of his effort was devoted to exposing both the "soft" and the "dark" sides of the movement. Populism was "soft," he claimed, because it rested on a nostalgic and unrealistic myth, because it romanticized the nation's agrarian past and refused to confront the realities of modern life. Farmers were, he argued, themselves committed to the values of the capitalist system they claimed to abhor. And Populism was "dark," he argued, because it was permeated with bigotry and ignorance. Populists, he claimed, revealed anti-Semitic tendencies, and they displayed animosity toward intellectuals, Easterners, and urbanites as well. He stopped short of comparing Populism directly to twentieth-century fascism, but other scholars, adopting elements of his approach, made such connections explicitly.

Almost immediately, historians more favorably

white Southern leaders displayed a notable willingness to foster interracial cooperation. But in the end, the influence of white racism proved stronger than the influence of common economic interests. Most white Populists were willing to accept the assistance of blacks only as long as it was clear that whites would remain indisputably in control. When conservatives began to attack the Populists for undermining white supremacy, the interracial character of the movement quickly faded.

Populist leaders, although easier to identify than their constituencies, are nevertheless also difficult to

WHERE HISTORIANS DISAGREE

disposed toward mass politics in general, and Populism in particular, began to challenge what became known as the "Hofstadter thesis." Norman Pollack argued in a 1962 study, *The Populist Response to Industrial America,* and in a number of articles, that the agrarian revolt had rested not on nostalgic, romantic concepts but on a sophisticated, farsighted, and even radical vision of reform—one that recognized, and even welcomed, the realities of an industrial economy, but one that sought to make that economy more equitable and democratic by challenging many of the premises of capitalism. Walter T. K. Nugent, in *Tolerant Populists* (1963), argued—as his title implies—that the Populists in Kansas were far from bigoted, that they not only tolerated but welcomed Jews and other minorities into their party, and that they offered a practical, sensible program.

It was not until 1976, however, that a comprehensive study of Populism emerged that could rival Hicks and Hofstadter in its influence. Lawrence Goodwyn, in *Democratic Promise* (and in a briefer version of the same work, *The Populist Moment,* published in 1978), described the Populists as members of a "cooperative crusade," battling against the "coercive potential of the emerging corporate state." Populists were more than the nostalgic bigots Hofstadter described, more even than the progressive reformers portrayed by Hicks. They offered a vision of truly radical change, widely disseminated through what Goodwyn called a "movement culture." They advocated an intelligent, and above all a democratic, alternative to the inequities of modern capitalism.

At the same time that historians were debating the question of what Populism meant, they were arguing as well over who the Populists were. Hicks, Hofstadter, and Goodwyn disagreed on many things, but they shared a general view of the Populists as victims of economic distress—usually one-crop farmers in economically marginal agricultural regions victimized by drought and debt. Other scholars, however, have suggested that the problem of identifying the Populists is more complex. Sheldon Hackney, in *Populism to Progressivism in Alabama* (1969), has argued that the Populists were not only economically troubled, but socially rootless, "only tenuously connected to society by economic function, by personal relationships, by stable community membership, by political participation, or by psychological identification with the South's distinctive myths." Peter Argersinger, Stanley Parsons, James Turner, and others have similarly suggested that Populists were characterized by a form of social and even geographical isolation. Steven Hahn's 1983 study *The Roots of Southern Populism* identifies poor white farmers in the "upcountry" as the core of Populist activity in Georgia; and he argues that they were reacting not simply to the psychic distress of being "left behind," but also to a real economic threat to their way of life—to the encroachments of a new commercial order in which they had never been and could never be a part.

There has, finally, been continuing debate over the legacy of Populism. Historians and politicians alike have argued repeatedly that a Populist tradition has survived throughout the twentieth century, influencing movements as disparate as those led by Huey Long in the 1930s and George Wallace in the 1960s. Others have maintained that the term "Populism" has been used (and misused) so widely as to have become virtually meaningless, that its only real value is in reference to the agrarian insurgents of the 1890s, who first gave meaning to the word.

categorize. Most were members of the rural middle class: professional people, editors and lawyers, or long-time politicians and agitators. Few were themselves marginal farmers. Almost all leaders were, like their constituents, Protestants. But beyond these basic characteristics, there were wide variations. Some Populist leaders were somber, serious theoreticians; others were semihysterical rabble-rousers. In the South, in particular, Populism produced the first generation of what was to become a distinctive and enduring political breed—the "Southern demagogue." Tom Watson in Georgia, Jeff Davis in Arkansas, and others attracted widespread popular support by arousing the resentment of poor Southerners against the entrenched Bourbon aristocracy. They were the beginning of a line of such figures that stretched well into the twentieth century. There were similarly flamboyant leaders in the Midwest: "Sockless" Jerry Simpson of Kansas, for example, or Ignatius Donnelly of Minnesota. Donnelly, in particular, seemed to exemplify the divided character of the movement: sincere idealism combined with crassness and opportunism. A committed, principled man who spoke eloquently on behalf of Populist ideals and appeared sincerely to believe in them, Donnelly was also at times something of a charlatan. As a member of Congress, he compiled a shabby legislative record marked, among other things, by a series of seamy, secret deals with railroad companies.

The Populist Ideology

The ideology of Populism, like the character of its leadership, was a complex combination of progressive idealism and bewildering rhetorical excess. There were three basic elements of that ideology: a concrete program of reform, a strident and at times almost hysterical denunciation of enemies, and a millennial vision of a just and stable society.

The reform program of the Populists was spelled out first in the Ocala Demands of 1890 and then, even more clearly, in the Omaha platform of 1892. Among the most prominent of the many issues included in these documents was a proposal for a system of "subtreasuries," which would replace and strengthen the cooperatives with which the Grangers and Alliances had been experimenting for years. The government would establish a network of warehouses, where farmers could deposit their crops. Using those crops as collateral, growers could then borrow money from the government at low rates of interest and wait for the price of their goods to go up before selling them. In addition, the Populists called for the abolition of national banks, which they believed were dangerous institutions of concentrated power; the end of absentee ownership of land; the direct election of United States senators (which would weaken the power of conservative state legislatures); and other devices to improve the ability of the people to influence the political process. They called as well for regulation and (after 1892) government ownership of railroads, telephones, and telegraphs. And they demanded a system of government-operated postal savings banks, a graduated income tax, the inflation of the currency, and later, the remonetization of silver. Some of the Pop-

ulist proposals were clearly unrealistic, but much of the platform was a serious and responsible effort to find solutions to difficult problems.

Less serious and responsible were the Populist denunciations of enemies, which at times became so strident and hysterical as to border on the irrational. A few Populists were openly anti-Semitic, pointing to the Jews as leaders of the obscure financial forces attempting to enslave them. Others were anti-intellectual, anti-Eastern, and antiurban. Some of the leading Populists gave an impression of personal failure, brilliant instability, and brooding communion with mystic forces. Ignatius Donnelly, for example, wrote one book locating the lost isle of Atlantis, another claiming that Bacon had written Shakespeare's plays, and still another—*Caesar's Column* (1891)—embodying an almost lunatic vision of bloody revolution and the creation of a Populist utopia. Tom Watson, once a champion of interracial harmony, ended his career baiting blacks and Jews.

Yet the occasional bigotry of the movement should not be allowed to dominate the image of Populism. The hysterical quality of some Populist "scapegoating" can be explained in part by the condition of many of the members of the movement—people whose personal distress was so great that some excesses were all but inevitable. Some of this denunciation of enemies, moreover, was not as irrational as critics often charged. The rhetoric may have been excessive, but the most frequent targets—banks, railroads, monopolies—were far from guiltless in creating the problems of the farmer.

The resentment against supposed villains existed alongside a well-developed view of a just and stable society. The Populists argued not only for the destruction of monopolistic power but for a new social morality. Society, they claimed, had an obligation to protect the well-being of its individual citizens. The rights of property ownership were, therefore, secondary to the needs of the community. Populists did not reject the idea of private property; most were themselves landowners or aspirants to land ownership. They did, however, emphatically reject the laissez-faire orthodoxies of their time, the idea that the rights of ownership are absolute. They raised, in short, one of the most overt and powerful challenges of the era to the direction in which American industrial capitalism was moving. Populism was not a challenge to industrialization or to capitalism itself, but to what the Populists considered the brutal and chaotic way in which the economy was developing. Progress and growth should continue, they urged,

Taking Arms Against the Populists
Kansas was a Populist stronghold in the 1890s, but the new party faced powerful challenges. In 1893 state Republicans disputed an election that the Populists believed had given them control of the legislature. When the Populists occupied the statehouse, Republicans armed themselves, drove out the Populists, and seized control of the state government. Republican members of the legislature pose here with their weapons in a photograph perhaps intended as a warning to any Populists inclined to challenge them. (Kansas State Historical Society, Topeka)

but it should be strictly defined by the needs of individuals and communities.

The Crisis of the 1890s

The emergence of a powerful movement of agrarian protest was only one of many factors that were combining by the early 1890s to create a national political crisis. There was a severe depression, which began in 1893 and which exacerbated the unhappiness of not only farmers but other groups as well. There was widespread labor unrest and violence, culminating in the tumultuous strikes of 1894, of which the Pullman strike was only the most prominent example. There was the continuing failure of either major party to respond to the growing distress. And there was the rigid conservatism of Grover Cleveland, who took office (for the second time) just at the moment that

the economy collapsed. Out of this growing sense of crisis came some of the most heated political battles in American history, culminating in the dramatic campaign of 1896, on which, many Americans came to believe, the future of the nation hung.

The Panic of 1893

Benjamin Harrison sent a message to Congress early in 1893, shortly before he left the White House, stating, "There has never been a time in our history when work was so abundant or when wages were so high." Only months later, with the second Cleveland administration hardly settled in office, the Panic of 1893 precipitated the most severe depression the nation had yet experienced.

The panic began in March 1893, when the Philadelphia and Reading Railroad declared bankruptcy. Two months later, the National Cordage Company (a new national corporation that was trying, but failing, to establish itself as the dominant force in the industry) collapsed as well. Together, the two corporate failures precipitated a collapse of the stock market. And since many of the major New York banks were heavy investors in the market, a wave of bank failures soon began. The problems of the banking system caused a contraction of credit, which meant that many of the new, aggressive businesses that had recently begun operations soon went bankrupt because they were unable to secure the loans they needed. There were other, longer-range causes of the financial collapse. Depressed prices in agriculture since 1887 had weakened the purchasing power of farmers, the largest group in the population. Depression conditions that had begun earlier in Europe were resulting in a loss of American markets abroad, a decline in the export trade, and a withdrawal by foreign investors of gold invested in the United States.

Above all, perhaps, the depression was a result of several structural flaws in the American economy. In the frenzied atmosphere of competition and growth of the 1880s, businessmen had made enormous capital investments in enterprises that could not possibly pay for themselves. Railroads, in particular, were expanding far too rapidly, well beyond market demand. The depression reflected, too, the degree to which the American economy was now interconnected, the degree to which failures in one area affected all other areas. And the depression showed how dependent the economy remained on the health of the railroads, which remained the nation's most powerful corporate and financial institutions. When the railroads suffered, as they did beginning in 1893, everything suffered.

Once the panic began, its effects spread with startling speed. In a period of six months, more than 8,000 business concerns failed, 156 railroads went into receivership, and 400 banks suspended operations. Agricultural prices tumbled to new lows. Perhaps as many as 1 million workers, 20 percent of the labor force, lost their jobs—the highest level of unemployment in American history to that point, a level comparable to that of the Great Depression of the 1930s. The leading financial newspaper of the time declared in the summer of 1893: "The month of August will long remain memorable in our industrial history. Never before has there been such a sudden and striking cessation of industrial activity. Nor is any section of the country exempt from the paralysis." There had been serious financial crises before, but the depression of the 1890s was unprecedented

The Panic of 1893
The 1893 depression was America's first experience of mass industrial unemployment. The New England illustrator Charles Dana Gibson, generally known for portraits of aristocratic women ("Gibson Girls"), produced this pen-and-ink sketch of an urban bread line in 1893. The costumes of the men suggest how the Depression affected working people and middle-class people alike. (Dover Publications)

in both its severity and its persistence. Although there was slight improvement beginning in 1895, real prosperity did not return until 1901.

The suffering caused by the depression naturally produced widespread economic and political unrest, not least among the enormous numbers of unemployed workers. In 1894, Jacob S. Coxey, an Ohio businessman and Populist, began advocating a massive public works program, through which the government would spend $500 million and hire the unemployed to do the work. He also advocated inflation of the currency.

When it became clear that his proposals were making no progress in Congress, Coxey announced that he would "send a petition to Washington with boots on"—a march of the unemployed to the capital to present their demands to the government. "Coxey's Army," as it was known, numbered only about 500 when it reached Washington, after having marched on foot from Massillon, Ohio. The marchers were barred from the Capitol by armed police. Coxey was arrested and later convicted (of walking on the grass). He and his followers were herded into camps because their presence supposedly endangered public health. Congress took no action on their demands.

Coxey's Army was only one of several industrial protest movements—some of them larger than Coxey's—to stage conspicuous marches and rallies in the 1890s. There were many signs of union unrest as well during the decade—the Homestead and Pullman strikes, for example. (See above, pp. 533–535.) To many Americans, the worker unrest seemed to augur a dangerous instability, even perhaps a revolution. Labor radicalism—some of it real, much of it imagined by the frightened middle class—was seldom far from the public mind, heightening the general sense of crisis.

The Silver Question

The financial panic weakened the government's monetary system, and in the minds of such people as Cleveland, the instability of the currency was the primary cause of the depression. The "money question," therefore, became the basis for some of the most dramatic political conflicts of the era. It had a long history.

The currency issue is a complicated and confusing one, and it has often been difficult for later generations to understand the enormous passions the controversy aroused. The heart of the debate was over what would form the basis of the dollar, what would lie behind it and give it value. Today, the value of the dollar rests on little more than public confidence in the government. But in the nineteenth century, currency was assumed to be worthless if there was not something concrete behind it—precious metal (specie), which holders of paper money could collect if they presented their currency to a bank or to the Treasury.

The United States during most of its existence as a nation had recognized two metals—gold and silver—as a basis for the dollar, a situation known as "bimetallism." By the 1870s, however, the system had begun to produce various problems. The official ratio of the value of silver to the value of gold for purposes of creating currency (the "mint ratio") was established at 16 to 1: Sixteen ounces of silver equaled one ounce of gold. But the actual commercial value of silver (the "market ratio") was, in fact, much higher than that. Owners of silver could get more by selling it for manufacture into jewelry and other objects than they could by taking it to the mint for conversion to coins. So they stopped taking it to the mint, and the mint stopped coining silver.

In 1873, Congress passed a law that seemed simply to recognize the long-existing situation by officially discontinuing silver coinage. Few objected at the time; but within a few years the measure began to create controversy. Silver prices in 1873 had already begun to fall, and it soon became clear that Congress had foreclosed a very real potential method of expanding the currency. Before long, many Americans concluded that a conspiracy of big bankers had been responsible for the "demonetization" of silver. Critics of the law referred to it as the "Crime of '73."

That very year, 1873, the silver price fell to a point at which the market ratio between silver and gold was the same as the mint ratio. In subsequent years, the market value of silver continued to fall—to well below the old mint ratio of 16 to 1. The drop was due simply to changes in demand and supply. The world demand for silver decreased as several European countries abandoned bimetallism and adopted the "gold standard"—defining their currencies only in terms of gold and issuing only gold coins. And at the same time that European governments were disposing of their holdings, huge new deposits of ore were being discovered and exploited in Nevada, Colorado, and other Western states.

Two groups of Americans were especially determined to undo the "Crime of '73." One consisted of the silver-mine owners, now understandably eager to have the government take their surplus silver and pay them much more than the market price. The other group consisted of discontented farmers, who wanted an increase in the quantity of money—an inflation of the currency—as a means of raising the prices of farm products and easing payment of the farmers' debts. The inflationists demanded that the government return at once to "free silver"—that is, to the "free and unlimited coinage of silver" at the old ratio of 16 to 1. In 1878, a coalition of Democrats and Republicans from the South, Midwest, and Far West attempted to push a free-silver bill through Congress. They had to settle for a compromise, the Bland-Allison Act, which directed the government to purchase and coin at the old ratio only a limited amount of silver (from $2 million to $4 million worth per month).

Later, in 1890, the Sherman Silver Purchase Act directed the Treasury to buy 4.5 million ounces of silver each month—an amount estimated to be the maximum domestic production—and to pay for the purchased bullion in Treasury notes. But the bill did little to appease the inflationists. Since the purchased silver was not to be coined, the amount of money in circulation did not increase materially, and the price of silver kept on falling.

Ever since the Resumption Act of 1875 (which had retired the Civil War greenbacks), the Treasury had tried to maintain a minimum gold reserve of $100 million to redeem its paper and silver dollars. During the prosperous 1880s, the reserve increased, and it reached the figure of $190 million by 1890. But in the last two years of the Harrison administration it declined sharply—as revenues declined because of the McKinley Tariff (whose prohibitively high duties kept foreign companies from sending their goods to America and hence from paying duties on them) and as government expenses increased to pay for pensions, internal improvements, and the purchase of silver required by the Sherman Silver Purchase Act. Those who continued to hold greenbacks and silver certificates grew nervous at rumors that the government might abandon the gold standard, which would, they feared, devalue the notes they held; thus they turned their currency in for gold at an increasing rate. When Cleveland returned to office in 1893, the reserve had shrunk to a little over $100 million.

The panic of that year intensified the rush for gold, and soon the reserve had sunk below the minimum deemed necessary to sustain the gold standard. Cleveland had always disliked the Sherman Silver Purchase Act, and now he was convinced that it was the chief factor draining gold from the Treasury, that it would, if allowed to stand, force the country off the gold standard and impair the government's financial honor. Early in his second administration, therefore, he summoned Congress into special session and demanded the repeal of the Sherman Act. He got his way, but only after a bitter and divisive battle that helped create a permanent split in the Democratic party. The president's gold policy had aligned the Southern and Western Democrats in a solid phalanx against him and his Eastern followers.

The division over the money question reflected more than a disagreement over currency. It revealed opposing views of the proper nature of society and government. To its supporters, the gold standard was essential to America's ability to engage in world trade. It was also an important emotional symbol. It stood for stability, fiscal soundness, and public morality. An assault on the gold standard, they believed, would be the same as an assault on the sanctity of contracts or the rights of property. It would be a threat to civilization itself.

Opponents of the gold standard, however, took a different view. To them, gold placed artificial restrictions on the currency, allowing far too little money to circulate for the needs of a growing economy. In particular, the gold standard made it difficult for debtors to repay their loans and for investors to find credit for new ventures. More than that, however, "free silver" became a symbol of liberation. Silver would be a "people's money," as opposed to gold, the money of oppression and exploitation. It would be a panacea that would eliminate the indebtedness of farmers and of whole regions of the country. A graphic illustration of the popularity of the silver issue was the enormous success of William H. Harvey's *Coin's Financial School,* published in 1894, which became one of the great best sellers of its age. The fictional Professor Coin ran a school, an imaginary institution specializing in finance, and the book reproduced his lectures and his dialogues with his students. The professor's brilliant discourses left even his most vehement opponents dazzled as he persuaded his listeners, with simple logic, of the almost miraculous restorative qualities of free silver: "It means the reopening of closed factories, the relighting of fires in darkened furnaces; it means hope instead of despair; comfort in place of suffering; life instead of death."

"A Cross of Gold"

The Populists at first did not pay a great deal of attention to the silver issue. But as the party developed strength, the money question developed an increasing importance, if only for tactical reasons. The Populists desperately needed money to finance their campaigns. Silver-mine owners were willing to provide it but insisted on an elevation of the money plank and the subordination of other proposals. And the Populists needed to form alliances with other political groups. The "money question" seemed a way to win the support of many people not engaged in farming but nevertheless starved for currency. The election of 1896 appeared to some Populists to provide an unmatched opportunity to expand their influence and reach for real national power.

As the election approached, Republicans—gloating over the failure of the Democrats to deal effectively with either the economic crisis or the social chaos that seemed to have emerged from it—were confident of success. The only apparent question of importance was the identity of the man they would anoint as the next president. Marcus A. Hanna, boss of the Ohio machine and soon to be national boss of the party, had picked out his man—

William Jennings Bryan
Bryan addresses a crowd late in his career, displaying the flamboyant oratorical style that characterized his public life from the beginning. The poster at the lower left of the platform shows him as he appeared in the 1890s, when, as a young congressman from Nebraska, he became known as the "Boy Orator of the Platte" and the leader of the national free-silver movement.
(Library of Congress)

William McKinley, governor of Ohio, who as a congressman had been the author of the tariff act of 1890. By calling him "Bill McKinley, the agent of prosperity," and the "champion of protection" for American producers, Hanna secured McKinley the Republican nomination. The party platform opposed the free coinage of silver except by international agreement with the leading commercial nations (which everyone realized was highly unlikely). Thirty-four delegates from the mountain and plains states walked out in protest. Their destination was the Democratic party.

The Democrats met amid scenes of drama seldom equaled in American politics. Southern and Western delegates came to the convention determined to seize control of the party from conservative Easterners. Eager to stem challenges from the Populist party in their sections, they hoped to incorporate some important Populist demands—among them free silver—into the Democratic platform. And they wanted as well to nominate a prosilver candidate.

The divided platform committee presented two reports to the convention—one expressing the majority opinion, the other a minority dissent. The majority report, reflecting the views of the Westerners and Southerners, demanded tariff reduction, endorsed the principle of the income tax, denounced the issuing of currency notes by the national banks, condemned the use of injunctions in industrial disputes, pledged a "stricter control" of trusts and railroads, and—most prominently—supported free silver: "We demand the free and unlimited coinage of both silver and gold at the present legal ratio of 16 to 1, without waiting for the aid or consent of any other nation." The minority report, the product of the party's Eastern wing, echoed the Republican platform by opposing the free coinage of silver except by international agreement. The debate over the two competing platforms dominated the convention.

Speakers on both sides debated the resolutions, and the defenders of the gold standard had the better of the argument—until the final address. Then a handsome young man from the Nebraska delegation walked to the platform to close the debate. He was William Jennings Bryan, thirty-six years old. His political experience was limited to two terms in the House of Representatives, but Bryan was widely known in the plains country as a magnetic orator. He eagerly (and not entirely secretly) hoped that his rhetorical talents might win him the presidential nomination. His magnificent, organlike voice echoed through the farthest reaches of the hall, as he delivered what became one of the most famous political speeches in American history. He ended with a passage that sent his audience into something close to a frenzy and that was repeated by later generations of schoolboys all over rural America: "If they dare to come out in the open and defend the gold standard as a good thing, we will fight them to the uttermost. Having behind us the producing masses of this nation and the world, supported by the commercial interests, the laboring interests and the toilers everywhere, we will answer their demand for a gold standard by saying to them: 'You shall not press down upon the brow of labor this crown of thorns; you shall not crucify mankind upon a cross of gold.' "

The convention voted to adopt the prosilver platform. The agrarians had found their leader. And the following day, Bryan was nominated for president on the fifth ballot. One Republican, Joseph Foraker, when asked if he thought the epithet Boy Orator of the Platte was an apt one for Bryan, replied that it was, because the Platte River was six inches deep and six miles wide at the mouth. But many of Bryan's admirers applied a more accurate label to their hero: the Great Commoner. Born in Illinois of typical middle-class stock, he had attended a small sectarian college, had practiced law with only average success, and then, repeating a normal American pattern, had moved to Nebraska, a frontier area, to try his fortune. He served as a potent symbol of rural, Protestant, middle-class America.

The choice of Bryan and the nature of the Democratic platform placed the Populists in a cruel quandary. They had expected both the major parties to adopt conservative programs and nominate conservative candidates, leaving the Populists to represent the growing forces of protest. But now the Democrats had stolen much of their thunder. The Populists faced the choice of naming their own candidate and splitting the protest vote or endorsing Bryan and losing their identity as a party. When the party assembled, the convention (amid considerable acrimony) voted to approve Bryan but nominated its own vice-presidential candidate, Tom Watson, whom they expected the Democrats to embrace but whom the Democrats ignored. Many Populists argued fervently that "fusion" with the Democrats—who had endorsed free silver, but ignored other and more important Populist demands—would destroy their party. But the majority concluded that there was no viable alternative.

The Conservative Victory

The campaign of 1896 produced both passion and desperation. The business and financial community, frightened beyond reason at the prospect of Bryan's sitting in the White House and taking advice from John P. Altgeld and Ignatius Donnelly, pressed lavish contributions on the Republicans—perhaps as much as $7 million. The Democrats, in contrast, reported expenditures of only $300,000, a sum only slightly larger than the contribution of a single firm, Standard Oil, to the Republican war chest.

Shrewdly, Hanna kept McKinley largely out of sight, knowing better than to pit his dull and solemn candidate against the matchless Bryan. From his home at Canton, Ohio, McKinley conducted a dignified "front-porch" campaign before pilgrimages of the Republican faithful, organized and paid for by Hanna. They came every day, and McKinley always had a speech ready for them. He stressed one theme: The Republican party was the only agency that could bring prosperity to the country.

No such decorous restraint marked the campaigning of the young and vital Bryan. Previous candidates had occasionally addressed audiences in campaigns and had even toured the country to speak at a few selected points. But Bryan was the first to stump every section systematically, to appear in villages and hamlets, indeed the first to say frankly to the voters that he wanted to be president. He traveled

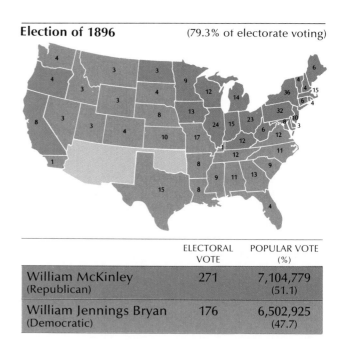

Election of 1896   (79.3% of electorate voting)

	ELECTORAL VOTE	POPULAR VOTE (%)
William McKinley (Republican)	271	7,104,779 (51.1)
William Jennings Bryan (Democratic)	176	6,502,925 (47.7)

18,000 miles, speaking several times a day, and addressed an estimated 5 million people.

Some businessmen grew almost hysterical at the thought of a possible Bryan victory. Many a company told its employees that if Bryan should win, the company would have to go out of business. Employers threatened to fire workers who voted for him. Bankers said they could not renew the mortgages of farmers who did so. Such threats, however, were less important than Bryan's own character in turning Democratic voters away from him. His revivalistic, camp-meeting style was pleasing enough to most Protestant sectarians of old native stock, but it antagonized many of the immigrant Catholics, who normally voted Democratic. Many of them decided to stay home on election day, if not to go out and vote Republican. Meanwhile, Bryan attracted fewer Republican farmers than he had hoped for—in part because shortly before the election the price of wheat suddenly rose, and Western farm discontent just as suddenly fell.

On election day, McKinley polled 271 electoral votes to Bryan's 176 and received 51.1 percent of the popular vote to Bryan's 47.7. Bryan won the Confederate South plus Missouri, swept the plains and mountain states except North Dakota, but lost California and Oregon on the Pacific coast. In short, he carried only the mining regions and the areas where staple farming was predominant and agricultural prices were lowest. He went down to defeat in all the Granger states in the Midwest. The Democratic program, like that of the Populists, had been designed to serve the needs of only one segment of one class—the most depressed fraction of agriculture—and this appeal was too narrow to win a national election.

Conservative Americans breathed a collective sigh of relief at the results of the 1896 election. What they had perceived as a radical threat to the nation's future had been averted—but only barely. It would be many years before they would forget that the "spirit of revolution" had seized control of one of the two major parties.

For the Populists and their allies, the election results were a disaster. They had gambled everything on their "fusion" with the Democratic party, and they had lost. The Populist movement stood exposed, it seemed, as a phenomenon too weak to influence national politics. And within months of the election, the People's party began to dissolve. Never again would American farmers unite so militantly to demand economic reform. And never again would so large a group of Americans raise so forceful a protest against the nature of the industrial economy.

McKinley and Prosperity

The administration of William McKinley, which began in the aftermath of turmoil, saw the nation return to a relative calm. One reason was simple exhaustion. By 1897, the labor unrest that had so frightened many middle-class Americans and so excited working-class people had subsided, victim of the internal weaknesses of the labor movement and of the strength of the corporate forces opposing it. And with the simultaneous decline of agrarian protest, the greatest destabilizing forces in the nation's politics were—temporarily at least—removed. Another reason was the character of the McKinley administration itself, which was politically shrewd and nothing if not committed to a reassuring stability. Most important, however, was the gradual easing of the economic crisis, a change that undercut many of those who were agitating for change.

William McKinley was the last of the long list of veteran officers of the Union army (beginning with Grant) to sit in the White House. Friendly and generous in nature, he was inclined to defer to stronger characters such as Hanna and to act in harmony with his party's leaders. His administration was passive, cautious, and conservative.

McKinley and his allies were eager to avoid inflaming the divisions they knew lurked beneath the surface of their party. They committed themselves fully to only one issue, one on which they knew virtually all Republicans were agreed: the need for higher tariff rates. Immediately after assuming office, McKinley summoned Congress into special session to consider tariff revision. With record brevity, the Republican majority whipped into shape and passed the Dingley Tariff, raising the duties to an average of 57 percent—the highest in history.

The administration dealt more gingerly with the explosive silver question (an issue that McKinley himself had never considered very important in any case). In accordance with the party's platform pronouncement that bimetallism could not be established except by international action, McKinley sent a commission to Europe to explore the possibility of a silver agreement with Great Britain and France. As he and everyone else anticipated, Britain refused to abandon its gold standard, thus effectively ending any hopes for international bimetallism. The administration could now argue that if the United States embarked on a silver program alone, it would be economically isolated from the rest of the world. Believing that their position was unassailable, the Republicans finally moved to enact currency legislation.

SIGNIFICANT EVENTS

The Currency, or Gold Standard, Act of 1900 confirmed the nation's commitment to the gold standard.

And so the "battle of the standards" ended in victory for the forces of conservatism. Economic developments at the time seemed to prove that the conservatives had been right in the struggle. In 1898 prosperity began to return to America. Foreign crop failures enlarged the farmers' market and sent farm prices surging upward. At the same time, business entered another cycle of booming expansion. Prosperity and gold had come hand in hand—the lesson seemed obvious.

But it was not quite that simple. Bryan and the silverites were essentially right in demanding currency inflation. In the quarter century before 1900, the countries of the Western world had experienced a spectacular growth in productive facilities and population. Yet the supply of money had not kept pace with economic progress, because the supply was tied to gold and the amount of gold had remained practically constant. Populist predictions of continuing financial distress might have proved correct had it not been for the fortuitous increase in the gold supply soon after the Republicans took over the government in 1897. A new technique for extracting gold from low-content ores, the cyanide process, made it possible to work mines previously considered marginal or unprofitable. At the same time, huge new gold deposits were discovered in Alaska, South Africa, and Australia. In 1898, two and a half times as much gold was produced as in 1890, and the currency supply was soon inflated far beyond anything proposed by Bryan.

The McKinley administration brought a tariff increase, the gold standard, and prosperity. It also brought a new departure in foreign policy, as the nation entered upon the path of overseas imperialism and took its place among the "great powers" of the world.

SUGGESTED READINGS

General Histories.   Nell Irvin Painter, *Standing at Armageddon: The United States, 1877–1919* (1987); R. Hal Williams, *Years of Decision: American Politics in the 1890s* (1978); John H. Dobson, *Politics in the Gilded Age* (1972); John A. Garraty, *The New Commonwealth* (1969); Harold U. Faulkner, *Politics, Reform, and Expansion* (1959); Samuel P. Hays, *The Response to Industrialism, 1885–1914* (1957); Robert Wiebe, *The Search for Order, 1877–1920* (1967); Sean Denis Cashman, *America and the Gilded Age* (1984); Alan Trachtenberg, *The Intercorporation of America: Culture and Society in the Gilded Age* (1982).

Politics, Reform and the States.   Morton Keller, *Affairs of State* (1977); Stephen Skowronek, *Building a New American State: The Expansion of National Administrative Capacities, 1877–1920* (1982); Martin J. Sklar, *The Corporate Reconstruction of American Capitalism, 1890–1916* (1988); Matthew Josephson, *The Politicos* (1963); David J. Rothman, *Politics and Power: The United States Senate, 1869–1901* (1966); Robert D. Marcus, *Grand Old Party* (1971); H. Wayne Morgan, *From Hayes to McKinley* (1969); Leonard D. White, *The Republican Era* (1958); Ari Hoogenboom, *Outlawing the Spoils* (1961); Walter T. K. Nugent, *Money and American Society* (1968); Allen Weinstein, *Prelude to Populism* (1970); Irwin Unger, *The Greenback Era* (1964); John Sproat, *"The Best Men"* (1968); Geoffrey Blodgett, *The Gentle Reformers* (1966); James Bryce, *The American Commonwealth*, 2 vols. (1888); Paul Kleppner, *The Cross of Culture: A Social Analysis of Midwestern Politics, 1850–1900* (1970) and *The Third Electoral System, 1853–1892* (1979); Richard Jensen, *The Winning of the Midwest: Social and Political Conflict, 1888–1896* (1971); Ruth Bourdin, *Women and Temperance: The Quest for Power and Liberty, 1873–1900* (1980); Michael E. McGerr, *The Decline of Popular Politics* (1986).

Party Leaders.   Harry Barnard, *Rutherford B. Hayes and His America* (1954); Kenneth Davison, *The Presidency of Rutherford B. Hayes* (1972); Allan Peskin, *Garfield* (1978); Margaret Leech and Harry J. Brown, *The Garfield Orbit* (1978); Thomas C. Reeves, *Gentleman Boss: The Life of Chester Alan Arthur* (1975); David Jordan, *Roscoe Conkling of New York* (1971); Allan Nevins, *Grover Cleveland: A Study in Courage* (1933); Horace Samuel Merrill, *Bourbon Leader:*

Grover Cleveland and the Democratic Party (1957); Harry J. Sievers, *Benjamin Harrison*, 3 vols. (1952–1968); H. Wayne Morgan, *William McKinley and His America* (1963); Lewis L. Gould, *The Presidency of William McKinley* (1981); Margaret Leech, *In the Days of McKinley* (1959); Herbert Croly, *Marcus Alonzo Hanna* (1912); Nick Salvatore, *Eugene V. Debs: Citizens and Socialist* (1982).

The Depression.   Samuel McSeveney, *The Politics of Depression* (1972); Donald McMurray, *Coxey's Army* (1929); Carlos A. Schwantes, *Coxey's Army* (1955); Ray Ginger, *The Bending Cross* (1949); Almot Lindsey, *The Pullman Strike* (1942); Ray Ginger, *Altgeld's America* (1958).

Populism.   John D. Hicks, *The Populist Revolt* (1931); Lawrence Goodwyn, *Democratic Promise* (1976) and *The Populist Moment* (1978), an abridgement of *Democratic Promise;* Norman Pollack, *The Populist Response to Industrial America* (1962) and *The Just Polity: Populism, Law, and Human Welfare* (1987); Allan Weinstein, *Prelude to Populism: Origins of the Silver Issue* (1970); Richard Hofstadter, *The Age of Reform* (1954); Sheldon Hackney, *Populism to Progressivism in Alabama* (1969); C. Vann Woodward, *Origins of the New South* (1972); Steven Hahn, *The Roots of Southern Populism* (1983); Robert McMath, *Populist Vanguard* (1975); Bruce Palmer, *Man over Money* (1980); Walter T. K. Nugent, *The Tolerant Populists* (1960); Theodore Saloutos, *Farmer Movements in the South, 1865–1933* (1960); Fred Shannon, *The Farmer's Last Frontier* (1945); Peter Argersinger, *Populism and Politics: William Alfred Peffer and the People's Party* (1974); Barton C. Shaw, *The Wool-Hat Boys: Georgia's Populist Party* (1984); Theodore R. Mitchell, *Political Education in the Southern Farmers Alliance, 1887–1900* (1987); C. Vann Woodward, *Tom Watson, Agrarian Rebel* (1938); Francis B. Simkins, *Pitchfork Ben Tillman* (1944).

The Election of 1896.   Paul Glad, *McKinley, Bryan, and the People* (1964) and *The Trumpet Soundeth* (1960); Stanley Jones, *The Presidential Election of 1896* (1964); J. Rogers Hollingsworth, *The Whirligig of Politics: The Democracy of Cleveland and Bryan* (1963); Paolo Coletta, *William Jennings Bryan: Political Evangelist* (1964).

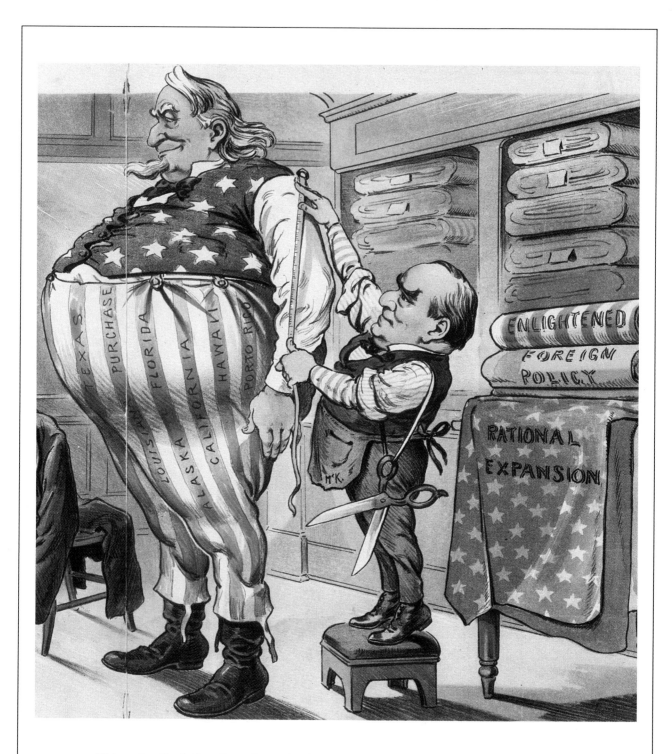

"Measuring Uncle Sam for a New Suit," by J. S. Pughe, in *Puck* Magazine, 1900
President William McKinley is favorably depicted here as a tailor, measuring his client for a suit large enough to accommodate the new possessions the United States obtained in the aftermath of the Spanish-American War. The cartoon tries to link this expansion with earlier, less controversial ones such as the Louisiana Purchase. (*Culver Pictures*)

CHAPTER 20

⟨symbols⟩

The Imperial Republic

⟨symbols⟩

The American republic had been an expansionist nation since the earliest days of its existence. Throughout the first half of the nineteenth century, as the population of the United States grew and pressed westward, the government continually acquired new territory for its citizens to occupy: the trans-Appalachian West, the Louisiana Territory, Florida, Texas, Oregon, California, New Mexico, Alaska, and more. It was the nation's "Manifest Destiny," many Americans believed, to expand into new realms.

In the last years of the nineteenth century, the United States had little room left in which to expand on the North American continent. And in those years, expansionism moved into a new phase. In the past, the nation had almost always annexed land contiguous to its existing boundaries, land that could provide new areas of settlement for the American people, land that could be organized as territories and, ultimately, admitted to the Union as states. But the expansionism of the 1890s, the new Manifest Destiny, involved acquiring possessions separate from the continental United States: island territories, many of which were already thickly populated, most of which were not suitable for massive settlement from America, few of which were expected ever to become states of the Union. The United States was acquiring colonies. It was joining England, France, Germany, and other expanding nations in the great imperial drive that was, by the end of the century, to bring much of the underdeveloped world under the control of the industrial powers of the West.

There had been some agitation in America for overseas expansion as early as the 1850s, agitation that continued after the Civil War and, to some extent, during the ensuing decades. Not until the 1890s, however, did the nation seriously embark on the new imperialism. In the wake of a brief, victorious war with Spain, the United States suddenly found itself in possession of a substantial empire and in the position of being a widely recognized "world power." Out of the imperial experience of the late nineteenth century emerged some of the premises that would dominate American foreign policy for many decades to come. And out of it, too, would emerge many of the problems that would accompany the nation's position as a great power.

Stirrings of Imperialism

For over two decades after the Civil War, the American people seemed to have abandoned the expansionist impulse that had been so powerful in the antebellum years. They were occupied with things closer to home—reconstructing the South, defeating the Plains Indians and settling the Far West, building a network of railroads, and expanding their great industrial system. By the 1890s, however, some Americans were ready—indeed, eager—to resume the course of Manifest Destiny that had inspired their forebears to wrest an empire from Mexico in the expansionist 1840s.

Imperialism at High Tide: The World in 1900

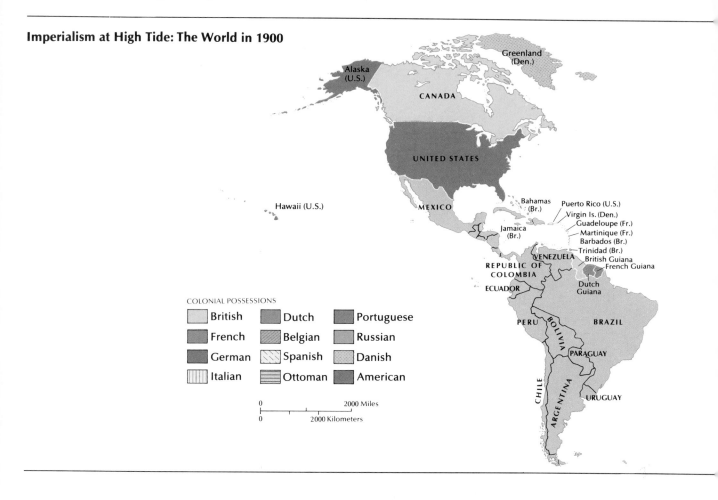

COLONIAL POSSESSIONS

British   Dutch   Portuguese
French   Belgian   Russian
German   Spanish   Danish
Italian   Ottoman   American

The New Manifest Destiny

Several developments played a part in shifting the attention of Americans from their own country to lands across the seas. The experience of subjugating the Indian tribes had established a precedent for exerting colonial control over dependent peoples. The "closing of the frontier," widely heralded by Frederick Jackson Turner and many others in the 1890s, produced fears that natural resources would soon dwindle and that alternative sources must be found abroad. The depression that began in 1893 convinced some businessmen that industry had overexpanded and was producing more goods than customers at home could buy. The bitter social protests of the time—the Populist movement, the free-silver crusade, the bloody labor disputes—led many people to believe that the nation was threatened with internal collapse; some politicians advocated a more aggressive foreign policy to provide an outlet for frustra-

tions that would otherwise destabilize domestic life.

Foreign trade was becoming increasingly important to the American economy in the late nineteenth century. The nation had exported about $392 million worth of goods in 1870; by 1890, the figure was $857 million; and by 1900, it had leaped to $1.4 billion. Once convinced of the great advantages of overseas markets, many Americans began to consider the possibility of acquiring colonies that might expand such markets further. "Today," Senator Albert J. Beveridge of Indiana cried in 1899, "we are raising more than we can consume. Today, we are making more than we can use. Therefore, we must find new markets for our produce, new occupation for our capital, new work for our labor."

Americans could not, moreover, insulate themselves entirely from the imperialist fever that was raging through Europe. In the last years of the century, the major powers of Europe were partitioning most of Africa among themselves and turning eager

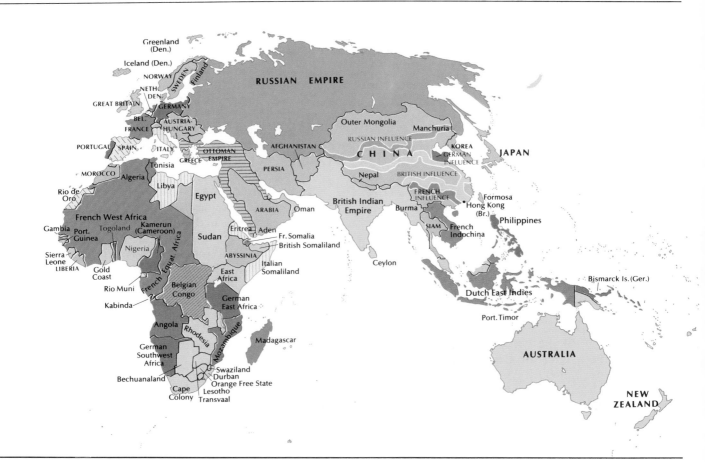

eyes on the Far East and the feeble Chinese Empire. Some Americans feared that their nation would soon be left out, that no territory would remain to be acquired. Senator Henry Cabot Lodge of Massachusetts, a leading imperialist, warned that the United States "must not fall out of the line of march."

A philosophic justification for expansionism was provided by historians, professors, clergymen, and others who found a basis for imperialism in their interpretations of Charles Darwin's theories (interpretations that Darwin himself never intended). These intellectuals contended that nations or "races," like biological species, struggled constantly for existence and that only the fittest could survive. For strong nations to dominate weak ones was, therefore, in accordance with the law of nature. This was an application to world affairs of the same distortion of Darwinism that industrialists and others had long been applying to domestic economic affairs in the form of Social Darwinism.

One of the first to advance this argument was the popular writer John Fiske, who predicted in an 1885 article in *Harper's Magazine* that the English-speaking peoples would eventually control every land that was not already the seat of an established civilization. The experience of white Americans in subjugating the native population of their own continent, Fiske argued, was "destined to go on" in other parts of the world. Support for Fiske's position came the same year from Josiah Strong, a Congregational clergyman and champion of overseas missionary work. In a book entitled *Our Country: Its Possible Future and Its Present Crisis,* Strong declared that the Anglo-Saxon "race," and especially its American branch, represented the great ideas of civil liberty and pure Christianity and was "divinely commissioned" to spread its institutions over the earth. John W. Burgess, founder of Columbia University's School of Political Science, gave the stamp of scholarly approval to imperialism. In his 1890 study *Political Sci-*

ence and Comparative Law, he flatly stated that the Anglo-Saxon and Teutonic nations possessed the highest political talents. It was the duty of these nations, he said, to uplift less fortunate peoples, even to force superior institutions on them if necessary: "There is no human right to the status of barbarism."

The ablest and probably the most effective apostle of imperialism was Alfred Thayer Mahan, a captain and later an admiral in the navy. Mahan presented his philosophy in three major works: *The Influence of Sea Power upon History, 1660–1783* (1890), *The Influence of Sea Power upon the French Revolution and Empire, 1793–1812* (1892), and *The Interest of America in Sea Power* (1897). His thesis was reasonably simple: The sea-power nations were the great nations of history, and the United States, a huge island, had to base its greatness on sea power. The essential links in sea power were a productive domestic economy, foreign commerce, a strong merchant marine, a navy to defend trade routes—and colonies, which would provide raw materials and markets and could serve as bases for the navy. Specifically, Mahan advocated that the United States construct a canal across the isthmus of Central America to join the oceans, acquire defensive bases on both sides of the canal in the Caribbean and the Pacific, and take possession of Hawaii and other Pacific islands. "Whether they will or no," he proclaimed, "Americans must now begin to look outward."

Mahan doubted that the United States would achieve its destiny, because its navy was not large enough to play the role he envisioned for it. But he did not accurately gauge the progress of the naval construction program launched in the Garfield-Arthur administration and continued by every succeeding administration. By 1898, the United States had advanced to fifth among the world's naval powers; and by 1900, to third.

Hemispheric Hegemony

The most ardent practitioner of the new, assertive diplomacy was Benjamin Harrison's secretary of state, James G. Blaine. Blaine believed that his country was destined to dominate the Caribbean and the Pacific. And he believed that it needed to do so because it had to find enlarged foreign markets for its surplus goods. The most likely foreign outlet, he thought, was Latin America, with whose countries he wanted advantageous commercial relations.

Blaine had served briefly as secretary of state once before—under James Garfield, in 1881. During his six months in office, he had invited the Latin nations to a Pan-American conference in Washington to discuss trade matters and the arbitration of disputes. Blaine left office after the Garfield assassination, and his successor withdrew the invitations. But sentiment for such a meeting survived, and the first Pan-American Congress finally took place in Washington in October 1889, with delegates from nineteen American nations in attendance. The Latin delegates rejected both of Blaine's principal proposals: the creation of an inter-American customs union and the establishment of arbitration procedures to resolve hemispheric disputes. They preferred to buy in the cheaper European market, and they feared the dominance of the United States in arbitration. But the meeting was not a total failure. Out of it arose the Pan-American Union, an agency in Washington that became a clearinghouse for distributing information to the member nations. Other congresses would meet in the future to discuss common hemispheric matters.

The Cleveland administration continued the newly aggressive approach to American interests in Latin America when it assumed office in 1893. Indeed, in 1895 President Cleveland and his secretary of state, Richard Olney, carried the country to the brink of war in a dispute with Great Britain over the boundary of Venezuela. Britain and Venezuela had been arguing for years about the boundary between Venezuela and British Guiana, and the dispute assumed new importance when gold was discovered in the disputed area. Both Cleveland and Olney, as well as the American public, were disposed to sympathize with Venezuela—the little underdog country confronting the great European power. The president and Congress both urged Britain to submit the matter to arbitration, but the British government took no action.

Olney drafted a harsh note to Lord Salisbury at the Foreign Office, charging that Britain was violating the Monroe Doctrine: "Today the United States is practically sovereign on this continent, and its fiat is law upon the subjects to which it confines its interposition." Salisbury waited four months before sending a curt and condescending reply. The Monroe Doctrine, he insisted, did not apply to boundary disputes or the present situation and had no standing as international law in any case. Britain would not submit to arbitration. Cleveland was enraged. In December 1895, he asked Congress for authority to create a special commission to determine the boundary line; if Britain resisted the commission's decision, he insisted, the United States should be willing to go to war to enforce it.

Congress supported Cleveland's plan with enthusiasm, and war talk raged all over the country. Belatedly, the British government realized that it had stumbled into a genuine diplomatic crisis and was on the verge of a war with the United States it did not want and could not afford. The British quickly backed down and agreed to arbitration. And the dusty Monroe Doctrine, to which few Europeans (and not many Americans) had paid much attention in recent decades, suddenly assumed new importance. Equally significant, the peaceful settlement of the dispute began a long era of friendship between America and Britain and made it possible for the United States to consider new imperialist ventures of its own without risking opposition from the British.

Hawaii and Samoa

The islands of Hawaii in the mid-Pacific had been an important stopover station for American ships in the China trade since the early nineteenth century and was the home of a growing number of American settlers. New England missionaries had arrived in Hawaii as early in 1820; and like their fellow missionaries elsewhere, they advertised the economic possibilities of the islands in the religious press. Soon other Americans arrived to become sugar planters and to found a profitable new industry. Eventually, officers of the growing navy looked longingly on the magnificent natural base of Pearl Harbor on the island of Oahu.

Gradually, the American residents of Hawaii came to dominate the economic and political life of the islands, despite the presence of native rulers. Commercial relations were inexorably pushing Hawaii into the American orbit and making it, as Blaine accurately contended, a part of the American economic system. A treaty signed in 1875 permitted Hawaiian sugar to enter the United States duty-free and obliged the Hawaiian kingdom to make no territorial or economic concessions to other powers. The trade arrangement tied the islands to the American economy, and the political clauses meant that, in effect, the United States was guaranteeing Hawaii's independence and hence was making the islands a protectorate. In 1887, a new treaty renewed the existing arrangements and granted the United States exclusive use of Pearl Harbor as a naval station. The course

Celebrating the Annexation of Hawaii
American residents of Hawaii gather in front of Iolani Palace, the principal government building of Honolulu, to celebrate the 1898 annexation of the islands by the United States. This drawing was based on a photograph of the actual scene. (Culver Pictures)

of events in the Pacific was rendering outright political union almost inevitable.

Sugar production in Hawaii boomed, and prosperity burgeoned for the American planters. Then the McKinley Tariff of 1890 dealt the planters a harsh blow; by removing the duty on foreign raw sugar and giving domestic producers a bounty, it deprived Hawaii of its privileged position in the American sugar market. Annexation (which would give Hawaiian planters the same bounty that American planters were receiving) seemed the only alternative to economic strangulation.

In the midst of growing sentiment among white Hawaiians for union with the United States, the passive native king, Kalakaua, died, to be succeeded in 1891 by Queen Liliuokalani, a nationalist determined to eliminate American influence in the government. Two years later, the American residents staged a revolution and called on the United States for protection. At a critical moment the American minister, John L. Stevens, an ardent annexationist and a friend of Blaine's, ordered 160 marines from a warship in Honolulu harbor to go ashore to aid the rebels. The queen yielded her authority, and a delegation representing the triumphant provisional government set out for Washington to negotiate a treaty of annexation. President Harrison happily signed an annexation agreement in February 1893, only weeks before leaving office. But the Senate refused to ratify the treaty, and Grover Cleveland, the new president, refused to support it. However disposed Cleveland was to upholding American rights under the Monroe Doctrine, his conservative ideas about the sanctity of property ownership made him wary of the proposed annexation. He withdrew the treaty and sent a special representative to the islands to investigate. When his agent reported that Americans had engineered the revolution, Cleveland endeavored to restore the queen to her throne. But Americans were now firmly in control of the kingdom and refused to budge. Reluctantly, the president had to recognize their government as the new "republic" of Hawaii. Cleveland had only delayed the inevitable. Debate over the annexation of Hawaii continued until 1898, when— with the Republicans again in power and with the United States constructing a colonial empire in both oceans— Hawaii was annexed by joint resolution of both houses of Congress.

Three thousand miles to the south of Hawaii, the Samoan islands dominated the sea lanes of the South Pacific and had long served as a way station for American ships in the Pacific trade. As American commerce with Asia increased after the completion of the first transcontinental railroad in 1869 and the extension of a steamship line from San Francisco to New Zealand, certain business groups regarded Samoa with new interest; and the navy eyed the harbor at Pago Pago on the island of Tutuila. In 1872, a naval officer visited the islands and negotiated a treaty granting the United States the use of Pago Pago; but the Senate rejected the agreement. President Grant nevertheless sent a special representative to Samoa to encourage American trading and business interests. A chain of events leading to greater American involvement was being set in motion. In 1878, the Hayes administration brought a native prince to Washington to sign a treaty, which was approved by the Senate, providing for an American naval station at Pago Pago and binding the United States to use its "good offices" to adjust any differences between a foreign power and Samoa. This treaty indicated that the American government meant to have a voice in Samoan affairs.

The opportunity to use that voice soon came. Great Britain and Germany were also interested in the islands, and they hastened to secure treaty rights from the native princes. For the next ten years the three powers scrambled and intrigued for dominance in Samoa, playing off one ruler against another and coming dangerously close to war. In 1889, warships of the contending nations appeared in one Samoan harbor, and a clash seemed imminent. But a tropical hurricane dispersed the vessels, and the German government, not wishing to antagonize the United States, suggested a conference of the interested powers in Berlin to settle the dispute. Germany and Britain would have preferred a division of the islands, but Secretary Blaine insisted on preserving native Samoan rule. The result was that the conferees agreed on a tripartite protectorate over Samoa, with the native chiefs exercising only nominal authority.

The three-way arrangement proved unsatisfactory, failing altogether to halt the intrigues and rivalries of the signatory members. It was abandoned in 1899, when the United States and Germany divided the islands between them, compensating Britain with territories elsewhere in the Pacific. Germany obtained the two largest islands, but the United States retained Tutuila with its incomparable harbor at Pago Pago.

War with Spain

Imperial ambitions had thus begun to stir within the United States well before the late 1890s. But it was the war with Spain in 1898 that turned those stirrings into an overt expansionism. The war transformed America's relationship to the rest of the world, and it left the nation with a far-flung overseas empire.

Controversy over Cuba

The immediate background of the Spanish-American War lay in the Caribbean island of Cuba, which with nearby Puerto Rico represented nearly all that was left of Spain's once extensive Latin American empire. The Cubans had long resented Spanish rule, and they had engaged in a notable but unsuccessful attempt to overthrow it between 1868 and 1878 (the Ten Years' War). During that revolt, many Americans were strongly sympathetic to the Cuban cause, but such feelings did not produce anything beyond vague of-

THE DUTY OF THE HOUR:—TO SAVE HER NOT ONLY FROM SPAIN BUT FROM A WORSE FATE.

The Duty of the Hour

This 1892 lithograph was no doubt inspired by the saying "Out of the frying pan and into the fire." A despairing Cuba, struggling to escape from the frying pan of Spanish misrule, contemplates an even more dangerous alternative: "anarchy" (or home rule). Cartoonist Louis Dalrymple here suggests that the only real solution to Cuba's problems is control by the United States, whose "duty" to Cuba is "To Save Her Not Only from Spain but from a Worse Fate."   (The Granger Collection)

ficial expressions of support. America even resisted strong provocations. In 1873, Spanish authorities had seized a ship carrying arms to the Cuban rebels and had executed fifty-three members of its crew as pirates. The vessel had flown an American flag (although its owners were Cuban), and some of its seamen were Americans. Popular indignation was intense, but Secretary of State Hamilton Fish had avoided a crisis by inducing the Spanish government to return the *Virginius* and pay an indemnity to the families of the executed men.

In 1895, the Cubans rose up again. Not only the continuing Spanish misrule but also the American tariff policy created conditions of misery that prepared the way for revolt. Cuba's principal export was sugar, and the bulk of the crop went to the United States. The Wilson-Gorman Tariff of 1894, with its high duties on raw sugar, shut off the island's chief source of wealth and prostrated its economy.

From the beginning, the struggle took on aspects of ferocity that horrified Americans. The Cubans deliberately devastated the island to force the Spaniards to leave. To put down the insurrection, the Spanish resorted to methods equally extreme. General Valeriano Weyler—or "Butcher" Weyler, as he soon came to be known in the American press—confined all civilians in certain areas to hastily prepared concentration camps, where they died by the thousands, victims of disease and malnutrition.

Many of the same savage techniques had been employed earlier in the Ten Years' War without shocking American sensibilities. But in the 1890s a wave of anger ran through the American public. The revolt of 1895 was reported more fully and floridly by the American press than the former outbreak—and so reported as to give the impression that all the cruelties were being perpetrated by the Spaniards.

At this time, Joseph Pulitzer with his New York

World and William Randolph Hearst with his New York *Journal* were revolutionizing American journalism. The new "yellow press" specialized in lurid and sensational news; when such news did not exist, editors were not above creating it. To Hearst and Pulitzer, engaged in a ruthless circulation war, the struggle in Cuba was a journalist's dream. Both sent batteries of reporters and illustrators to Cuba with orders to provide accounts of Spanish atrocities. "You furnish the pictures," Hearst supposedly told an overly scrupulous artist, "and I'll furnish the war."

A growing population of Cuban émigrés in the United States—concentrated in places as various as Florida, New York, Philadelphia, and Trenton, New Jersey—also played a role in arousing American public sentiment against the Spanish. The émigrés gave extensive support to the insurgents' Cuban Revolutionary Party (whose headquarters was in New York) and helped publicize its leader, Jose Marti, who was killed after returning to Cuba in 1895. Later, Cuban Americans formed other clubs and associations to support the cause of *Cuba Libre*. In many areas of the country, their efforts were at least as important as those of the yellow journalists in generating popular support for the revolution.

The mounting storm of indignation against Spain left President Cleveland unmoved. Convinced that both sides in Cuba were guilty of atrocities and that the United States had no interests justifying involvement in the struggle, he issued a proclamation of neutrality and attempted to stop the numerous filibustering expeditions being organized by a "junta" of Cuban refugees in New York City. When Congress, in a state of excitement, passed a resolution favoring recognition of Cuban belligerency, he ignored it. His only concession to the demands for intervention was to offer to mediate the conflict, a proposal that Spain declined.

When McKinley became president in 1897, he renewed the American mediation offer, which the Spanish again refused. Taking a stronger line than his predecessor, he protested to Spain against its "uncivilized and inhuman" conduct. The Spanish government, alarmed that McKinley's course might lead to American intervention in Cuba, recalled Weyler, modified the concentration policy, and took steps to grant the island a qualified autonomy. At the end of 1897, with the insurrection losing ground, it seemed that war might be averted.

But whatever chance might have existed for a peaceful settlement vanished as a result of two dramatic incidents in February 1898. The first occurred when a Cuban agent in Havana stole a private letter written by Dupuy de Lôme, the Spanish minister in Washington, and turned it over to the American press. Published first in Hearst's New York *Journal,* and later in newspapers across the land, the minister's letter described McKinley as a weak man and "a bidder for the admiration of the crowd." This was no more than many Americans, including some Republicans, were saying about their president (Theodore Roosevelt described McKinley as having "no more backbone than a chocolate éclair"), but because a foreigner had made the remark it was considered a national insult. Popular anger was intense, and Dupuy de Lôme resigned before McKinley could demand his recall.

While the excitement was still at fever pitch, even more sensational news hit the front pages: The American battleship *Maine* had been blown up in Havana harbor with a loss of more than 260 lives. The ship had been ordered to Cuban waters in January on a supposedly "friendly" visit but really to protect American lives and property against possible attacks by Spanish loyalists. Many Americans jumped to the conclusion that the Spanish had sunk the ship— "an act of dirty treachery," Theodore Roosevelt announced—and the imperialists and the jingoists screamed for war. This opinion seemed confirmed when a naval court of inquiry reported that an external explosion by a submarine mine had caused the disaster. In fact, the real cause of the *Maine* disaster was never determined. Later evidence suggested that it was the result of an accidental explosion inside one of the engine rooms. Nevertheless, war hysteria swept the country, and Congress unanimously appropriated $50 million for military preparations. "Remember the *Maine*!" became a national chant for revenge.

After the *Maine* incident, there was little chance that the government could suppress the popular demand for war, although McKinley still preferred to avoid a conflict. Others in his administration (including Assistant Secretary of War Theodore Roosevelt) were clamoring for America to join the hostilities. In March 1898, the president asked Spain to agree to an armistice, with negotiations for a permanent peace to follow, and an immediate ending of the concentration camps. After a slight delay, Spain accepted some of the American demands—an end to hostilities, the elimination of the concentration camps—on April 9. But it refused to agree to an armistice or to negotiations with the rebels; and it reserved the right to

The Yellow Press and the Wreck of the *Maine*

No evidence was ever found tying the Spanish to the explosion in Havana harbor that destroyed the American battleship *Maine* in February 1898. Indeed, most evidence indicated that the blast came from inside the ship, a fact that suggests an accident rather than sabotage. Nevertheless, the newspapers of Joseph Pulitzer and William Randolph Hearst ran sensational stories about the incident that were designed to arouse public sentiment in support of a war against the Spanish. This front page from Pulitzer's *New York World* is an example of the lurid coverage the event received. Circulation figures at the top of the page suggest, too, how successful the coverage was in selling newspapers. (The Granger Collection)

resume hostilities at its discretion. Two days later, McKinley asked Congress for authority to use military force to end the hostilities in Cuba—in short, for a declaration of war, "in the name of humanity, in the name of civilization, in behalf of endangered American interests." On April 25, Congress passed a formal declaration of war.

There was, as yet, only limited popular support for annexation of Cuba as a war aim. Some national leaders were calling openly for imperialism, and indeed some policy makers may have supported the war less out of revulsion at Spanish atrocities than out of fear that the insurgents might win and establish a genuinely independent Cuba in which the United States would have limited influence. But a powerful anti-imperialist movement more than counterbalanced the expansionists for the time. Evidence of the anti-imperialists' strength was the addition to the congressional resolution of the Teller Amendment, which disclaimed any intention on the part of the United States to annex Cuba.

"A Splendid Little War"

The Spanish-American conflict was, in the words of Roosevelt's friend John Hay, "a splendid little war." Indeed, to virtually all Americans—with the exception of many of the enlisted men who fought in it—it seemed almost an ideal conflict. It was the last small, short, individualistic war before the huge, protracted, impersonal struggles of the twentieth century. Declared in April, it was over in August, in part because Cuban rebels had already greatly weakened the Spanish resistance. The American intervention, therefore, was in many respects a "mopping up" exercise. Newspaper readers easily and eagerly followed the campaigns and the exploits of American soldiers and sailors. Only 460 Americans were killed in battle or died of wounds, but some 5,200 perished of disease: malaria, dysentery, typhoid, among others. Casualties among Cuban insurgents, who continued to bear the brunt of the struggle, were much higher.

Blithely and confidently, the United States embarked on a war it was not prepared to fight. The agencies responsible for supplying the troops, manned by elderly bureaucratic officers, proved incapable of meeting the modest wants of the armed forces during the war. There were not enough modern repeating rifles for all the troops, and many volunteers had to make do with old, single-shot Springfields. American soldiers fighting in tropical regions were clothed in the traditional heavy blue uniforms and fed canned rations that they called "embalmed beef." Medical supplies and services were inadequate, which contributed to the heavy impact of tropical diseases on the troops.

The regular army—numbering only 28,000 troops and officers scattered around the country at various posts—was a tough little force, skilled at quelling Indian outbreaks, but with no experience in large-scale warfare. Hastily Congress directed the president to increase the army to 62,000 and to call for 125,000 volunteers.

National Guard units, organized by local communities and commanded for the most part by local leaders, did the bulk of the fighting. Each unit considered itself a representative of its own town, and friends and relatives at home took a special pride in the performance of their "boys" and their unit. It was, in fact, the connection between the war and this pride in community that helped make the conflict so popular. More than 1 million young men volunteered for service, nearly ten times the number the president had requested. The invasion army also included several volunteer cavalry units, including the celebrated Rough Riders, nominally commanded by Leonard Wood but actually by Theodore Roosevelt, who was about to make the front pages as a war hero.

The character of the American war effort was determined in part by the nature of the opposition. The Spanish army numbered almost 130,000 men, of whom 80,000 were already in Cuba at the beginning of the war. Despite its size, however, its commanders seemed to be paralyzed by a series of reverses at the hands of the insurgents and by a conviction of certain defeat. The American navy, fifth largest in the

The Spanish-American War in Cuba, 1898

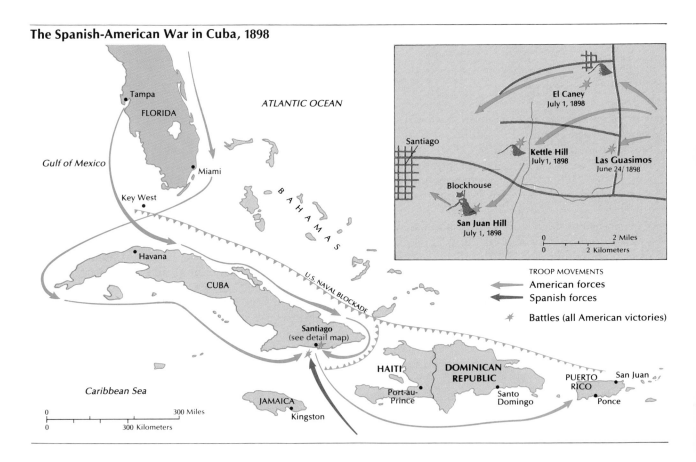

The Rough Riders

This volunteer cavalry regiment—organized in New York, commanded by Theodore Roosevelt, and christened the "Rough Riders"—was typical of the community-based, amateur military units with which the United States fought its first overseas conflict. (Culver Pictures)

world, was far superior to the Spanish in ships, guns, and personnel.

No agency in the American military had clear authority over strategic planning. Only the navy had worked out an objective, and its objective had little to do with freeing Cuba. The assistant secretary of the navy in the McKinley administration was Theodore Roosevelt, ardent imperialist, active proponent of war, and uninhibited by the fact that he was a relatively minor figure in the military hierarchy. In consultations with naval officers, Roosevelt prepared to seize Spain's Philippine Islands in the far Pacific. He strengthened the Asiatic squadron and instructed its commander, Commodore George Dewey, to attack the Philippines in the event of war.

Immediately after war was declared, Dewey left the China coast and headed for Manila, where an aging Spanish fleet was stationed. On May 1 he steamed into Manila Bay, and as his ships prepared to pass down the line of anchored enemy vessels he uttered the first slogan of the war: "You may fire when ready, Gridley." When the firing ended, the Spanish fleet had been completely destroyed, one American sailor lay dead (of a heat stroke) and George Dewey, immediately promoted to admiral, had become the first hero of the war. The Spaniards still held Manila, and Dewey had no troops with which to attack them.

While he waited nervously, the American government assembled an expeditionary force to relieve him and take the city. On August 13, the Americans received the surrender of Manila. In the rejoicing over Dewey's victory, few Americans paused to note that the character of the war was changing. What had begun as a war to free Cuba was becoming a war to strip Spain of its colonies.

But Cuba was not to be left out of the war picture. Late in April, the American government learned that a Spanish fleet under Admiral Pascual Cervera had sailed for the west, presumably for a Cuban harbor. Cervera's antique armada was no match for the powerful American Atlantic squadron, as the Spanish government well knew. The Atlantic squadron, commanded by Admiral William T. Sampson, was expected to intercept and destroy Cervera before he reached his destination. But the Spaniard eluded his pursuers and slipped into Santiago harbor, on the southern coast of Cuba, where he was not discovered by the Americans until ten days after his arrival. Immediately the Atlantic fleet moved to bottle him up.

While the navy was monopolizing the first phases of the war, the War Department was trying to mobilize and train an army. The volunteer and National Guard units were collected near Chattanooga, Tennessee, while the regulars, plus the Rough Rid-

"Smoked Yankees"
Nearly one-fourth of the American invasion force in Cuba consisted of black soldiers, many of whom had already served with distinction in campaigns against Indians in the West. Spanish troops called them "smoked Yankees" and often looked on them with more respect than did their American commanders, who kept black troops in rigidly segregated units. In this painting members of the all-black Tenth Cavalry support a charge by the Rough Riders. Members of the Twenty-fourth and Twenty-fifth Negro Infantry Divisions played a crucial role at the battle of San Juan Hill.   (Library of Congress)

ers, were assembled at Tampa, Florida, under the command of General William R. Shafter. The entire mobilization process was conducted with remarkable inefficiency.

There were also racial conflicts. A large proportion of the American invasion force consisted of black soldiers. Some were volunteer troops put together by black communities in several states (although some governors refused to allow the formation of such units). Others were members of the four black regiments in the regular army, who had been stationed on the frontier to defend white settlements against Indians and were now transferred east to fight in Cuba. As the black soldiers traveled through the

South toward the training camps, they chafed at the rigid segregation to which they were subjected and occasionally openly resisted the restrictions. Black soldiers in Georgia deliberately made use of a "whites only" park; in Florida, they beat a soda-fountain operator for refusing to serve them; in Tampa, white provocations and black retaliation led to a night-long riot that left thirty wounded. Although regiments and even troop ships were strictly segregated, black and white soldiers in the heat of battle often forgot the customary separation and fought together as equals. In some areas, black officers briefly took command of white troops.

Racial tensions continued in Cuba itself, where

American blacks played crucial roles in some of the important battles of the war (including the famous charge at San Juan Hill) and won many medals. Nearly half the Cuban insurgents fighting with the Americans were black, and unlike their American counterparts they were fully integrated into the rebel army. (Indeed, one of the leading insurgent generals, Antion Maceo, was a black man.) The sight of black Cuban soldiers fighting alongside whites as equals gave American blacks a stronger sense of the injustice of their own position. The Spanish-American War was one of many American military conflicts in which blacks played important roles and from which they derived a heightened sense of their rights as citizens.

The army's commanding general, Nelson A. Miles, veteran of the Civil War, had planned to train the troops until autumn, then to occupy Puerto Rico and, in conjunction with the Cuban rebels, attack Havana. But with a Spanish naval force at Santiago, plans hastily changed. In June, Shafter left Tampa with a force of 17,000 to take Santiago. The departure occurred amid scenes of fantastic incompetence, but it was efficiency itself compared to the landing. Five days were required to put the army ashore, and this with the enemy offering no opposition.

Once landed, Shafter moved his army toward Santiago, planning to surround and capture it. On the way he fought and defeated the Spaniards at the crossroads at Las Guasimas and, a week later, in two simultaneous battles, El Caney and San Juan Hill. In all the engagements the Rough Riders were in the middle of the fighting and on the front pages of the newspapers. Colonel Roosevelt, who had resigned from the Navy Department to get into the war and who had struggled with an almost desperate fury to ensure that his regiment made it to the front before the fighting ended, rapidly emerged as a hero of the conflict. His fame rested in large part on his role in leading a bold, even reckless charge up Kettle Hill (a charge that was a minor part of the larger battle for the adjacent San Juan Hill) directly into the face of Spanish guns. Roosevelt himself emerged unscathed, but nearly a hundred of his soldiers were killed or wounded. To the end of his life, he remembered the battle as "the great day of my life."

Having chased the Spaniards from the hills around Santiago, Shafter was now in position to assault the city. But his army was so weakened by sickness that he feared he might have to abandon his position. When he appealed to Sampson to unite with him in a joint attack on the city, the admiral answered that mines in the harbor made it too danger-

ous to take his big ships in. At this point, disaster seemingly confronted the Americans. But unknown to them, the Spanish government had decided that Santiago was lost. On July 3, Cervera, acting under orders from home, broke from the harbor to attempt an escape that he knew was hopeless. The waiting American squadron destroyed his entire fleet. Shafter then pressed the Spanish army commander to surrender, and that official, after bargaining for generous terms, including free transportation back to Spain for his troops, turned over Santiago on July 16. While the Santiago campaign was in its last stages, an American army landed in Puerto Rico and occupied it against virtually no opposition.

Spain was defeated (more as a result of its own weakness and incompetence and of the military successes of the Cuban rebels than because of American strength) and knew it. Through the French ambassador in Washington, the Spanish government asked for peace; and on August 12, an armistice ended the war.

Decision for Imperialism

The terms of the armistice confirmed what the military situation had already established. Spain recognized the independence of Cuba and ceded Puerto Rico (now occupied by American troops) to the United States. It also ceded to the victor the Pacific island of Guam, between Hawaii and the Philippines, and agreed to permit the Americans to hold Manila pending the final disposition of the Philippines.

The uncertainty of the provisions concerning the Philippines did not reflect Spanish resistance. It reflected the confusion in the McKinley administration as to what to do about the islands the United States now occupied. There was little controversy about the annexation of Puerto Rico and Guam. Puerto Rico was close enough to the mainland to seem a tempting acquisition to almost everyone. And Guam seemed too small and insignificant to be worthy of dispute. But the Philippines constituted a large and important territory; and American annexation of it would mean a major change in the nation's position in the world.

McKinley weighed a number of options for dealing with the Philippines. Returning them to Spain was politically impossible. Granting the islands independence appealed to almost no one; Americans believed the Filipinos unfit to rule themselves. Ultimately, McKinley decided that only actual annexation would do. He later said that he had arrived at his decision as a result of divine guidance, but growing popular sentiment for annexation in the country and the pressure of the imperialist leaders of his party undoubtedly influenced his thinking more.

In October 1898, commissioners from the United States and Spain met in Paris to negotiate a treaty formally ending the war. Spain readily agreed to recognize Cuba's independence, to assume the Cuban debt, and to cede Puerto Rico and Guam to the United States. Then the American commissioners, acting under instruction from McKinley, startled the conference by demanding the cession of all the Philippines. Stubbornly the Spanish resisted the American demand, although they realized they could retain the islands only by resuming the war. They yielded when the United States offered to pay $20 million for the islands. The Treaty of Paris was signed on December 10, 1898, and sent to the United States for ratification by the Senate.

When the treaty was submitted to the Senate, it encountered immediate and fierce criticism and occasioned in that body and throughout the country one of those "great debates" that frequently precede a departure in American foreign policy. The chief point at issue was the acquisition of the Philippines, denounced by many, including prominent Republicans, as a repudiation of America's high moral position in the war and a shameful occupation of a land that wanted to be free.

The anti-imperialists were a varied and powerful group and included some of the nation's wealthiest and most powerful figures: Andrew Carnegie, John Sherman, Mark Twain, Samuel Gompers, and others. Their opposition to annexation stemmed from various motives. Some feared the "pollution" of the American population by introducing "inferior" Asian races into the national community. Industrial workers feared a flood of cheap laborers from the new colonies who would undercut their wages and take their jobs. Conservatives feared annexation would produce a large standing army and entangling foreign alliances, which would threaten American liberties. Certain economic interests (most notably sugar growers) feared the new territories would provide unwelcome competition. Many Democrats opposed annexation because they considered it a Republican tactic to enhance the party's prestige. Others saw in annexation a repudiation of basic American principles of independence and self-determination: The United States could not impose colonial rule on other peoples without debasing its own democratic heritage.

The Anti-Imperialist League, established by upper-class Bostonians, New Yorkers, and others late in 1898 to fight against annexation, attracted a widespread following in the Northeast and waged a vigorous campaign against ratification of the Paris treaty. But the League, and the anti-imperialist movement as a whole, had a number of crippling weaknesses. Its appeal was limited for the most part to a few areas; it attracted little support in the West and the South. It suffered from internal divisions; some anti-imperialists opposed annexing any new possessions, while others opposed only the acquisition of the Philippines. Most important, however, the anti-imperialists, for all their strength, represented a distinct minority sentiment—both in the country and, of more immediate importance, in the Senate.

Favoring ratification was an equally varied group. There were the exuberant imperialists such as Theodore Roosevelt, who saw the acquisition of empire as a way to reinvigorate the nation, to keep alive the healthy, restorative influence of the war. "A nation cannot safely absorb itself in its own affairs," wrote one Midwestern annexationist. "It breeds strange and dangerous disorders." Other supporters of annexation included businessmen who saw economic potential in the Philippines and believed annexation would position the United States to dominate the Oriental trade; shipbuilders and others who stood to benefit from the creation of a larger navy, which the new empire would certainly require; the Protestant clergy, who saw in a colonial empire enlarged fields for missionary enterprise; and most Republicans, who saw clear partisan advantages in acquiring valuable new territories in the aftermath of a war fought and won by a Republican administration. Perhaps the strongest argument in favor of annexation, however, was the apparent ease with which it could be accomplished. The United States, after all, already possessed the islands as a result of its military triumph.

The imperialists argued, too, that annexation was fully in accord with American traditions. The United States had been an expansionist power from its earliest days, and it had long ago established its right not only to annex territory, but to subjugate peoples. When anti-imperialists warned of the danger of absorbing lands with large populations who might have to become citizens, the imperialists had a ready answer: The nation's longstanding policies toward Indians—treating them as dependents rather than as citizens—had created a precedent for annexing land without absorbing people. Senator Henry Cabot Lodge of Massachusetts, one of the leading imperialists in Congress, made the point explicitly:

> The other day . . . a great Democratic thinker announced that a Republic can have no subjects. He seems to have forgotten that this Republic not only has held subjects from the beginning, . . . but [that we have] acquired them by purchase. . . . [We] denied to the Indian tribes even the right to choose their allegiance, or to become citizens.

Other exponents of annexation argued that the "uncivilized" Filipinos "would occupy the same status precisely as our Indians. . . . They are, in fact, 'Indians'—and the Fourteenth Amendment does not make citizens of Indians."

After weeks of bitter wrangling, the Senate ratified the treaty on February 6, 1899, but only because it received an unexpected assist from William Jennings Bryan, a fervent anti-imperialist, who expected to be his party's candidate again in the election of 1900. Bryan persuaded a number of Democratic senators to vote for ratification. Some charged that he was looking for a campaign issue, but Bryan claimed that he wanted only to end the war. The question of the Philippines could, he believed, be decided by a national referendum. If the Democrats won in 1900, they would free the islands.

If the election of 1900 was such a referendum, it proved beyond doubt that the nation had decided in favor of imperialism. Once again, Bryan ran against McKinley; and once again, Bryan went down to defeat—an even more crushing defeat than he had experienced four years earlier. It was not only the issue of the colonies, however, that ensured McKinley's victory. The Republicans effectively exploited the money and tariff issues; they harped on the continuing prosperity in the country under a Republican administration; and they exploited to the full the colorful personality of their vice-presidential candidate, the hero of San Juan Hill, Colonel Theodore Roosevelt.

The Republic as Empire

The new colonial empire was a small one by the standards of the great imperial powers of Europe. But it spanned a vast area of the globe. It stretched from the Caribbean to the far reaches of the Pacific. It embraced Puerto Rico, Alaska, Hawaii, a part of Samoa, Guam, the Philippines, and a chain of minor Pacific islands.

But with the empire came new problems. Many of the predictions of the anti-imperialists proved accurate. Ultimately, as a colonial power, the United States had to maintain large stockpiles of armaments, concern itself with the complexities of Far Eastern international politics, and modify its traditional policy of holding aloof from alliances.

Governing the Colonies

A host of perplexing questions arose as the nation tried to decide how to administer its new possessions. Did Congress have to administer the colonies in accordance with the Constitution? Did the inhabitants of the new possessions have the rights of American citizens? Could Congress levy tariff duties on colonial imports? Or, in a phrase that pleased the public fancy, did the Constitution follow the flag? The Supreme Court suggested a solution in the so-called insular cases (*De Lima* v. *Bidwell, Downes* v. *Bidwell,* and others, 1900–1904), by distinguishing between "incorporated" and "unincorporated" territories. In legislating for "unincorporated" territories—the insular possessions—Congress had great latitude and need not be bound by all the provisions of the Constitution. The Constitution followed the flag, the Court implied, only if Congress so decided. The government could administer its colonies in almost any way it saw fit.

Three of the dependencies—Hawaii, Alaska, and Puerto Rico—received territorial status relatively quickly. A 1900 act granted American citizenship to all citizens of Hawaii, authorized an elective two-house legislature there, and vested executive authority in a governor appointed from Washington. Alaska (which had been purchased from Russia in 1869) was being governed by appointed civil officials. The discovery of gold there in 1896 caused the first substantial influx of Americans; and in 1912, Alaska received territorial status and a legislature, and its inhabitants were given the rights of citizenship. In Puerto Rico, the natives seemed readily to accept American rule. Military occupation of the island ended quickly, and a civilian government was established by the Foraker Act in 1900. The governor and upper house of the legislature were to be appointed from Washington, while only the lower house was to be elected. The 1900 act did not grant Puerto Ricans American citizenship, but a 1917 law did. Smaller possessions in the empire received more arbitrary treatment. Guam and Tutuila came under the control of naval officials; and some of the small Pacific islands, containing only a handful of inhabitants, experienced no form of American government at all.

American military forces, commanded by General Leonard Wood, remained in Cuba until 1902 under orders to prepare the island for the independence promised in the peace treaty of 1898. The occupiers built roads, schools, and hospitals, reorganized the legal, financial, and administrative systems, and introduced far-reaching sanitary reforms. They also laid the basis for years of American domination of the island—a domination that ultimately would become as intolerable to the Cuban people as the Spanish rule against which they had first rebelled.

At Wood's urging, a convention assembled to draft a constitution for independent Cuba. The document contained no provisions concerning relations with the nation responsible for Cuba's freedom. Many Americans considered this a significant oversight, for the United States, with its expanding interests in the Caribbean, expected to exercise some kind of control over the island republic. In 1901, therefore, Congress passed the Platt Amendment, as a rider to an army appropriations bill, and pressured Cuba into incorporating the terms of the amendment into its constitution. The Platt Amendment declared that Cuba could make no treaties with any foreign powers (this was equivalent to giving the United States a veto over Cuba's diplomatic policy); that the United States had the right to intervene in Cuba to preserve Cuba's independence, life, and property; and that Cuba must sell or lease to the United States lands for naval stations. The amendment left Cuba only nominally independent. With American capital taking over the island's economy—investments jumped from $50 million in 1898 to $220 million by 1914—Cuba was in fact, if not in name, an American appendage.

The Philippine War

Americans did not like to think of themselves as imperial rulers in the European mold. Their mission, they believed, was different—to enlighten and reform the societies they had acquired, to improve the lives of their newly subjugated peoples. Yet like other imperial powers, the United States soon discovered—as it had often discovered at home in its relations with the Indians—that subjugating another people required more than ideals; it also required strength, and often brutality. That, at least, was the lesson of the American experience in the Philippines, where American forces soon became engaged in a long and bloody war with insurgent forces fighting for independence.

The conflict in the Philippines is the least remembered of all American wars. It was also one of the longest (it lasted from 1898 to 1902) and one of the most vicious. It involved 200,000 American troops and resulted in 4,300 American deaths, nearly ten times the number who died in combat in the Spanish-American War. Controversy still rages over the number of Filipinos killed in the conflict, but it seems likely that more than 50,000 natives died. (Some claim the number is far higher than that.) The American occupiers faced guerrilla tactics in the Philippines very similar to those the Spanish occupiers had faced prior to 1898 in Cuba. And they soon found themselves drawn into the same pattern of brutality that had outraged so many Americans when employed by Weyler in the Caribbean.

The Filipinos had been rebelling against Spanish rule even before 1898, and they had hailed Admiral Dewey and the expeditionary force he sent to Manila as their deliverers from tyranny. When the hard fact sank in that the Americans had come to stay, the Filipinos resolved to expel the new invaders. Ably led by Emilio Aguinaldo, who claimed to head the legitimate government of the nation, Filipinos harried the American army of occupation from island to island for more than three years. At first, American commanders believed that the rebels represented only a small minority; but by early 1900, they were beginning to recognize otherwise. General Arthur MacArthur (father of Douglas), an American commander in the islands, wrote at the time: "I have been reluctantly compelled to believe that the Filipino masses are loyal to Aguinaldo and the government which he heads."

To MacArthur and others, however, that realization was not a reason to moderate American tactics or conciliate the rebels. It was a reason to adopt far more severe measures. Gradually, the American military effort became more systematically vicious and brutal. Captured Filipino guerrillas were treated not as prisoners of war, but as murderers. Most were summarily executed. On some islands, entire communities were evacuated—the residents forced into concentration camps while American troops destroyed their villages, farms, crops, livestock, and

Filipino Prisoners

American troops guard captured Filipino guerrillas in Manila. The suppression of the Filipino insurrection was a much longer and costlier military undertaking than the Spanish-American War, by which the United States first gained possession of the islands. By mid-1900 there were 70,000 American troops in the Philippines, under the command of General Arthur MacArthur (whose son, Douglas, won fame in the Philippines during World War II).   (Library of Congress)

everything else that might give sustenance to the "rebels." A spirit of savagery grew among American soldiers, who came to view the Filipinos as almost subhuman and at times seemed to take pleasure in killing almost arbitrarily. One American commander ordered his troops "to kill and burn, the more you kill and burn the better it will please me. . . . Shoot everyone over the age of 10." Over fifteen Filipinos were killed for every one wounded; in the Civil War— the bloodiest conflict in American history to that point—one person had died for every five wounded.

By 1902, reports of the brutality and the American casualties had soured the American public on the war. But by then, the rebellion had largely exhausted itself and the occupiers had established control over most of the islands. The key to their victory was the capture of Aguinaldo in March 1901 by five American soldiers who had used deception to enter the Filipino's remote camp in the mountains. They took Aguinaldo to Manila, where he signed a document urging his followers to stop fighting and declaring his own allegiance to the United States. (He then retired from public life and lived quietly until 1964.) Fighting continued in places for another year, and the war revived intermittently until as late as 1906; but American possession of the Philippines was now secure.

President McKinley had sent a special commission to the islands in 1900, under the direction of William Howard Taft, to establish a civilian government there; and in the summer of 1901, the military transferred final authority over the islands to Taft, who became the first civilian governor. He announced that the American purpose was to prepare the islands for independence, and he oversaw the creation of a civilian government that gave the Filipinos broad local autonomy. The Americans also built roads, schools, bridges, and sewers; instituted major administrative and financial reforms; and established

The American South Pacific Empire, 1900

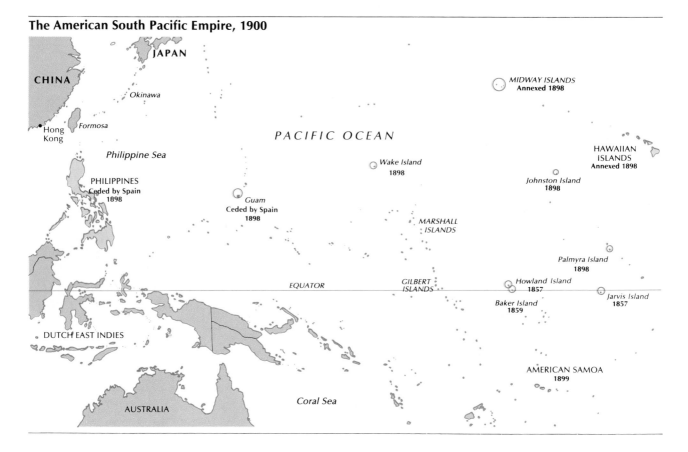

a public health system. Filipino autonomy gradually increased. On July 4, 1946, the islands finally gained their independence.

The Open Door

The acquisition of the Philippines made the United States an Asian power and greatly increased American interest in the Far East, which had already grown strong as a result of the increasing trade with China. But other nations more experienced in the ways of empire were casting covetous eyes on China, ancient, enfeebled, and seemingly open to exploitation by stronger countries. By the turn of the century, the great European imperialistic powers—England, France, Germany, and Russia—and one Asian power—Japan—were beginning to partition China into "spheres of influence." One nation would force the Chinese government to grant it "concessions" for developing a particular area; another would use pressure to secure a long-term lease to a specific region.

In some cases, the outside powers even asserted ownership of territory. The process, if continued, threatened to destroy American hopes for a vast trade with China.

The situation posed a delicate problem for the men directing American foreign policy. Knowing that public opinion would not support any use of force, they had to find a way to protect American interests in China without risking war. McKinley suggested the American answer in a statement in September 1898, when he said that the United States sought trade with China, but no special advantages there. "Asking only the open door for ourselves, we are ready to accord the open door to others." McKinley's secretary of state, John Hay, translated McKinley's words into policy a year later, in September 1899, when he addressed identical messages—what became known as the "Open Door notes"—to England, Germany, and Russia, and later to France, Japan, and Italy. The new policy that he asked them to approve embodied three principles: Each nation with a sphere of influence was to respect the rights and

The Boxer Rebellion

American troops march through the grounds of the Temple of Agriculture in Beijing's Imperial City during the Boxer Rebellion of 1900. They were among 5,000 American soldiers summoned to China. In mid-August, they joined British, Russian, Japanese and French soldiers to rescue diplomats, foreigners, and Christians who had barricaded themselves in the city's diplomatic quarter in June to protect themselves from the Boxers, a secret society committed to purging Chinese life of foreign influence. "The will of Heaven," the Boxers claimed, "is that the telegraph wires be first cut, the railways torn up and then shall the foreign devils be decapitated." The hostages were able to survive long enough to be rescued because the head of the American legation had stockpiled a large supply of food in anticipation of the siege. (The Bettmann Archive)

privileges of other nations in its sphere; Chinese officials were to continue to collect tariff duties in all spheres (the existing tariff favored the United States); and nations were not to discriminate against other nations in levying port dues and railroad rates within their own spheres.

The Open Door policy was appealing to the United States for a number of reasons. It would preserve at least the illusion of Chinese sovereignty, thus preventing formal colonial dismemberment of the empire. More important, it allowed the United States to trade freely with the Chinese without fear of interference and without the need for American military occupation.

Hay could hardly have expected an enthusiastic response to his notes, and he got none. Russia rejected the Open Door proposals, and the remaining powers gave evasive replies. Each one stated in effect that it approved Hay's ideas in principle but could make no commitment until the others had acted. Apparently, the United States had met a humiliating rebuff; but Hay boldly announced that since all the powers had accepted the principle of the Open Door, his government considered their assent to be "final and definitive." Although the American public applauded his diplomacy, Hay had won little more than a theoretical victory. Unless the United States was willing to resort to war, it could not prevent any nation that wanted to violate the Open Door from doing so.

No sooner had the diplomatic maneuvering over the Open Door ended than a secret Chinese society known as the Boxers instigated an uprising against foreigners in China. The movement came to a blazing climax when the Boxers and their supporters besieged the entire foreign diplomatic corps in the British embassy in Peking. At this point, the powers with interests in China decided to send an international expeditionary force to rescue the diplomats. The situation seemed to offer a perfect excuse to those nations with ambitions to dismember China.

The United States contributed 2,500 troops to the rescue force, which in August 1900 fought its way into Peking and broke the siege. McKinley and Hay had decided on American participation in order to secure a voice in the settlement of the uprising and to prevent the partition of China. Again Hay sent a note to the world powers. This time he called for the Open Door not only in the spheres of influence but in "all parts of the Chinese Empire." He also called for the maintenance of China's "territorial and administrative integrity," for a return to the situation preceding the rebellion. Hay won support for his approach from England and Germany and then induced the other participating powers to accept compensation from the Chinese for the damages the Boxer Rebellion had caused.

SIGNIFICANT EVENTS

1868–1878 Cubans revolt against Spanish rule in Ten Years' War (p. 598)

1889 First Pan-American Congress meets (p. 596)

1890 Alfred Thayer Mahan publishes *The Influence of Sea Power upon History* (p. 596)

1893 Harrison signs annexation agreement with Hawaii, but Cleveland rejects it (p. 598)

1894 Wilson-Gorman Tariff on sugar ravages Cuban economy (p. 574)

1895 United States and Britain dispute Venezuelan boundary (p. 596)

Insurrection against Spanish begins in Cuba (p. 599)

1896 Alaska gold rush begins (p. 607)

1897 McKinley offers to mediate Cuban conflict; Spain refuses (p. 600)

1898 William Randolph Hearst publishes de Lôme letter (p. 600)

U.S. battleship *Maine* explodes in Havana harbor (p. 600)

Congress declares war on Spain (April 25) (p. 601)

Spanish army in Cuba retreats (p. 605)

Dewey captures Philippines (p. 603)

United States and Spain sign armistice (August 12) (p. 605)

1898 Treaty of Paris cedes Puerto Rico, Philippines, and other Spanish possessions to United States; recognizes Cuban independence (p. 606)

United States formally annexes Hawaii (p. 598)

Anti-Imperialist League formed (p. 606)

1898–1902 Philippines revolt against American rule (pp. 608–610)

1899 Senate ratifies Treaty of Paris (p. 606)

Hay releases "Open Door notes" (p. 610)

1900 Foraker Act establishes civil government in Puerto Rico (p. 607)

Hawaii granted territorial status (p. 607)

Boxer Rebellion breaks out in China (p. 611)

McKinley reelected president (p. 607)

1901 Americans capture Emilio Aguinaldo in Philippines (p. 609)

Congress passes Platt Amendment (p. 608)

U.S. establishes civil government in Philippines (p. 609)

1912 Alaska given territorial status (p. 607)

1917 Puerto Ricans granted U.S. citizenship (p. 608)

1946 United States grants Philippines independence (p. 610)

A Modern Military System

The war with Spain had revealed glaring deficiencies in the American military system. The greatest weakness had appeared in the army, but there had been an absence of coordination in the entire military organization that might have resulted in disaster had the United States been fighting a more powerful nation. After the war, McKinley appointed Elihu Root, an extremely able administrator, as secretary of war to supervise a major overhaul of the armed forces. Between 1900 and 1903, Root put into effect, by congressional authorization or by executive order, a series of reforms that gave the United States what amounted to a new military system.

The Root reforms enlarged the regular army from its previous small size of about 25,000 to a maximum of 100,000. They established federal supervision of the National Guard, ensuring that never again would the nation fight a war with volunteer regiments over which the federal government had only limited control. They sparked the creation of a system of officer training schools, crowned by the Army Staff College (later the Command and General Staff School) at Fort Leavenworth, Kansas, and the Army War College at Washington. And they established, in 1903, a general staff headed by a chief of staff, to act as military adviser to the secretary of war.

It was this last reform that Root considered most important: the creation of a central planning agency modeled on the example of European staffs. The general staff was charged with many functions. It was to "supervise" and "coordinate" the entire army establishment, and it was to establish an office that would plan for possible wars. An Army and Navy Board, on which both services were represented, was to foster interservice cooperation.

As a result of the new reforms, the United States entered the twentieth century with something resembling a modern military system. The country would make use of it in the turbulent decades to come.

SUGGESTED READINGS

General Histories. Charles S. Campbell, *The Transformation of American Foreign Relations, 1865–1900* (1976); Robert L. Beisner, *From the Old Diplomacy to the New, 1865–1900* (1975); Julius W. Pratt, *Expansionists of 1898* (1936); Albert K. Weinberg, *Manifest Destiny: A Study in Nationalist Expansion in American History* (1935); Walter LeFeber, *The New Empire* (1963); William Appleman Williams, *The Tragedy of American Diplomacy* (rev. ed., 1972); Ernest May, *Imperial Democracy* (1961) and *American Imperialism: A Speculative Essay* (1968); David F. Healy, *U.S. Expansionism: Imperialist Urge in the 1890s* (1970); John Dobson, *America's Ascent: The United States Becomes a Great Power, 1880–1914* (1978); H. Wayne Morgan, *America's Road to Empire* (1965); J. A. S. Grenville and George Berkeley Young, *Politics, Strategy and American Diplomacy: Studies in Foreign Policy, 1873–1917* (1966); Milton Plesur, *America's Outward Thrust: Approaches to Foreign Affairs, 1865–1890* (1971); David M. Pletcher, *The Awkward Years: American Foreign Relations under Garfield and Arthur* (1962).

The Spanish-American War. David F. Trask, *The War with Spain in 1898* (1981); Frank Freidel, *The Splendid Little War* (1958); Joyce Milton, *The Yellow Journalists* (1989); Walter Millis, *The Martial Spirit* (1931); Louis A. Perez, Jr., *Cuba Between Empires, 1868–1902* (1983); Philip S. Foner, *The Spanish-Cuban-American War and the Birth of American Imperialism*, 2 vols. (1972); Graham A. Cosmas, *An Army for Empire: The United States Army in the Spanish-American War* (1971); Richard S. West, Jr., *Admirals of the American Empire* (1948); Richard Challener, *Admirals, Generals, and American Foreign Policy, 1889–1914* (1973); Willard B. Gatewood, Jr., *Black Americans and the White Man's Burden, 1898–1903* (1975) and *"Smoked Yankees": Letters from Negro Soldiers, 1898–1902* (1971); Edmund Morris, *The Rise of Theodore Roosevelt* (1979); Gerald F. Linderman, *The Mirror of War: American Society and the Spanish-American War* (1974).

Imperialism and Anti-Imperialism. Robert L. Beisner, *Twelve Against Empire* (1968); E. Berkeley Tompkins, *Anti-Imperialism in the United States, 1890–1920: The Great Debate* (1970); Thomas J. Osborne, *"Empire Can Wait": American Opposition to Hawaiian Annexation, 1893–1898* (1891); Kendrick A. Clements, *William Jennings Bryan* (1983); Frederick Merk, *Manifest Destiny and Mission in American History* (1963); Julius W. Pratt, *America's Colonial Empire* (1950); James H. Hitchman, *Leonard Wood and Cuban Independence, 1898–1902* (1971).

The Pacific Empire. Peter Stanley, *A Nation in the Making: The Philippines and the United States* (1974); Paul M. Kennedy, *The Samoan Tangle* (1974); Glenn May, *Social Engineering in the Philippines* (1980); Merze Tate, *The United States and the Hawaiian Kingdom* (1965); Richard E. Welch, Jr., *Response to Imperialism: The United States and the Philippine-American War, 1899–1902* (1979); Leon Wolff, *Little Brown Brother* (1961); Stuart Creighton Miller, *"Benevolent Assimilation": The American Conquest of the Philippines, 1899–1903* (1982); John Morgan Gates, *Schoolbooks and Krags: The United States Army in the Philippines, 1898–1902* (1971); Daniel B. Schirmer, *Republic or Empire? American Resistance to the Philippine War* (1972).

America and Asia. James C. Thomsen, Jr., Peter W. Stanley, and John Curtis Perry, *Sentimental Imperialists: The American Experience in East Asia* (1981); Marilyn B. Young, *The Rhetoric of Empire* (1968); Warren Cohen, *America's Response to China* (rev. ed., 1980); Akira Iriye, *Across the Pacific* (1967) and *Pacific Estrangement: Japanese and American Expansion* (1972); Robert McClellan, *The Heathen Chinese: A Study of American Attitudes Toward China* (1971); Jane Junter, *The Gospel of Gentility: American Women Missionaries in Turn-of-the-Century China* (1984); Charles Neu, *The Troubled Encounter* (1975); Paul Varg, *The Making of a Myth: The United States and China, 1897–1912* (1968) and *Missionaries, Chinese, and Diplomats* (1958); Patricia Hill, *The World Their Household: The American Women's Foreign Mission Movement and Cultural Transformation* (1985).

PITTSBURG: A CITY ASHAMED

McCLURE'S MAGAZINE

MAY

LINCOLN STEFFENS'S exposure of another type of municipal grafting; how Pittsburg differs from St. Louis and Minneapolis.

THE END OF THE WORLD, by Professor Newcomb. A powerful story, yet a scientific prediction; pictures by the famous French artist, Henri Lanos.

IDA M. TARBELL on the Standard tactics which brought on the famous oil crisis of 1878.

SIX SHORT STORIES

***McClure's* Magazine, May 1903**
McClure's was the leading outlet for a form of journalism known as "muckraking," which attempted to expose social and economic scandals in the hope of promoting reform. This issue contains articles by two of the leading muckrakers, Lincoln Steffens and Ida Tarbell. *(Culver Pictures)*

CHAPTER 21

The Rise of Progressivism

The last decades of the nineteenth century—and the tumultuous 1890s in particular—had a profound effect on the nation's social and political outlook. Well before 1900, a large number of Americans had become convinced that the rapid industrialization and urbanization and the other profound changes their nation was experiencing had created intolerable problems, that new measures would be necessary to impose order on the growing chaos and to curb industrial society's most glaring injustices. In the early years of the new century, that outlook acquired a name: progressivism.

Not even the progressives themselves could always agree on what the word really meant. To some, it suggested simply a broad cultural vision. To others, it meant a cluster of moral and humanitarian goals. To still others, it was a particular set of political reforms (and, later, a particular political party). At times, in fact, it seemed that virtually everyone had become a "progressive": middle-class reformers and machine bosses, big businessmen and small entrepreneurs, white segregationists and black activists, industrial workers and farmers, immigrants and immigration restrictionists. More than one historian has suggested that the word *progressive* ultimately came to mean so many different things to so many different people that it ceased to mean anything at all, that it should be dropped from our vocabulary. (See "Where Historians Disagree," pp. 616–617.)

Yet if progressivism was a phenomenon of remarkable scope and diversity, it was also one that rested on an identifiable set of central assumptions, assumptions that reflected both the hopefulness and the concern that were the legacy of the late nineteenth century. It was, first, an optimistic vision. Progressives believed, as their name implies, in the idea of progress. They believed that society was capable of improvement, even of perfection, that continued growth and advancement were the nation's destiny. There was in progressivism a heady, boisterous enthusiasm, a continuing excitement over possibilities.

But progressives believed, too, that growth and progress could not continue to occur recklessly, as they had in the nineteenth century. Order and stability, they claimed, were essential for social betterment. And direct, purposeful human intervention in social and economic affairs was essential to the creation of that order. The "natural laws" of the marketplace, and the doctrines of laissez faire and Social Darwinism that celebrated those laws, were not sufficient.

Progressives did not always agree on the form their intervention should take; but most believed that government could play an important role in the process. Only government could effectively counter the corrupt special interests that were responsible for social disarray. Only government could provide the services and the regulation that were necessary for future progress. It was essential, therefore, to rescue the nation's political institutions from the influence of corrupt party leaders and selfish interest groups; and it was vital that government expand its role in the society and in the economy. Not all progressive efforts required the assistance of government, but the

WHERE HISTORIANS DISAGREE

Progressivism

Few issues in the history of twentieth-century America have inspired more disagreement, even confusion, than the nature of progressivism. Until about 1950, most historians were in general accord about the nature of the progressive "movement." It was, they generally agreed, just what it had said it was: a movement by the "people" to curb the power of the "special interests." In particular, it was a protest by an aroused citizenry against the excessive power of urban bosses, corporate moguls, and tame corrupt elected officials.

In the early 1950s, however, a new interpretation emerged to challenge the traditional view. It retained the earlier view of progressivism as a largely political movement, but it offered a new explanation of who the progressives were and what they were trying to do. George Mowry, in *The California Progressives* (1951), described the reform movement in the state not as a protest by the mass of the people, but as an effort by a relatively small and privileged group of business and professional men to limit the overbearing power of large corporations and labor unions. Viewing themselves as natural social leaders, they resented their loss of political power to these new economic forces and envisioned reform as a way to restore both their economic fortunes and their social importance and self-esteem. Richard Hofstadter expanded on this idea in *The Age of Reform* (1955), in which he described progressives throughout the country as people suffering from "status anxiety"—old, formerly influential, upper-middle-class families seeking to restore their fading prestige by challenging the powerful new institutions that had begun to displace them. Like the Populists, Hofstadter suggested, the progressives were suffering from psychological, not economic, discontent.

The Mowry-Hofstadter thesis was for a time widely influential, but it was never without critics. In particular, it received strong challenges from historians who disagreed with two of the basic assumptions of the interpretation. First, these scholars maintained, Mowry and Hofstadter were mistaken in examining progressivism purely in terms of its visible political leaders. It was a movement with a far broader social and economic base. Second, they claimed, progressive reformers were not expressing a vague psychological malaise, but a clear recognition of their own self-interest. Beyond that, the new historians of progressivism often disagreed with one another as much as they disagreed with Mowry and Hofstadter.

Perhaps the harshest challenge to earlier interpretations came from the New Left historian Gabriel Kolko, whose influential 1963 study, *The Triumph of Conservatism*, dismissed the supposedly "democratic" features of progressivism as meaningless rhetoric and examined instead the impact of progressive economic reforms. Progressivism was, he agreed, an effort to regulate business. But it was not the "people" who were responsible for this regulation. It was the businessmen, who saw in government supervision a way to protect themselves from competition. Regulation, Kolko claimed, was "invariably controlled by the leaders of the regulated industry and directed towards ends they deemed acceptable or desirable."

A somewhat more moderate challenge to the "psychological" interpretation of progressivism came from historians embracing a new "organizational" view of history. Samuel P. Hays was among the first to suggest the approach in *The Response to Industrialism, 1885–1914* (1957) and other writings. Hays argued that progressives were indeed businessmen, as Kolko had suggested. But their impulse was not so much narrow self-interest as a broad desire to bring order and efficiency to political and, hence, economic life. The most important progressives, he claimed, were members of the upper class, who viewed a restoration of stability as essential to the preservation of their privileged position.

Even more influential was a 1967 study by Robert Wiebe, *The Search for Order, 1877–1920*. Wiebe saw progressivism as a response to dislocations in American life that had resulted from rapid changes in the nature of the economy unaccompanied by corresponding changes in social and political institutions. Economic power had moved to large, national organizations, while social and political life remained centered primarily on local communities. The result was widespread disorder and unrest, culminating in the turbulent 1890s. Progressivism, Wiebe argued, was the effort of a "new middle class"—a class tied to the emerging

WHERE HISTORIANS DISAGREE

national economy—to stabilize and enhance their position in society.

Yet despite all the challenges to the original view of progressivism as a democratic movement, some historians continued to produce evidence that the reform phenomenon was indeed a movement of the people against the special interests, although some identified the "people" somewhat differently from earlier such interpretations. J. Joseph Huthmacher argued in 1962 that much of the force behind progressivism came from members of the working class, especially immigrants, who pressed for such reforms as workmen's compensation and wage and hour laws. John P. Buenker strengthened this argument in *Urban Liberalism and Progressive Reform* (1973), which argues that political machines and urban "bosses" were important sources of reform energy and helped create twentieth-century liberalism.

David P. Thelen, in a 1972 study of progressivism in Wisconsin, *The New Citizenship,* offered an even broader challenge to both the "status anxiety" and the "conservatism-organizational" views. Thelen found a real clash between the "public interest" and "corporate privilege" in Wisconsin. The depression of the 1890s had mobilized a broad coalition of citizens of highly diverse backgrounds behind efforts to make both business and government responsible to the popular will. It marked the emergence of a new "consumer" consciousness that crossed boundaries of class and community, religion and ethnicity.

Other historians writing in the 1970s and 1980s tackled the question of the nature of progressivism less by looking at particular reformers or particular reforms than by trying to identify some of the broad processes of political change that had created the public battles of the era. Richard L. McCormick's *From Realignment to Reform* (1981), for example, studied political change in New York state and argued that the crucial change in this era was the decline of the political parties as the vital players in public life and the rise of interest groups working for particular social and economic goals. Progressivism, he and others have suggested, was not so much a coherent "movement" as part of a broader process of political adaptation to the realities of modern industrial society. At the same time, a large group of historians was focusing on the role of women in shaping and promoting progressive reform and seeing in their efforts concerns rooted in the female experience. Some progressive battles, they argued, were part of an effort by women to protect their interests within the domestic sphere in the face of jarring challenges to that sphere from the new industrial world. Others were attempts by women to expand their roles in the public world. In either case, they contend, progressivism cannot be understood without understanding the role of women and the importance of issues involving the family and the private world within it.

Given the range of disagreement over the nature of the progressive movement, it is hardly surprising that some historians have despaired of finding any coherent definition for the term at all. Peter Filene, for one, suggested in 1970 that the concept of progressivism as a "movement" had outlived its usefulness. "It is time," he suggested, "to tear off the familiar label and, thus liberated from its prejudice, see the history between 1890 and 1920 for what it was—ambiguous, inconsistent, moved by agents and forces more complex than a [single, uniform] progressive movement." Critics argued that Filene's view was an argument for abandoning the search for any historical meaning in the politics of the early twentieth century. But Daniel Rodgers, in an important 1982 article, "In Search of Progressivism," disagreed. Concluding a review of the new scholarship on the progressive era, he wrote:

> Whether historians of the 1980s will call off the search for that great, overarching thing called "progressivism" is hard to predict. Certainly historians in the 1970s manifestly failed to find it. In recompense they found out a vast amount about the world in which the progressives lived and the structures of social and political power shifting so rapidly around them. To acknowledge that these are the questions that matter and to abandon the hunt for the *essence* of the noise and tumult of that era may not be, as Filene's first critics feared, to lose the whole enterprise of historical comprehension. It may be to find it.

broad reordering of society that most progressives believed necessary would be impossible without such aid.

The Progressive Impulse

Beyond these central premises, progressivism flowed outward in a number of different directions, embodying several different approaches to reform. One powerful impulse shaping many progressive efforts was the spirit of "antimonopoly," the fear of concentrated power and the urge to limit and disperse authority and wealth. That impulse had, of course, a long history in American life and had been central, most recently, to the demands of the Populists. Many progressives absorbed it as well, although they often turned it to more moderate purposes than some earlier antimonopolists had done.

A second progressive impulse was a belief in the importance of social cohesion: the belief that individuals are not autonomous but part of a great web of social relationships, that the welfare of any single person is dependent on the welfare of society as a whole. This impulse suggested both that individuals had responsibilities to their society, and that society had responsibilities to the individual. It marked an open rejection of the laissez-faire orthodoxies of the late nineteenth century.

And a third progressive impulse was a belief in organization and efficiency: a belief that social order was a result of intelligent social organization, a belief in the importance of process, a belief in the need for rational procedures to guide social and economic life. Society was too complex, many progressives believed, to be left in the hands of party bosses, untrained amateurs, old-fashioned institutions. A new breed of leaders and organizations would be necessary to guide America to its future.

These varied reform impulses were not entirely incompatible with one another; and they did not exist in completely separate worlds. Progressives made use, at different times and in different ways, of the whole range of ideas available to them as they tried to restore order and stability to their turbulent society.

The Muckrakers

Historians looking for a starting point for progressivism have often pointed to the rise of a group of crusading journalists, who in the late nineteenth and early twentieth centuries began to direct public attention toward social, economic, and political injustices.

They became known as the "muckrakers," after Theodore Roosevelt, in a fit of pique, accused one of them of doing nothing but raking up muck through his writings. And they were committed above all to uncovering scandal, corruption, and injustice and exposing it as widely as possible. The work of the muckrakers achieved an extraordinary impact beginning in the late nineteenth century—in part because of the birth of mass-circulation newspapers and magazines, but also because their work reinforced some of the other reform currents of their time.

At first, their major targets were the trusts and particularly the railroads, whom the muckrakers believed to possess excessive power and to be the source of enormous corruption. Exposés of the great corporate organizations began to appear as early as the 1860s, when Charles Francis Adams, Jr., and others published revelatory magazine articles about nefarious doings among the railroad barons. Such inquiries continued into the twentieth century—the most notable, perhaps, being Ida Tarbell's enormous and influential study of the Standard Oil trust (published as a two-volume book in 1904).

By the turn of the century, many of the muckrakers were turning their attention to government and particularly to the urban political machines. The most influential, perhaps, was Lincoln Steffens, a reporter for *McClure's* magazine, who traveled through much of the country in the first years of the century and produced a series of articles on municipal corruption that aroused a major public outcry. His portraits of "machine government" and "boss rule," his exposures of "boodlers" in cities as diverse as St. Louis, Minneapolis, Cleveland, Cincinnati, Chicago, Philadelphia, and New York, his tone of studied moral outrage (as reflected in the title of his series and of the book that emerged from it, *The Shame of the Cities*)—all combined to persuade urban reformers of the need for a militant response. The alternative to leaving government in the hands of corrupt party leaders, the muckrakers argued, was for the people themselves to take a greater interest in public life. Indeed, some journalists seemed less outraged at the bosses themselves than at the apathetic public that seemed not to care about the corruption occurring in their midst.

The muckrakers reached their peak in the first decade of the twentieth century, when they published startling exposés of a wide range of problems. They investigated governments, labor unions, and corpo-

THE BOSSES OF THE SENATE.

"The Bosses of the Senate" (1889), by Joseph Keppler
Keppler was a popular political cartoonist of the late nineteenth century who shared the growing concern about the power of the trusts—portrayed here as bloated, almost reptilian figures standing menacingly over the members of a U.S. Senate, to whose chamber the "people's entrance" is "closed." (The Granger Collection)

rations. They explored the problems of child labor, immigrant ghettoes, prostitution, and family disorganization. They denounced the waste and destruction of natural resources, the subjugation of women, even occasionally the oppression of blacks. By bringing problems to the attention of the public, and by presenting those problems with indignation and moral fervor, they helped inspire other Americans to take action against their problems. In the process, they themselves expressed some of the most basic progressive impulses: the opposition to monopoly; the belief in the need for social unity in the face of corruption and injustice; even at times the cry for efficiency and organization.

The Social Gospel

The moralistic tone of the muckrakers' exposés reflected one important aspect of the emerging progressive sentiment: a sense of social responsibility and

a humanitarian concern for personal injustice. The pursuit of "social justice" became one of the central concerns of many progressive reformers. And perhaps the clearest expression of that concern emerged from an important segment of American religion, through the rise of what became known as the "Social Gospel." A powerful movement within American Protestantism (and, to a lesser extent, within American Catholicism and Judaism), the Social Gospel had emerged by the early twentieth century as a vigorous force in the effort to redeem the nation's cities. The Salvation Army, which had come to the United States from England, boasted a corps of 3,000 officers and 20,000 privates by 1900, offering both material aid and spiritual service to the urban poor. Ministers of many denominations, priests, and rabbis left traditional parish work to serve in the troubled cities, and their efforts soon became part of the folklore of their time. Charles Sheldon's *In His Steps*

(1898), the story of a young minister who abandoned a comfortable post to work among the needy, sold more than 15 million copies and established itself as the most successful novel of the era.

Walter Rauschenbusch, a Protestant theologian with socialist inclinations from Rochester, New York, published a series of influential discourses on the possibilities for human salvation through Christian reform. To him, the message of Darwinism was not that the individual was engaged in a brutal struggle for survival of the fittest, but that all individuals should work for a humanitarian evolution of the social fabric. "Translate the evolutionary themes into religious faith," he wrote, "and you have the doctrine of the Kingdom of God." Some American Catholics seized on the 1893 publication of Pope Leo XIII's encyclical *Rerum Novarum* as justification for their own crusade for social justice. Catholic liberals such as Father John A. Ryan took to heart the pope's warning that "a small number of very rich men have been able to lay upon the masses of the poor a yoke little better than slavery itself. . . . No practical solution of this question will ever be found without the assistance of religion and the church." For decades, he worked to expand the scope of Catholic social welfare organizations.

The Social Gospel was never the dominant element in the movement for urban reform. Some of the most influential progressives dismissed it as irrelevant moralization; others viewed it as little more than a useful complement to their own work. But the engagement of religion with reform helped bring to progressivism a powerful moral component and a commitment to redeem the lives of even the lowliest residents. Walter Rauschenbusch captured some of both the optimism and the spirituality of the Social Gospel with his proud comment, after a visit to a New York slum known as Hell's Kitchen, where Christian reformers were hard at work: "One could hear human virtue cracking and crashing all around."

The Settlement House Movement

Not all efforts to redeem the urban masses were as openly moralistic as those of the advocates of the Social Gospel. The settlement house movement, in particular, combined a humanitarian compassion for the poor with a strong belief in the importance of scientific methods of social organization.

One of the strongest elements of much progressive thought was the belief in the influence of the environment on individual development. Social Darwinists such as William Graham Sumner had argued that people's fortunes reflected their inherent "fitness" for survival; most progressive theorists disagreed. Ignorance, poverty, even criminality, they argued, were not the result of inherent moral or genetic failings or of the workings of divine providence. They were, rather, the effects of an unhealthy environment. To elevate the distressed, therefore, required an improvement of the conditions in which they lived.

Of particular interest to such reformers were the urban immigrant ghettoes, which publicists such as Jacob Riis were exposing through vivid photographs

Slum Babies
Orange Box Nursery

Salvation Army Day Care
The Salvation Army was founded in England in 1865 as a Protestant evangelical organization and given its name thirteen years later. The American branch began in Pennsylvania in 1880 and soon spread throughout the nation. Organized along semi-military lines (with "officers," "troops," and uniforms), it sought not only to promote Christian faith but also to minister to the physical needs of the poor. In this photograph, taken about 1910, Salvation Army women care for the babies of working mothers in an urban slum. (Salvation Army)

Tenement Cigarmakers

Jacob Riis included this photograph, "Bohemian Cigarmakers at Work in Their Tenement," in his first major exposé of life in the immigrant ghettoes—*How the Other Half Lives* (1890). Riis was himself an immigrant. Born in Denmark, he arrived in New York City in 1870 and for several years worked at the usual menial jobs open to newcomers. By the end of the decade, however, he was an established journalist; and after his work as a police reporter exposed him to conditions in the tenements, he developed the commitment that became his life's work: eliminating the slums of New York. (Museum of the City of New York)

and lurid descriptions. Riis himself usually took a callous approach to the problem; he urged the razing of the most offensive slums without making any provision for the relocation of displaced residents. (Later, he became an advocate of immigration restriction.) Other progressives, however, responded more sensitively. Borrowing ideas from reform movements in Europe, especially England, committed men and women established settlement houses in immigrant neighborhoods.

The most famous American settlement house, and one of the first, was Hull House. It opened in 1889 in Chicago as a result of the efforts of Jane Addams, a college graduate who had studied briefly for a career in medicine; and it became a model for more than 400 similar institutions throughout the nation. Staffed by members of the middle class, these institutions sought to help immigrant families adapt to the language and customs of their new country. Settlement houses offered educational services, staged community events, built libraries, and in general tried to enhance the lives of their neighborhoods without adopting the stance of disapproving moral superior-

ity that had hampered the success of earlier philanthropic efforts. But settlement houses often embodied, too, a belief that middle-class Americans had a responsibility to impart their own values to immigrants and to teach them how to live middle-class life styles. The name itself suggests their founders' outlook. The word *settlement* had connotations of the frontier: middle-class people "settling" in the inner city and bringing civilization to the urban frontier.

Central to the settlement houses were the efforts of college women, who found in the movement an outlet for their growing demand for useful, professional work. Indeed, the movement became a training ground for many important female leaders of the twentieth century, including Eleanor Roosevelt. The settlement houses provided these women with an environment that society could view as "appropriate" for women: urban "homes" where settlement workers helped immigrants to become better members of society. (The settlement house was "home" only to the reformers; their immigrant constituents did not live there.)

The settlement houses also helped spawn another important institution of reform: the profession of social work—another profession in which women were to play an important role. Workers at Hull House, for example, maintained a close relationship with the University of Chicago's pioneering work in the field of sociology; and a growing number of programs for the professional training of social workers began to appear in the nation's leading universities, partly in response to the activities of the settlements. The professional social worker combined a compassion for the poor with a commitment to the values of bureaucratic progressivism: scientific study, efficient organization, reliance on experts. The new profession produced elaborate surveys and reports, collected statistics, and published scholarly tracts on the need for urban reform.

The Allure of Expertise

As the emergence of the social work profession suggests, progressives involved in humanitarian efforts often placed high value on knowledge and expertise. Even nonscientific problems, they optimistically believed, could be analyzed and solved scientifically. The allure of expertise, in fact, became one of the most important aspects of many progressive efforts. Many reformers came to believe that only enlightened experts and well-designed bureaucracies could create the order that America so badly needed.

This belief found expression in innumerable ways, among them the writings of a new group of scholars and intellectuals. Unlike the Social Darwinists of the nineteenth century, these theorists were no longer content with merely justifying the existing industrial system. They spoke instead of the creation of a new civilization, one in which the expertise of scientists and engineers could be brought to bear on the problems of the economy and society. Among their most influential spokesmen was the social scientist Thorstein Veblen. Harshly critical of the industrial tycoons of the late nineteenth century—the "leisure class" as he satirically described them in his first major work, *A Theory of the Leisure Class* (1899)—Veblen proposed instead a new economic system in which power would reside in the hands of highly trained engineers. Only they, he argued, could fully understand the "machine process" by which modern society must be governed. Only they could provide the efficiency and order necessary for the industrial economy. By the end of his life, Veblen

was calling for government by a "soviet of technicians," who would impose on the economy their own instinct for rational process.

In practical terms, the impulse toward expertise and organization helped produce the idea of scientific management, or "Taylorism." (See p. 674.) It encouraged the development of modern mass-production techniques and, above all, the assembly line. It inspired a revolution in American education and the creation of a whole new area of inquiry—social science, the use of scientific techniques in the study of society and its institutions. It produced a generation of bureaucratic reformers concerned with the structure of organizations and committed to building new political and economic institutions capable of managing a modern society. It also helped to create a movement toward organization among the expanding new group of middle-class professionals.

The Professions

The late nineteenth century had seen not only a growth of the industrial work force but also a dramatic expansion in the number of Americans engaged in administrative and professional tasks. Industries needed managers, technicians, and accountants as well as workers. Cities required a growing range of commercial, medical, legal, and educational services. The demand for technology required scientists and engineers who, in turn, required institutions and instructors to train them. The industrial state, in short, had produced an enormous new infrastructure of specialized, professional services. And by the turn of the century, those performing these services had come to constitute a distinct social group—what some have called a new middle class.

More than the older middle class, whose position in society often derived from family background and stature within the local community, the new middle class placed a high value on education and individual accomplishment. By the early twentieth century, its millions of members were hard at work building organizations and establishing standards to secure and stabilize their position in society.

As their principal vehicle, they created the modern, organized professions. The idea of professionalism had been a frail one in America even as late as 1880. When every patent-medicine salesman could claim to be a doctor, when every frustrated politician could set up shop as a lawyer, when anyone who could read and write could pose as a teacher, it was clear that a professional label would by itself carry little weight. There were, of course, skilled and responsible doctors, lawyers, teachers, and others; but they had no way of controlling the charlatans and incompetents who presumed to practice their trades. As the demand for services increased, so did the pressures, from both within and without, for reform.

Among the first to respond was the medical profession. Throughout the 1890s, doctors who considered themselves true professionals—who had had formal training in medicine, who understood the new scientific discoveries that were revolutionizing their methods—began forming local associations and societies. In 1901, finally, they reorganized the American Medical Association into a modern, national, professional society. Between 1900 and 1910, membership increased from 8,400 to over 70,000; by 1920, nearly two-thirds of all American doctors were members. The first major effort of the AMA was to insist on strict, scientific standards for admission to the practice of medicine, with doctors themselves serving as protectors of the standards. State and local governments readily complied, passing new laws that required the licensing of all physicians and restricting licenses to those practitioners approved by the profession.

Accompanying the emphasis on strict regulation of the profession came a concern for rigorous scientific training and research. By 1900, medical education at a few medical schools—notably Johns Hopkins in Baltimore (founded in 1893)—compared favorably with that in the leading institutions of Europe. Doctors such as William H. Welch at Hopkins revolutionized the teaching of medicine by moving students out of the classrooms and into laboratories and clinics. Rigorous new standards forced many inadequate medical schools out of existence, and those that remained were obliged to adopt a strict scientific approach.

There was similar movement in other professions. By 1916, lawyers in all forty-eight states had established professional bar associations; and virtually all of them had succeeded in creating central examining boards, composed of lawyers, to regulate admission to the profession. Increasingly, aspiring lawyers found it necessary to enroll in graduate programs, and the nation's law schools accordingly expanded greatly, both in numbers and in the rigor of their curricula. Businessmen supported the creation of schools of business administration and created their own national organizations: the National Association of Manufacturers in 1895 and the United States Chamber of Commerce in 1912. Even farmers, long the symbol of the romantic spirit of individualism, responded to the new order by forming, through the National Farm Bureau Federation, a network of agricultural organizations designed to spread scientific farming methods, teach sound marketing techniques, and lobby for the interests of their members.

Among the most important purposes of the new professionalism was restricting entry into the professions. Professional organizations established rigorous standards for certifying new members and strove to keep control of admission in the hands of the professionals themselves. This was partly an effort to defend the professions from the untrained and incompetent; and the admission procedures served a valuable and important service in keeping out many of the inept doctors, lawyers, and others who had tainted the reputation of their fields in the past. But the admission requirements also served less altruistic purposes: to defend those already in the profession from excessive competition and to lend prestige and status to the professional label. Some professionals used their entrance requirements to exclude blacks, women, immigrants, and other "undesirables" from their ranks. Others used them simply to keep the numbers down, to ensure that demand for the services of existing members would remain high.

Women and the Professions

American women found themselves excluded—both by custom and by active barriers of law and prejudice—from most of the emerging professions. But a substantial number of middle-class women—particularly those emerging from the new women's colleges and from the coeducational state universities—were beginning to enter professional careers nevertheless.

A few women managed to establish themselves as physicians, lawyers, engineers, scientists, and corporate managers. Several leading medical schools (Johns Hopkins among them) admitted women, and about 5 percent of all American physicians were female in 1900 (a proportion that remained unchanged until the 1960s). Most, however, turned by necessity to those professions that society had somehow decided were "suitable" for women. The settlement houses and social work provided two "appropriate" professional outlets for women. The most important, however, was teaching. Indeed, in the late nineteenth century, more than two-thirds of all grammar

Maine School, c. 1900
With the growth of public schools in the late nineteenth century, women came to dominate a new profession: teaching.   (Culver Pictures)

it was still considered a menial occupation, akin to domestic service. But by the early twentieth century, it was adopting professional standards. Prospective nurses generally needed certification from schools of nursing and could not simply learn on the job. Women also found opportunities as librarians, another field beginning to define itself in modern, professional terms. And many women entered academia—often receiving advanced degrees at such predominantly male institutions as the University of Chicago, MIT, or Columbia, but usually finding professional opportunities in the new and expanding women's colleges.

The "women's professions" had much in common with other professions: the value they placed on training and expertise, the creation of professional organizations and a professional "identity," the monitoring of admission to professional work. But they also had distinctive qualities that set them apart from the male professional world. Female professions tended to involve activities that society could associate with traditionally female roles. Teaching, nursing, library work, and others were "helping" professions. They involved working primarily with other women or with children. Their activities occurred in places that seemed different from the offices that dominated the predominantly male business and professional worlds; such places as schools, hospitals, and libraries had a vaguely "domestic" image.

The Clubwomen

The great majority of American women did not take up professional careers. But many of those who did not found ways to play an active role in the effort to remake society. In the vanguard of many progressive social reforms was a large network of women's associations that proliferated rapidly beginning in the 1880s and 1890s. Large numbers of women gravitated to the growing temperance movement. (See below, pp. 631–632.) Others turned to the new women's clubs.

The women's clubs began largely as cultural organizations to provide middle- and upper-class women with an outlet for their intellectual energies. Gradually, however, they turned their attention to public matters and embraced a substantial reform agenda. In 1892, when women formed the General Federation of Women's Clubs to coordinate the activities of local organizations, there were more than 100,000 members in nearly 500 clubs. Eight years

school teachers were women; and perhaps 90 percent of all professional women were teachers. For educated black women, in particular, teaching was often the only professional opportunity they could hope to find. The existence of a large network of segregated black schools in the South created a substantial market for black teachers.

In many ways, the teaching profession behaved in these years much like other professions. It established new entrance requirements, policed by teachers' organizations, to keep unqualified people out. A growing network of teachers' colleges and schools of education emerged in the late nineteenth century to service the profession. And the National Education Association, founded in 1905, fought for, among other things, a government licensing process for teachers.

Women also came to dominate other activities that were beginning to achieve professional status. Nursing had become primarily a women's field when

later, there were 160,000 members; and by 1917, over 1 million.

By the early twentieth century, the clubs were becoming less concerned with cultural activities and more concerned with making a contribution to social betterment. Much of what they did was uncontroversial: planting trees; supporting schools, libraries, and settlement houses; building hospitals and parks. But clubwomen were not afraid to take positions on controversial public issues, and they adopted resolutions supporting such measures as child labor laws, worker compensation, pure food and drug legislation, occupational safety, and—beginning in 1914—woman suffrage. Because club members were so often from wealthy families, the organizations often had ample funds at their disposal and could make their influence felt.

Black women occasionally joined clubs dominated by whites. But blacks formed a network of clubs of their own, some of which affiliated with the General Federation, but more of which became part of the indeptendent National Association of Colored Women. They modeled themselves primarily on their white counterparts, but some black clubs also took positions on issues of particular concern to blacks. Some crusaded against lynching and called for congressional legislation to make lynching a federal crime. Others protested aspects of segregation.

The women's club movement raised few overt challenges to prevailing assumptions about the proper role of women in society. But it did represent an important effort by women to extend their influence beyond their traditional sphere within the home and the family. Few clubwomen were willing to accept the arguments of such committed feminists as Charlotte Perkins Gilman, who in her 1898 book *Women and Economics* argued that the traditional definition of sexual roles was exploitive and obsolete. The club movement, rather, allowed women to define a space for themselves in the public world without openly challenging the existing, male-dominated order.

But the importance of the club movement did not lie simply in what it did for middle-class women. It lay also in what those women did for the working-class people they attempted to help. The women's club movement was an important force in winning passage of state (and ultimately federal) laws that regulated the conditions of woman and child labor, that established government inspection of workplaces, that regulated the food and drug industries, and that applied new standards to urban housing.

In many of these efforts, the clubwomen formed alliances with other women's groups. Among them was the Women's Trade Union League, founded in 1903 by female union members and upper-class reformers and committed to persuading women to join unions. In addition to working on behalf of protective legislation for woman workers, WTUL members held public meetings on behalf of female workers, raised money to support strikes, marched on picket lines, and bailed woman strikers out of jail.

The Assault on the Parties

Sooner or later, most progressive goals required the involvement of government. Social workers wanted laws to protect woman and child workers and to improve conditions in the ghettos. Professionals advocated legal standards for admission to the practice of law or medicine. Others urged legislative solutions to such problems as the power of trusts or the destructive effects of cutthroat competition. Only government, progressives agreed, could provide the centralized regulation and control necessary to impose order and justice on modern society.

But American government at the dawn of the new century was, progressives believed, peculiarly ill adapted to perform these ambitious tasks. At every level, political institutions were outmoded, inefficient, often corrupt. Before society could be effectively reformed, it would be necessary to reform government itself. In the beginning, at least, many progressives considered one of their principal goals to be an assault on the domination of government and politics by the political parties, which they considered corrupt, undemocratic, and reactionary.

Early Attacks

Attacks on party dominance had emerged repeatedly in the late nineteenth century. Such third-party movements as Greenbackism and Populism had been, at least in part, efforts to break the hammerlock with which the Republicans and Democrats controlled public life. The Independent Republicans (or mugwumps; see p. 571) had attempted to challenge the grip of partisanship; and the mugwumps, in fact, became one of the important cores of progressive political reform activity in the 1890s and later.

The early assaults enjoyed some success. In the 1880s and 1890s, for example, most states adopted the secret ballot. Prior to that, the political parties themselves had printed ballots (or "tickets"), which they distributed to their supporters, who then simply went to the polls to deposit their "tickets" in the ballot box. The old system had made it possible for bosses to monitor the voting behavior of their constituents; it had also made it difficult for voters to "split" their tickets—to vote for candidates of different parties for different offices. The new secret ballot—printed by the government and distributed at the polls to be filled out and deposited in secret— helped chip away at the power of the parties over the voters.

By the late 1890s, critics of the parties had expanded their goals and were beginning to challenge directly some of the structures of government that they believed made possible the existence of bosses. Party rule could be broken, they believed, in one of two ways. It could be broken by increasing the power of the people, by permitting them to circumvent partisan institutions and express their will directly at the polls. Or it could be broken by placing more power in the hands of nonpartisan, nonelective officials, insulated from political life. Reformers promoted measures that moved along both those paths.

Municipal Reform

It was in the cities, many progressives believed, that the impact of party rule was most damaging. And it was municipal government, therefore, that became the first target of those working for political reform. Settlement houses, social workers, and scholars all attempted to focus attention on urban problems and the need for governmental changes to combat them. And muckraking journalists (see above, pp. 618–619) were especially successful in arousing public outrage at the rampant corruption and incompetence in city politics.

The muckrakers struck a responsive chord among a powerful group of urban middle-class progressives. For several decades after the Civil War, "respectable" citizens of the nation's large cities had avoided participation in municipal government. Viewing politics as a debased and demeaning activity, they shrank from contact with the "vulgar" elements who were coming to dominate public life. By the end of the century, however, a new generation of activists—some of them members of old aristocratic families, others a part of the new middle class—were taking a renewed interest in government. The nineteenth-century middle class had abdicated control of politics to the party organizations and the urban masses they manipulated; the twentieth-century middle class, appalled by the abuses and failures that had ensued, would win it back.

They faced a formidable array of opponents. In addition to challenging the powerful city bosses and their entrenched political organizations, they were attacking a large group of special interests: saloon owners, brothel keepers, and perhaps most significantly, those businessmen who had established cozy and lucrative relationships with the urban machines and viewed reform as a threat to their profits. Allied with these interests were many influential newspapers, which ridiculed the reformers as naïve do-gooders or prigs. Finally, there was the great constituency of urban working people, mostly of immigrant origin, to whom the machines were a source of needed jobs and services. To them, the progressives often seemed to be middle-class prudes attempting to impose an alien and unappealing life style. Gradually, however, the reformers gained in political strength—in part because of their own growing numbers, in part because of the conspicuous failures of the existing political leadership. And in the first years of the twentieth century, they began to score some important victories.

One of the first major successes came in Galveston, Texas, where the old city government collapsed in ineffectuality in the wake of a destructive tidal wave in 1900. Capitalizing on public dismay, reformers (many of them local businessmen) won approval of a new city charter. The mayor and council were replaced by an elected, nonpartisan commission whose five members would jointly enact ordinances and individually run the main city departments. In 1907, Des Moines, Iowa, adopted its own version of the commission plan, and other cities soon followed. Another approach to reform, similarly motivated by the desire to remove city government from the hands of the parties, was the city-manager plan, by which elected officials hired an outside expert— often a professionally trained business manager or engineer—to take charge of the government. Responsible not to the voters but to the councilors or commissioners who appointed him, the city manager would presumably remain untainted by the corrupting influence of politics. Staunton, Virginia, was one of the first municipalities to hire a city manager, in 1908. Five years later, Dayton, Ohio, attracted wider attention to the device when it adopted the new system after a major flood. By the end of the progressive era, almost 400 cities were operating under commissions, and another 45 employed city managers.

The commission governments and the city-manager systems removed municipal administration from party politics altogether. In most urban areas, and in the larger cities in particular, reformers had to settle for less absolute victories. They attempted to reform municipal elections in various ways. Some cities made the election of mayors nonpartisan (so that the parties could not choose the candidates) or moved them to years when no presidential or congressional races were in progress (to reduce the influence of the large turnouts that party organizations produced on such occasions). Reformers tried to make city councilors run at large, to limit the influence of ward leaders and district bosses. They tried to strengthen the power of the mayor at the expense of the city council, on the assumption that reformers were more likely to succeed in getting a sympathetic mayor elected than to win control of the entire council.

Some of the most successful reformers emerged not from the new commission and city-manager systems but from conventional political structures that progressives came to control. Tom Johnson, the celebrated reform mayor of Cleveland, waged a long and difficult war against the powerful streetcar interests in his city, fighting to raise the ridiculously low assessments on railroad and utilities properties, to lower streetcar fares to 3 cents, and ultimately to impose municipal ownership on certain basic utilities. After Johnson's defeat and death, his talented aide Newton D. Baker won election as mayor and helped maintain Cleveland's reputation as the best-governed city in America. Hazen Pingree of Detroit, Samuel "Golden Rule" Jones of Toledo, and other mayors effectively challenged local party bosses to bring the spirit of progressivism into city government.

Statehouse Progressivism

Often frustrated in their assault on boss rule in the cities, many progressives turned to state government as an agent for reform. Crusading district attorneys such as Hiram Johnson in California and Joseph W. Folk in Missouri left their cities to become reform governors. Elsewhere, progressive leaders arrived in the statehouse by other routes. Whatever their back-

Hiram Johnson and Gifford Pinchot

Johnson (at left, with cane) was elected governor of California in 1910 and quickly won passage of a program of railroad legislation that was among the nation's most stringent. In 1916 he was elected to the U.S. Senate and served until the 1940s. A leading progressive for many years, he became toward the end of his life a bitter conservative critic of the New Deal and a defender of isolationism. Gifford Pinchot (right), the first professional forester in the United States and the chief of the Division of Forestry, became a hero to progressives through his conflict with Interior Secretary Richard Ballinger and, as a result, with President Taft. The controversy helped to precipitate a rift between Theodore Roosevelt and Taft and Roosevelt's independent presidential candidacy in 1912, which both Johnson and Pinchot supported. Pinchot later served two terms as governor of Pennsylvania. (Culver Pictures)

grounds, however, such reformers agreed that state government must take a leading role in the task of stabilizing American life.

State-level progressives agreed on the unfitness of existing state governments to provide reform. They looked with particular scorn on state legislatures, whose ill-paid, relatively undistinguished

Robert La Follette Campaigning in Wisconsin
After three terms as governor of Wisconsin, La Follette began a long career in the United States Senate in 1906 during which he worked uncompromisingly for advanced progressive reforms—so uncompromisingly, in fact, that he was often almost completely isolated. He entitled a chapter of his autobiography "Alone in the Senate." La Follette had a greater impact on his own state, whose politics he and his sons dominated for nearly forty years and where he was able to win passage of many of the reforms that the federal government resisted. (State Historical Society of Wisconsin)

members were, they believed, generally incompetent, often corrupt, and totally controlled by party bosses. In the face of the debasement of the legislatures, they argued, it was necessary to circumvent the parties and return power directly to the people.

The result was a wave of reforms in state after state that attempted to "democratize" state government by limiting the influence of party organizations and the authority of elected officials, and increasing the influence of the electorate. Two of the most important changes were innovations first proposed by leaders of the Populist movement in the 1890s: the initiative and the referendum. The initiative gave reformers the ability to circumvent their legislatures altogether by submitting legislation directly to the voters in general elections. The referendum provided a method by which actions of the legislature could be returned to the electorate for approval. Oregon, in 1902, became the first state to enact such reforms. By 1918, nineteen other states had followed.

Progressives also attempted to improve the quality of elected officials, and for this purpose they created two more devices designed to limit the influence of traditional party politics: the direct primary and the recall. The primary election was an attempt to limit the influence of party machines on the selection of candidates. The recall gave voters the right to remove a public official from office at a special election, which could be called after a sufficient number of

citizens had signed a petition. Mississippi adopted the nation's first direct primary in 1902, and by 1915 every state in the nation had instituted primary elections for at least some offices. The recall encountered more strenuous opposition. No progressive measure so horrified conservatives as this effort to subject officeholders to voter censure before the end of their terms, and they blocked the adoption of the recall more effectively than any other reform.

Other reform measures attempted to clean up the legislatures themselves by limiting the influence of corporations on their activities and on the behavior of the parties. Between 1903 and 1908, twelve states passed laws restricting lobbying in state legislatures by business interests. In those same years, twenty-two states banned campaign contributions by corporations, and twenty-four states forbade public officials from accepting free passes from railroads.

Reform efforts proved most effective in states that elevated vigorous and committed politicians to positions of leadership. In New York, Governor Charles Evans Hughes exploited progressive sentiment to create a commission to regulate public utilities. In California, Governor Hiram Johnson used the new reforms to limit the political power of the Southern Pacific Railroad in the state. In New Jersey, Woodrow Wilson, the Princeton University president elected governor in 1910, used executive leadership to win a substantial array of reforms designed to end New Jersey's widely denounced position as the "mother of trusts."

The Laboratory of La Follette

The state that virtually all progressives came to view as the nation's leading center of reform was Wisconsin, the home of the great progressive hero Robert M. La Follette. La Follette had begun his career in Wisconsin as a conservative defender of free enterprise against its "radical" challengers. By the end of the 1890s, however, he had become convinced of the need for major reforms to curb the power of bosses, railroads, trusts, and financiers—the special interests that were, he argued, corrupting American life. Above all, perhaps, he had become convinced of the need for an alternative to the dominance of the traditional party organizations. Elected governor in 1900, he called for a new concept of politics: as the vehicle for enhancing the public interest, rather than as an arena in which special interests contended for favors.

In the years that followed, La Follette and his supporters turned Wisconsin into what reformers across the nation described as a "laboratory of progressivism." The Wisconsin progressives won approval of direct primaries, initiatives, and referendums. They secured effective regulation of railroads and utilities. They obtained the passage of laws to regulate the workplace and provide compensation for laborers injured on the job. They instituted graduated taxes on inherited fortunes, and they nearly doubled state levies on railroads and other corporate interests.

La Follette brought to progressivism his own fervent, almost evangelical, commitment to reform; and he used his personal magnetism to widen public awareness of progressive goals and to mobilize the energies of many previously passive groups. Reform was not simply the responsibility of politicians, he argued, but of newspapers, citizens' groups, educational institutions, and business and professional organizations. Progressivism, he suggested, must become a part of the fabric of American life. Ultimately, La Follette would find himself overshadowed by other national progressive leaders. In the early years of the century, however, few men were as effective in publicizing the message of reform. None was as successful in bending state government to that goal.

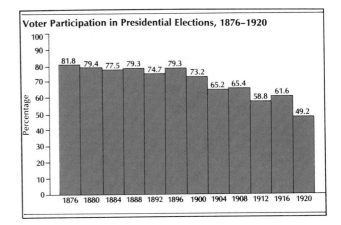

Parties and Interest Groups

The result of these reforms was not, of course, the elimination of party from American political life. Party organizations and party bosses remained enormously powerful for many years to come. But the many political reforms of the late nineteenth and early twentieth centuries did diminish the centrality of the parties in American life. By removing control of the electoral process from the hands of party leaders and placing it more securely with the government, reformers were beginning to wean Americans away from their once fervent party loyalties.

Evidence of that came from, among other things, the decline in voter turnout. In the late nineteenth century, up to 81 percent of eligible voters normally turned out for national elections. In the early twentieth century, while turnout remained very high by today's standards, the figure began to decline markedly. In the presidential election of 1900, 73 percent of the electorate voted. Four years later, the figure had dropped to 65 percent. By 1912, it had declined to about 59 percent. There were fluctuations from year to year, but never again did voter turnout reach as high as 70 percent.

At the same time that the influence of the parties was declining, another force was beginning to establish its power in American politics: what have become known as "interest groups." Indeed, one of the reasons for the assault on the parties had been the conviction of an increasing number of groups that they needed other avenues through which to influence the government. Beginning late in the nineteenth century and accelerating rapidly in the twentieth, a wide range of new organizations emerged, operating outside the party system, designed to pressure government to do the bidding of their members: trade associations, representing particular businesses and industries; labor organizations; farm lobbies; and many others. The new professional organizations saw as one of their central purposes lobbying in Washington and in state capitals for the interests of their members. Social workers, the settlement house movement, the women's clubs, and others learned to operate as interest groups to advance their demands.

Reform by Machine

One result of the assault on the parties was a change in the party organizations themselves, which attempted to adapt to the new realities so as to preserve their influence. Indeed, some of the most powerful party machines emerged from the progressive era almost as powerful as they had entered it. In large part, this was because the bosses themselves, who were usually intelligent men, recognized that they must change in order to survive. Thus they sometimes allowed their machines to become vehicles of social reform. The best example was New York's Tammany Hall, the nation's oldest and most notorious city machine. Its astute leader, Charles Francis Murphy, began in the early years of the century to fuse the techniques of boss rule with some of the concerns of social reformers. In the process, he ushered his organization into one of the most successful eras in its history.

Murphy did nothing to challenge the fundamental workings of Tammany Hall. The machine continued to mobilize working-class immigrant voters to support its candidates; it continued to offer them favors and services in return; its members continued to use patronage and even graft to strengthen their positions and expand their bank accounts. At the same time, however, Tammany began to take an increased interest in state and national politics, which it had traditionally scorned; and it used its political power on behalf of legislation to improve working conditions, protect child laborers, and eliminate the worst abuses of the industrial economy.

In 1911, a sudden fire swept the factory of the Triangle Shirtwaist Company in New York; 146 workers, most of them women, died. Many of them had been trapped inside the building because management had locked the emergency exits to prevent malingering. It was the worst industrial tragedy in the city's history, and the outrage it produced echoed across the nation. For the next three years, a broad-based state commission studied not only the background of the fire but the general condition of the industrial workplace; and by 1914, it had issued a series of reports calling for major reforms in the conditions of modern labor.

The report itself was a classic progressive document, based on the testimony of experts, replete with statistics and technical data. Yet when its recommendations reached the New York legislature, its most effective supporters were not middle-class progressives but two Tammany Democrats: Senator Robert

The Triangle Shirtwaist Fire
Policemen and investigators stand amid the coffins of victims of the 1911 fire in the Triangle Shirtwaist Factory in New York City, in which 146 workers (almost all of them women) died. Although the proprietors of the factory were acquitted of criminal charges in the deaths, the fire spurred reform and labor groups—most notably the International Ladies Garment Workers Union—to agitate for government action to improve conditions in the sweatshops.   (Culver Pictures)

F. Wagner and Assemblyman Alfred E. Smith. With the support of Murphy and the backing of other Tammany legislators, they steered through a series of pioneering labor laws that imposed strict regulations on factory owners and established effective mechanisms for enforcement. Tammany Hall, the incarnation of evil in the eyes of many progressives, had itself become a potent agent for reform.

Crusades for Order and Reform

Reformers directed many of their energies at the political process, in the belief that reshaping procedures and institutions would lead to greater justice and democracy. But they also crusaded on behalf of what they considered moral issues: particular reforms that would, they claimed, serve to remake the nation. Some were efforts to control private behavior: campaigns to eliminate alcohol from national life, to curb prostitution, to regulate divorce. Others were attempts to restore order to the public sphere: efforts to restrict immigration or curb the power of monopoly in the industrial economy. Still others were crusades to resolve what many considered longstanding injustices, of which the most prominent was the campaign for woman suffrage. Proponents of each of those reforms believed that success would mean a regeneration of society as a whole.

The Temperance Crusade

To some progressives, the elimination of alcohol from American life was a necessary step in the task of restoring order to society. Workers in settlement houses and social agencies abhorred the effects of drinking on working-class families: Scarce wages vanished as workers spent hours in the saloons. Drunkenness spawned violence, and occasionally murder, within urban families. Women, in particular, saw alcohol as a source of some of the greatest problems of working-class wives and mothers, and hoped through temperance to reform male behavior and thus improve women's lives. Employers, too, regarded alcohol as an impediment to industrial efficiency; workers often missed time on the job because of drunkenness or, worse, came to the factory intoxicated and performed their tasks sloppily and dangerously. Critics of economic privilege denounced the

liquor industry as one of the nation's most sinister trusts. And political reformers, who looked on the saloon (correctly) as one of the central institutions of the machine, saw an attack on drinking as part of an attack on the bosses. Out of such sentiments emerged the temperance movement.

Temperance had been a major reform movement before the Civil War, mobilizing large numbers of people (and particularly large numbers of women) in a crusade with strong evangelical overtones. Beginning in the 1870s, it experienced a major resurgence. As in the antebellum years, it was a movement led and supported primarily by women. In 1873, temperance advocates met in Chicago to form the Women's Christian Temperance Union (WCTU). And after 1879, when Frances Willard became its leader, the new organization became a militant, national organization. By 1911, it had 245,000 members and had become the largest single women's organization in American history to that point—and a model of administrative efficiency and political skill. The WCTU worked tirelessly to publicize the evils of alcohol and the connection between drunkenness and family violence, unemployment, poverty, and disease. In 1893, the Anti-Saloon League joined the temperance movement and, along with the WCTU, began to press for a specific legislative solution: the legal abolition of saloons. Gradually, that demand grew to include the complete prohibition of the sale and manufacture of alcoholic beverages.

Despite substantial opposition from immigrant and working-class voters, pressure for prohibition grew steadily through the first decades of the new century. By 1900, restrictions on the sale of alcohol were in effect in areas embracing more than a quarter of the population of the nation. By 1916, nineteen states had passed prohibition laws. But since the consumption of alcohol was actually increasing in many unregulated areas, temperance advocates were becoming convinced that what was necessary was a national prohibition law.

America's entry into World War I, and the moral fervor it unleashed, provided the last push to the advocates of prohibition. With the support of rural fundamentalists, who opposed alcohol on moral and religious grounds, progressive advocates of prohibition in 1917 steered through Congress a constitutional amendment embodying their demands. Two years later, after ratification by every state in the nation except Connecticut and Rhode Island (bastions of Catholic immigrants), the Eighteenth Amendment became law, to take effect in January 1920. The fed-

Crusading for Temperance

This unflattering painting by Ben Shahn portrays late-nineteenth-century women demonstrating in front of a saloon. It suggests the degree to which temperance and prohibition had fallen out of favor with liberals and progressives by the 1930s, when Shahn was working. In earlier years, however, temperance attracted the support of some of the most advanced American reformers.   (Museum of the City of New York)

eral government, many progressives believed, had taken an important step toward eliminating a major source of social instability and inefficiency. Only later did it become clear that prohibition would create new problems of its own.

Immigration Restriction

A similar concern for order fueled the movement demanding the restriction of immigration, which likewise gained force throughout the progressive era. While virtually all reformers agreed that the burgeoning immigrant population had created social problems, there was wide disagreement on how best to respond. Many progressives, convinced that open immigration was one of the nation's most valued traditions, believed that helping the new residents adapt to American society was the proper approach. Others, however, argued that efforts at assimilation had

failed and that the only solution was to limit the flow of new arrivals.

The first decades of the century, therefore, saw a steady growth in pressure on the federal government to close the nation's gates. New scholarly theories, designed to appeal to the progressive respect for expertise, argued that the introduction of immigrants into American society was polluting the nation's racial stock. The spurious "science" of eugenics spread the belief that human inequalities were hereditary and that immigration was contributing to the multiplication of the unfit. Skillful publicists such as Madison Grant, whose *The Passing of the Great Race* (1916) established him as the nation's most effective nativist, warned of the dangers of racial "mongrelization" and of the importance of protecting the purity of Anglo-Saxon and other Nordic stock.

As on other issues, progressives in Washington established a special commission of "experts," chaired by Senator William P. Dillingham of Vermont, to study the problem of immigration. Sup-

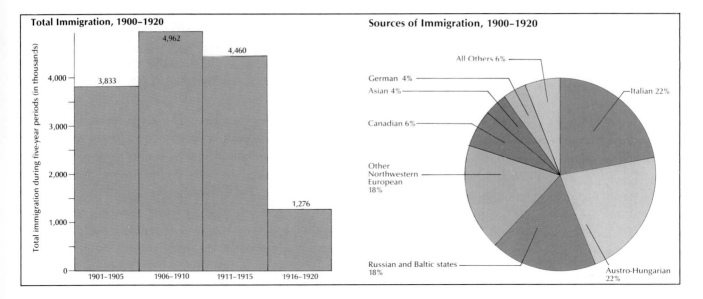

Total Immigration, 1900-1920

Total immigration during five-year periods (in thousands)

- 1901–1905: 3,833
- 1906–1910: 4,962
- 1911–1915: 4,460
- 1916–1920: 1,276

Sources of Immigration, 1900-1920

- Italian 22%
- Austro-Hungarian 22%
- Russian and Baltic states 18%
- Other Northwestern European 18%
- Canadian 6%
- Asian 4%
- German 4%
- All Others 6%

ported by elaborate statistics and scholarly testimony, the commission's report argued that the newer immigrant groups—largely southern and eastern Europeans— had proven themselves less assimilable than earlier immigrants. Immigration, the report implied, should be restricted by nationality.

Racial arguments helped mobilize impressive support behind the restriction movement, but even many who rejected such arguments supported limiting immigration. The continuing influx of foreigners was, they believed, creating unmanageable urban problems: overcrowding, unemployment, strained social services, social unrest. The combination of these concerns gradually won for the nativists the support of some of the nation's leading progressives: Theodore Roosevelt, Henry Cabot Lodge, and others. Powerful opponents—employers who saw immigration as a source of cheap labor, reformers who valued the ethnic culture of immigrant communities, immigrants themselves and their political representatives—managed to block the restriction movement for a time. But by the beginning of World War I (which itself effectively blocked immigration temporarily), the nativist tide was clearly gaining strength.

Suffrage for Women

Perhaps the largest single reform movement of the progressive era, indeed one of the largest of such movements in American history, was the fight for woman suffrage—a movement that attracted support from both women and men for many reasons. Women, in particular, often supported suffrage as a matter of simple justice or because they believed that the vote would enable them to increase the power and opportunities available to their sex. But many supported suffrage as well because of what they felt it could do to advance other causes. If the agitations for prohibition and immigration restriction were attempts to remove dangerous influences from American life, the suffrage movement was an attempt, its supporters believed, to inject into society a healthy new force. Giving women the right to vote, suffrage advocates claimed, was not only a matter of abstract principle; it was a practical measure to strengthen the forces of reform.

The movement for woman suffrage had already experienced a long and often frustrating history as the twentieth century began. Women had played an important role in the crusade for the abolition of slavery in the 1840s and 1850s, and they had included suffrage among their political demands after the Civil War (see pp. 361–362). Spurned by political leaders of the post–Civil War era, who insisted that this was "the Negro's hour," suffragists continued their efforts through the last decades of the nineteenth century, winning a few victories in some of the new Western states but lacking sufficient power to change national policy.

It is sometimes difficult for today's Americans to understand why the suffrage issue could have become the source of such enormous controversy in the

Suffragists
Suffrage activists hang posters along the boardwalk in the beachfront town of Long Branch, New Jersey. Twenty-nine states had permitted women at least some access to the ballot before ratification of the Nineteenth Amendment in 1920. New Jersey was not one of them. (Culver Pictures)

early years of this century. But at the time, suffrage seemed to many of its critics a very radical demand—in part because of the rationale some of its supporters used to advance it. Throughout the late nineteenth century, many suffrage advocates presented their views in terms of "natural rights," arguing that women deserved the same rights as men—including, first and foremost, the right to vote. Elizabeth Cady Stanton, one of the organizers of the 1848 women's rights convention at Seneca Falls (see pp. 361–362) and a suffrage leader for more than forty years, wrote in 1892 of woman as "the arbiter of her own destiny. . . . if we are to consider her as a citizen, as a member of a great nation, she must have the same rights as all other members." A woman's role as "mother, wife, sister, daughter" was "incidental" to her larger role as a part of society.

This was an argument that stood in stark contrast to prevailing views of women among men (and even among many women), who believed that society required a distinctive female "sphere" in which women would serve first and foremost as wives and mothers. To many men, and even to many women, the idea of women's rights seemed frightening and threatening. And so a powerful antisuffrage movement appeared, which challenged this apparent threat to the existing social order. There were antisuffrage organizations, some with substantial memberships; antisuffrage newspapers; rallies; petitions to legislatures; and widely circulated tracts. Opponents railed against the threat suffrage posed to the "natural order" of civilization. Woman, said one opponent, "was made man's helper, was given a servient place (not necessarily inferior) and man the dominant place (not necessarily superior) in the division of labor." Antisuffragists associated suffrage with divorce (not without some reason, since some suffrage advocates also supported revising the laws to make it easier for women to obtain a divorce). They linked suffrage with promiscuity, looseness, and neglect of children.

The suffrage movement began to overcome this opposition and to win some substantial victories in the first years of the twentieth century. That was in part because suffragists were becoming better organized and more politically sophisticated than their opponents. Under the leadership of Anna Howard Shaw, a Boston social worker, and Carrie Chapman Catt, a journalist from Iowa, the National American Woman Suffrage Association grew from a membership of about 13,000 in 1893 to over 2 million in 1917. The involvement of such well-known and widely admired women as Jane Addams gave added respectability to the cause.

But the movement also gained strength because many of its most prominent leaders began to justify suffrage in "safer," less theatening ways. Suffrage, some supporters began to argue, would not challenge the "separate sphere" in which women resided. It would allow women to bring their special and distinct virtues more widely to bear on society's problems. It was, they claimed, precisely because women occupied a distinct sphere—because as mothers and wives and homemakers they had special experiences and special sensitivities to bring to public life—that woman suffrage could make such an important contribution to politics. Jane Addams expressed this more conservative justification for suffrage in a 1909 article: "If women would effectively continue their old avocations, they must take part in the slow upbuilding of that code of legislation which is alone sufficient to protect the home from its dangers incident to modern life." In particular, many suffragists argued that enfranchising women would help the temperance movement, by giving its largest group of supporters a political voice. Some suffrage advocates claimed that once women had the vote, war would become a thing of the past, since women would—by their calming, peaceful influence—help curb the belligerence of men. It was perhaps unsurprising, therefore, that the outbreak of World War I gave the final, decisive push to the movement for suffrage.

Suffrage also attracted support for other, less optimistic reasons. Many middle-class people found persuasive the argument that if blacks, immigrants, and other "base" groups had access to the franchise, then it was not only a matter of justice but of common sense to allow educated, "well-born" women to vote. Some people supported woman suffrage, in fact, because they believed that it would add to the constituency that supported immigration restriction and racial disfranchisement. Florence Kelley, a prominent social reformer who was later to help organize the NAACP, remarked unhappily in 1906 on this aspect of the suffrage movement: "I have rarely heard a ringing suffrage speech which did not refer to the 'ignorant and degraded' men, or the 'ignorant immigrants' as our masters. This is habitually spoken with more or less bitterness."

Not all suffragists narrowed their arguments. Among working class, immigrant, and black women in particular, suffrage continued to generate substantial support precisely because it seemed so radical, because it promised to reshape the role of women and

reform the social order. But among members of the middle class, the separation of the suffrage movement from more radical feminist goals, and its association with other reform causes of concern to many Americans, helped it gain widespread support. Suffragists from a wide range of groups, embracing many different justifications for their cause, briefly converged behind the same issue to push it toward victory.

The principal triumphs of the suffrage movement began in 1910. That year, Washington became the first state in fourteen years to extend suffrage to women. California joined it a year later, and in 1912 four other Western states did the same. In 1913, Illinois became the first state east of the Mississippi to embrace woman suffrage. And in 1917 and 1918, New York and Michigan—two of the most populous states in the Union—gave women the vote. By 1919, thirty-nine states had granted women the right to vote in at least some elections; fifteen had allowed them full participation. In 1920, finally, suffragists won ratification of the Nineteenth Amendment, which guaranteed political rights to women throughtout the nation.

To some feminists, however, the victory seemed less than complete. Alice Paul, the head of the militant National Woman's party (founded in 1916) and a suffragist who had never accepted the relatively conservative "separate sphere" justification for suffrage, argued that the Nineteenth Amendment alone would not be sufficient to protect women's rights. Women needed more: a constitutional amendment that would provide clear, legal protection for their rights and would prohibit all discrimination on the basis of sex. Such an amendment would do what the suffrage amendment had not. It would provide legal affirmation of women's rights as individuals, of their rights to pursue their interests and abilities on the same terms as men. But Alice Paul's argument found limited favor even among many of the most important leaders of the recently triumphant suffrage crusade. Jane Addams, Florence Kelley, Carrie Chapman Catt, and others showed no interest in the Equal Rights Amendment. Some, such as Addams, denounced it bitterly, fearing it would invalidate the special protective legislation for women that they had fought so hard to have enacted. It would be many years before the divisions between these two wings of American feminism were healed.

As the controversy over the Equal Rights Amendment suggests, the suffrage movement did not, in the end, produce a coherent movement behind any issue other than securing women the vote. On most other issues, in fact, women were generally no more in agreement than men. Once enfranchised, the new voters did little to support the arguments of those suffragists who had claimed that women would operate in politics as a coherent force for reform.

The Dream of Socialism

Prohibition, immigration restriction, woman suffrage—these and other issues attracted large but limited constituencies. Of more general concern to progressives of all backgrounds was the state of the nation's economy. From the beginning, it had been animosity toward the great industrial combinations— the trusts—that had formed the core of progressive sentiment. It was to the task of limiting the power of the giant corporations, therefore, that many reformers devoted their greatest energies.

On how best to deal with the trusts, however, there was wide disagreement. Some reformers believed in the importance of careful government regulation, others in the necessity of destroying the trusts. But others, moving beyond the strictures of progressivism, argued that the problem lay not in the abuses of the economic system but in the system itself—that the solution lay in replacing capitalism with socialism.

At no time in American history to that point, and in few times after it, did radical critiques of the capitalist system attract more support than in the period between 1900 and 1914. Although never a force to rival, or even seriously threaten, the two major parties, the Socialist party of America grew during the progressive era into a force of considerable strength. In 1900, it had attracted the support of fewer than 100,000 voters; in 1912, its durable leader and perennial presidential candidate, Eugene V. Debs, received nearly 1 million ballots. Strongest in urban immigrant communities (particularly among Germans and Jews in New York, Chicago, Milwaukee, and elsewhere), it won the loyalties, too, of a substantial number of Protestant farmers in the South and Midwest. Socialists won election to over 1,000 state and local offices, and they attracted the admiring attention of some journalists and intellectuals as well as of members of the lower class. Lincoln Steffens, the crusader against municipal corruption, ultimately became a defender of socialism. So for a time did Walter Lippmann, the brilliant young journalist who was to become one of the nation's most important social critics. Florence

Kelley, Frances Willard, and other women reformers were attracted to socialism because of its support for pacifism and labor militancy.

Virtually all socialists agreed on the need for basic structural changes in the economy, but they differed widely on how drastic those changes should be. Some endorsed the sweepingly radical goals of European Marxists; others envisioned a more moderate reform that would allow small-scale private enterprise to survive but would nationalize the major industries. Debs spoke for the mainstream of the party in citing economic concentration as the greatest danger to democracy: "If we could but destroy the money monopoly, the land monopoly, all would be different." There was disagreement as well on tactics. Militant groups within the party favored drastic, even violent, action. Most conspicuous was the radical labor union the Industrial Workers of the World (IWW), known to opponents as the "Wobblies." Under the leadership of William ("Big Bill") Haywood, the IWW advocated a single union for all workers and abolition of the "wage slave" system; it rejected political action in favor of strikes—especially the general strike. Although few in number, the "Wobblies" struck terror into the hearts of the middle class with their inflammatory rhetoric. They were widely believed to have been responsible for the dynamiting of railroad lines and power stations and other acts of terror, although evidence of their actually engaging in such activities is slim.

More moderate socialists advocated peaceful change through political struggle, and it was they who dominated the party. They emphasized a gradual education of the public to the need for change and patient efforts within the system to enact it. It soon became clear, however, that the period before World War I was not the first stage of an effective socialist movement but the last. By the end of the war—in large part because the party had refused to support the war effort, in part too because of a growing wave of antiradicalism that subjected the socialists to enormous harassment and persecution—socialism was in decline as a significant political force.

Decentralization and Regulation

An ultimately more influential debate was raging at the same time between those who believed in the essential premises of capitalism but urged reforms to preserve it. The debate centered on two basic approaches: decentralization and regulation.

SIGNIFICANT EVENTS

1873 Women's Christian Temperance Union (WCTU) founded (p. 631)

1889 Jane Addams opens Hull House in Chicago (p. 621)

1892 General Federation of Women's Clubs founded (p. 624)

1893 Johns Hopkins Medical School established (p. 623)
Anti-Saloon League founded (p. 631)

1895 National Association of Manufacturers founded (p. 623)

1898 Charles Sheldon publishes *In His Steps* (pp. 619–620)
Charlotte Perkins Gilman publishes *Women and Economics* (p. 625)

1899 Thorstein Veblen publishes *A Theory of the Leisure Class* (p. 622)

1900 Galveston, Texas, establishes commission government (p. 626)
Robert La Follette elected governor of Wisconsin (p. 628)

1901 American Medical Association reorganized (p. 623)

1902 Oregon adopts initiative and referendum (p. 628)
Mississippi adopts direct primary (p. 628)

1903 Women's Trade Union League founded (p. 625)

1904 Ida Tarbell publishes exposé of Standard Oil (p. 618)

1905 National Education Association founded (p. 624)

1909 Herbert Croly publishes *The Promise of American Life* (p. 638)

1911 Fire kills 146 workers at Triangle Shirtwaist Company in New York City (p. 630)

1912 United States Chamber of Commerce founded (p. 623)

1913 Dayton, Ohio, establishes city-manager government (pp. 626–627)
Louis D. Brandeis publishes *Other People's Money* (p. 637)

1914 Walter Lippmann publishes *Drift and Mastery* (p. 638)

1916 Madison Grant publishes *The Passing of the Great Race* (p. 632)

1919 Eighteenth Amendment (prohibition) ratified (p. 631)

1920 Nineteenth Amendment (woman suffrage) ratified (p. 635)

To many progressives, the greatest threat to the nation's economy was excessive centralization and consolidation. The trusts had made it impossible for the free market to work as it should; only by restoring the economy to a more human scale could the nation hope for stability and justice. Few such reformers envisioned a return to a society of small, local enterprises; some consolidation, they recognized, was inevitable. They did, however, argue that the federal government should take forceful action to break up the largest combinations, to enforce a balance between the need for bigness and the need for competition. This viewpoint came to be identified with Louis D. Brandeis, the brilliant lawyer and later justice of the Supreme Court, who spoke and wrote widely (most notably in his 1913 book *Other People's Money*) about the "curse of bigness." "If the Lord had intended things to be big," Brandeis once wrote, "he would have made man bigger—in brains and character."

Brandeis and his supporters opposed bigness in part because they considered it inefficient. But their opposition had a moral basis as well. Bigness was a threat not just to efficiency but to freedom. It limited the ability of individuals to control their own destinies. It encouraged abuses of power. Government must, Brandeis insisted, regulate competition in such a way as to ensure that large combinations did not emerge.

To other progressives, competition was an overrated commodity. Far more important was efficiency. And since economic concentration tended to enhance efficiency, the government, they believed, should not discourage it. What government should do, however, was to ensure that "bigness" did not bring with it abuses of power. It should stand constant guard against irresponsibility and corruption in the great corporations. It should distinguish between "good trusts" and "bad trusts," encouraging the good while disciplining the bad. Such progressives argued that

America had entered a new era. Economic consolidation, they foresaw, would remain a permanent feature of society, but continuing oversight by a strong, modernized government would be vital.

The defenders of consolidation looked on the antimonopolists with condescension and some contempt. Brandeis and his allies were outmoded moralists, harking back to the ideals of a vanished age. America needed, instead, to look forward, to a bold new future. One of the most influential spokesmen for this emerging "nationalist" position was Herbert Croly, whose 1909 book *The Promise of American Life* became one of the most influential of all progressive documents. America's greatest need, Croly argued, was for unity—the kind of fervent unity that had made the great civilizations of the past (ancient Greece, the Roman Empire) flourish. And America's economic life, he claimed, needed unity as much as did its social life.

Opinions varied widely, even among national-

ists, on how that unity should be achieved. But increasingly, attention focused on some form of coordination of the industrial economy. Society must act, Walter Lippmann wrote in a notable 1914 book, *Drift and Mastery,* "to introduce plan where there has been clash, and purpose into the jungles of disordered growth." To some, the search for "plan" required businesses themselves to learn new ways of cooperation and self-regulation; some of the most energetic "progressive" reformers of the period, in fact, were businessmen searching eagerly for ways to bring order to their own troubled world. To others, the solution was for government to play a far more active role in regulating and planning economic life. One of those who came to endorse that position (although not fully until 1912) was Theodore Roosevelt, who said: "We should enter upon a course of supervision, control, and regulation of those great corporations—a regulation which we should not fear, if necessary, to bring to the point of control of monopoly prices."

SUGGESTED READINGS

Progressivism: Overviews. Richard Hofstadter, *The Age of Reform: From Bryan to FDR* (1955); Robert Wiebe, *The Search for Order, 1877–1920* (1967); Gabriel Kolko, *The Triumph of Conservatism* (1963); James Weinstein, *The Corporate Ideal in the Liberal State, 1900–1918* (1969); Arthur Link and Richard L. McCormick, *Progressivism* (1983); John Whiteclay Chambers, *The Tyranny of Change* (1980); Nell Irvin Painter, *Standing at Armageddon: The United States, 1877–1919* (1987).

The Muckrakers. Harold S. Wilson, *McClure's Magazine and the Muckrakers* (1970); C. C. Regier, *The Era of the Muckrakers* (1932); David Chambers, *The Social and Political Ideas of the Muckrakers* (1964); Justin Kaplan, *Lincoln Steffens* (1974); Leon Harris, *Upton Sinclair* (1975); Louis Filler, *The Muckrakers,* rev. ed. (1980).

Progressive Thought. Arthur Ekirch, *Progressivism in America* (1974); Morton White, *Social Thought in America* (1949); D. W. Marcell, *Progress and Pragmatism: James, Dewey, Beard and the American Idea of Progress* (1974); Charles Forcey, *The Crossroads of Liberalism: Croly, Weyl, Lippmann* (1961); Richard Abrams, *The Burdens of Progress* (1978); Sudhir Kakar, *Frederick Taylor* (1970); David W. Noble, ed., *The Progressive Mind,* rev. ed. (1981).

Social Work and the Social Gospel. Allen F. Davis, *Spearheads of Reform: The Social Settlements and the Progressive Movement, 1890–1914* (1968), and *American Heroine: The Life and Legend of Jane Addams* (1973); Roy Lubove, *The Progressives and the Slums: Tenement House Reform in New York City* (1962); Jane Addams, *Twenty Years at Hull House* (1910); C. H. Hopkins, *The Rise of the Social Gospel in American Protestantism* (1940); Henry May, *Protestant*

Churches and Industrial America (1949); William R. Hutchinson, *The Modernist Impulse in American Protestantism* (1982); Robert M. Cruden, *Ministers of Reform: The Progressives' Achievement in American Civilization, 1889–1920* (1982); Paul Boyer, *Urban Masses and Moral Order, 1820–1920* (1978); Timothy Miller, *Following in His Steps: A Biography of Charles M. Sheldon* (1987).

Education and the Professions. Burton Bledstein, *The Culture of Professionalism* (1976); Thomas L. Haskell, *The Emergence of Professional Social Science* (1977); Paul Starr, *The Social Transformation of American Medicine* (1982); Regina Markell Morantz-Sanchez, *Sympathy and Science: Women Physicians in American Medicine* (1985); Kenneth M. Ludmerer, *Learning to Heal: The Development of American Medical Education* (1985); David Tyack and Elizabeth Hansot, *Managers of Virtue: Public School Leadership in America, 1820–1980* (1982); Lawrence Veysey, *The Emergence of the American University* (1970); Barbara Miller Solomon, *In the Company of Educated Women: A History of Women in Higher Education in America* (1985); Barbara Harris, *Beyond Her Sphere: Women and the Professions in American History* (1978).

Municipal Reform. Zane Miller, *Boss Cox's Cincinnati* (1968); John D. Buenker, *Urban Liberalism and Progressive Reform* (1973); James B. Crooks, *Politics and Progress: The Rise of Urban Progressivism in Baltimore* (1968); Melvin G. Holli, *Reform in Detroit* (1969); J. Joseph Huthmacher, *Senator Robert F. Wagner and the Rise of Urban Liberalism* (1971); Oscar Handlin, *Al Smith and His America* (1958); Michael Kazin, *Barons of Labor: The San Francisco Building Trades and Union Power in the Progressive Era* (1981).

Women, Reform, and Suffrage. Eleanor Flexner, *Century of Struggle* (1959); Nancy Cott, *The Grounding of Modern*

Feminism (1987); Karen Blair, *The Clubwoman as Feminist* (1980); Anne F. Scott, *Making the Invisible Woman Visible* (1984); Nancy Shrom Dye, *As Equal as Sisters: Feminism, The Labor Movement, and the Women's Trade Union League of New York* (1981); Sheila M. Rothman, *Woman's Proper Place* (1978); Ellen C. Lagemann, *A Generation of Women: Education in the Lives of Progressive Reformers* (1979); Rosalind Rosenberg, *Beyond Separate Spheres: Intellectual Roots of Modern Feminism* (1982); Jacquelyn Dowd Hall, *The Revolt Against Chivalry* (1979); Elaine Tyler May, *Great Expectations: Marriage and Divorce in Post-Victorian America* (1980); Mari Jo Buhle, *Women and American Socialism* (1983); Aileen S. Kraditor, *Ideas of the Woman Suffrage Movement* (1965); Alan P. Grimes, *The Puritan Ethic and Woman Suffrage* (1967); David Morgan, *Suffragists and Democrats: The Politics of Woman Suffrage in America* (1972); Ellen C. DuBois, *Feminism and Suffrage: The Emergence of an Independent Women's Movement in America, 1848–1869* (1978); Ruth Rosen, *The Lost Sisterhood: Prostitutes in America, 1900–1918* (1982); William O'Neill, *Divorce in the Progressive Era* (1967) and *Everyone Was Brave: The Rise and Fall of Feminism in America* (1969); David M. Kennedy, *Birth Control in America: The Career of Margaret Sanger* (1970); Linda Gordon, *Woman's Body, Woman's Right: A Social History of Birth Control* (1976); Elyce J. Rotella, *From Home to Office: U.S. Women and Work, 1870–1930* (1981).

Racial Issues.   Louis Harlan, *Booker T. Washington: The Making of a Black Leader* (1856) and *Booker T. Washington: The Wizard of Tuskegee, 1901–1915* (1983); Elliott Rudwick, *W. E. B. Du Bois* (1969); August Meier, *Negro Thought in America, 1880–1915* (1963); Donald Spivey, *Schooling for the New Slavery: Black Industrial Education* (1978); Charles F. Kellogg, *NAACP* (1970); James M. McPherson, *The Abolitionist Legacy: From Reconstruction to the NAACP* (1975); George Fredrickson, *The Black Image in the White Mind* (1968); Joel Williamson, *The Crucible of Race: Black-White Relations in the American South Since Emancipation* (1985); John Dittmer, *Black Georgia in the Progressive Era, 1900–1920* (1977); Paula Giddings, *When and Where I Enter: The Impact of Black Women on Race and Sex in America* (1984); Cynthia Neverdon-Morton, *Afro-American Women of the South and the Advancement of the Race, 1885–1925* (1989).

State-Level Reform.   George E. Mowry, *California Progressives* (1951); David P. Thelen, *The New Citizenship: Origins of Progressivism in Wisconsin* (1972), *Robert M. La Follette and the Insurgent Spirit* (1976), and *Paths of Resistance: Tradition and Dignity in Industrializing Missouri* (1986); Sheldon Hackney, *Populism to Progressivism in Alabama* (1969); Robert S. Maxwell, *La Follette and the Rise of Progressivism in Wisconsin* (1944); Russel B. Nye, *Midwestern Progressive Politics* (1951); Richard M. Abrams, *Conservatism in a Progressive Era: Massachusetts* (1964); Robert F. Wesser, *Charles Evans Hughes: Politics and Reform in New York State, 1905–1910* (1967); Irwin Yellowitz, *Labor and the Progressive Movement in New York State* (1965); Richard L. McCormick, *From Realignment to Reform: Political Change in New York State, 1893–1910* (1981); Dewey Grantham, *Southern Progressivism: The Reconciliation of Progress and Tradition* (1983); C. Vann Woodward, *Origins of the New South* (1951).

National Issues.   Ruth Bourdin, *Women and Temperance: The Quest for Power and Liberty, 1873–1900* (1980); James T. Timberlake, *Prohibition and the Progressive Movement* (1963); Joseph Gusfield, *Symbolic Crusade: Status Politics and the Temperance Movement* (1963); John Higham, *Strangers in the Land* (1955); James Weinstein, *The Decline of Socialism in America* (1967); Robert Wiebe, *Businessmen and Reform* (1962); Sidney Fine, *Laissez Faire and the General Welfare State* (1956); Melvyn Dubofsky, *We Shall Be All* (1969); Michael E. McGerr, *The Decline of Popular Politics: The American North, 1865–1928* (1986).

" 'Terrible Teddy' Waits for 'The Unknown,' " by Joseph Keppler, Jr.
This cartoon conveys the widespread (and in the end correct) belief that Theodore Roosevelt was an unbeatable candidate for election to the presidency in 1904. To oppose him, the Democrats nominated Alton B. Parker, a New York appeals court judge who was indeed virtually "unknown" to most of the public. *(The Granger Collection)*

CHAPTER 22

❊ ❊ ❊

The Battle for National Reform

❊ ❊ ❊

The spirit of reform came relatively late to national politics, but come it did. As progressives encountered setbacks and frustrations in their efforts to win social and economic reforms at the state and local levels, they began increasingly to look to the federal government as a court of last resort. Efforts to reform the industrial economy, in particular, seemed to require action at the federal level. The great combinations were national in scope; only national action could effectively control their power.

But just as at the state and local levels, the national government seemed at first unable to respond to popular demands, mired as it was in the partisan politics of the nineteenth century. Progressives attempted to make it more responsive to their demands in various ways. They tried in Congress to limit the power of conservative party leaders and make the legislative process more responsive to the popular will. Some reformers, for example, urged an end to the system whereby United States senators were elected by the members of their state legislatures; they proposed instead a direct popular election, which they believed would force the Senate to react to public demands. The Seventeenth Amendment provided for that change; after conservatives had delayed action on it for years, it was finally passed by Congress in 1912 and ratified by the states in 1913.

Even a reformed Congress, however, could not be expected to provide the kind of coherent leadership that the progressive agenda required. If the federal government was truly to fulfill its mission, it would, most reformers agreed, have to do so largely through the executive branch. It would require, above all, strong leadership from the one office capable of providing it: the presidency.

Theodore Roosevelt and the Progressive Presidency

"Presidents in general are not lovable," Walter Lippmann, who had known many, said near the end of his life. "They've had to do too much to get where they are. But there was one President who was lovable—Teddy Roosevelt—and I loved him."

He was not alone. To a generation of progressive reformers, Theodore Roosevelt was more than an admired public figure; he was an idol. No president before and few since could match him in attracting attention and devotion. Yet for all his popularity among reformers, Roosevelt was not the era's most advanced progressive. In many respects he was decidedly conservative. He earned his extraordinary popularity less because of the extent of the reforms he championed than because of the vigor and dynamism with which he approached them. He brought to his office a broad conception of its powers, and he invested the presidency with something of its modern status as the center of national political life.

The Accidental President

Roosevelt was not intended by his party for the presidency. Republican leaders had nominated him to run for vice president with William McKinley in 1900 largely to remove him from the governorship of New York, to which he had been elected in 1898 and where he was proving troublesome to party bosses. When McKinley suddenly died in September 1901, the victim of an assassination, Roosevelt was only forty-two years old, the youngest man ever to assume the presidency. Already, however, he had achieved a notoriety that caused party leaders to feel something close to despair. "I told William McKinley that it was a mistake to nominate that wild man at Philadelphia," Mark Hanna was reported to have exclaimed. "I asked him if he realized what would happen if he should die. Now look, that damned cowboy is President of the United States!"

Roosevelt's reputation as a wild man was, characteristically, a result less of the substance than of the style of his early political career. As a young member of the New York legislature, he had displayed an energy seldom seen in that lethargic body. As a rancher in the Dakota Badlands (where he retired briefly after the sudden death of his first wife), he had helped capture outlaws. As New York City police commissioner, he had been a flamboyant battler against crime and vice. As commander of the Rough Riders, he had led a heroic, if militarily useless, charge in the battle of San Juan Hill in Cuba during the Spanish-American War.

Never, however, had Roosevelt openly rebelled against the leaders of his party; and once in the White House, he continued to balance his personal dynamism against the demands of the political establishment, becoming a champion of cautious, moderate change. Reform was, he believed, less a vehicle for remaking American society than for protecting it against more radical challenges.

Managing the Trusts

For all his cautiousness, however, Roosevelt did bring certain assumptions to the presidency that markedly differentiated him from his predecessors. Imbued with progressive ideas about the importance of the efficient, modern management of society, he envisioned the federal government not as the agent of any particular interest but as a mediator of the public good. The president would be the central figure in that mediation.

Such attitudes found expression in Roosevelt's policies toward the great industrial combinations. Like William McKinley, he was not opposed to the principle of economic concentration. Unlike McKinley, however, he acknowledged that consolidation produced abuses of power that could prove harmful to society. He allied himself, therefore, with those progressives who urged regulation (but not destruction) of the trusts.

At the heart of Roosevelt's policy was his desire to win for government the power to investigate the activities of corporations and to publicize the results. The pressure of educated public opinion, he believed, would alone eliminate most corporate abuses. Government could legislate solutions for those that remained. The new Department of Commerce and Labor, established in 1903 (and later to be divided into two separate departments), was to assist in this task through its investigatory arm, the Bureau of Corporations.

Roosevelt did make occasional flamboyant gestures on behalf of a more drastic approach to reform. Although not a trust buster at heart, he engaged in several highly publicized efforts to break up notorious combinations—actions that strengthened his credentials as a progressive without offering any fundamental challenge to the structure of the economy. In 1902, he ordered the Justice Department to invoke the Sherman Antitrust Act against a great new railroad monopoly in the Northwest, the Northern Securities Company, a $400 million enterprise pieced together by J. P. Morgan, E. H. Harriman, and James J. Hill. To Morgan, accustomed to a warm, supportive relationship with Republican administrations, the action was baffling. Hurrying to the White House with two conservative senators in tow, he told the president, "If we have done anything wrong, send your man to my man and they can fix it up." Roosevelt proceeded with the case nonetheless, and in 1904 the Supreme Court ruled that the Northern Securities Company must be dissolved. At the same time, however, he assured Morgan and others that the suit did not signal a general campaign to dissolve trusts. Other monopolistic corporations, such as United States Steel, he would challenge only if "they have done something we regard as wrong." Although he filed more than forty additional antitrust suits during the remainder of his presidency, and although he succeeded in dissolving several important combinations, Roosevelt made no serious effort to reverse the prevailing trend toward economic concentration. Regulation, with the government serving as mediator between corporate and public interests, remained his central goal.

Government and Labor

A similar commitment to establishing the government as an impartial regulatory mechanism shaped Roosevelt's policy toward labor. In the past, federal intervention in industrial disputes had almost always meant action on behalf of employers, as in the Pullman strike in 1894. Roosevelt, however, was willing to consider labor's position as well.

He displayed this willingness during a bitter strike in 1902 by members of the United Mine Workers employed in the anthracite coal industry. Miners, under the leadership of John Mitchell, were demanding a 20 percent wage increase, an eight-hour day, and recognition of their union. Management, represented by the combative George F. Baer, was responding with conspicuous contempt. When the strike threatened to drag on long enough to endanger coal supplies for the coming winter, Roosevelt decided to step in—not to assist management but to invite both the operators and the miners to the White House, where he asked them to accept impartial federal arbitration. Mitchell readily agreed. Baer balked.

Furious at the obstinacy of the mine owners (who had already alienated public opinion), Roosevelt threatened drastic action. He would, he told them, order 10,000 federal troops to seize the mines and resume coal production if the dispute was not resolved. Under pressure from politicians, the press, and perhaps most significantly, J. P. Morgan, the operators finally relented. Arbitrators awarded the strikers a 10 percent wage increase and a nine-hour day, but no recognition of the union. It was a meager reward for a long and costly strike, but it was more than the miners might have won without the government's intervention.

Despite such episodes, Roosevelt viewed himself as no more the champion of labor than of management. On several occasions, he ordered federal troops to intervene in strikes on behalf of employers—in Arizona in 1903 and in Colorado in 1904. And although he believed in the right of workers to join a union, he believed, too, in the right of employers to refuse to bargain with it.

The Square Deal

Even if Roosevelt had wished to move more quickly on economic reforms (and there was little evidence that he did), he would have been reluctant to do so during his first term as president. Much of his energy in those years he was devoting to the business of winning reelection. Above all, he was working to ensure that the conservative Republican Old Guard, which bristled at even the most modest of reforms, would not block his nomination in 1904. By skillfully dispensing patronage to conservatives and progressives alike, by reshuffling the leadership of unstable Republican organizations in the South, by winning the support of Northern businessmen while making adroit gestures to reformers, he succeeded in all but neutralizing his opposition within the party and won its presidential nomination with ease. And in the general election, where he faced a pallid conservative Democrat, Alton B. Parker, he stormed to one of the largest victories in the nation's history. Roosevelt captured over 57 percent of the popular vote and lost not one state outside the South. Now, relieved of immediate political concerns, he was free to display the full extent (and the real limits) of his commitment to reform.

During the 1904 campaign, Roosevelt boasted that he had worked in the anthracite coal strike to provide everyone with a "square deal." In his second term, he became more aggressive in his efforts to extend the square deal even further. Among his most important targets was the powerful railroad industry. The Interstate Commerce Act of 1887, establishing the Interstate Commerce Commission (ICC), had been an early effort to regulate the industry; but over the years, the courts had virtually nullified its influence. Roosevelt asked Congress for a law that would considerably increase the government's power to set railroad rates. In June 1906, the Hepburn Railroad Regulation Act became law, although not until after the Senate had greatly weakened a much stronger bill passed by the House. It was a classic example of the cautiousness with which Roosevelt, even after his 1904 mandate, approached reform. The bill satisfied even many conservatives; and it infuriated advanced progressives such as La Follette, who never forgave Roosevelt for the concessions he made.

The Hepburn Act was the most conspicuous reform legislation of Roosevelt's second term, but only one of many new regulatory measures. The president won approval of laws providing for compensation by employers to injured workers in the District of Columbia and certain other limited areas. He pressured Congress to enact the Pure Food and Drug Act, which, despite weaknesses in its enforcement mechanisms, did restrict the sale of some dangerous or ineffective medicines. When Upton Sinclair's powerful novel *The Jungle* appeared in 1906, featuring appalling descriptions of the preparation of meats in the nation's stockyards, Roosevelt insisted on passage of the Meat Inspection Act, which ultimately helped eliminate many diseases once transmitted in impure meat.

Starting in 1907, moreover, he seemed to expand his vision of regulation and began to propose even more stringent measures: an eight-hour day for workers, broader compensation for victims of industrial accidents, inheritance and income taxes, regulation of the stock market, and others. In the process, he started openly to criticize conservatives in Congress, who were blocking much of this legislation, and to denounce the judiciary, which was striking down or weakening many of the measures that did pass. The result was not only a general stalemate in Roosevelt's reform agenda, but a widening gulf between the president and the conservative wing of his party.

Conservation

Nothing contributed more to the creation of that gulf than Roosevelt's aggressive policies on behalf of conservation. An ardent sportsman and naturalist, he had long been concerned about the unregulated exploitation of America's natural resources and the despoiling of what remained of the nation's wilderness. Using executive powers, he began early in his presidency to restrict private development on millions of acres of undeveloped land still controlled by the government, adding them to the hitherto modest system of national forests. When vigorous conservative and Western opposition finally resulted in legislation in 1907 to restrict his authority over public lands, Roosevelt and his chief forester, Gifford Pinchot, worked furiously to seize all the forests and many of the water power sites still in the public domain, before the bill became law.

Making Sausages
Upton Sinclair's 1906 novel *The Jungle* contained, among other things, nauseating descriptions of the process by which meat factories (such as the one shown here) made sausages. Partly in response to the success of his book, Congress passed the Meat Inspection Act the same year, establishing federal standards for the industry. (The Bettmann Archive)

The Grand Canyon of the Yellowstone

The Philadelphia-born artist Thomas Moran painted this spectacular scene in 1893, twenty years after Yellowstone had become the first national park in the United States. Moran's passion for the West in general and Yellowstone in particular inspired him to make five Western trips in the 1870s, and his dramatic views of Yellowstone from those journeys played an important role in convincing Congress to establish the park system. (National Museum of American Art, Smithsonian Institution)

Roosevelt was the first president to take an active interest in the new and struggling American conservation movement, and his policies had a lasting effect on national environmental policies. More than most public figures, he was sympathetic to the concerns of the naturalists—those within the movement committed to protecting the natural beauty of the land and the health of its wildlife from human intrusion. Early in his presidency, Roosevelt even spent four days camping in the Sierras with John Muir, the nation's leading preservationist and the founder of the Sierra Club. In the end, however, Roosevelt's policy tended to favor less the preservationists than another faction within the conservation movement—those who believed in carefully managed development.

The leading conservation figure in government was Pinchot, who became the first director of the National Forest Service (which he helped to create). The first professionally trained American forester, Pinchot supported rational and efficient human use of the wilderness. The Sierra Club might argue for the "aesthetic" value of the forests; Pinchot insisted, in contrast, that "the whole question is a practical one." He and Roosevelt both believed that trained experts in forestry and resource management, such men as Pinchot himself, should apply to the landscape the same scientific standards that others were applying to the management of cities and industries. The president did side with the preservationists on certain issues, but the more important legacy of his conservation policy was to establish the government's role as manager of the continuing development of the wilderness.

To much of the Old Guard, the extension of government control over vast new lands smacked of socialism. Even worse, Roosevelt's use of executive powers to achieve that control smacked of dictatorship. Many of these same interests, however, displayed no such scruples in supporting another important aspect of Roosevelt's natural resource policy: public reclamation and irrigation projects. In 1902, the president supported the Newlands Reclamation Act, which provided federal funds for the

Establishment of National Parks and Forests

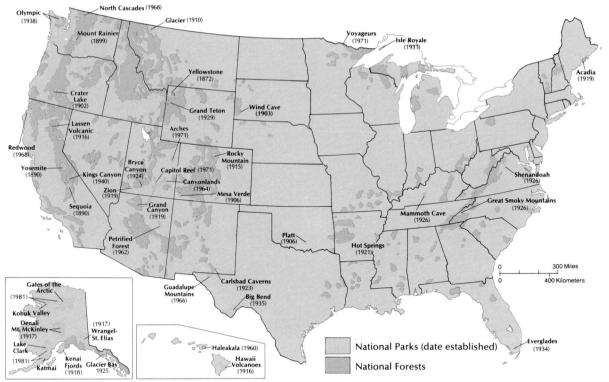

National Parks (date established)

National Forests

construction of huge dams, reservoirs, and canals in the West—projects to open new lands for cultivation and provide cheap electric power. It was the beginning of many years of federal aid for irrigation and power development in the Western states.

The Panic of 1907

The flurry of reforms Roosevelt was able to enact, and the enormous popularity he attracted as a result, made it easy for members of his administration to believe that finally the government had imposed a strong, effective set of regulations on the new industrial economy. But in fact, the Roosevelt record—although substantial when compared with that of his predecessors—was a relatively modest one, and the economy at large remained essentially uncontrolled. That truth was harshly brought home to Roosevelt and his allies in 1907, when a serious panic and recession revealed how flawed the nation's economic structure remained. The scenario was eerily familiar to those who remembered 1893. Once again, American industrial production had outrun the capacity of

either domestic or foreign markets to absorb it. Once again, the banking system and the stock market had displayed pathetic inadequacies. Once again, irresponsible speculation and rampant financial mismanagement had helped to shatter a prosperity that many had come to believe was now permanent. Banks failed; industries cut or ceased production; workers suffered layoffs and wage cuts.

To many conservatives, Roosevelt's "mad" economic policies were the obvious cause of the disaster. The president, naturally (and correctly), disagreed. But the panic was clearly unnerving to him, and he acted quickly to reassure business leaders that he would not interfere with their recovery efforts. J. P. Morgan, in a spectacular display of his financial power, helped construct a pool of the assets of several important New York banks to prop up shaky financial institutions. The key to the arrangement, Morgan told the president, was the purchase by U.S. Steel of the shares of the Tennessee Coal and Iron Company, currently held by a threatened New York bank. He would, he insisted, need assurances that no antitrust action would ensue. Roosevelt tacitly agreed, and the Morgan plan proceeded. Whether or not as a result, the panic soon subsided.

The Roosevelt Retirement

Theodore Roosevelt loved being president. He had made that plain during his first moments in office, when, torn between his excitement at his new position and his distress at McKinley's death, he had written, "It is a dreadful thing to come into the Presidency in this way; but it would be a far worse thing to be morbid about it." As his years in office produced increasing political successes, as his public popularity continued to rise, more and more observers began to doubt that he would happily stand aside in 1908.

Events, however, dictated otherwise. The Panic of 1907, combined with Roosevelt's growing "radicalism" during his second term, had deeply alienated conservatives in his own party. He would, he realized, have considerable difficulty winning the Republican nomination for another term. In 1904, moreover, he had made a public promise to step down four years later, a promise that would surely emerge to haunt him if he decided to run again. And so, after nearly eight energetic years in the White House, during which he had transformed the role of the presidency in American government, Theodore Roosevelt, fifty years old, retired from public life—briefly.

The Troubled Succession

It seemed at first that William Howard Taft, who assumed the presidency in 1909, would be that rare thing among politicians: a leader acceptable to virtually everyone. He had been Theodore Roosevelt's most trusted lieutenant and his hand-picked successor; progressive reformers believed him to be one of their own. But he had also been a restrained and moderate jurist, a man with a punctilious regard for legal process; conservatives expected him to abandon Roosevelt's aggressive use of presidential powers.

It was perhaps unsurprising, then, that in 1908 Taft won election to the White House with almost ridiculous ease. With the support of both Roosevelt and much of the Republican Old Guard, he received his party's nomination virtually uncontested. His victory in the general election in November—over

William Howard Taft
Taft could be a jovial companion in small groups, but his public image was of a dull, stolid man who stood in sharp and unfortunate contrast to his dynamic predecessor, Theodore Roosevelt. Taft also suffered public ridicule for his enormous size. He weighed as much as 350 pounds at times, and wide publicity accompanied his installation of a special, oversized bathtub in the White House.   (UPI/Bettmann Newsphotos)

William Jennings Bryan, running forlornly for the Democrats for the third time—was a foregone conclusion. Taft entered the White House on a wave of good feeling.

Four years later, however, Taft would leave office the most decisively defeated president of the twentieth century, with his party deeply divided and the government in the hands of a Democratic administration for the first time in twenty years.

It had been obvious from the start that Taft and Roosevelt were not at all alike, but it was not until Taft took office that the real extent of the differences became clear. Roosevelt had been the most dynamic public figure of his age; Taft was stolid and respectable and little more. Roosevelt was an ardent sportsman and athlete; Taft was sedentary and obese—he weighed over 300 pounds and required a special, oversized bathtub to be installed in the White House. Most of all, Roosevelt had taken an expansive view of the powers of his office; Taft, in contrast, was slow, cautious, even lethargic, insistent that the president take pains to observe the strict letter of the law.

Yet even had Taft been the most dynamic of political figures, he would still have had difficulties, for he quickly found himself in the middle of a series of political controversies from which no leader could emerge unscathed. Having come into office as the darling of progressives and conservatives alike, he soon found that he could not please them both. Gradually he found himself, without really intending it, pleasing the conservatives and alienating the progressives.

Congress and the Tariff

The first fiasco occurred in the opening months of the new administration, when Taft called Congress into special session to enact legislation lowering protective tariff rates. Tariff reduction had been a consistent demand of many progressives for nearly a decade. It had reflected less a belief in free trade than a conviction that foreign competition would weaken the power of the great trusts and thus lower domestic prices. Theodore Roosevelt had made several tentative gestures on behalf of tariff reform but had always pulled away from the issue in the end. Taft was determined to do more.

But the president soon proved completely ineffectual in challenging the power of the congressional Old Guard, which remained committed to protection. Progressives battling for revision needed help from the White House, but Taft believed it would violate the constitutional doctrine of separation of powers if he were to intervene in legislative matters. On August 5, 1909, the president signed the ineffectual Payne-Aldrich Tariff, which reduced tariff rates scarcely at all and in some areas actually raised them. It had been passed without the support of the Midwestern reformers.

The wedge between Taft and the Republican progressives was driven deeper as a result of the president's role in efforts to reform the House of Representatives. The almost dictatorial power of Speaker

Joseph Cannon had been a thorn in the side of progressives for many years; Taft himself harbored a strong dislike for the aging "Uncle Joe." So when reformers began a campaign during the 1909 special session to limit the Speaker's power, Taft at first expressed cautious approval. He soon found, however, that without Cannon's support, his tariff legislation faced almost certain death, and he backed away from the insurgent revolt. Again, congressional progressives watched their reform efforts collapse; again, they blamed Taft for betraying them. The following year, after a fierce debate that raged for nearly thirty hours, progressive Republicans under the leadership of George W. Norris finally succeeded in stripping Cannon of some of his most important powers. Even then, however, they acted without the president's support.

The Pinchot-Ballinger Affair

With Taft's standing among Republican progressives steadily deteriorating and with the party growing more and more deeply divided, a sensational controversy broke out late in 1909 that helped destroy for good Taft's popularity with admirers of Theodore Roosevelt. Many progressives had been unhappy when Taft replaced Roosevelt's secretary of the interior, James R. Garfield, an aggressive conservationist, with Richard A. Ballinger, a more conservative corporate lawyer. Suspicion of Ballinger grew when he attempted to invalidate Roosevelt's actions in removing nearly 1 million acres of forests and mineral reserves from the public lands available for private development.

In the midst of this mounting concern, Louis Glavis, an Interior Department investigator, uncovered information that he believed constituted proof that the new secretary had once connived to turn over valuable public coal lands in Alaska to a private syndicate in exchange for personal profit. Glavis took the evidence to Gifford Pinchot, who had remained as head of the Forest Service and had been appalled by Ballinger's retreat from Roosevelt's policies. Pinchot took the charges to the president. Taft listened to Pinchot, heard Ballinger's rebuttal, asked Attorney General George Wickersham to investigate, and finally announced his support for his interior secretary. The charges, he insisted, were groundless.

Pinchot, however, was not satisfied. Unhappy that Ballinger remained in office and angry when Taft fired Glavis for his part in the episode, he leaked the story to the press and appealed directly to Congress to investigate the scandal. The president quickly discharged him for insubordination, and the congressional committee appointed to study the controversy, dominated by the Old Guard, exonerated Ballinger. But Taft's victory had come at a high cost. Progressives throughout the country rallied to the support of Pinchot, whom they considered the defender of the public interest against selfish business interests. Taft, in contrast, appeared to have capitulated to conservatives and to have repudiated the legacy of Theodore Roosevelt. The controversy aroused as much public passion as any dispute of its time; and when it was over, Taft had alienated the supporters of Roosevelt as completely as his tariff actions had alienated the followers of La Follette.

The Return of Roosevelt

During most of Taft's first year in office, Theodore Roosevelt was far from the political fray. He embarked first on a long hunting safari in the jungles of Africa; from there he traveled to Europe for visits to the major heads of state. To the American public, however, Roosevelt remained a formidable presence. Reports of his triumphant European tour dominated the front pages of newspapers across the country. Rumors that he would return to retake control of his party abounded. His arrival in New York in the spring of 1910 was a major public event; and progressives noted that, although he turned down an invitation from Taft to visit the White House, he met at once with Gifford Pinchot (who had already traveled to England to see him several months before).

Roosevelt insisted that he had no plans to return to active politics, but his resolve lasted less than a week. Politicians began flocking immediately to his home at Oyster Bay, Long Island, for conferences; Roosevelt himself took an active role in several New York political controversies; and within a month, he announced that he would embark on a national speaking tour before the end of the summer. Furious with Taft, who had, he believed, "completely twisted around the policies I advocated and acted upon," he was becoming convinced that he alone was capable of reuniting the Republican party.

The real signal of Roosevelt's return to active leadership of the progressives was a speech on September 1, 1910, in Osawatomie, Kansas, where he outlined a set of principles that he labeled the "New Nationalism." The speech made clear how far

Roosevelt had moved from the cautious conservatism that had marked the first years of his presidency. Social justice, he argued, could be attained only through the vigorous efforts of a strong federal government whose executive acted as the "steward of the public welfare." Those who thought primarily of property rights and personal profit "must now give way to the advocate of human welfare, who rightly maintains that every man holds his property subject to the general right of the community to regulate its use to whatever degree the public welfare may require it." Such generalizations were frightening enough by themselves to the Republican Old Guard, but Roosevelt went beyond them with a list of "radical" specific proposals: graduated income and inheritance taxes, workers' compensation for industrial accidents, regulation of the labor of women and children, tariff revision, and firm regulation of corporations through a more powerful Bureau of Corporations and ICC.

Spreading Insurgency

The congressional elections of 1910 provided further evidence of how far the progressive revolt had spread. In primary elections, conservative Republicans suffered defeat after defeat at the hands of progressive insurgents—forty in the House of Representatives alone. Incumbent progressives, moreover, won renomination almost without exception. In the general election, the Democrats, who were increasingly offering progressive candidates of their own, won control of the House of Representatives for the first time in sixteen years and greatly strengthened their position in the Senate. Progressivism appeared to have become a tidal wave. Still, Roosevelt continued to deny any presidential ambitions and to claim that his real purpose was to pressure Taft to return to progressive policies. Two events, however, changed his mind.

The first was a 1911 decision by the Taft administration that became, in Roosevelt's eyes, the final indignity. With his strong respect for the letter of the law, Taft had been far more active than Roosevelt in enforcing the provisions of the Sherman Antitrust Act and had launched dozens of suits against corporate combinations. To Roosevelt, such actions were troubling by themselves, for they reflected what he believed to be a wholly unrealistic attempt to abolish trusts when the proper course was to regulate them. But what truly outraged him was the announcement

Roosevelt at Osawatomie
Roosevelt's famous speech at Osawatomie, Kansas, in 1910 was the most radical of his career and openly marked his break with the Taft administration and the Republican leadership. "The essence of any struggle for liberty," he told his largely conservative audience, "has always been, and must always be to take from some one man or class of men the right to enjoy power, or wealth, or position or immunity, which has not been earned by service to his or their fellows."
(Brown Brothers)

on October 27, 1911, that the administration was filing an antitrust suit against U. S. Steel, charging, among other things, that the 1907 acquisition of the Tennessee Coal and Iron Company had been illegal. Roosevelt had approved that acquisition in the midst of the 1907 panic, and he was enraged by the implication that he had acted improperly.

There remained, however, a major obstacle to Roosevelt's pursuit of the presidency. Since January 1911, Robert La Follette had been working through the newly formed National Progressive Republican League to secure the presidential nomination for himself. Many reformers believed he had established first claim to the leadership of any insurgent revolt, and Roosevelt was at first reluctant to challenge him. But La Follette's candidacy stumbled in February 1912,

when, exhausted and plagued by personal worries (including the illness of his daughter), he appeared to suffer a nervous breakdown during a speech in Philadelphia. With almost indecent haste, many of his supporters abandoned him and turned to Roosevelt, who finally announced his candidacy on February 22.

TR Versus Taft

La Follette never forgave Roosevelt for "using" and then "betraying" him, and some diehard loyalists refused to abandon their allegiance to the Wisconsin senator. But for all practical purposes, the campaign for the Republican nomination had now become a battle between Roosevelt, the champion of the progressives, and Taft, the candidate of the conservatives. Roosevelt scored overwhelming victories in every presidential preference primary (there were thirteen in all) and arrived at the convention convinced that he had proved himself the choice of the party rank and file. Taft, however, remained the choice of most party leaders, and in the end it was their preference that proved decisive.

The battle for the nomination at the Chicago convention revolved around an unusually large number of contested delegates: 254 in all. Roosevelt needed about 100 of the disputed seats to clinch the nomination. But the Republican National Committee, which ruled on credentials, was controlled by members of the Old Guard; and it awarded all but 19 of the disputed seats to Taft. Roosevelt and his followers responded bitterly. The decision to seat the Taft delegates, they claimed, was an example of the same corrupt politics that progressives had been fighting for years; once more the people had been thwarted by the special interests. At a rally the night before the convention opened, Roosevelt addressed 5,000 madly cheering supporters and announced that he would not feel bound by the decision of his party if it refused to seat his delegates, that he would continue to fight for a candidacy that had now, it seemed, become a holy cause. "We stand at Armageddon," he told the roaring crowd, "and we battle for the Lord." As good as his word, Roosevelt the next day led his supporters out of the convention, and out of the party. Taft was then quietly nominated on the first ballot.

With financial support from newspaper magnate Frank Munsey and industrialist George W. Perkins, Roosevelt summoned his supporters back to Chicago in August for another convention, this one to launch the new Progressive party and nominate Roosevelt as its presidential candidate. By now, even Roosevelt was aware that the cause was virtually hopeless, particularly when many of the leading insurgents who had supported him during the primaries refused to follow him out of the Republican party. Nevertheless, he approached the battle feeling, as he put it, "fit as a bull moose" (thus giving his new party an enduring nickname). At the meeting in Chicago, he delivered a resounding "Confession of Faith" in which he castigated both of the traditional parties for representing "government of the needy many by professional politicians in the interests of the rich few"; and he produced a platform that embodied a full array of the most advanced progressive reforms.

Woodrow Wilson and the New Freedom

Yet even while Roosevelt was constructing his New Nationalism as a challenge to conservatives within his own party, another powerful alternative was emerging from the ranks of the Democrats. The contest, it soon became clear, was not simply one between conservatives and reformers; it was also one between two brands of progressivism, expressing two apparently different views of America's future.

Woodrow Wilson

For most of the first decade of the century, the Republican party had often seemed the sole home of progressive reform. In fact, however, progressive sentiment had been gaining strength within the Democratic party as well; and by 1912 it was ready to assert its dominance. At the Democratic convention in Baltimore in June, Champ Clark, the conservative Speaker of the House, was the early favorite for the presidential nomination. He controlled a majority of the delegates; but on ballot after ballot he failed to assemble the two-thirds necessary to win. For days the battle dragged on until finally, on the forty-sixth ballot, Woodrow Wilson, the governor of New Jersey, emerged as the party's nominee. His victory was in part a result of the last-minute support of Senator Oscar Underwood of Alabama, who had himself been one of the leading contenders for the nomination, and of William Jennings Bryan, who was to become Wilson's secretary of state. It was also, however, a result of Wilson's position as the only genuinely progressive candidate in the race.

Born in Virginia and raised in Confederate Georgia and Reconstruction South Carolina, Wilson had risen to political prominence by an unusual path. An 1879 graduate of Princeton University, he attended law school and for a time engaged unhappily in practice in Atlanta. But he was really more interested in politics and government, and after a few years he enrolled at Johns Hopkins University, where he earned a doctorate in political science. By virtue of his effective teaching and his lucid if unprofound books on the American political system, he rose steadily through the academic ranks until in 1902 he was promoted from the faculty to the presidency of Princeton. There, he displayed both the strengths and the weaknesses that would characterize his later po-

Woodrow Wilson
Well-wishers congratulate Woodrow Wilson on his nomination for the presidency in 1912. Wilson spent much of the summer vacationing in Sea Girt, New Jersey, and preparing for the presidential campaign that fall. (Culver Pictures)

litical career. A champion of academic reform, he acted firmly and energetically to place Princeton on the road to becoming a great national university. At the same time, however, he displayed during controversies a self-righteous morality that at times made it nearly impossible for him to compromise.

It was a series of such stalemates that propelled him out of academia and into politics. Elected governor of New Jersey in 1910, he brought to his new office the same commitment to reform that he had displayed in the past; and during his two years in the statehouse, he compiled an impressive record of progressive legislation—one that earned him a wide national reputation. At the same time, however, he was gradually alienating conservative party leaders with his intransigence and self-righteousness, and greatly hampering his ability to govern. His nomination for president in 1912 rescued him from what might well have become a political disaster in New Jersey.

In later years, Wilson's personal characteristics would help polarize the nation. In 1912, however, he sparked controversy by presenting a brand of progressivism that was both forceful and sharply different from Theodore Roosevelt's New Nationalism. His supporters soon began to describe Wilson's pro-

gram as the "New Freedom"; and although in later years the two phrases began to seem like meaningless slogans, reflecting few important differences, the opposing philosophies—"nationalism" versus "freedom"—were in fact distinct from each other in important ways.

In its narrowest sense, Wilson's New Freedom differed from Roosevelt's New Nationalism in its approach to economic policy, in particular its approach to the trusts. Roosevelt had always believed in accepting economic concentration and using government to regulate and control it. Wilson, in contrast, appeared to be a disciple of Louis Brandeis's approach to economic reform. He sided with those who believed that bigness was both unjust and inefficient, that the proper response to monopoly was not to regulate it but to destroy it.

The Election of 1912

Despite the philosophical importance of the issues in 1912, the campaign itself was surprisingly uneventful. Voters seemed generally unaware of the ideological differences between Roosevelt and Wilson, and

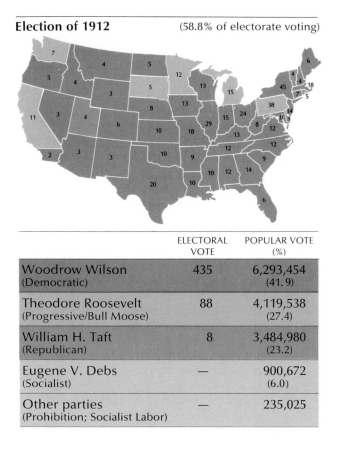

Election of 1912 (58.8% of electorate voting)

	ELECTORAL VOTE	POPULAR VOTE (%)
Woodrow Wilson (Democratic)	435	6,293,454 (41.9)
Theodore Roosevelt (Progressive/Bull Moose)	88	4,119,538 (27.4)
William H. Taft (Republican)	8	3,484,980 (23.2)
Eugene V. Debs (Socialist)	—	900,672 (6.0)
Other parties (Prohibition; Socialist Labor)	—	235,025

the election in the end reflected traditional party divisions.

It was a three-candidate election but a two-candidate campaign. William Howard Taft, resigned to defeat, delivered a few desultory, conservative speeches and then lapsed into silence. "There are so many people in the country who don't like me," he sadly explained. Roosevelt campaigned energetically (until a gunshot wound from a would-be assassin forced him to the sidelines during the last weeks before the election), and he continued to generate excitement among his Republican followers. He failed, however, to draw any significant numbers of Democratic progressives away from Wilson, who as the campaign wore on was beginning to evoke an enthusiastic national following of his own. The results in November were, therefore, predictable. Roosevelt and Taft split the Republican vote; Wilson held onto the Democratic vote and won. He polled only a plurality of the popular vote: 42 percent, to 27 percent for Roosevelt and a dismal 23 percent for Taft. Eugene Debs, the Socialist candidate, received 6 percent of the vote. But in the electoral college, Wilson won

by a landslide: 435 of the 531 votes. Roosevelt had carried only six states, Taft only two.

The Scholar as President

The administration of Woodrow Wilson ended unhappily. It began, however, in triumph. For nearly five years, until international problems turned his attention elsewhere, Wilson served as the most successful leader of domestic reform of his era.

Wilson brought to the White House a conception of the presidency based on long years of scholarly study. His first published book, *Congressional Government* (1898), expressed what remained a lifelong admiration for the British parliamentary system and a belief in its adaptability to American institutions. In his later writings, however, he began to display more interest in the possibilities of presidential leadership. "His is the only voice in national affairs," he wrote of the president only four years before he himself assumed the office. His must therefore be the voice of popular aspirations, the hand that guides public demands into legislative realities.

More than William Howard Taft, therefore, more even than Theodore Roosevelt, Wilson concentrated the powers of the executive branch in his own hands. He exerted firm control over his cabinet, and he delegated real authority only to those whose loyalty to him was beyond question. Perhaps the clearest indication of his style of leadership was the identity of the most powerful figure in his administration: Colonel Edward M. House, a man who held no office and whose only claim to authority was his personal intimacy with the president.

In legislative matters, he skillfully used his position as party leader and his appointive powers to weld together a coalition of conservatives and progressives who would, he believed, support his program. His task was eased by the existence of Democratic majorities in both houses of Congress and by the realization of many Democrats that the party must enact a progressive program in order to maintain those majorities.

Tariffs and Taxes

Wilson's first triumph as president was the fulfillment of an old Democratic and progressive promise—a substantial lowering of the protective tariff. Roosevelt had avoided the issue; Taft had failed at it. Wilson moved quickly and forcefully to succeed. On the day he took office, he called a special session of Congress. And when it met, he did what no president since Jefferson had done: He appeared before it in person to ask for genuine tariff reform. The Underwood-Simmons Tariff provided cuts substantial enough, progressives believed, to introduce real competition into American markets and thus to help break the power of trusts. It passed easily in the House; and despite Senate efforts to weaken its provisions, the bill survived more or less intact. Wilson's forceful exercise of party powers mobilized virtually the entire Democratic majority behind it.

To make up for the loss of revenue under the new tariff, Representative Cordell Hull of Tennessee drafted an amendment to the bill that provided for a graduated income tax, which the recently adopted Sixteenth Amendment to the Constitution now permitted. This first modern income tax imposed a 1 percent tax on individuals and corporations earning over $4,000, with rates ranging up to 6 percent on incomes over $500,000.

Banking Reform

President Wilson held Congress in session through the sweltering summer to begin work on a major reform of the American banking system. "The great monopoly in this country," he had declared in 1911, "is the money monopoly. So long as that exists, our old variety and freedom and individual energy of development are out of the question." Few progressives would have disagreed, but there were wide differences of opinion about how best to attack the problem.

Some legislators, of whom Representative Carter Glass of Virginia was one, wanted to decentralize control of the banking system so as to limit the power of the great Wall Street financiers but still leave ultimate authority over it with the bankers themselves. Others, whose hatred of the "money trust" was more intense—for example, William Jennings Bryan and fellow agrarians—wanted firm government control. After consultation with Louis Brandeis, Wilson accepted a plan that divided power in the system. The government would have substantial control at the national level; the bankers would retain control at the local level. With Bryan mediating and Wilson brandishing every presidential weapon in his arsenal, a banking reform bill passed both houses of

Congress and was signed by the president on December 23, 1913. It was the most important piece of domestic legislation of Wilson's administration.

The Federal Reserve Act of 1913 created twelve regional banks, each to be owned and controlled by the individual banks of its district. The regional Federal Reserve banks would hold a certain percentage of the assets of their member banks in reserve; they would use those reserves to support loans to private banks at an interest (or "discount") rate that the Federal Reserve system would set; they would issue a new type of paper currency—Federal Reserve notes—which would become the nation's basic medium of trade and be backed by the government. Most important, perhaps, they would serve as central institutions able to shift funds quickly to troubled areas—to meet increased demands for credit or to protect imperiled banks. Supervising and regulating the entire system was a national Federal Reserve Board, whose members were appointed by the president. All "national" banks were required to join the system; smaller banks were encouraged to do the same. Within a year, nearly half the nation's banking resources were represented in the system; by the late 1920s, the proportion had swelled to 80 percent.

The Problem of the Trusts

The cornerstone of Wilson's campaign for the presidency had been his promise to attack economic concentration, most notably to destroy monopolistic trusts. By the beginning of his second year in office, however, it was becoming clear that his thinking had changed significantly. He was moving away from his earlier insistence that government dismantle the combinations and toward a commitment to regulating them. On this issue, at least, the New Freedom was giving way to the New Nationalism.

Wilson's attitude toward several major pieces of economic legislation symbolized the trend. When in 1914 he began to promote a sweeping plan to deal with the problem of monopoly, two elements emerged at its core. There was a proposal to create a federal agency through which the government would help business police itself—in other words, a regulatory commission of the type Roosevelt had advocated in 1912. There were, in addition, proposals to strengthen the government's power to prosecute and dismantle the trusts—a decentralizing approach more characteristic of Wilson's campaign. The two measures took shape, ultimately, as the Federal Trade Commission Act and the Clayton Antitrust Act.

Wilson fought hard for the Federal Trade Commission Act, which created a regulatory agency of the same name, and he signed it happily when it arrived at the White House. The new commission would, he promised, remove "uncertainty" within the corporate community, allowing businesses to determine in advance whether their actions would be acceptable to the government. It would also have authority to launch prosecutions against "unfair trade practices," which the law did not define, and it would have wide power to investigate corporate behavior. The act, in short, increased the government's regulatory authority significantly. But Wilson seemed to lose interest in the Clayton Antitrust bill and showed a notable lack of vigor in fighting to protect it from conservative assaults, which greatly weakened its potential effectiveness. When the emasculated bill finally reached his desk, he lauded it as a major accomplishment. The vigorous legal pursuit of monopoly that Wilson had promised in 1912 never materialized. The future, he had apparently decided, lay with government supervision.

Retreat and Advance

By the fall of 1914, Wilson believed that the program of the New Freedom was essentially complete and that agitation for reform would now subside. As a result, he himself began a conspicuous retreat from political activism. Citing the doctrine of states' rights, he refused to support the movement for national woman suffrage (a movement to which he had earlier been openly hostile). Accepting the inclinations of the many Southerners in his cabinet, he condoned the reimposition of segregation in the agencies of the federal government (a sharp contrast to Theodore Roosevelt, who had ordered the elimination of many such barriers and had even taken the unprecedented step of inviting a black man—Booker T. Washington—to the White House). When congressional reformers attempted to enlist his support for new social legislation, he breezily dismissed their proposals as unconstitutional or unnecessary.

The president's complacency could not, however, long survive the congressional elections of 1914. It was disturbing enough that Democrats suffered major losses in the House of Representatives. But it was even more alarming that voters who had in 1912 supported the Progressive party were returning in droves to the Republicans. Wilson would not be able to rely on a divided opposition when he ran for reelection in 1916; he would need more than his 1912 total of 42 percent of the vote, and he would need the support of some of Theodore Roosevelt's former constituency to get it.

By the end of 1915, therefore, Wilson had shed his lethargy and begun to support a second flurry of reforms. In January 1916, he appointed Louis Brandeis to the Supreme Court, making him not only the first Jew but the most advanced progressive to be so named; and he weathered a conservative uproar in the Senate to obtain Brandeis's confirmation. Later, he supported a measure to make it easier for farmers to receive credit and one creating a system of workers' compensation for federal employees.

This renewed effort at reform revealed that Wilson seemed now to have capitulated to the New Nationalism almost entirely; indeed, he had moved beyond it. No longer was the president appealing for the restoration of a competitive, decentralized economy. No longer was he warning about excessive federal power. Instead, Wilson was sponsoring measures that expanded the role of the national government in important ways, giving it new instruments by which it could not only regulate the economy but help shape the economic and social structure itself.

In 1916, for example, Wilson supported the Keating-Owen Act, the first federal law regulating child labor. It was important not only for the problem it addressed but for the means it adopted. The measure prohibited the shipment of goods produced by underage children across state lines, thus giving an expanded importance to the constitutional clause assigning Congress the task of regulating interstate commerce. (It would be some years before the Supreme Court would uphold this interpretation of the clause; the Court invalidated the Keating-Owen Act in 1918.) The president similarly supported measures that used federal taxing authority as a vehicle for legislating social change. When the Court struck down Keating-Owen, a new bill attempted to achieve the same goal by imposing a heavy tax on the products of child labor. (The Court later struck it down too.) The government's spending authority likewise became an instrument of social control. The Smith-Lever Act, for example, had as early as 1914 offered matching federal grants to states that agreed to support agricultural extension education.

Louis Brandeis
Brandeis graduated from Harvard Law School in 1877 with the best academic record of any student in the school's previous or subsequent history. His success in his Boston law practice was such that by the early twentieth century he was able to spend much of his time in unpaid work for public causes. His investigations of monopoly power soon made him a major figure in the emerging progressive movement. Woodrow Wilson nominated him for the United States Supreme Court in January 1916. He was one of only three or four nominees in the Court's history never to have held prior public office, and he was the first Jew ever to have been nominated. The appointment aroused five months of bitter controversy in the Senate before Brandeis was finally confirmed. For the next twenty years, he was one of the Court's most powerful members—all the while lobbying behind the scenes on behalf of the many political causes (preeminent among them Zionism, the founding of a Jewish state) to which he remained committed.
(UPI/Bettmann Newsphotos)

The "Big Stick": America and the World, 1901–1917

American foreign policy during the progressive years reflected many of the same impulses that were motivating domestic reform. But it reflected far more clearly the nation's new sense of itself as a world power with far-flung economic and political interests. To the general public, foreign affairs remained largely remote. Walter Lippmann once wrote: "I cannot remember taking any interest whatsoever in foreign affairs until after the outbreak of the First World War." But to Theodore Roosevelt and later presidents, that made foreign affairs even more appealing. There the president could act with less regard for the Congress or the courts. There, he could free himself from concerns about public opinion. Overseas, the president could exercise power unfettered and alone.

Sea Power and Civilization

Theodore Roosevelt was well suited, both by temperament and by ideology, for an activist foreign policy. A vigorous athlete and once an enthusiastic college boxer, he spoke often of the virtues of the "strenuous life" and viewed physical combat as an ennobling, manly challenge. His fondness for battle had been greatly enhanced by his famous charge up San Juan Hill, a crucial event in the development of his political career.

Roosevelt believed, moreover, that an important distinction existed between the "civilized" and "uncivilized" nations of the world. "Civilized" nations, as he defined them, were predominantly white and Anglo-Saxon or Teutonic; "uncivilized" nations were generally nonwhite, Latin, or Slavic. But racism was only partly the basis of the distinction. At least as important was economic development. Thus it was that Japan, a rapidly industrializing society, seemed to Roosevelt to have earned admission to the ranks of the civilized.

There was another important aspect of this global division. Civilized nations were, by Roosevelt's definition, producers of industrial goods; uncivilized nations were suppliers of raw materials and markets. There was, he believed, an economic relationship between the two parts that was vital to both of them; and it was natural, perhaps, that he should come to believe in the right and duty of the civilized societies to intervene in the affairs of "backward" nations to

"The New Diplomacy"

This 1904 drawing by the famous *Puck* cartoonist Louis Dalrymple conveys the new image of America as a great power that Theodore Roosevelt was attempting to project to the world. Roosevelt the world policeman deals effectively with "less civilized" peoples (Asians and Latin Americans, seen clamoring at left) by using the "big stick" and deals equally effectively with the "civilized" nations (at right) by offering arbitration. (Culver Pictures)

preserve order and stability. The economic health of the globe might depend on the result.

Accordingly, Roosevelt early became an outspoken champion of the development of American sea power. A friend and admirer of Alfred Thayer Mahan, Roosevelt had believed since his days as assistant secretary of the navy in 1897 that the United States must move rapidly to expand the size and power of its fleet. By 1906, Roosevelt's support had enabled the American navy to attain a size and strength surpassed only by that of Great Britain (although Germany was fast gaining ground).

Challenges in Asia

The new strength was not, however, always enough to enable the president to have his way in global developments, as events in the Pacific soon illustrated. Roosevelt believed that the "Open Door" was vital for maintaining American trade in the Pacific and for preventing any single nation from establishing dominance there. (See above, pp. 610–611.) He looked with alarm, therefore, at the military rivalries involving Japan, Russia, Germany, and France in the region.

He was particularly concerned by Russian efforts to expand southward into Manchuria, a province of China; and when in 1904 the Japanese attacked the Russian fleet at Port Arthur in southern Manchuria, Roosevelt, like most Americans, was inclined to approve. Yet the president was no more eager for Japan to control Manchuria than for Russia to do so. In 1905, therefore, he eagerly agreed to a Japanese request to mediate an end to the conflict. Russia, far-ing badly in the war—and, as a result, already experiencing a domestic instability that twelve years later would culminate in revolution—had no choice but to agree.

At a peace conference in Portsmouth, New Hampshire, Roosevelt extracted from the embattled Russians a recognition of Japan's territorial gains—control of Korea, South Manchuria, and part of Sakhalin Island, formerly a Russian outpost. Japan, in return, agreed to cease the fighting and expand no further. At the same time, Roosevelt worked to secure American interests by negotiating a secret agreement with the Japanese to ensure that the United States could continue to trade freely in the region.

Roosevelt was pleased with his work at the Portsmouth Conference, particularly when it helped him win the Nobel Peace Prize in 1906. But his triumph was, in fact, a hollow one. In the years that followed, relations between the United States and Japan steadily deteriorated, and the careful assurances Roosevelt had won in 1905 proved all but meaningless. Having destroyed the Russian fleet at Port Arthur, Japan now emerged as the preeminent naval power in the Pacific and soon began to exclude American trade from many of the territories it controlled.

It did not help matters that in 1906 the school board of San Francisco voted to segregate Oriental schoolchildren in the city in separate schools; or that a year later, the California legislature attempted to pass legislation limiting the immigration of Japanese laborers into the state. Anti-Oriental riots in California and inflammatory stories in the Hearst papers about the "Yellow Peril" further fanned resentment in Japan. The president did his best to douse the flames. He quietly persuaded the San Francisco school board to rescind its edict in return for a Japanese agreement to stop the flow of agricultural immigrants into California. Then, lest the Japanese government construe his actions as a sign of weakness, he sent sixteen battleships of the new American navy on an unprecedented 45,000-mile voyage around the world that included a call on Japan. Despite fears by some members of Congress that a naval conflict might result, the "Great White Fleet," as the flotilla was called, received a warm reception when it arrived in Yokohama. For the moment, Roosevelt's foreign policy—which he once summarized with the African proverb: "Speak softly and carry a big stick"—seemed to have borne important fruit. But the problem of Japanese expansion in the Far East had not been resolved, and Japan continued to look for ways to extend its power in the region.

The Iron-Fisted Neighbor

Roosevelt took a special interest in events in what he (and most other Americans) considered the nation's special sphere of interest: Latin America. And very early in his presidency, he became concerned—some believed almost obsessed—by the possibility of German penetration into the region. Unwilling to share trading rights, let alone military control, with any other nation, Roosevelt embarked on a series of ventures in the Caribbean and South America that established a pattern of American intervention in the region that would long survive his presidency.

Crucial to Roosevelt's thinking was an incident early in his administration. When the government of Venezuela began in 1902 to renege on debts to European bankers, naval forces of Britain, Italy, and Germany erected a blockade along that country's coast. Roosevelt at first expressed little concern. But when German ships began to bombard a Venezuelan port and when rumors spread that Germany planned to establish a permanent base in the region, Roosevelt changed his mind. In 1903, he warned the Germans (according to his own later account) that Admiral Dewey and his fleet were standing by in the Caribbean and would act against any German effort to acquire new territory. The German navy finally withdrew.

The incident helped persuade Roosevelt that European intrusions into Latin America could result not only from aggression but from internal instability or irresponsibility (such as defaulting on debts) within the Latin American nations themselves. As a result, he added a new "corollary" to the Monroe Doctrine. In a 1904 message to Congress, he claimed that the United States had the right not only to oppose European intervention in the Western Hemisphere but to intervene itself in the domestic affairs of its neighbors if those neighbors proved unable to maintain order on their own.

The immediate motivation for the Roosevelt Corollary, and the first opportunity for putting the doctrine into practice, was a crisis in the Dominican Republic. A revolution had toppled the corrupt and bankrupt government of that nation in 1903, but the new regime proved no better able than the old to make good on the country's $22 million of debts to European nations. Both France and Italy were threatening to intervene to recover their losses, and the new Dominican leaders had turned to the United States for help. Using the rationale he had outlined in his address to Congress, Roosevelt established, in ef-

The United States in Latin America, 1895–1941

UNITED STATES

Gulf of Mexico

□○ U.S. possessions
□ U.S. interventions

0   400 Miles
0   400 Kilometers

Cuba
U.S. troops
1898–1902
1906–1909
1917–1922
Protectorate
1898–1934

ATLANTIC OCEAN

BAHAMAS

MEXICO
Military intervention
1914,
1916–1919
Mexico City ⊛   • Veracruz

VIRGIN ISLANDS
Purchased from Denmark
1917

Santo
Domingo

JAMAICA
(Br.)

Caribbean Sea

BRITISH
HONDURAS

HAITI
U.S. troops
1915–1934
Financial
supervision
1915–1941

**DOMINICAN
REPUBLIC**
U.S. troops
1916–1924
Financial
supervision
1905–1941

PUERTO RICO
Acquired from
Spain 1898

GUATEMALA

HONDURAS

EL SALVADOR

NICARAGUA
U.S. Troops 1909–1910
1912–1925
1926–1933
Financial supervision
1911–1924

CANAL ZONE*
Control over canal
beginning 1904

VENEZUELA
Settlement of boundary
dispute
1895–1896

BRITISH
GUIANA

COSTA RICA

PACIFIC OCEAN

PANAMA
Support of revolution
1903

COLOMBIA

* Canal Zone not a possession
but controlled through a lease
from Panama.

fect, an American receivership, assuming control of Dominican customs and distributing 45 percent of the revenues to Santo Domingo and the rest to foreign creditors. This arrangement lasted, in one form or another, for more than three decades.

Two years later, another opportunity for intervention in the Caribbean arose. In 1902, the United States had granted political independence to Cuba, but only after the new government had agreed to the so-called Platt Amendment to its constitution, giving the United States the right to prevent any foreign power from intruding into the new nation. When, in 1906, a series of domestic uprisings seemed to threaten the internal stability of the island, Roosevelt reasoned that America must intervene to "protect" Cuba from disorder. American troops landed in Cuba, quelled the fighting, and remained there for three years.

The Panama Canal

The most celebrated accomplishment of Roosevelt's presidency, and the one that illustrated most clearly his own expansive view of the powers of his office and the role of the United States abroad, was the construction of the Panama Canal. Creating a channel through Central America linking the Atlantic and the Pacific had been a dream of many nations since the mid-nineteenth century, but somehow the canal had never been built. Roosevelt was determined to do better.

The first step was the removal of an old obstacle. In 1850, the United States and Great Britain had agreed to a treaty under which the two nations would construct, operate, and defend any such canal together. The McKinley administration had already begun negotiations to cancel the agreement; Roosevelt completed the process. In 1901, the Hay-Pauncefote Treaty gave the United States the right to undertake the canal project alone.

The next question was where to locate the canal. At first, the Roosevelt administration (and many congressional leaders) favored a route across Nicaragua, which would permit a sea-level canal requiring no locks. A possible alternative was the Isthmus of Panama in Colombia, the site of an earlier, abortive effort by a French company to construct a channel. The Panama route was shorter (although not at sea level), and construction was already about 40 percent complete. When the French company lowered its price for its holdings from $109 million to $40 million, and when it combined this gesture with skillful lobbying efforts in Washington, the president and Congress changed their minds.

Roosevelt quickly dispatched John Hay, his secretary of state, to negotiate an agreement with Colombian diplomats in Washington that would allow construction to begin without delay. Under heavy American pressure, the Colombian chargé d'affaires, Tomas Herrán, signed an agreement considered highly unfavorable to his own nation. The United States would gain perpetual rights to a six-mile-wide "canal zone" across Colombia; in return, it would pay Colombia $10 million and an annual rental of $250,000. The treaty produced outrage in the Colombian Senate, whose members refused to ratify the agreement and sent a new representative to the United States with instructions to demand at least $20 million from the Americans plus a share of the payment to the French.

Roosevelt was furious. The Colombians, he charged, were "inefficient bandits" and "blackmailers." He began to contemplate ways to circumvent the Bogotá government. He found a ready ally in the person of Philippe Bunau-Varilla, chief engineer of the French canal project. Bunau-Varilla watched with dismay as the government of Colombia appeared ready to destroy his efforts, and in November 1903 he helped organize and finance a revolution in Panama. There had been many previous revolts, all of them failures. But this one had an important additional asset: the support of the United States. Using an 1846 American-Colombian treaty as justification, Roosevelt landed troops from the U.S.S. *Nashville* in Panama to "maintain order." Their presence prevented Colombian forces from suppressing the rebellion, and three days later the United States recognized Panama as an independent nation. The new Panamanian government, under the influence of Bunau-Varilla, quickly agreed to a treaty with the United States. It granted America a canal zone ten miles wide; the United States would pay Panama the $10 million fee and the $250,000 annual rental that the Colombian Senate had rejected. Work on the canal proceeded rapidly, despite the enormous cuts and elaborate locks (which alone cost $375 million) that the construction required. It opened in 1914, three years after Roosevelt had proudly boasted to a university audience, "I took the Canal Zone and let Congress debate!"

Taft and "Dollar Diplomacy"

Many of those who had admired Roosevelt's vigorous command of American foreign policy and his strenuous efforts to maintain a world balance of power were dismayed by William Howard Taft's performance in international affairs. Although the new president made no decisive break with the policies of his predecessor, and while in some areas he actually extended American involvement abroad, he was in general no readier to exert strong leadership internationally than he was domestically. He worked to advance the nation's economic interests overseas, but he seemed to lack Roosevelt's larger vision of world stability. Worst of all, several of his most important foreign policy initiatives were conspicuous failures.

The thrust of Taft's foreign policy was best symbolized by the man he chose to administer it: Secretary of State Philander C. Knox, a corporate lawyer committed to using his position to promote American business interests overseas. Roosevelt, of course, had promoted American economic interests too; but Knox seemed at times to regard the State Department as little more than an agent of the corporate community. He worked aggressively to extend American investments into underdeveloped regions, motivating critics to label his policies "Dollar Diplomacy."

The Taft-Knox foreign policy faced its severest test, and encountered its greatest failure, in the Far East. Ignoring Roosevelt's tacit 1905 agreement with Japan to limit American involvement in Manchuria, the new administration succumbed to the persuasive powers of American bankers and began to move aggressively to increase America's economic influence in the region. When British, French, and German bankers formed a consortium to finance a vast system of railroads in China, Knox insisted that Americans should also participate; and when in 1911 the Europeans finally agreed to include the United States in their venture, Knox proposed that an international syndicate purchase the South Manchurian Railroad to remove it from Japanese control. Japan responded by signing a treaty of friendship with Russia—a warning to the Europeans—and the entire railroad project quickly collapsed. Having attempted to expand its influence in Asia, America now found the door to Manchuria slammed in its face.

In the Caribbean, the new administration continued and even expanded upon Roosevelt's policies of maintaining order and stability in troubled areas, without regard for the national integrity of the nations involved. Limiting European influence in the region meant, Taft and Knox believed, not only preventing disorder but establishing a significant American economic presence there—replacing the investments of European nations with investments from the United States. In 1909, Knox tried (unsuccessfully) to arrange for American bankers to establish a financial receivership in Honduras. Later, he persuaded New York bankers to invest in the National Bank of Haiti.

But Dollar Diplomacy was not always so peaceful. When a revolution broke out in Nicaragua in 1909, the administration quickly sided with the insurgents (who had been inspired to revolt by an American mining company) and sent American troops into the country to seize the customs houses. As soon as peace was restored, Knox encouraged American bankers to move into Nicaragua and offer substantial loans to the new government, thus increasing Washington's financial leverage over the country. Within two years, however, the new pro-American government faced a revolt of its own; and Taft again landed American troops in Nicaragua, this time to protect the existing regime. The troops remained there for more than a decade.

Diplomacy and Morality

"It would be the irony of fate," Woodrow Wilson remarked shortly before assuming the presidency, "if my administration had to deal chiefly with foreign affairs." Ironic or not, Wilson faced international challenges of a scope and gravity unmatched by any president before him; and he brought to his treatment of them not only remarkable vision but an often inflexible, even self-righteous morality that would ultimately destroy both him and many of the goals for which he fought. Although the true ordeal of Wilsonian diplomacy did not occur until after World War I, many of the qualities that would help produce it were evident in his foreign policy from his first moments in office.

Through much of his administration, Wilson made strenuous but generally unsuccessful efforts to maintain an open door for American trade in China

and to resist the expansion of Japanese influence in the Pacific. At the same time, however, the United States was itself working energetically to close the door to all nations but itself in Latin America. Wilson presided over a foreign policy that not only continued but greatly increased American intervention in the Caribbean and in Latin America, justifying his actions by citing both economic necessity and moral imperative.

The list of American incursions was lengthy and impressive. Having already seized control of the finances of the Dominican Republic in 1905, the United States established a military government there in 1916 when the Dominicans refused to accept a treaty that would have made the country a virtual American protectorate. The military occupation lasted eight years. In Haiti, which shares the island of Hispaniola with the Dominican Republic, Wilson landed the marines in 1915 to quell a revolution in the course of which a mob had murdered an unpopular president. American military forces remained in the country until 1934, and American officers drafted the new Haitian constitution adopted in 1918. When Wilson began to fear that the Danish West Indies might be about to fall into the hands of Germany, he bought the colony from Denmark and renamed it the Virgin Islands. Concerned about the possibility of European influence in Nicaragua, he signed a treaty with that country's government ensuring that no other nation would build a canal there and winning for the United States the right to intervene in Nicaragua's internal affairs to protect American interests.

Mission in Mexico

It was in Mexico that Wilson's missionary view of America's role in the Western Hemisphere received its greatest test and suffered its greatest frustrations. For many years, under the friendly auspices of dictator Porfirio Díaz, American businessmen had been establishing an enormous economic presence in Mexico, with investments totaling more than $1 billion. In 1910, however, the corrupt and tyrannical Díaz had been overthrown by the popular leader Francisco Madero, who excited many of his countrymen by promising democratic reform but alarmed many American businessmen by threatening their investments in his country. With the approval of, among others, the American ambassador in Mexico, Madero was himself deposed early in 1913 by a reactionary general, Victoriano Huerta.

A relieved Taft administration prepared, in its last weeks in office, to recognize the new Huerta regime and welcome back a receptive environment for American investments in Mexico. Before it could do so, however, the new government murdered Madero. Wilson, once in office, displayed no hesitation in responding to the atrocity. He would never, he insisted, recognize Huerta's "government of butchers."

The problem dragged on for years. At first, Wilson hoped that simply by refusing to recognize Huerta he could help topple the regime and bring to power the opposing Constitutionalists, led by Venustiano Carranza. When Huerta established a full military dictatorship in October 1913, however, the president decided on a more forceful approach. First he pressured the British to stop supporting Huerta. Then he offered to send American troops to assist Carranza. Carranza, aware that such an open alliance with the United States would undermine his popular support in Mexico, declined the offer; but he did request and receive from Wilson the right to buy arms in the United States. Still the stalemate continued.

Finally, a minor naval incident provided the president with an excuse for more open intervention. In April 1914, an officer in Huerta's army briefly arrested several American sailors from the U.S.S. *Dolphin* who had gone ashore in Tampico. Although a superior officer immediately released them and apologized to the ship's commander, the American admiral demanded that the Huerta forces fire a twenty-one-gun salute to the American flag as a public display of penance. The Mexicans refused. Wilson seized on the trivial incident as a pretext for sending all available American naval forces into Mexican waters; and a few days later, eager to prevent a German ship from delivering munitions to the Huerta forces, he ordered the navy to seize the Mexican port of Veracruz.

Wilson had envisioned a bloodless action, but in a clash with Mexican troops in the city, the Americans killed 126 of the defenders and suffered 19 casualties of their own. With the two nations at the brink of war, Wilson now drew back and began to look for alternative measures to deal with the crisis. His show of force, however, had in the meantime helped strengthen the position of the Carranza faction, which captured Mexico City in August and forced Huerta to flee the country. At last, it seemed, the crisis might be over.

It was not to be. Wilson reacted angrily when Carranza refused to accept American guidelines for the creation of a new government, and he briefly considered throwing his support to still another aspirant to leadership: Carranza's erstwhile lieutenant Pancho Villa, who was now leading a rebel army of his own. When Villa's military position deteriorated, however, Wilson abandoned the scheme and finally, in October 1915, granted preliminary recognition to the Carranza government. But by now he had created yet another crisis. Angry at what he considered an American betrayal, Villa retaliated in January 1916 by taking sixteen Americans from a train in northern Mexico and shooting them. Two months later, he led his soldiers (or bandits, as the United States preferred to call them) across the border into New Mexico, where they killed nineteen more Americans. His goal, apparently, was to destabilize relations between Wilson and Carranza and provoke a war between them, which might provide him with an opportunity

Pancho Villa and His Soldiers
In 1913, when this photograph was taken, Pancho Villa (second from left) was still on good terms with the government of Woodrow Wilson, which viewed him as a fighter for democracy in Mexico. Three years later, Wilson declared Villa a "bandit" and sent American troops into Mexico in a futile effort to capture him.
(UPI/Bettmann Newsphotos)

SIGNIFICANT EVENTS

1898   Theodore Roosevelt elected governor of New York (p. 642)

1900   Roosevelt elected vice president (p. 642)

1901   McKinley assassinated; Roosevelt becomes president (p. 642)

Hay-Pauncefote Treaty ratified (p. 659)

1902   Northern Securities antitrust case filed (p. 642)

Roosevelt intervenes in anthracite coal strike (p. 643)

Newlands Reclamation Act passed (p. 645)

1903   Department of Commerce and Labor created (p. 642)

1904   Roosevelt mediates settlement of Russo-Japanese War (pp. 657–658)

"Roosevelt Corollary" announced (p. 658)

United States orchestrates Panamanian independence; new government signs treaty allowing United States to build Panama Canal (p. 660)

Roosevelt elected president (p. 643)

1906   Hepburn Railroad Regulation Act passed (p. 643)

Upton Sinclair publishes *The Jungle* (p. 644)

Meat Inspection Act passed (p. 644)

American troops intervene in Cuba (p. 659)

1907   Financial panic and recession (p. 646)

1908   William Howard Taft elected president (p. 647)

1909   Payne-Aldrich Tariff passed (p. 648)

Pinchot-Ballinger dispute begins (pp. 648–649)

U.S. troops intervene in Nicaragua (p. 661)

1910   Roosevelt's Osawatomie speech outlines "New Nationalism" (p. 649)

1910   Woodrow Wilson elected governor of New Jersey (p. 652)

Porfirio Díaz overthrown by Francisco Madero in Mexico (p. 661)

1911   Taft administration files antitrust suit against U.S. Steel (p. 650)

1912   Roosevelt challenges Taft for Republican nomination; wins all party primaries (p. 651)

Taft receives Republican nomination; Roosevelt and followers walk out (p. 651)

Roosevelt forms Progressive party (p. 651)

Woodrow Wilson elected president (p. 653)

1913   Thirteenth Amendment, establishing direct popular election of U.S. senators, ratified (p. 654)

Federal Reserve Act passed (p. 654)

Victoriano Huerta overthrows Madero in Mexico (p. 661)

1914   Federal Trade Commission Act passed (p. 655)

Clayton Antitrust Act passed (p. 655)

Panama Canal opens (p. 660)

U.S. troops intervene in Haiti (p. 661)

Tampico incident strains U.S. relations with Mexico (p. 662)

Venustiano Carranza deposes Huerta in Mexico (p. 662)

1916   Wilson appoints Louis Brandeis to Supreme Court (p. 655)

United States establishes military government in Dominican Republic (p. 661)

U.S. troops pursue Pancho Villa into Mexico (p. 663)

1917   United States recognizes Carranza government (p. 663)

---

to improve his own declining fortunes. He almost succeeded.

With the permission of the Carranza government, Wilson ordered General John J. Pershing to lead an American expeditionary force across the Mexican border in pursuit of Villa. The American troops, during their 300-mile penetration of Mexico, were never able to manage a clash with Villa. They did, however, engage in two ugly skirmishes with Car-

ranza's army, in which forty Mexicans and twelve Americans died. Again, the United States and Mexico stood at the brink of war. But at the last minute, Wilson agreed to the face-saving expedient of referring the dispute to an international commission, which debated for six months without agreeing on a solution. In the meantime, Wilson was quietly withdrawing American troops from Mexico; and in March 1917, having spent four years of effort and gained nothing but a lasting Mexican hostility toward the United States, he at last granted formal recognition to the Carranza regime.

By now, however, Wilson's attention was turning elsewhere—to the far greater international crisis engulfing the European continent and ultimately much of the world. The American response to the Great War transformed the nation's position in the world. It also provided Woodrow Wilson with his most important, and in the end most disastrous, opportunity to bring his strong sense of moralism to the conduct of international relations.

SUGGESTED READINGS

General Histories. George E. Mowry, *The Era of Theodore Roosevelt* (1958); Arthur Link, *Woodrow Wilson and the Progressive Era, 1910–1917* (1954); John Milton Cooper, Jr., *The Warrior and the Priest: Woodrow Wilson and Theodore Roosevelt* (1983). See also Suggested Readings for Chapter 21.

Theodore Roosevelt. Edmund Morris, *The Rise of Theodore Roosevelt* (1979); Henry F. Pringle, *Theodore Roosevelt* (1931); William H. Harbaugh, *Power and Responsibility* (1961), published in paperback as *The Life and Times of Theodore Roosevelt;* John Morton Blum, *The Republican Roosevelt* (1954); G. Wallace Chessman, *Theodore Roosevelt and the Politics of Power* (1969); John A. Garraty, *The Life of George W. Perkins* (1960); Horace S. Merrill and Marion G. Merrill, *The Republican High Command* (1971).

William Howard Taft. Henry F. Pringle, *The Life and Times of William Howard Taft*, 2 vols. (1939); Paolo E. Coletta, *The Presidency of Taft* (1973); Donald E. Anderson, *William Howard Taft* (1973); James L. Penick, *Progressive Politics and Conservation: The Ballinger-Pinchot Affair* (1968); Harold T. Pinkett, *Gifford Pinchot: Private and Public Forester* (1970); George Mowry, *Theodore Roosevelt and the Progressive Movement* (1946); Norman Wilensky, *Conservatives in the Progressive Era: The Taft Republicans of 1912* (1965).

Woodrow Wilson. Arthur S. Link, *Woodrow Wilson*, 5 vols. (1947–1965); John Morton Blum, *Woodrow Wilson and the Politics of Morality* (1956); Alexander George and Juliette George, *Woodrow Wilson and Colonel House* (1956); Edwin A. Weinstein, *Woodrow Wilson: A Medical and Psychological Biography* (1981); John Morton Blum, *Joseph Tumulty and the Wilson Era* (1951); L. J. Holt, *Congressional Insurgents and the Party System, 1909–1916* (1967).

National Issues. Samuel P. Hays, *The Gospel of Efficiency: The Progressive Conservation Movement, 1890–1920* (1962);

Elmo P. Richardson, *The Politics of Conservation* (1962); O. E. Anderson, *The Health of a Nation* (1958); Craig West, *Banking Reform and the Federal Reserve, 1863–1923* (1977).

Roosevelt's Foreign Policy. Howard K. Beale, *Theodore Roosevelt and the Rise of America to World Power* (1956); Richard Challener, *Admirals, Generals, and American Foreign Policy, 1898–1914* (1973); David H. Burton, *Theodore Roosevelt: Confident Imperialist* (1969); Julius W. Pratt, *Challenge and Rejection: The United States and World Leadership, 1900–1921* (1967); Richard Leopold, *Elihu Root and the Conservative Tradition* (1954); Akira Iriye, *Pacific Estrangement: Japanese and American Expansion, 1897—1911* (1972); Charles E. Neu, *An Uncertain Friendship: Roosevelt and Japan, 1906–1909* (1967); Charles Vevier, *United States and China* (1955).

America and the Caribbean. Dana G. Munro, *Intervention and Dollar Diplomacy in the Caribbean, 1900–1921* (1964); Louis A. Perez, Jr., *Cuba Under the Platt Amendment* (1988); Dwight C. Miner, *Fight for the Panama Route* (1966); Walter LaFeber, *The Panama Canal* (1978); David McCullough *The Path Between the Seas* (1977); Walter Scholes and Marie Scholes, *The Foreign Policies of the Taft Administration* (1970).

Wilson's Foreign Policy. Arthur Link, *Wilson the Diplomatist* (1957) and *Woodrow Wilson: Revolution, War, and Peace* (1979); Robert Freeman Smith, *The United States and Revolutionary Nationalism in Mexico, 1916–1932* (1972); Kenneth Grieb, *The United States and Huerta* (1969); Robert Quirk, *An Affair of Honor: Woodrow Wilson and the Occupation of Veracruz* (1962) and *The Mexican Revolution, 1914–1915* (1960); David Healy, *Gunboat Diplomacy in the Wilson Era: The U.S. Navy in Haiti, 1915–1916* (1976); Dana Munro, *Intervention and Dollar Diplomacy in the Caribbean, 1900–1914* (1964).

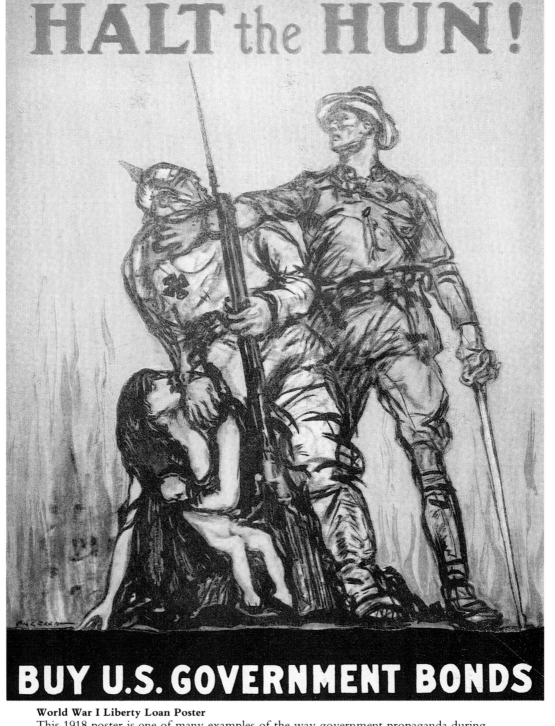

World War I Liberty Loan Poster
This 1918 poster is one of many examples of the way government propaganda during World War I encouraged Americans to think of Germans as savage beasts. An American soldier prevents a "Hun" from ravaging a young woman and her baby—a reference to the widespread and largely erroneous belief that German troops had massacred women and children in Belgium early in the war. *(The Granger Collection)*

CHAPTER 23

❖ ❖ ❖

America and the Great War

❖ ❖ ❖

The Great War, as it was known to a generation unaware that another, greater war would soon follow, began modestly in August 1914 when Austria invaded the tiny Balkan nation of Serbia. Within weeks, however, it had grown into a widespread conflagration, engaging the armies of all the major nations of Europe and shattering forever the delicate balance of power that had maintained a general peace on the Continent since the early nineteenth century. Americans looked on with horror but also at first with a conviction that the conflict had little to do with them. They were wrong.

After nearly three years of attempting to affect the outcome of the conflict without becoming embroiled in it, the United States formally entered the war in April 1917. In doing so, it joined the most savage conflict in history. The fighting had already dragged on for two and a half years, inconclusive, almost inconceivably murderous, engaging not only the armies of the contending nations but their civilian populations as well. Although the American Civil War had greatly increased the ferocity and extent of combat, World War I was the first truly "total" war. It pitted entire societies against one another, and it had by 1917 left Europe exhausted and on the brink of utter collapse. By the time it ended late in 1918, Germany had lost nearly 2 million soldiers in battle, Russia 1.7 million, France 1.4 million, Great Britain 900,000. A generation of European youth was decimated; centuries of political, social, and economic traditions were damaged and all but destroyed.

For America, however, the war was the source of a very different experience. As a military struggle, it was brief, decisive, and—in relative terms—without great cost. Only 112,000 American soldiers died in the conflict, half of them from disease rather than in combat. Economically, it was the source of a great industrial boom, which helped spark the years of prosperity that would follow. And the war propelled the United States into a position of international pre-eminence.

In other respects, World War I was a painful, even traumatic experience for the American people. At home, the nation became obsessed with a search not just for victory but also for social unity—a search that continued and even intensified in the troubled years following the armistice, and that helped shatter many of the progressive ideals of the first years of the century. And in the world at large, once the conflict ended, the United States encountered frustration and disillusionment. The "war to end wars," the war "to make the world safe for democracy," became neither. Instead, it led directly to twenty years of international instability that would ultimately generate another great conflict.

The Road to War

The causes of the war in Europe—indeed, the question of whether there were any significant causes at all, or whether the entire conflict was the result of a tragic series of blunders—have been the subject of continued debate for more than seven decades. What is clear is that the European nations had by 1914 created an unusually precarious international system that careened into war very quickly on the basis of what most historians agree was a minor series of provocations.

The Collapse of the European Peace

The major powers of Europe were organized in two great, competing alliances. The "Triple Entente" linked the fortunes of Britain, France, and Russia. The "Triple Alliance" united Germany, the Austro-Hungarian Empire, and Italy. The chief rivalry, however, was not between the two alliances, but between the great powers that dominated them: Great Britain and Germany—the former long established as the world's most powerful colonial and commercial nation, the latter ambitious to expand its own empire and become at least Britian's equal.

The Anglo-German rivalry, however, was not the direct cause of the outbreak of World War I. The conflict emerged out of an essentially local controversy involving nationalist movements within the Austro-Hungarian Empire. On June 28, 1914, the Archduke Franz Ferdinand, heir to the throne of the tottering empire, was assassinated while paying a state visit to Sarajevo. Sarajevo was the capital of Bosnia, a province of Austria-Hungary that Slavic nationalists wished to annex to neighboring Serbia; the Archduke's assassin was a Serbian nationalist.

This local controversy quickly created an international crisis through the workings of the system of entangling alliances that the great powers had constructed. Germany pressured Austria-Hungary to launch a punitive assault on Serbia. The Serbians called on Russia to help with their defense. The Russians began mobilizing their army on July 30. By August 3, Germany had declared war on both Russia and France and had invaded Belgium in preparation for a thrust across the French border. On August 4, Great Britain—ostensibly to honor its alliance with France, but more importantly to blunt the advance of its principal rival—declared war on Germany. Russia and the Austro-Hungarian Empire formally began hostilities on August 6. Italy, the Ottoman Empire (Turkey) and other, smaller nations all joined the fighting later in 1914. For reasons historians continue to debate, virtually the entire European continent was embroiled in a major war.

A False Neutrality

Wilson's determination to keep the United States isolated from the conflict reflected the overwhelming sentiment of the American people. But it rested on a false premise. The United States had nothing at stake in this war, he told the nation. In fact, America had a great deal at stake, and as the war continued that stake grew.

Wilson called on his fellow citizens in 1914 to remain "impartial in thought as well as deed." But that was impossible, for several reasons. For one thing, many Americans were not, in fact, genuinely impartial. Some sympathized with the German cause (German-Americans, because of affection for Germany, Irish-Americans, because of hatred of Britain). Many more sympathized with Britain. Wilson himself was only one of many Americans who fervently admired England—its traditions, its culture, its political system; almost instinctively, these Americans attributed to the cause of the Allies (Britain, France, Italy, Russia) a moral quality that they denied to the Central Powers (Germany, the Austro-Hungarian Empire, and the Ottoman—or Turkish—Empire). Lurid reports of German atrocities in Belgium and France, skillfully exaggerated by British propagandists, strengthened the conviction of many Americans that Germany was a brutal and autocratic culture threatening the democracies of Britain and France.

Economic realities also made it impossible for the United States to deal with the belligerents on equal terms. The neutral rights that Wilson so ardently sought to uphold included, among other things, the right of an impartial nation such as the United States to trade freely with both sides in the conflict. But the British, whose control of the seas was their most effective weapon, clamped a naval blockade on Germany to prevent munitions and supplies—from neutrals as well as belligerents—from reaching the enemy. The United States government had two choices. It could preserve a genuine American neutrality by denouncing the blockade and imposing an embargo on trade with Great Britain; or it could accept the situation and allow trade with England to continue and trade with Germany to cease.

Economic realities, combined with his own inclination to support the British, caused Wilson to choose the latter. The United States could survive an interruption of its relatively modest trade with the Central Powers. It could not, however, easily weather an embargo on its much more extensive trade with the Allies, particularly when war orders from Britain and France jumped from $824 million in 1914 to $3.2 billion two years later. The war had produced the greatest economic boom in the nation's history, and Wilson realized that it would be both economically and politically costly to cut off (or even substantially to limit) the extensive trade and financial ties the United States was developing with the belligerents.

By 1915, therefore, the United States had gradually transformed itself into the arsenal of the Allies. In the process, it had replaced its stance of genuine neutrality with something quite different. Americans acquiesced quietly, or with feeble protests, in violations of their rights by the British, who periodically seized American ships suspected of carrying supplies destined for Germany. When Germany infringed on neutral rights, however, the response of the United States was harsh and unyielding—even though the Germans had far better cause for objecting to the patterns of American trade than did the British.

The Germans intensified American antagonism by resorting to a new and, in American eyes, barbaric tactic: submarine warfare. Unable to challenge British domination on the ocean's surface, Germany began early in 1915 to use the newly improved submarine to try to stem the flow of supplies to England. Enemy vessels, the Germans announced, would be sunk on sight, prompting Wilson to declare that he would hold Germany to "strict accountability" for unlawful acts.

A test of this pronouncement came only months later, when on May 7, 1915, a German U-boat (short for *Unterseeboot*, undersea boat) sank the British passenger liner *Lusitania* without warning, causing the deaths of 1,198 people, 128 of them Americans. The ship was, it later became clear, carrying not only passengers but munitions; at the time, however, the attack seemed to most Americans to be what Theodore Roosevelt called it: "an act of piracy."

Wilson reacted by initiating an angry exchange of notes with Germany, demanding assurances that such outrages would not recur and that the Central Powers would respect the rights of neutral nations, among which, he insisted, was the right of their citizens to travel on the nonmilitary vessels of belligerents. (After one particularly threatening note, Secretary of State William Jennings Bryan—who argued that equally strenuous protests should be sent to the British in response to their blockade—resigned from office as a matter of principle, one of the few high government officials of the United States ever to do so.) The Germans finally agreed to Wilson's demands, but a pattern of relations had been established that would increasingly bring the two nations into conflict.

Early in 1916, American-German relations soured anew when, in response to an announcement that the Allies were now arming merchant ships to sink submarines, Germany proclaimed that it would fire on such vessels without warning. A few weeks

Submarine Warfare

A German submarine (or U-boat) stops a Spanish steamer for inspection on the North Sea in 1917. Germany claimed the right to search (and at times, the right to sink) all neutral vessels suspected of carrying war matériel to the Allied powers. (Culver Pictures)

later, it did just that, attacking the unarmed French steamer *Sussex* and injuring several American passengers. Again, Wilson demanded that Germany abandon its "unlawful" tactics; again, the German government relented. Lacking sufficient naval power to enforce an effective blockade against Britain, the Germans decided that the marginal advantages of unrestricted submarine warfare did not yet justify the possibility of drawing America into the war.

Preparedness Versus Pacifism

Despite the president's increasing bellicosity in 1916, he was still far from ready to commit the United States to war. One obstacle was American domestic politics. Facing a difficult battle for reelection, Wilson could not ignore the powerful factions that continued to oppose intervention. His policies, therefore, represented an effort to satisfy the demands both of those who, like Theodore Roosevelt, insisted that the nation defend its "honor" and economic interests and those who, like Bryan, La Follette, and others (including many German-Americans and Irish-Americans hostile to Britain), denounced any action that seemed to increase the chance of war.

The question of whether America should make military and economic preparations for war provided a preliminary issue over which the two coalitions could battle. Wilson at first sided with the anti–preparedness forces, denouncing the idea of an American military build-up as needless and provocative. As tensions between the United States and Germany grew, however, he changed his mind. In the fall of 1915, he endorsed an ambitious proposal by American military leaders for a large and rapid increase in the nation's armed forces, to cost more than half a billion dollars; and amid expressions of outrage from pacifists in Congress and elsewhere, he worked hard to win approval of it. He even embarked on a national speaking tour early in 1916 to arouse support for the proposal. By midsummer his efforts had in large part succeeded, and rearmament for a possible conflict was well under way.

Still, the peace faction wielded considerable political strength. How much strength became clear to Wilson at the Democratic Convention that met to renominate him in the summer of 1916. The keynote speaker turned his address into a litany of praise for Wilson's efforts to avoid American intervention. He evoked a remarkable response. As he recited the president's diplomatic accomplishments, the delegates

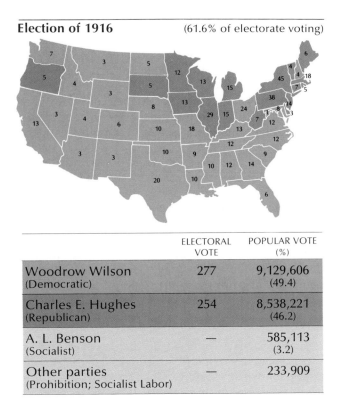

Election of 1916 (61.6% of electorate voting)

	ELECTORAL VOTE	POPULAR VOTE (%)
Woodrow Wilson (Democratic)	277	9,129,606 (49.4)
Charles E. Hughes (Republican)	254	8,538,221 (46.2)
A. L. Benson (Socialist)	—	585,113 (3.2)
Other parties (Prohibition; Socialist Labor)	—	233,909

chanted again and again, "What did we do? What did we do?" And the speaker shouted in response, "We didn't go to war! We didn't go to war!" Out of that almost hysterical exchange came one of the most prominent slogans of Wilson's reelection campaign (although one that he himself never used or approved): "He kept us out of war."

In the face of such pressures, therefore, Wilson remained highly cautious. When prowar rhetoric became particularly heated, Wilson spoke defiantly of the nation being "too proud to fight." And when the Republicans chose as their 1916 presidential candidate Charles Evans Hughes, a progressive who attracted the support of the bellicose Theodore Roosevelt, Wilson did nothing to discourage those who argued that Hughes was more likely than he to lead the nation into war. At times, he issued such warnings himself. Wilson's promises of progressivism and peace ultimately combined to give the Democrats, once again a minority party against the reunited Republicans, a narrow victory in November. Wilson won reelection by one of the smallest margins in American history: fewer than 600,000 popular votes and only 23 electoral votes, with the Democrats retaining a precarious control over Congress.

A War for Democracy

With the election behind him, and with tensions between the United States and Germany unabated, there remained for Wilson a final obstacle to involvement in the world war. He required a lofty justification for American intervention, one that would not only unite public opinion but satisfy his own sense of morality. The Germans had gone far toward providing such a justification with their "barbaric" tactics on the seas and their alleged atrocities on land (including, the American prowar press ardently claimed, the use of poison gas and the senseless butchering of women and children). Wilson himself, however, created the most important rationale. The United States, he insisted, had no material aims of its own in the conflict. The nation was, rather, committed to using the war as a vehicle for constructing a new world order, one based on the same progressive ideals that had motivated reform in America.

In a speech before Congress in January 1917, he presented a plan for a postwar order in which the United States would help maintain peace through a permanent league of nations—a peace that would include self-determination and equality for all nations, a "peace among equals," a "peace without victory."

In the first months of 1917, when new provocations once again inflamed German-American relations, Wilson was at last ready to fight. In January, after months of inconclusive warfare in the trenches of France, the military leaders of Germany decided on one last dramatic gamble to achieve a quick and decisive victory. They would launch a series of major assaults on the enemy's lines in France. At the same time, they would begin unrestricted submarine warfare in an effort to cut off vital supplies from Britain. The Allies would collapse, they hoped, before the United States had time to intervene. Beginning February 1, the German ambassador informed Wilson, U-boats would sink all ships, enemy and neutral alike, in a broad zone around the British Isles. If America chose to continue supplying the Allies, it would have to risk attack.

With that, the president recognized that war was inevitable; the only question remaining was the appropriate time to declare it. Two additional developments helped clear the way. On February 25, the British turned over to him an intercepted telegram from the German foreign minister, Arthur Zimmermann, to the government of Mexico. It proposed that in the event of war between Germany and the United States, the Mexicans should join the struggle against the Americans. In return, they would regain their "lost provinces" to the north when the war was over. Widely publicized by British propagandists and in the American press, the Zimmermann telegram inflamed public opinion and helped build up popular sentiment for war.

A second event, in March, provided Wilson with additional comfort. A revolution in Russia toppled the reactionary czarist regime, which had been tottering ever since the Russo-Japanese War in 1905. A new, republican government took its place. The United States would now be spared the embarrassment of allying itself with a despotic monarchy. The war for a progressive world order could proceed untainted.

On the rainy evening of April 2, two weeks after German submarines had torpedoed three American ships, Wilson appeared before a joint session of Congress and spoke words that brought to an end the years of uncertain waiting:

> It is a fearful thing to lead this great peaceful people into war, into the most terrible and disastrous of all wars, civilization itself seeming to be in the balance. But the right is more precious than peace, and we shall fight for the things which we have always carried nearest our hearts—for democracy, for the right of those who submit to authority to have a voice in their own Governments, for the rights and liberties of small nations, for a universal dominion of right by such a concert of free peoples as shall bring peace and safety to all nations and make the world itself at last free.

The audience in the House chamber roared its approval. In Europe, the Allied nations rejoiced at their deliverance. Even some of Wilson's bitterest enemies, men such as Theodore Roosevelt and Henry Cabot Lodge, offered warm words of praise.

The sentiment for war was not, however, unanimous. For four days, amid cries of treason and cowardice, pacifists in Congress carried on their futile struggle. When the declaration of war finally passed on April 6, fifty representatives and six senators had voted against it. America was entering a new era, but it was doing so divided and fearful. And Woodrow Wilson, perhaps aware of the ordeal that lay ahead, returned to the White House after his dramatic war address and, according to one account, broke down and wept.

"War Without Stint"

Armies on both sides in Europe were decimated and exhausted by the time of Woodrow Wilson's declaration of war. The German offensives of early 1917 had failed to produce an end to the struggle, and French and British counteroffensives had accomplished little beyond adding to the appalling number of casualties. The ghastly stalemate continued, and the Allies looked desperately to the United States to provide them with a chance for victory.

The Americans were eager to oblige. Wilson had called on the nation to wage war "without stint or limit." And in that spirit, the American government proceeded to launch massive campaigns against German submarines in the Atlantic and against German armies in France, and to mobilize the nation's economic resources on a grand scale.

The Military Struggle

The conflicts at sea had brought the United States into the war; and it was on the naval struggle that American participation had the most immediate effect. By the spring of 1917, Great Britain was suffering such vast losses from attacks by German submarines—one of every four ships setting sail from British ports never returned—that its ability to continue ferrying vital supplies across the Atlantic was coming into serious question. Within weeks of joining the war, the United States had begun to alter the balance. A fleet of American destroyers aided the British navy in its assault on the U-boats; other American warships escorted merchant vessels across the Atlantic; American assistance was crucial in sowing antisubmarine mines in the North Sea.

The results were dramatic. Sinkings of Allied ships had totaled nearly 900,000 tons in the month of April 1917; by December, the figure had dropped to 350,000; by October 1918, it had declined to 112,000. The flow of weapons and supplies from the United States to England and France continued; without it, the Allied cause would have been lost.

At first, most Americans believed that this naval assistance was all that would be required of them. It soon became clear, however, that a major commitment of American ground forces would be necessary as well. Britain and France by 1917 had few reserves left on which to draw. Russia was in even direr straits; and after the Bolshevik Revolution in November

1917, the new government, led by Vladimir Ilich, negotiated a hasty and costly peace with the Central Powers. Battalions of German troops were now free to fight on the western front. It would be up to American forces to counterbalance them.

In 1917, however, those forces barely existed. The regular army was pathetically small, and little thought had been given to an effective method for expanding it. Theodore Roosevelt, old and ill, swallowed his personal hatred of President Wilson and visited the White House, offering to raise a regiment to fight in Europe. Others, similarly, urged an entirely voluntary recruitment process. The president, however, decided otherwise. Only a national draft, he insisted, could provide the needed men; and despite the protests of those who agreed with House Speaker Champ Clark that "there is precious little difference between a conscript and a convict," he won passage of the Selective Service Act in mid-May. The draft brought nearly 3 million men into the army; another 2 million joined various branches of the armed services voluntarily.

The engagement of these forces in combat was intense but brief. Not until near the end of 1917 did most members of the American Expeditionary Force (AEF), as it was called, arrive in Europe. Not until the following spring were American troops there in significant numbers. Eight months later, the war was over.

Under the command of General John J. Pershing, whose unhappy experience in Mexico only a year before had not diminished his military reputation, the fresh American troops first joined the existing Allied forces in turning back a series of new German assaults. In early June, they assisted the French in repelling a bitter German offensive at Château-Thierry, near Paris. Six weeks later, the AEF helped turn away another assault, at Rheims, farther south. By July 18, the German advance had been halted; and for the first time in what seemed years, the Allies began a successful offensive of their own.

On September 26, an enormous American fighting force began to advance against the Germans in the Argonne Forest as part of a grand, 200-mile attack that was to last nearly seven weeks. Over 1 million American soldiers took part in the assault, using more ammunition than the entire Union army had used in four years of the Civil War; and by the end of October, they had helped push the Germans back toward their own border and had cut the enemy's major supply lines to the front.

America in World War I: The Western Front, 1918

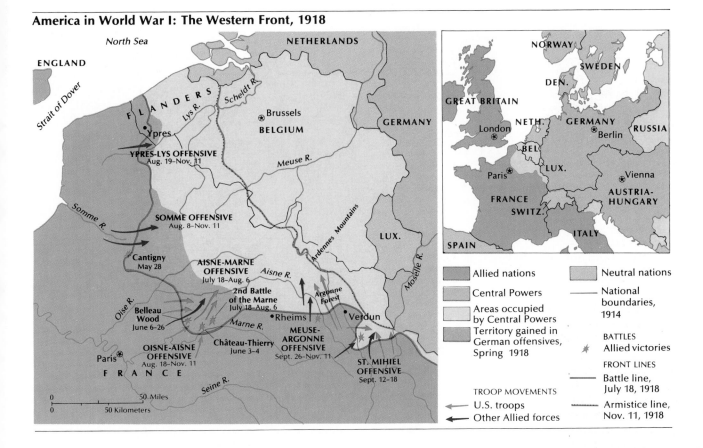

Faced with an invasion of their own country, German military leaders now began to seek an armistice—an immediate cease-fire that would, they hoped, serve as a prelude to negotiations among the belligerents. Pershing wanted to drive on into Germany itself; but other Allied leaders, after first insisting on terms so stringent as to make the agreement little different in effect from a surrender, accepted the German proposal. On November 11, 1918, the Great War shuddered to a close. And American troops, having fought in it for only about eight months of its four years, boasted proudly that it had been they who had won it. Whether or not the claim was militarily accurate, it was already clear that the United States was the only real victor in the conflict.

Financing the War

At home, in the meantime, the war was having profound economic and social effects. The conflict had begun to transform the American economy even be-

fore the United States joined the struggle. After the declaration of war, the pace of change quickly accelerated. Many government officials had scoffed at early predictions that the United States would need to spend $10 billion before the fighting ceased, but it soon became clear that even that figure was preposterously low. Before it was over, the federal government had appropriated $32 billion for expenses directly related to the war.

This was an enormous sum by the standards of the day; the entire federal budget had seldom exceeded $1 billion before 1915. To raise the money, the government relied on two devices. First, it launched a major drive to solicit loans from the American people by selling "Liberty Bonds" to the public. By 1920, the sale of bonds, which was accompanied by a carefully orchestrated appeal to patriotic fervor, had produced $23 billion. At the same time, new taxes were bringing in an additional sum of nearly $10 billion— some of it from levies on the "excess profits" of corporations, much of it from new, steeply graduated income and inheritance taxes

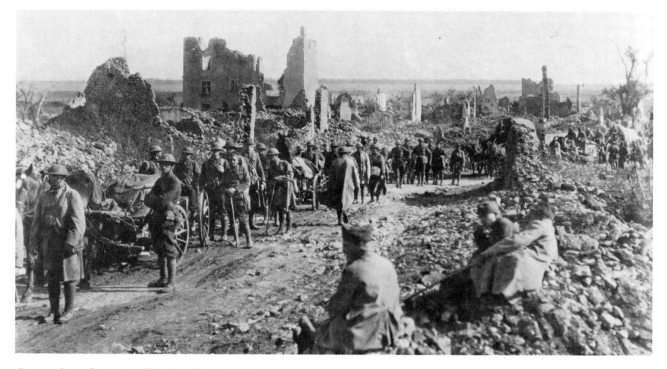

Capturing the St. Mihiel Salient, 1918
A convoy of American machine guns and supply wagons pauses on October 5, 1918, in a ruined French town, preparing to move ahead into the Moselle Valley. By then, German resistance was already crumbling, and only a few weeks later the war would come to an end. Although World War I was in many ways the last of the "old" wars (as suggested by the frequent use of horses for transport), it created widespread devastation of civilian areas (as this photograph illustrates) of the sort that would become characteristic of twentieth-century combat. (The Bettmann Archive)

that ultimately rose as high as 70 percent in some brackets. The nation financed the war by spreading the burden widely and reasonably efficiently.

The War Boards

An even greater challenge than raising the necessary funds was the task of organizing the nation's economy to ensure that war needs could be met. The administration made use of two very different approaches.

The first approach was in many ways reminiscent of Wilson's early commitment to the New Freedom concept of economic decentralization. In 1916, Wilson established a Council of National Defense, composed of members of his cabinet, to coordinate policy; connected with it was a Civilian Advisory Commission, which set up local defense councils in every state, county, and school district. Economic mobilization, according to this early plan, was to rest on a large-scale dispersal of power to local communities.

But this early administrative structure soon proved completely unworkable. And some members of the Council of National Defense, many of them disciples of the engineering gospel of Thorstein Veblen and the "scientific management" principles of Frederick Winslow Taylor, began to urge a more centralized approach. Instead of dividing the economy geographically, they proposed dividing it functionally by organizing a series of planning bodies, each to supervise a specific sector of the economy. Thus one agency would control transportation, another agriculture, another manufacturing. Associated with each agency would be "consulting boards," to encourage efficiency and standardization within industries.

The administrative structure that slowly emerged reflected many of the technocrats' assumptions, although it seldom worked as smoothly as they had envisioned. It was dominated by a series of "war

Financing the War
The Liberty Loan bond-selling drives, heavily promoted by the government in posters such as this one, raised $23 billion for the war effort, an almost unimaginable sum to Americans at the time. Prior to World War I, the total federal budget had seldom exceeded $1 billion.   (Culver Pictures)

boards." A Railroad War Board, under the direction of Treasury Secretary William McAdoo, attempted to run the nation's major transportation resource as a single unified system. Using a half-billion-dollar budget for improving equipment and raising wages, McAdoo succeeded in untangling the flow of rail traffic and dramatically increasing the transportation of goods to the East, where they could be shipped on to Europe. A new Fuel Administration was charged with allocating the increasingly scarce supplies of coal among the many contending groups seeking to buy it. Production increased, but the fuel shortage continued to intensify, forcing the agency to adopt drastic measures. Eastern industries were forced to endure several coal "holidays" early in 1918; some energy consumers were encouraged to forgo using coal altogether and convert to oil.

Perhaps the most dramatically effective of all the new war agencies was the Food Administration, headed by the brilliant young engineer and business executive Herbert Hoover. Hoover had supervised a famously successful effort earlier in the war to provide food and relief to Belgium, which had been devastated by the German invasion. He brought the same administrative skills to bear on the greater task of supervising the feeding of the nation, its armies, and its Allies—all of whom were dependent on the products of American agriculture. Hoover attempted to increase supplies by encouraging voluntary conservation. At the same time, he encouraged increased production of basic foodstuffs such as wheat by arranging for the government to purchase crops at high prices to stimulate farmers to plant as much as possible. The nation managed to supply many of the needs of Europe as well as to continue feeding itself. Hoover emerged from the war as one of the most admired figures in the country.

Government, Industry, and Labor

At the center of the effort to rationalize the economy was the War Industries Board, an agency created in July 1917 to coordinate government purchases of military supplies. Casually organized at first, it stumbled badly until March 1918, when Wilson restructured it and placed it under the control of the Wall Street financier Bernard Baruch. From then on, the board

Women War Workers
With much of the male work force fighting overseas, women moved into occupations that in other times would have been considered unsuitable for them. One such occupation, pictured here, was delivering huge blocks of ice daily to households to be used (in this age before refrigeration) in wooden iceboxes. (National Archives)

wielded powers greater (in theory at least) than any government agency had ever possessed. Baruch became, in popular legend, a virtual czar of American industry. Baruch decided which factories would convert to the production of which war materials; he set prices for the goods that resulted; he imposed standardized production procedures on industries to increase the efficiency of their operations and to promote interchangeability of parts among their products. When materials were scarce, Baruch decided to whom they should go. When corporations were competing for government contracts, he chose among them. He had become, it seemed, the ultimate expression of the progressive ideals of the New Nationalism. He was providing the centralized regulation of the economy that many reformers had long urged.

There were, however, substantial differences between the image and the reality. For one thing, the WIB never worked as well as Baruch and his admirers liked to claim. It performed better than it had earlier in the war; but confusion and mismanagement continued rampant. Only because American resources and productive capacities were so great was the nation able to meet its war needs. Nor was the WIB in any real sense an example of state control of the economy. Baruch viewed himself, openly and explicitly, as the partner of business; and within the WIB, businessmen themselves—the so-called dollar-a-year men, who took paid leave from their corporate jobs and worked for the government for a token salary—supervised the affairs of the private economy.

Indeed, the relationship between the public and private sectors during the war was so warm and mutually supportive that to many people it began to seem as though the line between the two had all but dissolved. Baruch ensured that manufacturers coordinating their efforts in accord with his goals would be exempt from antitrust laws. He helped major industries earn enormous profits from their efforts. Steel manufacturers, for example, saw their prices rise 300 percent during a single year of the war. Corporate profits as a whole increased threefold between 1914 and 1919. Rather than working to restrict private power and limit corporate profits, as many progressives had urged, the government was working to enhance the private sector through a mutually beneficial alliance. Business itself, once antagonistic to the idea of any government interference, was beginning to see the advantages of having the state control competition and sanction what were, in essence, collusive arrangements.

This growing link between the public and private sectors extended, although in greatly different form, to labor. The National War Labor Board, established in April 1918, served as a kind of supreme court for labor disputes. It pressured industry to grant important concessions to workers: an eight-hour day, the maintenance of minimal living standards, equal pay for women doing equal work, recognition of the right of unions to organize and bargain collectively. In return, it insisted that workers forgo all strikes and that employers not engage in lockouts. Samuel Gompers, president of the American Federation of Labor, sat on the board and supported its decisions; and he watched approvingly as membership in labor unions increased by more than 1.5 million between 1917 and

1919. Many of these organizational gains, however, would not long survive the armistice.

The Results of Organization

Despite the enthusiasm with which government and business alike greeted their new, cooperative relationship, the material results were often disappointing. The proliferation of government agencies at times created more confusion than order. Bureaucracies occasionally contradicted one another in the directives they issued. Lines of authority were never entirely clear. And excessive regulation sometimes slowed, rather than enhanced, production.

There were some spectacular accomplishments: Hoover's efficient organization of food supplies, McAdoo's success in untangling the railroads, and others. In some areas, however, progress was so slow that the war was over before many of the supplies ordered for it were ready. The Aircraft Production Board, for example, had promised to deliver 22,000 new planes to the western front by July 1918. By the time the armistice was signed, it had managed to produce only 1,185 of them. The Emergency Fleet Corporation, created to oversee production of a vast armada of merchant vessels, took more than a year to overcome the effects of its own incompetent management. By the end of the war, American shipbuilding facilities were beginning to produce new ships at a remarkable rate; but most were not completed in time to contribute to the war effort. Had the fighting continued another year, it is possible that the productive machinery the Wilson administration had so painstakingly constructed would have begun to accomplish great feats. As it was, the eighteen months of war were not enough time for the war economy to learn to function with real efficiency. Even so, many leaders of both government and industry emerged from the experience convinced of the advantages of a close, cooperative relationship between the public and private sectors. Some hoped to continue and extend the wartime experiments in the peacetime world.

The Search for Social Unity

The idea of unity—not only in the direction of the economy but in the nation's social purpose—had been the dream of many progressives for decades. To them, the war seemed to offer an unmatched opportunity. At last, America was to close ranks behind a great common cause. In the process, they hoped, society could achieve a lasting sense of mutual purpose. In fact, however, the search for unity became an experience of ugly hysteria and bitter repression. American society remained divided, both in its attitude toward the war and in its larger political and social goals.

Selling the War

Government leaders were painfully aware of how deeply divided public opinion had been up to the moment of America's declaration of war. They knew, too, that many pacifists and isolationists remained opposed to United States participation even after that participation had begun. It was easy to argue, therefore, that a crucial prerequisite for victory was the uniting of public opinion behind the war effort. The government approached that task in several ways.

Most conspicuous was a propaganda campaign far greater than any the government had ever undertaken. A Committee on Public Information (CPI), under the direction of journalist George Creel, supervised the distribution of innumerable tons of pro-war literature (75 million pieces of printed material in all). War posters plastered the walls of offices, shops, theaters, schools, churches, homes. Newspapers dutifully printed official government accounts of the reasons for the war and the prospects for quick victory. Creel encouraged reporters to exercise "self-censorship" when reporting news about the struggle; and although many people in the press resented the suggestion, the veiled threats that accompanied it persuaded most of them to comply.

The CPI attempted at first to distribute only the "facts," believing that the truth would speak for itself. As the war continued, however, their tactics became increasingly crude. Government-promoted films, at first relatively mild in tone, were by 1918 becoming vicious portrayals of the savagery of the Germans, bearing such titles as *The Prussian Cur*. CPI-financed advertisements in magazines appealed to citizens to report to the authorities any evidence among their neighbors of disloyalty, pessimism, or yearning for peace.

Legal Repression

The Wilson administration soon began not only to encourage public approval but to suppress opposition. The Espionage Act of 1917 imposed heavy fines and stiff jail terms on those convicted of spying, sabotage, or obstruction of the war effort. Those crimes were often broadly defined. The law also empowered the postmaster general to ban from the mails any "seditious" material—an authority he exercised enthusiastically and often capriciously. More repressive were two measures of 1918: the Sabotage Act of April 20 and the Sedition Act of May 16. These bills expanded the meaning of the Espionage Act to make illegal any public expression of opposition to the war; in practice, it allowed officials to prosecute anyone who criticized the president or the government.

The most frequent target of the new legislation (and one of the reasons for its enactment in the first place) were such anticapitalist groups as the Socialist party and the Industrial Workers of the World (IWW). Unlike their counterparts in Europe, American socialists had not dropped their opposition to the war after their country had decided to join it; the impact of this decision on them was devastating. Many Americans had favored the repression of socialists and radicals even before the war; now, the new government policies made it possible to move against them with full legal sanction. Eugene V. Debs, the humane leader of the party, an opponent of the war but no friend of Germany, was sentenced to ten years in prison in 1918. Only a pardon by President Warren G. Harding ultimately won his release in 1921. Big Bill Haywood and members of the IWW were especially energetically prosecuted. Only by fleeing to the Soviet Union did Haywood avoid long imprisonment. In all, more than 1,500 people were arrested in 1918 for the crime of criticizing the government.

Popular Repression

The federal government was not alone in fueling the hysteria of the war years. State governments, local governments, corporations, universities, and above all the actions of private citizens contributed as well to the climate of repression. Vigilante mobs sprang up to "discipline" those who dared challenge the war and occasionally inflicted terrible violence on dissenters. A dissident Protestant clergyman in Cincinnati was pulled from his bed one night by a mob, dragged to a nearby hillside, and whipped "in the name of the women and children of Belgium." An IWW organizer in Montana was seized by a mob and hanged from a railroad bridge.

A cluster of citizens' groups emerged to mobilize "respectable" members of their communities to root out disloyalty. The American Protective League, probably the largest of such groups, enlisted the services of 250,000 people, who served as "agents"—prying into the activities and thoughts of their neighbors, stopping men on the street and demanding to see their draft cards, opening mail, tapping telephones, and in general attempting to impose unity of opinion on their communities. Attorney General Thomas W. Gregory described them approvingly as a "patriotic organization." Other vigilante organizations—the National Security League, the Boy Spies of America, the American Defense Society—performed much the same function.

The most frequent victims of such activities were immigrants, who were already a source of concern to much of American society. Now they became the targets of special abuse. "Loyal" Americans described immigrant communities as spawning grounds for radicalism. Vigilantes devoted special attention to immigrant groups suspected of sympathizing with the enemy. Irish-Americans faced constant accusations because of their historic animosity toward the British and because they had, before 1917, often expressed hopes for a German victory. Jews aroused suspicion because many had expressed opposition to the anti-Semitic policies of the Russian government, until 1917 one of the Allies. Immigrant ghettoes were strictly policed by the "loyalist" citizens' groups. Even some settlement house workers, many of whom had once championed ethnic diversity, contributed to such efforts.

The German-Americans

The greatest target, perhaps the inevitable target, of abuse was the German-American community. Its members had unwittingly contributed to their plight; in the first years of the war in Europe, some had openly advocated American assistance to the Central Powers, and many had opposed United States intervention on behalf of the Allies. But while most German-Americans loyally supported the American war effort once it began, public opinion turned hostile.

A campaign to purge society of all things German quickly gathered speed, at times assuming ludicrous forms. Sauerkraut was renamed "liberty cabbage." Hamburger became "liberty sausage." Performances of German music were frequently banned; German books were removed from the shelves of libraries; courses in the German language were removed from school curricula. For Americans of German descent, moreover, life became a dangerous ordeal. Germans were routinely fired from jobs in war industries, lest they "sabotage" important tasks. Others were fired from positions entirely unrelated to the war; Karl Muck, the German-born conductor of the Boston Symphony Orchestra, was forced to resign his position and was interned for the last months of the war. Vigilante groups routinely subjected Germans to harassment and beatings; there was even a lynching—in southern Illinois in 1918. Relatively few Americans favored such extremes, but many came to agree with the belief of the eminent psychologist G. Stanley Hall (the man responsible for the first visit of Sigmund Freud to America in 1909) that "there is something fundamentally wrong with the Teutonic soul."

The Search for a New World Order

In the meantime, the United States was articulating a vision of a new international order based on lofty democratic principles. Woodrow Wilson had led the nation into war promising a more just and stable peace at its conclusion. Even before the armistice, therefore, he was beginning preparations to lead the fight for a postwar settlement based on principle, not selfish nationalism.

It was, he realized, a difficult task. America had barely joined the war when the new Bolshevik government in Russia began disclosing terms of secret treaties negotiated earlier among the Allies. Britain, France, and imperial Russia had already agreed, according to these reports, on how to divide the colonies of their enemies among them. To Wilson, such treaties ran counter to the idealistic vision for which he was exhorting Americans to fight. It was all the more important, he decided as a result, to build strong international support for his own war aims, which rested on an internationalist philosophy that became known as Wilsonianism.

The Fourteen Points

On January 8, 1918, Wilson appeared before a joint session of Congress to present the principles for which he claimed the nation was fighting. The war aims fell under fourteen headings, widely known as the Fourteen Points; but their essential elements clustered in three major categories. First, Wilson's proposals contained a series of specific recommendations for adjusting postwar boundaries and for establishing new nations to replace the defunct Austro-Hungarian and Ottoman empires, all reflecting his belief in the right of all peoples to self-determination. Second, it contained a set of general principles to govern international conduct in the future: freedom of the seas, open covenants instead of secret treaties, reductions in armaments, free trade, and impartial mediation of colonial claims. Finally, and most important of all to Wilson, there was a proposal for a league of nations that would help to implement these new principles and territorial adjustments, and serve to resolve future controversies. It would be, Wilson announced, "a general association of nations . . . formed under specific covenants for the purpose of affording mutual guarantees of political independence and territorial integrity to great and small states alike." Together, Wilson told Congress, the Fourteen Points would help make the world "fit to live in."

There were serious flaws in Wilson's proposals, a result more of what they omitted than of what they contained. He provided no formula for deciding how to implement the "national self-determination" he promised for subjugated peoples. He made no mention of the new Soviet government in Russia, even though its existence had struck fear in the hearts of all Western governments (and had helped spur Wilson to announce his own war aims in an effort to undercut Lenin's appeal). He said little about economic rivalries and their effect on international relations, even though it had been just such economic rivalries that had been in large part responsible for the war.

Nevertheless, Wilson's picture of the postwar world was a clear and eloquent expression of an international vision that would enchant not only much of his own generation but members of generations to come. It reflected his belief, strongly rooted in the ideas of progressivism, that the world was as capable of just and efficient government as were individual nations; that once the international community accepted certain basic principles of conduct, and once it constructed modern institutions to implement them, the human race could at last live in peace. The rule of law, he promised, would replace the rule of national passions and self-interested diplomacy.

The Fourteen Points came at a low moment in the war—before American troops had arrived in Europe in substantial numbers, at a time when many among the Allies believed the struggle might still be lost. It was greeted, therefore, with special yearning both in America and in Europe. The Allied leaders might have been cool toward the proposals, but there was an enthusiastic popular response among liberals, working people, and others throughout the world.

Early Obstacles

Wilson was confident, as the war neared its end, that this popular support would enable him to win Allied approval of his peace plan. He seemed at times to expect virtually to dictate a settlement. There were, however, ominous signs both at home and abroad that his path might be more difficult than he expected. In Europe, leaders of the Allied powers were marshaling their energies to resist him even before the armistice was signed. Most of them had long resented what they considered Wilson's tone of moral superiority. They had reacted unhappily when Wilson refused to make the United States their "ally" but had kept his distance as an "associate" of his European partners. They had been offended by his insistence on keeping American military forces separate from the Allied armies they were joining. Most of all, however, Britain and France, having suffered incalculable losses in their long years of war, and having stored up an enormous reserve of bitterness toward Germany as a result, were in no mood for a benign and generous peace. They were determined to gain something from the struggle to compensate them for the catastrophe they had suffered.

At the same time, Wilson was encountering problems at home. In 1918, with the war almost won, Wilson unwisely appealed to the American people to show their support for his peace plans by returning Democrats to Congress in the November elections. A Republican victory, he declared, would be "interpreted on the other side of the water as a repudiation of my leadership." Only days later, the Republicans captured majorities in both houses of Congress. Domestic economic troubles, more than international issues, had been the most important factor in the voting; but because of the president's ill-timed appeal, the results were interpreted both at home and abroad just as he had predicted: as a sign of his own political weakness.

The election fiasco contributed as well to another dangerous development: Wilson's alienation of the leaders of the Republican party. They were angry when he attempted to make the 1918 balloting a referendum on his war aims, especially since many Republicans had been loyally supporting the Fourteen Points. And Wilson further antagonized the Republican leadership when he refused to appoint any important Republicans to the negotiating team that would represent the United States in Paris, where a treaty was to be drafted. Although such men as Elihu Root and William Howard Taft had supported his war aims, Wilson named only one Republican—a little-known diplomat—to the group.

To the president, who was becoming almost obsessed with his own moral mission, such matters were unimportant. There would be only one member of the American negotiating team with any real authority: Wilson himself. And once he had produced a just and moral treaty, the weight of world and American opinion would compel his enemies to support him. Confident of his ability to create a new world, Woodrow Wilson stepped aboard the steamer *George Washington* and on December 3, 1918, sailed for Europe.

The Paris Peace Conference

Wilson arrived in Europe to a welcome such as few men in history have experienced. To the war-weary people of the Continent, he was nothing less than a savior, the man who would create a new and better world. And when he arrived in Paris on the afternoon of December 13, 1918, he saw clear evidence of their adulation in the form of the largest crowd in the history of France. It was the kind of demonstration that Wilson believed would make it impossible for other world leaders to oppose his peace plans. The negotiations themselves, however, proved less satisfying.

The meeting in Paris to draft a peace treaty was almost without precedent, and it entailed a sizable risk. International negotiations had traditionally been the province of diplomats; kings, presidents, and prime ministers had generally avoided direct encounters. In Paris there were four national leaders meeting face to face: David Lloyd George, the prime minister of Great Britain; Georges Clemenceau, the president of France; Vittorio Orlando, the prime minister of Italy; and Wilson, who hoped to dominate them all. Some of Wilson's advisers had warned him that if agreement could not be reached at the "summit," there would be nowhere else to go and that it would therefore be better to begin negotiations at a lower

The Big Four in Paris

Surface cordiality during the Paris Peace Conference disguised serious tensions among the so-called Big Four, the leaders of the victorious nations in World War I. As the conference progressed, the European leaders developed increasing resentment of Woodrow Wilson's high (and some thought sanctimonious) moral posture in the negotiations. Shown here in the library of the Hotel Crillon are, from left to right, Vittorio Orlando of Italy, David Lloyd-George of Great Britain, Georges Clemenceau of France, and Wilson. (The Bettmann Archive)

level. Wilson, however, was adamant; he alone would represent the United States.

Wilson's commitment to personal diplomacy encountered difficulties from the start. Heads of state in the glare of world publicity were, he soon found, reluctant to modify their nations' demands. The atmosphere of idealism he had sought to create was, therefore, competing with a spirit of national aggrandizement. There was, moreover, a pervasive sense of unease about the situation in eastern Europe, where starvation seemed imminent and the threat of communism menacing. Russia, whose new Bolshevik government was still fighting "White" counterrevolutionaries, was unrepresented in Paris; but the radical threat it seemed to pose to Western governments was never far from the minds of the delegates.

In this tense and often vindictive atmosphere, the Fourteen Points did not fare well. Wilson was unable to win approval of many of the broad principles he had espoused: freedom of the seas, which the British refused even to discuss; free trade; "open covenants openly arrived at" (the Paris negotiations themselves were often conducted in secret). Despite his support for "impartial mediation" of colonial claims, he was forced to accept a transfer of German colonies in the Pacific to Japan, to whom the British had promised them in exchange for Japanese assistance in the war. His pledge of "national self-determination" for all peoples suffered numerous assaults. Italy, for example, obtained new territory in which 200,000 Austrians lived, and then expressed outrage at not also receiving the port of Fiume,

which became part of the new nation of Yugoslavia. Poland received a corridor to the sea which ran through territory that was ethnically German. Economic and strategic demands were constantly coming into conflict with the principle of cultural nationalism.

Where the treaty departed most conspicuously from Wilson's ideals was on the question of reparations. As the conference began, the president was staunchly opposed to exacting reparations from the defeated Central Powers. The other Allied leaders, however, were intransigent, and slowly Wilson gave way. Although he resisted the demand of the French government that Germany be required to pay $200 billion to the Allies, he ultimately bowed to pressure and accepted the principle of reparations, the specific sum to be set later by a commission. The final figure, established in 1921, was $56 billion, supposedly to pay for civilian damages and military pensions. Although lower than some earlier demands, it was still far more than the crippled German economy could absorb. The reparations, combined with other territorial and economic penalties, constituted an effort to keep Germany not only weak but prostrate for the indefinite future. Never again, the Allied leaders believed, should the Germans be allowed to become powerful enough to threaten the peace of Europe.

Wilson did manage to win some important victories in Paris. He secured approval of a plan to place many former colonies in "trusteeship" to be supervised by the League of Nations—the so-called mandate system. He blocked a French proposal to break up western Germany into a group of smaller states, although in return he had to agree to a demilitarization and Allied occupation of the Rhineland. He oversaw the creation of the new nations of Yugoslavia and Czechoslovakia and the strengthening of Poland.

Such accomplishments were of secondary importance to Wilson, however, when compared with his most visible triumph: the creation of a permanent international organization to oversee world affairs and prevent future wars. On January 25, 1919, the Allies voted to accept the "covenant" of the League of Nations; and with that, Wilson believed, the peace treaty was transformed from a disappointment into a success. Whatever mistakes and inequities had emerged from the peace conference, he was convinced, could be corrected later by the League.

The covenant provided for an assembly of nations that would meet regularly to debate means of resolving disputes and protecting the peace. Authority to implement League decisions would rest with a nine-member Executive Council; the United States would be one of five permanent members of the council, along with Britain, France, Italy, and Japan. The covenant, like the larger treaty of which it was a part, left many questions unanswered, most notably how the League would enforce its decisions. Wilson, however, was confident that once established, the new organization would find suitable answers. The League of Nations, he believed, would become not only the centerpiece of the treaty, but the cornerstone of a new world order. Like other progressives considering other issues, the president was placing his hopes for the future in the process, rather than the substance, of international relations. If rational institutions could be established, then the actual conduct of world affairs would become rationalized as well.

The Ratification Battle

Wilson was well aware of the political obstacles awaiting him at home. Many Americans, accustomed to their nation's isolation from Europe, questioned the wisdom of this major new commitment to internationalism. Others had serious reservations about the specific features of the treaty and the covenant. On a brief trip to Washington in February 1919, during a recess in the peace conference, the president listened to harsh objections from members of the Senate and oth-

ers; and although he reacted angrily and haughtily to his critics, he returned to Europe and insisted on certain modifications in the covenant to satisfy them. The amendments provided that a nation need not accept a mandate (responsibility for overseeing a League territory) against its will, that a member could withdraw from the organization with two years' notice, and that the League would not infringe on the Monroe Doctrine. Beyond that, however, Wilson refused to go. When Colonel House, his close friend and trusted adviser, told him he must be prepared to compromise further, the president retorted sharply: "I have found that you get nothing in this world that is worth-while without fighting for it."

How bitter that fight would be soon became clear, for there was ample inflexibility and self-righteousness on both sides of the conflict. Wilson presented the Treaty of Versailles (which took its name from the palace outside Paris where the final negotiating sessions had taken place) to the Senate on July 10, 1919, asking: "Dare we reject it and break the heart of the world?" In the weeks that followed, he consistently refused to consider even the most innocuous compromise. (His deteriorating physical condition—he was suffering from hardening of the arteries and had apparently experienced something close to a stroke in Paris—may have contributed to his intransigence.)

The Senate, in the meantime, was raising a host of objections to the treaty. For the fourteen so-called "irreconcilables"—Western progressives who included Hiram Johnson, William Borah, and Robert La Follette—the Versailles agreement was totally unacceptable. The United States should never become embroiled in the sordid politics of Europe, they argued; not even the most generous compromise could have won their support for the League. Other opponents, with less fervent convictions, were more concerned with constructing a winning issue for the Republicans in 1920 and with embarrassing a president whom they had not yet forgiven for his political tactics in 1918. Most notable of these was Senator Henry Cabot Lodge of Massachusetts, the powerful chairman of the Foreign Relations Committee. A man of stunning arrogance and a close friend of Theodore Roosevelt (who had died early in 1919, spouting hatred of Wilson to the end), Lodge loathed the president with genuine passion. "I never thought I could hate a man as I hate Wilson," he once admitted. He used every possible tactic to obstruct, delay, and amend the treaty.

Public sentiment clearly favored ratification, so Lodge at first could do little more than play for time. When the document reached his committee, he spent two weeks slowly reading aloud each word of its 300 pages; then he held six weeks of public hearings to air the complaints of every disgruntled minority (Irish-Americans, for example, angry that the settlement made no provision for an independent Ireland). Gradually, Lodge's general opposition to the treaty crystallized into a series of "reservations"—amendments to the League covenant limiting American obligations to the organization.

Wilson might still have won approval at this point if he had agreed to some relatively minor changes in the language of the treaty. But the president refused to yield. The United States had a moral obligation, he claimed, to respect the terms of the agreement precisely as they stood. When one senator warned him that his position was becoming hopeless, that he would have to accept some of the Lodge reservations to have any hope of victory, Wilson retorted: "Never! Never! . . . I'll appeal to the country!"

Wilson's Ordeal

What followed was a political disaster and a personal tragedy. Against the stern warnings of his physician, Wilson decided to embark on a grueling, cross-country speaking tour to arouse public support for the treaty. For more than three weeks, he traveled by train from city to city, covering more than 8,000 miles, writing his own speeches as he went along, delivering them as often as four times a day, an hour at a time. He received little rest. In the beginning, the crowds were small and the speeches clumsy. As the tour progressed, however, both the size and the enthusiasm of the audiences grew; and Wilson's own eloquence and fervor increased. Had it been possible to sway the Senate through public opinion, the tour might have been a success. But it had long ago become plain that the opposition in Washington had little to do with popular sentiment. So the tour was not only an exhausting ordeal for Wilson but a futile one as well.

Finally, the president reached the end of his strength. After speaking at Pueblo, Colorado, on September 25, he collapsed with severe headaches. Canceling the rest of his itinerary, he rushed back to Washington, where, a few days later, he suffered a major stroke. For two weeks, he was close to death; for six weeks more, he was so seriously ill that he could conduct virtually no public business. His wife and his doctor formed an almost impenetrable barrier around him, shielding the president from any official pressures that might impede his recovery, preventing the public from receiving any accurate information about the gravity of his condition.

Wilson ultimately recovered fully enough to resume a limited official schedule, but he was essentially an invalid for the eighteen remaining months of his presidency. His left side was partially paralyzed; more important, his mental and emotional state was precarious and unstable. Like many stroke victims, he found it difficult to control his feelings, often weeping at the slightest provocation. And his condition only intensified what had already been his strong tendency to view public issues in moral terms and to resist any attempts at compromise. When the Senate Foreign Relations Committee finally reported the treaty, recommending nearly fifty amendments and reservations, Wilson refused to consider any of them. When the full Senate voted in November to accept fourteen of the reservations, Wilson gave stern directions to his Democratic allies: they must vote only for a treaty with no changes whatsoever; any other version must be defeated. On November 19, 1919, forty-two Democrats, following the president's instructions, joined with the thirteen Republican "irreconcilables" to reject the amended treaty. When the Senate voted on the original version without any reservations, thirty-eight senators, all but one a Democrat, voted to approve it; fifty-five voted no.

It did not seem so at the time, but Wilson's long and painful struggle for a new world order was now lost. There were sporadic efforts to revive the treaty over the next few months; on March 19, 1920, the day of the final vote, the amended version came as close as seven votes short of the necessary two-thirds majority. But Wilson's opposition to anything but the precise settlement he had negotiated in Paris remained too formidable an obstacle to surmount. He was, moreover, becoming convinced that the 1920 national election would serve as a "solemn referendum" on the League, that the force of public opinion could still compel ratification of the treaty. He even spoke, somewhat pathetically, of running for reelection himself. By now, however, public interest in the peace process had begun to fade—partly as a reaction against the tragic bitterness of the ratification fight, but more in response to a series of other crises.

A Society in Turmoil

Even during the Paris Peace Conference, the attention of many Americans was directed less toward international matters than toward events at home. There were increasing economic problems; there was widespread social unrest and violence; there was a growing fear of revolution. Some of this unease was a legacy of the almost hysterical social atmosphere of the war years; some of it was a response to issues that surfaced after the armistice. Whatever the reasons, however, America, in the immediate postwar years, was a turbulent place.

The Troubled Economy

Citizens of Washington, on the day after the armistice, found it impossible to place long-distance telephone calls. The lines were jammed with officials of the war agencies canceling government contracts. The fighting had ended sooner than anyone had anticipated; and without warning, without planning, the nation was launched into the difficult task of economic reconversion.

At first, to the surprise of almost everyone, the wartime boom continued. But it was a troubled and precarious prosperity, based largely on the lingering effects of the war (government deficit spending continued for some months after the armistice) and on sudden, temporary demands (a booming market for scarce consumer goods at home, a strong European market in the war-ravaged nations). It was accompanied, moreover, by raging inflation, a result in part of the precipitous abandonment of wartime price controls. Through most of 1919 and 1920, prices rose at an average of more than 15 percent a year.

Finally, late in 1920, the economic bubble burst, as many of the temporary forces that had created it disappeared and as inflation began killing the market for consumer goods. Between 1920 and 1921, the gross national product (GNP) declined nearly 10 percent; the index of wholesale prices fell from 227.9 to 150.6; 100,000 businesses went bankrupt; 453,000 farmers lost their land; nearly 5 million Americans lost their jobs.

Labor Unrest

Perhaps the most visible result of the postwar economic problems was a dramatic increase in labor unrest. American workers had generally refrained from strikes during the war. But with the fighting over, they were willing to be patient no longer. Many factors combined to produce labor discontent: the raging inflation, which wiped out what had been at best modest gains in wages during the war; concern about job security, heightened by the return to the labor force of hundreds of thousands of veterans; arduous working conditions—such as the perpetuation of the twelve-hour day in the steel industry. Employers aggravated the discontent by using the end of the war (and the end of government controls) as an excuse for taking back some of the benefits they had been forced to concede to workers in 1917 and 1918—most notably recognition of unions. Mine owners reneged on promised wage increases. In such a climate, conflict was virtually inevitable.

The year 1919, therefore, saw an unprecedented wave of strikes—more than 3,600 in all, involving over 4 million workers. Several of the strikes received wide national attention and raised particular alarm. In January, a walkout by shipyard workers in Seattle, Washington, evolved into a general strike that brought the entire city to a virtual standstill. The mayor requested and received the assistance of U.S. Marines to keep the city running, and eventually the strike failed. But the incident was widely cited as

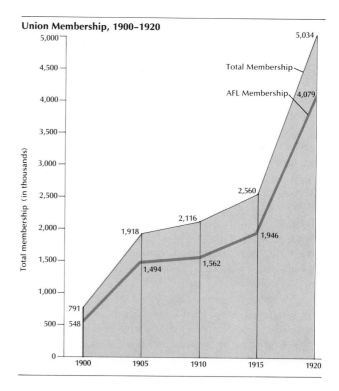

Union Membership, 1900–1920

The Great Steel Strike

Mounted police charge a group of striking steelworkers in Philadelphia during the steel strike of 1919. The strike lasted three and a half months and was the greatest single labor action in American history to that point. The strike centered around five demands: recognition of the steelworkers' union, the right of workers to bargain collectively with management through the union, abolition of the twelve-hour day, abolition of company unions, and wage increases. It finally dissolved in failure in early January 1920. (Culver Pictures)

evidence of the vulnerability of any community to disruption from labor agitation. In September, there was an even more alarming strike by the Boston police force, which was demanding recognition of its union. Seattle had remained generally calm; but with its police off the job, Boston erupted in violence and looting. Efforts by local businessmen, veterans, and college students to patrol the streets proved ineffective; and finally Governor Calvin Coolidge called in the National Guard to restore order. (His public statement at the time that "there is no right to strike against the public safety by anybody, anywhere, any time" attracted national acclaim.) Eventually, Boston officials dismissed the entire police force and hired a new one.

Of all the strikes of 1919, the greatest was the one, also in September, by 350,000 steelworkers in several Midwestern cities. They were demanding an eight-hour day and recognition of their union; but Elbert Gary, president of U.S. Steel, led the industry management in standing firm. The strike was long and bitter, marked by frequent violent conflicts, and climaxed by a riot in Gary, Indiana, in which eighteen strikers were killed. With the assistance of their own armed guards, steel executives managed to keep most plants running with nonunion labor; and by January, the strike had collapsed. Public opinion had turned so decisively against the strikers that Samuel Gompers and the AFL had finally and timidly repudiated them. It was a setback from which organized labor would not recover for more than a decade.

The Red Scare

The great wave of strikes seems notable in retrospect chiefly for its failure, for how it demonstrated the weakness of the American labor movement and the strength of the corporate establishment. To much of the public at the time, however, the industrial warfare appeared to be a frightening omen of social instability. More than that, it was a sign of a dangerous increase in domestic radicalism. The mayor of Seattle claimed that the general strike was an attempt by revolutionaries "to establish a Soviet government." The leaders of the steel industry insisted that "radical agitators" had stirred up trouble among their employees, who were, they claimed, content with things as they were.

This was in part because other evidence emerging at the same time seemed likewise to suggest the existence of a radical menace. The Russian Revolution of November 1917 had been disturbing enough by itself—so disturbing to Woodrow Wilson, in fact, that in 1918 he permitted the landing of American troops in the Soviet Union. They were there, he claimed, to help a group of 60,000 Czech soldiers trapped in Russia escape. But the Americans soon became involved, both directly and indirectly, in assisting the White Russians (the anti-Bolsheviks) in their fight against the new regime. Some American troops remained as late as April 1920. Wilson's actions failed to undermine Lenin's communist regime; they did, however, become a source of lasting Russian-American hostility and mistrust. American concerns about the communist threat grew even more intense in 1919 when the Soviet government announced the formation of the Communist International (or Comintern), whose purpose was to export revolution around the world.

In America, meanwhile, there was, in addition to the great number of imagined radicals, a modest number of real ones. And when they heard the frightened warnings that a revolution was imminent, they tended to believe them. Some engaged in sporadic acts of terrorism to speed the supposed crisis on its way. It was these small bands of radicals, presumably, who were responsible for a series of bombings in the spring of 1919 that produced great national alarm. In April, the post office intercepted several dozen parcels addressed to leading businessmen and politicians that were triggered to explode when opened; several reached their destinations, one of them severely injuring the servant of a Georgia public official. Two months later, eight bombs exploded in eight cities within minutes of one another, suggesting a nationwide conspiracy. One of them damaged the facade of Attorney General A. Mitchell Palmer's home in Washington.

In response to these and other provocations, the nation embarked on a crusade against radicalism that resembled in many ways its wartime crusade against disloyalty and dissent. Indeed, many of its targets were people whose principal "crime" had been their pacifism during the war. Nearly thirty states enacted new peacetime sedition laws imposing harsh penalties on those who promoted revolution; some 300 people went to jail as a result. Citizens in many communities removed "subversive" books from the shelves of libraries; administrators in some universities dismissed "radical" members from their faculties. A mob of off-duty soldiers in New York City ransacked the offices of a socialist newspaper and beat up its staff. Another mob, in Centralia, Washington, dragged an IWW agitator from jail and castrated him before hanging him from a bridge. Women's groups such as the National Consumers' League came under attack by antiradicals because so many feminists had opposed American intervention in the fighting in Europe.

Perhaps the greatest contribution to the Red Scare, as it later became known, came from the federal government. Attorney General Palmer ordered the Justice Department to take steps to quell what he later called the "blaze of revolution . . . sweeping over every American institution of law and order." On New Year's Day, 1920, he and his ambitious assistant, J. Edgar Hoover, orchestrated a series of raids on alleged radical centers throughout the country and arrested more than 6,000 people. The Palmer Raids had been intended to uncover huge caches of weapons and explosives; they netted a total of three pistols and no dynamite. Nevertheless, many of those arrested spent days and weeks in jail with no formal charges filed against them. Most were ultimately released, but about 500 who were not American citizens were summarily deported. For these violations of civil liberties, A. Mitchell Palmer, who harbored thinly concealed ambitions for the presidency, received a barrage of favorable publicity and enjoyed a period of intense (if brief) national popularity.

The ferocity of the Red Scare soon abated, but its effects lingered well into the 1920s, most notably in the celebrated case of Sacco and Vanzetti. In May of 1920, two Italian immigrants, Nicola Sacco and Bartolomeo Vanzetti, were charged with the murder of a paymaster in Braintree, Massachusetts. The ev-

Rallying to Save Sacco and Vanzetti
By the mid-1920s, the Sacco-Vanzetti case had aroused the anger of hundreds of thousands of Americans (and others around the world). The result was a series of large demonstrations attempting to pressure public officials in Massachusetts to stop the executions of the two Italian immigrants. (UPI/Bettmann Newsphotos)

idence against them was at best questionable; but because both men were confessed anarchists, they faced a widespread public presumption of guilt. The judge in their trial, Webster Thayer, was openly prejudiced; and it was perhaps unsurprising under the circumstances that they were convicted and sentenced to death. Over the next several years, however, public support for Sacco and Vanzetti grew to formidable proportions. But all requests for a new trial or a pardon were denied. On August 23, 1927, amid widespread protests around the world, Sacco and Vanzetti, still proclaiming their innocence, died in the electric chair. It was a cause that a generation of Americans never forgot, an episode that kept the bitter legacy of the Red Scare alive for many years.

Racial Unrest

No group suffered more from the inflamed climate of the postwar years than American blacks. To them more than to most, the war seemed to offer a major opportunity for social and economic advancement. Over 400,000 blacks served in the army, half of them in Europe, over 40,000 of them in combat. They had endured numerous indignities during the conflict. They had been placed in segregated units, under the command of white officers who often held them in contempt. They had put up with these humiliations, however, in the belief that their service would earn them the gratitude of the nation when they returned.

For many other American blacks, the war raised expectations in other ways. Nearly half a million migrated from the rural South to industrial cities (often enticed by Northern "labor agents," who offered them free transportation) in search of the factory jobs that the war was rapidly generating. This was the beginning of what became known as the "Great Migration." Almost overnight, the nation's racial demographics were transformed; suddenly there were enormous black communities crowding into the urban North, most of which had received only a relatively few blacks in the past. Just as black soldiers expected their military service to enhance their social status, so black factory workers regarded their move north as an escape from racial prejudice and an opportunity for economic gain.

Even before the war ended, however, the racial climate had begun to sour. In 1919, it turned savage and murderous. In the South, there was a sudden increase in lynchings: More than seventy blacks, some of them war veterans, died at the hands of white mobs in 1919 alone. In the North, conditions were in many respects even worse. When the war ended,

A Black Veteran

Residents of Harlem watch the 309th Colored Infantry parading through New York on the occasion of their return from Europe in March 1919. One little girl stares intently at a disabled veteran, still in uniform, who is standing somberly among the crowd—perhaps already aware of the disappointments awaiting other black veterans as they reentered civilian life. (UPI/Bettmann Newsphotos)

black factory workers faced widespread layoffs as returning white veterans displaced them from their jobs. Black veterans were cruelly disillusioned when they returned to find a society still unwilling to grant them any significant social or economic gains. These immediate economic problems helped inflame an already tense racial climate.

The Great Migration had thrown thousands of blacks into close proximity to Northern whites who were unfamiliar with and generally hostile to them. Many black migrants were unskilled and uneducated rural men and women, whose country ways made them seem even more alien to their new urban neighbors. As whites and blacks jostled together on the streets, trolleys, and subways of the overcrowded cities, tensions escalated; and as whites became convinced that black workers with their lower wage demands were hurting them economically, the animosity grew further. The result was a rash of urban disorders. As early as 1917, serious race riots had flared in cities as diverse as Houston, Philadelphia, and East St. Louis (where forty-nine people, thirty-nine of them blacks, were killed). In 1919, things grew worse. In Chicago, a black teen-ager swimming in Lake Michigan on a hot July day happened to drift toward a white beach. Whites on shore allegedly stoned him unconscious; he sank and drowned. The incident ignited the severe racial tensions in the city; for more than a week, Chicago was virtually at war. White mobs roamed into black neighborhoods, shooting, stabbing, and beating passers-by, destroying homes and properties. Blacks fought back and

Black Migration, 1910–1950

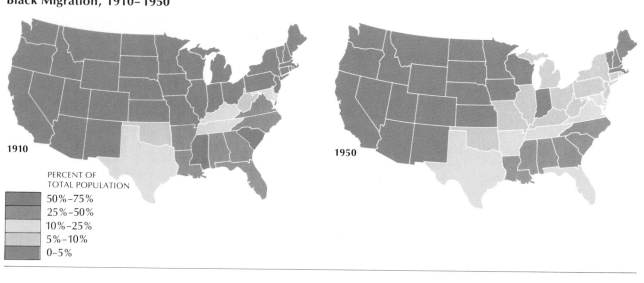

1910

PERCENT OF
TOTAL POPULATION

50%–75%
25%–50%
10%–25%
5%–10%
0–5%

1950

SIGNIFICANT EVENTS

1914	Austria invades Serbia; World War I begins
	Wilson declares American neutrality
1915	Wartime economic boom begins
	Great Migration of blacks to the North begins
	Germany begins submarine warfare
	Lusitania torpedoed
	Wilson launches preparedness program
1916	*Sussex* attacked
	Wilson reelected president
1917	Germany announces unrestricted submarine warfare
	Germans launch major offensive in France
	Zimmerman telegram
	Russian czar overthrown
	United States declares war on Central Powers
	Selective Service Act passed
	War Industries Board created
	Espionage Act passed
1918	Russia signs a separate peace with Central Powers
	Sedition Act passed
	U.S. troops repel Germans at Château Thierry and Rheims
	U.S. troops launch offensive in Argonne Forest

1918	Armistice ends war (November 11)
	Bernard Baruch takes over War Industries Board
	Wilson announces Fourteen Points
	American troops land in Soviet Union
	Republicans gain control of Congress
	Paris Peace Conference convenes
1919	Treaty of Versailles signed
	Senate proposes modifications to treaty
	Wilson suffers stroke
	Senate rejects treaty
	Economy experiences postwar inflation
	Race riots break out in Chicago and other cities
	Workers engage in steel strike and other unrest
	Soviet Union creates Comintern
	Theodore Roosevelt dies
1920	Economic recession disrupts economy
	United States reacts to "radicalism" with Palmer Raids and Red Scare
	Sacco and Vanzetti charged with murder
	Warren G. Harding elected president
1924	Woodrow Wilson dies
1927	Sacco and Vanzetti executed

---

inflicted violence and destruction of their own. In the end, 38 people died—15 whites and 23 blacks—and 537 were injured; over 1,000 people were left homeless. The Chicago riot was the worst but not the only racial violence during the so-called red summer of 1919; in all, 120 people died in such racial outbreaks in the space of little more than three months.

Blacks responded to the turmoil in various ways. Some were simply bewildered, deeply disillusioned at the shattering of their hopes, frightened by the savagery to which they were now exposed. Others were defiant. The NAACP urged blacks to fight back, to defend themselves and demand government protection. At the same time, a black Jamaican, Marcus Garvey, began to attract a wide American following with an ideology of black nationalism. Garvey encouraged American blacks to take pride in their own achievements and to develop an awareness of their African heritage—to reject assimilation into white society and develop pride in their own race.

Black culture was superior to white culture, Garvey told supporters; blacks should leave America and return to Africa, where they could create a new society of their own. At the peak of his popularity, Garvey claimed a following of 4 million. In the end, however, most blacks had little choice but to acquiesce in the social and economic subjugation being forced on them. Although they continued to make certain limited gains, it would be more than thirty years before they made any substantial progress toward social or economic equality.

The Retreat from Idealism

On August 26, 1920, after ratification by the necessary thirty-six states, the Nineteenth Amendment, guaranteeing women the right to vote, became part of the Constitution. To the woman suffrage movement, this was the culmination of nearly a century of struggle. To many progressives, who had seen the inclusion of women in the electorate as a way of bolstering their political strength, it seemed to promise new support for reform. The passage of the Nineteenth Amendment marked not the beginning of an era of reform, but the end of one.

The economic problems, the labor unrest, the fear of radicalism, the racial tensions—all had combined in the years immediately following the war to produce a general sense of disillusionment. By 1920, the American people seemed to have grown tired of idealism, reform, controversy, and instability. For decades, they had been living in turbulent times. Many now yearned for tranquility.

How many of them yearned for it became apparent in the election of 1920. Woodrow Wilson wanted the campaign to be a referendum on the League of Nations. The Democratic candidates, Ohio Governor James M. Cox and Assistant Secretary of the Navy Franklin D. Roosevelt, worked hard to keep Wilson's ideals alive. The Republican presidential nominee, however, offered a different vision. He was Warren Gamaliel Harding, an obscure Ohio senator whose only real asset seemed to be his pliability; party leaders had settled on him late one night in a "smoke-filled room" in a Chicago hotel, confident that he would do their bidding once in office. In the course of his brief and spiritless campaign, Harding offered no soaring ideals, only a vague and comfortable reassurance of stability, the promise of a return, as he later phrased it, to "normalcy." He won in a landslide. The Republican ticket received 61 percent of the popular vote and carried every state outside the South. The party made major gains in Congress as well.

Woodrow Wilson, for so long a symbol of the nation's ideals, stood repudiated. Early in 1921, he retired to a house on S Street in Washington, where for the next three years he lived quietly and inconspicuously. On February 3, 1924, he died.

SUGGESTED READINGS

The Road to War. Ernest R. May, *The World War and American Isolation* (1959); Patrick Devlin, *Too Proud to Fight: Woodrow Wilson's Neutrality* (1974); Jeffrey J. Sanford, *Wilsonian Maritime Diplomacy* (1978); Manfred Jonas, *The United States and Germany* (1984); John Milton Cooper, Jr., *The Vanity of Power: American Isolation and the First World War* (1969); Ross Gregory, *The Origins of American Intervention in the First World War* (1971); Daniel Smith, *Robert Lansing and American Neutrality* (1958); C. Roland Marchand, *The American Peace Movement and Social Reform* (1973); Thomas A. Bailey and Paul B. Ryan, *The Lusitania Disaster* (1975); Barbara Tuchman, *The Zimmerman Telegram* (1958).

Military Histories. Edward M. Coffman, *The War to End All Wars* (1969); Harvey A. De Weerd, *President Wilson Fights His War* (1968); A. E. Barbeau and Florette Henri, *The Unknown Soldiers: Black American Troops in World War I* (1974); J. Garry Clifford, *The Citizen Soldiers* (1972); Russell Weigley, *The American Way of War* (1973); Frank Freidel, *Over There* (1964); David Trask, *The United States in the Supreme War Council* (1961); John Whiteclay Chambers, *To Raise an Army* (1987); Donald Smythe, *Pershing* (1986).

Wartime Diplomacy. Arno Mayer, *Political Origins of the New Diplomacy* (1959); George F. Kennan, *Russia Leaves the War* (1956) and *Russia and the West Under Lenin and Stalin* (1961); W. B. Fowler, *British-American Relations, 1917–1918* (1969); Carl Parrini, *Heir to Empire: United States Economic Diplomacy, 1916–1923* (1969).

Domestic Impact. David M. Kennedy, *Over Here* (1980); Neil A. Wynn, *From Progressivism to Prosperity:* *World War I and American Society* (1986); Jordan Schwarz, *The Speculator* (1981); Robert D. Cuff, *The War Industries Board: Business-Government Relations During World War I* (1973); Valerie Jean Conner, *The National War Labor Board* (1983); Daniel Beaver, *Newton D. Baker and the American War Effort, 1917–1919* (1966); Seward Livermore, *Politics Is Adjourned* (1966); Charles Gilbert, *American Financing of World War I* (1970); George T. Blakey, *Historians on the Homefront* (1970); J. R. Mock and Cedric Larson, *Words That Won the War* (1939); Stephen Vaughn, *Holding Fast the Inner Lines: Democracy, Nationalism, and the Committee on Public Information* (1979); Richard Polenberg, *Fighting Faiths: The Abrams Case, the Supreme Court, and Free Speech* (1987); Zechariah Chaffee, Jr., *Free Speech in the United States* (1941); William Preston, Jr., *Aliens and Dissenters: Federal Suppression of Radicals, 1903–1933* (1963); H. C. Peterson and Gilbert Fite, *Opponents of War, 1917–1918* (1957); Harry N. Scheiber, *The Wilson Administration and Civil Liberties, 1917–1921* (1960); Donald Johnson, *The Challenge to America's Freedoms* (1963); John Higham, *Strangers in the Land* (1955); Frederick C. Luebke, *Bonds of Loyalty* (1974); Alfred W. Crosby, Jr., *Epidemic and Peace, 1918* (1976); Allan M. Brandt, *No Magic Bullet: A Social History of Venereal Disease in the United States* (1985); Maurine W. Greenwald, *Women, War, and Work* (1980); Barbara J. Steinson, *American Women's Activism in World War I* (1982); Carol S. Gruber, *Mars and Minerva* (1975); Charles Chatfield, *For Peace and Justice: Pacifism in America, 1914–1941* (1971); Sondra Herman, *Eleven Against War* (1969); Charles DeBenedettis, *Origins of the Modern Peace Movement* (1978); Otis L. Graham, Jr., *The Great Campaigns* (1971); Ellis W. Hawley, *The Great War and the Search for a Modern Order* (1979).

Wilson and the Peace.   Arthur S. Link, *Wilson the Diplomatist* (1957); N. Gordon Levin, Jr., *Woodrow Wilson and World Politics* (1968); Lloyd Ambrosius, *Woodrow Wilson and the American Diplomatic Tradition* (1987); Arthur Walworth, *Wilson and the Peacemakers* (1986); Robert H. Ferrell, *Woodrow Wilson and World War I* (1985); Arno Mayer, *Wilson vs. Lenin* (1959) and *Politics and Diplomacy of Peacemaking* (1965); Peter Filene, *Americans and the Soviet Experiment* (1967); Christopher Lasch, *The American Liberals and the Russian Revolution* (1962); Lloyd C. Gardner, *Safe for Democracy: The Anglo-American Response to Revolution, 1913–1923* (1984); Inga Floto, *Colonel House at Paris* (1980); John A. Garraty, *Henry Cabot Lodge* (1953); Ralph Stone, *The Irreconcilables* (1970); Warren F. Kuehl, *Seeking World Order* (1969); Denna Fleming, *The United States and the League of Nations* (1932); Arthur Link, *Woodrow Wilson: War, Revolution, and Peace* (1979); Gene Smith, *When the Cheering Stopped* (1964); George Kennan, *Decision to Intervene* (1958); John L. Gaddis, *Russia, the Soviet Union, and the United States* (1978); William C. Widenor, *Henry Cabot Lodge and the Search for an American Foreign Policy* (1980); Robert E. Osgood, *Ideals and Self-Interest in American Foreign Relations* (1953).

Postwar America.   Burl Noggle, *Into the Twenties* (1974); Stanley Coben, *A. Mitchell Palmer* (1963); Robert K. Murray, *The Red Scare* (1955); Roberta Strauss Feuerlicht, *Justice Crucified: The Story of Sacco and Vanzetti* (1977); David Brody, *Steelworkers in America* (1960) and *Labor in Crisis* (1965); Francis Russell, *A City in Terror* (1975); Robert L. Friedheim, *The Seattle General Strike* (1965); William M. Tuttle, Jr., *Race Riot: Chicago in the Red Summer of 1919* (1970); Elliott Rudwick, *Race Riot at East St. Louis* (1964); Robert V. Haynes, *A Night of Violence: The Houston Riot of 1917* (1976); Kenneth Kusmer, *A Ghetto Takes Shape* (1976); Alan Spear, *Black Chicago* (1967); David Cronon, *Black Moses* (1955); Amy J. Garvey, *Garvey and Garveyism* (1963); Judith Stein, *The World of Marcus Garvey* (1986); Theodore Vincent, *Black Power and the Garvey Movement* (1971); Wesley M. Bagby, Jr., *The Road to Normalcy* (1962); Stuart I. Rochester, *American Liberal Disillusionment in the Wake of World War I* (1977).

Saving the Forests

From the earliest days of European settlement in North America, people depended for their very survival on forests and the wood they contained. Lumber was essential not just for houses and farm buildings, but for fences and vehicles as well. Most Americans heated their homes with firewood until late in the nineteenth century, when coal finally gained ascendancy. The nation's early steam engines, including railroad locomotives and steamboats, were mainly fueled with wood, and iron was forged with charcoal. Tree bark was the major source of tannin, which was used in curing leather. When trees were burned to clear land, their ashes were turned into potash, which was used in making soap. Next to food, wood was the most basic resource in the American economy.

It was also the most wasted. The paradox of the American forest was that although its trees were essential to frontier settlements, they were also the chief obstacle those settlements faced. East of the Mississippi River, creating new farming communities usually meant cutting down forests. Although trees were cut for lumber and fuel, the main reason for their removal was simple clearing. To prepare land for crops, farmers "girdled" trees by removing a ring of bark from their base, stopping nutrients from reaching leaves and quickly killing them. With the leaves gone, sunlight reached the forest floor and corn could be planted amidst the stumps. In time, the dead trees could be cut and burned to fertilize the soil in preparation for plowing. Within a decade or two, few signs would remain that the new cornfield or pasture had ever been a forest at all.

The American forest was seemingly so endless that few worried about conserving it. As a result, the nineteenth-century inhabitants of the United States destroyed trees at an astonishing rate. By 1850, over 100 million acres of land—an area roughly the size of modern California—had been cleared since the time of the first colonists. Moreover, the rate of forest destruction was increasing, so that over the next ten years another 40 million acres were cleared—as if the entire state of Georgia had been deforested in a single decade. The 1850s saw fully one-third as many trees cut down as had been cleared during the preceding two centuries.

Although most Americans still regarded their forests as limitless, a few began to voice concern about what might happen if deforestation continued at this rapid

A Newly Cleared Farm, 1790s
Clearing forests was the essential first step toward establishing a new farm and thereby "improving" land. Farmers killed trees by stripping their bark and then planted crops amid the remaining stumps. Settlers used lumber to build houses and barns, erect fences, and supply fireplaces with fuel. (The Bettmann Archive)

pace. The most influential of these was a remarkable Vermonter named George Perkins Marsh. A scholar who read a dozen or more European languages, Marsh served as the U.S. ambassador to Turkey from 1849 to 1854, and to Italy from 1860 until his death in 1882. During his many years living on the shores of the Mediterranean, Marsh became interested in the environmental effects of classical civilizations. He gathered evidence from his travels and readings to demonstrate that deforestation had wreaked havoc with the earth.

The result was one of the most important books in the history of American conservation. Published in 1864, Marsh's *Man and Nature* warned of the dangerous consequences that might result if the United States did not stop destroying its forests. Losing access to lumber and fuel was the least of the problems he named. Much more important, he said, was the forest's role in stabilizing the natural environment. According to Marsh's theories, trees slowed the rate at which water drained from the soil. They prevented erosion, maintained soil fertility, and stabilized the flow of natural springs and streams. Removing them laid the groundwork for environmental disaster. In addition to promoting erosion, drying up rivers, and causing floods, forest destruction decreased the amount of water evaporating into the air and so reduced the total amount of rain that fell in an area. In the end, it would turn the landscape into a desert.

For proof of his claims, Marsh offered evidence from around the world. He described springs he had known as a child in Vermont that had since dried up as the trees around them were cleared. He listed floods that had become more frequent in lumbered areas of the northeastern United States. As evidence that cutting down forests could lead to desertification, he pointed to North Africa and the Middle East, holding them up as examples of what America might become if its citizens refused to heed his warnings. Only a strong commitment to conserving the forest and other natural resources could save the nation from its folly. "Man has too long forgotten," he wrote, "that the earth was given to him for usufruct alone, not for consumption, still less for profligate waste."

Marsh's book drew wide attention from scientists and politicians all over the United States. From the 1870s forward, increasing numbers of Americans began to express concern about the future of the nation's forests, and laws started to be passed

Early Lumbering in Michigan
As pioneer farmers moved west, a parallel migration of woodcutters took place. By the second half of the nineteenth century, pine lumber was being shipped by rail out of the north woods of Maine, New York, Michigan, and Minnesota to supply farmers on the treeless prairies with the construction materials and fuel that were essential to an agricultural economy. (The Bettmann Archive)

The Adirondack Forest: "Forever Wild"
By the closing decades of the nineteenth century, Americans had become so worried about the destruction of eastern forests that they increased their efforts to protect them. One important consequence was the creation of the Adirondack Forest Preserve in northern New York. A unique provision of the 1894 state constitution mandated that the Adirondacks were to be left "forever wild." (The Adirondack Museum, Blue Mountain Lake, N.Y.)

for their protection and restoration. Although Marsh's theories about the climatic influence of forests would eventually prove to be overstated or wrong, they became the basis for laws in the 1870s that offered free land on the Great Plains to settlers who planted trees there. Such stands of trees did not increase rainfall as the authors of the laws had hoped, but other early efforts at conserving forests were more effective.

The most important of these occurred in the state of New York. There, people worried that falling water levels in the Erie Canal might threaten the very lifeblood of the state's economy and might foreshadow problems for New York City's water supply as well. Following Marsh's theories, they attributed the problem to deforestation in the state's heavily lumbered Adirondack Mountains. Various citizens began to lobby for protection of the Adirondack forests, and the result was a law in 1885 creating a huge "forest reserve" there. To guarantee that the Adirondacks would remain "forever wild," defenders saw that a clause to this effect was inserted into the new state constitution in 1894.

The Adirondack Forest Reserve was a model for the nation as a whole. In 1891, seeking specifically to protect watersheds, Congress passed the Forest Reserve Act of 1891. It empowered the president to set aside any "public lands wholly or in part covered with timber or undergrowth," and became the basis for the National Forest system of the United States. Conservation of the forest reserves soon emerged as a chief political objective of Theodore Roosevelt's presidency. Saving the forests had become national policy, in no small measure because of the book Marsh had published four decades earlier.

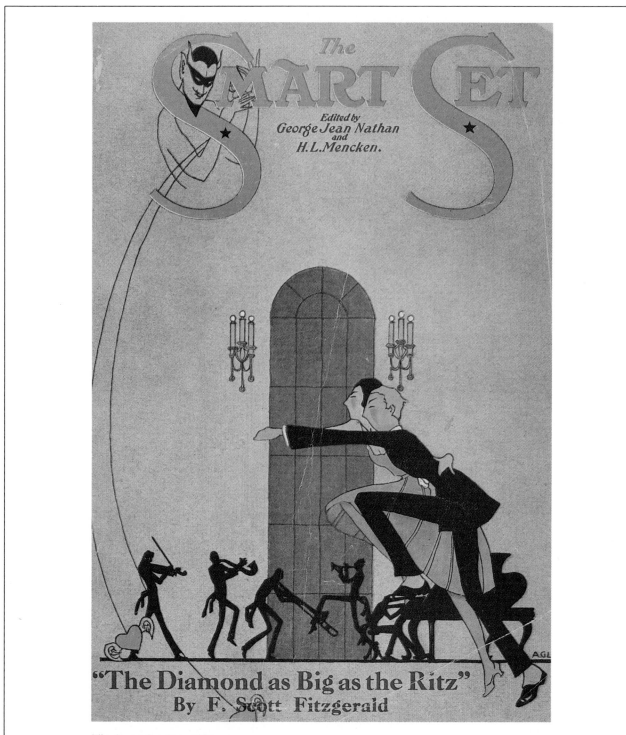

The Smart Set, June 1922
The Smart Set was one of the most fashionable magazines of the 1920s among young intellectuals and Bohemians and their admirers. Its editors, George Jean Nathan and H. L. Mencken, were leading exponents of the iconoclastic view of American society that characterized the intellectual life of the era. (*The Granger Collection*)

CHAPTER 24

⊠ ⚏ ⊠

The New Era

⊠ ⚏ ⊠

"America's present need is not heroics, but healing; not nostrums, but normalcy," Warren G. Harding, soon to become president of the United States, told the nation in 1920. "The world needs to be reminded that all human ills are not curable by legislation."

The 1920s have often been portrayed as an era fully in accord with Harding's conservative words—an era of affluence, conservatism, and cultural frivolity; the Roaring Twenties; the age of "normalcy." In reality, however, the decade was a time of significant, even dramatic social, economic, and political change. It was an era in which the American economy not only enjoyed spectacular growth but began to assume its modern forms of organization. It was a time in which American popular culture reshaped itself to reflect the realities of an urban, industrial, consumer-oriented society. And it was a decade in which American government, for all its conservatism, experimented with new approaches to public policy that helped pave the way for the important period of reform that was to follow. Contemporaries liked to refer to the 1920s as the "New Era"—an age in which America was becoming a modern nation. In many ways, it was an appropriate label.

At the same time, however, the decade saw the rise of a series of spirited and at times effective rebellions against the modern developments that were transforming American life. The intense cultural conflicts that characterized the 1920s were evidence of how much of American society remained unreconciled to the modernizing currents of the New Era.

The New Economy

Growth and affluence were the most striking and visible characteristics of American life in the 1920s; and the remarkable performance of the economy in those years lay at the heart of the many other social and cultural changes of the era. After the recession of 1921–1922, the United States began a long period of almost uninterrupted prosperity and economic expansion; indeed, American industry came to seem one of the wonders of the world. Less visible at the time, but equally significant, was the survival (and even extension) of serious inequalities and imbalances.

Economic Performance

No one could deny the remarkable, some believed miraculous, feats of the American economy in the 1920s. The nation's manufacturing output rose by more than 60 percent during the decade; the gross national product increased at an average of 5 percent a year; output per worker rose by more than 33 percent. Per capita income grew by a third. Inflation was negligible. A mild recession in 1923 momentarily interrupted the pattern of growth; but when it subsided early in 1924, the economy expanded with even greater vigor than before.

The economic boom was a result of many things. The most obvious immediate cause was the debilitation of Europe after World War I, leaving the United States for a time the only truly vigorous industrial power in the world. More important, however, was technology, and the great industrial expansion it made possible. The automobile industry, as a result of the development of the assembly line and other technological innovations, grew from a relatively modest size in the years before the war to become one of the most important forces in the nation's economy. Americans bought 1.5 million cars in 1921; in 1929 they purchased more than 5 million. Expansion in one industry meant, of course, expansion in others. Auto manufacturers purchased the products of steel, rubber, glass, and tool companies. Auto owners bought gasoline from the oil corporations. Road construction in response to the proliferation of motor vehicles became itself an important industry. The increased mobility that the automobile afforded increased the demand for suburban housing, fueling a boom in the construction industry.

Other new industries benefiting from technological innovations contributed as well to the economic growth. The new radio industry became a booming concern within a few years of its commercial debut in 1920. The motion picture industry expanded dramatically, especially after the introduction of sound in 1927. Aviation, electronics, and home appliances all helped sustain American economic growth. The invention of new plastics and synthetic fibers helped the chemical industry become an important force. Improved methods of extraction and transportation, as well as new production techniques, helped the aluminum and magnesium industries develop.

Cheap, readily available energy—from newly discovered oil reserves, from the expanded network of electric power, and from the nation's abundant coal fields—further enhanced the ability of industry to produce. Improvements in management techniques also played a role in increasing productivity. More and more industries were making deliberate efforts to improve the efficiency of their operations, some of them subscribing to the "scientific management" theories of Frederick Winslow Taylor.

Economic Organization

This quest for improved efficiency in the factory was only part of a larger trend. Large sectors of American business in the 1920s were making rapid strides toward national organization and consolidation. The

process had begun decades before; but the New Era witnessed an acceleration of such trends. By the end of the decade, 8,000 small mining and manufacturing companies had been swallowed up into larger combinations; 5,000 local utilities companies had disappeared, most of them into great holding companies. Local merchants foundered and vanished as national chain stores cornered more than a quarter of the nation's food, apparel, and general merchandise markets. In some industries, power resided in so few firms that competition had all but vanished. U.S. Steel, the nation's largest corporation, controlled its industry almost alone; its dominance was suggested by the widely accepted use of the term "Little Steel" to refer to all of its competitors.

This consolidation did not occur in all segments of the economy. Some industries—notably those dependent on large-scale mass production—seemed naturally to move toward concentrating production in a few large firms. Others—industries less dependent on technology, less susceptible to great economies of scale—proved resistant to consolidation, despite the efforts of many businessmen to promote it. By the end of the decade, it was becoming clear that the American economy would not be dominated by any single form of organization; that in some industries there would be a high degree of consolidation, while in others power would remain widely dispersed.

In those areas where industry did consolidate, new forms of corporate organization emerged to advance the trend. General Motors, which was by 1920 not only the largest automobile manufacturer but the fifth largest American corporation, was a classic example. Under the leadership of Alfred P. Sloan, GM developed a modern administrative system with an efficient divisional organization, which replaced a chaotic management structure. With the new system, not only was it easier for GM to control its many subsidiaries; it was also a simpler matter for it—and for the many other corporations that adopted similar administrative systems—to expand further.

Some industries less susceptible to domination by a few great corporations attempted to stabilize themselves not through consolidation, but through cooperation. An important vehicle was the trade association—a national organization created by various members of an industry to encourage coordination in production and marketing techniques. Trade associations often succeeded in limiting competition and stabilizing the market in industries dominated by a few large firms. But in industries such as cotton textiles, which remained highly decentralized, their effectiveness was limited.

The strenuous efforts by industrialists throughout the economy to find ways to curb competition through consolidation or cooperation reflected the survival of a basic corporate fear: the fear of overcapacity. Even in the booming 1920s, industrialists remembered how too-rapid expansion and overproduction had helped produce disastrous recessions in 1893, 1907, and 1920. The great dream of the New Era—a dream that remained unfulfilled—was to find a way to stabilize the economy so that such collapses would never occur again.

Labor's Dilemma

The remarkable economic growth was only one side of the American economy in the 1920s. Another was maldistribution of wealth and purchasing power, which persisted during the decade. New Era prosperity was real enough, but most of its benefits flowed to a minority of the population. More than two-thirds of the American people in 1929 lived at no better than what one study described as the "minimum comfort level." Half of those languished at or below the level of "subsistence and poverty." Large segments of society remained unable to organize, and they found themselves without sufficient power to protect their economic interests.

American labor experienced both the benefits and the deficiencies of the 1920s as much as any other group. On the one hand, most workers saw their standard of living rise during the decade; many enjoyed greatly improved working conditions and other benefits. Some employers in the 1920s, eager to avoid disruptive labor unrest and forestall the growth of unions, adopted paternalistic techniques that came to be known as "welfare capitalism." Industrialists such as Henry Ford shortened the work week for employees and instituted paid vacations. Manufacturers such as U.S. Steel spent millions of dollars installing safety devices and improving sanitation in the workplace. Most important, perhaps, many employers offered their workers substantial raises in pay and other financial benefits. By 1926, nearly 3 million industrial workers were eligible for pensions on retirement. In some companies, employees were permitted to buy stock at below-market value. When labor grievances surfaced despite these efforts, workers could voice them through the so-called company unions that were emerging in many industries—

The Steamfitter
Lewis Hine was among the first American photographers to recognize his craft as an art. In this photograph from the mid-1920s, Hine made a point that many other artists were making in other media: The rise of the machine could serve human beings, but might also bend them to its own needs. The steamfitter (carefully posed by the photographer) is forced to shape his body to the contours of his machine in order to complete his task. (International Museum of Photography at George Eastman House)

workers' councils and shop committees, organized by the corporations themselves. Welfare capitalism brought workers important economic benefits. It did not, however, offer employees any real control over their own fates. Company unions may have been psychologically comforting, but they were for the most part feeble vehicles for demanding benefits. In most companies, the workers' councils were forbidden to deal with questions of wages and hours. And welfare capitalism survived only as long as industry prospered. After 1929, with the economy in crisis, the entire system quickly collapsed.

Welfare capitalism affected only a relatively small number of workers, in any case. Most laborers worked for employers interested only in keeping their labor costs to a minimum, and workers as a whole, therefore, received wage increases that were proportionately far below the increases in corporate profits. Unskilled workers, in particular, saw their wages increase very slowly—by only a little over 2 percent between 1920 and 1926. Many workers, moreover, enjoyed no security in their jobs. Unemployment in the 1920s was lower than during most of the previous decades. But while historians and economists disagree about the levels of joblessness in these years, the most recent evidence suggests that an average of between 5 and 7 percent of nonfarm workers were unemployed between 1923 and 1929.

In the end, American workers remained in the 1920s a relatively impoverished and powerless group. Their wages rose; but the average annual income of a worker remained below $1,500 a year at a time when $1,800 was considered necessary to maintain a minimally decent standard of living. Only by relying on the earnings of several family members at once could many working-class families make ends meet. In some industries, such as coal mining and textiles, hours remained long and wages rose scarcely at all. Nor could workers do very much to counter the effects of technological unemployment. Total factory employment increased hardly at all during the 1920s, even while manufacturing output was soaring.

Some laborers continued to regard an effective union movement as the best hope for improving their position. But the New Era was a bleak time for labor organization. Part of the blame lay with the workers themselves, some of whom were seduced by the benefits of welfare capitalism and displayed no interest in organizing. Even more of the blame rested with the unions, which failed to adapt to the realities of the modern economy. The conservative American Federation of Labor remained wedded to the concept of the craft union, in which workers were organized on the basis of particular skills. In the meantime, a huge new segment of the work force was emerging: unskilled industrial workers, many of them immigrants from southern or eastern Europe. They received little sympathy or attention from the craft unions and found themselves, as a result, with no organizations to join. The AFL, moreover, remained painfully timid about supporting strikes throughout the 1920s—partly in reaction to the disastrous setbacks it had suffered in 1919. William Green, who became president of the organization in 1924, was committed to peaceful cooperation with employers and strident opposition to communism and socialism.

A growing proportion of the work force consisted of women, who were concentrated in what have since become known as "pink-collar" jobs—low-paying service occupations with many of the same problems as manufacturing employment. Large numbers of women worked as secretaries, salesclerks, and telephone operators, and in similar capacities. Because such positions were not technically industrial jobs, the AFL and other labor organizations were uninterested in organizing these workers.

Black workers were another group that could hope for little help from the unions. The half-million blacks who had migrated from the rural South into the cities during the Great Migration after 1914 constituted a small but significant proportion of the unskilled work force in industry; but as unskilled workers, they had few opportunities for union representation. The skilled crafts represented in the AFL often worked actively to exclude blacks from their trades and organizations. Most blacks worked in jobs in which the AFL took no interest at all—as janitors, dishwashers, and garbage collectors, and in other menial service jobs.

But however much the workers and unions themselves contributed to the weakness of the labor movement, corporate and government policies contributed more. If welfare capitalism was the carrot for inducing workers to accept the status quo, the antiunion policies of most industrialists constituted the stick. Corporate leaders worked hard after the turmoil of 1919 to spread the doctrine that unionism was somehow subversive and un-American, that a crucial element of democratic capitalism was the protection of the open shop (a shop in which no worker could be required to join a union). The crusade for the open shop, euphemistically titled the "American Plan," received the endorsement of the National Association of Manufacturers in 1920 and became a pretext for a harsh campaign of union busting across the country.

When such tactics proved insufficient to counter union power, government assistance often made the difference. In 1921, the Supreme Court upheld a ruling that declared picketing illegal and supported the right of lower courts to issue injunctions against strikers. In 1922, the Justice Department intervened to quell a strike by 400,000 railroad workers. In 1924, the courts refused protection to members of the United Mine Workers Union when mine owners launched a violent campaign in western Pennsylvania to drive the union from the coal fields.

As a result of these developments, union mem-

Farm Tenancy, 1910 and 1930

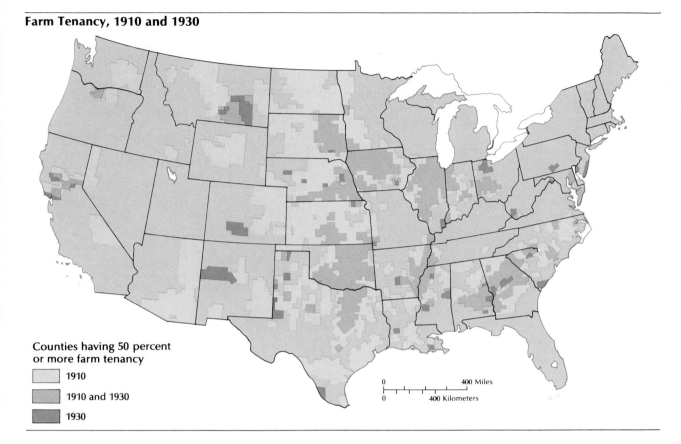

Counties having 50 percent or more farm tenancy
- 1910
- 1910 and 1930
- 1930

bership suffered a serious decline in the 1920s. Union membership as a whole fell from more than 5 million in 1920 to under 3 million in 1929. Not until the mid-1930s, when a combination of increased labor militancy and active government assistance added strength to the labor movement, would the antiunion syndrome be broken.

The Plight of the Farmer

Despite their other problems, many American workers gained at least an increase in income during the 1920s. In contrast, most American farmers of the New Era experienced only decline. Agriculture, like industry, was discovering the advantages of new technology for increasing production. The number of tractors at work on American farms, for example, quadrupled during the 1920s, helping to open 35 million new acres to cultivation. But while the increases in industrial production were matched by increases in consumer demand, the expansion of agricultural production was not. The European market for American foodstuffs contracted rapidly after the war, as European agriculture began to resume production. At the same time, domestic demand for food rose only slightly.

The result was a disastrous decline in food prices and a severe drop in income for farmers. The per capita annual income for Americans not engaged in agriculture in 1929 was $870. For farmers, it was $223. In 1920, farm income had been 15 percent of the national total; by 1929, it was 9 percent. More than 3 million people left agriculture altogether in the course of the decade. Of those who remained, many were forced into tenancy—losing ownership of their lands and having to rent instead from banks or other landlords.

In response, some farmers began to demand government relief. A few gravitated to such vaguely radical organizations as the Nonpartisan League of North Dakota or its successor, the Farmer-Labor party, which established a foothold as well in Minnesota and other Midwestern states. Most farmers, however, adopted a more moderate approach, agitating for some form of government price supports. Through such organizations as the Farm Bureau Federation, they put increasing pressure on Congress (where farmers continued to enjoy disproportionately high representation); and while reform sentiment in most other areas made little headway in the 1920s, the movement for agrarian reform rapidly gathered strength.

One price-raising scheme in particular came to dominate agrarian demands: the idea of parity. "Parity" referred to a price for crops determined by a complicated system. The parity price of agricultural goods was to reflect what farmers called a "fair exchange formula," which was based on the average price of the crop during the decade preceding the war (a good time for farmers) as compared with the general average of all prices during the same period. Its purpose was to ensure that farmers would earn back at least their production costs no matter how the national or world agricultural market might fluctuate. The government would guarantee parity to farmers in two ways: first, by maintaining a high tariff barrier against foreign competition, thus enabling American agriculture to sustain high prices at home; second, by buying up any surplus crops at parity and selling them abroad at whatever the world market would bring. An "equalization fee"—that is, a general tax on all crops—would compensate the government for any loss while spreading the burden evenly among all farmers.

The legislative expression of the demand for parity was the McNary-Haugen bill, named after its two principal sponsors in Congress and introduced repeatedly between 1924 and 1928. In 1924, a bill requiring parity only for grain failed in the House. Two years later, with cotton, tobacco, and rice added to win Southern support, the measure passed, only to fall victim to a veto by President Coolidge. In 1928, it won congressional approval again, only to succumb to another presidential veto. Although farmers had impressive political strength, as long as agrarian problems did not seem to affect the general prosperity there was little hope for reform.

Despite the inequities, and despite structural flaws that would ultimately contribute to the coming of a great crisis, the American economy in the 1920s did experience real and important growth. That growth helped spur the development of a host of new industries that would be of long-range importance to American economic health. It increased the size of the affluent middle class and thus helped create the

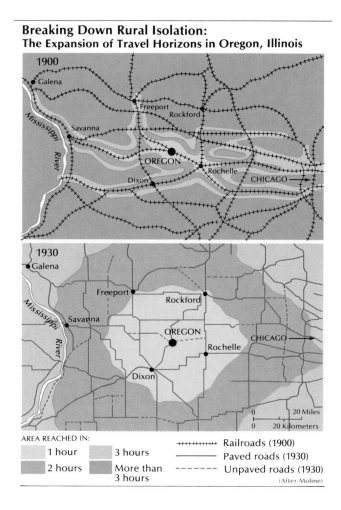

Breaking Down Rural Isolation:
The Expansion of Travel Horizons in Oregon, Illinois

AREA REACHED IN:

| 1 hour | 3 hours |
| 2 hours | More than 3 hours |

++++++++ Railroads (1900)
———— Paved roads (1930)
- - - - - Unpaved roads (1930)

(After Moline)

mass consumer market that would be so crucial to future economic growth. It changed the American landscape by producing new residential and travel patterns and, in the process, breaking down the isolation of rural areas. And it helped create the outlines of a new national culture, which reflected both the fruits of American industry and the growing importance of urban life.

The New Culture

Americans in the 1920s were in the midst of profound changes in the way they lived and thought. The nation's increasingly urban and consumer-oriented culture helped people in all regions to live their lives and perceive their world in increasingly

Urbanization in 1920

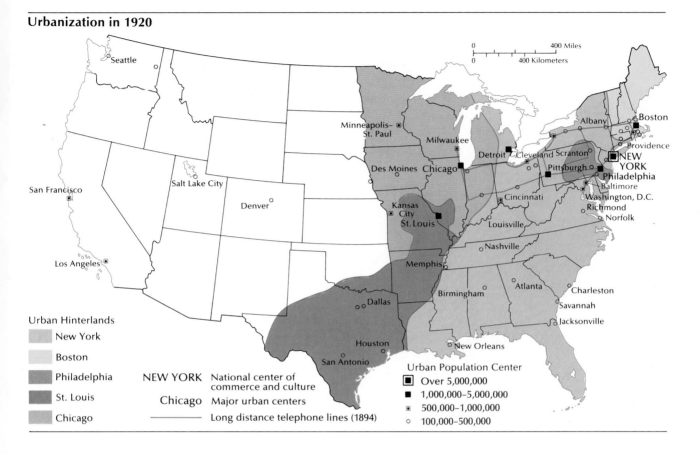

similar ways; and that same culture exposed them to a new set of values that reflected the prosperity and complexity of the modern economy.

Consumerism

The United States of the 1920s was for the first time becoming a true consumer society—a society in which not only the affluent but many ordinary men and women bought items not just because of need but for pleasure. What they bought, moreover, helped change the way they lived. Middle-class families rushed to purchase such new appliances as electric refrigerators, washing machines, and vacuum cleaners. Men and women wore wristwatches and smoked cigarettes. Women purchased cosmetics and mass-produced fashions. Americans in every part of the country ate commercially processed foods distributed nationally through chain stores and supermarkets. The clearest illustration of the new consumerism was the frenzied excitement with which Americans greeted the automobile, which was in the 1920s becoming more widely available and affordable than ever before. By the end of the decade, there were more than 30 million cars on American roads. Automobiles had, in the process, become not just a means of transportation but one of the first great national consumer obsessions.

No group was more aware of the emergence of consumerism (or more responsible for creating it) than a new and growing sector of the economy: the advertising industry. The first advertising and public relations firms (N. W. Ayer and J. Walter Thompson) had appeared well before World War I; but in the 1920s, partly as a result of techniques pioneered by wartime propaganda, advertising truly came of age. Publicists began to see themselves as more than purveyors of information. They viewed themselves, rather, as agents of the growing American economy; and they advertised products by attempting to invest them with glamour and prestige.

They also encouraged the public to absorb the values of promotion and salesmanship and to admire

It hasn't a single belt, fan or drain pipe....

It always works
perfectly and never
needs oiling . . . .

ONE of the first things that made me favor this General Electric Refrigerator was the fact that it was so unusually quiet. And I liked the idea of never having to oil it. All you have to do is plug it into an electric outlet . . . and then you can forget it. It hasn't any belts, drains, fans, or stuffing boxes.

But, of course, the thing that appeals to me most is the way it has cut my housekeeping job. I only market twice a week now, because I have plenty of space and just the right temperature to keep all sorts of foods in perfect condition.

We go away for week-ends without having to worry about ice. Everything is ready for use when we get back.

Cooking has become easier, too. Desserts, which used to be the most difficult part of the dinner to prepare, now are beautifully simple —and ever so much more attractive.

Expensive to run? Not a bit. It uses very little current to make all the ice we need and give us perfect refrigeration. And, do you know, it's quite remarkable the way the top

of this box never gets dusty. The circulation of air through those coils seems to drive the dust away.

✦ ✦ ✦ ✦

For fifteen years the vast laboratories of General Electric have been busy developing a simplified refrigerator that would be about

as easy to operate as an electric fan . . . and almost as portable. Four thousand models of nineteen different types were built, field-tested and improved before this new-day refrigerator was brought to its present simplicity and efficiency.

You will want to see the models. Let us send you the address of the dealer who has them on display and booklet 11-J, which is interesting and completely descriptive.

Electric Refrigeration Department
of General Electric Company

Hanna Building   Cleveland, Ohio

GE Refrigerator
GENERAL ELECTRIC

The New Kitchen and the New Woman
Manufacturers attempted to associate their new consumer appliances with the elegant life style of the affluent middle class. Advertisers tried to suggest that modern conveniences could liberate the "new woman" from the drudgery of housework and enable her to enter the glamorous world of society.   (Culver Pictures)

those who were effective "boosters" and publicists. One of the most successful books of the 1920s was the work of an advertising executive, Bruce Barton. In *The Man Nobody Knows,* Barton drew a portrait of Jesus Christ as not only a religious prophet but also a "super salesman" who "picked up twelve men from the bottom ranks of business and forged them into an organization that conquered the world." The parables, Barton argued, were "the most powerful advertisements of all time." Barton's message, a message apparently in tune with the new spirit of the consumer culture, was that Jesus had been a man concerned with living a full and rewarding life in this world; twentieth-century men and women should do

the same. "Life," Barton wrote on another occasion, "is meant to live and enjoy as you go along."

National Communications

The advertising industry could never have had the impact it did without the emergence of new vehicles of communication that made it possible to reach large audiences quickly and easily. Some of these vehicles were traditional media in changing guises. The number of local newspapers was shrinking rapidly; and those that survived often became members of great national chains—which meant that readers in widely scattered cities were reading the same material in their various newspapers. There was, as well, a growing number of national, mass-circulation magazines—*Time, Reader's Digest, The Saturday Evening Post,* and others—aimed at the widest possible audience. Fewer and fewer sources of information were servicing larger and larger groups of people.

Even more influential in shaping the popular culture of the 1920s was the growing popularity of the movies. Over 100 million people saw films in 1930, as compared to only 40 million in 1922. The addition of sound to motion pictures, beginning with the first "talkie" in 1927—*The Jazz Singer* with Al Jolson—created nationwide excitement. All across the nation, Americans were watching the same films, idolizing the same screen stars, and absorbing the same set of messages and values.

The most important communications vehicle of all, however, was the only one that was truly new to the 1920s: radio. The first commercial radio station in America, KDKA in Pittsburgh, began broadcasting on election night in 1920; and the first national radio network, the National Broadcasting Company, took form in 1927. By 1923, there were more than 500 radio stations, covering virtually every area of the country; by 1929, more than 12 million families owned radio sets. Broadcasting became the most important vehicle for linking the nation together, providing Americans everywhere with instant access to a common source of information and entertainment.

One result of the communications revolution was that America became in the 1920s a society in which fads and obsessions could emerge suddenly and powerfully. Radio helped elevate professional sports, and in particular professional baseball, from the level of limited local activities to that of a national craze. Men and women across the country enjoyed the same popular stunts—flagpole sitting, marathon dancing, goldfish swallowing. They shared an interest in national sensations, such as the famous murder trial of Leopold and Loeb or the tortuous progress of the Sacco-Vanzetti case. Frederick Lewis Allen, the celebrated chronicler of the 1920s, referred to the decade as the "ballyhoo years."

Modern Religion

It was not only fads that were engaging the attention of the nation. Americans in the 1920s were being exposed as well to a wide range of new standards of thought and behavior. Such changes affected some of the nation's most basic institutions, among them religion.

The scientific advances of the late nineteenth and early twentieth centuries had by the 1920s already produced profound changes in American theology. Liberal Protestant clergymen in particular had revised religious doctrine in an effort to reconcile traditional faith with the theories of Charles Darwin. Ministers in the progressive era had played an important role in promoting social issues; churches had become not only centers of worship but agents of reform. After World War I, the increasing secularism of American society worked even further changes on both religious faith and religious behavior. Theological modernists—among them Harry Emerson Fosdick and A. C. McGiffert—taught their followers to abandon some of the traditional tenets of evangelical Christianity (literal interpretation of the Bible, belief in the Trinity, attribution of human traits to the deity) and to accept a faith that would help individuals to live more fulfilling lives in the modern world. Critics considered the most advanced forms of this new, more secular Protestantism only one step removed from agnosticism.

The extremes of religious modernism found acceptance among only a relatively few people; Americans remained, by the standards of a later time, highly religious. Even so, changes in popular religious assumptions and patterns were widespread. The sociologists Robert and Helen Merrell Lynd discovered during a study of community life in Muncie, Indiana, for example, that while most people continued to attend church and express a belief in God, their faith was also experiencing important changes. Fewer people seemed to believe in hell; many admitted that they "think of Heaven less than they used to." "One infers," the Lynds reported in their famous study *Middletown* (1929), "that doubts and uneasiness among individuals may be greater than a generation ago."

The New Woman

The decade of the 1920s was particularly important in redefining the role of women, both within the family and within American society as a whole. The new economy and culture affected women in a number of ways. For many, it meant a turning away from the social activism of the progressive era and into a more personal, private search for satisfaction. For others, it meant new kinds of professional careers. And for still others, it meant political activism, an effort to keep feminism alive as a vital force after the victory of the suffrage crusade.

College-educated women were no longer pioneers in the 1920s. They were forming the second and third generations of graduates of women's or coeducational colleges and universities; and they were occasionally making their presence felt in professional areas that in the past they had rarely penetrated. A substantial group of women now attempted to combine marriage and careers; 25 percent of all woman workers were married in the 1920s. In the progressive era, middle-class women had generally had to choose between work and family. Still, professional opportunities remained limited by society's assumptions about what were suitable occupations for women. Although there were notable success stories about woman business executives, journalists, doctors, and lawyers, most professional women remained confined to such fields as fashion, education, social work, nursing, and the lower levels of business management.

The "new professional woman" was a vivid and widely publicized image in the 1920s. In reality, however, most employed women were nonprofessional, lower-class workers. Middle-class women, in the meantime, remained largely in the home. The number of employed women rose by several million in the 1920s, but the percentage of women employed rose scarcely at all. Society as a whole still had little tolerance for the idea of combining marriage and a career, and women who might otherwise have been inclined to try to do so found little support for their ambitions.

Yet the 1920s nevertheless constituted a new era for non-professional middle-class women. In particular, the decade saw a redefinition of motherhood. In the first years of the twentieth century, most Americans had believed that a woman's principal mission was to bear and raise children. They had assumed that women were uniquely and instinctively qualified for parenthood. After World War I, however, an influential group of psychologists—the "behaviorists," led by John B. Watson—began to challenge such assumptions. Maternal affection was not, they claimed, sufficient preparation for child rearing. Instead, mothers should rely on the advice and assistance of experts and professionals: doctors, nurses, and trained educators in nursery schools and kindergartens.

For many middle-class women, these changes devalued what had been an important and consuming activity. Motherhood and housekeeping continued to occupy a large proportion of most women's time (except for the affluent few able to afford servants). But it did not provide satisfaction commensurate with its costs. Some middle-class women turned to professional careers to find fulfillment. Many more, however, attempted to enrich their lives by devoting new attention to their roles as wives and companions. A woman's relationship with her husband assumed a greatly enhanced importance. She increasingly shared in her husband's social life; she devoted attention to cosmetics and seductive clothing in an effort to please her husband; she tried to prevent her children from interfering with the development of the marital relationship. Most of all, perhaps, a woman was encouraged to think of her sexual relationship with her husband not simply as a means of procreation, as earlier generations had been taught, but as an important and pleasurable experience in its own right, as the culmination of romantic love.

Thus it was that the 1920s saw important new advances in the creation of a national birth control movement. The pioneer of American birth-control was Margaret Sanger, who had spent most of her adult life promoting and publicizing new birth-control techniques (especially the diaphragm). At first, she had been principally concerned with birth control for working-class women, believing that large families were among the major causes of poverty and distress in poor communities. By the 1920s (partly because she had limited success in persuading working-class women to accept her teachings), she was becoming more concerned with persuading middle-class women of the benefits of birth control. Women should, Sanger argued, be free to enjoy the pleasures of sexual activity without relation to the bearing of children. Birth-control devices began to find a large market among middle-class women, even though some techniques remained illegal in many states (and abortion remained illegal nearly everywhere).

In some senses, these changes offered women a form of liberation. The declining birth rate meant that many women had to spend fewer years caring for children. The introduction of labor-saving appliances (washing machines, refrigerators, vacuum cleaners) in the home reduced some of the burdens of housework (although not always the amount of time devoted to housework, since standards of cleanliness rose simultaneously). Many middle-class women experienced a significant increase in their leisure time.

The new, more secular view of womanhood had effects on women beyond the middle class as well.

Some women concluded that in the "New Era" it was no longer necessary to maintain a rigid, Victorian female "respectability," that women could adopt less inhibited life styles. They could smoke, drink, dance, wear seductive clothes and make-up, and attend lively parties. The popular image of the "flapper"—the modern woman whose liberated life style found expression in dress, hair style, speech, and behavior—became one of the most widely discussed features of the era. The "flapper" life style had a particular impact on lower-middle-class and working-class single women, who were flocking to new jobs in industry and the service sector. (The young "Bohemian" women most often associated with the "flapper" image were, in fact, imitating a style that emerged among this larger group.) At night, such women flocked to clubs and dance halls in search of excitement and companionship. Yet despite the image of independence such life styles produced, single women living alone in cities—many of them far removed from their families and their original communities, most of them paid so little that they lived precariously—remained highly dependent on men and hence sexually vulnerable.

Even among more affluent middle-class women, the transformation of gender roles was not without cost. By placing more and more emphasis on their relationships with men, women were increasing their vulnerability to frustration and unhappiness when those relationships proved unsatisfactory. It was not surprising, perhaps, that the national divorce rate climbed dramatically in the 1920s; nor that many women who remained married experienced boredom and restlessness.

The realization that the "new woman" was as much myth as reality inspired some American feminists to continue their crusade for reform. The National Woman's party, under the leadership of Alice Paul, pressed onward with its campaign for the Equal Rights Amendment, although members found little support in Congress (and met continued resistance from other feminist groups such as the League of Women Voters). The campaign for the ERA made little headway in the 1920s.

Nevertheless, women's organizations and female political activities grew in many ways in the 1920s. The General Federation of Women's Clubs, the YWCA, and other female philanthropic and reform groups expanded. Responding to the suffrage victory, women organized the League of Women Voters and the women's auxiliaries of both the Democratic and Republican parties. Female-dominated consumer groups grew rapidly and increased the range and energy of their efforts.

Women activists won an apparent triumph in 1921 when they helped secure passage of a measure in keeping with the traditional feminist goal of securing "protective" legislation for women: the Sheppard-Towner Act. It provided federal funds to states to establish prenatal and child health care programs. From the start, however, it produced controversy both inside and outside women's ranks. Alice Paul and her supporters opposed the measure, complaining that it classified all women as mothers. Margaret Sanger complained that the new programs would discourage birth-control efforts. More important, the American Medical Association fought Sheppard-Towner, warning that it would introduce untrained outsiders into the health-care field, which should remain solely the province of doctors. In 1929, Congress terminated the program. On the whole, feminists willing to challenge the belief that women occupied a separate sphere and had special needs were relatively few in the 1920s. Most feminists continued to accept the idea of a distinct place for women in society; and with suffrage now achieved, many retreated from controversial political efforts and, like many other groups in American life, concentrated instead on working for personal fulfillment.

Education and Youth

The growing secularism of American culture and its expanding emphasis on training and expertise found reflection in the changing role of education, which was occupying an increasingly important role in the lives of American youth. The changes were evident in numerous ways. First, more people were going to school in the 1920s than ever before. High-school attendance more than doubled during the decade: from 2.2 million to over 5 million. Enrollment in colleges and universities increased threefold between 1900 and 1930, with much of that increase occurring after World War I. In 1918, there had been 600,000 college students; in 1930, there were 1.2 million, nearly 20 percent of the college-age population. Attendance was increasing as well at trade and vocational schools and in other institutions providing the specialized training that the modern economy demanded. Schools were, in addition, beginning to perform new and more varied functions. Instead of offering instruction simply in the traditional disciplines, they were providing training in modern technical skills: engineering, management, economics.

The growing importance of education was contributing as well to the emergence of a separate youth culture. The idea of adolescence as a distinct period in the life of an individual was for the most part new to the twentieth century. It was a result in some measure of the influence of Freudian psychology. But it was a result, too, of society's recognition that a more extended period of training and preparation was necessary before a young person was ready to move into the workplace. Schools and colleges provided adolescents with a setting in which they could develop their own social patterns, their own hobbies, their own interests and activities. An increasing number of students saw school as a place not just for academic training but for organized athletics, other extracurricular activities, clubs, and fraternities and sororities—that is, as an institution that allowed them to define themselves less in terms of their families and more in terms of their peer group.

The Decline of the "Self-Made Man"

The increasing importance of education and the changing nature of adolescence underscored one of the most important changes in American society: the gradual disappearance of the reality, and to some degree even of the ideal, of the "self-made man." The belief that any person could, simply through hard work and innate talent, achieve wealth and renown had always been largely a myth; but it had had enough basis in reality to remain a convincing myth for generations. By the 1920s, however, it was becoming difficult to believe any longer that success was possible without education and training. "The self-made manager in business," wrote *Century Magazine* in 1925, "is nearing the end of his road. He cannot escape the relentless pursuit of the same forces that have eliminated self-made lawyers and doctors and admirals."

The "Doom of the Self-Made Man," as *Century* described it, was a difficult development for Americans to accept. It suggested that individuals were no longer entirely in control of their own destinies, that a person's future depended in large part on factors over which he or she had only limited control. And like other changes of the decade, many Americans greeted this one with marked ambivalence. These mixed feelings were reflected in the identity of three men who became the most widely admired heroes of the New Era: Thomas Edison, the inventor of the

electric light bulb and many other technological marvels; Henry Ford, the creator of the assembly line and one of the founders of the automobile industry; and Charles Lindbergh, the first aviator to make a solo flight across the Atlantic Ocean. All received the adulation of much of the American public. Lindbergh, in particular, became a national hero the like of which the country had never seen before.

The reasons for their popularity indicated much about how Americans viewed the new epoch in which they were living. On the one hand, all three men represented the triumphs of the modern technological and industrial society. On the other hand, all three had risen to success without the benefit of formal education and at least in part through their own private efforts. They were, it seemed, genuinely self-made men. Even many Americans who were happily embracing a new society and a new culture were doing so without entirely diverting their gaze from a simpler past.

The Disenchanted

To a generation of artists and intellectuals coming of age in the 1920s, the new society in which they lived was even more disturbing. Many were experiencing a disenchantment with modern America so fundamental that they were often able to view it only with contempt. As a result, they adopted a role sharply different from that of most intellectuals of earlier eras. Rather than involving themselves with their society's popular or political culture and attempting to influence and reform the mass of their countrymen, they isolated themselves and embarked on a restless search for personal fulfillment. Gertrude Stein once referred to the young Americans emerging from World War I as a "Lost Generation." For many writers and intellectuals, at least, it was an apt description.

At the heart of the Lost Generation's critique of modern society was a sense of personal alienation, a belief that contemporary America no longer provided the individual with avenues by which he or she could achieve personal fulfillment. Modern life, they argued, was cold, impersonal, materialistic, and thus meaningless. The sensitive individual could find no happiness in the mainstream of American society.

This disillusionment had its roots in many things, but in nothing so deeply as the experience of World War I. To those who had fought in France and experienced the horror and savagery of modern warfare—and even to those who had not fought but who nevertheless had been aware of the appalling costs of the struggle—the aftermath of the conflict was shattering. Nothing, it seemed, had been gained. The war had been a fraud; the suffering and the dying had been in vain. Ernest Hemingway, one of the most celebrated (and most commercially successful) of the new breed of writers, expressed the generation's contempt for the war in his novel *A Farewell to Arms* (1929). Its hero, an American officer fighting in Europe, decides that there is no justification for his participation in the conflict and deserts the army with a nurse with whom he has fallen in love. Hemingway made it clear that he was to be admired for doing so.

At least equally dispiriting was the character of the nation these young intellectuals found on their return home at war's end. It was, they believed, a society utterly lacking in vision or idealism, obsessed with materialism, steeped in outmoded, priggish morality. Worst of all, it was one in which the individual had lost the ability to control his or her own fate. It was a sleek, new, industrialized and professionalized world that was organized in a dehumanizing way.

One result of this alienation was a series of savage critiques of modern society by a wide range of writers, some of whom were often described as the "debunkers." Particularly influential was the Baltimore journalist H. L. Mencken. In the pages of his magazines, first the *Smart Set* and later the *American Mercury,* he delighted in ridiculing everything Americans held dear: religion, politics, the arts, even democracy itself. He found it impossible to believe, he claimed, that "civilized life was possible under a democracy," because it was a form of government that placed power in the hands of the common people, whom he ridiculed as the "booboisie." When someone asked Mencken why he continued to live in a society he found so loathsome, he replied: "Why do people go to the zoo?"

Echoing Mencken's contempt was the novelist Sinclair Lewis, the first American to win a Nobel Prize in literature. In a series of savage novels, he lashed out at one aspect of modern society after another. In *Main Street* (1920), he satirized life in a small Midwestern town (much like the one in which he himself had grown up). In *Babbitt* (1922), he ridiculed life in the modern city. *Arrowsmith* (1925) attacked the medical profession (and by implication professionalism in general). *Elmer Gantry* (1927) satirized popular religion.

To those who held the values of their society in such contempt, the standard avenues for advance-

Mr. Lewis and the American Eagle
The novels of Sinclair Lewis were notable for their harsh, satiric tone. This 1931 caricature by William Cotton suggests the writer's dour view of his society. Lewis looks quizzically and somewhat sourly at an American eagle, just as he had looked with disdain on many aspects of national life in his writing. (Condé Nast Publications/ American Heritage)

ment held little appeal. Intellectuals of the 1920s turned their backs on the traditional goals of their parents. They claimed to reject the "success ethic" that they believed dominated American life (even though many of them hoped for—and a few achieved—commercial and critical success on their own terms). F. Scott Fitzgerald, whose first novel, *This Side of Paradise* (1920), established him as a spokesman for his generation, ridiculed the American obsession with material success in *The Great Gatsby* (1925). The novel's hero, Jay Gatsby, spends his life accumulating wealth and social prestige in order to win the woman he loves. The world to which he has aspired, however, turns out to be one of pretension, fraud, and cruelty, and Gatsby is ultimately destroyed by it. Fitzgerald and his intellectual contemporaries claimed to want nothing to do with conventional American society (although Fitzgerald himself seemed at the same time desperately to crave acceptance by it). They chose, instead, to search elsewhere for fulfillment.

A Refuge in Art

Their quest took them in several different directions, often at the same time. Many Lost Generation intellectuals left America to live in France, making Paris for a time a center of American artistic life. Some adopted hedonistic life styles, indulging in conspicuous debauchery: drinking, drugs, casual sex, wild parties, and a generally flamboyant way of life. (The publicity they received helped set the tone for other less alienated members of their generation, who began to imitate this uninhibited pursuit of pleasure.) Many intellectuals resorted to an outspoken self-absorption, openly repudiating any responsibility for anyone but themselves. For most of these young men and women, however, the only real refuge from the travails of modern society was art—not art for any social purpose, but art for its own sake. Only art, they argued, could allow them full individual expression; only the act of creation could offer them fulfillment.

The result of this quest for fulfillment through art was not, for the most part, personal satisfaction for the writers and artists involved. They remained throughout the 1920s a restless, usually unhappy generation, searching in vain for contentment. They did, however, produce a body of work that made the decade one of the great eras of American art. Most notable were the writers: Hemingway, Fitzgerald, Lewis, as well as others such as Thomas Wolfe, John Dos Passos, Ezra Pound, Gertrude Stein, Edna Ferber, and Eugene O'Neill—the first great American playwright and the only one ever to win a Nobel Prize. T. S. Eliot, a native of Boston who spent most of his adult life in England, led a generation of poets in breaking with the romanticism of the nineteenth century. His epic work *The Waste Land* (1922) brought to poetry much of the harsh tone of despair that was invading other areas of literature.

The writers of the 1920s were notable not only for the effectiveness of their critiques but for their success in pioneering new literary styles and techniques. Some incorporated Freudian psychology into their work, using literature to explore the workings of the psyche as well as the external actions of char-

acters. Others produced innovations in form, structure, and dialogue: Ernest Hemingway, with his spare, clean prose; Sinclair Lewis, with his biting satire; John Dos Passos, with his use of the techniques of journalism as well as of literature. The literature of the 1920s was escapist; but it was also intensely creative, even revolutionary.

Other Visions

Not all intellectuals of the 1920s, however, expressed such total alienation and despair. Some expressed reservations about their society not by withdrawing from it but by advocating reform. Older progressive theorists continued to expound the values they had celebrated in the years before the war. Thorstein Veblen, for example, attracted a wide audience with his argument that modern society should adopt the "discipline of the machine" and assign control to engineers and technocratic experts. John Dewey remained influential with his appeals for "practical" education and experimentation in social policy. Charles and Mary Beard, perhaps the most influential historians of their day, also promoted progressive principles. In their book *The Rise of American Civilization* (1927), they stressed economic factors in tracing the development of modern society and suggested the need for social and economic planning.

These progressive intellectuals were often harshly critical of the society of the 1920s; yet they were, indirectly, legitimizing some of its most important features. Society was not, they were saying, excessively routinized and disciplined, as members of the Lost Generation were complaining. If anything, it was not disciplined and organized enough.

To another group of intellectuals, the solution to contemporary problems lay neither in escapism nor in progressivism, but in an exploration of their own regional or cultural origins. In New York City, a new generation of black intellectuals created a flourishing Afro-American culture widely described as the "Harlem Renaissance." The Harlem poets, novelists, and artists drew heavily from their African roots in an effort to prove the richness of their own racial heritage (and not incidentally to prove to the white race that the black was worthy of respect). The poet Langston Hughes captured much of the spirit of the movement in a single sentence: "I am a Negro—and beautiful." Other black writers in Harlem and elsewhere—James Weldon Johnson, Countee Cullen,

Zora Neale Hurston, Claude McKay, Alain Locke—
as well as emerging black artists and musicians helped
to establish a thriving culture rooted in the historical
legacy of their race.

A similar effort was under way among an influential group of Southern intellectuals. Known first as
the "Fugitives" and later as the "Agrarians," these
young poets, novelists, and critics sought to counter
the depersonalization of industrial society by evoking
the strong rural traditions of their own region. In
their controversial manifesto *I'll Take My Stand*
(1930), a collection of twelve essays by twelve Southern intellectuals, they issued a simultaneously radical
and conservative appeal for a rejection of the doctrine
of "economic progress" and the spiritual debilitation
that had accompanied it. The supposedly "backward" South, they argued, could serve as a model for
a nation drunk with visions of limitless growth and
modernization.

One of the greatest of all American writers of
this era also expressed the Southerner's strong sense
of place and of cultural heritage. William Faulkner, in
a remarkable series of novels set in the fictional Mississippi county of Yoknapatawpha—*The Sound and
the Fury* (1929), *Absalom, Absalom* (1936), and
others—was, like many of his contemporaries, concerned with the problems of the individual seeking
fulfillment in the modern world. But unlike others,
he painstakingly re-created the bonds of region, family, and community, rather than expressing a detachment from society.

A Conflict of Cultures

The modern, secular culture of the 1920s was not
unchallenged. It grew up alongside an older, more
traditional culture, with which it continually and often bitterly competed. The new culture reflected the
values and aspirations of an affluent, largely urban
middle class, committed to a new, increasingly uninhibited life style, linked to a national cultural outlook. The older culture expressed the outlook of
generally less affluent, less urban, more provincial
Americans—men and women who continued to revere traditional values and customs and who feared
and resented the modernist threats to their way of
life. Beneath the apparent stability of the New Era
and its celebrated business civilization, therefore,
raged a series of harsh cultural controversies.

Prohibition

When the prohibition of the sale and manufacture of
alcohol went into effect in January 1920, it had the
support of most members of the middle class and
most of those who considered themselves progressives. Within a year, however, it had become clear
that the "noble experiment," as its defenders called
it, was not working well. Prohibition did substantially reduce drinking, at least in some regions of the
country. But it also produced conspicuous and grow-

Enforcing Prohibition
Despite widely publicized efforts by
federal agents to seize and destroy illegal alcohol, most Americans soon
came to view the "Noble Experiment"
of prohibition as a failure, impossible
to enforce effectively. (The Bettmann Archive)

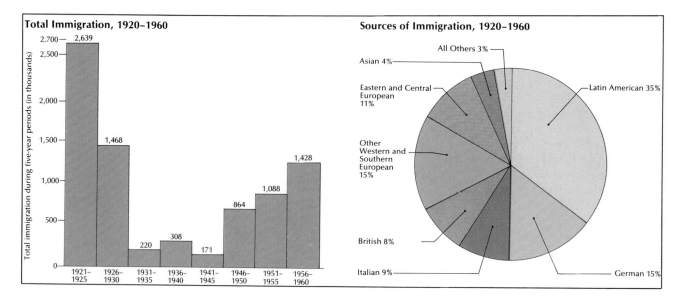

Total Immigration, 1920–1960

Total immigration during five-year periods (in thousands)

- 1921–1925: 2,639
- 1926–1930: 1,468
- 1931–1935: 220
- 1936–1940: 308
- 1941–1945: 171
- 1946–1950: 864
- 1951–1955: 1,088
- 1956–1960: 1,428

Sources of Immigration, 1920–1960

- Latin American 35%
- German 15%
- Italian 9%
- British 8%
- Other Western and Southern European 15%
- Eastern and Central European 11%
- Asian 4%
- All Others 3%

ing violations that made the law an almost immediate source of disillusionment and controversy.

The first prohibition commissioner promised rigorous enforcement of the new law. But violations were soon so rampant that the resources available to him proved ludicrously insufficient. The government hired only 1,500 agents to do the job. Before long, it was almost as easy to acquire illegal alcohol in much of the country as it had once been to acquire legal alcohol. More disturbing than the ineffectiveness of the law, however, was the role prohibition played in stimulating organized crime. An enormous, lucrative industry was now barred to legitimate businessmen; underworld figures quickly and decisively took it over. In Chicago, Al Capone built a criminal empire based largely on illegal alcohol. He guarded it against interlopers with an army of as many as 1,000 gunmen, whose zealousness contributed to the violent deaths of more than 250 people in the city between 1920 and 1927. Other regions produced gangsters and gang wars of their own. Prohibition, in short, became not only a national joke but a national scandal.

Nevertheless, it survived. The middle-class progressives who had originally supported prohibition may have lost interest; but an enormous constituency of provincial, largely rural, overwhelmingly Protestant Americans continued vehemently to defend it. To them, drinking and the general sinfulness with which they associated it were an assault on their conservative code of morality. Prohibition had always carried implications far beyond the issue of drinking itself. It represented the effort of an older America to

maintain its dominance in a society that was moving forward in spite of it.

As the decade proceeded, opponents of prohibition (or "wets," as they came to be known) gained steadily in influence. Not until 1933, however, when the Great Depression added weight to their appeals, were they finally able effectively to challenge the "drys" and win repeal of the Eighteenth Amendment.

Nativism and the Klan

Hostility to immigrants was not new to the 1920s. Nor was it restricted to the defenders of traditional, provincial society. Like prohibition (which was itself in part a result of old-stock Americans trying to discipline the new immigrant population), agitation for a curb on immigration had begun in the nineteenth century; and like prohibition, it had gathered strength in the years before the war largely because of the support of middle-class progressives. Such concerns had not been sufficient in the first years of the century to win passage of curbs on immigration; but when in the years immediately following the war immigration began to be associated with radicalism, popular sentiment on behalf of restriction grew rapidly.

In 1921, Congress passed an emergency immigration act, establishing a quota system by which annual immigration from any country could not exceed 3 percent of the number of persons of that nationality who had been in the United States in 1910. The new law cut immigration from 800,000 to

The Ku Klux Klan in Washington, 1926
So powerful was the Ku Klux Klan in the mid-1920s that its members felt emboldened to march openly and defiantly down the streets of major cities—even down Pennsylvania Avenue in Washington, in the shadow of the Capitol of the United States.   (Culver Pictures)

300,000 in any single year, but the nativists remained unsatisfied. In 1924, Congress enacted an even harsher law: the National Origins Act, which banned immigration from east Asia entirely (deeply angering Japan) and reduced the quota for Europeans from 3 to 2 percent. The quota would be based, moreover, not on the 1910 census, but on the census of 1890, a year in which there had been far fewer southern and eastern Europeans in the country. What immigration there was, in other words, would heavily favor northwestern Europeans—people of "Nordic" or "Teutonic" stock. The 1924 act cut the yearly flow almost in half, to 164,000. Five years later, a further restriction set a rigid limit of 150,000 immigrants a year. In the years that followed, immigration officials seldom permitted even half that number actually to enter the country.

The legislative expression of nativism reflected largely the doctrines of progressivism, even if a harsh and narrow progressivism. Restricting immigration, its proponents believed, would contribute to the efficient and productive operation of society. There were, however, other expressions of nativism that reflected very different sentiments. To defenders of an older, more provincial America, the growth of large communities of foreign peoples, alien in their speech, their habits, and their values, came to seem a direct threat to their own embattled way of life. This provincial nativism took a number of forms. But the most prominent was the rebirth of the Ku Klux Klan as a major force in American society.

The first Klan was the product of the years after the Civil War. That organization had died in the 1870s. But in 1915, shortly after the premiere of the film *The Birth of a Nation,* which celebrated the early Klan, a new group of Southerners gathered on Stone Mountain outside Atlanta, Georgia, to establish a modern version of the society. At first the new Klan, like the old, was largely concerned with intimidating blacks, who were, Klan leader William J. Simmons claimed, becoming dangerously insubordinate. After World War I, however, concern about blacks gradually became secondary to concern about Catholics, Jews, and foreigners. The Klan would devote itself, its leaders proclaimed, to purging American life of impure, alien influences.

It was then that the modern Klan experienced its greatest growth. Membership in the small towns and rural areas of the South soon expanded dramatically. More significantly, the Klan was now spreading northward, establishing a strong foothold particularly in the industrial cities of the Midwest. By 1923, there were reportedly 3 million members; by 1924, 4 million.

In some communities, where Klan leaders came from the most "respectable" segments of society, the organization operated much like a fraternal society, engaging in nothing more dangerous than occasional political pronouncements. Most Klan units (or "klaverns") tried to present themselves as patriots and defenders of morality. Many established women's and even children's auxiliaries to demonstrate their commitment to the family. Often, however, the Klan also operated as a brutal, even violent, opponent of "alien" groups and as a defender of traditional, fundamentalist morality. Klansmen systematically terrorized blacks, Jews, Catholics, and foreigners: boycotting their businesses, threatening their families, and attempting to drive them out of their communities. Occasionally, they resorted to violence: public whipping, tarring and feathering, arson, and lynching.

What the Klan most deeply feared, it soon became clear, was not simply "foreign" or "racially impure" groups; it was anyone who posed a challenge to traditional values. Klansmen persecuted not only immigrants and blacks but those white Protestants they considered guilty of irreligion, sexual promiscuity, or drunkenness. The Klan worked to enforce prohibition; it attempted to institute compulsory Bible reading in schools; it worked to punish divorce. The Ku Klux Klan, in short, was fighting not just to preserve racial homogeneity but to defend a traditional culture against the values and morals of modernity. The organization itself began to decline in influence after 1925, when a series of internal power struggles and several sordid scandals discredited some of its most important leaders. The issues it had raised, however, retained strength among some Americans for many years.

Religious Fundamentalism

Another great cultural controversy of the 1920s revealed even more starkly the growing gulf between the new culture and the old. It was a bitter conflict over questions of religious doctrine and, even more, over the place of religion in contemporary society. By 1921, American Protestantism was already divided into two warring camps. On one side stood the modernists: mostly urban, middle-class people who had attempted to adapt religion to the teachings of modern science and to the realities of their modern, secular society. On the other side stood the fundamentalists: provincial, largely (although not exclusively) rural men and women, fighting to preserve traditional faith and to maintain the centrality of religion in American life. The fundamentalists looked with horror at the new morality of the modern city. (They formed a substantial part of the constituency defending prohibition in the 1920s.) They expressed outrage at the abandonment of traditional beliefs in the face of scientific discoveries, insisting that the Bible was to be interpreted literally. Above all, they opposed the teachings of Charles Darwin, who had openly challenged the biblical story of the Creation. Human beings had not evolved from lower orders of animals, the fundamentalists insisted. They had been created by God, as described in Genesis.

Fundamentalism had been growing in strength in American Protestantism since the 1870s, but for many years it had found expression chiefly within its existing denominations. But it was also an evangelical movement, interested in spreading the doctrine to new groups. Evangelists, among them the celebrated Billy Sunday, traveled from state to state (particularly in the South and parts of the West) attracting huge crowds to their revival meetings.

Protestant modernists looked on much of this activity with condescension and amusement. But by the mid-1920s evangelical fundamentalism was beginning to take a form that many regarded with real alarm. In a number of states, fundamentalists were gaining political strength with their demands for legislation to forbid the teaching of evolution in the public schools. To the modernists, such laws were almost unthinkable. Darwinism had to them become indisputable scientific fact; to forbid the teaching of evolution, they believed, would be like forbidding teachers to tell their students that the world was round. Yet they watched with incredulity as one state after another seriously considered the fundamentalist demands. In Tennessee in March 1925, the legislature actually adopted a measure making it illegal for any public school teacher "to teach any theory that denies the story of the divine creation of man as taught in the Bible."

The result was one of the most celebrated events of the decade. When the American Civil Liberties

Bryan and Darrow in Dayton
Clarence Darrow (left) and William Jennings Bryan pose for photographers during the 1925 Scopes trial in Dayton, Tennessee. Both men are in shirt sleeves; Bryan is tieless and holding a fan—testimony to the intense heat that plagued the large crowd throughout the trial. (Brown Brothers)

Union offered free counsel to any Tennessee educator willing to defy the law and become the defendant in a test case, a twenty-four-year-old biology teacher in the town of Dayton, John T. Scopes, arranged to have himself arrested. And when the ACLU decided to send the famous attorney Clarence Darrow to defend Scopes, the aging William Jennings Bryan (now an important fundamentalist spokesman) announced that he would travel to Dayton to assist the prosecution. Journalists from across the country, among them H. L. Mencken, flocked to Tennessee to cover the trial, which opened in an almost circus atmosphere. Scopes had, of course, clearly violated the law; and a verdict of guilty was a foregone conclusion, especially when the judge refused to permit "expert" testimony by evolution scholars. Scopes was fined $100, and the case was ultimately dismissed in a higher court because of a technicality. Nevertheless, Darrow scored an important victory for the modernists by calling Bryan himself to the stand to testify as an "expert on the Bible." In the course of the cross-examination, which was broadcast by radio to much of the nation, Darrow made Bryan's stubborn defense of biblical truths appear increasingly foolish and finally tricked him into admitting the possibility that not all religious dogma was subject to only one interpretation.

The Scopes trial did not resolve the conflict between fundamentalists and modernists. Indeed, four other states soon proceeded to pass antievolution laws of their own. The issue continued to smolder for decades until it emerged once again in the form of the creationist movement of the early 1980s.

The Democrats' Ordeal

The anguish of provincial Americans attempting to defend an embattled way of life proved particularly troubling to the Democratic party, which suffered a serious debilitation during the 1920s as a result of tensions between its urban and rural factions. Far more than the Republicans, the Democrats consisted of a diverse coalition of interest groups, linked to the party more by local tradition than common commitment. Among those interest groups were prohibitionists, Klansmen, and fundamentalists on one side and Catholics, urban workers, and immigrants on the other.

In 1924, the tensions between them proved devastating. At the Democratic National Convention in New York that summer, bitter conflict broke out over the platform when the party's urban wing attempted to win approval of planks calling for the repeal of prohibition and a denunciation of the Klan. Both planks narrowly failed. More serious was a deadlock in the balloting for a presidential candidate. Urban Democrats supported Alfred E. Smith, the

Election of 1928   (56.9% of electorate voting)

	ELECTORAL VOTE	POPULAR VOTE (%)
Herbert Hoover (Republican)	444	21,391,381 (58.2)
Alfred E. Smith (Democratic)	87	15,016,443 (40.9)
Norman Thomas (Socialist)	—	267,835 (0.7)
Other parties (Socialist Workers, Prohibition)	—	62,890

Irish Catholic Tammanyite who had risen to become a progressive governor of New York; rural Democrats backed William McAdoo, Woodrow Wilson's Treasury secretary (and son-in-law), later to become a senator from California, who had skillfully positioned himself to win the support of Southern and Western delegates suspicious of Tammany Hall and modern urban life. For 103 ballots, the convention dragged on, until finally both Smith and McAdoo withdrew and the party settled on a compromise: the corporate lawyer John W. Davis.

In the years that followed, the schism between the two wings of the party continued to plague the Democrats. In 1928, Al Smith finally did manage to secure his party's nomination for president after another acrimonious but less prolonged battle. He was not, however, able to unite his divided party—largely because of strong anti-Catholic sentiment throughout much of Protestant America, especially in the South. As a result, he became the first Democrat since the Civil War to fail to carry the South. (He won only six of the eleven states of the former Confederacy.) Elsewhere, although he did well in the large cities, he carried no states at all except Massachusetts and Rhode Island.

Smith's opponent, and the victor in the presidential election, was a man who perhaps more than any other personified the modern, prosperous, middle-class society of the New Era: Herbert Hoover. The business civilization of the 1920s, with its new institutions, fashions, and values, continued to arouse the animosity of large portions of the population; but the majority of the American people appeared to have accepted and approved it. In 1928, at least, the New Era seemed to be permanently enshrined—as the success of the Republican party, its political embodiment, suggested.

Republican Government

For twelve years, beginning in 1921, both the presidency and the Congress rested securely in the hands of the Republican party—a party in which the power of reformers had greatly dwindled since the heyday of progressivism before the war. For most of those years, the federal government expressed a profound conservatism and enjoyed a warm and supportive relationship with the American business community. Yet the government of the New Era was more than the passive, pliant instrument that critics often described. It attempted to serve in many respects as an active agent of economic change.

Warren G. Harding

Nothing seemed more clearly to illustrate the death of crusading idealism in the 1920s than the characters of the two men who served as president during most of the decade: Warren G. Harding and Calvin Coolidge.

Harding was elected to the presidency in 1920, having spent many years in public life doing little of note. He had advanced from the editorship of a newspaper in his hometown of Marion, Ohio, to the state legislature by virtue of his good looks, polished speaking style, and geniality. He had moved from there to the United States Senate as a result of his party regularity. And he had moved from there to the White House as a result of a political agreement among leaders of his party who considered him, as one noted, a "good second-rater."

The new president had few illusions about his own qualifications for office. Awed by his new responsibilities, he made sincere efforts to perform them with distinction. He appointed capable men to the most important cabinet offices; he attempted to stabilize the nation's troubled foreign policy; and he displayed on occasion a vigorous humanity, as when he pardoned socialist Eugene V. Debs in 1921. Even as he attempted to rise to his office, however, he exhibited a sense of bafflement about his situation, as if he recognized his own unfitness. "I am a man of limited talents from a small town," he reportedly told friends on one occasion. "I don't seem to grasp that I am President." Unsurprisingly, perhaps, Harding soon found himself delegating much of his authority to others: to members of his cabinet, to political cronies, to Congress, to party leaders. In the meantime, the nation's press, overwhelmingly Republican, was portraying him as a wise and effective leader.

Harding's personal weaknesses as much as his political naïveté finally resulted in his demise. He realized the importance of capable subordinates in an administration in which the president himself was reluctant to act. At the same time, however, he lacked the strength to abandon the party hacks who had helped create his political success. One of them, Harry Daugherty, the Ohio party boss principally responsible for his meteoric political ascent, he appointed attorney general. Another, Albert B. Fall, he made secretary of the interior. Members of the so-called Ohio Gang filled important offices throughout the administration. It was widely known within the government that the president's cronies led active, illicit social lives; that they gathered nightly at the famous "House on K Street" to drink illegal alcohol, play poker, and entertain attractive women; and that the president himself often joined in all these activities.

The Harding Scandals

What remained for a time generally unknown was that Daugherty, Fall, and others were engaged in a widespread pattern of fraud and corruption. They sold government offices and favors, bribed congressmen and senators to support legislation favorable to their interests, and plundered the agencies and departments in which they worked.

The most spectacular scandal involved the rich naval oil reserves at Teapot Dome, Wyoming, and Elk Hills, California. At the urging of Albert Fall, Harding transferred control of those reserves from the Navy Department to the Interior Department. Fall then secretly leased them to two wealthy businessmen and received in return nearly half a million dollars in "loans" to ease his private financial troubles. Fall was ultimately convicted of bribery and sentenced to a year in prison; Harry Daugherty barely avoided a similar fate for his part in another scandal.

For several years, apparently, Harding himself remained generally unaware of the corruption infecting his administration. But by the summer of 1923, only months before Senate investigations and press revelations brought the scandals to light, he began to realize how desperate his situation had become. Tired and depressed, the president left Washington for a speaking tour in the West and a visit to Alaska. In Seattle late in July, he suffered severe pain, which his doctors wrongly diagnosed as food poisoning. A few days later, he seemed to rally and traveled on to San Francisco. There, on August 2, he died. He had suffered two major heart attacks.

Calvin Coolidge

In many ways, Calvin Coolidge, who succeeded to the presidency on the death of Harding, was utterly different from his predecessor. Where Harding was genial and garrulous, Coolidge was dour and silent. Where Harding embraced a loose, even debauched life style, Coolidge lived soberly and puritanically. And while Harding was if not personally corrupt then at least tolerant of corruption in others, Coolidge was honest beyond reproach. The image of stolid respectability he projected was so unassailable that the Republican party managed to avoid any lasting damage from Teapot Dome and related scandals. In other ways, however, Harding and Coolidge were similar figures. Both represented an unadventurous conservatism. Both took an essentially passive approach to their office.

Like Harding, Coolidge rose to the presidency on the basis of few substantive accomplishments. During his years in Massachusetts politics, he had won a reputation as a safe, trustworthy figure; and largely as a result of that, he had become governor in 1919. His response to the Boston police strike won him national attention and, in 1920, his party's vice-presidential nomination. Three years later, news of Harding's death reached him in Vermont; and there, by the light of a kerosene lamp on a kitchen table, he took the oath of office from his father, a justice of the peace.

"Thar She Blows!!!" Political Cartoon, 1924
This cartoon appeared in March 1924 on the cover of *Life* magazine (which was unrelated to the later photo magazine of the same name). It suggests Americans' preoccupation with the Teapot Dome scandal and other corruption in the Harding administration. Fortunately for the Republicans, Harding's successor, Calvin Coolidge, projected an image of total honesty and averted lasting damage to the party.   (Culver Pictures)

If anything, Coolidge was an even less active president than Harding, partly as a result of his conviction that government should interfere as little as possible in the life of the nation and partly as a result of his own personal lassitude. He took long naps every afternoon. He kept official appointments to a minimum and engaged in little conversation with those who did manage to see him. He proposed no significant legislation and took little part in the running of the nation's foreign policy. "He aspired," wrote one of his contemporaries, "to become the least President the country ever had. He attained his desire."

In 1924, he received his party's presidential nomination virtually unopposed. Running against Democrat John W. Davis, a wealthy corporate lawyer who had served in the Wilson administration, he won a comfortable victory: 54 percent of the popular vote and 382 of the 531 electoral votes. Robert La Follette, the candidate of the reincarnated Progressive party, received 16 percent of the popular vote but carried only his home state of Wisconsin. Coolidge's nega-

tive, custodial view of the presidency clearly had the approval of the majority of the American people. Four years later, it still did. The president could probably have won renomination and reelection easily in 1928. Instead, in characteristically laconic fashion, he walked into a press room one day and handed each reporter a slip of paper containing a single sentence: "I do not choose to run for president in 1928."

Government and Business

The story of Harding and Coolidge themselves, however, is only a part—and by no means the most important part—of the story of their administrations. However inert the New Era presidents may have been, much of the federal government was working effectively and efficiently during the 1920s to adapt public policy to the widely accepted goal of the time: helping business and industry operate with maximum efficiency and productivity. The close relationship between the private sector and the federal government that had been forged during World War I continued.

In the executive branch, the most active efforts came from members of the cabinet. Secretary of the Treasury Andrew Mellon, the wealthy steel and aluminum tycoon, became one of the most influential and respected figures in government. He devoted himself to working for substantial reductions in taxes on corporate profits and personal incomes and inheritances. Largely because of his efforts, Congress cut them all by more than half. The result, Mellon claimed, would be to stimulate investment and ensure general prosperity. Mellon also worked closely with President Coolidge after 1924 on a series of measures to trim dramatically the already modest federal budget. The administration even managed to retire half the nation's World War I debt.

The most prominent member of the cabinet was Commerce Secretary Herbert Hoover, who considered himself, and was considered by others, a notable progressive. Hoover was active in so many areas that he often seemed to be running the entire federal government single-handedly. He used his position to promote a better organized, more efficient national economy. Only thus, he claimed, could the nation hope to fulfill its most important task: the elimination of poverty.

During his eight years in the Commerce Department, Hoover constantly encouraged voluntary cooperation in the private sector as the best avenue to stability. But the idea of voluntarism did not require

Calvin Coolidge at Leisure
Although Coolidge was a silent man of
simple tastes, he was not really an out-
doorsman, despite his efforts to appear
so. He is shown here fishing in
Simsbury, Connecticut, carefully at-
tired in suit, tie, hat, and rubber boots.
(The Bettmann Archive)

the government to remain passive; on the contrary,
public institutions, Hoover believed, had a duty to
play an active role in creating the new, cooperative
order. Above all, he became the champion of the
concept of business associationalism—a concept that
envisioned the creation of national organizations of
businessmen in particular industries. Through such
trade associations, private entrepreneurs could,
Hoover believed, stabilize their industries and promote efficiency in production and marketing.
Hoover strongly resisted those who urged that the
government sanction collusion among manufacturers
to fix prices, arguing that competition was essential
to a prosperous economy. He did, however, believe
that shared information and limited cooperation
would keep that competition from becoming destructive and thus improve the strength of the economy as a whole.

The Supreme Court in the 1920s further confirmed the business orientation of the federal government, particularly after the appointment of William
Howard Taft as chief justice in 1921. The Court
struck down federal legislation regulating child labor
(*Bailey* v. *Drexel Furniture Company,* 1922); it nulli-

fied a minimum wage law for women in the District
of Columbia (*Adkins* v. *Children's Hospital,* 1923); and
it sanctioned the creation of trade associations, ruling
in *United States* v. *Maple Flooring Association* (1925)
that such organizations did not violate antitrust statutes as long as some competition survived within an
industry. Five years earlier, in *United States* v. *U.S.
Steel,* the Court had applied the same doctrine to the
monopolistic United States Steel Corporation; there
was no illegal "restraint of trade," it ruled, as long as
U.S. Steel continued to face any competition, no
matter how slight.

The probusiness policies of the Republican administrations were not without their critics. There
survived in Congress throughout the 1920s a large
and influential group of progressive reformers of the
old school, whose vision of public power as an antidote to private privilege remained very much alive.
They continued to criticize the monopolistic practices of big business, to attack government's alliance
with the corporate community, to decry social injustices, and to call for economic reform. Occasionally,
they were able to mobilize enough support to win
congressional approval of progressive legislation,

SIGNIFICANT EVENTS

1920	First commercial radio station, KDKA in Pittsburgh, begins broadcasting (p. 707)		**1925**	Congress passes McNary-Haugen bill; Coolidge vetoes it (p. 704)
	Prohibition begins (p. 713)			F. Scott Fitzgerald publishes *The Great Gatsby* (p. 711)
	Warren G. Harding elected president (p. 718)			Scopes trial in Dayton, Tennessee (p. 717)
1921	Sheppard-Towner Act funds maternity assistance (p. 709)		**1927**	First sound motion picture, *The Jazz Singer*, released (p. 707)
	Nation experiences economic recession (p. 699)			Charles Lindbergh makes solo transatlantic flight (p. 710)
1922	Sinclair Lewis publishes *Babbitt* (p. 711)		**1928**	Congress passes, and Coolidge vetoes, McNary-Haugen bill again (p. 704)
1923	Nation experiences mild recession (p. 699)			Herbert Hoover elected president (p. 722)
	Harding dies; Calvin Coolidge becomes president (p. 719)		**1929**	Sheppard-Towner program terminated (p. 709)
	Teapot Dome and other scandals revealed (p. 719)			William Faulkner publishes *The Sound and the Fury* (p. 713)
	Ku Klux Klan reaches peak membership (p. 716)			
1924	National Origins Act passed (p. 715)			
	Coolidge elected president (p. 720)			

most notably the McNary-Haugen plan for farmers and an ambitious proposal to use federal funds to develop public electric power projects on the Tennessee River at Muscle Shoals. But the progressive reformers were clearly no longer the dominant force in American political life. When the president vetoed the legislation they had promoted, as he almost always did, they lacked the strength to override him.

Some progressives derived encouragement from the results of the 1928 election, which elevated Herbert Hoover—widely regarded as the most progressive member of the Harding and Coolidge administrations—to the presidency. Hoover easily defeated Alfred Smith, the Democratic candidate. And he entered office promising bold new efforts to solve the nation's remaining economic problems. But Hoover had scant opportunity to demonstrate his commitment to extending American prosperity to those who had not shared in it. Because less than a year after his inauguration, the nation plunged into the severest and most prolonged economic crisis in its history—a crisis that brought many of the optimistic assumptions of the New Era crashing down and launched the nation into a period of unprecedented social innovation and reform.

SUGGESTED READINGS

General Studies. William Leuchtenburg, *The Perils of Prosperity* (1958); John D. Hicks, *Republican Ascendancy* (1960); Arthur M. Schlesinger, Jr., *The Crisis of the Old Order* (1957); Ellis Hawley, *The Great War and the Search for a Modern Order* (1979); Donald R. McCoy, *Coming of Age* (1973); Geoffrey Perrett, *America in the Twenties* (1982); John Braeman (ed.), *Change and Continuity in Twentieth Century America: The 1920s* (1968); Frederick Lewis Allen, *Only Yesterday* (1931); Isabel Leighton (ed.), *The Aspirin Age* (1949); George Soule, *Prosperity Decade* (1947).

Labor, Agriculture, and Economic Growth. George Soule, *Prosperity Decade* (1947); Alfred Chandler, *Strategy and Structure* (1962); Louis Galambos, *Competition and Co-operation* (1966); Louis Galambos and Joseph Pratt, *The Rise of the Corporate Commonwealth: U.S. Business and Public Policy in the Twentieth Century* (1988); Irving Bernstein, *The Lean Years: A History of the American Worker, 1920–1933* (1960); David Brody, *Steelworkers in America* (1960) and *Workers in Industrial America* (1980); Gerald Zahavi, *Workers, Managers, and Welfare Capitalism: The Shoe Workers and Tanners of Endicott Johnson, 1890–1950* (1988); Peter Gottlieb, *Making Their Own Way: Southern Blacks' Migration to Pittsburgh, 1916–1930* (1987); Robert Zieger, *Republicans and Labor* (1969); Leslie Woodcock, *Wage-Earning Women* (1979); Gilbert Fite, *George Peek and the Fight for Farm Parity* (1954); Theodore Saloutos and John D. Hicks, *Twentieth Century Populism* (1951).

The New Culture. Daniel Boorstin, *The Americans: The Democratic Experience* (1973); Ed Cray, *Chrome Colossus* (1980); James J. Flink, *The Car Culture* (1975) and *The Automobile Age* (1988); Bernard A. Weisberger, *The Dream Maker* (1979); Lary May, *Screening Out the Past* (1980); Robert Sklar, *Movie-Made America* (1975); Sumiko Higashi, *Virgins, Vamps, and Flappers: The American Silent Movie Heroine* (1978); Susan J. Douglas, *Inventing American Broadcasting* (1987); Erik Barnouw, *A Tower of Babel*, vol. 1 (1966); Philip T. Rosen, *The Modern Stentors: Radio Broadcasting and the Federal Government, 1920–1933* (1980); Robert Creamer, *Babe* (1974); Kenneth S. Davis, *The Hero: Charles A. Lindbergh* (1959); Randy Roberts, *Jack Dempsey, The Manassa Mauler* (1979); Robert Lynd and Helen Lynd, *Middletown* (1929); Paul Carter, *Another Part of the Twenties* (1977); Kathy Peiss, *Cheap Amusements* (1986); Stewart Ewen, *Captains of Consciousness* (1976); Roland Marchand, *Advertising the American Dream* (1985); Stephen Fox, *The Mirror Makers: A History of American Advertising and Its Creators* (1984); Daniel Horowitz, *The Morality of Spending: Attitudes Toward the Consumer Society in America, 1875–1940* (1985); Ronald Edsforth, *Class Conflict and Cultural Consensus: The Making of a Mass Consumer Society: Flint, Michigan* (1987).

Women and Family. Nancy Cott, *The Grounding of American Feminism* (1987); Alice Kessler-Harris, *Out to Work: A History of Wage-Earning Women in America* (1982); Sheila Rothman, *Woman's Proper Place* (1978); William Chafe, *The American Woman* (1972); Linda Gordon, *Woman's Body, Woman's Right* (1976); J. Stanley Lemons, *The Woman Citizen: Social Feminism in the 1920s* (1973); Winifred Wandersee, *Women's Work and Family Values, 1920–1940* (1981); Susan Strasser, *Never Done: A History of American Housework* (1982); Ruth Schwarz Cowan, *More Work for Mother* (1983); Lois Scharf, *To Work and to Wed* (1980); Paula Fass, *The Damned and Beautiful* (1977); Helen Lefkowitz Horowitz, *Campus Life: Undergraduate Cultures from the End of the Eighteenth Century to the Present* (1987); Susan Porter Benson, *Counter Cultures* (1986); Lois Banner, *American Beauty* (1983); John D'Emilio and Estelle B. Friedman, *Intimate Matters: A History of Sexuality in America* (1988); W. Andrew Achenbaum, *Shades of Gray: Old Age, American Values, and Federal Policies Since 1920* (1983); Howard P. Chudacoff, *How Old Are You? Age in American Culture* (1989); David H. Fischer, *Growing Old in America* (1977).

Intellectuals. Roderick Nash, *The Nervous Generation: American Thought, 1917–1930* (1969); Robert Crunden, *From Self to Society: Transition in American Thought, 1919–1941* (1972); Malcolm Cowley, *Exiles Return* (1934); Edmund Wilson, *The Twenties* (1975); Frederick J. Hoffman,

The Twenties (1949); Nathan I. Huggins, *Harlem Renaissance* (1971); David L. Lewis, *When Harlem Was in Vogue* (1981); Kenneth M. Wheeler and Virginia L. Lussier, eds., *Women and the Arts and the 1920s in Paris and New York* (1982); John Stewart, *The Burden of Time* (1965); Cleanth Brooks, *William Faulkner: The Yoknapatawpha Country* (1963).

Cultural Conflict. Norman Clark, *Deliver Us from Evil* (1976); Joseph Gusfeld, *Symbolic Crusade* (1963); Andrew Sinclair, *The Era of Excess* (1962); Herbert Asbury, *The Great Illusion* (1950); John Higham, *Strangers in the Land* (1963); David Chalmers, *Hooded Americanism* (1965); Kenneth Jackson, *The Ku Klux Klan in the City* (1965); Ray Ginger, *Six Days or Forever?* (1958); Norman Furniss, *The Fundamentalist Controversy* (1954); William G. McLoughlin, *Modern Revivalism* (1959); George M. Marsden, *Fundamentalism and American Culture* (1980); Lawrence Levine, *Defender of the Faith, William Jennings Bryan: The Last Decade, 1915–1925* (1965).

Politics and Government. Robert K. Murray, *The Politics of Normalcy* (1973) and *The Harding Era* (1969); Eugene Trani and David Wilson, *The Presidency of Warren G. Harding* (1977); Burl Noggle, *Teapot Dome* (1962); James N. Giglio, *H. M. Daugherty and the Politics of Expediency* (1978); Francis Russell, *The Shadow of Blooming Grove* (1968); Andrew Sinclair, *The Available Man* (1965); Donald McCoy, *Calvin Coolidge* (1967); William Allen White, *A Puritan in Babylon* (1940); James Gilbert, *Designing the Industrial State* (1972); John Hoff Wilson, *Herbert Hoover: Forgotten Progressive* (1975); David Burner, *Herbert Hoover* (1979); Robert F. Himmelberg, *The Origins of the National Recovery Administration: Business, Government, and the Trade Association Issue, 1921–1933* (1976); Ellis Hawley, *Herbert Hoover as Secretary of Commerce: Studies in New Era Thought and Practice* (1974); LeRoy Ashby, *Spearless Leader* (1972); Richard Lowitt, *George W. Norris*, vol. 2 (1971); David P. Thelen, *Robert M. La Follette and the Insurgent Spirit* (1978); George B. Tindall, *The Emergence of the New South* (1967); Christine Bolt, *American Indian Policy and American Reform* (1987); William Harbaugh, *Lawyer's Lawyer* (1973); David Burner, *The Politics of Provincialism* (1967); Alan Lichtman, *Prejudice and the Old Politics* (1979); Kristi Andersen, *The Creation of a Democratic Majority, 1928–1936* (1979); Oscar Handlin, *Al Smith and His America* (1958); Paula Elder, *Governor Alfred E. Smith: The Politician as Reformer* (1983); Elisabeth Israels Perry, *Belle Moskowitz: Feminine Politics and the Exercise of Power in the Age of Alfred E. Smith* (1987); Frank Freidel, *Franklin D. Roosevelt: The Ordeal* (1954) and *Franklin D. Roosevelt: The Triumph* (1956).

Detail from *Private Car* (1932), by Leconte Stewart
Thousands of men left their homes during the Great Depression and traveled from city to city looking for work, often hopping freight trains for an illegal but free ride. *(Museum of Church History & Art, Salt Lake City, Utah)*

CHAPTER 25

❧ ⚑ ❧

The Great Depression

❧ ⚑ ❧

Few Americans in the first months of 1929 saw any reason to question the strength and stability of the nation's economy. Most agreed with their new president that the booming prosperity of the years just past would not only continue but increase, and that dramatic social progress would follow in its wake. "We in America today," Herbert Hoover had proclaimed in August 1928, "are nearer to the final triumph over poverty than ever before in the history of any land. The poorhouse is vanishing from among us."

Only fifteen months later, those words would return to haunt him, as the nation plunged into the severest and most prolonged economic depression in its history. It began with a stock market crash in October 1929; it slowly but steadily deepened over the next three years until the nation's economy (and, many believed, its social and political systems) approached a total collapse; and it continued in one form or another for a full decade, not only in the United States but throughout much of the rest of the world, until war finally restored American prosperity.

America had experienced economic crises before. The Panic of 1893 had ushered in a prolonged era of economic stagnation, and there had been more recent recessions, in 1907 and in 1920. The Great Depression of the 1930s, however, affected the nation more profoundly than any economic crisis that had come before—not only because it lasted longer, but because its impact was far more widely felt. The American economy by 1929 had become so intercon-

nected, so dependent on the health of large national corporate institutions, that a collapse in one sector of the economy now reached out to affect virtually everyone. Even in the 1890s, large groups of Americans had lived sufficiently independent of the national economy to avoid the effects of economic crisis. By the 1930s, few such people remained.

The misery of the Great Depression was, then, without precedent in the nation's history. There was prolonged massive unemployment; over a quarter of the work force is estimated to have been without work in 1932, the worst year of the crisis. Even those who retained their jobs often had to accept drastic pay cuts, reduced hours, and continued uncertainty. On the nation's farms, the economic problems that had been growing in severity through the 1920s became far worse; great numbers of farmers lost their land, and many of them left the countryside altogether in search of work in other regions—work that generally did not exist. The Depression was not only a traumatic experience for individual Americans. It also placed great strains on the political and social fabric of the nation. And out of those strains emerged a series of fundamental reforms—most notably in the role of government in American life. Private institutions and local governments were completely unprepared to deal with a crisis of this magnitude; and despite occasionally strenuous attempts, their efforts gradually collapsed under the burden. Slowly, Americans began to look to the federal government for some solution to their problems.

Herbert Hoover was the first to expand the federal presence in the economy in response to the crisis. His innovative programs in the early 1930s made his the most activist peacetime administration in American history to that point. But Hoover's efforts, inhibited by conservative assumptions about the proper functions of government, were in the end insufficient. And so, in 1932, the American people turned to the Democratic party and to its presidential candidate Franklin Delano Roosevelt to show them the way out of the Depression.

The Coming of the Depression

The sudden financial collapse in 1929 came as an especially severe shock because it followed so closely a period in which the New Era seemed to be performing another series of economic miracles. In particular, the nation was experiencing in 1929 a spectacular boom in the stock market.

The Great Crash

In February 1928, stock prices began a steady ascent that continued, with only a few temporary lapses, for a year and a half. By the autumn of that year, the market had become a national obsession, attracting the attention not only of the wealthy but of millions of people of modest means. Many brokerage firms gave added encouragement to the speculative mania by offering absurdly easy credit to purchasers of stocks.

It was not hard to understand why so many Americans flocked to invest in the market. Stocks seemed to provide a certain avenue to quick and easy wealth. Between May 1928 and September 1929, the average price of stocks rose over 40 percent. The stocks of the major industrials—the stocks that are used to determine the Dow Jones Industrial Average—doubled in value in that same period. Trading mushroomed from 2 or 3 million shares a day to over 5 million, and at times to as many as 10 or 12 million. There was, in short, a widespread speculative fever that grew steadily more intense. A few economists warned that the boom could not continue, that the prices of stocks had ceased to bear any relation to the earning power of the corporations that were issuing them. But most Americans refused to listen.

In the autumn of 1929, the market began to fall apart. On October 21, stock prices dipped sharply, alarming those who had become accustomed to an uninterrupted upward progression. Two days later, after a brief recovery, an even more alarming decline began. J. P. Morgan and Company and other big bankers managed to stave off disaster for a while by conspicuously buying up stocks to restore public confidence. But on October 29, all the efforts to save the market failed. That day—"Black Tuesday," as it became known—saw a devastating panic. Sixteen million shares of stock were traded; the industrial index dropped 43 points; stocks in many companies became virtually worthless. In the weeks that followed, the market continued to decline, with losses in October totaling $16 billion. Despite occasional hopeful signs of a turnaround, the market remained deeply depressed for more than four years and did not fully recover for more than a decade.

Popular folklore has established the stock market crash as the beginning, and even the cause, of the Great Depression. But although October 1929 might have been the first visible sign of the crisis, the Depression had earlier beginnings and more important causes.

Causes of the Depression

Economists, historians, and others have argued for decades about the causes of the Great Depression. But most agree on several things. They agree, first, that what is remarkable about the crisis is not that it occurred; periodic recessions are a normal feature of capitalist economies. What is remarkable is that it was so severe and that it lasted so long. The important question, therefore, is not so much why was there a depression, but why was it such a bad one. Most observers agree, too, that a number of different factors account for the severity of the crisis, even if there is considerable disagreement about which was the most important.

One of those factors was a lack of diversification in the American economy in the 1920s. Prosperity had depended excessively on a few basic industries, notably construction and automobiles. In the late 1920s, those industries began to decline. Expenditures on construction fell from $11 billion to under $9 billion between 1926 and 1929. Automobile sales remained strong for a while longer, but in the first nine months of 1929 they fell by more than a third. Newer industries were emerging to take up the slack—

Panic on Wall Street
Anxious crowds gather outside the New York Stock Exchange in October 1929 to wait for news about the financial mayhem in progress inside.   (UPI/Bettmann Newsphotos)

among them petroleum, chemicals, and plastics—but had not yet developed enough strength to compensate for the decline in other sectors. Hence when the crucial construction and automobile industries weakened, no other area of the economy was ready to compensate for them.

A second important factor was the maldistribution of purchasing power and, as a result, a weakness in consumer demand. As industrial and agricultural production increased, the proportion of the profits going to farmers, workers, and other potential consumers was too small to create an adequate market for the goods the economy was producing. Demand was not keeping up with supply. Even in 1929, after nearly a decade of economic growth, more than half the families in America lived on the edge of or below the minimum subsistence level—too poor to share in the great consumer booms of the 1920s, too poor to

buy the houses, cars, and other goods the industrial economy was producing, too poor in many cases even to buy adequate food and shelter for themselves. As long as corporations had continued to expand their capital facilities (factories, warehouses, heavy equipment, and other investments), the economy had flourished. By 1929, however, capital investment had created more plant space than could profitably be used, and factories were producing more goods than consumers could purchase. And industries that were experiencing declining demand (construction, autos, coal, and others) began laying off workers, depleting mass purchasing power further. Even expanding industries often reduced their work forces because of new, less labor-intensive technologies; and in the sluggish economic atmosphere of 1929 and beyond, such workers had difficulty finding employment elsewhere.

A third major problem was the credit structure of the economy. Farmers were deeply in debt—their land mortgaged, and crop prices too low to allow them to pay off what they owed. Small banks, especially those tied to the agricultural economy, were in constant trouble in the 1920s as their customers defaulted on loans; there was a steady stream of failures among these smaller banks throughout the decade. The banking system as a whole, moreover, was only very loosely regulated by the Federal Reserve System. Although most American bankers in this era were intensely conservative, some of the nation's largest banks were failing to maintain adequate reserves and were investing recklessly in the stock market or making unwise loans. In other words, the banking system was not well prepared to absorb the shock of a major recession.

A fourth factor contributing to the coming of the Depression was America's position in international trade. The United States was far less dependent on overseas trade than it would later become, but exports formed a significant part of the economy in the 1920s. Beginning late in the decade, European demand for American goods began to decline. That was partly because European industry and agriculture were becoming more productive, and partly because some European nations (most notably Germany, under the government of the Weimar Republic) were suffering serious financial crises and could not afford to buy goods from overseas. But it was also because the European economy was being destabilized by the international debt structure that had emerged in the aftermath of World War I.

The international debt structure, therefore, was a fifth factor contributing to the Depression. When the war came to an end in 1918, all the European nations that had been allied with the United States owed large sums of money to American banks, sums much too large to be repaid out of their shattered economies. That was one reason why the Allies had insisted (over Woodrow Wilson's objections) on demanding reparation payments from Germany and Austria. Reparations, they believed, would provide them with a way to pay off their own debts. But Germany and Austria were themselves in deep economic trouble after the war; they were no more able to pay the reparations than the Allies were able to pay their debts.

The debtor nations put strong pressure on the United States in the 1920s to forgive the debts, or at least to reduce them. The American government refused. Instead, American banks began making large loans to the nations of Europe. Thus debts (and reparations) were being paid only by piling up new and greater debts. In the late 1920s, and particularly after the American economy began to weaken in 1929, the European nations found it much more difficult to borrow money from the United States. At the same time, high American protective tariffs were making it difficult for them to sell their goods in American markets. Without any source of foreign exchange with which to repay their loans, they began to default. The collapse of the international credit structure was one of the reasons the Depression spread to Europe (and grew much worse in America) after 1931. (See below, p. 741.)

Progress of the Depression

The stock market crash of 1929 did not so much cause the Depression, then, as help trigger a chain of events that exposed a large number of weaknesses that had long existed in the American economy. Over the next three years, the crisis grew steadily worse.

The collapse of the stock market meant, of course, that companies now found it far more difficult to raise money to expand their enterprises. That was one reason for the rapid decline in investment after 1929. More important, perhaps, was the collapse of the American banking system. Over 9,000 American banks either went bankrupt or closed their doors to avoid bankruptcy between 1930 and 1933. Depositors lost over $2.5 billion in deposits. Partly as a result of these banking closures, the nation's money supply greatly decreased. As banks stopped making loans, farmers, businessmen, and others found it more and more difficult to get money with which to invest. The total money supply, according to some measurements, fell by more than a third between 1930 and 1933. And the declining money supply meant a decline in purchasing power, and thus deflation. With fewer and fewer Americans able to buy, manufacturers and merchants began reducing prices, cutting back on production, and laying off workers. A cycle of economic contraction began early in 1930 that would not be reversed until 1933. Full recovery would not arrive until the 1940s.

Some economists argue that a severe depression could have been avoided if the Federal Reserve system had acted more responsibly. Instead of moving to increase the money supply so as to keep things from getting worse in the early 1930s, the Federal Reserve first did nothing and then did the wrong

Selling Apples, New York City
In the fall of 1931 and again in the fall of 1932, large numbers of the unemployed took to selling apples on the streets of major cities and became in the process a popular symbol of the economic despair of those years. Herbert Hoover later wrote bitterly of the phenomenon: "One incident of these times has persisted as the eternal damnation of Hoover. Some Oregon or Washington growers' association shrewdly appraised the sympathy of the public for the unemployed. They set up a system of selling apples on the street corners in many cities, thus selling their crop and raising their prices. Many persons left their jobs for the more profitable one of selling apples. When any leftwinger wishes to indulge in scathing oratory, he demands, 'Do you want to return to selling apples?' "
(Culver Pictures)

thing: Late in 1931 it raised interest rates, which contracted the money supply even further.

The collapse was so rapid and so devastating that at the time it created only bewilderment among many of those who attempted to explain it. The American gross national product plummeted from over $104 billion in 1929 to $76.4 billion in 1932—a 25 percent decline in three years. By 1933, Americans had virtually ceased making investments in productive enterprises. In 1929, they had spent $16.2 billion to promote capital growth; in 1933, they invested only a third of a billion. The consumer price index declined 25 percent between 1929 and 1933, the wholesale price index 32 percent. Farm prices, already depressed in the 1920s, fell even more dramatically. Gross farm income dropped from $12 billion to $5 billion in four years. With economic activity contracting so sharply, it was inevitable that industrial

unemployment would greatly increase. By 1932, according to the relatively crude estimates of the time, 25 percent of the American work force was unemployed. (Some believe the figure was even higher.) For the rest of the decade, unemployment averaged nearly 20 percent, never dropping below 15 percent.

The American People in Hard Times

Someone asked the British economist John Maynard Keynes in the 1930s whether he was aware of any historical era comparable to the Great Depression. "Yes," Keynes replied. "It was called the Dark Ages, and it lasted 400 years." The Depression did not last

400 years. It did, however, bring unprecedented despair to the economies of the United States and much of the Western world. And it had far-reaching effects on American society and culture.

Unemployment and Relief

The suffering extended into every area of society. In the industrial Northeast and Midwest, cities were becoming virtually paralyzed by unemployment. Cleveland, Ohio, for example, had an unemployment rate of 50 percent in 1932; Akron, 60 percent; Toledo, 80 percent. To the men and women suddenly without incomes, the situation was frightening and bewildering. Most had grown up believing that every individual was responsible for his or her own fate, that unemployment and poverty were signs of personal failure; and even in the face of national distress, many continued to believe it. Unemployed workers walked through the streets day after day looking for jobs that did not exist. When finally they gave up, they often just sat at home, hiding their shame.

An increasing number of families were turning in humiliation to local public relief systems, just to be able to eat. But that system, which had in the 1920s served only a small number of indigents, was totally unequipped to handle the new demands being placed on it. In many cities, therefore, relief simply collapsed. New York, which offered among the highest relief benefits in the nation, was able to provide families an average of only $2.39 per week. Private charities attempted to supplement the public relief efforts, but the problem was far beyond their capabilities as well.

With local efforts rapidly collapsing, state governments began to feel new pressures to expand their own assistance to the unemployed. Most resisted the pressure. Tax revenues were declining along with everything else, and state leaders balked at placing additional strains on already tight budgets. Many public figures, moreover, feared that any permanent welfare system would undermine the moral fiber of its clients.

As a result, American cities were experiencing scenes that a few years earlier would have seemed almost inconceivable. Bread lines stretched for blocks outside Red Cross and Salvation Army kitchens. Thousands of people sifted through garbage cans for scraps of food or waited outside restaurant kitchens in hopes of receiving plate scrapings. Nearly 2 million young men simply took to the roads, riding freight trains from city to city, living as nomads.

In rural areas conditions were in many ways even worse, especially in a large part of the South and Midwest known as the Dust Bowl. Between 1929 and 1932, not only did farm income decline by more than 60 percent; not only did an estimated one-third of all American farmers lose their land through mortgage foreclosures or eviction. Much of the farm belt was suffering as well from a catastrophic natural disaster: one of the worst droughts in the history of the nation. Beginning in 1930, a large area of the nation—and particularly a group of states stretching north from Texas into the Dakotas—began to experience a steady decline in rainfall and an accompanying increase in heat. The drought continued for a full decade, turning what had once been fertile farm regions into virtual deserts. In Kansas, the soil in some places was completely without moisture as far as three feet below the surface. In Nebraska, Iowa, and other states, summer temperatures were averaging over 100 degrees. Swarms of grasshoppers were moving from region to region, devouring what meager crops farmers were able to raise, often even devouring fenceposts or clothes hanging out to dry. Great dust storms—"black blizzards," as they were called—swept across the plains, blotting out the sun and suffocating livestock as well as any people unfortunate or foolish enough to stay outside. (See "The American Environment," pp. 819–822.)

It is a measure of how productive American farmers were and how depressed the market for agricultural goods had become that even with these disastrous conditions, the farm economy continued through the 1930s to produce far more than American consumers could afford to buy. With the domestic market dwindling and the international market having almost vanished, farmers were able to sell their goods only at prices so low as to make continued operations unprofitable for most of them. Thus many farmers, like many urban unemployed, left their homes and traveled to what they hoped would be better areas. In the South, in particular, many dispossessed farmers—black and white—simply wandered from town to town, hoping to find jobs or handouts. Hundreds of thousands of families from the Dust Bowl (often known as "Okies," since many came from Oklahoma) packed their belongings in rickety cars or trucks and traveled to California and other states, where they found conditions little better than those they had left. Owning no land of their

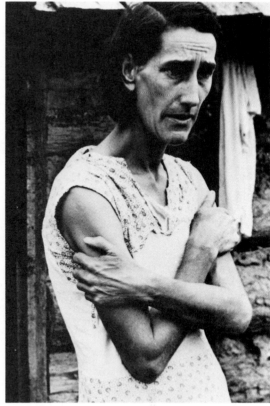

White Migrants
The plight of uprooted agricultural families from the South and Southwest captured the attention of many Americans in the 1930s. In particular, it captured the attention of some of the country's most talented photographers, many of whom worked for a time in the late 1930s for the Farm Security Administration recording the lives of migrant farmworkers. Russell Lee photographed a Texas family (above) moving west in search of work; and Ben Shahn recorded this portrait of a weary rural woman (right) and entitled it "Destitute." (Library of Congress)

own, many worked as agricultural migrants, traveling from farm to farm picking fruit and other crops at starvation wages.

For urban and rural Americans alike, malnutrition and homelessness became a growing problem. City hospitals reported an alarming increase in deaths by starvation. Although such deaths in rural areas often went unreported, they too were increasing. People who had lost their farms or their homes were often unable to afford any permanent shelter. Large shantytowns began to spring up on the outskirts of major cities, where homeless families lived in makeshift shacks constructed of flattened tin cans, scraps of wood, abandoned crates, and other debris. Many homeless Americans simply kept moving—sleeping in freight cars, in city parks, in subways, or in unused sewer ducts.

Black Americans and the Depression

Those Americans whose access to opportunities had been limited even in prosperity found the Depression especially devastating. Thus black Americans encountered special hardships in the 1930s. They had not generally shared in the prosperity of the previous decade; they now experienced the problems of unemployment, homelessness, malnutrition, and disease to a greater degree than in the past, and to a far greater degree than most whites.

As the Depression began, over half of all American blacks still lived in the South, most of them farmers. The collapse of prices for cotton and other staple crops left many with no income at all. Those who stayed on their farms had to grow their own food or scavenge or beg for it. Many left the land altogether—either by choice or because forced to by landlords who no longer found the sharecropping system profitable. Some migrated to Southern cities, where it was now difficult to secure even the menial jobs traditionally considered suitable for blacks. Unemployed whites believed they had first claim to all work, and some now began to take positions as janitors, street cleaners, and domestic servants, displacing the blacks who formerly occupied them.

Black Migrants
The Great Migration of blacks from the rural South into the cities had begun before World War I. But in the 1930s and 1940s the movement accelerated. Jacob Lawrence, an eminent black artist, created a series of paintings entitled, collectively, *The Migration of the Negro* to illustrate this major event in the history of American blacks.   (Phillips Collection, Washington, D.C.)

As the Depression deepened, whites in many Southern cities began to demand that all blacks be dismissed from their jobs. In Atlanta in 1930, an organization calling itself the Black Shirts organized a campaign with the slogan "No Jobs for Niggers Until Every White Man Has a Job!" In other areas, whites used intimidation and violence to drive blacks from jobs. By 1932, over half the blacks in the South were without employment. Even unemployed, blacks continued to encounter discrimination. What limited relief there was went almost invariably to whites first; benefits for blacks were consistently lower than those for whites. Some private organizations, and some local governments, refused to provide any assistance at all to blacks.

Unsurprisingly, therefore, many Southern blacks—perhaps 400,000 in all—left the South in the 1930s and journeyed to the cities of the North. There they found less direct discrimination, perhaps, but conditions that were in most respects little better than those in the South. In Harlem, the median income of skilled workers dropped by nearly half between 1929 and 1932. But most blacks, there and elsewhere, were unskilled workers; and as always, they tended to be the first fired when layoffs began. In New York, black unemployment was nearly 50 percent. In other cities, it was even higher. A black sociologist reported in 1932 that a third of all black Americans were unemployed and another third underemployed. Two million blacks—half the total black population of the country—were on some form of relief by 1932. But relief provided most of them with far less support than was necessary to sustain health.

Relatively few white Americans showed any sensitivity to the special plight of blacks during the 1930s. Traditional patterns of segregation and disfranchisement in the South survived largely unchallenged. The tragic phenomenon of lynching continued (although at a diminished rate), with all efforts to win passage of a law making the practice a federal crime frustrated by the opposition of national leaders afraid of antagonizing powerful white Southern politicians. But several particularly notorious examples of racism did attract the attention of the nation.

The most celebrated, perhaps, was the Scottsboro case. In March 1931, nine black teen-agers were taken off a freight train in Alabama (in a small town near Scottsboro) and arrested for vagrancy and disorder. Later, two white women who had also been riding the train accused them of rape. In fact, there was overwhelming evidence, medical and otherwise, that the women had not been raped at all; they may have made their accusations out of fear of being arrested themselves. Nevertheless, an all-white jury in Alabama quickly convicted all nine of the "Scottsboro boys" (as they were known to both friends and foes) and sentenced eight of them to death.

After the Supreme Court overturned the convictions in 1932, a series of new trials began that gradually attracted national attention. This was in part because the International Labor Defense, an organization associated with the Communist party, came to the aid of the accused youths and began to publicize the case. The trials continued throughout the 1930s. Although the white Southern juries who sat on the case never acquitted any of the defendants, all of them eventually gained their freedom—four because the charges were dropped, four because of early paroles, and one because he escaped. The last of the Scottsboro boys did not leave prison until 1950.

Although the Depression generally did little to alter white racial attitudes, it was a time of important changes in the role and behavior of the leading black organizations. The NAACP, for example, began to work diligently to win a position for blacks within the emerging labor movement, supporting the formation of the Congress of Industrial Organizations and helping to break down racial barriers within labor unions. Walter White, secretary of the NAACP, once even made a personal appearance at an auto plant to implore blacks not to work as strikebreakers. Partly as a result of such efforts, more than half a million blacks were able to join the labor movement. In the Steelworkers Union, for example, blacks constituted about 20 percent of the membership.

At the same time, many black leaders were beginning to question their traditional belief that patient lobbying in Congress and through the courts would ultimately produce racial equality. The economic distress of American blacks, combined with adverse judicial decisions and the continuing disinterest of Congress and state legislatures in their problems, caused many to contemplate more direct forms of protest.

Hispanics in America

Similar patterns of discrimination confronted many Mexicans and Mexican-Americans. The Hispanic population in the United States had been growing steadily since early in the century, largely in California and other areas of the Southwest through massive immigration from Mexico (which was specifically excluded from the immigration restriction laws of the 1920s). Some Chicanos (as Mexican-Americans are known) filled many of the same menial jobs there that blacks had traditionally filled in other regions. Others began to farm on small, marginal tracts. Still others became agricultural migrants, traveling from region to region harvesting fruit, lettuce, and other crops. Even during the prosperous 1920s, it had been a precarious existence. The Depression made things significantly worse. As in the South, so in the Southwest: Unemployed whites began to demand jobs held by Hispanics, jobs that whites had previously considered beneath them. Thus Mexicans and Mexican-Americans found themselves, like blacks in the South, the last to be hired and the first to be fired; and Mexican unemployment rose quickly to levels far higher than those for whites. Some Mexicans—those willing to move across the border into Mexico—were provided free transportation. Others were, in effect, forced to leave by officials who arbitrarily removed them from relief rolls or simply rounded them up and transported them across the border. Perhaps half a million Chicanos left the United States for Mexico in the first years of the Depression.

For those who remained, there were both economic hardships and increasing social discrimination. Most relief programs excluded Mexicans from their rolls or offered them benefits far below those available to whites. Hispanics generally had no access to American schools. Many hospitals refused them admission. Unlike American blacks, who had established certain educational and social facilities of their own in response to discrimination, Hispanics generally had nowhere to turn. Even those who possessed American citizenship found themselves treated like foreigners.

There were, occasionally, signs of organized resistance by Mexican-Americans themselves, most notably in California, where they attempted to form a union of migrant farm workers. But harsh repression by local growers and the public authorities allied with them prevented such organizations from making significant progress. Like black farm workers, many Hispanics began as a result to migrate to the cities. In Los Angeles and other Western cities, they lived in a poverty comparable to that of urban blacks in the South and Northeast.

Women in the Work Force

The Depression had conflicting effects on the ability and willingness of women to obtain paid employment. The economic crisis served in many ways to strengthen the widespread belief that a woman's proper place was in the home. Most men and also many women believed that with employment so scarce, what work there was should go to men—that female workers were taking jobs away from male

Women in the Work Force, 1900–1940

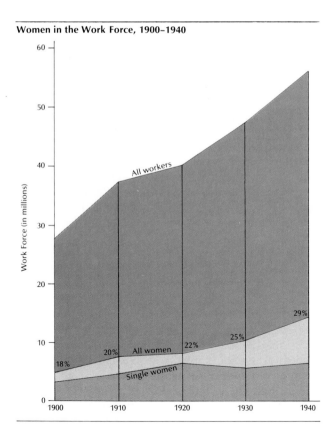

breadwinners. There was a particularly strong belief that no woman whose husband was employed should accept a job, that to do so would take income away from other, needier families. That belief, in fact, was for a time enshrined in law. From 1932 until 1937, it was illegal for more than one member of a family to hold a federal civil-service job. State and local governments often introduced similar restrictions. And in over twenty states, the legislatures considered (but never passed) laws prohibiting women from working in any paid jobs.

But the widespread assumption that married women, at least, should not work outside the home did not stop them from doing so. Both single and married women worked in the 1930s, despite public condemnation of the practice, because they or their families needed the money. In fact, the largest new group of female workers consisted of precisely those people who, according to popular attitudes, were supposed to be leaving the labor market: wives and mothers. Such women worked to supplement reduced family incomes or, often, because their husbands had lost their jobs. By the end of the Depression, 25 percent more women were working than had been doing so at the beginning.

Few of the new women workers were entering professional work. In fact, the Depression saw an erosion of the already limited professional opportunities for women. That was partly because unemployed men now began moving into professions such as teaching and social work that had previously been considered women's fields. It was also because the general prejudice against women taking jobs away from men operated particularly strongly in the professions. Female industrial workers suffered similar discrimination. They were far more likely to be laid off or to experience wage reductions than their male counterparts. But white women also had certain advantages in the workplace in the 1930s. The nonprofessional jobs that women traditionally held—as salesclerks and stenographers, and in other service positions—were less likely to disappear than the predominantly male jobs in heavy industry. Nor were many men, even unemployed men, likely to search for such jobs.

Black women, however, enjoyed few such advantages. In the South, in particular, they suffered massive unemployment because of a great reduction of domestic service jobs. Doing without paid servants was often one of the first economies that troubled white families imposed on themselves. Thus, as many as half of all black working women lost their jobs in the 1930s. Even so, at the end of the 1930s, 38 percent of black women were employed, as compared to 24 percent of white women. Married black women were twice as likely to be employed as married white women. That was because black women—both married and unmarried—had always been more likely to work than white women, less out of preference than out of economic necessity. And that pattern continued despite the setbacks of the Depression.

For American feminists, the Depression years were, on the whole, a time of frustration. Although economic pressures pushed more women into the work force, those same pressures helped to erode the frail support that feminists had won in the 1920s for the idea of women becoming economically and professionally independent. Most Americans could accept the idea of women working as a way to meet pressing family needs, but few could accept the idea of women working as an assertion of independence and individualism. In the difficult years of the 1930s, such aspirations seemed to many to be less important than dealing with economic hardship.

The Depression saw the virtual extinction of the National Woman's party, which had fought throughout the 1920s for the Equal Rights Amendment and for other egalitarian goals. Even more moderate feminists, committed to "protective" legislation for women, found their gains in decline by the end of the decade—although they did achieve some significant gains in the early years of the New Deal. (See below, pp. 775–776.) By the end of the 1930s, American feminism had reached its lowest ebb in nearly a century.

Depression Families

The economic hardships of the Depression years placed great strains on American families, particularly on the families of middle-class people who had become accustomed in the 1920s to a steadily rising standard of living and now found themselves plunged suddenly into uncertainty. It was not only unemployment that shook the confidence of middle-class families, although that was of course the worst blow. It was also the reduction of incomes among those who remained employed.

Economic circumstances forced many families, therefore, to retreat from the consumer patterns they had developed in the 1920s. Women often returned to sewing clothes for themselves and their families and to preserving their own food rather than buying such products in stores. Others engaged in home businesses—taking in laundry, selling baked goods, accepting boarders. Many households expanded to include more distant relatives. Parents often moved in with their children and grandparents with their grandchildren, or vice versa.

The Depression made family life in many ways more important economically. It also worked to erode the strength of many family units. There was a decline in the divorce rate, but that was largely because divorce was now too expensive for some. More common was the informal breakup of families, particularly the desertion of families by unemployed men bent on escaping the humiliation of being unable to earn a living. The marriage rate and the birth rate both declined.

The families whose structure and behavior were perhaps least affected by the onset of the Depression were those that had not shared in the affluence of the 1920s. Rural families, black families, and migrant families continued to survive in traditional ways. But in middle-class families the sudden deterioration of conditions often caused significant changes. Men, who had been accustomed to the role of breadwinner and central authority figure within the family and who now found themselves unemployed or underemployed, tended to experience strong feelings of failure and inadequacy. Married women who had not worked before the Depression might find the changes less jarring. Sociologists examining family structure in these years noted the frequent phenomenon of husbands becoming secondary to their wives as the center of family life. In some cases, it was the children who assumed leadership when their parents lost the ability to support the family. Young men and women sometimes managed to obtain paid employment when their parents could not, and their authority within the family rose as a result—often with disorienting results for everyone.

Social Values

Much of American culture in the 1920s had been a response to prosperity and industrial growth. It had celebrated affluence and consumerism and had stressed the importance of personal gratification through both. The economic crisis of the 1930s thus came as a special shock to those men and women who had come to expect continued and increasing prosperity. Many Americans assumed, therefore, that the experience of hard times would have profound effects on the nation's social values, on the way the society defined its goals.

In general, however, American social values seemed to change relatively little in response to the Depression. On the contrary, many people responded to hard times by redoubling their commitment to familiar ideas and goals. The sociologists Robert and Helen Merrell Lynd, who had published a celebrated study of Muncie, Indiana, in 1929 (*Middletown*), returned there in the mid-1930s to see how the city had changed. They described their findings in their 1937 book, *Middletown in Transition;* and they concluded that in most respects "the texture of Middletown's culture has not changed. . . . Middletown is overwhelmingly living by the values by which it lived in 1925." Above all, the men and women of "Middletown"—and by implication the people of the nation at large—remained committed to the traditional American emphasis on the individual.

No assumption would seem to have been more vulnerable to erosion during the Depression than the belief that the individual was in control of his or her own fate, that anyone displaying sufficient talent and industry could become a success. And in some respects, the economic crisis did work to undermine the traditional "success ethic" in America. People became more accustomed during the 1930s to looking to their government for assistance; they learned to blame corporate moguls, international bankers, "economic royalists," and others for their distress. Yet the Depression fell far short of destroying the success ethic.

The survival of the ideals of work and individual advancement was evident in many ways, not least in the reactions of those most traumatized by the Depression: responsible, conscientious working people of all economic levels who suddenly, bewilderingly, found themselves without employment. Some expressed anger and struck out at the economic system. More, however, blamed themselves—if not openly, at least subconsciously. Nothing so surprised foreign observers of America in the 1930s than the apparent passivity of the unemployed, many of whom were so ashamed of their joblessness that they refused to leave their homes. Perhaps that was why people who continued in the 1930s to work and to live more or less as they always had sometimes found it easy to forget that there was an economic crisis. The Depression was sometimes hard to see, because the unemployed tended to hide themselves, unwilling to display to the world what many of them considered their own personal failure.

At the same time, millions responded eagerly to reassurances that they could, through their own efforts, restore themselves to prosperity and success. Dale Carnegie's *How to Win Friends and Influence People* (1936), a self-help manual preaching individual initiative, was one of the best-selling books of the decade. Harry Emerson Fosdick, a Protestant theologian who similarly preached the virtues of positive thinking and individual initiative, attracted large audiences with his radio addresses. And although many of the great financial moguls fell into wide disrepute after 1929, the public continued to revere such "self-made men" as Thomas Edison and even, to some extent, Henry Ford.

The Depression also seemed to reinforce the belief of many Americans in the importance of conforming to the predominant standards of their society. If failure was, as many people believed, a result of personal inadequacies, then the best way to compensate for those inadequacies was to conform more and more tightly to the values of the community, to try harder to be like other, more successful people. Dale Carnegie's message was not only that personal initiative was the route to success; it was also that the best way for people to make something of themselves was to adapt to the world in which they lived, to understand the values and expectations of others and mold themselves accordingly. The way to get ahead, Carnegie taught, was to make other people feel important, to fit in.

Depression Culture

Not all Americans, of course, responded to the crisis of the Depression so passively. Large groups of men and women did come to believe that the economic problems of their time were the fault of society, not of individuals, and that some collective social response was necessary. Such beliefs found expression in, among other places, American artistic and intellectual life.

Just as many progressives had become alarmed when, early in the twentieth century, they "discovered" the existence of widespread poverty in the cities, so many Americans were shocked during the 1930s at their discovery of debilitating rural poverty. The plight of the farmer—and particularly of the Southern tenant farmer and sharecropper—became one of the leading themes of Depression intellectual life.

Perhaps most effective in conveying the dimensions of rural poverty was a group of documentary photographers, many of them employed by the Farm Security Administration in the late 1930s, who traveled through the South recording the nature of agricultural life. Men such as Roy Stryker, Walker Evans, Arthur Rothstein, and Ben Shahn and women such as Margaret Bourke-White and Dorothea Lange produced memorable studies of farm families and their surroundings, studies designed to show the savage impact of a hostile environment on its victims. Through their work, not only did the problems of poverty receive wider public attention but the art of photography earned new stature.

Many writers, similarly, turned away from the personal concerns of the 1920s and devoted themselves to exposés of social injustice. Erskine Caldwell exposed many of the same injustices that the documentary photographers had studied, in *Tobacco Road* (1932)—a novel about life in the rural South, which later became a long-running play. James Agee produced one of the most powerful portraits of the lives of sharecroppers, in *Let Us Now Praise Famous Men* (1941)—a careful, nonjudgmental description of the lives of three Southern families, illustrated with photographs by Walker Evans. Other writers and artists turned their gaze on social injustice in other settings. Richard Wright, a major black novelist, exposed the plight of residents of the urban ghetto, in *Native Son* (1940). James T. Farrell, in his Studs Lonigan trilogy (1932–1935), depicted the savage world of urban, lower-class white youth.

Other artists and intellectuals moved beyond social realism and combined an effort to expose social problems with a commitment to political solutions. Some were successful novelists of the 1920s who now turned to new themes. Ernest Hemingway, in *To Have and Have Not* (1937), displayed for the first time a concern with social issues by portraying a bitter labor struggle and advocating a collective solution; in *For Whom the Bell Tolls* (1940), he used the Spanish Civil War as a setting through which to illustrate the importance of solidarity in the face of oppression. Other writers were discussing similar themes. John Steinbeck's *The Grapes of Wrath* (1939) portrayed the trials of a migrant family in California, concluding with an open call for collective social action against injustice (although in an earlier novel, *In Dubious Battle,* in 1936, Steinbeck had expressed grave reservations about the most collective political effort of the 1930s: the Communist party). John Dos Passos's *U.S.A.* trilogy (1930) explicitly attacked modern capitalism. Playwright Clifford Odets provided a

particularly explicit demonstration of the appeal of political radicalism in *Waiting for Lefty* (1935).

For the most part, however, the cultural products of the 1930s that attracted wide popular audiences were those that diverted attention away from the Depression rather than those that illuminated its problems. The two most powerful instruments of popular culture in the 1930s—radio and the movies— were particularly careful to provide mostly light and diverting entertainment. The radio industry, still fearful of the possibility of nationalization (which was occurring in many other countries just establishing broadcasting systems), made every effort to avoid controversy. Although stations occasionally carried inflammatory programs, the staple of broadcasting was escapism: comedies such as *Amos 'n Andy,* adventures such as *Superman, Dick Tracy,* and *The Lone Ranger,* and other programs designed to be pure entertainment. Hollywood continued to exercise tight control over its products through its resilient censor Will Hays, who in response to growing pressure from the Catholic church's Legion of Decency, founded in 1934, redoubled his efforts to ensure that movies carried only safe, conventional messages. There were some films that did explore provocative political themes. The film version of *The Grapes of Wrath* (1940) faithfully evoked Steinbeck's social criticism. Director Frank Capra provided a muted social message in several of his comedies—*Mr. Deeds Goes to Town* (1936), *Mr. Smith Goes to Washington* (1939), and *Meet John Doe* (1941)—which celebrated the virtues of the small town and the decency of the common people in contrast to the selfish, corrupt values of the city and the urban rich. More often, however, the commercial films of the 1930s were deliberately and explicitly escapist: lavish musicals and "wacky" comedies designed to divert audiences from their troubles and, very often, satisfy their fantasies about quick and easy wealth.

Popular literature, similarly, offered Americans an escape from the Depression rather than an investigation of it. Two of the best-selling novels of the decade were romantic sagas set in bygone eras: Margaret Mitchell's *Gone with the Wind* (1936), which became the source of one of the most celebrated films of all time; and Hervey Allen's *Anthony Adverse* (1933). Leading magazines, and particularly such popular new photographic journals as *Life,* did offer occasional glimpses of the ravages of the Depression. But for the most part they concentrated on fashions, stunts, and eye-catching scenery. Even the newsreels distributed to movie theaters across the country

***Twenty Cent Movie,* by Reginald Marsh, 1936**
Although moviegoing declined in the 1930s from its peak levels of the previous decade, it remained the most popular (and affordable) form of entertainment for Depression-era Americans. This painting captures the riotous lights and colors at the Lyric Theater on Forty-second Street in New York. The stylish young women and cocky young men in front of the theater are juxtaposed against pictures of similarly flashy movie stars.   (Whitney Museum of American Art)

tended to give more attention to beauty contests and ship launchings than to the Depression itself. The American people lived through the 1930s without experiencing a radical change in their values in part because they managed so frequently and effectively to divert themselves from their problems.

The Allure of the Left

For a relatively small but important group of Americans—intellectuals, artists, workers, blacks,

and others who became disenchanted for various reasons with the prevailing values of American life—the Depression meant a commitment, for a time at least, to radical politics. Some became members of the American Communist party, which achieved a size and visibility in the 1930s it had never attained before and would never attain again. Others expressed sympathy for the party and its ideas without actually becoming members. The United States has always been distinctive for the weakness of radicalism in its political tradition; and even during the Depression, the left remained, by the standards of other nations, small and frail. But by America's own modest standards, the 1930s represented one of the high-water marks of radical activism.

For intellectuals, in particular, the left offered an escape from the lonely and difficult stance of detachment and alienation that many had embraced in the 1920s. It combined a harsh critique of mainstream American society with an intense commitment to a political movement that seemed to give meaning and purpose to their lives. The particular importance of the Spanish Civil War (see below, p. 788) to many American intellectuals was a good example of how the left's sense of commitment proved appealing. The battle against the Spanish fascists of Francisco Franco (who was receiving support from Hitler and Mussolini) attracted a substantial group of young Americans, more than 3,000 in all, who formed the Abraham Lincoln brigade and traveled to Spain to join in the fight. About a third of its members died in combat; but for those who survived, the experience was profoundly rewarding. Ernest Hemingway, who spent time in Spain as a correspondent, wrote in *For Whom the Bell Tolls* of how the war provided those Americans who fought in it with "a part in something which you could believe in wholly and completely and in which you felt an absolute brotherhood with others who were engaged in it."

Instrumental in creating the Lincoln brigade, and directing many of its activities throughout its existence, was the American Communist party. The Communist party of the 1930s remains the subject of considerable controversy among historians and many others. Its membership peaked at perhaps 100,000 during its heyday in the mid-1930s; and for a time it made efforts to present itself as a genuinely American organization, no more threatening or alien than any other political organization. For several years beginning in 1935, the party dropped its insistence on working completely apart from other organizations and began to advocate a great democratic alliance of all antifascist groups in the United States, a "Popular Front." It began to praise Franklin Roosevelt and John L. Lewis, a powerful (and strongly anticommunist) labor leader. It adopted the slogan "Communism is twentieth-century Americanism."

The party did perform functions in the 1930s that even many Americans unsympathetic to its long-range goals found appealing. It was active in organizing the unemployed in the early 1930s and staged a hunger march in Washington, D.C., in 1931. Party members worked in the labor movement, were in

fact often among the most effective union organizers in some industries. And the party was one of the few political organizations to take a firm, unequivocal stand in favor of racial justice; its active defense of the Scottsboro boys was but one example of its efforts to ally itself with the aspirations of blacks. It also helped organize a union of black sharecroppers in Alabama, which resisted—in several instances violently—efforts of white landowners and authorities to displace them from their farms.

But it is also clear that despite its efforts to appear as a humane, patriotic organization, the American Communist party was always under the close and rigid supervision of the Soviet Union. Its leaders took their orders from the Comintern in Moscow. Most members followed the "party line" or found themselves expelled from its ranks. The subordination of the party leadership to the Soviet Union was most clearly demonstrated in 1939, when Stalin signed a nonaggression pact with Nazi Germany. Moscow then sent orders to the American Communist party to abandon the Popular Front idea and return to its old stance of harsh criticism of American liberals; and the leaders in the United States immediately obeyed—although thousands of disillusioned members left the party as a result.

The Socialist party of America, now under the leadership of Norman Thomas, also cited the economic crisis as evidence of the failure of capitalism and sought vigorously to win public support for its own political program. In particular, it attempted to mobilize support among the most desperate elements of society—especially the rural poor. The Southern Tenant Farmers Union, supported by the party and organized by a young socialist, H. L. Mitchell, attempted to create a biracial coalition of sharecroppers, tenant farmers, and others to demand economic reform. Neither the Farmers Union nor the party itself, however, made any real progress toward establishing socialism as a major force in American politics. By 1936, in fact, membership in the Socialist party had fallen below 20,000.

In the end, what is most striking about American radicalism in the 1930s is less its unprecedented strength than its continuing limits. Neither the Communist party nor any other radical organization ever achieved dimensions during the Depression sufficient to make it a truly important political force. Even the most distressed Americans seemed to find the subordination of the Communists to Moscow unappealing. But the more moderate Socialist party, whose independence from foreign control was not in question, fared no better in increasing its membership in these years. However strong radical sentiment may have become, the strength of antiradicalism remained far stronger.

The Ordeal of Herbert Hoover

Herbert Hoover entered the presidency in March 1929 believing, like most Americans, that the nation faced a bright and prosperous future. For the first six months of his administration, he attempted to expand the policies he had advocated during his eight years as secretary of commerce, policies that would, he believed, complete the stable system of cooperative individualism that he thought would sustain a successful economy. The economic crisis that began before the year was out forced the president to deal with a new set of problems; but for most of the rest of his term, he continued to rely on the principles that had always governed his public life.

The Hoover Program

Hoover's first response to the Depression was to attempt to restore public confidence in the economy. "The fundamental business of this country, that is, production and distribution of commodities," he said in 1930, "is on a sound and prosperous basis." Subsequently, he held a series of highly publicized meetings, summoning leaders of business, labor, and agriculture to the White House and urging upon them a program of voluntary cooperation for recovery. He implored businessmen not to cut production or lay off workers; he talked labor leaders into forgoing demands for higher wages or better hours. For a few brief months, the president's efforts seemed to be having some effect; but by mid-1931, economic conditions had deteriorated so much that the structure of voluntary cooperation he had erected collapsed. Frightened industrialists soon began cutting production, laying off workers, and slashing wages. Hoover was powerless to stop them.

Hoover also attempted to use government spending as a tool for fighting the Depression. Rejecting the demands of some fiscal conservatives that the government cut back its own programs to ensure a balanced budget, the president proposed to Congress an increase of $423 million—a substantial sum

by the standards of the time—in federal public works programs; and he exhorted state and local governments to engage in the "energetic yet prudent pursuit" of public construction. Nevertheless, Hoover's spending programs were in the end no more effective than his efforts at persuasion; for he was not willing to spend enough money, or to spend it for a long enough time, to do any good. He viewed his public works program as a temporary expedient, something to promote a rapid recovery. When economic conditions worsened, he became less willing to increase government spending, worrying instead about maintaining federal solvency. In 1932, at the depth of the Depression, he proposed a tax increase to help the government avoid a deficit.

Even before the stock market crash, Hoover had begun to construct a program to assist the troubled agricultural economy. It embodied two major initiatives, which the president proposed to a special session of Congress in April 1929. The Agricultural Marketing Act established for the first time a major government bureaucracy to help farmers maintain prices. A federally sponsored Farm Board of eight members would administer a budget of $500 million, from which it could make loans to national marketing cooperatives or establish "corporations" to buy surpluses and thus raise prices. At the same time, Hoover attempted to protect American farmers from international competition by raising agricultural tariffs. The Hawley-Smoot Tariff of 1930 contained protective increases on seventy-five farm products and raised rates from the average of 26 percent established by the 1922 Fordney-McCumber Tariff to a new high of 50 percent.

Neither the Agricultural Marketing Act nor the Hawley-Smoot Tariff ultimately helped American farmers in any significant way. The Marketing Act relied on voluntary cooperation among farmers and gave the government no authority to do what the agricultural economy most badly needed: limit production. Hoover's call for a reduction of the wheat crop, for example, resulted in a drop in acreage of only 1 percent in Kansas. The Farm Board lacked sufficient funds to deal effectively with the crisis. Prices continued to fall despite its efforts. The Hawley-Smoot Tariff was an unqualified disaster—as 1,000 members of the American Economic Association had warned the president even before he signed it into law. It provoked foreign governments to enact trade restrictions of their own in reprisal, further diminishing the market for American agricultural goods. And it raised rates not only on farm

Herbert Hoover Receiving a Load of Potatoes
The Maine Potato Growers Association sent a team of oxen to Washington with a load of Maine potatoes in 1931. They presented them as a gift to President Hoover on the White House lawn on November 23, reminding him of the difficulties that faced the agricultural economy as the Great Depression worsened.   (UPI/Bettmann Newsphotos)

products but on 925 manufactured goods as well, making industrial products more expensive for farmers.

A Change of Direction

By the spring of 1931, Herbert Hoover's political position had deteriorated considerably. Democrats had made major gains in the 1930 congressional elections, winning control of the House and making substantial inroads in the Senate. Large portions of the public were beginning to hold the president personally to blame for the crisis, and Hoover's name soon became synonymous with economic distress. Shantytowns established on the outskirts of cities were known as "Hoovervilles." Progressive reformers both inside and outside the government urged the president to support more vigorous programs of relief and public spending. Hoover ignored the recommendations. Instead, he seized on a slight improvement in economic conditions early in 1931 as proof that his policies were working.

The international financial panic of the spring of 1931 destroyed the illusion that the economic crisis was coming to an end. The ability of European nations to secure loans from American banks, which had been so crucial to their solvency throughout the 1920s, largely disappeared after 1929; and shortly thereafter, the financial fabric of many European nations began to unravel. In May 1931, the largest bank in Austria collapsed. Over the next several months, panic gripped the financial institutions of neighboring countries. European governments, desperate for sound assets, withdrew their gold reserves from American banks. European investors, in need of dollars to pay off their loans and protect their solvency, dumped their shares of American stocks onto the market, further depressing prices. More and more European nations were abandoning the gold standard and devaluing their currencies, leaving the United States, which remained tied to gold, at a disadvantage in international trade. American economic conditions rapidly declined to new lows, and Herbert Hoover quickly adopted a new approach to the Depression.

It was not the domestic American economy that was to blame for the Depression, he now argued, but the structure of international finance. The proper response to the crisis, therefore, was not to adopt active social and economic programs at home but to work to restore international stability. Hoover's solution was to propose a moratorium—first on the payment of all war debts and reparations, then on the payment of international private debts as well. It was a sound proposal, but it came too late to halt the panic.

By the time Congress convened in December 1931, conditions had grown so desperate that Hoover finally decided to support an expanded federal role in the economy. He persuaded Congress to increase funding for federal land banks and to create a system of government home loan banks. Through them, financial institutions holding mortgages on farms, homes, and other properties could receive cash from the government for the mortgages instead of foreclosing on them—thus keeping the banks afloat and, incidentally, preventing many Americans from losing their homes and properties. Hoover also supported the Glass-Steagall Banking Act of 1932, designed to make it easier for American banks to meet the demands of overseas depositors who were withdrawing their gold from the United States. And he encouraged New York financiers to establish a $500 million fund to help troubled banks stay afloat.

The most important piece of legislation of his presidency, however, was a bill passed in January 1932 establishing the Reconstruction Finance Corporation (RFC), a government agency whose purpose was to provide federal loans to troubled banks, railroads, and other businesses. It even made funds available to local governments to support public works projects and assist relief efforts. It was an unprecedented use of federal power; and unlike some earlier Hoover programs, it operated on a large scale. In 1932, the RFC had a budget of $1.5 billion for public works alone.

Nevertheless, the new agency failed to deal directly or forcefully enough with the real problems of the economy to produce any significant recovery. Because the RFC was permitted to lend funds only to those financial institutions with sufficient collateral, much of its money went to large banks and corporations, prompting some critics to dub it a "bread line for big business." The RFC could only provide loans; it could not purchase stock or otherwise provide capital to troubled institutions, even though that was what they most desperately needed. And at Hoover's insistence, it helped finance only those public works projects that promised ultimately to pay for themselves (toll bridges, public housing, and others), thus severely limiting the scope of its efforts. Its chairman, the conservative Texas banker Jesse Jones, prided himself on the solvency of his agency and followed sound, prudent banking practices. This meant that the RFC itself remained healthy by refusing to make loans to those institutions that most desperately needed them. Above all, the RFC did not have enough money to make any real impact on the Depression; and it did not even spend all the money it had. Of the $300 million available to support local relief efforts, the RFC lent out only $30 million in 1932. Of the $1.5 billion public works budget, it released only about 20 percent. Even Hoover's most vigorous and expansive program had been crippled by the cautiousness and fiscal conservatism of his administration.

Agrarian Unrest

For the first several years of the Depression, most Americans were either too stunned or too confused to raise any effective protest. By the middle of 1932, however, the crisis had continued so long and had grown so severe that dissident voices began to be heard.

In the Midwest, farmers sensing themselves near economic extinction raised new and louder demands for government assistance. In particular, they called for legislation similar to the McNary-Haugen bill of the 1920s by which the government would guarantee them a return on their crops at least equal to the cost of production. Lobbyists from the larger farm organizations converged on Washington to pressure members of Congress to act. Some disgruntled farmers staged public protests in the capital. But when neither the president nor Congress showed any signs of movement, they adopted a more drastic approach. In the summer of 1932, a group of unhappy farm owners gathered in Des Moines, Iowa, to establish a new organization: the Farm Holiday Association. Under the leadership of Milo Reno, the association endorsed the withholding of farm products from the market— in effect a farmers' strike. The strike began in August in western Iowa, spread briefly to a few neighboring areas, and succeeded in blockading several markets; but in the end it dissolved in failure. The scope of the effort was too modest to affect farm prices, and many farmers in the region refused to cooperate in any case. When clashes between strikers and local authorities resulted in several episodes of violence, Reno called off the strike. Nevertheless, the uprising created considerable consternation in state governments in the farm belt and even more in Washington, where the president and much of Congress were facing a national election.

Bonus Marchers, 1932
Although the Bonus March of 1932 would end in violence, it began optimistically, as well-dressed World War I veterans demonstrated in Washington in favor of early payment of a bonus that Congress had already voted them. Bonus Marchers are seen here en route to the Capitol from the Washington Monument in July 1932, only days before President Hoover ordered the army to clear them out of their encampments.   (The Bettmann Archive)

The Bonus March

A more celebrated protest movement emerged from a less likely quarter: American veterans. In 1924, Congress had approved the payment of a bonus to all those who had served in World War I, the money to be distributed in 1945. By 1932, however, economic distress had mobilized a widespread demand among veterans that the bonus be paid immediately. Hoover would not consider the request, fearing that acquiescence would ruin his hopes for a balanced budget; but the veterans refused to accept his arguments. In June, more than 20,000 veterans, members of the self-proclaimed "Bonus Army," marched into Washington, built crude camps in the city and its environs, and promised to stay until Congress approved legislation to pay the bonus. A few of the veterans departed in July, after Congress had voted down their proposal. Most, however, remained where they were.

Their continued presence in Washington was an irritant and an embarrassment to Herbert Hoover, who had problems enough already and who gradually became defensive and even paranoid about the protesters. Finally, in mid-July, he ordered police to clear the marchers out of several abandoned federal buildings in which they had been staying. The police arrived; a few marchers threw rocks at them; someone opened fire; and two veterans fell dead. To

Hoover, the incident seemed proof of dangerous radicalism, and he ordered the U.S. Army to assist the police in clearing out the buildings.

General Douglas MacArthur, the army chief of staff, chose to carry out the mission himself; in doing so, he greatly exceeded the president's orders. In full battle dress, he led the Third Cavalry (under the command of George S. Patton), two infantry regiments, a machine-gun detachment, and six tanks down Pennsylvania Avenue in pursuit of the motley Bonus Army. The veterans fled in terror as the troops hurled tear gas canisters and flailed at them with their bayonets. MacArthur followed them across the Anacostia River, where he ordered the soldiers to burn their camp to the ground. More than 100 marchers were injured. One baby died.

The incident served as perhaps the final blow to Hoover's already battered political standing. Many American newspapers (owned by conservative publishers) applauded the use of troops; but to much of the public, he now stood confirmed as an aloof and insensitive figure, locked in the White House, uncomprehending of the distress around him. Hoover's own cold and gloomy personality did nothing to change the public image, and some of his embattled public statements at the time made his plight even worse. "Nobody is actually starving," he assured reporters (inaccurately) in 1932. "The hoboes, for example, are better fed than they have ever been." The Great Engineer, the personification of the optimistic days of the 1920s, had become a symbol of the nation's failure to deal effectively with its startling reversal of fortune.

The Election of 1932

Most of the American people looked to the 1932 presidential election as their most effective vehicle of protest. Almost no one had any doubts about the outcome. The Republican party dutifully renominated Herbert Hoover for a second term in office, but the lugubrious atmosphere of their convention made it clear that few delegates believed he could carry the November election. The Democrats, in the meantime, gathered jubilantly in Chicago to nominate a candidate who, they were certain, would be the next president of the United States. Their choice was the governor of New York, Franklin Delano Roosevelt.

Roosevelt had been a well-known figure in the party for many years already. The son of a wealthy Hudson Valley railroad tycoon, schooled at Harvard and at Columbia Law School, Roosevelt had begun his political career in 1910 in the New York State legislature. Because he was handsome, charming, and articulate, and because he was a distant cousin of Theodore Roosevelt (a connection strengthened by his marriage in 1904 to the president's niece, Eleanor), he attracted increasing attention. He served as assistant secretary of the navy under Woodrow Wilson during World War I; and in 1920, he received his party's nomination for vice president on the ill-fated ticket with James M. Cox.

Less than a year later, however, his public career appeared to come to an end when he was stricken with polio and lost the use of his legs. For seven years, Roosevelt worked hard at his recovery, but he was never again able to walk without the use of crutches and braces. Nevertheless, he built up sufficient physical strength to make a courageous appearance at the 1924 Democratic Convention to nominate Al Smith for president. In 1928, when Smith finally received the Democratic nomination and left Albany to run for president, Roosevelt succeeded him as governor. In 1930, he easily won reelection.

Roosevelt worked no miracles in New York as the state suffered through the first years of the Depression. He did, however, initiate enough positive programs of government assistance to be able to

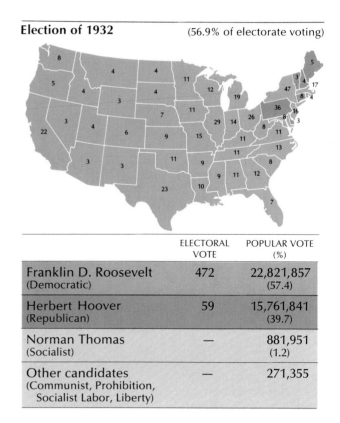

Election of 1932   (56.9% of electorate voting)

	ELECTORAL VOTE	POPULAR VOTE (%)
Franklin D. Roosevelt (Democratic)	472	22,821,857 (57.4)
Herbert Hoover (Republican)	59	15,761,841 (39.7)
Norman Thomas (Socialist)	—	881,951 (1.2)
Other candidates (Communist, Prohibition, Socialist Labor, Liberty)	—	271,355

present himself as a more energetic and imaginative leader than Herbert Hoover. At least as important to his political future, however, was his astute effort to win support from both the urban and rural wings of his party. By avoiding such divisive cultural issues as religion and prohibition, and by emphasizing the economic grievances that most Democrats shared, he assembled a coalition within the party that enabled him to win his party's nomination. And the next day, in a dramatic break with tradition, he flew to Chicago to address the convention in person and accept the nomination.

In the course of his acceptance speech, Roosevelt aroused the delegates with his ringing promise: "I pledge you, I pledge myself, to a new deal for the American people," giving his program a name that would long endure. Neither then nor in the subsequent campaign, however, did Roosevelt give much indication of what that program would be. In part, of course, it was because there was no need to be specific. Herbert Hoover's unpopularity virtually ensured Roosevelt's election; his only real concern was to avoid offending any voters unnecessarily. In part, however, it was because Roosevelt had no firm or coherent program to describe. Surrounded by advisers

SIGNIFICANT EVENTS

1929   Stock market crash signals onset of Great Depression (p. 726)

Agricultural Marketing Act passed (p. 740)

1930   Hawley-Smoot Tariff enacted (p. 740)

Ten-year drought begins in South and Midwest (the Dust Bowl) (p. 730)

1931   Federal Reserve raises interest rates (p. 729)

Depression spreads to Europe and deepens in United States (pp. 728, 741)

Scottsboro defendants arrested (p. 733)

1932   Erskine Caldwell publishes *Tobacco Road* (p. 737)

Glass-Steagall Banking Act passed (p. 742)

Reconstruction Finance Corporation established (p. 742)

Farm Holiday Association formed in Iowa (p. 742)

Bonus Marchers come to Washington, D.C. (p. 743)

Banking crisis (pp. 728, 742)

Franklin D. Roosevelt elected president (p. 745)

1935   American Communist party proclaims Popular Front (p. 739)

1936   Dale Carnegie publishes *How to Win Friends and Influence People* (p. 736)

Margaret Mitchell publishes *Gone with the Wind* (p. 737)

1939   John Steinbeck publishes *The Grapes of Wrath* (p. 737)

Nazi-Soviet pact weakens American Communist party (p. 739)

1940   Richard Wright publishes *Native Son* (p. 737)

Ernest Hemingway publishes *For Whom the Bell Tolls* (p. 737)

1941   James Agee and Walker Evans publish *Let Us Now Praise Famous Men* (p. 737)

---

holding widely disparate views, the candidate seemed at times to be little more than a genial mediator—listening to everyone, disagreeing with no one.

There was, however, evidence of important differences between Roosevelt and Hoover. Drawing from the ideas of a talented team of university professors (whom the press quickly dubbed the "Brains Trust"), Roosevelt espoused an amalgam of ideas that combined old progressive reform principles with some of the newer ideas of associationalism that had gained currency in the 1920s (although he also called for a balanced budget and attacked Hoover for his failure to provide one). Hoover liked to insist that the Depression was international in origin and that any attempt to combat it must be international as well. Roosevelt, in contrast, portrayed the crisis as a domestic (and Republican) problem and argued that the most important solutions could be found at home. Above all, perhaps, Roosevelt's style—his dazzling smile, his floppy broad-brimmed hat, his cigarette holder held at a jaunty angle between his teeth, his skillful oratory, his lively wit—all combined to win him a wide personal popularity only vaguely related to the specifics of his programs.

In November, to the surprise of no one, Roosevelt won by a landslide. He received 57.4 percent of the popular vote to Hoover's 39.7. The Socialist party, in this year of despair, garnered only 1.2 percent of the ballots. The Communist party polled a meager 103,000 votes. In the electoral college, the result was even more overwhelming. Hoover carried Pennsylvania, Connecticut, Vermont, New Hampshire, and Maine. Roosevelt won everything else. Democrats won majorities in both houses of Congress. It was a broad and convincing mandate, but it was not yet clear what Roosevelt intended to do with it.

The Interregnum

The period between the election and the inauguration (which in the early 1930s still lasted more than four months) was traditionally a time of quiet planning and federal inaction. The winter of 1932–1933, however, was a season of growing economic crisis; and traditional patterns seemed to many Americans to be inappropriate. Among those who believed that the president-elect should act forcefully even before tak-

Mar. 4, 1933   THE NEW YORKER   Price 15 cents

The Changing of the Guard

Long before the event actually occurred, Peter Arno of the *New Yorker* magazine drew this image of Franklin D. Roosevelt and Herbert Hoover traveling together to the Capitol for Roosevelt's inauguration. It predicted with remarkable accuracy the mood of the uncomfortable ride—Hoover glum and uncommunicative, Roosevelt buoyant and smiling. This was to have been the magazine's cover for the week of the inauguration; but after an attempted asassination of the president-elect several weeks earlier in Florida (in which the mayor of Chicago was killed), the editors decided to substitute a more subdued drawing. (© 1933, 1961 Peter Arno/Franklin D. Roosevelt Library)

ing office was Herbert Hoover, who argued that international economic stability depended on a clear affirmation by the United States of the sanctity of the gold standard. He argued as well that fear of "radical" economic measures by the new administration was unsettling the domestic financial climate. In a series of brittle exchanges with Roosevelt in the months following the election, Hoover tried to exact from the president-elect a pledge to maintain policies of economic orthodoxy. Roosevelt genially refused.

In February, only a month before the inauguration, a new crisis developed. The American banking system had been in desperate trouble since the middle of 1930. By 1932, it was beginning to collapse. Public confidence in the banks was ebbing; depositors were withdrawing their money in panic; and one bank after another was closing its doors and declaring bankruptcy. In mid-February, the governor of Michigan, one of the states hardest hit by the panic, ordered all banks temporarily closed. Other states soon followed, and by the end of the month banking activity

was restricted drastically in every state but one. Once again, Hoover wrote to Roosevelt insisting that the problem was a result of "steadily degenerating confidence" in the incoming administration. The only way to restore calm, he insisted, was for Roosevelt to give prompt public assurances that there would be no tinkering with the currency, no heavy borrowing, no unbalancing of the budget. "I realize," he wrote a Republican senator at the time, "that if these declarations be made by the president-elect, he will have ratified the whole major program of the Republican Administration." Roosevelt realized the same thing and refused to comply.

March 4, 1933, was, therefore, a day not only of economic crisis but of considerable personal bitterness. The nation waited anxiously as Herbert Hoover, convinced that the United States was headed for disaster, rode glumly down Pennsylvania Avenue with a beaming, buoyant Franklin Roosevelt, who would shortly be sworn in as the thirty-second president of the United States.

SUGGESTED READINGS

The Coming of the Depression. Michael Bernstein, *The Great Depression: Delayed Recovery and Economic Change in America, 1929–1939* (1987); Robert Sobel, *The Great Bull Market* (1968); John Kenneth Galbraith, *The Great Crash* (1954); Milton Friedman and Anna Schwartz, *The Great Contraction* (1965) or Chapter 7 of *A Monetary History of the United States* (1963); Peter Temin, *Did Monetary Forces Cause the Great Depression?* (1976); Broadus Mitchell, *Depression Decade* (1947); Lester V. Chandler, *America's Greatest Depression* (1970); Charles Kindelberger, *The World in Depression* (1973); Susan E. Kennedy, *The Banking Crisis of 1933* (1973).

The Impact of the Depression. Irving Bernstein, *The Lean Years* (1960); Arthur M. Schlesinger, Jr., *The Crisis of the Old Order* (1957); Robert S. McElvaine, ed., *Down and Out in the Great Depression: Letters from the Forgotten Man* (1983); Studs Terkel, *Hard Times* (1970); Federal Writers' Project, *These Are Our Lives* (1939); Tom Terrill and Jerrold Hirsch, *Such as Us* (1978); Ann Banks, *First-Person America* (1980); Janet Poppendieck, *Breadlines Knee-Deep in Wheat: Food Assistance in the Great Depression* (1986); Donald Worster, *Dust Bowl* (1979); Walter Stein, *California and the Dust Bowl Migration* (1973); James N. Gregory, *American Exodus: The Dust Bowl Migration and Okie Culture in California* (1989).

Depression Culture and Society. Robert Lynd and Helen Merrell Lynd, *Middletown in Transition* (1935); Frederick Lewis Allen, *Since Yesterday* (1940); Richard Pells, *Radical Visions and American Dreams: Culture and Social Thought in the Depression Years* (1973); Warren Susman, *Culture as History* (1984); Richard Krickus, *Pursuing the American Dream* (1976); Gilman Ostrander, *American Civilization in the First Machine Age* (1970); Andrew Bergman, *We're in the Money: Depression America and Its Films* (1971); Alice Goldfarb Marquis, *Hopes and Ashes: The Birth of Modern Times, 1929–1939* (1986); David P. Peeler, *Hope Among Us Yet: Social Criticism and Social Thought in the Depression Years* (1987). See Suggested Readings at the end of Chapter 26 for literature on blacks, Hispanics, Indians, and labor during the Depression.

Women and the Depression. Julia K. Blackwelder, *Women of the Depression: Caste and Culture in San Antonio, 1919–1939* (1984); William Chafe, *The American Woman* (1972); Lois Scharf, *To Work and to Wed: Female Employment, Feminism, and the Great Depression* (1980); Joan Jensen and Lois Scharf, eds., *Decades of Discontent: The Women's Movement, 1920–1940* (1983); Susan Ware, *Holding Their Own: American Women in the 1930s* (1982); Jeane Westin, *Making Do: How Women Survived the '30s* (1976).

The Hoover Presidency. Albert Romasco, *The Poverty of Abundance* (1965); Joan Hoff Wilson, *Herbert Hoover* (1975); David Burner, *Herbert Hoover* (1978); Harris Warren, *Herbert Hoover and the Great Depression* (1959); Jordan Schwarz, *The Interregnum of Despair* (1970); Herbert Hoover, *The Great Depression* (1952); James S. Olsen, *Herbert Hoover and the Reconstruction Finance Corporation* (1977) and *Saving Capitalism: The Reconstruction Finance Corporation and the New Deal, 1933–1940* (1988); Martin Fausold and George Mazuzun (eds.), *The Hoover Presidency* (1974); Martin Fausold, *The Presidency of Herbert C. Hoover* (1985); William J. Barber, *From New Era to New Deal: Herbert Hoover, The Economists, and American Economic Policy, 1921–1933* (1985).

Politics and Protest. John Shover, *Cornbelt Rebellion* (1965); Roger Daniels, *The Bonus March* (1971); Donald Lisio, *The President and Protest* (1974); Harvey Klehr, *The Heyday of American Communism: The Depression Decade* (1984); Mark Naison, *Communists in Harlem During the Depression* (1983); Arthur M. Schlesinger, Jr., *The Crisis of the Old Order* (1957); David Burner, *The Politics of Provincialism* (1967); Frank Freidel, *The Triumph* (1956) and *Launching the New Deal* (1973); Eliot Rosen, *Hoover, Roosevelt, and the Brains Trust* (1977); Rexford G. Tugwell, *The Brains Trust* (1968).

WPA Poster, 1930s
The Works Progress Administration, which this striking poster celebrates, was the New Deal's most prominent experiment in work relief. In addition to providing jobs for unemployed farmers and industrial workers (as depicted here), it created programs to assist writers, artists, actors, and others. (*Library of Congress*)

CHAPTER 26

▨ ◈ ▧

The New Deal

◨ ◈ ▨

Franklin Roosevelt not only served longer as president than any man in American history. He became during his years in office more central to the life of the nation than any chief executive before him. Most important, perhaps, his administration constructed a series of programs that permanently altered the federal government. The accomplishments of the New Deal, and their impact on all subsequent discussions of the role of government in American society, have helped shape the nation's political life ever since.

And yet the Roosevelt administration itself was never firmly committed to any particular philosophy of government. Pragmatic, experimental, unwedded to any single set of social or economic beliefs, the New Deal defied easy classification or neat description. Roosevelt himself gave perhaps the clearest statement of the New Deal's political philosophy. "Try something," he once exhorted the nation. "If it works, keep doing it. If it doesn't, try something else."

By the end of the 1930s, when the outbreak of war in Europe finally brought the crusade for domestic reform temporarily to a close, the Roosevelt administration had created many of the broad outlines of the political world we know today. It had constructed the beginnings of a modern welfare system. It had extended federal regulation over new areas of the economy. It had presided over the birth of the modern labor movement. It had made the government a major force in the agricultural economy. It had created a powerful coalition within the Democratic party that would dominate American politics for most of the

next thirty years. And it had produced the beginnings of a new liberal ideology that would govern reform efforts for several decades after the war.

One thing the New Deal had not done, however, was end the Great Depression. It had, to be sure, helped stabilize the economy in the desperate early months of 1933 and had kept things from getting worse. And there had been a limited, if erratic, recovery in many areas of economic life. But by the end of 1939, many of the basic problems of the Depression remained unsolved. An estimated 15 percent of the work force remained unemployed. The gross national product was no larger than it had been ten years before.

Inevitably, these long years of economic stagnation took their toll on the nation's political and social life. And the Roosevelt administration faced repeated challenges throughout the 1930s from groups impatient with its programs. The political fortunes of the New Deal ebbed and flowed throughout the 1930s, and at times a major political upheaval seemed to be at hand. But in the end, Franklin Roosevelt managed, despite the challenges, to retain a firm grip on the loyalties of a majority of the public.

Launching the New Deal

Roosevelt's first task, he knew, was to alleviate the crisis that was threatening in early 1933 to bring the financial system and the economy as a whole to its

The Roosevelt Smile

The battered hat, the uptilted cigarette holder, the jaunty smile—all were hallmarks of Franklin Roosevelt's ebullient public personality. In part, at least, the president's hearty optimism was a deliberate pose, adopted to distract attention from the paralysis that had denied him the use of his legs since 1921. Roosevelt took elaborate precautions to hide signs of his affliction from the public. He learned to "walk" short distances with the aid of metal braces, a cane, and the support of an aide (or, often, one of his sons). He appeared often in public (as seen in this 1939 photograph) driving a specially designed automobile with hand controls. In private, however, Roosevelt was largely confined to a wheelchair; he had to be lifted in and out of cars, even in and out of bed; and as the years passed and his strength ebbed, he seldom ventured from the White House. (AP/Wide World Photos)

knees. In particular, he had to stop the panic that was rapidly gripping the nation. He did so remarkably quickly—in part by sheer force of personality and in part by constructing, in a few months, an ambitious and diverse program of legislation. This "First New Deal," as many historians have called it, embraced many different approaches to reform (as well as some intensely conservative measures).

Restoring Confidence

Much of Roosevelt's success was a result of his ebullient personality. Beginning with his inaugural address—in which he assured the American people that "the only thing we have to fear is fear itself"—he projected an infectious optimism that helped dispel the growing despair. He was the first president to make regular use of the radio, and his friendly "fireside chats," during which he explained his programs and plans to the people, helped to build public confidence in the administration. Roosevelt was also a master at handling his relations with the press. He held frequent informal press conferences,

and he won both the respect and the friendship of most reporters. Their regard for him was such that by unwritten agreement, no journalist ever photographed the president getting into or out of his car or being wheeled in his wheelchair. Much of the American public remained unaware throughout the Roosevelt years that their president's legs remained completely paralyzed.

Image alone, however, could not solve the serious economic problems of March 1933; and within twenty-four hours of his inauguration, Roosevelt was moving forcefully to construct a program that would restore at least momentary stability to the nation. With the banking crisis at a fever pitch and with Congress apparently in a mood to do virtually anything the new president suggested, Roosevelt might well have taken drastic steps, such as nationalizing the banking system. Instead, he worked to shore up existing financial institutions and to revive business faith in the economy. On March 6, two days after taking office, he issued a proclamation closing all American banks for four days until Congress could meet in special session. Under other circumstances, shutting down the nation's banks would have created wide alarm. But since many states had already closed their banks before Roosevelt's proclamation, the "bank holiday," as the president euphemistically described it, created a general sense of relief. Finally, the federal government was stepping in to stop the alarming pattern of bank failures.

Three days later, Roosevelt sent to Congress the Emergency Banking Act, a generally conservative bill (much of it drafted by holdovers from the Hoover administration) designed primarily to protect the larger banks from being dragged down by the weakness of smaller ones. The bill provided for Treasury Department inspection of all banks before they would be allowed to reopen, for federal assistance to some troubled institutions, and for a thorough reorganization of those in the greatest difficulty. A confused and frightened Congress passed the bill within four hours of its introduction. "I can assure you," Roosevelt told the public on March 12, in his first fireside chat, "that it is safer to keep your money in a reopened bank than under the mattress." The public apparently believed him. Three-quarters of the banks in the Federal Reserve system reopened within the next three days, and $1 billion in hoarded currency and gold flowed back into them within a month. The immediate banking crisis was over.

On the morning after passage of the Emergency Banking Act, Roosevelt sent to Congress another measure—the Economy Act—designed to convince the public (and especially the business community) that the federal government was in safe, responsible hands. The act proposed to balance the federal budget by cutting the salaries of government employees and reducing pensions to veterans by as much as 15 percent. Otherwise, the president warned, the nation faced a $1 billion deficit. The bill seemed to confirm what Roosevelt had maintained throughout the 1932 campaign: that he was as much a fiscal conservative as his predecessor. And like the banking bill, it passed through Congress almost instantly—despite heated protests from some congressional progressives.

Roosevelt also moved in his first days in office to put to rest one of the divisive issues of the 1920s. He supported and then signed a bill to legalize the manufacture and sale of beer with a 3.2 percent alcohol content—an interim measure pending the repeal of prohibition, for which a constitutional amendment (the Twenty-first) was already in process. The amendment was ratified later in 1933.

Agricultural Adjustment

Roosevelt realized that these initial actions were nothing but stopgaps, that more comprehensive government programs would be necessary. The first such program was on behalf of the troubled agricultural economy, and it established an important and long-lasting federal role in the planning of the entire agricultural sector of the economy.

The Agricultural Adjustment Act, which Congress passed in May 1933, reflected the desires of leaders of various farm organizations and the ideas of Roosevelt's secretary of agriculture, Henry A. Wallace. It included scraps and reworkings of many long-cherished agricultural schemes, but its most important feature was its provision for crop reductions.

Under the "domestic allotment" system of the act, producers of seven basic commodities (wheat, cotton, corn, hogs, rice, tobacco, and dairy products) would decide on production limits for their crops. The government would then, through the Agricultural Adjustment Administration (AAA), tell individual farmers how much they should plant and would pay them subsidies for leaving some of their land idle. A tax on food processing (for example, the milling of wheat) would provide the funds for the new payments. Farm prices were to be subsidized up to the point of parity.

Because the 1933 agricultural season was already under way by the time the AAA began operations, the agency oversaw a large-scale destruction of existing crops and livestock to reduce surpluses. Six million pigs and 220,000 sows were slaughtered. Cotton farmers plowed under a quarter of their crop. In a society plagued by want, in which many families were suffering from malnutrition and starvation, it was difficult for the government to explain the need for destroying surpluses, and the crop and livestock destruction remained controversial for many years. Beginning in 1934, however, crop and livestock limitations were accomplished in less provocative ways.

The results of the AAA efforts were in many ways heartening. Prices for farm commodities did indeed rise in the years after 1933, and gross farm income increased by half in the first three years of the New Deal. The relative position of farmers in the nation, therefore, improved significantly for the first time in twenty years; and the agricultural economy as a whole emerged from the 1930s much more stable and prosperous than it had been in the past. The AAA did, however, tend to favor larger farmers over smaller ones, particularly since local administration of its programs often fell into the hands of the most powerful producers in a community. At times, even if unintentionally, the New Deal farm program actually dispossessed some struggling farmers. In the cotton belt, for example, planters who were reducing their acreage evicted their tenants and sharecroppers and fired many field hands.

In January 1936, the Supreme Court struck down the crucial provisions of the Agricultural Adjustment Act, arguing that the government had no constitutional authority to require farmers to limit production. But the essence of the AAA programs survived, because within a few weeks the administration had secured passage of new legislation (the Soil Conservation and Domestic Allotment Act), which permitted the government to pay farmers to reduce production so as to "conserve soil," prevent erosion, and accomplish other secondary goals. The new law apparently met the Court's objections.

It also attempted to correct one of the most glaring injustices of the original act: its failure to protect sharecroppers and tenant farmers. Now landlords were required to share the payments they received for cutting back production with those who worked their land. (The new requirements were, however, largely evaded.) The administration launched other efforts to assist poor farmers as well. The Resettlement Administration, established in 1935, and its successor, the Farm Security Administration, created in 1937, attempted through short- and long-term loans to help farmers cultivating submarginal soil to relocate on better lands. But the programs never moved more than a few thousand farmers. Of more importance was the Rural Electrification Administration, created in 1935, which worked to make electric power available to farmers through utility cooperatives. Because of the REA, thousands of rural families gained access to electricity for the first time.

Industrial Recovery

The industrial economy in 1933 was, as it had been for nearly three years, suffering from a vicious cycle of deflation. Ever since 1931, leaders of the U.S. Chamber of Commerce and many others had been urging the government to adopt an antideflation scheme that would permit trade associations to cooperate in stabilizing prices within their industries. Existing antitrust laws clearly forbade such practices, but businesspeople argued that the economic emer-

gency justified a suspension of the restrictions. Herbert Hoover had long been a supporter of the trade association movement, but he had refused to endorse suspension of the antitrust laws.

The Roosevelt administration was more receptive to the idea of cooperation among producers, and even to the demands of some businesspeople that the government enforce trade association agreements on pricing and production. But New Dealers insisted on additional provisions that would deal with other economic problems as well. Businesspeople would have to make important concessions to labor to ensure that the incomes of workers would rise along with prices. And lest consumer buying power lag behind and defeat the scheme, the administration added another ingredient: a major program of public works spending designed to pump needed funds into the economy. The result of these many impulses was the National Industrial Recovery Act, which Congress passed in June 1933. Roosevelt, signing the bill, called it "the most important and far-reaching legislation ever enacted by the American Congress." Businesspeople hailed it as the beginning of a new era of cooperation between government and industry. Labor leaders praised it as a "Magna Carta" for trade unions. There was, it seemed, something in the bill for everyone.

At first, moreover, the new program appeared to work miracles. At its center was a new federal agency, the National Recovery Administration (NRA); and to head it, Roosevelt chose the flamboyant and energetic Hugh S. Johnson, a retired general and successful businessman. Johnson envisioned himself as a kind of evangelist, whose major mission was to generate public enthusiasm for the NRA. He did so in two ways. First, he called on every business establishment in the nation to accept a temporary "blanket code": a minimum wage of between 30 and 40 cents an hour, a maximum workweek of 35 to 40 hours, and the abolition of child labor. The result, he claimed, would be to raise consumer purchasing power, increase employment, and eliminate the infamous sweatshop. To generate enthusiasm for the blanket code, Johnson devised a symbol—the famous NRA Blue Eagle— which employers who accepted the provisions could display in their windows. Soon Blue Eagle flags, posters, and stickers, carrying the NRA slogan "We Do Our Part," were decorating commercial establishments in every part of the country.

At the same time, Johnson was busy negotiating another, more specific set of codes with leaders of the

The NRA Blue Eagle on Parade, 1933
Hugh Johnson, the first director of the New Deal's National Recovery Administration, was a brilliant publicist who recognized from the start that the wage-price programs of his new agency required broad popular support. Among other things, he staged an enormous parade in New York City—one of the biggest in the city's history—to generate public enthusiasm for the NRA and its famous symbol, the Blue Eagle, and to forge a link between support for the program and patriotism. Merchants and householders displayed the eagle emblem (accompanied by the NRA slogan "We Do Our Part") on posters and stickers in their windows.   (UPI/Bettmann Newsphotos)

nation's major industries. These industrial codes set floors below which no company would lower prices or wages in its search for a competitive advantage, and they included agreements on maintaining employment and production. The extraordinary public support Johnson had managed to generate for the blanket code gave him substantial bargaining strength; in a remarkably short time, he won agreements from almost every major industry in the country. A nation eager for positive action was giving the NRA its fervent support.

From the beginning, however, the New Deal's bold experiment in economic cooperation encountered serious difficulties, and the entire effort ultimately dissolved in failure. The codes themselves were hastily and often poorly written. Administra-

tion of them proved to be a bureaucratic nightmare, far beyond the capacities of federal officials with no prior experience in administering so vast a program. Large producers consistently dominated the code-writing process and ensured that the new regulations would work to their advantage and to the disadvantage of smaller firms. And the codes often did more than simply set floors under prices; they actively and artificially raised them—at times to levels higher than was necessary to ensure a profit and far higher than market forces would have dictated.

A closely related problem was that attempts to increase consumer purchasing power did not progress as quickly as the efforts to raise prices. Section 7(a) of the National Industrial Recovery Act—the NRA's charter—gave legal protection to the right

Working for the Government, 1933
Work relief programs were among the most distinctive features of the New
Deal. They embodied a combination of commitment to helping the unemployed and uneasiness about welfare (or "the dole") that virtually all reformers
in the 1930s shared. Here men working for the Public Works Administration
build a street near the White House in Washington. (UPI/Bettmann Newsphotos)

of workers to form unions and engage in collective
bargaining. Partly as a result, many new workers
joined unions in the ensuing months; but actual recognition of unions by employers (and thus the significant wage increases the unions were committed to
winning) did not follow. The Public Works Administration (PWA), established by the bill to administer
spending programs, was placed in the hands of Interior Secretary Harold Ickes, a self-described "cur-
mudgeon" who only gradually allowed the $3.3
billion in public works funds to trickle out. Not until
1938 was the PWA budget pumping an appreciable
amount of money into the economy.

For a while, most Americans enthusiastically
supported the NRA experiment, expecting a major
industrial revival to result. But the revival did not
come. Indeed, industrial production actually declined in the months after the establishment of the
NRA—from an index of 101 in July 1933 to 71 in
November—despite the rise in prices that the codes
had helped to create. By the spring of 1934, therefore, the NRA was besieged by criticism. Busi-

nesses were beginning once again to cut wages and
prices or to violate agreements on levels of
production—claiming as they did so that the wage
requirements of the codes were making it impossible to earn adequate profits. They were also openly
flaunting the provisions requiring them to bargain
with unions, which attracted increasing labor hostility to the NRA. Economists were charging that
the price fixing encouraged by the codes was undermining efforts to raise purchasing power. Reformers were complaining that the NRA was
encouraging economic concentration and monopoly. A national Recovery Review Board, chaired by
the famous criminal lawyer Clarence Darrow, reported in the spring of 1934 that the NRA was excessively dominated by big business and unduly
encouraging monopoly; and Hugh Johnson's vitu-
perative response served only to undermine the
agency's prestige even further.

Finally, in the fall of 1934, Roosevelt pressured
Johnson to resign and established a new board of
directors to oversee the NRA. Then in 1935, the Su-

preme Court intervened to bring an end to the troubled experiment. The constitutional basis for the NRA had been Congress's power to regulate commerce among the states, a power the administration had interpreted very broadly. The case before the Court involved alleged code violations by the Schechter brothers, who operated a wholesale poultry business confined to one locality: Brooklyn, New York. The Court ruled unanimously that the Schechters were not engaged in interstate commerce and, further, that Congress had unconstitutionally delegated legislative power to the president to draft the NRA codes. The legislation establishing the agency, therefore, was declared void; the NRA was forced to cease its operations.

Roosevelt expressed outrage at what became known as the "sick chicken" decision and denounced the justices for their "horse-and-buggy" interpretation of the interstate commerce clause. He was rightly concerned, for the reasoning in the *Schechter* case threatened many other New Deal programs as well. But the destruction of the NRA itself was probably more a blessing than a catastrophe for the New Deal, providing it with a face-saving way to abolish the failed experiment.

Regional Planning

The AAA and the NRA largely reflected the beliefs of New Dealers who favored economic planning but wanted private interests (farmers or business leaders) to dominate the planning process. In some areas, however, other reformers—those who believed that the government itself should be the chief planning agent in the economy—managed to establish dominance. Their most conspicuous success, and one of the most celebrated accomplishments of the New Deal as a whole, was an unprecedented experiment in regional planning: the Tennessee Valley Authority (TVA).

The TVA had its roots in a political controversy that had surfaced repeatedly in the 1920s. Throughout that decade, one of the cherished goals of progressive reformers (above all Senator George Norris of Nebraska) had been public development of the nation's water resources as a source of cheap electric power. In particular, they had urged completion of a great dam at Muscle Shoals on the Tennessee River in Alabama—a dam begun during World War I but left unfinished when the hostilities concluded. The nation's utility companies, predictably opposed to the concept of public power in any form, had fought desperately and successfully against completion of the project.

In 1932, however, one of the great utility empires—that of the electricity magnate Samuel Insull—had collapsed spectacularly, amid widely publicized exposés of corruption. That and other scandals had combined by 1933 to create indignation against the private power interests so intense that they were no longer able to block the public power movement. The result was legislation supported by the president and enacted by Congress in May 1933 creating the Tennessee Valley Authority, a public corporation whose mandate was "national planning for a complete river watershed." The TVA was intended not only to complete the dam at Muscle Shoals and build others in the region, and not only to generate and sell electricity from them to the public at reasonable rates. It was also to be the agent for a comprehensive redevelopment of the entire region: for stopping the disastrous flooding that had plagued the Tennessee Valley for centuries, for encouraging the development of local industries, for supervising a substantial program of reforestation, and for helping farmers to improve productivity.

On the whole, it succeeded quite well. Although opposition by conservatives within the administration ultimately blocked some of the most ambitious social planning projects proposed by the more visionary TVA administrators, the project did revitalize the region in numerous ways. It improved five existing dams, built twenty new ones, and constructed an extensive (and heavily trafficked) system of inland waterways. It managed as a result virtually to eliminate flooding in the region and to provide electricity to thousands who had never before had it. Indeed, the TVA soon became the greatest producer of electric power in the United States, as well as one of the cheapest suppliers. Throughout the country, largely because of the yardstick provided by the TVA, private power rates soon declined as well. The TVA also produced inexpensive phosphate fertilizers, helped farmers to prevent soil erosion, and generally raised agricultural productivity—and through it the standard of living—for the entire region. But the Authority worked no miracles. The Tennessee Valley remained a generally impoverished region despite its efforts. And like many other New Deal programs, it made no serious effort to challenge local customs and racial prejudices.

The Tennessee Valley Authority

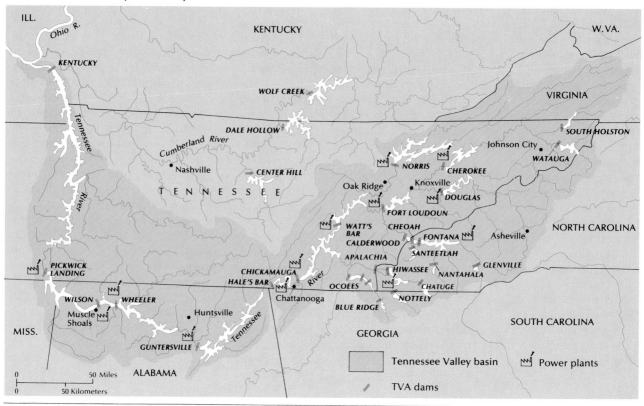

Financial Reforms

For more than half a century, many Americans concerned about the health of their economy had believed that the nation's monetary system—its currency—was the key to solving most problems. In the early days of the New Deal, this preoccupation with the currency continued to affect policy and helped produce a number of important initiatives. In particular, the administration made the controversial decision to take the country off the gold standard.

Roosevelt was not an inflationist at heart, but he soon came to consider the gold standard a major obstacle to the restoration of adequate prices. On April 18, 1933, the president made the shift off the gold standard official with an executive order (over the warnings of his budget director, Lew Douglas, who had predicted the action would lead to "the end of Western civilization"). A few weeks later, Congress passed legislation confirming his decision. By itself,

the repudiation of the gold standard meant relatively little. But both before and after the April decision, the administration experimented in various ways with manipulating the value of the dollar—by making substantial purchases of gold and silver and later by establishing a new, fixed standard for the dollar (reducing its gold content substantially from the 1932 amount). The resort to government-managed currency—that is, to a dollar whose value could be raised or lowered by government policy according to economic circumstances—created an important precedent for future federal policies and permanently altered the relationship between the public and private sectors. It did not, however, have any immediate impact on the depressed American economy.

Through other legislation, the early New Deal increased federal authority over previously unregulated or weakly regulated areas of the economy. The Glass-Steagall Act of June 1933 gave the government authority to curb irresponsible speculation by banks. More important, in the public mind at least, it established the Federal Deposit Insurance Corporation, which guaranteed all bank deposits up to $2,500. In other words, even should a bank fail, small depositors would be able to recover their money. Roosevelt opposed the FDIC during congressional debate over the bill, but once in operation it proved so successful that he later approved a gradual raising of the limit on guaranteed deposits, which by the end of the decade had reached $15,000. (It is now $100,000.) Finally, in 1935, Congress passed a major banking act that transferred much of the authority once wielded by the regional Federal Reserve banks to the Federal Reserve Board in Washington, whose seven members now exercised direct control over interest rates. By lowering the rates, the board could make it easier to borrow money from banks and thus, in most cases, encourage prices to rise.

To protect investors in the once popular and now mistrusted stock market, Congress passed the so-called Truth in Securities Act of 1933, requiring corporations issuing new securities to register them with the Federal Trade Commission and provide full and accurate information about them to the public. In June 1934, Congress went further and established the Securities and Exchange Commission (SEC) to police the stock market. Among other things, the establishment of the SEC was an indication of how far the financial establishment had fallen in the estimation of the public. In earlier years, J. P. Morgan and other important financiers could have wielded enough influence to stop such government interference in the financial world. Now Morgan could not even get a respectful hearing on Capitol Hill. The criminal trials of a number of once respected Wall Street figures for grand larceny and fraud (including the conviction and imprisonment of Richard Whitney, one-time head of the New York Stock Exchange and a close Morgan associate) eroded the public stature of the financial community still further.

The Growth of Federal Relief

The most important purpose of the New Deal, Franklin Roosevelt and his colleagues believed, was to reform and revive the economy—to restore stability and enhance productivity so that general prosperity would return. In the meantime, however, millions of Americans were in desperate need of assistance, and the administration recognized the necessity of providing them with relief.

Like his predecessor, Roosevelt believed that aid to the indigent was primarily a local responsibility and should remain so. But he also recognized that under the circumstances of the Depression, localities were unable to fulfill that responsibility. Among his first acts as president, therefore, was the establishment of the Federal Emergency Relief Administration (FERA), which provided cash grants to states (rather than loans, as the Hoover administration had favored) to prop up bankrupt relief agencies. To administer the program, he chose the director of the New York State relief agency, Harry Hopkins, who was ultimately to become one of the most important members of his administration. Hopkins, unlike Harold Ickes, realized the importance of speed in distributing government funds, and he disbursed the FERA grants widely and rapidly. Even he, however, shared Roosevelt's basic misgivings about establishing a government dole. "It is probably going to undermine the independence of hundreds of thousands of families," he once lamented.

Both Roosevelt and Hopkins felt somewhat more comfortable with another form of government assistance: work relief. Unlike the dole, Hopkins believed, work relief "preserves a man's morale. It saves his skill. It gives him a chance to do something socially useful." Thus when it became clear that the FERA grants would not be sufficient to pull the country through the winter, the administration established a second program: the Civil Works Administration. Between November and April, it put more than 4 million people to work on temporary projects: some of them of real value, such as the construction of roads, schools, and parks; others little more than make-work. The important thing, however, was that the 400,000 CWA projects (with a budget of $1 billion) were pumping money into an economy badly in need of it and were providing assistance to people with nowhere else to turn. This use of government spending to stimulate the economy—later to be known as Keynesian economics (see below, p. 857)— was one of the New Deal's most important contributions to public policy. But in 1933, at least, members of the administration were only vaguely aware of the broad effects of this spending on the economy as a whole; most thought of it more as a way to help particular people than as a way to stimulate a broader recovery.

Evidence of this limited view of the value of government spending was that most of these early relief programs had short lives. Like the FERA, the CWA was intended to be only a temporary expedient. In the spring of 1934, the president began to dismantle the agency, and he ultimately disbanded it altogether. Most economists now agree that massive and sustained government spending would have been the most effective way to end the Depression. Few policymakers in the 1930s shared that belief.

Of all the New Deal relief projects, the one Roosevelt had the least difficulty reconciling with his conservative beliefs was the Civilian Conservation Corps. Established in the first weeks of the new administration, the CCC was designed to provide employment to the millions of urban young men who could find no jobs in the cities and who, in many cases, were moving restlessly from one region of the country to another in search of work. At the same time, it was intended to advance the work of conservation and reforestation—goals Roosevelt had long cherished. The CCC created a series of camps in national parks and forests and in other rural and wilderness settings. There young men worked in a semimilitary environment on such projects as planting trees, building reservoirs, developing parks, and improving agricultural irrigation. As with the CWA, many of the CCC projects were of only marginal value. But the president took great pride in the success of the corps in providing jobs to over 500,000 young men, offering them not only incomes but an opportunity to work in a "healthy and wholesome" atmosphere.

Mortgage relief was a pressing need of millions of farm owners and homeowners. The New Deal had provided some assistance to farmers in danger of losing their land, through the AAA and particularly through the Farm Credit Administration, which within two years refinanced one-fifth of all farm mortgages in the United States. The Frazier-Lemke Farm Bankruptcy Act of 1933 went further, enabling some farmers to regain their land even after the foreclosure of their mortgages. Despite such efforts, however, small farmers continued to lose their property in many regions; by 1934, 25 percent of all American farm owners had lost their land.

Homeowners were similarly troubled, and in June 1933 the administration established the Home Owners' Loan Corporation, which in a three-year period loaned out more than $3 billion to refinance the mortgages of more than 1 million householders. Altogether, it carried about one-sixth of the nation's urban mortgage burden. A year later, Congress established the Federal Housing Administration to insure mortgages for new construction and home repairs—a measure that combined an effort to provide relief with a program to stimulate lasting recovery of the construction industry.

The relief efforts of the first two years of the New Deal were intended to be limited and temporary. Few of these early programs survived as a permanent part of the federal government. But they helped stimulate interest in other forms of social protection. Ultimately, the creation of a permanent welfare system would be one of the New Deal's most important and lasting accomplishments.

The New Deal in Transition

Seldom has an American president enjoyed such remarkable popularity as Franklin Roosevelt during his first two years in office. By early 1935, however, the New Deal was faced with serious problems. The Depression continued—softened, perhaps, by government programs, but generally unabated. And as a result, the New Deal was beginning to find itself the target of fierce public criticism. For a time, the president's political future seemed in doubt. Roosevelt himself, however, appeared unperturbed by the problems; and in the spring of 1935, he launched a forceful campaign of new legislation designed to preempt his critics and move the government more forcefully into the fight against the Depression.

Attacks from Right and Left

In the first heady days of 1933, critics of the New Deal (of whom there were, even then, considerable numbers) had difficulty finding any substantial public support for their position. But by the time two years had passed and the economy still had not revived, the situation had changed. Attacks on the New Deal were now generating a large response.

Some of the most strident attacks came from critics on the right. Roosevelt had for a time tried to conciliate conservatives and had allowed corporate leaders to play a major role in shaping some of his early policy initiatives—most notably by allowing business executives themselves to control most aspects of the NRA. By the end of 1934, however, it was clear that the American right in general, and much of the corporate world in particular, had become irreconcilably hostile to the New Deal. Indeed, so intense was conservative animosity toward the New Deal's "reckless spending," "economic crackpots," and "socialist" reforms that some of

Roosevelt's critics could not even bear to say the president's name. They called him, simply and bitterly, "that man in the White House."

In August 1934, a group of the most fervent (and wealthiest) Roosevelt opponents, led by members of the Du Pont family, formed the American Liberty League, designed specifically to arouse public opposition to the New Deal's "dictatorial" policies and its supposed attacks on free enterprise. The new organization generated wide publicity and caused some concern within the administration. In fact, however, it was never able to expand its constituency much beyond the Northern industrialists who had founded it. At its peak, membership in the organization numbered only about 125,000.

The real impact of the Liberty League and other conservative attacks on Roosevelt was not to undermine the president's political strength. It was, rather, to convince Roosevelt that his efforts to conciliate the business community had failed. By 1936, he no longer harbored any illusions about cooperation with conservatives. The forces of "organized money," he said near the end of his campaign for reelection, "are unanimous in their hate for me—and I welcome their hatred."

Roosevelt's critics on the far left also managed to produce alarm among some supporters of the administration; but like the conservatives, they proved to have only limited strength. The Communist party, the Socialist party, and other radical and semiradical organizations were at times harshly critical of the New Deal. But not only did they fail ever to attract genuinely widespread support; they proved at times uncertain about how best to combine their commitment to radical change with their fervent opposition to the growth of fascism elsewhere in the world. The Communist party, in particular, spent much of the 1930s tacitly and at times explicitly supporting the Roosevelt programs.

Popular Protest

More menacing to the New Deal than either the far right or the far left was a group of dissident political movements that defied easy ideological classification. Some were marginal "crackpot" organizations with little popular following, but others gained substantial public support within particular states and regions. Three men, in particular, succeeded in mobilizing genuinely national followings.

Dr. Francis E. Townsend, an elderly California physician, rose from obscurity to lead a movement of more than 5 million members with his plan for federal pensions for the elderly. According to the Townsend plan, all Americans over the age of sixty would receive monthly government pensions of $200, provided they retired from their current employment (thus freeing jobs for younger, unemployed Americans) and spent the money in full each month (which would pump needed funds into the economy). The movement expanded quickly from its founding in 1933, and within two years it had attracted the support of a formidable block of voters, most of them older men and women. The Townsend plan made little progress in Congress when it was introduced by sympathetic representatives. But the public sentiment behind the plan helped build support for the Social Security system, which Congress did approve in 1935.

Father Charles E. Coughlin, a Catholic priest in the small Detroit suburb of Royal Oak, Michigan, achieved even greater renown by means of his weekly sermons broadcast nationally over the radio. Drawing on Populism and other earlier political movements, as well as on what he claimed were the teachings of his church, he proposed a series of monetary reforms—remonetization of silver, issuing of greenbacks, and nationalization of the banking system—that he insisted would restore prosperity and provide economic justice. At first a warm supporter of Franklin Roosevelt, he had by 1934 become disheartened by what he claimed was the president's failure to deal harshly enough with the "money powers." In the spring of 1935, he established his own political organization, the National Union for Social Justice, which many people believed was the first step toward the formation of a third party. He was also displaying an apparently remarkable influence in Congress. (An avalanche of telegrams inspired by a Coughlin radio sermon was generally believed to have been responsible for the defeat in the Senate of a treaty admitting the United States to the World Court.) And he was attracting public support throughout much of the nation—primarily from Catholics, but from others as well. He was widely believed to have one of the largest regular radio audiences of anyone in America.

Most alarming of all to the administration was the growing national popularity of Senator Huey P. Long of Louisiana. Long had risen to power in his home state through his strident attacks on the banks, oil companies, and utilities, and on the conservative political oligarchy allied with them that had for de-

Huey Long

Few public speakers could arouse a crowd more effectively than Huey Long of Louisiana, known to many as
"the Kingfish" (a nickname borrowed from the popular
radio show "Amos 'n Andy"). It was Long's effective
use of radio, however, that contributed most directly to
his spreading national popularity in the early 1930s. (Culver Pictures)

because of his flamboyant personality and in part because of his record of accomplishment: building
roads, schools, and hospitals; revising the tax codes;
distributing free textbooks; lowering utility rates; and
more. Barred by law from succeeding himself as governor, he ran in 1930 for a seat in the U.S. Senate,
won easily, and left the state government in the hands
of loyal, docile allies.

Once in Washington, Long, like Coughlin, soon
became harshly critical of Herbert Hoover's ineffectual policies for dealing with the Depression. And
also like Coughlin, he supported Franklin Roosevelt
for president in 1932. Far more rapidly than the
priest, however, Long broke with the New Deal—a
break that was all but complete within six months of
the inauguration. As an alternative, he advocated a
drastic program of wealth redistribution, a program
he ultimately named the Share-Our-Wealth Plan. According to Long, the government could end the Depression easily and quickly simply by confiscating
through taxation the surplus riches of the wealthiest
men and women in America, whose fortunes were,
he claimed, so bloated that not enough wealth remained to satisfy the needs of the great mass of citizens. By limiting incomes to $1 million annually and
by limiting capital accumulation and inheritances to
$5 million, the government would soon acquire
enough assets to guarantee every family a minimum
"homestead" of $5,000 and an annual wage of $2,500.

Long made little effort to disguise his interest in
running for president. In 1934, he established his own
national organization: the Share-Our-Wealth Society,
which soon attracted a large following—not only in
Long's native South but in New York, Pennsylvania,
parts of the Midwest, and above all California. There
were no accurate figures to indicate the movement's
precise size, but even Long's critics admitted it might
have as many as 4 million members. A poll by the
Democratic National Committee in the spring of
1935 disclosed that Long might attract more than 10
percent of the electorate if he ran as a third-party
candidate, enough to tip a close election to the Republicans.

Observers in the 1930s hotly debated the significance of these dissident movements. Some believed
they represented the rise of fascism in America; others claimed they were dangerously close to socialism
or communism. In fact, they were neither. They represented, rather, two competing popular sentiments:
the urgent desire of many Americans for government
assistance in this time of need, and an equally strong
desire to protect their ability to control their own

cades dominated the Louisiana government. Elected
governor in 1928, he launched an assault on his opposition so thorough and forceful that they were soon
left with virtually no political power whatever. Long
dominated the legislature, the courts, and the executive departments; and he brooked no interference.
When opponents accused him of violating the Louisiana constitution, he brazenly replied, "I'm the Constitution here now." Many claimed that he had, in
effect, become a dictator.

If so, he was a dictator who maintained the overwhelming support of the Louisiana electorate, in part

lives from the encroachments of large and powerful organizations. Long, Coughlin, Townsend, and others spoke harshly of the "plutocrats," "international bankers," and other remote financial powers who were, they claimed, not only impoverishing the nation but exercising tyrannical power over individuals and communities. They spoke equally harshly, however, of the dangers of excessive government bureaucracy, attacking the New Deal for establishing a menacing, "dictatorial" state. They envisioned a society in which government would, through a series of simple economic reforms, guarantee prosperity to every American without exercising intrusive control over private and community activities.

However much their critics may have disagreed about the merits of these programs, most agreed on one thing: the specter of dissident politics seemed in 1935 to have become a genuine threat to the established political parties. An increasing number of advisers were warning the president that he would have to do something dramatic to counter their strength.

The "Second New Deal"

In response both to the growing political pressures and to the continuing economic crisis, Roosevelt embarked in 1935 on a set of new initiatives that together became known as the "Second New Deal." In some respects, the new proposals were simply an attempt to steal the thunder of the administration's critics. But they also represented, if not a new direction, at least a change in the emphasis of New Deal policy.

Perhaps the most conspicuous change in New Deal policy in 1935 was its new attitude toward big business. Rhetorically at least, the president was now openly attacking the great corporate interests. In March, for example, he proposed to Congress an act to combat the concentration of power in the great utility holding companies. In 1935, thirteen such companies controlled three-quarters of the nation's electric power; and Roosevelt spoke harshly of the injustices inherent in their monopolistic position. The companies fought desperately against the "death-sentence" bill; one of them spent $700,000 to lobby against the measure. In the end, neither side emerged entirely victorious. Congress did indeed pass the Holding Company Act of 1935, but the bill contained amendments favored by the companies that sharply limited its effects.

Equally alarming to affluent Americans was a series of tax reforms proposed by the president in 1935, a program conservatives quickly labeled a "soak the rich" scheme. Apparently designed to undercut the appeal of Huey Long's Share-Our-Wealth Plan, the Roosevelt proposals called for establishing the highest and most progressive peacetime tax rates in history. Rates in the upper brackets reached 75 percent on income, 70 percent on inheritances, and 15 percent on corporate incomes. In fact, the actual impact of these taxes was far less radical than the president liked to claim (as Huey Long quickly pointed out). Like the Holding Company Act, the New Deal's tax legislation served progressive political purposes; but in terms of its actual impact on the economy, it had only modest results.

The Supreme Court decision in 1935 to invalidate the National Industrial Recovery Act solved some problems for the administration, but it also created others. The now defunct act had contained, among other things, the important clause—Section 7(a)—guaranteeing to workers the right to organize and bargain collectively. Supporters of labor, both in the administration and in Congress, advocated quick action to restore that protection. With the president himself slow to respond, the initiative fell to a group of progressives in Congress led by Senator Robert F. Wagner of New York, who in 1935 introduced what was to become the National Labor Relations Act. The new bill, popularly known as the Wagner Act, provided workers with far more federal protection than Section 7(a) of the National Industrial Recovery Act had offered. It specifically outlawed a group of "unfair practices" by which employers had been fighting unionization. And it created a National Labor Relations Board (NLRB) to police employers, with power to compel them to recognize and bargain with legitimate unions. The president was not happy with the bill as it moved through Congress. But when the measure reached his desk, he signed it. That was in large part because American workers themselves had by 1935 become so important and vigorous a force that Roosevelt realized his own political future would depend in part on responding to their demands.

Labor Militancy

The emergence of a powerful American trade union movement in the 1930s was perhaps the most important social development of the decade, and one of the most significant political developments as well. It occurred in part in response to government efforts to enhance the power of unions; but it was primarily a result of the increased militancy of American workers and their leaders.

During the 1920s, most workers had displayed relatively little militancy in challenging employers or demanding recognition of their unions. They had faced a powerful and highly popular business establishment. They were often coopted by the system of welfare capitalism, which provided them with increased wages and benefits. And they had been saddled with conservative labor organizations, unwilling to risk the modest gains already won. Working-class militancy was visible at times at the local level. But without national support, local efforts rarely succeeded.

In the 1930s, these inhibiting factors began to vanish. Business leaders and industrialists lost (if only temporarily) the high public standing they had enjoyed in the New Era; and on matters of labor policy at least, they lost the support of the government. Both Section 7(a) of the National Industrial Recovery Act of 1933 and the Wagner Act of 1935 were passed over the strong objections of corporate leaders. The "welfare capitalism" of the 1920s had vanished almost overnight; with the economy in sharp decline, employers had quickly rescinded most of the gains offered to labor in the preceding years. Those workers who kept their jobs often did so only by accepting reduced wages and fewer benefits. Finally, as the decade progressed, new labor organizations emerged to challenge the established, conservative unions. The result was, among other things, an important change in the outlook of many workers: a growing resentment of conditions as they were, and an increasing commitment to the idea of organizing to rectify them.

The new militancy first became obvious in 1934, when newly organized workers (many of them inspired by the collective bargaining provisions of the National Industrial Recovery Act) staged a series of strikes to demand recognition of their unions. In Minneapolis, Toledo, and San Francisco, in particular, striking workers demonstrated a militancy and radicalism seldom seen in recent years and became involved at times in violent confrontations with employers and local authorities. Both the strength and the failure of these labor uprisings were important in promoting passage of the Wagner Act of 1935. Industrial workers were, it was clear, becoming too militant to ignore any longer. But it was equally clear that without stronger legal protection, their organiz-

ing drives would end in frustration. Once the Wagner Act became law, the search for more effective forms of organization rapidly gained strength in labor ranks.

Even though the American Federation of Labor, under the leadership now of William Green, increased its activities in response to the Depression, it proved in most cases inadequate to the task at hand. The AFL remained committed to the idea of the craft union: the idea of organizing workers on the basis of their skills. As a result, the Federation offered little hope to unskilled laborers, even though it was the unskilled who now constituted the bulk of the industrial work force.

During the 1930s, therefore, another concept of labor organization challenged the traditional craft union ideal: industrial unionism. Advocates of this approach argued that all the workers in a particular industry should be organized in a single union, regardless of what functions the workers performed. All auto workers should be in a single automobile union; all steel workers should be in a single steel union. Workers divided into many small unions would lack the strength to deal successfully with the great corporations. United into a single great union, however, they would wield considerable power.

Leaders of the AFL craft unions for the most part opposed the new concept. But industrial unionism found a number of important advocates, most prominent among them John L. Lewis. Lewis was the talented, flamboyant, and eloquent leader of the United Mine Workers—the oldest major union in the country organized along industrial rather than craft lines. He was also a charismatic public figure, whose personal magnetism alone helped win thousands of recruits to his cause.

At first, Lewis and his allies attempted to work within the AFL, but friction between the new industrial organizations and the older craft unions grew rapidly as a result. At the 1935 AFL convention, Lewis became embroiled in a series of angry confrontations (and one celebrated fistfight) with craft union leaders before finally walking out. A few weeks later, he created the Committee on Industrial Organization—a body officially within the AFL but unsanctioned by its leadership. After a series of bitter jurisdictional conflicts, the AFL finally expelled the new committee from its ranks, and along with it all the industrial unions it represented. In response, Lewis renamed the committee the Congress of Industrial Organizations (CIO), established it in 1936 as an organization directly rivaling the AFL, and be-

John L. Lewis
Lionized by industrial workers but despised by business-men, conservatives, and at times New Deal liberals, John L. Lewis—president of the United Mine Workers and, beginning in 1935, of the Congress of Industrial Organizations (CIO)—dominated the public image of the American labor movement in the 1930s. He is shown here speaking to a rally of the American Labor Party in 1936, exhorting them to do their best to defeat Republican presidential candidate Alf Landon and to "awaken" labor's political power.   (AP/Wide World photos)

came its first president. The schism clearly weakened the labor movement as a whole in many ways. But by freeing the advocates of industrial unionism from the restrictive rules of the Federation, it gave important impetus to the creation of powerful new organizations.

The CIO also expanded the constituency of the labor movement in important ways. Membership in most AFL craft unions had been limited not only to skilled workers, but to white male workers. The CIO, in reaching out to the great mass of unskilled laborers, was much more receptive to women and to blacks than the AFL had been. CIO organizing drives also reached out to new, previously unorganized industries where women and minorities constituted much of the work force: textiles, laundries, tobacco factories, and others. The labor schism, in short, involved issues of race and gender as well as questions of economics.

Organizing Battles

The new organizations had been struggling for recognition even before the schism of 1936. Major battles were under way, in particular, in the automobile and steel industries. Out of a myriad of competing auto unions, the United Auto Workers (UAW) was gradually becoming preeminent during the early and mid-1930s. But through 1936, although steadily gaining recruits, it was making little progress in winning recognition from the corporations.

In December 1936, however, auto workers employed a controversial and dramatically effective technique for challenging corporate opposition: the sit-down strike. Employees in several General Motors plants in Detroit simply sat down inside the plants, refusing either to work or to leave, thus preventing the company from making use of strikebreakers. The tactic quickly spread to other locations, so that by February 1937 strikers had occupied seventeen GM plants. The strikers ignored court orders to vacate the buildings, and they successfully resisted sporadic efforts by local police to remove them. When Michigan's governor, Frank Murphy, a liberal Democrat, refused to call out the National Guard to clear out the strikers, and when the federal government refused as well to intervene on behalf of employers, the company had little choice but to relent. In February 1937 General Motors became the first major manufacturer to recognize the UAW; other automobile companies soon did the same. The sit-down strike proved effective for rubber workers (who, in fact, were the first to use the technique in 1936) and workers in other industries as well, but it survived only briefly as a labor technique. Its apparent illegality aroused widespread public outrage and alarm, so labor leaders ultimately abandoned it.

In the steel industry, the battle for unionization was less easily won. In 1936, the CIO had appropriated $500,000 to support the Steel Workers' Organizing Committee (later United Steelworkers of America) in a major campaign. Over the next few months, the onslaught began, with the SWOC quickly recruiting tens of thousands of workers and staging a series of prolonged and often bitter strikes. The conflicts were notable not only for the militancy of the (predominantly male) steel workers themselves, but for the involvement of thousands of women (often wives or relatives of workers), who provided important logistical support for the strikers and who at times took direct action by creating a buffer between strikers and the police.

In March 1937, to the amazement of almost everyone, United States Steel, the giant of the industry, relented. Rather than risk a costly strike at a time when it sensed itself on the verge of recovery from the Depression, the company signed a contract with the SWOC, the new organization's first important victory. But the lesser companies (known collectively as "Little Steel") were not ready to surrender. On Memorial Day 1937, a group of striking workers from Republic Steel gathered with their families for a picnic and demonstration in South Chicago; and when they attempted to march peacefully (and legally) toward the steel plant, police opened fire on them. Ten demonstrators were killed; another ninety were wounded. Despite a public outcry against the "Memorial Day Massacre," the harsh tactics of "Little Steel" ultimately proved successful. The 1937 strike failed.

But the victory of Little Steel was the exception rather than the rule; it was, in fact, one of the last gasps of the kind of brutal strikebreaking that had proved so effective in the past. In the course of 1937, one of the most turbulent years in the history of American labor, there were 4,720 strikes—over 80 percent of them settled in favor of the unions. By the end of the year, more than 8 million workers were members of unions recognized as official bargaining units by employers (as compared with 3 million in 1932). By 1941, that number had expanded to 10 million and included the workers of Little Steel, which had finally relented. Workers were slower to win major new wage increases and benefits than they were to achieve union recognition. But the organizing battles of the 1930s had established the labor movement as a powerful force in the American economy.

Social Security

From the first moments of the New Deal, important members of the administration, most notably Secretary of Labor Frances Perkins, had been lobbying patiently for a system of federally sponsored social insurance for the elderly and the unemployed. The popularity of the Townsend movement added strength to their cause, and in 1935, finally, Roosevelt gave public support to what became the Social Security Act. It established a variety of programs. For the elderly, there were two types of assistance. Those who were presently destitute could receive up to $15 a month in federal assistance (depending on what matching sums the state might provide). More important for the future, Americans presently working were incorporated into a pension system, to which they and their employers would contribute by paying a payroll tax and which would provide them with an income on retirement. There were severe limits on the program. Pension payments would not begin until 1942 and even then would provide only $10 to $85 a month to recipients. And broad categories of workers (including domestic servants and agricultural laborers, many of whom were blacks and women) were excluded from the program. But the act was a crucial first step in creating the nation's most important social program for the elderly.

In addition, the Social Security Act expanded the government's activities on behalf of the unemployed and dispossessed. It provided for a system of unemployment insurance, to which employers alone would contribute and which made it possible for workers laid off from their jobs to receive government assistance for a limited period of time. It also established a system of federal aid to disabled people and to dependent children.

New Dealers did not like to think of Social Security as a "welfare" system; even the strongest supporters of the new program continued to oppose the idea of a "dole." They insisted, rather, that Social Security was an "insurance" system, most of whose recipients would earn their benefits. Those assumptions were reflected in the structure of the programs the act created. The pensions to the elderly were to be based not on need but on contributions to the system. Even the wealthiest retired Americans would be entitled to their Social Security payments. Unemployment insurance, similarly, was not to be "welfare," with benefits based on economic need. Any unemployed person would be eligible to receive assistance, no matter what his or her financial situation. Where the Social Security Act did provide direct assistance based on need—to the elderly poor, to the disabled, to dependent children—it was servicing groups widely perceived to be small and genuinely unable to support themselves.

In the years to come, however, Social Security

was to evolve in ways its planners neither foresaw nor desired. The old-age pension program would ultimately become far more expensive (and far more generous) than the founders of the system had expected. Aid to Dependent Children, envisioned as a relatively modest program to aid a small number of needy people, would in the 1950s (renamed Aid to Families with Dependent Children) expand to become one of the cornerstones of the modern welfare system. However one evaluates the long-range effects of Social Security, however, it is clear that the 1935 act was the most important single piece of social welfare legislation in American history.

New Directions in Relief

Social Security was designed primarily to fulfill long-range goals. Of more immediate concern were the millions of Americans who remained unemployed and who had not yet found relief through existing government programs. To meet their needs (and not incidentally to replace such early New Deal programs of direct relief as the FERA, with which the president had always felt uncomfortable), the administration established in 1935 the Works Progress Administration (WPA). Like the Civil Works Administration and other earlier efforts, the WPA established a system of work relief for the unemployed. It far surpassed all earlier agencies, however, both in the size of its budget ($5 billion at first) and in the energy and imagination of its operations.

Under the direction of Harry Hopkins, who had by now emerged as the New Deal's "minister of relief," the WPA employed an average of 2.1 million workers at any given moment between 1935 and 1941. The agency was responsible ultimately for the erection or renovation of 110,000 public buildings (schools, post offices, office buildings) and for the construction of almost 600 airports, more than 500,000 miles of roads, and over 100,000 bridges. More important, however, the WPA provided incomes to those it employed and helped stimulate the economy in general by increasing the flow of money into it.

The WPA also displayed remarkable flexibility and imagination in offering assistance to those whose occupations did not fit into any traditional category of relief. The Federal Writers Project of the WPA, for example, offered unemployed writers support to pursue their own creative endeavors and to work on projects initiated by the agency itself. The Federal Art Project, similarly, provided aid to painters, sculptors, and others to continue their careers. The Federal Music Project and the Federal Theater Project oversaw the production of concerts and of plays, skits, and even a controversial review of public affairs known as the "Living Newspaper," thus creating work for unemployed musicians, actors, directors, and others.

Other relief agencies emerged alongside the WPA. The National Youth Administration provided assistance to those between the ages of sixteen and twenty-five, largely in the form of scholarship assistance to high-school and college students. The Emergency Housing Division of the Public Works Administration (the agency that had been established in 1933 along with the NRA, but whose benefits were slow to be felt) began federal sponsorship of public housing. It cleared some of the nation's most notorious slums and built instead some fifty new housing developments, containing nearly 22,000 units—most of them priced too high for those who had been displaced by slum clearance. Not until 1937, when Congress approved Senator Wagner's bill creating the United States Housing Authority, did the government begin to provide a substantial amount of housing for the truly poor.

The hiring practices of the WPA, the NYA, and other work-relief programs revealed another important, if at the time largely unrecognized, feature of the New Deal welfare system. Men and women alike were in distress in the 1930s (as in all times). But the new welfare system dealt with members of the two sexes in very different ways. For men, the government concentrated mainly on work relief—on such programs as the CCC, the CWA, and the WPA, all of which were overwhelmingly male. The WPA did provide some jobs for women, although usually in such domestic settings as sewing rooms, nursery schools, and handicraft programs. Even these few jobs tended to be quickly eliminated when WPA funds became tight.

The principal government aid to women, therefore, came to be not work relief, but cash assistance—most notably through the Aid to Dependent Children program of Social Security, which was designed largely to assist single mothers. This disparity in treatment reflected a widespread assumption, which was already in conflict with economic reality, that men constituted the bulk of the paid work force and that women needed to be treated within the context of the family. In fact, millions of women were already employed by the 1930s, and many millions

WPA Mural Art
The Federal Arts Project of the Works Progress Administration commissioned an impressive series of public murals from the artists it employed. Many of these murals adorned post offices, libraries, and other public buildings constructed by the WPA. William Gropper's *Construction of a Dam,* a detail of which is seen here, is typical of much of the mural art of the 1930s in its celebration of the workingman. Workers are depicted in heroic poses, laboring in unison to complete a great public project.   (Department of the Interior)

more would enter the work force thereafter. The tension between the nature of the welfare system and the realities of employment would, therefore, trouble American society for decades.

The 1936 "Referendum"

The presidential election of 1936, it was clear from the start, was to be a national referendum on Franklin Roosevelt and the New Deal. And whereas in 1935 there had been reason to question the president's political prospects, by the middle of 1936 there could be little doubt that he would win a second term.

The conservative opposition to Roosevelt had always been intense but never large. In 1936, it was not even strong enough to win control of the Republican party. Ignoring the anguished pleas of Herbert Hoover and others who detested all aspects of the New Deal, the party nominated the moderate governor of Kansas, Alf M. Landon, who had supported Theodore Roosevelt's 1912 crusade (see pp. 649–651) and who had never abandoned his progressive commitments. The Republican platform promised, in ef-

fect, to continue the programs of the New Deal—but constitutionally, and without running a deficit.

As for the dissidents, their strength seemed to evaporate as quickly as it had emerged. One reason was the violent death of their most effective leader, Huey Long, who was assassinated in a corridor of the Louisiana state capitol in September 1935 by a young Baton Rouge doctor. (No one ever had a chance to discover the motives of the assailant; he was gunned down on the spot by Long's bodyguards.) Another reason was the ill-fated alliance among several of the remaining dissident leaders in 1936. Father Coughlin, Dr. Townsend, and Gerald L. K. Smith (a sycophantic henchman of Huey Long trying unsuccessfully to establish himself as Long's political heir) joined forces that summer to establish a new political movement—the Union party. But the incessant squabbling among them combined with the colorlessness of their presidential candidate—a mediocre North Dakota congressman, William Lemke—made the new party a sorry spectacle. It polled only 890,000 votes. The most important reason for the dissidents' collapse, however, was their failure ever to turn their supporters fully against Franklin Roosevelt, who had skillfully undercut the appeal of his critics by espousing many of their ideas.

The campaign was a lopsided contest. Roosevelt drew huge crowds and evoked widespread enthusiasm with his impassioned attacks on the "economic royalists." Landon's muted rhetoric and moderate platform could not effectively compete. The result was the greatest landslide in American history to that point. Roosevelt polled just under 61 percent of the vote to Landon's 36 percent. The Republican candidate carried only Maine and Vermont. The Democrats increased their already large majorities in both houses of Congress.

In addition to ensuring Roosevelt a second term, the election displayed the fundamental party realignment that the New Deal had managed to produce. The Democrats now controlled a broad coalition of Western and Southern farmers, the urban working classes, the poor and unemployed, and the black communities of the Northern cities, as well as traditional progressives and committed new liberals—a coalition that constituted a substantial majority of the electorate. It would be many years before the Republican party could again muster anything approaching a true majority coalition of its own.

The New Deal in Disarray

Roosevelt emerged from the 1936 election at the zenith of his popularity. Within months, however, the New Deal was mired in serious new difficulties—a result of continuing opposition, of the president's own political errors, and of major economic setbacks. His administration would never fully recover. Throughout Roosevelt's second term, recovery from the Depression remained elusive; and the New Deal, stumbling from one policy to another, was unable to regain the initiative it had once had.

The Court Fight and the "Purge"

If the 1936 election had been a mandate for anything, Franklin Roosevelt believed, it was a mandate to do something about the Supreme Court. No program of reform, he had become convinced, could long survive the ravages of the obstructionist justices, who had already struck down the NRA and the AAA and threatened to invalidate even more legislation. Foes

of such New Deal measures as the National Labor Relations Act, the Social Security Act, and the Holding Company Act were openly flouting the new laws, confident that the Supreme Court would soon disallow them. Through its narrow interpretation of the federal power over interstate commerce and taxation, and through its broad interpretation of freedom of contract, the Court seemed to have created an economic no man's land within which neither the federal government nor the state governments could act. Early in 1937, Roosevelt proposed a solution: expanding the Supreme Court through the addition of new justices—justices he would appoint and whose liberal views would presumably counterbalance the conservatism of the existing justices.

It was a bold measure, but not, the administration insisted, a radical one. The Constitution called for no specific number of Supreme Court justices, and Congress had from time to time changed the size of the Court in the past (although not since the late nineteenth century). Nevertheless, the plan aroused a great public furor, largely because Roosevelt displayed what was, for him at least, an astounding political ineptitude in proposing and promoting it. Without informing congressional leaders in advance, he sent a surprise message to Capitol Hill in February proposing a general overhaul of the federal court system and including, among many provisions, one to add up to six new justices to the Supreme Court. The courts were "overworked," he claimed, and needed additional manpower and younger blood to enable them to cope with their increasing burdens. The explanation fooled almost no one.

Conservatives throughout the country expressed outrage at the "court-packing plan," warning that such constitutional shortcuts were the common route by which dictators seized power. And while in the past few Americans had been disposed to heed such warnings, now, as a result of Roosevelt's heavy-handed tactics, much of the public seemed to agree. Still the president had considerable political clout at his disposal; and he might well have forced Congress to approve at least a compromise measure had not the Supreme Court itself intervened in the controversy.

Even before the court-packing fight began, the ideological balance of the Court had been a precarious one. Four conservative justices could be relied on to oppose the New Deal on almost all occasions; three were generally inclined to support it. The remaining two tended to waver, with Chief Justice Hughes often siding with the progressives and Associate Justice Owen J. Roberts more often voting with the conservatives. Were Hughes and Roberts both to side with the liberals, there would be a 5-to-4 majority in support of the New Deal without the appointment of additional justices. That is precisely what happened. On March 29, 1937, Roberts, Hughes, and the three progressive justices voted together to uphold a state minimum wage law—in the case of *West Coast Hotel v. Parrish*—thus reversing a 5-to-4 decision of the previous year invalidating a similar law. Two weeks later, again by a 5- to 4-margin, the Court upheld the Wagner Act; and in May, it validated the Social Security Act. The necessity for Roosevelt's judicial reform bill had vanished. The Supreme Court had prudently moderated its position in order to avert what it considered a disastrous precedent. "You may have saved the country," Hughes jubilantly told Owen Roberts after the first decision favorable to the New Deal in March.

On one level, the affair was a significant victory for Franklin Roosevelt. No longer would the Court serve as an obstruction to New Deal reforms, particularly after a group of older justices began retiring in the following months, to be replaced by Roosevelt appointees. On another level, however, the court-packing episode was a serious defeat for the president, and one that did lasting damage to his administration. By generating public suspicion of his motives, he had reinvigorated the conservative opposition, which only months before had been in disarray. By giving members of his own party an excuse to oppose him, he had helped destroy his congressional coalition. From 1937 on, Southern Democrats and other conservatives voted against his measures with alarming consistency; never again would the president enjoy the freedom of legislative action he had had during his first years in office. Roosevelt was not even spared the embarrassment of having his Court plan publicly voted down by Congress.

A year later, the president's political situation deteriorated further. Determined to regain the initiative in his legislative battles, Roosevelt launched an ill-considered effort to "purge" Congress of some of its most conservative members. In Democratic primaries that spring, he openly campaigned against members of his own party who had opposed his programs. The effort was a humiliating failure. Not only was Roosevelt unable to unseat any of the five Democratic senators against whom he campaigned, but his "purge" efforts drove an even deeper wedge between the administration and its conservative opponents, ensuring that Roosevelt would suffer more legislative frustrations in the future.

Retrenchment and Recession

Hard on the heels of the court-packing fiasco came another economic crisis: a severe recession that began in the fall of 1937, continued for more than nine months, and plunged the nation into its worst suffering since 1932. It was a bitter pill for a society that was just beginning to believe that true recovery was under way; and it was a particularly bitter pill for Franklin Roosevelt, whose policies seemed to have contributed to the new collapse.

By the summer of 1937, it no longer seemed fanciful to believe that prosperity was about to return. The national income, which had dropped from $82 billion in 1929 to $40 billion in 1932, had risen to nearly $72 billion. Other economic indices showed similar improvements. To the president, the time seemed ripe for a retrenchment in government spending, for allowing the business community, as Secretary of the Treasury Henry Morgenthau put it, to stand once again on its own two feet. Not incidentally, it also seemed to be a good time to balance the federal budget, whose mounting deficits had never ceased to trouble the president. Many economists believed that the real danger now was no longer depression but inflation.

As a result, the administration moved on several fronts to cut back its recovery programs. Roosevelt persuaded the Federal Reserve Board to tighten credit by raising interest rates. At the same time, he reduced government spending by slashing the budget for one relief program after another. Between January and August 1937, for example, he cut the WPA in half, sending 1.5 million relief workers on unpaid "vacations." A few weeks later, the fragile boom collapsed. The index of industrial production dropped from 117 in August 1937 to 76 in May 1938. Four million additional workers lost their jobs.

The recession of 1937 was a result of many factors. But to many observers at the time (including, apparently, Franklin Roosevelt), it seemed to be a direct result of the administration's unwise decision to reduce spending. And so the new crisis forced yet another reevaluation of policies by the president and his advisers and produced yet another shift of emphasis within the New Deal. The advocates of government spending as an antidote to the Depression had always had to struggle for the president's favor against those who believed in more conservative fiscal policies. Now, it seemed, they stood vindicated; and the notion of using government deficits to stimulate the economy—an idea coming to be associated with the great British economist John Maynard Keynes—had established its first, timid foothold in American public policy. In April 1938, the president asked Congress for an emergency appropriation of $5 billion for public works and relief programs, and government funds soon began pouring into the economy once again. Within a few months, another tentative recovery seemed to be under way, and the advocates of spending pointed to it as proof of the validity of their approach.

At the same time, advocates of another approach to the economic crisis began to win Franklin Roosevelt's ear: a group of younger liberals who saw the recession as the result of excessively concentrated corporate power and who wanted the government to move forcefully to curb that power and restore competition. It was time, they said, to launch a genuine assault on monopoly. There had been antimonopoly advocates in New Deal circles from the beginning, but until now their position had been weak. By 1937, however, the president was sufficiently disillusioned with the American business community (a disillusionment only strengthened by the 1937 recession, which he too tried to blame on "selfish interests") that he was willing to experiment with their approach. In April 1938, Roosevelt sent a stinging message to Congress, vehemently denouncing what he called an unjustifiable concentration of economic power and asking for the creation of a commission to examine that concentration with an eye to major reforms in the antitrust laws. In response, Congress established the Temporary National Economic Committee (TNEC), including representatives of both houses of Congress and of several executive agencies. At about the same time, Roosevelt appointed a new head of the antitrust division of the Justice Department: Thurman Arnold, a Yale Law School professor who soon proved to be the most vigorous director ever to serve in that office. Making new and sophisticated use of the Sherman and Clayton acts, Arnold filed (and won) almost as many antitrust cases in the next three years as the Justice Department had filed in its entire previous history.

Despite the apparent triumph of antimonopoly advocates, the policies of the late New Deal did not really represent a frontal assault on economic concentration. For one thing, neither the TNEC nor, in the end, Thurman Arnold's crusades had very much lasting impact. The TNEC investigation ran on for nearly three years and produced volumes of testimony, but in the end it made no important recommendations for action. And Arnold's vigorous tenure

in the Justice Department came to an end when wartime pressures convinced the president and others that the time for antitrust activity was over. But even at its peak, these antimonopoly efforts were not in any real sense attempts to restore a small-scale, decentralized economy. Arnold himself admitted that such efforts would be nostalgic nonsense and explained that he was using the antitrust laws not to break up combinations but to regulate their behavior. That, in fact, was the principal ideological commitment of many New Dealers in the late 1930s: not destroying monopoly, but increasing the regulatory functions of the federal government. Roosevelt's much vaunted (and only partially successful) effort to reorganize the executive branch of the federal government was motivated in part by the idea that a streamlined state would be able to exert its influence more effectively in the economy.

By the end of 1938, however, it was becoming clear that these ambitious new goals faced an uncertain future. For the New Deal had by then essentially come to an end. Congressional opposition now made it difficult for the president to enact any major new programs. But more important, perhaps, the threat of world crisis hung heavy in the political atmosphere, and Roosevelt was gradually growing more concerned with persuading a reluctant nation to prepare for war than with pursuing new avenues of reform.

The New Deal: Limits and Legacies

To some of Roosevelt's embittered conservative contemporaries, the New Deal was a dangerous, radical break with the past, a time in which constitutional safeguards were abandoned, in which the president sought to establish a dictatorship, in which the American economy fell under the control of a meddlesome and intrusive federal bureaucracy. To critics on the left, both in the 1930s and since, the New Deal was little more than a painfully timid defense of traditional capitalism, a bulwark of conservatism against demands for more fundamental change. (See "Where Historians Disagree," pp. 770–771.) There are elements of truth in both those views, although neither captures the essence of the New Deal experiment in reform. Any evaluation of this crucial episode in the history of American government must take into consideration both the extent and the limits of its legacy.

—————— WHERE HISTORIANS DISAGREE ——————

The New Deal

For many years, debate among historians over the nature of the New Deal mirrored the debate among Americans in the 1930s over the achievements of the Roosevelt administration. Historians struggled, just as contemporaries had done, to answer the question of whether the New Deal was a good thing or a bad thing. Did it go too far in expanding the size and power of the government? Did it go far enough in helping the dispossessed and reforming capitalism?

The conservative critique of the New Deal has received relatively little scholarly expression. Edgar Robinson, in *The Roosevelt Leadership* (1955), and John T. Flynn, in *The Roosevelt Myth* (1956), attacked Roosevelt as both a radical and a despot; but few historians have ever taken such charges seriously. By far the dominant view of the New Deal among scholars has been an approving, liberal interpretation—one that has appeared in various forms but that rests on several common assumptions. First, liberals maintain, the New Deal was not a radical, socialistic, or communistic program. It was firmly within the mainstream of the American political tradition. Second, they argue, the New Deal represented a powerful (and overdue) response by government to glaring social needs that had long gone unmet. And third, it marked a decisive repudiation of old orthodoxies about the proper relationships among government, business, labor, and other groups in society.

The leading voice in the liberal chorus has long been Arthur M. Schlesinger, Jr., who argued in the three volumes of *The Age of Roosevelt* (1957–1960) that the New Deal marked a continuation of the long struggle between public power and private interests, but that Roosevelt had moved that struggle to a new level. The unrestrained power of the business community was finally confronted with an effective challenge, and what emerged was a system of reformed capitalism, with far more protection for workers, farmers, consumers, and others than in the past.

Other liberals have gone further. Carl Degler, in *Out of Our Past* (1959), called the Roosevelt years a "Third American Revolution" (the first two being the Revolution of 1776 and the Civil War). It marked, he claimed, "the crossing of a divide from

which, it would seem, there could be no turning back." Eric Goldman, in *Rendezvous with Destiny* (1952) and later works, called the New Deal the culmination of a "Half-Century of Revolution." Although Roosevelt drew heavily on the traditions of the progressive past, "there was something more to New Deal liberalism" because it included unprecedented new departures such as Social Security.

Richard Hofstadter offered a more skeptical assessment of the New Deal in the 1950s, but one that fell largely within the liberal framework. In *The Age of Reform* (1955), he emphasized the New Deal's discontinuities with the past. It was, he said, a "drastic new departure . . . different from anything that had yet happened in the United States"—a program that even many old progressives found alarming, and opposed. The New Deal had largely abandoned the old progressive concern about reshaping the corporate world, what Hofstadter called "entrepreneurial" reform. Instead, New Deal liberalism took on a "social-democratic tinge that had never before been present in American reform movements" and raised a new set of issues to prominence: "social security, unemployment insurance, wages and hours, and housing."

Hofstadter not only echoed the view of other liberals that the New Deal marked an important break with the past; he also gave early expression to some of the criticisms that historians in the 1960s would begin to offer. In *The American Political Tradition* (1948) and again in *The Age of Reform,* he complained that the New Deal's fragmented, "pragmatic" approach had lacked a central, guiding philosophy. James MacGregor Burns, in *Roosevelt: The Lion and the Fox* (1956), raised other objections: that Roosevelt's wily political methods had often led him away from the proper goals to reform; that he had failed to make full use of his potential as a leader but had accommodated himself unnecessarily to existing patterns of political power. The first systematic "revisionist" interpretation of the New Deal came in 1963, in William Leuchtenburg's *Franklin D. Roosevelt and the New Deal.* Leuchtenburg was a sympathetic critic, arguing that most of the limitations of the New Deal were a result of the restrictions im-

————— WHERE HISTORIANS DISAGREE —————

posed on Roosevelt by the political and ideological realities of his time—that the New Deal probably could not have done much more than it did. Nevertheless, Leuchtenburg openly challenged earlier views of the New Deal as a revolution in social policy. He was able to muster only enough enthusiasm to call it a "halfway revolution," one that enhanced the positions of some previously disadvantaged groups (notably farmers and workers) but did little or nothing for many others (including blacks, sharecroppers, and the urban poor). Ellis Hawley augmented these moderate criticisms of the Roosevelt record in *The New Deal and the Problem of Monopoly* (1966). In examining 1930s economic policies, Hawley challenged liberal assumptions that the New Deal acted as the foe of private business interests. On the contrary, he argued, New Deal efforts were in many cases designed to enhance the position of private entrepreneurs—even, at times, at the expense of some of the liberal, reform goals that administration officials espoused.

Other historians in the 1960s, writing from the perspective of the New Left, expressed much harsher criticisms of the New Deal. Barton Bernstein, in a 1968 essay, compiled a dreary chronicle of missed opportunities, inadequate responses to problems, and damaging New Deal initiatives. The Roosevelt administration may have saved capitalism, Bernstein charged, but it failed to help—and in many ways actually harmed—those groups most in need of assistance. Paul Conkin, in *The New Deal* (1967), similarly chastised the government of the 1930s for its policies toward marginal farmers, its failure to institute meaningful tax reform, and its excessive generosity toward certain business interests.

The New Left attack on the New Deal never developed very far beyond these preliminary statements. Instead, by the 1970s and 1980s, scholars seemed largely to have accepted the revised liberal view: that the New Deal was a significant (and most agree valuable) chapter in the history of reform, but one that worked within rigid, occasionally crippling limits. Much of the recent work on the New Deal, therefore, has been less interested in the question of whether it was a "conservative" or "revolutionary" phenomenon than in the question of the constraints within which it was operating. The sociologist Theda Skocpol, in an important series of articles, has emphasized (along with others) the issue of "state capacity" as an important New Deal constraint; ambitious reform ideas often foundered, she argued, because of the absence of a government bureaucracy with sufficient strength and expertise to shape or administer them. James T. Patterson, Barry Karl, Mark Leff, and others have emphasized the political constraints the New Deal encountered. Both in Congress and among the public, conservative inhibitions about government remained strong; the New Deal was as much a product of the pressures of its conservative opponents as of its liberal supporters. Frank Freidel, Ellis Hawley, Herbert Stein, and many others point as well to the ideological constraints affecting Franklin Roosevelt and his supporters. Alan Brinkley has described a transition in New Deal thinking from a regulatory view of the state to one that envisioned relatively little direct interference by government in the corporate world; a movement toward an essentially "compensatory" state centered on Keynesian welfare state programs.

The phrase "New Deal liberalism" has come in the postwar era to seem synonymous with modern ideas of aggressive federal management of the economy, elaborate welfare systems, a powerful bureaucracy, and large-scale government spending. The "Reagan Revolution" of the 1980s often portrayed itself as a reaction to the "legacy of the New Deal." Many historians of the New Deal, however, would argue that the modern idea of "New Deal liberalism" bears only a limited relationship to the ideas that New Dealers themselves embraced. The liberal accomplishments of the 1930s can only be understood in the context of their own time; later liberal efforts drew from that legacy but also altered it to fit the needs and the assumptions of a very different era.

The Idea of the "Broker State"

In 1933, many New Dealers dreamed of using their new popularity and authority somehow to remake American capitalism—to produce new forms of cooperation and control that would create a genuinely harmonious, ordered economic world. By 1939, it was clear that what they had created was in fact something quite different. But rather than bemoan the gap between their original intentions and their ultimate achievements, New Deal liberals, both in 1939 and in later years, chose to accept what they had produced and to celebrate it—to use it as a model for future reform efforts.

What they had created was something that in later years would become known as the "broker state." Instead of forging all elements of society into a single, harmonious unit, as some reformers had once hoped to do, the effect of the New Deal was to elevate and strengthen new interest groups so as to allow them to compete more effectively in the national marketplace. And it was to make the federal government a mediator in that constant competition—a force that could intercede when necessary to help some groups and limit the power of others.

In 1933, there had been only one great interest group with genuine power in the national economy (albeit a varied and divided one): the corporate world. By the end of the 1930s, American business found itself competing for influence with an increasingly powerful labor movement, with an organized agricultural economy, and with aroused consumers. In later years, the "broker state" idea would expand to embrace other groups as well: racial and ethnic minorities, women, and many others. One of the enduring legacies of the New Deal, in other words, was to make the federal government a protector of interest groups and a supervisor of the competition among them, rather than an instrument attempting to create a universal harmony of interests.

What determines which interest groups receive government assistance in a "broker state"? The experience of the New Deal suggests that such assistance goes largely to those groups able to exercise enough political or economic power to demand it. Thus in the 1930s, farmers—after decades of organization and agitation—and workers—as the result of militant action and mass mobilization—won from the government new and important protections. Other groups, less well organized perhaps but politically important because so numerous and visible, won more limited assistance as well: imperiled homeowners, the unemployed, the elderly.

By the same token, the interest-group democracy that the New Deal came to represent offered much less to those groups either too weak to demand assistance or not visible enough to arouse widespread public support. And yet those same groups were often the ones most in need of help from their government. One of the important limits of the New Deal, therefore, was its very modest record on behalf of several important social groups.

Black America and the New Deal

One such group was black Americans, whose economic problems were accompanied by widespread

---

MAJOR ACHIEVEMENTS OF THE NEW DEAL

1933	Emergency Banking Act	**1935**	Works Progress Administration
	Economy Act		National Youth Administration
	Civilian Conservation Corps		Social Security Act
	Agricultural Adjustment Act		National Labor Relations Act
	Tennessee Valley Authority		Public Utilities Holding Company Act
	National Industrial Recovery Act		Resettlement Administration
	Banking Act		Rural Electrification Administration
	Federal Emergency Relief Act		Revenue Act ("wealth tax")
	Home Owners' Refinancing Act	**1936**	Soil Conservation and Domestic Allotment Act
	Civil Works Administration	**1937**	Farm Security Administration
	Federal Securities Act		National Housing Act
1934	National Housing Act	**1938**	Second Agricultural Adjustment Act
	National Labor Relations Board		Fair Labor Standards Act
	Securities and Exchange Act	**1939**	Executive Reorganization Act
	Home Owners' Loan Act		

Eleanor Roosevelt and Mary McLeod Bethune
Mrs. Roosevelt was a leading champion of racial equality within the administration of her husband, and her commitment had an important impact on the behavior of the government even though she held no official post. She is seen here meeting in 1937 with Aubrey Williams, executive director of the National Youth Administration, and Mary McLeod Bethune, the agency's director of black affairs. Founder and president of Bethune-Cookman College in Florida, Mrs. Bethune became a member of the New Deal's informal "Black Cabinet" and, with the encouragement of the First Lady and others, attempted to ensure that blacks participated equally in the NYA and other government relief programs. (UPI/Bettmann Newsphotos)

political disfranchisement and who were subjected throughout the nation to forms of discrimination that prevented them from making any significant advances. The New Deal did relatively little to improve their lot.

It was not that the administration was hostile to blacks. On the contrary, the New Deal was probably more sympathetic to the cause of racial justice than any previous government of the twentieth century. Indeed, the cause of racial equality had one of its greatest champions in the White House itself: the first lady. Eleanor Roosevelt spoke throughout the 1930s on behalf of racial justice. She put continuing pressure on her husband and others in the federal government to ease discrimination against blacks. She

was also in part responsibile for what was, symbolically at least, one of the most important events of the decade for American blacks. When the black opera singer Marian Anderson was refused permission in the spring of 1939 to give a concert in the auditorium of the Daughters of the American Revolution (Washington's only concert hall), Eleanor Roosevelt resigned from the organization and then (along with Interior Secretary Harold Ickes, another champion of racial equality) helped secure government permission for her to sing on the steps of the Lincoln Memorial. Anderson's Easter Sunday concert attracted 75,000 people and became, in effect, the first modern civil-rights demonstration.

The president himself made some important gestures to blacks as well. Unlike his Democratic predecessor, Woodrow Wilson, he did not move to increase government discrimination against blacks; on the contrary, he worked to repeal certain particularly glaring racial restrictions within the federal government. He appointed a number of blacks to significant second-level positions in his administration, creating a network of officeholders that became known as the "Black Cabinet." Roosevelt appointees such as Robert Weaver, William Hastie, and Mary McLeod Bethune consulted with one another frequently and served as an active lobby for the interests of their race. Blacks also benefited in significant though limited ways from New Deal relief programs. Eleanor Roosevelt, Harold Ickes, and Harry Hopkins all made efforts to ensure that such programs did not exclude blacks. By 1935, an estimated 30 percent of all blacks were receiving some form of government assistance. One result of all this was a historic change in black electoral behavior. As late as 1932, the great majority of American blacks were voting Republican, as they had since the Civil War. By 1936, more than 90 percent of them were voting Democratic—the beginnings of a political alliance that would endure for many decades.

Blacks supported Franklin Roosevelt because they knew he was not their enemy. And they supported him because the New Deal created relief agencies and other programs of public assistance that were of great economic importance to this particularly impoverished group. But they had few illusions that the New Deal represented a millennium in American race relations. The president was generally sympathetic to the plight of blacks, but he believed that other problems were far more pressing; he was never willing, therefore, to risk losing the support of Southern Democrats by becoming too much identified with the issue of race. Typical of his equivocal attitude was his harsh denunciation of lynching combined with his refusal to support legislation making lynching a federal crime. He declined as well to support efforts to enact legislation banning the poll tax, one of the most potent tools by which white Southerners kept blacks from voting.

Similarly, Roosevelt refused to use the relief agencies he was creating to challenge local patterns of discrimination. On the contrary, he permitted them to reinforce such patterns. The Civilian Conservation Corps established separate black camps. The NRA codes tolerated the widespread practice of paying blacks less than whites doing the same jobs. The FERA, the CWA, and other relief agencies permitted discriminatory practices in hiring and paying their workers. Blacks were largely excluded from employment in the TVA. The Federal Housing Administration refused to provide mortgages to blacks moving into white neighborhoods, and the first public housing projects financed by the federal government were racially segregated. The AAA and its successor agencies were almost entirely ineffectual in protecting the interests of black sharecroppers and tenant farmers, thousands of whom were evicted from their land. The WPA routinely relegated black and Hispanic workers to the least skilled and lowest paying jobs; when funding ebbed, blacks, like women, were among the first to be dismissed.

The New Deal was not often actively hostile to black Americans, and it did much—both directly and indirectly—to help them advance. But the Roosevelt years did not see American blacks emerge as a potent interest group capable of seriously challenging the discriminatory forces arrayed against them. That emergence would await the development of a powerful movement among blacks themselves during and after World War II.

The New Deal and the "Indian Problem"

In many respects, government policies toward the Indian tribes in the 1930s were simply a continuation of the long-established effort to encourage Native Americans to assimilate. Senator Burton K. Wheeler of Montana expressed the sentiments of many members of Congress (and many other white Americans) when he said in 1934, in the midst of a hearing on an Indian reform bill, "What we are trying to do is get rid of the Indian problem rather than add to it." By that he meant that the purpose of reforms should be to reduce the numbers of Native Americans who identified themselves as members of tribes and increase the number of those who attempted to become part of the larger society and culture.

Yet the principal elements of federal policy in the New Deal years worked to advance a very different goal, largely because of the efforts of the extraordinary commissioner of Indian affairs in those years, John Collier. Collier was a former social worker who had become committed to the cause of the Indians after exposure to tribal cultures in New Mexico in the 1920s. More important, perhaps, he was a man greatly influenced by the work of twentieth-century anthropologists who promoted the idea of cultural relativism—the idea that every culture should be accepted and respected on its own terms and that no culture was inherently superior to another. Cultural relativism was clearly a challenge to the three-centuries-old assumption among white Americans that Indians were "savages" and that white society was inherently superior and more "civilized."

Once appointed commissioner of Indian affairs, Collier promoted legislation that would, he hoped, reverse the pressures on Native Americans to assimilate and allow them the right to remain Indians. Not all tribal leaders agreed with Collier. Some believed in assimilation and favored government programs that would assist the process. Indeed, Collier's belief in the importance of preserving Indian culture would not find its greatest support among the tribes until the 1960s. Nevertheless, Collier effectively promoted legislation—which became the Indian Reorganization Act of 1934—to advance his goals.

The act did not go as far as Collier had hoped, but it did have a substantial impact. It returned significant political authority to the tribes themselves (including the right to form tribal governments and draft tribal constitutions). It provided government funds to support education, health care, and cultural activities. Most important, it restored to the tribes the right to own land collectively (reversing the allotment policy adopted in 1887, which encouraged the breaking up of tribal lands into individually owned plots—a policy that led to the loss of over 90 million acres of tribal lands to white speculators and others). In the thirteen years after passage of the 1934 bill, tribal land increased by nearly 4 million acres, the first such increase in fifty years. In those same years, Indian agricultural income increased dramatically (from under $2 million in 1934 to over $49 million in 1947). Some of that reflected a general growth in agricultural income, which most American farmers shared. But much of it was a result of government assistance and of allowing tribes greater control of their own lands.

While New Deal Indian policies, unlike those of most earlier administrations, were generally beneficial (rather than harmful) to the interests of the tribes, they fell far short of solving the grave problems of Native Americans. Even with the redistribution of lands under the 1934 act, Indians continued to possess, for the most part, only territory whites did not want—much of it arid, some of it desert. They continued to lack full authority to govern their own social and economic relationships, even within their reservations. And as a group, they continued to con-stitute the poorest segment of the population. The efforts of the 1930s did not, as Senator Wheeler had hoped, "get rid of the Indian problem." They did, however, provide Indians with some important tools in the work of rebuilding the viability of the tribes.

Women and the New Deal

American women, too, failed to emerge in the 1930s as an interest group powerful enough to challenge the obstacles to female advancement. This was not because the New Deal was especially hostile to feminist aspirations; it was because those aspirations did not yet attract sufficiently widespread support to make it politically necessary for the administration to back them.

There were, to be sure, important symbolic gestures on behalf of women. Roosevelt appointed the first female member of the cabinet in the nation's history, Secretary of Labor Frances Perkins. He also named more than 100 other women to positions at lower levels of the federal bureaucracy; they created an active female network within the government and cooperated with one another in advancing causes of interest to women. Such appointments were in part a response to pressure from Eleanor Roosevelt, who was a committed advocate of women's rights and a champion of humanitarian causes. Mary Dewson, head of the Women's Division of the Democratic National Committee, was also influential in securing federal appointments for women as well as in increasing their role within the Democratic party. Several women received appointments to the federal judiciary. And one, Hattie Caraway of Arkansas, became the first woman ever elected to a full term in the U.S. Senate. (She was running to succeed her husband, who had died in office.)

But New Deal support for women operated within strict limits, partly because New Deal women themselves often had limited views of what was appropriate for their sex. Frances Perkins and many others in the administration emerged out of the old feminist tradition of the progressive era, which emphasized not so much sexual equality as special protections for women. Perkins herself had been instrumental in fighting for passage of various state laws safeguarding female workers. She opposed the National Woman's party and its goal of securing the Equal Rights Amendment because she feared the amendment would threaten the protective mechanisms that she had helped to establish.

Unemployment, 1920–1945

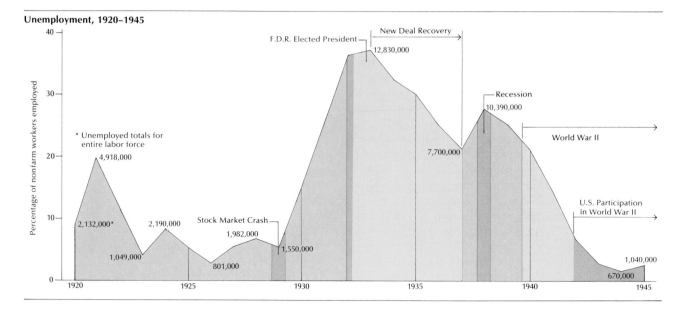

The New Deal also generally supported the prevailing belief that in hard times women should withdraw from the workplace to open up more jobs for men. Frances Perkins herself spoke out against what she called the "pin-money worker"—the married woman working to earn extra money for the household. Such women, the secretary of labor said, were a "menace to society." New Deal relief agencies offered relatively little employment for women. The NRA sanctioned sexually discriminatory wage practices. The Social Security program excluded domestic servants, waitresses, and other predominantly female occupations.

As with blacks, so also with women: The New Deal was not actively hostile; in many ways, it was unprecedentedly supportive. It did, however, accept prevailing cultural norms. There was not yet sufficient political pressure from women themselves to persuade the administration to do otherwise.

The "broker state" approach to reform, therefore, provided important opportunities for some groups to advance their interests. But for other, less powerful but at least equally imperiled interests—blacks, women, Native Americans, Hispanics, small farmers, small entrepreneurs, and many others—the New Deal offered relatively little. It did, however, help establish a pattern in American politics—individual interest groups mobilizing themselves to demand assistance from the government—that would govern the nation's public life for many decades.

The New Deal and the Economy

The most frequent criticisms of the New Deal involve its failure genuinely to revive or reform the American economy. New Dealers never fully recognized the value of government spending as a vehicle for recovery, and their efforts along other lines never succeeded in ending the Depression. Unemployment remained high throughout the New Deal years; consumption, investment, and economic growth remained low. It was the economic boom sparked by World War II, not the New Deal, that finally ended the crisis. Nor did the New Deal substantially alter the distribution of power within American capitalism; and it had only a small impact on the distribution of wealth among the American people. Large economic organizations continued to dominate the American economy at the end of the New Deal; in many respects, in fact, their power was greater than it had been a decade before.

Nevertheless, the New Deal did have a number of important and lasting effects on both the behavior and the structure of the American economy. It may not have ended the Depression, but it created a large array of protections for various groups of citizens who suffered from the crisis, and it helped prevent the economy from decaying further. It may not have altered the face of capitalism, but it helped elevate new groups—workers, farmers, and others—to positions from which they could on occasion effectively

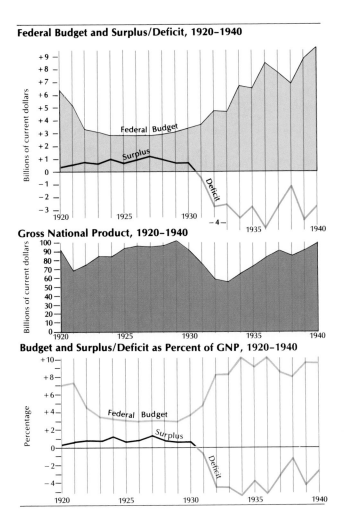

Federal Budget and Surplus/Deficit, 1920–1940

Gross National Product, 1920–1940

Budget and Surplus/Deficit as Percent of GNP, 1920–1940

American welfare state, through its many relief programs and above all through the Social Security system. The conservative inhibitions New Dealers brought to this task ensured that the welfare system that ultimately emerged would be limited in its impact (at least in comparison with those of other industrial nations), would reinforce some traditional patterns of gender and racial discrimination, and would be expensive and cumbersome to administer. But for all its limits, the new system marked a historic break with the nation's traditional reluctance to offer any public assistance whatever to indigent citizens.

The New Deal and American Politics

Perhaps the most dramatic effect of the New Deal was on the structure and behavior of American government and politics. Franklin Roosevelt helped enhance the power of the federal government as a whole. By the end of the 1930s, state and local governments were clearly of secondary importance to the government in Washington; in the past, that had not always been clear. Roosevelt also established the presidency as the preeminent center of authority within the federal government. Never again would Congress be able to wield as much independent power as it had in the years before the New Deal. And never again would it have the same control over presidential authority.

Finally, the New Deal had a profound impact on how the American people defined themselves politically. It took a weak, divided Democratic party, which had been a minority force in American politics for many decades, and turned it into a mighty coalition that would dominate national party competition for more than forty years. It turned the attention of many voters away from some of the cultural issues that had preoccupied them in the 1920s and awakened in them an interest in economic matters of direct importance to their lives. And it created among the American people at large greatly increased expectations of government—expectations that the New Deal itself did not always fulfill but that survived to become the basis of new liberal crusades in the postwar era.

challenge the power of the corporations. It increased the regulatory functions of the federal government in ways that helped stabilize previously troubled areas of the economy: the stock market, the banking system, among others. And although the New Dealers themselves did not fully realize it at the time, the administration helped establish the basis for new forms of federal fiscal policy, which in the postwar years would give the government a series of important tools for promoting and regulating economic growth.

The New Deal also created the rudiments of the

SIGNIFICANT EVENTS

1933 Franklin Roosevelt inaugurated (p. 750)

"First New Deal" legislation enacted (pp. 750–758)

United States officially abandons gold standard (p. 756)

Prohibition ends with repeal of Twenty-first Amendment (p. 751)

Dr. Francis Townsend begins campaign for old-age pensions (p. 759)

1934 Conservatives create American Liberty League (p. 759)

Huey Long establishes Share-Our-Wealth Society (p. 760)

Labor militancy increases (p. 762)

Indian Reorganization Act passed (p. 775)

1935 Supreme Court invalidates NRA (p. 755)

"Second New Deal" legislation passed (p. 761)

Father Charles Coughlin establishes National Union for Social Justice (p. 759)

John L. Lewis and allies break with AFL (p. 762)

Huey Long assassinated (p. 766)

1936 Supreme Court invalidates Agricultural Adjustment Act (p. 752)

CIO established (p. 762)

Sit-down strikes begin (p. 763)

Roosevelt wins reelection by record margin (p. 767)

1937 U.S. Steel recognizes Steel Workers' Organizing Committee (p. 764)

Roosevelt proposes "court-packing" plan (p. 767)

Supreme Court validates Wagner Act (p. 768)

"Memorial Day Massacre" in Chicago (p. 764)

New Deal spending reduced (p. 768)

Severe recession begins (p. 768)

1938 Roosevelt proposes new spending measures (p. 769)

Temporary National Economic Committee established (p. 769)

Executive reorganization plan proposed (p. 769)

1939 Marian Anderson sings at Lincoln Memorial (p. 773)

SUGGESTED READINGS

General and Biographical Studies.   William E. Leuchtenburg, *Franklin D. Roosevelt and the New Deal* (1963) and *In the Shadow of FDR* (1983); Robert S. McElvaine, *The Great Depression* (1984); Anthony J. Badger, *The New Deal* (1989); Arthur M. Schlesinger, Jr., *The Age of Roosevelt,* 3 vols. (1957–1960); Paul Conkin, *The New Deal* (1967); Edgar Robinson, *The Roosevelt Leadership* (1955); James MacGregor Burns, *Roosevelt: The Lion and the Fox* (1956); Gerald Nash, *The Great Depression and World War II* (1979); Frank Freidel, *Franklin D. Roosevelt,* 4 vols. (1952–1973) and *Franklin D. Roosevelt: A Rendezvous with Destiny* (1990); Geoffrey Ward, *Before the Trumpet: Young Franklin Roosevelt, 1882–1905* (1985) and *A First-Class Temperament: The Emergence of Franklin Roosevelt* (1989); Kenneth Davis, *FDR: The New York Years: 1928–1933* (1985) and *FDR: The New Deal Years, 1933–1937* (1986); Joseph P. Lash, *Eleanor and Franklin* (1971); J. H. Wilson and Marjorie Lightman, eds., *Without Precedent: The Life and Career of Eleanor Roosevelt* (1984); Steve Fraser and Gary Gerstle, eds., *The Rise and Fall of New Deal Liberalism* (1988); Harvard Sitkoff, ed., *Fifty Years Later: The New Deal Evaluated* (1985); John Braeman et al., eds., *The New Deal,* 2 vols. (1975); Katie Louchheim, *The Making of the New Deal* (1983); Peter Fearon, *War, Prosperity, and Depression* (1987).

New Deal Politics and Programs.   Frank Freidel, *Launching the New Deal* (1973); Raymond Moley and Eliot Rosen, *The First New Deal* (1966); Herbert Feis, *Characters in Crisis* (1966); Otis Graham, *Encore for Reform* (1967); Ellis Hawley, *The New Deal and the Problem of Monopoly* (1966); Bernard Bellush, *The Failure of the NRA* (1975); Sidney Fine, *The Automobile Under the Blue Eagle* (1963); Peter H. Irons, *The New Deal Lawyers* (1982); Susan Ware, *Beyond Suffrage* (1981) and *Partner and I: Molly Dewson, Feminism, and New Deal Politics* (1987); Thomas K. McCraw, *TVA and the Power Fight* (1970); Michael Parrish, *Securities Regulation and the New Deal* (1970); Ralph F. De Bedts. *The New Deal's SEC* (1964); Mark Leff, *The Limits of Symbolic Reform: The New Deal and Taxation, 1933–1939* (1984); Albert U. Romasco, *The Politics of Recovery: Roosevelt's New Deal* (1983); Searle Charles, *Minister of Relief* (1963); George McJimsey, *Harry Hopkins: Ally of the Poor and Defender of Democracy* (1987); John Salmond, *The Civilian Conservation Corps* (1967); Bonnie Fox Schwartz, *The Civil Works Administration, 1933–1934* (1984); James T. Patterson, *America's Struggle Against Poverty, 1900–1980* (1981); Mimi Abramowitz, *Regulating the Lives of Women* (1988); William R. Brock, *Welfare, Democracy, and the New Deal* (1987).

Agriculture. Van L. Perkins, *Crisis in Agriculture* (1969); Richard S. Kirkendall, *Social Scientists and Farm Politics in the Age of Roosevelt* (1966); Christina Campbell, *The Farm Bureaus* (1962); Gilbert Fite, *George M. Peek and the Fight for Farm Parity* (1954); David Conrad, *The Forgotten Farmers* (1965); Paul Mertz, *The New Deal and Southern Rural Poverty* (1978); Lowell K. Dyson, *Red Harvest: The Communist Party and American Farmers* (1982).

Depression Dissidents. Arthur M. Schlesinger, Jr., *The Politics of Upheaval* (1960); George Wolfskill, *Revolt of the Conservatives* (1962); Donald Grubbs, *Cry from the Cotton* (1971); Donald McCoy, *Angry Voices* (1958); R. Alan Lawson, *The Failure of Independent Liberalism* (1971); Alan Brinkley, *Voices of Protest: Huey Long, Father Coughlin, and the Great Depression* (1982); David H. Bennett, *Demagogues in the Depression* (1969); Leo Ribuffo, *The Old Christian Right: The Protestant Far Right from the Great Depression to the Cold War* (1983); Abraham Holzman, *The Townsend Movement* (1963); Charles J. Tull, *Father Coughlin and the New Deal* (1965); T. Harry Williams, *Huey Long* (1969).

The "Second New Deal." J. Joseph Huthmacher, *Senator Robert Wagner and the Rise of Urban Liberalism* (1968); W. D. Rowley, *M. L. Wilson and the Campaign for Domestic Allotment* (1970); Sidney Baldwin, *Poverty and Politics: The Farm Security Administration* (1968); Roy Lubove, *The Struggle for Social Security* (1968); Paul Conkin, *Tomorrow a New World* (1971); Jane deHart Matthews, *The Federal Theater* (1967); Jerre Mangione, *The Dream and the Deal* (1972); William F. McDonald, *Federal Relief Administration and the Arts* (1968).

The Late New Deal. James T. Patterson, *Congressional Conservatism and the New Deal* (1967); Frank Freidel, *FDR and the South* (1965); George Wolfskill and John Hudson, *All But the People* (1969); Leonard Baker, *Back to Back* (1967); William Leuchtenburg, "The Origins of Franklin D. Roosevelt's 'Court-Packing' Plan," in Philip B. Kurland (ed.), *The Supreme Court Review* (1966); Richard Polenberg, *Reorganizing Roosevelt's Government* (1966); Barry Karl, *Executive Reorganization and Reform in the New Deal* (1963); James T. Patterson, *The New Deal and the States* (1969); Charles Trout, *Boston: The Great Depression and the New Deal* (1977); Herbert Stein, *The Fiscal Revolution in America* (1969); Dean May, *From New Deal to New Economics* (1981); Theodore Rosenof, *Patterns of Political Economy in America* (1983).

Blacks, Hispanics, Indians. Harvard Sitkoff, *A New Deal for Blacks* (1978); Nancy Weiss, *Farewell to the Party of Lincoln: Black Politics in the Age of FDR* (1983) and *The National Urban League* (1974); John B. Kirby, *Black Americans in the Roosevelt Era* (1980); Raymond Wolters, *Negroes and the Great Depression* (1970); Ralph Bunche, *The Political Status of the Negro in the Age of FDR* (1973); John Dollard, *Caste and Class in a Southern Town*, 3rd ed. (1957); Dan T. Carter, *Scottsboro* (1969); Robert L. Zangrando, *The NAACP Crusade Against Lynching* (1980); Abraham Hoffman, *Unwanted Mexican Americans in the Great Depression* (1974); Francisco E. Balerman, *In Defense of La Raza* (1982); Rodolfo Acuña, *Occupied America* (rev. ed. 1981); Carey McWilliams, *Factories in the Field* (1939); Sarah Deutsch, *No Separate Refuge: Culture, Class, and Gender on the Anglo-Hispanic Frontier in the American Southwest, 1880–1940* (1987); Donald L. Parman, *The Navajos and the New Deal* (1976); Laurence M. Hauptman, *The Iroquois and the New Deal* (1981); Laurence C. Kelly, *The Assault on Assimilation: John Collier and the Origins of Indian Policy Reform* (1983); Vine DeLoria, Jr., *The Nations Within* (1984); Clifford Lytle, *American Indians, American Justice* (1983); Kenneth R. Philp, *John Collier's Crusade for Indian Reform, 1920–1954* (1977); Graham D. Taylor, *The New Deal and American Indian Tribalism* (1980).

Labor. Irving Bernstein, *Turbulent Years* (1970) and *A Caring Society: The New Deal, the Worker, and the Great Depression* (1985); Gary Gerstle, *Working-Class Americanism: The Politics of Labor in a Textile City, 1914–1960* (1989); Bruce Nelson, *Workers on the Waterfront: Seamen, Longshoremen, and Unionism in the 1930s* (1988); Joshua Freeman, *In Transit: The Transport Workers Union in New York City, 1933–1966* (1989); Melvyn Dubofsky and Warren Van Tine, *John L. Lewis* (1977); Daniel Nelson, *American Rubber Workers and Organized Labor, 1900–1941* (1988); Robert H. Zieger, *John L. Lewis: Labor Leader* (1988) and *American Workers, American Unions, 1920–1985* (1986); Christopher L. Tomlins, *The State and the Unions* (1985); George G. Suggs, Jr., *Union Busting in the Tristate: The Oklahoma, Kansas, and Missouri Metal Workers Strike of 1935* (1986); John W. Hevener, *Which Side Are You On? The Harlan County Coal Miners, 1931–1939* (1978); David Brody, *Workers in Industrial America* (1980); Jerold Auerbach, *Labor and Liberty* (1966); Sidney Fine, *Sit-Down* (1969); Bert Cochran, *Labor and Communism* (1977); Peter Friedlander, *The Emergence of a UAW Local* (1975); John Barnard, *Walter Reuther and the Rise of the Auto Workers* (1983); Ronald W. Schatz, *The Electrical Workers* (1983); David Milton, *The Politics of U.S. Labor: From the Great Depression to the New Deal* (1980); August Meier and Elliott Rudwick, *Black Detroit and the Rise of the UAW* (1979).

Allied Unity, World War II
This U.S. government poster celebrates the wartime unity of America, Britain, China, the Soviet Union, and other allies. It was also an expression of hope that the great powers could sustain the alliance in the postwar world and create a stable, lasting peace. (*West Point Museums Collection, United States Military Academy*)

CHAPTER 27

The Global Crisis, 1921–1945

Henry Cabot Lodge of Massachusetts, chairman of the Senate Foreign Relations Committee and one of the most powerful figures in the Republican party, led the fight against ratification of the Treaty of Versailles in 1918 and 1919. In part because of his efforts, the treaty was defeated; the United States failed to join the League of Nations; and American foreign policy embarked on an independent course that for the next two decades would attempt, but ultimately fail, to expand American influence and maintain international stability without committing the United States to any lasting relationships with other nations.

Lodge was not an isolationist. He recognized that America had emerged from World War I the most powerful nation in the world. He believed the United States should use that power and should exert its influence internationally. But he believed, too, that America's expanded role in the world should reflect the nation's own interests and its own special virtues; it should leave the nation unfettered with obligations to anyone else. He said in 1919:

> We are a great moral asset of Christian civilization. . . . How did we get there? By our own efforts. Nobody led us, nobody guided us, nobody controlled us. . . . I would keep America as she has been—not isolated, not prevent her from joining other nations for . . . great purposes—but I wish her to be master of her own fate.

Lodge was not alone in voicing such sentiments. Throughout the 1920s, those controlling American foreign policy attempted continually to increase America's role in the world while at the same time keeping the nation free of burdensome commitments that might limit its own freedom of action. In 1933, Franklin Roosevelt became president, bringing with him his own legacy as a leading Wilsonian internationalist and an erstwhile supporter of the League of Nations. But for more than six years, Roosevelt also attempted to keep America the "master of her own fate," to avoid important global commitments that might reduce the nation's ability to pursue its own ends.

In the end, the cautious, limited American internationalism of the interwar years proved insufficient either to protect the interests of the United States or to create global stability. In the 1920s and 1930s, the fragile international order established in the aftermath of World War I suffered a series of devastating blows—economic, political, and military. By the late 1930s, a new world crisis had emerged, which threatened to create another world war. The United States moved slowly to respond to the emerging dangers—partly because the government itself was not certain how to act, partly because it was aware of how strongly much of the public opposed any involvement in international conflicts. But after war broke out in Europe in 1939, the nation found it increasingly difficult to maintain a detached stance. By the fall of 1941, the United States was deeply involved in the conflict in countless ways. The Japanese attack on Pearl Harbor on December 7, 1941, only made official what had been growing obvious for some time:

that America would play a critical role in the greatest war in human history.

The Diplomacy of the New Era

Critics of American foreign policy in the 1920s often used a single word to describe the cause of their disenchantment: *isolationism*. Having rejected the Wilsonian vision of a new world order, the nation had, many charged, turned its back on the rest of the globe and repudiated its international responsibilities. But in reality, the United States played a more active role in world affairs in the 1920s than it had at almost any previous time in its history.

Replacing the League

It was clear when the Harding administration took office in 1921 that American membership in the League of Nations was no longer a realistic possibility. As if finally to bury the issue, Secretary of State Charles Evans Hughes secured legislation from Congress in 1921 declaring the war with Germany at an end and then proceeded to negotiate separate peace treaties with the former Central Powers. Through these treaties, American policymakers believed, the United States would receive all the advantages of the Versailles Treaty with none of the burdensome responsibilities. Hughes was, however, committed to finding something to replace the League as a guarantor of world peace and stability. He embarked, therefore, on a series of efforts to build safeguards against future wars—but safeguards that would not hamper American freedom of action in the world.

The most important of such efforts was the Washington Conference of 1921—an attempt to prevent what was threatening to become a costly and destabilizing naval armaments race among America, Britain, and Japan. Hughes startled the delegates by proposing in his opening speech a plan for dramatic reductions in the fleets of all three nations and a ten-year moratorium on the construction of large warships. He envisioned the actual scrapping of nearly 2 million tons of existing shipping. Far more surprising than the proposal was that the conference ultimately agreed to accept most of its terms, something that Hughes himself apparently had not anticipated. The Five-Power Pact of February 1922 established

both limits for naval tonnage and a ratio of armaments among the signatories. For every 5 tons of American and British capital warships, Japan would maintain 3 and France and Italy 1.75 each. (Although the treaty seemed to confirm the military inferiority of Japan, in fact it sanctioned Japanese dominance in East Asia. America and Britain had to spread their fleets across the globe; Japan was concerned only with the Pacific.) The Washington Conference also produced two other, related treaties: the Nine-Power Pact, pledging a continuation of the Open Door policy in China, and the Four-Power Pact, by which the United States, Britain, France, and Japan promised to respect one another's Pacific territories and cooperate to prevent aggression.

The Washington Conference began the New Era effort to protect the peace (and to protect the international economic interests of the United States) without accepting active international duties. The Kellogg-Briand Pact of 1928 concluded it. When the French foreign minister, Aristide Briand, asked the United States in 1927 to join an alliance against a resurgent Germany, Secretary of State Frank Kellogg (who had replaced Hughes in 1925) proposed instead a multilateral treaty outlawing war as an instrument of national policy. Fourteen nations signed the agreement in Paris on August 27, 1928, amid great solemnity and wide international acclaim. Forty-eight other nations later joined the pact. It contained no instruments of enforcement but rested, as Kellogg put it, on the "moral force" of world opinion.

Debts and Diplomacy

The first responsibility of diplomacy, Hughes, Kellogg, and others agreed, was to ensure that American overseas trade faced no obstacles to expansion and that, once established, it would remain free of interference. Preventing a dangerous armaments race and reducing the possibility of war were two steps to that end. So were the new financial arrangements that emerged at the same time. Most important to the United States was Europe, on whose economic health American prosperity in large part depended. Not only were the major industrial powers there suffering from the devastation of war; they were also staggering under a heavy burden of debt. The Allied powers were struggling to repay $11 billion in loans they had contracted with the United States during and shortly after the war, loans that the Republican administrations were unwilling to reduce or forgive. "They hired the money, didn't they?" Calvin Coolidge replied when queried about the debts. At the same time, an even more debilitated Germany was attempting to pay the enormous reparations levied against it by the Allies. With the financial structure of Europe on the brink of collapse as a result, the United States stepped in with a solution.

Charles G. Dawes, an American banker, negotiated an agreement in 1924 among France, Britain, Germany, and the United States under which American banks would provide enormous loans to the Germans, enabling them to meet their reparations payments; in return, Britain and France would agree to reduce the amount of those payments. The Dawes Plan became the centerpiece of a growing American economic presence in Germany. It also became the source of a troubling circular pattern in international finance. America would lend money to Germany, which would use that money to pay reparations to France and England, which would in turn use those funds (as well as large loans they themselves were receiving from American banks) to repay war debts to the United States. The flow was able to continue only by virtue of the enormous debts Germany and the other European nations were acquiring to American banks and corporations.

Those banks and corporations were doing more than providing loans. They were becoming a daily presence in the economic life of Europe. American automobile manufacturers were opening European factories, capturing a large share of the overseas market. Other industries in the 1920s were establishing subsidiaries worth more than $10 billion throughout the Continent, taking advantage of the devastation of European industry and the inability of domestic corporations to recover. Some groups within the American government warned that the reckless expansion of overseas loans and investments, many in enterprises of dubious value, threatened disaster; that the United States was becoming too dependent on unstable European economies. The high tariff barriers that the Republican Congress had erected (through the Fordney-McCumber Act of 1922) were creating additional problems, such skeptics warned. European nations unable to export their goods to the United States were finding it difficult to earn the money necessary to repay their loans. Such warnings fell, for the most part, on deaf ears; and American economic expansion in Europe continued until disaster struck in 1931.

The government felt even fewer reservations about assisting American economic expansion in Latin America. The United States had, after all, long considered that region its exclusive sphere of influence; and its investments there had become large even before World War I. During the 1920s, American military forces maintained a presence in numerous countries in the region, despite Hughes's withdrawal of troops from the Dominican Republic. United States investments in Latin America more than doubled between 1924 and 1929; American corporations built roads and other facilities in many areas—partly, they argued, to weaken the appeal of revolutionary forces in the region, but at least equally to increase their own access to Latin America's rich natural resources. American banks were offering large loans to Latin American governments, just as they were in Europe; and just as in Europe, the Latin Americans were having great difficulty earning the money to repay them, in the face of the formidable United States tariff barrier. By the end of the 1920s, resentment of "Yankee imperialism" was already reaching alarming proportions; the economic troubles after 1929 would only accentuate such problems.

Hoover and the World Crisis

After the relatively placid international climate of the 1920s, the diplomatic challenges facing the Hoover administration must have seemed ominous and bewildering. The world financial crisis that had begun in 1929 and greatly intensified after 1931 was not only creating economic distress; it was producing a heightened nationalism that threatened the weak international agreements established during the previous decade. Above all, the Depression was toppling some existing political leaders and replacing them with powerful, belligerent governments bent on expansion as a solution to their economic problems. Hoover was confronted, therefore, with the beginning of a process that would ultimately lead to war, and he was finding himself without sufficient tools to deal with it.

In Latin America, Hoover worked studiously to repair some of the damage created by earlier American actions. He made a ten-week good-will tour through the region before his inauguration. Once in office, he attempted to abstain from intervening in the internal affairs of neighboring nations and moved to withdraw American troops from Nicaragua and Haiti. When economic distress led to the collapse of one Latin American regime after another, Hoover announced a new policy: America would grant diplomatic recognition to any sitting government in the region without questioning the means it had used to obtain power. He even repudiated the Roosevelt Corollary to the Monroe Doctrine by refusing to permit American intervention when several Latin American countries defaulted on debt obligations to the United States in October 1931.

In Europe, the administration enjoyed few successes in its efforts to promote economic stability. When Hoover's proposed moratorium on debts in 1931 failed to attract broad support or produce financial stability (see above, pp. 742–744), many economists and political leaders appealed to the president to cancel all war debts to the United States. Like his predecessors, Hoover refused; and several European nations promptly went into default, severely damaging an already tense international climate. American efforts to extend the disarmament agreements of the 1920s met with similar frustration. At a conference in London in January 1930, American negotiators reached agreement with European and Japanese delegates on extending the limits on naval construction established at the Washington Conference of 1921. But France and England, fearful of a resurgent Germany and an expanding Japan, insisted on so many loopholes as to make the treaty virtually meaningless. The increasing irrelevance of the New Era approach to diplomacy became even clearer at the World Disarmament Conference that opened in Geneva in January 1932. France rejected the idea of disarmament entirely and called for the creation of an international army to counter the growing power of Germany. Hoover continued to urge major reductions in armaments, including an immediate abolition of all "offensive" weapons (tanks, bombers) and a 30 percent reduction in all land and naval forces. The conference ultimately dissolved in failure.

The ineffectiveness of diplomacy in Europe was particularly troubling in view of the character of some of the new governments coming to power on the Continent. Benito Mussolini's Fascist party had been in control of Italy since the early 1920s; by the 1930s, the regime was growing highly nationalistic and militaristic, and fascist leaders were loudly threatening an active campaign of imperial expansion. Even more ominous was the growing power of the National Socialist (or Nazi) party in Germany. The Weimar Republic, the nation's government since the end of World War I, had by the late 1920s lost virtually all popular support; it was discredited by, among other things, a ruinous inflation. Adolf Hitler, the stri-

dently nationalistic leader of the Nazis, was rapidly growing in popular favor. Although he lost a 1932 election for president, Hitler would sweep into power less than a year later. His belief in the racial superiority of the Aryan (German) people, his commitment to providing *Lebensraum* (living space) for his "master race," his pathological anti-Semitism, and his passionate militarism—all posed a threat to European peace.

More immediately alarming was a major crisis in Asia—one that proved to be an early step toward World War II. The Japanese, reeling from an economic depression of their own, had developed an intense concern about the increasing power of the Soviet Union and of Chiang Kai-shek's nationalist China. In particular, they were alarmed at Chiang's insistence on expanding his government's power in Manchuria, which remained officially a part of China but over which the Japanese had maintained effective economic control since 1905. When the moderate government of Japan failed to take forceful steps to counter Chiang's ambitions, Japan's military leaders staged what was, in effect, a coup in the autumn of 1931—seizing control of foreign policy from the weakened liberals. Only weeks later, they launched a major invasion of northern Manchuria.

The American government had few options. For a while, Secretary of State Henry Stimson (who had served as secretary of war under Taft) continued to hope that Japanese moderates would regain control of the Tokyo government and halt the invasion. The militarists, however, remained in command; and by the beginning of 1932, the conquest of Manchuria was complete. Hoover permitted Stimson to issue warnings to Japan and attempt to use moral suasion to end the crisis. He forbade him, however, to cooperate with the League of Nations in imposing economic sanctions against the Japanese. Stimson's only real tool in dealing with the Manchurian invasion was a refusal to grant diplomatic recognition to the new Japanese territories. Japan was unconcerned and early in 1932 expanded its aggression farther into China, attacking the city of Shanghai and killing thousands of civilians.

By the time Hoover left office early in 1933, therefore, it was clear that the international system the United States had attempted to create in the 1920s—a system based on voluntary cooperation among nations and on an American refusal to commit itself to the interests of other countries—had collapsed. The United States faced a choice. It could adopt a more energetic form of internationalism and

Hitler and Mussolini in Berlin
The German and Italian dictators (shown here reviewing Nazi troops in Berlin in the mid-1930s) acted publicly as if they were equals. Privately, Hitler treated Mussolini with contempt, and Mussolini complained constantly of being treated as a junior partner in the relationship. (The Bettmann Archive)

enter into firmer and more meaningful associations with other nations. Or it could resort to nationalism and rely on its own devices for dealing with its problems. For the next six years, it experimented with elements of both approaches.

Isolationism and Internationalism

The administration of Franklin Roosevelt faced, therefore, a dual challenge as it entered office in 1933. It had to deal with the worst economic crisis in the nation's history; and it had to deal as well with the effects of a decaying international structure. The two problems were not unrelated. It was the worldwide

Depression itself that was producing much of the political chaos throughout the globe.

Through most of the 1930s, however, the United States was unwilling to make more than the faintest of gestures toward restoring stability to the world. Like many other peoples suffering economic hardship, Americans were turning inward. Yet the realities of world affairs were not to allow the nation to remain isolated for very long—as Franklin Roosevelt realized earlier than many other Americans.

Depression Diplomacy

From Herbert Hoover, Roosevelt inherited a foreign policy less concerned with issues of war and peace than with matters of economic policy. And although the New Deal rejected some of the initiatives the

Republicans had begun, it continued for several years to base its foreign policy almost entirely on the nation's immediate economic needs.

Perhaps Roosevelt's sharpest break with the policies of his predecessor was on the question of American economic relations with Europe. Hoover had argued that only by resolving the question of war debts and reinforcing the gold standard could the American economy hope to recover. He had, therefore, agreed to participate in the World Economic Conference, to be held in London in June 1933, to attempt to resolve these issues. By the time the conference assembled, however, Roosevelt had already become convinced that the gold value of the dollar had to be allowed to fall in order for American goods to be able to compete in world markets. Shortly after the conference convened, Roosevelt released a famous "bombshell" message repudiating the orthodox views of most of the delegates and rejecting any agreement on currency stabilization. The conference quickly dissolved without reaching agreement, and not until 1936 did the administration finally agree to new negotiations to stabilize Western currencies.

At the same time, Roosevelt was moving to abandon the commitments of the Hoover administration to settle the issue of war debts through international agreement. In effect, he simply let the issue die. Not only did he decline to negotiate a solution at the London Conference, but in April 1934 he signed a bill to forbid American banks from making loans to any nation in default on its debts. The result was to stop the old, circular system by which debt payments continued only by virtue of increasing American loans; within months, war-debt payments from every nation except Finland stopped for good.

If the new administration had no interest in international currency stabilization or settlement of war debts, it did have an active interest in improving America's position in world trade. Roosevelt approved the Reciprocal Trade Agreement Act of 1934, authorizing the administration to negotiate treaties lowering tariffs by as much as 50 percent in return for reciprocal reductions by other nations. The immediate effects of the reciprocal trade agreements negotiated as a result of the act were not impressive. Most agreements in the 1930s were carefully drafted to admit only products not competitive with American industry and agriculture. By 1939, Secretary of State Cordell Hull, a devoted advocate of free trade, had succeeded in negotiating new treaties with twenty-one countries. The result was an increase in American exports to them of nearly 40 percent, but imports

into the United States continued to lag. Thus other nations were not obtaining the American currency needed to buy American products, and foreign debts to the United States increased considerably.

America and the Soviet Union

America's hopes of expanding its foreign trade produced particular efforts by the administration to improve its diplomatic posture in two areas: the Soviet Union and Latin America. The United States and Russia had viewed each other with mistrust and even hostility since the Bolshevik Revolution of 1917, and the American government still had not officially recognized the Soviet regime by 1933. But powerful voices within the United States were urging a change in policy—less because the revulsion with which most Americans viewed communism had diminished than because the Soviet Union appeared to be a possible source of trade. The Russians, too, were eager for a new relationship. They were hoping for American cooperation in containing the power of Japan on Russia's southeastern flank. In November 1933, therefore, Soviet Foreign Minister Maxim Litvinov reached an agreement with the president in Washington. The Soviets would cease their propaganda efforts in the United States and protect American citizens in Russia; in return, the United States would recognize the communist regime.

Despite this promising beginning, however, relations with the Soviet Union soon soured once again. American trade failed to establish a foothold in Russia, disappointing hopes in the United States; and the American government did little to reassure the Soviets that it was interested in stopping Japanese expansion in Asia, dousing expectations in Russia. By the end of 1934, the Soviet Union and the United States were once again viewing each other with considerable mistrust. And Stalin, having abandoned whatever hopes he might once have had of cooperation with America, was beginning to consider making agreements of his own with the fascist governments of Japan and Germany.

The Good Neighbor Policy

Somewhat more successful were American efforts to enhance both diplomatic and economic relations with Latin America through what became known as the "Good Neighbor Policy." Latin America was one of the most important targets of the new policy of trade reciprocity, and the United States succeeded during the 1930s in increasing both exports to and imports from the other nations of the Western Hemisphere by over 100 percent. Closely tied to these new economic relationships was a new American attitude toward intervention in Latin America. The Hoover administration had unofficially abandoned the earlier American practice of using military force to compel Latin American governments to repay debts, respect foreign investments, or otherwise behave "responsibly." The Roosevelt administration went further. At the Inter-American Conference in Montevideo in December 1933, Secretary of State Hull signed a formal convention declaring: "No state has the right to intervene in the internal or external affairs of another." Roosevelt respected that pledge throughout his years in office.

The Good Neighbor Policy did not mean, however, that the United States had abandoned its influence in Latin America. On the contrary, it had simply replaced one form of leverage with another. Instead of military force, Americans would now use economic influence. The new reliance on economic pressures eased tensions between the United States and its neighbors considerably, eliminating the most abrasive and conspicuous irritants in the relationship. It did little, however, to stem the growing American domination of the Latin American economy.

The Rise of Isolationism

The first years of the Roosevelt administration marked not only the death of Hoover's hopes for international economic agreements. They marked, too, the end of any hopes for world peace through treaties and disarmament. That the international arrangements of the 1920s were no longer suitable for the world of the 1930s became obvious in the first months of the Roosevelt presidency, when the new administration attempted to stimulate movement toward world disarmament. The arms control conference in Geneva had been meeting, without result, since 1932; and in May 1933, Roosevelt attempted to spur it to action by submitting a new American proposal for arms reductions. Negotiations stalled and then broke down on the Roosevelt proposal; and only a few months later, first Hitler and then Mussolini withdrew from the talks altogether. The Geneva Conference, it was clear, was a failure. Two years later, Japan withdrew from the London Naval Conference, which was attempting to draw up an agreement to continue the limitations on naval armaments negotiated at the Washington Conference of 1921.

Faced with a choice between more active efforts to stabilize the world or more energetic attempts to isolate the nation from it, most Americans unhesitatingly chose the latter. Support for isolationism emerged from many quarters. Old Wilsonian internationalists had grown disillusioned with the League of Nations and its inability to stop Japanese aggression in Asia; internationalism, they were beginning to argue, had failed. Other Americans were listening to the argument that powerful business interests—Wall Street, munitions makers, and others—had tricked the United States into participating in World War I. An investigation by a Senate committee chaired by Senator Gerald Nye of North Dakota revealed exorbitant profiteering and blatant tax evasion by many corporations during the war, and it suggested that bankers had pressured Wilson to intervene in the war so as to protect their loans abroad.

Roosevelt himself shared some of the suspicions voiced by the isolationists and claimed to be impressed by the findings of the Nye investigation. Nevertheless, he continued to hope for at least a modest American role in maintaining world peace. In 1935, he proposed to the Senate a treaty to make the United States a member of the World Court—a treaty that would have expanded America's symbolic commitment to internationalism without increasing its actual responsibilities in any important way. Nevertheless, isolationist opposition (spurred by a passionate broadcast by Father Coughlin on the eve of the Senate vote) resulted in the defeat of the treaty. It was a devastating political blow to the president, and he would not soon again attempt to challenge the isolationist tide.

That tide seemed to grow stronger with every passing month. Through the summer of 1935, it became clear to the world that Mussolini's Italy was preparing to invade Ethiopia in an effort to expand its colonial holdings in Africa. Fearing that a general European war would ensue, American legislators began to design legal safeguards to prevent the United States from being dragged into the conflict. The result was the Neutrality Act of 1935.

The 1935 act, and the Neutrality Acts of 1936 and 1937 that followed, were designed to prevent a recurrence of the events that many Americans now believed had pressured the United States into World War I. The 1935 law established a mandatory arms embargo against both victim and aggressor in any military conflict and empowered the president to warn American citizens that they might travel on the ships of warring nations only at their own risk. Thus, isolationists believed, the "protection of neutral rights" could not again become an excuse for American intervention in war. The 1936 Neutrality Act renewed these provisions. And in 1937, with world conditions growing even more precarious, Congress passed a yet more stringent measure. The new Neutrality Act established the so-called cash-and-carry policy, by which belligerents could purchase only nonmilitary goods from the United States and had to pay cash and ship their purchases themselves.

The American stance of militant neutrality was reinforced in October 1935 when Mussolini finally launched his long-anticipated attack on Ethiopia. When the League of Nations protested, Italy simply resigned from the organization, completed its conquest of Ethiopia, and formed an alliance (the "Axis") with Nazi Germany. Americans responded to the news with renewed determination to isolate themselves from European instability. Two-thirds of those responding to public-opinion polls at the time opposed any American action to deter aggression.

Isolationist sentiment showed its strength once again in 1936–1937 in response to the civil war in Spain. The Falangists of General Francisco Franco, a group much like the Italian fascists, revolted in July 1936 against the existing government, a moderate republic. Hitler and Mussolini supported Franco, both vocally and with weapons and supplies. Some individual Americans traveled to Spain to assist the republican cause (see above, p. 739); but the United States government joined with Britain and France in an agreement to offer no assistance to either side— although all three governments were sympathetic to the loyalists. In effect, then, the agreement denied what might otherwise have been crucial aid to the anti-Franco forces.

Growing Dangers

Franklin Roosevelt, in the meantime, was viewing the events of 1935 and 1936 with alarm. Slowly, cautiously, he attempted to challenge the grip of the isolationists on the nation's foreign policy; yet for a time, it seemed to be a hopeless cause. The United States was unable to do much more than watch as a series of new dangers emerged that brought the world closer to war.

Particularly disturbing was the deteriorating sit-

uation in Asia. Japan's aggressive designs against China had been clear since the invasion of Manchuria in 1931. In the summer of 1937, Tokyo launched an even broader assault, attacking China's five northern provinces. The United States could not, Roosevelt believed, allow the Japanese aggression to go unremarked or unpunished. In a speech in Chicago in October 1937, therefore, the president warned forcefully of the dangers that Japanese aggression posed to world peace. Aggressors, he proclaimed, should be "quarantined" by the international community to prevent the contagion of war from spreading.

The president was deliberately vague about what such a "quarantine" would mean; and there is evidence that he was contemplating nothing more drastic than a break in diplomatic relations with Japan, that he was not considering economic or military sanctions. Nevertheless, public response to the speech was disturbingly hostile. As a result, Roosevelt drew back. Although his strong words encouraged the British government to call a conference in Brussels to discuss the crisis in Asia, the United States refused to make any commitments to collective action; and the conference produced no agreement.

Only months later, another episode gave renewed evidence of how formidable the obstacles to Roosevelt's efforts remained. On December 12, 1937, Japanese aviators bombed and sank the U.S. gunboat *Panay* as it sailed the Yangtze River in China. The attack was almost undoubtedly deliberate. It occurred in broad daylight, with clear visibility; and a large American flag had been painted conspicuously on the *Panay*'s deck. Even so, the American public seized eagerly on Japanese protestations that the bombing had been an accident and pressured the administration to accept Japan's apologies and overlook the attack.

The Failure of Munich

In the meantime, Roosevelt was unable to find any politically acceptable way to increase American influence in Europe. It was not yet clear, moreover, that he believed the United States should become involved there in any case, even though the forces of war were rapidly gathering momentum. In 1936, Hitler had moved the now powerful German army into the Rhineland, rearming an area that France had, in effect, controlled since World War I. In March 1938, German forces marched into Austria; and Hit-

Germany Invades Poland

On September 1, 1939, after staging an incident at the border that he claimed was a provocation, Adolf Hitler sent his armies into Poland and began World War II. This photograph shows working-class homes in Warsaw burning in the aftermath of German incendiary bombing, as citizens scramble for shelter. (UPI/Bettmann Newsphotos)

ler proclaimed a union (or *Anschluss*) between Austria, his native land, and Germany, his adopted one. Neither in America nor in most of Europe was there much more than a murmur of opposition.

The Austrian invasion, however, soon created another crisis; for Hitler had by now occupied territory surrounding three sides of western Czechoslovakia, a region he dreamed of annexing to provide Germany with the *Lebensraum* (living space) he believed it needed. In September 1938, he demanded that Czechoslovakia cede to him part of that region, the Sudetenland, an area on the Austro-German border in which many ethnic Germans lived. Czechoslovakia, which possessed substantial military power of its own, was prepared to fight rather than submit. But it realized it could not hope for success without assistance from other European nations. That assistance it did not receive. Most Western nations, including the United States, were appalled at the prospect of another war and were willing to pay almost any price to settle the crisis peacefully. On September 29, Hitler met with the leaders of France and Great Britain at Munich in an effort to resolve the crisis. The French and British agreed to accept the German demands in Czechoslovakia in return for Hitler's promise to expand no farther. "This is the last territorial claim I have to make in Europe," the Führer solemnly declared. And Prime Minister Neville Chamberlain returned to England to a hero's welcome, assuring his people that the agreement ensured "peace in our time." Among those who had cabled

him with encouragement at Munich was Franklin Roosevelt.

The Munich accords were the most prominent element of a policy that came to be known as "appeasement" and that came to be identified (not altogether fairly) almost exclusively with Chamberlain. Whoever was to blame, however, it became clear almost immediately that the policy was a failure. In March 1939, Hitler occupied the remaining areas of Czechoslovakia, violating the Munich agreement unashamedly. And in April, he began issuing threats against Poland. At that point, both Britain and France gave assurances to the Polish government that they would come to its assistance in case of an invasion; they even flirted, too late, with the Stalinist regime in Russia, attempting to draw it into a mutual defense agreement. Stalin, however, had already decided that he could expect no protection from the West; he had, after all, not even been invited to attend the Munich Conference. Accordingly, he signed a nonaggression pact with Hitler in August 1939, freeing the Germans for the moment from the danger of a two-front war.

For a few months, Hitler had been trying to frighten the Poles into submitting to German rule. When that failed, he staged an incident on the border to allow him to claim that Germany had been attacked; and on September 1, 1939, he launched a full-scale invasion of Poland. Britain and France, true to their pledges, declared war on Germany two days later. World War II had begun.

Neutrality Tested

"This nation will remain a neutral nation," the president declared shortly after the hostilities began in Europe, "but I cannot ask that every American remain neutral in thought as well." It was a statement that stood in stark and deliberate contrast to Woodrow Wilson's 1914 plea that the nation remain neutral in both deed and thought; and it was clear from the start that among those whose opinions were decidedly unneutral in 1939 was the president himself. There was never any question that both he and the majority of the American people favored Britain, France, and the other Allied nations in the contest. The question was how much the United States was prepared to do to assist them.

At the very least, Roosevelt believed, the United States should make armaments available to the Allied armies to help them counteract the remarkably productive German munitions industry. As a result, in September 1939, he asked Congress for a revision of the Neutrality Acts. The original measures had forbidden the sale of American weapons to any nation engaged in war; Roosevelt wanted the arms embargo lifted. Powerful isolationist opposition forced him to accept a weaker revision than he would have liked; as passed by Congress, the 1939 measure maintained the prohibition on American ships entering war zones. It did, however, permit belligerents to purchase arms on the same cash-and-carry basis that the earlier Neutrality Acts had established for the sale of nonmilitary materials.

For a time, it was possible to believe that little more would be necessary. After the German armies had quickly subdued Poland, the war in Europe settled into a long, quiet lull that lasted through the winter and spring—a "phony war," as it was beginning to be termed. The only real fighting during this period occurred not between the Allies and the Axis, but between Russia and its neighbors. Taking advantage of the situation in the West, the Soviet Union overran first the small Baltic republics of Latvia, Estonia, and Lithuania and then, in late November, Finland. Americans were, for the most part, outraged; but neither Congress nor the president was willing to do more than impose a "moral embargo" on the shipment of armaments to Russia. By March 1940, the Soviet advance was complete. The American sanctions had had no effect.

Whatever illusions Americans had harbored about the war in Western Europe were shattered in the spring of 1940 when Germany launched an invasion to the west—first attacking Denmark and Norway, sweeping next across the Netherlands and Belgium, and driving finally deep into the heart of France. Allied efforts proved futile against the Nazi *blitzkrieg*. One western European stronghold after another fell into German hands. On June 10, Mussolini brought Italy into the war, invading France from the south as Hitler was attacking from the north. On June 22, finally, France fell to the German onslaught. Nazi troops marched into Paris; a new collaborationist regime began to assemble in Vichy; and in all Europe, only the shattered remnants of the British army, which had been miraculously rescued from the beaches of Dunkirk, remained to oppose the Axis forces.

Roosevelt had already begun to expand not only American aid to the Allies but preparations to resist a possible Nazi invasion of the United States. On May 16, he asked Congress for an additional $1 billion for defense (much of it for the construction of an enormous new fleet of warplanes) and received it quickly. With France tottering a few weeks later, he proclaimed that the United States would "extend to the opponents of force the material resources of this nation." And on May 15, Winston Churchill, the new British prime minister, sent Roosevelt the first of many long lists of requests for ships, armaments, and other assistance without which, he insisted, England could not long survive. Many Americans (including the United States ambassador to London, Joseph P. Kennedy) argued that the British plight was already hopeless, that any aid to the English was a wasted effort. The president, however, disagreed and made the bold and politically dangerous decision to "scrape the bottom of the barrel" to make war materials available to Churchill. He even circumvented the cash-and-carry provisions of the Neutrality Act by trading fifty American destroyers (most of them left over from World War I) to England in return for the right to build American bases on British territory in the Western Hemisphere; and he returned to the factories a number of new airplanes purchased by the American government so that the British could buy them instead.

Roosevelt was able to take such steps in part because of a major shift in American public opinion. Before the invasion of France, most Americans had believed that a German victory in the war would not be a threat to the United States. By July, with France defeated and Britain threatened, more than 66 percent of the public (according to opinion polls) believed that Germany posed a direct threat to the

The Global Crisis, 1921–1945   791

The Blitz, London

The German Luftwaffe terrorized London and other British cities in 1940–1941 and again late in the war by bombing civilian areas indiscriminately in an effort to break the spirit of the English people. The effort failed, and the fortitude of the British in the face of the attack did much to arouse support for their cause in the United States. St. Paul's Cathedral, miraculously undamaged throughout the raids, looms in the background of this photograph, as other buildings crumble under the force of German bombs. (Brown Brothers)

United States. Congress was aware of the change and was becoming more willing to permit expanded American assistance to the Allies. It was also becoming more concerned about the need for internal preparations for war, and in September it approved the Burke-Wadsworth Act, inaugurating the first peacetime military draft in American history.

But while the forces of isolation may have weakened, they were far from dead. On the contrary, there began in the summer of 1940 a spirited and often vicious debate between those who advocated expanded American involvement in the war (who were termed, often inaccurately, "interventionists") and those who continued to insist on neutrality. The celebrated journalist William Allen White served as

chairman of a new Committee to Defend America, whose members lobbied actively for increased American assistance to the Allies but opposed actual intervention. Others went so far as to urge an immediate declaration of war (a position that as yet had little public support) and in April created an organization of their own, the Fight for Freedom Committee. Opposing them was a powerful new lobby entitled the America First Committee, which attracted some of America's most prominent leaders. Its chairman was General Robert E. Wood, until recently the president of Sears Roebuck; and its membership included Charles Lindbergh, General Hugh Johnson, Senator Gerald Nye, and Senator Burton Wheeler. It won the editorial support of the Hearst chain and other influential newspapers; and it had at least the indirect support of a large proportion of the Republican party. (It also, inevitably, attracted a small fringe of Nazi sympathizers and anti-Semites.) The debate between the two sides was loud and bitter. Through the summer and fall of 1940, moreover, it was complicated by a presidential campaign.

The Third-Term Campaign

Much of the political drama of 1940 revolved around the question of Franklin Roosevelt's intentions. Would he break with tradition and run for an unprecedented third term? The president himself was deliberately coy and never publicly revealed his own wishes. But by refusing to withdraw from the contest, he made it impossible for any rival Democrat to establish a foothold within the party. And when, just before the Democratic Convention in July, he let it be known that he would accept a "draft" from his party, the issue was virtually settled. The Democrats quickly renominated him and even reluctantly swallowed his choice for vice president: Agriculture Secretary Henry A. Wallace, a man too liberal for the taste of many party leaders.

The Republicans, again, faced a far more difficult task. With Roosevelt effectively straddling the center of the defense debate, favoring neither the extreme isolationists nor the extreme interventionists, the Republicans had few viable alternatives. Their solution was to compete with the president on his own ground. Succumbing to the carefully orchestrated pressure of a remarkable grass-roots movement, they nominated for president a politically inexperienced businessman, Wendell Willkie. Both the candidate and the party platform took positions little different from Roosevelt's: They would keep the country out of war but would extend generous assistance to the Allies. Willkie was left, therefore, with the unenviable task of defeating Roosevelt by outmatching him in personal magnetism and by trying to arouse public fears of the dangers of an unprecedented third term. An appealing figure and a vigorous campaigner, he managed to evoke more public enthusiasm than any Republican candidate in decades. In the end, however, he was no match for Franklin Roosevelt. The election was closer than in either 1932 or 1936, but Roosevelt nevertheless won decisively. He received 55 percent of the popular vote to Willkie's 45 percent, and he won 449 electoral votes to Willkie's 82.

Neutrality Abandoned

With the election behind him and with the situation in Europe deteriorating, Roosevelt began in the last months of 1940 to make subtle but profound changes in the American role in the war. To the public, he claimed that he was simply continuing the now established policy of providing aid to the embattled Allies. In fact, that aid was taking new and more decisive forms.

In December 1940, Great Britain was virtually bankrupt. No longer could the British meet the cash-and-carry requirements imposed by the Neutrality Acts; yet England's needs, Churchill insisted, were greater than ever. The president, therefore, suggested a method that would "eliminate the dollar sign" from all arms transactions while still, he hoped, pacifying those who opposed blatant American intervention in the war. The new system was labeled "lend-lease." It would allow the government not only to sell but to lend or lease armaments to any nation deemed "vital to the defense of the United States." In other words, America could funnel weapons to England on the basis of no more than Britain's promise to return them when the war was over. Isolationists attacked the measure bitterly, arguing (correctly) that it was simply a device to tie the United States more closely to the Allies; but Congress enacted the bill by wide margins.

With lend-lease established, Roosevelt soon faced another serious problem: ensuring that the American supplies would actually reach Great Britain. Shipping lanes in the Atlantic had become extremely dangerous, as German submarines destroyed as much as a half-million tons of shipping each month. The British navy was losing ships more rapidly than it could replace them and was finding it difficult to transport materials across the Atlantic from America. Secretary of War Henry Stimson (who had been Hoover's secretary of state and who returned to the cabinet at Roosevelt's request in 1940) argued that the United States should itself convoy vessels to England; but Roosevelt decided to rely instead on the concept of "hemispheric defense." He argued that the western Atlantic was a neutral zone and the responsibility of the American nations. By July 1941, therefore, American ships were patrolling the ocean as far east as Iceland, escorting convoys of merchant ships, and radioing information to British vessels about the location of Nazi submarines.

At first, Germany did little to challenge these

obviously hostile American actions. By September 1941, however, the situation had changed. Nazi forces had invaded the Soviet Union in June of that year, driving quickly and forcefully deep into Russian territory. When the Soviets did not surrender, as many had predicted, Roosevelt persuaded Congress to extend lend-lease privileges to them—the first step toward creating a new relationship with Stalin that would ultimately lead to a formal Soviet-American alliance. Now American industry was providing the lifeblood to Hitler's foes on two fronts, and the navy was playing a more active role than ever in protecting the flow of goods to Europe. In September, Nazi submarines began a concerted campaign against American vessels. Early that month, a German U-boat fired on the American destroyer *Greer* (which was radioing the U-boat's position to the British at the time). Roosevelt responded by ordering American ships to fire on German submarines "on sight." In October, Nazi submarines actually hit two destroyers and sank one of them, the *Reuben James,* killing many American sailors in the process. An enraged Congress now voted approval of a measure allowing the United States to arm its merchant vessels and to sail all the way into belligerent ports. The United States had, in effect, launched a naval war against Germany.

At the same time, a series of meetings, some private and one public, were tying the United States and Great Britain ever more closely together. In April 1941, senior military officers of the two nations had met in secret and agreed on the joint strategy they would follow were the United States to enter the war. In August, Roosevelt met with Winston Churchill aboard a British vessel anchored off the coast of Newfoundland. The president made no military commitments, but he did join with Churchill in releasing a document that became known as the Atlantic Charter, in which the two nations set out "certain common principles" on which to base "a better future for the world." It was, in only vaguely disguised form, a statement of war aims that called openly for, among other things, "the final destruction of the Nazi tyranny."

By the fall of 1941, therefore, it seemed only a matter of time before the United States became an official belligerent. Roosevelt remained convinced that public opinion would support a declaration of war only in the event of an actual enemy attack. But an attack seemed certain to come, if not in the Atlantic, then in the Pacific.

The Road to Pearl Harbor

The Japanese had not been idle during the crisis in Europe. With Great Britain preoccupied with Germany, and with Soviet attention diverted to the west, Japan sensed an opportunity to extend its empire in the Pacific. In September 1940, Japan signed the Tripartite Pact, a loose defensive alliance with Germany and Italy that seemed to extend the Axis into Asia. (In reality, the European Axis powers never developed a very strong relationship with Japan.)

Roosevelt had already displayed his animosity toward Japanese policies by harshly denouncing their continuing assault on China and by terminating a longstanding American commercial treaty with the Tokyo government. Still the Japanese drive continued. In July 1941, imperial troops moved into Indochina and seized the capital of Vietnam, a colony of France. The United States, having broken Japanese codes, knew that their next target would be the Dutch East Indies; and when Tokyo failed to respond to Roosevelt's stern warnings, the president froze all Japanese assets in the United States, severely limiting Japan's ability to purchase needed American supplies.

Tokyo now faced a choice. It would either have to repair relations with the United States to restore the flow of supplies, or it would have to find those supplies elsewhere, most notably by seizing British and Dutch possessions in the Pacific. At first, the Tokyo government seemed willing to compromise. The Japanese prime minister, Prince Konoye, had begun negotiations with the United States even before the freezing of his country's assets; and in August he increased the pace by requesting a personal meeting with President Roosevelt. On the advice of Secretary Hull, who feared that Konoye lacked sufficient power within his own government to be able to enforce any agreement, Roosevelt replied that he would meet with the prime minister only if Japan would give guarantees in advance that it would respect the territorial integrity of China. Konoye could give no such assurances, and the negotiations collapsed. In October, the militants in Tokyo forced Konoye out of office and replaced him with the leader of the war party, General Hideki Tojo. There seemed little alternative now to war.

The Tojo government maintained for several weeks a pretense of wanting to continue negotiations. On November 20, 1941, Tokyo proposed a *modus vivendi* highly favorable to itself and sent its diplomats in Washington to the State Department to discuss it. But Tokyo had already decided that it would

The Japanese Attack Pearl Harbor, December 7, 1941

The destroyer U.S.S. *Shaw*, immobilized in a floating drydock in Pearl Harbor in December 1941, survived the first wave of Japanese bombers unscathed. But in the second attack, the Japanese scored a direct hit and produced this spectacular explosion, which blew off the ship's bow. Damage to the rest of the ship, however, was slight. Just a few months later the *Shaw* was fitted with a new bow and rejoined the fleet.   (U.S. Navy Photo)

not yield on the question of China, and Washington had made clear that it would accept nothing less than a reversal of that policy. Hull rejected the Japanese overtures out of hand; on November 27, he told Secretary of War Henry Stimson, "I have washed my hands of the Japanese situation, and it is now in the hands of you and [Secretary of the Navy Frank] Knox, the Army and Navy." He was not merely speculating. American intelligence had already decoded Japanese messages which made clear that war was imminent, that after November 29 an attack would be only a matter of days.

What Washington did not know was where the attack would take place. Most officials were convinced that the Japanese would move first not against American territory but against British or Dutch possessions to the south. American intelligence took note of a Japanese naval task force that began sailing east from the Kurile Islands in the general direction of Hawaii on November 25; and a routine warning was sent to the United States naval facility at Pearl Har-

bor, near Honolulu. Officials were paying far more attention, however, to a large Japanese convoy moving southward through the China Sea. A combination of confusion and miscalculation caused the government to overlook indications that Japan intended a direct attack on American forces.

At 7:55 A.M. on Sunday, December 7, 1941, a wave of Japanese bombers attacked the United States naval base at Pearl Harbor. A second wave came an hour later. Because the military commanders in Hawaii had taken no precautions against such an attack, allowing ships to remain bunched up defenselessly in the harbor and airplanes to remain parked in rows on airstrips, the results of the raid were catastrophic. Within two hours, the United States lost 8 battleships, 3 cruisers, 4 other vessels, 188 airplanes, and several vital shore installations. More than 2,000 soldiers and sailors died, and another 1,000 were injured. The Japanese suffered only light losses.

American forces were now greatly diminished in the Pacific (although by sheer accident, none of the four American aircraft carriers—the heart of the Pacific fleet—had been at Pearl Harbor on December 7). Nevertheless, the raid on Pearl Harbor did overnight what more than two years of effort by Franklin Roosevelt had been unable to do: It unified the American people in a fervent commitment to war. On December 8, the president traveled to Capitol Hill, where he grimly addressed a joint session of Congress: "Yesterday, December 7, 1941—a date which will live in infamy—the United States of America was suddenly and deliberately attacked by the naval and air forces of the Empire of Japan." Within four hours, the Senate unanimously and the House 388 to 1 (the lone dissenter being Jeanette Rankin of Montana, who had voted against war in 1917 as well) approved a declaration of war against Japan. Three days later, Germany and Italy, Japan's European allies, declared war on the United States; and on the same day, December 11, Congress reciprocated without a dissenting vote. For the second time in less than twenty-five years, the United States had joined in a terrible international conflagration.

War on Two Fronts

Whatever political disagreements and social tensions there may have been among the American people during World War II, there was from the beginning of the nation's formal involvement a remarkable unity of opinion about the conflict itself—"a unity," as one member of Congress proclaimed shortly after Pearl Harbor, "never before witnessed in this country." That unity and confidence were severely tested in the first, troubled months of 1942. For despite the impressive display of patriotism and the dramatic flurry of activity, the war was going very badly. Britain appeared ready to collapse. The Soviet Union was staggering. One after another, Allied strongholds in the Pacific were falling to the forces of Japan. The first task facing the United States, therefore, was less to achieve victory than to stave off defeat.

Containing the Japanese

Ten hours after the strike at Pearl Harbor, Japanese airplanes attacked the American airfields at Manila in the Philippines, destroying much of America's re-

maining air power in the Pacific. Three days later Guam, an American possession, fell to Japan; then Wake Island and Hong Kong. The great British fortress of Singapore in Malaya surrendered in February 1942, the Dutch East Indies in March, Burma in April. In the Philippines, exhausted Filipino and American troops finally surrendered on May 6, not long after General Douglas MacArthur left the islands defiantly promising "I shall return."

Alone among the warring nations, the United States was committed to major military endeavors in both Europe and the Pacific. But despite the setbacks in the struggle with Japan, American policymakers remained committed to a decision they had made in 1940. The defeat of Germany would be the nation's first priority. Nevertheless, American strategists planned two broad offensives against the Japanese after the fall of the Philippines. One, under the command of General MacArthur, would move north from Australia, through New Guinea, and eventually back to the Philippines. The other, under Admiral Chester Nimitz, would move west from Hawaii toward major Japanese island outposts in the central Pacific. Ultimately, the two offensives would come together to invade Japan itself.

The first test of this strategy came just northwest of Australia, which in mid-1942 stood almost undefended. (Only weak outposts in southern New Guinea stood between the Australian mainland and the Japanese forces.) There the Allies at last achieved their first important victory. In the Battle of Coral Sea on May 7–8, 1942, American aircraft carriers and other forces turned back the hitherto unstoppable Japanese.

A month later, there was an even more important turning point northwest of Hawaii. The American navy had broken the Japanese codes and knew that an enormous enemy offensive was taking shape there; it rushed every available airplane and vessel into the area. An enormous battle raged for four days, June 3–6, 1942, near the small American outpost at Midway Island. Both sides suffered great losses, but the encounter was, in the end, a significant American victory. Nimitz's forces had not only prevented the Japanese from securing their original objectives—the capture of Midway and the destruction of what was left of American naval power in the Pacific. They had also destroyed four Japanese aircraft carriers (the United States lost only one) and regained control of the central Pacific for the United States.

The Americans took the offensive for the first time several months later in the southern Solomon

——————— WHERE HISTORIANS DISAGREE ———————

The Question of Pearl Harbor

The phrase "Remember Pearl Harbor!" became a rallying cry during World War II—reminding Americans of the surprise Japanese attack on the American naval base in Hawaii, and arousing the nation to even greater efforts to exact revenge. But within a few years of the end of hostilities, some Americans remembered Pearl Harbor for different reasons and began to challenge the official version of the attack on December 7, 1941. Their charges sparked a debate that has never fully subsided. Was the Japanese attack on Pearl Harbor unprovoked, and did it come without warning, as the Roosevelt administration claimed at the time? Or was it part of a deliberate plan by the president to have the Japanese force a reluctant United States into the war? Most controversial of all, did the administration know of the attack in advance? Did Roosevelt deliberately refrain from warning the commanders in Hawaii so that the air raid's effect on the American public would be more profound?

Among the first to challenge the official version of Pearl Harbor was the historian Charles A. Beard, who maintained in *President Roosevelt and the Coming of the War, 1941* (1948) that the United States had deliberately forced the Japanese into a position where they had no choice but to attack. By cutting off Japan's access to the raw materials it needed for its military adventure in China, by stubbornly refusing to compromise, the United States ensured that the Japanese would strike out into the southwest Pacific to take the needed sup-

plies by force—even at the risk of war with the United States. Not only was American policy provocative in effect, Beard suggested. It was also *deliberately* provocative. More than that, the administration, which had some time before cracked the Japanese code, must have known weeks in advance of Japan's plans to attack. Beard supported his argument by citing Secretary of War Henry Stimson's comment in his diary: "The question was how we should maneuver them into the position of firing the first shot."

A partial refutation of the Beard argument appeared in 1950 in Basil Rauch's *Roosevelt from Munich to Pearl Harbor*. The administration did not know in advance of the planned attack on Pearl Harbor, he argued. It did, however, expect an attack somewhere; and it made subtle efforts to "maneuver" Japan into firing the first shot in the conflict. But Richard N. Current, in *Secretary Stimson: A Study in Statecraft* (1954), offered an even stronger challenge to Beard. Stimson did indeed anticipate an attack, Current argued, but not an attack on American territory; he anticipated, rather, an assault on British or Dutch possessions in the Pacific. The problem confronting the administration was not how to maneuver the Japanese into attacking the United States, but how to find a way to make a Japanese attack on British or Dutch territory *appear* to be an attack on America. Only thus, he believed, could Congress be persuaded to approve a declaration of war.

Islands, to the east of New Guinea, where the Japanese were establishing a base for air raids against American communications with Australia. In August 1942, American forces assaulted three of the islands: Gavutu, Tulagi, and Guadalcanal. A struggle of unprecedented ferocity (and, before it was over, terrible savagery) developed at Guadalcanal and continued for six months, inflicting heavy losses on both sides. In the end, however, the Japanese were forced to abandon the island—and with it their last chance of launching an effective offensive to the south.

In both the southern and central Pacific, therefore, the initiative had shifted to the United States by

mid-1943. The Japanese advance had been halted. The Americans, with aid from the Australians and the New Zealanders, now began the slow, arduous process of moving toward the Philippines and Japan itself.

Holding Off the Germans

In the European war, the United States was less able to shape military operations to its liking. It had to cooperate with Britain and with the exiled "Free French" forces in the west; and it had to conciliate its

---

WHERE HISTORIANS DISAGREE

Roberta Wohlstetter took a different approach to the question, in *Pearl Harbor: Warning and Decision* (1962), the most thorough scholarly study to appear to that point. De-emphasizing the question of whether the American government *wanted* a Japanese attack, she undertook to answer the question of whether the administration *knew* of the attack in advance. Wohlstetter concluded that the United States had ample warning of Japanese intentions and should have realized that the Pearl Harbor raid was imminent. But government officials failed to interpret the evidence correctly, largely because their preconceptions about Japanese intentions were at odds with the evidence they confronted. Admiral Edwin T. Layton, who had been a staff officer at Pearl Harbor in 1941, also blames political and bureaucratic failures for the absence of advance warning of the attack. In a 1985 memoir, *And I Was There*, he argues that the Japanese attack was not only a result of "audacious planning and skillful execution" by the Japanese, but of "a dramatic breakdown in our intelligence process . . . related directly to feuding among high-level naval officers in Washington."

Probably the most thorough study of Pearl Harbor appeared in 1981 in the form of Gordon W. Prange's *At Dawn We Slept*. Like Wohlstetter, Prange concluded that the Roosevelt administration was guilty of a series of disastrous blunders in interpreting Japanese strategy; the American government had possession of enough information to predict the attack, but failed to do so. But Prange dismissed the arguments of the "revisionists" (Beard and his successors) that the president had deliberately maneuvered the nation into the war by permitting the Japanese to attack. Instead, he emphasized the enormous daring and great skill with which the Japanese orchestrated an ambitious operation that few Americans believed possible.

But the revisionist claims have not been laid to rest. John Toland revived the charge of a Roosevelt betrayal in 1982, in *Infamy: Pearl Harbor and Its Aftermath*, claiming to have discovered new evidence (the testimony of an unidentified seaman) that proves the navy knew at least five days in advance that Japanese aircraft carriers were heading toward Hawaii. From that, Toland concluded that Roosevelt must have known that an attack was forthcoming and that he allowed it to occur in the belief that a surprise attack would arouse the nation. Warning the commanders in Hawaii in advance, Roosevelt feared, might cause the Japanese to cancel their plans. The president was gambling that American defenses would be sufficient to repel the attack; but his gamble failed—and resulted in the deaths of over 2,000 people and the crippling of the American Pacific fleet. But like the many previous writers who have made the same argument, Toland was unable to produce any direct evidence of Roosevelt's knowledge of the planned attack.

---

new ally, the Soviet Union, which was engaged in a remarkably costly conflict with Hitler in the east. The army chief of staff, George C. Marshall, supported a plan for a major Allied invasion of France across the English Channel in the spring of 1943; and he placed a hitherto little known general, Dwight D. Eisenhower, in charge of planning the operation. But Marshall and Eisenhower faced strong and conflicting pressures from their allies. The Soviet Union, which was absorbing (as it would throughout the war) the brunt of the German war effort, was desperate for relief and wanted the Allied invasion to proceed at the earliest possible moment. The British,

however, wanted to wait. Winston Churchill, in particular, argued strenuously for a series of Allied offensives around the edges of the Nazi empire—in northern Africa and southern Europe—before undertaking the major invasion in France itself.

The conflicting pressures came to a head in the spring of 1942. By then, the German Afrika Korps under the command of General Erwin Rommel had advanced to El Alamein, only seventy-five miles west of Alexandria, Egypt, threatening the Suez Canal and the Middle East, still under British control. At the same time, German armies in Russia were plunging toward the Caucasus. In May the Russian foreign

World War II in the Pacific

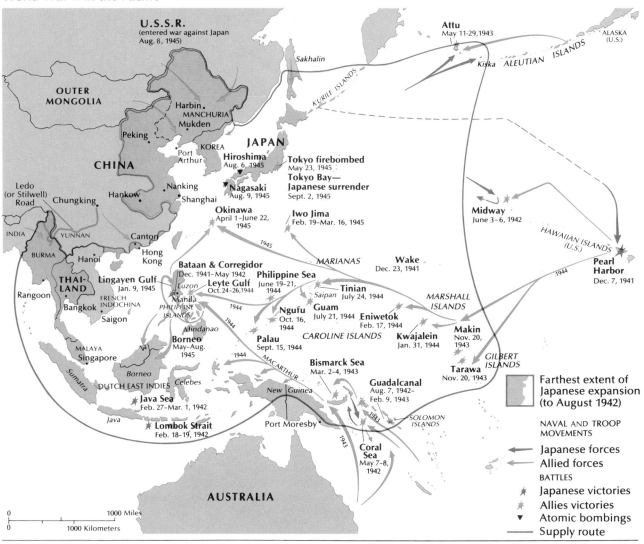

U.S.S.R. (entered war against Japan Aug. 8, 1945)

Attu
May 11-29, 1943

ALASKA (U.S.)

Sakhalin

Kiska ALEUTIAN ISLANDS

KURILE ISLANDS

OUTER MONGOLIA

Harbin
MANCHURIA
Mukden

Peking

KOREA

Port Arthur

CHINA

JAPAN

Hiroshima
Aug. 6, 1945

Tokyo firebombed
May 23, 1945

Nanking

Hankow

Nagasaki
Aug. 9, 1945

Tokyo Bay—
Japanese surrender
Sept. 2, 1945

Midway
June 3-6, 1942

HAWAIIAN ISLANDS (U.S.)

Chungking

Shanghai

Ledo
(or Stilwell)
Road

Okinawa
April 1-June 22, 1945

Iwo Jima
Feb. 19-Mar. 16, 1945

Pearl Harbor
Dec. 7, 1941

INDIA

YUNNAN

Canton

Hong Kong

MARIANAS

Wake
Dec. 23, 1941

1945

BURMA

Hanoi

Bataan & Corregidor
Dec. 1941-May 1942

Philippine Sea
June 19-21, 1944

1944

THAI-
LAND

Lingayen Gulf
Jan. 9, 1945

Leyte Gulf
Oct. 24-26, 1944

Tinian
July 24, 1944

Saipan

FRENCH INDOCHINA

Luzon

MARSHALL ISLANDS

Rangoon

Bangkok

Manila

PHILIPPINE ISLANDS

Ngufu
Oct. 16, 1944

Guam
July 21, 1944

Eniwetok
Feb. 17, 1944

Saigon

1944

Kwajalein
Jan. 31, 1944

Mindanao

CAROLINE ISLANDS

Makin
Nov. 20, 1943

MALAYA

Singapore

Borneo
May-Aug. 1945

Palau
Sept. 15, 1944

Sumatra

Borneo

1944

GILBERT ISLANDS

DUTCH EAST INDIES Celebes

MACARTHUR

Bismarck Sea
Mar. 2-4, 1943

Tarawa
Nov. 20, 1943

Java Sea
Feb. 27-Mar. 1, 1942

New Guinea

Guadalcanal
Aug. 7, 1942-
Feb. 9, 1943

Java

Lombok Strait
Feb. 18-19, 1942

Port Moresby

1943

SOLOMON ISLANDS

1943

Coral Sea
May 7-8, 1942

AUSTRALIA

| 0 | 1000 Miles |
| 0 | 1000 Kilometers |

Farthest extent of Japanese expansion (to August 1942)

NAVAL AND TROOP MOVEMENTS

→ Japanese forces
→ Allied forces

BATTLES

✳ Japanese victories
✳ Allies victories
▼ Atomic bombings
— Supply route

minister, Vyacheslav Molotov, visited Washington to demand an immediate second front that would divert at least forty German divisions from Russia; otherwise, he warned, the Soviet effort might collapse. A month later, however, Churchill arrived in Washington to urge an invasion of North Africa instead. Roosevelt knew that a Mediterranean offensive would be of less value than an invasion of the Continent, but he also concluded that an invasion of Europe would require many months of preparation. Eager to engage American forces in combat as soon as possible, he supported Churchill and ordered

American forces to join the British in the defense of northern Africa.

At the end of October 1942, the British opened a counteroffensive against Rommel at El Alamein and sent the Afrika Korps reeling back from Egypt. On November 8, Anglo-American forces landed at Oran and Algiers in Algeria and at Casablanca in Morocco—areas under the Nazi-controlled French government at Vichy. A controversial deal with French admiral Jean Darlan (a notorious collaborator with the Nazis) halted what was for a time fierce fighting between Vichy forces and the Americans at

World War II in North Africa and Italy: The Allied Counteroffensive, 1942–1943

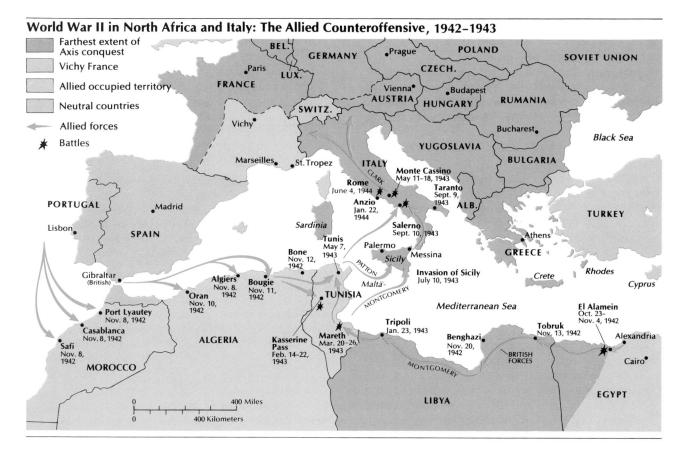

Casablanca and enabled Eisenhower to begin moving his forces east toward Rommel. The Germans, having moved west from Egypt across Libya, now threw the full weight of their forces in Africa against the inexperienced Americans and inflicted a serious defeat on them at the Kasserine Pass in Tunisia. General George S. Patton, however, regrouped the American troops and began an effective counteroffensive. With the help of Allied air and naval power and of British forces attacking from the east under Field Marshall Bernard Montgomery (the hero of El Alamein), the American offensive finally drove the last Germans from Africa in May 1943.

The North African campaign, combined with continuing shipping losses from German submarine attacks in the Atlantic, had tied up so large a proportion of the Allied resources that the planned May 1943 cross-channel invasion of France had to be postponed, despite angry complaints from the Soviet Union. By now, however, the threat of a Soviet collapse seemed much diminished; for during the winter

of 1942–1943, the Red Army had successfully held off a major German assault at Stalingrad in southern Russia. Hitler had committed such enormous forces to the battle, and had suffered such appalling losses, that his ability to continue his eastern offensive was now shattered.

The Soviet victory had come at a terrible cost. The German siege of Stalingrad had decimated the civilian population of the city and devastated the surrounding countryside. Indeed, throughout the war, the Soviet Union absorbed losses far greater than any other warring nation—a fact that generations later continued to haunt the Russian memory and affect Soviet policy. But by beating back the German offensive, the Soviets persuaded Roosevelt to agree to Churchill's plan for an Allied invasion of Sicily, a plan the two men worked out together in January 1943 at a meeting in Casablanca. General Marshall opposed the plan, fearing that it would further delay the vital invasion of France. But Churchill prevailed with his argument that the operation in Sicily might knock Italy out of the war and force the Germans to tie up many divisions in defense of Italy and the Balkans. On the night of July 9, 1943, American and British armies landed in the extreme southeast of Sicily; thirty-eight days later, they had conquered the island and begun moving onto the Italian mainland. In the face of these setbacks, Mussolini's government collapsed and the dictator himself fled north to Germany. But although Mussolini's successor, Marshal Pietro Badoglio, moved quickly to commit Italy to the Allies, Germany moved eight divisions into the country and established a powerful defensive line south of Rome. The Allied offensive on the Italian peninsula, which began on September 3, 1943, soon bogged down against the powerful, entrenched Nazi forces, particularly after a serious Allied setback at Monte Cassino early in 1944. Not until May 1944 did the Allies finally capture Cassino and resume their northward advance. On June 4, 1944, they captured Rome.

The invasion of Italy contributed to the Allied war effort in several important ways, but on the whole it was probably a strategic mistake. It postponed the invasion of France by as much as a year. It deeply embittered the Soviet Union, which was convinced that America and Britain were deliberately delaying in order to force the Russians to absorb the bulk of the German offensive. And it gave the Soviets time to reverse the course of battle and begin moving toward the countries of Eastern Europe.

America and the Holocaust

In the midst of this intensive fighting, the leaders of the American government found themselves confronted with one of history's great tragedies: the Nazi campaign to exterminate the Jews of Europe—the Holocaust. As early as 1942, high officials in Washington had incontrovertible evidence that Hitler's forces were rounding up Jews and others (including Poles, homosexuals, and communists) from all over Europe, transporting them to concentration camps in eastern Germany and Poland, and systematically murdering them. (The death toll would ultimately reach 6 million Jews and approximately 4 million others.) News of the atrocities was reaching the public as well, and pressure began to build for some Allied response, some effort to end the killing or at least to rescue some of the surviving Jews.

The American government consistently resisted almost all such entreaties. Although Allied bombers were flying missions within a few miles of the most notorious death camp at Auschwitz in Poland, pleas that the planes try to destroy the crematoria at the camp were rejected as militarily unfeasible. So were similar requests that the Allies try to destroy railroad lines leading to the camp.

The United States also resisted entreaties that it admit large numbers of the Jewish refugees attempting to escape the horrors of Europe. One ship, the *St. Louis,* arrived off Miami in 1939 carrying nearly 1,000 escaped German Jews, only to be refused entry and forced to return to Europe. Throughout the war, the State Department did not even use up the number of visas permitted by law; almost 90 percent of the quota remained untouched. One opportunity after another to assist the imperiled Jews was either ignored or rejected.

In fairness to American leaders, there was probably little they could have done to save the majority of Hitler's victims. But more forceful action by the United States (and Britain, which was even less amenable to Jewish requests for assistance) might well have saved at least some lives. The failure to take such action is difficult to understand; but in the midst of a terrible conflict, policymakers found it possible to justify abandoning the Jews to their fate by concentrating their attention solely on the larger goal of winning the war. Any diversion of energy and attention to other purposes, they apparently believed, would distract them from the overriding goal of victory.

The American People in Wartime

"War is no longer simply a battle between armed forces in the field," an American government report of 1939 concluded. "It is a struggle in which each side strives to bring to bear against the enemy the coordinated power of every individual and of every material resource at its command. The conflict extends from the soldier in the front line to the citizen in the remotest hamlet in the rear."

The United States had experienced the demands of "total war" before. But never had the nation experienced so consuming a military experience as World War II. American armed forces engaged in combat around the globe—not just for a few months, as during World War I, but for nearly four years.

American society, in the meantime, experienced changes and distortions that reached into virtually every corner of the nation.

The War Economy

World War II had its most profound impact on American domestic life by ending at last the Great Depression. By the middle of 1941, the economic problems of the 1930s—unemployment, deflation, industrial sluggishness—had virtually vanished before the great wave of wartime industrial expansion.

The most important agent of the new prosperity was federal spending, which after 1939 was pumping more money into the economy each year than all the New Deal relief agencies combined had done. In 1939, the federal budget had been $9 billion; by 1945, it had risen to $100 billion. Largely as a result, the gross national product soared: from $91 billion in 1939 to $166 billion in 1945. The index of industrial production doubled. Seventeen million new jobs were created.

Perhaps most striking was the increase in personal income. In New York, the average family income in 1938 had been $2,760; by 1942, it had risen to $4,044. In Boston, the increase was from $2,455 to $3,618; in Washington, D.C., from $2,227 to $5,316. There were limits on what the recipients of these expanded incomes could do with their money. Many consumer goods—automobiles, radios, and appliances, even many types of food and clothing—were in short supply. Wage earners diverted much of their new affluence, therefore, into savings, which would later help keep the economic boom alive in the postwar years.

The war years not only increased the total wealth of the nation; it produced the only significant change of the century in the distribution of wealth among the population. Almost everyone's income grew during the war; but the incomes of the poorest 20 percent rose by nearly 70 percent—substantially more than those of the wealthiest 20 percent, which rose by only 20 percent. Farmers, whose earnings had risen very slightly if at all during the previous two decades, saw their incomes rise by 400 percent. Industrial workers enjoyed somewhat less substantial gains; union leaders agreed to limit wage increases to 15 percent during the war. But workers who had been unemployed or underemployed in the 1930s were now fully employed, often working substantial overtime.

Labor and the War

Instead of the prolonged and debilitating unemployment that had been the most troubling feature of the Depression economy, the war created a serious labor shortage. The armed forces diverted over 15 million men and women from the civilian work force at the same time that the demand for labor was rising rapidly. Nevertheless, the civilian work force jumped from 46.5 million at the beginning of the war to over 53 million at the end. The 7 million who had previously been unemployed accounted for some of the increase; the employment of many people previously considered inappropriate for the work force—the very young, the elderly, and perhaps most important, several million women—accounted for the rest of it.

The war gave an enormous boost to union membership, which rose from about 10.5 million in 1941 to over 13 million in 1945. But it also created important new restrictions on the ability of unions to win increased wages for their members. The government was determined to prevent strikes, which might disrupt war production, and to forestall large wage increases, which might contribute to inflation. It managed to win from union leaders important concessions on both issues. One was the "no-strike" pledge, by which unions agreed not to stop production in wartime. Another was the so-called Little Steel formula, which set a 15 percent limit on wage increases. That limit was the result of negotiations conducted by the National War Labor Board, which included representatives of labor, management, and government and which was charged with settling all labor disputes. In return for these agreements, the government provided labor with a "maintenance-of-membership" agreement, which promised that the thousands of new workers pouring into defense plants would be automatically enrolled in unions that had previously established bargaining rights there. The agreement ensured the continued health of the union organizations, but in return workers had to give up the right to demand major economic gains during the war.

Many rank-and-file union members, and some union leaders, resented the restrictions imposed on them by the government and the labor hierarchy. Despite the no-strike pledge, there were nearly 15,000 work stoppages during the war. When the United Mine Workers defied the government by striking in May 1943, Congress reacted by passing a month later, over Roosevelt's veto, the Smith-

Connally Act (War Labor Disputes Act), which required unions to wait thirty days before striking and empowered the president to seize a struck war plant. A far more drastic proposal, a bill to conscript workers into government service, made considerable progress in Congress before the administration managed to block it. In the meantime, public animosity toward labor rose rapidly, and many states passed laws to limit union power. By the end of the war, pressure was growing for federal action to limit the influence of the unions.

Stabilizing the Boom

The fear of deflation, which had been the central concern of most American economists in the 1930s, gave way during the war to an at times equally serious fear of inflation. Fueling that fear was a rapid and destabilizing 25 percent increase in prices in the two years before Pearl Harbor.

In response to growing public concern, the Office of Price Administration (the war agency charged with stabilizing prices) began freezing prices and rents in certain areas of particularly rapid economic growth. But with farm prices still rising rapidly, the OPA's policies failed to reduce pressure from workers for further wage increases. In October 1942, therefore, Congress grudgingly responded to the president's request and passed the Anti-Inflation Act, which gave the administration authority to freeze agricultural prices, wages, salaries, and rents throughout the country.

The first director of the OPA, the vigorous New Dealer Leon Henderson, resigned exhausted and frustrated in mid-1943. To replace him, Roosevelt appointed Chester Bowles, a former advertising executive with remarkable administrative talents, who managed to hold the increase in living costs during the next two years to 1.4 percent. In part because of his success, inflation was a much less serious problem during World War II than it had been during World War I.

Even so, the OPA was never popular. There was widespread resentment of its "meddlesome" controls over wages and prices. And there was only grudging acquiescence in its complicated system of rationing scarce consumer goods: coffee, sugar, meat, butter, canned goods, shoes, tires, gasoline, and fuel oil. Black-marketing and overcharging grew in proportions far beyond OPA policing capacity.

Among the most important methods of controlling inflation were the government's revenue-raising programs: borrowing and taxation. The government borrowed about half the revenues it needed from the American people, by selling $100 billion worth of bonds. Most of the rest it raised by radically increasing taxes on incomes. The Revenue Act of 1942, which Roosevelt hailed as "the greatest tax bill in American history," levied a 94 percent tax on the highest incomes; and for the first time, the income tax fell as well on those in lower income brackets. To simplify payment for these new millions, Congress enacted a withholding system of payroll deductions in 1943.

From 1941 to 1945, the federal government spent a total of $321 billion—twice as much as it had spent in the entire 150 years of its existence to that point, and ten times as much as the cost of World War I. The national debt rose from $49 billion in 1941 to $259 billion in 1945, yet the black warnings of national bankruptcy that had punctuated the New Deal years were almost entirely muted.

Mobilizing Production

America's great productive capacity was its most important weapon in the fight against the Axis; it was ultimately a decisive factor in the Allied victory. But that capacity, and its importance, also created difficult challenges, which the government was never entirely successful in meeting.

The search for an effective mechanism to mobilize the economy for war began as early as 1939 and continued for nearly four years. One failed agency after another attempted to bring order to the mobilization effort: the National Defense Advisory Commission, the Office of Production Management, the Supply Priorities and Allocation Board. Finally, in January 1942, the president responded to widespread criticism by creating the War Production Board (WPB), under the direction of former Sears Roebuck executive Donald Nelson. In theory, the WPB was to be a "superagency," controlling government purchases of war matériel and supervising the allocation of materials and manpower. In fact, it never had as much authority as its World War I equivalent, the War Industries Board. And the genial Donald Nelson never displayed the administrative or political strength of his 1918 counterpart, Bernard Baruch.

Throughout its troubled history, therefore, the WPB found itself constantly outmaneuvered and

African-American Troops in Germany, 1945
Many black Americans served in the military during World War II, almost all of them in segregated units. Relatively few black soldiers were sent into combat, but those who were fought with distinction. This platoon of the 104th Division—all of them volunteers—captured twenty-four SS troops near this spot (Scherfide, Germany) in the last weeks of the war. (UPI/Bettmann Newsphotos)

frustrated. It was never able to win complete control over military purchases; the army and navy often circumvented the board entirely in negotiating contracts with producers. It was never able to satisfy the complaints of small business, which charged (correctly) that most contracts were going to large corporations. Gradually, the president transferred much of the authority he had originally delegated to Nelson to a new office located within the White House: the Office of War Mobilization, directed by a former South Carolina senator, James F. Byrnes. But the OWM was only modestly more successful than the WPB.

Despite the administrative problems, however, the war economy managed to meet almost all of the nation's critical war needs. Enormous new factory complexes were constructed in the space of a few months, many of them funded by the federal government's Defense Plants Corporation. An entire new industry producing synthetic rubber was created to make up for the loss of access to natural rubber in the Pacific. By the beginning of 1944, American factories were, in fact, producing more than the government needed. Their output was twice that of all the Axis countries combined. There were even complaints late in the war that military production was becoming excessive, that a limited resumption of civilian production should now begin. (The military staunchly and successfully opposed such demands.)

Blacks and the War

During World War I, many American blacks had eagerly seized the chance to serve in the armed forces, believing that their patriotic efforts would win them an enhanced position in postwar society. They had been cruelly disappointed. As World War II approached, blacks were again determined to use the conflict to improve the position of their race—this time, however, not by currying favor but by making demands.

In the summer of 1941, with preparedness efforts at their height, A. Philip Randolph, president of the Brotherhood of Sleeping Car Porters, an important black union, began to insist that the government require those companies receiving defense contracts to integrate their work forces. To mobilize support for the demand, Randolph planned a massive march on Washington, which threatened to bring more than 100,000 protesting blacks into the capital. Roosevelt, fearful of both the possibility of violence and the certainty of political embarrassment, finally persuaded Randolph to cancel the march in return for a promise to establish a Fair Employment Practices Commission. Its purpose was to investigate discrimination against blacks in war industries; and although its enforcement powers, and thus its effectiveness, were limited, it was a visible step toward a government commitment to racial equality.

The economic realities of the war years greatly

increased the migration of blacks from the rural areas of the South into the industrial cities, where there were suddenly factory jobs available in war plants. In the South, the migration produced white resentment and suspicion, including the false rumor among white homeowners that blacks were engaged in a conspiracy to deprive the region of domestic servants. In the North, the migration produced much more severe tensions. In Detroit in 1943 violence erupted when black families began moving into the new Sojourner Truth housing project near a Polish neighborhood. The following year, racial tensions in the city produced a major riot in which thirty-four people died, twenty-five of them blacks.

Despite such tensions, the leading black organizations redoubled their efforts during the war to challenge the system of segregation. The Congress of Racial Equality (CORE), organized in 1942, mobilized mass popular resistance to discrimination in a way that the older, more conservative organizations had never done. Randolph, Bayard Rustin, James Farmer, and other, younger black leaders helped organize sit-ins and demonstrations in segregated theaters and restaurants. In 1944, they won a much publicized victory by forcing a Washington, D.C., restaurant to agree to serve blacks. In other areas, their victories were few. Nevertheless, the war years aroused a defiant public spirit among many blacks that would survive into the 1950s and help produce the civil-rights movement.

Racial agitation was most pronounced in civilian institutions, but pressure for change was growing within the military as well. At first, the armed forces maintained their traditional practice of limiting blacks to the most menial assignments, keeping them in segregated training camps and units, and barring them entirely from the Marine Corps and the Army Air forces. Gradually, however, military leaders were forced to make adjustments—in part because of public and political pressures, but also because they recognized that these forms of segregation were wasting manpower. By the end of the war, the number of black servicemen had increased sevenfold, to 700,000; some training camps were being at least partially integrated; blacks were being allowed to serve on ships with white sailors; and more black units were being sent into combat. But tensions remained. In some of the partially integrated army bases—Fort Dix, New Jersey, for example—riots occasionally broke out when blacks protested having to serve in segregated divisions. Substantial discrimination survived in all the services until well after the war. But within the military, as within the society at large, the traditional pattern of race relations was slowly eroding.

Indians and the War

The military was somewhat more receptive to Indian participation in the war, and Native Americans suffered less overt discrimination than did blacks while serving in the armed forces. Approximately 25,000 Indians performed military service during World War II (among them Ira Hayes, one of the men who raised the American flag at Iwo Jima and became part of a legendary photograph and, later, war memorial). Other Indians served as "code-talkers," working in military communications and speaking their own languages over the radio and the telephones. Enemy forces intercepting the messages, the military concluded, would be unlikely to know Indian dialects.

The war had important effects on the Indians who served in the military, bringing them into intimate contact (often for the first time) with white society and awakening among some of them a taste for the material benefits of life in capitalist America that they would retain after the war. Some never returned to the reservations, but chose to remain in the non-Indian world and assimilate to its ways.

But the war had important effects, too, on those Native Americans who stayed on the reservations. Little war work reached the tribes, who had developed almost no industrial capacity. Government subsidies dwindled. Talented young men left the reservations to serve in the military or work in war production, creating manpower shortages in some tribes. The wartime emphasis on national unity undermined support for the revitalization of tribal autonomy that the Indian Reorganization Act of 1934 had launched. New pressures emerged to eliminate the reservation system and require the tribes to assimilate into white society—pressures so severe that John Collier, the energetic director of the Bureau of Indian Affairs who had done so much to promote the reinvigoration of the reservations, resigned in 1945.

Mexican-American War Workers

Large numbers of Mexican workers entered the United States during the war in response to labor shortages on the Pacific Coast and in the Southwest. The American and Mexican government agreed in 1942 to a program by which *braceros* (contract laborers) would be admitted to the United States for a limited time to work at specific jobs, and American employers in some parts of the Southwest began actively recruiting Hispanic workers.

Before 1940, Mexicans had come to the United States mainly as farm workers. During the Depression, many had been deported to make room for desperate white workers. The wartime labor shortage caused farm owners to begin hiring them again. More important, however, Mexican–Americans were able for the first time to find significant numbers of factory jobs. They formed the second largest group of migrants (after blacks) to American cities in the 1940s. Hispanics encountered much the same kind of discrimination that blacks faced in many industries, from both employers and unions. But the Fair Employment Practices Commission forced some industries to hire significant numbers of Hispanics. More than 17,000 found jobs in shipyards in Los Angeles.

The sudden expansion of the Mexican–American communities of American cities created tensions and occasionally open conflict. White residents of Los Angeles became alarmed at the activities of Mexican–American teenagers, many of whom were joining street gangs (*pachucos*). They were particularly distinctive because of what whites considered their outrageous style of dress: long, loose jackets with padded shoulders, baggy pants tied at the ankles, long watch chains, broad-brimmed hats, and greased, ducktail hairstyles. (It was a style borrowed in part from fashions in Harlem.) The outfit was known as a "zoot suit," and those Mexican–Americans who wore them as "zoot suiters." For them, as for many other adolescents, their style of dress became a symbol of rebellion and defiance.

In June 1943, animosity toward the zoot suiters produced a series of riots in Los Angeles. For four days, white sailors stationed at a base in Long Beach invaded Mexican–American communities and attacked zoot suiters (in response to alleged attacks by them on servicemen). The police did little to restrain the sailors, who grabbed Hispanic teenagers, tore off and burned their clothes, cut off their ducktails, and beat them. When Hispanics tried to fight back, however, the police moved in and arrested them. In the aftermath of the "zoot suit riots," Los Angeles passed a law prohibiting the wearing of zoot suits.

The conflict revealed the tension built into the social position of Mexican–Americans. Although they were moving into the United States in ever larger numbers, they continued to be treated as a despised minority: barred them from all but the poorest and most squalid residential areas, consigned to the lowest-paying jobs, and often offered no schooling for their children. Since many of the wartime immigrants stayed in the United States after 1945, their experiences helped shaped the culture and outlook of enduring Mexican–American communities in many areas of the country.

"Rosie the Riveter"

The war was also an important event in the modern history of American women, who found themselves because of social and economic necessity suddenly thrust into roles long considered inappropriate for them. With so many men serving in the military, women became even more crucial to the successful operation of industry. And so the number of women in the work force increased by over 6 million, or by nearly 60 percent, in the course of the war. The new working women were far more likely to be married and were on the whole considerably older than those who had entered the work force in the past. They were also more likely to work in heavy industrial jobs that had previously been reserved for men. The famous wartime image of "Rosie the Riveter" symbolized the new importance of the female industrial work force.

But the "Rosie the Riveter" image also tended to obscure the significant limits that remained on the ability of women to participate fully in the workplace. Indeed, in the first years of war production, when popular hostility to hiring women for war work was still strong, female unemployment and under-employment actually increased in some areas. Economic and military necessity eroded many of the objections after 1941, but never entirely. Factory owners were convinced that women could not do certain kinds of work and categorized jobs in the factories by sex. (Female work, like male work, was also categorized by race: black women were usually assigned more menial tasks, and paid at a lower rate, than their white counterparts.) Employers also made substantial investments in automated assembly lines to reduce the need for heavy labor. Special recruiting materials presented factory work to women through domestic analogies that male employers assumed females would find easily comprehensible. Cutting airplane wings was compared to making a dress pattern, mixing chemicals to making a cake. Many employers treated women in the war plants with a combination

U. S. ARMY
OFFICIAL POSTER

SOLDIERS *without guns*

Women at War
Late in the war, during a meeting with Roosevelt and Winston Churchill, Josef Stalin offered a toast: "To American production, without which the war would have been lost." The American military was well aware of how important production was to the war effort, and it gave evidence of its concern in official posters, such as this one exhorting American women to perform vital tasks in the civilian economy. (Library of Congress)

of solicitude and patronization, which was helpful to them in some respects but was also an obstacle to winning genuine equality within the work force. Still, women did make important inroads in industrial employment during the war. They joined unions in substantial numbers, and they helped erode at least some of the prejudice, including the prejudice against mothers working, that had previously kept many of them from paid employment.

Most women workers during the war were employed not in factories but in service-sector jobs. Above all, they worked for the government, whose bureaucratic needs expanded dramatically alongside its military and industrial needs. Washington, D.C.,

in particular, was flooded with young female clerks, secretaries, and typists—known as "government girls"—most of whom lived in cramped quarters in boarding houses, private homes, and government dormitories and worked long hours in the war agencies. Public and private clerical employment for women expanded in other urban areas as well, creating high concentrations of young women in places largely depleted of young men. The result was the development of distinctively female communities, in which women, often separated for the first time from home and family, adjusted to life in the work force through their association with other female workers.

But if working women encountered less popular

hostility than they had in previous decades, the new opportunities produced new problems of their own. Many mothers whose husbands were in the military tried to combine jobs with caring for their children and found the task extraordinarily difficult. The scarcity of child-care facilities or other community services meant that some women had no choice but to leave young children—often known as "latch-key children" or "eight-hour orphans"—at home alone (or sometimes locked in cars in factory parking lots) while they worked. The search for wartime employment also required many women to move to new communities. This geographical mobility often had beneficial economic results, but it also took its toll on family stability.

Perhaps in part because of the family dislocations the war produced, juvenile crime rose markedly in the war years. Young boys were arrested at rapidly increasing rates for car theft and other burglary, vandalism, and vagrancy. The arrest rate for prostitutes, many of whom were teen-age girls, rose too, as did the incidence of venereal disease. For many children, however, the distinctive experience of the war years was not crime but work. More than a third of all teen-agers between the ages of fourteen and eighteen were employed late in the war, causing some reduction in high-school enrollments.

The return of prosperity helped increase the rate and lower the age of marriage, but many of these young marriages were unable to survive the pressures of wartime separation. The divorce rate rose rapidly. The rise in the birth rate that accompanied the increase in marriages was the first sign of what would become the great postwar "baby boom."

The Internment of the Japanese-Americans

World War I had produced in America a virtual orgy of hatred, vindictiveness, and hysteria, as well as widespread and flagrant violations of civil liberties. World War II did not. A few papers, among them Father Coughlin's anti-Semitic and pro-fascist *Social Justice,* were barred from the mails as seditious; but there was no general censorship of dissident publications. A few Nazi agents and American fascists were jailed; but there was no major assault on those suspected of sympathizing with the Axis. Indeed, the most ambitious effort to punish domestic fascists, a sedition trial of twenty-eight people, ended in a mistrial, and the defendants went free. Unlike during

World War I, socialists and communists (most of whom strongly supported the war effort) were left unpunished and largely unpersecuted.

Nor was there much of the ethnic or cultural animosity that had characterized World War I. Americans continued to eat sauerkraut without calling it "liberty cabbage." They displayed little hostility toward German- and Italian-Americans. Instead, they seemed to share the view of government propaganda that the enemy was less the German and Italian people than the vicious political systems to which they had been subjected.

But there was a glaring exception to the general rule of tolerance: the treatment of the small, politically powerless group of Japanese-Americans. From the beginning, Americans adopted a different attitude toward their Asian enemy than they did toward their European foes. They attributed to the Japanese people certain racial and cultural characteristics that made it easier to hold them in contempt. The Japanese, both government and private propaganda encouraged Americans to believe, were a devious, malign, and cruel people. The infamous attack on Pearl Harbor seemed to many to confirm that assessment.

It was perhaps unsurprising, therefore, that this growing racial animosity soon extended to Americans of Japanese descent. There were not many Japanese-Americans in the United States—only about 127,000, most of them concentrated in a few areas in California. About a third of them were unnaturalized, first-generation immigrants (Issei); two-thirds were naturalized or native-born citizens of the United States (Nisei). Because they generally kept to themselves and preserved traditional Japanese cultural patterns, it was easy for others to imagine that the Japanese-Americans were engaged in conspiracies on behalf of their ancestral homeland. Wild stories circulated about sabotage at Pearl Harbor and plots to aid a Japanese landing on the coast of California—all later shown to be entirely without foundation. Public pressure to remove the "threat" grew steadily.

Finally, in February 1942, in response to pressure from military officials and political leaders on the West Coast and recommendations from the War Department, the president authorized the army to "intern" the Japanese-Americans. More than 100,000 people (Issei and Nisei alike) were rounded up, told to dispose of their property however they could (which often meant simply abandoning it), and taken to what the government euphemistically termed "relocation centers" in the "interior." In fact, they were facilities little different from prisons, many of them located in the desert. Conditions in the internment camps were not brutal, but they were harsh and uncomfortable. More important, a large group of loyal, hard-working Americans were forced to spend up to three years in grim, debilitating isolation, barred from lucrative employment, provided with only minimal medical care, and deprived of decent schools for their children. (Some young men, however, were encouraged to join a Nisei army unit, which fought with distinction in Europe.) The Supreme Court upheld the evacuation in a 1944 decision; and although most of the Japanese-Americans were released later that year (after the reelection of the president), they were largely unable to win any compensation for their losses until Congress finally acted to redress the wrongs in the late 1980s.

The Retreat from Reform

Late in 1943, Franklin Roosevelt publicly suggested that "Dr. New Deal," as he called it, had served its purpose and should now give way to "Dr. Win-the-War." The statement reflected the president's own genuine shift in concern: that victory was now more important than reform. But it reflected, too, the political reality that had emerged during the first two years of war. Liberals in government were finding themselves unable to enact new programs. They were even finding it difficult to protect existing ones from conservative assault.

Within the administration itself, many of the liberals who in the late 1930s had established positions of influence found themselves displaced by the new managers of the wartime agencies, who were drawn overwhelmingly from large corporations and conservative Wall Street law firms. The greatest assault on liberal reform, however, came from Congress. The war provided conservatives there with the excuse they had been waiting for to dismantle many of the achievements of the New Deal, which they had always mistrusted. By the end of 1943, Congress had eliminated the Civilian Conservation Corps, the National Youth Administration, and the Works Progress Administration; and the Farm Security Administration was left virtually impotent. With budget deficits mounting because of war costs, liberals made no headway in their efforts to increase Social Security benefits and otherwise extend social welfare programs.

Even had Roosevelt had the inclination to resist this conservative trend, his awareness of political realities would have been enough to stop him from trying very hard. In the congressional elections of 1942, Republicans gained 47 seats in the House and 10 in the Senate. Increasingly, the president quietly accepted the defeat or erosion of New Deal measures in order to win support for his war policies and peace plans. He also accepted the changes, however, because he realized that his chances for reelection in 1944 depended on his ability to identify himself less with domestic issues than with world peace.

Republicans approached the 1944 election determined to exploit what they believed was a smoldering national resentment of wartime regimentation and privation and a general unhappiness with the pattern of Democratic reform. Also hoping to play on concerns about the deteriorating health of the president, they nominated as their candidate the young and vigorous governor of New York, Thomas E. Dewey. Roosevelt faced no opposition for the Democratic nomination for president; but because he was so visibly in poor health, there was great pressure on him to abandon Vice President Henry Wallace, an advanced New Dealer and hero of the CIO, and replace him with a more moderate figure, acceptable to conservative party bosses and Southern Democrats. Roosevelt reluctantly succumbed to the pressure and acquiesced in the selection of Senator Harry S. Truman of Missouri, who had won national acclaim as chairman of the Senate War Investigating Committee (known as the Truman Committee), which had compiled an impressive record uncovering waste and corruption in wartime production.

Republican and Democratic leaders agreed in advance that the conduct of the war and the plans for the peace would not be an issue in the campaign. Instead, the campaign revolved around domestic economic issues and, indirectly, the president's health. In reality, the president was suffering from a range of very serious physical maladies (including arteriosclerosis) and also, apparently, from intermittent depression. It may not be too much to say that he was dying. But the campaign seemed momentarily to revive him. At the end of September, he addressed a raucously appreciative audience of members of the Teamsters Union and was at his sardonic best. He followed this triumph with strenuous campaign appearances in Chicago and a day-long drive in an open car through New York City in a soaking rain.

Roosevelt's apparent capacity to serve four more years, his stature as an international leader, and his promise to workers to revive the New Deal after the war combined to ensure him a substantial victory.

He captured 53.5 percent of the popular vote to Dewey's 46 percent; and he won 432 electoral votes to Dewey's 99. Democrats lost 1 seat in the Senate, gained 20 in the House, and maintained control of both.

The Defeat of the Axis

By the middle of 1943, America and its allies had succeeded in stopping the Axis advance both in Europe and in the Pacific. In the next two years, the Allies themselves seized the offensive and launched a series of powerful drives that rapidly led the way to victory.

The Liberation of France

In the fall of 1943, Germany was already reeling under incessant blows from Allied air power. By early 1944, American and British bombers were attacking German industrial installations and other targets almost around the clock, drastically cutting production and impeding transportation. Especially devastating was the massive bombing of such German cities as Leipzig, Dresden, and Berlin. A February 1945 incendiary raid on Dresden created a great firestorm that destroyed three-fourths of the previously undamaged city and killed over 100,000 people, mostly civilians.

The morality of such attacks has been much debated in the years since the war, but military leaders argued that the bombing had cleared the way for the great Allied invasion of France in the late spring. An enormous invasion force had been gathering in England for two years: almost 3 million troops, and perhaps the greatest array of naval vessels and armaments ever assembled in one place in the history of warfare. On the morning of June 6, 1944, after several delays, this vast invasion force moved into action. The landing came not at the narrowest part of the English Channel, where the Germans had expected and prepared for it, but along sixty miles of the Cotentin peninsula on the coast of Normandy. While airplanes and battleships offshore bombarded the Nazi defenses, 4,000 vessels, stretching as far as the eye could see, landed troops and supplies on the beaches. (Three divisions of paratroopers had been dropped behind the German lines the night before.)

Fighting was intense along the beach, but the superior manpower and equipment of the Allied forces gradually prevailed. Within a week, the German forces had been dislodged from virtually the entire Normandy coast; but for more than a month further progress remained slow.

The Battle of Saint-Lô, late in July, was an important turning point. General Omar Bradley's First Army smashed the German lines after a heavy bombardment. George S. Patton's Third Army, spearheaded by heavy tank attacks, then broke through the hole Bradley had created and began a steady drive into the heart of France. On August 25, amid scenes of great popular joy, Free French forces arrived in Paris and liberated the city from four years of German occupation. By mid-September the Allied armies had driven the Germans almost entirely out of France and Belgium. But then they came to a halt at the Rhine River against a firm line of German defenses.

Cold weather, rain, and floods provided the Germans with a temporary respite from the Allied advance in late 1944. Then, in mid-December, the German forces struck in desperation along fifty miles of front in the Ardennes Forest. In the ensuing Battle of the Bulge (named for a large bulge that appeared in the American lines as the Germans pressed forward), they drove fifty-five miles toward Antwerp before they were finally stopped at Bastogne. The battle marked the end of serious German resistance in the west.

While the Allies were fighting their way through France, Soviet forces were sweeping westward into Central Europe and the Balkans. In late January 1945, the Russians launched an offensive of more than 150 divisions toward the Oder River, far inside Germany. By early spring, they were ready to launch a final offensive against Berlin. Omar Bradley pushed on in the meantime toward the Rhine and early in March captured the city of Cologne, on the river's west bank. The next day, through a remarkable stroke of luck, he discovered and seized an undamaged bridge over the river at Remagen; and Allied troops were soon pouring across the Rhine. In the following weeks the British commander, Montgomery, with a million troops, pushed into Germany in the north while the First Army, sweeping through central Germany, completed the encirclement of 300,000 German soldiers in the Ruhr.

The German resistance was finally broken on both fronts, and the only real questions remaining involved how the Allies would divide the final tasks

Americans in Paris, 1944
American troop transports roll into Paris in August 1944 to a delirious welcome from French citizens, who had by then lived under Nazi occupation for more than four years. They had given an even warmer greeting to the Free French forces under General Charles De Gaulle, which had arrived in the city a few days earlier.   (UPI/Bettmann Newsphotos)

of conquest. American forces under General Eisenhower were moving eastward much faster than they had anticipated and could have beaten the Russians to Berlin and Prague. The American and British high commands decided, instead, to halt the advance along the Elbe River in central Germany to await the Russians. That decision enabled the Soviets to occupy eastern Germany and Czechoslovakia, with major consequences for the future of both countries and the world.

On April 30, with Soviet forces on the outskirts of Berlin, Adolf Hitler killed himself in his bunker in the capital. And on May 8, 1945, the remaining German forces surrendered unconditionally. V-E (Victory in Europe) Day prompted great celebrations in Western Europe and in the United States, tempered by the knowledge of the continuing war against Japan.

The Pacific Offensive

The victory in Europe had come more quickly than most military leaders had expected; less than a year

after the Normandy landing, the war against Germany was over. The victory in the Pacific was expected to take far longer, but events there proceeded with unanticipated speed as well.

In February 1944, American naval forces under Admiral Nimitz won a series of victories in the Marshall Islands and cracked the outer perimeter of the Japanese Empire. Before the month was out, the navy had plunged far within it to destroy other Japanese bastions. American submarines, in the meantime, were wreaking havoc on Japanese shipping and crippling the nation's domestic economy. By the summer of 1944, the already skimpy food rations for the Japanese people had been reduced by nearly a quarter; there was also a critical gasoline shortage.

A more frustrating struggle was in progress in the meantime on the Asian mainland. In 1942, the Japanese had forced General Joseph H. Stilwell out of Burma and had moved their own troops as far west as the mountains bordering on India. Stilwell organized an aerial ferry over the Himalayas to supply the isolated Chinese forces continuing to resist Japan and

World War II in Europe: The Allied Counteroffensive, 1943–1945

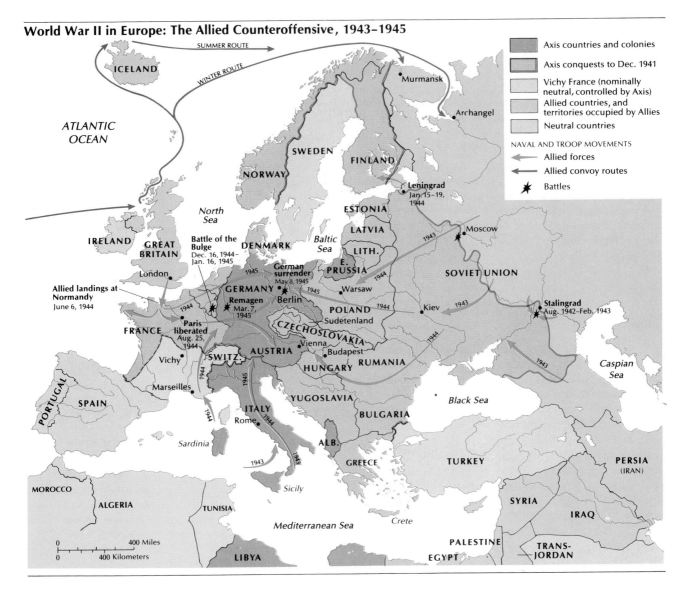

to bring Chinese troops out for Stilwell to train and arm. In 1943, Stilwell led Chinese, Indian, and a few American troops back through northern Burma, constructing a road and a parallel pipeline across the rugged mountains into Yunnan province of China. The Burma Road (also known as the Ledo Road or Stilwell Road) finally opened in the fall of 1944. By then, however, the Japanese had launched a major counteroffensive, capturing some of the bases from which American air strikes against the Japanese mainland had been launched and driving so deep into the Chinese interior that they threatened the terminus of the

Ledo Road and the center of government at Chungking.

The great Japanese offensive precipitated a long-simmering crisis in Chinese-American affairs, centering on the relations between General Stilwell and Premier Chiang Kai-shek. Stilwell was contemptuous of Chiang and indignant because the Chinese leader was using many of his troops to maintain an armed frontier against the Chinese communists and would not deploy those troops against the Japanese.

The decisive battles of the Pacific War, however, occurred not on the mainland but in the central and western Pacific. In mid-June 1944, an enormous American armada struck the heavily fortified Mariana Islands and, after some of the bloodiest operations of the war, captured Tinian, Guam, and Saipan, 1,350 miles from Tokyo. In September, American forces landed on the western Carolines. And on October 20, General MacArthur's troops landed on Leyte Island in the Philippines. The Japanese now mobilized their remaining strength for a last defense of their empire and employed virtually their entire fleet against the Allied invaders in three major encounters—which together constituted the decisive Battle of Leyte Gulf, the largest naval engagement in history. American forces held off the Japanese onslaught and sank four Japanese carriers, all but destroying Japan's capacity to continue a serious naval war.

Toward Final Victory

The defeat of Japan now seemed inevitable, but the war was not yet over. As American forces advanced steadily closer to the Japanese mainland early in 1945, the imperial forces seemed only to increase their resistance. Fighting continued in the Philippines. In the meantime, American marines moved in February to seize the tiny volcanic island of Iwo Jima, only 750 miles from Tokyo, a potentially valuable base for future air strikes against Japan. The Japanese defended the island so ferociously that the marines suffered over 20,000 casualties. It was the costliest battle in the history of the Marine Corps.

The battle for Okinawa, an island only 370 miles south of Japan, was further evidence of the strength of the Japanese resistance in these last desperate days. Week after week, the Japanese sent Kamikaze suicide planes against American and British ships, sacrificing 3,500 of them while inflicting great damage. Japanese troops on shore launched equally desperate nighttime attacks on the American lines. The United States and its allies suffered nearly 50,000 casualties on land and sea before finally capturing Okinawa in late June 1945. Over 100,000 Japanese died in that encounter.

The same kind of bitter fighting seemed to await the Americans when they invaded Japan. But there were signs early in 1945 that such an invasion might not be necessary. The Japanese had almost no ships or planes left with which to fight and seemed unable to mount even token resistance to American challenges at sea. In July 1945, for example, American warships stood off the shore of Japan and shelled

industrial targets (many already in ruins from aerial bombings) with impunity. The brutal firebombing of Tokyo in May, in which American bombers dropped napalm on the city and created a firestorm in which over 80,000 died, had further weakened the will to resist.

Moderate Japanese leaders, who had long since decided that the war was lost, were in the meantime increasing their power within the government. After the invasion of Okinawa, Emperor Hirohito appointed a new premier and gave him instructions to sue for peace. Although the new leader could not persuade military leaders to give up the fight, he did try, along with the emperor himself, to obtain mediation through the Soviet Union. The Russians showed little interest in playing the role of arbitrator, but other developments made their participation superfluous in any case. For at a meeting of Allied leaders in Potsdam, Germany, in mid-July 1945, President Harry S. Truman (who had succeeded to the office on the death of Franklin Roosevelt three months earlier; see below, p. 832) received news of the first successful test of an atomic weapon.

The Manhattan Project

Reports had reached the United States in 1939, through the Italian physicist Enrico Fermi and the German mathematician Albert Einstein (then living in exile in America), that Nazi scientists had learned how to produce atomic fission in uranium. That knowledge, they warned, could be the first step toward the creation of a bomb more powerful than any weapon ever devised. The United States and Britain immediately began a race to develop the weapon before the Germans did.

In December 1942, American physicists produced a controlled chain reaction in an atomic pile at the University of Chicago, solving the first great problem in producing an atomic weapon. There remained the enormous technical problems of achieving the release of this power in a bomb. Over the next three years, the government secretly poured nearly $2 billion into the so-called Manhattan Project—a massive scientific effort conducted at hidden laboratories in Oak Ridge, Tennessee, Los Alamos, New Mexico, and other sites. (Its name had emerged earlier, when many of the atomic physicists had been working at Columbia University in New York.) Hundreds of scientists, many of them not fully aware of what they were working on, labored

Hiroshima After the Bomb
Where once a bustling city stood, only rubble remains. This photograph shows the center of Hiroshima shortly after it was devastated by the first of two atomic bombs the United States dropped on Japan in the last days of World War II.   (Brown Brothers)

feverishly to complete two complementary projects. One (at Oak Ridge) was the production of fissionable plutonium, the fuel for an atomic explosion; the other (at Los Alamos, under the supervision of J. Robert Oppenheimer) was the construction of a bomb that could employ the fuel. The scientists pushed ahead far faster than anyone had predicted. Even so, the war in Europe had ended by the time they were ready to test the first bomb. (Only later did they discover that the Germans had never come close to constructing a usable atomic device.)

On July 16, 1945, the Manhattan Project scientists stood on a hill near Alamogordo, New Mexico, watching a tower several miles away on which was suspended the fruits of their labor. And just before dawn, they witnessed the first atomic explosion in history: a blinding flash of light brighter than any ever seen on earth, and a huge, billowing mushroom cloud. Some were exhilarated by their success. Others, among them J. Robert Oppenheimer, were already troubled by the implications of what they had done. Standing on the New Mexico desert watching the terrible explosion, Oppenheimer thought grimly of the words from Hindu Scripture: "Now I am become death, the destroyer of worlds."

Atomic Warfare

As soon as news of the explosion reached Truman in Potsdam, he issued an ultimatum to the Japanese (signed jointly by the British) demanding that they surrender immediately or face utter devastation. He set a deadline of August 3. The Japanese premier wanted to accept the Allied demand, but by the time the deadline arrived he had not yet been able to persuade the military leaders to agree. There was some reason to believe that the government might be willing to surrender, in return for a promise that the Japanese could retain their emperor (who was, even then, a largely symbolic ruler). The American government apparently disregarded those overtures; and when the August 3 deadline came and went without a settlement, Truman ordered the air force to use the new atomic weapons against Japan.

Controversy has raged for decades over whether Truman's decision to use the bomb was justified and what his motives were. Some have argued that the atomic attack was unnecessary, that had the United States agreed to the survival of the emperor (which it ultimately did agree to in any case), or had it waited only a few more weeks, the Japanese would have surrendered anyway. Others argue that nothing less than the atomic bombs could have persuaded the Japanese to surrender without an American invasion.

Some critics of the decision, including some of the scientists involved in the Manhattan Project, have argued that whatever Japanese intentions, the United States, as a matter of moral conviction, should not have used the terrible new weapon. One horrified physicist wrote the president shortly before the at

SIGNIFICANT EVENTS

1921 Washington Conference leads to reductions in naval armaments (p. 782)

1922 Fordney-McCumber Tariff passed (p. 783)

1924 Dawes Plan renegotiates European debts, reparations (p. 783)

1928 Kellogg-Briand Pact signed (p. 782)

1931 Economic crisis spreads worldwide (p. 783)
Japan invades Manchuria (p. 784)

1932 World Disarmament Conference held in Geneva (p. 784)

1933 Adolf Hitler becomes chancellor of Germany (p. 784)
United States scuttles London Economic Conference (p. 786)
United States establishes diplomatic relations with Soviet Union (p. 786)
Roosevelt proclaims Good Neighbor Policy (p. 786)

1935 Senate defeats World Court treaty (p. 787)
Neutrality Act passed (p. 787)
Italy invades Ethiopia (p. 788)

1936 Spanish Civil War begins (p. 788)
Germany reoccupies Rhineland (p. 788)
A second Neutrality Act passed (p. 788)

1937 Japan launches new invasion of China (p. 788)
Roosevelt gives "quarantine" speech (p. 788)
Japan attacks U.S. gunboat *Panay* (p. 788)
A third Neutrality Act passed (p. 788)

1938 Germany annexes Austria (*Anschluss*) (p. 789)
Munich Conference (p. 789)

1939 Nazi-Soviet nonaggression pact signed (p. 789)
Germany invades Czechoslovakia (p. 789)
Germany invades Poland (p. 789)
World War II begins (p. 789)

1940 Soviet Union invades Baltic nations, Finland (p. 790)
German *blitzkrieg* conquers most of Western Europe (p. 790)
Germany, Italy, Japan sign Tripartite Pact (p. 793)
Fight for Freedom Committee founded (p. 791)

1940 America First Committee founded (p. 791)
Roosevelt reelected president (p. 792)
United States makes destroyers-for-bases deal with Britain (p. 790)

1941 A. Philip Randolph proposes march on Washington (p. 803)
Roosevelt establishes Fair Employment Practices Commission (p. 803)
Lend-lease plan provides aid to Britain (p. 792)
American ships confront German submarines in North Atlantic (p. 793)
Germany invades Soviet Union (p. 793)
Atlantic Charter signed (p. 793)
Japan attacks Pearl Harbor (p. 794)
United States enters war (p. 795)

1942 Japanese capture Philippines (p. 795)
Battle of Midway (p. 795)
North Africa campaign begins (p. 798)
News of Holocaust reaches United States (p. 800)
War Production Board created (p. 802)
Japanese-Americans interned (p. 807)
Manhattan Project begins (p. 812)

1943 Americans capture Guadalcanal (p. 796)
Soviets defeat Germans at Stalingrad (p. 799)
Allies launch invasion of Italy (p. 800)
Smith-Connally Act passed (pp. 801–802)
Race riot breaks out in Detroit (p. 804)
Sailors battle Mexican-Americans in "zoot suit" riots in Los Angeles (p. 805)

1944 Allies invade Normandy (p. 809)
Roosevelt reelected president (p. 808)
Americans recapture Philippines (p. 812)

1945 Roosevelt dies; Truman becomes president (p. 812)
Hitler kills himself (p. 810)
Allies capture Berlin (p. 810)
Germany surrenders (p. 810)
Americans capture Okinawa (p. 812)
Atomic bomb tested in New Mexico (p. 813)
United States drops atomic bombs on Hiroshima and Nagasaki (p. 815)
Japan surrenders (p. 815)

tack: "This thing must not be permitted to exist on this earth. We must not be the most hated and feared people in the world." The nation's military and political leaders, however, showed little concern about such matters. Truman, through no fault of his own, had not even been aware of the bomb's existence until a few weeks before he was called on to decide whether to use it. And knowing so little about it, he could hardly have been expected to recognize the full implications of its power. He was, apparently, making what he believed to be a simple military decision. A weapon was available that would end the war quickly; he could see no reason not to use it.

Still more controversy has existed over whether there were other motives at work in Truman's decision as well. With the Soviet Union poised to enter the war in the Pacific, did the United States want to end the conflict quickly to forestall an expanded communist presence in Asia? Did Truman use the bomb as a weapon to intimidate Stalin, with whom he was engaged in difficult negotiations, so the Soviet leader would accept American demands? Little direct evidence is available to support either of these accusations, but historians continue to disagree on the issue.

Whatever the reasons, the decision was made. On August 6, 1945, an American B-29, the *Enola Gay,* dropped an atomic weapon on the Japanese industrial center at Hiroshima. With a single bomb, the United States completely incinerated a four-square-mile area at the center of the previously undamaged city. More than 80,000 civilians died, according to later American estimates. Many more survived to suffer the painful and crippling effects of radioactive fallout or to pass those effects on to their children in the form of serious birth defects.

The Japanese government, stunned by the attack, was at first unable to agree on a response. Two days later, on August 8, the Soviet Union declared war on Japan. And the following day, another American plane dropped another atomic weapon—this time on the city of Nagasaki—inflicting horrible damage on yet another unfortunate community. Finally, the emperor intervened to break the stalemate in the cabinet; and on August 14, the government announced that it was ready to give up. On September 2, 1945, on board the American battleship *Missouri,* anchored in Tokyo Bay, Japanese officials signed the articles of surrender.

The greatest war in the history of mankind had come to an end, and the United States had emerged from it not only victorious, but in a position of unprecedented power, influence, and prestige. It was a victory, however, that few could greet with unambiguous joy. Fourteen million men under arms had died in the struggle. Many more civilians had perished. The United States had suffered only light casualties in comparison with some other nations, but the totals were frightful nevertheless: 322,000 dead, another 800,000 injured. And in spite of having paid so high a price for peace, the world continued to face an uncertain future. The menace of nuclear warfare hung like a black cloud on the horizon. And already the world's two strongest nations—the United States and the Soviet Union—were developing antagonisms toward one another that would darken the peace for many decades to come.

SUGGESTED READINGS

The 1920s. L. Ethan Ellis, *Republican Foreign Policy, 1921–1933* (1968); Merlo J. Pusey, *Charles Evans Hughes,* 2 vols. (1963); Joan Hoff Wilson, *American Business and Foreign Policy, 1920–1933* (1968) and *Ideology and Economics* (1974); William Appleman Williams, *The Tragedy of American Diplomacy* (1962); Frank Costigliola, *Awkward Dominion: American Political, Economic, and Cultural Relations with Europe, 1919–1933* (1984); Akira Iriye, *After Imperialism* (1965); Warren Cohen, *America's Response to China* (1971) and *Empire Without Tears* (1987); Roger Dingman, *Power in the Pacific* (1976); Thomas Buckley, *The United States and the Washington Conference* (1970); Robert H. Ferrell, *Peace in Their Time* (1952); Joseph Tulchin, *The Aftermath of War* (1971); William Kamman, *A Search for Stability* (1968); Michael J. Hogan, *Informal Entente: The Private Structure of Cooperation in Anglo-American Economic Diplomacy, 1918–1928* (1977); Melvyn P. Leffler, *The Elusive Quest* (1979).

The Hoover Years. Robert H. Ferrell, *American Diplomacy in the Great Depression* (1970); Elting Morison, *Turmoil and Tradition* (1960); Alexander DeConde, *Hoover's Latin American Policy* (1951); Raymond O'Connor, *Perilous Equilibrium* (1962); Armin Rappaport, *Stimson and Japan* (1963).

New Deal Diplomacy. Robert Dallek, *Franklin D. Roosevelt and American Foreign Policy, 1932–1945* (1979); Lloyd Gardner, *Economic Aspects of New Deal Diplomacy* (1964); Frank Freidel, *Launching the New Deal* (1973); Beatrice Farnsworth, *William C. Bullitt and the Soviet Union* (1967); Robert Browder, *The Origins of Soviet-American Diplomacy* (1953); Peter Filene, *Americans and the Soviet Experiment, 1917–1933* (1967); Edward E. Bennett, *Recognition of Russia* (1970); Walter LaFeber, *Inevitable Revolutions* (1983); Bruce J. Calder, *The Impact of Intervention* (1984); Lorenzo Meyer, *Mexico and the United States in the Oil Controversy* (1977); Bryce Wood, *The Making of the Good Neighbor Pol-*

icy (1961); Irwin F. Gellman, *Good Neighbor Diplomacy: United States Policies in Latin America, 1933–1945* (1979); David Green, *The Containment of Latin America* (1971); Dorothy Borg, *The United States and the Far Eastern Crisis of 1933–1938* (1964).

Isolationism and Pacifism.   Selig Adler, *The Uncertain Giant* (1966) and *The Isolationist Impulse* (1957); Robert Divine, *The Reluctant Belligerent* (1965); William Langer and S. Everett Gleason, *The Challenge to Isolation* (1952); *The Undeclared War* (1953); Manfred Jonas, *Isolationism in America* (1966); Wayne S. Cole, *America First* (1953), *Senator Gerald P. Nye and American Foreign Relations* (1962), *Charles A. Lindbergh and the Battle Against American Intervention in World War II* (1974), and *Roosevelt and the Isolationists, 1932–1945* (1983); Warren I. Cohen, *The American Revisionists* (1967); Thomas C. Kennedy, *Charles A. Beard and American Foreign Policy* (1975); Richard Lowitt, *George W. Norris*, 3 vols. (1963–1978); John K. Nelson, *The Peace Prophets* (1967); Lawrence Wittner, *Rebels Against War* (1984); Charles Chatfield, *For Peace and Justice: Pacifism in America, 1914–1941* (1971); Charles DeBenedetti, *Origins of the Modern American Peace Movement, 1915–1929* (1978) and *The Peace Reform in American History* (1980).

The Coming of World War II.   Arnold Offner, *The Origins of the Second World War* (1975); Bernard F. Donahoe, *Private Plans and Public Dangers* (1965); Garry Clifford and Samuel R. Spencer, Jr., *The First Peacetime Draft* (1986); Waldo H. Heinrichs, Jr., *Threshold of War* (1988); Manfred Jonas, *The United States and Germany* (1984); James Leutze, *Bargaining for Supremacy* (1977); Michael S. Sherry, *The Rise of American Airpower* (1987); Joseph Lash, *Roosevelt and Churchill* (1976); Warren Kimball, *The Most Unsordid Act: Lend-Lease, 1939–1941* (1970); David Reynolds, *The Creation of the Anglo-American Alliance, 1937–1941* (1982); David F. Schmitz, *The United States and Fascist Italy, 1922–1944* (1988); Roger Dingman, *Power in the Pacific* (1976); Akira Iriye, *Across the Pacific* (1967), *After Imperialism: The Search for a New Order in the Far East, 1921–1933* (1965), and *The Origins of the Second World War in Asia and the Pacific* (1987); Hebert Feis, *The Road to Pearl Harbor* (1950); Jonathan Utley, *Going to War with Japan* (1985); James MacGregor Burns, *Roosevelt: The Soldier of Freedom* (1970); Roberta Wohlstetter, *Pearl Harbor: Warning and Decision* (1962); Gordon Prange, *At Dawn We Slept* (1981) and *Pearl Harbor* (1986); Martin V. Melosi, *The Shadow of Pearl Harbor* (1977).

War and American Society.   John Morton Blum, *V Was for Victory* (1976); Richard Polenberg, *War and Society* (1972); Mark J. Harris et al., *The Homefront* (1984); Alan Clive, *State of War: Michigan in World War II* (1979); Gerald D. Nash, *The American West Transformed: The Impact of the Second World War* (1985); Richard R. Lingeman, *Don't You Know There's a War On?* (1970); Studs Terkel, *"The Good War": An Oral History of World War II* (1984).

War Mobilization and Wartime Politics.   Donald Nelson, *Arsenal of Democracy* (1946); Bruce Catton, *War Lords of*

Washington (1946); David Brinkley, *Washington Goes to War* (1987); Eliot Janeway, *Struggle for Survival* (1951); Joel Seidman, *American Labor from Defense to Reconversion* (1953); Nelson Lichtenstein, *Labor's War at Home* (1982); Howell John Harris, *The Right to Manage* (1982); Leslie R. Groves, *Now It Can Be Told* (1962); Oscar E. Anderson, Jr., *The New World* (1962); Chester Bowles, *Promises to Keep* (1971); Lester V. Chandler, *Inflation in the United States, 1940–1948* (1951); Richard Steele, *Propaganda in an Open Society* (1985); Patrick S. Washburn, *A Question of Sedition: The Federal Government's Investigation of the Black Press During World War II* (1986); Alan Winkler, *The Politics of Propaganda* (1978); Philip Knightley, *The First Casualty* (1975); James MacGregor Burns, *Roosevelt: The Soldier of Freedom* (1970); Ellsworth Barnard, *Wendell Willkie* (1966); Maurice Isserman, *Which Side Were You On? The American Communist Party During World War II* (1982).

The War and Race.   Louis Ruchames, *Race, Jobs, and Politics* (1953); Neil Wynn, *The Afro-American and the Second World War* (1976); Herbert Garfinkel, *When Negroes March* (1959); Richard M. Dalfiume, *Desegregation of the U.S. Armed Forces* (1969); Domenic J. Capeci, Jr., *The Harlem Riot of 1943* (1977) and *Race Relations in Wartime Detroit* (1987); Philip McGuire, ed., *Taps for a Jim Crow Army: Letters from Black Soldiers in World War II* (1982); August Meier and Elliott Rudwick, *CORE* (1973); Mauricio Mazon, *The Zoot-Suit Riots* (1984); Roger Daniels, *The Politics of Prejudice* (1962) and *Concentration Camps, USA* (1971); Audrie Girdner and Anne Loftis, *The Great Betrayal* (1969); Bill Hosokawa, *Nisei* (1969); Peter Irons, *Justice at War* (1983); Thomas James, *Exiles Within: The Schooling of Japanese-Americans, 1942–1945* (1987).

Women and the War.   Ruth Milkman, *Gender at Work: The Dynamics of Job Segregation by Sex During World War II* (1987); Susan M. Reverby, *Ordered to Care: The Dilemma of American Nursing, 1850–1945* (1987); Karen Anderson, *Wartime Women: Sex Roles, Family Relations, and the Status of Women During World War II* (1981); D'Ann Campbell, *Women at War with America* (1984); Sherna B. Gluck, *Rosie the Riveter Revisited* (1987); Maureen Honey, *Creating Rosie the Riveter: Class, Gender, and Propaganda During World War II* (1984); Margaret R. Higgonet et al., *Behind the Lines: Gender and the Two World Wars* (1987); Susan Hartmann, *The Homefront and Beyond: American Women in the 1940s* (1982); Leila Rupp, *Mobilizing Women for War* (1978).

Wartime Military and Diplomatic Experiences.   James MacGregor Burns, *Roosevelt: The Soldier of Freedom* (1970); Robert Divine, *Roosevelt and World War II* (1969) and *Second Chance* (1967); Albert Russell Buchanan, *The United States and World War II*, 2 vols. (1962); Fletcher Pratt, *War for the World* (1951); Margaret Hoyle, *A World in Flames* (1970); Kenneth Greenfield, *American Strategy in World War II* (1963); Samuel Eliot Morison, *Strategy and Compromise* (1958), *History of United States Naval Operations in World War II*, 14 vols. (1947–1960), and *The Two Ocean War* (1963); Winston S. Churchill, *The Second World War*, 6 vols.

(1948–1953); Chester Wilmot, *The Struggle for Europe* (1952); Charles B. McDonald, *The Mighty Endeavor* (1969); Stephen Ambrose, *The Supreme Commander* (1970) and *Eisenhower: Soldier, General of the Army, President-Elect* (1983); Michael Howard, *The Mediterranean Strategy in World War II* (1968); Dwight D. Eisenhower, *Crusade in Europe* (1948); Forrest Pogue, *George C. Marshall*, 2 vols. (1963–1966); D. Clayton James, *A Time for Giants: Politics of the American High Command in World War II* (1987); Max Hastings, *Overlord: D-Day and the Battle for Normandy* (1984); Russel F. Weigley, *The American Way of War* (1973); Cornelius Ryan, *The Last Battle* (1966); John Toland, *The Last Hundred Days* (1966); Ronald Schaffer, *Wings of Judgment: American Bombing in World War II* (1985); David S. Wyman, *The Abandonment of the Jews: America and the Holocaust, 1941–1945* (1984); Gaddis Smith, *American Diplomacy During the Second World War* (1964); E. J. Kind and W. M. Whitehill, *Fleet Admiral King* (1952); Barbara Tuchman, *Stilwell and the American Experience in China* (1971); John W. Dower, *War Without Mercy: Race and Power in the Pacific War* (1986); John Toland, *The Rising Sun* (1970); Ronald Spector, *Eagle Against the Sun: The American War with Japan* (1985); William Manchester, *American Caesar* (1979).

Atomic Warfare. Martin Sherwin, *A World Destroyed* (1975); Gar Alperovitz, *Atomic Diplomacy* (1965); Robert Jungk, *Brighter Than a Thousand Suns* (1958); Nuel Davis, *Lawrence and Oppenheimer* (1969); Gregg Herken, *The Winning Weapon* (1980); W. S. Schoenberger, *Decision of Destiny* (1969); Robert Donovan, *Conflict and Crisis* (1977); John Hersey, *Hiroshima* (1946); Herbert Feis, *The Atomic Bomb and the End of World War II* (1966); Richard Rhodes, *The Making of the Atomic Bomb* (1987); Leon V. Sigal, *Fighting to a Finish* (1988).

Dust Bowl

T he Dust Bowl of the 1930s was one of the great environmental disasters of American history. Although historians have often attributed it solely to an especially severe natural drought, it was in fact a much more complicated event that had as much to do with people as with nature.

The origins of the Dust Bowl stretched back more than half a century. As American settlers moved out onto the Western plains after the Civil War, they encountered a more arid climate than any they had known in the East. Farming techniques that had been successful elsewhere failed as rain became scarcer. The biggest problem with the plains was the unreliability of rainfall from year to year: years of above-average rainfall alternated at unpredictable intervals with years of drought. The prosperity farmers enjoyed during good years encouraged them to hang on even if they might face economic ruin when the rains failed.

To deal with the problem of too little rain, farmers experimented with new ways of farming. By plowing the soil deeply, stirring up a fine layer of dust on the surface, and leaving fields bare to gather moisture when not being cropped, they sought to conserve water as best they could. At the same time, they grew less corn and introduced winter wheats from central Europe that were especially well adapted to dry conditions. These techniques worked well enough to encourage farmers to expand into new areas.

The great period of expansion for plains farmers came during World War I. European demand and government subsidies sent the price of wheat soaring past $2 per bushel, and other grains rose as well. Farmers responded by planting as never before. By 1919, Colorado, Nebraska, Kansas, Oklahoma, and Texas had expanded their wheat acreage by 13.5 million acres—11 million acres of which had been covered with native grasses. To handle this vast new cropland, farmers invested in new mechanical equipment: disk plows, combines, and tractors. Tractors quickly replaced horses as the universal power source on Great Plains farms, and their total numbers grew accordingly. In 1915, there had been approximately 3,000 tractors in all of Kansas. Five years later, there were over 17,000, and by 1930 the number had risen to more than 66,000. More and more of the basic work of the farm was performed by internal combustion engines burning gasoline.

Dust Storm, Southwest Plains, 1937
The dust storms of the 1930s were a terrifying experience for all who lived through them. Appearing as a black wall sweeping in from the western horizon, such a storm engulfed farms and towns alike, blotting out the light of the sun and covering everything with fine dirt. (UPI/Bettmann Newsphotos)

The new machinery enabled farm families to produce more grain per capita than ever before, but also exposed them to new risks. Equipment was expensive: a typical tractor in the 1920s cost several hundred dollars, and a typical combine two or three thousand. Most farmers financed such purchases with loans. They also planted larger acreages to take advantage of the new equipment, and incurred additional debts for their new land. Paying off debts was no problem during good years, but could become a nightmare if economic or climatic conditions became unfavorable. Unfortunately, they both went bad at once during the 1920s.

By 1930, the world wheat market was in deep trouble, and farmers had no choice but to plant as many acres as possible in a desperate effort to earn enough to pay their debts. At the same time, rain failed up and down the plains. Starting in 1931, areas in the southern plains that ordinarily received eighteen inches of rain each year—the bare minimum for many types of farming—had annual deficits of three to seven inches. Crops died. The parched soil baked and cracked in the sun as thermometers rose above 100 degrees each day for weeks on end. Even many native grasses eventually succumbed. The region was entering its worst drought in recorded history, and it would be a decade before rainfall became abundant once again.

Drought was nothing new to the plains, but the new human regime was unprecedented. Never before had so many farmers carried so high a burden of debt. The collapse of crop prices meant that thousands of acres stood naked in the sun. The native grasses of the plains had once formed a tight natural sod that could withstand a drought even if many individual plants died. Now the sod was gone, and nothing remained to protect soil from the wind.

Dust storms had been part of life on the plains for centuries, especially in western Kansas, Oklahoma, and the Texas panhandle, where the soil was sandy and especially susceptible to blowing. Now, however, they fueled themselves in a vicious cycle of ecological and economic disaster. A single famous storm in May 1934 carried 300 million tons of Great Plains soil all the way to the Atlantic Ocean, dropping dust in New York and Washington and even on ships 300 miles at sea. On the Southern plains, such storms became a regular occurrence for the better part of the 1930s. They darkened the sky at midday, seeped dust into houses, blew drifts along fencerows, even killed animals and people who were unlucky enough to be caught in their midst. "Three little words," wrote a reporter for the Associated Press in 1935, "achingly familiar on a Western farmer's tongue—rule life today in the dust bowl of the continent. . . . If it rains." And so the Southern plains gained a new name: Dust Bowl.

There were 22 dust storms in 1934, 40 in 1935, 68 in 1936, 72 in 1937, 61 in 1938, 30 in 1939, and 17 each in 1940 and 1941. Unplanted soil made conditions

Contour Plowing

Farmers responded to the dust storms by adopting new cultivation practices designed to prevent soil from blowing away in the wind. Among the most important techniques was contour plowing, which raised furrows in the soil to break the wind's velocity as it moved across the surface. Contour plowing also discouraged water erosion. (The Bettmann Archive)

perfect for dust storms when the drought finally hit, and the combined force of economic depression and too little rain left farmers with few defenses once the cycle got going. Many families eventually abandoned their farms and took to the road, becoming the "Okies" who migrated to California in search of a better life. A number of New Deal agencies stepped in to try to help with a variety of programs. The Resettlement Administration sought to buy up farms on soils that were too marginal for safe agricultural production. The Forest Service planted over 200 million trees as "shelter belts" designed to slow the dusty winds. And the Soil Conservation Service promoted new forms of tillage that held the soil better.

All these things helped, but it was not until 1941, when the rains returned in earnest and World War II began to generate massive new demand for crops, that the Dust Bowl came to an end. New farming techniques, including irrigation systems that tapped underground water supplies, have prevented the return of dust storms on anything like the scale of the 1930s, though lesser storms have from time to time blown through the region. Whether they return in the future depends on whether farmers remember the lessons of the Dust Bowl and adapt their methods to the special needs of their land.

The Communist Triumph in Beijing
This Chinese wall poster shows Mao Zedong's Communist forces entering Beijing in January 1949 as the long struggle for control of China came to an end.

CHAPTER 28

America and the Cold War

The immediate aftermath of World War II was a trying time for the United States. Having emerged from the struggle indisputably the greatest power in the world, America assumed that the peace would take a form to its liking. It did not. Almost immediately, it became clear that another great power—a nation not yet as strong as the United States, but strong enough to make its influence felt—had a very different vision of the postwar order. Even before the war ended, there were signs of tension between the United States and the Soviet Union, who had fought together so effectively as allies. Once the hostilities were over, those tensions quickly grew to create an enduring "Cold War" between the two nations that would cast its shadow over the entire course of international affairs for decades.

At the same time, the American people were experiencing the predictable upheavals of readjustment to civilian life. The economy was undergoing a difficult transformation in preparation for the remarkable growth that was soon to follow. Politics was in some confusion, partly as a result of the death of Franklin Roosevelt in April 1945. And the specter of the Cold War was having profound effects on American domestic life, ultimately producing the most corrosive outbreak of antiradical hysteria of the century. America in the postwar years was both powerful and prosperous; but it was also for a time troubled and uncertain about its future.

Origins of the Cold War

No issue in twentieth-century American history has aroused more debate than the question of the origins of the Cold War. Two questions, in particular, have provoked controversy: When did it begin? Who was to blame? Some have argued that the Cold War could have been avoided as late as 1947 or 1948, others that it was virtually inevitable long before the end of World War II. Some have claimed that Soviet duplicity and expansionism created the international tensions, others that American provocations and imperial ambitions were at least equally to blame. On virtually every aspect of the history of the Cold War, disagreement remains rampant. (See "Where Historians Disagree," pp. 826–827.)

But if historians have reached no general accord on these questions, they have gradually arrived at something approaching a consensus on some of the outlines of the debate. Most would agree that the origins of the Cold War can be understood only by looking at both the historic background of Soviet-American relations and the specific events of 1945 through 1948. And most would also agree that, wherever the preponderance of blame may lie, both the United States and the Soviet Union contributed to the atmosphere of hostility and suspicion that quickly clouded the peace.

WHERE HISTORIANS DISAGREE

Origins of the Cold War

No issue in recent American history has produced more controversy than that of the origins of the Cold War between the United States and the Soviet Union. In particular, historians have disagreed over the question of who was responsible for the breakdown of American-Soviet relations, and on whether the conflict between the two superpowers was inevitable or could have been avoided.

For more than a decade after the end of World War II, few historians saw any reason to challenge the official American interpretation of the beginnings of the Cold War. Thomas A. Bailey spoke for most students of the conflict when he argued, in *America Faces Russia* (1950), that the breakdown of relations was a direct result of aggressive Soviet policies of expansion in the immediate postwar years. Stalin's government violated its solemn promises in the Yalta Accords, imposed Soviet-dominated governments on the unwilling nations of Eastern Europe, and schemed to spread communism throughout the world. American policy was the logical and necessary response: a firm commitment to oppose Soviet expansionism and to retain its armed forces in a continual state of preparedness.

It was the American involvement in Vietnam that finally disillusioned many historians with the premises of the containment policy and, thus, with the traditional view of the origins of the Cold War. But even before the conflict in Asia had reached major proportions, the first works in what would become known as the "revisionist" interpretation began to appear. William Appleman Williams challenged the accepted wisdom as early as 1952; in 1959 he published *The Tragedy of American Diplomacy*, which studied the Cold War in the context of American foreign policy throughout the twentieth century. The United States had operated in world affairs, Williams argued, in response to

one overriding concern: its commitment to maintaining an "open door" for American trade in world markets. The confrontation with the Soviet Union, therefore, was less a response to Russian aggressive designs than an expression of the American belief in the necessity of capitalist expansion.

Later revisionists modified many of Williams's claims, but most accepted some of the basic outlines of his thesis: that the United States had been primarily to blame for the Cold War; that the Soviet Union had displayed no aggressive designs toward the West (and was so weak and exhausted at the end of World War II as to be unable to pose any serious threat to America in any case); that the United States had used its nuclear monopoly to attempt to threaten and intimidate Stalin; that Harry Truman had recklessly abandoned the conciliatory policies of Franklin Roosevelt and taken a provocative hard line against the Russians; and that the Soviet response had reflected a legitimate fear of capitalist encirclement. Walter LaFeber, in *America, Russia, and the Cold War, 1945–1967* (1967), maintained that America's supposedly idealistic internationalism at the close of the war—its vision of "One World," with every nation in control of its own destiny—was in reality an effort to ensure a world shaped in the American image, with every nation open to American influence (and to American trade).

Crucial to many revisionist arguments has been the American decision to use atomic weapons against Japan in the closing days of World War II. As early as 1948, a British physicist, P. M. S. Blackett, wrote in *Fear, War, and the Bomb* that the destruction of Hiroshima and Nagasaki was "not so much the last military act of the second World War as the first major operation of the cold diplomatic war with Russia." Gar Alperovitz expanded that idea in *Atomic Diplomacy* (1965), in

A Legacy of Mistrust

The wartime alliance between the United States and the Soviet Union was an aberration from the normal tenor of Soviet-American relations. Ever since the

Bolshevik Revolution of 1917, the two nations had viewed each other with deep mutual mistrust.

The reasons for American hostility toward the Soviet Union were both obvious and many. There was, of course, the fundamental American animosity

WHERE HISTORIANS DISAGREE

which he claimed that American decision makers used the bombs on an already defeated Japan not to win the war (for the war was already won) but to impress and intimidate the Soviets, to make them more "manageable." In fact, Alperovitz argued, this atomic diplomacy had the opposite effect: it convinced the Soviet Union of America's hostile intentions and helped speed the beginning of the Cold War.

Ultimately, the revisionist interpretation began to produce a reaction of its own, what some have called the "counter-" or "post-revisionist" view of the conflict. Some manifestations of this reaction have consisted of little more than a reaffirmation of the traditional view of the Cold War. Herbert Feis, for example, argued in *The Atomic Bomb and the End of World War II* (1966) that the revisionist claim that the use of nuclear weapons on Japan was a tactic to intimidate the Soviets was unfounded, that Truman had made his decision on purely military grounds—to ensure a speedy American victory and eliminate the need for what was expected to be a long and costly invasion of Japan. Others challenged the revisionists by accepting some of their findings but rejecting their most important claims. Arthur M. Schlesinger, Jr., admitted in a 1967 article that the Soviets may not have been committed to world conquest, as most earlier accounts had claimed. Nevertheless, the Soviets (and Stalin in particular) were motivated by a deepseated paranoia about the West, which made them insistent on dominating Eastern Europe and rendered any amicable relationship between them and the United States impossible.

But the dominant works of post-revisionist scholarship have attempted to strike a balance between the two camps, to identify areas of blame and misconception on both sides of the conflict. Thomas G. Paterson, in *Soviet-American Confron-*

tation (1973), viewed Russian hostility and American efforts to dominate the postwar world as equally responsible for the Cold War. John Lewis Gaddis, in *The United States and the Origins of the Cold War, 1941–1947* (1972), similarly maintained that "neither side can bear sole responsibility for the onset of the Cold War." American policymakers, he argued, had only limited options because of the pressures of domestic politics. And Stalin was immobilized by his obsessive concern with maintaining his own power and ensuring absolute security for the Soviet Union. But if neither side is entirely to blame, Gaddis concluded, the Soviets must be held at least slightly more accountable for the problems; for Stalin was in a much better position to compromise, given his broader power within his own government than the politically hamstrung Truman.

Out of the post-revisionist literature has begun to emerge a new and more complex view of the Cold War, which deemphasizes the question of who was to blame and adopts a more detached view of the conflict. The Cold War, recent historians suggest, was not so much the fault of one side or the other as it was the natural result, perhaps the inevitable result, of the predictable tensions between the world's two most powerful nations; two nations that had been suspicious of, if not hostile toward, one another for nearly a century. As Ernest May wrote in a 1984 essay:

> After the Second World War, the United States and the Soviet Union were doomed to be antagonists. . . . There probably was never any real possibility that the post-1945 relationship could be anything but hostility verging on conflict. . . . Traditions, belief systems, propinquity, and convenience . . . all combined to stimulate antagonism, and almost no factor operated in either country to hold it back.

toward communism, which had strong roots in the nation's past and had been a powerful force in society since well before the Russian Revolution. But there were more specific reasons as well. America's first image of the Soviet regime had been of a government that negotiated a separate peace with Germany in

1917, leaving the West to fight the Central Powers alone. Many Americans had chafed at the strident attacks on the American capitalist system emanating from Moscow—attacks that proved particularly grating during the 1930s, when that system was under duress. They had long been concerned about the Soviet regime's open avowal of the need for world revolution. They had felt a deep and understandable revulsion at the bloody Stalinist purges of the 1930s. And they had been deeply embittered in 1939 when Stalin and Hitler agreed to the short-lived Nazi-Soviet Pact.

But Soviet hostility toward the United states had deep roots as well. Russian leaders were well aware of the American opposition to their revolution in 1917, and they remembered that the United States had sent troops into the Soviet Union at the end of World War I to work, they believed, to overthrow their new government. They resented their exclusion from the international community throughout the two decades following World War I; Russia had been invited to participate in neither the Versailles Conference in 1919 nor the Munich Conference in 1938. The Stalin regime remembered, too, the long delay by the United States in recognizing the Soviet government; the two nations did not exchange ambassadors until 1933, sixteen years after the Revolution. And just as most Americans viewed communism with foreboding and contempt, so did most Russian communists harbor deep suspicions of and a genuine distaste for industrial capitalism. There was, in short, a powerful legacy of mistrust on both sides.

In some respects, the wartime experience helped to abate that mistrust. Both the United States and the Soviet Union tended to focus during the war less on the traditional image of a dangerous potential foe and more on the image of a brave and dauntless ally. Americans expressed open admiration for the courage of Soviet forces in withstanding the Nazi onslaught and began to depict Stalin less as the bloody ogre of the purges than as the wise and persevering "Uncle Joe." The Soviet government, similarly, praised both the American fighting forces and the wisdom and courage of Franklin Roosevelt.

In other respects, however, the war deepened the gulf between the two nations. Americans were hostile to the Soviet invasion of Finland and the Baltic states late in 1939, once the war with Germany had begun in the west. Many were aware, as the war continued, of Soviet brutality—not only toward the fascist enemies but toward supposedly friendly forces: for example, the Polish resistance fighters. Stalin harbored even greater resentments toward the American approach to the war. Despite repeated assurances from Roosevelt that the United States and Britain would soon open a second front on the European continent, thus drawing German strength away from the assault on Russia, the Allied invasion

did not finally occur until June 1944, more than two years after Stalin had first demanded it. In the meantime, the Russians had suffered appalling casualties— some estimates put them as high as 20 million; and it was easy for Stalin to believe that the West had deliberately delayed the invasion to force the Soviets to absorb the brunt of the German strength. So although in most respects the wartime alliance worked well, with both sides making serious efforts to play down their differences, an undercurrent of tension and hostility remained.

Two Visions of the World

At least as important as these deep-seated suspicions was a fundamental difference in the ways the great powers envisioned the postwar world—a difference that was not at first immediately obvious, but one that ultimately shattered any hope for international amity. The first vision was that of many people in the United States, one perhaps best expressed by the title of a famous book by Wendell Willkie, *One World* (1943). First openly outlined in the Atlantic Charter, drafted by Roosevelt and Churchill in 1941, it was a vision of a world in which nations abandoned their traditional belief in military alliances and spheres of influence. Instead, the world would govern itself through democratic processes, with an international organization serving as the arbiter of disputes and the protector of the peace. No nation would control any other. Every people would have the right "to choose the form of government under which they will live."

The other vision was that of the Soviet Union and to some extent, it gradually became clear, of Great Britain. Both Stalin and Churchill had agreed to sign the Atlantic Charter espousing the "One World" principles. But neither man truly shared them. Britain had always been uneasy about the implications of the self-determination ideal for its own empire, which remained at the close of World War II the largest in the world. The Soviet Union was determined to create a secure sphere for itself in Eastern Europe as protection against possible future aggression from the West. Both Churchill and Stalin, therefore, tended to envision a postwar structure in which the great powers would control areas of strategic interest to them, in which something vaguely similar to the traditional European balance of power would reemerge.

This difference of opinion was particularly serious because the internationalist vision of Roosevelt had, by the end of the war, become a fervent commitment among many Americans. It was a vision composed equally of expansive idealism and national self-interest. Roosevelt had never abandoned his youthful enthusiasm for the principles of Wilsonian idealism, and he saw his mission in the 1940s as one of bringing lasting peace and genuine democracy to the world. But it was clear, too, that the "One World" vision would enhance the position of the United States in particular. As the world's greatest industrial power, and as one of the few nations unravaged by the war, America stood to gain more than any other country from opening the entire world to unfettered trade.

Thus when Britain and the Soviet Union began to balk at some of the provisions the United States was advocating, the debate seemed to become more than a simple difference of opinion. It became an ideological struggle for the future of the world. And on that rock the hope for a harmonious peace would ultimately founder. By the end of the war Roosevelt was able to win at least the partial consent of Winston Churchill to his principles; but although he believed at times that Stalin would similarly relent, he never managed to steer the Soviets from their determination to control Eastern Europe, from their vision of a postwar order in which each of the great powers would dominate its own sphere. Gradually, the irreconcilable differences between these two positions would turn the peacemaking process into a form of warfare.

Wartime Diplomacy

Almost from the moment of Pearl Harbor, the Roosevelt administration devoted nearly as much attention to planning the peace as it did to winning the war. Indeed, the president himself realized that the conduct of the war—the relationships among the Allies in coordinating their efforts—would go far toward determining the shape of the postwar world.

Throughout 1942, Roosevelt had engaged in inconclusive discussions with the Soviet Union, and particularly with Foreign Minister Vyacheslav Molotov, about how best to implement the principles of the Atlantic Charter, to which all the Allies had in theory subscribed. Until 1943, however, neither nation was ready for any specific commitments. In the meantime, serious strains in the alliance were beginning to appear as a result of Stalin's irritation at delays in opening the second front and his resentment of the Anglo-American decision to invade North Africa before Europe.

It was in this deteriorating atmosphere that the president called for a meeting of the "Big Three"—Roosevelt, Churchill, and Stalin—in Casablanca, Morocco, in January 1943. Stalin declined the invitation, but Churchill and Roosevelt met nevertheless. Because the two leaders agreed that they could not accept Stalin's most important demand—the immediate opening of a second front—they reached another decision designed to reassure the Soviet Union. The Allies, Roosevelt announced, would accept nothing less than the unconditional surrender of the Axis powers. The announcement was a signal to Stalin that the Americans and British would not negotiate a separate peace with Hitler and leave the Soviets to fight on alone.

In November 1943, Roosevelt and Churchill traveled to Teheran, Iran, for their first meeting with Stalin. By now, however, Roosevelt's most effective bargaining tool—Stalin's need for American assistance in his struggle against Germany—had been largely removed. The German advance against Russia had been halted; Soviet forces were now launching their own westward offensive. Meanwhile, new tensions had emerged in the alliance as a result of the refusal by the British and Americans to allow any Soviet participation in the creation of a new Italian government following the fall of Mussolini. To Stalin, at least, the "One World" doctrine was already embodying a double standard: America and Britain expected to have a voice in the future of Eastern Europe, but the Soviet Union was to have no voice in the future of the West.

Nevertheless, the Teheran Conference seemed in most respects a success. Roosevelt and Stalin established a cordial relationship, one that the president hoped would eventually produce the same personal intimacy he enjoyed with Churchill. Stalin agreed to an American request that the Soviet Union enter the war in the Pacific soon after the end of hostilities in Europe. Roosevelt, in turn, promised that an Anglo-American second front would be established within six months. More important to Roosevelt, all three leaders agreed in principle to a postwar international organization and to efforts to prevent a resurgence of German expansionism.

On other matters, however, the origins of future disagreements could already be discerned. Most important was the question of the future of Poland. Roosevelt and Churchill were willing to agree to a movement of the Soviet border westward, thus allowing Stalin to annex some historically Polish territory. But on the nature of the postwar government in the portion of Poland that would remain independent, there were sharp differences. Roosevelt and Churchill supported the claims of the Polish government-in-exile that had been functioning in London since 1940; Stalin wished to install another, procommunist exiled government that had spent the war in Lublin, in the Soviet Union. The three leaders avoided a bitter conclusion to the Teheran Conference only by leaving the issue unresolved.

Yalta

For more than a year, during which the Soviet Union began finally to destroy German resistance and the British and Americans launched their successful invasion of France, the Grand Alliance among the United States, Britain, and the Soviet Union alternated between high tension and warm amicability. In the fall of 1944, Churchill flew by himself to Moscow for a meeting with Stalin to resolve issues arising from a civil war in Greece. In return for a Soviet agreement to cease assisting Greek communists, who were challenging the British-supported monarchical government, Churchill consented to a proposal whereby control of Eastern Europe would be divided between Britain and the Soviet Union. "This memorable meeting," Churchill wrote Stalin after its close, "has shown that there are no matters that cannot be adjusted between us when we meet together in frank and intimate discussion." To Roosevelt, however, the Moscow agreement was evidence of how little the Atlantic Charter principles seemed to mean to his two most important allies.

It was in an atmosphere of some gloom, therefore, that Roosevelt joined Churchill and Stalin for a great peace conference in the Soviet city of Yalta in February 1945. The American president sensed resistance to his internationalist dreams. The British prime minister was already dismayed by Stalin's willingness to make concessions and compromises, warning even before the conference met that "I think the end of this war may well prove to be more disappointing than was the last." Stalin, whose armies were now only miles from Berlin and who was well aware of how much the United States still wanted his assistance in the Pacific, was confident and determined.

On a number of issues, the Big Three reached amicable and mutually satisfactory agreements. In return for Stalin's promise to enter the war against Japan, Roosevelt agreed that the Soviet Union should receive the Kurile Islands north of Japan; should regain southern Sakhalin Island and Port Arthur, both of which Russia had lost in the 1904 Russo-Japanese War; and could exercise some influence (along with the government of China) in Manchuria.

The negotiators agreed as well on a plan for a new international organization: the United Nations. Tentative plans for the UN had been hammered out the previous summer at a conference in Washington, D.C., at the Dumbarton Oaks estate. At Yalta, the leaders ratified the Dumbarton plan to create (1) a General Assembly, in which every member would be represented, and (2) a Security Council, on which would sit permanent representatives of the five major powers (the United States, Britain, France, the Soviet Union, and China), along with temporary delegates from several other nations. They accepted, too, the provision giving each of the major powers a veto over all Security Council decisions. These agreements became the basis for the drafting of the United Nations charter at a conference of fifty nations beginning April 25, 1945, in San Francisco. The United States Senate ratified the charter in July by a vote of 80 to 2 (a striking contrast to the slow and painful defeat it had administered to the charter of the League of Nations twenty-five years before).

On other issues, however, the Yalta Conference produced no real agreement, either leaving fundamental differences unresolved or papering them over with weak and unstable compromises. As at Teheran, the most important stumbling block remained Poland. Fundamental disagreement remained about the postwar Polish government, with each side continuing to insist on the rights of its own government-in-exile. Stalin, whose armies had by now occupied Poland, had already installed a government composed of the procommunist "Lubin" Poles, to the chagrin of the British and Americans.

Roosevelt and Churchill protested strongly at Yalta against Stalin's unilateral establishment of a new Polish government, insisting that the pro-Western "London" Poles must be allowed a place in the Warsaw regime. Roosevelt envisioned a complete restructuring of the Soviet-controlled government, based on free, democratic elections—which both he and Stalin recognized the pro-Western forces would win. Stalin agreed only to a vague compromise by which an unspecified number of pro-Western Poles would be granted a place in the government. Although he reluctantly consented to hold "free and unfettered elections" in Poland, he made no firm

The Big Three at Yalta

Churchill, Roosevelt, and Stalin meet in the Soviet Crimea at Yalta to discuss the shape of the postwar order. Churchill and Stalin were alarmed by Roosevelt's gaunt appearance and his apparent weariness during the meeting—evidence of a physical deterioration that would lead to the president's death only months later. By the time the Allied leaders next met—at Potsdam, Germany, in July—only Stalin would remain in power. By then, Truman had succeeded Roosevelt, and Clement Atlee had succeeded Churchill as prime minister of Great Britain after Atlee's Labour party won a postwar election.   (Franklin D. Roosevelt Library)

commitment to a date for them. They did not take place.

Nor was there agreement about one of the touchiest issues facing the three leaders: the future of Germany. All three leaders were determined to ensure that Germany could not soon again become a major military power, but there were wide differences in their views of how to accomplish that goal. Stalin wanted to impose $20 billion in reparations on the Germans, of which Russia would receive half. Churchill protested, arguing that the result would be that Britain and America would have to feed the German people. Roosevelt finally accepted the $20 bil-

lion figure as a "basis for discussion" but left final settlement to a future reparations commission. To Stalin, whose hopes for the reconstruction of Russia rested in part on tribute from Germany, it was an unsatisfactory compromise.

Roosevelt was uncertain at first about how he wished to resolve the German question. In 1944, he and Churchill had met in Quebec and agreed on what became known as the Morgenthau Plan—a plan for dismantling much of Germany's industrial capacity and turning that country into a largely agricultural society. But by accepting the principle of reparations at Yalta, he was clearly abandoning the idea of destroying German industry; without it, the Germans would have no means by which to pay. Instead, he seemed to be hoping for a reconstructed and reunited Germany—one that would be permitted to develop a prosperous, modern economy, but one that would remain under the careful supervision of the Allies. Stalin, in contrast, wanted a permanent dismemberment of Germany, a proposal the British and Americans firmly rejected. The final agreement was, like the Polish agreement, a vague and unstable one. The United States, Great Britain, France, and the Soviet Union would each control its own "zone of occupation" in Germany—the zones to be determined by the position of troops at the time when the war would end. (Berlin, the German capital, was already well inside the Soviet zone, but because of its symbolic importance it would itself be divided into four sectors, one for each nation to occupy.) At an unspecified date, the nation would be reunited; but no specific agreement was reached on how the reunification would occur.

As for the rest of Europe, the conference produced a murky accord on the establishment of interim governments "broadly representative of all democratic elements." They would be replaced ultimately by permanent governments "responsible to the will of the people" and created through free elections. Once again, no specific provisions or timetables accompanied the agreements.

The Yalta accords, in other words, were less a settlement of postwar issues than a general set of loose principles that sidestepped the most divisive issues. Roosevelt, Churchill, and Stalin returned home from the conference each apparently convinced that he had signed an important agreement. But the Soviet interpretation of the accords differed so sharply from the Anglo-American interpretation that the illusion endured only briefly. Stalin continued to believe that Soviet control of Eastern Europe was essential and considered the Yalta accords little more than a set of small concessions to Western punctiliousness. Roosevelt, in contrast, thought the agreements represented a mutual acceptance of the idea of an "open" Europe, under the direct control of no single nation. In the weeks following the Yalta Conference, therefore, he watched with horror as the Soviet Union moved systematically to establish procommunist governments in one Eastern European nation after another and as Stalin refused to make the changes in Poland that the president believed he had promised.

Still, Roosevelt did not abandon hope. His personal relationship with Stalin was such, he believed, that a settlement of these issues remained possible. Continuing to work to secure his vision of the future, he left Washington early in the spring for a vacation at his retreat in Warm Springs, Georgia. There, on April 12, 1945, he suffered a sudden, massive stroke and died.

The Collapse of the Peace

Harry S. Truman, who succeeded Roosevelt in the presidency, inherited an international predicament that would have taxed the most experienced and patient statesman. He did not, however, inherit Roosevelt's familiarity with the world situation. (He had served in the administration only three months and had received few substantive briefings on foreign policy.) Nor did he share Roosevelt's belief in the flexibility of the Soviet Union. Roosevelt had insisted until the end that the Russians could be bargained with, that Stalin was, essentially, a reasonable man with whom an ultimate accord could be reached. Truman, in contrast, sided with those in the government (and there were many) who considered the Soviet Union fundamentally untrustworthy and viewed Stalin himself with deep suspicion and basic dislike.

There was also a significant contrast between the personalities of the two men. Roosevelt had always been a wily, even devious public figure, using his surface geniality to disguise his intentions. He had, as a result, been an unusually effective negotiatior. Truman, on the other hand, was a sharp, direct, and impatient leader, a man who said what he thought and seldom wavered from decisions once he had made them. They were qualities that would win him the admiration of many of his contemporaries and of an even larger proportion of later generations of Americans. They were not, however, always qualities well suited to patient negotiation.

The Failure of Potsdam

Truman had been in office only a few days before he decided on his approach to the Soviet Union. He would "get tough." Stalin had made what the new president considered solemn agreements with the United States at Yalta. The United States, therefore, would insist that he honor them. Dismissing the advice of Secretary of War Stimson that the Polish question was a lost cause and not worth a world crisis, Truman met on April 23 with Soviet Foreign Minister Molotov and sharply chastised him for violations of the Yalta accords. "I have never been talked to like that in my life," a shocked Molotov reportedly replied. "Carry out your agreements and you won't get talked to like that," said the president.

In fact, however, Truman had only limited leverage by which to compel the Soviet Union to carry out its agreements. Russian forces already occupied Poland and much of the rest of Eastern Europe. Germany was already divided among the conquering nations. The United States was still engaged in a war in the Pacific and was neither able nor willing to engage in a second conflict in Europe. Despite Truman's professed belief that the United States should be able to get "85 percent" of what it wanted, he was ultimately forced to settle for much less.

He conceded first on Poland. When Stalin made a few minor concessions to the pro-Western exiles, Truman recognized the Warsaw government, hoping that noncommunist forces might gradually expand their influence there. (Until the 1980s, they did not.) Other questions remained. To settle them, Truman met in July with Churchill (who was replaced as prime minister by Clement Atlee in the midst of the negotiations) and Stalin. The meeting took place in Potsdam, near Berlin, in Russian-occupied Germany. The British and Americans hoped to use the Potsdam Conference to resolve the question of Germany, and in one sense they succeeded. But the resolution was not, ultimately, to the liking of the Western leaders. Truman reluctantly accepted the adjustments of the Polish-German border that Stalin had long demanded; he refused, however, to permit the Russians to claim any reparations from the American, French, and British zones of Germany. The result, in effect, was to confirm that Germany would remain divided, with the western zones united into one nation, friendly to the United States, and the Russian zone surviving as another nation, with a pro-Soviet, communist government. Stalin had failed to receive the reparations he wanted, and he had been unable to secure other forms of financial assistance from the West (a failure symbolized by the abrupt termination by the Truman administration in May of all lend-lease assistance). He would, therefore, use eastern Germany to help rebuild the shattered Russian economy. Soon, the Soviet Union was siphoning between $1.5 and $3 billion a year out of its zone of occupation.

A Dilemma in Asia

Throughout the frustrating course of its negotiations over the future of Europe, the United States was facing an equally troubling dilemma in Asia. Central to American hopes for an open, peaceful world "policed" by the great powers was a strong, independent China. But even before the war ended, the American government was aware that those hopes faced a major, perhaps insurmountable obstacle: the Chinese government of Chiang Kai-shek. Chiang was generally friendly to the United States, but he had few other virtues. His government was corrupt and incompetent. His popular legitimacy was feeble. And Chiang himself lived in a world of surreal isolation, unable or unwilling to face the problems that were threatening to engulf him. Ever since 1927, the nationalist government he headed had been engaged in a prolonged and bitter rivalry with the communist armies of Mao Zedong. So successful had the communist challenge grown that Mao was in control of one-fourth of the population by 1945.

Truman had managed at Potsdam to win Stalin's agreement that Chiang would be recognized as the legitimate ruler of China; but Chiang himself was rapidly losing his grip on his country. Some Americans urged the government to try to find a third faction to support as an alternative to either Chiang or Mao. A few argued that America should try to reach some accommodation with Mao. Truman, however, decided reluctantly that he had no choice but to continue supporting Chiang, despite the weakness of Chiang's position. American forces in the last months of the war diverted attention from the Japanese long enough to assist Chiang against the communists in Manchuria. For the next several years, as the long struggle between the nationalists and the communists erupted into a full-scale civil war, the United States continued to pump money and weapons to Chiang. By late 1947, however, it was clear to the president that the cause was lost. Although he did not abandon China entirely or immediately, he was not prepared to intervene to save the nationalist regime.

Instead, the American government was beginning to consider an alternative to China as the strong, pro-Western force in Asia: a revived Japan. During the first years of American occupation of Japan after the war, the United States commander, Douglas MacArthur, provided a firm and restrictive administration of the island. A series of purges removed what remained of the warlord government of the Japanese

Empire. Americans insisted, too, on dismantling the nation's munitions industry. But after two years of occupation, American policy toward Japan shifted. All limitations on industrial development were lifted, and rapid economic growth was encouraged. The vision of an open, united Asia had been replaced, as in Europe, with an acceptance of the necessity of developing a strong, pro-American sphere of influence.

The Containment Doctrine

By the end of 1945, the Grand Alliance was in shambles, and with it any realistic hope of a postwar world constructed along the lines Roosevelt and others had urged. Although few policymakers were willing to admit openly that the United States must abandon its "One World" ideals, a new American policy was slowly emerging to replace them. Rather than attempting to create a unified, "open" world, the West would work to "contain" the threat of further Soviet expansion. The United States would be the leading force in that effort.

The new doctrine received one test before it was even fully formulated. When Stalin refused in March 1946 to follow the British and American lead in pulling his occupation forces out of Iran, the Truman administration issued a strong and threatening ultimatum. Stalin relented and withdrew. But new crises were emerging—in Turkey, where Stalin was exerting heavy pressure to win some control over the vital straits to the Mediterranean, and in Greece, where communist forces were again threatening the pro-Western government and where the British had announced they could no longer provide assistance. Faced with these challenges, the president finally decided to enunciate a firm new policy.

For some time, Truman had been convinced that the Soviet Union, like Nazi Germany before it, was an aggressor nation bent on world conquest. He had accepted the arguments of the influential American diplomat George F. Kennan, who warned that the United States faced "a political force committed fanatically to the belief that with the U.S. there can be no permanent *modus vivendi*," and that the only answer was "a long-term, patient but firm and vigilant containment of Russian expansive tendencies." On March 12, 1947, Truman appeared before Congress and used Kennan's warnings as the basis of what became known as the Truman Doctrine. "I believe," he argued, "that it must be the policy of the United

States to support free peoples who are resisting attempted subjugation by armed minorities or by outside pressures." In the same speech he requested $400 million—part of it to bolster the armed forces of Greece and Turkey, another part to provide economic assistance to Greece. Congress quickly approved the measure.

The American commitment ultimately eased Soviet pressure on Turkey and helped the Greek government to defeat the communist insurgents. More important, it established a fundamental new doctrine that would become the basis of American foreign policy for more than two decades—a doctrine that pushed Kennan's concept of containment in directions he had never intended. Communism, Truman seemed to claim, was an ideological threat; it was indivisible; its expansion anywhere was a threat to democracy because, as Secretary of State Dean Acheson had argued, the fall of one nation to communism would have a "domino effect" on surrounding nations. It was, therefore, the policy of the United States to assist pro-Western forces in any struggle against communism anywhere in the world, whether that struggle directly involved the Soviet Union or not. The Truman Doctrine marked the final American abandonment of the "One World" vision of a generation of idealists. But it replaced it with another, equally powerful vision—a vision of two worlds, one enslaved and one free, in which every rivalry and every conflict could be defined as a struggle between the United States and the Soviet Union. In the years to come, the ideology of the Truman Doctrine would at times blind Americans to local or regional particularities, with the result that the United States would on more than one occasion interpret an internal revolution as an expression of Soviet expansionism.

The Marshall Plan

The Truman Doctrine was only one half—the military half—of the new containment doctrine. The second part of the new American policy was a proposal to aid in the economic reconstruction of Western Europe. There were a number of motives for the assistance. One was a simple humanitarian concern for the European peoples, whose economies lay in ruins and whose future appeared bleak. But there was powerful self-interest at work as well. Until Europe could support itself economically, it would remain a drain on the United States, which was endeavoring in the

George C. Marshall at Harvard, 1947

Secretary of State George C. Marshall is escorted through Harvard Yard en route to the commencement ceremony, where he received an honorary degree. Later that day, in a speech to Harvard alumni, he presented the Truman administration's proposal to aid in the postwar reconstruction of Europe. Its official name was the European Recovery Program, but it was always known as the Marshall Plan. (UPI/Bettmann Newsphotos)

meantime to feed it. And without a strong European market for American goods, most policymakers believed, the United States economy would be unable to sustain the prosperity it had achieved during the war. Above all, unless something could be done to strengthen the perilous position of the pro-American governments in Western Europe, they might fall under the control of domestic communist movements, which were gaining strength as a result of the economic misery.

In June 1947, therefore, Secretary of State George C. Marshall spoke before a commencement gathering at Harvard University and announced a plan to provide economic assistance to all European nations (including the Soviet Union) that would join in drafting a program for recovery. Although Russia and its Eastern satellites quickly rejected the plan, claiming that it represented an American attempt to reshape Europe in its own image, sixteen Western European nations eagerly participated. There was substantial opposition at first to Truman's request for an enormous appropriation to fund the effort; but congressional opponents lost power quickly, embarrassed by the unwelcome support of the American Communist party and shocked by a sudden seizure of power by communists in Czechoslovakia, which had hitherto remained at least nominally free of Soviet control. In April 1948, the president signed a bill

establishing the Economic Cooperation Administration and providing an initial budget of $4 billion. Over the next three years, the Marshall Plan, as it soon became known, channeled over $12 billion of American aid into Europe, sparking what many viewed as a miraculous economic revival. By the end of 1950, European industrial production had risen 64 percent, communist strength in the member nations was declining, and the opportunities for American trade had revived.

Mobilization at Home

That the United States had fully accepted a continuing commitment to the containment policy became clear in 1947 and 1948 through a series of measures designed to maintain American military power at near wartime levels. Although the government had moved rapidly in 1945 to release almost 7 million men from the armed forces in the space of a few months, it was not long before the president began to demand a renewal of universal military training through a continuing draft. Congress finally restored the Selective Service System in 1948. The United States had announced, shortly after the surrender of Japan, that it was prepared to accept an international agreement banning nuclear weapons

Divided Europe After World War II

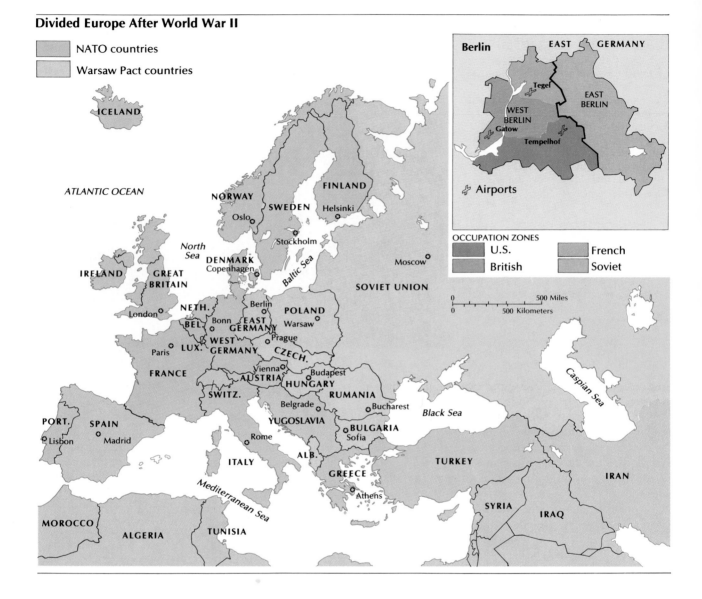

NATO countries

Warsaw Pact countries

Berlin

EAST GERMANY

Tegel

EAST BERLIN

WEST BERLIN

Gatow

Tempelhof

✈ Airports

OCCUPATION ZONES

U.S.   French

British   Soviet

ATLANTIC OCEAN

ICELAND

NORWAY   SWEDEN   FINLAND
Oslo   Helsinki
Stockholm

North Sea

DENMARK   Baltic Sea
Copenhagen   Moscow

IRELAND   GREAT BRITAIN   SOVIET UNION

London   NETH.   Berlin   POLAND
BEL.   Bonn   EAST GERMANY   Warsaw
Paris   LUX.   WEST   Prague
GERMANY   CZECH.
FRANCE   Vienna   Budapest
AUSTRIA   HUNGARY
SWITZ.   RUMANIA
Belgrade   Bucharest   Caspian Sea
PORT.   SPAIN   YUGOSLAVIA   Black Sea
Lisbon   Madrid   Rome   BULGARIA
Sofia
ALB.   TURKEY   IRAN
ITALY
GREECE
Mediterranean Sea   Athens   SYRIA
MOROCCO   IRAQ
ALGERIA   TUNISIA

0   500 Miles
0   500 Kilometers

(through a proposal known as the Baruch Plan). Few American policymakers believed the Soviets would agree to the proposal. And as they expected, Moscow, arguing that since only America had developed a bomb, America alone should abandon it, resisted any system of international inspection and controls. In response, the United States simply redoubled its own efforts in atomic research, elevating nuclear weaponry to a central place in its military arsenal. The Atomic Energy Commission, established in 1946, became the supervisory body

charged with overseeing all nuclear research, civilian and military alike.

Perhaps the clearest indication of America's continuing concern with military power, however, came through the National Security Act of 1947. It created a new Department of Defense, whose secretary would combine the traditional functions of the secretary of war and the secretary of the navy and preside over all branches of the armed services. The National Security Council (NSC), operating out of the White House and including the president, several

The Berlin Airlift
Children standing in the rubble of a still unreconstructed West Berlin watch an American plane bringing food and supplies to the beleaguered city in 1948. The Soviet blockade of West Berlin was intended to force the western Allies to abandon the city, but it only increased their resolve, and that of the Berliners themselves. (The Bettmann Archive)

members of his cabinet, and others, would govern foreign and military policy. The Central Intelligence Agency (CIA) would be responsible for collecting information through both open and covert methods and, as the Cold War continued, for engaging secretly in active political and military operations on behalf of American goals.

The National Security Act effected important changes in the nation's ability to conduct a cold war. It transferred to the president expanded powers over all defense activities, centralizing in the White House control that had once been widely dispersed; it enabled the administration to take warlike actions without an open declaration of war; and it created vehicles by which the government could at times act politically and militarily overseas behind a veil of secrecy.

The Road to NATO

At about the same time, the United States was moving to strengthen the military capabilities of Western Europe. Convinced that only a reconstructed Germany could serve as the necessary bulwark against communist expansion, Truman abandoned earlier polices designed to restrain German power and forged an agreement with England and France to merge the three western zones of occupation into a new West German republic (which would include the American, British, and French sectors of Berlin, even though that city lay well within the Soviet zone.)

Stalin interpreted the move (correctly) as a direct challenge to his hopes for a subdued Germany and a docile Europe. At almost the same moment, he was facing a challenge from inside what he considered his own sphere. The government of Yugoslavia, under the leadership of Marshall Josip Broz Tito, broke openly with the Soviet Union and declared the nation an unaligned communist state. The United States offered Tito assistance.

Stalin's response came quickly. On June 24, 1948, taking advantage of the lack of a written guarantee of Western transit through eastern Germany, he imposed a tight blockade around the western sectors of Berlin. If Germany was to be officially divided, he was implying, then the country's Western government would have to abandon its outpost in the heart of the Soviet-controlled eastern zone. He was attempting to give the United States a choice between dropping its plan for a united West Germany and surrendering Berlin. Truman refused to do either. He was unwilling to risk war by responding militarily to the blockade; but he ordered a massive airlift to supply the city with food, fuel, and supplies. The airlift continued for more than ten months, transporting nearly 2.5 million tons of material, keeping alive a city of 2 million people, and transforming West Berlin into a symbol of the West's resolve to resist communist expansion. Finally, late in the spring of 1949, Stalin lifted the now ineffective blockade. And in October, the division of Germany into two nations—the Federal Republic in the west and the Democratic Republic in the East—became official.

The crisis in Berlin accelerated the consolidation of what was already in effect an alliance of the United States and the countries of Western Europe. On April 4, 1949, twelve nations signed an agreement establishing the North Atlantic Treaty Organization (NATO) and declaring that an armed attack against one member would be considered an attack against all. The NATO countries would, moreover, maintain a standing military force in Europe to defend against what many believed was the threat of a Soviet invasion. The American Senate quickly ratified this first peacetime alliance between the United States and Europe since the eighteenth century—an agreement that fused European nations that had been fighting one another for centuries into a strong and enduring alliance. Whatever effects NATO may have had on the global balance of power, it created a stable peace in Western Europe. (It also spurred the Soviet Union to create an alliance of its own with the communist governments in Eastern Europe—an alliance formalized in 1955 by the Warsaw Pact.)

The NATO alliance also greatly increased American influence in Europe. The United States quickly became the most important supplier of the NATO military forces; and an American officer, General Dwight D. Eisenhower, assumed the position of supreme commander of Allied forces in Europe.

The Enduring Crisis

The Berlin blockade, the offer of aid to Yugoslavia, the creation of NATO—all had in most respects been expressions of American confidence. Truman had believed, along with most other policymakers, that the United States was easily the more powerful of the two great rivals, that the Soviet Union would not dare provoke war because of the certainty of defeat. For a time, it had seemed that the battle against communism was being won.

But a series of events in 1949 began seriously to erode that confidence and launched the Cold War into a new and more enduring phase. An announcement in September that the Soviet Union had successfully exploded its first atomic weapon, years

before most Americans had considered it possible, came as a severe shock to the nation. So did the collapse of Chiang Kai-shek's nationalist government in China, which occurred with startling speed in the last months of 1949. Chiang fled with his political allies and the remnants of his army to the offshore island of Formosa (Taiwan), and the entire Chinese mainland came under the control of a communist government that many Americans believed to be a mere extension of the Soviet Union. The United States, powerless to stop the communists without a major military commitment that virtually no one wanted, had no choice but to watch the collapse of its ill-chosen ally. Few policymakers shared the belief of the so-called China lobby that the United States should now commit itself to the rearming of Chiang Kai-shek. But neither would the administration recognize the new communist regime, particularly after the Maoist government began expropriating American property, expelling American businesspeople, and strengthening its ties to the Soviet Union. The Chinese mainland would remain almost entirely closed to the West for a full generation. The United States, in the meantime, would devote increased attention to the revitalization of Japan as a buffer against Asian communism, ending the American occupation of that island nation, finally, in 1952.

With the containment policy in apparent disarray, and with political opposition mounting at home, Truman called for a thorough review of American foreign policy. The result was a National Security Council report, commonly known as NSC-68, which outlined a shift in the American position. The April 1950 document argued that the United States could no longer rely on other nations to take the initiative in resisting communism. It must itself establish firm and active leadership of the noncommunist world. Among other things, the report called for a major expansion of American military power, with a defense budget almost four times the previously projected figure. It also reinforced what was already a strong sense of mission in the formulation of American foreign policy. Upon the United States, the report maintained, lay the responsibility of defending freedom in the world.

America After the War

The dangers overseas were only a part of the frustrations facing the United States after the wars. The nation also encountered serious difficulties in adapt-

Surviving Nuclear War

Preoccupation with the possibility of a nuclear war reached a fever pitch in the first years of the atomic era. The Federal Civil Defense Agency, which in 1950 issued these simple rules for civilians to follow in dealing with an atomic attack, was one of many organizations attempting to convince the American public that a nuclear war was survivable. (Federal Civil Defense Agency)

Survival Secrets for Atomic Attacks

ALWAYS PUT FIRST THINGS FIRST

Try to Get Shielded
If you have time, get down in a basement or subway. Should you unexpectedly be caught out-of-doors, seek shelter alongside a building, or jump in any handy ditch or gutter.

Drop Flat on Ground or Floor
To keep from being tossed about and to lessen the chances of being struck by falling and flying objects, flatten out at the base of a wall, or at the bottom of a bank.

Bury Your Face in Your Arms
When you drop flat, hide your eyes in the crook of your elbow. That will protect your face from flash burns, prevent temporary blindness and keep flying objects out of your eyes.

NEVER LOSE YOUR HEAD

ing its complex economy to the new demands of peace; the instability that resulted contributed to the creation of a heated political climate.

The Problems of Reconversion

The bombs that destroyed Hiroshima and Nagasaki ended the war months earlier than almost anyone had predicted and propelled the nation precipitously into a process of reconversion. The lack of planning was soon compounded by a growing popular impatience for a return to normal. Under intense public pressure, the Truman administration attempted to hasten that return, despite dire warnings by some planners and economists. The result was a period of economic problems.

They were not, however, the problems that most Americans had feared. There had been many predictions that peace would bring a return of Depression unemployment, as war production ceased and returning soldiers flooded the labor market. But there was no general economic collapse in 1946—for several reasons. Government spending dropped sharply and abruptly, to be sure; $35 billion of war contracts were canceled at a stroke within weeks of the Japanese surrender. But increased consumer demand soon compensated. Consumer goods had been generally unavailable during the war, so many workers had saved a substantial portion of their wages and were now ready to spend. A $6 billion tax cut pumped additional money into general circulation. The Servicemen's Readjustment Act of 1944, better known as the GI Bill of Rights, provided economic and educational assistance to veterans, increasing spending even further.

But while the sudden flood of consumer demand ensured that there would be no new depression, it also created rampant inflation. For more than two years inflation continued, with prices rising at rates of 14 or 15 percent annually. In the summer of 1946, the president vetoed an extension of the authority of the wartime Office of Price Administration because Congress had weakened the agency's authority. In so doing, he permitted government price controls, which were already having difficulty holding down price increases, to be removed altogether. A month later, he relented and signed a bill little different from the one he had rejected. But in the meantime inflation had soared briefly to 25 percent.

Compounding the economic difficulties was a sharp rise in labor unrest. Most unions had grudgingly accepted government-imposed restraints on their demands during the war, but now they were willing to wait no longer, particularly as inflation cut into the existing wage scales with painful force. By the end of 1945, there had already been major strikes in the automobile, electrical, and steel industries. Government intervention had helped settle the strikes relatively quickly, but the agreements fueled inflation even further.

In April 1946, a fresh crisis emerged when John L. Lewis led the United Mine Workers out on strike, shutting down the coal fields for forty days. The economic impact was devastating. Freight and shipping activity declined by 75 percent; the steel industry made plans to shut down operations; fears grew that without vital coal supplies, the entire nation might virtually grind to a halt. Truman finally forced coal production to resume by ordering government seizure of the mines. But in the process, he induced mine owners to concede to the union most of its demands, which he had earlier denounced as inflationary. Almost simultaneously, the nation's railroads suffered a total shutdown—the first in the nation's history—as two major unions walked out on strike. By threatening to use the army to run the trains, Truman pressured the workers back to work after only a few days.

Reconversion had a particularly dramatic effect on the millions of women and minorities who had entered the work force during the war. With veterans returning home and looking for jobs in the industrial economy, employers tended to push women, blacks, Hispanics, and others out of the plants to make room for white males. Some of the war workers, particularly women, left the work force voluntarily, out of a desire to return to their former domestic lives. But public opinion surveys of the time suggest that most women (as many as 80 percent) and virtually all black and Hispanic males wanted to continue working. The postwar inflation, the pressure to meet the rising expectations of a high-consumption society, the rising divorce rate (which left many women responsible for

their own economic well-being)—all combined to create a high demand for paid employment among women. As they found themselves excluded from many industrial jobs, therefore, women workers moved increasingly into other areas of the economy (above all, the service sector). Popular mythology to the contrary, there was not a mass movement of women out of the work force after the war—only a movement from one area of the economy to another.

The Fair Deal Rejected

On September 16, 1945, only fourteen days after the formal Japanese surrender, Truman submitted to Congress a twenty-one-point domestic program outlining what he later termed the "Fair Deal." It called for expansion of Social Security benefits, the raising of the legal minimum wage from 40 to 65 cents an hour, a program to ensure full employment, a permanent Fair Employment Practices Act, public housing and slum clearance, long-range environmental and public works planning, and government promotion of scientific research. Weeks later he added other proposals: federal aid to education, government health insurance, prepaid medical care, funding for the St. Lawrence Seaway, and nationalization of atomic energy. The president was, it was clear, declaring an end to the wartime moratorium on reform and creating an impressive new liberal agenda. The announcement of the Fair Deal, he later wrote, symbolized "for me my assumption of the office of President in my own right."

Truman's proposals greatly heartened Democratic liberals, who had continued to wonder whether the new president would prove a satisfactory successor to Franklin Roosevelt. But the Fair Deal made little progress in Congress. Truman's programs fell victim to the same general public and congressional conservatism that had crippled the last years of the New Deal and had increased during the war. The economic problems and labor unrest of 1946 only intensified congressional resistance to further spending and reform. And what little hope there had been for legislative progress died in November 1946, when the Republican party—making use of the simple but devastating slogan "Had Enough?"—won control of both houses of Congress.

With the new Congress in place, the retreat from reform rapidly became a stampede. The president bowed to what he claimed was the popular mandate to lift most remaining wage and price controls, and

Congress moved further to deregulate the economy. Inflation rapidly increased. When a public outcry arose over the soaring prices for meat, Senator Robert Taft, perhaps the most influential Republican conservative in Congress, advised consumers to "Eat less," and added, "We have got to break with the corrupting idea that we can legislate prosperity, legislate equality, legislate opportunity." True to the spirit of Taft's words, the Republican Congress quickly applied what one congressman described as a "meat- axe to government frills." It refused to appropriate funds to aid education, increase Social Security, or support reclamation and power projects in the West. It defeated a proposal to raise the minimum wage. It passed tax measures that cut rates dramatically for high-income families and moderately for those with lower incomes. Only vetoes by the president finally forced a more progressive bill.

The most notable action of the Eightieth Congress was an open assault on one of the cornerstones of Depression reform: the Wagner Act of 1935. Conservatives had always resented the enormous powers the legislation had granted unions; and in the light of the labor difficulties during and after the war, such resentments intensified sharply. The result was the Labor-Management Relations Act of 1947, better known as the Taft-Hartley Act, which loosened several of the earlier restrictions on employers and added some important new prohibitions against the unions. The act made illegal the so-called closed shop (a workplace in which no one could be hired without first being a member of a union). And although it continued to permit the creation of so-called union shops (in which workers must join a union after being hired), it permitted states to pass "right-to-work" laws prohibiting even that. This provision, the controversial Section 14(b), remained a particular target of the labor movement for decades. The act also empowered the president to call for a "cooling-off" period before a strike by issuing an injunction against any work stoppage that endangered national safety or health.

These and other provisions delighted conservatives, who viewed union power as one of the nation's greatest social evils. But they outraged workers and union leaders, who denounced the measure as a "slave labor bill" and called on the president to veto it. Truman needed little persuading. He had opposed the Taft-Hartley Act from the beginning and on June 20, 1947, returned it to Congress with a stinging veto message. Both houses easily overruled him the same day.

The Taft-Hartley Act did not destroy the labor movement, as many union leaders had predicted. But it did seriously damage the position of weaker unions in relatively lightly organized industries such as chemicals and textiles; and it made far more difficult the organizing of workers who had never been union members at all, especially in the South. Powerful unions remained powerful, for the most part; but unorganized or loosely organized workers now faced serious obstacles. Equally important in the short run, the passage of Taft-Hartley served as a symbol of the repudiation of New Deal reform by the Republican party and its Congress, a warning that government innovations that many had come to take for granted were now in jeopardy. "Victories fought and won years ago were suddenly in doubt," a columnist for the *New Republic* wrote at the time. "Everything was debatable again."

The Election of 1948

Truman and his advisers were convinced that the American public was not ready to abandon the achievements of the New Deal, that the 1946 election had not been a mandate for a surrender to conservatism. As they planned strategy for the 1948 campaign, therefore, they placed their hopes in an appeal to enduring Democratic liberalism. Throughout 1948, Truman proposed one reform measure after another (including, on February 2, the first major civil-rights bill of the century). Congress ignored or defeated them all; but the president was effectively building a campaign issue for the fall.

There remained, however, the serious problem of Truman's personal unpopularity—the assumption among much of the electorate that he lacked stature, that his administration was weak and inept. Many of the qualities that made him such an admired figure in later years—his outspokenness, his impatience, his common-man demeanor—seemed at the time to be evidence of his unfitness to fill the shoes of Franklin Roosevelt. Liberals within his own party were actively looking for an alternative candidate. Conservatives were regarding the president with disgust.

All of these tensions came to a head at the Democratic Convention that summer. Two factions abandoned the party altogether. Southern conservatives were angered by Truman's proposed civil-rights bill and outraged by the approval at the convention of a civil-rights plank in the platform (engineered by Hubert Humphrey, the mayor of Minneapols). They

Harry and Bess Truman at Home
Senator Harry Truman and his wife Bess pose for photographers in the kitchen of their Washington apartment, suggesting the "common man" image that Truman retained throughout his public life. The picture was taken shortly before the 1944 Democratic National Convention, which would nominate Truman for vice president. Less than a year later, the Trumans would be living in the White House. (UPI/Bettmann Newsphotos)

walked out and formed the States' Rights (or "Dixiecrat") party, with Governor Strom Thrumond of South Carolina as its nominee. At the same time, the party's left wing formed a new Progressive party, with Henry A. Wallace as its candidate. Wallace supporters objected to what they considered the slow and ineffective domestic policies of the Truman administration, but they resented even more the president's confrontational stance toward the Soviet Union.

In addition, many Democrats unwilling to leave the party attempted to dump the president in 1948. The Americans for Democratic Action (ADA), a coalition of liberals, tried to entice Dwight D. Eisenhower, the popular war hero, to contest the nomination, certain that he could win the November election while Truman could not. Only after Eisenhower had refused did the party bow to the inevitable and, in near despair, give the nomination to Truman. The Republicans, in the meantime, had once again nominated Governor Thomas E. Dewey of New York, whose substantial reelection victory in 1946 had made him one of the nation's leading political figures. Austere, dignified, and competent, he seemed to offer an unbeatable alternative to the president. That his views on most issues were only marginally different from Truman's appeared further to strengthen his chances of victory.

Nothing, it seemed, could save the president

from certain defeat. His party was seriously splintered. Polls showed him trailing so far behind Dewey that late in September public-opinion analysts stopped taking surveys. Dewey was conducting a quiet, statesmanlike campaign, behaving much as if he were already president. Only Truman, it seemed, believed he could win. As the campaign gathered momentum, he became ever more aggressive, turning his fire away from himself and toward Dewey and the "do-nothing, good-for-nothing" Republican Congress, which was, he told the voters, responsible for fueling inflation and abandoning workers and common people. To dramatize his point, he called Congress into special session in July to give it a chance, he said, to enact the liberal measures the Republicans had recently written into their platform. Congress met for two weeks and, predictably, did almost nothing. Truman was delighted.

Before the campaign was over, the president had traveled nearly 32,000 miles and made 356 speeches, delivering blunt, extemporaneous attacks. He had told Alben Barkley, his running mate, "I'm going to fight hard. I'm going to give them hell." He called for repeal of the Taft-Hartley act, increased price supports for farmers, and strong civil-rights protection for the blacks. (He was the first president to campaign in Harlem.) He sought, in short, to re-create much of Franklin Roosevelt's New Deal coalition. And to the surprise of virtually everyone, he suc-

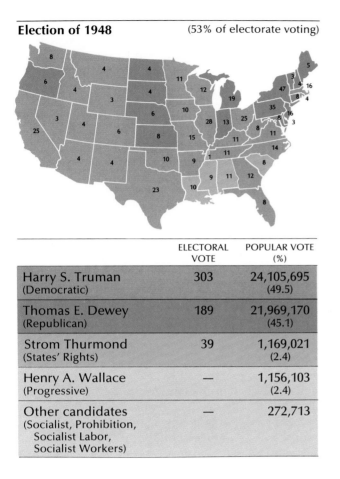

Election of 1948   (53% of electorate voting)

	ELECTORAL VOTE	POPULAR VOTE (%)
Harry S. Truman (Democratic)	303	24,105,695 (49.5)
Thomas E. Dewey (Republican)	189	21,969,170 (45.1)
Strom Thurmond (States' Rights)	39	1,169,021 (2.4)
Henry A. Wallace (Progressive)	—	1,156,103 (2.4)
Other candidates (Socialist, Prohibition, Socialist Labor, Socialist Workers)	—	272,713

ceeded. When the returns came in, the nation was stunned to learn that Truman had won a narrow but decisive victory: 49.5 percent of the popular vote to Dewey's 45.1 percent (with the two splinter parties dividing the small remainder between them), and an electoral margin of 303 to 189. Democrats, in the meantime, had regained both houses of Congress by substantial margins. It was the most dramatic upset in the history of presidential elections.

The Fair Deal Revived

Truman interpreted the 1948 election as a mandate for the revival of liberal reform. But despite the Democratic victories, the Eighty-first Congress was often no more hospitable to reform than its Republican predecessor. Truman failed once again to win approval of such major new reforms as aid to education and national health insurance. Nevertheless, his administration managed in the first two years of its second term to consolidate and extend a number of already established New Deal reforms that before the election had seemed to be in jeopardy.

On three issues, in particular, Truman won important victories. Congress raised the legal minimum wage from 40 cents to 75 cents an hour. It approved an expansion of the Social Security system, increasing benefits by 75 percent and extending them to 10 million additional people. And it strengthened the federal commitment to public housing. The National Housing Act of 1949 called for the construction of 810,000 units of low-income housing over six years, to be accompanied by long-term rent subsidies. (Inadequate funding plagued the program for years, and the initial goal was reached only in 1972.)

While many of the other initiatives Truman had sponsored before 1948 gradually faded from view, he continued to press strenuously on what was perhaps the most controversial domestic issue of all: civil rights. The president had little luck persuading Congress to accept the civil-rights legislation he proposed in 1949, legislation that would have made lynching a federal crime, provided federal protection of black voting rights, abolished the poll tax, and established a Fair Employment Practices Commission to curb discrimination in hiring. Although a majority of the Senate appeared ready to support at least some aspects of this package, a vigorous filibuster by Southern Democrats (who also controlled crucial committees) managed to block the legislation. Nevertheless, Truman proceeded on his own to battle several forms of racial discrimination. He had appointed a federal Civil Rights Commission in 1946, whose 1947 report became the first important government call for the total elimination of segregation. Truman publicly approved its recommendations, although he was as yet unable to implement them. He ordered an end to discrimination in the hiring of government employees. He began to dismantle segregation within the armed forces. And he allowed the Justice Department to become actively involved in court battles against discriminatory statutes. The Supreme Court, in the meantime, signaled its own growing awareness of the issue by ruling, in *Shelley* v. *Kraemer* (1948), that the courts could not be used to enforce private "covenants" meant to bar blacks from residential neighborhoods. The Truman record, and the judicial decisions that accompanied it, made only minor dents in the structure of segregation. They did, however, signal the beginning of a commitment by liberal Democrats—and by the federal government as a whole—finally to confront the problem of race.

The Korean War

Truman's domestic policies had had a difficult time from the beginning in competing against the nation's obsession with the Soviet threat in Europe. In 1950, a new and more dangerous element of the Cold War emerged and all but killed hopes for further Fair Deal reform. On June 24, 1950, the armies of communist North Korea swept across their southern border and began a major invasion of the pro-Western half of the Korean peninsula to the south. Suddenly, the United States found itself embroiled in a new kind of conflict. The nation was neither fully at war nor fully at peace. It was, rather, discovering the peculiar demands of "limited war."

The Divided Peninsula

Korea had long been a source of international controversy. A peninsula of strategic importance in Asia, it was easily accessible to the Soviet Union, Japan, and China. At the end of World War II, therefore, neither the United States nor the Soviet Union—both of which had sent troops into Korea against the Japanese—was willing to leave. As a result, the nation had been divided, supposedly temporarily, along the 38th parallel. The Russians departed in 1949, leaving behind a communist government in the north with a strong, Soviet-equipped army. The Americans left only months later, handing control to the pro-Western government of Syngman Rhee, a ruthless and only nominally democratic leader. He possessed a far less imposing army than his northern counterparts, and he used it primarily to strengthen his own position against internal political opposition.

The situation proved a strong temptation to the nationalists in the North Korean government and, apparently, to the Soviet leadership. The communist government of the north, recognizing its military superiority, was eager to invade the south and reunite the nation—particularly after the American government had implied that it did not consider South Korea within its own "defense perimeter." The evidence remains murky as to how much the Soviet Union was involved in initiating the invasion; there is some reason to believe that the North Koreans acted without Stalin's approval. But the Soviets supported the offensive once it began.

The Truman administration was quick to respond. On June 27, 1950, the president ordered American air and naval forces to assist the South Korean army against the invaders; and on the same day he appealed to the United Nations to intervene. Because the Soviet Union was boycotting the Security Council at the time (to protest the council's refusal to recognize the new communist government of China), American delegates were able to avoid a Soviet veto and win UN agreement to a resolution calling for international assistance to the embattled Rhee government. On June 30, the United States ordered its own ground forces into Korea, and Truman appointed General Douglas MacArthur to command the UN operations there. (Several other nations offered some assistance, including troops, to the effort, but the "UN" armies were, in fact, overwhelmingly American.)

The intervention in Korea was the first expression of the newly militant American foreign policy outlined in NSC-68. Very quickly, the administration decided that the war would be an effort not simply at containment but also at "liberation." After a surprise American invasion at Inchon in September had routed the North Korean forces from the south and sent them fleeing back across the 38th parallel, Truman gave MacArthur permission to pursue the communists into their own territory. His aim, as an American-sponsored UN resolution proclaimed in October, was to create "a unified, independent and democratic Korea." (Paralleling this decision came new American initiatives in other areas: efforts to strengthen the Chiang regime in Taiwan for a possible future assault on the Chinese mainland; and assistance to the French, who were attempting to rout communist forces from Vietnam and Laos.)

From Invasion to Stalemate

For several weeks, MacArthur's invasion of North Korea proceeded smoothly. On October 19, the capital, Pyongyang, fell to the UN forces. At the same time, parachutists managed to trap and immobilize much of the rest of the North Korean army. Victory seemed near. Slowly, however, the United States was

The Korean War, 1950–1953

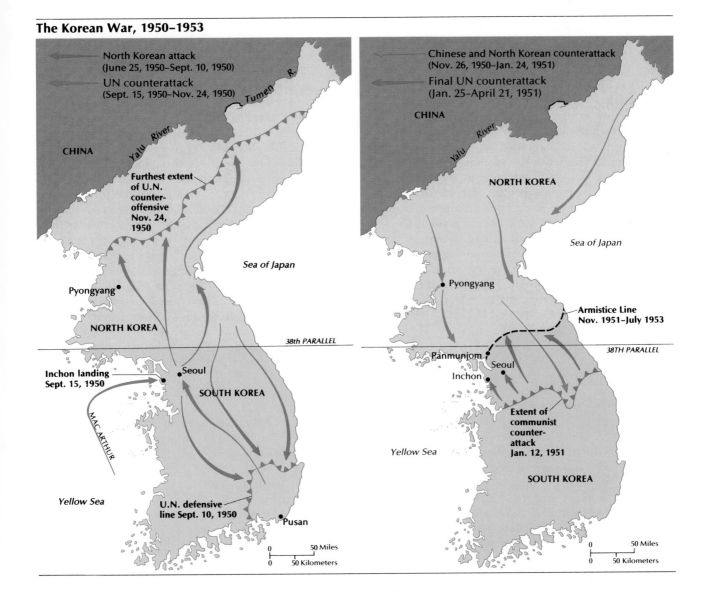

becoming aware of the growing presence of forces from communist China; and by November 4, it was clear that eight Chinese divisions had entered the war. Suddenly, the UN offensive stalled and then collapsed. Through December 1950, American forces fought a bitter, losing battle against far more numerous Chinese divisions, retreating at almost every juncture. Within weeks, communist forces had pushed the Americans back below the 38th parallel once again and had captured the South Korean capital of Seoul. By mid-January 1951 the rout had ceased; and by March the UN armies had managed to regain

much of the territory they had recently lost, taking back Seoul and pushing the communists north of the 38th parallel for the second time. But with that, the war degenerated into a protracted stalemate.

It was then that the nation first began to experience the true dilemmas of limited war. Truman had been determined from the beginning to avoid embroiling the nation in a direct conflict with China, a conflict that would, he believed, lead to a world conflagration. As early as December 1950, he had begun seeking a negotiated solution to the struggle; and he continued through the next two years to insist that there would be no wider war. He faced, however, a formidable opponent in General MacArthur, a soldier of the old school who could not accept the idea of any limits on a military endeavor. The United States was fighting the Chinese, he argued. It should, therefore, attack China itself, if not through an actual invasion, then at least by bombing communist forces massing north of the Chinese border. In March 1951 he gave a public indication of his unhappiness with the administration's policy, sending to House Republican leader Joseph W. Martin a message that concluded: "There is no substitute for victory." His position quickly won wide popular support from a nation frustrated by the long, inconclusive war.

For nine months, Truman had chafed at MacArthur's resistance to his decisions about the conduct of the war. More than once, he had warned him to keep his objections to himself. The release of the Martin letter, therefore, struck the president as intolerable insubordination. On April 11, 1951, he relieved MacArthur of his command.

The result was a storm of public outrage. Sixty-nine percent of the American people supported MacArthur in the controversy, a Gallup poll reported. When the general returned to the United States in 1951, the first time he had set foot in the country since 1935, he was greeted with wild enthusiasm. His televised farewell appearance before a joint session of Congress attracted an audience of millions. Public criticism of Truman finally abated somewhat when a number of prominent military figures, including General Omar Bradley, publicly supported the president's decision. But not until many years later would most Americans come to see the decision to fire MacArthur as one of Truman's finest moments.

In the meantime, the Korean stalemate continued for what seemed interminable months. In July 1951, negotiations began between the opposing forces at Panmunjom, near the 38th parallel; but they produced no swift resolution. Instead, the talks—and the war—dragged on until 1953.

Limited Mobilization

Just as the war in Korea produced only a limited American military commitment abroad, so it created only a limited economic mobilization at home. Although the Truman administration drew heavily on the experiences of World War II in meeting the demands for armaments and supplies, never was it necessary to create the enormous bureaucracy and pervasive controls that had been required a decade earlier.

Nevertheless, the Korean War did place pressure on the government to control the economy in several important ways. First, Truman attempted to halt a new wave of inflation by setting up the Office of Defense Mobilization to hold down prices and discourage high union wage demands. Then, confronted with the failure of these cautious regulatory efforts, the president took more drastic action. When railroad workers walked off the job in 1951, Truman ordered the government to seize control of the railroads. But while the dramatic gesture helped keep the trains running, it was of no effect in restraining union demands. Workers ultimately got most of what they had demanded before the railroads were returned to their owners. In 1952, a nationwide steel strike threatened to interrupt vital war production; and again Truman moved to seize the steel mills, citing his powers as commander in chief. This time, however, the courts intervened. In a 6-to-3 decision, the Supreme Court ruled that the president had exceeded his authority, and Truman was forced to relent. A lengthy and costly strike followed.

The effects of the war on American society at large were mixed. The conflict gave a significant boost to national prosperity. Just at the point when some economists believed the postwar consumer demand was about to decline, a new surge of funds was being pumped into the economy by the federal government, which increased military expenditures more than fourfold, to $60 billion in 1953. Unemployment declined. Industry embarked on a new wave of capital expansion. But the war had other, less healthy effects on American life. Coming at a time of rising insecurity about the position of the United States in the world, it intensified anxiety about communism. As the long stalemate continued, producing 140,000 American casualties (and more than 1 million South Korean dead and wounded), frustration increasingly turned to anger. The United States, which had recently won the greatest war in history, seemed unable to conclude what many Americans considered a minor border skirmish in an unimportant country. Many began to believe that something must be deeply wrong—not only in Korea but within the United States as well. Such fears became one of many factors contributing to the rise of the second major campaign of the century against domestic communism.

The Crusade Against Subversion

There has never been a single, satisfactory explanation of why, in the years following World War II, the American people developed a growing fear of internal communist subversion that by the early 1950s had reached the point of near hysteria. Only by looking at the convergence of many factors at once is it possible to understand the era of the "great fear."

One factor was obvious. Communism was not an imagined enemy in the 1950s. It had tangible shape, in the person of Joseph Stalin and the Soviet Union. It was a dark and menacing threat to America's hopes for the world. The continuing setbacks overseas, the frustrations in Korea, the "loss" of China, the shocking realization that Russia had developed an atomic bomb—all created a sense of unease and a need to find someone to blame. The idea of a communist conspiracy within American borders became a natural outlet for such feelings. But there were other factors as well, rooted in events in American domestic politics.

HUAC and Alger Hiss

Much of the anticommunist furor emerged out of the search by the Republican party for an issue with which to attack the Democrats, and out of the efforts of the Democrats to take that issue away. Beginning in 1947, the House Un-American Activities Committee (HUAC), established by the Democrats in 1938 to uncover malign foreign influences in the United States and now under the control of conservative Republicans, launched a series of widely publicized and inflammatory investigations to prove that, under Democratic rule, the nation had allowed communist subversion to reach alarming levels. The committee turned first to the movie industry, arguing that communists had so infiltrated Hollywood that American films were being tainted with Soviet propaganda. A parade of writers and producers was summoned to testify; and when some of them ("the Hollywood Ten") refused to answer questions about their own political beliefs and those of their colleagues, they were sent to jail for contempt. Others were barred from employment in the industry when Hollywood, attempting to protect its public image, adopted a blacklist of those of "suspicious loyalty."

Far more frightening to much of the public, however, was HUAC's investigation into charges of disloyalty leveled against a former high-ranking member of the State Department: Alger Hiss. Whittaker Chambers, a self-avowed former communist agent, now an editor at *Time* magazine, told the committee in 1948 that Hiss had passed classified documents to him in 1937 and 1938. When Hiss sued him for slander, Chambers produced microfilms of the documents (called the "pumpkin papers," because Chambers had kept them hidden in a pumpkin in his garden). Hiss could not be tried for espionage because of the statute of limitations (a law that protects individuals from prosecution for most crimes after seven years have passed). But as a result of the committee's efforts (and particularly because of the relentless pursuit of the case by Richard M. Nixon, a freshman Republican congressman from California), Hiss was charged with lying to the HUAC inquisitors. After a sensational trial, in which a number of leading Democratic liberals—including Adlai Stevenson, Felix Frankfurter, and Dean Acheson— testified as character witnesses for Hiss, the jury was unable to reach a verdict. A second trial produced a conviction for perjury, and Hiss served several years in prison, still proclaiming his innocence. The Hiss case not only discredited a prominent young diplomat; it cast suspicion on an entire generation of liberal Democrats and made it possible for the public to believe that communists had actually infiltrated the government.

The Federal Loyalty Program

The Truman administration, in the meantime, was making its own contribution to increasing the popular fear. Partly to protect itself against Republican attacks, partly to encourage support for the president's foreign policy initiatives, the executive branch in 1947 initiated a widely publicized program to review the "loyalty" of federal employees. A series of "loyalty boards" undertook a sweeping investigation of the government; and in August 1950, the president authorized the dismissal in sensitive departments of even those deemed no more than "bad security risks." The faintest suspicion of disloyalty could cause a federal employee to lose his or her job. By 1951, more than 2,000 government employees had resigned and 212 had been dismissed.

Not only was the employee loyalty program itself being abused; the program also served as a signal throughout the executive branch to launch a major

The Rosenbergs
Julius and Ethel Rosenberg leave federal court in a police van after being convicted in March 1951 of transmitting atomic secrets to the Soviet Union. A week later, Judge Irving Kaufman sentenced them to death. (UPI/Bettmann Newsphotos)

assault on subversion. The attorney general established a list of dissident organizations and, in 1948, obtained indictments of eleven American communists for "conspiring to teach the violent overthrow of the government." The Federal Bureau of Investigation (FBI)—whose director, J. Edgar Hoover, had been obsessed with the issue of communism for years (and had been one of the principal organizers of the notorious "Palmer Raids" after World War I; see p. 686)—launched major crusades to investigate and harass alleged radicals. Federal information and education programs began to become tinged with strident anticommunist propaganda.

By now, the anticommunist frenzy was growing so intense that even a Democratic Congress was bowing to it. In 1950, over the objections of the Department of Defense, the Department of Justice, and the CIA, it enacted the McCarran Internal Security Act. The bill required all communist organizations to register with the government and to publish their records. Americans were now liable for prosecution on grounds as vague as "fomenting revolution." Communists were barred from working in defense plants and denied passports. Members of overseas "subversive organizations" were denied visas to enter the country. Truman vetoed the bill. Congress easily overrode his veto.

Of particular importance in fanning public fears

were the efforts of the FBI and the Justice Department to prove a communist conspiracy to steal America's atomic secrets for the Soviet Union. The early explosion of a Russian nuclear weapon made such charges credible. And the testimony in 1950 of Klaus Fuchs, a young British scientist, that he had delivered to the Russians full details of the manufacture of the bomb gave the charges substance. Through an arcane series of connections, the case ultimately settled on an obscure New York couple, Julius and Ethel Rosenberg, members of the Communist party, whom the government claimed had been the masterminds of the conspiracy. The Rosenbergs had allegedly received the information from Ethel's brother, a machinist who had worked on the Manhattan Project, and passed it on to the Soviet Union through other agents (including Fuchs). Several witnesses corroborated the story. Although the Rosenbergs vehemently denied any guilt, they were convicted and, on April 5, 1951, sentenced to death. A rising chorus of public protests and a long string of appeals failed to save them. On June 19, 1953, they died in the electric chair.

All these factors—the HUAC investigations, the Hiss trial, the loyalty investigations, the McCarran Act, the Rosenberg case—combined with other concerns by the early 1950s to create a fear of communist subversion that seemed to grip the entire country.

State and local governments launched loyalty programs of their own, dismissing thousands of employees. Local courts began handing down extraordinarily harsh sentences to defendants convicted of anything resembling subversion. Schools and universities rooted out teachers suspected of teaching "un-American" ideas. Unions found themselves under continuing assault for suspected (and sometimes real) communist leanings. And a pervasive fear settled on the country—not only the fear of communist infiltration but the fear of being suspected of communism. It was a climate that made possible the rise of an extraordinary public figure, whose behavior at any other time might have been dismissed as preposterous.

McCarthyism

Joseph McCarthy was an undistinguished, first-term, Republican senator from Wisconsin when, in February 1950, he suddenly burst into national prominence. In the midst of a speech in Wheeling, West Virginia, he raised a sheet of paper into the air and claimed to "hold in my hand" a list of 205 known communists currently working in the American State Department. No person of comparable stature had ever made so bold a charge against the federal government; and in the weeks to come, as McCarthy repeated and expanded on his accusations, he emerged as the nation's preeminent leader of the crusade against communism.

He had seized on the issue less out of a deep concern about domestic subversion than because he needed something with which to run for reelection in 1952. And he continued to exploit the issue for the next four years because, to his surprise, it won him fame and notoriety beyond his wildest dreams. His rise was meteoric. Within weeks of his charges against the State Department he was expanding his accusations to other agencies. After 1952, with the Republicans in control of the Senate and McCarthy the chairman of a special subcommittee, he conducted highly publicized investigations of subversion—investigations that probed virtually every area of the government. His unprincipled assistants, Roy Cohn and David Schine, sauntered arrogantly through federal offices and American embassies overseas looking for evidence of communist influence. One hapless government official after another found himself summoned before McCarthy's subcommittee, where the senator belligerently and often cruelly badgered witnesses and destroyed public careers.

In the course of this extraordinary crusade, not once did McCarthy produce conclusive evidence that any federal employee had communist ties. But much of the public seemed not to care. A growing constituency adored him for his coarse, "fearless" assaults on a government establishment that many considered arrogant, effete, even effeminate. They admired his efforts to expose the "traitors" who had, he claimed, riddled the Truman administration. They even tolerated his attacks on public figures who earlier would have been considered unassailable, men such as General George C. Marshall and Governor Adlai Stevenson. Republicans, in particular, rallied to his claims that the Democrats had been responsible for "twenty years of treason," that only a change of parties could rid the country of subversion. McCarthy, in short, provided his followers with an issue into which they could channel a wide range of resentments: fear of communism, animosity toward the country's "Eastern establishment," and frustrated partisan ambitions.

For several years, McCarthy terrorized American public life, intimidating all but a very few from speaking out in opposition to him. In 1952, when some Democratic senators dared to denounce him, McCarthy openly campaigned against their reelection; several went down to defeat. Journalists and intellectuals, with some notable exceptions, drew back from challenging him for fear of being themselves discredited by his attack. Even the highly popular Dwight D. Eisenhower, running for president in 1952, did not dare to oppose him. Outraged at McCarthy's attacks on General Marshall, Eisenhower briefly considered issuing a public protest. In the end, however, he remained silent.

The Republican Revival

Public frustration over the stalemate in Korea and popular fears of internal subversion combined to make 1952 an inhospitable year for the Democratic party. Truman, whose own popularity had diminished almost to the vanishing point, wisely withdrew from the year's presidential contest, creating the first open battle for the nomination since 1932. Senator Estes Kefauver of Tennessee launched a spirited campaign, performing well in the primaries. But party leaders ultimately settled on Governor Adlai E.

SIGNIFICANT EVENTS

1941   Roosevelt and Churchill draft Atlantic Charter (p. 828)

1943   Wendell Willkie publishes *One World* (p. 828)

Roosevelt, Churchill, Stalin meet at Teheran (p. 829)

1944   G.I. Bill of Rights enacted (p. 839)

1945   Yalta Conference (p. 830)

Roosevelt dies; Harry S. Truman becomes president (p. 832)

Potsdam Conference (p. 833)

United Nations founded (p. 830)

1946   Atomic Energy Commission established (p. 836)

Postwar inflation (p. 839)

Coal and railroad strikes (p. 840)

Republicans win control of Congress (p. 840)

Crisis in Iran (p. 834)

1947   Truman Doctrine announced (p. 834)

Marshall Plan proposed (p. 835)

National Security Act passed (p. 836)

Taft-Hartley Act passed (p. 841)

HUAC begins investigating Hollywood (p. 847)

Federal employee loyalty program launched (p. 847)

1948   Communists stage coup in Czechoslovakia (p. 835)

Economic Cooperation Administration established (p. 835)

Selective Service System restored (p. 835)

Berlin blockade prompts U.S. airlift (p. 837)

Truman elected president (p. 843)

Hiss case begins (p. 847)

1949   NATO established (p. 838)

Soviet Union explodes atomic bomb (p. 837)

Communists seize power in China (p. 838)

1950   NSC-68 outlines new U.S. policy toward communism (p. 838)

Korean War begins (p. 844)

American troops enter North Korea (p. 844)

Chinese troops enter war (p. 845)

McCarran Act passed (p. 848)

Fuchs-Rosenberg case begins (p. 848)

Joseph McCarthy begins campaign against communists in government (p. 849)

1951   Truman removes MacArthur from command in Korea (p. 846)

Railroad workers strike (p. 846)

Negotiations begin in Korea (p. 846)

1952   American occupation of Japan ends (p. 837)

Steelworkers strike (p. 846)

Dwight D. Eisenhower elected president (p. 851)

Stevenson of Illinois, whose early reluctance to run seemed only to enhance his attractiveness.

Stevenson's dignity, wit, and eloquence quickly made him a beloved figure to many liberals and intellectuals, who developed a devotion to him that they had never offered Harry Truman. But those same qualities seemed only to fuel Republican charges that Stevenson lacked the strength or the will to combat communism sufficiently. McCarthy described him as "soft" and took delight in deliberately confusing him with Alger Hiss.

Stevenson's greatest problem, however, was the candidate the Republicans chose to oppose him. Rejecting the efforts of conservatives to nominate either Robert Taft or Douglas MacArthur, the Republicans turned to a man who had had so little previous identification with the party that some liberal Democrats

had tried to draft him four years earlier. Their choice was General Dwight D. Eisenhower, military hero, former commander of NATO, and president of Columbia University in New York. Despite a vigorous struggle by the Taft forces, Eisenhower won nomination on the first ballot. He chose as his running mate the young California senator who had won national prominence through his crusade against Alger Hiss: Richard M. Nixon.

Eisenhower and Nixon proved to be a powerful combination in the autumn campaign. While Eisenhower attracted support by virtue of his geniality and his statesmanlike pledges to settle the Korean conflict (at one point dramatically promising to "go to Korea" himself), Nixon effectively exploited the issue of domestic anticommunism. After surviving early accusations of financial improprieties (which he effec-

CHAPTER 29

◩◩◪

The Affluent Society

◩◩◪

In later decades, Americans have tended to look back on the 1950s and early 1960s as something of a golden age: an era of boundless prosperity, of social stability, of national optimism and confidence. To some extent, that image has simply been the result of the nostalgia with which most generations view earlier, apparently happier times. But to a remarkable degree, it was also the image that many Americans of the 1950s held of their own society. Seldom before had the United States experienced an era of such pride and self-satisfaction.

Two major phenomena in particular shaped the mood of the decade. One was a booming national prosperity, which profoundly altered the social, economic, and even physical landscape of the United States as well as the way many Americans thought about their lives and their world. The other was the continuing struggle against communism, a struggle that created an undercurrent of anxiety but that also encouraged Americans to look even more approvingly at their own society.

These two compelling realities blinded many Americans to other aspects of their society—to serious problems that continued to plague large groups of the population. Prosperity, real as it was, did not extend to everyone. More than 30 million Americans, according to some estimates, continued to live in poverty in the 1950s. And despite the smug belief in the essential virtuousness of American life, large minorities within the population—most prominently the 10 percent of the American people who were black—continued to suffer from a vicious system of social, political, and economic discrimination. Gunnar Myrdal, a Swedish sociologist well acquainted with life in the United States, wrote at the time: "American affluence is heavily mortgaged. America carries a tremendous burden of debt to its poor people." The efforts to pay that debt would ultimately help move the nation out of the complacency of the 1950s and into a far more turbulent era in the 1960s.

For a time, however, such problems seemed far away to most members of the rapidly growing American middle class, who were enjoying an era of rising living standards without precedent in history. And to some degree, they seemed far away to America's political leaders as well, who attempted in the 1950s to limit the role of the federal government in American life and even, in some respects, to limit the role of the United States in the world.

The Economic "Miracle"

Perhaps the most striking feature of American society in the 1950s and early 1960s, one that virtually no observer could ignore, was prosperity—a booming, almost miraculous economic growth that made even the heady 1920s seem pale by comparison. It was a prosperity far better balanced and far more widely distributed than that of thirty years earlier. It was not, however, as universal as some Americans liked to believe.

Economic Growth

By 1949, despite the continuing problems of postwar reconversion, what some called the "miracle" of American economic expansion had begun. It would continue with only minor interruptions for almost twenty years. The gross national product, the most basic indicator of economic growth, alone provides ample evidence of the prosperity of the era. The GNP had doubled in the five years of World War II. Between 1945 and 1960, it grew by 250 percent, from $200 billion to over $500 billion. That growth appears even more remarkable in view of widespread public expectations in 1945 that the GNP would soon decline once the extraordinary demands of war production subsided. Unemployment, which during the Depression had averaged between 15 and 25 percent, remained throughout the 1950s and early 1960s at above 5 percent or lower. Inflation, in the meantime, hovered at about 3 percent a year or less.

There was no single cause. Government spending, which had ended the Depression in the 1940s, continued to stimulate growth. There was increasing public funding of schools, housing, veterans' benefits, welfare, and interstate highways (for which the government spent over $100 billion in the two decades following passage of the Interstate Highway Act of 1956)—all helping to sustain prosperity. Above all, there was military spending. The Korean War, in particular, helped to spark the economic boom. During the first half of the 1950s, when military spending was at its peak, the annual growth rate was 4.7 percent. For the second half of the decade, with the Korean War concluded and spending on armaments in decline, the rate of growth was only 2.25 percent.

Technological progress also contributed to the boom. Because of advances in production techniques and mechanical efficiency, worker productivity increased more than 35 percent in the first decade after the war, a rate far higher than that of any previous era. The development of electronic computers, which first became commercially available in the mid-1950s, began to improve the performance of some American corporations. And technological research and development itself became an increasingly important sector of the economy, expanding the demand for scientists, engineers, and other highly trained experts.

The national birth rate reversed a long pattern of decline. The so-called baby boom, which had begun during the war, peaked in 1957. The nation's popu-

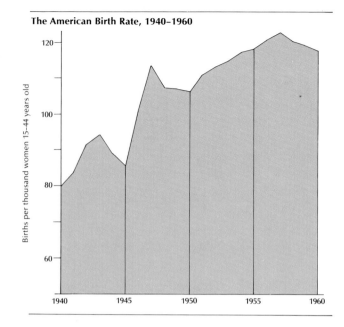

The American Birth Rate, 1940–1960

Births per thousand women 15–44 years old

lation rose almost 20 percent in the decade, from 150 million in 1950 to 179 million in 1960. This growth mirrored a worldwide demographic explosion that would ultimately place great strains on the resources of the planet. In the United States of the 1950s, however, the baby boom meant increased consumer demand and expanding economic growth.

The rapid expansion of suburbs—whose population grew 47 percent in the 1950s, more than twice as fast as the population of the nation as a whole—helped stimulate growth in several important sectors of the economy. The automobile industry experienced the greatest boom in its history, as the number of privately owned cars more than doubled in a decade. The demand for new homes helped sustain a vigorous housing industry. The construction of roads, which was both a cause and a result of the growth of suburbs, stimulated the economy even further.

Perhaps the most striking result of this long period of sustained economic growth was the rising standard of living for the majority of the population. In the thirty years after the war, the economy grew nearly ten times as fast as the population. And while that growth was far from equally distributed, it was great enough to affect most of society. The average American in 1960 had over 20 percent more purchasing power than in 1945, and more than twice as much as during the prosperous 1920s. By 1960, per capita income (the average income for every individual man, woman, and child) was over $1,800—$500 more than it had been fifteen years before. Family incomes had risen even more. The American people had achieved the highest standard of living of any society in the history of the world.

The New Economics

The exciting (and to some surprising) discovery of the power of the American economic system was a central element in the confident tone of American political life in the 1950s. During the Depression, some had questioned the viability of capitalism. In the 1950s, such doubts all but disappeared. Two features in particular made the postwar economy a source of national confidence.

First was the belief that Keynesian economics made it possible for government to regulate and stabilize the economy without intruding directly into the private sector. The British economist John Maynard Keynes had argued as early as the 1920s that by varying the flow of government spending and managing the supply of currency, the state could stimulate the economy to cure recession, and dampen growth to prevent inflation. The experience of the last years of the Depression and the first years of the war had seemed to confirm this argument. And by the mid-1950s. Keynesian theory was rapidly becoming a fundamental article of faith—not only among professional economists but among much of the public at large. The most popular economics textbook of the 1950s and 1960s, Paul Samuelson's *Economics,* imbued generations of college students with Keynesian ideas. Armed with these fiscal and monetary tools, economists now believed, it was possible for the government to maintain a permanent prosperity. The dispiriting boom-and-bust cycle that many had long believed to be a permanent feature of industrial capitalism could now be banished forever. Never again would it be necessary for the nation to experience another Depression.

If any doubters remained, they found ample evidence to dispel their misgivings during the brief recessions the economy experienced during the era. When the economy slackened in late 1953, Secretary of the Treasury George M. Humphrey and the Federal Reserve Board worked to ease credit and make money more readily available. The economy quickly recovered, seeming to confirm the value of Keyne-

sian tactics. A far more serious recession began late in 1957 and continued for more than a year. This time, the Eisenhower administration ignored the Keynesians and adopted such deflationary tactics as cutting the budget. The slow, halting nature of the recovery, in contrast with the rapid revival in 1954, seemed further to support the Keynesian philosophy. The new economics finally won official acceptance in 1963, when John Kennedy proposed a tax cut to stimulate economic growth, Although it took Kennedy's death and the political skills of Lyndon Johnson to win passage of the measure in 1964, the result seemed to be all that the Keynesians had predicted: an increase in private demand, which stimulated economic growth and reduced unemployment.

In addition to the belief in the possibility of permanent economic stability was the equally exhilarating belief in permanent economic growth. As the economy continued to expand far beyond what any observer had predicted was possible only a few years before, more and more Americans assumed that such growth was now without bounds—that there were few effective limits on the abundance available to the nation. This was not only a comforting thought in itself; it also provided a new outlook on social and economic problems. In the 1930s, many Americans had argued that the elimination of poverty and injustice would require a redistribution of wealth—a limitation on the fortunes of the rich and a distribution of this wealth to the poor. By the mid-1950s, reformers concerned about economic deprivation were arguing that the solution lay in increased production. The affluent would not have to sacrifice in order to eliminate poverty. The nation would simply have to produce more abundance, thus raising the quality of life of even the poorest citizens to a level of comfort and decency.

Capital and Labor

The prosperity of the 1920s had been accompanied by a rapid increase in economic centralization and concentration. The prosperity of the 1950s brought with it a similar consolidation. There were more than 4,000 corporate mergers in the course of the 1950s; and more than ever, a few large corporations controlled an enormous proportion of the nation's economic activity. This was particularly true in industries benefiting from government defense spending. As during World War II, the federal government tended to award military contracts to large corporations. In 1959, for example, half of all defense contracts went to only twenty firms. But the same pattern repeated itself in many other areas of the economy, as corporations moved from being single-industry firms to becoming diversified conglomerates. By the end of the decade, half of the net corporate income in the nation was going to only slightly more than 500 firms, or one-tenth of 1 percent of the total number of corporations.

A similar consolidation was in process in the agricultural economy. Increasing mechanization reduced the need for farm labor, and the agricultural work force declined by more than half in the two decades after the war. Mechanization rewarded economies of scale, as did the higher productivity that new fertilizers and improved irrigation techniques made possible. As a result, many farms began to come under the control of corporations or very large landowners. The rise of what became known as "agribusiness" challenged the survival of one of the most cherished American institutions: the family farm. By the 1960s, relatively few individuals could any longer afford to buy and equip a modern farm; and much of the nation's most productive land had been purchased by financial institutions and corporations.

Unlike the 1920s, the increase in corporate consolidation was accompanied by a rise in the power of labor organizations. Corporations enjoying such remarkable growth were reluctant to allow strikes to interfere with their operations; and since the most important unions were now so large and entrenched that they could not easily be suppressed or intimidated, business leaders made important concessions to them. As early as 1948, Walter Reuther, president of the United Automobile Workers, obtained from General Motors, a contract that included a built-in "escalator clause"—an automatic cost-of-living increase pegged to the consumer price index. The provision set a crucial precedent—not only for the rest of the automobile industry but for the economy as a whole. In 1955, Reuther received a guarantee from Ford Motor Company of continuing wages to auto workers even during layoffs (although not the guaranteed annual wage he had demanded). A few months later, steelworkers in several corporations did receive guarantees of an annual salary. By the mid-1950s, factory wages in all industries had risen substantially, to an average of $80 per week.

Not all laborers shared in such gains. The labor movement enjoyed great success in winning new benefits for workers already organized in strong

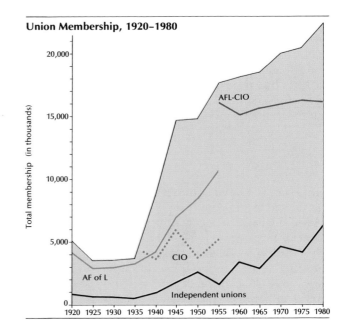

Union Membership, 1920–1980

unions. For the majority of laborers who were as yet unorganized, there were fewer advances. Total union membership remained relatively stable, at about 16 million, throughout the 1950s; and while this was in part a result of a shift in the work force from blue-collar to white-collar jobs, it was at least as much a result of new obstacles to organization. The Taft-Hartley Act and the state right-to-work laws that it spawned made more difficult the creation of new unions powerful enough to demand recognition from employers.

The economic successes of the entrenched unions in the 1950s helped pave the way for the reunification of the labor movement. In December 1955, the American Federation of Labor and the Congress of Industrial Organizations ended their twenty-year rivalry and merged to create a giant new federation, the AFL-CIO, under the leadership of George Meany. But the climate of the era produced other, less welcome changes in the nature of the labor movement. Some large unions, no longer required to engage in the militant crusades against corporate resistance that had dominated the 1930s, were themselves becoming wealthy, powerful bureaucracies. Most continued to operate responsibly and effectively; but some of the most important unions began to face accusations of corruption and indifference.

The powerful Teamsters Union became in 1957

the focal point of a congressional investigation in which its president, David Beck, was charged with the misappropriation of over $320,000 in union funds. Beck ultimately stepped down from his office to be replaced by Jimmy Hoffa, who was widely believed to have close ties to organized crime. Government investigators pursued Hoffa for nearly a decade before finally winning a conviction against him (for tax evasion) in 1967. After his release from prison in 1971 (on a pardon from President Richard Nixon), he attempted to regain his position in the union. But before he could succeed, he disappeared and was generally presumed to have been murdered. The United Mine Workers, the union that had spearheaded the industrial movement in the 1930s, similarly became tainted by suspicions of corruption and by violence. John L. Lewis's last years as head of the union were plagued with scandals and dissent within the organization. His successor, Tony Boyle, was ultimately convicted of complicity in the 1969 murder of Joseph Yablonski, the leader of a dissident faction within the union.

Even more troubling, perhaps, was the growing belief among union members that the leaders of these and other labor organizations had lost touch with the rank and file, that they had become more concerned with the internal bureaucratic and political struggles of the union organization itself than with the welfare of the members.

A People of Plenty

The most striking social development of the immediate postwar era was the rapid extension of a middle-class life style and outlook to large groups of the population previously insulated from it. The new prosperity of social groups that had previously lived on the margins; the growing availability of consumer products at affordable prices and the rising public fascination with such products; and perhaps above all, the massive population movement from the cities to the suburbs: All helped make the American middle class a much larger, more powerful, more homogeneous, and more dominant force than it had ever been before.

The new prosperity, in fact, inspired some Americans to see abundance as the key to understanding the American past and the American character. Leading intellectuals argued that American

history had been characterized by a broad "consensus" of agreement about the value and necessity of competitive, capitalist growth. "However much at odds on specific issues," the historian Richard Hofstadter wrote in *The American Political Tradition* (1948), Americans have "shared a belief in the rights of property, the philosophy of economic individualism, the value of competition; they have accepted the economic virtues of capitalist culture as necessary qualities of man." David Potter, another leading American historian of the era, published an influential examination of "economic abundance and American character" in 1954. He called it *People of Plenty*. For the American middle class in the 1950s, at least, it seemed an appropriate label.

The Consumer Culture

At the center of middle-class culture in the 1950s was a growing absorption with consumer goods. It was a result not just of the new prosperity and the increasing variety and availability of products but also of the adeptness of advertisers in creating a demand for those products. It was also a result of the growth of consumer credit, which increased by 800 percent between 1945 and 1957. Easily available credit cards, revolving charge accounts, and easy-payment plans made immediate gratification of consumer yearnings not only desirable but possible. Affluent Americans in the 1950s and 1960s showed renewed interest in such longtime consumer crazes as the automobile, and Detroit responded to the boom with ever-flashier styling and accessories. Consumers also responded eagerly to the development of such new products as dishwashers, garbage disposals, television, and "hi-fis" and stereos. To a striking degree, the prosperity of the 1950s and 1960s was consumer-driven (as opposed to investment-driven).

Because consumer goods were so often marketed (and advertised) nationally, the 1950s were notable for the rapid spread of great national consumer crazes. Children, adolescents, and even some adults became entranced in the late 1950s with the "hula-hoop"—a large plastic ring kept spinning around the waist. The popularity of the Walt Disney-produced children's television show, *The Mickey Mouse Club*, created a national demand for related products such as Mickey Mouse watches and hats. (It also helped produce the stunning success of Disneyland, an amusement park near Los Angeles that re-created many of the characters and events of Disney enter-

tainment programs.) The Disney technique of turning an entertainment success into an effective tool for marketing consumer goods was not an isolated event. Many other entertainers and producers did the same.

The Suburban Nation

A third of the nation's population lived in suburbs by 1960. The growth of suburbs was a result not only of increased affluence, but of important innovations in homebuilding, which made single-family houses affordable to millions of new people. The most famous of the suburban developers, Arthur Levitt, began what became a national trend with his use of mass-production techniques to construct a large housing development on Long Island, near New York City. This first "Levittown" (there would later be others in New Jersey and Pennsylvania) consisted of several thousand two-bedroom Cape Cod style houses, with identical interiors and only slightly varied facades, each perched on its own concrete slab (to eliminate excavation costs), facing curving, treeless streets.

Levittown, 1949

Young mothers struggle to manage their children and their groceries as they shop at a supermarket in Levittown, New York, in 1949. The suburbs that sprang up after World War II (of which Levittown served as something of a prototype) helped create a new style of life for middle-class Americans. So did the rapid rise in the birth rate, which produced the postwar "baby boom."   (UPI/Bettmann Newsphotos)

Levittown houses sold for under $10,000, and they helped meet an enormous demand for housing that had been developing for more than a decade. Young couples—often newly married war veterans eager to start a family—rushed to purchase the inexpensive homes, not only in the Levittowns but in similar developments that soon began appearing throughout the country.

Why did so many Americans want to move to the suburbs? One reason was the enormous importance postwar Americans placed on family life after five years of war in which families had often been separated or otherwise disrupted. Suburbs provided new families with larger homes than they could find (or afford) in the cities, and thus made it easier to bring up larger numbers of children. They provided privacy. They provided security from the noise and dangers of urban living. They offered space for the

new consumer goods—the appliances, cars, boats, outdoor furniture, and other products—that most Americans craved.

For many Americans, suburban life helped provide a sense of community that was sometimes difficult to develop in large, crowded, impersonal urban areas. In later years, the "conformity" and "homogeneity" of the surburbs would be blamed for a wide range of social ills. But in the 1950s, many people were attracted by the idea of living in a community populated largely by people of similar age and background. Not all suburbs were as homogeneous as they sometimes appeared; a famous study of one of the Levittowns, for example, revealed a striking variety of occupations, ethnic backgrounds, and incomes within a single neighborhood. Nevertheless, suburban societies tended to attract people looking for a similar life style. Women in particular often

Chicago's Annexations and the Suburban Noose

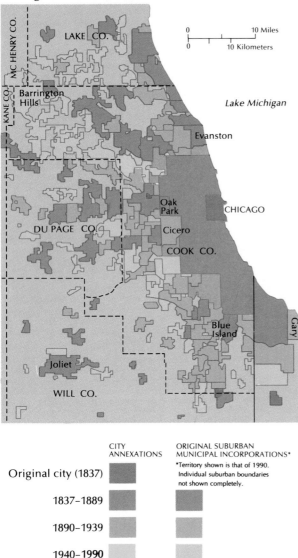

	CITY ANNEXATIONS	ORIGINAL SUBURBAN MUNICIPAL INCORPORATIONS*
		*Territory shown is that of 1990. Individual suburban boundaries not shown completely.
Original city (1837)		
1837–1889		
1890–1939		
1940–1990		

as urban school systems began to include increasing numbers of blacks (especially after the Supreme Court desegragation decisions of the mid-1950s), many white families fled to the suburbs to escape the integration of urban neighborhoods and schools.

One of the striking aspects of suburban life was how similar it often was from one area of the country to another. Because so many suburbs were built at about the same time, using similar construction techniques, the physical similarities alone were often striking. And because in the 1950s and 1960s many middle-class professionals were living increasingly mobile lives—moving from one city to another as the national corporations for which they worked demanded—suburban populations often did not consist of people with strong local roots. On the other hand, suburban neighborhoods, just like urban neighborhoods, were not uniform. The Levittowns ultimately became the homes of mainly lower-middle-class people, one step removed from the inner city. Other, more affluent suburbs became enclaves of far wealthier families. Around virtually every city, a clear hierarchy emerged of "good" suburban neighborhoods and more modest ones, just as such gradations had emerged years earlier within the cities themselves.

The Suburban Family

The growth of suburbs was not only a response to the growing demand for stable family life among the American middle class. It also helped shape the nature of that life. The suburban family was isolated from the activities of the city. To a large degree, it was even isolated from other suburban families. Homes were designed to maximize privacy; a distinctive feature of many new suburbs was that the back yard of each house, not the front yard, was the center of family activity. Moreover, since commercial and social facilities were generally distant enough from residential areas that they could be reached only by automobile, many suburban neighborhoods did not even include sidewalks; developers assumed that residents would seldom walk anywhere. The nature of the suburbs, in other words, encouraged families to turn inward, to focus their attention on the nuclear family unit.

For professional men (who tended to work at some distance from their homes, in the city), suburban life generally meant a rigid division between their working and personal worlds. For many middle-class

valued the presence of other nonworking mothers living nearby to share the tasks of child raising.

Another factor motivating white Americans to move to the suburbs was race. Most suburbs were restricted to white inhabitants—both because relatively few blacks could afford to live in them and because of formal and informal barriers to keep even affluent blacks out. As the black population of the nation's cities grew rapidly in the postwar years, and

women, it meant an increased isolation from the workplace. The enormous emphasis on family life of the 1950s created a particularly strong prejudice against women entering the professions, or occupying any paid job at all. Many husbands considered it demeaning for their wives to be employed; they feared it would be seen as a sign of their own inability to provide for their families. And many women themselves shied away from the workplace when they could afford to, in part because of new ideas about motherhood that seemed to require them to stay at home with their children.

One of the most influential books in postwar American life was a famous guide to child rearing: Dr. Benjamin Spock's *Baby and Child Care,* first published in 1946 and reissued repeatedly for years thereafter. Dr. Spock's approach to raising babies was child-centered, as opposed to the parent-centered theories of many previous child-care experts. The purpose of motherhood, he taught, was to help children learn and grow and realize their potential. All other considerations, including the mother's own physical and emotional requirements, must be subordinated to the needs of the child. Dr. Spock envisioned only a very modest role for fathers in the process of child rearing.

Affluent women, then, faced heavy pressures—both externally and internally imposed—to remain in the home and concentrate on raising their children. Many women, however, had to balance these pressures against other, contradictory ones. In a society that was increasingly coming to prize the accumulation of consumer goods as a badge of success, many middle-class families found that a second income was essential for the maintenance of the standard of living they desired. As a result, the number of married women working outside the home increased in the postwar years—even as the social pressure for them to stay out of the workplace grew. By 1960, nearly a third of all married women were part of the paid work force. Many of those, of course, were women from working-class families, whose incomes were often essential to family survival. But many were also middle-class women, working to supplement the family income to permit a more comfortable life style.

The experiences of the 1950s worked in some ways to diminish the power of feminism, which for a time ebbed to its lowest point in nearly a century. But they also helped create conditions that would only a decade later create the most powerful feminist movement in American history. The increasing num-

bers of women in the workplace laid the groundwork for demands for equal treatment that became an important part of the feminist crusades of the 1960s and 1970s. Some middle-class women who were not employed became deeply involved in the public world through work in such organizations as the League of Women Voters, the Red Cross, YWCAs, and PTAs, gaining organizational and political skills that they would later be able to use in more explicitly feminist causes. And the growing frustrations of other women, who remained in the home, created a heightened demand for female professional opportunities, a demand that would also soon help to fuel the women's liberation movement.

The Birth of Television

The postwar era witnessed the birth of perhaps the most powerful medium of mass communication in history: television. Experiments in broadcasting pictures (along with sound) over the airwaves had begun as early as the 1920s, but commercial television did not come into existence until shortly after World War II. It experienced a phenomenally rapid growth. In 1946, there were only 17,000 sets in the entire country; by 1953, two-thirds of all American homes had televisions; and by 1957, there were 40 million television sets in use—almost as many sets as there were families. More people had television sets, according to one report, than had refrigerators.

The television industry emerged directly out of the radio industry, and all three of the major networks—the National Broadcasting Company, the Columbia Broadcasting System, and the American Broadcasting Company—had begun their lives as radio companies. The television business, like radio, was driven by advertising. Programming decisions were made largely on the basis of how best to attract advertisers; and in the early days of television, sponsors often played a direct, powerful, and continuing role in determining the content of the programs they chose to sponsor. Many early television shows came to bear the names of the corporations that were paying for them: the "GE Television Theater," the "Chrysler Playhouse," the "Camel News Caravan," and others.

The impact of television on American life was rapid, pervasive, and profound. Television news had by the end of the 1950s replaced newspapers, magazines, and radios as the nation's most important vehicle of information. Television advertising exposed

Eisenhower and Dulles
Although President Eisenhower himself was a somewhat colorless television personality, his was the first administration to make extensive use of the new medium to promote its policies and dramatize its actions. The president's press conferences were frequently televised, and on several occasions Secretary of State John Foster Dulles reported to the president in front of the cameras. Dulles is shown here in the Oval Office on May 17, 1955, reporting on the occasion of his return from Europe, where he had signed the treaty restoring sovereignty to Austria. (AP/Wide World Photos)

the entire nation to new fashions and products. Televised sports events gradually made professional and college sports one of the important sources of entertainment (and one of the biggest businesses) in America. Television entertainment programming, almost all of it controlled by the three national networks (and their corporate sponsors), replaced movies and radio as the principal source of diversion for American families.

The content of television entertainment programming has been the object of widespread ridicule and contempt through much of its history. But whatever its quality, it has been undeniably important in reflecting and shaping social values and even political ideas. Much of the programming of the 1950s and early 1960s created a common image of American life—an image that was predominantly white,

middle-class, and suburban, an image epitomized by such popular situation comedies as *Ozzie and Harriet* and *Leave It to Beaver*. But television also conveyed other images: the gritty, urban working-class families in Jackie Gleason's *The Honeymooners;* the childless show-business family of the early *I Love Lucy;* the unmarried professional women in *Our Miss Brooks* and *My Little Margie*. Television not only sought to create an idealized image of a homogeneous suburban America; it also sought to convey experiences at odds with that image, but to convey them in warm, unthreatening terms. Throughout its history, the television entertainment industry has not so much avoided social diversity and cultural conflict as domesticated them, turned them into something benign and even comic.

Yet even if inadvertently, television also created

conditions that could accentuate social conflict. Even those unable to share in the affluence of the era could, through television, acquire a vivid picture of how the rest of their society lived. Thus, television ultimately became a force that, as it encouraged homogeneity among members of the white middle class, also contributed to the sense of alienation and powerlessness of groups excluded from the world it portrayed.

Science and Space

In 1961, *Time* magazine chose as its "man of the year," not a specific person but "the American Scientist." It was an indication of the widespread fascination with which Americans in the age of atomic weapons viewed science and technology. Major medical advances accounted for much of that fascination. In 1955, Jonas Salk's vaccine to prevent polio was made available to the public, free, by the federal government, and within a few years it had virtually eliminated polio from American life. Other dread diseases such as diphtheria and tuberculosis also all but vanished from society as new drugs and treatments were discovered. Infant mortality declined by nearly 50 percent in the first twenty-five years after the war; the death rate among young children declined significantly as well (although both such rates were lower in Western Europe). Average life expectancy in those same years rose by five years, to seventy-one.

The centrality of science in American life owed at least as much to other technological innovations—such as the jet plane, the computer, synthetics, and new types of commercially prepared foods. But nothing better illustrated the nation's veneration of scientific expertise than the popular enthusiasm for the American space program.

The program began in large part because of the Cold War. When the Soviet Union announced in 1957 that it had launched a satellite—*Sputnik*—into outer space, the United States reacted with shock and alarm. Strenuous efforts began—to improve scientific education in the schools, to develop more research laboratories, and above all, to speed the development of America's own exploration of outer space. The centerpiece of that exploration was the manned space program, established in 1958 with the selection of the first American space pilots. For several years, the original seven "astronauts" were the nation's most widely revered heroes. Millions of people sat by their television on May 5, 1961, as Alan Shepard became the first American launched into

space (several months after a Soviet "cosmonaut," Yuri Gagarin, had made a similar, if longer, flight). John Glenn, who on February 2, 1962, became the first American to orbit the globe (again, only after Gagarin had already done so), was soon an even more celebrated national idol. Yet for all the hero worship, Americans marveling at space exploration were reacting less to the individual men involved than to the enormous scientific effort that lay behind their exploits.

Ultimately, some Americans began to tire of the space program, which never managed to convince everyone that it offered any practical benefits. But interest remained high as late as the summer of 1969, when Neil Armstrong and Edwin Aldrin became the first men to walk on the surface of the moon. Not long after that, the government began to cut the funding for future missions. Even in leaner times, however, the space program continued to exercise a unique grip on the popular imagination. In the late 1970s and 1980s, the National Aeronautics and Space Administration (NASA) managed to revive some of the earlier enthusiasm for space exploration with the development of a reusable "space shuttle," which performed various commercial functions (such as launching communications satellites) as well as research and military ones. Early in 1986, an explosion destroyed one of the shuttles shortly after it took off. Seven astronauts died. The incident sparked a wave of national grief and anguish that made clear the degree to which the space program continued to embody some of the nation's most romantic hopes. It also stalled further development of the shuttle program.

Organized Society and Its Detractors

Even more than in the 1920s, Americans in the 1950s and 1960s were aware of the importance of organizations and bureaucracies in their lives. White-collar workers, who in the 1950s came to outnumber blue-collar laborers for the first time, found employment predominantly in corporate settings with rigid hierarchical structures. Industrial workers confronted ponderous bureaucracies in their own unions. Consumers discovered the frustrations of bureaucracy in dealing with the large national companies from whom they bought goods and services. More and more Americans were becoming convinced that the key to a successful future lay in acquiring the specialized training and skills necessary for work in large organizations, where every worker performed a particular, well-defined function.

The American educational system, in particular, began to respond to the demands of this increasingly organized society by experimenting with changes in curriculum and philosophy. Elementary and secondary schools gave increased attention to the teaching of science, mathematics, and foreign languages—all of which were believed to be important for the development of skilled, specialized professionals. The National Defense Education Act of 1958 (passed in response to the Soviet Union's *Sputnik* success) provided federal funding for development of programs in those areas. Universities in the meantime were expanding their curricula to provide more opportunities for students to develop specialized skills. The idea of the "multiversity"—a phrase first coined by the chancellor of the University of California at Berkeley to describe his institution's diversity—represented a commitment to making higher education a vehicle for training specialists in a wide variety of fields.

As in earlier eras, Americans reacted to these developments with ambivalence, often hostility. The debilitating impact of bureaucratic life on the individual slowly became one of the central themes of popular and scholarly debate. William H. Whyte, Jr., produced one of the most widely discussed books of the decade: *The Organization Man* (1956), which attempted to describe the special mentality of the worker in a large, bureaucratic setting. Self-reliance, Whyte claimed, was losing place to the ability to "get along" and "work as a team" as the most valuable trait in modern character. Sociologist David Riesman made similar observations in *The Lonely Crowd* (1950), in which he argued that the traditional "inner-directed" man, who judged himself on the basis of his own values and the esteem of his family, was giving way to a new "other-directed" man, more concerned with winning the approval of the larger organization or community. Even those who lived and worked outside bureaucratic settings, some critics argued, were subjected to the homogenizing pressures of a "mass culture," dominated by television and designed to appeal to the "lowest common denominator."

The most derisive critics of the culture of the affluent society were a number of young poets and writers generally known as the "beats" (or, by derisive critics, as "beatniks"). To them, the conventional society of the American middle class was a world to be avoided and despised. They wrote harsh critiques of the sterility and conformity of American life, the meaninglessness of American politics, and the banality of popular culture. Allen Ginsberg, one of the most celebrated of the beats, attracted wide acclaim with his dark, bitter poem *Howl* (1955), decrying the "Robot apartments! invincible suburbs! skeleton treasuries! blind capitals! demonic industries!" of modern life. Jack Kerouac, a talented novelist whose severe alcoholism and early death sharply limited his creative output, nevertheless produced what may have been the leading document of the Beat Generation: *On the Road* (1957)—an account of a cross-country automobile trip that depicted the rootless, iconoclastic life style of Kerouac and his friends.

Other, less starkly alienated writers also used their work to express misgivings about the enormity and impersonality of modern society. Saul Bellow produced a series of novels—*The Adventures of Augie March* (1953), *Seize the Day* (1956), *Herzog* (1964), and others—that chronicled the difficulties of modern, urban Jews in finding fulfillment in the dehumanizing environment in which they lived. J. D. Salinger, one of the most popular writers of the era, wrote in *The Catcher in the Rye* (1951) of the crushing impact of modern life on vulnerable, sensitive individuals. The novel described the dilemma of prep-school student Holden Caulfield, unable to find any area of society—school, family, friends, city—in which he could feel secure or committed. In the 1950s and early 1960s, such warnings remained relatively muted, as in the writings of Bellow and Salinger, or had only a limited impact on the culture at large, as with the work of Ginsberg and Kerouac. By the late 1960s, however, these concerns were becoming crucial to the creation of a widespread and at least briefly influential "counterculture."

The Other America

Middle-class Americans in the 1950s liked to believe that their growing prosperity was reaching virtually every area of society. It was not. Important groups continued to struggle on the fringes of the economic boom, unable to share in the abundance.

Between 1948 and 1956, while national income increased 50 percent, farm prices dropped 33 percent—the victim of enormous surpluses in basic staples. In 1948, farmers had received 8.9 percent of the national income; in 1956, they received only 4.1 percent. In part, this decline reflected the steadily shrinking farm population; in 1956 alone, one out of

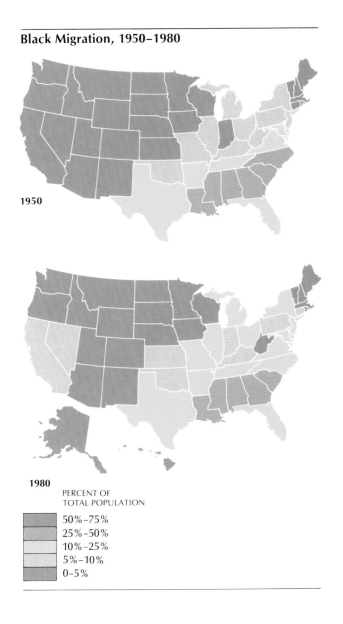

Black Migration, 1950–1980

1950

1980

PERCENT OF
TOTAL POPULATION

50%–75%
25%–50%
10%–25%
5%–10%
0–5%

Black ghettoes were expanding rapidly in the 1950s, as black farmers joined the general exodus from country to city and as the black population as a whole expanded rapidly. Continuing racial discrimination helped doom large proportions of these communities to ever-increasing poverty. In New York City, Los Angeles, and elsewhere, growing Puerto Rican, Mexican, and other Hispanic communities were also earning less than what the government considered the minimum necessary for "adequate" living.

Urban ghettoes were becoming so isolated from the economic mainstream that many of their residents were finding it almost impossible to obtain employment. Thus some "inner cities" were turning into virtual prisons for poor people, who had neither the resources to move to areas where jobs were more plentiful nor the political power to force development of their own communities. A similar predicament faced residents of several particularly destitute rural regions—most notably the Appalachian areas of the Southern and border states, which were experiencing an almost total economic collapse. Lacking adequate schools, health care, and services, the residents of Appalachia, like the residents of the urban ghettoes, were almost entirely shut off from the mainstream of American economic life. Not until the 1960s, when such exposés as Michael Harrington's *The Other America* (1962) began drawing attention to the continuing existence of poverty in the nation, did the middle class begin to recognize the seriousness of the problem.

The Rise of the Civil-Rights Movement

The prosperous 1950s helped produce a mood of cautious moderation among many Americans. On at least one issue, however, these years were a time in which a major social revolution commenced. After decades of skirmishes, there began in the 1950s an open battle against racial segregation and discrimination, a battle that would prove to be one of the longest and most difficult of the century.

The emergence of civil rights as a national issue was a slow and painful process, but it was speeded along its way by several important developments. The Cold War—and the pressures it created at home to remove social blights that might serve communist propaganda purposes—helped force many white

every eleven rural residents moved into or was absorbed by a city. But it also reflected the deteriorating economic condition of those farmers who remained in agriculture. They experienced not only a decline in their own income but a steady increase in the prices they paid for consumer goods.

Farmers, at least, were able to attract some public attention to their plight. Other, poorer groups languished in virtual obscurity. As middle-class Americans left the cities for the suburbs, it became easier for them to ignore the existence of severe poverty in the heart of the major industrial metropolises.

Americans to confront racial injustice with special urgency. The federal government—slowly, at times reluctantly—began moving into position to play a crucial role in fighting for civil rights, beginning in 1954 with one of the most important Supreme Court decisions in American history. The increasingly urban character of the black population sped the growth of black protest by creating large communities in which ideas and organizational efforts could expand. It was pressure from blacks themselves that was the crucial element in raising civil rights to prominence.

The Brown *Decision and "Massive Resistance"*

In 1954, years of patient legal efforts finally bore fruit when, on May 17, the Supreme Court announced its decision in the case of *Brown* v. *Board of Education of Topeka.* In considering the legal segregation of a Kansas public school system, the Court rejected the doctrine of the 1896 *Plessy* v. *Ferguson* decision, which had established that communities could provide blacks with separate facilities as long as the facilities were equal to those of whites.

The *Brown* decision was the culmination of many decades of effort by black opponents of segregation. Above all, perhaps, it was the result of efforts by a group of talented black lawyers, many of them trained at Howard University in Washington by the great legal educator Charles Houston. Thurgood Marshall, William Hastie, James Nabrit, and others (working under the aegis of the NAACP) spent years filing legal challenges to segregation in one state after another, nibbling at the edges of the system, exposing its weaknesses and contradictions, and accumulating precedents to support their assault on the "separate but equal" doctrine itself. It was these NAACP lawyers who filed the suits against the school boards of Topeka, Kansas, and several other cities that became the basis for the *Brown* decision.

The Topeka suit involved the case of a black girl who had to travel several miles to a black public school every day even though she lived virtually next door to a white elementary school. When the case finally arrived before the Supreme Court, the justices examined it not simply in terms of legal precedent but in terms of history, sociology, and psychology. And they concluded that school segregation inflicted unacceptable damage on those it affected, regardless of the relative quality of the separate schools. Chief Justice Earl Warren explained the unanimous opinion of his colleagues: "We conclude that in the field of public education the doctrine of 'separate but equal' has no place. Separate educational facilities are inherently unequal."

The original decision offered no guidance as to how desegregation was to be accomplished, and the justices apparently believed that any such change would have to be accomplished gradually. The following year, they issued another decision (known as "*Brown* II") to provide rules for the implementation of the 1954 order. They ruled that communities must work to desegregate their schools "with all deliberate speed," but they set no timetable and left specific decisions up to lower courts.

It was not to be an easy process. In some communities, compliance came relatively quickly and relatively painlessly, as in Washington, D.C. More often, however, strong local opposition (what came to be known in the South as "massive resistance") produced long delays and bitter conflicts. Some school districts ignored the ruling altogether. Others attempted to circumvent it with purely token efforts to integrate. The "pupil placement laws" that many school districts enacted allowed school officials to place students in schools according to their scholastic abilities and social behavior. Such laws were transparent devices for maintaining segregation; but in 1958, the Supreme Court (in *Shuttlesworth* v. *Birmingham Board of Education*) refused to declare them unconstitutional.

Southern politicians encouraged the growth of massive resistance. More than 100 Southern members of Congress signed a "manifesto" in 1956 denouncing the *Brown* decision and urging their constituents to defy it. Southern governors sometimes blocked sincere efforts by local officials to implement desegregation. Local school boards themselves occasionally took drastic action; in one county in Virginia, the school board simply closed public schools for several years rather than accede to court-ordered desegregation. White citizens' councils grew up in many Southern communities to place pressure on local officials (and parents) to resist the courts.

By the fall of 1957, only 684 of 3,000 affected school districts in the South had even begun to desegregate their schools. In those that had complied, white resistance often produced angry mob actions and other violence. Many white parents simply withdrew their children from the public schools and enrolled them in all-white "segregation academies," some of them poorly staffed and equipped. The *Brown* decision, far from ending segregation,

**Rosa Parks in
the Front of the Bus**
In December 1955 Rosa Parks was arrested in Montgomery, Alabama, for
refusing to obey a law that required
her to give up her seat to a white passenger and move to the back of the
bus. Her defiance sparked an almost
total boycott of Montgomery's transit
system by black citizens. Just over a
year later, the U.S. Supreme Court
ruled that racial segregation of public
transit systems was unconstitutional,
and Mrs. Parks proudly posed for photographers sitting near the front of a
city bus. (UPI/Bettmann Newsphotos)

launched a prolonged battle between federal authority and state and local governments. In the years to
come, federal courts would have to play an ever-
increasing role in public education to ensure compliance with the desegregation rulings. And the
executive branch, whose responsibility it was to enforce the decisions of the courts, found itself frequently pitted against local authorities attempting to
defy the law.

The first such confrontation occurred in September 1957 in Little Rock, Arkansas. The courts had
ordered the desegregation of that city's Central High
School. Governor Orval Faubus, a rabid and ambitious segregationist, ordered the National Guard to
intervene to stop it. Faubus finally called off the
Guard in response to the orders of a federal judge; but
an angry mob quickly took its place in blocking integration of the school. Faced with this open defiance
of federal authority (and with real danger to the safety
of the black students involved), President Eisenhower finally responded by sending federal troops to
Little Rock to restore order and ensure that the court
orders would be obeyed. Central High School admitted its first black students; but controversy continued to plague the Little Rock school system for
several years.

Eisenhower was a reluctant convert to the

civil-rights cause. He had greeted the 1954 *Brown*
decision with open skepticism (and once said it had
set back progress on race relations by "at least fifteen years"). He had hoped not to have to intervene
on behalf of such a controversial issue. But events
in Little Rock forced his hand. Faubus's use of the
state National Guard to resist enforcement of a federal court order, and his subsequent refusal to protect the safety of citizens exercising their rights, was
too direct a threat to constitutional law for the president to ignore.

The Expanding Movement

The legal assault on school segregation was only one
part of the war against racial discrimination in the
1950s. The *Brown* decision helped spark a growing
number of popular challenges to segregation in one
community after another. The first and most celebrated occurred in Montgomery, Alabama. On December 1, 1955, Rosa Parks, a black woman, was
arrested when she refused to give up her seat on a
Montgomery bus to a white passenger (as required
by the Jim Crow laws that regulated race relations in
the city and throughout most of the South). Parks,
who had been active for years within the black com-

munity as an advocate of civil rights, had apparently decided spontaneously to resist the order to move. Her feet were tired, she later explained. The arrest of this admired woman produced outrage in the city's black community, which organized a successful boycott of the bus system to demand an end to segregated seating.

The bus boycott was one of the first examples of a black community mobilizing itself en masse to resist segregation. It owed much of its success to the prior existence of a number of well-organized black citizens' groups committed to advancing the cause of racial justice. A black women's political caucus had, in fact, been developing plans for some time for a boycott of the segregated buses and had, along with other local civil rights leaders, been looking for an incident they could use to challenge the law. Rosa Parks was not the first black woman to defy the law; but she was, community leaders decided, the best suited to serve as a symbol of the movement.

Once launched, the boycott was almost completely effective. Black workers who needed to commute to their jobs (the largest group of which consisted of female domestic servants) formed car pools to ride back and forth to work, or simply walked, even at times over long distances. The boycott put economic pressure not only on the bus company (a private concern) but on many Montgomery merchants. The bus boycotters found it difficult to get to downtown stores and tended to shop instead in their own neighborhoods. Even so, the boycott might well have failed had it not been for a Supreme Court decision in 1955, inspired in part by the protest, that declared segregation in public transportation to be illegal. The buses in Montgomery abandoned their discriminatory seating policies, and the boycott came to a close.

The most important accomplishments of the Montgomery boycott were probably less its immediate victories than its success in establishing a new form of racial protest and, perhaps above all, in elevating to prominence a new figure in the movement for civil rights. The man chosen to lead the boycott movement once it was launched was a local Baptist pastor, Martin Luther King, Jr., son of a prominent Atlanta minister and the possessor of an oratorical power and leadership ability that even he had not previously suspected. King was reluctant at first to accept the leadership of the movement. He was new in Montgomery and feared that he would be seen as an outsider. But once he accepted the role, he became consumed by it. His life would never again be the same.

King's approach to black protest was based on the doctrine of nonviolence—that is, of passive resistance even in the face of direct assaults by white segregationists. He drew from the teachings of Mahatma Gandhi, the legendary Indian nationalist leader, whose life he had studied while a student in Boston; from Henry David Thoreau, and his doctrine of civil disobedience; and from Christian dogma. And he produced an approach to racial struggle that captured the moral high ground for the members of his race in a way that made it increasingly difficult for most white Americans to support his opponents. He urged blacks to engage in peaceful demonstrations; to allow themselves to be arrested, even beaten, if necessary; and to respond to hate with love. King's unparalleled rhetorical talents ensured that his message would be widely heard. And for the next thirteen years—as leader of the Southern Christian Leadership Conference, an interracial group he founded shortly after the bus boycott—he would be the most influential and most widely admired black leader in the country. After his tragic death in 1968, King became a revered hero, first to American blacks and gradually to most of the nation. In the 1980s, his birthday became a national holiday—making him the only American other than George Washington and Abraham Lincoln to be so honored.

Pressure from the courts, from Northern liberals, and from blacks themselves also speeded the pace of racial change in other areas. As early as 1947, one important color line had been breached when the Brooklyn Dodgers signed the great Jackie Robinson as the first black to play major-league baseball. By the mid-1950s, blacks had established themselves as a powerful force in almost all professional sports. Within the government, President Eisenhower completed the integration of the armed forces, attempted to desegregate the federal work force, and in 1957 signed a civil-rights act (passed, without active support from the White House, by a Democratic Congress) providing federal protection for blacks who wished to register to vote. It was a weak bill, with few mechanisms for enforcement; but it was the first civil-rights bill of any kind to win passage since the end of Reconstruction, and it served as a signal that the executive and legislative branches were beginning to join the judiciary in the federal commitment to the "Second Reconstruction."

Eisenhower Republicanism

It was appropriate, perhaps, that Dwight D. Eisenhower, a man who had risen to prominence as a great military leader, should preside over an era in which the American people were preoccupied with international tensions. And it was fitting, too, that this essentially conservative man, who enjoyed the company of wealthy business executives, should serve as president in a period when most Americans wanted nothing so much as a lasting stabilization of their newly prosperous economy. It should not have been surprising, therefore, that Eisenhower, the least experienced politician to serve in the White House in the twentieth century, was nevertheless among the most politically successful presidents of the postwar era. At home, he pursued essentially moderate policies, avoiding most new initiatives but accepting the work of earlier reformers. Abroad, he continued and even intensified American commitments to oppose communism but brought to some of those commitments a measure of restraint that his successors did not always match.

A Business Government

The first Republican administration in twenty years staffed itself with men drawn from the same quarter as those who had staffed Republican administrations in the 1920s: the business community. But the apparent similarities to the "New Era" governments are misleading, for much of the American business community had acquired a very different social and political outlook by the 1950s from that of their predecessors of earlier decades. Above all, many of the nation's leading businessmen and financiers had reconciled themselves to at least the broad outlines of the Keynesian welfare state the New Deal had launched and, indeed, had come to see it as something that actually benefited them—by helping maintain social order, by increasing mass purchasing power, and by stabilizing labor relations.

To his cabinet the president appointed a leading corporation lawyer (Secretary of State John Foster Dulles), the president of General Motors (Defense Secretary Charles E. Wilson), the head of a major financial firm (Treasury Secretary George Humphrey), a New England manufacturer, two automobile distributors, a farm marketing executive, and other wealthy corporate figures. Only Secretarty of

Labor Martin P. Durkin, president of the plumbers' union, stood apart. "Eight millionaires and a plumber," the *New Republican* caustically remarked. Members of the new administration were not apologetic about their backgrounds. Charles Wilson assured senators considering his confirmation that he foresaw no conflict of interest because he was certain that "what was good for our country was good for General Motors, and vice versa." But missing from most members of this business-oriented administration was the deep hostility to "government interference" that had so dominated corporate attitudes three decades before.

Eisenhower's leadership style, which stressed delegation of authority to subordinates, helped enhance the power of his cabinet officers and others. Secretary of State John Foster Dulles was widely believed to be running American foreign policy almost single-handedly (although subsequently released evidence made it clear that the president was far more deeply involved in international decisions than was often apparent at the time). Treasury Secretary Humphrey and Defense Secretary Wilson enjoyed wide latitude in imposing their own standards of stringency on federal fiscal policy and defense spending. The president's White House chief of staff, former New Hampshire governor Sherman Adams, exercised broad authority over relations with Congress and strictly controlled access to the president. (Late in the Eisenhower presidency, he left office in disgrace after he was discovered to have accepted gifts from a wealthy businessman, presumably in exchange for official favors).

The inclination of the Eisenhower government to limit federal activities and encourage private enterprise received clear illustration in its policies toward government power development. The president referred to the Tennessee Valley Authority in 1953 as an example of "creeping socialism" and once talked wistfully of selling "the whole thing" (although he made no effort to do so). He supported the private rather than public development of natural resources. Throughout his administration, he opposed federal public works projects in favor of private ventures.

Eisenhower moved in other areas as well to limit government involvement in the economy. To the chagrin of farmers, he lowered federal support for farm prices. He also removed the last limited wage and price controls maintained by the Truman administration. He opposed the creation of new social service programs such as national health insurance (although he did support a bill to underwrite private insurance programs, a bill that never passed). He strove constantly to reduce federal expenditures (even during the recession of 1958) and balance the budget. He ended 1960, his last full year in office, with a $1 billion surplus.

The Survival of Social Welfare

Eisenhower's philosophy of "dynamic conservatism," as he termed it, may not have been hospitable to new social programs. But it did permit the survival, and even on occasion the expansion, of some existing ones. The president resisted pressure from the right wing of his party to dismantle those welfare policies of the New Deal that had survived the conservative assaults of the war years and after. During his term, a Republican Congress agreed to extend the Social Security system to an additional 10 million people and unemployment compensation to an additional 4 million people. The minimum hourly wage increased from 75 cents to $1. And the president supported the combination of existing federal education and social welfare programs in the new Department of Health, Education, and Welfare, which began its life in 1953.

In economic terms, the most significant legislative accomplishment of the Eisenhower administration was the Federal Highway Act of 1956, which launched a government program of vast dimensions. It authorized $25 billion for a ten-year building effort to construct over 40,000 miles of interstate highways; the program was to be funded through a highway "trust fund," which would raise revenues through a new tax on the purchase of fuel, automobiles, trucks, and tires. The cost of the program would ultimately expand far beyond that figure and would have a major impact—both directly and indirectly—in spurring economic growth.

That Eisenhower did not launch a stronger assault on existing social programs and that he actually supported some liberal reforms and spending programs resulted partly from political realities. During his first two years in office, although Congress was nominally under Republican control, a coalition of Democrats and liberal Republicans limited the freedom of conservatives to act. And from 1954 to the end of Eisenhower's years in office (indeed, until 1980), both houses of Congress remained securely in Democratic hands.

Not even Eisenhower's personal popularity was sufficient to bring his party back to power in Congress. In 1956, Eisenhower ran for a second term, even though he had suffered a serious heart attack the previous year. With Adlai Stevenson opposing him once again, he won by another, even greater landslide, receiving nearly 57 percent of the popular vote and 442 electoral votes to Stevenson's 89. Still, Democrats retained control of both houses of Congress. And in 1958—on the heels of a serious recession—they increased that control by substantial margins. The American people had endorsed Eisenhower's inclination to moderate the reforming zeal of earlier years, to "hold the line." But they were not ready, apparently, to accept the belief of others in his party that the nation should adopt an even more militantly conservative policy.

The Decline of McCarthyism

The Eisenhower administration did little in its first years in office to discourage the anticommunist furor that had gripped the nation. Indeed, it helped to sustain it. The president actually intensified the already much abused hunt for subversives in the government, which Truman had begun several years earlier. More than 2,220 federal employees resigned or were dismissed as a result of security investigations. Among them were most of the leading Asian experts in the State Department, many of whom were harried from office because they had shown inadequate enthusiasm for the now exiled regime of Chiang Kai-shek. Their absence was later to prove costly, as the government expanded its commitments in Asia without sufficient knowledge of the political realities within the region.

Among the most celebrated controversies of the first year of the new administration was the case of J. Robert Oppenheimer, director of the Manhattan Project during the war and one of the nation's most distinguished and admired physicists. Although Oppenheimer was now out of government service, he continued as a consultant to the Atomic Energy Commission. But he had angered some officials by his public opposition to development of the new, more powerful hydrogen bomb. In 1953, the FBI distributed a dossier within the administration detailing Oppenheimer's prewar association with various left-wing groups. The president responded by ordering a "blank wall" to be placed between Oppenheimer and government secrets. A federal investigation, requested by Oppenheimer himself and conducted in an inflamed and confused atmo-

COMMUNIST PARTY ORGANIZATION U.S.A-FEB. 9,1950

The Army-McCarthy Hearings

Senator Joseph McCarthy uses a map to show the supposed distribution of communists throughout the United States during the televised 1954 Senate hearings to mediate the dispute between McCarthy and the U.S. Army. Joseph Welch, chief counsel for the army, remains conspicuously unimpressed. (UPI/Bettmann Newsphotos)

sphere, confirmed the decision to deny him a security clearance. The episode deeply embittered much of the scientific community and caused a major public outcry.

The strong opposition to the persecution of Oppenheimer was one indication that the anticommunist hysteria of the early 1950s was beginning to abate. A more important signal of the change was the political demise of Senator Joseph McCarthy. McCarthy continued during the first year of the Eisenhower administration to operate with almost total impunity. The president, who privately loathed him, nevertheless refused to speak out in public. "I will not get into the gutter with that guy," he reportedly explained. But McCarthy finally overreached himself in January 1954 when he began launching oblique attacks against the president and a direct assault on Secretary of the Army Robert Stevens and the armed services in general. In the face of McCarthy's provocative accusations, the administration and influential members of Congress decided together that no

choice remained but to stage a special investigation of the charges. They became known as the Army-McCarthy hearings, and they were among the first congressional hearings to be nationally televised. The result was devastating to McCarthy. Day after day, the public watched McCarthy in action—bullying witnesses, hurling groundless (and often cruel) accusations, evading issues, and offering churlish objections at every point. He began to appear less a hero than a villain, and ultimately less that than a mere buffoon. In December 1954, the Senate voted 67 to 22 to condemn him for "conduct unbecoming a senator." Three years later, with little public support left, he died—a victim, apparently, of complications arising from his serious alcoholism.

The Supreme Court, in the meantime, was also beginning to restrict the official harassment of suspected "subversives." Many people had expected the Court to become more conservative once the new president began to appoint new members. In fact, quite the opposite occurred. In 1953, Eisenhower nominated the former Republican governor of California, Earl Warren, to be the new chief justice. And to the surprise of many, including Eisenhower, Warren became the moving force behind the most strenuous judicial effort to protect and expand civil liberties in the nation's history. (See below, pp. 943–944). In 1957, the Warren Court limited the FBI's latitude in using secret evidence against an opponent. More important, that same year it struck down the Smith Act, ruling that it was not a crime to urge the overthrow of the government unless a person was directly inciting illegal actions. The following year, the Court forbade the State Department to deny passports to members of the Communist party.

Eisenhower, Dulles, and the Cold War

A strong undercurrent of anxiety tinged the domestic events of the Eisenhower years, for Americans were well aware throughout the affluent 1950s how dangerous was the world in which they lived. Above all, they were aware of the horrors of a possible nuclear war, as both the United States and the Soviet Union began to make atomic weapons more and more central to their foreign policies. Yet the nuclear threat had another effect as well. With the costs of war now so enormous, both superpowers began to edge away from direct confrontations. Increasingly, the attention of the United States began to turn to the rapidly escalating instability in the nations of the Third World.

Dulles and "Massive Retaliation"

Eisenhower's secretary of state, and (except for the president himself) the dominant figure in the nation's foreign policy in the 1950s, was John Foster Dulles, an aristocratic corporate lawyer with a stern moral revulsion to communism. A deeply religious man, Dulles detested the atheistic dogmas of Marxism; a man closely tied to the nation's financial establishment, he feared the communist challenge to world free enterprise. He entered office denouncing the containment policies of the Truman years as excessively passive, arguing that the United States should pursue an active program of "liberation," which would lead to a "rollback" of communist expansion. Once in power, however, he had to defer to the far more moderate views of the president himself. Dulles began, instead, to develop a new set of doctrines that reflected the impact of nuclear weapons on the world.

The most prominent of those doctrines was the policy of "massive retaliation," which Dulles announced early in 1954. The United States would, he explained, respond to communist threats to its allies not by using conventional forces in local conflicts (a policy that had led to so much frustration in Korea) but by relying on "the deterrent of massive retaliatory power . . . a great capacity to retaliate instantly, by means and at times of our choosing." He left little doubt that the retaliation he was envisioning was a nuclear one. The new doctrine reflected in part Dulles's inclination for tense confrontations, an approach he once defined as "brinksmanship"—pushing the Soviet Union to the brink of war in order to exact concessions. But the greater force behind the massive retaliation policy was economics. With pressure growing both in and out of government for a reduction in American military expenditures, an increasing reliance on atomic weapons seemed to promise, as some advocates put it, "more bang for the buck." Many argued further that smaller, so-called tactical nuclear weapons could replace conventional forces even in limited wars. The "new look" in American defense policy seemed at first to please almost everyone. It maintained the national commitment (and, its advocates argued, the national ability) to counter communist expansion throughout the world. Yet it did so at greatly reduced cost, satisfying those who were demanding new efforts to balance the budget.

At the same time, Dulles intensified the efforts of Truman and Acheson to "integrate" the entire noncommunist world into a system of mutual defense pacts. During his years in office, he logged almost 500,000 miles in foreign travels to cement new alliances that were modeled on NATO—but that were, without exception, far weaker than the European pact. By the end of the decade, the United States had become a party to almost a dozen such treaties in all areas of the world. In Southeast Asia, there was the SEATO alliance, which included Thailand and the Philippines but few other Asian nations. In the Middle East, there was the Baghdad Pact, soon renamed the CENTO alliance (for Central Treaty Organization), which tied the United States to Turkey, Pakistan, Iraq, and Iran. Other, smaller agreements pledged American aid to additional areas.

Challenges in Asia

What had been the most troubling foreign policy concern of the Truman years—the war in Korea—plagued the Eisenhower administration only briefly. The new president did indeed "go to Korea" as he had promised in his campaign—visiting briefly in the months between the election and his inauguration. But peace came as a result of other things, primarily a softening of both the American and communist positions. On July 27, 1953, negotiators at Panmunjom finally signed an agreement ending the hostilities. Each antagonist was to withdraw its troops a mile and a half from the existing battle line, which ran roughly along the 38th parallel, the prewar border between North and South Korea. A conference in Geneva was to consider means by which to reunite the nation peacefully—although in fact the 1954 meeting produced no agreement and left the cease-fire line as the apparently permanent border between the two countries.

In the meantime, however, American attention was being drawn to problems in other parts of Asia. There was, first, continuing pressure on the administration from the so-called China lobby, or "Asia firsters," who insisted on active American efforts to restore Chiang Kai-shek to the Chinese mainland. Such demands were wholly unrealistic. Chiang had nothing approaching sufficient military strength to launch an effective invasion. Even had he been able to muster the forces, he would have found virtually no popular following within China itself. Nevertheless, the administration continued to supply him with weapons and other assistance.

Almost simultaneously, the United States was becoming drawn into a long, bitter struggle in Southeast Asia. Ever since the end of World War II, France had been attempting to restore its authority over Vietnam, its one-time colony, which it had had to abandon to the Japanese during World War II. Opposing the French, however, were the powerful nationalist forces of Ho Chi Minh, determined to win independence for their nation.

Much of the later controversy over American involvement in Vietnam centered on the question of Ho Chi Minh's intentions and commitments. At the end of World War II, Ho had appealed to the United States on several occasions for support but had received no reply. Some Americans have argued that Ho was eager at that point to develop a close relationship with the United States and that the Truman administration squandered the opportunity. But

whatever Ho's views of the United States in 1945, he was then, as he had been for many years, a communist; he had been trained in Moscow, and his commitment to Marxism appears to have been genuine and important to him. At least equally important, however, was Ho's nationalism. He believed in an independent and united Vietnam, and that goal, at least, he was never willing to compromise.

By 1954, Ho was receiving substantial aid from communist China and the Soviet Union. America, in the meantime, had been paying most of France's war costs since 1950 (largely because of fears of Ho's communist connections). A crisis emerged in early 1954 when 12,000 French troops became surrounded in a disastrous siege at the city of Dienbienphu, which they were incapable of defending. Only American intervention, it was clear, could prevent the total collapse of the French military effort.

Eisenhower spoke out strongly about the importance of preserving a "free" Vietnam, using the analogy once employed by Acheson of a row of dominoes. If Vietnam fell to communism, he implied, the rest of Asia would soon follow. Yet despite the urgings of Secretary of State Dulles, Vice President Nixon, and others, Eisenhower refused to permit direct American military intervention in Vietnam, claiming that neither Congress nor America's other allies would support such action. In fact, Eisenhower seemed to sense how difficult and costly such intervention would be.

Without American aid, the French defense of Dienbienphu finally collapsed on May 7, 1954; and France quickly agreed to a settlement of the conflict at a conference in Geneva that summer. The Geneva accords of July 1954, to which the United States was not a party, established a supposedly temporary division of Vietnam along the 17th parallel. The north would be governed by Ho Chi Minh, the south by a pro-Western regime. Democratic elections would serve as the basis for uniting the nation in 1956. The agreement marked the effective end of the French commitment to Vietnam, but it became the basis for an expanded American presence. Realizing that Ho Chi Minh would win any election in Vietnam, Eisenhower and Dulles decided almost immediately that they could not accept the agreement. Instead, they helped establish a pro-American government in the south, headed by Ngo Dinh Diem, a wealthy, corrupt member of his country's Roman Catholic minority. Diem, it was clear from the start, would not permit elections. He felt secure in his refusal because the United States had promised to provide him

The Nation of Israel, 1948
David Ben Gurion, the first prime minister of the newly created nation of Israel (standing at left center, wearing a jacket), accepts a salute on the docks at Haifa as the last British troops prepare to leave. British soldiers had been a presence in Palestine since 1907. After their departure, Israel built up its own military strength for its long, bitter struggle with Palestinian Arabs for control of the historically contested land. (UPI/Bettmann Newsphotos)

with ample military assistance against any attack from the north. (There is some evidence that the Soviet Union, eager to avoid a confrontation with the United States at this point, was at the same time pressuring Ho and his regime not to press for an election.)

Crises in the Middle East

The redirection of America's international attention toward the problems of the Third World and its growing preoccupation with threats of communism there (threats both real and imagined) were nowhere more clearly illustrated than in the Middle East. The region was a volatile and important one for two reasons: Israel and oil.

The establishment of a Jewish state in Palestine had been the dream of a powerful Zionist movement that had gained strength in many parts of the world for more than half a century before World War II. The plight of the hundreds of thousands of homeless Jews uprooted by the war, and the international outrage that followed revelations of the Holocaust, gave new strength to Zionist demands in the late 1940s. Palestine had been a British protectorate since the end of World War I; and in deference to local Arab opposition, the British after 1945 had attempted to limit Jewish immigration there. But despite the British efforts to stop them, Jews had come to Palestine in such enormous numbers that they could not be ignored.

Finally, Britain brought the problem to the United Nations, which responded by recommending the partition of Palestine into a Jewish and an Arab state. On May 14, 1948, the British mandate ended, and Jews proclaimed the existence of the nation of Israel. President Truman recognized the new government the following day, thus effectively blocking a UN proposal to keep the area under a temporary trusteeship. But the creation of Israel was only the beginning of the battle for a Jewish homeland. Palestinian Arabs, unwilling to accept being displaced from what they considered their own country, fought determinedly against the new state in 1948—the first of several Arab–Israeli wars. And the United States found itself with a new ally whose survival would require years of extensive American aid.

The interest of the United States in the Middle East involved much more than its strong support of Israel. America was also concerned about the stability and friendliness of the Arab regimes in the area. The reason was simple: The region contained the richest oil reserves in the world, reserves in which American companies had already invested heavily, reserves on which the health of the American (and world) economy would ultimately come to depend. Thus the United States reacted with alarm as it watched Mohammed Mossadegh, the nationalist prime minister of Iran, begin to resist the presence of Western corporations in his nation. In 1951, he ordered the seizure of Iran's oil wells from the British companies that had been developing them. During the next two years, American observers began to claim that Mossadegh was becoming friendly with the Soviet Union. In 1953, the American Central Intelligence Agency (CIA) joined forces with conservative Iranian military leaders to engineer a coup that drove Mossadegh from office. To replace him, the United States favored elevating the young Shah of Iran, Mohammed Reza Pahlevi, from his position as a token constitutional monarch to that of a virtually absolute ruler. In return, the Shah allowed American companies to share in the development of Iranian oil reserves; and he remained closely tied to the United States for the next twenty-five years, even as his regime was becoming increasingly despotic and unpopular.

American policy was less effective in dealing with the nationalist government of Egypt, under the leadership of General Gamal Abdel Nasser. Nasser pressured the British in 1954 to remove their remaining troops from his country, an effort the United States accepted and even assisted. But Dulles and other policymakers were less willing to tolerate Nasser's flirtations with the Soviet Union, which took the form of Soviet shipments of armaments in return for Egyptian cotton. To punish Nasser for his transgressions, Dulles suddenly withdrew American offers of assistance in building the great Aswan Dam across the Nile. A week later, Nasser retaliated by seizing control of the Suez Canal from the British, saying that he would use the income from it to build the dam himself.

On October 29, 1956, Israeli forces struck a preemptive blow against Egypt; and the British and French followed the next day by landing troops to drive the Egyptians from the canal. Dulles and Eisenhower reacted with alarm, fearing that the Suez crisis would drive the Arab states toward the Soviet Union and precipitate a new world war. By refusing to support the Suez invasion, and by joining in a United Nations denunciation of it, the United States helped pressure the French and British to withdraw. When Egypt and Israel agreed to a cease-fire, a precarious truce was in place. In the following years, just as Dulles had feared, the government of Egypt turned to the Soviet Union for assistance, accepting Russian financing of the Aswan Dam and giving the Soviets an important (if temporary) foothold in the Middle East.

In Washington, the president responded in 1957 by enunciating the so-called Eisenhower Doctrine, which proclaimed that the United States would offer economic and military aid "to secure and protect the territorial independence" of Middle Eastern nations "against overt armed aggression from any nation controlled by international communism." In practice, that meant more than simply opposing Soviet aggression. It meant working to prevent the spread of pan-Arab nationalism: Nasser's efforts to unite all the Arab states into a single nation, in which he would be the dominant force. Egypt and Syria merged to form the United Arab Republic in February 1958, causing modest concern in Washington. But that concern soon turned to alarm as pan-Arab forces began to challenge the pro-Western governments of Lebanon, Jordan, and Iraq. The United States could do little about Iraq, which fell under the control of a pro-Nasser military government in July (although only temporarily). But in Lebanon and Jordan, the situation was different. At the request of the embattled Beirut government, Eisenhower ordered 5,000 American marines to land on the beaches of Lebanon in mid-July 1958; British troops entered Jordan at about the same time. The effect of the interventions was negligible. The governments of both countries managed to stabilize their positions on their own, and within months both the American and British forces withdrew.

Latin America and "Yankee Imperialism"

Similar difficulties were arising in an area important to, but generally neglected by, American foreign policy: Latin America. American economic interests in the region were vast; in some countries, United States corporations were the dominant force in the economy. The United States government, in the meantime, had all but abandoned even the limited initiatives of Franklin Roosevelt's Good Neighbor Policy and was sending most of its foreign aid to Europe and Asia rather than to Latin America.

Animosity toward the United States, therefore, grew steadily during the 1950s, as many Latin Americans began to regard the influence of United States business in their countries as an insidious form of imperialism. Some nationalists in the region had once believed that the United States would support popular efforts to overthrow undemocratic governments. But in 1954, the Eisenhower administration suggested otherwise when it ordered the CIA to help topple the new, leftist government of Jacobo Arbenz Guzman in Guatemala, a regime that Dulles (responding to the entreaties of the United Fruit Company, a major investor in Guatemala fearful of

Fidel Castro
After a long struggle in the Cuban countryside, Castro's rebel forces marched toward Havana in the last days of 1958 and, as the government of Fulgencio Batista fled the country, seized control of the capital city on New Year's Day, 1959. Castro is shown here shortly before he led his troops into Havana.   (UPI/Bettmann Newsphotos)

Arbenz) argued was potentially communist. Four years later, the depths of anti-American sentiment became clear when Vice President Richard Nixon visited the region, to be greeted in city after city by angry, hostile, occasionally dangerous mobs.

Americans were shocked by the outburst of animosity, and the administration began hasty, belated efforts to improve relations with its neighbors. But the legacy of more than fifty years of casual exploitation of Latin America was too strong to prevent the rise of other nationalist movements hostile to the United States. No nation in the region had been more closely tied to America than Cuba. Its leader, Fulgenico Batista, had ruled as a military dictator since 1952, when with American assistance, he had toppled a more moderate government. Cuba's economy (generally a relatively prosperous one) had become a virtual fiefdom of American corporations, which controlled almost all the island's natural resources and had cornered over half of the vital sugar crop. Be-

ginning in 1957, a popular movement of resistance to the Batista regime began to gather power under the leadership of Fidel Castro. By late 1958, the Batista forces were in almost total disarry. And on January 1, 1959, with Batista now in exile in Spain (having taken millions of dollars in government funds along with him), Castro marched into Havana and established a new government.

Despite its long support of the Batista government, the United States had long been vaguely embarrassed by its ties to that corrupt regime. At first, therefore, Americans reacted warmly to Castro, particularly since there was little evidence that he was tied to any communist elements. But once Castro began implementing drastic policies of land reform and expropriating foreign-owned businesses and resources, Cuban-American relations rapidly deteriorated.

The new government was causing particular concern to Eisenhower and Dulles by its growing interest in communist ideas and tactics. When Castro began accepting assistance from the Soviet Union in 1960, the United States cut back the "quota" by which Cuba could export sugar to America at a favored price. Early in 1961, as one of its last acts, the Eisenhower administration severed diplomatic relations with Castro. The American CIA had already begun secretly training Cuban expatriates for an invasion of the island to topple the new regime. Isolated by the United States, Castro soon cemented a close and lasting alliance with the Soviet Union.

Europe and the Soviet Union

The problems of the Third World would soon become the central focus of American foreign policy. Through most of the 1950s, however, the United States remained chiefly concerned with its direct relationship with the Soviet Union and with the possibility of communist expansion in Europe. The massive retaliation doctrine was the first American effort to deter such expansion. The rearming of West Germany was another. Beginning in 1954, the West German government began to develop its first armed forces since the end of World War II; and in 1957, the first German forces joined NATO, making the nation a full military ally of the United States.

In the meantime, however, many Americans continued to hope that the United States and the Soviet Union would be able to negotiate solutions to some of their remaining problems. Such hopes were buoyed when, after the death of Stalin in 1953, signs began to emerge of a new Russian attitude of conciliation. The Soviet Union extended a peace overture to the rebellious Tito government in Yugoslavia; it returned a military base to Finland; it signed a peace treaty with Japan; and it agreed at last to terminate its long military occupation of Austria (which, like Germany, had been partitioned into four zones of occupation by the Allies at the end of World War II), allowing that nation to become an independent, neutral state. Pressure for negotiation intensified when, in 1953–1954, both the United States and the Soviet Union successfully tested the new hydrogen bomb, a nuclear device of vastly greater power than those developed during the war. These factors seemed briefly to bear fruit in 1955, when Eisenhower and other NATO leaders met with the Soviet premier, Nicolai Bulganin, at a cordial summit conference in Geneva. But when a subsequent conference of foreign ministers met to try to resolve specific issues, the "spirit of Geneva" quickly dissolved, as neither side could agree to the terms of the other.

Relations between the Soviet Union and the West soured further in 1956 in response to the Hungarian Revolution. Inspired by riots in Poland a year earlier, Hungarian dissidents had launched a great popular uprising in November of that year to demand democratic reforms. For several days, they had control of the Hungarian government. But before the month was out, Soviet tanks and troops entered Budapest to crush the uprising and restore an orthodox, pro-Soviet regime. The United States had encouraged the uprising (through broadcasts over its Radio Free Europe network and other means), and some Hungarians had come to expect American intervention on their behalf. The Eisenhower administration, however, refused to risk a direct confrontation with the Soviets in what it had long ago implicitly conceded was their "sphere of influence." The suppression of the uprising convinced many American leaders that Soviet policies had not softened as much as the events of the previous two years had at times suggested.

The failure of conciliation brought renewed vigor to the Cold War. It not only helped produce tensions between the superpowers in the Third World; it also spurred a vastly increased Soviet–American arms race. Both nations engaged in extensive nuclear testing in the atmosphere, causing alarm among many scientists and environmentalists. Both nations redoubled efforts to develop effective intercontinental ballistic missiles, which could deliver

atomic warheads directly from one continent to another. The apparent Russian lead in such development caused wide alarm in the United States. The American military, in the meantime, developed a new breed of atomic-powered submarines, capable of launching missiles from under water anywhere in the world.

The arms race not only increased tensions between the United States and Russia; it increased tensions within each nation as well. In America, public concern about nuclear war was becoming an obsessive national nightmare, a preoccupation never far from popular thought. Movies, television programs, books, popular songs all expressed the pervasive fear. Government studies began to appear outlining the hideous casualties that a nuclear war would inflict on the nation. Schools, local governments, and individual families built a network of bomb shelters for protection against atomic blasts and radioactive fallout. Fear of communism, therefore, combined with fear of atomic war to create a widespread national unease.

The U-2 Crisis

In this tense and fearful atmosphere, new Soviet challenges in Berlin in 1958 created a particularly troubling crisis. The linking of West Germany first to NATO and then to the new European Common Market, establishing that nation as a full partner of the West, made the continuing existence of an anticommunist West Berlin a galling irritation to the Soviets. In November 1958, therefore, Nikita Khrushchev, who had succeeded Bulganin as Soviet premier and Communist party chief earlier that year, renewed the demands of his predecessors that the NATO powers abandon the city, threatening vaguely to cut its ties to the West if they did not. The United States and its allies refused, and America and Russia were locked in another tense confrontation.

Khrushchev declined to force the issue when it became apparent that the West was unwilling to budge. Instead, he suggested that he and Eisenhower engage in personal discussions, both by visiting each other's countries and by conferring at a summit meeting in Paris in 1960. The United States eagerly agreed. Khrushchev's 1959 visit to America produced a cool but polite response, and plans proceeded for the summit conference and for Eisenhower's visit to Moscow shortly thereafter. Only days before the scheduled beginning of the Paris meeting, however, the Soviet Union announced that it had shot down an

SIGNIFICANT EVENTS

1946   Dr. Benjamin Spock publishes *Baby and Child Care* (p. 863)

1947   Jackie Robinson becomes first black to play in major leagues (p. 870)

Construction begins on Levittown, New York (p. 860)

1948   UAW and General Motors agree to automatic cost-of-living increases for auto workers (p. 858)

United Nations votes to partition Palestine and create state of Israel (p. 876)

1950   David Riesman publishes *The Lonely Crowd* (p. 866)

1951   J.D. Salinger publishes *The Catcher in the Rye* (p. 866)

1952   Eisenhower elected president (p. 871)

1953   Economic recession sets in (p. 857)

Saul Bellow publishes *The Adventures of Augie March* (p. 866)

Department of Health, Education, and Welfare established (p. 872)

Earl Warren becomes chief justice (p. 874)

Truce ends Korean War (p. 875)

CIA helps engineer coup in Iran (p. 877)

Oppenheimer denied security clearance (p. 873)

Stalin dies (p. 879)

1954   Supreme Court rules on *Brown* v. *Board of Education* (p. 868)

Democrats regain control of Congress (p. 872)

Army-McCarthy hearings (p. 873)

Senate censures McCarthy (p. 873)

France surrenders at Dienbienphu (p. 875)

Geneva agreement partitions Vietnam (p. 875)

United States helps topple Arbenz regime in Guatemala (p. 877)

1955   Labor organizations reconcile and form AFL-CIO (p. 858)

Supreme Court announces "Brown II" decision (p. 868)

1955   Montgomery bus boycott begins (p. 870)

Ngo Dinh Diem becomes president of South Vietnam (p. 875)

Eisenhower and Bulganin meet in Geneva (p. 879)

1956   Federal Highway Act passed (p. 872)

Eisenhower reelected president (p. 872)

Suez crisis (p. 877)

Hungarian revolution (p. 879)

1957   Postwar baby boom peaks (p. 856)

Economic recession begins (p. 857)

Labor racketeering investigations focus on Teamsters (p. 859)

Soviet Union launches *Sputnik* (p. 865)

Jack Kerouac publishes *On the Road* (p. 866)

Little Rock school desegregation crisis (p. 869)

Civil-rights act passed (p. 870)

Germany joins NATO (p. 878)

1958   American manned space program founded (p. 865)

National Defense Education Act passed (p. 866)

American marines land in Lebanon (p. 877)

1959   Castro seizes power in Cuba (p. 878)

Nikita Khrushchev visits United States (p. 879)

1960   U-2 incident precedes collapse of Paris summit (p. 880)

1961   Yuri Gagarin of Soviet Union becomes first man in space (p. 865)

Alan Shepard becomes first American in space (p. 865)

United States breaks diplomatic relations with Cuba (p. 878)

Eisenhower gives farewell address (p. 881)

1962   Michael Harrington publishes *The Other America* (p. 867)

1969   Americans land on moon (p. 865)

American U-2, a high-altitude spy plane, over Russian territory. Its pilot, Francis Gary Powers, was in captivity. The Eisenhower administration responded clumsily, at first denying the allegations and then, when confronted with incontrovertible proof, awkwardly admitting the circumstances of Powers's mission and attempting to explain them. Khrushchev lashed back angrily, breaking up the Paris summit almost before it could begin and withdrawing his invitation to Eisenhower to visit the Soviet Union. But the U-2 incident was really only a pretext. By the spring of 1960, Khrushchev knew that no agreement was possible on the Berlin issue; and he, therefore, was eager for an excuse to avoid what he believed would be fruitless negotiations.

The events of 1960 provided a somber backdrop for the end of the Eisenhower administration. After eight years in office, Eisenhower had failed to eliminate the tensions between the United States and the Soviet Union. He had failed to end the costly and dangerous armaments race. And he had presided over a transformation of the Cold War from a relatively limited confrontation with the Soviet Union in Europe to a global effort to resist communist subversion.

Yet Eisenhower had brought to these matters his own sense of the limits of American power. He had refused to commit American troops to anticommunist crusades except in carefully limited and generally low-risk situations, such as Guatemala and Lebanon. He had resisted pressures from the British, from the French, and from hard-liners in his own government to place American force behind efforts to maintain colonial power in Vietnam and in the Suez or to intervene in Hungary. He had placed a measure of restraint on those who urged the creation of an enormous American military establishment, warning in his farewell address in January 1961 of the "unwarranted influence" of a vast "military-industrial complex." His caution, both in domestic and in international affairs, stood in marked contrast to the attitudes of his successors, who argued that the United States must act far more boldly and aggressively on behalf of its goals at home and abroad.

SUGGESTED READINGS

General Studies. William Leuchtenburg, *A Troubled Feast* (1979); Carl Degler, *Affluence and Anxiety* (1968); John Brooks, *The Great Leap* (1966); Godfrey Hodgson, *America in Our Time* (1976); William Chafe, *The Unfinished Journey* (1986); Eric Goldman, *The Crucial Decade and After* (1960); John P. Diggins, *The Proud Decades* (1989); Douglas T. Miller and Marion Novak, *The Fifties* (1977); William O'Neill, *American High* (1986).

The Postwar Economy. John K. Galbraith, *The Affluent Society* (1958) and *The New Industrial State* (1967); Loren J. Okroi, *Galbraith, Harrington, Heilbroner* (1986); C. Wright Mills, *The Power Elite* (1956); Harold G. Vatter, *The U.S. Economy in the 1950s* (1963); Robert Heilbroner, *The Limits of American Capitalism* (1965); Joel Seidman, *American Labor from Defense to Reconversion* (1953); John Hutchinson, *The Imperfect Union* (1970).

Culture and Society. Paul Carter, *Another Part of the Fifties* (1983); Marty Jezer, *The Dark Ages: Life in the U.S. 1945–1960* (1982); George Lipsitz, *Class and Culture in Cold War America* (1981); Douglas T. Miller and Marion Novak, *The Fifties* (1977); Herbert Gans, *The Levittowners* (1967); Kenneth Jackson, *The Crabgrass Frontier* (1985); Ruth Cowan, *More Work for Mother: The Irony of Household Technology* (1983); Elaine Tyler May, *Homeward Bound: American Families in the Cold War* (1988); Eugenia Kaledin, *Mothers and More: American Women in the 1950s* (1984); Edward J. Epstein, *News from Nowhere* (1973); David Halberstam, *The Powers That Be* (1979); Tom Wolfe, *The Right Stuff* (1979); Waltert A. McDougall, *. . . the Heavens and the Earth: A Political History of the Space Age* (1985); R. L. Rosholt, *An Administrative History of NASA* (1966); Walter Sullivan (ed.), *America's Race for the Moon* (1962); Barbara B.

Clowse, *Brainpower for the Cold War: The Sputnik Crisis and the National Defense Education Act of 1958* (1981); Paul Boyer, *By the Bomb's Early Light* (1986); David Riesman, *The Lonely Crowd* (1950); William Whyte, *The Organization Man* (1956); C. Wright Mills, *White Collar* (1956); Bruce Cook, *The Beat Generation* (1971); John Tytell, *Naked Angels* (1976); Ann Charters, *Kerouac* (1973); Dennis McNally, *Desolate Angel* (1979); Arthur M. Schlesinger, Jr., *The Vital Center* (1949); Daniel Bell, *The End of Ideology* (1960); Howard Brick, *Daniel Bell and the Decline of Intellectual Radicalism* (1986); Richard H. Pells, *The Liberal Mind in a Conservative Age* (1985); David Potter, *People of Plenty* (1954); Richard Hofstadter, *The Age of Reform* (1954); Mary Sperling McAuliffe, *Crisis on the Left* (1978); Daniel Bell, ed., *The Radical Right* (1963).

The Eisenhower Presidency. Stephen Ambrose, *Eisenhower the President* (1984); Piers Brendon, *Ike* (1986); Robert F. Burk, *Dwight D. Eisenhower* (1986); Fred Greenstein, *The Hidden-hand Presidency* (1982); Charles C. Alexander, *Holding the Line* (1975); Herbert S. Parmet, *Eisenhower and the American Crusades* (1972); Peter Lyon, *Eisenhower: Portrait of a Hero* (1974); Dwight D. Eisenhower, *The White House Years,* 2 vols. (1963–1965); Emmet John Hughes, *The Ordeal of Power* (1963); Sherman Adams, *Firsthand Report* (1961); Richard Nixon, *Six Crises* (1962); Nicol C. Rae, *The Decline and Fall of the Liberal Republicans* (1989); Gary Reichard, *The Reaffirmation of Republicanism* (1975); David W. Reinhard, *The Republican Right Since 1945* (1983); Mark H. Rose, *Interstate: Express Highway Politics, 1941–1956* (1979).

Foreign Policy. Robert Divine, *Eisenhower and the Cold War* (1981); Townsend Hoopes, *The Devil and John Foster*

Dulles (1973); Louis Gerson, *John Foster Dulles* (1967); Stephen Ambrose, *Ike's Spies* (1981); Michael Beschloss, *MAYDAY* (1986); Chester Cooper, *Lost Crusade* (1970); Frances Fitzgerald, *Fire in the Lake* (1972); John T. McAlister, Jr., *Vietnam: The Origins of Revolution* (1969); George Herring, *America's Longest War* (1979); Chester Cooper, *The Lion's Last Roar* (1978); Hugh Thomas, *Suez* (1967); Mira Wilkins, *The Maturing of Multinational Enterprise* (1974); Kermit Roosevelt, *Counter-coup* (1980); Burton Kaufman, *The Oil Cartel Case* (1978); Richard Immerman, *The CIA in Guatemala* (1982); Walter LaFeber, *Inevitable Revolutions* (1983); Stephen G. Rabe, *Eisenhower and Latin America* (1988); Robert A. Divine, *Foreign Policy and U.S. Presidential Elections,* 2 vols. (1974) and *Blowing in the Wind: The Nuclear Test Ban Debate, 1954–1960* (1978); Blanche W. Cooke, *The Declassified Eisenhower* (1981); Richard A. Melanson and David A. Mayers, ed., *Reevaluating Eisenhower* (1986); Burton I. Kaufman, *Trade and Aid* (1982); Howard Ball, *Justice Downwind: America's Nuclear Testing Program in the 1950s* (1986); Gregg Herken, *Counsels of War* (1985); Richard G. Hewlett and Jack M. Hall, *Atoms for Peace and War, 1953–1961* (1989); Richard Smoke, *National Security and the Nuclear Dilemma* (1988).

Legal and Constitutional Issues.   Philip Stern, *The Oppenheimer Case* (1969); Michael Straight, *Trial by Television* (1954); Paul Murphy, *The Constitution in Crisis Times* (1972); Alexander Bickel, *Politics and the Warren Court* (1965) and *The Supreme Court and the Idea of Progress* (1970); Philip Kurland, *Politics, the Constitution, and the Warren Court* (1970); John Weaver, *Earl Warren* (1967).

Civil Rights.   Richard Kluger, *Simple Justice* (1975); Anthony Lewis, *Portrait of a Decade* (1964); Martin Luther King, Jr., *Stride Toward Freedom* (1958); William Chafe, *Civilities and Civil Rights* (1980); Harvard Sitkoff, *The Struggle for Black Equality, 1954–1980* (1981); John W. Anderson, *Eisenhower, Brownell, and the Congress* (1964); Robert F. Burk, *The Eisenhower Administration and Black Civil Rights* (1984); Numan V. Bartley, *The Rise of Massive Resistance* (1969); Elizabeth Huckaby, *Crisis at Central High* (1980); David Garrow, ed., *The Montgomery Bus Boycott and the Women Who Started It: A Memoir of Jo Ann Gibson Robinson* (1987); Robert J. Norrell, *Reaping the Whirlwind: The Civil Rights Movement in Tuskegee* (1985); Howell Raines, *My Soul Is Rested* (1977).

The War in Vietnam
An American soldier awaits evacuation from Dak To, Vietnam, in November 1967. Heavy American bombing and artillery finally halted the communist offensive at Dak To in the largest battle of the war to that point. The American commander, General William Westmoreland, announced that "the enemy's hopes are bankrupt," but his confidence turned out to be unfounded. (*UPI/Bettmann Newsphotos*)

CHAPTER 30

⊠ ⛊ ⊠

The Ordeal of Liberalism

⊠ ⛊ ⊠

The calm, reassuring presence of Dwight D. Eisenhower seemed perfectly to match the political mood of the 1950s—a mood that combined a desire for domestic stability with a concern for international security. By the end of the decade, however, many Americans were beginning to clamor for a more active and assertive approach to public policy. The United States had, liberals complained, been allowed to "drift." It was time for an energetic assault on both domestic and world problems. Such sentiments helped produce two presidents whose activism transformed the nature of their office and the thrust of American politics.

Those same sentiments helped make the 1960s one of the most turbulent eras of the twentieth century. For several years after the inauguration of John F. Kennedy as president, the nation seemed to move firmly and confidently to combat the expansion of communism; and it seemed to act decisively to confront its most serious social problems at home: racial inequality, economic deprivation, and others. By 1968, however, the United States was embroiled in a major social, cultural, and political crisis. In extending the containment doctrine to dictate a deepening American involvement in the civil war in Vietnam, the United States was embroiling itself in a conflict it did not fully understand and was ultimately unable to resolve. And in assaulting the problems of racial injustice and poverty, the nation was undertaking a far more difficult and wrenching task than most reformers at first realized. These and other pressures produced social and political turmoil so profound that

those who described them as a "revolution" exaggerated only slightly.

Expanding the Liberal State

The presidency had been growing steadily more important in American public life throughout the twentieth century. The development of atomic weapons—the means of ultimate destruction, which remained (at least in theory) under the personal and exclusive control of the president—added a new dimension to the powers of the office in the 1950s. By 1960, more and more Americans were looking to the presidency as the source of all initiatives and were calling for more assertive leadership. The political scientist Richard Neustadt, for example, published an influential book that year entitled *Presidential Power,* which stressed the importance of presidential action in confronting national problems. Presidents faced many constraints, he argued, but effective presidents must learn to break free of them. Such exhortations found a receptive audience in the two men who served in the White House from 1961 until 1969: John F. Kennedy and Lyndon B. Johnson.

John Kennedy

The campaign of 1960 produced two young candidates who claimed to offer the nation active leadership. The Republican nomination went almost uncontested to Vice President Richard Nixon, who for the occasion abandoned the strident anticommunism that had characterized his earlier career and adopted a centrist position in favor of moderate reform. The Democrats, in the meantime, emerged from a spirited primary campaign united, somewhat uneasily, behind John Fitzgerald Kennedy, an attractive and articulate senator from Massachusetts who had narrowly missed being the party's vice-presidential candidate in 1956.

Kennedy's road to national leadership was an unusual one. He was the son of one of the most powerful and controversial public figures of the 1930s: Joseph P. Kennedy, who had made a large personal fortune in the stock market, who had served as the first chairman of the Securities and Exchange Commission, who had been the American ambassador to Great Britain in the first years of World War II, and who had transferred his own frustrated ambitions for the presidency to his children. John Kennedy grew up in a world of ease and privilege, although he himself suffered from a series of physical ailments throughout his life. He attended Harvard and then served in the navy during World War II. He attracted attention during the war after the PT boat he commanded was sunk at sea; he was decorated for heroism for his efforts to save members of the crew.

Kennedy returned to Massachusetts after the war and, making liberal use of both his own war record and his family's money, won a seat in Congress in 1946. Six years later, he was elected to the United States Senate, and in 1958 reelected by a record margin. Within days of his triumph, he was planning his campaign for the White House. He had by then attracted considerable national attention for his eloquence, his poise, and what was later widely described as his "charisma." In 1956, he had published a successful book, *Profiles in Courage,* which won the Pulitzer Prize for history and which celebrated American leaders who had displayed notable political bravery. But Kennedy himself had compiled a very cautious and modest political record up to that point and had inspired enthusiasm among relatively few liberals.

His presidential campaign, however, was notable for its strong endorsement of the idea of dynamic governmental activism. Kennedy had read and admired Richard Neustadt's book on the presidency, and he seemed committed to energetic use of the office. He had premised his campaign, he said, "on the single assumption that the American people are

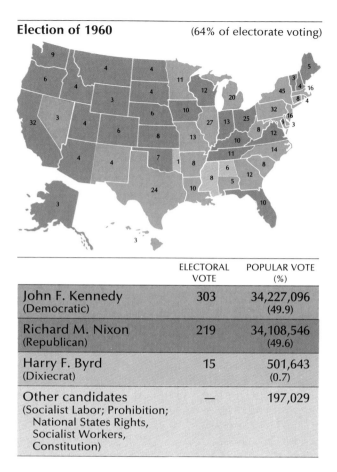

Election of 1960   (64% of electorate voting)

	ELECTORAL VOTE	POPULAR VOTE (%)
John F. Kennedy (Democratic)	303	34,227,096 (49.9)
Richard M. Nixon (Republican)	219	34,108,546 (49.6)
Harry F. Byrd (Dixiecrat)	15	501,643 (0.7)
Other candidates (Socialist Labor; Prohibition; National States Rights, Socialist Workers, Constitution)	—	197,029

uneasy at the present drift in our national course." He was, wrote *New Republic* columnist TRB, "a young man offering positive leadership and presidential power to the uttermost."

He was also a Catholic, a political liability that had almost cost him the nomination and that continued to dog him throughout the campaign. Kennedy compensated for that with a remarkably appealing public image—one that seemed perfectly suited for television—and with an unusually sophisticated and capable campaign. The crucial moment, perhaps, came when he met Vice President Nixon in the first of a series of televised debates. Cool, poised, and relaxed, Kennedy stood in marked contrast to the haggard and somewhat nervous Nixon, who was recovering from an illness. The favorable response Kennedy received from the debate helped propel him to victory.

It was, however, one of the narrowest victories in the history of presidential elections. A vigorous

John Kennedy
The new president and his wife, Jacqueline, attend one of the five balls in Washington marking Kennedy's inauguration in 1961. (Paul Schutzer, *Life* Magazine, © 1961 Time, Inc.)

The narrowness of Kennedy's victory placed a serious constraint on his ability to accomplish his goals. He had campaigned promising a program of domestic legislation more ambitious than any since the New Deal, a program he described as the "New Frontier." He was able to steer little of it to completion during his presidency.

Kennedy's most serious problem from the beginning was Congress. Although Democrats remained in control of both houses, they owed little to the new president, whose coattails in 1960 had been exceedingly short. Nor did the presence of Democratic majorities ensure a sympathetic reception for reform proposals; those majorities consisted in large part of conservative Southerners, who were far more likely to vote with the Republicans than with Kennedy. Moreover, many of those same Southerners maintained control, by virtue of their seniority, of the most important congressional committees. One after another of Kennedy's legislative proposals, therefore, found themselves hopelessly stalled long before they reached the floor of the House or Senate.

As a result, the president had to look elsewhere for opportunities to display forceful, positive leadership. One such area was the economy, which from the beginning of his administration had been among his primary concerns. Economic growth was sluggish in 1961 when Kennedy entered the White House, with unemployment hovering at about 6 percent of the work force. In addition to such legislative initiatives as requesting tax credits for businesses investing in capital growth, Kennedy attempted to use his executive powers to improve the economy. With congressional approval, he initiated a series of tariff negotiations with foreign governments—the "Kennedy Round"— to reduce barriers to international trade, in an effort to stimulate American exports. He began to consider the use of Keynesian fiscal and monetary tools in more direct and positive ways than those used by any previous administrations—culminating in his 1962 proposal for a substantial federal tax cut to stimulate the economy.

He even put his personal prestige on the line in a battle to curb inflation. In 1962, several steel companies, led by U.S. Steel, announced that they were raising their prices by $6 a ton, a move certain to trigger similar action by the rest of the steel industry. Angrily denouncing the steel companies both publicly and privately, the president exerted enormous pressure on U.S. Steel to rescind its decision— threatening the company with lawsuits and the can-

effort on behalf of Nixon by President Eisenhower in the closing days of the campaign, combined with continuing doubts about Kennedy's youth (he turned forty-three in 1960) and religion, almost enabled the Republicans to close what had at one time been a substantial Democratic lead. But in the end, Kennedy held on to win a tiny plurality of the popular vote— 49.9 percent to Nixon's 49.6 percent—and only a slightly more comfortable electoral majority—303 to 219. If a few thousand voters in Illinois and Texas had voted differently, Nixon would have won the election.

cellation of government contracts. He even called the president of U.S. Steel, Roger Blough, to the White House for an impassioned tongue-lashing. Finally, the steel companies relented and abandoned the price rise. But the president had won only a fleeting victory. His relationship with the business community was a strained one from that moment on, and a few months later the steel companies quietly raised prices again. The president did not protest.

Kennedy found the greatest opportunities to display his vision of presidential leadership in two areas: foreign policy and personal style. In his capacity as a world leader, he discovered—like other presidents both before and after him—that he could act without the constraints that hampered his domestic initiatives. And in adopting a new presidential style, he was able to employ his own most effective political skills. More than any other president of the century (excepting perhaps the two Roosevelts and, later, Ronald Reagan), Kennedy made his own personality an integral part of his presidency and a central focus of national attention.

Nothing more clearly illustrates how important Kennedy and the presidency had become to the American people than the tragedy of November 22, 1963, and the popular reaction to it. Already, the president was beginning to campaign for reelection the following year; and in November, he traveled to Texas with his wife and Vice President Lyndon Johnson for a series of political appearances. While the presidential motorcade rode slowly through the streets of Dallas, shots rang out. Two bullets struck the president—one in the throat, the other in the head. He was sped to a nearby hospital, where minutes later he was pronounced dead.

The circumstances of the assassination seemed clearer at the time than they did from the vantage point of later years. Lee Harvey Oswald, who appeared to be a confused and embittered Marxist, was arrested for the crime later that day, on the basis of strong circumstantial evidence. (Among other things, Oswald had shot and killed a police officer who had tried to apprehend him.) Two days later, as Oswald was being moved from one jail to another, Jack Ruby, a Dallas nightclub owner, stepped from a crowd of reporters and fired a pistol into Oswald's abdomen, an event that was broadcast graphically around the world on television. Oswald died only hours later. The popular assumption at the time was that Oswald had acted alone, expressing through the murder his personal frustration and anger, and that Ruby had acted out of grief and out of a desire to make himself a popular

hero. These assumptions received what seemed to be conclusive confirmation by a federal commission, chaired by Chief Justice Earl Warren, that was appointed to review the events surrounding the assassination. In later years, however, more and more questions and doubts arose about the circumstances of the shooting; and an increasing number of Americans became convinced that the Warren Commission report had not revealed the full story. For more than two decades, alternative theories of the assassination continued to surface—some of them based on lurid conspiracy theories, some based on real discrepancies in the evidence. In 1978, a congressional subcommittee raised the first official challenge from within the federal government to the findings of the Warren Commission by concluding, on the basis of controversial acoustical evidence, that more than one gunman had been involved in the shootings in Dallas. But the committee had no answer to the question of who the other assassins might have been.

The death of President Kennedy was one of those traumatic episodes in national history that have left a permanent mark on all who experienced it. Millions of Americans suspended their normal activities for four days to watch the televised events surrounding the presidential funeral. Images of Kennedy's widow, his small children, his funeral procession, his dramatic grave site at Arlington Cemetery with its symbolic eternal flame—all became deeply embedded in the public mind. When in later times Americans would look back at the optimistic days of the 1950s and early 1960s and wonder how everything had subsequently seemed to unravel, many would think of November 22, 1963, as the beginning of the change.

Lyndon Johnson

At the time, however, much of the nation took comfort in the personality and performance of Kennedy's successor in the White House, Lyndon Baines Johnson. Johnson was a native of the poor "hill country" of west Texas, the son of a once-prominent state politician who ended his days in poverty and obscurity. Johnson himself had risen to eminence by dint of extraordinary, even obsessive effort and ambition. He entered public life in the 1930s, first as an aide to a Texas congressman, then as the director of the New Deal's National Youth Administration in Texas, then as a young congressman with close personal ties to Franklin Roosevelt. After twelve years in the House,

Retroactive I, 1964

Within months of his death, John Kennedy had become transformed in the American imagination to a figure larger than life, a symbol of the nation's thwarted aspirations. The artist Robert Rauschenberg gave evidence of Kennedy's new mythological importance by making him the centerpiece of this evocation of contemporary American society.   (Wadsworth Atheneum, Hartford)

he narrowly won election in 1948 to the United States Senate. And there, by carefully cultivating the favor of party leaders, he rose steadily in influence to become the Senate majority leader. He brought to that post, as he would bring to the presidency, a remarkable level of energy and a legendary ability to persuade and cajole his colleagues into following his lead. He had failed in 1960 to win the Democratic nomination for president; but he had surprised many who knew him by agreeing to accept the second position on the ticket with Kennedy. The events in Dallas thrust him into the White House.

Johnson's personality could hardly have been more different from Kennedy's. Tall, gawky, inelegant in his public speech, he was the antithesis of the modern media politician. Where Kennedy had been smooth and urbane, Johnson was coarse, even crude. Where Kennedy had been personally reticent and almost unfailingly polite, Johnson was effusive, garrulous, and at times viciously cruel. But like Kennedy, Johnson was a man who believed in the active use of power. And he proved, in the end, more effective than his predecessor in translating his goals into reality.

Johnson the Candidate
Johnson never evoked the sort of personal adulation that John Kennedy had attracted. But in the course of the 1964 campaign, at least, his ebullient style generated considerable popular enthusiasm. (Popperfoto)

Johnson's ability to manage the Congress provided perhaps the most vivid contrast with Kennedy. Between 1963 and 1966, he compiled the most impressive legislative record of any president since Franklin Roosevelt. He was aided by the tidal wave of emotion that followed the death of President Kennedy, which helped win passage of many New Frontier proposals as a memorial to the slain leader. But Johnson also constructed a remarkable reform program of his own, one that he ultimately labeled the "Great Society." And he won approval of much of it through the same sort of skillful lobbying that had made him an effective majority leader.

Johnson envisioned himself, as well, as a great "coalition builder," drawing into the Democratic fold as many different constituencies as possible. Even more than Kennedy, he tried to avoid the politics of conflict—that is, of winning the support of one group by attacking another. Johnson wanted the support of everyone, and for a time he very nearly got it. His first year in office was, by necessity, dominated by the campaign for reelection. From the beginning, there was little doubt that he would win. As a Democrat in an era of wide support for liberal reform, as the successor of a beloved and martyred president, and as a personification of the same energetic activism that had helped make Kennedy so popular, he was an almost unbeatable candidate. He received considerable assistance from the Republican party, which in 1964 fell under the sway of its right wing and nominated the conservative Senator Barry

Goldwater of Arizona. Liberal Republicans abandoned Goldwater and openly supported Johnson.

In the fall campaign, Johnson avoided specific, detailed promises, concentrating instead on attracting support from as wide a range of voters as possible and letting Goldwater's rigid conservatism drive even more Americans into the Democratic fold. The strategy worked. Johnson received more votes, over 43 million, than any candidate before him, and a larger plurality, over 61 percent, than any candidate before or since. Goldwater managed to carry only his home state of Arizona and five states in the Deep South. Record Democratic majorities in both houses of Congress, many of whose members had been swept into office only because of the margin of Johnson's victory, ensured that the president would be able to fulfill many of his goals. On election night, Johnson told the nation that he regarded his victory as a "mandate for unity." For a time, that unity seemed to survive; and Johnson seemed well on his way to achieving his own most cherished aim: becoming the most successful reform president of the century.

The Assault on Poverty

The domestic programs of Kennedy and Johnson shared two basic goals: maintaining the strength of the American economy and expanding the responsibilities of the federal government for the general social welfare. In the first, the two presidents were largely continuing a commitment that had been central to virtually every administration since early in the century. In the second, however, they were responding to a marked change in public assumptions. In particular, they were responding to what some described as the "discovery of poverty" in the late 1950s and early 1960s—the realization by Americans who had been glorying in prosperity that there were substantial portions of the population that remained destitute.

For the first time since the 1930s, therefore, the federal government took steps in the 1960s not only to strengthen and expand existing social welfare programs but to create important new ones. The effort had begun in the Kennedy administration, although at first without great result. Kennedy did manage to win approval of important changes in existing welfare programs. A revision of the minimum wage law extended coverage to an additional 3.6 million workers and raised the minimum hourly wage from $1.00 to $1.25. Another measure increased Social Security benefits. Kennedy's most ambitious proposals, however, remained unfulfilled until after his death.

The most important of these, perhaps, was Medicare: a program to provide federal aid to the elderly for medical expenses. Its enactment in 1965 came at the end of a bitter, twenty-year debate between those who believed in the concept of national health assistance and those who denounced it as "socialized medicine." But the program as it went into effect removed many objections. For one thing, it avoided the stigma of "welfare" in much the same way the Social Security system had done: by making Medicare benefits available to all elderly Americans, regardless of need. That created a large middle-class constituency for the program. More important, perhaps, it defused the opposition of the medical community. Doctors serving Medicare patients continued to practice privately and to charge their normal fees; Medicare simply shifted responsibility for paying a large proportion of those fees from the patient to the government.

With that barrier now hurdled, advocates of national health insurance pushed for even more extensive coverage; and in 1966, President Johnson steered to passage the Medicaid program, which extended federal medical assistance to welfare recipients of all ages. Criticism of both programs continued. National health insurance advocates continued to insist that coverage be extended to all Americans, young and old, rich and poor. Others spoke harshly of the bureaucratic problems Medicare and Medicaid created, and of the corruption these programs seemed to encourage.

Still more complained bitterly of the tremendous costs the reforms were imposing on the government and the taxpayer. Beginning in 1969, as a result, the government began attempting to limit eligibility for assistance in order to reduce expenses. But public support for the programs was by now too powerful to allow very much limitation, especially on the benefits to the middle class. Medicare costs, in particular, continued to spiral. In 1970, expenditures for the program totaled $6.2 billion. By 1984, they had risen to over $60 billion. The average annual Medicare expenditure per person in that same period rose from $64 to $259, reflecting the dramatic increase in health costs in general.

Medicare and Medicaid were first steps in a much larger assault on poverty—one that Kennedy had been contemplating in the last months of his life and one that Johnson brought to fruition. Determined to eradicate the "pockets of poverty" that were receiving wide public attention, Johnson announced to Congress only weeks after taking office the declaration of an "unconditional war on poverty." The Economic Opportunity Act he then steered to passage provided for, among other things, the establishment of an Office of Economic Opportunity—the centerpiece in Johnson's vision of the Great Society. From the OEO stemmed an array of educational programs: vocational training, remedial education, college work-study grants, and others. The office funneled government money as well into programs to provide employment for unemployed youths—through the Job Corps, the Neighborhood Youth Corps, and other agencies. And it established VISTA (Volunteers in Service to America), a program reminiscent of the paternal reform efforts of the progressive era. VISTA volunteers moved out across the country into troubled communities to provide educational and social services. Other OEO programs financed housing assistance, health care, neighborhood improvements, and many more antipoverty efforts.

The OEO's Community Action programs were particularly controversial. The idea of community action (an idea promoted by, among others, Robert Kennedy) was to involve members of poor communities themselves in the planning and administration of the programs designed to help them, to promote what some of its advocates called "maximum feasible participation." The Community Action agencies at the local level varied widely. In some places, they were staffed and administered by community activists, who often challenged established political organizations. In other places, the established political organizations seized control of community action and made it part of the existing system.

It seems clear in retrospect that these programs provided a number of important benefits to poor communities that more conventional programs never did. Perhaps most important, they served in effect as a jobs program for poor people, giving them training and experience in administrative and political work. Many people who went on to important careers in politics or community organizing, including many black politicians who would rise to prominence in the 1970s and 1980s, got their start in Community Action programs.

Community Action had a dramatic impact, too, on American Indians, many of whom were already mobilizing to demand greater self-determination. The OEO programs allowed tribal leaders to design and run programs for themselves and to apply for funds from the federal government on an equal basis with state and municipal authorities. Administering these programs helped produce a new generation of tribal leaders who learned a great deal about political and bureaucratic power from the experience.

Despite its achievements, the Community Action approach proved impossible to sustain. Most local officials felt uncomfortable watching the creation of a new layer of government competing with, and often challenging, them. Many programs fell victim either to local mismanagement or to cumbersome federal supervision, problems that frequently resulted in a substantial waste of funds. The activists in Community Action agencies employed tactics to advance their aims that mainstream politicians considered frighteningly radical; and as is often the case, the seeming excesses of a few agencies shaped the popular image of the program as a whole.

The nearly $3 billion that the OEO spent during its first two years of existence did much to assist those who managed to qualify for funds. It helped to reduce poverty significantly in certain areas. It fell far short, however, of its goal of eliminating poverty altogether. The job-training programs that formed so important a part of the war on poverty produced generally disappointing results, particularly among the urban black unemployed; blacks continued, once trained, to be barred from many jobs because of racial discrimination or because the jobs simply did not exist in their communities. Whatever the strengths or weaknesses of particular approaches to the problem, the war on poverty never really approached the dimensions necessary to achieve its goals. From the beginning, funds were inadequate. And as the years passed and a costly war in Southeast Asia became the nation's first priority, even those limited funds began to dwindle.

Cities and Schools

Closely tied to the antipoverty program were federal efforts to promote the revitalization of decaying cities and to strengthen the nation's schools. Again, many such programs had received support from the Kennedy administration but won passage under Johnson. President Kennedy himself had managed to steer through Congress the Housing Act of 1961, which offered $4.9 billion in federal grants to cities for the preservation of open spaces, the development of mass-transit systems, and the subsidization of middle-income housing. Johnson went further. He established the Department of Housing and Urban Development to symbolize the government's commitment to the cities. (The first secretary of this department, Robert Weaver, was the first black ever to serve in the cabinet.) And Johnson also inaugurated the Model Cities program, which offered federal subsidies for urban redevelopment.

Kennedy had fought long and in vain to win congressional passage of a program to provide federal aid to public education. Like the idea of federal health insurance, the concept of aid to education aroused deep suspicion in many Americans, who saw it as the first step in a federal effort to take control of the schools from localities. Conservatives argued forcefully that once the government began paying for education, it would begin telling the schools how and what they must teach. Opposition arose from another quarter as well: Catholics insisted that aid to education must extend to parochial as well as public schools, something that President Kennedy had refused to consider and that many Americans believed was unconstitutional. Johnson managed to circumvent both objections with the Elementary and Secondary Education Act of 1965 and a series of subsequent measures. Such bills extended aid to both private and parochial schools—aid that was based on the economic conditions of their students, not the needs of the schools themselves. The formula met criteria established earlier by the Supreme Court, and it satisfied some, although not all, conservatives. Total federal expenditures for education and technical training rose from $5 billion to $12 billion between 1964 and 1967.

Legacies of the Great Society

The great surge of reform of the Kennedy–Johnson years reflected a new awareness of the nation's social problems. It also reflected the confidence of liberals that America's resources were virtually limitless and that purposeful public effort could solve any problem. By the time Johnson left office, legislation had been either enacted or initiated to deal with a remarkable number of social issues: poverty, health care, education, cities, transportation, the environment, consumer protection, agriculture, science, the arts. The Great Society produced the National Endowment for the Arts and the National Endowment for the Humanities, bringing government assistance to scholarship and the arts in America for the first time since the New Deal. It set aside millions of acres of land to be preserved as wilderness. It established new environmental regulations to improve the quality of the air and water. It banned billboards and other forms of advertising from the interstate highway system (as part of a "beautification" program much favored by the First Lady, Lady Bird Johnson).

Finally, the Great Society enacted the most important reform of American immigration policy in forty years. The Immigration Act of 1965 maintained a strict limit on the number of newcomers admitted to the country each year (170,000), but it eliminated the "national origins" system established in the 1920s, which gave preference to immigrants from northern Europe over those from other parts of the world. The new bill, one of the most important pieces of legislation of the 1960s even if largely unnoticed at the time, continued to restrict immigration from some parts of Latin America, but it allowed people from all parts of Europe, Asia, and Africa to enter the United States on an equal basis. It meant that large new categories of immigrants—and especially large numbers of Asians—would begin entering the United States by the early 1970s and changing the character of the American population.

Taken together, the Great Society reforms meant a dramatic increase in federal spending. For a time, rising tax revenues from the growing economy nearly compensated for the new expenditures. In 1964, Lyndon Johnson managed to win passage of the $11.5 billion tax cut that Kennedy had first proposed in 1962. Although the cut increased an already sizable federal deficit, it produced substantial economic growth over the next several years that made up for much of the revenue initially lost. But as the Great Society programs began to multiply, and particularly as they began to compete with the escalating costs of America's military ventures, the federal budget rapidly outpaced increases in revenues. In 1961, the federal government had spent $94.4 billion. By

---

MAJOR ACHIEVEMENTS OF THE GREAT SOCIETY

1964 Civil Rights Act (prohibiting discrimination in public accommodations and hiring)
Twenty-fourth Amendment (abolishing poll tax)
Tax Reduction Act
Urban Mass Transportation Act (subsidizing urban mass transit)
Economic Opportunity Act (creating OEO, Job Corps, VISTA)
Wilderness Preservation Act
1965 Elementary and Secondary Education Act (providing aid to schools)
Medicare
Civil Rights Act (protecting voting rights)
Omnibus Housing Act (providing rent supplements to poor)

1965 Department of Housing and Urban Development
National Endowments of the Arts and Humanities
Water Quality Act
Immigration law reform
Air Quality Act
Higher Education Act (offering federally financed scholarships)
1966 Medicaid
National Traffic and Motor Vehicle Safety Act
Highway Safety Act
Minimum wage increase
Department of Transportation
Model Cities
1967 Food Stamps
Corporation for Public Broadcasting

1970, that sum had more than doubled, to $196.6 billion. And except for 1969, when there was a modest surplus, the budget throughout the decade showed a deficit, which in 1968 rose to $25.1 billion—the highest in history to that point.

The vast costs of the programs of the Great Society, and the apparent inability of American society to raise the government revenues to pay for them, contributed to a growing disillusionment in later years with the idea of federal efforts to solve social problems. By the 1980s, many Americans had become convinced that the Great Society social programs had not worked; that the federal government lacked the expertise or the administrative capacity to make them work; that what progress there had been toward eliminating poverty in the 1960s and 1970s had been a result of economic growth, not government assistance. Others, however, argued equally fervently that social programs had made important contributions both to the welfare of the specific groups they were designed to help and to the health of the economy as a whole. They pointed, in particular, to the reduction of hunger in America, the inclusion of poor people in health-care programs, and the increased services available to young children.

Whatever the reason, the decade of the 1960s—a decade marked both by stunning economic growth and ambitious government antipoverty efforts—saw the most substantial decrease in poverty in the United States of any period in the nation's history. In 1959, according to the most widely accepted estimates, 21 percent of the American people lived below the officially established poverty line. By 1969, only 12 percent remained below that line. The improvements affected blacks and whites in about the same proportion: 56 percent of the black population had lived in poverty in 1959, only 32 percent did so ten years later—a 42 percent reduction; 18 percent of all whites had been poor in 1959, but only 10 percent were poor a decade later—a 44 percent reduction.

The Battle for Racial Equality

The nation's most important domestic initiative in the 1960s was the new national commitment to provide justice and equality to American blacks. It was also the most difficult commitment, the one that produced the severest strains on American society. Yet despite the initial reluctance of many whites, includ-

ing even many liberals, to confront the problem, it was an issue that could no longer be ignored. Black Americans were themselves ensuring that the nation would have to deal with the problem of race.

Expanding Protests

John Kennedy had long been sympathetic to the cause of racial justice, but he was hardly a committed crusader. His intervention during the 1960 campaign to help win the release of Martin Luther King, Jr., from a Georgia prison won him a large plurality of the black vote. Once in office, however, he was—like many presidents before him—reluctant to jeopardize his legislative program by openly committing himself to racial reform, fearing that he would alienate key Democratic senators. Resisting the arguments of those who urged new civil-rights legislation, the Kennedy administration worked instead to expand the enforcement of existing laws and to support litigation to overturn existing segregation statutes. Both efforts produced only limited results. Still, the administration hoped to contain the issue of race and resisted pressure to do more.

But that pressure was rapidly growing too powerful to ignore. In February 1960, black college students in Greensboro, North Carolina, staged a sit-in at a segregated Woolworth's lunch counter—an event that received wide national attention. In the following months, such demonstrations spread throughout the South, forcing many merchants to integrate their facilities. The sit-in movement had two important consequences. It mobilized large groups of blacks throughout the country, and particularly in the South, to take direct action to protest discrimination. Some of those who had participated in the sit-ins formed, in the fall of 1960, the Student Nonviolent Coordinating Committee (SNCC), which worked to keep the spirit of resistance alive. The sit-ins also aroused the support of a substantial number of Northern whites.

In 1961, students of both races, working with the Congress of Racial Equality (CORE), began what they called "freedom rides." Traveling by bus throughout the South, they went from city to city attempting to force the desegregation of bus stations. They were met in some places with such savage violence on the part of whites that the president finally dispatched federal marshals to help keep the peace and ordered the integration of all bus and train stations. In the meantime, SNCC workers began fan-

Sitting In
Black students stage a sit-in at a Woolworth's lunch counter in Charlotte, North Carolina, in 1960, after being refused service by the waitresses there. A similar demonstration at a Woolworth's in Greensboro several weeks earlier sparked a wave of sit-ins across the South.   (Bruce Roberts/Rapho-Photo Researchers)

ning out through black communities and even into remote rural areas to encourage blacks to challenge the obstacles to voting that white society had created. The SCLC also created citizen education and other programs (many of them organized by the indefatigable Ella Baker, one of the great grass-roots leaders of the movement) in an effort to mobilize black workers, farmers, housewives, and others to participate more fully in the challenge to segregation and discrimination.

Continuing judicial efforts to enforce the integration of public education increased the pressure on national leaders to respond to the civil-rights movement. In October 1962, a federal court ordered the University of Mississippi to enroll its first black stu-

dent, James Meredith; Governor Ross Barnett, a strident segregationist, refused to enforce the order. When angry whites in Oxford, Mississippi, began rioting to protest the court decree, President Kennedy sent federal troops to the city to restore order and protect Meredith's right to attend the university.

Events in Alabama the following year proved even more influential. In April 1963, Martin Luther King, Jr., launched a series of extensive nonviolent demonstrations in Birmingham, Alabama, a city unsurpassed in the strength of its commitment to segregation. Local officials responded brutally. Police Commissioner Eugene "Bull" Connor personally supervised measures to break up King's peaceful marches, arresting hundreds of demonstrators and using attack dogs, tear gas, electric cattle prods, and fire hoses—at times even against small children—as much of the nation watched televised reports in horror. Two months later, Governor George Wallace stood in the doorway of a building at the University of Alabama to prevent the court-ordered enrollment of several black students. Only after the arrival of federal marshals did he give way. The same night, NAACP official Medgar Evers was murdered in Mississippi.

A National Commitment

The events in Alabama and Mississippi were both a personal shock and a political warning to the president. He could not, he realized, any longer avoid the issue of race. In a historic television address the night of the University of Alabama confrontation, Kennedy spoke eloquently of the "moral issue" facing the nation. "If an American," he asked, "because his skin is dark, . . . cannot enjoy the full and free life which all of us want, then who among us would be content to have the color of his skin changed and stand in his place? Who among us would then be content with the counsels of patience and delay?" Days later, he introduced a series of new legislative proposals prohibiting segregation in "public accommodations" (stores, restaurants, theaters, hotels), barring discrimination in employment, and increasing the power of the government to file suits on behalf of school integration.

Congressional opposition to the new proposals was strong, and it was clear from the start that winning passage of the legislation would be difficult. Black Americans themselves, however, made clear that there could be no retreat from the effort. In August 1963, more than 200,000 demonstrators marched down the Mall in Washington, D.C., and gathered before the Lincoln Memorial for the greatest civil-rights demonstration in the nation's history. President Kennedy, who had at first opposed the idea of the march, in the end gave it his open support. And the peaceful gathering, therefore, seemed at the time to denote less the existence of a bitter racial struggle than the birth of a new national commitment to civil rights. Martin Luther King, Jr., in one of the greatest speeches of his distinguished oratorical career—indeed one of the most memorable speeches of any public figure of the century—aroused the crowd with a litany of images prefaced again and again by the phrase "I have a dream." The march was

the high-water mark of the peaceful, interracial civil-rights movement—and one of the high points of liberal optimism as well.

The assassination of President Kennedy three months later gave new impetus to the battle for civil-rights legislation. The ambitious measure that Kennedy had proposed in June 1963 had passed through the House of Representatives with relative ease; but it seemed hopelessly stalled in the Senate, where a determined filibuster by Southern conservatives continued to prevent a vote. Early in 1964, after Johnson had applied both public and private pressure, supporters of the measure finally mustered the two-thirds majority necessary to close debate; and the Senate passed the most comprehensive civil-rights bill in the history of the nation.

The Battle for Voting Rights

At the very moment of passage of the Civil Rights Act of 1964, however, new efforts were under way in the South to win even greater gains for blacks. During the "freedom summer" of that year, thousands of civil-rights workers, black and white, Northern and Southern, spread out through the South, but primarily in Mississippi, establishing "freedom schools," staging demonstrations, and demanding not only an end to segregation but the inclusion of blacks in the political process. Like earlier civil-rights activists, they met a hostile response—in some cases, a murderous response. Three of the first freedom workers to arrive in the South—two whites, Andrew Goodman and Michael Schwerner, and one black, James Chaney—disappeared; several weeks later, the FBI found their bodies buried under an earthen dam. Local law enforcement officials were later found to have participated in the murders.

The "freedom summer" also helped produce a political challenge to the established white order: the creation of the Mississippi Freedom Democratic party, an integrated alternative to the regular party organization. Under the leadership of Fannie Lou Hamer and others, the MFDP challenged the regular party's right to its seats at the Democratic National Convention that summer. President Johnson, eager to avoid conflicts at a convention that many likened to a "coronation," pressured both sides to accept a compromise, by which the MFDP could be seated as observers, with promises of party reforms later on, but the regular party would retain its official stand-

King Marches Through Selma

Martin Luther King, Jr., and his wife, Coretta (right), lead demonstrators on a march through Selma, Alabama, during his turbulent campaign for black voting rights in 1965. Selma was one of the last of the great interracial crusades on behalf of civil rights. Subsequent campaigns, such as King's frustrated effort in Chicago in 1966, attracted much less support from Northern whites and far less attention in the media. (Bruce Davidson/Magnum)

ing. Both sides grudgingly accepted the agreement, but both were embittered by it.

Black demands continued to escalate during 1965, and government efforts to satisfy them continued to intensify. In Selma, Alabama, in March, Martin Luther King, Jr., helped organize a major demonstration by blacks demanding the right to register to vote. Confronted with official resistance, the demonstators attempted a peaceful protest march; but Selma sheriff Jim Clark led local police in a brutal attack on the demonstrators—which, as in Birmingham, was televised to a horrified nation. Two Northern whites participating in the Selma march were murdered in the course of the effort there—one, a minister, beaten to death in the streets of the town; the other, a Detroit housewife, shot as she drove along a highway at night. The national outrage that followed the events in Alabama helped push Lyndon Johnson to propose and win passage of the Civil Rights Act of 1965, which provided federal protection to blacks attempting to exercise their right to vote. The traditional criteria for limiting the franchise to whites—literacy tests, knowledge of the Constitution, "good character," and others—were now illegal. (Another, similar device—the poll tax—had been abolished by constitutional amendment in 1964.)

But the civil-rights acts, the Supreme Court decisions, the new social welfare programs designed to help poor blacks, and other government efforts—all were insufficient. Important as such gains were, they failed to satisfy the rapidly rising expectations of American blacks, whose vision of equality included not only an end to segregation but access to economic prosperity. What had once seemed to many liberals a simple moral commitment was becoming a far more complex and demanding issue. Gradually, the generally peaceful, largely optimistic civil-rights movement of the early 1960s was evolving into what would become a major racial crisis.

The Changing Movement

It was inevitable, perhaps, that the focus of the racial struggle would shift away from the issue of segregation to the far broader and more complex demands of poor urban blacks. For decades, the nation's black population had been undergoing a major demographic shift; and by the 1960s, the problem of race was no longer a primarily Southern or rural one, as it had been earlier in the century. In 1910, only 25 percent of all blacks had lived in cities and only 10 percent outside the South. By 1966, 69 percent were living in metropolitan areas and 45 percent outside the South. In several of the largest cities, the proportion of blacks at least doubled between 1950 and 1968. Blacks constituted 30 percent or more of the population of seven major cities and nearly 70 percent of the population of Washington, D.C.

Conditions in the black ghettoes of most cities were abysmal. And although the economic condition of much of American society was improving, in many poor urban communities—which were experiencing both a rapidly growing population and the flight of white businesses—things were getting worse. More than half of all American nonwhites lived in poverty at the beginning of the 1960s; black

unemployment was twice that of whites. And although conditions improved for many blacks during the decade, the residents of the inner cities were usually the last to benefit. Black ghetto residents were far more likely than whites to be victimized by crime, to be enticed into drug addiction, and to be subjected to substandard housing at exploitive prices. They were far less likely than whites to receive an adequate education or to have access to skilled employment.

As the battle against legal segregation progressed in the early 1960s with the passage of the landmark Civil Rights Acts of 1964 and 1965, even such relatively moderate black leaders as Martin Luther King, Jr., began to turn their attention to the deeper, less immediately visible problems of their race. By the mid-1960s, the legal battle against school desegregation had moved beyond the initial assault on de jure segregation (segregation by law) to an attack on de facto segregation (segregation by practice, as through residential patterns), thus carrying the fight into Northern cities. Such attacks would lead (beginning in 1970) to the busing of students from one area of a community to another to achieve integration—an issue that would prove deeply divisive.

Many black leaders (and their white supporters) were demanding, similarly, that the battle against job discrimination move beyond the prohibition of overtly racist practices. Employers should not only abandon negative measures to deny jobs to blacks; they should adopt positive measures to recruit minorities, thus compensating for past injustices. Lyndon Johnson gave his support to the concept of "affirmative action" in 1965. Three years later, the Department of Labor ruled that all contractors doing business with the federal government must submit "a written affirmative action compliance program" to the government. Affirmative action guidelines gradually extended to all institutions doing business with or receiving funds from the federal government (including schools and universities). Yet another issue had arisen that would soon anger and alienate many whites.

And civil-rights activists were now, increasingly, directing their attention toward racism in the North. Martin Luther King, Jr. organized a major campaign in the summer of 1966 (a year after Selma) in Chicago. He hoped to direct national attention to housing and employment discrimination in Northern industrial cities in much the same way he had exposed legal racism in the South. But the Chicago campaign not only evoked vicious and at times violent opposition from white residents of that city; it failed to arouse the national conscience to anything approaching the degree the events in the South had done.

Urban Violence

As the Chicago campaign suggested, the most important black problem by the mid-1960s was less legalized segregation than urban poverty. Beginning in 1964, moreover, the problem thrust itself into public prominence when residents of black ghettoes in major cities participated in a series of riots that shocked and terrified much of the nation's white population. There were a few scattered disturbances in the summer of 1964, most notably in New York City's Harlem. But the first major race riot since the end of World War II occurred the following summer in the Watts section of Los Angeles. In the midst of a more or less routine traffic arrest, a white police officer struck a protesting black bystander with his club. The apparently minor incident unleashed a storm of pent-up anger and bitterness that resulted in a full week of mounting violence. As many as 10,000 rioters were estimated to have participated—attacking white motorists, burning buildings, looting stores, and sniping at policemen. As in most race riots, it was blacks who suffered most; of the thirty-four people who died during the Watts uprising, which was eventually quelled by the National Guard, twenty-eight were black. In the summer of 1966, there were forty-three additional outbreaks, the most serious of them in Chicago and Cleveland. And in the summer of 1967, there were eight major riots, including the most serious of them all—a racial clash in Detroit in which forty-three people (thirty-three of them black) died.

Televised reports of the violence alarmed millions of Americans and created both a new sense of urgency and a growing sense of doubt among those whites who had embraced the cause of racial justice only a few years before. After the Detroit uprising, President Johnson expressed the ambivalence of many white liberals about the riots, calling sternly on the one hand for a restoration of law and order, and appealing simultaneously for an attack on the social problems that were causing despair and violence. A special Commission on Civil Disorders echoed the latter impulse. Its celebrated report, issued in the spring of 1968, recommended massive spending to eliminate the abysmal conditions of the ghettoes. "Only a commitment to national action on an un-precedented scale," the commission concluded, "can shape a future compatible with the historic ideals of American society." To much of the nation, however, the lesson of the riots was that racial change was moving too quickly and that stern, coercive measures were necessary to stop violence and lawlessness.

Black Power

Disillusioned with the ideal of peaceful change in cooperation with whites, an increasing number of blacks were turning to a new approach to the racial issue: the philosophy of "black power." Black power could mean many different things. In its most moderate form, it was simply a belief in the importance of black self-reliance. In its more extreme guises, black power could mean complete separatism and even violent revolution. In all its forms, however, black power suggested a move away from interracial cooperation and toward increased awareness of racial distinctiveness.

The most important and lasting impact of the black-power ideology was a social and psychological one: the instilling of racial pride in black Americans who had long been under pressure from their nation's dominant culture to think of themselves as somehow inferior to whites. It encouraged the growth of "black studies" in schools and universities. It helped stimulate important black literary and artistic movements. It produced a new interest among many blacks in their African roots. It led to a rejection by some blacks of certain cultural practices borrowed from white society: "Afro" hair styles began to replace artificially straightened hair; some blacks began to adopt African styles of dress, even to change their names.

But black power had political manifestations as well, most notably in creating a deep schism within the civil-rights movement. Traditional black organizations that had emphasized cooperation with sympathetic whites—groups such as the NAACP, the Urban League, and King's Southern Christian Leadership Conference (SCLC)—now faced competition from younger, more radical groups. The Student Nonviolent Coordinating Committee (SNCC) and the Congress of Racial Equality (CORE) had both begun as relatively moderate, interracial organizations. SNCC, in fact, had been a student branch of the SCLC. By the mid-1960s, however, these and other groups were calling for more radical and occasionally even violent action against the "racism" of

Malcolm X
Malcolm X, a leader of the militant Black Muslims, arrives in Washington, D.C., in May 1963 to set up a headquarters for the organization there. Malcolm was hated and feared by many whites during his lifetime. After he was assassinated in 1965, he came to be widely revered by black Americans.   (UPI/Bettmann Newsphotos)

them, was Malcolm Little, who adopted the name Malcolm X ("X" to denote his lost African surname). His *Autobiography* (1965)—written in collaboration with Alex Haley—became one of the most influential documents of the 1960s. Malcolm X himself died shortly before publication of his book when black gunmen, presumably under orders from rivals within the Nation of Islam, burst into a meeting he was addressing and assassinated him. But he remained an important figure in many black communities long after his death—as important and revered a symbol to some blacks as Martin Luther King, Jr., was to others.

From "Flexible Response" to Vietnam

In international affairs as much as in domestic reform, the optimistic liberalism of the Kennedy and Johnson administrations dictated a more positive, more active approach to dealing with the nation's problems than in the past. Just as social difficulties at home required a search for new solutions, so the threat of communism overseas seemed to call for new methods and strategies. And just as the new activism in domestic reform ultimately produced frustration and disorder, so did the new activism overseas gradually pull the nation toward disaster.

white society and were openly rejecting the approaches of older, more established black leaders.

Other groups were emerging entirely outside the established civil-rights movement. Particularly alarming to whites were such overtly revolutionary organizations as the Black Panthers, based in Oakland, California, and the separatist group, the Nation of Islam, which denounced all whites as "devils" and appealed to blacks to embrace the Islamic faith and work for complete racial separation. The most celebrated of the Black Muslims, as whites often termed

Diversifying Foreign Policy

John Kennedy's stirring inaugural address was a clear indication of how central opposition to communism was to his and the nation's thinking. "In the long history of the world," he proclaimed, "only a few generations have been granted the role of defending freedom in its hour of maximum danger. I do not shrink from this responsibility; I welcome it." Yet the speech—which significantly made no mention whatever of domestic affairs—was also an indication of Kennedy's belief that the United States had not done enough to counter Soviet expansion. The defense policies of the new administration, therefore, emphasized not only strengthening existing implements of warfare but developing new ones—a strategy that came to be known as "flexible response."

Kennedy had charged repeatedly during his campaign that the United States was suffering from a "missile gap," that the Soviet Union had moved ahead of America in the number of missiles and warheads it could deploy. Even before the election, Kennedy received information indicating that whatever missile gap there was favored the United States. Nevertheless, once in office, he insisted on substantial increases in the nation's nuclear armaments. The Soviet Union, which had several years earlier decided to slow the growth of its atomic arsenal, responded with a new missile-building program of its own.

At the same time, Kennedy expressed dissatisfaction with the nation's ability to meet communist threats in "emerging areas" of the Third World—the areas in which, Kennedy believed, the real struggle against communism would be waged in the future. A nuclear deterrent might prevent a Soviet invasion of Western Europe; but in the Middle East, in Africa, in Latin America, in Asia, where insurgent forces had learned to employ methods of jungle and guerrilla warfare, different methods would be necessary. Kennedy gave enthusiastic support to the development of new counter insurgency forces—a million soldiers trained specifically to fight modern, limited wars. He even chose their uniforms, which included the distinctive green beret from which the Special Forces derived their nickname.

Along with military diversification, Kennedy favored the development of methods for expanding American influence through peaceful means. To repair the badly deteriorating relationship with Latin America, he proposed an "Alliance for Progress": a series of projects undertaken cooperatively by the United States and Latin American governments for peaceful development and stabilization of the nations of that region. Its purpose was both to spur social and economic development and to inhibit the rise of Castro-like movements in other Central or South American countries. Poor coordination and inadequate funding sharply limited the impact of the program, but relations between the United States and some Latin American countries did improve. Kennedy also inaugurated the Agency for International Development (AID) to coordinate foreign aid. And he established what became one of his most popular innovations: the Peace Corps, which trained and sent abroad young volunteers to work in developing areas.

Fiasco in Cuba

Kennedy's efforts to improve relations with developing countries were not aided by a hopelessly bungled (and, many believed, ill-conceived) assault on the Castro government in Cuba. Convinced that "communist domination in this hemisphere can never be negotiated" and that Castro represented a threat to the stability of other Latin American nations, Kennedy agreed in the first weeks of his presidency to continue a project the Eisenhower administration had begun. For months, the CIA had been helping secretly to train a small army of anti-Castro Cuban exiles in Central America. On April 17, 1961, with the approval of the president, 2,000 of the armed exiles landed at the Bay of Pigs in Cuba, expecting first American air support and than a spontaneous uprising by the Cuban people on their behalf. They received neither. At the last minute, Kennedy withdrew the air support, fearful of involving the United States too directly in the invasion. And the expected uprising did not occur. Instead, well-armed Castro forces easily crushed the invaders, and within two days the entire mission had collapsed.

A somber President Kennedy took full responsibility for the fiasco. Governments around the world—not only communist but neutral and pro-Western as well—joined in condemning the United States. But despite the humiliation, Kennedy refused to abandon the principle of overthrowing Castro by force. "We do not intend to abandon Cuba to the Communists," he said only three days after the Bay of Pigs.

Confrontations with the Soviet Union

In the grim aftermath of the Bay of Pigs, Kennedy traveled to Vienna in June 1961 for his first meeting with Soviet Premier Nikita Khrushchev. Their frosty exchange of views did little to reduce tensions between the two nations. Nor did Khrushchev's continuing irritation over the existence of a noncommunist West Berlin in the heart of East Germany.

Particularly embarrassing to the communists was the mass exodus of residents of East Germany to the West through the easily traversed border in the center of Berlin. Before dawn on August 13, 1961, the Soviet Union stopped the exodus by directing East Germany to construct a wall between East and West Berlin. Guards fired on those who continued to try to escape. For nearly thirty years, the Berlin Wall served as the most potent physical symbol of the tensions between the communist and noncommunist worlds.

The rising tensions culminated the following

Taking the Cuban Missile Crisis to the UN
Adlai Stevenson (seated at far right), the American ambassador to the United Nations, presents evidence to the Security Council on October 25, 1962, in support of President Kennedy's claim that the Soviet Union was installing offensive nuclear weapons in Cuba. At the same time, an American naval blockade was preparing to intercept any Soviet ships bringing military supplies to the island. (UPI/Bettmann Newsphotos)

October in the most dangerous and dramatic crisis of the Cold War. During the summer of 1962, American intelligence agencies had become aware of the arrival of Soviet technicians and equipment in Cuba and of military construction in progress. At first, the administration assumed that the new weapons system was, as the Soviets claimed, purely defensive. On October 14, however, aerial reconaissance photos produced clear evidence that in fact the Soviets were constructing missile sites on the island. The reasons for the Russian effort were not difficult to discern. The existence of offensive nuclear missiles in Cuba would go far toward compensating for the American lead in deployable atomic weapons, giving the Soviet Union the same easy access to enemy territory that the United States had long possessed by virtue of its missile sites in Europe and the Middle East. The weapons would, moreover, serve as an effective deterrent against any future American invasion of Cuba—a possibility that seemed very real both to Castro and to the Soviet leadership.

To Kennedy, and to most other Americans, the missile sites represented an unconscionable act of aggression by the Soviets toward the United States.

Almost immediately, he decided that the weapons could not be allowed to remain. On October 22, after nearly a week of tense deliberations by a special task force in the White House, the president announced on television that he was establishing a naval and air blockade around Cuba, a "quarantine" against all offensive weapons. Soviet ships bound for the island slowed course or stopped before reaching the point of confrontation. But work on the missile sites continued at full speed. Preparations were under way for an American air attack on the missile sites when, late in the evening of October 26, Kennedy received a message from Khrushchev implying that the Soviet Union would remove the missile bases in exchange for an American pledge not to invade Cuba. Ignoring other, tougher Soviet messages, the president agreed; privately, moreover, he gave assurances that the United States would remove its missiles from Turkey (a decision he had already reached months before but had not yet implemented). On October 27, the agreement became public. The crisis was over.

The Cuban missile crisis brought the world closer to nuclear war than at any time since World War II. It exposed in dangerous fashion the perils that both the Soviet Union and the United States were creating by allowing their own rivalry to extend into Third World countries. But it also, ironically, helped produce at least a momentary alleviation of Cold War tensions. Both the United States and the Soviet Union had been forced to confront the momentous consequences of war, and both seemed ready in the following months to move toward a new accommodation. In June 1963, President Kennedy addressed a commencement audience at American University in Washington, D.C., with a message starkly different from those of his earlier speeches. The United States did not, he claimed, seek a "Pax Americana enforced on the world by American weapons of war." And he seemed for the first time to offer hope for a peaceful rapprochement with the Soviet Union. "If we cannot now end our differences," he said, "at least we can help make the world safe for diversity." That same summer, the United States and the Soviet Union concluded years of negotiation by agreeing to a treaty to ban the testing of nuclear weapons in the atmosphere. It was the first step toward mutual arms reduction since the beginning of the Cold War—a small step, but one that seemed to augur a new era of international relations.

In the longer run, however, the missile crisis had more ominous consequences. The humiliating retreat forced upon the Soviet leadership undermined the position of Nikita Khruschev and contributed to his fall from power a year later. His replacement, Leonid Brezhnev, was a much more orthodox party figure, less interested in reform than Khruschev had been. Perhaps more important, the graphic evidence the crisis gave the Soviets of their military inferiority helped produce a dramatic Soviet arms buildup over the next two decades, a buildup that contributed to a comparable increase in the United States in the early 1980s and that for a time undermined American support for a policy of rapprochement.

Johnson and the World

Lyndon Johnson entered the presidency lacking even John Kennedy's limited prior experience with international affairs. He had never been much involved with foreign relations during his years in the Senate. He had traveled widely while vice president, but he had been included in few important decisions. He was eager, therefore, not only to continue the policies of his predecessor but to prove quickly that he too was a strong and forceful leader. As a result,

he quickly came to depend on those members of the Kennedy administration with the most assertive view of the proper uses of American power.

Johnson was even less adept than his predecessor—who had displayed little sensitivity on the subject—at distinguishing between nationalist insurgency and communist expansion. His response to an internal rebellion in the Dominican Republic was a clear illustration. A 1961 assassination had toppled the repressive dictatorship of General Rafael Trujillo, and for the next four years various factions in the country had struggled for dominance. In the spring of 1965, a conservative military regime began to collapse in the face of a revolt by a broad range of groups (including some younger military leaders) on behalf of the left-wing nationalist Juan Bosch. For Johnson, the situation seemed an ideal opportunity to display the effectiveness of American force. Arguing (without any evidence) that Bosch planned to establish a pro-Castro, communist regime, he dispatched 30,000 American troops to quell the disorder. The troops remained—although later they came under the auspices of the Organization of American States—until the Johnson administration had assurances that the Dominican Republic would establish a pro-American, anticommunist regime. Only after a conservative candidate defeated Bosch in a 1966 election were the forces withdrawn.

From Johnson's first moments in office, however, his foreign policy was almost totally dominated by the bitter civil war in Vietnam and by the expanding involvement of the United States there. That involvement had been growing slowly for more than a decade by the time Johnson assumed the presidency. In many respects, therefore, he was simply the unfortunate legatee of commitments initiated by his predecessors. But the determination of the new president, and of others within his administration, to prove their resolve in the battle against communism helped produce the final, decisive steps toward a full-scale commitment.

Guns and Advisers

The American involvement in Vietnam had developed so slowly and imperceptibly that when it began spectacularly to expand, in 1964 and 1965, few could remember how it had originated. The first steps toward intervention, certainly, had seemed at the time to be little more than minor events on the periphery of the larger Cold War. American aid to French forces

The United States in Latin America, 1954–1990

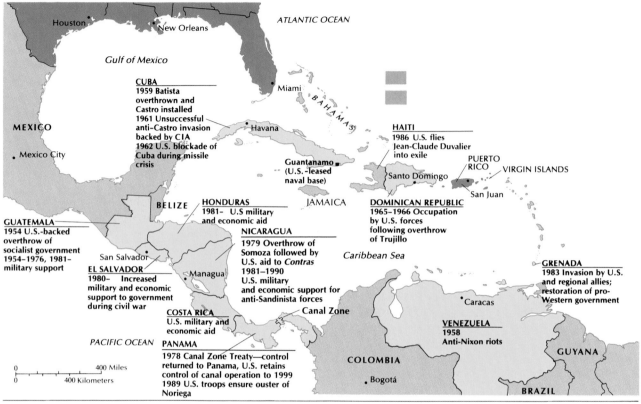

CUBA
1959 Batista overthrown and Castro installed
1961 Unsuccessful anti-Castro invasion backed by CIA
1962 U.S. blockade of Cuba during missile crisis

HAITI
1986 U.S. flies Jean-Claude Duvalier into exile

MEXICO

Guantanamo (U.S.-leased naval base)

HONDURAS
1981– U.S military and economic aid

DOMINICAN REPUBLIC
1965–1966 Occupation by U.S. forces following overthrow of Trujillo

GUATEMALA
1954 U.S.-backed overthrow of socialist government 1954–1976, 1981– military support

NICARAGUA
1979 Overthrow of Somoza followed by U.S. aid to *Contras*
1981–1990 U.S. military and economic support for anti-Sandinista forces

EL SALVADOR
1980– Increased military and economic support to government during civil war

GRENADA
1983 Invasion by U.S. and regional allies; restoration of pro-Western government

COSTA RICA
U.S. military and economic aid

VENEZUELA
1958 Anti-Nixon riots

PANAMA
1978 Canal Zone Treaty—control returned to Panama, U.S. retains control of canal operation to 1999
1989 U.S. troops ensure ouster of Noriega

in Indochina before 1954 had been limited and indirect; the nation's involvement with the Diem regime thereafter, while more substantial, seemed for several years no greater than its involvement with many other Third World governments. But as Diem began to face growing internal opposition, and as the threat from the communists to the north appeared to grow, the United States found itself drawn ever deeper into what would ultimately become widely known as the "quagmire."

Ngo Dinh Diem had been an unfortunate choice as the basis of American hopes for a noncommunist South Vietnam. Autocratic, aristocratic, and corrupt, he staunchly resisted any economic reforms that would weaken the position of the Vietnamese upper class and the power of his own family. A belligerent Roman Catholic in a nation with many Buddhists, he invited dissent through his efforts to limit the influence of the Buddhist religion.

Diem's own limitations intensified problems that would have faced any South Vietnamese ruler,

for the partition of the country in 1954 had never satisfied Ho Chi Minh and his supporters, many of whom had remained in the South. By the late 1950s, therefore, a powerful insurgency was growing in strength in South Vietnam—an insurgency encouraged and supplied in large part by the government of the north. By 1958, a fierce civil war was in progress. And two years later, that war intensified, as communist guerrillas (or Viet Cong, as they were known to their opponents) organized the National Front for the Liberation of South Vietnam (NLF). The NLF had close ties to the government of Ho Chi Minh and, as the war expanded in the ensuing years, received increasing assistance from the north.

Faced with a steadily deteriorating political and military position, Diem appealed to the United States for assistance. The Eisenhower administration increased the flow of weapons and ammunition to South Vietnam during its last years in office and introduced the first few American military advisers to the area—about 650 in all. The Kennedy administration, with its fervent belief in the importance of fighting communism in emerging areas, expanded that assistance into a major commitment. Despite misgivings about the reliability of Diem, Kennedy substantially increased the flow of munitions into South Vietnam. More important, he raised the number of American military personnel to 15,500.

But the real depth of the American commitment to the war became clear in 1963, when the Diem regime stood on the brink of collapse. The military struggle against the Viet Cong was going badly. Diem's brutal tactics in dispersing Buddhist demonstrators in Saigon had produced a religious crisis as well. Several Buddhist monks burned themselves to death in the streets of the capital, arousing further popular resistance to the government and horrifying the American public, which witnessed the immolations on television. Early in November, after receiving tacit assurances of support from the United States, South Vietnamese military leaders seized control of the government from Diem, executing the deposed president, his brother, and other associates. The Americans had not sanctioned the killings, but they had been instrumental in instigating the coup. Faced with what he considered a choice between allowing South Vietnam to fall and expanding the American involvement, John Kennedy had chosen the latter. Before he could indicate what further steps he was prepared to take, he himself fell victim to an assassin on November 22.

From Aid to Intervention

Lyndon Johnson, therefore, inherited what was already a substantial American commitment to the survival of an anticommunist South Vietnam. During his first two years in office, he expanded that commitment into a full-scale American war. Why he did so has long been a subject of debate. (See "Where Historians Disagree," pp. 906–907.)

Many factors played a role in Johnson's fateful decision. But the most obvious explanation is that the new president faced many pressures to expand the American involvement and only a very few to limit it. As the untested successor to a revered and martyred president, he felt obliged to prove his worthiness for the office by continuing the policies of his predecessor. Aid to South Vietnam had been one of the most prominent of those policies. Johnson also felt it necessary to retain in his administration many of the important figures of the

Kennedy years. In doing so, he surrounded himself with a group of foreign policy advisers—Secretary of State Dean Rusk, Secretary of Defense Robert McNamara, National Security Adviser McGeorge Bundy—who believed not only that the United States had an obligation to resist communism in Vietnam but that it possessed the ability and resources to make that resistance successful. As a result, Johnson at times lacked access to information making clear how difficult the new commitment might become. A compliant Congress raised little protest to, and indeed at one point openly endorsed, Johnson's use of executive powers to lead the nation into war. And for several years at least, public opinion remained firmly behind him—in part because Barry Goldwater's bellicose remarks about the war during the 1964 campaign made Johnson seem by comparison to be a moderate on the issue. Above all, intervention in South Vietnam was fully consistent with nearly twenty years of American foreign policy. An anticommunist ally was appealing to the United States for assistance; all the assumptions of the containment doctrine, as it had come to be defined by the 1960s, seemed to require the nation to oblige. Johnson seemed unconcerned that the government of South Vietnam existed largely because the United States had put it there and that the regime had never established full legitimacy among its own people. Vietnam, he believed, provided a test of American willingness to fight communist aggression, a test he was determined not to fail.

During his first months in office, Johnson expanded the American involvement in Vietnam only slightly, introducing an additional 5,000 military advisers there and preparing to send 5,000 more. Then, early in August 1964, the president announced that American destroyers on patrol in international waters in the Gulf of Tonkin had been attacked by North Vietnamese torpedo boats. Later information raised serious doubts as to whether one of the attacks had actually occurred and, if it had, whether it had been, as the president insisted, "unprovoked." At the time, however, virtually no one questioned Johnson's portrayal of the incident as a serious act of aggression or his insistence that the United States must respond. By a vote of 416 to 0 in the House and 88 to 2 in the Senate (with only Wayne Morse of Oregon and Ernest Gruening of Alaska dissenting), Congress hurriedly passed the Gulf of Tonkin Resolution, which authorized the president to "take all necessary measures" to protect American forces and "prevent further aggression" in Southeast Asia. The resolution

— WHERE HISTORIANS DISAGREE —

The Vietnam Commitment

In 1965 the Department of Defense released a film, intended for American soldiers about to embark for service in Vietnam and designed to explain why the United States had found it necessary to commit so many lives and resources to the defense of a small and distant land. The film was entitled *Why Vietnam?* The question it asked is one many Americans have pondered, and debated, in the two decades since. The debate has proceeded on two levels. At one level, it is an effort to assess the broad objectives that Americans believed they were pursuing in Vietnam. At another, it is an effort to explain how and why policymakers made the specific decisions that led to the American commitment.

The Defense Department film itself offered one answer to the question of America's broad objectives, an answer that for a time most Americans tended to accept: The United States was fighting in Vietnam to defend freedom and stop aggression; and it was fighting in Vietnam to prevent the spread of communism into a new area of the world, to protect not only Vietnam but also the other nations of the Pacific that would soon be threatened if Vietnam itself were to fall. That explanation—that America intervened in Vietnam to defend its ideals and its legitimate interests—continues to attract support. Journalist Norman Podhoretz's 1982 book *Why We Were in Vietnam* argues that America was in Vietnam "to save the Southern half of that country from the evils of communism" and that the tragic events in Indochina since 1975 prove the essential morality of the American cause. Political scientist Guenter Lewy contends, in *America in Vietnam* (1978), that the

United States entered Vietnam to help an ally combat "foreign aggression." R. B. Smith has argued that Vietnam was a vital American interest, that the global concerns of the United States required a commitment there. And historian Ernest R. May has stated: "The paradox is that the Vietnam War, so often condemned by its opponents as hideously immoral, may well have been the most moral or at least the most selfless war in all of American history. For the impulse guiding it was not to defeat an enemy or to serve a national interest; it was simply not to abandon friends."

Others have argued that America's broad objectives in Vietnam were less altruistic, that the intervention was a form of imperialism—part of a larger effort by the United States after World War II to impose a particular political and economic order on the world. "The Vietnam War," historian Gabriel Kolko wrote in *Anatomy of a War* (1985), "was for the United States the culmination of its frustrating postwar effort to merge its arms and politics to halt and reverse the emergence of states and social systems opposed to the international order Washington sought to establish." Economist Robert Heilbroner, writing in 1967, saw the American intent as somewhat more defensive; the intervention in Vietnam was a response to "a fear of losing our place in the sun," to a fear that a communist victory "would signal the end of capitalism as the dominant world order and would force the acknowledgement that America no longer constituted the model on which the future of world civilization would be mainly based."

Those who have looked less at the nation's broad objectives than at the internal workings of

became, in Johnson's view at least, an open-ended legal authorization for escalation of the conflict.

Publicly committed now to the defense of what the United States claimed was an independent, democratic government in the south, the administration had to confront the failure of any faction to establish a stable regime there to replace Diem. With the South Vietnamese leadership in disarray, more and more of the burden of opposition to the Viet Cong fell on the United States. In February 1965, seven marines died

when communist forces attacked an American military base at Pleiku. Johnson retaliated by ordering the first United States bombings of the north, attempting to destroy the depots and transportation lines that were responsible for the flow of North Vietnamese soldiers and supplies into South Vietnam. The bombing continued until 1972, even though there was little evidence that it was effective in limiting North Vietnamese assistance to the NLF.

A month later, in March 1965, two battalions of

WHERE HISTORIANS DISAGREE

the policymaking process have likewise produced competing explanations. Journalist David Halberstam's *The Best and the Brightest* (1972) argues that policymakers deluded themselves into thinking they could achieve their goals in Vietnam by ignoring, suppressing, or dismissing the information that might have suggested otherwise. The foreign policy leaders of the Kennedy and Johnson administrations were so committed to the idea of American activism and success that they refused to consider the possibility of failure; the Vietnam disaster was thus, at least in part, a result of the arrogance of the nation's leaders.

Larry Berman, a political scientist, offers a somewhat different view in *Planning a Tragedy* (1982). Lyndon Johnson never believed that American prospects in Vietnam were bright or that a real victory was within sight, Berman argues. Johnson was not misled by his advisers. He committed American troops to the war in Vietnam in 1965 not because he expected to win but because he feared that allowing Vietnam to fall would ruin him politically. To do otherwise, Johnson believed, would destroy his hopes for winning approval of his Great Society legislation at home.

Leslie H. Gelb (who as an official in the Defense Department in the 1960s directed the writing of the official study of the war that became known as the Pentagon Papers) has produced another, related explanation for American intervention, which sees the roots of the involvement in the larger imperatives of the American foreign policy system. In *The Irony of Vietnam: The System Worked,* published in 1979 and written in collaboration with political scientist Richard K. Betts,

Gelb argues that intervention in Vietnam was the logical, perhaps even inevitable result of a political and bureaucratic order shaped by certain ideological assumptions. The American foreign policy system was wedded to the doctrine of containment and operated, therefore, in response to a single, overriding imperative: the need to prevent the expansion of communism.

The United States, Gelb maintains, stumbled into a commitment to a shaky government in South Vietnam in the 1950s, and the unvarying policy of every subsequent administration until 1975 was to do what was necessary to prevent the collapse of that government. They were doing so not because they anticipated victory but because they saw no alternative. However high the costs of intervention, they believed, the costs of not intervening, of allowing South Vietnam to fall, would be higher. At every step, American presidents did the minimum they thought necessary to stave off the collapse of South Vietnam. In the 1950s and early 1960s, that meant modest economic and military assistance. In the mid-1960s, as the military situation worsened, the same commitment required the introduction of American troops in large numbers. Only when the national and international political situation had shifted to the point where it was possible for American policymakers to reassess the costs of the commitment—to conclude that the costs of allowing Vietnam to fall were less than the costs of continuing the commitment (a shift that began to occur in the early 1970s)—was it possible for the United States to begin disengaging.

American marines landed at Da Nang in South Vietnam. Although Johnson continued to insist that he was not leading the United States into a ground war in Southeast Asia, there were now more than 100,000 American troops in Vietnam. The following July, finally, the president publicly admitted that the character of the war had changed. American soldiers would now, he announced, begin playing an active role in the conduct of the war. By the end of the year, there were more than 180,000 American combat

troops in Vietnam; in 1966, that number doubled; and by the end of 1967, there were nearly 500,000 American soldiers fighting on the ground, while the air war had intensified until the tonnage of bombs dropped ultimately exceeded that in Europe during World War II. Meanwhile, American casualties were mounting. In 1961, 14 Americans had died in Vietnam; in 1963, the toll was 489. By the spring of 1966, more than 4,000 Americans had been killed; and they were continuing to die at a faster rate than soldiers in

The War in Vietnam and Indochina, 1964–1975

CHINA

Lao Cai

Than Uyen

Yen Bay

Dienbienphu

NORTH VIETNAM

BURMA

Red River

Hanoi

Haiphong

Red River Delta

Gulf of Tonkin

Pak Seng

Luang Prabang

Ban Ban

Plain of Jars

Vang Vieng

Hainan

L A O S

Vinh

Vientiane

Mekong River

Udon Thani

Phanom

Dong Hoi

Partition Line 1954

Vinh Linh

DMZ (Demilitarized Zone)

QUANG TRI PROVINCE

Khesanh

Hue

Phu Bai

Da Nang

Hoi An

FRIENDSHIP HIGHWAY

THAILAND

Tamky

Chulai

My Lai

Quang Ngai

Takhli

Don Muang

Udon Ratchathani

Dak To

South China Sea

Lop Buri

Ratchasima

Kontum

Plateau of Kontum

Ankhe

Pleiku

Quinhon

Bangkok

Angkor Wat

Plateau of Darlac

Tonle Sap

CAMBODIA

Battambang

Ban Me Thout

Nhatrang

Sattahip

Mekong River

Kompong Cham

Bo Duc

Da Lat

Camranh Bay

Phnom Penh

Prey Veng

1970: U.S. and South Vietnam troops entered Viet Cong strongholds inside Cambodia

Tay Ninh

Phanrang

SOUTH VIETNAM

Gulf of Thailand

Ben Cat

Sihanoukville

Tan Son Nhut Airbase

Bienhua

Saigon

Rach Gia

Cantho

Vung Tau

Mekong Delta

Quan Long

Ca Mau Peninsula

Con Son

0   150 Miles

0   150 Kilometers

■   U.S. bases

←   U.S. and South Vietnam invasion of Cambodia

←   Ho Chi Minh Trail (communist supply route)

"Walking the High Ground" in Vietnam

An American patrol makes its way along the raised earthen pathways that thread through flooded rice paddies in South Vietnam. The Vietnamese landscape, unfamiliar to American soldiers (and to the commanders planning tactics and strategy), was itself a significant factor in frustrating American war aims.   (UPI/Bettmann Newsphotos)

the ineffective South Vietnamese army. Yet the gains resulting from the carnage had been negligible. The United States had finally succeeded in 1965 in creating a reasonably stable government in the south under General Nguyen Van Thieu. But the new regime was hardly less corrupt or brutal than its predecessors, and no more able than they to maintain control over its own countryside. The Viet Cong, not the Thieu regime, controlled the majority of South Vietnam's villages and hamlets.

The Quagmire

For more than seven years, therefore, American combat forces remained bogged down in a war that the United States was never able either to win or fully to understand. Combating a foe whose strength lay not in weaponry but in a pervasive infiltration of the population, the United States responded with the kind of heavy-handed technological warfare designed for conventional battles against conventional armies. American forces succeeded in winning most of the major battles in which they became engaged, routing the Viet Cong and their North Vietnamese allies from such strongholds as Dak To, Con Thien, and later, Khe Sanh. There were astounding (if not always reliable) casualty figures showing that far more communists than Americans were dying in combat—statistics that the United States military referred to as a "favorable kill ratio." There was a continuing

stream of optimistic reports, from American military commanders, civilian officials, and others, that the war was progressing—including the famous words of Secretary of Defense McNamara that he could "see the light at the end of the tunnel." But if the war was not actually being lost, neither was it being won. It was, moreover, becoming a war that critics argued could not be won.

At the heart of the problem was that the United States was not fighting an army as much as a popular movement. The Viet Cong derived their strength in part from the aid they received from North Vietnam and, indirectly, from the Soviet Union and China. Equally important, however, was their success in mobilizing members of the native population—men, women, and even children—who were indistinguishable from their neighbors and who fought not only openly in major battles but covertly through sabotage, ambush, and terror. American troops might drive Viet Cong forces from a particular village or city; but as soon as the Americans left, the NLF forces would return. The frustrations of this kind of warfare mounted steadily, until the United States found itself involved in a series of desperate strategies.

Central to the American war effort was the heralded "pacification" program, designed in part by General William Westmoreland, whose purpose was to rout the Viet Cong from particular regions and then "pacify" those regions by winning the "hearts and minds" of the people. Routing the Viet Cong was often possible, but the subsequent pacification was more difficult. American forces were usually incapable of establishing the same kind of rapport with provincial Vietnamese that the highly nationalistic Viet Cong forces were able to achieve.

Gradually, therefore, the pacification program gave way to the more desperate "relocation" strategy. Instead of attempting to win the loyalty of the peasants in areas in which the Viet Cong were operating, American troops would uproot the villagers from their homes, send them fleeing to refugee camps or into the cities (producing by 1967 more than 3 million refugees), and then destroy the vacated villages and surrounding countryside. Saturation bombing, bulldozing of settlements, chemical defoliation of fields and jungles—all were designed to eliminate possible Viet Cong sanctuaries. But the Viet Cong responded simply by moving to new sanctuaries elsewhere. The futility of the United States effort was suggested by the statement of an American officer after flattening one such hamlet that it had been "necessary to destroy [the village] in order to save it."

As the war dragged on and victory remained elusive, some American officers and officials began to urge the president to expand military efforts in Indochina. Some argued for heavier bombing and increased troop strength; others insisted that the United States attack communist enclaves in surrounding countries; a few began to urge the use of nuclear weapons. The Johnson administration, however, resisted. Unwilling to abandon its commitment to South Vietnam for fear of destroying American "credibility" in the world, the government was also unwilling to expand the war too far, for fear of provoking direct intervention by the Chinese, the Soviets, or both. Caught in a trap largely of his own making, the president began to encounter additional obstacles and frustrations at home.

The War at Home

Few Americans, and even fewer influential ones, had protested the American involvement in Vietnam as late as the end of 1965. But as the war dragged on and its futility began to become apparent, political support for it began to erode. At first, the attack emerged from the perimeters of politics: for intellectuals, from students, and from the press. By the end of 1967, the debate over the war had moved fully into the mainstream of national public life.

Many of the earliest objections to the war emerged on college and university campuses. Political scientists, historians, Asian experts, and others began in 1965 to raise questions about both the wisdom and the morality of the Vietnam adventure, arguing that it reflected, among other things, a fundamental American misunderstanding of politics and society in Southeast Asia. A series of "teach-ins" on university campuses, beginning at the University of Michigan in 1965, sparked a national debate over the war, before such debate developed inside the government. Such pacifist organizations as the American Friends Service Committee and the Women's International League for Peace and Freedom organized early protests. By the end of 1967, American students opposed to the war had grown so numerous and so vocal as to form a major political force. Enormous peace marches in New York, Washington, D.C., and other cities drew increasing public attention to the antiwar movement. Campus demonstrations occurred almost daily. A growing number of journalists, particularly reporters who had spent time in Vietnam, helped sustain the movement with their frank revelations about the brutality and apparent futility of the war.

The chorus of popular protest soon began to stimulate opposition to the war from within the government itself. Senator J. William Fulbright of Arkansas, chairman of the powerful Senate Foreign Relations Committee, became one of the earliest influential public figures to turn against the war. Beginning in January 1966, he began to stage highly publicized and occasionally televised congressional hearings to air criticisms of the war, summoning as witnesses such distinguished public figures as George F. Kennan and General James Gavin. Other prominent members of Congress joined Fulbright in opposing Johnson's policies—including, in 1967, Robert F. Kennedy, brother of the slain president, then a senator from New York. Even within the administration, the consensus seemed to be crumbling. Secretary of State Rusk remained a true believer until the end; but McGeorge Bundy and Robert McNamara, both of whom had used their political and intellectual talents to extend the American involvement in Vietnam, quietly left the government in 1967 and 1968. Bundy's successor, Walt W. Rostow, was if anything even more committed to the war than his predecessor and one-time mentor. But the new secretary of defense, Clark Clifford, became a powerful voice within the administration on behalf of a cautious scaling down of the commitment.

Other factors weakened the position of supporters of the war as well. America's most important allies—Great Britain, France, West Germany, and Japan—all began to criticize the Vietnam involvement. Of more immediate concern, the American economy was beginning to suffer. Johnson's commitment to fighting the war while continuing his Great Society reforms—his promise of "guns and butter"—proved impossible to maintain. The inflation rate, which had remained at 2 percent through most of the early 1960s, rose to 3 percent in 1967, 4 percent in 1968, and 6 percent in 1969. In August 1967, Johnson asked Congress for a tax increase—a 10 percent surcharge that was widely labeled a "war tax"—which he knew was necessary if the nation was to avoid even more ruinous inflation. In return, congressional conservatives demanded and received a $6 billion reduction in the funding for Great Society programs. The war in Vietnam, in other words, was now not only a source of concern for its own sake. It had also become a direct threat to liberal efforts to redress social injustices at home.

The Traumas of 1968

By the end of 1967, the twin crises of the war in Vietnam and the deteriorating racial situation at home, crises that fed upon and inflamed each other, had helped create deep social and political tension. In the course of 1968, those tensions seemed suddenly to burst to the surface and threaten national chaos. Not since World War II had the United States experienced so profound a sense of crisis. Perhaps never before in its history had the nation suffered as many traumatic shocks in such short order.

The Tet Offensive

On January 31, 1968, the first day of the Vietnamese New Year (Tet), Viet Cong forces launched an enormous, concerted attack on American strongholds throughout South Vietnam. The attack displayed a strength that American commanders had long insisted the Viet Cong did not possess. Some major cities, most notably Hue, fell to the communists. Others suffered major disruptions. But what made the Tet offensive genuinely shocking to the American people, who saw vivid reports of it on television, was what happened in Saigon. If any place in South Vietnam had seemed secure from enemy attack, it

was the capital city. Now, suddenly, Viet Cong forces were in the heart of Saigon, setting off bombs, shooting down South Vietnamese officials and troops, and holding down fortified areas.

Even more chilling was the evidence the Tet offensive gave of the brutality of the fighting in Vietnam, of the savagery it seemed to have aroused in those who became involved in it. In the midst of the Tet offensive, television cameras recorded the sight of a captured Viet Cong guerrilla being led up to a South Vietnamese officer in the streets of Saigon. Without a word, the officer pulled out his pistol and shot the young guerrilla through the head, leaving him lying dead with his blood pouring onto the street. No single event did more to undermine support in the United States for the war. American forces soon dislodged the Viet Cong from most of the positions they had seized, and the Tet offensive in the end cost the communists such appalling casualties that they were significantly weakened for months to come. Indeed, the Tet defeats permanently depleted the ranks of the NLF and forced North Vietnamese troops to take on a much larger share of the subsequent fighting. But all that had little impact on American opinion. Tet may have been a military victory for the United States; but it was a political defeat for the administration, a defeat from which it would never fully recover.

In the weeks that followed, many of the pillars of American public opinion finally began to move into opposition to the war. Leading newspapers began taking editorial stands in favor of deescalation of the conflict. *Time, Newsweek,* and other national magazines began running searing exposés and urging American withdrawal. Network commentators began voicing open doubts about the wisdom of American policies. Within weeks of the Tet offensive, public opposition to the war had almost doubled. And Johnson's personal popularity rating had slid to 35 percent, the lowest of any president since Harry Truman.

The Political Challenge

As early as the summer of 1967, dissident Democrats had been attempting to mobilize support behind an antiwar candidate who would challenge Lyndon Johnson in the 1968 primaries. For many months, they tried to enlist Senator Robert Kennedy, the most widely known critic of the war. But mindful of the difficulties in challenging an incumbent president,

Kennedy declined. In his stead, the dissidents recruited Senator Eugene McCarthy of Minnesota, a subdued, cerebral candidate who avoided heated rhetoric in favor of carefully reasoned argument and attracted a particularly devoted following among college students. A brilliantly orchestrated campaign by young volunteers in the New Hampshire primary produced a startling showing by McCarthy in March; he polled nearly as many votes as the president.

A few days later, Robert Kennedy finally entered the campaign, deeply embittering many of those who had dedicated themselves to the cause of McCarthy, but bringing his own substantial strength among blacks, poor people, and workers to the antiwar cause. Polls showed the president trailing badly in the next scheduled primary, in Wisconsin. Public animosity toward Johnson was such that he did not dare venture from the White House to campaign. On March 31, Johnson went on television to announce a limited halt in the bombing of North Vietnam—his first major concession to the antiwar forces—and, much more surprising, his withdrawal from the presidential contest.

For a moment, it seemed as though the antiwar forces had won—that nothing could stop them from seizing the Democratic presidential nomination and even the presidency itself. Robert Kennedy quickly established himself as the champion of the Democratic primaries, winning one election after another. In the meantime, however, Vice President Hubert Humphrey, with the support of President Johnson, entered the contest and began to attract the support of party leaders and of the many delegations that were selected not by popular primaries but by state party organizations. He soon appeared to be the front runner in the race.

The King Assassination

In the midst of this bitter political battle, in which the war had been the dominant issue, the attention of the nation suddenly turned again to the matter of race in response to a shocking tragedy. On April 4, Martin Luther King, Jr., who had traveled to Memphis, Tennessee, to lend his support to a strike by black sanitation workers in the city, was shot and killed while standing on the balcony of his motel. The assassin, James Earl Ray, who was captured days later in London, had no apparent motive. Later evidence suggested that he had been hired by others to do the

killing, but he himself never revealed the identity of his employers.

The tragic death of King, who had remained the most widely admired black leader among both blacks and whites, deeply affected Americans of all races, producing an outpouring of grief matched in recent memory only by the reaction to the death of John Kennedy. Among blacks, however, it also produced widespread anger. In the days after the assassination, major riots broke out in more than sixty American cities. Forty-three people died; more than 3,000 suffered injuries; as many as 27,000 people were arrested. None of these riots was as intense as some earlier disturbances, but together the disorders were the greatest single manifestation of racial unrest in the nation's history.

The Kennedy Assassination and Chicago

Robert Kennedy continued his campaign for the presidential nomination. Late in the night of June 6, he appeared in the ballroom of a Los Angeles hotel to acknowledge the cheers of his supporters for his victory in that day's California primary. Waiting for him in a back room, in the meantime, was Sirhan Sirhan, a young Palestinian who had become enraged, apparently, by pro-Israeli remarks Kennedy had made several days earlier in a televised debate with Eugene McCarthy. As Kennedy was leaving the ballroom after his victory statement, Sirhan emerged from a crowd and shot him in the head. Early the next morning, Kennedy died.

By the time of his death, Robert Kennedy—who earlier in his career had been widely considered a cold, ruthless agent of his more appealing brother—had emerged as a figure of enormous popular appeal. More than John Kennedy, Robert identified his hopes with the American "underclass"—with blacks, Hispanics, Indians, the poor—and with the many American liberals who were coming to believe that the problems of such groups demanded attention. Indeed, it was Robert Kennedy more than John who shaped what some would later call the "Kennedy legacy" and what would for a time become central to American liberalism: the fervent commitment to using government to help the powerless. In addition, Robert had an impassioned following among many people who saw in him (and his family) the kind of glamour and hopefulness they had come, at least in retrospect, to identify with the martyred president.

The Battle of Chicago, 1968
City police battle young antiwar demonstrators in downtown Chicago on August 28, 1968, while the Democratic National Convention was meeting to nominate a presidential candidate less than a mile away. The media expressed horror at the violence of the police, but opinion polls later revealed that a majority of the American people was more hostile toward the demonstrators.   (UPI/Bettmann Newsphotos)

His campaign appearances inspired outbursts of public enthusiasm rarely seen in political life.

The passions Kennedy aroused made his violent death a particularly shattering experience for the American people. In reality, he had been the victim of a single, apparently crazed individual. But to much of the nation, stunned and bewildered by yet another public tragedy, Kennedy seemed to have been a victim of national social chaos.

The presidential campaign continued gloomily during the last weeks before the convention. Hubert Humphrey, who had seemed likely to win the nomination even before Robert Kennedy's death, now faced only minor opposition. Despite the embittered claims of many Democrats that Humphrey would simply continue the bankrupt policies of the Johnson administration, there seemed no possibility of stopping him. The approaching Democratic Convention, therefore, began to take on the appearance of an exercise in futility; and antiwar activists, despairing of winning any victories within the convention, began to plan major demonstrations outside it.

When the Democrats finally gathered in Chicago in August, even the most optimistic observers were predicting a turbulent convention. Inside the hall, carefully sealed off from all demonstrators by Mayor Richard Daley, delegates engaged in a long, bitter debate over an antiwar plank that both Kennedy and McCarthy supporters wanted to insert in the platform. Miles away, in a downtown park, thousands of students and other antiwar protesters had set up camps and were staging demonstrations. On the third night of the convention, as the delegates were beginning their balloting on the now virtually inevitable nomination of Hubert Humphrey, demonstrators and police clashed in a bloody riot in the streets of Chicago. Hundreds of protesters were injured as police attempted to disperse them with tear

Election of 1968   (60.6% of electorate voting)

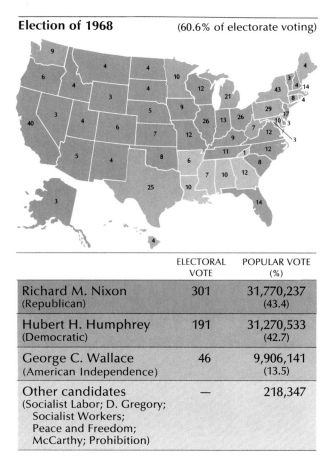

	ELECTORAL VOTE	POPULAR VOTE (%)
Richard M. Nixon (Republican)	301	31,770,237 (43.4)
Hubert H. Humphrey (Democratic)	191	31,270,533 (42.7)
George C. Wallace (American Independence)	46	9,906,141 (13.5)
Other candidates (Socialist Labor; D. Gregory; Socialist Workers; Peace and Freedom; McCarthy; Prohibition)	—	218,347

gas and billy clubs. Aware that the violence was being televised to the nation, the demonstrators taunted the authorities with the chant, "The whole world is watching!" And Hubert Humphrey, who had spent years dreaming of becoming his party's candidate for president, received a nomination that night which appeared at the time to be almost worthless.

The Conservative Response

The turbulent events of 1968 persuaded many observers that American society was on the verge of a fundamental social upheaval. Newspapers, magazines, the press—all helped create the impression of a nation in the throes of revolutionary change. In fact, however, the prevailing response of the American people to the turmoil was a conservative one.

The most visible sign of the conservative backlash was the surprising success of the campaign of

George Wallace for the presidency. Wallace had established himself in 1963 as one of the leading spokesmen for the defense of segregation when, as governor of Alabama, he had attempted to block the admission of black students to the University of Alabama. In 1968, he became a third-party candidate for president, basing his campaign on a host of conservative grievances. Although he tempered some of his earlier positions on the race issue, he continued to appeal to those who resented the intrusion of the federal government into local affairs. He denounced the forced busing of students, the proliferation of government regulations and social programs, and the permissiveness of authorities toward race riots and antiwar demonstrations. He chose as his running mate a retired air force general, Curtis LeMay, who was a bellicose advocate of expanding the war in Vietnam. There was never any serious chance that Wallace would win the election; but his remarkable standing in the polls over many months—rising at times to over 20 percent of those interviewed—was a clear indication that he had struck a responsive chord.

A more effective effort to mobilize the "silent majority" in favor of order and stability was under way within the Republican party. Richard Nixon, whose political career had seemed at an end after his losses in the presidential race of 1960 and a California gubernatorial campaign two years later, reemerged as the preeminent spokesman for "Middle America." Although he avoided the crudeness and stridency of the Wallace campaign, he skillfully exploited many of the same concerns that were sustaining the Alabama governor. Nixon was more perceptive than many other leaders in realizing that many Americans were now tired of hearing about their obligations to the poor, tired of hearing about the sacrifices necessary to achieve racial justice, tired of judicial reforms that seemed designed to help criminals. By offering a vision of stability, law and order, government retrenchment, and "peace with honor" in Vietnam, he easily captured the nomination of his party for the presidency. And after the spectacle of the Democratic Convention, he and his running mate, Governor Spiro Agnew of Maryland, enjoyed a commanding lead in the polls as the November election approached.

That lead diminished greatly in the last weeks before the voting. Old doubts about Nixon's character—doubts based in part on the sometimes vicious anticommunism of his earlier career—continued to haunt the Republican candidate. A skillful last-minute surge by Hubert Humphrey, who

SIGNIFICANT EVENTS

somehow managed to restore at least a tenuous unity to the Democratic party, narrowed the gap further. And the continuing appeal of George Wallace appeared to be hurting the Republicans more than the Democrats. In the end, however, Nixon eked out a victory almost as narrow as his defeat in 1960. He received 43.4 percent of the popular vote to Humphrey's 42.7 percent (a margin of only about 500,000 votes), and 301 electoral votes to Humphrey's 191.

George Wallace, who like most third-party candidates faded in the last weeks of the campaign, still managed to poll 13.5 percent of the popular vote and to carry five Southern states with a total of 46 electoral ballots. Nixon had hardly won a decisive mandate. But the election had made one thing clear. The majority of the American people were more interested in the restoration of stability than in fundamental social change.

SUGGESTED READINGS

General Studies.   Godfrey Hodgson, *America in Our Time* (1976); Charles R. Morris, *A Time of Passion* (1984); Allen J. Matusow, *The Unraveling of America* (1984); Theodore H. White, *America in Search of Itself* (1982); William Chafe, *The Unfinished Journey* (1986).

Kennedy and Johnson.   Theodore H. White, *The Making of the President, 1960* (1961); Arthur M. Schlesinger, Jr., *A Thousand Days* (1965); Theodore Sorensen, *Kennedy* (1965); Richard N. Goodwin, *Remembering America* (1988); Herbert Parmet, *Jack* (1980) and *JFK* (1983); Henry Fairlie, *The Kennedy Promise* (1973); David Burner, *John F. Kennedy and a New Generation* (1988); Lewis Paper, *The Promise and the Performance* (1975); Bruce Miroff, *Pragmatic Illusions* (1976); Garry Wills, *The Kennedy Imprisonment* (1982); Thomas Brown, *JFK: The History of an Image* (1988); *The Report of the Warren Commission* (1964); William Manchester, *The Death of a President* (1967); Anthony Summers, *Conspiracy* (1980); Edward J. Epstein, *Inquest* (1966) and *Legend* (1978); Henry Hurt, *Reasonable Doubt* (1985); Doris Kearns, *Lyndon Johnson and the American Dream* (1976); Eric Goldman, *The Tragedy of Lyndon Johnson* (1968); Ronnie Dugger, *The Politician* (1982); Robert Caro, *The Years of Lyndon Johnson: The Path to Power* (1982), and *Means of Ascent* (1990); Lyndon B. Johnson, *Vantage Point* (1971); George Reedy, *The Twilight of the Presidency* (1970); Jim Heath, *Decade of Disillusionment* (1975); Vaughn D. Bornet, *The Presidency of Lyndon B. Johnson* (1983); Paul K. Conkin, *Big Daddy from the Pedernales* (1986).

Domestic Policies.   Tom Wicker, *JFK and LBJ* (1968); Jim Heath, *John F. Kennedy and the Business Community* (1969); Victor Navasky, *Kennedy Justice* (1971); James Sundquist, *Politics and Policy* (1968); Sar Levitan, *The Great Society's Poor Law* (1969); Sar Levitan and Robert Taggart, *The Promise of Greatness* (1976); Daniel Knapp and Kenneth Polk, *Scouting the War on Poverty* (1971); Robert H. Haveman, ed., *A Decade of Federal Antipoverty Programs* (1977); Greg J. Duncan, *Years of Poverty, Years of Plenty* (1984); Charles Murray, *Losing Ground* (1984); Frances Fox Piven and Richard Cloward, *Regulating the Poor* (1971); Hugh Davis Graham, *Uncertain Trumpet* (1984); Allen J. Matusow, *The Unraveling of America: A History of Liberalism in the 1960s* (1984); James T. Patterson, *America's Struggle Against Poverty, 1900–1980* (1981); Henry J. Aaron, *Politics and the Professors* (1978); John E. Schwarz, *America's Hidden Success* (1983).

Race Relations.   David Lewis, *King* (1970); Carl Brauer, *John F. Kennedy and the Second Reconstruction* (1977); Martin Luther King, Jr., *Why We Can't Wait* (1964); David Garrow, *Protest at Selma* (1978), *The FBI and Martin Luther King* (1981), and *Bearing the Cross* (1986); Taylor Branch, *Parting the Waters* (1988); William Chafe, *Civilities and Civil Rights* (1980); Hugh Davis Graham, *The Civil Rights Era* (1990); Steven Lawson, *Black Ballots: Voting Rights in the South, 1966–1969* (1976); Abigail Thernstrom, *Whose Votes Count?*

Affirmative Action and Minority Voting Rights (1987); Harris Wofford, *Of Kennedy and Kings* (1980); Stephen Oates, *Let the Trumpet Sound* (1982); Doug McAdam, *Freedom Summer* (1988); Stokely Carmichael and Charles Hamilton, *Black Power* (1967); Alex Haley, *The Autobiography of Malcolm X* (1966); Benjamin Muse, *The American Negro Revolution* (1969); Eugene Wolfenstein, *The Victims of Democracy: Malcolm X and the Black Revolution* (1981); Robert Fogelson, *Violence as Protest* (1971); Joe R. Feagin and Harlan Hahn, *Ghetto Revolts* (1973); *Report of the National Advisory Commission on Civil Disorders* (1968); Paul Burstein, *Discrimination, Jobs, and Politics* (1985).

Foreign Policy.   Richard Walton, *Cold War and Counterrevolution* (1972); Louise Fitzsimmons, *The Kennedy Doctrine* (1972); Roger Hilsman, *To Move a Nation* (1965); Philip Geyelin, *Lyndon B. Johnson and the World* (1966); Richard Barnet, *Intervention and Revolution* (1968); Haynes Johnson, *The Bay of Pigs* (1964); Peter Wyden, *Bay of Pigs* (1969); Trumbull Higgins, *The Perfect Failure: Kennedy, Eisenhower, and the CIA at the Bay of Pigs* (1987); Elie Abel, *The Missile Crisis* (1966); Graham Allison, *Essence of Decision* (1971); Robert Kennedy, *Thirteen Days* (1969); Herbert Dinerstein, *The Making of a Missile Crisis* (1976); Dan Kurzman, *Santo Domingo* (1966); Jerome Slater, *Intervention and Negotiation* (1970); Richard D. Mahoney, *JFK: Ordeal in Africa* (1983); Warren Cohen, *Dean Rusk* (1980); Gerald T. Rice, *The Bold Experiment: JFK's Peace Corps* (1985).

Vietnam.   George C. Herring, *America's Longest War*, rev. ed. (1986); Stanley Karnow, *Vietnam* (1983); R. B. Smith, *An International History of the Vietnam War: The Kennedy Strategy* (1985); *The Pentagon Papers,* Senator Gravel edition (1975); David Halberstam, *The Best and the Brightest* (1972); Neil Sheehan, *A Bright Shining Lie* (1988); Guenter Lewy, *America in Vietnam* (1978); John Galloway, *The Gulf of Tonkin Resolution* (1970); Alexander Kendrick, *The Wound Within* (1974); Norman Podhoretz, *Why We Were in Vietnam* (1982); Leslie Gelb and Richard Betts, *The Irony of Vietnam: The System Worked* (1979); Larry Berman, *Planning a Tragedy* (1982); George McT. Kahin, *Intervention* (1986); Gabriel Kolko, *The Anatomy of a War* (1985); Wallace J. Thies, *When Governments Collide* (1980); Michael Herr, *Dispatches* (1977); Lawrence Baskir and William Strauss, *Chance and Circumstance* (1978); Gloria Emerson, *Winners and Losers* (1976); Mark Baker, *Nam* (1982); Al Santoli, *Everything We Had* (1981); Wallace Terry, *Bloods* (1984); William Broyles, Jr., *Brothers in Arms: A Journey from War to Peace* (1986); Thomas Powers, *Vietnam: The War at Home* (1973); Irwin Unger, *The Movement* (1974); Peter Braestrup, *Big Story* (1977, abridged ed. 1978); Don Oberdorfer, *Tet* (1971); Bruce C. Palmer, Jr., *The 25-Year War* (1984); Col. Harry Summers, *On Strategy* (1981); Thomas C. Thayer, *War Without Fronts* (1985); Robert W. Komer, *Bureaucracy at War* (1986); Ronald Spector, *Advice and Support* (1983).

1968. David Caute, *The Year of the Barricades* (1988); Lewis Chester, Godfrey Hodgson, and Lewis Page, *American Melodrama* (1969); David Farber, *Chicago '68* (1988); Charles Kaiser, *1968 in America* (1988); Godfrey Hodgson, *America in Our Time* (1976); Arthur M. Schlesinger, Jr., *Robert Kennedy and His Times* (1978); Norman Mailer, *Miami and the Siege of Chicago* (1968); Ben Stavis, *We Were the Campaign* (1969); Marshall Frady, *Wallace,* rev. ed. (1976); Theodore White, *The Making of the President, 1968* (1969).

Richard Nixon Resigns, August 9, 1974
Richard Nixon strikes an incongruously jubilant pose as he boards a helicopter on the White House
lawn, bound for political exile in California after resigning the presidency in the wake of the
Watergate scandals. (*UPI/Bettmann Newsphotos*)

CHAPTER 31

⬚ ⬚ ⬚

The Crisis of Authority

⬚ ⬚ ⬚

The election of Richard Nixon in 1968 was the result of more than the unpopularity of Lyndon Johnson's policies and the divisions within the Democratic party. It was the result, too, of a widespread public reaction against what many believed was a frontal assault on the foundations of American culture. Throughout the late 1960s and early 1970s, new interest groups were mobilizing to demand protections and benefits. New values and assumptions were emerging to challenge traditional patterns of thought and behavior. The United States was in the throes, some believed, of a genuine cultural revolution.

At the same time, however, many Americans—a clear majority, it seemed, on the basis of the 1968 election returns—were tired of and frightened by the social turmoil. They were coming to resent the attention directed toward minorities and the poor, the federal social programs that were funneling billions of dollars into the inner cities to help the poor and unemployed, the increasing tax burden on the middle class, the "hippies" and radicals who were dominating public discourse with their bitter critiques of everything middle-class Americans held dear. It was time, such men and women believed, for a restoration of stability.

In Richard Nixon they found a man who seemed perfectly to match their mood. Himself a product of a hard-working, middle-class family, he had risen to prominence on the basis of his own unrelenting ef-forts. His public demeanor displayed nothing of the flashiness of the Kennedys or the stridency of the Democratic left. He projected instead an image of stern dedication to traditional values. The extraordinary narrowness of his margin of victory in 1968 suggested that many Americans continued to consider him sanctimonious, "tricky," and unappealing. To much of the nation, however, he was the embodiment of the search for a new, more placid social order.

Yet the presidency of Richard Nixon, far from returning calm and stability to American politics, produced more years of crisis. The new president inherited many problems from his predecessor that would have plagued any leader. The war in Vietnam, the social conflicts of the 1960s, the failure of major institutions to perform as the public had come to expect—all had combined by 1969 to make Americans suspicious of their leaders and mistrustful of their government. Yet it was the performance of Nixon's own administration that caused the most rapid erosion of that public respect for authority. By the early 1970s, the once vigorous American economy had begun a long descent into crisis; and the failure of government to reverse its course raised serious questions about the ability of elected officials to govern. Of more immediate importance, beginning in 1972, the administration found itself embroiled in a series of scandals that not only resulted in Nixon's untimely departure from office but further increased public cynicism about the nation's leadership.

The Turbulent Society

What was perhaps most alarming to conservative Americans in the 1960s and 1970s was a pattern of social and cultural protest that seemed to produce constant turmoil and uncertainty. Younger Americans, in particular, were raising a direct and wide-ranging challenge to the conventions of national life; and they were doing so by giving vent to two related impulses.

One was the impulse, emerging from the political left, to create a great new community of "the people," which would rise up to break the power of corrupt elites and would force the nation to end the war, pursue racial and economic justice, and transform its political life. The other, at least equally powerful impulse was not entirely compatible with the first: the vision of individual "liberation." It found expression in part through the efforts of particular groups—blacks, Indians, Hispanics, women, and others—to define and assert themselves as coherent interests and to make demands on the larger society. It also found expression through the efforts of individuals to create a new culture—one that would allow them to escape from what many considered the dehumanizing pressures of the modern "technocracy."

The New Left

Among the products of the racial crisis and the war in Vietnam was a radicalization of many American students, who in the course of the 1960s formed what became known as the New Left. The New Left emerged from many sources, but from nothing so much as the civil-rights movement, in which many idealistic young white Americans had become involved in the early 1960s. (Black Americans had, of course, been committed to the quest for racial justice for many years.) Exposed as a result to evidence of social injustice, enraged by the violence and racism they encountered at the hands of segregationists and others, some civil-rights activists were by the mid-1960s beginning to consider more radical political commitments than they once had embraced. As early as 1962, a group of students (most of them white) gathered in Michigan to form an organization to give voice to their political demands: Students for a Democratic Society (SDS). Their declaration of beliefs, the Port Huron Statement, signaled much of what was to come. "Many of us began maturing in com-

placency," the statement (most of it the work of student activist Tom Hayden) declared. "As we grew, however, our comfort was penetrated by events too troubling to dismiss." In the following years, as the racial crisis grew more intense and the war in Vietnam expanded, members of SDS became even more troubled, extending the scope of their demands and the range of their activities until they had become the cutting edge of student radicalism.

For a time, that radicalism centered on issues related to the modern universities, with which most members of the New Left were associated. A 1964 dispute at the University of California at Berkeley over the rights of students to engage in political activities on campus was the first outburst of what was to be nearly a decade of campus turmoil. The tumultuous Berkeley Free Speech Movement soon moved beyond the immediate issue of pamphlet distribution and produced far more fundamental protests against the depersonalized nature of the modern "multiversity" and against the role of educational institutions in sustaining corrupt or immoral public policies. The antiwar movement greatly inflamed and expanded the challenge to the universities; and beginning in 1968, campus demonstrations, riots, and building seizures became almost commonplace. At Columbia University in New York, students seized the offices of the president and other members of the administration, occupying them for days until local police forcibly ejected them. At Harvard University a year later, the seizure of administrative offices resulted in an even more violent confrontation with police. Over the next several years, hardly any major university was immune to some level of disruption from radicals and activists among its own student body. Occasionally, there were more serious episodes. Small groups of particularly fervent radicals— most notably the "Weathermen," an offshoot of SDS—were responsible for instances of arson and bombing that destroyed some campus buildings and claimed several lives.

The New Left never succeeded in attracting the support of more than a relatively small number of students to its most radical tactics and demands. It succeeded brilliantly, however, in elevating the antiwar movement to the status of a major national crusade. Among other things, student activists were instrumental in organizing some of the largest political demonstrations in American history to protest the war in Vietnam. The march on the Pentagon of October 1967, where demonstrators were met by a solid line of armed troops; the "spring mobilization" of April 1968, which attracted hundreds of thousands of demonstrators in cities around the country; the Vietnam "moratorium" of the fall of 1969, during which millions of opponents of the war gathered in major rallies across the nation; and countless other demonstrations, large and small—all helped thrust the issue of the war into the center of American politics.

Closely related to opposition to the war—and another issue that helped fuel the New Left—was opposition to military conscription. Since the early 1950s, the government had relied on the draft to staff its peacetime army, generally without controversy. But when in the 1960s draftees began to be called on to fight in a stalemated, unpopular war, dissent grew quickly. The gradual abolition of many traditional deferments—for students, teachers, husbands, fathers, and others—swelled the ranks of those faced with conscription (and thus likely to oppose it). And the autocratic manner in which the draft was being administered by General Lewis Hershey spawned even greater bitterness. The shadow of the draft—the possibility of being compelled to join a despised military and fight in a hated war—loomed large over an entire generation of American youth. Draft card burnings became common features of antiwar rallies on college campuses. Many draft-age Americans simply refused induction, accepting what were occasionally long terms in jail as a result. Thousands of others fled to Canada, Sweden, and elsewhere (where they were joined by many deserters from the armed forces) to escape conscription, even though they realized it might be years before they could return home without facing prosecution. Not until 1977, when President Jimmy Carter issued a general pardon to draft resisters and a far more limited amnesty for deserters, did the Vietnam exiles begin to return to the country in substantial numbers.

The Counterculture

Closely allied to the emergence of the New Left was the growth of a new youth culture openly scornful of the values and conventions of middle-class society. The most visible characteristic of the counterculture, as it became known, and the one that seemed to have the widest influence, was a change in life style. As if to display their contempt for conventional standards, young Americans flaunted long hair, shabby or flamboyant clothing, and a rebellious disdain for traditional speech and decorum. Central to the coun-

terculture were drugs: marijuana smoking—which after 1966 became almost as common a youthful diversion as beer drinking had once been—and the use of other, more potent hallucinogens, such as LSD. There was also a new, more permissive view of sex among members of the counterculture.

Parents and others found these open challenges to traditional life the most disturbing aspect of the counterculture, and there was a temptation among many in the older generation to dismiss such youths simply as iconoclasts and hedonists. That was no doubt true of many. But the counterculture also encompassed a philosophy, one that offered a more fundamental challenge to the American mainstream than the changes in appearance and social behavior. Like the New Left, with which it in many ways overlapped, the counterculture challenged the very structure of modern American society, attacking its banality, its hollowness, its artificiality, its isolation from nature. Among the heroes of the counterculture were some of the beat poets and writers of the 1950s—Allen Ginsberg and others—who had been making similar criticisms years before, when few would listen.

The most committed adherents of the counterculture—the hippies, who came to dominate the Haight-Ashbury neighborhood of San Francisco and whose influence spread to many other areas, and the "dropouts," who retreated to rural communes in Colorado, New Hampshire, and elsewhere—rejected modern society altogether and attempted to find refuge in a simpler, more natural existence. But even those whose commitment to the counterculture was less dramatic shared a pervasive commitment to the idea of personal fulfillment. Popular phrases such as "Do your own thing" and "If it feels good, do it" seemed to capture much of the spirit of the counterculture. In a corrupt and alienating society, the new creed seemed to suggest, the first responsibility of the individual is cultivation of the self, the unleashing of one's own full potential for pleasure and fulfillment.

Theodore Roszak, whose book *The Making of a Counter Culture* (1969) became a central document of the era, captured much of the spirit of the movement in his frank admission that "the primary project of our counter culture is to proclaim a new heaven and a new earth so vast, so marvelous that the inordinate claims of technical expertise must of necessity withdraw to a subordinate and marginal status in the lives of men." Charles Reich, in *The Greening of America* (1970), was even more explicit, arguing that the individual should strive for a new form of conscious-

An Icon of the Counterculture
Milton Glaser, a commercial artist who became a major figure in the transformation of American magazine design in the 1960s, produced this poster of folk singer Bob Dylan in 1966. It suggests not only the importance of Dylan and other musicians to the emerging youth culture of the 1960s, but also the flamboyance that would soon become a hallmark of the counterculture. (Milton Glaser, *Dylan,* 1966. Offset lithograph, 33″ x 22″. Collection, The Museum of Modern Art, New York. Gift of the designer.)

ness—"Consciousness III," as he called it—in which the self would be the only reality.

The effects of the counterculture were not restricted to rebellious youths. They reached out as well to the society at large and provided a set of social norms that many young people (and some adults) chose to imitate. Long hair and freakish clothing became the badge not only of hippies and radicals but of an entire generation. The use of marijuana, the freer attitudes toward sex, the iconoclastic (and often obscene) language—all spread far beyond the realm of the true devotees of the counterculture. And perhaps the most pervasive element of the new youth society was one that even the least radical members of the generation embraced: rock music.

Rock-'n'-roll had first achieved wide popularity in the 1950s, on the strength of such early performers as Buddy Holly and, above all, Elvis Presley. Early in the 1960s, its influence began to spread, a result in large part of the phenomenal popularity of the Beatles, whose music was first heard in the United States in 1964. For a time, most rock musicians—like most popular musicians before them—concentrated largely on uncontroversial romantic themes. But rock's driving rhythms, its undisguised sensuality, its often harsh and angry tone—all made it an appropriate vehicle for expressing the themes of the social and political unrest of the late 1960s. By the end of the decade, therefore, rock had begun to reflect many of the new iconoclastic values of its time. Once again, the Beatles helped lead the way by abandoning their once simple and seemingly innocent style for a new, experimental, even mystical approach that reflected the growing popular fascination with drugs and Eastern religions. Others, such as the Rolling Stones, turned even more openly to themes of anger, frustration, and rebelliousness. Many popular musicians used their music to express explicit political radicalism as well—especially some of the leading folk singers of the era, such as Bob Dylan and Joan Baez.

Even those Americans who had no interest in rock music or other aspects of the counterculture could not avoid the evidence of how rapidly the norms of their society were changing. Those who attended movies saw a gradual disappearance of the banal, conventional messages that had dominated films since the 1920s. Instead, they saw explorations of political issues, of new sexual mores, of violence, of social conflict. The most influential source of entertainment of all, television, began similarly to turn away (even if more slowly than the other media) from its evocation of the stable, middle-class, suburban family. Beginning in the early 1970s, it started to offer programming imbued with social conflict—as exemplified by the enormously popular *All in the Family,* whose protagonist, Archie Bunker, was a lower-middle-class bigot.

The Mobilization of Minorities

The growth of black protest, and of a significant white response to it, both preceded the political and cultural upheavals of the 1960s and helped to produce them. It also encouraged other minorities to assert themselves and demand redress of their grievances. For Indians, Hispanic Americans, gay men and women, and others, the late 1960s and 1970s were a time of growing self-expression and political activism.

Seeds of Indian Militancy

Few minorities had deeper or more justifiable grievances against the prevailing culture than American Indians—or Native Americans, as many began to call themselves in the 1960s. Indians were in those years the least prosperous, least healthy, and least stable group in the society. Average annual family income for Indians was $1,000 less than that for blacks. The Native American unemployment rate was ten times the national rate. Joblessness was particularly high on the reservations, where nearly half the Indians lived and where few industries or other sources of employment existed. But even the many Indians who left the reservations for the cities found only limited opportunities. Many had received limited education and training and were qualified only for menial jobs. Life expectancy among Indians was more than twenty years less than the national average. Suicides among Indian youths were a hundred times more frequent than among white youths. And while black Americans attracted the attention (for good or for ill) of many whites, Indians for many years remained largely ignored.

For much of the postwar era, and particularly after the resignation of John Collier as Commissioner of Indian Affairs in 1946, federal policy toward the tribes had been shaped by a determination to incorporate Indians into mainstream American society whether Indians wanted to assimilate or not. Two laws passed in 1953 established the basis of a new policy, which became known as "termination." Through termination, the federal government withdrew all official recognition of the tribes as legal entities, administratively separate from the states in which their reservations existed, and made them subject to the same local jurisdictions as white residents. Indian property was to be managed not by tribal councils, but by private organizations, mostly private banks, which served as trustees of the tribe's resources. At the same time, the government encouraged Indians to assimilate into the white world and funneled many Native Americans into cities, where, presumably, they would adapt themselves to the white world and lose their cultural distinctiveness.

To some degree, the termination and assimilation policies achieved their objectives. The tribes grew weaker as legal and political entities. Many Na-

Aboriginal Territories and Modern Reservations of Western Indian Tribes

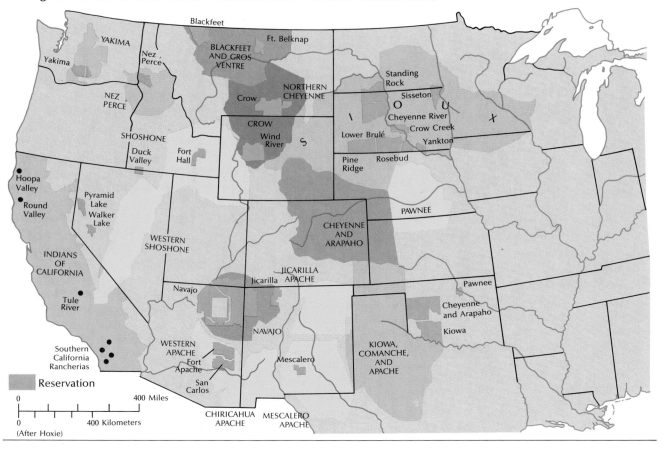

Reservation

0   400 Miles

0   400 Kilometers

(After Hoxie)

tive Americans adapted to life in the cities, at least to a degree; and even though these "urban Indians" remained in many ways distinctive, they were no longer as culturally separate from the larger society as their counterparts on the reservations. On the whole, however, the new policies were a disaster for the tribes and a failure for the white reformers who had created them. Termination led to widespread corruption and abuse. Indians themselves considered it a tragedy and fought so bitterly against it that in 1958 the Eisenhower administration barred further "terminations" without the consent of the affected tribes. In the meantime, the struggle against termination had mobilized a new generation of Indian militants and had breathed life into the principal Native American organization, the National Congress of American Indians (NCAI), which had been created in 1944.

The Democratic administrations of the 1960s did not disavow the termination policy, but neither did they make any effort to revive it. Indeed, the federal government in these years, to the degree that it involved itself in Indian affairs at all, worked to restore at least some degree of tribal autonomy. The funneling of OEO money to tribal organizations through the Community Action program was one prominent example. In the meantime, the tribes themselves were beginning to mobilize to fight for self-determination and liberation—partly in response to the black civil-rights movement and partly in response to other social and cultural changes (among them, the expanding mobility and rising educational levels of younger Indians, who were becoming more aware of the world around them and of their own anomalous place within it). The new militancy also benefited from the rapid increase in the Indian population, which was growing much faster than that of the rest of the nation (nearly doubling between 1950 and 1970 to a total of about 800,000).

The Indian Civil-Rights Movement

In 1961, more than 400 members of 67 tribes gathered in Chicago to discuss ways of bringing all Indians together in an effort to redress common wrongs. The manifesto they issued, the Declaration of Indian Purpose, reflected the same impulse toward cultural liberation that other segments of the population would soon adopt. It stressed the "right to choose our own way of life" and the "responsibility of preserving our precious heritage." Many considered this Chicago meeting the beginning of an Indian civil-rights movement that would gain in strength over the next decade.

The 1961 meeting was only one example of a growing Indian self-consciousness that found expression in countless ways. Indians and others began writing books (for example, Vine Deloria, Jr.'s *Custer Died for Your Sins* and Dee Brown's *Bury My Heart at Wounded Knee*) and otherwise drawing renewed attention to the wrongs inflicted on the tribes by white people in past generations. The National Indian Youth Council, created in the aftermath of the 1961 Chicago meeting, became an important source of activism behind the idea of Indian nationalism and intertribal unity. In 1968, a group of young, militant Indians established the American Indian Movement (AIM), which drew its greatest support from those Indians who lived in urban areas but soon established a significant presence on the reservations as well.

The new activism succeeded in winning some government attention to the plight of the tribes. Congress included Indians in the benefits of the Economic Opportunity Act, and Lyndon Johnson promised in 1968 a "new goal" for Indian programs that "stresses self-determination" and "erases old attitudes of paternalism." That same year, Congress passed the Indian Civil Rights Act, which guaranteed reservation Indians many of the protections accorded other citizens by the Bill of Rights, but which also recognized tribal laws as having legitimacy within the reservations.

But leaders of AIM and other insurgent groups, not satisfied with the cautious official responses to their demands, turned increasingly to direct action. In 1968, Indian fishermen, seeking to exercise old treaty rights on the Columbia River and in Puget Sound, clashed with officials of the state of Washington. The following year, members of several tribes occupied the abandoned federal prison on Alcatraz Island in San Francisco Bay, claiming the site "by right of discovery." In response to the growing pressure, the new Nixon administration appointed a Mohawk-Sioux to the position of Commissioner of Indian Affairs in 1969; and in 1970, the president promised both increased tribal self-determination and an increase in federal aid. Many of these promises were not fulfilled, but the change in direction in federal policy toward support for Indian self-determination was a lasting one—although in the 1970s and 1980s, both the Carter and Reagan administrations showed signs of wanting to limit tribal autonomy and to treat Indians like all other citizens.

Continuing Indian frustration produced the most forceful protests in decades in the winter of 1972–1973. In November 1972, nearly a thousand protesters, most of them Sioux Indians, forcibly occupied the building of the Bureau of Indian Affairs in Washington for six days. A more celebrated protest occurred later that winter at Wounded Knee, South Dakota, the site of the 1890 massacre of Sioux by federal troops.

In the early 1970s, Wounded Knee was part of a large Sioux reservation, two-thirds of which had been leased to white ranchers for generations as an outgrowth of the Dawes Act. Conditions for the Indian residents were desperate and might in themselves have been sufficient to spark resistance. Passions among younger and more militant tribal members were aroused further after the 1972 murder of a Sioux by a group of whites, who were not, many Indians believed, adequately punished. In February 1973, members of AIM seized and occupied the town of Wounded Knee for two months, demanding radical changes in the administration of the reservation and insisting that the government honor its long-forgotten treaty obligations. A brief clash between the occupiers and federal forces left one Indian dead and another wounded. Shortly thereafter the siege came to an end.

More immediately effective than these militant protests were the victories that various tribes were achieving in the 1970s in a wave of lawsuits in the federal courts. Citing violations by the federal government of ancient treaty obligations, Native Americans began winning judicial approval of their demands for restitution. Beginning with a case in Alaska in 1969, the legal actions spread quickly across the country, establishing a possible basis for a major change in the economic status of many tribes. In 1985, the U.S. Supreme Court, in

Wounded Knee
Wounded Knee, South Dakota, had been the site of a conflict between American soldiers and Teton Sioux in 1890. The soldiers had attempted to suppress Indian religious rites ("Ghost Dances"), which whites considered threatening. The result had been a substantial massacre of the tribespeople. In 1973 armed members of the new American Indian Movement seized the village of Wounded Knee (now part of a Sioux reservation) and occupied it for over two months to press their demands for reform in federal Indian policy and tribal government.   (Michael Abramson/Black Star)

County of Oneida v. *Oneida Indian Nation,* supported Indian claims to 100,000 acres in upstate New York that the Oneida tribe claimed by virtue of treaty rights long forgotten by whites. In doing so, the Court raised the possibility that even ancient wrongs could be redressed through judicial action.

The Indian civil-rights movement, like other civil-rights movements of the same time, fell far short of winning full justice and equality for the most oppressed of American minorities. At the same time, it helped the tribes win a series of new legal rights and protections that, together, gave them a stronger position than they had enjoyed at any previous time in this century. It also helped many Indians gain a renewed awareness of and pride in their identity as Indians. Native Americans were demanding not only an end to discrimination against them but also the right to remain a distinct community within the larger United States.

Hispanic-American Activism

More numerous and more visible than Indians were Hispanic-Americans, the fastest-growing minority group in the United States. Large numbers of Mexican-Americans (or Chicanos) had entered the country during World War II in response to the wartime labor shortage, and many had remained in the cities of the Southwest and the Pacific Coast. After the war, when the legal agreements that had allowed Mexican contract workers to enter the country expired, large numbers of immigrants continued to move to the United States illegally. In 1953, the government launched what it called Operation Wetback to deport the illegals, but the effort failed to stem the flow of new arrivals.

By 1960, there were already substantial Chicano neighborhoods (*barrios*) in many American cities, from El Paso to Detroit. The largest (with more than 500,000 people, according to Census figures) was in Los Angeles, which by then had a bigger Mexican population than anyplace except Mexico City. But the greatest expansion in the Hispanic population of the United States was yet to come. In 1960, the Census reported slightly more than 3 million Hispanics living in the United States. In 1970, that number had grown to 9 million, and by 1980 to 14.6 million. Hispanics constituted more than a third of all legal immigrants to the United States after 1960. Since there was also an uncounted but very large number of illegal immigrants in those years (estimates ranged from 7 million to 12 million), the real percentage of Hispanic immigrants was undoubtedly much larger.

They were not, of course, a single, homogeneous group. Large numbers of Puerto Ricans (who were entitled to American citizenship by birth) migrated to eastern cities, particularly New York. South Florida's substantial Cuban population began with a wave of middle-class refugees who had fled the Castro regime in the early 1960s and had moved primarily to Miami. These first Cuban migrants quickly established themselves as a successful and increasingly assimilated part of Miami's middle class. In 1980, a second, much poorer wave of Cuban immigrants—the so-called Marielistas, named for the port from which they left Cuba—arrived in Florida when Castro temporarily relaxed exit restrictions. (This group included a large number of criminals, whom Castro had, in effect, expelled from the country.) This second wave was less easily assimilated and produced severe social tensions in Florida. In the 1980s, large numbers of immigrants (both legal and illegal) began to arrive from the troubled nations of Central and South America—from Guatemala, Nicaragua, El Salvador, Peru, and others. The most numerous Hispanic group, however, remained the Mexican-Americans, who were concentrated in the Southwest and California.

Many Hispanic-Americans were affluent and successful people (for example, the first wave of Cuban exiles in Miami and the long-time Hispanic residents of the Southwest, some of whom were descendants of families who had been living in Mexican territory when it was incorporated into the United States). However, newly arrived Chicanos and others were generally less well educated than either "Anglo" or black Americans and hence less well prepared for high-paying jobs. The fact that many spoke English poorly or not at all further limited their employment prospects. As a result, they found themselves concentrated in poorly paid service jobs.

Like blacks and Indians, Hispanic-Americans responded to the highly charged climate of the 1960s by developing their own sense of ethnic identification and by organizing for political and economic power. Their successes were impressive. The affluent Hispanics in Miami operated major businesses and filled influential positions in the professions and local government; in Los Angeles, Hispanic-Americans organized as an influential political group; and in the Southwest, they elected Mexican-Americans to seats in Congress and to several governorships. A Mexican-American political organization, La Raza Unida, exercised significant influence in southern California and elsewhere in the Southwest in the 1970s and beyond.

For the majority of Hispanics, however, the path to economic and political power was more arduous. Partly because of language barriers and partly because the family-centered culture of many Hispanic communities discouraged effective organization, Mexican-Americans and others were slow to develop political influence in proportion to their numbers. In the meantime, Hispanics formed one of the poorest segments of the U.S. population. In New York, Puerto Rican immigrants were crammed into the city's worst slums, including the notorious South Bronx, which became in the 1970s a national symbol of urban decay. In other cities, Hispanics suffered economic deprivation and overt discrimination; in many areas, they became involved in bitter and violent rivalries with blacks, especially in large cities where teen-aged gangs repeatedly clashed with one another.

One Hispanic group, at least, brought the power of organization and political action strongly to bear against problems of poverty and oppression. In California, an Arizona-born Mexican-American farm worker, César Chávez, succeeded where generations of migrants before him had tried and failed: he created an effective union of itinerant farm workers. His United Farm Workers (UFW), a largely Hispanic organization, launched a prolonged strike in 1965 against growers to demand, first, recognition of their union and, second, increased wages and benefits. When employers resisted, Chávez enlisted the cooperation of college students, churches, and civil-rights groups (including CORE and SNCC) and organized a nationwide boycott, first of table grapes and then of lettuce. In 1968, Chávez campaigned openly for Robert Kennedy, bringing his farm workers into the co-

César Chávez
As the leader of the United Farm Workers, the first Chicano-dominated labor organization to attract national attention, Chávez became for a time the most visible spokesman for and symbol of the needs of Hispanic-Americans. He is shown here leading a demonstration outside the headquarters of the Safeway supermarket chain in San Diego, California, in 1973, protesting the arrest of other UFW members several days earlier. (UPI/Bettmann Newsphotos)

alition of the dispossessed that the senator was attempting to establish and, more important, winning national recognition of the UFW's cause. Two years later, Chávez won a substantial victory when the growers of half of California's table grapes signed contracts with his union. In the following years, his union suffered less from the opposition of growers than from competition with the powerful Teamsters Union, which attempted to entice farm workers into its own vast labor network.

Hispanic Americans also became the focus of another dispute that was to prove divisive in the 1970s: the issue of bilingualism. It was a question that aroused the opposition not only of many whites but of some Hispanics as well. Supporters of bilingualism in education argued that Spanish-speaking Americans were entitled to schooling in their own language, that only thus could they achieve an equal footing with English-speaking students. Opponents cited not only the cost and difficulty of bilingualism but the dangers it posed to the ability of Spanish-speaking students to become assimilated into the mainstream of American culture. Even many Hispanics feared that bilingualism would isolate their communities further from the rest of America and increase resentments toward them.

Challenging the "Melting Pot" Ideal

The efforts of blacks, Hispanics, Indians, and others to forge a clearer group identity ran counter to a longstanding premise of American political thought—the idea of the "melting pot." Older, European immigrant groups liked to believe that they had advanced in American society by assimilating, by adopting the values and accepting the rules of the world to which they had moved and advancing within it on its own terms. The newly militant ethnic groups of the 1960s seemed less willing to accept the standards of the larger society and demanded instead recognition of their own ethnic identity. Advocates of black power specifically rejected cultural assimilation and celebrated the particular achievements of their own race. Mexican-Americans had been calling for a "culturally pluralist" (as opposed to assimilationist) society since the 1920s. The League of United Latin American Citizens, created soon after World War I, not only fought segregated schools and public facilities but also promoted the survival of a Hispanic cultural and political identity.

To a large degree, the advocates of cultural pluralism succeeded. Recognition of the special character of particular groups was embedded in federal law through a wide range of affirmative action programs, which extended not only to blacks, but to Indians, Hispanics, and others as well. The rise of "black studies" programs in schools and universities helped pave the way for new attention to Hispanic and Indian culture and heritage in many institutions as well. The Ethnic Heritage Act of 1972 appropriated federal funds to set up such ethnic studies programs and in the process gave federal recognition to the idea that preservation of "ethnicity" was a "positive constructive force in our society," rather than an obstacle to be overcome by the workings of the "melting pot."

Gay Liberation

The last important liberation movement to emerge in the 1960s, and the most unexpected, was the effort by homosexuals and lesbians to win political and economic rights and, more important, social acceptance. Homosexuality had been an unacknowledged reality throughout American history. Nonheterosexual men and women had long been forced as a result either to suppress their sexual preferences, to exercise them surreptitiously, or to live within isolated and often persecuted communities.

By the late 1960s, the liberating impulses that had affected other groups began to mobilize gay men and women (as homosexuals and lesbians had come to term themselves) to fight for their own rights. A single incident greatly strengthened that impulse. On June 27, 1969, police officers raided the Stonewall Inn, a gay nightclub in New York City, and began arresting patrons simply for frequenting the place. The raid was not unusual, but the response was. Gay onlookers began taunting the police, then attacking them. Someone started a blaze in the Stonewall Inn itself. The fire almost trapped the policemen inside. Rioting continued throughout Greenwich Village (the center of New York's gay community) through much of the night.

The "Stonewall Riot," as it came to be known, marked the beginning of the gay liberation movement—one of the most controversial challenges to traditional values and assumptions of the time. New organizations—among them the Gay Liberation Front, founded in New York in 1969—sprang up around the country. Public discussion and media coverage of homosexuality, long subject to an unofficial taboo, quickly and dramatically increased. Gradually, some cities and states began to consider laws forbidding discrimination on the basis of sexual preference in an effort to end a longstanding practice of treating homosexuals as "aberrant" people who should be barred from contact with the "normal" population.

Most of all, however, the gay liberation movement transformed the outlook of gay men and women themselves. It helped them to "come out," to express their preferences openly and unapologetically, and to demand from society a recognition that gay relationships could be as significant and worthy of respect as heterosexual ones. Many gays, like some radical feminists, hoped for a genuinely revolutionary change in attitudes, not only for an acceptance of homosexuality as a valid and "normal" preference, but for a redefinition of personal identity to give much greater importance to erotic impulses. Those changes did not quickly occur. But by the early 1980s, no one could deny that the gay liberation movement had made remarkable strides.

The New Feminism

American women in the 1960s were hardly a minority. They constituted 51 percent of the population. In the course of the decade, however, many women began to identify with members of other, smaller oppressed groups and to demand a liberation of their own. Sexual discrimination was so deeply embedded in the fabric of society that when feminists first began to denounce it, many Americans responded with bafflement and anger. By the 1970s, however, public awareness of the issue had increased dramatically, and the role of women in American life had changed more radically than that of any other group in the nation.

The Rebirth

Feminism was a weak and often embattled force in American life for more than forty years after the adoption of the woman suffrage amendment in 1920. A few determined women kept feminist political demands alive in the National Woman's Party and other organizations. Many more women expanded the acceptable bounds of female activity by entering the workplace or engaging in political activities. Nevertheless, through the 1950s and early 1960s, it seemed at times as if feminism was almost extinct. Yet within a very few years, it evolved from an almost invisible remnant to one of the most powerful social movements in American history.

The 1963 publication of Betty Friedan's *The Feminine Mystique* is often cited as the first event of contemporary women's liberation. Friedan had graduated from Smith College in 1947. Fifteen years later she traveled around the country to interview her classmates—the great majority of whom were suburban housewives and mothers—and to ask them about the state of their lives. These women were living out the dream that postwar American society had created for them, what Friedan called the "mystique of feminine fulfillment." And yet many of them were deeply frustrated and unhappy. The suburbs, Friedan claimed, had become a "comfortable concentration camp," providing the women who inhabited them with no outlets for their intelligence, talent, and education. The "feminine mystique" was responsible for "burying millions of women alive." The only escape was for them to begin to fulfill "their unique possibilities as separate human beings."

Friedan's book did not so much cause the revival of feminism as help give voice to a movement that was already stirring. By the time the book appeared, John Kennedy had already established the President's Commission on the Status of Women; and although the president's motives in creating it probably had more to do with deflecting more substantive feminist demands than with real commitment to women's goals, the commission brought widespread attention to sexual discrimination and helped create important networks of feminist activists who would lobby for legislative redress. Also in 1963, the Kennedy administration secured passage of the Equal Pay Act, which barred the pervasive practice of paying women less than men for equal work.

A year later, Congress incorporated into the Civil Rights Act of 1964 an amendment—Title VII—that extended to women many of the same legal protections against discrimination that were being extended to blacks. It had been introduced by Southern Democrats attempting to discredit the entire civil-rights package; but it survived the legislative debate and became the basis for a major federal assault on sexual discrimination in later years.

The events of the early 1960s helped expose a contradiction that had been developing for decades between the image and the reality of women's roles in America. The image was what Friedan had called the "feminine mystique"—the ideal of women living happy, fulfilled lives in purely domestic roles. The reality was that increasing numbers of women (including, by 1963, over a third of all married women) had already entered the workplace and were encountering widespread discrimination there; and the reality was, too, that many other women were finding their domestic lives suffocating and frustrating. The conflict between the ideal and the reality was crucial to the rebirth of feminism.

In 1966, three years after publishing her book, Friedan joined with other feminists to create the National Organization for Women (NOW), which was to become the nation's largest and most influential feminist organization. "The time has come," the founders of NOW maintained, "to confront with concrete action the conditions which now prevent women from enjoying the equality of opportunity and freedom of choice which is their right as individual Americans and as human beings." Like other movements for liberation, feminism drew much of its inspiration from the black struggle for freedom. "There is no civil rights movement to speak for women," the NOW organizers claimed, "as there has been for Negroes and other victims of discrimination."

The new organization reflected the varying constituencies of the emerging feminist movement. It responded to the complaints of the women Friedan's book had examined—affluent suburbanites with no outlet for their interests—by demanding greater educational opportunities for women and denouncing the domestic ideal and the traditional concept of marriage. But the heart of the movement, at least in the beginning, was directed toward the needs of women in the workplace. NOW denounced the exclusion of women from professions, from politics, and from countless other areas of American life because of ancient male prejudices about the proper role of women. It decried legal and economic discrimination, including the practice of paying women less than men for equal work (a practice the Equal Pay Act had not eliminated). The organization called for "a fully equal partnership of the sexes, as part of the worldwide revolution of human rights." By the end of the decade, its membership had expanded to 15,000.

Women's Liberation

By the late 1960s, new feminist demands had attracted a large following among affluent, white, educated women—although generally not among the older women whose lives Friedan had studied. The

Women in the Work Force, 1940–1985

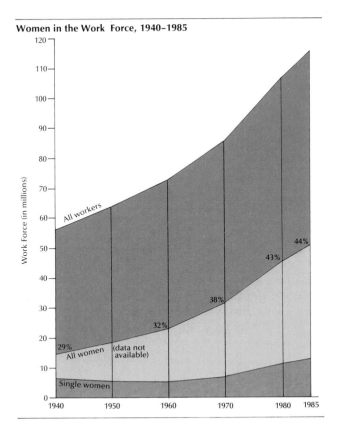

structure. Shulamith Firestone's *The Dialectic of Sex* (1970) was subtitled "The Case for Feminist Revolution."

In its most radical form, the new feminism rejected the whole notion of marriage, family, and even heterosexual intercourse (a vehicle, some women claimed, of male domination). Not many women, indeed not even many feminists, embraced such extremes. But women's growing sense of themselves as an exploited group banding together to force social change was by the early 1970s becoming one of the most powerful phenomena in American life. National magazines and the television networks helped legitimize the women's movement by giving it extensive and increasingly respectful attention. *Ms.* magazine, founded by Gloria Steinem and others, had attracted 200,000 subscribers by 1973.

Perhaps more significant, the women's liberation movement had inspired the creation of countless grass-roots organizations and activities through which women not only challenged sexism and discrimination but created communities of their own. In cities and towns across the country, feminists opened women's bookstores, bars, and coffee shops. They founded local feminist newspapers and magazines. They created centers to assist victims of rape and abuse, women's health clinics (and, particularly after 1973, abortion clinics), and day-care centers.

new feminists were younger, the vanguard of the baby-boom generation; many of them drew inspiration from the New Left and the counterculture. Some were involved in the civil-rights movement, others in the antiwar crusade. Many had found that even within those movements, they faced discrimination and exclusion, that they were constantly subordinated to male leaders. Moving from those experiences, they embraced a more radical feminism than the founders of NOW had envisioned.

By the early 1970s, a significant change was visible in the tone and direction of the organization and of the women's movement as a whole. New books by younger feminists expressed a harsher critique of American society than Friedan had offered. Kate Millett's *Sexual Politics* (1969) signaled the new direction by complaining that "every avenue of power within the society is entirely within male hands." The answer to women's problems, in other words, was not, as Friedan had suggested, for individual women to search for greater personal fulfillment; it was for women to band together to assault the male power

Expanding Achievements

By the early 1970s, both the public and private achievements of the women's movement were already substantial. In 1971, the government extended its affirmative action guidelines to include women—linking sexism with racism as an officially acknowledged social problem. Women were making rapid progress, in the meantime, in their efforts to move into the economic and political mainstream. The nation's major educational institutions began in the late 1960s to open their doors to women for the first time. Princeton and Yale, two of the most prestigious all-male colleges, accepted women undergraduates in 1969. Within a few years, all but a few major academic institutions had done the same. Some women's colleges, in the meantime, began accepting male students.

Women were becoming an important force in business and in the professions. Nearly half of all married women held jobs by the mid-1970s, and almost nine-tenths of all women with college degrees worked. The two-career family, in which both the husband and the wife maintained active professional lives, was becoming a widely accepted norm; many women were postponing marriage or motherhood for the sake of their careers. There were also important symbolic changes, such as the refusal of many women to adopt their husbands' names when they married and the use of the term "Ms." in place of "Mrs." or "Miss"—the latter change intended to denote the irrelevance of a woman's marital status in the professional world.

Women were also advancing in some of the most visible areas of American life. In politics, they were by the early 1970s beginning to compete effectively with men for both elected and appointive positions. In 1980 and again in 1986, two women won seats in the United States Senate—all elected in their own right rather than, like all woman senators before them, to succeed their husbands. A substantial number of women served in the United States House of Representatives throughout the 1970s and 1980s, and two won election to state governorships. The number of female appointments in the executive branch rose steadily; women held cabinet positions in the Carter, Reagan, and Bush administrations. The first female justice of the Supreme Court, Sandra Day O'Connor, took her seat in 1981. And in 1984, the Democratic party chose a woman, Representative Geraldine Ferraro of New York, as its vice-presidential candidate.

In professional athletics, in the meantime, women were beginning to compete with men both for attention and for an equal share of prize money. Billie Jean King spearheaded the most effective female challenge to male domination of sports. Under her leadership, professional woman tennis players established their own successful tours and demanded equal financial incentives when they played in the same tournaments as men. By the late 1970s, the federal government was pressuring colleges and universities to provide women with athletic programs equal to those available to men. In academia, women were expanding their presence in traditional scholarly fields; they were also creating a wholly new field of their own—women's studies, which by the early 1980s was the fastest-growing area of American scholarship. Women even joined what had previously been the most celebrated all-male fraternity in American culture: the space program. Sally Ride became the first woman astronaut to fly in space in 1983.

Of all the feminist crusades of the 1960s and 1970s, none united more women from more different backgrounds than the campaign for passage of the Equal Rights Amendment (ERA). Congress approved the amendment in 1972 and sent it to the states; and for a while it seemed that eventual ratification was only a matter of time. By the end of the 1970s, however, the momentum behind the amendment had died. Approval of the ERA remained several states short of the three quarters necessary for enactment; and some state legislatures that had earlier voted in favor were trying to rescind their approval. In 1979, Congress granted a three-year extension of the time permitted for ratification.

The ERA was in trouble not because of indifference but because of a rising chorus of objections to it from those who feared it would create a major disruption of traditional social patterns. In 1980, the Republican party—after forty years of support for the idea of the ERA—wrote into its platform a new plank opposing the amendment. And two years later, the amendment finally died when the time allotted for ratification expired.

The Abortion Controversy

A vital element of American feminism since the 1920s has been the effort by women to win greater control of their own physical and sexual lives. In its least controversial form, this impulse helped produce an increasing awareness in the 1960s and 1970s of the problems of rape, sexual abuse, and wife beating. Far more divisive, however, was the desire of many women to control their reproductive function in new ways. There continued to be some controversy over the dissemination of contraceptives and birth-control information; but that issue, at least, seemed to have lost much of the explosive character it had possessed in the 1920s, when Margaret Sanger had become a figure of public scorn for her efforts on its behalf. A related issue, however, stimulated as much popular passion as any question of its time: abortion.

Abortion had once been legal in much of the United States, but by the beginning of the twentieth century it was banned by statute in most of the country and remained so into the 1960s (although abortions continued to be performed quietly, and at times dangerously, out of sight of the law). But the growing strength of the women's movement increased pressure on behalf of the legalization of abortion. Several states had abandoned restrictions on abortion by the end of the 1960s. And in 1973, the Supreme Court's decision in *Roe* v. *Wade*, based on a new theory of a constitutional "right to privacy" first recognized by the Court only a few years earlier, invalidated all laws prohibiting abortion during the "first trimester"—the first three months of pregnancy. The issue, it seemed, had been settled. But it soon became clear that it was not (see below, pp. 983–984).

The women's movement was at once the most potent symbol and the most glaring exception to the general impulse toward political and cultural "liberation" of the late 1960s. Feminism expressed both a desire to win social justice through collective political action—a desire that characterized the New Left— and a concern for individual fulfillment and personal freedom—a concern that typified much of the counterculture. But it differed from both in one fundamental respect: its success. The women's movement may not have fulfilled all its goals. But it achieved fundamental and permanent changes in the position of women in American life, and it had itself become a lasting political and social force.

Nixon, Kissinger, and the War

Richard Nixon assumed office in 1969 committed not only to restoring stability at home but to creating a new and more stable order in the world. Few presidents have entered the White House with such well-developed ideas about foreign policy; few have moved as decisively to translate those ideas into practice.

Central to Nixon's hopes for international stability was a resolution of the stalemate in Vietnam. Yet the new president felt no freer than his predecessor to abandon the American commitment in Indochina. He realized that the endless war was undermining both the nation's domestic stability and its position in the world. But he feared that a precipitous retreat would destroy American honor and "credibility."

During the 1968 campaign, Nixon claimed to have formulated a plan to bring "peace with honor" in Vietnam. He had refused to disclose its details. Once in office, however, he soon made clear that the plan consisted of little more than a vague set of general principles, not of any concrete measures to extricate the United States from the quagmire. American involvement in Indochina continued for four more years, during which the war expanded

both in its geographic scope and in its bloodiness. And when a settlement finally emerged early in 1973, it produced neither peace nor honor. It succeeded only in removing the United States from the wreckage.

Vietnamization

Nixon had long considered himself an expert in foreign affairs, and as president he was far more drawn to international matters than to domestic ones. But despite his own passionate interest in diplomacy, he brought with him into government a public figure who ultimately seemed to overshadow the president himself in the conduct of international affairs: Henry Kissinger.

Kissinger was a respected and prolific professor of international politics at Harvard when Nixon tapped him to serve as his special assistant for national security affairs. Both Secretary of State William Rogers, who had served as Eisenhower's attorney general, and Secretary of Defense Melvin Laird, who had been an influential member of Congress, were far more experienced in public life. But Kissinger quickly outshone them both. Nixon's passion for concentrating decision making in the White House was in large measure responsible, but Kissinger's keen intelligence and his remarkable adeptness both in fighting for bureaucratic influence and in currying favor with the press were at least equally important. Together, Nixon and Kissinger set out to find an acceptable solution to the stalemate in Vietnam.

The new Vietnam policy moved along several fronts. One was an effort to limit domestic opposition to the war so as to permit the administration more political space in which to maneuver. Aware that the military draft was one of the most visible targets of dissent, the administration devised a new "lottery" system, through which only a limited group—those nineteen-year-olds with low lottery numbers—would be subject to the draft. The new system would continue to supply the military with its manpower needs while removing millions of potential critics from the danger of conscription. Later, the president urged the creation of an all-volunteer army that would permit the abolition of the draft altogether. By 1973, the Selective Service System was on its way to at least temporary extinction.

More important in stifling dissent, however, was the new policy of "Vietnamization" of the war—that is, the training and equipping of the South Vietnam-

Kent State University, May 4, 1970
On May 3, 1970, aroused by the announcement of the American invasion of Cambodia, students at Kent State University in Ohio attacked and burned an ROTC building on campus. Ohio Governor James Rhodes, calling the demonstrators "worse than the [Nazi] brownshirts," ordered National Guard forces to the campus to restore order. During the next day's tense confrontation—shown here, with a student hurling a tear-gas canister back at National Guardsmen—nervous guardsmen fired into the crowd, killing four students. (UPI/Bettmann Newsphotos)

ese military to assume the burden of combat in place of American forces. In the fall of 1969, Nixon announced the withdrawal of 60,000 American ground troops from Vietnam, the first reduction in U.S. troop strength since the beginning of the war. The withdrawals continued steadily for more than three years, so that by the fall of 1972 relatively few American soldiers remained in Indochina. From a peak of more than 540,000 in 1969, the number had dwindled to about 60,000.

Vietnamization did help undermine domestic opposition to the war. It did nothing, however, to break the stalemate in the negotiations with the North Vietnamese in Paris. The new administration quickly decided that new military pressures would be necessary to do that.

Escalation

By the end of their first year in office, Nixon and Kissinger had decided that the most effective way to tip the military balance in America's favor was to destroy the "staging areas" in Cambodia from which the North Vietnamese had been launching many of their attacks. Very early in his presidency, Nixon ordered the air force to begin a series of secret bombings of Cambodian territory to destroy the enemy sanctuaries. He withheld information about the raids from Congress and the public. In the spring of 1970,

with what some have claimed was American encouragement and support, conservative military leaders overthrew the neutral government of Prince Norodom Sihanouk, Cambodia's leader for two decades, and established a new, pro-American regime under General Lon Nol. Lon Nol quickly gave his approval to American incursions into his territory; and on April 30, Nixon went on television to announce that he was ordering American troops across the border into Cambodia to "clean out" the bases that the enemy had been using for its "increased military aggression."

So successful had Nixon been in seeming to de-escalate the war that the once-powerful peace movement had by mid-1970 begun to lose much of its strength. The Cambodian invasion, however, restored it to life. The first days of May saw the most widespread and vocal antiwar demonstrations ever. Hundreds of thousands of protesters gathered in Washington to denounce the president's policies. Millions, perhaps, participated in countless smaller demonstrations on campuses nationwide. Antiwar frenzy was reaching so high a level that it became possible briefly to believe that a genuine revolution was imminent.

The mood of crisis intensified on May 4, when four college students were killed and nine others injured when members of the National Guard opened fire on antiwar demonstrators at Kent State University in Ohio. The incident seemed to many young

Americans to confirm their worst suspicions of their government and their society. Ten days later, police killed two black students at Jackson State University in Mississippi during a demonstration there.

The clamor against the war quickly spread beyond the campuses and into the government and the press. Congress angrily repealed the Gulf of Tonkin Resolution in December, stripping the president of what had long served as the legal basis for the war. Nixon ignored the action, claiming that he had the authority to continue military efforts in Vietnam to protect American troops already there. Then, in June 1971, first the *New York Times* and later other newspapers began publishing excerpts from a secret study of the war prepared by the Defense Department during the Johnson administration. The so-called Pentagon Papers, leaked to the press by former Defense official Daniel Ellsberg, provided confirmation of what many had long believed: that the government had often been dishonest, both in reporting the military progress of the war and in explaining its own motives for American involvement. The administration went to court to suppress the documents, but to no avail. The Supreme Court ruled that the press had the right to publish them.

Particularly troubling, both to the public and to the government itself, were signs of decay within the American military. Morale and discipline among U.S. troops in Vietnam, who had been fighting a savage and inconclusive war for more than five years, was rapidly deteriorating. The trial and conviction in 1971 of Lieutenant William Calley, who was charged with overseeing a massacre of more than 100 unarmed South Vietnamese civilians, attracted wide public attention to the dehumanizing impact of the war on those who fought it. Less publicized were other, more widespread problems among American troops in Vietnam: desertion, drug addiction, refusal to obey orders, even the occasional killing of unpopular officers by enlisted men. Among the disenchanted—deserters, draft resisters, and others—were not simply the radical college students so unpopular with most Americans but many otherwise conventional sons of middle- and lower-class families. The continuing carnage, the increasing savagery, and the social distress at home were drawing an ever-larger proportion of the population into opposition to the war. By 1971, nearly two-thirds of those interviewed in public-opinion polls were urging American withdrawal from Vietnam.

From Richard Nixon, however, there came no sign of retreat. On the contrary, the events of the spring of 1970 left him more convinced than ever of the importance of resisting what he once called the "bums" who opposed his military policies. With the approval of the White House, both the FBI and the CIA intensified their surveillance and infiltration of antiwar and radical groups, often resorting to blatant illegalities in the process. Administration officials sought to discredit prominent critics of the war by leaking damaging personal information about them. At one point, White House agents broke into the office of a psychiatrist in an unsuccessful effort to steal files on Daniel Ellsberg. During the congressional campaign of 1970, Vice President Spiro Agnew, using the acid rhetoric that had already made him the hero of many conservatives, stepped up his attack on the "effete" and "impudent" critics of the administration. The president himself once climbed on top of an automobile to taunt a crowd of angry demonstrators.

In Indochina, meanwhile, the fighting raged on. In February 1971, the president ordered the air force to assist the South Vietnamese army in an invasion of Laos—a test, as he saw it, of his Vietnamization program. Within weeks, the badly mauled South Vietnamese scrambled back across the border in defeat. American bombing in Vietnam and Cambodia continued to increase, despite its apparent ineffectiveness, so that by the end of 1971 the Nixon administration had dropped more explosives on the region in three years than the Johnson administration had done in five. When in March 1972 the North Vietnamese mounted their biggest offensive since 1968, Nixon responded by escalating the bombing once again, ordering attacks on targets near Hanoi, the capital of North Vietnam, and Haiphong, its principal port. He called as well for the mining of seven North Vietnamese harbors (including Haiphong) to stop the flow of supplies from China and the Soviet Union.

"Peace with Honor"

The approach of the 1972 presidential election, in which the war promised to be the leading issue, seemed finally to do what years of military frustration and escalating public protests had failed to do: convince the administration that it must alter its terms for the withdrawal of American forces. In April 1972, the president dropped his longtime insistence on a removal of North Vietnamese troops from the south before any American withdrawal. In July, word leaked out that Henry Kissinger had been meeting privately in Paris with the North Vietnamese foreign secretary, Le Duc Tho, and rumors abounded that a cease-fire was near. On October 26, only days before the presidential election, Kissinger announced that "peace is at hand."

Several weeks later (after the election), negotiations broke down once again. Although both the American and the North Vietnamese governments were ready to accept the Kissinger-Tho plan for a cease-fire, the Thieu regime balked, still insisting that the full withdrawal of North Vietnamese forces from the south be a prerequisite to any agreement. Kissinger tried to win additional concessions from the communists to meet Thieu's objections, but on December 16—despite the American insistence that the agreement was "99 percent complete"—talks broke off.

The next day, December 17, American B-52s began twelve days of bombing of North Vietnamese cities, the heaviest and most destructive raids of the entire war. The Pentagon announced that the bombers were attacking docks, airfields, railyards, power plants, and the like; but many of those targets were located in the middle of heavily populated urban areas, and civilian casualties were high. So were American losses. Fifteen of the giant bombers were shot down by the North Vietnamese; in the entire war to that point, the United States had lost only one B-52. Then, on December 30, Nixon terminated the "Christmas bombing" as quickly as he had begun it. The United States and the North Vietnamese returned to the conference table. And on January 27, 1973, representatives of the four interested parties (the governments of the United States, North Vietnam, and South Vietnam, together with the "Provisional Republican Government" of the south—the Viet Cong) signed an "agreement on ending the war and restoring peace in Vietnam." Nixon liked to claim that the Christmas bombing had forced the North Vietnamese to relent. But a more important factor was the increasing American pressure on Thieu to accept the cease-fire and Nixon's promise to him that the United States would respond "with full force" to any violation of the agreement. Some have suggested that the Christmas bombing was designed more to convince Thieu of American resolve than to break the will of the North.

The terms of the Paris accords were little different from those that Kissinger and Tho had accepted in principle the previous fall. There would be an immediate cease-fire, and the North Vietnamese would release several hundred American prisoners of war, whose fate had become an emotional issue of great importance within the United States. After that, the agreement descended quickly into murky and plainly unworkable political arrangements. The Thieu regime would survive for the moment—perhaps the only major concession Kissinger was able to wrest from Tho. But there would be no withdrawal of North Vietnamese forces from the south and no abandonment of the communist commitment to a reunified Vietnam. What Nixon described as a "peace with honor" turned out to be little more than a formula for allowing the United States to extricate itself from the quagmire before the South Vietnamese regime collapsed.

Defeat in Indochina

The American forces were hardly out of Indochina and the prisoners of war barely reunited with their families before the Paris accords collapsed. During the first year after the cease-fire, the contending Vietnamese armies suffered greater battle losses than the Americans had endured during ten years of fighting. In Laos, fighting came to an end only after communist forces had established control of more than half the country. In Cambodia, the war raged on, and American planes continued to bomb communist installations in that country until Congress compelled the president to desist in August 1973. In March 1975, finally, the North Vietnamese launched a full-scale offensive against the now hopelessly weakened forces of the south. Thieu appealed to Washington for assistance; the president (by now, Gerald Ford) appealed to Congress for additional funding; Congress refused. Late in April 1975, communist forces marched into Saigon, shortly after officials of the Thieu regime and the American embassy had fled the country in humiliating disarray. Communist forces quickly occupied the capital, renamed it Ho Chi Minh City, and began the process of reuniting Vietnam under the harsh and often brutal rule of Hanoi. At about the same time, the Lon Nol regime in Cambodia fell to the Khmer Rouge, the Cambodian equivalent of the Viet Cong.

Still the war in Indochina did not end. Although Vietnam was soon reunited after more than thirty years of civil war, conflict continued in the surrounding nations. In Cambodia, the Khmer Rouge government of Pol Pot (who renamed the country Kampuchea) launched a reign of terror perhaps unparalleled in modern history. Their vision of an

The Fall of Saigon
The chaotic evacuation of Americans from Saigon in the spring of 1975, only hours before victorious North Vietnamese troops entered the city, was a humiliating spectacle. Desperate South Vietnamese soldiers and officials fought with American soldiers and diplomats for space on the few airplanes and helicopters available. (UPI/ Bettmann Newsphotos)

agrarian society, unpolluted by urban or Western influences, caused them literally to empty the nation's cities and towns and force virtually the entire population to move to the countryside. The result was the death—by murder, exhaustion, or starvation—of more than a third of the country's residents. In 1978, the communist government of the now united Vietnam launched an invasion of Cambodia and drove Pol Pot and the Khmer Rouge from power. The war, however, did little to resolve the problems of that unhappy country.

Vietnam, in the meantime, faced an invasion of its territory by the forces of communist China, which supported Pol Pot and feared the extension of Russian influence in the region. The two sides established an uneasy truce after several weeks of fighting, but there remained no stable peace between the ancient adversaries. American officials had claimed for years that the collapse of South Vietnam would lead quickly to coordinated communist domination of all of Southeast Asia. In fact, the new regimes were soon fighting each other as bitterly as they had once fought against the West.

Such were the dismal results of more than a decade of direct American military involvement in Vietnam. More than 1.2 million Vietnamese soldiers had died in combat, along with countless civilians throughout the region. A beautiful land had been ravaged; an ancient culture had been all but destroyed. The agrarian economy of much of Indochina lay in ruins. Even in the mid- 1980s, Vietnam remained one of the poorest nations in the world. And a country the United States had attempted in vain to make into a viable democratic nation was now under the control of a repressive, authoritarian regime closely tied to the Soviet Union.

The United States had paid a heavy price as well. The war had cost the nation almost $150 billion in direct costs and much more indirectly. It had resulted in the deaths of over 55,000 young Americans and the injury of 300,000 more, some of whom were permanently maimed or crippled. An entire generation had been scarred by the experience, many of them cruelly disillusioned, some of them deeply and permanently embittered toward their government and their political system. And the nation had suffered a blow to its confidence and self-esteem from which it would not soon recover. A decade before, Americans had believed that they could create a great society at home and maintain peace and freedom in the world. Now many harbored serious doubts about their ability to do either.

Nixon, Kissinger, and the World

The continuing war in Vietnam provided a dismal backdrop to what Nixon considered his larger mission in world affairs: the construction of a new international order. The president had become convinced that old assumptions of a "bipolar" world—in which the United States and the Soviet Union were the only truly great powers—were now obsolete. The rise of China, Japan, and Western Europe, the increasing nationalism of the Third World, the growing disunity within the communist alliance—all augured a new, "multipolar" international structure. To deal with this changing world, Nixon drew on the theories of Henry Kissinger, a longtime student of the nineteenth-century European balance of power. The United States must, Nixon and Kissinger believed, work for a new equilibrium. "It will be a safer world and a better world," the president proclaimed in 1971, "if we have a strong, healthy United States, Europe, Soviet Union, China, Japan—each balancing the other, not playing one against the other, an even balance."

Nixon and Kissinger believed it was possible to construct something like the "balance of power" that had permitted nineteenth-century Europe to enjoy nearly a century of relative stability. To do that, America would need to do several things. It would need to encourage what became known as "trilateralism," recognizing that the noncommunist world was not a single bloc dominated by the United States, but three major power centers (America, Europe, and Japan), each with its own role to play in the world. America would also have to bring China out of its isolation so that it too could play its proper role as one of the major elements in the international balance. And the United States would have to find some means of reaching accommodation with the Soviet Union, by recognizing that country's legitimate interests in the world and by trying to induce the Soviets to defend those interests with restraint and responsibility in a multipolar world.

The China Initiative

For more than twenty years, ever since the fall of Chiang Kai-shek in 1949, the United States had treated China, the second largest nation on earth, as if it did not exist. One of the world's greatest powers, a nation now in possession of nuclear weapons, was living in almost total isolation from the West, while the United States continued to recognize the decaying regime-in-exile on Taiwan as the legitimate government of China.

Nixon and Kissinger were determined to forge a new relationship with the Chinese communists. A rapprochement would, among other things, strengthen China's position as a counterbalance to the Soviet Union, thus inducing the Russians to adopt a more conciliatory attitude toward the United States. The Chinese, for their part, were at least equally eager for a new relationship with the United States. Their own dispute with the Soviet Union had grown far more bitter than any rivalry they had with the West. By 1970, Soviet and Chinese forces were massed along both sides of the border, poised, it seemed, for a war between the two communist powers. The Beijing government was eager, therefore, both to forestall the possibility of a Soviet-American alliance against China and to end China's own isolation from the international arena.

In July 1971, Nixon sent Henry Kissinger on a secret mission to Beijing. When Kissinger returned, the president made the startling announcement that he would visit China himself within the next few months. That fall, the United States dropped its long opposition to the admission of communist China to the United Nations; and in October that body admitted the communist delegation and expelled the representatives of the Taiwan regime. Finally, in February 1972, Nixon arrived in China for a week-long visit. American television broadcast vivid pictures of presidential tours of famous Chinese landmarks, which had been invisible to much of the West for more than two decades, of meetings with Zhou Enlai and Mao Zedong, and of gracious and friendly exchanges of toasts during elaborate state dinners. At a single stroke, Nixon managed to erase much of the deep animosity toward China that the American people had developed over the course of a generation.

The summit meeting did not produce any agreement on establishing formal diplomatic relations between the United States and China. Nixon was not yet prepared openly to repudiate the Chiang regime, which the United States had supported for so long. But a year after the Nixon visit, the two countries set up "liaison offices" in Washington and Beijing that served as embassies in all but name.

The Birth of Détente

The initiatives in China helped pave the way as well for a new relationship with the Soviet Union, which was as eager to prevent a Chinese-American alliance as Beijing was to prevent a Soviet-American one. The road to what soon became known as détente had actually begun in 1968, the last year of the Johnson administration, when the United States and the Soviet Union signed a treaty agreeing to discourage the further proliferation of nuclear weapons in the world. More important, however, was the beginning of talks between American and Russian diplomats in Helsinki in 1969 on a strategic arms limitation treaty (SALT). The negotiations continued for two and a half years, and the result was the conclusion in 1972 of the first phase of a new arms control accord: the so-called SALT I. In May of that year, the president traveled to Moscow for a cordial meeting with the Soviet leadership and a glittering ceremony to sign the agreement. The Moscow summit produced as well a series of accords establishing new trade and other exchanges between the two nations—including the soon to be infamous Soviet-American wheat deal, by which the United States would sell nearly one quarter of the total American grain supply to the Russians at a cost below the world market price. The federal government would make up the price difference through subsidies to American farmers.

Nixon returned from Moscow in triumph, boasting of dramatic progress toward bringing the arms race to an end. In fact, SALT I did less to end the arms race (or even slow it) than to move it in a different direction. The two nations agreed to limit themselves to their existing number of intercontinental ballistic missiles (ICBMs), thus institutionalizing Soviet superiority in total missile strength. But the United States continued to possess a substantial lead in the total number of its warheads; it had almost twice as many submarines equipped with nuclear missiles as the Soviets. Each country would, in addition, curtail its construction of antiballistic missile systems (ABMs). The treaty thus limited the quantity of certain weapons on both sides. It said nothing, however, about limiting quality or about forestalling the creation of entirely new weapons systems.

SALT I had always been intended as the first step toward a more comprehensive arms control agreement. In June 1973, during a visit by the Soviet premier, Leonid Brezhnev, to Washington, the Russian and American governments pledged renewed efforts to speed the completion of the next phase of the

Détente at High Tide
The visit of Soviet Premier Leonid Brezhnev to Washington in 1973 was a high-water mark in the search for détente between the two nations, a search that had begun as early as 1962, that continued through parts of five presidential administrations, and that collapsed in disarray in the late 1970s. Here, Brezhnev and Nixon share friendly words while standing on the White House balcony.   (J. P. Laffont/Sygma)

negotiations. Nixon and Brezhnev agreed in principle to abstain from nuclear war, to work for a permanent freeze on offensive nuclear weapons, and to extend Soviet-American cooperation in other areas as well.

The Problems of Multipolarity

The policies of rapprochement with communist China and détente with the Soviet Union reflected several basic assumptions of the Nixon-Kissinger foreign policy. The communist world was no longer a monolithic bloc, the administration believed, and the situation required a more flexible and varied diplomatic approach than the situation in the 1950s. The Soviet threat to Western Europe, American officials were convinced, was much abated, removing the most serious source of tension from the Cold War. Above all, the new policies reflected a belief that world stability depended primarily on the relationships among the great powers, that the pervasive concern of previous administrations with "emerging areas" had diverted American policy from pursuit of its most important goals. By the last years of the Nixon administration, however, it had become clear that the Third World remained the most volatile and dangerous source of world instability; that tensions in developing countries had the capacity not only to produce local turmoil but to erode the new relationships among the superpowers.

Central to the Nixon-Kissinger policy toward the Third World was the effort to maintain a stable status quo without involving the United States too deeply in local disputes. In 1969 and 1970, the president laid out the elements of what became known as the Nixon Doctrine, by which the United States would "participate in the defense and development of allies and friends" but would leave the "basic responsibility" for the future of those "friends" to the nations themselves. In practice, the Nixon Doctrine meant a declining American interest in contributing to Third World development; a growing contempt for the United Nations, where underdeveloped nations were gaining influence through their sheer numbers; and increasing support to authoritarian regimes attempting to withstand radical challenges from within. In 1970, for example, the CIA poured substantial funds into Chile to help support the established government against a communist challenge. When the Marxist candidate for president, Salvador Allende, came to power through an honest election, the United States began funneling more money to opposition forces in Chile to help "destabilize" the new government. In 1973, a military junta seized power from Allende, who was subsequently murdered under mysterious circumstances. The new regime of General Augusto Pinochet, which was as brutally repressive as any in the Western Hemisphere, received warm approval and increased military and economic assistance from the United States.

More troubling than Latin America was the Middle East. Long an area of interest to the United States because of its strategic position between the Soviet Union and the Mediterranean, the region was now also of vital economic importance to the West, which beginning in the 1960s had become highly dependent on the purchase of oil from the Arab states. For the United States, this energy dependence presented special problems. As the most important ally and defender of Israel, America was standing squarely in opposition to the Islamic states, which were unanimous in their condemnation of Zionism.

Hostility toward Israel had grown particularly intense after the humiliating Arab defeat in the Six-Day War of 1967, in which Israeli forces had routed the opposing armies of Egypt, Jordan, and Syria and had seized territory from all three nations. For many years thereafter, Israel refused to relinquish the newly occupied territories.

Conditions in the region grew more volatile as a result of the desperate plight of hundreds of thousands of Palestinian Arab refugees, some of whom had been virtually homeless since 1948 and whose numbers had increased drastically after the 1967 war. Many of them lived in Jordan, whose ruler, King Hussein, was eager to maintain stable relations with the United States. Disturbed by the activities of the new Palestinian Liberation Organization (PLO) and other radical or terrorist groups, Hussein used his own armies to attack the Palestinians and expel them from Jordan after a series of uprisings in 1970, almost precipitating another general war in the region. Many of the exiled Palestinians moved to Lebanon, helping to precipitate many years of instability and civil war there.

In October 1973, on the Jewish high holy day of Yom Kippur, Egyptian and Syrian forces suddenly attacked Israel. The ensuing conflict was very different from the 1967 war, during which Israel had quickly and decisively overwhelmed its opponents. For ten days, the Israelis struggled to recover from the surprise attack; finally, they launched an effective counteroffensive against Egyptian forces in the Sinai. Only then did the United States intervene to bring an end to the fighting in the region. Under heavy American pressure, the government of Israel agreed not to press its advantage and accepted a cease-fire.

The imposed settlement of the Yom Kippur War reflected a significant change in the American position in the Middle East. Above all, perhaps, it served as evidence of the growing dependence of the United States and its allies on Arab oil. Permitting Israel to continue its drive into Egypt might have jeopardized the ability of the United States to purchase needed

Crises in the Middle East

1974 Fighting between Turkey and Greece over Cyprus threatens NATO unity

IRAN
1953 U.S. supports shah, helps put down anti-U.S. Socialist government
1979 Shah overthrown
1979–1981 Hostage crisis

AFGHANISTAN
1979 – U.S. supports guerrillas fighting Soviet invaders

LIBYA
1969 Qaddafi seizes power
1977 Abortive border war with Egypt
1986 U.S. responds to Libyan-backed terrorism by bombing Tripoli

IRAQ
1980 – Iran-Iraq war

EGYPT
1978 Egypt and Israel agree to Camp David accords
1979 Formal peace treaty signed between Egypt and Israel
1981 Sadat assassinated

LEBANON
1958 U.S. intervention supports pro-West government
1981–1984 U.S. joins UN peacekeeping force, suffers series of violent attacks

1982 Sinai peninsula returned to Egypt by Israel

U.S. allies

Israel before 1967

Territory occupied by Israel since Six-Day War, 1967

Oilfields (U.S. supporters involved)

The Arab-Israeli Wars
1948 War of Independence
1956 Sinai War
1967 Six-Day War
1973 Yom Kippur War
1982 Invasion of Lebanon
(occupied 1982–1985)

0   400 Miles
0   500 Kilometers

0   50 Miles
0   50 Kilometers

petroleum from the Arab states. A brief but painful embargo by the Islamic governments on the sale of oil to America in 1973 provided an ominous warning. (See p. 946.) The lesson of the Yom Kippur War, therefore, was that the United States could no longer ignore the interests of the Arab nations in its efforts on behalf of Israel.

A larger lesson of 1973 was even more disturbing. The Yom Kippur War and the oil embargo had given clear evidence of the new limits facing the United States in its effort to construct a stable world order. The nations of the Third World could no longer be depended on to act as passive, cooperative "client states." The easy access to raw materials on which the American economy had come to depend was becoming a thing of the past. The United States could not even rely any longer on the automatic support of its NATO allies. None of the principal nations of Western Europe had joined the United States in providing military support for Israel in the 1973 war, and most had complained bitterly when American policies had resulted in their own temporary loss of access to vital Middle Eastern oil.

Politics and Economics Under Nixon

For a time in the 1960s, it had seemed to many Americans that the forces of chaos and radicalism were taking control of the nation. The domestic policy of the Nixon administration was an attempt to restore balance: between the needs of the poor and the desires of the middle class, between the power of the federal government and the interests of local communities. The president himself described the effort as the "New Federalism"—a series of programs to "reverse the flow of power and resources from the states and communities to Washington and start power and resources flowing back . . . to the people." In the end, however, economic and political crises sharply limited the administration's ability to fulfill its domestic goals.

Domestic Initiatives

Many of Nixon's domestic policies were a response to what he believed to be the demands of his constituency—conservative Middle America or what he liked to call the "silent majority"—for retreat from federal interference with local affairs. He tried, unsuccessfully, to persuade Congress to pass legislation prohibiting school desegregation through the use of forced busing. He forbade the Department of Health, Education, and Welfare to cut off federal funds from school districts that had failed to comply with court orders to integrate (precipitating the resignation of Secretary Robert Finch and other HEW officials). At the same time, he began to reduce or dismantle many of the social programs of the Great Society and the New Frontier. He cut off hundreds of federal grants for urban renewal, social welfare, job training, and educational assistance. He attempted to reduce funding for dozens of other social programs, only to be blocked by the Democratic Congress; on occasion, he attempted to defy congressional opposition by simply impounding funds for programs he considered unnecessary. In 1973, he abolished the Office of Economic Opportunity, the centerpiece of the anti-poverty program of the Johnson years.

Yet Nixon's effort to satisfy the demands of Middle Americans were not entirely negative. One of the administration's boldest efforts was an attempt to overhaul the nation's enormous welfare system. The cumbersome, expensive, and inefficient welfare bureaucracy was the most glaring symbol of what Nixon and his supporters considered the excessive intrusiveness of the federal government. The primary vehicle for federal relief—Aid to Families with Dependent Children—was not only costly; it required a large, awkward infrastructure of caseworkers, administrators, and others, and it extended the authority of the federal government directly into the daily lives of families and communities. As an alternative, Nixon proposed what he called the Family Assistance Plan. Designed in large part by the president's urban adviser, Daniel Patrick Moynihan, the FAP proposed what would in effect have been a guaranteed annual income for all Americans: $1,600 in federal grants, which could be supplemented by outside earnings up to $4,000. Even many liberals applauded the proposal as an important step toward expanding federal responsibility for the poor. To Nixon, however, the appeal of the plan was its simplicity. It would reduce the supervisory functions of the federal government and transfer to welfare recipients themselves daily responsibility for their own lives. Although the FAP won approval in the House in 1970, concerted attacks by welfare recipients (who considered the benefits inadequate) and members of the welfare bureaucracy (whose own influence stood to be sharply diminished by the bill) helped kill it in the Senate.

Nixon appealed to conservative and provincial sentiments in other ways as well. He issued strident denunciations of protesters and radicals, ordered the Justice Department to arrest demonstrators and dissidents, and unleashed Vice President Agnew to attack not only youthful critics of the administration but the liberal news media and the "biased" television networks. He rejected as "morally bankrupt" the recommendations of a special commission on pornography, which saw no reason for the government to suppress the distribution of obscene materials. He expressed sympathy for those who opposed abortion. He refused to consider extending amnesty to draft resisters. He was, in short, establishing a new stance for the federal government: one that balanced its commitments to the poor and minorities against a larger concern for preserving traditional values and protecting the status of the middle class.

From the Warren Court to the Nixon Court

One of the loudest cheers during Richard Nixon's acceptance speech at the 1968 Republican Convention greeted his pledge to change the composition of the Supreme Court. The reaction was unsurprising. Of all the liberal institutions that had aroused the enmity of the "silent majority" in the 1950s and 1960s, none had evoked more anger and bitterness than the Warren Court. Not only had its rulings on racial matters disrupted traditional social patterns in both the North and the South, but its staunch defense of civil liberties had, in the eyes of many Americans, contributed directly to the increase in crime, disorder, and moral decay. One after another landmark decision seemed to tread on the sensibilities of provincial and conservative Americans. In *Engel* v. *Vitale* (1962), the Court had ruled that prayers in public schools were unconstitutional, sparking outrage among religious fundamentalists and others, who began a long battle against the edict. In *Roth* v. *United States* (1957), the Court had sharply limited the authority of local governments to curb pornography. In a series of decisions, the Court had greatly strengthened the civil rights of criminal defendants and had, in the eyes of many Americans, greatly weakened the power of law-enforcement officials to do their jobs. For example, in *Gideon* v. *Wainwright* (1963), the Court had ruled that every felony defen-

dant was entitled to a lawyer regardless of his or her ability to pay. In *Escobedo* v. *Illinois* (1964), it had ruled that a defendant must be allowed access to a lawyer before questioning by police. Above all, in *Miranda* v. *Arizona* (1966), the Court had confirmed the obligation of authorities to inform a criminal suspect of his or her rights.

Other examples of "judicial activism" had antagonized both local and national political leaders. In *Baker* v. *Carr* (1962), the Warren Court, in its most influential decision since *Brown* v. *Board of Education*, had ordered state legislatures to apportion representation so that the votes of all citizens would carry equal weight. In dozens of states, systems of legislative districting that had given disproportionate representation to rural areas were thus rendered invalid. The reapportionment that resulted greatly increased the political voice of blacks, Hispanics, and other poor urban residents. By 1968, the Warren Court had become the target of Americans of all kinds who felt that the balance of power in the United States had shifted too far toward the poor and dispossessed at the expense of the middle class.

Richard Nixon shared such sentiments, and he was determined to use his judicial appointments to give the Court a more conservative cast. His first opportunity came almost as soon as he entered office. Chief Justice Earl Warren, who had tried to resign during the last months of the Johnson administration only to be stymied by the refusal of Congress to approve the appointment of liberal Associate Justice Abe Fortas as his successor, announced his resignation early in 1969. Nixon replaced him with a federal appeals court judge of known conservative leanings, Warren Burger.

The president had less success in filling the next Court opening to become available. In May 1969, Abe Fortas resigned his seat after the disclosure of a series of alleged financial improprieties. To replace him, Nixon named Clement F. Haynsworth, a respected federal circuit court judge from South Carolina. Haynsworth received the endorsement of the American Bar Association, but he came under fire from Senate liberals, black organizations, and labor unions for his conservative record on civil rights. The revelation that he had sat on cases involving corporations in which he himself had a financial interest finally doomed his nomination; the Senate rejected him. Nixon's next choice was a particularly unfortunate one. G. Harold Carswell, a judge of the Florida federal appeals court, was almost entirely lacking in distinction and widely considered unfit for the Supreme Court. After weeks of damaging revelations about Carswell's record, the Senate rejected his nomination too.

An enraged President Nixon announced that the votes had been a result of prejudice against the South. But he was careful thereafter to choose men of standing within the legal community to fill vacancies on the Supreme Court. Harry Blackmun, a moderate jurist from Minnesota; Lewis F. Powell, Jr., a respected judge from Virginia; and William Rehnquist, a member of the Nixon Justice Department—all met with little opposition from the Senate. And the Warren Court gradually gave way to what many observers came to describe as the "Burger Court" but which others termed the "Nixon Court."

The new Court, however, fell short of what the president and many conservatives had hoped. Rather than retreating from its commitment to social reform, the Court in many areas actually extended its reach. In *Swann* v. *Charlotte-Mecklenburg Board of Education* (1971), it ruled in favor of the use of forced busing to achieve racial balance in schools. Not even the intense and occasionally violent opposition of local communities as diverse as Boston and Louisville, Kentucky, was able to weaken the judicial commitment to integration. In *Furman* v. *Georgia* (1972), the Court overturned existing capital punishment statutes and established strict new guidelines for such laws in the future. In *Roe* v. *Wade* (1973), it struck down laws forbidding abortions (see above, pp. 932–933).

In other decisions, however, the Burger Court did signal a marked withdrawal from the crusading commitment to civil liberties and reform. It attempted instead to follow a moderate path. Although the justices approved busing as a tool for achieving integration, they rejected, in *Milliken* v. *Bradley* (1974), a plan to transfer students across district lines (in this case, between Detroit and its suburbs) to achieve racial balance. While the Court upheld the principle of affirmative action in its celebrated 1978 decision *Bakke* v. *Board of Regents of California,* it established restrictive new guidelines for such programs in the future. In *Stone* v. *Powell* (1976), the Court agreed to certain limits on the right of a defendant to appeal a state conviction to the federal judiciary.

The Election of 1972

However unsuccessful the Nixon administration may have been in achieving some of its specific goals, by 1972 it had scored a series of triumphs in enlisting the loyalties of the electorate. The "real majority"—what a 1970 book of that name by Richard Scammon and Ben Wattenberg called the "unyoung, unblack, and unpoor"—responded enthusiastically to the president's attacks on liberals and radicals as well as to his apparent diplomatic successes in China and the Soviet Union.

Nixon entered the presidential race in 1972, therefore, with a substantial reserve of strength. The events of that year improved his position immeasurably. His energetic reelection committee collected enormous sums of money to support the campaign. The president himself made full use of the powers of incumbency, refraining from campaigning in the primaries (in which he faced, in any case, only token opposition) and concentrating on highly publicized international decisions and state visits. Agencies of the federal government dispensed funds and favors to communities around the country in a concerted effort to strengthen Nixon's political standing in questionable areas.

Nixon was most fortunate in 1972, however, in his opposition. The return of George Wallace to the presidential fray caused some early concern, for Nixon's own reelection strategy rested on the same appeals to the troubled middle class that Wallace was so skillfully expressing. But although Wallace showed significant strength in the early Democratic primaries, the possibility of another third-party campaign in the fall vanished in May, when a would-be assassin shot the Alabama governor during a rally at a Maryland shopping center. Paralyzed from the waist down, Wallace was unable to continue campaigning.

The Democrats, in the meantime, were making the greatest contribution to the Nixon cause by nominating for president a representative of their most liberal faction: Senator George S. McGovern of South Dakota. An outspoken critic of the war, a forceful advocate of advanced liberal positions on virtually every social and economic issue, McGovern seemed to embody those aspects of the turbulent 1960s that middle-class Americans were most eager to reject. McGovern profited greatly from party reforms (which he himself had helped to draft) that gave increased influence to women, blacks, and young people in the selection of the Democratic ticket. But those same reforms helped make the Democratic Convention of 1972 an unappealing spectacle to much of the public. The candidate then disillusioned even some of his own

Inflation, 1960–1989

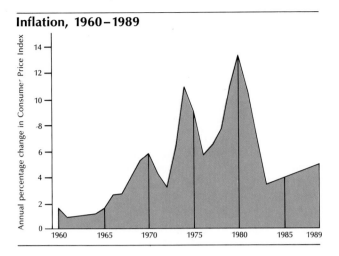

supporters by his confused response to revelations that his running mate, Senator Thomas Eagleton of Missouri, had undergone treatment for an emotional disturbance. McGovern first announced that he supported Eagleton "1,000 percent," then suddenly dropped him from the ticket. The remainder of the Democratic presidential campaign was an exercise in futility.

For Nixon, in contrast, the fall campaign was an uninterrupted triumphal procession. After a Republican Convention utterly devoid of controversy, the president made a few carefully planned appearances in strategic areas of the country. Most of his time, however, he devoted to highly publicized work on behalf of "world peace." And in October, although by then it was clearly unnecessary politically, he sealed the victory with a skillfully orchestrated demonstration that a settlement of the war in Vietnam was near. On election day, Nixon won reelection by one of the largest margins in history: 60.7 percent of the popular vote compared with 37.5 percent for the forlorn McGovern, an electoral margin of 520 to 17. The Democratic candidate had carried only Massachusetts and the District of Columbia. The new commitments that Nixon had so effectively expressed—to restraint in social reform, to decentralization of political power, to the defense of traditional values, and to a new balance in international relations—had clearly won the approval of the American people. But other problems, some beyond the president's control and some of his own making, were already lurking in the wings.

The Troubled Economy

Although it was political scandal that would ultimately destroy the Nixon presidency, an even more serious national crisis was emerging in the early 1970s: the decline of the American economy. For three decades, the American economy had been the envy of the world. The United States had been responsible for as much as a third of the world's industrial production and had dominated international trade. The American dollar had been the strongest currency in the world, the yardstick by which other nations measured their own monetary health. The American standard of living, already high at the end of World War II, had improved dramatically in the years since. Most Americans had begun to assume that this remarkable prosperity was the normal condition of their society. In fact, however, it had rested in part on several artificial conditions that were by the late 1960s rapidly disappearing.

The most disturbing economic problem, one that was symptomatic of all the others, was inflation, which had been creeping upward for several years when Richard Nixon took office and which shortly thereafter began to soar. Its most visible cause was the performance of the federal government in the mid-1960s. At the same time that President Johnson had persuaded Congress to accept a tax cut in 1964, he was rapidly increasing spending both for domestic social programs and for the war in Vietnam. The result was a major expansion of the money supply, resting largely on government deficits, that pushed prices rapidly upward.

But there were other, equally important causes of the inflation and of the economic problems that lay behind it. Much of America's economic strength in the 1950s and 1960s had rested on the nation's unquestioned supremacy in international trade. This meant that the United States enjoyed easy access to raw materials and a substantial market for its goods abroad. More important, it meant that American industrial goods faced little competition at home. The United States had its vast domestic market to itself.

By the late 1960s, however, the world economic picture had changed. No more did the United States have exclusive access to cheap raw materials around the globe; not only were other industrial nations now competing for increasingly scarce raw materials, but Third World suppliers of those materials were beginning to realize their value and demand higher prices for them. And American manufacturers of automobiles, steel, and other industrial products were facing

America and World Industrial Production, 1950–1980

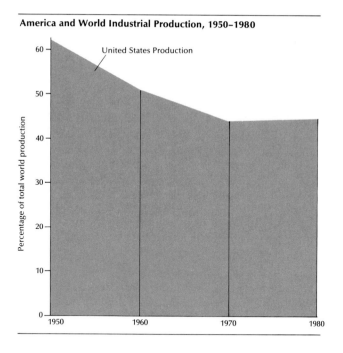

would no longer ship petroleum to nations supporting Israel—that is, to the United States and its allies in Western Europe. At about the same time, the OPEC nations agreed to raise their prices 400 percent.

These twin shocks produced momentary chaos in the West. The United States suffered its first fuel shortage since World War II, and the disruptive effects were a painful reminder to the American people of their dependence on plentiful energy. Motorists faced long lines at gas stations; schools and offices closed down to save on heating oil; factories cut production and laid off workers for lack of sufficient fuel. A few months later, the crisis eased. But the price of energy continued to skyrocket in the following years, both because of OPEC's new militant policies and because of the weakening competitive position of the dollar in world markets. No single factor did more to produce the soaring inflation of the 1970s.

more intense competition—in the world market and in the domestic market—from Japanese and Western European producers.

But the greatest immediate blow to the American economy was the interruption of its access to sources of energy. More than any nation on earth, the United States had based its economy on the easy availability of cheap and plentiful fuels. No society was more dependent on the automobile; none was more profligate in its use of oil and gas in its homes, schools, and factories. As the economy expanded in the 1960s, an already high demand for energy soared much higher. And with domestic petroleum reserves beginning to dwindle, the nation increased its dependence on imports from the Middle East and Africa.

For many years, the Organization of Petroleum Exporting Countries (OPEC) had operated as an informal bargaining unit for the sale of oil by Third World nations. Not until the early 1970s, however, did it begin to display its strength. Aware of the growing dependence of Western economies on the resources of its member nations, OPEC was no longer willing to follow the direction of American and European oil companies. Instead, it began to use its oil both as an economic tool and as a political weapon. In 1973, in the midst of the Yom Kippur War, Arab members of OPEC announced that they

The Nixon Response

Richard Nixon, therefore, inherited an economy in which growth was already sluggish, in which inflation was already troubling, and in which even greater new problems lurked. Within weeks of taking office, he announced a "game plan" for dealing with these various woes. He would, he promised, spend less and tax more. But such policies were easier announced than implemented, evoking as they did both congressional and popular protest. As a result, Nixon turned increasingly to an economic tool more readily available to him: control of the currency. Placing conservative economists at the head of the Federal Reserve Board, he ensured sharply higher interest rates and a contraction of the money supply. But the tight money policy did little to curb inflation. The cost of living rose a cumulative 15 percent during Nixon's first two and a half years in office. In 1971, moreover, the United States recorded its first balance-of-trade deficit (an excess of imports over exports) in nearly eighty years. With inflation unabated and economic growth in decline, the United States was encountering a new and puzzling dilemma: "stagflation," a combination of rising prices and general economic stagnation.

By the summer of 1971, therefore, the president was under strong public pressure to act decisively to reverse the economic tide. First, he released the dollar from the fluctuating gold standard that had controlled its worth since the end of World War II, allowing its value to fall in world markets. The devaluation helped stimulate exports, but it also made more expensive the American purchase of vital raw materials abroad. At the same time, the president announced an even bolder and more startling new policy. For years, he had denounced the idea of using government controls to curb inflation. On August 15, 1971, however, he reversed himself. Under the provisions of the Economic Stabilization Act of 1970, the president imposed a ninety-day freeze on all wages and prices at their existing levels. Then, in November, he launched Phase II of his economic plan: mandatory guidelines for wage and price increases, to be administered by a federal agency. Inflation subsided temporarily, but the recession continued. The unemployment rate for 1971 was 6 percent, compared with 4 percent two years earlier.

Fearful that the recession would be more damaging than inflation in an election year, the administration reversed itself once again late in 1971: Interest rates were allowed to drop sharply, and government spending was increased—producing the largest budget deficit since World War II. The new tactics served their purpose. By election day, personal incomes were up and unemployment was down. But there were disastrous side effects. Even though wage and price controls managed to hold down inflation in some areas, consumers were soon paying drastically higher prices for food and other basic goods. At this critical moment, with both domestic and world inflation on the verge of skyrocketing, Nixon abandoned the strict Phase II controls and replaced them with a set of flexible, largely voluntary, and almost entirely ineffective guidelines—Phase III of the administration's economic program. With the end of wage and price controls, inflation quickly resumed its upward course. In 1973, it rose to 9 percent; in 1974, after the Arab oil embargo and the OPEC price increases, it soared to 12 percent—the highest rate since shortly after the end of World War II. The value of the dollar continued to slide, and the nation's international trade continued to decline.

Nixon now turned his attention to solving the new "energy crisis," which had become America's most pressing preoccupation. But the administration seemed to have no clearer idea of how to deal with that problem than it had of how to deal with the general inflation. The president spoke vaguely of conservation, of increasing production, of restoring "energy independence." But there were few concrete proposals for accomplishing them. And Nixon, in the mean-

time, was becoming so embroiled in his own political problems that he would have had great difficulty winning approval of a major new program in any case.

The stumbling and erratic economic programs of the Nixon administration were indicative of a broader national confusion about the future prospects for American prosperity. With little understanding of the international forces creating the economic problems, both the government and the people focused on immediate issues and short-range solutions. The Nixon pattern—of lurching from a tight money policy to curb inflation at one moment to a spending policy to cure recession at the next—repeated itself during the two administrations that followed. These erratic policies had little effect, ultimately, either on inflation or on the general economic stagnation.

The Watergate Crisis

Although economic problems greatly concerned the American people in the 1970s, another stunning development almost entirely preoccupied the nation beginning early in 1973: the fall of Richard Nixon. The president's demise was a result in part of his own personality. Defensive, secretive, resentful of his critics, he brought to his office an element of mean-spiritedness that helped undermine even his most important accomplishments. But the larger explanation lay in Nixon's view of American society and the world, and of his own role in both. Far more than most of his compatriots, the president was convinced that the United States faced grave dangers from the radicals and dissidents who were challenging his policies. Obsessed with his mission to create a new "structure of peace" in the world, he came increasingly to consider any challenge to his policies a threat to "national security." By identifying his own political fortunes with those of the nation, in other words, Nixon was creating a climate in which he and those who served him could justify to stifle dissent and undermine opposition.

The White House Autocracy

Nixon's outlook was in part a culmination of decades of changes in the nature of the presidency. Public expectations of the president had increased dramatically in the years since World War II; yet the constraints on the authority of the office had grown as well. Congress had become more difficult to control; the bureaucracy had become cumbersome and unmanageable; the press, particularly in light of the war in Vietnam, had become suspicious and increasingly hostile. In response, a succession of presidents had sought new methods for the exercise of power, often stretching the law, occasionally breaking it.

Nixon not only continued but greatly accelerated these trends. Facing a Democratic Congress hostile to his goals, he attempted to find ways to circumvent the legislature whenever possible. Saddled with a federal bureaucracy unresponsive to his wishes, he constructed a hierarchy of command in which virtually all executive power became concentrated in the White House. A few cabinet members retained direct access to the president—among them Attorney General John Mitchell, a longtime personal friend, and Henry Kissinger, who became secretary of state in 1973. For the most part, however, Nixon isolated himself almost completely, relying on a few trusted advisers through whom he exercised his power. At the head of what critics sometimes called the "palace guard" stood two particularly influential aides: H. R. Haldeman, the president's chief of staff, and John Ehrlichman, his chief domestic adviser.

Operating within this rigid, even autocratic structure, the president became a solitary, brooding figure, whose contempt for his opponents and impatience with obstacles to his policies festered and grew. Insulated from criticism, surrounded by flatterers, he became increasingly blatant in his defiance of the normal constraints on his office. Unknown to all but a few intimates, he also became mired in a pattern of illegalities and abuses of power that late in 1972 began to break through to the surface.

The Scandals

Early on the morning of June 17, 1972, police arrested five men who had broken into the offices of the Democratic National Committee, located in the Watergate office building in Washington, D.C. Two others were seized a short time later and charged with supervising the break-in. When reporters for the *Washington Post* began researching the backgrounds of the culprits, they discovered a series of startling facts. Among those involved in the burglary were former employees of the Committee for the Re- Election of the President (CRP). One of them had worked in the White House itself. They had, moreover, been paid for the break-in from a secret fund of the reelection committee, a fund controlled by members of the White House staff. The further the reporters looked, the more evidence they found that the burglary had been part of a larger pattern of illegalities, planned and financed by the president's closest associates.

Public interest in the disclosures grew only slowly in the last months of 1972. Few Americans, apparently, chose to question the president's assurances that neither he nor his staff had any connection with what he called "this very bizarre incident." Early in 1973, however, the Watergate burglars went on trial; and under relentless prodding from federal judge John J. Sirica, one of the defendants, James W. McCord, agreed to cooperate both with the grand jury and with a special Senate investigating committee recently established under Senator Sam J. Ervin of North Carolina. McCord's testimony opened a floodgate of confessions, and for months a parade of White House and campaign officials exposed one illegality after another. Foremost among them was a member of the inner circle of the White House, Counsel to the President John Dean, who leveled allegations against Nixon himself.

Two different sets of scandals were emerging from the investigations. One was a general pattern of abuses of power involving both the White House and the Nixon campaign committee. Every week, it seemed, there was a new, even more damaging revelation. White House "plumbers"—under the direction of John Ehrlichman—had established illegal wiretaps, intercepted mail, and engaged in burglaries, (including the attempt to steal files from Daniel Ellsberg's psychiatrist) in an effort to prevent leaks of sensitive or politically embarrassing information or, as in Ellsberg's case, to discredit critics of the administration. Members of the reelection committee had solicited illegal contributions, "laundered" the money through accounts in Mexico, and used the funds to support a variety of "dirty tricks" against Democratic presidential candidates and to pay for other maneuvers to sabotage the campaigns of Nixon's opponents. In addition, associates of the president had created devious opportunities for Nixon to increase his personal wealth, including several real-estate transactions and income-tax dodges of dubious legality.

The other scandal, and the one that became the major focus of public attention for nearly two years, was the Watergate break-in itself and the events that it had set in motion. There was never any conclusive evidence that the president had planned or approved the burglary in advance. John Dean and others testi-

Haldeman Testifies

White House Chief of Staff H. R. Haldeman, who had been an advertising executive in California before joining Richard Nixon's administration, was one of the most powerful (and feared) figures in Washington in the early 1970s. He and other White House officials became known to their critics as "the Prussians," a label derived from their reputation for toughness bordering on ruthlessness. Here Haldeman testifies before the special Senate committee investigating the Watergate scandals in 1973. He would later resign from the White House, stand trial for his part in the scandals, and serve time in federal prison. (J. P. Laffont/Sygma)

fied that then Attorney General Mitchell had ordered the break-in, hoping to plant electronic bugs in and steal copies of files from the Democratic offices. (Mitchell had resigned from the Justice Department shortly after the burglary to head the president's re-election committee; then, after the scandals began to break, he resigned from CRP as well, citing "personal problems.")

But if there was no proof that Nixon had planned the break-in, there was mounting suspicion that he had been involved in what became known as the "cover-up"—illegal efforts to obstruct investigations of and withhold information about the episode. Testimony before the Ervin committee provided evidence of the complicity not only of Dean and Mitchell but of Haldeman, Ehrlichman, and other key White House figures. As interest in the case grew to something approaching a national obsession, only one question remained: In the words of Senator Howard Baker of Tennessee, a member of the Ervin committee, "What did the President know and when did he know it?"

Nixon, in the meantime, steadfastly denied knowing anything. One by one, he accepted the departure of those members of his administration implicated in the scandals: first a string of lower-level aides; then, with great reluctance, Haldeman and Ehrlichman, who resigned on the same day that Nixon dismissed John Dean. But the president himself continued to insist on his own innocence. At one news conference he declared, "I am not a crook."

There the matter might have rested had it not been for the disclosure during the Senate hearings of a White House taping system that had recorded virtually every conversation in the president's office during the period in question. All the various groups investigating the scandals sought access to the tapes; Nixon, pleading "executive privilege," refused to release them. A special prosecutor appointed by the president to handle the Watergate cases, Harvard law professor Archibald Cox, took Nixon to court in October 1973 in an effort to force him to relinquish the recordings. Nixon, now clearly growing desperate, fired Cox and suffered the humiliation of watching both Attorney General Elliot Richardson (who had succeeded Mitchell) and his deputy resign in protest. This "Saturday night massacre" made the president's predicament infinitely worse. Not only did public pressure force him to appoint a new special prosecutor, Texas attorney Leon Jaworski, who proved just as determined as Cox to subpoena the tapes; but the episode precipitated an investigation by the House of Representatives into the possibility of impeachment.

The Fall of Richard Nixon

Nixon's situation deteriorated further in the following months. Late in 1973, Vice President Agnew became embroiled in a scandal of his own when evidence surfaced that he had accepted bribes and kickbacks while serving as governor of Maryland and even as vice president. In return for a Justice Department agreement not to press the case, Agnew pleaded *nolo contendere* (no contest) to a lesser charge of income-tax evasion and resigned from the government. With the controversial Agnew no longer in line to succeed to the presidency, the prospect of removing Nixon from the White House became less worrisome to his opponents. The new vice president (the first appointed under the terms of the Twenty-fifth Amendment, which had been adopted in 1967) was House Minority Leader Gerald Ford, an amiable and popular Michigan congressman whom most Nixon critics considered more acceptable. The im-

peachment investigation quickly gathered pace. In April 1974, in an effort to head off further subpoenas of the tapes, the president released transcripts of a number of relevant conversations, claiming that they proved his innocence. Investigators and much of the public felt otherwise. Even these edited tapes seemed to suggest not only appalling ill will on Nixon's part but also his complicity in the cover-up.

In July, finally, the crisis came to a boil. First the Supreme Court ruled unanimously, in *United States v. Richard M. Nixon,* that the president must relinquish the tapes to Special Prosecutor Jaworski. Days later, the House Judiciary Committee voted to recommend three articles of impeachment, charging that Nixon had, first, obstructed justice in the Watergate cover-up; second, misused federal agencies to violate the rights of citizens; and third, defied the authority of Congress by refusing to deliver tapes and other materials subpoenaed by the committee. Even without additional evidence, Nixon might well have been impeached by the full House and convicted by the Senate. Early in August, however, he provided at last the "smoking gun"—the concrete proof of his guilt that his defenders had long contended was missing from the case against him. Among the tapes that the Supreme Court compelled Nixon to relinquish were several that offered incontrovertible evidence of his involvement in the Watergate cover-up. Only days after the burglary, the recordings disclosed, the president had ordered the FBI to stop investigating the break-in. Impeachment and conviction now seemed inevitable.

For several days, Nixon brooded in the White House, on the verge, some claimed, of a breakdown. Many of the normal operations of the government ground to a virtual halt as the nation waited tensely for a resolution of the greatest constitutional crisis since Reconstruction. Finally, on August 8, 1974, Nixon addressed the nation and announced his resignation—the first president in American history ever to do so. At noon the next day, while Nixon and his family were flying west to their home in California, Gerald Ford took the oath of office as president.

Americans expressed both relief and exhilaration that, as the new president put it, "Our long national nightmare is over." They were relieved to be rid of Richard Nixon, who had lost virtually all of the wide popularity that had won him his landslide reelection victory only two years before. And they were exhilarated that, as some boasted, "the system had worked." A president had been held accountable to the law, and the transfer of power had been smooth and orderly. But the wave of good feeling could not

SIGNIFICANT EVENTS

1962 Students for a Democratic Society formed at Port Huron, Michigan (p. 920)

Supreme Court decides *Baker* v. *Carr* (p. 943)

1963 Betty Friedan publishes *The Feminine Mystique* (p. 930)

1964 Free Speech Movement begins at UC Berkeley (p. 920)

Beatles come to America (p. 923)

1965 United Farm Workers strike (p. 927)

1966 National Organization for Women (NOW) formed (p. 930)

Miranda v. *Arizona* expands rights of criminal suspects (p. 943)

1967 Antiwar protesters march on Pentagon (p. 920)

Israel and Arabs clash in Six-Day War (p. 940)

1968 Campus riots break out at Columbia University and elsewhere (p. 920)

Antiwar "mobilization" day (p. 920)

American Indian Movement (AIM) launched (p. 925)

Nuclear nonproliferation treaty signed (p. 939)

1969 Antiwar movement stages Vietnam "moratorium" (p. 921)

Theodore Roszak publishes *The Making of a Counter Culture* (p. 921)

Nixon orders secret bombing of Cambodia (p. 934)

Nixon begins withdrawing American troops from Vietnam (p. 934)

"Stonewall Riot" in New York City launches gay liberation movement (p. 929)

1970 American troops enter Cambodia (p. 934)

Antiwar protests increase; students killed at Kent State and Jackson State universities (p. 934)

Palestinians expelled from Jordan (p. 940)

1971 Pentagon Papers published (p. 935)

Supreme Court decides *Swann* v. *Charlotte-Mecklenburg Board of Education* (p. 944)

1971 Nixon imposes wage-price freeze and controls (p. 947)

1972 Congress approves Equal Rights Amendment (p. 932)

Nixon visits China (p. 938)

SALT I treaty signed (p. 939)

United States mines Haiphong harbor in North Vietnam (p. 935)

Nixon orders "Christmas bombing" of North Vietnam (p. 936)

Supreme Court decides *Furman* v. *Georgia* (p. 944)

Burglary interrupted in Watergate office building (p. 948)

Nixon reelected president (p. 945)

1973 Indians demonstrate at Wounded Knee (p. 925)

Supreme Court decides *Roe* v. *Wade* (p. 932)

Paris accords produce cease-fire, American withdrawal from Vietnam (p. 936)

Israel and Arabs clash in Yom Kippur War (p. 940)

Arab oil embargo produces first American energy crisis (p. 946)

Watergate scandal expands (p. 948)

1974 Impeachment proceedings begin against Nixon (p. 950)

Vice President Spiro Agnew resigns; Gerald Ford appointed to replace him (p. 950)

Nixon resigns; Ford becomes president (p. 950)

1975 South Vietnam falls (p. 936)

Khmer Rouge seize control of Cambodia (p. 936)

1978 Vietnam invades Cambodia (p. 937)

Supreme Court hands down *Bakke* decision (p. 944)

1982 Equal Rights Amendment fails to be ratified (p. 932)

obscure the deeper and more lasting damage of the Watergate crisis. In a society in which distrust of leaders and of institutions of authority was already widespread, the fall of Richard Nixon seemed to confirm the most cynical assumptions about the character of American public life. The depths of that cynicism were evident in the widespread belief, documented in public-opinion polls, that what Nixon had done, bad as it was, was little worse than what other presidents had done undetected before him.

SUGGESTED READINGS

General Studies. William O'Neill, *Coming Apart* (1971); Ronald Berman, *America in the Sixties* (1968); Allen J. Matusow, *The Unraveling of America* (1984); Peter N. Carroll, *It Seemed Like Nothing Happened* (1982).

The New Left and the Counterculture. James Miller, *"Democracy in the Streets": From Port Huron to the Siege of Chicago* (1987); Maurice Isserman, *"If I Had a Hammer . . . : The Death of the Old Left and the Birth of the New Left* (1987); Milton Viorst, *Fire in the Streets* (1979); Todd Gitlin, *The Whole World Is Watching* (1981) and *The Sixties: Years of Hope, Days of Rage* (1987); Irwin Unger, *The Movement* (1974); Lawrence Lader, *Power on the Left* (1979); Kirkpatrick Sale, *SDS* (1973); Sara Evans, *Personal Politics* (1979); W. J. Rorabaugh, *Berkeley at War* (1989); Peter Clecak, *Radical Paradoxes* (1973); Kenneth Keniston, *Young Radicals* (1968); Lewis Feuer, *The Conflict of Generations* (1969); Paul Goodman, *Growing Up Absurd* (1960); Theodore Roszak, *The Making of a Counter Culture* (1969); Charles Reich, *The Greening of America* (1970); Ronald Berman, *America in the Sixties* (1968); Joan Didion, *Slouching Towards Bethlehem* (1967) and *The White Album* (1979); John Diggins, *The American Left in the Twentieth Century* (1973); Richard Flacks, *Youth and Social Change* (1971); Morris Dickstein, *Gates of Eden* (1977); Jon Wiener, *Come Together: John Lennon in His Time* (1984).

Indians and Hispanics. Larry W. Burt, *Tribalism in Crisis: Federal Indian Policy, 1953–1961* (1982); Charles F. Wilkinson, *American Indians, Time, and the Law* (1987); Wilcomb Washburn, *Red Man's Land/White Man's Land* (1971); Vine Deloria, Jr., *Behind the Trail of Broken Treaties* (1974) and *Custer Died for Your Sins* (1969); D'Arcy McNickle, *Native American Tribalism* (1973); Stan Steiner, *The New Indians* (1968); Peter Iverson, *The Navajo Nation* (1981); Rodolfo Acuña, *Occupied America*, 2nd ed. (1981); Julian Samora, *Los Mojados* (1971); Oscar Lewis, *La Vida* (1969); Matt Meier and Feliciano Rivera, *The Chicanos* (1972); Ronald Taylor, *Chávez and the Farm Workers* (1975).

Feminism. Susan M. Hartmann, *From Margin to Mainstream: Women and American Politics Since 1960* (1989); Winifred Wandersee, *On the Move: American Women in the 1970s* (1988); William Chafe, *The American Woman* (1972); Sheila Rothman, *Woman's Proper Place* (1978); Jo Freeman, *The Politics of Women's Liberation* (1975); Gayle Yates, *What Women Want* (1975); Betty Friedan, *The Feminine Mystique* (1963); Carol Gilligan, *In a Different Voice* (1982); Alice Kessler-Harris, *Out to Work: A History of Wage-Earning Women in the United States* (1982); Robin Morgan, ed., *Sisterhood Is Powerful* (1970); Ethel Klein, *Gender Politics* (1984); Kristin Luker, *Abortion and the Politics of Motherhood* (1984);

Rosalind Petchesky, *Abortion and Women's Choice* (1984); Marian Faux, *Roe v. Wade* (1988); Nancy Cott, *The Grounding of Modern Feminism* (1987).

Nixon and the World. Franz Schurman, *The Foreign Policies of Richard Nixon* (1987); Richard Stevenson, *The Rise and Fall of Détente* (1985); Robert S. Litwak, *Détente and the Nixon Doctrine: Amerian Foreign Policy and the Pursuit of Stability* (1984); Henry A. Kissinger, *White House Years* (1979) and *Years of Upheaval* (1982); Gareth Porter, *A Peace Denied* (1975); William Shawcross, *Sideshow: Nixon, Kissinger, and the Destruction of Cambodia* (1978); Roger Morris, *Uncertain Greatness* (1977); Seyom Brown, *The Crisis of Power* (1979); David Landau, *Kissinger: The Uses of Power* (1972); Marvin Kalb and Bernard Kalb, *Kissinger* (1974); Seymour Hersh, *The Price of Power* (1983); Tad Szulc, *The Illusion of Peace* (1978); Roger Hilsman, *The Crouching Future* (1975); Harland Moulton, *From Superiority to Parity* (1973); John Newhouse, *Cold Dawn* (1973); John Stockwell, *In Search of Enemies* (1977); Thomas Powers, *The Man Who Kept the Secrets* (1979); Michael Oksenberg and Robert Oxnam (eds.), *Dragon and Eagle* (1978); William Quandt, *Decade of Decision* (1977); Robert Stookey, *America and the Arab States* (1975).

Nixon's Domestic Policies. Herbert Parmet, *Richard Nixon and His America* (1989); Stephen Ambrose, *Nixon: The Triumph of a Politician, 1962–1972* (1989); William Safire, *Before the Fall* (1975); Raymond Price, *With Nixon* (1977); Daniel P. Moynihan, *The Politics of a Guaranteed Income* (1973); Vincent Burke and Vee Burke, *Nixon's Good Deed* (1974); R. L. Miller, *The New Economics of Richard Nixon* (1972); R. P. Nathan et al., *Monitoring Revenue Sharing* (1975); John Ehrlichman, *Witness to Power* (1982); Bob Woodward and Scott Armstrong, *The Brethren* (1980); Theodore H. White, *The Making of the President, 1972* (1973); Richard Barnet, *The Lean Years* (1980); Joan Edelman Spero, *The Politics of International Economic Relations* (1977); J. C. Hurewitz (ed.), *Oil, the Arab–Israeli Dispute, and the Industrial World* (1976).

Nixon and Watergate. Garry Wills, *Nixon Agonistes* (1970); Fawn Brodie, *Richard Nixon* (1981); Bruce Mazlish, *In Search of Nixon* (1972); Jonathan Schell, *The Time of Illusion* (1975); Stanley J. Kutler, *The Wars of Watergate* (1990); Richard M. Nixon, *RN: The Memoirs of Richard Nixon* (1978); Theodore H. White, *Breach of Faith* (1975); Anthony Lukas, *Nightmare* (1976); Bob Woodward and Carl Bernstein, *All the President's Men* (1974) and *The Final Days* (1976); John Dean, *Blind Ambition* (1976); Richard Cohen and Jules Witcover, *A Heartbeat Away* (1974); Arthur M. Schlesinger, Jr., *The Imperial Presidency* (1973).

Crossing the Berlin Wall, November 9, 1989
Jubilant Germans swarm over the infamous Berlin Wall, which had divided the city since 1961, on the day the East German government began allowing free passage in both directions between east and west. (*D. Aubert/Sygma*)

CHAPTER 32

❈ ❈ ❈

Toward a New Century

❈ ❈ ❈

The 1970s inflicted damaging blows to the confident, optimistic nationalism that had characterized so much of the postwar era. The war in Vietnam and the Watergate crisis had brought disrepute to the institution Americans had earlier made central to their hopes: the presidency. The problems of the economy, which grew steadily more serious in the second half of the 1970s, cast doubt on the assumption that abundance was a natural and permanent feature of American life. Growing international frustrations raised questions about the nation's ability to control, or even significantly influence, the course of world affairs. Many Americans responded to these problems by announcing the arrival of an "age of limits," in which America would have to learn to live with increasingly constricted expectations.

By the end of the decade, however, the contours of another response to these challenges had become visible in both American culture and American politics. It was a response that combined a conservative retreat from some of the heady visions of the 1960s with a reinforced commitment to the idea of economic growth, international power, and American exceptionalism. The same fervent belief in the nation's special virtues that had fueled the liberal crusades of the New Frontier and the Great Society became the basis for the Reagan administration's commitment to a reduced federal presence in national life and a more forceful American role in the world. At the same time, many Americans seemed to be embracing a new cultural outlook that focused less on the direction of society than on the hopes of the individual.

For much of the 1980s, these new assumptions seemed to dominate American politics and culture. The personal popularity of Ronald Reagan, the most conservative president of the postwar era, was one indication of that. So was the inability of the liberal opposition to articulate a consistent alternative to the policies of the administration. Yet those who were tempted to compare the 1980s to the 1950s, an earlier era of apparent calm and political stasis, could do so only by ignoring much of the world around them. By the end of the decade, the American economy—despite a surface buoyancy—had undergone profound and troubling changes. The complexity and diversity that had always characterized American society, and the problems associated with them, were straining the fabric of national life in new ways. And the international system, which had experienced a dismal stability for more than forty years, was in the throes of a genuinely revolutionary transformation.

Politics and Diplomacy After Watergate

The Watergate crisis—and the war in Vietnam, which had helped produced that crisis—shook the nation's confidence in its elected leaders; and in the aftermath of Richard Nixon's ignominious departure from of-

955

fice, many wondered whether faith in the presidency, and in the government as a whole, could easily be restored. The administrations of the two presidents who succeeded Nixon did little to answer those questions.

The Ford Custodianship

Gerald Ford inherited the presidency under unenviable circumstances. He had to try to rebuild confidence in the presidency in the face of the widespread cynicism the Watergate scandals had unleashed. And he had to try to restore national prosperity in the face of increasing domestic and international challenges to the American economy. He enjoyed modest success in the first of these efforts but very little in the second.

Few Americans considered Ford a brilliant or an overwhelmingly skillful leader. But for a time, his candor and unpretentiousness, and the apparent contrast those qualities provided to his predecessor, won him a wide popularity. The new president's effort to establish himself as a symbol of political integrity suffered a severe setback only a month after he took office, however, when he suddenly granted Richard Nixon "a full, free, and absolute pardon . . . for all offenses against the United States" during his presidency. Ford explained that he was attempting to spare the nation the ordeal of years of litigation and to spare Nixon himself any further suffering. It was, he insisted, an act of "compassion," an effort "to firmly shut and seal this book." To much of the public, however, it was evidence of bad judgment at best and a secret deal with the former president at worst. It caused a decline in his popularity from which he never fully recovered.

Nevertheless, relatively few Americans actively disliked Gerald Ford in the way so many had come to dislike Lyndon Johnson and Richard Nixon. Most believed him to be a decent man, even if many considered him a weak leader. His attractive and outspoken wife, Betty, became one of the most active and popular first ladies in recent history. Ford's honesty and amiability did much to reduce the bitterness and acrimony of the Watergate years.

The Ford administration enjoyed less success in its effort to deal with the other challenge it inherited: solving the problems of the American economy. In particular, the president was unable to devise an effective strategy for dealing with the related problems of inflation and energy. In his efforts to curb infla-

tion, the president rejected the idea of wage and price controls and called instead for largely ineffective voluntary efforts. Of somewhat greater impact was the government's pursuit of the familiar path of tightening the money supply (through the Federal Reserve Board) to curb inflation, and then struggling to deal with the recession that resulted. By supporting high interest rates, opposing increased federal spending (by use of frequent presidential vetoes), and resisting pressures for a tax reduction, Ford helped produce in 1974 and 1975 a severe recession. Production declined more than 10 percent in the first months of 1975, and unemployment rose to nearly 9 percent of the labor force. There was a temporary abatement of inflation, which dropped briefly below 5 percent in 1976; but by then, the administration was already beginning to reverse its course and support new measures to stimulate the economy.

Central to these problems was the continuing energy crisis. In the aftermath of the Arab oil embargo of 1973, the OPEC cartel began dramatically and suddenly to raise the price of oil—a 400 percent increase in 1974 alone. At the same time, American dependence on OPEC supplies continued to grow. By 1976, the United States was importing almost a third of its energy supply from OPEC. That was one of the principal reasons why inflation in that year reached 11 percent. The Ford administration responded as tentatively to the energy crisis as it did to the problem of inflation.

At first it seemed that the foreign policy of the new administration would differ little from that of its predecessor. The new president retained Henry Kissinger as secretary of state and continued the general policies of seeking rapprochement with China, détente with the Soviet Union, and stability in the Middle East. There were signs of progress in all these areas.

In particular, there appeared to be major progress in the effort to produce another arms control agreement with the Soviet Union. Ford met with Leonid Brezhnev late in 1974 at Vladivostok in Siberia and signed a new arms control accord that was to serve as the basis for SALT II. The following summer, a European security conference in Helsinki, Finland, produced an agreement that seemed to advance détente even further. The Soviet Union and Western nations finally agreed to ratify the borders that had divided Europe since the end of World War II; and the Russians accepted the so-called Basket Three clause, which pledged increased respect for human rights. In the Middle East, in the meantime, the ef-

Election of 1976   (53.5% of electorate voting)

	ELECTORAL VOTE	POPULAR VOTE (%)
Jimmy Carter (Democratic)	297	40,828,587 (50.0)
Gerald R. Ford (Republican)	240	39,147,613 (47.9)
Ronald Reagan (Independent Republican)	1	—
Other candidates McCarthy (Ind.), Libertarian	—	1,575,459 (2.1)

forts of Henry Kissinger produced a new accord by which Israel agreed to return large portions of the occupied Sinai to Egypt; the two nations pledged not to resolve future differences by force. In China, finally, the death of Mao Zedong in 1976 brought to power a new, apparently more moderate government, eager to expand its ties with the United States.

Nevertheless, as the 1976 presidential election approached, Ford's policies were coming under attack from both the right and the left. In the Republican primary campaign, Ford faced a powerful challenge from former California governor Ronald Reagan, leader of the party's conservative wing, who spoke for many on the right unhappy with any conciliation of communists. He only barely survived the assault to win his party's nomination. The Democrats, in the meantime, were gradually uniting behind a new and, before 1976, almost entirely unknown candidate: Jimmy Carter, a former governor of Georgia who organized a brilliant primary campaign and appealed to the general unhappiness

with Washington by offering honesty, piety, and an outsider's skepticism of the federal government. Capitalizing on the momentum of his early primary victories, Carter secured the Democratic nomination before most Americans had developed any very distinct impression of him. And while the tentativeness of Carter's support became clear when his early, mammoth lead dwindled to almost nothing by election day, unhappiness with the economy and a general disenchantment with Ford enabled the Democrat to hold on for a narrow victory. Carter emerged with 50 percent of the popular vote to Ford's 47.9 percent and 297 electoral votes to Ford's 240.

The Trials of Jimmy Carter

Jimmy Carter assumed the presidency at a moment when the nation faced problems of staggering complexity and difficulty. No leader could have avoided antagonizing much of the public under such inhospitable circumstances. But Carter seemed at times to make his predicament worse by a style of leadership that evoked little popular enthusiasm and, as time went on, increasing derision. He left office in 1981 as one of the least popular presidents of the century.

Carter had campaigned for the presidency as an "outsider," a representative of ordinary Americans who were deeply suspicious of the entrenched bureaucracies and complacent officials who had dominated American government for decades. He carried much of that suspiciousness with him to Washington. He surrounded himself in the White House with a group of close-knit associates from Georgia; and in the beginning, at least, he seemed deliberately to spurn assistance from more experienced political figures. Carter was among the most intelligent and quick-witted men ever to serve in the White House, but his critics charged that he provided no overall vision or direction to his government. His was, a disenchanted member of his own White House staff once charged, a peculiarly "passionless presidency."

Like his two immediate predecessors, Carter devoted the bulk of his domestic efforts to the problems of the economy, which remained linked to the problem of energy. Entering office in the midst of a severe recession, Carter moved first to reduce unemployment through an increase in public spending for public works and public services and a substantial cut in federal taxes. Unemployment soon began to decline—from nearly 8 percent late in 1976 to slightly above 5 percent by the end of 1978. But inflation in

Jimmy and Rosalynn Carter, January 20, 1977
Jimmy Carter startled the crowds (and alarmed the Secret Service) on his Inauguration Day by walking down Pennsylvania Avenue from the Capitol to the White House after taking the oath of office. Not since Jefferson, whose effort to identify with the "common man" Carter hoped to emulate, had a president walked in his inaugural parade.   (Owen Franken/Sygma)

the meantime soared. The Ford administration had left behind an inflation rate of slightly under 5 percent. In 1977, it rose to 7 percent, and in 1978 to nearly 10 percent. During Carter's last two years in office, things grew even worse, with prices rising at well over a 10 percent annual rate ("double-digit inflation," it began to be called) and at times rising by as much as 18 percent. Like Nixon and Ford before him, Carter responded with a combination of tight money and calls for voluntary restraint. He appointed first G. William Miller and then Paul Volcker, conservative economists both, to head the Federal Re-

serve Board, thus ensuring a policy of high interest rates and reduced currency supplies. By 1980, interest rates had risen to the highest levels in American history; at times, they exceeded 20 percent.

The problem of energy also grew steadily more troublesome in the Carter years. One of the president's first acts was to present to the public what he called a "comprehensive energy program," whose success, he insisted, was vital to the nation's future. But the specific features of the Carter plan—which relied largely on energy conservation—were less dramatic than the rhetoric, and Congress took this already modest program and substantially weakened it. The energy bill it passed in 1978 was almost entirely without substance or effect. In the summer of 1979, the energy battle moved into a new and more desperate phase. Increasing instability in the Middle East produced a second major fuel shortage, forcing American motorists to wait in long gasoline lines once again and creating problems for businesses, industries, and homeowners. In the midst of the crisis, OPEC announced another major price increase, clouding the economic picture still further.

Faced with increasing pressure to act (and with public-opinion polls showing his approval rating at a dismal 26 percent, lower than Richard Nixon's in his worst moments), Carter went to Camp David, the presidential retreat in the Maryland mountains, and invited a string of visitors to advise him—not only on a new energy program but on the revitalization of his administration as a whole. Ten days later, he emerged to deliver a remarkable television address. It included a series of proposals for resolving the energy crisis (including the creation of a vast new synthetic fuels industry to reduce American reliance on imported oil). But the speech was most notable for Carter's broad assessment of the national condition. Speaking with unusual fervor, he complained of a "crisis of confidence" that had reduced the nation to confusion and despair and had struck "at the very heart and soul of our national will." The address became known as the "malaise" speech (although Carter himself had never used that word), and it helped fuel attacks that the president was trying to blame his own problems on the American people. Carter's sudden firing of several members of his cabinet a few days later deepened his political problems.

Human Rights and National Interests

Among Jimmy Carter's most frequent campaign promises was a pledge to build a new basis for American foreign policy, one in which the defense of "human rights" would replace the pursuit of "selfish interests" as the cornerstone of America's role in the world. Rhetorically, at least, Carter maintained that commitment during his first months in office, speaking out sharply and often about violations of human rights in many countries (including, most prominently, the Soviet Union). Beyond that general commitment, the Carter administration focused on several more traditional concerns—the same areas, essentially, that had been the focus of the Nixon-Kissinger era. Carter's first major diplomatic accomplishment was the completion of negotiations on a pair of treaties that would turn over control of the Panama Canal to the government of Panama. In exchange for Panamanian agreements to maintain the neutrality of the canal, the United States would gradually hand over control of the Canal Zone, which it had administered since Theodore Roosevelt's bold maneuvers at the beginning of the century, to Panama. Domestic opposition to the treaties was intense, especially among conservatives who viewed the new arrangements as part of a general American retreat from international power. (Unhappiness over the treaty had fueled the 1980 conservative challenge to Gerald Ford, who had begun the negotiations, by Ronald Reagan, who opposed them.) Supporters argued that relinquishing the canal was the best way to improve relations with Latin America and avoid the possibility of years of violence. After an acrimonious debate, the Senate ratified the treaties by 68 to 32, only one vote more than the necessary two-thirds.

Less controversial, within the United States at least, was Carter's success in arranging a peace treaty between Egypt and Israel—the crowning diplomatic accomplishment of his presidency. Middle East negotiations had seemed hopelessly stalled when a dramatic breakthrough occurred in November 1977. The Egyptian president, Anwar Sadat, accepted a formal invitation to visit Israel from Prime Minister Menachem Begin and declared in Tel Aviv that Egypt was now willing to accept the state of Israel as a legitimate political entity. There remained, however, the difficult task of translating these good feelings into an actual peace treaty. When talks between Israeli and Egyptian negotiators stalled, Carter invited Sadat and Begin to a summit conference at Camp David in September 1978, holding them there for two weeks while he, Secretary of State Cyrus Vance, and others mediated the disputes between them. On September 17, Carter escorted the two leaders into the White House to announce agreement

on a "framework" for an Egyptian–Israeli peace treaty. Final agreement, the two sides promised, would be completed within three months.

But serious obstacles to the treaty emerged in those months, a result in part of the insistence of the Begin government that Israel continue to establish new Jewish settlements in the disputed territory of the West Bank of the Jordan River (which Israel had seized during the 1967 war and which Palestinian Arabs insisted should become part of a homeland for them). Only after Carter himself had intervened again, persuading Sadat to agree to a postponement of resolution of the sensitive Palestinian refugee issue, did the negotiations finally bear fruit. On March 26, 1979, Begin and Sadat returned together to the White House to sign a formal peace treaty between their two nations in the presence of Jimmy Carter, whose personal diplomacy had been largely responsible for the moment.

In the meantime, Carter attempted to continue improving relations with China and Soviet Union and to complete a new arms agreement. He responded eagerly to the overtures of Deng Xiaoping, the new Chinese leader who was attempting to open his nation to the outside world. On December 15, 1978, Washington and Beijing issued a joint communiqué announcing that formal diplomatic relations between the two nations would be restored on January 1, 1979.

Only a few months later, Carter traveled to Vienna to meet with the aging and visibly ailing Brezhnev to complete the final steps in the drafting of the new SALT II arms control agreement. The treaty set limits on the number of long-range missiles, bombers, and nuclear warheads on each side. Almost immediately, however, SALT II met with fierce conservative opposition in the United States. A powerful group of Senate Republicans denounced the treaty as excessively favorable to the Soviet Union, citing in particular provisions that restricted development of the American cruise missile while leaving the Soviets free to proceed with their new backfire bomber. Others denounced concessions permitting increases in certain Soviet missile systems that would, they charged, increase an already large Russian advantage in that area. Central to the arguments of the opposition, however, was a larger issue: a fundamental distrust of the Soviet Union that nearly a decade of détente had failed to destroy. Pointing to Soviet activities in Third World countries in Africa, to increasing Russian influence among the radical governments of the Middle East, and to allegations of Soviet

Parading for Khomeini
Iranians staged massive demonstrations on behalf of the Ayatollah Khomeini in Teheran, the capital of Iran, in 1979. The ayatollah's religious militancy and hatred of the West (especially of the United States) appealed to fundamentalist Muslims and helped sustain the Iranian revolution.   (C. Spengler/Sygma)

support of international terrorism, conservatives argued for the "linkage" of arms control agreements with agreements about Soviet behavior in other areas. By the fall of 1979, with the Senate scheduled to begin debate over the treaty shortly, ratification was already in jeopardy. Events in the following months would provide the final blow, both to the treaty and to the larger framework of détente.

The Year of the Hostages

The accumulated frustrations of more than a decade seemed to culminate in the events of the last months of 1979 and the full year that followed. Not since 1968 had the United States experienced such a sense of cascading crisis.

Ever since the early 1950s, the United States had provided political support and, more recently, massive military assistance to the government of the Shah of Iran, hoping to make his nation a bulwark against Soviet expansion in the Middle East. By 1979, however, the Shah was in deep trouble with his own people, reaping the harvest of years of brutal and unpopular policies. Iranians resented the repressive, authoritarian tactics through which the Shah had maintained his autocratic rule. At the same time, the Shah was earning the animosity of the Islamic clergy (and much of the fiercely religious populace) through his rapid efforts to modernize and Westernize his fundamentalist society. The combination of resentments produced a powerful revolutionary movement. In January 1979, finally, the Shah fled the country.

The United States, which had supported the Shah unswervingly until very near the end, was caught almost by surprise when he fell from power.

The Carter administration was even less aware, apparently, of the deep resentments that the Iranian people continued to harbor toward America, which had become a hated symbol of Western intrusion into their society. The president made cautious efforts in the first months after the Shah's abdication to establish cordial relations with the succession of increasingly militant regimes that followed. By late 1979, however, such efforts were beginning to appear futile. Not only did revolutionary chaos in the nation make any normal relationships impossible, but what power there was in Iran resided with a zealous religious leader, the Ayatollah Ruhollah Khomeini, whose hatred of the West in general and the United States in particular was intense.

In late October 1979, the deposed Shah entered the United States and checked into a hospital in New York, where he was treated for cancer. Days later, on November 4, an armed mob invaded the American embassy in Teheran, seized the diplomats and military personnel inside, and held them as hostages, demanding the return of the Shah to Iran in exchange for their freedom. Although the militants released a few of the hostages within days, fifty-three Americans remained prisoners in the embassy for over a year.

This was not the first time American citizens had been held hostage by a foreign government. In 1968, eighty-two members of the crew of the *Pueblo,* a navy intelligence-gathering ship, had been captured and held prisoner by the government of North Korea. It took eleven months for the Johnson administration to win their release, during which time the American public all but forgot about the problem. But the reaction of the nation to the events in Teheran was radically different. Coming after years of what many Americans considered international humiliations and defeats, the hostage seizure released a deep well of anger and emotion. President Carter, facing a difficult reelection battle, worked for a time to keep alive the sense of crisis. But even without his efforts, it was clear, the American people would have reacted strongly. Television newscasts relayed daily pictures of angry anti-American mobs outside the embassy, chanting such slogans as "Death to America," "Death to Carter," and "the U.S. can do nothing." The nation responded with anger and with emotional displays of patriotism.

Only weeks after the hostage seizure, on December 27, 1979, Soviet troops invaded Afghanistan, the mountainous nation lying between the USSR and Iran. The Soviet Union had, in fact, been a power in Afghanistan for years, and the dominant force since April 1978, when a coup had established a Marxist government there with close ties to the Kremlin. But while some observers claimed that the Soviet invasion was a Russian attempt to secure the status quo, others—most notably the president—viewed the situation differently. The invasion of Afghanistan, Carter claimed, was a Russian "stepping stone to their possible control over much of the world's oil supplies." It was also the "gravest threat to world peace since World War II." The war in Afghanistan was a crippling blow to the already badly weakened structure of détente. Carter angrily imposed a series of economic sanctions on the Russians, canceled American participation in the 1980 summer Olympic Games in Moscow, and announced the withdrawal of SALT II from Senate consideration.

The Campaign of 1980

By the time of the crises in Iran and Afghanistan, Jimmy Carter was in desperate political trouble. His standing in popularity polls was lower than that of any president in history. His economic policies were in shambles. Senator Edward Kennedy, younger brother of John and Robert Kennedy and one of the most magnetic figures in the Democratic party, was preparing to challenge him in the primaries. For a short while, the seizure of the hostages and the stern American response to the Soviet invasion revived Carter's candidacy. The president scored a series of impressive victories in the early primaries. But Carter's troubles were far from over.

As month followed month without any discernible progress in efforts to secure the release of the hostages in Iran, public impatience grew. In April, after the collapse of one round of negotiations, the president ordered a secret rescue attempt by American commandos. It ended in failure when several military helicopters broke down in the desert. Secretary of State Cyrus Vance, who had opposed both the rescue mission and much of the new belligerence in the nation's foreign policy, resigned in protest. Kennedy, in the meantime, managed to revive his flagging campaign and win a series of victories over the president in the later primaries.

Carter continued to benefit greatly from the many personal controversies surrounding Edward Kennedy (most notably a 1969 automobile accident at Chappaquiddick Island in Massachusetts that had left a young woman dead), and he managed in the

Election of 1980   (52.6% of electorate voting)

	ELECTORAL VOTE	POPULAR VOTE (%)
Ronald Reagan (Republican)	489	43,901,812 (50.7)
Jimmy Carter (Democratic)	49	35,483,820 (41.0)
John B. Anderson (Independent)	—	5,719,722 (6.6)
Other candidates (Libertarian)	—	921,299 (1.1)

end to stave off the challenge and win his party's nomination. But it was an unhappy convention that heard the president's listless call to arms, and Carter's campaign aroused little popular enthusiasm as he prepared to face a powerful challenge.

The Republican party had, in the meantime, rallied enthusiastically behind a man whom, not many years before, many Americans had considered a frightening reactionary. Ronald Reagan, a one-time film actor, a former California governor, and a poised and articulate campaigner, seemed in 1980 to be a man in tune with his times. Like Carter before him, he was a strident critic of the excesses of the federal government. More important, he championed a restoration of American "strength" and "pride" in the world. Although he refrained from discussing the issue of the hostages, Reagan clearly benefited from the continuing popular frustration at Carter's inability to resolve the crisis. In a larger sense, he benefited as well from the accumulated frustrations of more than a decade of domestic and international disappointments.

Election day was the anniversary of the seizure of the hostages in Iran. It was also the day on which the conservative forces that had been gathering strength in American life for more than a decade finally seized control of the nation's political life as Ronald Reagan swept to victory in the presidential election. His popular margin was decisive: 51 percent of the ballots cast to 41 percent for Jimmy Carter, and 7 percent for John Anderson—a moderate Republican congressman who had mounted an independent campaign. Reagan's electoral margin was overwhelming. Carter carried only five states and the District of Columbia, for a total of 49 electoral votes to Reagan's 489. At least as startling was the tidal wave of Republican victories in the congressional races. The party won control of the Senate for the first time since 1952; and although the Democrats retained a diminished majority in the House, the lower chamber too seemed firmly in the hands of conservatives.

On the day of Reagan's inauguration, the American hostages remaining in Iran were boarding an airplane en route to freedom after their 444-day ordeal. Jimmy Carter, in the last hours of his presidency, had concluded months of negotiations by agreeing to release several billion dollars in Iranian assets that he had frozen in American banks shortly after the seizure of the embassy. The government of Iran, desperate for funds to support its floundering war effort against neighboring Iraq, had ordered the hostages freed in return. The next few days produced a remarkable display of national emotion, as Americans welcomed the hostages home with mingled relief, joy, and anger. Not since the end of World War II had there been such demonstrations of joy and patriotism. But while the celebration in 1945 had marked a great American triumph, the euphoria in 1981 marked something quite different—a troubled nation grasping for reassurance. Ronald Reagan set out to provide it.

The "Reagan Revolution"

Ronald Reagan assumed the presidency in January 1981 promising a change in government more fundamental than any since the New Deal of fifty years before. While his eight years in office produced a significant shift in public policy, they brought nothing so fundamental as many of his supporters had

Reagan at the Ranch
Ronald Reagan relaxes at his ranch in the mountains near Santa Barbara, California, demonstrating the informal geniality that accounted for much of his remarkable popularity. (Michael Evans/Sygma)

hoped or his opponents had feared. But if the record of the new administration on matters of policy was a mixed one, there was no ambiguity about its purely political achievements. Ronald Reagan succeeded brilliantly in making his own engaging personality the central fact of American politics in the 1980s.

Reagan as President

Even many people who disagreed with the president's policies found themselves drawn to his attractive and carefully honed public image. Reagan was a master of television, a warm and appealing raconteur, a gifted public speaker, and—in public at least—rugged, fearless, and seemingly impervious to misfortune. He turned seventy only weeks after taking office and was the oldest man ever to serve as president. But his public image was of a vigorous, resilient, even youthful man. He spent vacations on a California ranch, where he chopped wood and rode horses. When he was wounded in an assassination attempt in 1981, he joked with doctors on his way into surgery and appeared to bounce back from the ordeal with remarkable speed. Four years later, he seemed to rebound from cancer surgery with similar zest. He had few visible insecurities. He seldom displayed the anger or vindictiveness or humorlessness that had plagued his predecessors. Even when things went wrong, as they often did, the blame seemed seldom to attach to Reagan himself (inspiring some Democrats to begin referring to him as "the Teflon president"). Reagan managed to stand above the fray, a symbol of America's search to regain confidence in itself.

Reagan was not much involved in the day-today affairs of running the government; he surrounded himself with tough, energetic administrators who insulated him from many of the pressures of the office and apparently relied on him largely for general guidance, not specific decisions. At times, the president revealed a startling ignorance about the nature of his own policies or the actions of his subordinates; aides often had to step in to "clarify" or correct presidential misstatements. But Reagan did make active use of his office to generate support for his administration's programs, by appealing repeatedly to the public over television and through public appearances and by fusing his proposals to a nationalistic rhetoric that seemed perfectly to match the public mood.

"Supply-Side" Economics

Reagan's 1980 campaign for the presidency had centered on several goals. It had promised to end the drift in American foreign policy and restore the nation's military strength. It had promised to reduce the intrusive influence of government on American life. And it had promised to restore the economy to health by a bold experiment that became known as "supply-side" economics or, to some, "Reaganomics." It was this last pledge that the new administration attempted to fulfill first and that, initially at least, became the source of its most conspicuous triumphs.

Supply-side economics operated from the assumption that the woes of the American economy were in large part a result of excessive taxation, which left inadequate capital available to investors to stimulate growth. The solution, therefore, was to reduce taxes, with particularly generous benefits to corporations and wealthy individuals, in order to encourage new investments. The result would be a general economic revival that would affect all levels of the population. But cutting taxes was only one part of the supply-side program. Because a tax cut would reduce government revenues, it would also be necessary to reduce government expenses. Otherwise, large federal deficits might negate the effects of the tax cut by requiring the government to borrow in the marketplace, thus raising interest rates and drying up capital for investment once again. A cornerstone of the Reagan economic program, therefore, was a drastic cut in the federal budget, one intended to produce, within four years, a balance between government revenues and expenditures for the first time since 1969.

In his first months in office, accordingly, Reagan hastily assembled a legislative program that would enact the basic features of the supply-side program. His energetic budget director, David Stockman, proposed new budget reductions that would cut expenditures by some $40 billion; and despite opposition from liberals, special-interest groups, and constituencies threatened by the loss of social services, the new budget cuts passed through Congress with relative ease, almost in the form the administration had proposed. In addition, the president proposed a bold, three-year rate reduction on both individual and corporate taxes. In the summer of 1981, it too was passed, generally in the form presented by the administration. No president since Lyndon Johnson had compiled so impressive a legislative record in his first months in office.

By early 1982, however, the Reagan economic program was beset with difficulties. The nation was experiencing the most severe recession since the 1930s, with unemployment approaching 10 percent of the work force. Some regions of the country, most notably the industrial Midwest, had descended into virtual depression conditions. The Reagan economic program was not directly to blame for the problems, but critics claimed in 1982 that the administration's policies were doing nothing to improve the situation.

In fact, however, the economy recovered more rapidly and impressively than almost anyone had expected. By the middle of 1983, unemployment (which had reached nearly 11 percent in 1982, the highest level in over forty years) had fallen to 8.2 percent. The gross national product grew 3.6 percent, the largest increase since the mid-1970s. Inflation was below 5 percent. And despite the continuing claims of many economists that the recovery was weak, erratic, and artificial, the economy continued to grow, and both inflation and unemployment remained low (at least by the new and more pessimistic standards the nation seemed now to have accepted) through the remainder of the decade.

Opinions differed as to the causes of the recovery. Some credited Reagan's "supply side" fiscal policies. Others attributed it to the long-term effects of the Federal Reserve Board's tight-money policies, which some economists claimed had "wrung" inflation out of the economy. Having done that, the Board altered its course in 1983 and began reducing interest rates and expanding the money supply—in effect subordinating concern about inflation to concern about unemployment and declining investment. The recovery was also a result of a radical drop in oil prices, the result of a worldwide "energy glut" that

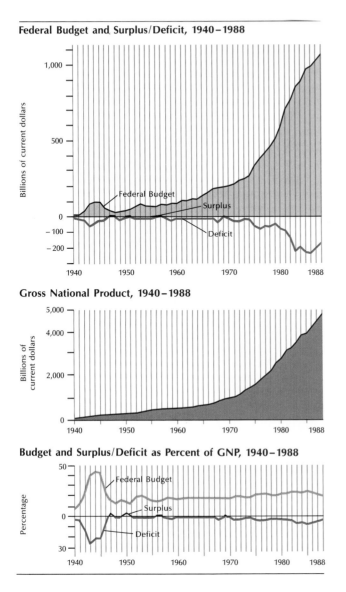

Federal Budget and Surplus/Deficit, 1940–1988

Gross National Product, 1940–1988

Budget and Surplus/Deficit as Percent of GNP, 1940–1988

led to the virtual collapse of the OPEC cartel and an at least temporary end to the inflationary pressures of spiraling fuel costs. And the recovery was a result, too, of staggering budget deficits that pumped billions of dollars into the flagging economy but that also, many warned, threatened ultimately to destroy the recovery they were helping to create.

The Fiscal Crisis

By the mid-1980s, this growing fiscal crisis had become one of the central issues in American domestic politics. Having entered office promising a balanced budget within four years, Reagan presided over record budget deficits and accumulated more debt in his eight years in office than the American government had accrued in its entire previous history. Before the 1980s, the highest single-year budget deficit in American history had been $66 billion (in 1976). Throughout the 1980s, the annual budget deficit consistently exceeded $100 billion (and in 1986 peaked at $221 billion). The national debt rose from $907 billion in 1980 to over $2 trillion by 1986 and just under $3 trillion by early 1990.

Even those who had always believed in the value of deficit spending as an economic stimulus found the dimensions of the fiscal crisis of the 1980s alarming. The deficits, economists argued, were keeping interest rates high and were threatening to push them higher; the government was forced to borrow so much money itself to pay its own bills that it was leaving too little for investors and thus driving up the price of borrowing. Should that continue, new private investment would dry up and the economy would once again sag. For much the same reason, the deficits were also keeping the American dollar overvalued. The high cost of the dollar made it more difficult for foreigners to buy American goods and more tempting for Americans to buy products from overseas. One result was a large and growing imbalance in American trade. Once the world's leading creditor, the United States had become by the mid-1980s the world's largest debtor. Among the causes of these difficulties were the increasing problems of such fundamental American industries as automobiles and steel, which not only found it difficult to export their goods abroad, but which faced growing competition within the American market as well.

The enormous deficits had many causes, some of them stretching back over decades of American public policy decisions. But some of the most important causes lay in the policies of the Reagan administration. The 1981 tax cuts, the largest in American history, sharply eroded the revenue base of the federal government and accounted for a large percentage of the deficit. The massive increase in military spending (a proposed $1.6 trillion over five years) on which Reagan and his defense secretary, Casper Weinberger, fervently insisted added more to the federal budget than the administration's cuts in domestic spending removed.

In his efforts to reduce the deficit, the president steadfastly refused to consider raising income taxes (or even reducing the 25 percent reduction in tax rates he had himself initiated), although he did agree to several major "revenue enhancements" that increased taxes indirectly and to a substantial increase in Social Security taxes, which shifted much of the revenue burden from upper- to lower- and middle-income groups. He refused to reduce military expenditures (despite rising demands from leaders of both major parties to do so). He resisted any substantial revision of the major "entitlement" programs (Social Security, Medicare, federal and military pensions, and others), whose spiraling costs accounted for a large part of the budget. He could not, by law, reduce the growing proportion of the budget devoted to interest payments on the enormous national debt. Instead, he concentrated largely on reducing the relatively small portion of the budget devoted to "discretionary" domestic spending. That meant significant cuts in many programs aimed at the poorest (and politically weakest) Americans: reductions in funding for food stamps, a major cut in federal subsidies for low-income housing (which contributed to the radical increase in homelessness that by the late 1980s was plaguing virtually all American cities), strict new limitations on Medicare and Medicaid payments, reductions in student loans, school lunches, and other educational programs.

By the end of Reagan's third year in office, however, funding for domestic programs had been cut nearly as far as the Congress (and, apparently, the public) was willing to tolerate. Congress responded with the so-called Gramm-Rudman bill, passed late in 1985, which mandated major deficit reductions over five years and provided for automatic budget cuts in all areas of government spending should the president and Congress fail to agree on an alternative solution. It attracted support from leaders of both parties and even, somewhat uneasily, from the president. Under Gramm-Rudman, the budget deficit did steadily decline from its 1983 high. But much of that decline was a result of a substantial surplus in the Social Security trust fund (which the sharply increased Social Security taxes had produced), not of any larger fiscal successes.

Reagan and the World

Reagan encountered a similar combination of triumphs and difficulties in international affairs. Determined to restore American pride and prestige in the world, he attacked what he claimed was the weakness and "defeatism" of previous administrations,

which had allowed Vietnam, Watergate, and other crises to paralyze their will to act. The United States, he argued, should once again become active and assertive in opposing communism throughout the world and in supporting friendly governments whatever their internal policies.

Relations with the Soviet Union, which had been steadily deteriorating in the last years of the Carter administration, grew still more chilly after Reagan took office. Both the president and his first secretary of state, Alexander Haig, spoke harshly of the Soviet regime, accusing it of sponsoring world terrorism and declaring that any armaments negotiations must be "linked" to negotiations about Soviet behavior in other areas. Relations with the Russians deteriorated further after the government of Poland (under strong pressure from Moscow) imposed martial law on the country in the winter of 1981 to crush a growing challenge from an independent labor organization, Solidarity.

Although the president had long denounced the SALT II arms control treaty as unfavorable to the United States, he continued to honor its provisions. But the Reagan administration at first made little progress toward arms control in other areas, despite the growing political power of a popular antinuclear movement in both Europe and the United States. In fact, the president proposed the most ambitious new military program in many years: the so-called Strategic Defense Initiative (SDI), widely known as "Star Wars" (after the popular movie of that name). Reagan claimed that SDI, through the use of lasers and satellites, could provide an impenetrable shield against incoming missiles and thus make nuclear war obsolete. The Soviet Union reacted with anger and alarm and insisted that the new program would elevate the arms race to new and more dangerous levels. For nearly four years, Soviet leaders insisted that any arms control agreement begin with an American abandonment of SDI; the president refused even to consider it.

In other respects, American foreign policy in the early and mid-1980s embraced once again many of the assumptions that had fueled its international activities in the 1950s and early 1960s. In particular, the Reagan administration began, rhetorically at least, to commit itself to supporting opponents of communism anywhere in the world, whether or not the regimes they were challenging were directly allied to the Soviet Union. This became known as the Reagan Doctrine, and it meant, above all, a new American activism in the Third World.

The most conspicuous examples of the new activism came in Latin America. In October 1982, the administration sent American soldiers and Marines into the tiny Caribbean island of Grenada to oust an anti-American Marxist regime that showed signs of forging a relationship with the Soviet Union. The invasion was brief and not particularly costly. It was highly popular with the American public (and, apparently, with many of the residents of Grenada). In El Salvador, where first a repressive military regime and later a moderate civilian one were engaged in murderous struggles with left-wing revolutionaries (who were supported, according to the Reagan administration, by Cuba and the Soviet Union), the president committed himself to increased military and economic assistance, although he insisted that this assistance would not extend to the introduction of American forces into the region. In neighboring Nicaragua, a pro-American dictatorship had fallen to the revolutionary "Sandinistas" in 1979; the new government had grown increasingly anti-American (and increasingly Marxist) throughout the early 1980s. The administration gave both rhetorical and material support to the so-called *contras,* a guerrilla movement drawn from several antigovernment groups and fighting (without great success) to topple the Sandinista regime. Indeed, support of the contras became a mission of special importance to the president, and later the source of some of his greatest difficulties.

In other parts of the world, the administration's bellicose rhetoric seemed to hide an instinctive restraint. In June 1982, the Israeli army launched an invasion of Lebanon in an effort to drive guerrillas of the Palestinian Liberation Organization from the country. The United States supported the Israelis rhetorically but also worked to reduce the violence and to permit PLO forces to leave Lebanon peacefully. An American peacekeeping force entered Beirut to supervise the evacuation. Later, American Marines remained in the city, apparently to protect the fragile Lebanese government, which was embroiled in a vicious civil war. Once they were identified with one faction in the struggle, Americans became the targets of increasing violence, including a 1983 terrorist bombing of a Marine barracks in Beirut that left 241 Americans dead. In the face of this difficult situation, Reagan chose to withdraw American forces rather than become more deeply involved in the Lebanese struggle.

The tragedy in Lebanon was a sign of the new character of Third World struggles: an increasing reliance on terrorism by otherwise powerless groups to advance their political aims. A series of terrorist acts—attacks on airplanes, cruise ships, commercial and diplomatic posts, the seizing of American and other Western hostages—did precisely what they were intended to do: alarmed and frightened much of the Western world. The Reagan administration spoke bravely about its resolve to punish terrorism; and at one point in 1986, the president ordered American planes to bomb sites in Tripoli, the capital of Libya, whose controversial leader Muammar al-Qaddafi was widely believed to be a leading sponsor of terrorism. In general, however, terrorists remained virtually impossible to identify or control.

The Election of 1984

Reagan approached the campaign of 1984 at the head of a united Republican partly firmly committed to his candidacy. The Democrats, as had become their custom, followed a more fractious course. Former Vice President Walter Mondale established an early and commanding lead in the race by soliciting support from a wide range of traditional Democratic interest groups, including the politically powerful AFL-CIO and National Education Association. But while many Democrats liked Mondale, few found him exciting. And for a time, he seemed to lose the initiative to a younger and apparently more dynamic candidate, Senator Gary Hart of Colorado, who presented himself as a leader of a "new generation" and the spokesman for vaguely defined "new ideas." Hart scored a series of stunning upsets in the early primaries and left the Mondale campaign reeling. The dynamic and controversial black leader, Jesse Jackson, also staged an impressive primary campaign that drew substantial minority support away from Mondale and weakened him further against Hart. But with the help of the AFL-CIO and other established groups, and as a result of a series of blunders by the Hart campaign, Mondale revived and managed to capture the nomination. At the Democratic Convention in San Francisco that summer, he brought momentary excitement to the campaign by selecting a woman, Representative Geraldine Ferraro of New York, to be his running mate and the first female candidate ever to appear on a national ticket.

The Democratic Convention displayed to the public a parade of diverse constituencies asking for greater representation in the political process: blacks, Hispanics, women, the handicapped, gays, the poor,

Election of 1984 (53.3% of electorate voting)

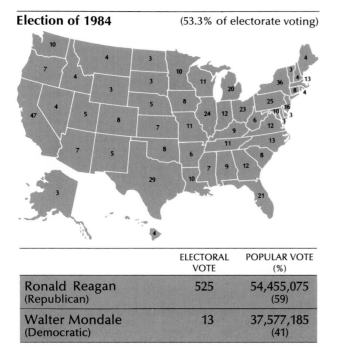

	ELECTORAL VOTE	POPULAR VOTE (%)
Ronald Reagan (Republican)	525	54,455,075 (59)
Walter Mondale (Democratic)	13	37,577,185 (41)

and others. The Republican Convention, by contrast, presented an image of a united, homogeneous society rallying comfortably behind a revered leader. The meeting in Dallas was, in fact, a tribute to the "new spirit" the Reagan administration was attempting to create: a celebration of American strength and pride. Few Republicans gave more than passing attention to the nation's social problems.

Reagan's victory in 1984 was one of the most decisive in American political history. His popular majority was impressive; he won approximately 59 percent of the vote. His electoral majority was overwhelming; he carried every state but Mondale's native Minnesota and the District of Columbia. Only 53.3 percent of the electorate voted, the lowest figure in over fifty years. Republicans liked to claim that the 1984 election confirmed that a historic realignment of partisan loyalties had taken place, that the Republican party was now the dominant voice in American politics. The results of the presidential election alone would seem to confirm that claim. But the wider pattern of voter behavior in the 1980s suggested less a fundamental realignment than a weakening of partisan loyalties on both sides. While Reagan was carrying forty-nine states, Democrats gained a seat in the Senate and main-

tained only slightly reduced control of the House of Representatives.

The Reagan Scandals

For a time, Reagan's personal popularity deflected attention from a series of scandals that might well have destroyed another administration—scandals that together created what critics of the government liked to call the Reagan presidency's "sleaze factor." Top officials in the Environmental Protection Agency resigned when it was disclosed that they were flouting the laws they had been appointed to enforce. Officials of the CIA and the Defense Department resigned after revelations of questionable stock transactions. Reagan's secretary of labor left office after being indicted for racketeering (although he was later acquitted of the charges). Edwin Meese, the White House counsel and later attorney general, was the subject of almost ceaseless attacks for controversial financial arrangements that many believed had compromised his office; Meese finally resigned in 1988.

Unnoticed at the time were two far greater scandals that surfaced only as Reagan was about to leave office. One involved misuse of funds by the Department of Housing and Urban Development, abuses so widespread that by 1990 the survival of the agency itself was in question. Another, more serious scandal involved the savings and loan industry. The Reagan administration, true to its philosophy of removing government from the marketplace, had sharply reduced its regulatory controls over the savings and loans, which were already in serious difficulties because of the unusual volatility of interest rates in the 1980s. Many had responded to the relaxation of controls by rapidly and often recklessly expanding. In some cases, the speculation was combined with personal corruption. By the end of the decade, the industry was in chaos, and the government was forced to step in to prevent a complete collapse. In 1990, estimates of the eventual cost to taxpayers of rescuing the banks ran as high as $500 billion. Some predicted the cost would eventually be even higher.

In 1986, however, the nation became aware of a scandal that even Reagan could not explain away. In November of that year, after reports of the episode had begun appearing in foreign newspapers, the White House conceded that it had entered secret negotiations with the revolutionary government of Iran to secure the release of several Americans being held hostage by radical Islamic groups in the Middle East.

That alone seemed to contradict the president's repeated promises that he would "never negotiate with terrorists." The revelation that the United States had been selling arms to Iran in exchange for its assistance (which, with one exception, failed to materialize) triggered even greater public outrage. But what turned the affair into a major scandal was the revelation that some of the money from the arms deal with Iran had been covertly funneled into a fund to aid the contras in Nicaragua.

In the months that followed, aggressive reporting and a highly publicized series of congressional hearings exposed a remarkable and previously unsuspected feature of the Reagan White House: the existence within it of something like a "secret government," unknown to the State Department, the Defense Department, perhaps even the CIA, dedicated to advancing the administration's foreign policy aims through secret and at times illegal means. The principal figure in this covert world appeared to be an obscure Marine lieutenant colonel assigned to the staff of the National Security Council, Oliver North. North was a magnetic personality who believed fervently in the righteousness of his efforts and who, in an extraordinary appearance before a congressional investigating committee, defiantly admitted having circumvented the law—insisting both that he was right to do so and that he was following the orders of superiors. North became a popular figure, even something of a folk hero, to many Americans at the time. But the Iran-contra scandal, as it became known, did serious damage to the Reagan presidency—even though the investigations were never able to tie the president himself to the most serious violations of the law. If nothing else, the affair exposed a pattern of remarkable inattention by the president to the activities of his staff and raised questions about both his competence and his integrity.

There were other signs in the late 1980s that the glow of the "Reagan Revolution" was beginning to fade. In October 1987, the American stock market—whose spectacular success had been one of the most conspicuous features of the economic boom—experienced the greatest single-day decline in its history; and although stock prices gradually recovered over the next two years, the crash inflicted a severe blow on the heady confidence that had fueled the financial markets over the previous five years. At about the same time, one of the most popular financial innovations of the 1980s, the "leveraged buyout," which had permitted a wave of corporate takeovers financed by huge loans, began to unravel. Some of the nation's largest corporations, unable to carry the enormous debt they had acquired in their takeover efforts, began to flounder. Several declared bankruptcy. The new breed of traders spawned by the 1980s boom—aggressive, brash, many believed greedy and arrogant, committed to making enormous profits quickly—suddenly seemed the architects of financial disasters. The collapse of the market for "junk bonds," the high-risk, high-interest loan instruments that facilitated many corporate takeovers in the 1980s, was one sign of the new investment climate. So too was the 1989 indictment of the most powerful "junk bond" trader, Michael Milken, and the collapse in early 1990 of his company, Drexel Burnham Lambert. Together, such events suggested that the speculative wave had created not only quick profits, but enormous instability.

Public opinion polls, in the meantime, suggested that a majority of Americans were becoming alarmed at the failure of government to address social problems that were becoming increasingly serious: the rapid decline of the inner cities, the dramatic increase in homelessness, the inadequacy of the American educational system, the decay of the nation's physical infrastructure, and most of all, as the decade came to a close, the ravages of a massive drug epidemic, fueled by the widespread availability of the new, relatively inexpensive, and highly addictive form of cocaine known as "crack."

The Election of 1988

The fraying of the Reagan administration helped the Democrats regain control of the United States Senate in 1986 and fueled hopes in the party for a presidential victory in 1988. Even so, several of the most popular figures in the Democratic party—New York Governor Mario Cuomo, New Jersey Senator Bill Bradley, and Edward Kennedy—all refused to run. And the early front runner, Senator Gary Hart of Colorado, withdrew from the race in May 1987 after embarrassing revelations of an extramarital relationship with a young model. That left the field to a group of lesser-known candidates and to Jesse Jackson, whose fervent support in the black community made him a major force in the party.

The man who finally emerged from the pack had been almost entirely unknown to the American public a year earlier: Michael Dukakis, who was be-

Election of 1988   (50% of electorate voting)

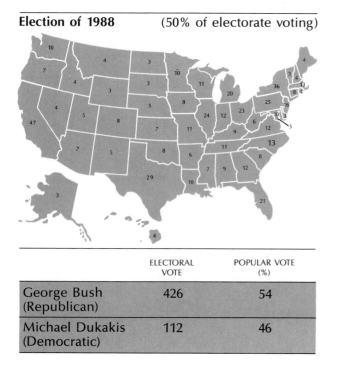

	ELECTORAL VOTE	POPULAR VOTE (%)
George Bush (Republican)	426	54
Michael Dukakis (Democratic)	112	46

ginning his third term as governor of Massachusetts and who capitalized on his reputation as an effective, honest administrator and as a leader who had overseen a dramatic turnaround in the New England economy (a revival frequently described as "the Massachusetts miracle"). Dukakis was a dry, even somewhat dull campaigner who created little real excitement. But Democrats remained optimistic about their prospects in 1988, largely because of the identity of their opponent, Vice President George Bush.

In nearly thirty years in public life—as a member of Congress from Texas, as ambassador to the United Nations and China, as director of the CIA, head of the Republican National Committee, and finally vice president—Bush had never identified himself clearly with any major issue and could take credit for no major accomplishments. He had been an ineffective campaigner in 1980, when he ran for president, and had attracted wide derision for his performance in the 1984 campaign, when he was running for reelection as vice president. *Time* magazine, early in 1988, devoted its cover to Bush's political problems, which it described as "the wimp factor." Capitalizing on his ties to the still-popular Reagan, Bush captured the Republican nomination without great difficulty, but he entered the last months of the campaign substantially behind Dukakis.

Beginning at the Republican convention, however, Bush staged a remarkable turnaround. He survived controversy over his choice of a vice presidential running mate, Senator J. Danforth Quayle of Indiana, a young and relatively inexperienced candidate whom even many Republicans considered alarmingly callow and uninformed. And he made his campaign into a long, relentless attack on Michael Dukakis as an exemplar of all the unpopular social and cultural stances Americans had come to identify with "liberals." Bush described Dukakis as "soft" on crime, inadequately patriotic, and incompetent as an administrator. Indeed, the Bush campaign was almost certainly the most negative, and many believed among the most dishonest and discreditable, of the twentieth century. It was also, apparently, one of the most effective, although the listless, indecisive character of the Dukakis campaign contributed to the Republican cause as well. Having trailed Dukakis by a substantial margin as late as August, Bush moved ahead early in the fall and won a substantial victory in November. He received 54 percent of the popular vote to Dukakis's 46, and he won 426 electoral votes to Dukakis's 111. But Bush carried few Republicans into office with him; the Democrats retained secure majorities in both houses of Congress.

Launching the Bush Presidency

The first eighteen months of the Bush presidency were notable above all for the absence of important initiatives or compelling new ideas emanating from the White House. That reflected, in part, the president's own innate caution and his reluctance to compete with his dynamic predecessor for public acclaim. It reflected, too, the absence of any real sense of crisis in American life, as the economy continued to avoid a recession and international affairs underwent a series of dizzying transformations that left the United States largely on the sidelines.

Bush surrounded himself with moderate conservatives—pragmatists, largely uninterested in the grand ideological missions many Reagan supporters had embraced. He committed himself to a fiscal stringency that foreclosed virtually any new programs. He expressed more sympathy than had his predecessor toward efforts to improve education, protect the environment, and tackle such pressing social problems as homelessness and drug

Three Presidents, 1988
President-elect George Bush and President Ronald Reagan stand with Soviet President Mikhail Gorbachev before the Statue of Liberty on December 7, 1988, during Gorbachev's visit to the United Nations. (Reuters/Bettmann Newsphotos)

abuse. But in the absence of funding, he could offer little more than rhetorical support to any of these causes. In the meantime, debate continued over how to reduce the nation's enormous budget deficits, which were declining only because of the controversial diversion of large surpluses in the Social Security trust fund into general revenues and because the enormous sums being spent in the savings and loan bailout were not included in budget calculations. Neither the Bush administration nor the Democratic Congress seemed willing to act to resolve the deficit crisis.

Nevertheless, Bush enjoyed broad and continuing popularity during his first year and a half in office. That was partly because of his low-key, unthreatening public image; partly because of continuing general contentment with the state of the economy; and partly because of his decision to dispatch American troops into Panama late in 1989 to overthrow the unpopular military leader Manuel Noriega, who was under indictment in the United States for drug trafficking and whose contemptuous defiance of American pressures had embarrassed the government in Washington for two years. The Panama invasion was larger and more costly than the Grenada excursion of 1983, but no less popular. It installed an elected, pro-American, civilian government in Panama, captured Noriega, and brought him to the United States to stand trial.

But Bush's popularity also owed a great deal to events over which he had virtually no control, a series of genuinely revolutionary transformations in the international order that made 1989 and 1990 one of the truly epochal moments in modern world history.

The End of the Cold War?

In the midst of the turbulent changes that were enveloping the world as the 1980s came to a close, it was difficult to identify the point at which it all began. Some pointed to the upheavals in Poland in 1981, the first broad challenge to communist rule in eastern Europe in over a decade. Some pointed to the Soviet war in Afghanistan, a long, stalemated conflict that proved in many ways more disastrous to the Soviet economy and the Soviet government than the Vietnam War had been to the United States. Some pointed to the long-term economic troubles of the Eastern bloc nations; by the late 1980s, some were experiencing something close to collapse, and even the most successful were falling further and further behind the dynamically expanding economies of Western Europe.

The most frequent explanation, however, centered on a single man: Mikhail Gorbachev, who succeeded to the leadership of the Soviet Union in 1985 and, to the surprise of almost everyone, very quickly became the most revolutionary figure in world politics in at least four decades. Benefiting from widespread frustration in the Soviet Union with the rigid and ineffective policies of the preceding twenty years (now labeled the "time of stagnation"), Gorbachev transformed Soviet politics by introducing two dramatic new policies. The first he called *glasnost* (openness). *Glasnost* meant the dismantling of many of the repressive mechanisms that had been among the most conspicuous features of Soviet life for over half a century. Suddenly it became possible for Soviet citizens to express themselves freely, to criticize the government, even to organize politically in opposition to official policy. The other policy Gorbachev called *perestroika* (reform, or restructuring). Through it, he attempted to remake the rigid and unproductive Soviet economy by introducing, among other things, such elements of capitalism as private ownership and the profit motive.

The forces Gorbachev unleashed changed Soviet life more quickly than even he had imagined. By early 1990, nationalist movements in several of the republics (including Lithuania, Azerbaijan, even the Russian Republic itself) were threatening to tear apart the Soviet nation. The country's economic problems, severe even before the reforms, grew significantly worse; Soviet citizens faced massive shortages of basic items and increasing unemployment. Throughout it all, Gorbachev managed not only to maintain, but apparently to strengthen, his grip on power; and as the instability grew, he endorsed more and more radical reforms—including, in February 1990, a formal renunciation by the Communist party of its guaranteed monopoly of political power.

To the rest of the world, however, the most dramatic result of the Gorbachev reforms was the transformation of Soviet foreign policy and the dramatic collapse of the Soviet empire. That the Gorbachev regime was committed to moving in bold new directions had been clear almost from the start, when the new leader began reaching out to Ronald Reagan for major arms control agreements. At a summit meeting with Reagan in Reykjavik, Iceland, in 1986, Gorbachev proposed an across-the-board reduction in the nuclear arsenals of both sides by 50 percent or more, although continuing disputes over Reagan's commitment to the SDI program derailed agreements. But in 1988, after Reagan and Gorbachev exchanged cordial visits to each other's capitals, the two superpowers signed a treaty eliminating American and Soviet intermediate-range nuclear forces (INF) from Europe.

These important developments seemed to pale, however, in light of the dramatic events of 1989, a year that saw what many believed was nothing less than the collapse of world communism. In the space of a few months, every nation in the so-called Soviet bloc in Eastern Europe—Poland, Hungary, Czechoslovakia, Bulgaria, Romania, and East Germany—either overthrew its government or forced it to transform itself into an essentially noncommunist (and in some cases, actively anticommunist) regime. The Communist parties of Eastern Europe all but collapsed. And in every case, Gorbachev and the Soviet Union not only refused to oppose, but actively encouraged, the changes. Perhaps the most dramatic moment in the transformation of Europe came on November 9, 1989, when the government of East Germany began dismantling the infamous Berlin Wall, for nearly thirty years a symbol of the Cold War, and allowed free passage between the two Germanys. Within a few weeks, German reunification—which only a few months earlier had seemed at best a distant dream—appeared both inevitable and imminent.

The challenges to communism were not successful everywhere. In May 1989, students in China had begun staging large demonstrations calling for greater democratization, which the post-Mao government had long been promising but had never delivered. A visit by Gorbachev to Beijing in late May inspired even greater demonstrations. By the beginning of June, the demonstrations had grown so large and widespread, and had attracted the support of so

A Pro-democracy Demonstration in Tiananmen Square, Beijing

The "democracy movement" in China, launched by students early in 1989, was attracting support from millions of Chinese by June 1989 and was threatening to topple the country's communist government. Here students demonstrate in the central square of Beijing, China's capital city, before a portrait of Mao Zedong, whose harsh revolutionary dogma they were challenging. A few days later, government troops entered the square, crushing both the demonstration and, for a time at least, the movement behind it. (Sygma)

much of the population, that the communist regime seemed likely to topple. Instead, hard-line leaders seized control and sent military forces to crush the uprising. The result was a bloody massacre on June 3, 1989, in Tiananmen Square in Beijing, in which hundreds, perhaps thousands, of student demonstrators died. The assault crushed the democracy movement, restored the hard-liners to power, and inaugurated a period of harsh repression and international ostracism.

But the events in China had no counterpart in the rest of the communist world. The attempt by the Romanian dictator, Nicolae Ceausescu, to crush a dissident revolt in his country in December 1989 produced a popular revolution that drove him from power and led to his capture and execution and to the installation of a new, noncommunist regime. In all other Eastern European nations, the toppling of communist regimes occurred remarkably peacefully.

There were even signs of democratization in parts of the world far removed from the Soviet empire. Early in 1990, the government of South Africa, long an international pariah for its rigid enforcement of white supremacy through the "apartheid" system, began a cautious retreat from its traditional policies. Among other things, it legalized the major black opposition movements, most prominently the African National Congress, which had been banned for decades. And on February 11, 1990, it released from prison the leader of the ANC, Nelson Mandela, a revered hero to black South Africans, who had been in jail for twenty-seven years. Mandela pledged to continue the struggle for the complete destruction of apartheid.

In the face of these dramatic changes, American foreign policy, which had for over four decades remained securely tied to the premises of "containment" first outlined in the late 1940s, suddenly seemed obsolete. The Bush administration responded cautiously to the changes. After the massacre in Beijing, the president sent two of his principal aides to China to try to restore cordial relations with the communist government—a decision that provoked bitter criticism from Republicans and Democrats alike. Bush expressed warm (if at times muted) praise for many of Gorbachev's initiatives, voiced his approval of the changes in Eastern Europe, but warned that the precariousness of Soviet reforms required the United States to move slowly toward a new order.

Still, by early 1990 American foreign policy was in the throes of change almost despite itself. After years of resistance, the United States expressed a willingness to negotiate major reductions in the number of American troops stationed in Western Europe; and in mid-February, the Soviet Union agreed to Bush's proposal to reduce troop strength on both sides, while leaving the United States with a 30,000-troop edge. Other arms control initiatives, including major cuts in the strategic (or nuclear) arsenals on both sides, suddenly seemed not only possible, but imminent. Also in February 1990, the United States and the Soviet Union (along with Britain and France) reached an agreement with East and West Germany to support the process of German reunification, a process by then already far advanced.

In the meantime, policymakers, scholars, and others engaged in a spirited debate over the meaning of the bewildering international changes for the future of American foreign policy. What role would America play in the world in the absence of a Cold War? If the Soviet Union ceased to be a menacing adversary, what justification would there be for America's great military establishment or for NATO? Would economic rivalries now replace ideological ones? Would a multipolar world be more or less stable than the bipolar world it was replacing? Seldom in history had such momentous changes occurred so quickly. Building any new approach to international relations, let alone one as coherent as the collapsing containment doctrine, was a daunting task.

Modern Times

Much of the anxiety that beset American life in the 1970s, and much of the conservative sentiment that emerged to dominate American politics in the 1980s,

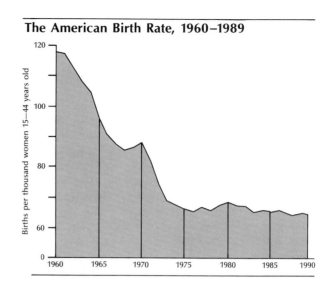

The American Birth Rate, 1960–1989

was a result of jarring public events that left many men and women shaken and uncertain. But much of it was a result as well of significant changes in the nature and behavior of American society. Old assumptions were called into question. New strains and new challenges were forcing significant adjustments in belief.

The New Demography

One of the most fundamental changes in American life in the postliberal era was the new profile of the American population. After decades of steady growth, the nation's birth rate began to decline in the 1970s and remained low through the 1980s. In 1970, there were 18.4 births for every 1,000 people in the population. By 1975, the rate had declined to 14.6, the lowest in the twentieth century. And despite a modest increase in the 1980s, the rate remained below 16 throughout the decade.

The declining birth rate had several causes. Many men and women were marrying later, were postponing having children because of professional pressures, and were having fewer children because of financial stringencies. (The dramatic increase in housing costs across the country in the 1970s and 1980s undoubtedly played a role in discouraging large families.) The greater availability of contraceptive and sterilization procedures also reduced births, as did the legalization of abortion. There is no way to know

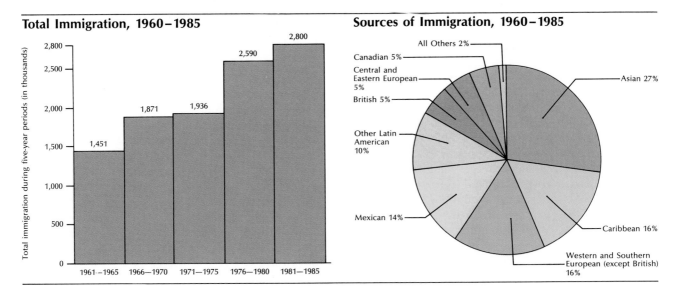

Total Immigration, 1960–1985

Total immigration during five-year periods (in thousands)

Period	Value
1961–1965	1,451
1966–1970	1,871
1971–1975	1,936
1976–1980	2,590
1981–1985	2,800

Sources of Immigration, 1960–1985

All Others 2%
Canadian 5%
Central and Eastern European 5%
British 5%
Other Latin American 10%
Mexican 14%
Asian 27%
Caribbean 16%
Western and Southern European (except British) 16%

how many abortions were performed illegally before the Supreme Court's 1973 decision invalidating most restrictions on them; but there was almost certainly an increase in the number of abortions once the process became legal. There were approximately 1.3 million legal abortions reported in the United States during each year of the 1980s.

One result of the declining birth rate was a marked increase in the proportion of elderly citizens. Over 12 percent of the population was more than sixty-five years old by the end of the 1980s, as compared with 8 percent in 1970. That figure was projected to rise to over 20 percent by the end of the century. The median age in 1988 was 32.3 years, as compared with 28.0 in 1970. The "graying" of America, as some described it, was a result not only of the declining birth rate, but of higher life expectancy. The American death rate declined from 9.5 per thousand in 1970 to 8.8 in 1988; the average life expectancy at birth rose from 67.1 years to 71.5 for males in the same period, and from 74.7 to 78.3 for females. The aging of the population had important, if still not fully understood, implications. It was, for example, the cause of the increasing costliness of Social Security pensions; the ratio of people paying into the system versus people drawing out of it was shifting rapidly to favor the latter. It meant rapidly increasing health costs, both for the federal Medicare system and for private hospitals and insurance companies.

Hispanics, Asians, and the New Immigration

Perhaps the most striking demographic change in America in the 1970s and 1980s, and the one likely to have the farthest-reaching consequences, was the enormous change in both the extent and the character of immigration. The nation's immigration quotas expanded significantly in those years (partly to accommodate refugees from Southeast Asia and other nations), allowing more newcomers to enter the United States legally than at any point since the beginning of the nineteenth century. In the 1970s, more than 4 million legal immigrants entered the United States. In the 1980s, that number rose to more than 6 million. Throughout those decades, according to most estimates, almost as many immigrants entered the country illegally as came legally. When these estimates are included in the total, the wave of immigration in the twenty years after 1970 is the largest of the twentieth century.

Equally striking was the character of the new immigration. The Immigration Reform Act of 1965 (see p. 893) had eliminated quotas based on national origin; from then on, newcomers were generally admitted on a first-come, first-served basis. In 1965, 90 percent of the immigrants to the United States came from Europe. Twenty years later, only 10 percent of the new arrivals were Europeans. The extent and character of the new immigration promised to bring about a dramatic change in the composition of the American population as a whole. Already by the end of the 1980s, people of white European background constituted under 80 percent of the population (as opposed to 90 percent a half century before). It seemed likely that by the middle of the twenty-first century, whites would constitute less than 50 percent of the population.

Through most of the nation's history, Americans had been accustomed to thinking of themselves as essentially a society of two races: whites and blacks. Indians, Asians, Hispanics, and others had been either too few or too isolated from the rest of society to challenge that assumption. In the late twentieth century, however, it was no longer possible to think of America in that way. *Time* magazine ran a cover story in 1990 entitled "America's Changing Colors." It was an indication of how important a presence in American life new immigrant groups from all parts of the world were becoming.

Particularly important to the new immigration were two groups: Hispanics and Asians. Both had been significant segments of the American population for many decades: Hispanics since the very beginning of the nation's history, Asians since the waves of Chinese and Japanese immigration in the nineteenth century. But both groups experienced enormous, indeed unprecedented, growth after 1965.

People from Latin America constituted more than a third of the total number of legal immigrants to the United States in every year since 1965—and a much larger proportion of the total number of illegal immigrants. In California and the Southwest, in particular, they became a major presence. By the late 1980s, Hispanics formed over a third of the population of New Mexico, about a quarter of the population of Texas, and more than 10 percent of the populations of California, Arizona, and Colorado. There were also substantial Hispanic populations in Illinois, New York, and Florida (concentrated mainly in Chicago, New York City, and Miami). High birth rates among Hispanic communities already in the United States further increased their numbers. In the 1980 census, 6 percent of the population was listed as being of Hispanic origin. The 1990 census was not yet complete when this volume went to press, but it was certain to show another significant increase. By the end of the twentieth century, many experts predicted, Hispanics would pass African-Americans as the largest minority group in the United States.

The growing Hispanic presence became a political issue of increasing importance in the 1980s, both to "Anglos" and, of course, to Hispanics themselves. The Immigration Reform and Control (or Simpson-Mazzoli) Act of 1987 reflected the political power of both groups. Its principal goal was to respond to the demands of whites in the Southwest and California by stemming the flow of illegal immigrants (mostly from Mexico). To that end, it placed the burden on employers for the first time to confirm the legal status of their employees. Those who failed to do so faced economic and even criminal penalties. Hispanics charged that the bill would increase discrimination in hiring, and there was considerable evidence in the first years after its passage that such charges were well-founded. At the same time, the act responded to the growing political influence of Hispanics by offering amnesty to all undocumented workers who had entered the country before 1982. By the end of the decade, however, it seemed clear that the law was failing. Illegal immigration from Mexico and elsewhere was continuing at near record levels.

White residents of areas in which the Hispanic communities were growing rapidly often reacted with alarm, fearing that they would soon become a minority in what they considered their own cities. Such fears lay behind efforts to bar the use of the Spanish language in public schools and other measures to force Hispanic immigrants to assimilate more quickly and completely. And while the strenuous effort to combat Hispanic street gangs in Los Angeles and other cities was motivated mainly by the desire to fight crime, it was also an effort to halt the creation of an "alien" culture within America.

These white fears prompted angry and defiant responses from many Hispanics. "You hear all the ravings and complaints like, 'In the year 2000 Los Angeles is going to become a minority city! The Mexicans are going to take over!'" a Mexican-American film producer said in 1989. "I'd like to remind them that we're just going to reinstate the original composition of the city—like it was a hundred years ago, before they showed up."

By the 1980s, Asian immigrants were arriving in even greater numbers than Hispanics, constituting more than 40 percent of the total of legal newcomers. They came in particularly large numbers from Vietnam, Thailand, Cambodia, Laos, the Philippines, Korea, and India. By the end of the decade, there were nearly 7 million Asian-Americans in the United States. Like Hispanics, they were concentrated mainly in large cities and in the West. Aside from Hawaii (where the native population was Asian and where whites had always been a minority), Asians established their most significant presence in the Western states of California, Washington, Oregon, Nevada, Utah, Alaska, and Colorado. There were also significant Asian communities in Chicago, New York City, northern New Jersey, Washington, D.C., and northern Virginia.

Many of the new Asian immigrants were refugees, including many Vietnamese driven from their homes in the aftermath of the disastrous war in which the United States had so long been involved. Large numbers of "boat people"—Vietnamese refugees who put to sea in crowded boats without any clear destination—ultimately found their way to the United States, usually after enduring terrible dangers and hardships. Other Asian immigrants were highly educated professionals seeking greater opportunities in the United States.

As with most new immigrant groups, Asian-Americans found adjustment to the very different culture of the United States difficult and disorienting. "When I think how lonely I am in America," a Vietnamese immigrant wrote in the late 1980s, "I wonder why I am here, and what I have to live for." They also suffered substantial discrimination. Whites feared Asian competition in economic activities that they had been accustomed to controlling. There were, for example, heated disputes between white and Vietnamese shrimpers on the Gulf Coast in Texas, Mississippi, and Louisiana. African-Americans at times resented the success of Asian merchants in black neighborhoods (as the black filmmaker Spike Lee noted in *Do the Right Thing* in 1989). In New York, for example, Koreans established a large network of produce and grocery stores throughout the city in the 1980s, including many in black neighborhoods. Racial tensions led to a black boycott of some of these Korean markets in 1990.

Resentment of Asian-Americans may have been a result, in part, of their remarkable economic success. Indeed, some Asian groups (most notably Indians, Japanese, and Chinese) were by the 1980s earning larger average annual incomes than were whites. Chinese- and Japanese-Americans consistently ranked at or near the top of high school and college classes in the 1980s. Many universities were forced to defend themselves against charges that they limited their admissions of Asian students in order to prevent their numbers on campus from becoming disproportionately large; some institutions acknowledged that if they were to admit students on the basis of grades and test scores alone, they would have to admit more Asians than they did.

Asian-American communities were not all alike, but many shared certain cultural traits that seemed to contribute to their success. They contained significant numbers of people who had been involved in business and the professions before coming to America and had arrived with a high degree of expertise. They placed an unusually high value on education; Asian children, most evidence suggested, spent many more hours on schoolwork than did their non-Asian counterparts. Asian communities also had the benefit of an especially strong work ethic.

The Sunbelt

As striking as the change in the racial composition were the changes in the geographic distribution of the American population. The most widely discussed demographic phenomenon of the 1970s was the rise of what became known as the "Sunbelt" or "Southern Rim"—the Southeast, the Southwest, and above all, California, which became the nation's most populous state (surpassing New York) in 1964 and continued to grow in the years that followed. By 1980, the population of the Sunbelt had risen to exceed that of the industrial regions of the North and East, which were experiencing not only a relative, but in some cases an absolute, decline in their numbers.

In addition to shifting the nation's economic focus from one region to another, the rise of the Sunbelt was, for the moment at least, producing a change in the political climate. The South and the West had always been more conservative than many other regions of the country. The changes in both areas seemed, if anything, to strengthen that conservatism. In the 1970s and early 1980s, the boom mentality of this growing region conflicted sharply with the concerns of the Northeast, which—saddled with a declining economic base, highly congested, and home to large, impoverished minority groups—remained more committed to social programs and more interested in regulated growth than the more wide-open areas of the Sunbelt. By the mid-1980s, the collapse of energy prices (and hence of much of the oil industry) suddenly brought near-depression conditions to large areas of the Southwest, most notably Texas and Louisiana. But other regions of the Sunbelt (particularly California) continued to grow. Indeed California's growth was so precipitous that by 1990 Los Angeles and other southern California communities were considering radical restrictions on further growth to protect the region's imperiled environment.

Growth of the Sunbelt: Population and Urban Center Shifts

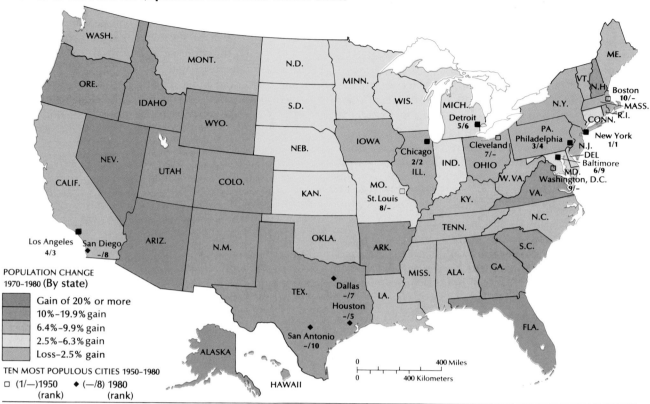

POPULATION CHANGE
1970-1980 (By state)

- Gain of 20% or more
- 10%–19.9% gain
- 6.4%–9.9% gain
- 2.5%–6.3% gain
- Loss–2.5% gain

TEN MOST POPULOUS CITIES 1950-1980
- □ (1/—)1950 ◆ (—/8) 1980
  (rank)   (rank)

Urban Growth and Urban Crises

Acutely affected by the changing distribution of population were the major industrial cities, particularly those in the Northeast and Midwest (which some now termed the "Frostbelt" or "Rustbelt"), which continued to confront the specter of social and financial decay. As more and more industries and corporate headquarters moved from the older urban centers to the suburbs or to the beckoning Sunbelt, many cities experienced a major contraction of their economic bases. Unemployment increased. Tax bases declined as municipalities lost the revenues from those enterprises that had departed. And the demand for social services increased as members of minorities found it ever more difficult to find even menial employment. Under the twin burdens of shrinking economic bases and expanding demands for social services, one city after another encountered fiscal crises. New York City barely averted bankruptcy in

1975, and then only after federal assistance and an unprecedented arrangement to finance municipal loans. By the late 1980s, it was in the midst of fiscal crisis again. Cleveland, Ohio, became, in late 1978, the first major metropolis in the nation to go into receivership since the Great Depression.

The crusading liberal urban leaders of the 1960s—people such as New York's Mayor John Lindsay, who served from 1966 to1974—seemed to have no place in the cities of the late 1970s and 1980s. Successful urban politicians were now far more likely to be people such as Edward I. Koch, who became mayor of New York in 1978 and who was overwhelmingly reelected (almost without opposition) in both 1981 and 1985. Koch openly subordinated concern for the poor to a commitment to fiscal stability and to the welfare of the middle class. Koch was ultimately defeated in 1989 (largely as a result of a series of scandals in his administration) by David Dinkins, who became the first black mayor in New

York history. But saddled with significant budget deficits and apparently intractable problems, Dinkins appeared unlikely to have much latitude to launch major new initiatives.

Despite the continuing, and indeed accelerating, problems of many cities, many observers were by the early 1980s pointing to signs of an urban renaissance. Affluent men and women were beginning to abandon the suburbs (which were developing urban problems of their own) and return to downtown areas, where they often bought up declining real estate, refurbished it, and created prosperous new communities—a process that became known as gentrification. The phenomenon had many obvious benefits for cities. It helped restore a viable tax base. It attracted new businesses. And it meant that the community's most affluent members would now have a direct stake in the well-being of the city. But gentrification was not a panacea to the woes of cities. The return of affluent, middle-class people to urban neighborhoods usually meant a displacement of poorer residents, who found it increasingly difficult and expensive to find decent housing. And the gentrification process increased the social stratification within many urban areas. The economic profile of some cities was one of a large group of the least affluent members of society, a growing group of the most affluent, and often little in between.

Despite the positive effects of gentrification on some neighborhoods, moreover, urban dwellers continued to struggle with a gradual decay of services and a rise in social disorder. Urban public schools suffered an increase in violence, drug addiction, and truancy; and the white middle class looked upon the school system as a virtually hopeless morass and showed little inclination to improve it. Public high-school graduates in some major cities were found to be virtually illiterate. City streets became zones of increasing danger.

The New Epidemics: Drug Abuse and AIDS

The rising crime rate in many major cities could be traced above all to the ravages of the drug epidemic that by the end of the 1980s was penetrating nearly every community in the nation. The enormous demand for drugs, and particularly for "crack" cocaine, spawned what was in effect a multi-billion-dollar industry; and those reaping the enormous profits of the illegal trade fought strenuously and often savagely to protect their positions. In Washington, D.C., for example, violence among warring drug dealers produced a wave of murders in the late 1980s that made the capital a national symbol of the crisis. When the city's long-time mayor, Marion Barry, was himself arrested in early 1990 for illegal drug use, the alarming dimensions of the epidemic seemed even clearer. (Barry was convicted in August 1990 of a cocaine-possession misdemeanor.) The Bush administration, and virtually all political figures, spoke heatedly about the need for a "war on drugs," but in the absence of significant funding for such programs, public efforts appeared to be having little effect. There were signs at the end of the 1980s that drug use was in decline among middle-class people, but the epidemic showed no signs of abating in the poor urban neighborhoods where it was doing the most severe damage.

The drug epidemic was directly related to another scourge of the cities in the 1980s: the epidemic spread of a new and lethal disease first documented in 1981, and soon named AIDS (acquired immune deficiency syndrome). AIDS is the product of a virus transmitted by the exchange of bodily fluids (blood or semen). The virus destroys the body's immune system and makes its victims highly vulnerable to a number of diseases (particularly to various forms of cancer and pneumonia) to which they would otherwise have a natural resistance. Although not everyone infected with the virus necessarily develops the disease, those who do are virtually certain to die from it. The first victims of AIDS (and in 1990 the group among whom cases remained the most numerous) were homosexual men. But by the late 1980s, as the gay community began to take preventive measures, the most rapid increase in the spread of the disease occurred among intravenous drug users, many of them heterosexuals, who spread the virus by sharing contaminated hypodermic needles. By the end of 1989, more than 90,000 cases of AIDS had been reported in the United States (and more than 300,000 worldwide). Because of the long incubation period of the disease, most experts predicted the number of victims would almost certainly rise. Although by 1990 researchers had discovered several drugs that could delay or limit the effects of AIDS, neither a cure nor a vaccine seemed in sight.

Comparison of Black and White Occupational Distribution, 1985

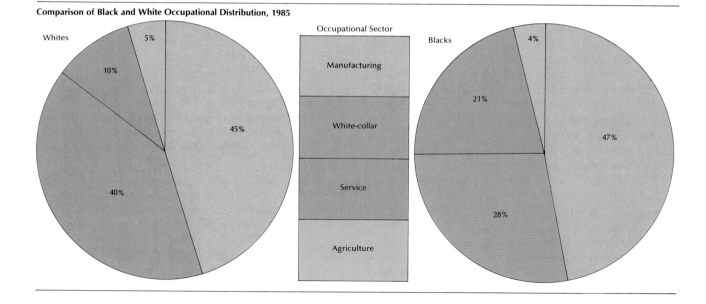

Whites: 45%, 5%, 10%, 40%

Occupational Sector: Manufacturing, White-collar, Service, Agriculture

Blacks: 4%, 21%, 47%, 28%

The Homeless

The increasing scarcity of housing for low-income people contributed to another of the most widely discussed phenomena of the 1980s: homelessness. There were no reliable figures to show how many men and women in the country were now living without housing, sleeping on streets or in municipal shelters, depending on handouts or public agencies for food and protection from the cold. There had always been some such men and women in most major cities; but their numbers were clearly increasing at an alarming rate. Homelessness was in part a product of new policies for care of the mentally ill—the trend toward deinstitutionalization, which apparently released into society many men and women unable to care for themselves. But even many of the mentally ill homeless had previously managed to support themselves. Now—in the face of rising housing costs, severe cutbacks in federal support for public housing, reduced welfare assistance, the declining availability of unskilled jobs, and the increasing weakness of family structures—many had somehow "fallen through the cracks" and found themselves on the streets. Entire families, even some in which one or more members had jobs, at times found themselves without homes. The phenomenon of tens of thousands of homeless people at large in the cities confronted municipal governments with a vexing problem. There were strong public pressures to pro-vide shelter and assistance for the indigent; but in an age of fiscal stringency and greatly reduced federal aid, city governments generally found it difficult to produce responses adequate to the dimensions of the crisis.

Nonwhites in the Postliberal Era

The civil-rights movement and the other liberal efforts of the 1960s had two very different effects on nonwhites in America. On the one hand, there were increased opportunities for advancement available to those who were in a position to take advantage of them. On the other hand, as the industrial economy declined and government services dwindled, there was a growing sense of helplessness and despair among the larger groups of nonwhites who continued to find themselves barred from upward mobility.

For the black middle class, which by the late 1970s constituted nearly a third of the entire black population of America, the progress was at times astonishing. Economic disparities between black and white professionals did not vanish, but they diminished substantially. Black families moved into more affluent urban communities and, in many cases, into suburbs—at times as neighbors of whites, more often into predominantly black suburban communities. The number of blacks attending college rose by 350 percent in the decade following the passage of the civil-rights acts (as opposed to the 150 percent increase among whites); by the 1980s the percentage of black high-school graduates going on to college was virtually the same as that of white high-school graduates (although a far smaller proportion of blacks than whites managed to complete high school). Middle-class blacks, in other words, had realized great gains from the legislation of the 1960s, from the changing national mood on race, and from the creation of controversial affirmative action programs.

But the rise of a black middle class served also to accentuate the increasingly desperate plight of other black Americans, whom many of the liberal programs of the 1960s had never reached. This growing "underclass," made up not only of blacks but increasingly of people from the various Hispanic backgrounds, felt the impact of the economic troubles of the 1970s and 1980s with special force. By the late 1980s, more than one-third of all black families lived in poverty. More than one-fourth of all the Hispanic families counted by the government likewise lived in poverty (as well as many more who undoubtedly remained uncounted). At the same time, just under 11 percent of white families could be officially classified as poor.

The black family structure suffered as well from the dislocations of urban poverty. There was a radical increase in the number of single-parent, female-headed black households in the 1970s and 1980s. At the end of the 1980s, over half of all black children were born into single-parent families, as opposed to only 15 percent of white children. In 1960, only 20 percent of black children had lived in single-parent homes.

Nonwhites were victimized by many things in the changing social and economic climate of the 1980s. Among them was a growing impatience with affirmative action and other programs designed to advance their fortunes, as symbolized by the *Bakke* case in 1978 (see above, p. 944) and by a growing reluctance among federal officials after 1980 to move aggressively to enforce affirmative action guidelines. Nonwhites suffered as well from a steady decline in the number of unskilled jobs in the economy. They suffered from the deterioration of public education and of other social services, which made it more difficult for them to find opportunities for advancement. And they suffered, in some cases, from a sense of futility and despair, born of years of entrapment in brutal urban ghettoes. By the early 1990s, whole generations of nonwhites had grown to maturity living in destitute neighborhoods where welfare, drug dealing, and other crimes were virtually the only means of support for many people.

The New Religion and the New Right

In the 1960s, many social critics had predicted the virtual extinction of religious influence in American life. *Time* magazine had reflected such assumptions in 1966 with a celebrated cover emblazoned with the question "Is God Dead?" Nevertheless, America in the 1970s entered the throes of a major religious revival, perhaps the most powerful since the second Great Awakening of the early nineteenth century, which made it clear that religion remained an enormously powerful force in American life as it headed into the twenty-first century.

Some of the new religious enthusiasm found expression in the rise of various cults and pseudofaiths: the Church of Scientology; the Unification Church of the Reverend Sun Myung Moon; even the tragic People's Temple, whose members committed mass suicide in their jungle retreat in Guyana in 1978. But the most important impulse of the revival of religion was the rise of evangelical Christianity. It was not a sudden phenomenon. It had, in fact, been in progress since the 1870s; and in its modern form, it had been visible since the early 1950s, when fundamentalists such as Billy Graham and pentecostals such as Oral Roberts had begun to attract huge national (and international) followings for their energetic revivalism.

For many years, the new religion had gone unnoted by much of the media, which had dismissed it as a limited, provincial phenomenon. By the early 1980s, they could no longer do so. More than 70 million Americans now described themselves as "born-again" Christians—men and women who had established a "direct personal relationship with Jesus." Christian evangelicals owned their own newspapers, magazines, radio stations, and television networks. They operated their own schools and universities. They occupied positions of eminence in the worlds of entertainment and professional sports. And one of their number ultimately occupied the White House itself—Jimmy Carter, who during the 1976 campaign had talked proudly of his own "conversion experience" and who continued openly to proclaim his "born-again" Christian faith during his years in office.

For Jimmy Carter, evangelical Christianity had served as a prod to social commitment and public service; it had formed the basis for his commitment to racial and economic justice and to world peace. To others, the message of the new religion was very different—but no less political. Some Christian revivalism had by the 1980s become closely tied to deep political and social conservatism. Such organizations as the Reverend Jerry Falwell's Moral Majority expressed the political sentiments of many fundamentalist evangelicals. They opposed federal interference in local affairs, denounced abortion, defended unrestricted free enterprise, and supported a strong American posture in the world. Some even reopened issues that had long seemed closed. For example, many fundamentalist Christians questioned the scientific doctrine of evolution and urged the teaching in schools of the biblical story of the Creation instead. Others drew criticism from defenders of civil liberties by demanding stricter censorship of television, movies, and printed materials.

Closely tied to the new religion was a new political right, many of whose members were themselves evangelical Christians. The New Right drew heavily on the conservative dogmas of earlier eras, but in addition to doctrinal enthusiasm, it displayed a remarkable organizing zeal. While earlier right-wing political groups, such as the John Birch Society, had stumbled along in administrative chaos, the new organizations marshaled their influence with awesome skill and effectiveness. Mass-mailing campaigns of staggering size, such as those orchestrated by Richard Viguerie, raised great sums of money to support conservative efforts. The National Conservative Political Action Committee, for example, spent millions of dollars in support of its chosen political candidates in 1980 and claimed credit for the defeat of many liberal senators and representatives.

The power of the New Right in the early 1980s represented the culmination of many decades of steadily growing conservative sentiment. Such sentiment had surfaced occasionally in the 1950s in the form of militantly anticommunist political organizations; it had shown itself in 1964, when it helped to engineer the Republican nomination of Barry Goldwater for president. And it had triumphed, finally, in 1980, when it became a central force in propelling Ronald Reagan into the White House. But the phenomenon was, despite its conspicuous strength, difficult to define with any precision. The most active groups within the New Right were not conservatives of traditional stripe—people associated with and supportive of the business community, defending the position of established economic and social elites. They were, rather, middle-class and lower-middle-

class people, whose political demands centered more around social and cultural issues than economic ones, who seemed to exhibit not so much a staid conservatism as a right-wing populism.

By the beginning of the 1990s, the power of the New Right seemed to be in decline in some areas. A series of scandals discredited several leading evangelical ministers—most notably Jim Bakker, who was convicted of fraud in 1989 and sentenced to prison, and Jimmy Swaggart, whose powerful ministry was shaken by revelations of his sexual improprieties. Late in 1989, Jerry Falwell announced the dissolution of the Moral Majority. Other factions of the New Right also began to experience hard times after the election of the determined centrist George Bush. The right remained a significant force within the Republican party and a constant factor in the calculation of all those (among them President Bush) who hoped to secure a base within it. But "movement conservatives" no longer had the same access to the government that they had enjoyed under Reagan.

The New Right continued, however, to display impressive strength in managing to keep alive a spirited debate over what they called "family" issues. In reality, the new conservative groups were launching an intense assault on feminism. Leaders of the New Right campaigned fervently (and successfully) against the proposed Equal Rights Amendment to the Constitution. They claimed that it would force radical changes in the relationships between men and women and would threaten the structure of the family. When the amendment died in 1982, New Right leader Phyllis Schlafly—an outspoken critic of feminism—claimed much of the credit.

The most divisive issue of the late 1980s and early 1990s, and the one on which the two sides seemed the most evenly matched, was the controversy over abortion rights. (See above, pp. 932–933.) For those who favored allowing women to choose to terminate unwanted pregnancies, the Supreme Court's decision in *Roe* v. *Wade* (1973) had seemed to settle the question. But the opposition gradually gained strength and by the mid-1980s had become a powerful grass-roots movement. The right-to-life movement, as it called itself, found its most fervent supporters among Catholics; and indeed, the Catholic Church itself lent its institutional authority to the battle against legalized abortion. By the early 1990s, some Church leaders (among them Cardinal John O'Connor of New York) were threatening elected officials with excommunication for supporting abortion rights. Religious doctrine also motivated the

Abortion Rights: The Continuing Battle

Demonstrators representing both the "pro-life" and "pro-choice" movements demonstrate on the steps of the Supreme Court in 1989 as the justices inside consider a challenge to the 1973 *Roe* v. *Wade* decision. Their decision in the case (*Webster* v. *Reproductive Health Services*) stopped short of overturning *Roe,* but gave states considerable new latitude in restricting access to abortions. One result was that the battle over abortion rights began moving increasingly out of the courts and into state legislatures. (UPI/Bettmann Newsphotos)

anti-abortion stance of Mormons, fundamentalist Christians, and other groups. The opposition of other anti-abortion activists had less to do with religion than with their commitment to traditional notions of family and sexual relations. To them, abortion was a particularly offensive part of a much larger assault by feminists on the role of women as wives and mothers. It was also, most foes contended, a form of murder. Fetuses, they claimed, were human beings who had a "right to life" from the moment of conception.

Although the right-to-life movement was persistent in its demand for a reversal of *Roe* v. *Wade* or, barring that, a constitutional amendment banning abortion, it also attacked abortion in more limited ways, at its most vulnerable points. In 1976, Representative Henry Hyde of Illinois forced passage of an amendment barring the use of Medicaid funds to pay for abortions for poor women, even if doctors asserted that such an abortion was medically necessary. The Supreme Court upheld the law four years later. The Reagan administration imposed further restrictions on federal funding. In one state after another, the movement forced passage of legislation barring the use of public funds for abortions.

The changing composition of the Supreme Court in the 1980s (which saw three new conservative justices named by President Reagan) renewed the right-to-life movement's hopes for a reversal of *Roe* v. *Wade.* In *Webster* v. *Reproductive Health Services* (1989), the Court upheld a Missouri law that forbade any institution receiving state funds from performing abortions, whether or not those funds were used to finance the abortions. The Court stopped short of

overturning its 1973 decision, although it left open the possibility it might do so later.

Through much of the 1970s and 1980s, supporters of abortion rights had remained confident that *Row* v. *Wade* protected their right to choose abortion and that the anti-abortion movement was unlikely to prevail. But the changing judicial climate of the late 1980s mobilized defenders of abortion as never before. They called themselves the "pro-choice" movement, because they were defending not so much abortion itself as every woman's right to choose whether and when to bear a child. Just as abortion opponents had been doing for years, defenders of abortion rights urged their supporters to vote for or against political candidates on the basis of their position on that issue alone. It quickly became clear that the pro-choice movement was in many parts of the country at least as strong as, and in some areas much stronger than, the right-to-life movement. Public opinion polls were ambiguous, but most suggested that a majority of Americans favored the right of women to choose abortion in at least some circumstances. Battles over this deeply emotional issue seemed certain to continue for many years.

The controversy in 1989 and 1990 over federal support for the arts again revealed the New Right's ability to inject its moral concerns into public debate. Several provocative art exhibits—one a collection of photographs by Robert Mapplethorpe, some of which contained graphic depictions of homosexual behavior; another an exhibit by André Serrano, which contained (among many other things) a piece consisting of a crucifix immersed in a jar of the artist's urine—offended conservatives (as well as others). It sparked calls for closing the exhibits or limiting access to them. The Corcoran Gallery in Washington, D.C., cancelled the Mapplethorpe exhibit. Later, a smaller gallery in Cincinnati displayed the Mapplethorpe photographs, defying a city ordinance that had banned them as obscene.

The controversy over the content of the Mapplethorpe and Serrano exhibits soon extended to a dispute over their funding. Both the artists and the museums displaying their work had received grants from the National Endowment for the Arts, although not for the controversial works in question. Senator Jesse Helms of North Carolina, one of the most prominent figures of the New Right, led a concerted attack on the NEA. At first he demanded strict new "moral" guidelines for all grants to the arts. When members of the arts community responded defiantly, insisting that any such guidelines would amount to censorship, Helms changed his course. He and other members of Congress began arguing that the NEA should be abolished altogether because funding the arts was not an appropriate activity for the federal government.

At the same time, conservatives were mobilizing behind another, purely symbolic issue: the American flag. In two decisions, one in 1989 and one in 1990, the Supreme Court struck down laws forbidding the burning of the American flag. The justices ruled that flag burning was a legitimate form of political protest and was protected by the First Amendment to the Constitution. President Bush and other Republicans quickly called for a constitutional amendment allowing Congress and the states to legislate against "desecration" of the flag. Congress soundly defeated this first-ever attempt to amend the Bill of Rights.

Despite the energy of these conservative crusades of the late 1980s and early 1990s, the power of the New Right generally appeared by then to be in decline.

The Changing Left

The New Left of the 1960s and early 1970s did not disappear after the end of the war in Vietnam, but it faded rapidly. Many of the students who had fought in its battles grew up, left school, and entered conventional careers. Some radical leaders, disillusioned by the unresponsiveness of American society to their demands, resignedly gave up the struggle and chose instead to work "within the system." Marxist cri-

tiques continued to flourish in academic circles, but to much of the public they came to appear dated and irrelevant. Yet a left of sorts did survive in the late 1970s and even through the 1980s, giving evidence in the process of how greatly the nation's political climate had changed. Where 1960s activists had rallied to protest racism, poverty, and war, their 1970s and 1980s counterparts more often fought to save the wilderness, protect endangered species, limit reckless economic development, and stop the proliferation of nuclear weapons and power plants.

The spread of atomic power plants in the 1950s and 1960s had aroused little controversy at the time; but by the late 1970s, a well-organized and often militant antinuclear movement had emerged in almost every region of the country to oppose new plant construction and to warn of the dangers of existing facilities. A frightening accident in 1979 at a nuclear power plant at Three Mile Island in Pennsylvania seemed to expose serious deficiencies in the safety mechanisms that both government and private industry had assured the public were in place, and the result was an intensification of antinuclear activity.

A related movement seemed to surface almost overnight in 1981 and 1982: a movement to stop the spread of nuclear weapons and to promote world disarmament. Opposition to atomic weapons had never entirely vanished in America. But for most of the first thirty-five years after the detonation of atomic bombs in New Mexico and Japan in 1945, such protests had remained muted and isolated. Then, beginning in the late 1970s, a powerful antinuclear movement emerged in Europe, gaining in numbers and intensity so rapidly that by 1980 it had become a formidable political force. And in 1981, partly in response to the European movement, partly in response to the deteriorating international climate, and partly, it seemed, in response to bellicose statements by officials of the federal government, the antinuclear movement gained forced in the United States as well.

It took many forms. Some advocated a return to the disarmament negotiations that had produced the SALT II treaty, which the Senate had never ratified. Others called for an American commitment to "no first use" of atomic weapons. Still others agitated for a "nuclear freeze," for halting production of any new weapons or weapons systems (a position that the Reagan administration opposed because it would, they claimed, leave the United States in a position of military inferiority toward the Soviet Union). By 1982, the nuclear-freeze movement in particular had at-

Earth Day, 1990
Demonstrators gather in front of the United States Capitol in one of thousands of rallies held across the country to mark Earth Day, April 22, 1990. The containers shown here reflect one of the most conspicuous achievements of the environmental movement, the steady increase in recycling as a method of reducing waste. (Atlan/Sygma)

tracted wide support. State and local governments in widely scattered areas of the country (including parts of the supposedly conservative South) were going on record in support of the idea. Influential members of Congress (among them Senator Edward M. Kennedy) were publicly endorsing the idea. Referendum questions on the issue were being placed on ballots in several states. Within three years, however, the new movement had faded—a victim in part of the relaxation of world tensions in the Gorbachev era and the resumption of serious arms control negotiations between the superpowers. The 1984 presidential campaign saw the nuclear question relegated largely to the sidelines; in 1988, it played no role at all.

The New Environmentalism

By the late 1980s, the most compelling issue to most activists on the left (and to others as well) was the effort to protect the environment. Public concerns about the environment had arisen intermittently since the beginning of the industrial era and had been growing in intensity ever since 1962, when the publication of Rachel Carson's *Silent Spring* had aroused widespread public concern about the effect of insecticides on the natural world. (See "The American Environment," pp. 991–994.) A major oil spill off the coast of Santa Barbara, California, early in 1969—which befouled the city's beaches and destroyed wildlife for miles along the coast—triggered even greater public alarm. So did the discovery of large deposits of toxic wastes, improperly disposed of at sites all over the country. Some toxic waste dumps were alongside residential neighborhoods, schoolyards, and playgrounds and posed immediate dangers to residents. These and other revelations of the extent to which human progress threatened the natural world helped produce a major popular movement.

In the spring of 1970, a nationwide "Earth Day" had signaled the beginning of the environmental movement. It differed markedly from the "conservation" movements of earlier years (see pp. 644–646). Modern environmentalists shared the concerns of such earlier figures as John Muir and Gifford Pinchot about preserving some areas of the wilderness and carefully managing the exploitation of resources. But the new activists went much further, basing their positions on the developing field of ecology, the study of the connections among all components of an environment. Toxic wastes, air and water pollution, the destruction of forests, the extinction of species: these were not separate, isolated problems. They were signs of the growing threat that human society was posing to the natural world. All elements of the earth's environment were intimately and delicately linked together, ecologists claimed. Damaging any one of those elements risked damaging all the others. Only by adopting a new social ethic, in which economic growth became less important than ecological health, could the human race hope to survive in a healthy world.

Throughout the 1970s and 1980s, environmental issues gained increasing attention and support. Although the federal government displayed limited interest in the subject, environmentalists won a series of significant battles, mostly at the local level. They blocked the construction of roads, airports, and other

Doonesbury

Cartoonist Garry Trudeau created his celebrated comic strip in the 1960s while he was an undergraduate at Yale University. Since then, he has used the strip to offer political commentary and to chronicle the changing values and life styles of his own generation and those that have followed it. In this 1984 cartoon, Trudeau uses his title character, Mike Doonesbury, to illustrate the transformation of 1960s idealists into 1980s "yuppies." (© 1984 G. B. Trudeau. Universal Press Syndicate)

projects (including American development of the supersonic transport airplane, or SST) that they claimed would be ecologically dangerous. By the end of the decade, the sense of urgency had grown, as scientists began warning that the release of certain industrial pollutants (most notably chlorofluorocarbons) into the atmosphere was depleting the ozone layer of the earth's atmosphere, which protects the globe from the sun's most dangerous rays. They warned, too, of the related danger of global warming, a rise in the earth's temperature as a result of emissions from the burning of fossil fuels (coal and oil). On April 22, 1990, twenty years after the first Earth Day, millions of Americans gathered across the nation to demonstrate their allegiance to what was becoming one of the largest and most broadly supported movements in the nation's history.

The Challenge to "Progress"

The concern for the environment, the opposition to nuclear power, the fear of nuclear war—all were reflections of a more fundamental assumption of the post–Vietnam left. In a sharp break from the nation's long commitment to growth and progress, some dissidents argued that only by limiting growth and curbing traditional forms of progress could society hope to survive. Industrial society had, they claimed, created a desperate threat to the planet's ecological balance. Continued growth would place intolerable strains on the world's finite resources. Some of these critics of the "idea of progress" expressed a gloomy resignation, urging a lowering of social expectations and foreseeing an inevitable deterioration in the quality of life. Other advocates of restraint believed that change did not require decline: human beings could live more comfortably and more happily if they simply learned to respect the limits imposed on them by their environment. But in either case, such arguments evoked strong opposition from conservatives and others, who ridiculed the no-growth ideology as an expression of defeatism and despair. Ronald Reagan, in particular, made an attack on the "limits" idea central to his political success.

For many Americans, however, the answer to the dilemmas of living in uncertain times lay not in religion or politics but in the cultivation of the self.

No aspect of the era aroused more comment than this tendency of individuals to "turn inward," that is, to replace social concerns with personal ones. Among affluent Americans, at least, there emerged a pervasive concern with personal "life styles." Newspapers introduced special sections devoted to such newly popular pursuits as gourmet cooking, physical fitness, and home decorating. Magazines specialized in helping Americans achieve personal fulfillment through a satisfying life style. In the booming 1980s, which greatly increased the affluence of the upper middle class, such concerns became a central theme of popular culture. The "yuppie"—the young, urban professionals with large disposable incomes, intent on ever greater material comforts—became a common image of the Reagan years (often as a contrast to the ever more desperate poverty that was becoming visible in the same urban communities the "yuppies" were "gentrifying").

The American Future

The American people had suffered many trials and disappointments since the heady days at the end of World War II when an "American Century" seemed about to dawn, when the United States appeared poised for a prolonged era of domestic tranquility and international preeminence. By the early 1990s, America, like much of the rest of the world, was faced with the problems of a faltering economy, an increasingly diverse population, a domestic social fabric showing signs of strain, and growing dangers to the environment that threatened the health of the entire world. Many feared the United States was on the road toward a major, perhaps irreversible decline; that the future promised only an increase in the nation's seeming economic frailty and its apparent international impotence. Books chronicling or predicting the "fall" of the United States as a great power became best sellers.

At the same time, however, the great changes in world affairs of the late 1980s seemed to vindicate some of America's most important assumptions: that democratic political and economic systems are better suited to the modern world than totalitarian ones; that even decades of repressive government cannot extinguish the yearning for liberty that Americans have always insisted every human being shares. The dramatically different world order that was emerging from the upheavals of the late twentieth century was not without dangers. But many of the traditional tensions that had plagued international relations for the previous forty years were rapidly abating. The forces of democracy seemed newly vigorous throughout the world as communist regimes everywhere wavered and toppled. And the United States, despite its many problems, remained what it had long been: one of the stablest, wealthiest, and most resilient societies in modern history. At the dawn of a new era, the United States—whose example had done much to fuel the forces of change—faced the challenge of preserving and extending its own democracy in the face of major new perils and great new opportunities.

SIGNIFICANT EVENTS

1974 OPEC raises oil prices (p. 956)

"Stagflation" (recession and inflation together) begins (p. 956)

Ford pardons Nixon (p. 956)

Ford meets Brezhnev at Vladivostok summit (p. 956)

1976 Jimmy Carter elected president (p. 957)

Mao Zedong dies (p. 957)

1977 Panama Canal treaties signed (p. 959)

1978 Camp David accords signed (p. 959)

Panama Canal treaties ratified (p. 959)

1979 Energy crisis jolts United States (p. 958)

U.S. and China restore diplomatic relations (p. 959)

Iranian revolution overthrows Shah (p. 960)

American diplomats taken hostage in Iran (p. 961)

Soviet Union invades Afghanistan (p. 961)

Sandinista revolution triumphs in Nicaragua (p. 967)

Nuclear accident at Three Mile Island (p. 984)

SALT II treaty signed (p. 959)

1980 U.S. boycotts Moscow Olympics (p. 961)

Attempt to rescue American hostages in Iran fails; Secretary of State Cyrus Vance resigns in protest (p. 961)

Edward Kennedy challenges Carter in Democratic primaries (p. 961)

Ronald Reagan elected president (p. 962)

1981 American hostages in Iran released (p. 962)

Reagan wins major tax and budget cuts (p. 964)

U.S. military build-up begins (p. 965)

Soviet Union forces imposition of martial law in Poland (p. 966)

Existence of AIDS reported in United States (p. 980)

United States begins supporting *contra* rebellion in Nicaragua (p. 967)

1982 Severe recession (p. 964)

Inflation and interest rates decline (p. 964)

Israel invades Lebanon (p. 967)

1983 U.S. Marines killed in terrorist attack in Beirut (p. 967)

United States invades Grenada (p. 967)

Nuclear freeze movement expands in United States (p. 984)

Unemployment reaches 10.2 percent (p. 964)

Economic recovery begins (p. 964)

1984 Jesse Jackson campaigns for Democratic presidential nomination (p. 967)

Democrats nominate Geraldine Ferraro for vice president (p. 967)

Reagan defeats Walter Mondale in presidential election (p. 968)

1985 Mikhail Gorbachev chosen as leader of the Soviet Union (p. 972)

Reagan and Gorbachev meet in Geneva (p. 972)

Congress passes Gramm-Rudman bill to limit deficits (p. 966)

Homeless crisis worsens (p. 980)

Crack cocaine appears in American cities (p. 979)

1986 U.S. planes bomb targets in Libya (p. 967)

Reagan and Gorbachev meet in Reykjavik, Iceland (p. 972)

Insider trading scandals on Wall Street (p. 969)

Democrats regain control of U.S. Senate (p. 969)

Iran-contra scandal revealed (p. 968)

Glasnost and *perestroika* expand in Soviet Union (p. 972)

1987 Gorbachev visits Reagan in Washington (p. 972)

Congress investigates Iran-contra scandal (p. 969)

Stock market falls by record 508 points (p. 969)

Televangelist scandals begin (p. 982)

Congress passes Immigration Reform and Control Act (p. 976)

1988 INF Treaty signed (p. 972)

Gorbachev announces Soviet troop reductions in Europe (p. 974)

George Bush elected president (p. 970)

SIGNIFICANT EVENTS

1989 Democracy movement in China crushed by government (p. 973)

Communist regimes fall in Eastern Europe (p. 972)

Congress passes savings and loan bailout plan (p. 968)

Scandals in Department of Housing and Urban Development revealed (p. 968)

Berlin Wall dismantled (p. 972)

Gorbachev proposes far-reaching reforms in Soviet Union (p. 972)

United States invades Panama (p. 971)

1990 Soviet Union strips Communist party of guaranteed monopoly (p. 972)

Nationalist movements erupt within Soviet Union (p. 972)

East and West Germany move toward reunification (p. 972)

Drexel Burnham Lambert investment house declares bankruptcy (p. 969)

Nelson Mandela released from prison in South Africa (p. 973)

SUGGESTED READINGS

The Ford Presidency. Gerald Ter Horst, *Gerald Ford* (1975); Robert T. Hartmann, *Palace Politics* (1980); Richard Reeves, *A Ford Not a Lincoln* (1976); Gerald Ford, *A Time to Heal* (1979); James L. Sundquist, *The Decline and Resurgence of Congress* (1981); A. James Reichley, *Conservatives in an Age of Change: The Nixon and Ford Administrations* (1981).

The Carter Presidency. Jimmy Carter, *Why Not the Best?* (1975) and *Keeping Faith* (1982); Rosalynn Carter, *First Lady from Plains* (1984); Erwin Hargrove, *Jimmy Carter as President* (1989); Jules Witcover, *Marathon* (1977); James Wooten, *Dasher* (1978); Clark Mollenhoff, *The President Who Failed* (1980); Jack Bass and Walter Devries, *The Transformation of Southern Politics* (1976); Hamilton Jordan, *Crisis* (1982); Haynes Johnson, *In the Absence of Power* (1980); Charles O. Jones, *The Trusteeship Presidency* (1988); Zbigniew Brzezinski, *Power and Principle* (1983); Cyrus Vance, *Hard Choices* (1983); Gaddis Smith, *Morality, Reason, and Power* (1986); James Bill, *The Eagle and the Lion* (1988); Walter LaFeber, *Panama Canal* (1978); A. Glenn Mower, Jr., *Human Rights and American Foreign Policy* (1987); William B. Quandt, *Camp David* (1986).

The New Right. Peter Steinfels, *The Neo-Conservatives* (1979); Sidney Blumenthal, *The Rise of the Counter-Establishment*(1986); Burton Yale Pines, *Back to Basics* (1982); David W. Reinhard, *The Republican Right Since 1945* (1983); John K. White, *The New Politics of Old Values* (1988).

The Reagan Presidency. Theodore H. White, *American in Search of Itself* (1982); William Boyarsky, *The Rise of Ronald Reagan* (1968); Anne Edwards, *Early Reagan* (1987); Garry Wills, *Reagan's America* (1987); Hedrick Smith et al., *Reagan: The Man, the President* (1980); Hedrick Smith, *The Power Game* (1988); Lou Cannon, *Reagan* (1982); Robert Dallek, *Ronald Reagan: The Politics of Symbolism* (1984); Ronnie Dugger, *On Reagan* (1983); Richard Reeves, *The Reagan Detour* (1985); Laurence I. Barrett, *Gambling with History* (1984); Rowland Evans and Robert Novak, *The Reagan Revolution* (1981); Fred I. Greenstein, ed., *The Reagan Presidency* (1983); John L. Palmer and Isabel V. Sawhill, eds., *The Reagan Experiment* (1982); Joan Claybrook, *Retreat from Safety* (1984); Jonathan Lash, *A Season of Spoils* (1984); Jane Mayer and Doyle McManus, *Landslide: The Unmaking of the President, 1984–1988* (1988); George Gilder, *Wealth and Poverty* (1981); Frank Ackerman, *Reaganomics* (1982); Thomas Byrne Edsall, *The New Politics of Inequality* (1984); Sidney Weintraub and Marvin Goodstein, eds., *Reaganomics in the Stagflation Economy* (1983); Michael J. Piore and Charles F. Sabel, *The Second Industrial Divide* (1984); David Stockman, *The Triumph of Politics* (1986); William Greider, *The Education of David Stockman and Other Americans* (1982); Donald T. Regan, *For the Record* (1988); Nancy Reagan, *My Turn* (1989).

Reagan and the World. Alexander Haig, *Caveat: Realism, Reagan and Foreign Policy* (1984); Strobe Talbott, *Deadly Gambits* (1984) and *The Master of the Game: Paul Nitze and the Nuclear Peace* (1988); Walter LaFeber, *Inevitable Revolutions,* rev. ed. (1984); Raymond Bonner, *Weakness and Deceit: U.S. Policy and El Salvador* (1984); Tom Buckley, *Violent Neighbors* (1984); Robert O. Pastor, *Condemned to Repetition: The United States and Nicaragua* (1987); Bob Woodward, *Veil: The Secret Wars of the CIA* (1987); Seweryn Bialer and Michael Mandelbaum, eds., *Gorbachev's Russia and American Foreign Policy* (1988); John Newhouse, *War and Peace in the Nuclear Age* (1989).

Politics After Reagan. Thomas Ferguson and Joel Rogers, *Right Turn* (1986); Adolph L. Reed, Jr., *The Jesse Jackson Phenomenon* (1986).

Post-Liberal Culture. Peter N. Carroll, *It Seemed Like Nothing Happened* (1982); Peter Clecak, *America's Quest for the Ideal Self* (1983); Jim Hougan, *Decadence: Radical Nos-*

talgia, *Narcissism, and Decline in the Seventies* (1975); Christopher Lasch, *The Culture of Narcissism* (1978); Edwin Schur, *The Awareness Trap* (1976).

Society and Culture. Kirkpatrick Sale, *Power Shift* (1975); John Woodridge, *The Evangelicals* (1975); Marshall Frady, *Billy Graham* (1979); Jonathan Schell, *The Fate of the Earth* (1982); Randy Shilts, *And the Band Played On: Politics, People, and the AIDS Epidemic* (1987); John Langone, *AIDS: the Facts* (1988); Frank Levy, *Dollars and Dreams: The Changing American Income Distribution* (1987); Studs Terkel, *The Great Divide* (1988).

Gender and Family. Andrea Dworkin, *Right-Wing Women* (1983); Barbara Enrenreich, *The Hearts of Men: American Dreams and the Flight from Commitment* (1983); Susan M. Bianchi, *American Women in Transition* (1987); Mary Francis Berry, *Why ERA Failed* (1986); Jane Mansbridge, *Why We Lost the ERA* (1986); Kristin Luker, *Abortion and the Politics of Motherhood* (1984); Rosalind Pechesky, *Abortion and Woman's Choice* (1984); Winifred D. Wandersee,

On the Move: American Women in the 1970s (1988); Jonathan Kozol, *Rachel and Her Children: Homeless Families in America* (1988); Ruth Sidel, *Women and Children Last* (1986); Harrell R. Rodgers, Jr., *Poor Women, Poor Families* (1986); Hilda Scott, *Working Your Way to the Bottom: The Feminization of Poverty* (1985).

Nonwhites in the 1970s and 1980s. Derrick Bell, *And We Are Not Saved: The Elusive Quest for Racial Justice* (1987); Douglas Glasgow, *The Black Underclass* (1980); Leslie W. Dunbar, ed., *Minority Report* (1984); Marian Wright Edelman, *Families in Peril* (1987); William Julius Wilson, *The Truly Disadvantaged* (1987); Frank D. Bean and Marta Tienda, *The Hispanic Population of the United States* (1987); James D. Cockcroft, *Outlaws in the Promised Land: Mexican Immigrant Workers and America's Future* (1986); David M. Reimers, *Still the Golden Door* (1985); John Crewden, *The Tarnished Door* (1983); Stan Steiner, *The New Indians* (1968); Vine Deloria, Jr., *American Indian Policy in the Twentieth Century* (1985).

Silent Spring

O ne summer day in 1957, a small plane flew over the nature sanctuary behind Olga Huckins's house in Duxbury, Massachusetts. It sprayed the land below with an oily mist and then vanished. The next day, Huckins found seven dead songbirds, their beaks gaping in apparent agony. She was so furious that she wrote an angry letter to a local paper, and, as an after-thought, sent a copy to her friend Rachel Carson. It was one of those small events that can alter the course of history.

Carson was a biologist and a gifted writer. Educated at Johns Hopkins University at a time when few women became scientists, she had gone to work for the government as an aquatic biologist. Although extremely shy, her skills as a writer quickly led her colleagues to rely on her to communicate their work to a wider public. She eventually became chief editor for the U.S. Fish and Wildlife Service in 1949. In the meantime, she began to write popular essays about her special love, the ocean. A first book proved only marginally successful, but in 1951 she published *The Sea Around Us*. It instantly became an international best seller, bringing Carson a fame she never imagined and enough income to retire. By 1957, she was one of the most popular nature writers of her generation. Huckins's letter would turn her life onto an entirely new path.

The mist that the plane had sprayed behind Huckins's house was a mixture of ordinary fuel oil and a chemical called dicholoro-diphenyl-trichloroethane: DDT. In 1939, a Swiss chemist named Paul Muller had discovered that although DDT seemed harmless to human beings and other mammals, it was extremely toxic to insects. American scientists learned of Muller's discovery in 1942, just as the army was grappling with the special problems of tropical warfare. Unless something could be done to exterminate the mosquitoes that carried malaria and the lice that carried typhus, thousands of soldiers seemed likely to die from disease.

Under these circumstances, DDT seemed a godsend. First used on a large scale during a typhus outbreak in Italy during 1943–1944, it quickly helped end the epidemic. It was soon being sprayed in mosquito-infested areas of Pacific islands where American troops were fighting the Japanese. No soldiers suffered any appar

Pesticide Spraying
When pesticides first became available to farmers, they proved so effective against agricultural pests that they were soon being sprayed on most crops. Although scientists and consumers have raised many questions about the safety of such chemicals, they continue to play an important role in the farm economy. Most foods grown in the United States are still treated with pesticides to some degree. (The Bettmann Archive)

ent ill effects from the sprayings, but the incidence of malaria dropped precipitously. DDT quickly gained a reputation as a miraculous tool for controlling insects, and it undoubtedly saved thousands of lives. For its discovery, Paul Muller was awarded the Nobel Prize in medicine in 1948.

With so many benefits and no obvious drawbacks, the new chemical was first released for public use in 1945. Scientists in the Food and Drug Administration noted only one disturbing fact about DDT: it tended to accumulate in the fatty tissues of large animals, including humans, and was passed on in the milk of cows and humans alike. In large doses, it damaged the central nervous system. But data on the effects of chronic exposure were lacking, and the FDA could not legally restrict its use while waiting for further research. DDT thus entered the marketplace billed as an extraordinarily safe and effective poison, the ultimate weapon against destructive insects.

For the next decade, the new chemical continued to live up to its early billing. It helped farmers eliminate chronic pests and was widely used to control mosquitoes. One of its most impressive successes was against the gypsy moth, a voracious insect that had been stripping the leaves from northeastern forests ever since it was accidentally introduced to the Boston area in 1868. All previous efforts to control the destructive moth had come to naught, but it virtually vanished from forests that were sprayed with DDT.

By the time Rachel Carson received Olga Huckins's letter, however, signs of trouble were beginning to appear in areas that had been sprayed with the chemical. For one, its effectiveness against certain insects declined as they developed resistance to its effects, so that higher doses were needed to produce the same lethal effect. A resistant housefly had appeared as early as 1948, and a resistant mosquito by 1949.

More worrisome were the effects of the chemical on larger animals. Some were killed outright, like the birds in Olga Huckins's back yard. But DDT also seemed to inhibit the ability of some animals to reproduce. It would later turn out that the eggshells of certain birds were so thinned by the chemical that young birds were crushed in their nests before they even hatched. The extraordinary persistence of DDT in the environment, and its tendency to accumulate in fatty tissues, meant that animals could concentrate surprising quantities in their flesh. This was especially true of those at the top of food chains—eagles, trout, and, not least, people. What this meant remained unclear, but many bird lovers were noting a general reduction in bird populations, and people who fished were catching fewer fish. As the woods became emptier and more silent, DDT seemed the mostly likely culprit.

Rachel Carson had worried about pesticides for years, but it was not until reading Olga Huckins's letter that she decided to do something about them. Meticulously gathering the best available data, she eventually wrote a book that was published in 1962, *Silent Spring*. In it, she warned that the indiscriminate use of pesticides was wreaking havoc with the web of life, destroying wildlife populations, and even threatening human health. She wrote of a landscape in which sickness and death threatened animals and people alike, and "a strange stillness" had replaced the familiar songs of birds. Her eloquence was made all the more urgent by her private knowledge that she herself was dying of cancer as she finished the book.

Silent Spring became one of the most controversial books of the 1960s. It sold nearly half a million copies within six months of its publication and was discussed everywhere. The chemical industry responded with cries of outrage. After first trying to suppress the book's publication altogether and threatening lawsuits against its author and publisher, pesticide manufacturers began a long campaign to discredit Carson and repair the damage her book had done. They attacked her, often unfairly, for being unscientific, for distorting facts, and for being hostile to technological progress. In the end, though, Carson won at least a partial victory: the U.S. finally banned the sale of DDT in 1972. More important, her book raised public awareness about the threats human activities pose to the natural environment. Although she died in 1964, no single person would be more important in shaping environmental policies over the next quarter century.

Rachel Carson
Rachel Carson, who began her career as a marine biologist, became the world's best-selling author about the ocean environment in the 1950s. Carson's abiding love for the creatures of shore and surf led to her concern about the harm pesticides might do them. (The Bettmann Archive)

Appendices

United States Political Map

CANADA

WASHINGTON
- Seattle
- Tacoma
- Olympia
- Spokane
- Portland
- Salem
- Eugene

OREGON

IDAHO
- Boise

MONTANA
- Helena
- Billings

NORTH DAKOTA
- Bismarck

SOUTH DAKOTA
- Pierre
- Rapid City

WYOMING
- Casper
- Laramie
- Cheyenne

NEBRASKA

NEVADA
- Reno
- Carson City

- Salt Lake City
- Provo

UTAH

Lincc

Sacramento
- Berkeley
- Oakland
- San Francisco
- Stockton
- Sunnyvale
- San Jose
- Modesto
- Fresno

CALIFORNIA
- Bakersfield

COLORADO
- Boulder
- Denver
- Aurora
- Lakewood
- Colorado Springs
- Pueblo

KANSAS

- Las Vegas

ARIZONA

- Taos
- Santa Fe
- Albuquerque

NEW MEXICO

W

- Amarillo

OKLAHC
- Oklahoma City

- Oxnard
- Glendale
- Pasadena
- Los Angeles
- San Bernardino
- Torrance
- Riverside
- Long Beach
- Anaheim
- Huntington Beach
- Santa Ana

- Phoenix
- Mesa
- Tempe

- Tucson

- Lubbock

Ga
Dallas
Irving
Fort Worth
Arlington

W

- San Diego

- El Paso

PACIFIC OCEAN

TEXAS
- Austin

- San Antonio

Kauai
HAWAII
- Honolulu
Oahu
- Ewa
Maui
Hawaii

0   100 Miles

0   100 Kilometers

U.S.S.R.

ALASKA
- Fairbanks

CANADA

- Anchorage

MEXICO

Corp
Chris

0   300 Miles

0   300 Kilometers

- Juneau

CANADA

Lake Superior

MAINE

MINNESOTA

MICHIGAN

Lake Huron

VERMONT

Augusta ☆

Burlington

Montpelier ☆

NEW HAMPSHIRE

Portland

nneapolis

St. Paul

WISCONSIN

Lake Michigan

Concord ☆

Manchester

Lake Ontario

Rochester

NEW YORK

Albany

Syracuse

Worcester

Boston

Springfield

MASSACHUSETTS

Providence

Milwaukee

Grand Rapids

Flint

Sterling Heights

Hartford

CONNECTICUT

RHODE ISLAND

Madison

Warren

Lansing

Detroit

Lake Erie

New Haven

Bridgeport

Stamford

Rockford

Ann Arbor

Livonia

Buffalo

IOWA

Cedar Rapids

Chicago

South Bend

Cleveland

PENNSYLVANIA

Youngstown

Allentown

Newark

New York

Jersey City

Moines

Davenport

Gary

Toledo

Akron

Erie

Harrisburg

Trenton

a

Peoria

Fort Wayne

OHIO

Dayton

Pittsburgh

Baltimore

Philadelphia

NEW JERSEY

Dover

Springfield

Urbana

Indianapolis

Cincinnati

Columbus

WASHINGTON D.C.

Annapolis

DELAWARE

MISSOURI

ILLINOIS

INDIANA

Louisville

Frankfort ☆

Alexandria

MARYLAND

ansas City

Independence

Evansville

Lexington

WEST VIRGINIA

VIRGINIA

Hampton

Norfolk

Kansas City

St. Louis

KENTUCKY

Charleston

Richmond

Newport News

Virginia Beach

Jefferson City

Roanoke

Portsmouth

Chesapeake

Springfield

Greensboro

Durham

Knoxville

Winston-Salem

Raleigh

ARKANSAS

Nashville

TENNESSEE

Asheville

NORTH CAROLINA

Charlotte

Chattanooga

Little Rock

Memphis

Huntsville

Greenville

Columbia

ATLANTIC OCEAN

Atlanta

Augusta

SOUTH CAROLINA

Birmingham

University

GEORGIA

Charleston

MISSISSIPPI

ALABAMA

Macon

Shreveport

Jackson

Montgomery

Columbus

Savannah

Beaumont

LOUISIANA

Baton Rouge

Biloxi

Mobile

Pensacola

Tallahassee

Jacksonville

uston

Galveston

New Orleans

Orlando

Gulf of Mexico

Tampa

FLORIDA

St. Petersburg

Hialeah

Fort Lauderdale

Hollywood

Miami

URBAN POPULATION CENTERS

◼ Over 5,000,000

■ 1,000,000–5,000,000

▣ 500,000–1,000,000

○ 100,000–500,000

☆ State capitals

| 0 | | 300 Miles |
| 0 | | 300 Kilometers |

United States Physical Map

Puget Sound

Ranges

Columbia R.

Cascade Range

Coast

Willamette R.

Columbia R.

Columbia Plateau

Snake R.

Owyhee

Snake R.

Kootenai R.

Columbia R.

Snake R.

Marias R.

Milk R.

Missouri R.

Yellowstone R.

Bighorn R.

Tongue R.

Powder R.

Assiniboine R.

ROCKY MOUNTAINS

Little Missouri R.

Belle Fourche R.

Black Hills

Cheyenne

James R.

Missouri

GREAT

Humboldt R.

Sacramento R.

Sierra Nevada

GREAT BASIN

Great Salt Lake

Sevier R.

Green R.

White

Yampa R.

N. Platte R.

Laramie R.

Niobrara R.

N. Platte R.

Loup R.

Missouri

Platte R.

San Joaquin R.

Central Valley

Coast Ranges

Death Valley

Virgin R.

Colorado R.

Gunnison R.

S. Platte R.

Lodgepole Cr.

Republican R.

Smoky Hill R.

Arkansas R.

Kan

PLAINS

Mohave Desert

Colorado Plateau

Colorado R.

Verde R.

Gila R.

ROCKY MOUNTAINS

Rio Grande

Pecos R.

Cimarron R.

Canadian R.

N. Canadian R.

Red R.

Colorado R.

Trinity R.

Brazos

PACIFIC OCEAN

Rio Grande

Pecos R.

Nueces R.

Rio Grande

Inset — Hawaii

PACIFIC OCEAN

PACIFIC OCEAN

20°

160°

Inset — Alaska

ARCTIC OCEAN

Brooks Range

70°

Arctic Circle

Yukon R.

Alaska Range ▲ Mt. McKinley

60°

BERING SEA

PACIFIC OCEAN

180°

170°

160°

150°

140°

125°

120°

115°

110°

105°

100°

50°

65°

St. Lawrence R.

45°

Lake Superior

Kennebeck R.

Mississippi R.

St. Croix R.

Adirondack
Mts.

Lake Huron

Mohawk R.

Connecticut R.

Lake Michigan

Lake Ontario

Hudson R.

40°

Iowa R.

Cedar R.

Rock R.

Fox R.

Lake Erie

APPALACHIAN MOUNTAINS

Delaware R.

Susquehanna R.

Des Moines R.

Kankakee R.

Allegheny R.

Illinois R.

Wabash R.

Scioto R.

Ohio R.

COASTAL PLAIN

CENTRAL PLAINS

Potomac R.

Mts.

Shenandoah Valley

Missouri R.

Kanawha R.

James R.

Chesapeake
Bay

Osage R.

Mississippi R.

Ohio R.

Allegheny

APPALACHIAN MOUNTAINS

Roanoke R.

35°

Ozark Plateau

70°

White R.

Cumberland R.

Blue Ridge Mountains

S. Francis R.

Arkansas R.

Tennessee R.

Saluda R.

ATLANTIC

Ouachita R.

Yazoo R.

Tombigbee R.

Savannah R.

Red R.

Pearl R.

Alabama R.

Chattahoochee R.

Altamaha R.

30°

Sabine R.

Mississippi R.

ATLANTIC OCEAN

COASTAL PLAIN

Galveston
Bay

Gulf of Mexico

25°

95°

90°

85°

80°

75°

World Political Map

United States and
its possessions

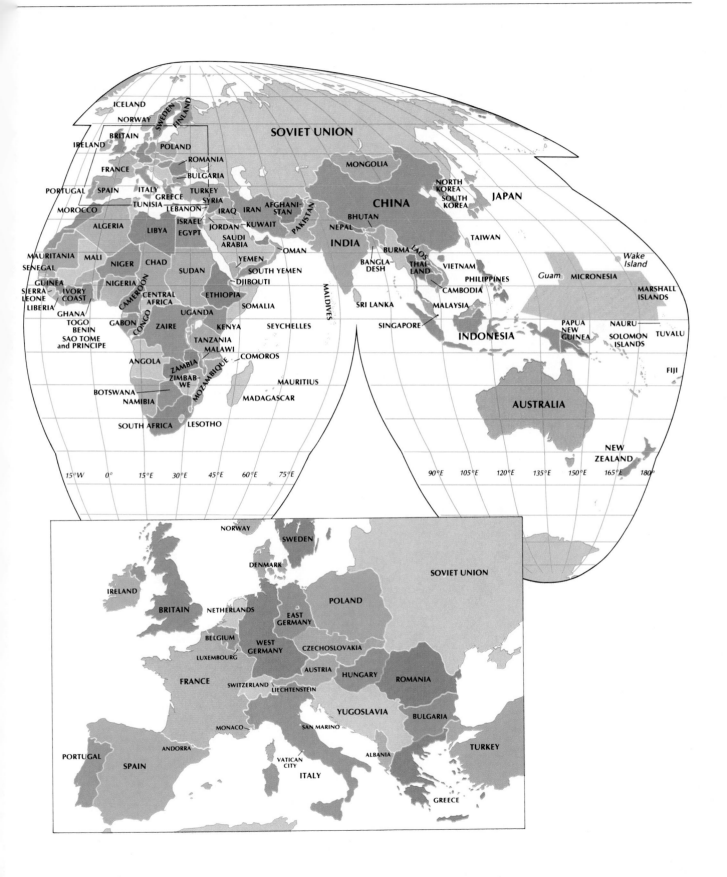

United States Territorial Expansion, 1783–1898

Legend:

(1820) Date of statehood

The United States in 1783

Louisiana Purchase, 1803

1819 Treaty with Spain defined border of Oregon and Louisiana

Florida: East Florida cession by Spain, 1819; West Florida annexation, 1810, 1813

Texas Annexation, 1845

Texas boundary claimed by U.S., 1845–1848

Oregon Country, 1846

Mexican Cession, 1848

Gadsden Purchase, 1853

The Declaration of Independence

In Congress, July 4, 1776,

THE UNANIMOUS DECLARATION OF THE THIRTEEN UNITED
STATES OF AMERICA

When, in the course of human events, it becomes necessary for one people to dissolve the political bands which have connected them with another, and to assume, among the powers of the earth, the separate and equal station to which the laws of nature and of nature's God entitle them, a decent respect to the opinions of mankind requires that they should declare the causes which impel them to the separation.

We hold these truths to be self-evident, that all men are created equal; that they are endowed by their Creator with certain unalienable rights; that among these, are life, liberty, and the pursuit of happiness. That, to secure these rights, governments are instituted among men, deriving their just powers from the consent of the governed; that, whenever any form of government becomes destructive of these ends, it is the right of the people to alter or to abolish it, and to institute a new government, laying its foundation on such principles, and organizing its powers in such form, as to them shall seem most likely to effect their safety and happiness. Prudence, indeed, will dictate that governments long established, should not be changed for light and transient causes; and, accordingly, all experience hath shown, that mankind are more disposed to suffer, while evils are sufferable, than to right themselves by abolishing the forms to which they are accustomed. But, when a long train of abuses and usurpations, pursuing invariably the same object, evinces a design to reduce them under absolute despotism, it is their right, it is their duty, to throw off such government and to provide new guards for their future security. Such has been the patient sufferance of these colonies, and such is now the necessity which constrains them to alter their former systems of government. The history of the present King of Great Britain is a history of repeated injuries and usurpations, all having, in direct object, the establishment of an absolute tyranny over these States. To prove this, let facts be submitted to a candid world:

He has refused his assent to laws the most wholesome and necessary for the public good.

He has forbidden his governors to pass laws of immediate and pressing importance, unless suspended in their operation till his assent should be obtained; and, when so suspended, he has utterly neglected to attend to them.

He has refused to pass other laws for the accommodation of large districts of people, unless those people would relinquish the right of representation in the legislature; a right inestimable to them, and formidable to tyrants only.

He has called together legislative bodies at places unusual, uncomfortable, and distant from the depository of their public records, for the sole purpose of fatiguing them into compliance with his measures.

He has dissolved representative houses repeatedly for opposing, with manly firmness, his invasions on the rights of the people.

He has refused, for a long time after such dissolutions, to cause others to be elected; whereby the legislative powers, incapable of annihilation, have returned to the people at large for their exercise; the state remaining, in the meantime, exposed to all the danger of invasion from without, and convulsions within.

He has endeavored to prevent the population of these States; for that purpose, obstructing the laws for naturalization of foreigners, refusing to pass others to encourage their migration hither, and raising the conditions of new appropriations of lands.

He had obstructed the administration of justice, by refusing his assent to laws for establishing judiciary powers.

He has made judges dependent on his will alone, for the tenure of their officers, and the amount and payment of their salaries.

He has erected a multitude of new offices, and sent hither swarms of officers to harass our people, and eat out their substance.

He has kept among us, in time of peace, standing armies, without the consent of our legislatures.

He has affected to render the military independent of, and superior to, the civil power.

He has combined, with others, to subject us to a jurisdiction foreign to our Constitution, and unacknowledged by our laws; giving his assent to their acts of pretended legislation:

For quartering large bodies of armed troops among us:

For protecting them by a mock trial, from punishment, for any murders which they should commit on the inhabitants of these States:

For cutting off our trade with all parts of the world:

For imposing taxes on us without our consent:

For depriving us, in many cases, of the benefit of trial by jury:

For transporting us beyond seas to be tried for pretended offences:

For abolishing the free system of English laws in a neighboring province, establishing therein an arbitrary government, and enlarging its boundaries, so as to render it at once an example and fit instrument for introducing the same absolute rule into these colonies:

For taking away our charters, abolishing our most valuable laws, and altering, fundamentally, the powers of our governments:

For suspending our own legislatures, and declaring themselves invested with power to legislate for us in all cases whatsoever.

He had abdicated government here, by declaring us out of his protection, and waging war against us.

He has plundered our seas, ravaged our coasts, burnt our towns, and destroyed the lives of our people.

He is, at this time, transporting large armies of foreign mercenaries to complete the works of death, desolation, and tyranny, already begun, with circumstances of cruelty and perfidy scarcely paralleled in the most barbarous ages, and totally unworthy the head of a civilized nation.

He has constrained our fellow citizens, taken captive on the high seas, to bear arms against their country, to become the executioners of their friends, and brethren, or to fall themselves by their hands.

He has excited domestic insurrections amongst us, and has endeavored to bring on the inhabitants of our frontiers, the merciless Indian savages, whose known rule of warfare is an undistinguished destruction of all ages, sexes, and conditions.

In every stage of these oppressions, we have petitioned for redress, in the most humble terms; our repeated petitions have been answered only by repeated injury. A prince, whose character is thus marked by every act which may define a tyrant, is unfit to be the ruler of a free people.

Nor have we been wanting in attention to our British brethren. We have warned them, from time to time, of attempts made by their legislature to extend an unwarrantable jurisdiction over us. We have reminded them of the circumstances of our emigration and settlement here. We have appealed to their native justice and magnanimity, and we have conjured them, by the ties of our common kindred, to disavow these usurpations, which would inevitably interrupt our connections and correspondence. They, too, have been deaf to the voice of justice and consanguinity. We must, therefore, acquiesce in the necessity which denounces our separation, and hold them as we hold the rest of mankind, enemies in war, in peace, friends.

We, therefore, the representatives of the United States of America, in general Congress assembled, appealing to the Supreme Judge of the world for the rectitude of our intentions, do, in the name, and by the authority of the good people of these colonies, solemnly publish and declare, that these united colonies are, and of right ought to be, free and independent states: that they are absolved from all allegiance to the British Crown, and that all political connection between them and the state of Great Britain is, and ought to be, totally dissolved; and that, as free and independent states, they have full power to levy war, conclude peace, contract alliances, establish commerce, and to do all other acts and things which independent states may of right do. And, for the support of this declaration, with a firm reliance on the protection of Divine Providence, we mutually pledge to each other our lives, our fortunes, and our sacred honor.

The foregoing Declaration was, by order of Congress, engrossed, and signed by the following members:

JOHN HANCOCK

New Hampshire
Josiah Bartlett
William Whipple
Matthew Thornton

Massachusetts Bay
Samuel Adams
John Adams
Robert Treat Paine
Elbridge Gerry

Rhode Island
Stephen Hopkins
William Ellery

Connecticut
Roger Sherman
Samuel Huntington
William Williams
Oliver Wolcott

New York
William Floyd
Philip Livingston
Francis Lewis
Lewis Morris

New Jersey
Richard Stockton
John Witherspoon
Francis Hopkinson
John Hart
Abraham Clark

Pennsylvania
Robert Morris
Benjamin Rush
Benjamin Franklin
John Morton
George Clymer
James Smith
George Taylor
James Wilson
George Ross

Delaware
Caesar Rodney
George Read
Thomas M'Kean

Maryland
Samuel Chase
William Paca
Thomas Stone
Charles Carroll,
  of Carrollton

Virginia
George Wythe
Richard Henry Lee
Thomas Jefferson
Benjamin Harrison
Thomas Nelson, Jr.
Francis Lightfoot Lee
Carter Braxton

North Carolina
William Hooper
Joseph Hewes
John Penn

South Carolina
Edward Rutledge
Thomas Heyward, Jr.
Thomas Lynch, Jr.
Arthur Middleton

Georgia
Button Gwinnett
Lyman Hall
George Walton

Resolved, That copies of the Declaration be sent to the several assemblies, conventions, and committees, or councils of safety, and to the several commanding officers of the continental troops; that it be proclaimed in each of the United States, at the head of the army.

The Constitution of the United States of America[1]

We the People of the United States, in Order to form a more perfect Union, establish Justice, insure domestic Tranquility, provide for the common defence, promote the general Welfare, and secure the Blessings of Liberty to ourselves and our Posterity, do ordain and establish this CONSTITUTION for the United States of America.

Article 1

Section 1.

All legislative Powers herein granted shall be vested in a Congress of the United States, which shall consist of a Senate and House of Representatives.

Section 2.

The House of Representatives shall be composed of Members chosen every second Year by the People of the several States, and the Electors in each State shall have the Qualifications requisite for Electors of the most numerous Branch of the State Legislature.

No Person shall be a Representative who shall not have attained to the Age of twenty-five Years, and been seven Years a Citizen of the United States, and who shall not, when elected, be an Inhabitant of that State in which he shall be chosen.

[Representatives and direct Taxes[2] shall be apportioned among the several States which may be included within this Union, according to their respective Numbers, which shall be determined by adding to the whole Number of free Persons, including those bound to Service for a Term of Years, and excluding Indians not taxed, three fifths of all other Persons.][3] The actual Enumeration shall be made within three Years after the first Meeting of the Congress of the United States, and within every subsequent Term of ten Years, in such Manner as they shall by Law direct. The Number of Representatives shall not exceed one for every thirty Thousand, but each State shall have at Least one Representative; and until such enumeration shall be made, the State of New Hampshire shall be entitled to chuse three, Massachusetts eight, Rhode-Island and Providence Plantations one, Connecticut five, New York six, New Jersey four, Pennsylvania eight, Delaware one, Maryland six, Virginia ten, North Carolina five, South Carolina five, and Georgia three.

When vacancies happen in the Representation from any State, the Executive Authority thereof shall issue Writs of Election to fill such Vacancies.

The House of Representatives shall chuse their Speaker and other Officers; and shall have the sole Power of Impeachment.

Section 3.

The Senate of the United States shall be composed of two Senators from each State, chosen by the Legislature thereof, for six Years; and each Senator shall have one Vote.

Immediately after they shall be assembled in Consequence of the first Election, they shall be divided as equally as may be into three Classes. The Seats of the Senators of the first Class shall be vacated at the Expiration of the second Year, of the second Class at the Expiration of the fourth Year, and of the third Class at the Expiration of the sixth Year, so that one-third may be chosen every second Year; and if Vacancies happen by Resignation, or otherwise, during the Recess of the Legislature of any State, the Executive thereof may make temporary Appointments until the next Meeting of the Legislature, which shall then fill such Vacancies.

No Person shall be a Senator who shall not have attained to the Age of thirty Years, and been nine Years a Citizen of the United States, and who shall not, when elected, be an Inhabitant of that State for which he shall be chosen.

The Vice President of the United States shall be President of the Senate, but shall have no vote, unless they be equally divided.

The Senate shall chuse their other Officers, and also a President pro tempore, in the absence of the Vice President, or when he shall exercise the Office of President of the United States.

---

[1] This version, which follows the original Constitution in capitalization and spelling, was published by the United States Department of the Interior, Office of Education, in 1935.

[2] Altered by the Sixteenth Amendment.

[3] Negated by the Fourteenth Amendment.

The Senate shall have the sole Power to try all Impeachments. When sitting for that purpose they shall be on Oath or Affirmation. When the President of the United States is tried, the Chief Justice shall preside: And no person shall be convicted without the Concurrence of two thirds of the Members present.

Judgment in Cases of Impeachment shall not extend further than to removal from Office, and disqualification to hold and enjoy any Office of honor, Trust, or Profit under the United States: but the Party convicted shall nevertheless be liable and subject to Indictment, Trial, Judgment, and Punishment, according to Law.

Section 4.

The Times, Places and Manner of holding Elections for Senators and Representatives, shall be prescribed in each State by the Legislature thereof; but the Congress may at any time by Law make or alter such Regulations, except as to the Places of Chusing Senators.

The Congress shall assemble at least once in every Year, and such Meeting shall be on the first Monday in December, unless they shall by Law appoint a different Day.

Section 5.

Each House shall be the Judge of the Elections, Returns and Qualifications of its own Members, and a Majority of each shall constitute a Quorum to do Business; but a smaller number may adjourn from day to day, and may be authorized to compel the Attendance of absent Members, in such Manner, and under such Penalties, as each House may provide.

Each House may determine the Rules of its Proceedings, punish its Members for disorderly Behaviour, and, with the Concurrence of two thirds, expel a Member.

Each House shall keep a Journal of its Proceedings, and from time to time publish the same, excepting such Parts as may in their Judgment require Secrecy; and the Yeas and Nays of the Members of either House on any question shall, at the Desire of one fifth of those Present, be entered on the Journal.

Neither House, during the Session of Congress, shall, without the Consent of the other, adjourn for more than three days, nor to any other Place than that in which the two Houses shall be sitting.

Section 6.

The Senators and Representatives shall receive a Compensation for their Services, to be ascertained by Law, and paid out of the Treasury of the United States. They shall in all Cases, except Treason, Felony, and Breach of the Peace, be privileged from Arrest during their Attendance at the Session of their respective Houses, and in going to and returning from the same; and for any Speech or Debate in either House, they shall not be questioned in any other Place.

No Senator or Representative shall, during the Time for which he was elected, be appointed to any civil Office under the Authority of the United States, which shall have been created, or the Emoluments whereof shall have been increased, during such time; and no Person holding any Office under the United States shall be a Member of either House during his continuance in Office.

Section 7.

All Bills for raising Revenue shall originate in the House of Representatives; but the Senate may propose or concur with Amendments as on other bills.

Every Bill which shall have passed the House of Representatives and the Senate, shall, before it become a Law, be presented to the President of the United States; If he approve he shall sign it, but if not he shall return it, with his Objections, to that House in which it shall have originated, who shall enter the Objections at large on their Journal, and proceed to reconsider it. If after such Reconsideration two thirds of that House shall agree to pass the bill, it shall be sent, together with the objections, to the other House, by which it shall likewise be reconsidered, and if approved by two thirds of that House, it shall become a Law. But in all such Cases the Votes of both Houses shall be determined by Yeas and Nays, and the Names of the Persons voting for and against the Bill shall be entered on the Journal of each House respectively. If any Bill shall not be returned by the President within ten Days (Sundays excepted) after it shall have been presented to him, the Same shall be a Law, in like Manner as if he had signed it, unless the Congress by their Adjournment prevent its Return, in which Case it shall not be a Law.

Every Order, Resolution, or Vote to which the Concurrence of the Senate and House of Representatives may be necessary (except on a question of Adjournment) shall be presented to the President of the United States; and before the Same shall take

Effect, shall be approved by him, or being disapproved by him, shall be repassed by two thirds of the Senate and House of Representatives, according to the Rules and Limitations prescribed in the Case of a Bill.

Section 8.

The Congress shall have Power To lay and collect Taxes, Duties, Imposts and Excises, to pay the Debts and provide for the common Defence and general Welfare of the United States; but all Duties, Imposts and Excises shall be uniform throughout the United States;

To borrow money on the credit of the United States;

To regulate Commerce with foreign Nations, and among the several States, and with the Indian Tribes;

To establish an uniform rule of Naturalization, and uniform Laws on the subject of Bankruptcies throughout the United States;

To coin Money, regulate the Value thereof, and of foreign Coin, and fix the Standard of Weights and Measures;

To provide for the Punishment of counterfeiting the Securities and current Coin of the United States;

To establish Post Offices and post Roads;

To promote the Progress of Science and useful Arts, by securing for limited Times to Authors and Inventors the exclusive Right to their respective Writings and Discoveries;

To constitute Tribunals inferior to the Supreme Court;

To define and punish Piracies and Felonies committed on the high Seas, and Offenses against the Law of Nations;

To declare War, grant Letters of Marque and Reprisal, and make Rules concerning Captures on Land and Water;

To raise and support Armies, but no Appropriation of Money to that Use shall be for a longer Term than two Years;

To provide and maintain a Navy;

To make Rules for the Government and Regulation of the land and naval forces;

To provide for calling forth the Militia to execute the Laws of the Union, suppress Insurrections and repel Invasions;

To provide for organizing, arming, and disciplining the Militia, and for governing such Part of them as may be employed in the Service of the United States, reserving to the States respectively, the Appointment of the Officers, and the Authority of training the Militia according to the discipline prescribed by Congress;

To exercise exclusive Legislation in all Cases whatsoever, over such District (not exceeding ten Miles square) as may, by Cession of particular States, and the acceptance of Congress, become the Seat of the Government of the United States, and to exercise like Authority over all Places purchased by the Consent of the Legislature of the State in which the Same shall be, for the Erection of Forts, Magazines, Arsenals, Dock-yards, and other needful Buildings;—And

To make all Laws which shall be necessary and proper for carrying into Execution the foregoing Powers, and all other Powers vested by this Constitution in the Government of the United States, or in any Department or Officer thereof.

Section 9.

The Migration or Importation of such Persons as any of the States now existing shall think proper to admit, shall not be prohibited by the Congress prior to the Year one thousand eight hundred and eight, but a tax or duty may be imposed on such Importation, not exceeding ten dollars for each Person.

The privilege of the Writ of Habeas Corpus shall not be suspended, unless when in Cases of Rebellion or Invasion the public Safety may require it.

No bill of Attainder or ex post facto Law shall be passed.

No capitation, or other direct, Tax shall be laid unless in Proportion to the Census or Enumeration herein before directed to be taken.

No Tax or Duty shall be laid on Articles exported from any State.

No Preference shall be given by any Regulation of Commerce or Revenue to the Ports of one State over those of another: nor shall Vessels bound to, or from, one State, be obliged to enter, clear, or pay Duties in another.

No Money shall be drawn from the Treasury, but in Consequence of Appropriations made by Law; and a regular Statement and Account of the Receipts and Expenditures of all public Money shall be published from time to time.

No Title of Nobility shall be granted by the United States: And no Person holding any Office of Profit or Trust under them, shall, without the Consent of the Congress, accept of any present, Emolument, Office, or Title, of any kind whatever, from any King, Prince, or foreign State.

Section 10.

No State shall enter into any Treaty, Alliance, or Confederation; grant Letters of Marque and Reprisal; coin Money; emit Bills of Credit; make any Thing but gold and silver Coin a Tender in Payment of Debts; pass any Bill of Attainder, ex post facto Law, or Law impairing the Obligation of Contracts, or grant any Title of Nobility.

No State shall, without the Consent of the Congress, lay any Imposts or Duties on Imports or Exports, except what may be absolutely necessary for executing its inspection Laws; and the net Produce of all Duties and Imposts, laid by any State on Imports or Exports, shall be for the use of the Treasury of the United States; and all such Laws shall be subject to the Revision and Control of the Congress.

No state shall, without the Consent of Congress, lay any duty of Tonnage, keep Troops, or Ships of War in time of Peace, enter into any Agreement or Compact with another State, or with a foreign Power, or engage in War, unless actually invaded, or in such imminent Danger as will not admit of delay.

Article II

Section 1.

The executive Power shall be vested in a President of the United States of America. He shall hold his Office during the Term of four years, and, together with the Vice President, chosen for the same Term, be elected, as follows:

Each State shall appoint, in such Manner as the Legislature thereof may direct, a Number of Electors, equal to the whole Number of Senators and Representatives to which the State may be entitled in the Congress: but no Senator or Representative, or Person holding an Office of Trust or Profit under the United States, shall be appointed an Elector.

[The Electors shall meet in their respective States, and vote by Ballot for two persons, of whom one at least shall not be an Inhabitant of the same State with themselves. And they shall make a List of all the Persons voted for, and of the Number of Votes for each; which List they shall sign and certify, and transmit sealed to the Seat of the Government of the United States, directed to the President of the Senate. The President of the Senate shall, in the Presence of the Senate and House of Representatives, open all the Certificates, and the Votes shall then be counted. The Person having the greatest Number of Votes shall be the President, if such Number be a Majority of the whole Number of Electors appointed; and if there be more than one who have such Majority, and have an equal Number of Votes, then the House of Representatives shall immediately chuse by Ballot one of them for President; and if no Person have a Majority, then from the five highest on the List the said House shall in like Manner chuse the President. But in chusing the President, the Votes shall be taken by States, the Representation from each State having one Vote; a quorum for this Purpose shall consist of a Member or Members from two-thirds of the States, and a Majority of all the States shall be necessary to a Choice. In every Case, after the Choice of the President, the Person having the greatest Number of Votes of the Electors shall be the Vice President. But if there should remain two or more who have equal votes, the Senate shall chuse from them by Ballot the Vice President.][4]

The Congress may determine the Time of chusing the Electors, and the Day on which they shall give their Votes; which Day shall be the same throughout the United States.

No person except a natural-born Citizen, or a Citizen of the United States, at the time of the Adoption of this Constitution, shall be eligible to the Office of President; neither shall any Person be eligible to that Office who shall not have attained to the Age of thirty-five years, and been fourteen Years a Resident within the United States.

In Case of the Removal of the President from Office, or of his Death, Resignation, or Inability to discharge the Powers and Duties of the said Office, the same shall devolve on the Vice President, and the Congress may by Law provide for the Case of Removal, Death, Resignation, or Inability, both of the President and Vice President, declaring what Officer shall then act as President, and such Officer shall act accordingly, until the disability be removed, or a President shall be elected.

The President shall, at stated Times, receive for his Services a Compensation, which shall neither be increased nor diminished during the Period for which he shall have been elected, and he shall not receive within that Period any other Emolument from the United States, or any of them.

Before he enter on the execution of his Office, he shall take the following Oath or Affirmation:—"I do solemnly swear (or affirm) that I will faithfully execute the Office of President of the United States, and

---

[4] Revised by the Twelfth Amendment.

will, to the best of my Ability, preserve, protect, and defend the Constitution of the United States."

Section 2.

The President shall be Commander in Chief of the Army and Navy of the United States, and of the Militia of the several States, when called into the actual Service of the United States; he may require the Opinion, in writing, of the principal Officer in each of the executive Departments, upon any subject relating to the Duties of their respective Offices, and he shall have Power to Grant Reprieves and Pardons for Offenses against the United States, except in Cases of Impeachment.

He shall have Power, by and with the Advice and Consent of the Senate, to make Treaties, provided two-thirds of the Senators present concur; and he shall nominate, and by and with the Advice and Consent of the Senate, shall appoint Ambassadors, other public Ministers and Consuls, Judges of the supreme Court, and all other Officers of the United States, whose Appointments are not herein otherwise provided for, and which shall be established by Law: but the Congress may by Law vest the Appointment of such inferior Officers, as they think proper, in the President alone, in the Courts of Law, or in the Heads of Departments.

The President shall have Power to fill up all Vacancies that may happen during the Recess of the Senate, by granting Commissions which shall expire at the End of their next Session.

Section 3.

He shall from time to time give to the Congress Information of the State of the Union, and recommend to their Consideration such Measures as he shall judge necessary and expedient; he may, on extraordinary occasions, convene both Houses, or either of them, and in Case of Disagreement between them, with respect to the Time of Adjournment, he may adjourn them to such Time as he shall think proper; he shall receive Ambassadors and other public Ministers; he shall take care that the Laws be faithfully executed, and shall Commission all the Officers of the United States.

Section 4.

The President, Vice President and all civil Officers of the United States, shall be removed from Office on

Impeachment for, and Conviction of, Treason, Bribery, or other high Crimes and Misdemeanors.

Article III

Section 1.

The judicial Power of the United States, shall be vested in one supreme Court, and in such inferior Courts as the Congress may from time to time ordain and establish. The Judges, both of the supreme and inferior Courts, shall hold their Offices during good Behaviour, and shall, at stated Times, receive for their Services, a Compensation, which shall not be diminished during their Continuance in Office.

Section 2.

The judicial Power shall extend to all Cases, in Law and Equity, arising under this Constitution, the Laws of the United States, and Treaties made, or which shall be made, under their Authority;—to all Cases affecting ambassadors, other public ministers and consuls;—to all cases of admiralty and maritime Jurisdiction;—to Controversies to which the United States shall be a Party;—to Controversies between two or more States;—between a State and Citizens of another State;[5]—between Citizens of different States—between Citizens of the same State claiming Lands under Grants of different States, and between a State, or the Citizens thereof, and foreign States, Citizens, or Subjects.

In all Cases affecting Ambassadors, other public Ministers and Consuls, and those in which a State shall be Party, the supreme Court shall have original Jurisdiction. In all the other Cases before mentioned, the supreme Court shall have appellate Jurisdiction, both as to Law and Fact, with such Exceptions, and under such Regulations as the Congress shall make.

The trial of all Crimes, except in Cases of Impeachment, shall be by Jury; and such Trial shall be held in the State where the said Crimes shall have been committed; but when not committed within any State, the Trial shall be at such Place or Places as the Congress may by Law have directed.

Section 3.

Treason against the United States, shall consist only in levying War against them, or in adhering to their

---

[5] Qualified by the Eleventh Amendment.

Enemies, giving them Aid and Comfort. No Person shall be convicted of Treason unless on the Testimony of two Witnesses to the same overt Act, or on Confession in open Court.

The Congress shall have power to declare the Punishment of Treason, but no Attainder of Treason shall work Corruption of Blood, or Forfeiture except during the Life of the Person attainted.

Article IV

Section 1.

Full Faith and Credit shall be given in each State to the public Acts, Records, and judicial Proceedings of every other State. And the Congress may by general Laws prescribe the Manner in which such Acts, Records and Proceedings shall be proved, and the Effect thereof.

Section 2.

The Citizens of each State shall be entitled to all Privileges and Immunities of Citizens in the several States.

A Person charged in any State with Treason, Felony, or other Crime, who shall flee from Justice, and be found in another State, shall on demand of the executive Authority of the State from which he fled, be delivered up, to be removed to the State having Jurisdiction of the crime.

No Person held to Service or Labour in one State, under the Laws thereof, escaping into another, shall, in Consequence of any Law or Regulation therein, be discharged from such Service or Labour, but shall be delivered up on Claim of the Party to whom such Service or Labour may be due.

Section 3.

New States may be admitted by the Congress into this Union; but no new State shall be formed or erected within the Jurisdiction of any other State; nor any State be formed by the Junction of two or more States, or parts of States, without the Consent of the Legislatures of the States concerned as well as of the Congress.

The Congress shall have Power to dispose of and make all needful Rules and Regulations respecting the Territory or other Property belonging to the United States; and nothing in this Constitution shall be so construed as to Prejudice any Claims of the United States, or of any particular State.

Section 4.

The United States shall guarantee to every State in this Union a Republican Form of Government, and shall protect each of them against Invasion; and on Application of the Legislature, or of the Executive (when the Legislature cannot be convened) against domestic Violence.

Article V

The Congress, whenever two-thirds of both Houses shall deem it necessary, shall propose Amendments to this Constitution, or, on the Application of the Legislatures of two-thirds of the several States, shall call a Convention for proposing Amendments, which, in either Case, shall be valid to all Intents and Purposes, as part of this Constitution, when ratified by the Legislatures of three-fourths of the several States, or by Conventions in three-fourths thereof, as the one or the other Mode of Ratification may be proposed by the Congress; Provided that no Amendment which may be made prior to the Year One thousand eight hundred and eight shall in any Manner affect the first and fourth Clauses in the Ninth Section of the first Article; and that no State, without its Consent, shall be deprived of its equal Suffrage in the Senate.

Article VI

All Debts contracted and Engagements entered into, before the Adoption of this Constitution, shall be as valid against the United States under this Constitution, as under the Confederation.

This Constitution, and the Laws of the United States which shall be made in Pursuance thereof; and all Treaties made, or which shall be made, under the Authority of the United States, shall be the supreme Law of the Land; and the Judges in every State shall be bound thereby, any Thing in the Constitution or Laws of any State to the Contrary notwithstanding.

The Senators and Representatives before mentioned, and the Members of the several State Legislatures, and all executive and judicial Officers, both of the United States and of the several States, shall be bound by Oath or Affirmation to support this Constitution; but no religious Tests shall ever be required as a qualification to any Office or public Trust under the United States.

Article VII

The Ratification of the Conventions of nine States shall be sufficient for the Establishment of this Constitution between the States so ratifying the same.

George Washington
President and deputy and deputy from Virginia

New Hampshire
John Langdon
Nicholas Gilman

Massachusetts
Nathaniel Gorham
Rufus King

Connecticut
William Samuel
    Johnson
Roger Sherman

New York
Alexander Hamilton

New Jersey
William Livingston
David Brearley
William Paterson
Jonathan Dayton

Pennsylvania
Benjamin Franklin
Thomas Mifflin
Robert Morris
George Clymer
Thomas FitzSimons
Jared Ingersoll
James Wilson
Gouverneur Morris

Done in Convention by the Unanimous Consent of the States present the Seventeenth Day of September in the Year of our Lord one thousand seven hundred and Eighty seven, and of the Independence of the United States of America the Twelfth. In Witness whereof We have hereunto subscribed our Names.[6]

Delaware
George Read
Gunning Bedford, Jr.
John Dickinson
Richard Bassett
Jacob Broom

Maryland
James McHenry
Daniel of
    St. Thomas Jenifer
Daniel Carroll

Virginia
John Blair
James Madison, Jr.

North Carolina
William Blount
Richard Dobbs
    Spaight
Hugh Williamson

South Carolina
John Rutledge
Charles Cotesworth
    Pinckney
Charles Pinckney
Pierce Butler

Georgia
William Few
Abraham Baldwin

Articles in Addition to, and Amendment of, the Constitution of the United States of America, Proposed by Congress, and Ratified by the Legislatures of the Several States, Pursuant to the Fifth Article of the Original Constitution[7]

[Article I]

Congress shall make no law respecting an establishment of religion, or prohibiting the free exercise thereof; or abridging the freedom of speech, or of the press; or the right of the people peaceably to assemble, and to petition the Government for a redress of grievances.

[Article II]

A well regulated Militia, being necessary to the security of a free State, the right of the people to keep and bear Arms shall not be infringed.

[Article III]

No Soldier shall, in time of peace, be quartered in any house, without the consent of the Owner, nor in time of war, but in a manner to be prescribed by law.

[Article IV]

The right of the people to be secure in their persons, houses, papers, and effects, against unreasonable searches and seizures, shall not be violated, and no

---

[6] These are the full names of the signers, which in some cases are not the signatures on the document.

[7] This heading appears only in the joint resolution submitting the first ten amendments.

Warrants shall issue, but upon probable cause, supported by Oath or affirmation, and particularly describing the place to be searched, and the persons or things to be seized.

[Article V]

No person shall be held to answer for a capital or otherwise infamous crime, unless on a presentment or indictment of a Grand Jury, except in cases arising in the land or naval forces, or in the Militia, when in actual service in time of War or public danger; nor shall any person be subject for the same offence to be twice put in jeopardy of life or limb; nor shall be compelled in any criminal case to be a witness against himself, nor be deprived of life, liberty, or property, without due process of law; nor shall private property be taken for public use, without just compensation.

[Article VI]

In all criminal prosecutions, the accused shall enjoy the right to a speedy and public trial, by an impartial jury of the State and district wherein the crime shall have been committed, which district shall have been previously ascertained by law, and to be informed of the nature and cause of the accusation; to be confronted with the witnesses against him; to have compulsory process for obtaining witnesses in his favour, and to have the Assistance of Counsel for his defence.

[Article VII]

In suits at common law, where the value in controversy shall exceed twenty dollars, the right of trial by jury shall be preserved, and no fact tried by a jury, shall be otherwise reexamined in any Court of the United States, than according to the rules of the common law.

[Article VIII]

Excessive bail shall not be required, nor excessive fines imposed, nor cruel and unusual punishments inflicted.

[Article IX]

The enumeration of the Constitution, of certain rights, shall not be construed to deny or disparage others retained by the people.

[Article X]

The powers not delegated to the United States by the Constitution, nor prohibited by it to the States, are reserved to the States respectively, or to the people.
[Amendments I-X, in force 1791.]

[Article XI][8]

The Judicial power of the United States shall not be construed to extend to any suit in law or equity, commenced or prosecuted against one of the United States by Citizens of another State, or by Citizens or Subjects of any Foreign State.

[Article XII][9]

The Electors shall meet in their respective States and vote by ballot for President and Vice-President, one of whom, at least, shall not be an inhabitant of the same State with themselves; they shall name in their ballots the person voted for as President, and in distinct ballots the person voted for as Vice-President, and they shall make distinct lists of all persons voted for as President, and of all persons voted for as Vice-President, and of the number of votes for each, which lists they shall sign and certify, and transmit sealed to the seal of the government of the United States, directed to the President of the Senate;—The President of the Senate shall, in the presence of the Senate and House of Representatives, open all the certificates and the votes shall then be counted;—The person having the greatest number of votes for President, shall be the President, if such number be a majority of the whole number of Electors appointed; and if no person have such majority, then from the persons having the highest numbers not exceeding three on the list of those voted for as President, the House of Representatives shall choose immediately, by ballot, the President. But in choosing the President, the votes

[8] Adopted in 1798.
[9] Adopted in 1804.

shall be taken by states, the representation from each state having one vote; a quorum for this purpose shall consist of a member or members from two-thirds of the states, and a majority of all the states shall be necessary to a choice. And if the House of Representatives shall not choose a President whenever the right of choice shall devolve upon them, before the fourth day of March next following, then the Vice-President shall act as President, as in the case of the death or other constitutional disability of the President.—The person having the greatest number of votes as Vice-President, shall be the Vice-President, if such number be a majority of the whole number of Electors appointed, and if no person have a majority, then from the two highest numbers on the list, the Senate shall choose the Vice-President; a quorum for the purpose shall consist of two-thirds of the whole number of Senators, and a majority of the whole number shall be necessary to a choice. But no person constitutionally ineligible to the office of President shall be eligible to that of Vice-President of the United States.

[Article XIII][10]

Section 1.

Neither slavery nor involuntary servitude, except as a punishment for crime whereof the party shall have been duly convicted, shall exist within the United States, or any place subject to their jurisdiction.

Section 2.

Congress shall have power to enforce this article by appropriate legislation.

[Article XIV][11]

Section 1.

All persons born or naturalized in the United States, and subject to the jurisdiction thereof, are citizens of the United States and of the State wherein they reside. No State shall abridge the privileges or immunities of citizens of the United States; nor shall any State deprive any person of life, liberty, or property, without due process of law; nor deny to any person within its jurisdiction the equal protection of the laws.

Section 2.

Representatives shall be apportioned among the several States according to their respective numbers, counting the whole number of persons in each State, excluding Indians not taxed. But when the right to vote at any election for the choice of electors for President and Vice-President of the United States, Representatives in Congress, the Executive and Judicial officers of a State, or the members of the Legislature thereof, is denied to any of the male inhabitants of such State, being twenty-one years of age, and citizens of the United States, or in any way abridged, except for participation in rebellion, or other crime, the basis of representation therein shall be reduced in the proportion which the number of such male citizens shall bear to the whole number of male citizens twenty-one years of age in such State.

Section 3.

No person shall be a Senator or Representative in Congress, or elector of President and Vice-President, or hold any office, civil or military, under the United States, or under any State, who, having previously taken an oath, as a member of Congress, or as an officer of the United States, or as a member of any State legislature, or as an executive or judicial officer of any State, to support the Constitution of the United States, shall have engaged in insurrection or rebellion against the same, or given aid or comfort to the enemies thereof. But Congress may by a vote of two-thirds of each House, remove such disability.

Section 4.

The validity of the public debt of the United States, authorized by law, including debts incurred for payment of pensions and bounties for services in suppressing insurrection or rebellion, shall not be questioned. But neither the United States nor any State shall assume or pay any debts or obligation incurred in aid of insurrection or rebellion against the United States, or any claim for the loss or emancipation of any slave; but all such debts, obligations, and claims shall be held illegal and void.

Section 5.

The Congress shall have the power to enforce, by appropriate legislation, the provisions of this article.

---

[10] Adopted in 1865.
[11] Adoped in 1868.

[Article XV][12]

Section 1.

The right of citizens of the United States to vote shall not be denied or abridged by the United States or by any State on account of race, color, or previous condition of servitude—

Section 2.

The Congress shall have power to enforce this article by appropriate legislation.

[Article XVI][13]

The Congress shall have power to lay and collect taxes on incomes, from whatever source derived, without apportionment among the several States, and without regard to any census or enumeration.

[Article XVII][14]

The Senate of the United States shall be composed of two Senators from each State, elected by the people thereof, for six years; and each Senator shall have one vote. The electors in each State shall have the qualifications requisite for electors of the most numerous branch of the State legislatures.

When vacancies happen in the representation of any State in the Senate, the executive authority of such State shall issue writs of election to fill such vacancies: *Provided,* That the legislature of any State may empower the executive thereof to make temporary appointments until the people fill the vacancies by election as the legislature may direct.

This amendment shall not be so construed as to affect the election or term of any Senator chosen before it becomes valid as part of the Constitution.

[Article XVIII][15]

Section 1.

After one year from the ratification of this article the manufacture, sale, or transportation of intoxicating

---

[12] Adopted in 1870.
[13] Adopted in 1913.
[14] Adopted in 1913.
[15] Adopted in 1918.

liquors within, the importation thereof into, or the exportation thereof from the United States and all territory subject to the jurisdiction thereof for beverage purposes is hereby prohibited.

Section 2.

The Congress and the several States shall have concurrent power to enforce this article by appropriate legislation.

Section 3.

This article shall be inoperative unless it shall have been ratified as an amendment to the Constitution by the legislatures of the several States, as provided in the Constitution, within seven years from the date of the submission hereof to the States by the Congress.

[Article XIX][16]

The right of citizens of the United States to vote shall not be denied or abridged by the United States or by any State on account of sex.

Congress shall have power to enforce this article by appropriate legislation.

[Article XX][17]

Section 1.

The terms of the President and Vice-President shall end at noon on the 20th day of January, and the terms of Senators and Representatives at noon on the 3d day of January, of the years in which such terms would have ended if this article had not been ratified; and the terms of their successors shall then begin.

Section 2.

The Congress shall assemble at least once in every year, and such meeting shall begin at noon on the 3d day of January, unless they shall by law appoint a different day.

Section 3.

If, at the time fixed for the beginning of the term of the President, the President elect shall have died, the

---

[16] Adopted in 1920.
[17] Adopted in 1933.

Vice-President elect shall become President. If a President shall not have been chosen before the time fixed for the beginning of his term or if the President elect shall have failed to qualify, then the Vice-President elect shall act as President until a President shall have qualified; and the Congress may by law provide for the case wherein neither a President elect nor a Vice-President elect shall have qualified, declaring who shall then act as President, or the manner in which one who is to act shall be selected, and such person shall act accordingly until a President or Vice-President shall have qualified.

Section 4.

The Congress may by law provide for the case of the death of any of the persons from whom the House of Representatives may choose a President whenever the right of choice shall have devolved upon them, and for the case of the death of any of the persons from whom the Senate may choose a Vice-President whenever the right of choice shall have devolved upon them.

Section 5.

Sections 1 and 2 shall take effect on the 15th day of October following the ratification of this article.

Section 6.

This article shall be inoperative unless it shall have been ratified as an amendment to the Constitution by the legislatures of three-fourths of the several States within seven years from the date of its submission.

[Article XXI][18]

Section 1.

The eighteenth article of amendment to the Constitution of the United States is hereby repealed.

Section 2.

The transportation or importation into any State, Territory, or possession of the United States for delivery or use therein of intoxicating liquors, in violation of the laws thereof, is hereby prohibited.

---

[18] Adopted in 1933.

Section 3.

This article shall be inoperative unless it shall have been ratified as an amendment to the Constitution by conventions in the several States, as provided in the Constitution, within seven years from the date of the submission hereof to the States by the Congress.

[Article XXII][19]

No person shall be elected to the office of the President more than twice, and no person who has held the office of President, or acted as President, for more than two years of a term to which some other person was elected President shall be elected to the office of the President more than once.

But this Article shall not apply to any person holding the office of President when this Article was proposed by the Congress, and shall not prevent any person who may be holding the office of President, or acting as President, during the term within which this Article becomes operative from holding the office of President or acting as President during the remainder of such term.

This article shall be inoperative unless it shall have been ratified as an amendment to the Constitution by the legislatures of three-fourths of the several states within seven years from the date of its submission to the states by the Congress.

[Article XXIII][20]

Section 1.

The District constituting the seat of Government of the United States shall appoint in such manner as the Congress may direct:

A number of electors of President and Vice-President equal to the whole number of Senators and Representatives in Congress to which the District would be entitled if it were a State, but in no event more than the least populous State; they shall be in addition to those appointed by the States, but they shall be considered, for the purposes of the election of President and Vice-President, to be electors appointed by a State; and they shall meet in the District and perform such duties as provided by the twelfth article of amendment.

---

[19] Adopted in 1961.
[20] Adopted in 1961.

Section 2.

The Congress shall have power to enforce this article by appropriate legislation.

[Article XXIV][21]

Section 1.

The right of citizens of the United States to vote in any primary or other election for President or Vice President, for electors for President or Vice President, or for Senator or Representative in Congress, shall not be denied or abridged by the United States or any state by reason of failure to pay any poll tax or other tax.

Section 2.

The Congress shall have the power to enforce this article by appropriate legislation.

[Article XXV][22]

Section 1.

In case of the removal of the President from office or of his death or resignation, the Vice President shall become President.

Section 2.

Whenever there is a vacancy in the office of the Vice President, the President shall nominate a Vice President who shall take office upon confirmation by a majority vote of both Houses of Congress.

Section 3.

Whenever the President transmits to the President Pro Tempore of the Senate and the Speaker of the House of Representatives his written declaration that he is unable to discharge the powers and duties of his office, and until he transmits to them a written declaration to the contrary, such powers and duties shall be discharged by the Vice President as Acting President.

Section 4.

Whenever the Vice President and a majority of either the principal officers of the executive departments or of such other body as Congress may by law provide, transmit to the President Pro Tempore of the Senate and the Speaker of the House of Representatives their written declaration that the President is unable to discharge the powers and duties of his office, the Vice President shall immediately assume the powers and duties of the office as Acting President.

Thereafter, when the President transmits to the President Pro Tempore of the Senate and the Speaker of the House of Representatives his written declaration that no inability exists, he shall resume the powers and duties of his office unless the Vice President and a majority of either the principal officers of the executive departments or of such other body as Congress may by law provide, transmit within four days to the President Pro Tempore of the Senate and the Speaker of the House of Representatives their written declaration that the President is unable to discharge the powers and duties of his office. Thereupon Congress shall decide the issue, assembling within forty-eight hours for that purpose if not in session. If the Congress, within twenty-one days after receipt of the latter written declaration, or, if Congress is not in session, within twenty-one days after Congress is required to assemble, determines by two-thirds vote of both Houses that the President is unable to discharge the powers and duties of his office, the Vice President shall continue to discharge the same as Acting President; otherwise, the President shall resume the powers and duties of his office.

[Article XXVI][23]

Section 1.

The right of citizens of the United States, who are eighteen years of age or older, to vote shall not be denied or abridged by the United States or by any State on account of age.

Section 2.

The Congress shall have power to enforce this article by appropriate legislation.

---

[21] Adopted in 1964.
[22] Adopted in 1967.

---

[23] Adopted in 1971.

Presidential Elections

Year	Candidates	Parties	Popular Vote	Percentage of Popular Vote	Electoral Vote	Percentage of Voter Participation
1789	**GEORGE WASHINGTON (Va.)**★				69	
	John Adams				34	
	Others				35	
1792	**GEORGE WASHINGTON (Va.)**				132	
	John Adams				77	
	George Clinton				50	
	Others				5	
1796	**JOHN ADAMS (Mass.)**	Federalist			71	
	Thomas Jefferson	Democratic-Republican			68	
	Thomas Pinckney	Federalist			59	
	Aaron Burr	Dem.-Rep.			30	
	Others				48	
1800	**THOMAS JEFFERSON (Va.)**	Dem.-Rep.			73	
	Aaron Burr	Dem.-Rep.			73	
	John Adams	Federalist			65	
	C. C. Pinckney	Federalist			64	
	John Jay	Federalist			1	
1804	**THOMAS JEFFERSON (Va.)**	Dem.-Rep.			162	
	C. C. Pinckney	Federalist			14	
1808	**JAMES MADISON (Va.)**	Dem.-Rep.			122	
	C. C. Pinckney	Federalist			47	
	George Clinton	Dem.-Rep.			6	
1812	**JAMES MADISON (Va.)**	Dem.-Rep.			128	
	De Witt Clinton	Federalist			89	
1816	**JAMES MONROE (Va.)**	Dem.-Rep.			183	
	Rufus King	Federalist			34	
1820	**JAMES MONROE (Va.)**	Dem.-Rep.			231	
	John Quincy Adams	Dem.-Rep.			1	
1824	**JOHN Q. ADAMS (Mass.)**	Dem.-Rep.	108,740	30.5	84	26.9
	Andrew Jackson	Dem.-Rep.	153,544	43.1	99	
	William H. Crawford	Dem.-Rep.	46,618	13.1	41	
	Henry Clay	Dem.-Rep.	47,136	13.2	37	
1828	**ANDREW JACKSON (Tenn.)**	Democratic	647,286	56.0	178	57.6
	John Quincy Adams	National Republican	508,064	44.0	83	
1832	**ANDREW JACKSON (Tenn.)**	Democratic	687,502	55.0	219	55.4
	Henry Clay	National Republican	530,189	42.4	49	
	John Floyd	Independent			11	
	William Wirt	Anti-Mason	33, 108	2.6	7	

★ State of residence at time of election.

Year	Candidates	Parties	Popular Vote	Percentage of Popular Vote	Electoral Vote	Percentage of Voter Participation
1836	**MARTIN VAN BUREN (N.Y.)**	Democratic	765,483	50.9	170	57.8
	W. H. Harrison	Whig			73	
	Hugh L. White	Whig	739,795	49.1	26	
	Daniel Webster	Whig			14	
	W. P. Magnum	Independent			11	
1840	**WILLIAM H. HARRISON (Ohio)**	Whig	1,274,624	53.1	234	80.2
	Martin Van Buren	Democratic	1,127,781	46.9	60	
	J. G. Birney	Liberty	7,069		—	
1844	**JAMES K. POLK (Tenn.)**	Democratic	1,338,464	49.6	170	78.9
	Henry Clay	Whig	1,300,097	48.1	105	
	J. G. Birney	Liberty	62,300	2.3	—	
1848	**ZACHARY TAYLOR (La.)**	Whig	1,360,967	47.4	163	72.7
	Lewis Cass	Democratic	1,222,342	42.5	127	
	Martin Van Buren	Free-Soil	291,263	10.1	—	
1852	**FRANKLIN PIERCE (N.H.)**	Democratic	1,601,117	50.9	254	69.6
	Winfield Scott	Whig	1,385,453	44.1	42	
	John P. Hale	Free-Soil	155,825	5.0	—	
1856	**JAMES BUCHANAN (Pa.)**	Democratic	1,832,955	45.3	174	78.9
	John C. Frémont	Republican	1,339,932	33.1	114	
	Millard Fillmore	American	871,731	21.6	8	
1860	**ABRAHAM LINCOLN (Ill.)**	Republican	1,865,593	39.8	180	81.2
	Stephen A. Douglas	Democratic	1,382,713	29.5	12	
	John C. Breckinridge	Democratic	848,356	18.1	72	
	John Bell	Union	592,906	12.6	39	
1864	**ABRAHAM LINCOLN (Ill.)**	Republican	2,213,655	55.0	212	73.8
	George B. McClellan	Democratic	1,805,237	45.0	21	
1868	**ULYSSES S. GRANT (Ill.)**	Republican	3,012,833	52.7	214	78.1
	Horatio Seymour	Democratic	2,703,249	47.3	80	
1872	**ULYSSES S. GRANT (Ill.)**	Republican	3,597,132	55.6	286	71.3
	Horace Greeley	Democratic; Liberal Republican	2,834,125	43.9	66	
1876	**RUTHERFORD B. HAYES (Ohio)**	Republican	4,036,298	48.0	185	81.8
	Samuel J. Tilden	Democratic	4,300,590	51.0	184	
1880	**JAMES A. GARFIELD (Ohio)**	Republican	4,454,416	48.5	214	79.4
	Winfield S. Hancock	Democratic	4,444,952	48.1	155	
1884	**GROVER CLEVELAND (N.Y.)**	Democratic	4,874,986	48.5	219	77.5
	James G. Blaine	Republican	4,851,981	48.2	182	
1888	**BENJAMIN HARRISON (Ind.)**	Republican	5,439,853	47.9	233	79.3
	Grover Cleveland	Democratic	5,540,309	48.6	168	
1892	**GROVER CLEVELAND (N.Y.)**	Democratic	5,556,918	46.1	277	74.7
	Benjamin Harrison	Republican	5,176,108	43.0	145	
	James B. Weaver	People's	1,041,028	8.5	22	
1896	**WILLIAM McKINLEY (Ohio)**	Republican	7,104,779	51.1	271	79.3
	William J. Bryan	Democratic-People's	6,502,925	47.7	176	
1900	**WILLIAM McKINLEY (Ohio)**	Republican	7,207,923	51.7	292	73.2
	William J. Bryan	Dem.-Populist	6,358,133	45.5	155	
1904	**THEODORE ROOSEVELT (N.Y.)**	Republican	7,623,486	57.9	336	65.2
	Alton B. Parker	Democratic	5,077,911	37.6	140	
	Eugene V. Debs	Socialist	402,283	3.0	—	

Year	Candidates	Parties	Popular Vote	Percentage of Popular Vote	Electoral Vote	Percentage of Voter Participation
1908	**WILLIAM H. TAFT (Ohio)**	Republican	7,678,908	51.6	321	65.4
	William J. Bryan	Democratic	6,409,104	43.1	162	
	Eugene V. Debs	Socialist	420,793	2.8	—	
1912	**WOODROW WILSON (N.J.)**	Democratic	6,293,454	41.9	435	58.8
	Theodore Roosevelt	Progressive	4,119,538	27.4	88	
	William H. Taft	Republican	3,484,980	23.2	8	
	Eugene V. Debs	Socialist	900,672	6.0	—	
1916	**WOODROW WILSON (N.J.)**	Democratic	9,129,606	49.4	277	61.6
	Charles E. Hughes	Republican	8,538,221	46.2	254	
	A. L. Benson	Socialist	585,113	3.2	—	
1920	**WARREN G. HARDING (Ohio)**	Republican	16,152,200	60.4	404	49.2
	James M. Cox	Democratic	9,147,353	34.2	127	
	Eugene V. Debs	Socialist	919,799	3.4	—	
1924	**CALVIN COOLIDGE (Mass.)**	Republican	15,725,016	54.0	382	48.9
	John W. Davis	Democratic	8,386,503	28.8	136	
	Robert M. LaFollette	Progressive	4,822,856	16.6	13	
1928	**HERBERT HOOVER (Calif.)**	Republican	21,391,381	58.2	444	56.9
	Alfred E. Smith	Democratic	15,016,443	40.9	87	
	Norman Thomas	Socialist	267,835	0.7	—	
1932	**FRANKLIN D. ROOSEVELT (N.Y.)**	Democratic	22,821,857	57.4	472	56.9
	Herbert Hoover	Republican	15,761,841	39.7	59	
	Norman Thomas	Socialist	881,951	2.2	—	
1936	**FRANKLIN D. ROOSEVELT (N.Y.)**	Democratic	27,751,597	60.8	523	61.0
	Alfred M. Landon	Republican	16,679,583	36.5	8	
	William Lemke	Union	882,479	1.9	—	
1940	**FRANKLIN D. ROOSEVELT (N.Y.)**	Democratic	27,244,160	54.8	449	62.5
	Wendell L. Willkie	Republican	22,305,198	44.8	82	
1944	**FRANKLIN D. ROOSEVELT (N.Y.)**	Democratic	25,602,504	53.5	432	55.9
	Thomas E. Dewey	Republican	22,006,285	46.0	99	
1948	**HARRY S TRUMAN (Mo.)**	Democratic	24,105,695	49.5	304	53.0
	Thomas E. Dewey	Republican	21,969,170	45.1	189	
	J. Strom Thurmond	State-Rights Democratic	1,169,021	2.4	38	
	Henry A. Wallace	Progressive	1,156,103	2.4	—	
1952	**DWIGHT D. EISENHOWER (N.Y.)**	Republican	33,936,252	55.1	442	63.3
	Adlai E. Stevenson	Democratic	27,314,992	44.4	89	
1956	**DWIGHT D. EISENHOWER (N.Y.)**	Republican	35,575,420	57.6	457	60.6
	Adlai E. Stevenson	Democratic	26,033,066	42.1	73	
	Other	—	—	—	1	
1960	**JOHN F. KENNEDY (Mass.)**	Democratic	34,227,096	49.9	303	62.8
	Richard M. Nixon	Republican	34,108,546	49.6	219	
	Other	—	—	—	15	
1964	**LYNDON B. JOHNSON (Tex.)**	Democratic	43,126,506	61.1	486	61.7
	Barry M. Goldwater	Republican	27,176,799	38.5	52	

Year	Candidates	Parties	Popular Vote	Percentage of Popular Vote	Electoral Vote	Percentage of Voter Participation
1968	**RICHARD M. NIXON (N.Y.)**	Republican	31,770,237	43.4	301	60.6
	Hubert H. Humphrey	Democratic	31,270,533	42.7	191	
	George Wallace	American Indep.	9,906,141	13.5	46	
1972	**RICHARD M. NIXON (N.Y.)**	Republican	47,169,911	60.7	520	55.2
	George S. McGovern	Democratic	29,170,383	37.5	17	
	Other	—	—		1	
1976	**JIMMY CARTER (Ga.)**	Democratic	40,828,587	50.0	297	53.5
	Gerald R. Ford	Republican	39,147,613	47.9	241	
	Other	—	1,575,459	2.1	—	
1980	**RONALD REAGAN (Calif.)**	Republican	43,901,812	50.7	489	52.6
	Jimmy Carter	Democratic	35,483,820	41.0	49	
	John B. Anderson	Independent	5,719,722	6.6	—	
	Ed Clark	Libertarian	921,188	1.1	—	
1984	**RONALD REAGAN (Calif.)**	Republican	54,455,075	59.0	525	53.3
	Walter Mondale	Democratic	37,577,185	41.0	13	
1988	**GEORGE BUSH (Texas)**	Republican	47,946,422	54.0	426	50.2
	Michael S. Dukakis	Democratic	41,016,429	46.0	112	

Vice Presidents and Cabinet Members

The Washington Administration (1789–1797)

Vice President	John Adams	1789–1797
Secretary of State	Thomas Jefferson	1789–1793
	Edmund Randolph	1794–1795
	Timothy Pickering	1795–1797
Secretary of Treasury	Alexander Hamilton	1789–1795
	Oliver Wolcott	1795–1797
Secretary of War	Henry Knox	1789–1794
	Timothy Pickering	1795–1796
	James McHenry	1796–1797
Attorney General	Edmund Randolph	1789–1793
	William Bradford	1794–1795
	Charles Lee	1795–1797
Postmaster General	Samuel Osgood	1789–1791
	Timothy Pickering	1791–1794
	Joseph Habersham	1795–1797

The John Adams Administration (1797–1801)

Vice President	Thomas Jefferson	1797–1801
Secretary of State	Timothy Pickering	1797–1800
	John Marshall	1800–1801
Secretary of Treasury	Oliver Wolcott	1797–1800
	Samuel Dexter	1800–1801
Secretary of War	James McHenry	1797–1800
	Samuel Dexter	1800–1801
Attorney General	Charles Lee	1797–1801
Postmaster General	Joseph Habersham	1797–1801
Secretary of Navy	Benjamin Stoddert	1798–1801

The Jefferson Administration (1801–1809)

Vice President	Aaron Burr	1801–1805
	George Clinton	1805–1809
Secretary of State	James Madison	1801–1809
Secretary of Treasury	Samuel Dexter	1801
	Albert Gallatin	1801–1809
Secretary of War	Henry Dearborn	1801–1809
Attorney General	Levi Lincoln	1801–1805
	Robert Smith	1805
	John Breckinridge	1805–1806
	Caesar Rodney	1807–1809
Postmaster General	Joseph Habersham	1801
	Gideon Granger	1801–1809
Secretary of Navy	Robert Smith	1801–1809

The Madison Administration (1809–1817)

Vice President	George Clinton	1809–1813
	Elbridge Gerry	1813–1817
Secretary of State	Robert Smith	1809–1811
	James Monroe	1811–1817
Secretary of Treasury	Albert Gallatin	1809–1813
	George Campbell	1814
	Alexander Dallas	1814–1816
	William Crawford	1816–1817
Secretary of War	William Eustis	1809–1812
	John Armstrong	1813–1814
	James Monroe	1814–1815
	William Crawford	1815–1817
Attorney General	Caesar Rodney	1809–1811
	William Pinkney	1811–1814
	Richard Rush	1814–1817
Postmaster General	Gideon Granger	1809–1814
	Return Meigs	1814–1817
Secretary of Navy	Paul Hamilton	1809–1813
	William Jones	1813–1814
	Benjamin Crowninshield	1814–1817

The Monroe Administration (1817–1825)

Vice President	Daniel Tompkins	1817–1825
Secretary of State	John Quincy Adams	1817–1825
Secretary of Treasury	William Crawford	1817–1825
Secretary of War	George Graham	1817
	John C. Calhoun	1817–1825
Attorney General	Richard Rush	1817
	William Wirt	1817–1825
Postmaster General	Return Meigs	1817–1823
	John McLean	1823–1825
Secretary of Navy	Benjamin Crowninshield	1817–1818
	Smith Thompson	1818–1823
	Samuel Southard	1823–1825

The John Quincy Adams Administration (1825–1829)

Vice President	John C. Calhoun	1825–1829
Secretary of State	Henry Clay	1825–1829
Secretary of Treasury	Richard Rush	1825–1829
Secretary of War	James Barbour	1825–1828
	Peter Porter	1828–1829
Attorney General	William Wirt	1825–1829
Postmaster General	John McLean	1825–1829
Secretary of Navy	Samuel Southard	1825–1829

The Jackson Administration (1829–1837)

Vice President	John C. Calhoun	1829–1833
	Martin Van Buren	1833–1837
Secretary of State	Martin Van Buren	1829–1831
	Edward Livingston	1831–1833
	Louis McLane	1833–1834
	John Forsyth	1834–1837
Secretary of Treasury	Samuel Ingham	1829–1831
	Louis McLane	1831–1833
	William Duane	1833
	Roger B. Taney	1833–1834
	Levi Woodbury	1834–1837
Secretary of War	John H. Eaton	1829–1831
	Lewis Cass	1831–1837
	Benjamin Butler	1837
Attorney General	John M. Berrien	1829–1831
	Roger B. Taney	1831–1833
	Benjamin Butler	1833–1837
Postmaster General	William Barry	1829–1835
	Amos Kendall	1835–1837
Secretary of Navy	John Branch	1829–1831
	Levi Woodbury	1831–1834
	Mahlon Dickerson	1834–1837

The Van Buren Administration (1837–1841)

Vice President	Richard M. Johnson	1837–1841
Secretary of State	John Forsyth	1837–1841
Secretary of Treasury	Levi Woodbury	1837–1841
Secretary of War	Joel Poinsett	1837–1841
Attorney General	Benjamin Butler	1837–1838
	Felix Grundy	1838–1840
	Henry D. Gilpin	1840–1841
Postmaster General	Amos Kendall	1837–1840
	John M. Niles	1840–1841
Secretary of Navy	Mahlon Dickerson	1837–1838
	James Paulding	1838–1841

The William Harrison Administration (1841)

Vice President	John Tyler	1841
Secretary of State	Daniel Webster	1841
Secretary of Treasury	Thomas Ewing	1841
Secretary of War	John Bell	1841
Attorney General	John J. Crittenden	1841
Postmaster General	Francis Granger	1841
Secretary of Navy	George Badger	1841

The Tyler Administration (1841–1845)

Vice President	None	
Secretary of State	Daniel Webster	1841–1843
	Hugh S. Legaré	1843
	Abel P. Upshur	1843–1844
	John C. Calhoun	1844–1845
Secretary of Treasury	Thomas Ewing	1841
	Walter Forward	1841–1843
	John C. Spencer	1843–1844
	George Bibb	1844–1845
Secretary of War	John Bell	1841
	John C. Spencer	1841–1843
	James M. Porter	1843–1844
	William Wilkins	1844–1845
Attorney General	John J. Crittenden	1841
	Hugh S. Legaré	1841–1843
	John Nelson	1843–1845
Postmaster General	Francis Granger	1841
	Charles Wickliffe	1841
Secretary of Navy	George Badger	1841
	Abel P. Upshur	1841
	David Henshaw	1843–1844
	Thomas Gilmer	1844
	John Y. Mason	1844–1845

The Polk Administration (1845–1849)

Vice President	George M. Dallas	1845–1849
Secretary of State	James Buchanan	1845–1849
Secretary of Treasury	Robert J. Walker	1845–1849
Secretary of War	William L. Marcy	1845–1849
Attorney General	John Y. Mason	1845–1846
	Nathan Clifford	1846–1848
	Isaac Toucey	1848–1849
Postmaster General	Cave Johnson	1845–1849
Secretary of Navy	George Bancroft	1845–1846
	John Y. Mason	1846–1849

The Taylor Administration (1849–1850)

Vice President	Millard Fillmore	1849–1850
Secretary of State	John M. Clayton	1849–1850
Secretary of Treasury	William Meredith	1849–1850
Secretary of War	George Crawford	1849–1850
Attorney General	Reverdy Johnson	1849–1850
Postmaster General	Jacob Collamer	1849–1850
Secretary of Navy	William Preston	1849–1850
Secretary of Interior	Thomas Ewing	1849–1850

The Fillmore Administration (1850–1853)

Vice President	None	
Secretary of State	Daniel Webster	1850–1852
	Edward Everett	1852–1853
Secretary of Treasury	Thomas Corwin	1850–1853

The Fillmore Administration (1850–1853) *continued*

Secretary of War	Charles Conrad	1850–1853
Attorney General	John J. Crittenden	1850–1853
Postmaster General	Nathan Hall	1850–1852
	Sam D. Hubbard	1852–1853
Secretary of Navy	William A. Graham	1850–1852
	John P. Kennedy	1852–1853
Secretary of Interior	Thomas McKennan	1850
	Alexander Stuart	1850–1853

The Pierce Administration (1853–1857)

Vice President	William R. King	1853–1857
Secretary of State	William L. Marcy	1853–1857
Secretary of Treasury	James Guthrie	1853–1857
Secretary of War	Jefferson Davis	1853–1857
Attorney General	Caleb Cushing	1853–1857
Postmaster General	James Campbell	1853–1857
Secretary of Navy	James C. Dobbin	1853–1857
Secretary of Interior	Robert McClelland	1853–1857

The Buchanan Administration (1857–1861)

Vice President	John C. Breckinridge	1857–1861
Secretary of State	Lewis Cass	1857–1860
	Jeremiah S. Black	1860–1861
Secretary of Treasury	Howell Cobb	1857–1860
	Philip Thomas	1860–1861
	John A. Dix	1861
Secretary of War	John B. Floyd	1857–1861
	Joseph Holt	1861
Attorney General	Jeremiah S. Black	1857–1860
	Edwin M. Stanton	1860–1861
Postmaster General	Aaron V. Brown	1857–1859
	Joseph Holt	1859–1861
	Horatio King	1861
Secretary of Navy	Isaac Toucey	1857–1861
Secretary of Interior	Jacob Thompson	1857–1861

The Lincoln Administration (1861–1865)

Vice President	Hannibal Hamlin	1861–1865
	Andrew Johnson	1865
Secretary of State	William H. Seward	1861–1865
Secretary of Treasury	Samuel P. Chase	1861–1864
	William P. Fessenden	1864–1865
	Hugh McCulloch	1865
Secretary of War	Simon Cameron	1861–1862
	Edwin M. Stanton	1862–1865
Attorney General	Edward Bates	1861–1864
	James Speed	1864–1865
Postmaster General	Horatio King	1861
	Montgomery Blair	1861–1864
	William Dennison	1864–1865
Secretary of Navy	Gideon Welles	1861–1865
Secretary of Interior	Caleb B. Smith	1861–1863
	John P. Usher	1863–1865

The Andrew Johnson Administration (1865–1869)

Vice President	None	
Secretary of State	William H. Seward	1865–1869
Secretary of Treasury	Hugh McCulloch	1865–1869
Secretary of War	Edwin M. Stanton	1865–1867
	Ulysses S. Grant	1867–1868
	Lorenzo Thomas	1868
	John M. Schofield	1868–1869
Attorney General	James Speed	1865–1866
	Henry Stanbery	1866–1868
	William M. Evarts	1868–1869
Postmaster General	William Dennison	1865–1866
	Alexander Randall	1866–1869
Secretary of Navy	Gideon Welles	1865–1869
Secretary of Interior	John P. Usher	1865
	James Harlan	1865–1866
	Orville H. Browning	1866–1869

The Grant Administration (1869–1877)

Vice President	Schuyler Colfax	1869–1873
	Henry Wilson	1873–1877
Secretary of State	Elihu B. Washburne	1869
	Hamilton Fish	1869–1877
Secretary of Treasury	George S. Boutwell	1869–1873
	William Richardson	1873–1874
	Benjamin Bristow	1874–1876
	Lot M. Morrill	1876–1877
Secretary of War	John A. Rawlins	1869
	William T. Sherman	1869
	William W. Belknap	1869–1876
	Alphonso Taft	1876
	James D. Cameron	1876–1877
Attorney General	Ebenezer Hoar	1869–1870
	Amos T. Ackerman	1870–1871
	G. H. Williams	1871–1875
	Edwards Pierrepont	1875–1876
	Alphonso Taft	1876–1877
Postmaster General	John A. J. Creswell	1869–1874
	James W. Marshall	1874
	Marshall Jewell	1874–1876
	James N. Tyner	1876–1877
Secretary of Navy	Adolph E. Borie	1869
	George M. Robeson	1869–1877
Secretary of Interior	Jacob D. Cox	1969–1870
	Columbus Delano	1870–1875
	Zachariah Chandler	1875–1877

The Hayes Administration (1877–1881)

Vice President	William A. Wheeler	1877–1881
Secretary of State	William M. Evarts	1877–1881
Secretary of Treasury	John Sherman	1877–1881
Secretary of War	George W. McCrary	1877–1879
	Alex Ramsey	1879–1881
Attorney General	Charles Devens	1877–1881
Postmaster General	David M. Key	1877–1880
	Horace Maynard	1880–1881
Secretary of Navy	Richard W. Thompson	1877–1880
	Nathan Goff, Jr.	1881
Secretary of Interior	Carl Schurz	1877–1881

The Garfield Administration (1881)

Vice President	Chester A. Arthur	1881
Secretary of State	James G. Blaine	1881
Secretary of Treasury	William Windom	1881
Secretary of War	Robert T. Lincoln	1881
Attorney General	Wayne MacVeagh	1881
Postmaster General	Thomas L. James	1881
Secretary of Navy	William H. Hunt	1881
Secretary of Interior	Samuel J. Kirkwood	1881

The Arthur Administration (1881–1885)

Vice President	None	
Secretary of State	F. T. Frelinghuysen	1881–1885
Secretary of Treasury	Charles J. Folger	1881–1884
	Walter Q. Gresham	1884
	Hugh McCulloch	1884–1885
Secretary of War	Robert T. Lincoln	1881–1885
Attorney General	Benjamin H. Brewster	1881–1885
Postmaster General	Timothy O. Howe	1881–1883
	Walter Q. Gresham	1883–1884
	Frank Hatton	1884–1885
Secretary of Navy	William H. Hunt	1881–1882
	William E. Chandler	1882–1885
Secretary of Interior	Samuel J. Kirkwood	1881–1882
	Henry M. Teller	1882–1885

The Cleveland Administration (1885–1889)

Vice President	Thomas A. Hendricks	1885–1889
Secretary of State	Thomas F. Bayard	1885–1889
Secretary of Treasury	Daniel Manning	1885–1887
	Charles S. Fairchild	1887–1889
Secretary of War	William C. Endicott	1885–1889
Attorney General	Augustus H. Garland	1885–1889
Postmaster General	William F. Vilas	1885–1888
	Don M. Dickinson	1888–1889
Secretary of Navy	William C. Whitney	1885–1889
Secretary of Interior	Lucius Q. C. Lamar	1885–1888
	William F. Vilas	1888–1889
Secretary of Agriculture	Norman J. Colman	1889

The Benjamin Harrison Administration (1889–1893)

Vice President	Levi P. Morton	1889–1893
Secretary of State	James G. Blaine	1889–1892
	John W. Foster	1892–1893
Secretary of Treasury	William Windom	1889–1891
	Charles Foster	1891–1893
Secretary of War	Redfield Proctor	1889–1891
	Stephen B. Elkins	1891–1893
Attorney General	William H. H. Miller	1889–1891
Postmaster General	John Wanamaker	1889–1893
Secretary of Navy	Benjamin F. Tracy	1889–1893
Secretary of Interior	John W. Noble	1889–1893
Secretary of Agriculture	Jeremiah M. Rusk	1889–1893

The Cleveland Administration (1893–1897)

Vice President	Adlai E. Stevenson	1893–1897
Secretary of State	Walter Q. Gresham	1893–1895
	Richard Olney	1895–1897
Secretary of Treasury	John G. Carlisle	1893–1897
Secretary of War	Daniel S. Lamont	1893–1897
Attorney General	Richard Olney	1893–1895
	James Harmon	1895–1897
Postmaster General	Wilson S. Bissell	1893–1895
	William L. Wilson	1895–1897
Secretary of Navy	Hilary A. Herbert	1893–1897
Secretary of Interior	Hoke Smith	1893–1896
	David R. Francis	1896–1897
Secretary of Agriculture	Julius S. Morton	1893–1897

The McKinley Administration (1897–1901)

Vice President	Garret A. Hobart	1897–1901
	Theodore Roosevelt	1901
Secretary of State	John Sherman	1897–1898
	William R. Day	1898
	John Hay	1898–1901
Secretary of Treasury	Lyman J. Gage	1897–1901
Secretary of War	Russell A. Alger	1897–1899
	Elihu Root	1899–1901
Attorney General	Joseph McKenna	1897–1898
	John W. Griggs	1898–1901
	Philander C. Knox	1901

The McKinley Administration (1897–1901) *continued*

Postmaster General	James A. Gary	1897–1898
	Charles E. Smith	1898–1901
Secretary of Navy	John D. Long	1897–1901
Secretary of Interior	Cornelius N. Bliss	1897–1899
	Ethan A. Hitchcock	1899–1901
Secretary of Agriculture	James Wilson	1897–1901

The Theodore Roosevelt Administration (1901–1909)

Vice President	Charles Fairbanks	1905–1909
Secretary of State	John Hay	1901–1905
	Elihu Root	1905–1909
	Robert Bacon	1909
Secretary of Treasury	Lyman J. Gage	1901–1902
	Leslie M. Shaw	1902–1907
	George B. Cortelyou	1907–1909
Secretary of War	Elihu Root	1901–1904
	William H. Taft	1904–1908
	Luke E. Wright	1908–1909
Attorney General	Philander C. Knox	1901–1904
	William H. Moody	1904–1906
	Charles J. Bonaparte	1906–1909
Postmaster General	Charles E. Smith	1901–1902
	Henry C. Payne	1902–1904
	Robert J. Wynne	1904–1905
	George B. Cortelyou	1905–1907
	George von L. Meyer	1907–1909
Secretary of Navy	John D. Long	1901–1902
	William H. Moody	1902–1904
	Paul Morton	1904–1905
	Charles J. Bonaparte	1905–1906
	Victor H. Metcalf	1906–1908
	Truman H. Newberry	1908–1909
Secretary of Interior	Ethan A. Hitchcock	1901–1907
	James R. Garfield	1907–1909
Secretary of Agriculture	James Wilson	1901–1909
Secretary of Labor and Commerce	George B. Cortelyou	1903–1904
	Victor H. Metcalf	1904–1906
	Oscar S. Straus	1906–1909
	Charles Nagel	1909

The Taft Administration (1909–1913)

Vice President	James S. Sherman	1909–1913
Secretary of State	Philander C. Knox	1909–1913
Secretary of Treasury	Franklin MacVeagh	1909–1913
Secretary of War	Jacob M. Dickinson	1909–1911
	Henry L. Stimson	1911–1913
Attorney General	George W. Wickersham	1909–1913
Postmaster General	Frank H. Hitchcock	1909–1913
Secretary of Navy	George von L. Meyer	1909–1913
Secretary of Interior	Richard A. Ballinger	1909–1911
	Walter L. Fisher	1911–1913
Secretary of Agriculture	James Wilson	1909–1913
Secretary of Labor and Commerce	Charles Nagel	1909–1913

The Wilson Administration (1913–1921)

Vice President	Thomas R. Marshall	1913–1921
Secretary of State	William J. Bryan	1913–1915
	Robert Lansing	1915–1920
	Bainbridge Colby	1920–1921
Secretary of Treasury	William G. McAdoo	1913–1918
	Carter Glass	1918–1920
	David F. Houston	1920–1921
Secretary of War	Lindley M. Garrison	1913–1916
	Newton D. Baker	1916–1921
Attorney General	James C. McReynolds	1913–1914
	Thomas W. Gregory	1914–1919
	A. Mitchell Palmer	1919–1921
Postmaster General	Albert S. Burleson	1913–1921
Secretary of Navy	Josephus Daniels	1913–1921
Secretary of Interior	Franklin K. Lane	1913–1920
	John B. Payne	1920–1921
Secretary of Agriculture	David F. Houston	1913–1920
	Edwin T. Meredith	1920–1921
Secretary of Commerce	William C. Redfield	1913–1919
	Joshua W. Alexander	1919–1921
Secretary of Labor	William B. Wilson	1913–1921

The Harding Administration (1921–1923)

Vice President	Calvin Coolidge	1921–1923
Secretary of State	Charles E. Hughes	1921–1923
Secretary of Treasury	Andrew Mellon	1921–1923
Secretary of War	John W. Weeks	1921–1923
Attorney General	Harry M. Daugherty	1921–1923
Postmaster General	Will H. Hays	1921–1922
	Hubert Work	1922–1923
	Harry S. New	1923
Secretary of Navy	Edwin Denby	1921–1923
Secretary of Interior	Albert B. Fall	1921–1923
	Hubert Work	1923
Secretary of Agriculture	Henry C. Wallace	1921–1923
Secretary of Commerce	Herbert C. Hoover	1921–1923
Secretary of Labor	James J. Davis	1921–1923

The Coolidge Administration (1923–1929)

Vice President	Charles G. Dawes	1925–1929
Secretary of State	Charles E. Hughes	1923–1925
	Frank B. Kellogg	1925–1929

Secretary of Treasury	Andrew Mellon	1923–1929
Secretary of War	John W. Weeks	1923–1925
	Dwight F. Davis	1925–1929
Attorney General	Henry M. Daugherty	1923–1924
	Harlan F. Stone	1924–1925
	John G. Sargent	1925–1929
Postmaster General	Harry S. New	1923–1929
Secretary of Navy	Edwin Derby	1923–1924
	Curtis D. Wilbur	1924–1929
Secretary of Interior	Hubert Work	1923–1928
	Roy O. West	1928–1929
Secretary of Agriculture	Henry C. Wallace	1923–1924
	Howard M. Gore	1924–1925
	William M. Jardine	1925–1929
Secretary of Commerce	Herbert C. Hoover	1923–1928
	William F. Whiting	1928–1929
Secretary of Labor	James J. Davis	1923–1929

The Hoover Administration (1929–1933)

Vice President	Charles Curtis	1929–1933
Secretary of State	Henry L. Stimson	1929–1933
Secretary of Treasury	Andrew Mellon	1929–1932
	Ogden L. Mills	1932–1933
Secretary of War	James W. Good	1929
	Patrick J. Hurley	1929–1933
Attorney General	William D. Mitchell	1929–1933
Postmaster General	Walter F. Brown	1929–1933
Secretary of Navy	Charles F. Adams	1929–1933
Secretary of Interior	Ray L. Wilbur	1929–1933
Secretary of Agriculture	Arthur M. Hyde	1929–1933
Secretary of Commerce	Robert P. Lamont	1929–1932
	Roy D. Chapin	1932–1933
Secretary of Labor	James J. Davis	1929–1930
	William N. Doak	1930–1933

The Franklin D. Roosevelt Administration (1933–1945)

Vice President	John Nance Garner	1933–1941
	Henry A. Wallace	1941–1945
	Harry S. Truman	1945
Secretary of State	Cordell Hull	1933–1944
	Edward R. Stettinius, Jr.	1944–1945
Secretary of Treasury	William H. Woodin	1933–1934
	Henry Morgenthau, Jr.	1934–1945
Secretary of War	George H. Dern	1933–1936
	Henry A. Woodring	1936–1940
	Henry L. Stimson	1940–1945
Attorney General	Homer S. Cummings	1933–1939
	Frank Murphy	1939–1940
	Robert H. Jackson	1940–1941

Attorney General	Francis Biddle	1941–1945
Postmaster General	James A. Farley	1933–1940
	Frank C. Walker	1940–1945
Secretary of Navy	Claude A. Swanson	1933–1940
	Charles Edison	1940
	Frank Knox	1940–1944
	James V. Forrestal	1944–1945
Secretary Interior	Harold L. Ickes	1933–1945
Secretary of Agriculture	Henry A. Wallace	1933–1940
	Claude R. Wickard	1940–1945
Secretary of Commerce	Daniel C. Roper	1933–1939
	Harry L. Hopkins	1939–1940
	Jesse Jones	1940–1945
	Henry A. Wallace	1945
Secretary of Labor	Frances Perkins	1933–1945

The Truman Administration (1945–1953)

Vice President	Alben W. Barkley	1949–1953
Secretary of State	Edward R. Stettinius, Jr.	1945
	James F. Byrnes	1945–1947
	George C. Marshall	1947–1949
	Dean G. Acheson	1949–1953
Secretary of Treasury	Fred M. Vinson	1945–1946
	John W. Snyder	1946–1953
Secretary of War	Robert P. Patterson	1945–1947
	Kenneth C. Royall	1947
Attorney General	Tom C. Clark	1945–1949
	J. Howard McGrath	1949–1952
	James P. McGranery	1952–1953
Postmaster General	Frank C. Walker	1945
	Robert E. Hannegan	1945–1947
	Jesse M. Donaldson	1947–1953
Secretary of Navy	James V. Forrestal	1945–1947
Secretary of Interior	Harold L. Ickes	1945–1946
	Julius A. Krug	1946–1949
	Oscar L. Chapman	1949–1953
Secretary of Agriculture	Clinton P. Anderson	1945–1948
	Charles F. Brannan	1948–1953
Secretary of Commerce	Henry A. Wallace	1945–1946
	W. Averell Harriman	1946–1948
	Charles W. Sawyer	1948–1953
Secretary of Labor	Lewis B. Schwellenbach	1945–1948
	Maurice J. Tobin	1948–1953
Secretary of Defense	James V. Forrestal	1947–1949
	Louis A. Johnson	1949–1950
	George C. Marshall	1950–1951
	Robert A. Lovett	1951–1953

The Eisenhower Administration (1953–1961)

Vice President	Richard M. Nixon	1953–1961
Secretary of State	John Foster Dulles	1953–1959
	Christian A. Herter	1959–1961
Secretary of Treasury	George M. Humphrey	1953–1957
	Robert B. Anderson	1957–1961

The Eisenhower Administration (1953–1961)
continued

Attorney General	Herbert Brownell, Jr.	1953–1958
	William P. Rogers	1958–1961
Postmaster General	Arthur E. Summerfield	1953–1961
Secretary of Interior	Douglas McKay	1953–1956
	Fred A. Seaton	1956–1961
Secretary of Agriculture	Ezra T. Benson	1953–1961
Secretary of Commerce	Sinclair Weeks	1953–1958
	Lewis L. Strauss	1958–1959
	Frederick H. Mueller	1959–1961
Secretary of Labor	Martin P. Durkin	1953
	James P. Mitchell	1953–1961
Secretary of Defense	Charles E. Wilson	1953–1957
	Neil H. McElroy	1957–1959
	Thomas S. Gates Jr.	1959–1961
Secretary of Health, Education, and Welfare	Oveta Culp Hobby	1953–1955
	Marion B. Folsom	1955–1958
	Arthur S. Flemming	1958–1961

The Kennedy Administration (1961–1963)

Vice President	Lyndon B. Johnson	1961–1963
Secretary of State	Dean Rusk	1961–1963
Secretary of Treasury	C. Douglas Dillon	1961–1963
Attorney General	Robert F. Kennedy	1961–1963
Postmaster General	J. Edward Day	1961–1963
	John A. Gronouski	1963
Secretary of Interior	Stewart L. Udall	1961–1963
Secretary of Agriculture	Orville L. Freeman	1961–1963
Secretary of Commerce	Luther H. Hodges	1961–1963
Secretary of Labor	Arthur J. Goldberg	1961–1962
	W. Willard Wirtz	1962–1963
Secretary of Defense	Robert S. McNamara	1961–1963
Secretary of Health, Education, and Welfare	Abraham A. Ribicoff	1961–1962
	Anthony J. Celebrezze	1962–1963

The Lyndon Johnson Administration (1963–1969)

Vice President	Hubert H. Humphrey	1965–1969
Secretary of State	Dean Rusk	1963–1969
Secretary of Treasury	C. Douglas Dillon	1963–1965
	Henry H. Fowler	1965–1969
Attorney General	Robert F. Kennedy	1963–1964
	Nicholas Katzenbach	1965–1966
	Ramsey Clark	1967–1969
Postmaster General	John A. Gronouski	1963–1965
	Lawrence F. O'Brien	1965–1968
	Marvin Watson	1968–1969
Secretary of Interior	Stewart L. Udall	1963–1969
Secretary of Agriculture	Orville L. Freeman	1963–1969
Secretary of Commerce	Luther H. Hodges	1963–1964
	John T. Connor	1964–1967
	Alexander B. Trowbridge	1967–1968
	Cyrus R. Smith	1968–1969
Secretary of Labor	W. Willard Wirtz	1963–1969
Secretray of Defense	Robert F. McNamara	1963–1968
	Clark Clifford	1968–1969
Secretary of Health, Education, and Welfare	Anthony J. Celebrezze	1963–1965
	John W. Gardner	1965–1968
	Wilbur J. Cohen	1968–1969
Secretary of Housing and Urban Development	Robert C. Weaver	1966–1969
	Robert C. Wood	1969
Secretary of Transportation	Alan S. Boyd	1967–1969

The Nixon Administration (1969–1974)

Vice President	Spiro T. Agnew	1969–1973
	Gerald R. Ford	1973–1974
Secretary of State	William P. Rogers	1969–1973
	Henry A. Kissinger	1973–1974
Secretary of Treasury	David M. Kennedy	1969–1970
	John B. Connally	1971–1972
	George P. Shultz	1972–1974
	William E. Simon	1974
Attorney General	John N. Mitchell	1969–1972
	Richard G. Kleindienst	1972–1973
	Elliot L. Richardson	1973
	William B. Saxbe	1973–1974
Postmaster General	Winton M. Blount	1969–1971
Secretary of Interior	Walter J. Hickel	1969–1970
	Rogers Morton	1971–1974
Secretary of Agriculture	Clifford M. Hardin	1969–1971
	Earl L. Butz	1971–1974
Secretary of Commerce	Maurice H. Stans	1969–1972
	Peter G. Peterson	1972–1973
	Frederick B. Dent	1973–1974
Secretary of Labor	George P. Shultz	1969–1970
	James D. Hodgson	1970–1973
	Peter J. Brennan	1973–1974
Secretary of Defense	Melvin R. Laird	1969–1973
	Elliot L. Richardson	1973
	James R. Schlesinger	1973–1974
Secretary of Health, Education, and Welfare	Robert H. Finch	1969–1970
	Elliot L. Richardson	1970–1973
	Caspar W. Weinberger	1973–1974

Secretary of Housing and Urban Development	George Romney James T. Lynn	1969–1973 1973–1974
Secretary of Transportation	John A. Volpe Claude S. Brinegar	1969–1973 1973–1974

The Ford Administration (1974–1977)

Vice President	Nelson A. Rockefeller	1974–1977
Secretary of State	Henry A. Kissinger	1974–1977
Secretary of Treasury	William E. Simon	1974–1977
Attorney General	William Saxbe Edward Levi	1974–1975 1975–1977
Secretary of Interior	Rogers Morton Stanley K. Hathaway Thomas Kleppe	1974–1975 1975 1975–1977
Secretary of Agriculture	Earl L. Butz John A. Knebel	1974–1976 1976–1977
Secretary of Commerce	Frederick B. Dent Rogers Morton Elliot L. Richardson	1974–1975 1975–1976 1976–1977
Secretary of Labor	Peter J. Brennan John T. Dunlop W. J. Usery	1974–1975 1975–1976 1976–1977
Secretary of Defense	James R. Schlesinger Donald Rumsfeld	1974–1975 1975–1977
Secretary of Health, Education, and Welfare	Caspar Weinberger Forrest D. Mathews	1974–1975 1975–1977
Secretary of Housing and Urban Development	James T. Lynn Carla A. Hills	1974–1975 1975–1977
Secretary of Transportation	Claude Brinegar William T. Coleman	1974–1975 1975–1977

The Carter Administration (1977–1981)

Vice President	Walter F. Mondale	1977–1981
Secretary of State	Cyrus R. Vance Edmund Muskie	1977–1980 1980–1981
Secretary of Treasury	W. Michael Blumenthal G. William Miller	1977–1979 1979–1981
Attorney General	Griffin Bell Benjamin R. Civiletti	1977–1979 1979–1981
Secretary of Interior	Cecil D. Andrus	1977–1981
Secretary of Agriculture	Robert Bergland	1977–1981
Secretary of Commerce	Juanita M. Kreps Philip M. Klutznick	1977–1979 1979–1981
Secretary of Labor	F. Ray Marshall	1977–1981
Secretary of Defense	Harold Brown	1977–1981
Secretary of Health, Education, and Welfare	Joseph A. Califano Patricia R. Harris	1977–1979 1979
Secretary of Health and Human Services	Patricia R. Harris	1979–1981
Secretary of Education	Shirley M. Hufstedler	1979–1981
Secretary of Housing and Urban Development	Patricia R. Harris Moon Landrieu	1977–1979 1979–1981
Secretary of Transportation	Brock Adams Neil E. Goldschmidt	1977–1979 1979–1981
Secretary of Energy	James R. Schlesinger Charles W. Duncan	1977–1979 1979–1981

The Reagan Administration (1981–1989)

Vice President	George Bush	1981–1989
Secretary of State	Alexander M. Haig George P. Shultz	1981–1982 1982–1989
Secretary of Treasury	Donald Regan James A. Baker III Nicholas F. Brady	1981–1985 1985–1988 1988–1989
Attorney General	William F. Smith Edwin A. Meese III Richard Thornburgh	1981–1985 1985–1988 1988–1989
Secretary of Interior	James Watt William P. Clark, Jr. Donald P. Hodel	1981–1983 1983–1985 1985–1989
Secretary of Agriculture	John Block Richard E. Lyng	1981–1986 1986–1989
Secretary of Commerce	Malcolm Baldrige C. William Verity, Jr.	1981–1987 1987–1989
Secretary of Labor	Raymond Donovan William Brock Ann D. McLaughlin	1981–1985 1985–1987 1987–1989
Secretary of Defense	Caspar Weinberger Frank C. Carlucci	1981–1987 1987–1989
Secretary of Health and Human Services	Richard Schweiker Margaret Heckler Otis R. Bowen	1981–1983 1983–1985 1985–1989
Secretary of Education	Terrel H. Bell William J. Bennett Laura F. Cavazos	1981–1985 1985–1988 1988–1989
Secretary of Housing and Urban Development	Samuel Pierce	1981–1989
Secretary of Transportation	Drew Lewis Elizabeth Dole James H. Burnley	1981–1983 1983–1987 1987–1989
Secretary of Energy	James Edwards Donald P. Hodel John S. Herrington	1981–1982 1982–1985 1984–1989

The Bush Administration (1989–)		
Vice President	J. Danforth Quayle	1989–
Secretary of State	James A. Baker III	1989–
Secretary of Treasury	Nicholas F. Brady	1989–
Attorney General	Richard Thornburgh	1989–
Secretary of Interior	Manuel Lujan	1989–
Secretary of Agriculture	Clayton K. Yeutter	1989–
Secretary of Commerce	Robert A. Mosbacher	1989–
Secretary of Labor	Elizabeth Dole	1989–
Secretary of Defense	Richard B. Cheney	1989–
Secretary of Health and Human Services	Louis W. Sullivan	1989–
Secretary of Education	Laura F. Cavazos	1989–
Secretary of Housing and Urban Development	Jack F. Kemp	1989–
Secretary of Energy	James D. Watkins	1989–
Secretary of Veterans Affairs	Edward J. Derwinski	1989–

Population of the United States, 1790–1988

Year	Population	Percent Increase	Population Per Square Mile	Percent Urban/ Rural	Percent White/ Nonwhite	Median Age
1790	3,929,214		4.5	5.1/94.9	80.7/19.3	NA
1800	5,308,483	35.1	6.1	6.1/93.9	81.1/18.9	NA
1810	7,239,881	36.4	4.3	7.3/92.7	81.0/19.0	NA
1820	9,638,453	33.1	5.5	7.2/92.8	81.6/18.4	16.7
1830	12,866,020	33.5	7.4	8.8/91.2	81.9/18.1	17.2
1840	17,069,453	32.7	9.8	10.8/89.2	83.2/16.8	17.8
1850	23,191,876	35.9	7.9	15.3/84.7	84.3/15.7	18.9
1860	31,443,321	35.6	10.6	19.8/80.2	85.6/14.4	19.4
1870	39,818,449	26.6	13.4	25.7/74.3	86.2/13.8	20.2
1880	50,155,783	26.0	16.9	28.2/71.8	86.5/13.5	20.9
1890	62,947,714	25.5	21.2	35.1/64.9	87.5/12.5	22.0
1900	75,994,575	20.7	25.6	39.6/60.4	87.9/12.1	22.9
1910	91,972,266	21.0	31.0	45.6/54.4	88.9/11.1	24.1
1920	105,710,620	14.9	35.6	51.2/48.8	89.7/10.3	25.3
1930	122,775,046	16.1	41.2	56.1/43.9	89.8/10.2	26.4
1940	131,669,275	7.2	44.2	56.5/43.5	89.8/10.2	29.0
1950	150,697,361	14.5	50.7	64.0/36.0	89.5/10.5	30.2
1960	179,323,175	18.5	50.6	69.9/30.1	88.6/11.4	29.5
1970	203,302,031	13.4	57.4	73.5/26.5	87.6/12.4	28.0
1980	226,545,805	11.4	64.0	73.7/26.3	86.0/14.0	30.0
1985	237,839,000	5.0	64.0	NA/NA	85.0/15.0	31.3
1988	246,113,000	3.0	NA	NA/NA	84.0/16.0	NA

NA = Not available.

Employment, 1870–1988

Year	Number of Workers (in Millions)	Male/Female Employment Ratio	Percentage of Workers in Unions
1870	12.5	85/15	—
1880	17.4	85/15	—
1890	23.3	83/17	—
1900	29.1	82/18	3
1910	38.2	79/21	6
1920	41.6	79/21	12
1930	48.8	78/22	7
1940	53.0	76/24	27
1950	59.6	72/28	25
1960	69.9	68/32	26
1970	82.1	63/37	25
1980	108.5	58/42	23
1985	108.9	57/43	19
1988	114.9	55/45	17

Production, Trade, and Federal Spending/Debt, 1790–1988

Year	Gross National Product (GNP) (in billions $)	Balance of Trade (in millions $)	Federal Budget (in billions $)	Federal Surplus/Deficit (in billions $)	Federal Debt (in billions $)
1790	—	− 3	.004	+ 0.00015	.076
1800	—	− 20	.011	+ 0.0006	.083
1810	—	− 18	.008	+ 0.0012	.053
1820	—	− 4	.018	− 0.0004	.091
1830	—	+ 3	.015	+ 0.100	.049
1840	—	+ 25	.024	− 0.005	.004
1850	—	− 26	.040	+ 0.004	.064
1860	—	− 38	.063	− 0.01	.065
1870	7.4	− 11	.310	+ 0.10	2.4
1880	11.2	+ 92	.268	+ 0.07	2.1
1890	13.1	+ 87	.318	+ 0.09	1.2
1900	18.7	+ 569	.521	+ 0.05	1.2
1910	35.3	+ 273	.694	− 0.02	1.1
1920	91.5	+ 2,880	6.357	+ 0.3	24.3
1930	90.7	+ 513	3.320	+ 0.7	16.3
1940	100.0	− 3,403	9.6	− 2.7	43.0
1950	286.5	+ 1,691	43.1	− 2.2	257.4
1960	506.5	+ 4,556	92.2	+ 0.3	286.3
1970	992.7	+ 2,511	196.6	+ 2.8	371.0
1980	2,631.7	+ 24,088	579.6	− 59.5	914.3
1985	4,087.7	− 148,480	946.3	− 212.3	1,827.5
1988	4,880.6	− 120,913	1,064.1	− 155.1	2,602.3

Illustrations

Maps

Charts

Index

⬙ ⬘ ⬙

Note: Some pages are in *italics* and are preceded by letters. These refer to (*i*) illustrations, (*m*) maps, and (*c*) charts.

World Political Map

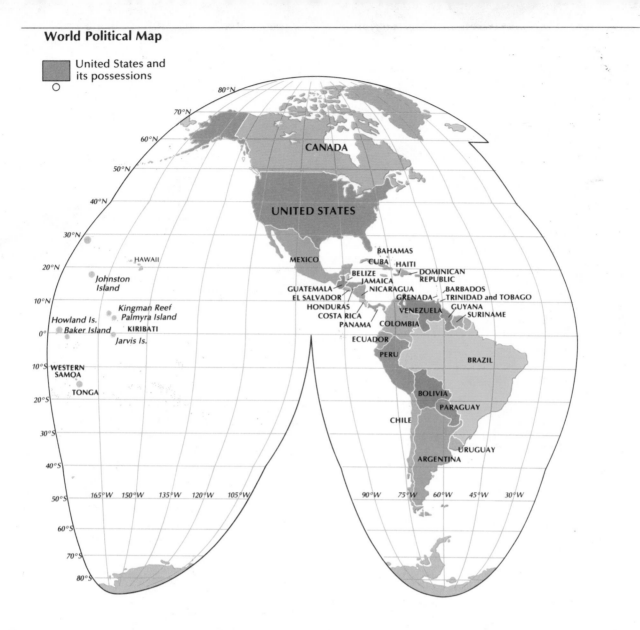

United States and its possessions

80°N
70°N
60°N
50°N
40°N
30°N
20°N
10°N
0°
10°S
20°S
30°S
40°S
50°S
60°S
70°S
80°S

CANADA

UNITED STATES

HAWAII

Johnston Island

Kingman Reef
Palmyra Island

Howland Is.
Baker Island   KIRIBATI

Jarvis Is.

WESTERN SAMOA

TONGA

165°W   150°W   135°W   120°W   105°W

MEXICO

BAHAMAS
CUBA   HAITI
BELIZE   DOMINICAN REPUBLIC
JAMAICA
GUATEMALA   NICARAGUA   BARBADOS
EL SALVADOR   GRENADA   TRINIDAD and TOBAGO
HONDURAS   VENEZUELA   GUYANA
COSTA RICA   SURINAME
PANAMA   COLOMBIA

ECUADOR

PERU   BRAZIL

BOLIVIA
PARAGUAY

CHILE

URUGUAY

ARGENTINA

90°W   75°W   60°W   45°W   30°W